American State Government

FOURTH

EDITION

AMERICAN STATE GOVERNMENT

W. Brooke Graves

Legislative Reference Service, Library of Congress; Adjunct Professor of Political Science, The American University

D. C. HEATH AND COMPANY Boston

Offices: *Boston New York Chicago San Francisco Dallas Atlanta London*

Preface to the fourth edition

This Fourth Edition of a text long familiar to the members of the profession attempts to report and analyze significant developments in the forward movement of the states in the period since World War II. Author and publisher have cooperated in the effort to produce a better book, the former by a serious attempt to condense and shorten some discussions while introducing new material in others, the latter by completely resetting the type in an attractive new format. While all of the chapters have been thoroughly revised in the effort to bring them up to date, a few of the more important changes may be specifically mentioned.

Three new chapters have been added: (1) "Legislative Service Agencies"; (2) "The Military Establishment and Civilian Defense"; (3) "County and Municipal Government." Two chapters appearing in the previous edition have been omitted: (1) "The Legislature in Action," and (2) "The States in the War and the Postwar." Reference lists have been restricted, for the most part, to relatively recent books (periodical references have been omitted, except in some footnotes). The lists have been materially shortened and scope notes or other descriptive phrases have been supplied for each entry. By rearrangement of chapters, the number of Parts has been reduced by one. The *Model State Constitution*, still an important document, is readily available in pamphlet form; it has not seemed necessary, therefore, to continue to run it in the Appendix. These changes have been made in the hope of producing a somewhat shorter and less bulky volume, without impairing such merits as the previous editions may have had.

The Introduction and many of the chapters have been entirely rewritten. The recent extension of legislative services, and the importance of these services to the effective functioning of representative assemblies, has seemed to require that more attention be given to them (see Chapter 7). Several new studies of the governorship have made possible substantial revision and strengthening of Chapter 9. The continued existence of the cold war and the generally uncertain conditions abroad have indicated the necessity of emphasizing, as is done in Chapter 11, the role of the states in the field of military affairs and civil defense. The chapters on fiscal management and the revenue system, both having been — as usual — thoroughly revised, are now included in Part Four on executive and administrative problems. The chapter on constitutional protections has been extensively revised to take account of a large number of Supreme Court decisions handed down during the postwar years. The treatment of local government has been expanded into two chapters. The remaining chapters on intergovernmental relations, particularly the one on interstate relations, have been extensively revised and rewritten.

One never completes a task of this kind without incurring indebtedness to more public officials, professional colleagues, and associates than he can recall or adequately acknowledge. Most of all, I am once again indebted to my wife, Hazel W. Graves, for encouragement and assistance at many points along the way.

— W. Brooke Graves
Library of Congress

Contents

Preface to the Fourth Edition v

INTRODUCTION

State Government at Mid-Century 1

General Considerations. The Training Function of the States. The States as Laboratories. Fundamental Position of the States in the Federal System. New Duties and Responsibilities. General Sources of Information about the States.

PART ONE

Constitutional Bases of State Government

1 **THE STATES IN THE FEDERAL UNION** 15

The Nature of the Federal System. Relation of the States to the Federal Government. Expansion of Federal Power. Constitutional Limitations on State Power. Admission of New States. Relations of the States with Foreign Governments. Selected References.

2 **STATE CONSTITUTIONS** 43

History and Characteristics. Essential Elements of a State Constitution. The Role of the Legislature in Constitutional Amendment. Other Methods of Constitutional Amendment. Operation of the Amending Procedures. Current Needs for Constitutional Revision. Selected References.

3 **STATE CONSTITUTIONAL CONVENTIONS** 69

The Calling and Composition of Conventions. Preparation for the Convention. Powers of the Convention.

The Work of the Convention. Motivation and Control of Constitutional Conventions. Ratification of the Constitution. Selected References.

PART TWO

Political Parties and Popular Control

4 PARTIES AND ELECTIONS 95

The American Party System. The Suffrage. Registration. Nominating Systems. The Conduct of Elections. Selected References.

5 POPULAR CONTROL OF GOVERNMENT 142

Direct Legislation. A Workable Electoral System. Types of Weighted Voting. The Influence of Civic Organizations. Popular Participation in Government. Selected References.

PART THREE

The Process of Lawmaking

6 STATE LEGISLATIVE ORGANIZATION 187

Historical Development. Bicameral and Unicameral Systems. Representative Character. Place of the Legislatures in Popular Esteem. Descriptive Features of the Two Houses. Sessions. The Committee System. Cost of Legislation. Improvements in Organization. Selected References.

7 LEGISLATIVE SERVICE AGENCIES 241

Reference and Information Services. Research and Planning Services. Bill-Drafting Services. Statutory Revision and Codification. Budgetary and Fiscal Analysis. Problems of Over-all Organization. Selected References.

8 STATE LEGISLATIVE PROCEDURE 280

Lawmaking Powers. Selection of Legislative Subjects. The Passage of Bills. Informal Aspects of Lawmaking. Improvements in Procedure. Selected References.

PART FOUR
Executive and Administrative Problems

9 **THE GOVERNOR** 317

History and Development of the Office. General Characteristics of the Office. Executive and Administrative Powers. Legislative Powers of the Governor. Judicial Powers. Actual Functioning of the Office. Selected References.

10 **ADMINISTRATIVE ORGANIZATION AND REORGANIZATION** 362

State Administrative Organization. State Administrative Reorganization. Characteristics of Structural Reorganization. Forms of Control over Administration. The Problem of Boards and Commissions. Current Problems and Tendencies. Selected References.

11 **THE MILITARY ESTABLISHMENT AND CIVILIAN DEFENSE** 395

Military Powers of the Governor. The National Guard. Civilian Defense. The States and the Veteran. Selected References.

12 **STATE ADMINISTRATIVE SERVICES** 422

General Government. Control over Business and Industry. Agriculture and Natural Resources. Transportation Facilities. Public Health and Social Welfare. Education. Selected References.

13 **PERSONNEL MANAGEMENT** 457

The Spoils System. The Civil Service System. The Merit System. Fundamental Problems in Personnel Administration. Selected References.

14 **FINANCIAL MANAGEMENT** 486

Financial Administration. The Budget System. Control of State Expenditures. The Borrowing Power. Selected References.

15 **THE REVENUE SYSTEM** 515

Sources of State Income. Some Fundamental Aspects of the Tax Problem. General Property Tax — Real and

Personal. Corporation and Business Taxes. General Sales, Use, and Gross Receipts Taxes. Excise Taxes. Income Taxes. Inheritance and Estate Taxes. Some Current Tax Problems. Selected References.

PART FIVE
Judicial and Legal Problems

16 THE LEGAL SYSTEMS OF THE STATES 559

The Common Law. Equity. Civil Law. Criminal Law. Other Types of Law. The Nature of the Judicial Process. The Doctrine of Judicial Review. Selected References.

17 STATE COURTS: ORGANIZATION AND JURISDICTION 590

Historical Development of the State Courts. State Court Organization. The Selection of Judges. Characteristics of the Judicial Office. The Judicial Council Movement. Problems of Administrative Reorganization. Relations of State and Federal Courts. Selected References.

18 STATE COURTS: PROCEDURE 636

The Powers and Duties of Courts. Procedure in Civil Cases. Procedure in Criminal Cases. The Jury System. Improving Judicial Procedure. Selected References.

19 CONSTITUTIONAL PROTECTIONS 668

The War Amendments. Due Process of Law. Equal Protection of the Law. Constitutional Protections of Personal Rights. Statutory Protection of Personal Rights. Protection of Property Rights. Selected References.

20 STATE POLICE POWER 707

Protection of the Public Health. Protection of the Public Safety. Protection of the Public Convenience. Protection of the Public Morals. The Prevention of Fraud. The Suppression of Public Nuisances. Selected References.

PART SIX

Intergovernmental Relations

21 LOCAL GOVERNMENT 743

History of American Local Government. The Units of Local Government. Original Functions of Local Government. Newer Functions of Local Government. Selected References.

22 COUNTY AND MUNICIPAL GOVERNMENT 767

County Government. Municipal Government. Municipal Administration. Selected References.

23 STATE-LOCAL RELATIONS 793

Reasons for State Centralization. State Relations with Local Governments. State Supervision of Local Finances. State Supervision of School Administration. State Supervision over Public Health. State Supervision of Public Welfare. General Conclusions. Selected References.

24 INTERSTATE RELATIONS 834

Federal Constitutional Provisions. Uniform State Action. Interstate Compacts and Agreements. Legislative Uniformity. Administrative Cooperation. The Council of State Governments. Uniformity as a Possible Substitute for Centralization. Selected References.

25 COOPERATIVE FEDERALISM 874

Some Historical Considerations. The Indictment of the States. Federal-State Relations in Emergency Periods. Federal-Municipal Relations. Regionalism: Sub-National and Metropolitan. The Emerging Pattern of Intergovernmental Relations. Selected References.

INDEX 913

American State Government

INTRODUCTION

State Government at Mid-Century

It would be difficult to overemphasize the importance of state government in the American tradition, for it is now recognized that the effective functioning of state and local units is essential to the preservation of the American type of democratic, federal government. At the same time, significant improvements in personnel management, in financial management, and in structural organization have served to stimulate interest in the problems of state government and administration.

Various factors contribute to the growing importance of the states. First, there are such general ones as expanding services, increased costs, and the close relationship of the states to the individual citizen. In addition there are factors peculiar to the states — the training they provide for those who are later to become officials of the Federal government, their function as laboratories for political experimentation, and their position as fundamental units in our federal system.

General Considerations

Our government does for us dozens of things that no one ever thought of asking it to do in the days of our fathers and grandfathers. These services are only a natural and normal response to modern needs,[1] resulting from the great advances in preventive medicine and the treatment of disease, in agriculture and forestry, in new techniques and skills in industry, in the development of transportation and communication. At the same time industrialization, which has been accompanied by a trend toward urbanism, has created a vast number of new demands upon government.

As the services of the states have expanded, the costs of government have

[1] Theodore Roosevelt well described this transformation when he wrote: "The government has been forced to take the place of the individual in a hundred ways; in, for instance, such matters as the prevention of fires, the construction of drainage systems, the supply of water, light, and transportation. In a primitive community every man or family looks after his or its interests in all these matters. In a city it would be an absurdity to expect every man to continue to do this, or to say that he had lost the power of individual initiative because he relegated any or all of these matters to the province of public officers." Quoted by Beard, Charles A., *American Government and Politics*, Ninth Edition, p. 346 (Macmillan, New York, 1944).

increased by leaps and bounds. Two states now have annual budgets hovering around the billion dollar mark, and expenditures in most other states doubled in the first four postwar years. A considerable part of this increase may be attributed to efforts to catch up on highway construction and other capital outlays which were neglected during the war, but there has also been a rapid upswing in aid to local governments for schools and for many other purposes.

In the third place, the state is increasingly important because of its close relationship to its citizens. The application of its authority is sometimes direct, sometimes so indirect that the individual is unaware of it. Sometimes it is exercised by the state itself or its officers, and sometimes by the local units of government which have been created by the state authority and which are, to some extent, responsible to it. This is true from the moment the individual is born until the moment he is laid in his final resting place. It is especially true of the business or professional man from the time he leaves his home each morning until he returns at the close of the day.

These three aspects of the state problem — expanding services, increased costs, and intimate relationship to the citizens — are grouped here under the heading "General Considerations," not because they are of minor significance but because they apply alike to all other major units of government. At both the Federal and the municipal levels services have also increased in number, in scope and effectiveness, and in cost. Citizens have always had close contacts with their local governments; in late decades they have come to have similarly close contacts with the Federal government — the Post Office Department, the Internal Revenue Service, the Federal Security Agency, the Veterans Administration, and many other Federal departments and agencies.

The Training Function of the States

The states render the Federal government a service of inestimable value in the practical training they provide for those who later become Federal officials. Many serve first in local offices and then move on to the state legislature or to some position in the administrative end of the state government. Two thirds of our Presidents have served in the legislatures of their respective states. Of the seven Presidents elected since the beginning of World War I in 1914, Wilson, Coolidge, and Roosevelt had previously served as governors. Of the defeated candidates in the same period, Hughes, Cox, Smith, Landon, Dewey, and Stevenson had served or were serving as governors. It is still true, as Woodrow Wilson wrote in his *Constitutional Government* many years ago, that "the governorship of a state is very like a smaller Presidency; or, rather, the Presidency is very like a big governorship. Training in the duties of one fits for the duties of the other."

Many men who have been schooled in state politics eventually find their way into the Senate, the House of Representatives, the Cabinet, the foreign service, the Federal courts, and the various departments and agencies of the Federal government. During recent Congresses approximately one third of the members of the Senate have been former governors of the states from which they came, while in the House nearly half of the membership has had previous experience in state legislatures. Included in this number are many former speakers, majority and minority floor leaders, and others with extensive periods of legislative service.[2] Thus it is that the states (and the local units which perform a similar service for both the states and the Federal government) serve as a training school for the development of Federal office holders and the leaders in national affairs.

The States as Laboratories

One of the most interesting aspects of state government is the function of these units as laboratories for the trial of new political policies and the development of new administrative techniques. This phase of state government has rarely been adequately emphasized. In 1910 Justice Holmes referred to "the insulated laboratories of the states" in the course of his opinion in the case of Noble State Bank v. Haskell,[3] in which the Court upheld the validity of an Oklahoma statute creating a state banking board and directing it to levy upon every bank existing under the laws of the state an assessment of 1 per cent of the bank's average daily deposits, with certain deductions, for the purpose of creating a depositors' guarantee fund.

The history of American government is replete with illustrations of problems with regard to which either the Federal government or the states have asserted leadership; the experience thus obtained has been promptly utilized by the other as a basis for the formulation of a relatively permanent policy. In a number of instances the initial leadership has come from the Federal government. In 1935, when the Federal Social Security Act was passed, only Wisconsin had an unemployment compensation law; by 1940 all the states,

[2] John Brown Mason has made a number of interesting studies in this field; see especially his "State Legislatures: The Proving-Grounds of American Statesmanship," in *State Government*, December 1938, pp. 230–231, 239; and "The State Legislature as Training for Further Public Service," in *Annals* of the American Academy of Political and Social Science (cited hereafter as *Annals*), January 1938, pp. 172–186. At one time there were 195 former state legislators in Congress; see *State Government*, January 1933, pp. 23–24. The following year Professor Mason showed (in "184 of Us in Congress," *State Government*, June 1934, pp. 126–128) "that 34% of the nation's present Senators, 36% of its Representatives, have learned the ropes 'back home.' " The 184 (35% of all the members) included had 35 Senators and 149 Representatives who had had previous state legislative experience, the average length of which was: Senators, 3.2 years, Representatives, 5.6 years. The average length of service in the home capitol was 4.4 years. Many members of Congress have served as prosecuting attorneys, as judges in the state courts, and in various administrative positions.

[3] 219 U.S. 104, 1910. For general comment, see Caldwell, Lynton K., "Laboratories for Democratic Government," *State Government*, April 1950, pp. 76–80; Handlin, Oscar and Mary F., *Commonwealth: A Study of the Role of Government in the American Economy — Massachusetts* (New York University Press, 1947); Radin, Max, "The Function of the States," *Oregon Law Review*, February 1946, pp. 83–102.

Alaska, Hawaii, and the District of Columbia had such statutes. The same thing happened with planning legislation in the states.

On the other hand, the states have pioneered in direct legislation, the direct primary, the guaranty of bank deposits, liquor control, workmen's compensation, and other fields. Eleven states, for instance, adopted bank deposit guaranty laws, but none of these proved notably successful. They were, in fact, so unsatisfactory in operation that, one by one, they were repealed. Yet in 1933 Congress was able, on the basis of this experience, to frame and adopt the Federal Deposit Guarantee Act, which has functioned in a satisfactory manner ever since.

The Federal Budget and Accounting Act of 1921 provides another illustration. For years students of government had been urging the adoption of budgetary legislation. Such systems had long been in use in the more important European countries, and in this country there had been one commission and investigating committee after another through the forty years preceding the passage of the act, all recommending such legislation. During the administration of President Wilson a budget act was passed, but for technical reasons he felt obliged to veto it. The Republicans made budget legislation a campaign issue in 1920, and the original act was adopted early in the Harding administration. Meanwhile, however, the states had been experimenting with every conceivable type of budgetary procedure, and the executive budget had come to be recognized as the most desirable.

The whole matter was well stated by Mr. Hoover before a joint session of the Illinois General Assembly, at Springfield, June 17, 1931[4]:

> Our state legislatures occupy a position of dominant importance to the Nation as a whole . . . for the legislatures are the laboratories in which new ideas are developed and in which they are tried out.
>
> A study of national legislation and national action will show that an overwhelming proportion of the ideas which have been developed nationally have first been born in the state legislatures, as the result of problems which have developed within the states. . . . It is true that not all of the ideas come through this successfully, but even the negative values of the trial . . . are of themselves of inestimable value to the Nation, and the ideas which develop with success become of vital importance to our people at large.

The philosophy which underlies this interesting aspect of American governmental procedure has nowhere been better stated than in the dissenting opinion of Mr. Justice Brandeis in the case of the New State Ice Company v. Liebmann,[5] in which a majority of the Court held invalid, as an unreasonable interference with private business, an Oklahoma statute forbidding the State Corporation Commission to license persons or corporations for the manu-

[4] It has been suggested that "the old function of the states as originators and experimenters" may have been lost and that "the new practices and ideas come chiefly from national and interest group sources. Certainly, few states have displayed the initiative in recent decades which the theory of their role as originators would call for." See Gaus, John M., "The States Are in the Middle," *State Government*, June 1950, pp. 138–142.

[5] 285 U.S. 262, 1932.

facture, sale, or distribution of ice, except on proof of necessity, and authorizing the denial of license where existing facilities were sufficient.

The attorneys for the defendant, and the majority opinion of the Court, argued that the manufacturing of ice for sale and distribution is a common calling and that the right to engage in a common calling is one of the fundamental liberties guaranteed by the due process clause in Amendment XIV. To this Mr. Brandeis replied: "To think of the ice-manufacturing business as a common calling is difficult, so recent is it in origin and so peculiar in character. Moreover, the Constitution does not require that every calling which has been common shall ever remain so. The liberty to engage in a common calling, like other liberties, may be limited in the exercise of the police power." And elsewhere: "The business of supplying to others, for compensation, any article or service whatsoever may become a matter of public concern. Whether it is, or is not, depends upon the conditions existing in the community affected." And in this connection he quotes with approval: "Plainly circumstances may so change in time or so differ in space as to clothe with such an [public] interest what at other times or in other places would be a matter of purely private concern." [6]

This brilliant dissenting opinion discusses at length the local situation which prompted the enactment of this Oklahoma statute, and the history of previous efforts at control by the State Corporation Commission. It traces the gradual and comparatively recent extension of the practice, among the states, of requiring the issuance of certificates of public convenience and necessity in an increasing number and for a variety of types of business. It points out, under the due process clause, the Court has by unanimous decisions ruled that a state or a city may engage "in the business of supplying its inhabitants with articles in general use, when it is believed that they cannot be secured at reasonable prices from the private dealers," and it continues:

> As states may engage in a business, because it is a public purpose to assure to their inhabitants an adequate supply of necessary articles, may they not achieve this public purpose, as Oklahoma has done, by exercising the lesser power of preventing single individuals from wantonly engaging in the business and thereby making impossible a dependable private source of supply? As a state so entering upon a business may exert the taxing power, all individual dealers may be driven from the calling by the unequal competition. If states are denied the power to prevent the harmful entry of a few individuals into a business, they may thus, in effect, close it altogether to private enterprise.

The significance of the opinion can best be shown by a further quotation from its concluding paragraphs. Mr. Brandeis reviews the seriousness of the then existing economic emergency, noting how unusual situations give rise to the warranted exercise of unusual governmental powers. He reviews the suggestions for economic planning and the various proposals for economic

[6] Block v. Hirsh, 256 U.S. 135, 155, 1920.

control, and then raises the fundamental question whether the act before the Court may not be a step in this direction. His conclusions on the planning program in general and its relations to the states, are significant:

> Whether that view [concerning economic planning] is sound nobody knows. The objections to the proposal are obvious and grave. The remedy might bring evils worse than the present disease. The obstacles to success seem insuperable. The economic and social sciences are largely uncharted seas. We have been none too successful in the modest essays in economic control already entered upon. The new proposal involves a vast extension of the area of control. Merely to acquire the knowledge essential as a basis for the exercise of this multitude of judgments would be a formidable task; and each of the thousands of these judgments would call for some measure of prophecy. Even more serious are the obstacles to success inherent in the demands which execution of the project would make upon human intelligence and upon the character of men. Man is weak and his judgment is at best fallible.
>
> Yet the advances in the exact sciences and the achievements in invention remind us that the seemingly impossible sometimes happens. There are many men now living who were in the habit of using the age-old expression: "It is as impossible as flying." The discoveries in physical science, the triumphs in invention, attest the value of the process of trial and error. In large measure, these advances have been due to experimentation. In those fields experimentation has, for two centuries, been not only free but encouraged. Some people assert that our present plight is due in part, to the limitations set by courts upon experimentation in the fields of social and economic science; and to the discouragement to which proposals for betterment there have been subjected otherwise. There must be power in the states and the nation to remould, through experimentation, our economic practices and institutions to meet changing social and economic needs. I cannot believe that the framers of the Fourteenth Amendment, or the states which ratified it, intended to deprive us of the power to correct the evils of technological unemployment and excess productive capacity, which have attended progress in the useful arts.
>
> To stay experimentation in things social and economic is a grave responsibility. Denial of the right to experiment may be fraught with serious consequences to the nation. It is one of the happy incidents of the federal system that a single courageous state may, if its citizens choose, serve as a laboratory; and try novel social and economic experiments without risk to the rest of the country. This Court has the power to prevent an experiment. We may strike down the statute which embodies it on the ground that, in our opinion, the measure is arbitrary, capricious, or unreasonable. We have power to do this, because the due process clause has been held by the Court applicable to matters of substantive law as well as to matters of procedure. But, in the exercise of this high power, we must ever be on our guard, lest we erect our prejudices into legal principles. If we would guide by the light of reason, we must let our minds be bold.

Fundamental Position of the States in the Federal System

From the point of view of our governmental structure as a whole, the states are perhaps the most important units. It should not be forgotten that the Federal government was established by, and is still maintained through, the cooperation of the states; that in many particulars the Constitution of the United States was based on the original state constitutions; and that the

Federal constitution limits the powers of the Federal government to those subjects upon which the states thought it necessary or desirable that the Federal government should be authorized to act. In the course of the years, particularly in the older sections of the country, it is to the states that the people have developed, to a high degree, a kind of sentimental attachment. Many individuals and families pride themselves upon being natives of some particular state and upon the part which that state has played in the history of the nation.

From a more practical point of view, the states have in our own time come to be important as administrative areas for many of the undertakings of the Federal government. In many instances the states have cooperated with Federal agencies, sometimes upon their own initiative and sometimes upon that of the agencies. The nature of modern government is such, in fact, that there are no longer any important domestic functions that can be performed as a sole responsibility of any one unit or level of government. All require the cooperation of units at two or more such levels, while at the same time the cooperation of different units at the same level is often essential to effective administration. These interlevel and interjurisdictional relationships have in recent years become so numerous and so important that a new term, "cooperative federalism," has been developed to describe them. This system makes possible the maximum degree of adaptability to local conditions.

On the other hand it is important to remember that the local units have been created by the action of the states and that the nature and extent of their powers are defined by enactments of the state legislature, at whose will the powers and duties of these units may be changed or the units themselves modified or abolished (subject to constitutional restrictions on the freedom of the legislatures to change the boundary lines of the counties). Likewise, in every state, laws or codes of laws have been enacted for the government of these several types of local unit, specifying what officers shall be chosen, what their duties shall be, by what method and how much they shall be paid, and so on. In the more progressive states nearly all the services rendered by these units are subject to state supervision and control. While this aspect of state government is discussed at length in a later chapter, what has been said here is sufficient to emphasize the point that the powers of local government rest in the states and that the powers exercised by the local units are powers which the states have delegated to them or permitted or required them to exercise.

Clearly, the states are the key units in our system of government. Both the Federal government on the one hand and the local units of government on the other owe their origins, powers, and continued existence largely to the governments of the states. In carrying on the numerous cooperative programs, the state legislatures are usually called upon to enact legislation providing both for the relations between the state and the Federal government and for the organization and administration of the program within the state, including relations with the political subdivisions. Administrative relationships both upward and downward may then develop.

New Duties and Responsibilities

The new and unprecedented demands made upon the states extend into many fields — housing, education, highways, mental health, construction and modernization of institutions, to mention only a few of the more costly.[7] But the states are still pioneering, and many more fields offer almost unlimited opportunities for service. One example is seen in the Barter Theater of Virginia. Although in European countries public funds have long been used in support of the arts, Virginia is the first American state to use state funds to help professional actors take first-rate legitimate theater to every interested city and town in the state.[8]

Organized in 1932 as a relief measure for stranded actors in the depths of the depression, it has grown steadily until it now claims to be "the largest professional stage organization outside of New York as well as the only traveling repertory company in America." State assistance — in small amounts, to be sure — has been given annually since 1946 to help the company expand both its repertoire and its itinerary. In 1948 the company consisted of sixty-five actors, technicians, and others, divided into three troupes. Two of these tour Virginia while the third makes a nationwide circuit, including altogether scheduled appearances in some five hundred cities and towns. From June through August the group produces summer theater at Abingdon, Virginia. The actors belong to Equity and are paid union wages while on tour.

In 1945, the Wisconsin Idea Theater was established at the state University; its stage is said to be "as large as all the stages in the state put together; its audiences number in the millions and its participants are the thousands of actors, directors, technicians, and playwrights within the boundaries of the state." Still another example is found in North Carolina whose "people's symphony orchestra" is partially supported by state appropriation; it plays well over 100 concerts a year in approximately sixty towns and cities.[9]

In a totally different field, at least four states — Rhode Island beginning in 1943, California, New Jersey, and New York — are pioneering in disability insurance. It has long been recognized that one of the major weaknesses of the unemployment compensation program has been its failure to protect

[7] See, for instance, Linen, John S., "Demands on States Grow," *National Municipal Review*, March 1949, pp. 121–125.

[8] Davis, Virginia M., "Barter Theater of Virginia," *State Government*, April 1948, pp. 86–88.

[9] Kamarck, Edward L., "Wisconsin Idea Theatre," *New York Times*, September 25, 1949; Selden, Samuel, "America's Open-Air Dramas," *State Government*, April 1952, pp. 86–88, 94–95; and Boyden, Lucile K., "North Carolina's State Symphony," *ibid.*, February 1948, pp. 34–36.

workers against hazards. These laws are designed to provide workers, by a tax on their own paychecks, an insurance plan against unemployment in time of sickness or disability. The results have been highly satisfactory so far and have demonstrated the possibility of broadening the coverage of the social security program as it now generally exists.[10]

The tremendous growth of services suggests the question of the so-called welfare state at the state level. Professor John F. Sly, who made an analysis of legislative proposals in twenty-eight states in the 1949 legislative sessions,[11] concludes that "this survey plus any review of recent and long-range developments would seem to support the belief that great pressures exist in favor of the development and extension of the welfare state in America." He points out that some of the historical precedents such as the internal improvements policy of John Quincy Adams and Henry Clay, the development of regulatory agencies in the late nineteenth century, the Square Deal of Theodore Roosevelt, the New Freedom of Woodrow Wilson, and the New Deal of Franklin Delano Roosevelt, each represented nationalizing influences which changed the character of the federal system, but none of them — he contends — carried the great economic and social implications of the present trend.

In still another area, the states are being subjected to tremendous pressure for change — change resulting from population growth and population shifts. The intercensal growth from 1920 to 1930 was 17 million; from 1930 to 1940, it was 9 million; and "that since 1940 exceeded 14 million by July 1, 1948 and probably will exceed 17 million when the 1950 census" returns are all in. By 1975 the population is likely to be between 165 million and 170 million.[12] Population shifts of enormous significance have occurred during and since World War II, the former as the result of opportunities for employment at high wages in war industries, the latter because many war workers failed to return to their former locations, and many new families settled in states often far removed from their former homes. Such migrations create enormous problems for states and cities in schools, housing, welfare, and many other essential services.[13]

This new era of the service state in a period of great population growth and adjustment imposes many new responsibilities upon the states themselves.

[10] See Newton, Mortimer W., "The Rhode Island Cash Sickness Compensation Program, a Pioneer Venture in Social Security," *State Government*, September 1945, pp. 156–159, 161, and Leary, Mary E., "California's Disability Insurance Program," *ibid.*, April 1948, pp. 89–90.

[11] "The 'Welfare State' at the State Level," *Tax Review*, June 1949, entire issue; on the general question, see Achinstein, Asher, *The Welfare State: The Case For and Against* (Public Affairs Bulletin, Legislative Reference Service, Library of Congress, 1950).

[12] Whelpton, P. K., "A History of Population Growth in the United States," *The Scientific Monthly*, October 1948, pp. 277–288.

[13] For illustrative comments see Stanbery, Van Beuren, "What Population Growth Is Doing to the Pacific Coast States," *State Government*, September 1948, pp. 189–191, 195, and Warren, Earl, "California's Biggest Headache," an interview with Frank J. Taylor in the *Saturday Evening Post*, August 14, 1948, pp. 20–21, 74 ff.

Overlapping and duplication of effort between different levels of government must be eliminated, and suitable divisions of functions between them must be worked out.[14] Something effective must be done, for instance, about the earmarking of funds, the establishment of four-year terms for the governor and other important elected officials, the reduction of the number of such officials, provision for annual legislative sessions, the solution of the problem of legislative apportionment and of state-local relations, and a careful appraisal of the courts and the administration of justice.

Even so, there is no reason to entertain any serious doubts as to the future of the states. They have been here for a very long time, and they will be here for a long time to come. They are considerably different now from what they once were, and they are still changing. Like all human institutions they have had their periods of progress and retrogression. The mid-period of the twentieth century finds them operating as going concerns, relatively strong and vigorous, performing many new functions at a high standard of administrative efficiency, needing many important changes and improvements, but nevertheless looking forward with confidence to the years that lie ahead.

General Sources of Information about the States

Serious students of state government will do well to provide themselves with, or make certain that they have access to, such important working tools as are listed below.

STATE CONSTITUTIONS. Obtain a copy of the constitution of your own state. The full text is usually available in pamphlet form upon application to the Secretary of State, or in the state legislative manual, blue book, or red book. The current edition of the *Model State Constitution* may be obtained in pamphlet form, at small cost, with explanatory articles, from the National Municipal League, 299 Broadway, New York 7, N. Y.

Analysis of the provisions of all state constitutions on constitutional conventions and constitutional revision will be regularly found in *The Book of the States*, while biennial summaries of developments in the field of state constitutional law appear in the *American Political Science Review*. The biennial *State Law Index*, published by the Library of Congress, 1925 to 1950, gave citations to all constitutional changes.

CONSTITUTIONAL CONVENTION PUBLICATIONS. Studies prepared for, or in anticipation of, constitutional conventions contain a vast amount of information on various aspects of state government. Most extensive compilation and analysis is found in the twelve-volume report of the New York State Constitutional Convention Committee of 1938; others, prepared since that date, have appeared in Hawaii, Missouri, New Jersey, Oklahoma. These are cited in Chapters 2 and 3.

STATE MANUALS. In most states, a state manual is published, usually on a biennial basis (check your own state in Hotaling, Donald O., "State Manual Procurement Guide," *Special Libraries*, July–August, 1948, pp. 184–191). Copies are obtainable free from your state senator or state representative, or at small cost from the Secretary of State, or the state division or bureau of documents and/or publica-

[14] See Chatters, Carl H., "20th Century Public Service," *National Municipal Review*, October 1947, pp. 503–507.

tions. In a few states where manuals are privately printed, they must be purchased from the publishers.

THE BOOK OF THE STATES. This volume is issued biennially by the Council of State Governments, 1313 East 60th Street, Chicago 37, Illinois, and is kept up to date by frequent supplements. It is available in any good library, and is an absolutely indispensable working tool for any student or any state government official. For comparable information on cities, see *Municipal Yearbook*, issued annually by the International City Managers Association at the above address.

PROFESSIONAL JOURNALS. There are occasional articles dealing with various aspects of state government in the current periodicals and professional journals, among them:

American Political Science Review (American Political Science Association, Washington, D.C., quarterly)
Journal of Politics (Southern Political Science Association, Gainesville, Florida, quarterly)
National Municipal Review (National Municipal League, New York, monthly)
New York Times, Sunday edition ("A Report on the Nation," in Section 4, weekly)
Public Administration Review (American Society for Public Administration, Chicago, quarterly)
State Government (Council of State Governments, Chicago, monthly)
Western Political Quarterly (Western Political Science Association, Salt Lake City, quarterly)

BIBLIOGRAPHIES. In the reference lists of books at the close of the various chapters of this volume, emphasis is placed on works of general interest, preferably fairly recent, and ordinarily accessible or obtainable. The only available bibliography presenting references of significant state studies on a state by state basis is: Graves, W. Brooke, Small, Norman J., and Dowell, E. Foster, *American State Government and Administration, a State by State Bibliography* (Council of State Governments, Chicago, 1949).

There are several bibliographies dealing with state documents: Brown, Everett S., *Manual of Government Publications* (Appleton-Century-Crofts, New York, 1950); a bibliography of bibliographies of state publications in Lloyd, Gwendolyn, "The Status of State Document Bibliography," *Library Quarterly*, July 1948, pp. 192–199; Jenkins, William S., "Records of the States of the United States, a Microfilm Compilation," Library of Congress *Journal of Acquisitions*, May 1949, pp. 3–7.

The bureaus of public administration, bureaus of governmental or municipal research connected with the state universities, particularly in the South and West, likewise the research divisions of the state legislative councils, are a prolific source of special studies of state and local governmental problems, in the states in which they exist. Your college or university library doubtless has a complete file of these publications for your own state, perhaps for others, or you may obtain a list of available publications by writing to the agency.

STATE DOCUMENTS. The public document systems of the states are well organized in only a few states. The best available key to the use of such documents is Wilcox, Jerome K., Ed., *Manual on the Use of State Publications* (American Library Association, Chicago, 1940), and for current information, the *Monthly Checklist of State Publications*, issued by the Library of Congress.

READINGS. In years past, there were a number of volumes of readings on state government, although some items relating to the states are included in most of the currently available volumes of readings in American government. The only volume of state readings now available is: Lancaster, Lane W., and Breckenridge, A. C., *Readings in American State Government* (Rinehart & Company, New York, 1950).

Two volumes of readings dealing with individual states have appeared recently: Farrelly, David, and Hinderacker, Ivan H., Eds., *The Politics of California* (Ronald Press, New York, 1951) and Asseff, Emmett, and Owen, Kimbrough, Eds., *Readings and Materials in Louisiana Government* (Edwards Brothers, Ann Arbor, 1951).

GENERAL COMMENT. See Peel, Roy V., *State Government Today* (University of New Mexico Press, 1948). This little book, which is not intended to be a text, modestly "aspires to nothing more than raising some questions about our American system of state governments." This is done in an interesting and challenging way. There is a considerable bibliography and comment on source materials.

VOLUMES ON STATE GOVERNMENTS. There are few volumes — and still fewer good ones — now available on government and administration in the individual states. A few of the more acceptable ones are listed below:

California: Crouch, Winston W., and McHenry, Dean E., *California Government: Politics and Administration*, Revised Edition (University of California Press, 1949)

Indiana: Sikes, Pressly S., *Indiana State and Local Government*, Revised Edition (Principia Press, Bloomington, 1946)

New Mexico: Donnelly, Thomas C., *Government of New Mexico* (University of New Mexico Press, 1947)

Pennsylvania: Tanger, Jacob, Alderfer, Harold F., and McGeary, M. Nelson, *Pennsylvania's Government, State and Local*, Third Edition (Penns Valley Publishers, State College, 1950)

Tennessee: Combs, William H., and Cole, William E., *Tennessee — a Political Study* (University of Tennessee Press, 1940)

Texas: MacCorkle, Stuart A., and Smith, Dick, *Texas Government*, Second Edition (McGraw-Hill, New York, 1952)

Patterson, C. Perry, and others, *State and Local Government in Texas*, Third Edition (Macmillan, New York, 1948)

Stewart, Frank M., and Clark, Joseph L., *The Constitution and Government of Texas*, Fourth Edition (Heath, Boston, 1949)

Washington: Webster, Donald H., and others, *Washington State Government: Its Administrative Organization and Functions* (University of Washington Press, 1948)

West Virginia: Lambert, Oscar D., *West Virginia and Its Government* (Heath, Boston, 1951)

AMERICAN COMMONWEALTHS SERIES. A series of substantial volumes in this field is now in course of preparation, under the general editorship of the author of this volume. Ultimately, all states and major territories will be covered. Publication of these books by the Thomas Y. Crowell Company, New York, began in 1953, under the title: The American Commonwealths Series. First volumes to appear were:

Florida: Doyle, Wilson K., Laird, Angus, and Weiss, S. Sherman, *Florida Government and Administration* (Crowell, New York, 1953)

New York: Caldwell, Lynton K., *New York Government and Administration* (Crowell, New York, 1953)

Wyoming: Trachsel, Herman H., and Wade, Ralph M., *Wyoming Government and Administration* (Crowell, New York, 1953)

PART ONE

Constitutional Bases of State Government

Your ordinary constitution will last you hardly ten years without repairs or additions. . . . Whoever would effect a change in a modern constitutional government must first educate his fellow-citizens to want some *change. That done, he must persuade them to want the particular change he wants. He must first make public opinion willing to listen and then see to it that it listens to the right things. He must stir it up to search for an opinion, and then manage to put the right opinion in its way.*

— WOODROW WILSON

I

The States in the Federal Union

The Nature of the Federal System

Before considering certain characteristics of the American federal system, it seems desirable to note briefly the meaning of several terms used in describing different types of governmental organization. First among these is the concept of a federal system. Professor Ogg once defined a federal government as one in which "the political sovereign has made a distribution of the powers of government among certain agencies, central and divisional, and has done so through the medium of constitutional provisions which neither the central nor the divisional government has made, and which are beyond the power of either to alter or rescind." [1] If one restates this in the terms of American conditions, it is evident that "We, the people" have, in the Federal Constitution, made a division of the powers of government between the Federal government in Washington and the governments of the several states. The division of powers so prescribed was not devised by either the previously existing central government or the states acting alone, nor can it be amended or abrogated by the action of either type of governmental agency acting alone.

In this connection it should be noted that the American use of the term "state" is somewhat confusing, at least to beginners in the study of government. A state is technically regarded as a governmental unit possessing full powers of sovereignty and recognized as a regular member of the family of nations. This concept is obviously inapplicable to the forty-eight subdivisions of the American Union. The confusion in terminology might have been avoided had the majority of the states chosen to follow the example of Kentucky, Massachusetts, Pennsylvania, and Virginia, all of which are officially known as Commonwealths. The term "commonwealth" is more accurately descriptive of the kind of governmental unit which the so-called states represent. It implies a separate political entity but does not necessarily indicate the existence of a complete sovereignty. It is, in fact, generally applied to self-governing bodies which are a part of a whole. While at this late date it

[1] Ogg, Frederic A., *Governments of Europe*, p. 53 (Macmillan, New York, 1924), and in revised form in Ogg and Zink, Revised Edition, p. 37 (Macmillan, New York, 1950).

is impossible to consider seriously the changing of a national practice supported by a century and a half of usage, it is essential that one understand the manner in which the everyday use of the term "state" differs from what might be called a scientific connotation.

The Tenth Amendment. In settling the apportionment of powers between the central and the local governments of a federal system, any one of several principles is conceivably available. In the United States, as in the Australian Commonwealth, the principle originally adopted was that the national government should possess only those powers which were conferred upon it in more or less definite terms by the Constitution, while the remaining powers should, unless otherwise specified, be reserved to the states, or — as Professor Corwin has said [2] — the national government was a government of enumerated powers, while the states were governments of residual powers.

In other words, in the American federal system the sum total of all the powers of government is divided between the Federal government and the states under the principle set forth in Amendment X, which provides that "the powers not delegated to the United States by the Constitution, nor prohibited by it to the States, are reserved to the States respectively, or to the people." It is thus apparent that those powers of government not conferred upon the Federal government in Article I, Section 8, in Article IV, and elsewhere, nor denied to the states in Article I, Section 10, belong to the states or to the people. Under this theory the Federal government may do those things and only those things which are expressly authorized by the Constitution or which, under the doctrine of implied powers set forth by Chief Justice Marshall in McCulloch v. Maryland,[3] may be reasonably implied therefrom; while the states may exercise all the powers of government except those definitely denied them by the provision of Amendment X or Article I, Section 10.

Under these conditions the powers of the states may be determined by a process of elimination. If it be found that any given power has been neither conferred upon the Federal government nor prohibited to the states, it may properly be assumed that this subject is one falling within the scope of state power. Take, for instance, the power over education. Search of those sections of the Constitution which confer powers upon the Federal government does not reveal that the control over this important activity has been vested in the central government. Search of the provisions of Article I, Section 10, does not reveal that this power has been denied to the states. Therefore it may be assumed that this power, like that over health, welfare, highways, and many other activities, has been left to the states. These powers are all examples of residuary or inherent powers.

This suggests at least one fundamental distinction between the unitary and the federal types of government. Under the latter, the administrative

[2] Corwin, Edward S., "The Passing of Dual Federalism," *Virginia Law Review*, February 1950, pp. 1–24.

[3] 4 Wheaton 316, 1819.

areas (states) possess powers which cannot be alienated from them except by Constitutional amendment. Even here, unless there is specific provision for such change, the Court assumes, as in the Slaughter House cases [4] involving the interpretation of Amendment XIV, that it was not the intention of the Congress nor of the states to disturb in any fundamental way the existing governmental structure by a general redistribution of the powers of government. Similarly, in interpreting the sweeping phrase of Amendment XVI, "from whatever source derived," the Court long refused to sanction the taxation of Federal judges' salaries, on the ground that to do so would result in a diminution of their salaries, contrary to the Constitutional guarantee as then understood.[5]

It should be remembered too that the Constitution contemplated an "indestructible union of indestructible states" — to use the famous phrase from Chief Justice Chase.[6] It may be that a terrible civil war was necessary to secure a full realization of this intention, but the reality of such a union can now be scarcely questioned. Looking toward the permanency of the Federal government, on the one hand, one finds established, as a result of the supreme law clause (Article VI, Section 2), the principle of a constitutional review of state laws and the imposing of definite duties upon the states as members of the Federal Union. Looking toward the permanency of the states, on the other, one finds the whole doctrine of delegated powers for the Federal government and of residuary powers for the states. Not only has the system enjoyed an uninterrupted existence since the date of its establishment, but during this time it has been subjected to few drastic changes in form. There have been some amendments, and of course changes have been made in practice through the operation of the system of grants-in-aid and through other extensions of Federal power.

Advantages and Disadvantages of the Federal System. The arguments for and against such a form of federalism as exists in the United States have been well stated by Professor Benson.[7] The federal plan insures "(1) the prevention, by division of the agencies possessing political power, of the acquisition by any one agency of power sufficient to overthrow democratic, constitutional government; (2) opportunity for experimentation in governmental matters; (3) an opportunity to adapt governmental programs to needs of different localities; (4) an opportunity to train our citizenry in state institu-

[4] 16 Wallace 36, 1873.

[5] In O'Malley v. Woodrough, 307 U.S. 277, 1939, the Court overruled Miles v. Graham, 268 U.S. 501, 1925, and virtually overruled the parent case, Evans v. Gore, 253 U.S. 245, 1920.

[6] Texas v. White, 7 Wallace 700, 1868. For contemporary statements of the arguments on the secession question, see Perkins, Howard C., *Northern Editorials on Secession*, 2 vols., and Dumond, Dwight L., *Southern Editorials on Secession* (both, Appleton-Century, New York, 1942).

[7] Benson, George C. S., "Federal-State Personnel Relations," *Annals*, January 1940, pp. 38–43.

tions before selecting them for national responsibilities; (5) the administrative advantages attendant upon a forced administrative decentralization."

Professor Benson goes on to say that "recognition of the desirability of these goals does not, however, deny the validity of certain basic criticisms of a federal form of government. The most obvious disadvantages are: (1) The tendency of freedom of commerce — almost universal within federal systems — to place economic handicaps on progressive social legislation by members of the system. These handicaps frequently operate to prevent the establishment of even minimum nationwide standards. (2) The great variations in fiancially feasible governmental programs of member states which result from the unequal economic resources of different members of federal systems. These variations adversely affect establishment of nationwide minimum levels of government personnel. (3) The central government almost inevitably possesses a predominance in financial resources over most of the member units, simply because most taxes can be collected more effectively over an entire economic area than over portions of such an area. (4) A problem, if not a disadvantage, arises from the fact that the financial strength of the federal government often exceeds its responsibilities. Federal financial supremacy often results in higher-salaried personnel and hence better administrative standards."

Federalism in Other Lands. The student of American government should be aware of the fact that this is only one of the plans in accordance with which a federal government may be constructed. In addition to those of the United States and Canada, the best known federal systems are found in Australia and Switzerland; others exist in Brazil, Russia, and South Africa. Germany, under the Weimar Constitution, had a federal system.[8] The American federal system is much older than any of the others; other peoples have, therefore, been able to profit to some extent by the experience of the United States. The British North America Act, which serves as a constitution for the Dominion of Canada, was drafted in 1867. Its framers had before them the then very recent and very distressing spectacle of the American Civil War. It is only natural that they should have sought to prevent the occurrence in Canada of an experience similar to that occurring in this country. In their effort to do this they provided that the powers not delegated to the provinces should be reserved to the government of the Dominion. In this way they sought to avoid many of the difficulties experienced in the United States in

[8] *State Government* published in 1945 a series of articles on federalism abroad. Bland, F. A., "Federalism in Australia," November, pp. 204–207; Hazard, John N., "Federalism in the U.S.S.R.," June, pp. 92–94; Hodgetts, John E., "Problems of Canadian Federalism," *ibid.*, pp. 95–99; Lipson, Leslie, "Centralization in New Zealand," November, pp. 208–210, 218: May, Henry H., "The Union of South Africa: the Provinces and the Central Government," July, pp. 115–119; Walker, Harvey, "Federalism in Brazil," March, pp. 43–44, 52; and Aspaturian, Vernon V., "The Theory and Practice of Soviet Federalism," *Journal of Politics*, February 1950, pp. 20–51.

the effort to distinguish, in commerce and in other fields, between interstate and intrastate matters.[9]

Relation of the States to the Federal Government

The position of the states in the federal system involves several reciprocal relationships. While the states have certain definite duties and responsibilities, they receive from the Federal government guarantees of assistance and protection with regard to several vital matters. Among the duties of the states should be noted the requirement that they participate in the election of representatives to both houses of Congress and of Presidential electors; that they maintain the public peace within their borders; and that they maintain a republican form of government.

Duties and Responsibilities of the States. It is definitely to the advantage of the states to discharge promptly their duty of participation in the choice of Presidential electors and of members of Congress. While it is of course true that the Federal government could not continue to function for any considerable length of time as the government of a united people, if any large number of states refrained from the discharge of this responsibility, it is also true that the states would by such failure be denying themselves their proper influence in the conduct of the affairs of the Federal government. This is especially true in the case of the selection of Senators, where a failure to choose one Senator deprives a state of 50 per cent of its voting strength in the upper chamber. This fact is so well recognized throughout the country that Senatorial vacancies are rarely permitted to exist for any considerable time.

The states are responsible also for establishing by law appropriate districts for the election of that number of members of the House of Representatives to which each is entitled. Since there appears to be a general lack of standards imposed by either the Federal or the state governments to govern their formation, there is wide variation in the extent to which the traditional standards of equal population and of contiguous and compact territory are followed. All but about half a dozen states have been redistricted during or since 1931. As a result of the 1950 Census, redistricting was necessary because of reduced representation in nine states and was urgently needed if not required in seven others. All of the states in the first group and all but two in the second were redistricted during the 1951 and 1952 sessions.[10]

[9] Corwin reports, *op. cit.*, that "surprisingly enough, when New Deal programs were being tested judicially under the two constitutions a decade and a half ago, it was the United States Constitution which proved to be, in the final upshot, the more commodious vehicle of national power, the reason being that the draftsmen of the British North America Act, besides generally using more precise language than did the Framers, designated certain of the powers which they assigned the Canadian provinces as "exclusive," with the result of rendering them logically restrictive of the powers of the Dominion — or at least the Judicial Committee of the House of Lords so ruled."

[10] Todd, James E., "The Apportionment Problem Faced by the States," *Law and Contemporary Problems*, Spring 1952, pp. 314–337. This article is one of a symposium on legislative apportionment.

If, however, the legislature fails to make such apportionment when due, there appears to be no legal method by which it may be compelled to do so. In the case of Colegrove v. Green, the Supreme Court dismissed a suit brought by three qualified voters in Illinois to restrain election officials from proceeding, in 1946, under the provisions of a state statute of 1901, under which Congressional districts varied greatly in size. The petitioners claimed violation of: (1) the Federal Reapportionment Act of 1911; (2) both Article I, Section 2, and Amendment XIV of the Constitution.[11]

The Court had held in a prior decision [12] that the Reapportionment Act of 1911 was superseded by the Reapportionment Act of 1929, and now reaffirmed that position. It dismissed the constitutional questions on the basis that the case was not justiciable, holding that the Constitution does not guarantee a citizen the right to vote and have his vote counted. A divided Court regarded the question before it as a political one, a decision with regard to which would involve the judiciary in politics in a manner "hostile to the democratic system." One can only wonder how the majority of the Court believed that by using its influence to perpetuate an obviously undemocratic electoral system, they were strengthening the democratic system.

The states are definitely responsible for the maintenance of peace and order within their borders, for the protection of the lives and property of persons (not merely citizens) within their jurisdictions. The principle has, however, been established that in instances where an individual state may be unable to discharge this responsibility, the Federal government may, either with or without the consent of the state, send in Federal troops. The Constitution, in Article IV, Section 4, authorizes the President to dispatch troops for the purpose of quieting domestic violence, at the request of the legislature or the governor of the state concerned. An illustration of the use of this power occurred in West Virginia when Governor John J. Cornwall requested assistance from President Harding in 1921 for the quieting of disturbance in the coal fields. Such a request from the governor of a state makes for harmonious relations between the states and the Federal government. It is, however, well established that in case of necessity Federal troops may be sent into a state to preserve order, not only without the request of the governor, but in spite of his protest and opposition. The most famous illustration of this is found in the decision of President Cleveland to send Federal troops into Illinois at the time of the Pullman strike, against the vigorous protest of Governor John P. Altgeld.[13]

[11] 66 Sup. Ct. 1198, 1946; for an analysis of the case, see Burdette, Franklin L., "The Illinois Congressional Redistricting Case," *American Political Science Review*, October 1946, pp. 958–962.

[12] Wood v. Broom, 287 U.S. 1, 1932.

[13] The power of the President in this case was upheld by the Supreme Court in its opinion in *In re Debs* (158 U.S. 564, 1894), on the ground that the interference of the strikers with the free flow of interstate commerce and with transportation of the mail justified this exercise of Federal power.

It is the duty of the states to maintain a republican form of government. No particular government is designated as republican, nor is the exact form to be guaranteed in any manner described; the question as to what constitutes such government is in most cases a political one, coming within the authority of Congress, or perhaps of the President, rather than a judicial one coming within the power of the courts. In repeated instances where the question has been under consideration in Congress, it has been decided that the guarantee is in effect a guarantee of a representative form of government. In the Pacific States Telephone and Telegraph Company v. Oregon,[14] a public service corporation succeeded in getting this question before the Supreme Court. The voters of Oregon enacted by use of the initiative a tax law affecting this corporation. The company paid the tax under protest, filing suit to recover the tax money on the ground that the law under which the tax was paid was a violation of the clause guaranteeing a republican form of government. The opinion of the Court took the position that the Constitutional guarantee was being fulfilled as long as the state maintained its representative institutions. If, in any state, the citizens should decide that they wished to supplement the work of these representative institutions by resort to methods of direct legislation, the Court said that they would be entirely within the limits of their authority. The Oregon decision seems reasonable, but under the conditions existing at the time, it was no less expedient politically than it was wise.

The States and Amendment of the Constitution. Finally, the states must on occasion participate in the procedure of amending the Federal Constitution. The two methods by which amendments may be proposed, and the two methods either of which may be designated by Congress for their ratification, are set forth in Article V.[15]

[14] 223 U.S. 118, 1912; see also Ohio v. Hildebrant, 241 U.S. 565, 1916. "All of the States had governments when the Constitution was adopted. In all, the people participated to some extent, through their representatives elected in the manner specially provided. These governments the Constitution did not change. They were accepted precisely as they were, and it is therefore to be presumed that they were such as it is the duty of the States to provide. Thus we have unmistakable evidence of what was republican in form, within the meaning of that term as employed in the Constitution." From *Constitution of the United States of America*, revised and annotated, pp. 533–534 (Government Printing Office, 1924) — hereafter referred to as *Constitution.*

[15] "The Congress, whenever two-thirds of both Houses shall deem it necessary, shall propose Amendments to this Constitution, or, on the Application of the Legislatures of two-thirds of the several States, shall call a Convention for proposing Amendments, which, in either Case, shall be valid to all Intents and Purposes, as Part of this Constitution, when ratified by the Legislatures of three-fourths of the several States, or by Conventions in three-fourths thereof, as the one or the other Mode of Ratification may be proposed by the Congress; Provided that no Amendment which may be made prior to the Year One thousand eight hundred and eight shall in any Manner affect the first and fourth Clauses in the Ninth Section of the first Article; and that no State, without its Consent, shall be deprived of its equal Suffrage in the Senate." *Constitution*, p. 539.

Methods of Amending the Federal Constitution

PROPOSAL	RATIFICATION
1. By two-thirds vote of both houses of Congress	1. By affirmative action of the legislatures of three fourths of the states
2. By a convention called by Congress at request of the legislatures of two thirds of the states	2. By affirmative action of conventions called in at least three fourths of the states for the purpose of considering the proposed amendment

While our Constitution was framed by the second method of proposal and put in effect by the second method of ratification, all the amendments thus far have been proposed by the first method, and all except Amendment XXI have been ratified by the first method. In the case of Amendment XXI Congress specified the second method, ratification by convention, in order to avoid the recurrence of the charges so frequently made concerning Amendment XVII — that it had been "put over" by a powerful and aggressive minority and that it did not represent the will of a majority of the people at any given time.[16]

Use Made of the Amending Procedure

PERIOD	AMENDMENT NUMBER	SUBJECT MATTER
1791–1804	I–X	Bill of Rights
	XI	Limiting Power of Federal Courts
	XII	Election of the President
1865–1870	XIII–XV	War Amendments
1913–1933	XVI	Income Tax
	XVII	Direct Election of Senators
	XVIII, XXI	Liquor Control
	XIX	Woman Suffrage
	XX	Lame Duck Amendment
1951–	XXII	Two-Term Limitation for President

It thus appears that for long periods of time no amendments have been added to the Constitution. After some necessary changes immediately following the establishment of the government under it, none were made for a period of sixty-one years, from 1804 to 1865. Again, after the changes incorporated in the Constitution by the War Amendments, no changes were made during a period of forty-three years, from 1870 to 1913. Since the latter date

[16] See published proceedings of these conventions, and monograph by Brown, Everett S., *Ratification of the Twenty-first Amendment to the Constitution of the United States* (University of Michigan Press, 1938).

the amending process was used more or less frequently for a period of twenty years. Only one has been adopted since 1933, and at the time of writing, no other proposal (with the dubious exception of the child labor amendment) was officially pending.

In the course of the years the courts have been called upon to answer many questions involving the interpretation of the provisions of Article V. The first was presented to the Supreme Court as early as 1797; most of them, however, arose in connection with the interpretation of Amendment XVIII, as is evident from the data in the table on page 24.

Guarantees of Assistance and Protection to the States. Such are the duties of the states as members of the Federal Union. On the other hand, the states receive certain compensations for the discharge of their duties. If they cannot or do not maintain a republican form of government, the Federal government will intervene to see that such a government is established. If they are unable to maintain domestic peace or to protect themselves against invasion, there is a guarantee of assistance from the Federal government. After providing that Congress shall have the power to admit new states into the Union, the Constitution says in Article IV, Section 3, that "no new State shall be formed or erected within the jurisdiction of any other States; nor shall any State be formed by the junction of two or more States, or parts of States, without the consent of the legislatures of the States concerned as well as of the Congress." Thus the states have a guarantee of territorial integrity. Again, there is the assurance of equal representation in the Senate, based upon the guarantee in Article V. Certain other clauses attempt to insure an equality of the states in the possession of the same kinds and degrees of political power. Finally, the adoption in 1798 of Amendment XI brought to the states the promise of immunity from suits in the Federal courts, at least without their own consent.[17]

Expansion of Federal Power

Largely because of the changing character of modern civilization, the power of the Federal government has in recent decades been very greatly increased — often at the expense of the states. There are a number of ways in which this has happened, each of which will be discussed in turn.

Through Legislative Influence. The expansion of Federal power through Congressional influence has developed most notably under exercise of the commerce power and the tax power, the Federal police power and the Federal spending power. Another notable example has been legislation based on the grant-in-aid or subsidy principle, under which, as originally operated, Federal funds were offered to the states under two conditions: (1) the Federal grant must be matched, dollar for dollar; (2) the full amount must be expended for

[17] Orth, Samuel P., and Cushman, Robert E., *American National Government*, pp. 709–712 (Crofts, New York, 1931).

Judicial Interpretation of Article V on the Amending Process

QUESTION	DECISION	CASE(S)
1. What does $\frac{2}{3}$ mean — $\frac{2}{3}$ of those present, or $\frac{2}{3}$ of those elected?	$\frac{2}{3}$ of those present.	Missouri Pacific Railway Company v. Kansas, 248 U.S. 276, 1919, and National Prohibition Cases, 253 U.S. 350, 1920.
2. Is approval of the proposing resolution by the President necessary?	No.	Hollingsworth v. Virginia, 3 Dallas 378, 1798.
3. Is an amendment effective when the last state ratifies, or when proclaimed by the Secretary of State?	When the last state ratifies, but proclamation usually follows promptly last ratification.	Dillon v. Gloss, 256 U.S. 368, 1921.
4. Can a time limit be placed on ratification?	Yes, in order to insure majority support during a specified period of time.	*Ibid.*
5. May a state ratify a proposed amendment after prior rejection?	Yes.	Coleman v. Miller, 307 U.S. 463, 1939.
6. Does a proposed amendment, without a time limitation, lose its potency because of the lapse of time?	No (example: proposed Child Labor Amendment)	*Ibid.*
7. Are there limitations, other than the one on Senate representation, to what an amendment may contain?	No.	National Prohibition Cases, 253 U.S. 350, 1920.
8. May an amendment properly proposed and properly ratified be itself unconstitutional?	No.	United States v. Sprague, 282 U.S. 716, 1931.
9. May a state require a popular referendum on proposed amendments?	It may, but the results thereof have no binding effect, since no such requirement appears in Article V.	Hawke v. Smith, 253 U.S. 231, 1921.
10. May a state withdraw a ratification once officially made?	No.	*Ibid.*
11. May a state refuse to observe an amendment it has failed to approve?	No.	Leser v. Garnet, 258 U.S. 130, 1922.
12. May a state actually, although not specifically, violate an amendment to the Constitution?	No.	Guinn and Beal v. United States, 238 U.S. 347, 1915.

the exact purposes specified in the act, and in accordance with the conditions prescribed.

In later years the principle of the matching grant has gradually given way to other allocation formulae. It is no longer essential that the states should make any contribution, some grants being made outright. Some are for specified periods of limited duration, while others presumably continue indefinitely. The types of formula employed (in addition to the matching grant) include lump-sum, uniform, variable, and open-end, which forms may be employed simultaneously in varying combinations. Lump-sum grants are usually outright grants. Under the uniform grants, each state receives the same amount.

The variable grant fixes the amount that each state receives by a factor or combination of factors such as general population or population of a particular type, area and mileage, need and fiscal ability, cost of service, administrative discretion, and special needs. In the open-end grant Congress makes no appropriation in advance; the amount is determined later when, as in the case of public assistance grants, the actual costs of administration have been determined. The result of this system, regardless of the method of allocation used, has been gently to coerce the states into making expenditures which they might not have made otherwise or into increasing the amount of their expenditures for the purposes specified in the act. In spite of vigorous criticism of this policy in some quarters and a certain amount of resentment on the part of some of the states, it has been steadily extended over the years, and particularly since 1912, with regard to both the amount of the expenditures and the number of purposes to which the money has been applied.

The total amounts expended increased from $6,000,000 in 1912 to $215,000,000 a year at the close of the Hoover administration. During the depression years they increased rapidly in response to needs for unemployment relief and public works. The social security program was set up in this way, but in spite of these considerable increases the total still constituted less than 10 per cent of the national budget. The amount expended in 1930 was $134,802,944; in 1935 it was $343,030,546; while in 1940 it rose to $582,519,-319 for twenty-one different purposes. The amount had increased to $676,-089,112 by 1945 and to a total of approximately $2,000,000,000 in 1950, expended in connection with fifty-seven different programs, of which social security, highways, and agriculture, in that order, received the largest allocations. The result of this policy has been in practically every case to diminish the power of the states and to extend the policy-determining power of the Federal government to a large number of subjects formerly thought to be exclusively within the power and control of the state governments.[18]

[18] Grants-in-aid literature continues to grow; in addition to the titles cited in Chapter 2, and in previous editions of this volume, see: Council of State Governments, *Federal Aid to the States* (Chicago, 1949), and in particular fields: Bray, Ruth, *Federal Grants-in-Aid in Health-Education-Social Security: Selected References, 1938–1948* (Federal Security

There has never been any centralized responsibility for the administration of Federal grants, some eight or ten different departments and agencies sharing therein. The number and the agencies vary with changes in the Federal administrative structure, many of which have occurred as a result of action taken on Hoover Commission recommendations beginning in 1949. A list of the major programs, classified according to the Federal department or agency responsible for their administration, is shown in the table on this page. A

Major Federal Grant Programs and Their Administration

FEDERAL SECURITY AGENCY

Social Security Administration:
- Old Age Assistance
- Aid to Dependent Children
- Aid to the Blind
- Aid to the Permanently and Totally Disabled
- Unemployment Compensation

Public Health Service:
- Venereal Disease Control
- Tuberculosis Control
- General Health Service
- Hospital Survey and Construction
- Mental Health Activities

Children's Bureau:
- Maternal and Child Health Service
- Services for Crippled Children
- Child Welfare Services

Office of Education:
- Colleges for Agriculture and Mechanic Arts
- Cooperative Vocational Education

Other Agencies and Programs:
- Office of Vocational Rehabilitation
- American Printing House for the Blind
- Public Employment Offices

DEPARTMENT OF AGRICULTURE
- Agricultural Experiment Stations
- Agricultural Extension Work
- School Milk and Lunch Program
- Forest Program
- Marketing and Marketing Research

DEPARTMENT OF COMMERCE
- Highway Construction
- Airport Program
- State Maritime Schools

DEPARTMENT OF THE INTERIOR
- Wildlife Restoration

VETERANS ADMINISTRATION
- State and Territorial Homes for Disabled Soldiers and Sailors

FEDERAL PUBLIC HOUSING AUTHORITY
- Housing and Home Finance Agency annual contributions

glance at this list will convince one that, while the objectives of these programs have all been highly commendable, most of them relate to subjects that have always been regarded as within the scope of state activity, into which they have made great inroads.

Agency, Washington, 1948); National Education Association, *One Hundred and Sixty Years of Federal Aid to Education* and *The Facts on Federal Aid for Schools* (Washington, 1946 and 1948); Quattlebaum, Charles A., *Federal Aid to Elementary and Secondary Education* (Public Affairs Bulletin, Legislative Reference Service, Library of Congress, 1948); Mountin, Joseph W., and others, *Ten Years of Federal Grants-in-Aid for Public Health, 1936–1946* (Public Health Bulletin, Federal Security Agency, Washington, n.d.); and American Association of State Highway Officials, *The History and Accomplishment of Twenty-five Years of Federal Aid for Highways* (Washington, 1945), giving an examination of policies from state and national viewpoints.

Through Executive Influence. In the executive departments the prestige if not the power of the Federal government has been enhanced at the expense of the states through the leadership and initiative of its administrative agencies. This has happened in one field after another; sometimes the Federal agencies have had their hand strengthened by subsidy legislation, and sometimes not. In the collection of crop estimates and market statistics the United States Department of Agriculture took the lead in inducing the state departments to render a more efficient service and to secure uniform reports. The Office of Agricultural Experiment Stations in similar manner cooperates with the experiment stations in the several states. The Bureau of Public Roads supervises the layout of roads under subsidy appropriations and has cooperated with the National Highway Users Conference and the American Association of State Highway Officials for the purpose of securing a uniform traffic code, uniform numbering of important highways, and uniform highway markings. The Food and Drug Administration has taken the initiative in calling sectional and regional conferences of food and drug administrators, as well as national and state conferences for the purpose of securing cooperation and, where possible, a uniform handling of common administrative problems.

Illustrations of this type might be continued almost indefinitely. The United States Public Health Service assumed the initiative in organizing the Conference of State and Territorial Health Officers and, largely through the Surgeon General of the United States, it has retained the leadership and control of this organization. The Bureau of the Census has worked for the development of the Federal Registration Service, through cooperation with the states, until it achieved a uniform system for the reporting of vital statistics that is nationwide. The United States Department of Labor had a powerful influence in the organization and development of what is now the Association of Government Officials in Industry. It has cooperated with the state officials for the improvement of labor legislation, and with the aid of the subsidy it has worked with them for the improvement of the system of public employment offices. It has developed informal cooperative arrangements with state administrative agencies on a highly successful basis, in the handling of a number of problems in areas where no grants-in-aid were available. For example, in the enforcement of the Walsh-Healey Public Contracts Act of 1936 plans of informal cooperation for enforcing safety and health standards in plants covered by contracts coming under the provisions of this Act have been signed by officials of the Bureau of Labor Standards and the corresponding state officials.

The needs for coordinating this work are recited in the agreements as follows: (1) reduce duplication of activities and inspections; (2) secure compliance with the safety and health provisions of both Federal and state laws; (3) reduce lost time in contract plants caused by industrial accidents and injuries; and (4) utilize to the fullest extent available trained safety and health inspection personnel. Other sections of the agreement outline the safety and health provisions of the Walsh-Healey Act, make provision for the utilization of state staff to make Federal safety and health inspections within the state, and the procedures to be observed by the cooperating agencies. The greatest difficulty experienced by this and other departments in carrying out such agreements arises from the rotation of personnel in states still ridden by the spoils system.

Cooperative and concerted action between the Interstate Commerce Commission and the state railroad commissions in the regulation of railroads and other public utilities has been advocated at every convention of the National Association of Railroad and Utility Commissioners since that Association was organized in 1889. Judge Thomas M. Cooley, first chairman of the Interstate Commerce Commission and first president of the Association, at the initial meeting urged that "it is of the highest importance that there should be harmony in the legislation of control, so that the system . . . . as nearly as local conditions" will permit, may operate harmoniously as a unit.[19]

It is clear that of late a large number of Federal departments have been attempting to exert a more positive influence on the course of legislation in the states; an investigator, however, is confronted by a curious situation. With rare exceptions Federal agencies will vigorously deny any attempt to influence state legislation. A few agencies, however, frankly point out that the very nature of the subsidy system has made it necessary for them from time to time to call the attention of state authorities to conditions in the Federal law. For instance, the Chief of the Bureau of Public Roads explained:

> In several instances it has been necessary to direct the attention of State legislatures to provisions of the Federal act requiring the enactment of concurrent or complying State legislation. One example is the provision of the Federal Highway Act requiring: "That before any project shall be approved by the Secretary of Agriculture for any State such State shall make provisions for State funds required each year of such States by this act for construction and maintenance of Federal-aid highways within the State, which funds shall be under the direct control of the State Highway Department."
>
> It was necessary to draw attention to this provision in several States in which under existing laws the funds provided for construction and maintenance of Federal-aid highways were obtained from county and other local sources and were not "under the direct control of the State Highway Department."[20]

In cases of this sort the procedure seems to be quite simple. The Federal agency sees something which needs to be done and which only a few states are doing well. The appeal is made to Congress for aid through a subsidy. Having secured the law and being anxious to get the work done, the agency

[19] McChord, C. C., *Twentieth Report*, National Association of Railroad and Utility Commissioners, p. 10. See also Baum, Robert D., *The Federal Power Commission and State Utility Regulation* (American Council of Public Affairs, Washington, 1942) and Fesler, James W., *The Independence of State Regulatory Agencies* (Public Administration Service, Chicago, 1942).

[20] Letter from the Chief of the Bureau of Public Roads, August 10, 1934.

then faces the task of getting the states to qualify under the terms of the act. No one will deny that the objectives of these Federal agencies have been laudable and that, in the main, they have worked for the enactment of laws of a desirable type. Even so, some questions important to the student of government arise.[21]

Through Judicial Influence. The influence of the Federal courts in the gradual expansion of Federal power has long been recognized. In an excellent article on this subject Professor Oliver P. Field makes the following observations:

> The Supreme Court of the United States has been as impartial an umpire in national-state disputes as one of the members of two contending teams could be expected to be. This is not to impugn the wisdom or the fairness of the Supreme Court, but it is to say that the Supreme Court has been partial to the national government during the past one hundred and forty-four years of our experience with a federal system in the United States. The states, as members of the federal system, have had to play against the umpire as well as against the national government itself. The combination has long been too much for them.[22]

After pointing out the fact that the distribution of powers between the Federal government and the states has in fact been greatly modified, compared with the original provisions of the Constitution and the intentions of the Fathers, he continues:

> This increase in Federal power, and this place of dominance of the national government in the Federal system, has been aided by the Supreme Court. For the time being, such changes do not necessarily mean that the states lose power, although they have already lost position, so far as the Federal system is concerned.

Somewhat facetiously, perhaps, he suggests that the rule on express, implied, and delegated powers might be restated in some such form as the following: "The national government has all those powers of government not specifically denied it. In case of doubt, the national government shall be deemed to have the power. In case of conflict between national and state power, the national government shall be deemed superior. In case of war or emergency, these rules apply particularly, but in case of doubt a state of emergency shall be deemed to exist."

This attitude on the part of the Court toward the states has been illustrated in numerous ways and with regard to numerous subjects. In Texas v. White [23] the Court accepted the results of the Civil War, taking the constitutionally logical position that the Southern states had never been out of the

[21] For a fuller discussion of these questions, see Graves, W. Brooke, "Stroke Oar," *State Government*, December 1934, pp. 259–262; "Federal Leadership in State Legislation," *Temple Law Quarterly*, July 1936, pp. 385–405; and "Influence of Congressional Legislation on Legislation in the States," *Iowa Law Review*, May 1938, pp. 519–538; also Key, V. O., Jr., "State Legislation Facilitative of Federal Action," *Annals*, January 1940, pp. 7–13.

[22] Field, Oliver P., "States versus Nation, and the Supreme Court," *American Political Science Review*, April 1934, pp. 233–245.

[23] 7 Wallace 700, 1868.

Union, and that, in future, states once in could not leave the Union unless by a general dissolution. The Federal government may bring actions against the states in the Supreme Court, but the states may not sue the Federal government without its consent. This distinction appears to rest "upon the assumption that the national government is sovereign and therefore not subject to suit, while the states are assumed not to be sovereign, and therefore are subject to the indignity of being made parties defendant in the Supreme Court." Again, the states as such may not challenge the actions of the Federal government, having to rely rather upon suits instituted by individual citizens whose interests are injured by such actions. This attitude has been further illustrated by the manner in which the Court has handled various questions in the fields of taxation, control over commerce, questions involving the health, safety, and welfare of citizens, and the like. It is significant also that this attitude is not new — it was first expressed by the Court as early as 1793 in Chisholm v. Georgia,[24] in which it was held that suit might be brought against the states in the Federal courts. The fact that the effect of this decision was overcome by the provisions of Amendment XI does not in any way diminish the importance of the case as an indicator of the attitude of the Court toward the states. An examination of the cases in the intervening years indicates clearly that the general attitude of the Court has not greatly changed.

Through Constitutional Amendment. Another influence toward the expansion of Federal power is the transfer of power from the states to the Federal government by the amendment of the Federal Constitution. Amendments XV and XIX imposed certain limitations upon the powers of the states with respect to the suffrage. The income tax amendment gave the Federal government a new source of revenue; it was supposed at the time that the states gave up their claim to this type of tax, but later developments indicate that they have not done so. Amendment XVIII, while it was in effect, greatly extended the powers of the Federal government with regard to control over the manufacture and sale of intoxicating liquors — a subject always supposed to fall within the police powers of the states. The amendment to prohibit child labor, if it had been ratified, would have represented a similar invasion of the rights of the states as previously interpreted. Most important of all, the powers of the states have been definitely limited, and those of the Federal government frequently indirectly enlarged, through the interpretation which has been given to the due process and equal protection clauses of Amendment XIV. These are discussed at some length in a later chapter.

Through Exercise of the Treaty Power. The treaty power of the United States "extends to all proper subjects of negotiation between this Government and those of other nations, and to protecting the ownership, transfer, and inheritance of property which citizens of one country may have in another. It is unlimited under the Constitution, except as to restraints found in that in-

[24] 2 Dallas 419, 1793.

strument," and those which arise from the nature of the federal system.[25] It occasionally happens, however, that the Federal government negotiates and ratifies treaties with regard to subjects that are proper in themselves but which, under the American system of allocation of powers, are commonly regarded as state powers. An illustration is that of the Migratory Bird Treaty between the United States and Great Britain, certain questions with regard to which were considered by the Supreme Court in Missouri v. Holland.[26] Under the terms of this treaty Congress passed the Act of July 3, 1918, which prohibited the destruction of migratory birds passing between the United States and Canada. The act authorized the Secretary of Agriculture to execute the law and to make the necessary regulations. The Missouri authorities objected to the activities of one Holland, United States Game Warden, who was proceeding under the terms of the treaty, the act of Congress, and the regulations of the Secretary of Agriculture. The state contended that the Federal act was unconstitutional, since the control of wild game was a subject reserved to the states or to the people under the terms of Amendment X. Mr. Justice Holmes, at the conclusion of an opinion upholding the act and emphasizing the fact that the Federal power to make treaties was broader and covered a wider range of subjects than the lawmaking power, used the following significant language:

> Here a national interest of very nearly the first magnitude is involved. It can be protected only by national action in concert with that of another power. The subject-matter is only transitory within the State and has no permanent habitat therein. But for the treaty and the statute there soon might be no birds for any powers to deal with. We see nothing in the Constitution that compels the Government to sit by while a food supply is cut off and the protectors of our forests and our crops are destroyed. It is not sufficient to rely upon the States. The reliance is vain, and were it otherwise, the question is whether the United States is forbidden to act. We are of opinion that the treaty and statute must be upheld.

Constitutional Limitations on State Power

The Federal Constitution in various ways imposes restrictions and limitations upon the powers of the states; the latter are diminished to the extent that powers are granted to the Federal government. These powers include the various types listed in Article I, Section 8, as well as certain others noted in other parts of the Constitution. The states may not make treaties or alliances with foreign nations, nor even formal agreements in the form of compacts among themselves, unless sanctioned by Congress. They may not keep troops or ships of war in time of peace, nor unless confronted by an imminent danger. The Federal government is given power to collect taxes, duties, imposts, and excises. The states may regulate and control intrastate commerce; but when such control in any way interferes with the control of Congress

[25] *Constitution*, p. 391.
[26] 252 U.S. 416, 1920, and United States v. Oregon, 295 U.S. 1, 1935.

over interstate commerce, they are likely to find that they have exceeded the bounds of their authority. So one might continue through all the clauses of the Constitution conferring power upon the Federal government, showing in turn how each indirectly imposes limitations upon the powers of the states.

Further limitations are to be found in the list of prohibitions in Article I, Section 10. No state, for instance, may make or enforce any law impairing the obligation of contract. If the states had not found ways of evading the declared intentions of the Court as expressed in Dartmouth College v. Woodward,[27] they would have been unable to control the corporate bodies which they had created. By constitutional provisions prohibiting the granting of unconditional charters and in other ways the states have succeeded in protecting themselves in spite of the decision. Other limitations forbid the states to issue letters of marque and reprisal (also prohibited to the Federal government); to coin money and emit bills of credit (which the states succeeded in evading through the operations of state banks, prior to the decision in Veazie Bank v. Fenno);[28] to make anything but gold or silver coin a legal tender in the payment of debts; and to pass any bill of attainder or ex post facto law, or confer any title of nobility. These latter prohibitions are also applied to the Federal government.[29]

Other restrictions prohibit the states from levying any imposts, or duties upon imports and exports, except such as may be necessary for the execution of their inspection laws, without the consent of Congress. At the time the Constitution was adopted this provision was urgently required in order to prevent the recurrence of the trade barriers which had so hampered the commercial and economic development of the colonies. States like New Jersey and North Carolina, with no ports of their own, were entirely at the mercy of their neighbors who imposed high duties on exports. It was also provided that no state should, without the consent of Congress, lay any duty on tonnage.

In still another field the powers of the states are restricted by grants of power to the central government. In Article I, Section 8, Clause 17, and in Article IV, Section 3, Paragraph 2, Congress is given broad powers over "the territories and other property belonging to the United States." As a result of these provisions no one of the forty-eight states has jurisdiction over

[27] 4 Wheaton 518, 1819.

[28] 8 Wallace 533, 1869.

[29] Letters of marque and reprisal and bills of attainder are no longer important. The first was an authorization to private parties to conduct private warfare against a public enemy; the second was a legislative act declaring an individual to be guilty of a crime and prescribing his punishment, all in the same act and without opportunity on his part to be heard or to offer testimony in his own defense. An ex post facto law may still be a matter of practical and vital importance; such an act is one which, in the field of the criminal law, applies retroactively, with the effect of making criminal an act which was innocent at the time it was committed, which increases the penalty imposed, which removes defenses permissible at the time the act was committed, or which in some other way operates to the disadvantage of the accused, as compared with his position at the time the act was committed.

all of the territory within its borders. Each has surrendered to the Federal government some territory over which it once exercised its general governmental power. There are, in fact, a few states which never possessed this power over all the territory within their borders. "In each of the states are enclaves, some small, some very large, over which the Federal government has a power fully as broad as that of the state, and to the exclusion of the latter." [30]

Still other limitations are, in various ways, either implied or inferred. When, for instance, the Constitution guarantees to each state a republican form of government, "it necessarily follows that every other form of government is prohibited." Although it is not expressly prohibited by the Constitution, the Supreme Court long held that for the states to impose taxes upon the officers, agencies, or instrumentalities of the Federal government was inherently opposed to the nature of the Federal system. After the Civil War the Supreme Court gave its approval to the doctrine of the constitutional impossibility of secession from the Union. Some of these restrictions are designed to prevent state encroachment on Federal authority, while certain others are intended to restrict the states for the purpose of protecting the civil liberties of the individual.

To the original meager list of restrictions upon the states for the purpose of protecting these civil rights — the passage of bills of attainder, ex post facto laws, and laws impairing the obligations of contract — the War Amendments made important additions; these are discussed at some length in later chapters, but the general nature of their contents may be noted here. The prohibition of slavery and involuntary servitude, contained in Amendment XIII, applies to the states as well as to the Federal government and individuals. Amendment XIV attempts to guarantee the privileges and immunities of citizens as well as their right to due process of law and the equal protection of the laws. A second section of this amendment, which has never been enforced, attempted to guarantee to the newly created group of Negro citizens the right to vote. This effort to prevent discrimination, so far as race, color, and previous condition of servitude were concerned, was continued in Amendment XV; so far as sex was concerned, it was continued much later in Amendment XIX.

Confusion sometimes arises when the states attempt to exercise power over matters granted to the Federal government but concerning which the Federal government has not acted. In general, it is assumed that the states may act in a given area unless or until the Federal government acts. Thus

[30] Colorado State Planning Commission, *Public Land Ownership in Colorado* (Denver, 1944); Ferina, Elizabeth, and Staniford, Edward F., *Federally Owned Property in California* (Bureau of Public Administration, University of California, 1949); Michigan State Planning Board, *State and Federal Lands in Michigan* (Lansing, 1943); Nichols, Ralph R., and King, Morton B., Jr., *Social Effects of Government Land Purchase* (Agricultural Experiment Station, Mississippi State College, 1943); and Flowers, J. N., "The Purchase by the Federal Government of Lands within the States," *Mississippi Law Journal*, March 1945, pp. 20–29.

while the power to regulate interstate and foreign commerce is unquestionably a Federal power, the Court held, before Congress assumed control of the matter, that the states and even cities might impose reasonable regulations designed to promote the public safety.[31] In many cases the states may act after the Federal government has acted, provided that the action taken by them is supplementary to or at least not in conflict with that taken by the Federal government. The regulation of the sale of food and drugs represents such an area.

Occasionally, however, it is assumed that when no action is taken by the Congress under a particular grant of power, the very failure to take action is to be construed as indicating a desire on the part of the Congress that no action be taken. The same decision has been made when Congress has acted and when the administrative department has refrained from taking the action contemplated by Congress. By following such a policy, it is possible to create governmental voids — areas in which the Federal government does not act and in which it will not permit the states to act, even though it would appear that somebody ought to do something.

Admission of New States

On the basis of the fact that nearly three fourths of the states came into the Union by the process of admission, it has commonly been assumed that Congress has the power to deny statehood to any territory seeking admission to the Union; and apparently it may compel a territory to become a state even though the people thereof prefer to retain the territorial status. The original thirteen states were the charter members of the Federal Union; the other thirty-five have come into the Union since the date of its establishment, through a process now to be described. Many years ago Mr. Justice Lamar said that while the states were in 1789 in a very real sense the creators of the Federal government, by 1861 or later the Federal government had created most of the states.

Admission Procedure. There has been little uniformity through the years regarding the requirements as to size or population essential to a territory in order to qualify for admission as a state. The process of admission has begun in a formally organized territory when its inhabitants have become impatient at a further continuance of their territorial status. Under such circumstances the territorial legislature has addressed a petition to Congress, requesting authority to hold an election of delegates to a constitutional convention and to submit the work of such convention to the citizens of the territory. In the instances in which Congress has considered such petitions favorably, the result has been the passage of an enabling act authorizing the voters to call a convention and to apply for admission. These enabling acts have sometimes specified that certain things should be included in the constitution;

[31] Cooley v. Port Wardens of Philadelphia, 12 Howard 299, 1824.

in Utah, for instance, it was required that polygamy should forever be prohibited.[32]

Thus authorized by Congress, the residents of the territory may proceed, upon proper notice, to elect the delegates to the convention. This body meets in due time and drafts a constitution which includes any conditions that may have been prescribed by Congress. If the constitution so framed is satisfactory to the electorate of the territory, it is then submitted to Congress with the plea that it be accepted and that the state be formally admitted as a member of the Union. This Congress does by the passage of a resolution.

New problems were presented in the years following World War II as both Alaska and Hawaii pressed their claims for statehood. Although Hawaii had a larger population than any other territory except Oklahoma at the time of admission, and although it met every other test previously imposed, it raised new and difficult questions, chiefly because of its overseas location. It has had a much longer period in territorial status than most other territories, and the question of its admission as a state has been before the Congress no less than sixteen different times since 1903. Numerous committees of both Houses have held hearings and made on-the-spot investigations. Almost without exception, favorable reports have been presented.

After meeting with so many disappointments when favorable action by the Congress seemed almost assured, citizens of the Territory in 1950 elected delegates to a constitutional convention which drafted a state constitution for submission to the electorate in November of that year.[33] It was pointed out at the time that an enabling act was not an indispensable prerequisite to the holding of a convention and that fifteen states had entered the Union without the aid of enabling acts.[34] Two states as early as 1791 and two others as recently as 1890 acquired statehood through Congressional acts of admission, after drafting constitutions in the absence of enabling acts.[35] It was hoped that if Congress was still unwilling to approve the statehood bill, it might be possible to achieve statehood by obtaining Congressional approval of the new constitution. While most of the controversy in the postwar years centered on Hawaii, there was considerable discussion of the Alaskan problem as well. It was generally assumed that when one was admitted as a state, the other would be also.[36]

[32] This irrevocable ordinance is found in Article III; compare the compacts with the United States in the constitutions of New Mexico (Article XXI) and North Dakota (Article XVI).

[33] For complete text, see Senate Report No. 1928, Part 2 (81st Congress, 2nd Session, 1950); for analytical comment, Roberts, Harold S., "Sound Prelude to Statehood," *National Municipal Review*, September 1950, pp. 377–382.

[34] These are: Arkansas, California, Florida, Idaho, Iowa, Kansas, Kentucky, Maine, Michigan, Oregon, Tennessee, Texas, Vermont, West Virginia, Wyoming.

[35] In the first group, Kentucky and Vermont; in the second, Idaho and Wyoming; see Hawaii Legislative Reference Bureau, *Procedures Followed by States Admitted into the Union Without Congressional Enabling Acts* (Mimeographed Memorandum, February 15, 1949).

[36] On the general problem, see: Huddle, Frank P., "Admission of New States," *Editorial Research Reports*, March 20, 1946, entire issue, and Lerche, Charles O., Jr., "The

Enforcement of Conditions of Admission. A number of questions regarding the power of Congress to impose conditions upon a state at the time of its admission have arisen and have been decided by the courts. For example, when Oklahoma was admitted to the Union in 1907, Congress specified that the state capital should not be removed from Guthrie before 1913. The purpose of this provision was to prevent the recurrence in Oklahoma of a practice common in a number of the western states — namely, the moving of the capital as an aid to land speculation. In 1910 the capital was removed from Guthrie to Oklahoma City. This change was tested in the case of Coyle v. Smith,[37] in which the Court ruled that the condition imposed by Congress could not be enforced, since the matter which Congress sought to regulate was one of internal and domestic concern. Arizona and New Mexico were admitted in 1912; in the constitution of the former as drafted and submitted to Congress were provisions for the initiative, referendum, and recall. Congress passed a resolution admitting these states, but this was vetoed by President Taft in a vigorous message presenting in classic form the arguments against the recall as applied to the judiciary. The objectionable clauses were removed by the Territory, only to be reinstated after the condition of statehood had been achieved. On the basis of the doctrine in the Oklahoma case it would have been useless to contest the state's right to make such reinstatement.

If this rule had not been adopted, it would have been possible for Congress to expand its power tremendously, in a manner and to an extent never intended by the Constitutional Fathers. The adoption of any other policy would, in addition, have resulted in the creation of different classes of states, or at least of states having different degrees of control over their own problems. It is obvious that this would have resulted in a lack of uniformity with regard to the powers of the states, as well as in the creation of other undesirable conditions. As one writer has observed,[38] this decision does not mean "that the states are free to do whatever they wish, once inside the Union, but holds that one state may do whatever the other states may do, politically, despite bargains to the contrary with Congress in connection with admission. This still leaves the states subject to all of the restrictions which rested upon the original thirteen which formed the Union, in addition to such other restrictions as have been imposed on them since." In the later case of United States v. Sandoval [39] the Court was obliged to deal again with the same funda-

---

Guarantee of a Republican Form of Government and the Admission of New States," *Journal of Politics*, August 1949, pp. 578–604. Also, on Hawaii: Tansill, William R., *Hawaii and Statehood* (Public Affairs Bulletin, Legislative Reference Service, Library of Congress, 1948), and on Alaska: Gruening, Ernest, "Why Alaska Needs Statehood," *State Government*, February 1948, pp. 31–33, 47, and Sundberg, George, "Statehood for Alaska," *ibid.*, January 1947, pp. 3–4.

[37] 221 U.S. 559, 1911.

[38] Field, *op. cit.*, p. 235.

[39] 231 U.S. 28, 1913.

mental problem. In this decision it was held that Congressional regulation in an enabling act which a state is required to accept as a condition of admission into the Union remains in force after such admission if, and only if, the subject is one within the regulatory power of Congress. It thus seems clear that the obligation imposed on the newly created state is an ethical or moral one, not enforceable at law after the territory has achieved the coveted position of statehood. The state ought to recognize the obligation and respect it, but if it ignores it there is not much that can be done about it.

Another phase of the question of the extent of the power which Congress may exercise over members of the Federal Union is illustrated by Ervien v. United States [40] — a case which might be considered with equal propriety under the heading of the subsidy system. While this is not a problem growing out of conditions of admission, it does involve matters of internal policy. New Mexico had been given a liberal grant of land by Congress, the proceeds from it to be used only for schools, highways, and other definitely specified purposes. The state accepted the grant and then proceeded to use 3 per cent of the annual income from this land for the purpose of advertising and publicizing the state, with the idea of attracting new settlers. The Court held that a property fund granted by Congress under a condition or with reservations was to be distinguished from the police power which a state possesses over its own affairs. The legal doctrine here is in harmony with a well-established principle of law; namely, that gifts, grants, and bequests may ordinarily be accepted and used only in accordance with the conditions accompanying them.

Similar judgments have been rendered in cases involving matters of a commercial character or a promise concerning tax exemptions.[41] Under the Homestead Act of 1863, Minnesota Territory sold tax-exempt homestead land for ten years. Then Minnesota was admitted into the Union as a state. Did she have the right to tax the land? In passing upon this question, the Supreme Court invoked the longstanding principle of international law that, when a government enters into agreement with private parties, the succeeding government is bound thereby. This same principle had been relied upon in the Dartmouth College Case. The point is that the equality of the states — important as that is — is not the only consideration involved in the determination of some of these cases.

Interesting constitutional questions with regard to the admission of new states developed in connection with the partition of Virginia and the admission of West Virginia in 1863. Aside from the somewhat irregular procedure by which this separation was effected during the troublous days of the Civil War, these questions were not peculiar to the Virginia–West Virginia situation; they had occurred in earlier instances and might easily occur again — if, for instance, Texas were to exercise the option contained in the resolution

[40] 251 U.S. 41, 1919.
[41] Stearns v. Minnesota, 179 Minn. 223, 1900.

of Congress for its annexation, that four more states might eventually be formed from it. Most important of these questions, perhaps, was the apportionment of the debt. For more than fifty years West Virginia failed to assume its equitable portion, quite in contrast to the arrangements with regard to this matter when Maine was separated from Massachusetts and admitted into the Union in 1820. Virginia was in fact forced "to resort to a long and painful litigation before the United States Supreme Court in order to overcome an obstructive attitude on the part of the younger commonwealth which at times verged upon defiance." Again, there was the question of the boundary. Since Virginia was not consulted on the terms of the separation and since the provisions of the Constitution on this point in Article IV, Section 3, were not complied with (although they are quite definite), the final arrangement was in some respects unfair to the older state. This also was quite in contrast to the Massachusetts-Maine separation. Questions of this character provide an interesting field for study in those states whose history provides incidents of somewhat parallel character.[42]

Relations of the States with Foreign Governments

The states are prohibited by a clause in Article I, Section 10 of the Federal Constitution from entering into treaties with foreign nations. They have had in the past and still have little occasion to conduct relations with such nations, yet as Ambassador Austin has pointed out, their power and influence in foreign affairs has always been greater than has been popularly supposed. Their influence arises mainly from two sources. They can and sometimes do seriously imperil the peaceful relations of the Federal government with foreign nations by their failure to cooperate in the enforcement of Federal treaty obligations. Their influence has of late increased greatly in new and unexpected ways as a result of obligations flowing from the establishment of a considerable number of agencies of world government.

The States and Federal Treaty Obligations. Significant instances of Federal embarrassment because of the failure of states to cooperate in the enforcement of treaty obligations include the numerous controversies with foreign governments over repudiated state debts, the Italian Mafia incident in Louisiana in 1891, the California School Case in 1906, and, most recently, the *Bremen* incident in New York in 1935.

The controversies over repudiated state debts grew out of extensive loans negotiated abroad for internal improvements in the period following the War of 1812 and out of loans made in the reconstruction period following the Civil War. As a result of these loans there were numerous state defaults in the forties and in the seventies and eighties; for almost a century those in the first group have been the subject of international controversy. They raise in

[42] These questions are discussed in Randall, James G., *Constitutional Problems under Lincoln*, Chapter 18 (Appleton, New York, 1926).

pointed fashion the question of the international responsibility of states (in the technical sense) for the acts of their political subdivisions — a basic question of international law which the United States was long able to evade. The question was squarely presented to the Supreme Court in 1934, when the Principality of Monaco brought suit against Mississippi on bonds issued by that state. The motion was denied by the Court in an opinion written by Chief Justice Hughes, holding that Article III, Section 2, Clause 1, of the Constitution gives the Supreme Court jurisdiction of such suits only in the event of the state's consent to be sued. Thus a state of the Union is immune from suits which are brought against it by a foreign state without its consent.[43]

The Italian Mafia incident grew out of the murder of the Chief of Police of New Orleans, John C. Hennessey. Investigation revealed the fact that certain Italian residents of the city, members of the Black Hand or Mafia Society, were guilty of the crime. These persons were arrested and confined in the parish jail. One morning prior to the date of their trial, one of the local papers announced that there would be a meeting of citizens on the plaza in front of the jail at four o'clock that afternoon. The crowd assembled, and after a series of harangues descended upon the jail, battered down the gates, went inside and seized five of the accused persons, carried them off, and lynched them. Since some of these persons were citizens of Italy, the Italian government protested. While the identity of the leaders of the mob was known, both the governor and the local authorities were in sympathy with the lynchers and refused to take any effective action looking toward their arrest and conviction. Secretary of State Blaine was placed in the painful and embarrassing position of having to explain to the Italian government that, reprehensible as the crime was and much as the Federal authorities regretted its occurrence, there was nothing they could do about it, since under our federal system it was a matter falling entirely within the authority of the state government. Even though the Secretary of State literally begged the state authorities to take action for the purpose of avoiding complications between the United States and Italy, they obdurately refused. Italy severed diplomatic relations and recalled its ambassador. For some time there was serious danger of war between the United States and Italy.[44]

In the California school case a controversy between the United States and Japan developed through the refusal of California to comply with certain treaty arrangements existing between Japan and the United States. In

[43] Monaco v. Mississippi, 292 U.S. 313, 1934. See McGrane, Reginald C., *Foreign Bondholders and American State Debts* (Macmillan, New York, 1935), and "Some Aspects of American State Debts in the Forties," *American Historical Review*, July 1933, pp. 673–686; also Ratchford, B. U., "An International Debt Settlement: the North Carolina Debt to France," *American Historical Review*, October 1934, pp. 63–69, and *American States Debts* (Duke University Press, 1941).

[44] This account is based upon a study of the State Papers made by the author some years ago; a fuller printed summary appears in Curtis, William E., *The United States and Foreign Powers*, Chapter 16 (Scribner's, New York, 1900).

these treaties the United States had agreed to accord to Japanese citizens equality of treatment. The San Francisco Board of Education passed, and attempted to enforce, a race segregation ordinance in its public schools. In this case also the Secretary of State, Elihu Root, was obliged to plead with the California officials for such a modification of the resolution as would enable the United States to live up to its treaty obligations and as would avoid a possible conflict with Japan.[45]

Even more embarrassing to the government of the United States was an incident which occurred in New York City in the summer and fall of 1935. The German liner *Bremen* arrived in New York harbor on July 26, flying the new flag of the Nazi government. A riot occurred, in the course of which the flag was hauled down and treated with disrespect. The German government filed a vigorous formal protest with the Department of State, and relations between the two governments became somewhat strained. In due course six prisoners charged with participation in the riot were brought for a hearing before Magistrate Louis B. Brodsky. Five of them he discharged, commenting, as he did so, upon the Nazi regime in language "offensive to another government with which we have official relations" — as Secretary of State Hull was to say shortly after in an official apology to the German government, whose protest at the words of the magistrate was even more vigorous than before. Three paragraphs from the statement of Secretary Hull to the Counselor of the German Embassy are worthy of quotation:

> The complaint of the German Government is specifically directed at the statements made by the magistrate in rendering his decision which that Government interprets as an unwarranted reflection upon it.
>
> The Department is constrained to feel that the magistrate, in restating contentions of the defendants in the case and in commenting upon the incident, unfortunately so worded his opinion as to give the reasonable and definite impression that he was going out of his way adversely to criticize the government, which criticism was not a relevant or legitimate part of his judicial decision.
>
> I may explain that State and municipal officials are not instrumentalities of the Federal Government. Although in this country the right of freedom of speech is well recognized by our fundamental law, it is to be regretted that an official having no responsibility for maintaining relations between the United States and other countries should, regardless of what he may personally think of the laws and policies of other governments, thus indulge in expressions offensive to another government with which we have official relations.

It is a serious weakness of our federal system that it should be possible for a state so to conduct its affairs as to involve the Federal government in diplomatic difficulties with other nations. The question has often been dis-

[45] See Root, Elihu, "The Real Question under the Japanese Treaty and the San Francisco School Board Resolution," *American Journal of International Law*, April 1907, pp. 274–283. For a valuable discussion of the background and the constitutional aspects of the race problem in California, see Swisher, Carl Brent, *Motivation and Political Technique in the California Constitutional Convention, 1878–1879*, Chapter 6 (Pomona College, Claremont, California, 1930).

cussed but no remedial measures have ever been adopted. Perhaps the most promising solution is one proposed by Attorney General Daugherty in 1922; his suggestion was that Congress should by law provide that all cases involving questions arising under the treaty obligations of the United States, regardless of the subject with which they dealt, should be taken immediately and automatically into the Federal courts for adjudication. This proposal has the merit of being simple and effective and of not requiring any modification of the Constitution; it should be adopted.

World Government and New Obligations. The states have, in the years since World War II, been confronted with a number of new and unusual problems. They were obliged, as a practical matter, to enact legislation to make the securities of the International Bank marketable. New York in 1946 authorized by law the investment of state funds in debentures of this bank. Meantime, the Council of State Governments prepared a model act for this purpose, submitting it to the states with recommendations for its adoption in the legislative sessions of 1947.

New York, within whose limits the headquarters of the United Nations have been established, has been faced with problems even more unusual. After the offer of John D. Rockefeller, Jr., to donate land in New York City as a United Nations site, there still remained the necessity of conferring upon the United Nations by law, limited territorial sovereignty over its headquarters and diplomatic immunity for its representatives. The Joint Legislative Committee on Affairs of United Nations took the position that the Federal government could not, without the consent of New York, cede to any international organization sovereign rights over any territory within the State of New York, and only such sovereign rights should be ceded as were necessary to effectuate the purposes of the United Nations and as were consistent with the moral, political, and economic welfare of the people of the state.[46] The New York Attorney General ruled in 1948 that immunity from arrest and conviction for crimes and traffic infractions within the state must be accorded members of delegations to the United Nations because they are listed by the State Department as entitled to diplomatic privileges and immunities in the United States.

Still another important question affects all the states. Do the provisions of the United Nations Charter, to which the United States subscribes, take precedence over state laws when provisions of the two are inconsistent or in conflict? At the time of writing, this question seems still undetermined. On April 24, 1950, the California Court of Appeals, in Fujii v. California, ruled that the United Nations Charter was, as a treaty duly ratified by the United States Senate in 1945, the supreme law of the land, superseding state laws that conflicted with its provisions. Taking quite a different view, Professor Manley O. Hudson contended that, while treaties are under the Constitution the

[46] *Report* (Legislative Document No. 66, Albany, 1949).

supreme law of the land, the only features of treaties that are automatically incorporated into American law are the "self-executing" provisions that do not require legislative implementation.[47]

SELECTED REFERENCES

Bitterman, Henry J., *State and Federal Grants-in-Aid* (Mentzer, Bush, Chicago, 1938). A good general treatise.

Clark, Jane Perry, *The Rise of a New Federalism* (Columbia University Press, 1938). An excellent pioneer study of Federal-state relationships with special reference to social security.

Council of State Governments, *Federal Aid to the States* (Chicago, 1949). Best and most recent study of the growth and development, and the significance of the grant-in-aid system.

Graves, W. Brooke, Ed., "Intergovernmental Relations in the United States," *Annals*, January, 1940, entire issue. Twenty-five authors contribute to a comprehensive survey of the whole field.

Key, Vladimer O., Jr., *The Administration of Federal Grants to States* (Public Administration Service, Chicago, 1937). Best treatment of the administrative aspects of the subject.

McLaughlin, Andrew C., *Confederation and Constitution* (Harpers, New York, 1905). Standard treatise on constitutional aspects of the problem during the formative period.

Maxwell, James A., *The Fiscal Impact of Federalism in the United States* (Harvard University Press, 1946). Covers extensively the financial aspects of the grant-in-aid program.

Mitchell, Nicholas P., *State Interests in American Treaties* (Garrett & Massie, Richmond, 1936). Significant study of the relation of the states to American foreign affairs.

Quattlebaum, Charles A., *Federal Aid to Elementary and Secondary Education* (Legislative Reference Service, Library of Congress, 1948, and Public Administration Service, Chicago, 1948). Analysis of the financial impact of federalism, as related to a particular governmental function.

Swisher, Carl B., *American Constitutional Development* (Houghton Mifflin, Boston, 1943). Standard treatise on American constitutional history including discussion of many problems considered in this chapter.

Thompson, Walter, *Federal Centralization* (Harcourt, Brace, New York, 1923). An excellent early study of the trend toward centralization; for a later one, see Benson, George C. S., *The New Centralization* (Farrar & Rinehart, New York, 1941).

Wendell, Mitchell, *Relations Between the Federal and State Courts* (Columbia University Press, 1949). Considers the problem of dual jurisdiction, and the proper method of dividing jurisdiction between the Federal and state courts.

[47] See *New York Times*, May 14, 1950, and Hudson, Manley O., *Charter Provisions of Human Rights in American Law*, a memorandum supplied in advance of publication to Fred N. Howser, Attorney General of California.

2

State Constitutions

History and Characteristics

Article VI of the Federal Constitution provides that this Constitution shall be "the supreme law of the land." The states are bound by the provisions of this document, but at the same time each of them has an instrument of government of its own. These state constitutions serve as the fundamental law of the states in somewhat the same manner in which the Federal Constitution serves as the fundamental law of the Federal government, or the municipal charter as the fundamental law of a municipality. It is important, therefore, that one be familiar with the characteristics of the original state constitutions, with their development, with the essential elements of the present state constitutions, and with recent tendencies in constitution making.

Background of the Original Constitutions. A study of the origins of the American state constitutions carries one back into the history of the Middle Ages; these constitutions are in reality the oldest instruments of government on this continent. The trading companies of the Middle Ages were obliged eventually to establish trading posts, for they discovered that it was too difficult for the operators of their vessels to sell the cargoes which they brought with them and buy up a new cargo of goods to take back to their native land. In the effort to expedite the trading process, outposts were established at which the cargo was sold and a new cargo of native products collected. As these posts increased in size, questions arose as to the exercise of governmental authority. The companies exercised such authority as seemed necessary without much supervision. As the significance of the problem was recognized, the charters of trading companies were amended to include provisions regarding the government of such outposts as the company might establish.

Characteristics of the Original Constitutions. The ideas of government in the original state constitutions were very similar. They were all based upon the conception, then new, that all governmental powers were vested in and consequently derived from the people, and most of them contained expressed provisions to that effect. Eight of them contained a bill of rights, and all provided for three branches of government and severe restrictions on the exercise of the suffrage. Provision for amendment was made in eight constitutions but was omitted in five. An authority in the history of this period describes the original constitutions in the following terms:

> . . . In all there were the three departments, — the Executive, Legislative, and Judicial; and these were rendered independent of one another. In most of the States the executive was hampered by a council. In Pennsylvania and Georgia the legislature consisted of one branch; in the others of two branches, according to the custom of the colonial period. In four States the Governor was to be chosen by the people; in the others, by the legislature.
>
> These constitutions were said to be "ordained, declared, established," and were not to be altered except in the manner pointed out. Thus they assume to be modes of action different from ordinary acts of legislation. They were universally recognized and held to be such. They were really decrees of the people as constituting the sovereignty. They prescribed the degrees and spheres of power by which their agents or "trustees" periodically chosen to make or administer the laws were to be governed in their various departments. Their sphere is internal government. Their provisions give validity and continuity to the body of local law. In no instance is there power conferred on these local agents to deal with foreign nations. This function had been vested by the same sovereignty in a congress; and the constitutions contain provisions for the appointment of members to compose it.
>
> These governments went immediately into operation. Well-known characters were selected to fill the high offices. . . These names gave *éclat* to the new governments. This field of labor and honor proved more attractive than the national council; and the work of enfranchising the local law from features derived from European traditions — the abolition of entails, primogeniture, and an established church — worthily employed the time and thought of the most able statesmen. The spectacle of republican order was a novelty in the political world.[1]

Even a cursory examination of the early constitutions reveals that the legislative branch was preeminent in the minds of the people, who evidently considered it the depository of all democratic principles. In all but three states (Georgia, Pennsylvania, and Vermont) it consisted of two houses, the upper house usually designated as the Senate, the lower one then as now by a variety of names among which House of Representatives was most common. Members were elected annually, except in South Carolina, where the term was two years. In one state members of the upper house were chosen by the members in office at the time of the election. The term in the upper house was usually three or five years. Property qualifications for members of the upper house were high, and religious qualifications for governor and for members of the legislature were prescribed. In most of the states the executive powers were vested in a governor and executive council, although in Delaware, New Hampshire, and Pennsylvania the chief executive was called the President. In all but three states — Massachusetts, New Hampshire, and New York, where the executives were elected by the people — the governor was elected by the legislature. Because of the abiding faith which the people had in the

[1] Frothingham, Richard, *The Rise of the Republic of the United States*, pp. 567–568 (Little, Brown, Boston, 1899).

legislative branch, the powers of the governor were severely curtailed; Massachusetts was the only state to give him even a limited veto power. All through these original constitutions one finds the governor authorized to perform duties clearly executive in character only with the "advice and consent of the executive council."

The judiciary was not, as a rule, fully provided for in the original state constitutions, the completion of the court plan being left to the legislatures. These early state court systems were modeled very largely after the colonial judiciary which had long administered the statutory law of the colonies and the common law of England. In one important respect they differed from earlier practice; they were placed, not under either the executive or the legislative branch, but alongside them, upon a basis of complete equality. None of the constitutions conferred express authority upon the courts to declare acts of the legislature unconstitutional, but earlier precedents of long standing encouraged the courts to exercise this power when in their judgment a statute contravened the provisions of the state constitution. Georgia was the only state to elect its judges by popular vote. The term of judges was usually during good behavior. Their salary was fixed by the legislature, a provision which, under conditions then existing, made the judiciary lacking in independence and security.

Although the original constitutions were alike in their recognition of three distinct branches of government, the principle of the separation of powers was not always fully observed in practice. The framers believed that the check and balance system would prevent the concentration of power in the hands of any one officer or department of government. They were greatly worried lest such a concentration of power should lead to the establishment of a dictatorship or an oligarchy. Consequently, all of them conferred extensive powers upon the legislative branch, while limiting those of the executive. The courts were to serve as a check upon both the governor and the legislature. It is conceivable that this system of checks and balances, if used extensively enough, might undermine the separation of powers. This, however, the framers of these early constitutions avoided, resorting to the check and balance system only to such an extent as would in practice strengthen and protect the separation of powers. Both of these principles are still in evidence in the present-day constitutions, although many governmental practices have developed which make them much less effective than they were originally intended to be and although the confidence of students in their soundness has greatly diminished.

In accordance with these practices, developed over a period of many years, trading companies exercised governmental authority over colonies and trading posts established in America. Many of these charters continued in use with slight modification during the entire colonial period. When it became apparent that the struggle for independence would be a long one, the colonies realized that they must have a better organization. Before the Declaration of

Independence had actually been adopted, seven of the states had independent governments; four of them were contemplating changes. Massachusetts retained its provisional government until 1780, at which date it adopted a constitution which remained in effect — with many amendments — for more than 140 years. Upon the recommendation of Congress, all the colonies applied themselves to the task of establishing state governments. New Hampshire and South Carolina adopted such plans on January 5 and March 26, 1776, respectively; they proved defective and were soon replaced.

When the states acquired a status of independence, several of them continued to use their previously existing charters as instruments of government under the new regime. This was true of Connecticut and Rhode Island; a few changes were made with reference to the King and short bills of rights were added, but Connecticut did not adopt a new constitution until 1819, nor Rhode Island until 1842. The student of American constitutional development must be impressed by two significant facts in this general situation. In the first place, there was no sharp break in the development of our institutions before and after the achievement of independence. The original constitutions were, like most things governmental, a result of generations — and in some cases centuries — of human experience. They were, in fact, little more than the previous constitutions adapted to changed conditions. In the second place, it is significant that the state constitutions antedated the Constitution of the Federal government. Accustomed to acknowledging the debt of the states to the Federal government, one may forget that originally the situation was reversed — that the provisions of the Federal Constitution were based upon the experience of the states and the provisions of their constitutions in effect when the Federal Convention met.

Present-Day Constitutions. The general characteristics of the original state constitutions and of those now in effect can best be presented by a series of comparisons and contrasts, covering such points as length, content, and relations of executive and legislative branches. The basic principles remain much the same. The original constitutions were brief and concise; the modern ones are lengthy and verbose, being padded with great quantities of legislative material. The original constitutions were confined to the statement of fundamental principles, whereas present-day constitutions include great numbers of detailed provisions on an ever-increasing number of subjects. Many of them have been expanded until they would fill a moderate-sized volume if the same size type and format were used as in trade publications.

The California Constitution fills more than 150 printed pages; that of Oklahoma, 115 printed pages; that of Louisiana, 306 pages. What happened in this extreme form in a few states happened also to a lesser degree in many others. Maryland, for example, has a relatively short constitution, but the present Constitution of 1867 (forty-seven pages) is more than three times as long as the original Constitution of 1776 (fifteen pages). Its Constitution of

1851 had twenty-nine pages; that of 1864, thirty-eight pages. The growth in this and other states has been gradual, extending over the entire period of the history of the states.

This excessive length can be traced to the steadily diminishing confidence with which, over a period of many years, the people regarded their legislative bodies and to the increasing number and complexity of governmental functions. Innumerable restrictions limit the subject matter with which the legislature may deal, the number of its sessions, and the number of days the sessions may last. They impose restrictions upon corporations, and limitations upon the financial powers of both states and cities with regard to methods of raising money, tax limits, debt limits, and other matters.

Certain basic principles of government generally accepted by the framers of the original state constitutions have become firmly imbedded in the American political tradition. Among them are the bill of rights, the principle of the separation of powers, the check and balance system, the concept of the relation of the executive and legislative branches of the government, and the general distrust of popular control. Many of those who participated in the framing of the Federal Constitution had previously given similar service in their respective states; their adherence to the principle of the separation of powers, under the influence of the writing of the French political philosopher Montesquieu, was in evidence in the state conventions as well as in the Federal Convention. Their respect for and knowledge of English institutions prompted them to adopt what they believed to be an essential element in the success of the English system. Professor Becker wrote of the attitude of the colonists in general toward the mother country:

> It is this aspect of the Revolution that gives it its chief significance for modern democracy. The privileged classes in the Colonies, generally speaking, never really desired separation from Great Britain. They took old England as their ideal. Outside of New England most educated men were educated in England, and wished for nothing better than to fashion their clothes, their houses, their minds, and their manners on the best English models. They opposed parliamentary taxation because they wanted to manage their own affairs in miniature parliaments, where they could carry on miniature contests with the governors for control of the purse, after the manner of the English Parliament in the seventeenth century. In no sense were they democrats; and they were as much afraid of radical movements in the Colonies as they were of British oppression. They wanted to preserve their *liberties* against parliament, without sharing their *privileges* with the people in the Colonies. They wanted home rule, but they wanted to rule at home. Left to themselves, the governing classes in America would never have carried the contest to the point of rebellion, would never have created an independent state.[2]

It is in the relations of the executive and legislative branches of the government that the greatest contrasts are to be found between the original and present-day constitutions. The framers of the early constitutions had a pro-

[2] Becker, Carl, *The United States, An Experiment in Democracy*, pp. 45–46 (Harper, New York, 1920).

found distrust of the executive authority. When one recalls their experience during the years preceding the Revolution, this is not difficult to explain. The Royal Governors were the agents of the King and of Parliament in America. In their efforts to enforce the orders of the Crown and the acts of Parliament in America, these governors came to be a veritable personification of the idea of oppression. Whether the acts to which the colonists objected were in fact oppressive or whether the colonists merely believed that they were makes no difference — the psychological effect is the same in either case. In view of this experience it is not strange that the framers of these early constitutions sought by every means at their command to limit and restrict the powers of their governors. They were determined that these officials should no longer have the power to do wrong; the fact that the withholding of such power inevitably withheld from them the power to do things necessary and proper for the effective functioning of their government had not yet impressed itself upon them.

At the same time that the inhabitants of these newly established states were seeking to curb the exercise of executive power, they were conferring almost unlimited powers upon their legislative bodies. The historical background of this fact is likewise easy to discover.[3] Time and time again throughout the period preceding the Revolution, it had been the representative assemblies that had offered protest against the oppressive acts of the Crown, the Parliament, and the Royal Governors. On one occasion after another these bodies had drafted and adopted resolutions of protest, had organized committees of correspondence, and finally had organized and contributed to the financing of the troops in the Revolutionary War. It was therefore quite natural that the framers of the early constitutions should confer broad powers upon their legislative bodies. In doing so they did nothing different from what present-day Americans might be expected to do under similar circumstances.

In the course of the last century and a half, significant changes have occurred in the relative positions of the executive and legislative branches of the government. While the prestige of the executive has steadily increased, that of the legislature has constantly declined. This change has been due largely to the failure of the legislatures to respond to the trust imposed in them; their personnel included too many persons lacking either the intellectual and educational requirements or the integrity essential to the operation of government on an honest and effective basis. They failed so often to deal adequately with pressing problems that they gradually lost the confidence of

[3] Former Senator George Woodward had a very simple explanation: "We all know that it was Thomas Jefferson or someone of the Fathers who could read French who read M. Montesquieu's essay on three compartments in government. The Father thought it over in English and put it in all our constitutions. It is therefore customary for the legislative, executive and judicial compartments to abstain from one another's society and to try to misunderstand one another as far as possible. This promotes business in the art of government and adds zest to elections." *The Pennsylvania Legislator*, May 1935.

the public. Instances of fraud and dishonesty were not rare. As the prestige of the legislatures declined, the people were more and more disposed to regard the executive as their champion. This tendency has been accentuated since the inauguration of the movement for administrative reorganization — a movement which has tended to make governors of states, in fact as well as in name, the responsible heads of their respective state governments.

The early constitutions differ from modern ones also in their attitude toward popular participation in government. The Founding Fathers were exceedingly cautious in this respect. Their conception of democracy bore a striking resemblance to what might now be called "mobocracy." They did not believe in "government of the people, by the people, and for the people," preferring rather a government of the people by the best people. They took extreme care in their effort to protect the people from what they feared might be the results of their own folly. The election of many officials was placed on an indirect basis. In New Jersey, which may be taken as a typical example, nearly all the state officials were chosen by the Council and Assembly in joint meeting; they were commissioned by the governor after such election. A very small number of minor officials were elected by the direct vote of the people.[4]

In most states the suffrage was restricted to men who were members in good standing, contributing to the support of the predominant religious sect of the state in which they lived, and to those who owned property. Even the majority of white persons could not vote. South Carolina limited the suffrage to those who believed in God and a future state of rewards and punishments. Property qualifications were higher to vote for senator than to vote for a member of the lower house. Although religious freedom was granted, there was everywhere a close connection between Church and State. In contrast, modern state constitutions, free from religious and property qualifications for voting, provide for a suffrage that is almost universal.

Essential Elements of a State Constitution

A constitution is a body of *fundamental law*. It is established for the purpose of providing a set of governmental machinery, on the one hand, and of protecting citizens from an unfair or improper use of governmental authority, on the other. There are in all constitutions certain essential features which must be included if the constitution is to meet the needs which led to its adoption. These fundamentals may be grouped under four headings: the bill of rights, the framework of government, its powers, and provision for piecemeal amendment and/or revision.

[4] The list of the New Jersey officers indirectly chosen, together with their terms of office, follows: Judges and Clerks of the Supreme Court and of the Inferior Court of Common Pleas, and Justices of the Peace — all seven years; Attorney General and Provincial Secretary, both five years; Provincial Treasurer, one year; and field and general officers of the State Militia.

Bill of Rights. In the United States the people have become definitely attached to the idea of a written bill of rights incorporated in the body of a constitution. The idea of the bill of rights owes its origin to a period of political philosophy during which great stress was laid upon the doctrine of natural rights. Its purpose was then, and is now, to guarantee to the individual the enjoyment of certain rights and privileges against possible infringement by governmental authority. Eight of the Revolutionary constitutions had bills of rights, either as a preamble or as a postscript. The first bill of rights in America was drafted by George Mason, who presented it to the Virginia Constitutional Convention of 1776, by which it was adopted and from which the idea spread rapidly to the other states.

In general, it may be said that provisions of the bills of rights in the state constitutions run parallel to the provisions of the Bill of Rights of the Federal Constitution, and that they were designed to serve the same purpose of protecting the individual from infringement of his rights by the state governments. An analysis made for the Missouri Constitutional Convention of 1943 revealed that the several states consider in their bills of rights some eighty odd diverse rights and privileges which had been regarded as essential. The basic rights, upon which all agree, are as follows[5]:

BASIC RIGHTS

Political power inherent in the people
Due process of law
Right to assemble and petition
Freedom of speech
Right of privacy
No privileges or immunities
Safeguarding the rights of accused persons
Protection of private property
Bail, no excessive bail, no cruel punishment
Subordination of the military
Trial by jury — methods of indictment
Power to suspend laws; where placed
No ex post facto laws
Freedom of religion
No slavery
Recognition of rights other than positive rights
Enumeration of foregoing rights not intended to deny or disparage others retained by the people

While these basic rights, enumerated in the constitutions, are everywhere regarded as fundamental, they are subject to some modification with the passage of time. Rights which are vital to the people of one age may become

[5] Kies, Harry B., *Manual on the Bill of Rights and Suffrage and Elections,* p. 13 (Missouri Constitutional Convention of 1943, Jefferson City, 1943); see also Heckel, C. Willard, *The Bill of Rights* (Governor's Committee on Preparatory Research for the New Jersey Constitutional Convention, Trenton, 1947), and Owen, Kimbrough, *Constitutional Problems No. 5, Bill of Rights* (Constitution Revision Project, Louisiana State University, 1947).

either unimportant or so widely recognized that they are rarely if ever questioned in another. Similarly, new conditions give rise to the demand for the protection of new rights. Present-day Americans are little concerned with some of the older rights, but they are interested in the protection of such social and economic rights growing out of an industrial civilization as old age pensions, unemployment insurance, public assistance, elimination of child labor, maximum hours, minimum wages and conditions of labor, housing conditions, and programs of social and economic planning. Such questions have assumed an importance comparable to that of ancient rights won in the long struggle for human liberty.

The bill of rights protects both personal and property rights. With regard to personal rights, its provisions are of two types: those relating to the protection of individuals in the normal course of life, and those relating to the protection of persons accused of crime. Among the former are the ordinary personal and civil rights, the substantive rights, such as religious freedom, freedom of speech, freedom of assemblage, freedom of the press, and other rights once much more important than they are now: freedom from the quartering of troops in times of peace, freedom from unreasonable searches and seizures, the right to bear arms. Most of the rights accorded to persons accused of crime fall under the heading of procedural rights, involving due process of law — the right to indictment by grand jury, to trial where the offense was committed, to trial by jury, to a speedy and public trial; freedom from the necessity for self-incrimination and from double jeopardy, from excessive bails and fines, and from cruel and unusual punishments. In addition to all these, there are miscellaneous safeguards of accused persons, which vary according to the jurisdiction in which the offense is being tried.

In connection with the protection of property, the clauses with regard to due process and eminent domain are most important. Although the due process clause in Amendment XIV applies only to the states, the majority of the state constitutions contain a provision of similar purpose and intent — often in the identical words: "No person shall be deprived of life, liberty, or property without due process of law." There is also the provision that private property shall not be taken for public use without just compensation. These guarantees are so essential that the repetition does no harm.

Framework of Government. The second essential of a state constitution includes the provisions outlining the framework of government. These must provide for the establishment of the three branches of government and should provide for necessary extensions of government service by legislative act and for the means by which incumbents of higher offices should be selected. The most frequent difficulty had been that the framers of constitutions have attempted to establish specific offices — a practice which has made it difficult to adapt the machinery of government to changed conditions and changing needs. Essential services should be provided for in such general terms that the legislature will be free to provide such organization and personnel as it may deem necessary. The progress of the reorganization movement has been hampered in many states by constitutional officers, provisions as to salaries, and other matters.

The framers of state constitutions might well take a leaf from the experience of the nation under the Federal Constitution dealing with such essential subjects as the three branches of government with the same clarity and brevity. Chief Justice Marshall well expressed this concept of the fundamental purpose of a constitution when, in the decision of McCulloch v. Maryland,[6] he wrote:

> A constitution, to contain an accurate detail of all the subdivisions of which its great powers will admit, and of all the means by which they may be carried into execution . . . could scarcely be embraced by the human mind. It would probably never be understood by the public. Its nature, therefore, requires that only its great outlines should be marked, its important objects designated, and the minor ingredients which compose those objects be deduced from the nature of the objects themselves.

Powers of the Government. The third essential relates to the powers which shall be exercised by the machinery so established. Either the constitution should enumerate the several types of power to be entrusted to the government agencies or it should state definitely and clearly some principle by means of which these powers may be determined. In some cases a combination of these two methods might be used. The result should be that the state is free to exercise all the powers belonging to it under our federal system, minus only such powers as the convention sees fit to deny to the state government altogether. Such an ideal solution of this problem has rarely, if ever, been achieved. Many of the constitutions now in effect were framed in the latter half of the last century. The movement to increase the power and responsibility of the governor had not yet begun. For reasons to be discussed more fully later, the legislatures were at a low ebb in public esteem, and every effort was made, not to give them power to perform their task well, but to limit their powers in such a way that they might be able to do a minimum amount of harm. During this period the judicial branch suffered less than either of the other two.

This question has much more than a mere theoretical significance. The constitutions have, in fact, gone into such great detail in the enumeration of the powers which the government might exercise and of those which were prohibited that it has been found repeatedly that this practice, coupled with prevailing doctrines of judicial interpretation, has prevented the enactment of desirable social and economic legislation. Illustrations were numerous during the depression in states whose constitutions were more than a quarter of a century old.

Provisions for Amendment. The fourth essential of a state constitution is a workable method of piecemeal amendment. This item is, in fact, so important that the remainder of this chapter is devoted to its consideration, while

[6] 4 Wheaton 316, 1819.

the following chapter is devoted to the problem of general revision by means of the convention.

The unworkable amending provisions found in many states constitute a serious barrier to their progress. Government is a changing, growing, developing, dynamic institution, in need of continuous adaptation to changed social and economic conditions. A constitution whose amending provisions make it impossible to make necessary modifications comes to be a sort of straitjacket. Governmental changes cannot be prevented merely by failing to make adequate constitutional provision for them. The alternative method is likely to be a revolutionary upheaval caused when the accumulation of grievances and social and economic maladjustments is no longer bearable. This alternative, even when carried on without violence and bloodshed, is not pleasing to a society whose governmental tradition is based upon the orderly processes characteristic of Anglo-Saxon institutions.

There are important questions to be considered by the people of a state when they are called upon to select the amending procedure under which they are to live. Will the plan or combination of plans work? Can practical use be made of it, so that actual changes in the fundamental law may be secured? If not, the plan is defective. In Tennessee, for instance, the Constitution of 1870, although containing provisions for amendment, has not been changed during the eighty years of its existence. Between 1870 and 1935 ten amendments were proposed, but only the first of these received an affirmative vote more than one fourth of that cast for governor. With the exception of Tennessee, however, there is not a state whose organic law has not been amended since 1912 — although many are in serious need of general revision.[7]

In the second place, does the plan recognize and tend to maintain the distinction between ordinary statutory law on the one hand and the fundamental law of the constitution on the other? If not, again the plan is defective. Finally, is the plan of such a nature as to be reasonably responsive to the popular will? This does not necessarily mean that the initiative method of proposal must be included in the plan, for there are methods of legislative proposal in connection with which effective popular control is possible. But it does mean that a plan under which popular control is impossible or ineffective is a poor plan for the American states.

The amending procedure provided in the *Model State Constitution* may serve as a standard for comparison. This would permit proposal of amendments either by use of the initiative or by the legislature (Article XII). In the latter case a simple majority vote in either a regular or a special session is sufficient, while the proposal from either source may be ratified by a majority of the voters voting thereon if 20 per cent of those participating in the election vote in the affirmative. The question of a constitutional convention may

[7] See Combs, William H., "An Unamended State Constitution: The Tennessee Constitution of 1870," *American Political Science Review*, June 1938, pp. 514–524.

emanate either from the legislature or from the people by initiative petitions, which must be signed by 5 per cent of the total number voting in the last election, the signers to reside in not less than half the counties of the state.

Contents of Existing Constitutions. With a view to getting a picture of the scope of the constitutions now in force, the headings of the various articles, as they appeared in the New York compilation of 1938, were classified under thirty-seven headings. The results, including those items found in one-third or more of the states, are indicated in the table below.[8]

CONTENTS OF EXISTING CONSTITUTIONS

Agriculture and Public Lands — 16 articles in 12 states
Amending Provisions — 48 articles in 44 states
Corporations Other Than Municipal — 39 articles in 37 states
Counties (see Local Government) — 21 articles in 19 states
Declaration of Rights — 49 articles in 48 states
Education (School Taxes, Funds, and Lands) — 44 articles in 42 states
Executive Department — 51 articles in 48 states
Impeachment (see Removal from Office) — 21 articles in 21 states
Institutions and Public Buildings — 22 articles in 22 states
Judiciary — 50 articles in 48 states
Legislative Department — 52 articles in 48 states
Militia — 39 articles in 37 states
Miscellaneous Provisions — 57 articles in 41 states
Municipal Corporations — 27 articles in 24 states
Officers of Government — 27 articles in 20 states
Powers of Government, Distribution of — 34 articles in 33 states
Public Debt (State) — 18 articles in 18 states
State and County Boundaries, State Capital — 28 articles in 24 states
Suffrage and Elections — 52 articles in 46 states
Taxation and Revenue, Finance — 41 articles in 37 states

In the framing of a modern constitution an effort at brevity should be made. This will mean less legislative matter in the constitution and greater discretion for the legislature. There should be an easier and more workable amending process, although it is also likely that, if other provisions are properly framed, there will be less need for using it. The aim should be, in the words of Mr. Justice Cardozo, to "state principles of government for an expanding future."

The Role of the Legislature in Constitutional Amendment

Legislative Proposal Subject to Restrictions. In more than half of the states constitutional amendments may be proposed by the legislature subject to popular approval, but with the amending process subject to such restrictions as to make amendment difficult. These restrictions are of three types.

[8] Other subjects appearing were banking and insurance; Federal-state relations; health; homesteads and exemptions; intoxicating liquors; labor; local government; mines and mining; oath of office; public salaries; public works; railroads, canals and turnpikes; removal from office, apportionment of representation; road bond issues and taxes; water rights and harbors.

The first requires the action of two successive legislatures for the proposal of amendments, upon the theory that such proposals will be of sufficient importance to influence the selection of legislative personnel. In ten of the fifteen states in which this requirement exists, a majority of the members elected is sufficient.

The second imposes limitations upon the number, frequency, and character of proposals. Thus it may happen, as was the case in Pennsylvania for many years, that amendments may not be voted upon oftener than once in five years; that, as in Indiana, only one proposal may be voted on at a time; or, as in Illinois, that the legislature may not propose amendments to more than one article of the constitution; or that the same proposal may not be re-submitted within a specified period of time. In some cases any other proposal to amend the same article is prohibited within a specified period of time. One serious disadvantage of permitting amendments only at periodic intervals is the fact that often ten, twelve, or more amendments appear on a ballot to be voted upon at a single election.

The third requires a popular vote greater than that of a majority of all persons voting on the amendment. In other words, instead of permitting the ratification of an amendment by a majority of the persons voting thereon, this provision requires the affirmative vote of a majority of those participating in the election. It is a matter of common knowledge that not many more than half the people who participate in an election of public officials vote on referendum proposals submitted at the same time. When, in addition to this, one recalls the general tendency of voters to vote "No" on propositions submitted in this way, it is possible to get some idea of the handicaps that such a system imposes upon the use of the amending process. It is also significant that some states have all three of these restrictive measures in force in their constitutions, thereby making any piecemeal amendment exceedingly difficult, if not practically impossible.

Other Methods of Legislative Proposal. Some states permit the unrestricted proposal of amendments by one legislative action only, and adoption by the majority of the persons voting thereon. If constitutions must be weighed down by great masses of detail, this is, of all the possible methods of amendment, the most satisfactory. If state constitutions were better framed, the question of the nature of the amending provisions would not be so important. This method has the merit of preserving the worthwhile distinction between constitutional and statutory law, without at the same time erecting impossible barriers to the use of the amending procedure.

Delaware permits amendment by two successive legislatures without a direct popular vote. This method, like amendment by special convention, preserves the valuable distinction between constitutional provisions and ordinary statutory law; its chief defect lies in the fact that it violates an almost universal practice of the American states of submitting proposed constitutional changes to a popular referendum for approval or rejection.

Still another method of legislative proposal involves technicalities which have fortunately appeared in only two states. In South Carolina amendments may be proposed by the legislature, with a popular vote upon the proposal but with the ultimate approval or rejection of the proposal left to the legislature. A similar provision exists in Mississippi. The objection to this procedure is obvious. There would seem to be little justification for the expenditures incident to the conduct of a referendum if, after the people have rendered their decision, the legislature is at liberty to disregard it.

General Observations. Of the forty-seven states providing for the proposal of amendments by the legislature (New Hampshire is the exception; see page 57), all but eight authorize introduction in either house.[9] In five states — Arkansas, Florida, Kentucky, New Mexico, and Texas — proposals for amendment may be introduced only at regular sessions of the legislature. Louisiana prescribes that no proposal may be considered unless introduced within the first thirty days of the session, whether regular or special. Provision is regularly made with regard to the size of the vote necessary to approve proposals for amendment. A two-thirds vote of each house is necessary in nineteen states. In eighteen states the requirement is a majority of those elected. Six states require a three-fifths majority. Nebraska requires a favorable vote of three fifths of those elected to its single-chambered legislative body.[10]

The Legislature in the Role of a Convention. The role of the legislature in the business of constitution making is always important. In addition to the submission of individual amendments for the consideration of the electorate, it must ordinarily put in motion the machinery of a referendum on the question of revision. It must make legislative provision for the convention or commission and must appropriate the funds necessary for the payment of expenses. It must approve the draft of the revised constitution to be submitted to the electorate.

The attempt to revise the Constitution of New Jersey, concluded unsuccessfully in 1944, brings the legislature to light in a new role — that of a legislature itself serving in the role of a constitutional convention. In November 1941, the legislature created a seven-man Commission on Revision of the New Jersey Constitution. After a winter of hard work the Commission reported in May 1942, a sample draft of a thoroughly revised constitution.

[9] Connecticut permits introduction in the lower house only; Vermont in the upper house only. Minnesota, Mississippi, Missouri, North Carolina, Rhode Island, and Texas are silent on this subject.

[10] *Two-thirds vote:* California, Colorado, Connecticut, Delaware, Georgia, Idaho, Illinois, Kansas, Louisiana, Maine, Michigan, Montana, South Carolina, Tennessee, Texas, Utah, Washington, West Virginia, and Wyoming. *Majority of those elected:* Arizona, Arkansas, Indiana, Iowa, Missouri, Nevada, New Jersey, New Mexico, New York, North Dakota, Oklahoma, Oregon, Pennsylvania, Rhode Island, South Dakota, Vermont, Virginia, and Wisconsin. *Three-fifths vote:* Alabama, Florida, Kentucky, Maryland, North Carolina, and Ohio. See Steinbicker, Paul G., and Faust, Martin L., *Manual on the Amending Procedure and the Initiative and Referendum* (Missouri Constitutional Convention of 1943, Columbia, 1943).

No hearings were held, but the Commission invited and received suggestions from citizens and civic associations and availed itself of the technical assistance of the Princeton Government Surveys. In its report the Commission suggested "that the people be asked at a referendum whether or not they wished to direct the legislature, acting as a constitutional convention, to submit a revised constitution for adoption or rejection at the following general election." Such a vote was held in November 1943, the result being overwhelmingly in favor of revision. The legislature proceeded to appoint a joint committee to hold public hearings and to prepare a draft of a constitution. The constitution was endorsed by the legislature in January 1944.

Here was a revision commission doing preliminary work, not for a convention as had been attempted in Pennsylvania in 1919–1920, but for the legislature, and here was the legislature of a state acting in the role of a constitutional convention. The experiment worked out successfully — that is to say, the legislature did an adequate job, presenting an instrument vastly superior to the century-old existing constitution. The defeat of the proposed constitution at the polls in November 1944, was in no wise attributable to the fact that the legislature had assumed a new and unusual role in the revision procedure.[11]

Other Methods of Constitutional Amendment

Proposal of Amendments by Conventions. A constitutional convention may, in any state, propose amendments to the existing fundamental law. In some instances, as in New York in 1938, a general revision has been accomplished through a series of amendments submitted to the electorate by a convention. In New Hampshire, however, constitutional amendment is possible only through the medium of a convention. Against this method must be noted its extreme costliness and its time-consuming and cumbersome nature. What happens in practice is that individual changes are not made when needed but are permitted to accumulate, since it is impractical to place upon the state the financial burden of a convention for relatively minor changes. Nevertheless, conventions have been held at frequent intervals — in 1930, 1938, 1941, and 1948.

It is assumed that the work of a constitutional convention will ordinarily result in a proposed new instrument of government, but this does not necessarily follow. Very often a convention will propose the retention of the existing constitution and will propose a series of amendments thereto. Even when the number of amendments is so extensive as to result in a thorough revision of the constitution, it may still be held by the courts that the original constitution, as amended, is in effect. Thus the New York Constitution of 1938 is still referred to as the Constitution of 1894.

The Constitutional Commission. The appointive commission may be used

[11] See Bebout, John E., "New Task for a Legislature," *National Municipal Review*, January 1944, pp. 17–21.

either for general revision or for the proposal of individual amendments. There has been a good deal of argument regarding the merits of this method of general revision, as compared with the convention. While the history of revision commissions goes back approximately a century, less than one third of the states have ever made use of them. Professor Rich, who has recently made a careful analysis of experience with them, reports that of twenty-six known commissions in fifteen states, seven were in New Jersey, with two each in California, Michigan, New York, North Carolina, and Rhode Island.[12] While there are specific cases like the ones in Georgia and Virginia [13] in which important advantages are claimed for the use of the method, its failures in other states far outnumber its successes. Professor Rich found that few of these commissions in any state measure up to expectations, that their members appear to be subject to the same prejudices and the same political pressures as the members of a legislature or a convention. In addition, they have, he believes, "one inherent and fatal weakness in that their every act is measured in terms of what they believe the legislature will accept." The fact that a commission must report to the legislature is regarded as an almost insurmountable barrier to thoroughgoing revision.

The commission system, however, is not without merit as a device for incidental changes, especially those of a technical character. Governor Arnall praised it in the circumstances under which he had used it, though he believed that if a wholly new constitution were to be written, "the commission method would be undesirable and perhaps impractical." [14] The commission can, like the convention, be of great value as an educational device in stimulating public discussion of constitutional issues and in helping in the formulation of policy. This use might be greatly facilitated by a general understanding that the commission should do a preliminary and exploratory job. Free from fear of legislative veto, it could do a constructive piece of work.

The Constitutional Initiative. The final method of amendment exists in fourteen states, which, in addition to the legislative power of proposal, permit the popular initiation of constitutional amendments.[15] One's judgment con-

[12] Rich, Bennett M., "Convention or Commission?" *National Municipal Review*, March 1948, pp. 133–139.

[13] The following are among the advantages claimed by Governor Byrd and other supporters of the commission plan: A commission, being a smaller body, can command the services of the ablest men, thereby making possible informal discussion and thorough deliberation. It costs a small fractional part of the cost of a convention (although, as Professor Rich points out, it is cheaper only if it works — and it seldom does). It is not as susceptible to political pressures and to logrolling as a convention. It can work more expeditiously, and is likely to turn out a superior final product, as compared with a convention.

[14] Arnall, Ellis, "Twenty Five Study Georgia Basic Law," *National Municipal Review*, January 1944, p. 12; Lloyd M. Short describes the Minnesota experience in "Constitutional Revision in Minnesota," *State Government*, May 1950, pp. 97–99; also Minnesota Constitution Review Commission, *Report* (St. Paul, 1950).

[15] See New York State Constitutional Convention Committee, *Problems Relating to Legislative Organization and Powers*, Chapter 9 (Albany, 1938), on the constitutional initiative; also Crouch, Winston W., "The Constitutional Initiative in Operation," *American*

cerning the desirability of this supplementary amending procedure will depend largely upon his attitude toward direct legislation in general. If he regards the initiative, referendum, and recall as devices vital to effective popular control of government, he will doubtless approve their application to the problem of constitutional amendment. If, on the other hand, he has serious objections to the use of these methods in other fields, he is not likely to approve their application to this problem.

Under the initiative plan any individual or group of individuals may draft a proposed amendment and, by securing the signatures of a certain number of qualified voters to a petition, bring about its submission to a popular vote. This method originated in Oregon in 1902 and has now spread to fourteen states. The percentage of signatures that must be secured varies from eight to fifteen, and other limitations have been imposed. These involve such matters as the geographical distribution of the signatures to the petition (Missouri), scrutiny of the proposal by the legislature (Massachusetts), and requirements as to the size of the popular vote necessary for approval. Except in California and Oregon, no very extensive use has been made of this device.

There appears to be a general tendency for voters to reject more amendments submitted by petition than amendments submitted by the legislature. This is true for California (29 per cent as against 57 per cent since 1911) and, according to Professor Gosnell, for the country as a whole (27 per cent as against 64 per cent).

Operation of the Amending Procedures

It is difficult to make generalizations that are either accurate or meaningful regarding the use made of the amending process. Tennessee, on the one hand, has never amended its Constitution of 1870. The Illinois Constitution has been amended only seven times since 1870, only twice since 1890. California and Louisiana, on the other hand, have adopted so many constitutional amendments that it is extremely difficult to keep track of all of them. By 1949 California had adopted 306 amendments to its Constitution of 1879. In the general election of 1948 the voters added to an already overlong document amendments containing more words than are to be found in the entire Constitution of the United States. Louisiana's twenty-seven year old Constitution has been amended 254 times; the late Professor Alden Powell reported of it in 1948[16]:

> Since 1937, 101 amendments have been ratified by the voters: twenty-eight in 1938, nineteen in 1940, ten in 1942, nineteen in 1944, and twenty-five in 1946.

Political Science Review, August 1939, pp. 634–645, and "Direct Legislation Laboratory," *National Municipal Review*, February 1951, pp. 81–87; Fordham, Jefferson B., and Leach, J. Russell, "The Initiative and Referendum in Ohio," *Ohio State Law Journal*, Autumn 1950, pp. 495–532.

[16] Powell, Alden L., "Constitutional Growth and Revision in the South," *Journal of Politics*, May 1948, pp. 354–384.

Constitutional amendments seldom fail of adoption at the polls in Louisiana, for two reasons. First, a proposal needs the approval of only a majority of those voting thereon. Second, amendments ordinarily receive the support of members of the Democratic faction in control of the state administration, from the governor on down. Posters, advertisements, stump speakers, and radio appeals may be used. If administration leaders, on the other hand, should give only lukewarm support to an amendment, or should they decide at the last moment they do not need it after all, the proposal is likely to fail.

These facts make it apparent that in the past much of the emphasis in the discussion of constitutional change has been misdirected. Having in mind states like Illinois and Tennessee whose amending procedures simply will not work, it has been customary to dwell at length on the importance of an amending process that is not too difficult to operate. This consideration is still important, but it is equally important to remember that in other jurisdictions the amending process appears to be too easy to operate, with the result that, as in California and Louisiana, the constitution ceases to be the body of fundamental law that it is supposed to be and becomes a haphazard collection of statutory enactments relating to any and all subjects. This abuse of the amending power and its accompanying violation of the whole basic concept of a written constitution is just as objectionable as is a constitutional straitjacket of the type exemplified by the constitutions of Illinois and Tennessee.

Use Made of the Amending Process. Most of the changes made by individual amendments grow out of problems and situations arising in the states and their local units, but pressure groups also contribute to the grist of constitutional amendments, as they do to the volume of legislation. While the number of proposals voted on in many states is small, there are exceptions; the totals for all of the states run, in even-numbered years (following legislative sessions in most states in the odd-numbered years), into sizable figures.

In 1944 voters were asked to pass upon more than 100 proposals in approximately thirty states. Rejection of the "$60 at 60" old-age assistance plans by Arizona, California, Oregon, and Washington, and approval of anti-closed-shop amendments in Arkansas and Florida, were conspicuous in the results of the voting in November of that year. The anti-closed-shop proposal was defeated in California. Other proposals had to do with airports and airways development, poll taxes and voting, taxation, prohibition, municipal retirement plans, horse and dog racing, postwar planning, veterans' preference, and bank operations.

Thus it is that practically all the usual types of subject matter are represented each year by one or more proposals. The number of proposals in some states is confusing to the voters and, if the proposals are approved, may have a serious effect upon the constitutions involved. In 1938 the voters of Georgia had to pass upon thirty-three proposals. In 1939 the voters of Louisiana had to pass upon twenty-eight, those of California on twenty-five, those of

Georgia on twenty-three.[17] While these may be extreme cases, they indicate a serious problem that has developed in a few states. The average number of amendments added per biennium in Louisiana is nineteen; in California, nine. A more moderate state like Kentucky has adopted thirteen amendments and rejected sixteen since 1891. Texas, between 1876 and 1948, passed on 181 proposed amendments, adopted 104, rejected seventy-five. Two were not submitted.[18]

An analysis of the relative frequency with which constitutions are amended, made by the Hawaii Legislative Reference Bureau, showed that use of the amending procedures varies even more than the procedures themselves. There appears to be no direct relationship between the number of authorized procedures for originating amendments and the number of amendments actually adopted. Of the ten states which make provision for all three methods of initiating amendments — legislature, convention, and initiative — only one, California, has a rate of amendment appreciably higher than the average for all of the constitutions now in effect. "No single procedural requirement," writes the Hawaii Bureau, "can be identified as *the* means of reducing the number of amendments to a state's constitution, or of encouraging timely changes in the organic law." Certain procedures, jointly employed, may, however, not only discourage the initiation of amendments but may in effect prevent the adoption of any amendments at all, as in Illinois and Tennessee.

Popular Referenda on Proposed Changes. In the early days of the Republic promulgated constitutions were not uncommon. In the years since, it has become universal practice to submit the work of constitutional conventions and proposals for constitutional amendment, no matter how initiated, to a popular referendum. Following the adoption of an amendment by the legislature, every state but Delaware requires a popular vote on the measure, the usual requirement being that the referendum shall be held at the next general election. Ten states, however, explicitly leave the setting of the time of the election to the legislature. All of the state constitutions which provide for the proposal of amendments by popular initiative require that such amendments be ratified by the general electorate. Only sixteen of the thirty-six constitutions which establish the convention as a means of originating amendments contain no provision requiring popular ratification of such amendments.

It is normally required that such proposals must be advertised; thus the Pennsylvania Constitution of 1873 provides (Article XVIII): ". . . and the Secretary of the Commonwealth shall cause the same to be published three months before the next general election, in at least two newspapers in every

[17] On the Georgia situation, see Saye, Albert B., *A Constitutional History of Georgia*, Chapter 15, "Amendments and More Amendments" (University of Georgia Press, 1948). Chapter 15 deals with the new Constitution of 1945.

[18] Keith, John P., *Methods of Constitutional Revision*, p. 59 (Bureau of Municipal Research, University of Texas, 1949).

county in which such newspapers shall be published." Submission must usually take place at a general election, although a few states permit submission at special elections. In some states a simple majority of those present and voting thereon is sufficient to ratify; others specify a majority of those voting in the election, while Rhode Island requires three fifths and New Hampshire two thirds of those present and voting in the election. Such provisions make the use of the amending process too difficult.

Public Interest in the Amending Process. Most of the amendments to state constitutions that are adopted receive the approval of only a minority of the population — often even a minority of the voting population — and that approval is given in a perfunctory and halfhearted manner by voters who know little or nothing about the nature of the proposals upon which they are voting. One has no cause for wonder at this when he examines a typical list of the propositions submitted such as the one for New York in 1927, which is reproduced here for reasons that will presently be explained.[19] The manner in which propositions are presented on the ballot apparently has a great deal to do with the extent of voter participation, if Illinois experience may be taken as a guide.[20] In a period of twenty years from 1870 to 1890, during which

State of New York —

Constitutional Amendments Submitted, 1927

NO.	SUBJECT OF PROPOSAL
1.	Establishing a state executive budget system
2.	Authorizing New York City to borrow $300,000,000 outside its existing debt limit for rapid transit construction and equipment purposes; also expanding the debt-incurring power of certain other cities
3.	Making counties, instead of towns and villages, the local units in the apportionment of costs in grade crossing eliminations
4.	Fixing the salary of the governor at $25,000, that of the lieutenant governor at $10,000, and that of the members of the legislature at $2,500
5.	Designating the governor as the head of the executive department of the state
6.	Providing four-year terms for elective state officers and state senators and two-year terms for assemblymen, the first election thereunder to be held in 1928
7.	Authorizing the construction of a state highway in Essex County, from Wilmington to the top of Whiteface Mountain
8.	Authorizing the legislature to confer upon counties powers of excess condemnation in connection with public improvements
9.	Providing that no territory shall be annexed to a city without the consent of a majority in the territory obtained by a referendum vote

[19] For a comment on the campaign for these amendments, see Godshall, W. Leon, "Amendment of State Constitutions in 1927," *American Political Science Review*, February 1929, pp. 102–106.

[20] From Illinois Legislative Council, Research Department, *Problems of Constitutional Revision in Illinois*, p. 13 (Springfield, November 1941).

the party ballot was used, the percentage of nonvoting ranged from 17.1 to 31.6. In a seven-year period from 1891 to 1898, when amendments were printed at the bottom of the ballot, nonvoting ranged from 75.4 to 79.6 per cent. From 1899 to 1928 amendments were printed on separate ballots; during this period, nonvoting dropped to from 24.1 to 57.3 per cent. In 1929, when the ballot was changed again, to its present form with amendments printed in the upper lefthand corner, the percentage of nonvoting increased again, the range being from 56.5 to 62.1 per cent.

The series of amendments advocated by Governor Smith during his last term were designed to make possible effective reorganization of the state government. In this list Proposals No. 1, 4, 5, and 6 relate definitely to the reorganization plan; they involve important structural changes in the government and are proper subjects for referendum. There is serious question as to the wisdom of constitutional salaries (see Proposal No. 4), but in this case an amendment was necessary to change similar provisions already in the constitution. Proposals No. 3, 7, and 9 involve matters of general interest but less fundamental than the structure and powers of the government, and might well have been left to the legislature by the framers of the constitution. With regard to Proposal No. 2, which relates chiefly to the debt limits of the City of New York, one wonders why the people in the up-state counties should be consulted, for it is a question which concerns them remotely if at all.

The fault, of course, was not with the framers of the amendments, but with the constitution itself, which, by dealing with these subjects in detail, made amendment necessary if the provisions were to be changed. Proposal No. 8 deals with excess condemnation, a highly technical and difficult subject concerning which the ordinary voter could scarcely be expected to have any real comprehension. Under ordinary circumstances these proposals would have aroused little popular interest, but in this case the interest was tremendous in New York City and throughout the state. It was estimated that there were between 40,000 and 50,000 people in Times Square on election night watching the returns on these various proposals as they were flashed on the screen. This interest was due almost solely to the genius which Mr. Smith showed as governor in presenting in an interesting manner, abstract principles and problems of government. In the absence of such leadership, the public is neither interested nor informed. Under such circumstances, it may even be difficult to ascertain what the final results of the voting were.

Piecemeal Amendment v. General Revision. What are the relative merits of constitutional change through piecemeal amendment and general revision by means of a constitutional convention? If one's judgment on this question were governed wholly by regard for logic, he would undoubtedly choose the second method. When, however, one faces the practical situation involved in securing the adoption of a new constitution where a thoroughgoing revision has been made, he is apt to prefer the energetic and continuous use of the provisions for piecemeal amendment, provided these are workable. The experience of New York in 1915, of Illinois in 1919, of New Jersey in 1944, and of other states shows conclusively the difficulty of securing popular approval for a new constitution, no matter how well drafted or how modern the ideas upon which it is based. General revisions widely recognized as good may be defeated at the polls through the cumulative effect of various disgruntled elements objecting to individual provisions. No one of these groups alone would be powerful enough to defeat the proposed constitution; all of them together, though they may have little or nothing in common, can defeat it by their united opposition.

Piecemeal amendment would therefore seem to be more practical for those who wish to get things done — unless, of course, the proposals are split up as was done in New York in 1938. The procedure followed in Massachusetts is interesting; the Constitution of 1780 remained in force without general revision until 1919, when a rearrangement of the document was effected in which obsolete provisions were struck out and the remaining portions still in effect were arranged in accordance with a logical and coherent plan. This revision was approved by the voters of the Commonwealth, with the assurance that the substance of the constitution had not been modified. The Supreme Court held that this rearrangement was for convenience only, and that in case of conflict the wording of the original constitution should control.

Current Needs for Constitutional Revision

Nature and Extent of the Need. The nation has, for a period of approximately one third of a century, been almost continuously in a period of emergency. These critical conditions have served repeatedly to illustrate the dangers that arise in the absence of workable provisions for piecemeal amendment. In many states, in the period of the depression, funds needed for relief were held up and desirable social legislation delayed because of the difficulty or the impossibility of getting necessary constitutional changes with any reasonable speed. The more detailed matter the constitution contains, the more urgent is the need for an easy amending process; this is clearly evident even in so-called normal times. Some years ago the Holland Tunnel between New York and New Jersey and the Delaware River Bridge between Camden and Philadelphia were under construction at the same time. The cost of the two projects was about the same. New Jersey promptly provided its part of the money for both of them, but the construction of the bridge was repeatedly delayed because Pennsylvania could not provide the necessary funds out of current revenues and could not operate an antiquated amending procedure with sufficient speed. In this state, loans for more than $1,000,000 may not be made except by amending the constitution; amendments require the action of two successive legislatures and, for a period of sixteen years, could not be submitted oftener than once in five years. This was frequently referred to as the time-lock provision.

The Pennsylvania Constitution of 1873 guarantees that soldiers shall not be quartered in the homes of citizens in time of peace, that canals shall ever be held open as public highways, that citizens shall not be denied the right to bear arms; but it has no word to say on the vital issues of our time. Again and again, as the people of this state have tried to cope with these issues, they have found themselves prevented from taking effective action by the dead hand of the past — by the constitutional convention of a generation which in its own time exercised the power to make a fundamental law, but which, by the adoption of a rigid and inelastic constitution, sought to withhold from future generations powers which it itself had enjoyed.[21] Other states find themselves in a similar situation, as regards both state and local government. In many states, the cities and counties as well as the states themselves are virtually in a straitjacket, while the provisions of antiquated state constitutions maintain barriers in the way of efforts to meet present-day needs for great economy and efficiency in government. Time and again, conscientious officials are "stymied by a horse-and-buggy charter." In ways that are sometimes fantastic, these outmoded constitutions thwart the will of the people.[22]

Numerous illustrations may be gathered from the recent history of many states. The urgency of the situation in California was most effectively stated in a concurrent resolution adopted by the legislature of that state in 1947; the language in the first paragraph was used by the California Constitutional Committee in 1930, in reporting to Governor Young:

> WHEREAS, The Constitution of California, while in its substantive provisions it affords a logical record of the struggle of the people to preserve their rights, by constant amendment has grown to be bad in form, inconsistent in many particulars, loaded with unnecessary detail, encumbered with provisions of no permanent value and replete with matter which might more properly be contained in the statue law of the State; and
>
> WHEREAS, This Constitution, adopted in 1879, has grown from a document of some 16,000 words to an instrument exceeding 72,000 words in length, as contrasted with the Federal Constitution of about 7,500 words, the California Constitution having one section which alone contains more words than will be found in the entire Constitution of the United States; and
>
> WHEREAS, The Constitution of this State since 1879 has been amended no less than 256 times, not to mention numerous amendments proposed either by the Legislature or by initiative which were submitted to the people and defeated, strikingly in contrast with the Federal Constitution which has been amended no more than twenty-one times since 1787 and but in eleven particulars since 1791; and . . .

[21] William A. Schnader, an able former Attorney General of the Commonwealth, said in 1935: "I consider we have a dangerous Constitution at the present moment as it is hamstringing the legislature from making immediate and important changes demanded by the electorate."

[22] Neuberger, Richard L., "States in Straitjackets," *American Magazine*, April 1951, pp. 34–35, 121–124, and Satterfield, Millard H., "Counties in a Straitjacket," *National Municipal Review*, February 1948, pp. 81–85, 124.

The Constitution of Minnesota has a complete description of the highway system of the state, route by route, placed there in 1916 in order "to keep the highways out of politics." If any prizes were to be awarded, however, for lengthy constitutions cluttered up with all manner of extraneous matter, probably Louisiana should come first[23]:

> The Louisiana Constitution of 1921 contains all the essentials and most of the nonessentials of a fundamental law, from "absentee voting" to the "zoological garden" of New Orleans. Partly because 219 amendments have been adopted since 1921, its length now exceeds some 300 pages. . . .
>
> The text of Louisiana's Constitution probably should be made available to future conventions everywhere as a model to be avoided. Some provisions are duplications. Others are contradictory. Many sections are long and vague in meaning. For example, an amendment of 1946 extended exemption from gasoline taxes to tractor fuel, "whether or not such product has a flash point below 110 degrees F. . ." and after prescribing the "distillation range," the "end point" of which must be "not less than 500 degrees F.," the amendment further provided:
>
> "Maximum Baume Gravity 50 degrees, Tractor Fuel or Distillate base stock shall have a plus 10 minimum Saybolt color, to which shall be added two grams per 100 gallons of base stock of green dye, such as Petrol Green 3-W and Petrol Green D., as manufactured by Patent Chemicals, Inc., or Oilfast Green GLB, as made by American Aniline Products or their equivalents."

Obstacles to Be Overcome. The longer these obviously needed changes are postponed or delayed, the more acute the need for them becomes. Three fourths of the constitutions now in effect were framed more than half a century ago, one fourth of them more than eighty years ago. They are weighted down with provisions that are useless, obsolete, and extraneous, and with great quantities of statutory matter, on the one hand, while on the other they lack provisions essential for the proper handling of present-day questions.

The need, as has been said, is for the framing of constitutions which state principles of government for an expanding future. In a new era it is essential that the provisions of the fundamental law in the several states should be so revised as to make it possible for the people to deal effectively with the problems which confront them. In doing so, that which time has proved to be suited to our needs must be preserved, but there must be no hesitation in breaking new trails in order to make suitable provision for the handling of the newer social and economic problems of our time and to modernize our governmental machinery in keeping with the needs of an industrial civilization. One writer who had the Federal Constitution particularly in mind, made some observations which are equally applicable to the constitutions of the states. He recommends that a new constitution should contain five things: provision for economic liberty, social security, more efficient government, personal liberty and the protection of property, and a planned economy.[24] It will take years to work out and secure the adoption of pro-

[23] Powell, *op. cit.*

[24] Wallace, William Kay, *Our Obsolete Constitution* (John Day, New York, 1932).

visions of this character in the constitutions, but the need for the effort is very plain.

Constitutional revision is urgently needed, not in one state but in many, and the time to act is now. In World War II and five years later in the Korean campaign, American soldiers fought in distant parts of the world to preserve the democratic way of life. It will avail little to save democracy in lands far away, only to discover that we have failed to preserve it at home. The democratic tradition will not be strengthened by declaring a moratorium on progress in state and local affairs.

Thomas Jefferson wrote many years ago:

> Some men look at constitutions with sanctimonious reverence, and deem them like the ark of the covenant — too sacred to be touched. They ascribe to the men of the preceding age a wisdom more than human, and suppose what they did to be beyond amendment. I knew that age well; I belonged to it and labored with it. It deserved well of its country. It was very like the present but without the experience of the present. . . . I am certainly not an advocate of frequent and untried changes in laws and constitutions. . . . But I know also that laws and institutions must go hand in hand with the progress of the human mind.

The obstacles to be overcome are tremendous — an undue reverence for the past, fear of the loss of existing privileges, fear of "radical" ideas, popular indifference and inertia, not to mention an almost unbelievable number of constitutional and legal hurdles and barriers.[25] To some the time for revision is never ripe. If existing economic conditions are favorable, if employment and wages are high, they see no need of "rocking the boat"; if existing conditions are bad, they feel that the serious task of revision should not be undertaken when men's minds are disturbed. If one were to be guided by these prophets of disaster, a long period of constitutional stagnation would certainly result. Dr. George Woodward, veteran of many an attempt to modify the Constitution of Pennsylvania, must have felt this strongly when, in whimsical mood, he wrote:

> There is a well known hymn with the title, "Abide with Me." It is a great favorite for funerals. One line says, "change and decay in all around I see. O Thou who changest not, abide with me." I always hum this hymn whenever I try to amend the Pennsylvania Constitution. We may be filled with a noble discontent. We may be burning with a crusader zeal to put a patch on the covenant of the Commonwealth but believe me, our Constitution seems to be immutable, immobile, and immortal.[26]

The task of constitutional revision requires competent and aggressive leadership, courage, and initiative on the part of both leaders and citizens. It requires time — a great deal of time, for the task may require years of continuous and sustained effort. It requires infinite patience and tact. Finally, it requires reasonably adequate financial support. Unless there are on hand

[25] Hindman, Wilbert L., "Road-Blocks to Conventions," *National Municipal Review*, March 1948, pp. 129–132, 144, discusses three hurdles — legal, political, psychological.

[26] *The Pennsylvania Legislator*, May 1941.

suitable leaders, financial support, and a determination to keep everlastingly at it, no matter how long it takes, there is little use of starting at all.

Model State Constitution. The Fifth Edition of the Model State Constitution appeared in 1948. The use of the word "model" is unfortunate, but there seems to be no alternative. The instrument itself is by no means perfect and it has sometimes been severely criticized, but it represents the judgment of some of the ablest students of state government. Frequent reference to it in connection with the various topics to be considered will be helpful. That it has had a great influence on the development of state institutions in the last thirty years there can be no doubt. While no state has adopted, and probably no state will try to adopt, its provisions in their entirety, various recommendations contained in it have gained wide acceptance. Specific mention might be made of the proposals for legislative councils and judicial councils, as well as of the establishment of the unicameral legislature in Nebraska.

SELECTED REFERENCES

Dodd, Walter F., *Revision and Amendment of State Constitutions* (Johns Hopkins Press, 1922). Latest of several available volumes on this subject.

Ethridge, William N., Jr., *Modernizing Mississippi's Constitution* (Bureau of Public Administration, University of Mississippi, 1950). Shows how present constitution affects both state and local government, presenting factual deficiencies in the state's organic law.

Faust, Martin L., *Five Years Under the New Missouri Constitution* (Missouri Public Expenditure Survey, Jefferson City, 1950). A progress report.

Graves, W. Brooke, Small, Norman J., and Dowell, E. Foster, *American State Government and Administration: a State by State Bibliography* (Council of State Governments, Chicago, 1949). Contains numerous references on state constitutions and constitutional revision.

Keith, John P., *Methods of Constitutional Revision* (Bureau of Municipal Research, University of Texas, 1949). Excellent summary of three major methods of revision — legislative, convention, commission — plus discussion of research and citizen participation. See also his *Public Relations Program for a Citizen Committee* (Bureau of Municipal Research, University of Texas, 1950). An excellent guide to citizen action in this field, and the only one available.

Kettleborough, Charles, Ed., *The State Constitutions* (Bobbs-Merrill, Indianapolis, 1928), and Mott, Rodney L., Ed., *Constitutions of the States and United States*, being Vol. III of the report of the New York State Constitutional Convention Committee. These are the two most recent compilations of state constitutions, both now very much out of date.

McCarthy, Sister M. Barbara, *The Widening Scope of American Constitutions* (Catholic University of America, Washington, 1928). Doctoral dissertation emphasizing constitutional aspects of the growth of government services.

New York State Constitutional Convention Committee, *Report*, 12 vols. (Albany, 1938). Most valuable single source of information on problems relating to American state constitutions.

Sturm, Albert L., *The Need for Constitutional Revision in West Virginia* (Bureau for Government Research, West Virginia University, 1950). A study of the constitutional basis of most of the governmental difficulties confronting the state.

For additional references, see pages 90–91 at the end of Chapter 3.

3

State Constitutional Conventions

State constitutions, generally speaking, have been much longer lived than is commonly supposed. They remain in force for an average of more than sixty-five years. The table on the following page shows that twelve of the present constitutions were drafted prior to 1870 (average age, 103.3 years); that twenty-three were drafted in the last thirty years of the nineteenth century (average age, sixty-seven years); while only thirteen have been drawn up during the twentieth century (average age, twenty-seven years). Thus one fourth of the states fall in the first group, one half in the second, one fourth in the third. Three fourths of the constitutions now in effect are more than seventy-five years old. This does not mean, of course, that these constitutions have not been amended many times — most of them have — or that various unsuccessful attempts may not have been made to revise them.

The states have been and still are extremely conservative in the matter of constitutional revision. Approximately one third of them have never had but one constitution; this group is made up chiefly of states most recently admitted, although three New England states are included. One fourth have had only two constitutions. Seven have had three constitutions, six states have had four, Alabama and New York have had five each, South Carolina has had seven, and Louisiana nine. Of the ten states that have had four or more, all but New York and Pennsylvania have some claim to being classified as southern; the changes in constitutions in these states are accounted for by the disturbances of the Civil War period. In some cases constitutions bearing a relatively recent date are not really new. The Massachusetts Constitution of 1919, for instance, was merely a rearrangement of the Constitution of 1780; the Supreme Court held that the rearrangement was for convenience only and that, in any case of conflict, the wording of the original constitution should control.

The Calling and Composition of Conventions

Exactly one fourth of the states fail to make provision for the calling of constitutional conventions. In the absence of such specific provisions, most states derive authority to revise their constitutions under that section usually

Dates of Adoption of Existing State Constitutions [1]

I. *Prior to 1870 — twelve states*
  Prior to 1800 — one state
    New Hampshire (1784)
  1800–1840 — one state
    Connecticut (1818)
  1840–1849 — two states
    Rhode Island (1843); Wisconsin (1848)
  1850–1859 — five states
    Indiana and Ohio (1851); Iowa and Minnesota (1857); Oregon (1859)
  1860–1869 — three states
    Kansas (1861); Nevada (1864); Maryland (1867)

II. *1870–1899 — twenty-three states*
  1870–1879 — eleven states
    Illinois and Tennessee (1870); West Virginia (1872); Arkansas and Pennsylvania (1874); Nebraska (1875); Colorado, Maine,[2] North Carolina, and Texas (1876); California (1879)
  1880–1889 — six states
    Florida (1887); Montana, North Dakota, South Dakota, Washington, and Wyoming (1889)
  1890–1899 — six states
    Idaho and Mississippi (1890); Kentucky (1891); South Carolina and Utah (1895); Delaware (1897)

III. *1900–1949 — thirteen states*
  1900–1909 — three states
    Alabama (1901); Oklahoma (1907); Michigan (1909)
  1910–1919 — four states
    Arizona and New Mexico (1912); Vermont [2] (1913); Massachusetts [2] (1919)
  1920–1929 — two states
    Louisiana (1921); Virginia [2] (1929)
  1930–1939 — one state
    New York [2] (1938)
  1940–1949 — three states
    Missouri (1944); Georgia (1945); New Jersey (1948)

contained in the bill of rights, which states that the people have "an inalienable and indefeasible right to alter, reform, or abolish their government in such manner as they may deem proper." This point of view is well stated in Ruling Case Law [3]:

[1] Follows, to 1938, Mott, Rodney L., Ed., *Constitutions of the States and United States* (New York State Constitutional Convention Committee, Albany, 1938).

[2] The Maine Constitution of 1876 is still regarded as the Constitution of 1820, the Massachusetts Constitution of 1919 as the Constitution of 1780, the New York Constitution of 1938 as the Constitution of 1894, the Vermont Constitution of 1913 as the Constitution of 1793, and the Virginia Constitution of 1929 as the Constitution of 1902. The Maine and Vermont rearrangements were made by the Supreme Court of the states concerned, those in Massachusetts and New York by conventions, and that in Virginia by a commission.

[3] Kentucky Constitution, Bill of Rights, Section 4, and *Ruling Case Law*, Section 17, p. 27; these twelve states are: Arkansas, Connecticut, Indiana, Louisiana, Massachusetts, Mississippi, New Jersey, North Dakota, Pennsylvania, Rhode Island, Texas, and Vermont.

It seems to be an almost universal custom in all of the states, where the constitution itself does not provide for the calling of a constitutional convention, to ascertain first the will of the people and procure from them a commission to call a convention, before the Legislature proceeds to do so. The people being the repository of the right to alter or reform its government, its will and wishes must be consulted before the Legislature can proceed to call a convention.

In all but two of the remaining thirty-six states — Georgia and Maine — a vote of the people is required. In these two exceptions a convention may be called by the legislature alone. In nine states a majority vote of the legislature and the referendum are sufficient, but Nebraska requires a three-fifths vote and the referendum. Seventeen states require a vote of two thirds and the referendum,[4] but New Mexico requires a three-fourths vote plus the referendum. A majority vote of two successive legislatures plus a referendum is necessary in Kentucky, and a convention may be brought about by initiative petition in Oregon. Eight constitutions contain provisions in accordance with which the voters may, at periodic intervals, indicate whether or not they consider revision necessary.[5]

Just as there is no uniformity in the practice of the several states with regard to the calling of conventions, so likewise one finds none within particular states. Pennsylvania is one of those states which have had four constitutions. The first of these, that of 1776, was framed by what was essentially a revolutionary body chosen at the call of an informal committee of gentlemen who had no legal mandate to speak for the people. The convention which drafted the Constitution of 1790 was called into being by the legislature of the state. First the legislature passed a resolution expressing the opinion that the constitution was in need of amendment and declaring that, if the people concurred in this opinion, it would call a convention. About six months later, without actually submitting the question to a popular vote, the legislature concluded that the people favored a convention and provided for the election of convention delegates. The conventions of 1837–1838 and 1872–1873 were called by the legislature after it had submitted to the people the question whether there should be a convention and the people had voted affirmatively thereon.

In any case, the decision to revise the constitution by means of a convention having been made, it is the legal obligation of the legislature to provide for the holding of the convention. Unfortunately, however, the fact that the people have voted for a convention provides little assurance that the legislature will properly discharge its responsibility, as the experience of Iowa well illustrates. Since the legislature cannot be mandamused, there is ap-

[4] *Majority vote:* Alabama, Arizona, New York, Oklahoma, Oregon, Tennessee, Virginia, West Virginia, and Wisconsin. *Two-thirds vote:* California, Colorado, Delaware, Florida, Idaho, Illinois, Kansas, Minnesota, Montana, Nevada, North Carolina, Ohio, South Carolina, South Dakota, Utah, Washington, and Wyoming.

[5] The submission of the question of calling a convention is mandatory every seven years in New Hampshire, every ten years in Iowa, every sixteen years in Michigan, and every twenty years in Maryland, Missouri, New York, Ohio, and Oklahoma.

parently no effective legal remedy. Professor Trachsel, formerly at the State University of Iowa, writes[6]:

> The vote of the people in 1920 was 279,652 for and 221,763 against calling a convention. On January 20, 1921, a bill was introduced into the House of Representatives making provision "for a convention to revise and amend the constitution, naming the number of delegates and districts. . . ." This bill passed the House on March 15 and was messaged to the Senate the following day. On March 30, it passed the Senate with amendments which the House refused to accept. A conference committee was appointed; but the House rejected its report on April 2, which was the last day of the session. Thus the General Assembly adjourned without making any provision for a constitutional convention.
>
> In support of the position taken by the General Assembly, some of the members and others insisted that there was no popular demand for a revision of the constitution. One representative, however, did not believe the General Assembly "should override the wishes of the people." Another said "the people expressed a wish for the convention and it is for the Assembly to make necessary machinery for it." However, nothing was done and there has been no constitutional convention since 1857. Every ten years, the question is submitted to the voters on a separate ballot.

The provisions of the acts providing for a constitutional convention depend in part on the nature of the constitutional provisions regarding conventions. Twenty-six constitutions require that the legislature provide for the convention, and twenty-one specify that this must be done at the next session after the popular referendum at which the proposition for holding the convention was approved. Fourteen constitutions specify the time at which the convention shall assemble; if the constitution does not do so, the legislative act must. The place at which the convention will meet is specified as the state capitol in Delaware, Kentucky, Michigan, and New York; elsewhere this question is determined by legislative act, the usual provision being that the convention will assemble in the hall of the House. The legislative act must make provision for the nomination and election of delegates, the manner of filling vacancies, the compensation of delegates to the convention (unless, as in seven states, this point is covered in the constitution), the necessary expenses of the convention,[7] and its temporary organization.

Conventions vary greatly in size; most of them are larger than they would be if the size of the membership were restricted to the limits of an effective working group. How should the delegates be chosen? The usual practice is to select one or more members from each senatorial district; in the larger states, from each Congressional district or from each county. The practice may not be uniform, however, even within a single state. To refer again to the experience of Pennsylvania, eight of the delegates to the Convention of 1776 were from the city of Philadelphia, while eight more were elected from each county

[6] Trachsel, Herman H., from a letter to the National Municipal League, July 26, 1947.

[7] Conventions cost money; the New York legislature in 1938 appropriated $1,300,000 on the basis of the estimate of a session of 150 days. Governor Harry F. Byrd of Virginia estimated in 1929 that a convention would have cost that state half a million dollars.

by the then qualified voters. Those who framed the Constitution of 1790 were the same in number and were elected and apportioned in the same manner as the members of the General Assembly, which at that time consisted of only one chamber. The delegates to the Convention of 1837–1838 were also the same in number and were elected and apportioned in the same manner as the members of the legislature; but the legislature was then, as it is now, a two-chambered body. The Convention of 1872–1873 was composed of 133 delegates, 28 elected at large, 6 from Philadelphia at large, and 99 from senatorial districts. Representation of minority parties was made possible by limiting the number of candidates a voter could vote for to less than the total number of delegates to be elected.[8]

The caliber of the personnel of conventions is usually higher than that of the legislature for the reason that the work of framing a constitution is regarded as being highly important. Since it does not have to be done often, and since the duration of the convention is not great, it is possible to enlist the services of outstanding business and professional men who often would not be willing to serve as members of the legislature.

Preparation for the Convention

In a day when American life was relatively simple and when the tasks imposed upon government were correspondingly fewer in number and less technical in nature, the work of framing a constitution was not nearly so difficult as it is under modern conditions. Under these conditions it would be impossible for any group of men possessing anything less than omniscient wisdom to deal intelligently and wisely with the multitude of problems confronting them, on the basis of their own information. Consequently it is necessary to prepare, in advance of the meeting, information and working materials for the members. Until after World War I such preparation consisted largely in making collections of state constitutions, from which members of the convention might determine how the questions facing them had been handled by the constitution makers of other states. Of late a more thorough and detailed preparation has been made.

Thus in Illinois in 1919 an extensive series of bulletins was prepared by the Legislative Reference Bureau for the use of the constitutional convention in that state. These bulletins dealt with such subjects as the procedure and problems of the constitutional convention; the amending article of the constitution; the executive, legislative, and judicial branches of the government; problems of finance and local government. Each of them analyzed provisions of the then existing constitution on the subject with which it dealt, pointing out their merits and defects; each called attention to significant practices in other states and made clear the different methods by which these various problems might be handled. It is a prerequisite to a high grade of work by a constitutional convention that information of this character should be care-

[8] Philadelphia Bureau of Municipal Research, *Citizens' Business*, November 6, 1934.

fully collected and made available in convenient form for the use of the delegates.

Not long after the voters of New York had decided in 1937 that a convention should be held, Governor Herbert H. Lehman appointed the New York State Constitutional Convention Committee, composed of forty-two members distinguished for their public service. This Committee, organized in August 1937, created six smaller working subcommittees, each of which, with a research staff, made a study of one or two specific subjects likely to be considered at the convention. Upon each of these subjects a volume of the resultant research was published. In addition, the chairman was authorized to initiate five general reference volumes. In all, a set of twelve volumes was published, the titles of which appear in the table on page 75, to provide the factual basis for discussion by the delegates.[9] The Committee had less than a year in which to complete its work, which followed in general the pattern established by the New York Convention of 1915, and of other states in recent years.

Similar procedures, on a much restricted scale, were followed in Missouri in 1943, in Georgia in 1944, in Hawaii in 1950. The University of Missouri assumed responsibility for the preparation of a series of eight manuals for the information of the delegates, while the Legislative Reference Bureau at the University of Hawaii performed a similar service for the delegates to the 1950 convention in that Territory. The titles appearing in both of these series are shown in the table on page 75. In Georgia the Constitutional Revision Commission of twenty-five members was broken up into a series of seven subcommittees, each of which made a report with recommendations. The subcommittees were assigned to bill of rights and judiciary, suffrage and elections, taxation and finance, the executive, the legislature, education, and county and local government.[10]

A great deal of preparatory work has been done in Louisiana, New Jersey, and Oklahoma for conventions either held, as in New Jersey, or contemplated. These states have followed a procedure at once similar and different. It has been similar in that the best available authorities in the state have cooperated in the preparation of a series of informative bulletins for the use of delegates; it has been different in that the bulletins have been much smaller and more numerous, thereby providing at least a minimum of information on a far larger number of subjects.

[9] The first five volumes were for general reference; the last six (exclusive of the general index) contained the studies and reports of the six subcommittees. Three thousand copies were prepared for distribution. For a description of the procedure followed, see Poletti, Charles, "First Steps in Streamlining a Constitution," *State Government*, August 1938, pp. 148–149, 157.

[10] Reports of each of these subcommittees were published. See also Arnall, Governor Ellis, "Twenty-five Study Georgia Basic Law," *National Municipal Review*, January 1944, pp. 11–13, and "A New Constitution for Georgia," *State Government*, July 1945, pp. 109–110; also Saye, Albert B., "Georgia's Proposed New Constitution," *American Political Science Review*, June 1945, pp. 459–463. For complete bibliography, see Saye, Albert B., *A Constitutional History of Georgia* (University of Georgia Press, 1948).

Preparation for a Constitutional Convention

NEW YORK — 1938

TWELVE BOUND VOLUMES

Vol. I *The New York State Constitution Annotated*
Vol. II *Amendments Proposed to New York Constitution, 1895–1937*
Vol. III *Constitutions of the States and United States*
Vol. IV *State and Local Government in New York*
Vol. V *New York City Government — Functions and Problems*
Vol. VI *Problems Relating to Bill of Rights and General Welfare*
Vol. VII *Problems Relating to Legislative Organization and Powers*
Vol. VIII *Problems Relating to Executive Administration and Powers*
Vol. IX *Problems Relating to Judicial Administration and Organization*
Vol. X *Problems Relating to Taxation and Finance*
Vol. XI *Problems Relating to Home Rule and Local Government*
Vol. XII *General Index*

MISSOURI — 1943

EIGHT PAMPHLET MANUALS

1. *Organization Manual*
2. *County Government Manual*
3. *Manual on Federal-State Relations*
4. *Manual on the Executive Article*
5. *Manual on Education*
6. *Manual on the Legislative Article*
7. *Manual on the Bill of Rights, and Suffrage and Elections*
8. *Manual on the Amending Procedure, and the Initiative and Referendum*

HAWAII — 1950

FOURTEEN PAMPHLETS

1. *Bill of Rights and General Welfare*
2. *Constitutional Amendment and Revision*
3. *Suffrage and Elections*
4. *The Initiative, Referendum, and Recall*
5. *Structure of State Legislatures*
6. *Legislative Organization and Procedure*
7. *Constitutional Provisions for Legislative Apportionment and Reapportionment*
8. *Legislative Aids*
9. *Executive Officers in State Constitutions*
10. *Fiscal Provisions of State Constitutions*
11. *Budgetary and Appropriation Provisions*
12. *State Judicial Systems*
13. *Home Rule*
14. *Selected References (on each of above topics)*

Extensive compilations of basic information on the many problems with which a constitutional convention must deal are not only a necessary prerequisite to a high grade of work by the bodies for which they are prepared; they are valuable for years to come as reference works for citizens and public officials of the state and for students and research workers in state government in other states throughout the country.[11] There would seem to be little excuse, however, in a federal system such as that in the United States, for imposing upon each state the necessity for expending the money and effort to compile this basic information anew every time a constitutional convention is authorized or given serious consideration. The central government can and should be prepared to perform services of this type which the individual states cannot or should not be expected to perform for themselves.

A comprehensive plan to provide this information for all the states on a current and up-to-date basis has been under consideration for some time, its fulfillment awaiting the necessary financial support either by the Federal government or through the use of private funds. Such a constitutional revision service would involve three specific types of publication: (1) the text of all existing state constitutions; (2) a new index-digest of state constitutions; (3) a series of monographs covering major topics to be considered in constitutional revision.

In the past, compilations of the texts of the existing state constitutions have been printed only at long and irregular intervals, the last appearing in the New York report in 1938. The texts of all state constitutions now in effect should be included, as amended to date, with an analytical index. Such an edition as is proposed here would be printed on thin paper punched for a ring binder, with replacement sheets sold annually on a subscription basis so that the compilation would at all times be accurate and up to date.

The second component of such a program would be a new and up-to-date edition of the *Index-Digest of State Constitutions*, prepared by the Legislative Drafting Fund of Columbia University in 1914–1915 for the use of the delegates to the New York Convention of 1915. This invaluable working tool in the field of constitutional law has long been out of date and long since out of print. Such a work does not require frequent revision, but thirty-five or forty years is much too long a time to leave it without revision.

The third component would be a series of ten or a dozen monographs dealing with major problems confronting any state constitutional convention, such as the three main branches of the government, constitutional amendment and revision, suffrage and elections, taxation and finance, and other subjects. These manuals would be strictly factual and unbiased, presenting in tabular form (where practicable) an analysis of the provisions of all the state constitutions on a particular subject, these tables to be supplemented by interpretative, comparative, and explanatory comment indicating the basis of classification of existing constitutional provisions, their strength and weakness.

[11] See Owen, Kimbrough, "Blazing the Constitution Trail," *National Municipal Review*, March 1948, pp. 140–144, showing how experience in six states proves the value of well-planned research to drafters of new state constitutions.

Powers of the Convention

Questions as to the scope of the powers of a constitutional convention and as to the relations of the convention to the legislature may arise in any state when a constitutional convention meets. These are troublesome questions. In powers, as well as in form, constitutional conventions differ from state legislatures. As Professor Walker observes:

> The convention is universally unicameral, the legislature is almost universally bicameral. Otherwise the two bodies are similar. Each chooses its own officers and prescribes its rules of procedure. The powers of the convention relate to a single object, the framing and submission to the people of a new constitution or a series of amendments. The legislature's powers relate to general purposes of government. The convention in no way supersedes or suspends the operation of any of the regular organs of government. These continue to function as before. The convention may propose that these be changed, but such changes go into effect only when approved by the people. Constitutional conventions do not meet, as do legislatures, at stated times; nor do they serve for a fixed term, as two or four years. They convene for a special task. When this is accomplished they adjourn *sine die*. Even if a new constitution were deemed necessary soon after, the old convention would not serve. The whole process of calling the convention would begin anew.[12]

As a practical matter, a convention once seated is hard to control. Its delegates are likely to feel that they have a direct and unlimited mandate from the sovereign people. The law may be against them on this, but the law may be one thing and practice quite another. A convention can usually find ways of doing what it wants to do. Its proposals may be submitted in such form that the good must be taken with the bad, or by the promulgation procedure may become effective without being submitted to the people.

Relation of a Convention to the Legislature. J. F. Jameson, in his work on constitutional conventions, asserts that such a body is absolutely bound by any restrictions which may appear in the legislative act by which it is called, but even he admits that these limitations "must be in harmony with the principles of the convention system, or, rather, not inconsistent with the exercise by the convention, to some extent, of its essential and characteristic function."[13] An important decision with regard to this question was handed down by the Supreme Court of Pennsylvania many years ago in the case of Wood's Appeal, which revolved around certain acts of the convention which framed the Pennsylvania Constitution of 1873.[14] An act of the General Assembly of Pennsylvania, passed in 1871, submitted to the people the question of constitutional revision. The popular vote being in the affirmative, an act passed the following year provided for the election of delegates and authorized the convention to propose "a new constitution or amendments to the present one,

[12] Walker, Harvey, *The Legislative Process: Lawmaking in the United States*, pp. 54–55 (Ronald Press, New York, 1948).

[13] Jameson, J. F., *The Constitutional Convention*, Section 338, p. 310 (Scribner's, New York, 1867). Cited by Walker, *op. cit.*, p. 72.

[14] 75 Pa. 59, 1874.

or specific amendments to be voted for separately." The act also required that the election for passing upon the work of the convention should be held according to the general election law of the Commonwealth. The convention chose to prepare a new constitution, and passed an ordinance providing for the submission of this document to the voters according to the general election law (except in Philadelphia, where different provisions were made).

The plaintiffs sought an injunction in the Allegheny County Court of Common Pleas to prevent various state officers from holding the election under the convention ordinance, alleging that the ordinance was illegal. The Court was faced with the question of the extent to which the legislature could impose restrictions upon a constituent assembly. In its opinion it distinguished clearly between the constitution-making power of a convention on the one hand, and the statute-making power of a legislative body on the other. Each is supreme within its own field when acting within the limits of its powers. If the convention felt, as it did, that there was adequate reason for prescribing a special election in all or part of the state for the purpose of passing upon the proposals which it wished to submit, the convention was — so far as this court was concerned — acting entirely within its rights, and attempts at the restriction of such action on the part of the legislature were without effect.

The Work of the Convention

When the convention assembles, its first problem is that of organization. It has the same power as a legislature to determine its rules, choose its officers and employees, and provide for its printing; it is, however, dependent upon the legislature for its funds, since it has no appropriating or taxing power. On the organization and work of the convention, Professor Walker says [15]:

> When the convention meets, it usually organizes in much the same manner as the lower house of a state legislature. Officers are elected, rules adopted, and committees appointed. There is usually a committee for each article of the existing constitution, with others to consider special questions. There were thirty-one committees in the New York convention in 1894; sixteen in that of Virginia in 1901–1902; twenty-nine in Michigan in 1907–1908; twenty-five in Ohio in 1912; and thirty-nine in Illinois in 1869–1870. The same reasons for few committees of small size apply in a constitutional convention as in a state legislature. Parts of the existing constitution are referred to the committees as are also proposals from the floor for new sections or for the amendment of old ones.
>
> When the committees are ready to report, they present their recommendations to the convention, where they are usually debated in committee of the whole. Then, after amendment, they are usually referred to a special committee on arrangement and phraseology, which is responsible for presenting the final draft of the constitutional document to the convention for its approval.

[15] Walker, *op. cit.*, p. 61; for a brief account of organization and methods in the Missouri Convention of 1943, see Blake, Robert E., and Bradshaw, William L., "The Convention Goes to Work," *National Municipal Review*, March 1948, pp. 145–149.

Usually the first committee to report is the committee on rules; these are commonly based upon those of the lower house of the legislature but may be modified in such manner as to provide more ample opportunity for discussion and deliberation. Party groups may set up unofficial steering committees to aid in determining their stand on proposals. The regular procedure for proposals adopted by the Michigan Convention of 1907 was as follows:

1. Introduction, first reading, and reference to a committee
2. Report of committee and placing in the general order
3. Consideration in committee of the whole in order of reference
4. Report by committee of the whole, and reference to the committee on arrangement and phraseology
5. Report of committee on arrangement and phraseology
6. Second reading, vote on passage by roll call
7. Reference to committee on arrangement and phraseology
8. Report of the complete revision by the committee on arrangement and phraseology
9. Consideration of the complete revision in committee of the whole, by sections
10. Report of the committee of the whole
11. Third reading and passage (on roll call) by articles and as a whole.[16]

The size of the vote necessary for the submission of amendments by the convention is ordinarily left to the decision of the convention. Upon the conclusion of its business, the convention may adjourn, the convention itself being the sole judge — except in Kentucky, Michigan, and New York — of whether or not its business has been completed.

Problems of Draftsmanship. Many state constitutions show slight evidence of care in arrangement of material or in draftsmanship. That the Federal Constitution has continued to be reasonably satisfactory during a century and a half is due in no small measure to the work of the Committee on Style and Arrangement. The failure of state conventions to exert similar care, through the use of like committees, has been productive of much uncertainty and litigation. Many questions present themselves: Should the convention rewrite or merely amend? How much detail should be included? Should changes be made solely for the purpose of achieving more effective expression?

As a general principle it may be urged that changes in the existing constitution should not be made unless it is desired to change the meaning. Most of the provisions of the old constitution have been interpreted and clarified by the courts; to the extent, therefore, that these provisions, as interpreted, are satisfactory, they should be permitted to remain unchanged. To rewrite them for any reason, however worthy, is likely to result only in substituting the unknown and the uncertain for what is known and relatively certain. The old wording may sometimes seem quaint and antiquated as compared with

[16] Fairlie, John A., "The Michigan Constitutional Convention," *Michigan Law Review,* May 1908, pp. 533–551.

modern usage. Many of these phrases, however, have come down through generations; to change them will necessitate new litigation to interpret them, while the time-honored phrases have already been interpreted.

Just as old phrases are to be preferred where applicable and satisfactory, so should the draftsmen of a new constitution strive for brevity. This objective is more difficult to achieve as the functions of the states increase in number and complexity. But unnecessary details are likely to cause a lack of flexibility, to encourage a rigidity which may become a distinct handicap to the effective functioning of the government. They will likewise assure the need for numerous amendments in the future and increase the probability of an extensive amount of litigation. The more details the constitution includes, the more opportunities there are for doubt, change, modification, and interpretation.

Extreme care must be exercised in the effort to have the text say what the framers wanted to have said — nothing more and nothing less. Where, in two or more different places in the constitution, it is intended to convey the same idea, the same phraseology should be used; for the courts are likely to assume that where the wording is different, a different meaning was intended. Some language permits or leads to technical constructions; some may grant more or less power than was intended. A bulletin prepared for the Illinois Convention of 1919 aptly illustrates these points.[17] In the Illinois Constitution of 1870 frequent reference is made to the requirement of a two-thirds vote on certain types of legislative measures. In some cases the wording indicated that the usual interpretation of the two-thirds rule was intended — namely, two thirds of the members present, providing that the number present constituted a quorum. In another case the wording was not clear, although it did not seem that any difference in meaning had been intended.

In the same constitution boards of county commissioners of three members each were provided for each of the counties of the state except Cook County, in which Chicago is located. The powers and duties of these boards were definitely described. The convention evidently believed that Cook County should be treated differently and provided in this case for a board of county commissioners consisting of fifteen members. They failed, however, to specify that the powers and duties of the Cook County Board should be the same as the powers and duties of the smaller boards created for the other counties of the state. In both of these cases litigation resulted to determine the meaning of these carelessly drawn provisions — litigation which would never have occurred had the convention exerted sufficient care in draftsmanship. It is essential that, where the same meaning is intended, the same language shall be consistently used, and that every effort shall be made to state in clear, accurate, and concise form the purpose and intent of the convention.

The same constitution contains a number of provisions — no less than eight — with respect to popular votes. "In some of these provisions differ-

[17] See Illinois Constitutional Convention, *Bulletin* No. 1, pp. 15–22.

ences in language were clearly intended to adopt different rules, but this was not true in all cases." The Illinois pamphlet continues:

> For example, Article X, Section 5, provides for the adoption of the township system "by a majority of the legal voters of such county, voting at any general election," and for the abolition of the township system if at a general election "a majority of all the votes cast upon that question shall be against township organization." It seems pretty clear that no difference in meaning was intended here, and that the purpose of the Constitutional Convention of 1870 was that merely of adding a provision for the abolition of the township system by the same vote as that required to establish the system. . . .

Similarly, there are six different provisions with respect to private legislation. "To find what is prohibited as special legislation therefore requires a search of the whole text of the Constitution." In some cases judicial construction of these clauses has restricted their application; in others it has made them mean much more than the language seems to mean.

Spotlighting Major Issues. Whether or not a state gets a new constitution as a result of a convention, the convention itself may be worth while if it serves to spotlight major issues and focus public attention upon them. Before the New York Convention met in 1938, the *National Municipal Review* said editorially that the constitution of that state was "in fair shape, far ahead of the constitutions of most of the forty-eight states." [18] The *Review* went on to say that major issues of our time should have a thorough airing, with able advocates on both sides. What are these major issues — the issues with which a state convention should now concern itself? While such a list may vary in different states and sections of the country, and with time and circumstance, the following is suggested:

1. Reorganization of the state administrative departments, and a review of the merits of proposals for new departments
2. Improvement of the functioning of the legislature, which is at the very core of the democratic process
3. Reorganization of the judicial system, in order to provide more efficient machinery for the administration of justice
4. City-county relations and the reorganization of the system of local government, including consolidation, reallocation of functions, long-range planning, and proper land utilization
5. Popular control of government, including the short ballot principle and proportional representation
6. Budgetary methods and procedure, including the possibility of provision for a capital outlay budget, a reserve fund, and an annual budget
7. The question of the extent, method, and purposes of state aid to political subdivisions as well as the relation of this question to the tax burden on real estate
8. An increasing burden of Federal taxes and overlapping of state levies with both Federal and local levies deserves careful study.
9. In view of extended Federal activity in the labor field, what should be the function of the states? Should unions be incorporated? Should "a bill of rights for labor" be written into the constitution?

[18] October 1937, p. 465.

10. Extensions of governmental activity in social welfare may well receive consideration. Should housing be dealt with in the constitution, and if so, in what manner?

If the convention finally accomplishes nothing more than to arouse public interest and discussion of these and other issues, it will have served a useful purpose. If the proposed new constitution should be defeated, there is still the possibility of securing the desired changes by individual amendments.

In its treatment of the major issues a convention naturally reflects the temper of the time. This is particularly noticeable in states that have had a number of constitutions, where the movement from liberalism to conservatism and back again operates with an almost pendulumlike regularity. The Pennsylvania Constitution of 1776 was a liberal, almost a revolutionary, document. That of 1790 was conservative. A liberal constitution of 1838 was followed by the conservative one of 1873, which is still in force. The experience of New York has been similar. Its Constitution of 1777 was conservative; the conventions of 1821 and 1846 were devoted largely to undoing the work of the first convention. The reform of the judiciary was the chief work of the Convention of 1867. The Convention of 1894 showed a more conservative tone, while the conventions held in 1915 and 1938 were generally liberal in their point of view.[19]

Trends in Types of Changes. In a comprehensive review of substantive changes in state constitutions during the forties, Professor Lloyd M. Short observes that (1) the changes adopted during the decade are on the whole less significant than the structural and procedural changes; (2) the amendment of state constitutions is in most states a slow and difficult process, and in consequence states find it possible and perhaps desirable to achieve by statute the changes which otherwise might be made by constitutional action; (3) the most significant and expensive changes have come in those states which have undertaken a thorough-going revision of their constitutions by means of constitutional conventions; and (4) constitutional changes which have been made reveal a mixture of attempts at controlling or modifying legislative action and of efforts to increase and strengthen legislative powers. "It is difficult," continues Professor Short, "to assess the effect of our failure to arrive at satisfactory bases of legislative representation upon the amending process, but it seems reasonably certain that many substantive changes in state constitutions suggested by present-day urban and industrial conditions are postponed more or less indefinitely because of the lack of interest and an understanding of those conditions by legislators from rural areas, however sincere and well-intentioned they may be." [20]

[19] There is no point in arguing here the meaning of "liberal" and "conservative"; an examination of the constitutions mentioned will show differences which justify the use of these or similar terms.

[20] Short, Lloyd M., "Substantive Changes in State Constitutions," in *Papers Delivered at the Panel on State Constitutional Developments, Forty-fourth Annual Meeting, American Political Science Association, Chicago, 1948* (Mimeographed, Louisiana State University, 1949).

At the same time the author undertook to review recent trends in the type of procedural changes, finding such changes neither numerous nor epoch-making. Most significant, perhaps, is the tendency to make as much of the constitution as possible self-executing, to make it function automatically. This is an interesting refinement of the older practice of hamstringing the legislature by all manner of restrictive provisions because of a general lack of confidence. Now, while claiming to recognize the importance of the elected representative assembly in democratic government, the attempt is made to by-pass it for fear that it will not perform its duties adequately or perhaps not perform them at all.

> Because the legislatures have not called constitutional conventions when they should, we tried first to compel them to do so by inserting in the constitution provisions requiring them to submit the question to the electorate at periodic intervals, and when that did not work, we seek to make the submission of the question a mandatory act on the part of a legislative or administrative officer.
>
> Because the legislatures have so habitually either bungled the job or refrained from taking action at all on the subject of executive organization and reorganization, we now seek to impose constitutional limitations on the number of executive departments, and to give the responsibility for maintaining an orderly administrative structure to the executive, subject to legislative review.
>
> Because the legislatures have failed so utterly in the matter of reapportionment, we seek now to make that process automatic also.
>
> Because the legislatures have so often either failed to act or refused to grant a reasonable latitude of home rule to their political subdivisions, we seek to find here too some magic formula by which local units may achieve home rule without legislative aid or in spite of legislative opposition.

It may be that on the basis of the record these efforts are justified. At the same time it may be well to consider whether such procedures are compatible with the theory of elected representative government.

Motivation and Control of Constitutional Conventions

Much has been written on the influence of pressure groups and propagandist methods on legislative bodies, but almost nothing has been said on the influence of these groups and methods upon the deliberations of constituent assemblies. It appears, in fact, to have been assumed that the members of conventions are in some way drawn from a different species than that from which the members of other law-making bodies are selected, and that they function in another sphere, quite remote from the mundane influence of political parties, lobbies, and pressure groups. Such clearly is not the case. Professor Dorr notes that, despite traditions to the contrary, politics always forms an important factor in constitutional conventions [21]:

> Fact and fiction have conspired over the years to destroy public confidence in state legislatures. Yet, by some strange magic, these same factors have glorified another popular assembly beyond its institutional significance. Myth,

[21] Dorr, Harold M., "The Myth of the Constitutional Convention," *Michigan Alumnus Quarterly Review*, December 6, 1947, pp. 22–33.

legend, and fiction attribute to the constitutional convention all the virtues of popular assemblies, leaving to its institutional cousin, the state legislature, only the dregs of virtue. "It is assumed," said a convention delegate, "that when we depart from this hall all the virtue and all the wisdom of this state will have departed with us. We have assumed that we alone are honest and wise."

The late Russell M. Story pointed out in his introduction to Professor Swisher's excellent study of pressure group influences in the California Convention of 1878 [22] that "the ability of man to identify the public welfare with his own desire and to rationalize the latter in terms of the former is almost unlimited." This work is intended to "provide the reader with perspective and generate insight into the life process by which constitutions come into being."

It is interesting to compare Mr. Swisher's findings with those of Charles A. Beard in his analysis of the Federal Convention of 1787. In California also there was the conflict between the established propertied classes and the representatives of the "plain people"; the legal profession was likewise heavily represented. The convention met in a period of rapid corporate development, and the representatives of the property-owning group had the moral and ethical standards that characterized the railroad and other corporate organizations throughout the country at that time. The state was greatly disturbed by the then recent organization of a so-called Workingmen's Party, led by the irresponsible agitator, Dennis Kearney.

These two groups clashed in the choice of delegates and again when the convention met and attempted to organize and select its officers. There was a bitter struggle on the effort to regulate corporations, particularly the railroads. In this the small business interests sided with the popular party. There were others, not extensive property owners, who supported the conservative group because they felt the railroads had been largely responsible for the rapid development of the state and that therefore they ought to be allowed a good deal of freedom. There was much dissatisfaction with the existing system of taxation, for the economic depression in the decade of the seventies had thrown added weight upon those who bore the burden of the taxes levied in the state. The taxation of mortgagers had been unfair, and a large part of the mortgager group was made up of farmers. Then there was the clash of interests over the taxation of the mining industry, which may have been inspired in part by the hostility of the farmers toward the mines, due to their pollution of streams. There were also questions of race relations, involving land ownership and the competition of Asiatic with white labor in agriculture and elsewhere. This situation was made more difficult by the agitation of Kearney and his supporters. In addition there were numerous lesser problems. The purpose of this comment is simply to call attention to the fact that in every convention there is a conflict of economic interests and that these interests resort to the same use of the press and of other types of pressure

[22] Swisher, Carl B., *Motivation and Political Technique in the California Constitutional Convention, 1878–1879* (Pomona College, Claremont, California, 1930).

group influence that is characteristic of their dealings with other governmental agencies.

The New York Convention of 1938. That pressure groups as well as citizen organizations can take an active and helpful interest in the work of a constitutional convention is well illustrated by the experience in New York in 1938. One state association after another established a constitutional convention committee. This was due largely to the leadership of the New York State Committee of the National Municipal League. Much of the work of these committees was done before the convention met, simultaneously with that of the official New York State Constitutional Convention Committee appointed by the Governor. The League's Committee performed a twofold function — first, in promoting organization throughout the state for the study of the problems of the convention, and second, in the development of certain recommendations of its own. This Committee included the presidents of all the universities and colleges of the state. In each institution a speaker's committee was set up to send interested faculty members and specially trained students to discuss and debate constitutional questions before ready-made audiences in churches, schools, and lodges and before farm organizations, chambers of commerce, and other similar groups. This work was tremendously valuable in stimulating interest among both the speakers and the audiences, and in informing citizens of the nature and importance of the work of the convention.

Not only the League's Committee but numerous other civic organizations like the Citizens Union formulated recommendations for the consideration of the convention. The League's Committee sponsored regional conferences of leaders interested in constitutional revision and mimeographed numerous papers and addresses for general circulation.[23] Members of university faculties prepared several special studies dealing with constitutional questions. The *New York Times* issued a *Constitutional Convention Almanac* containing much useful information. The New York League of Women Voters put out a pamphlet on convention issues and carried constant reference to these problems in its monthly bulletin. The Women's City Club and the State Federation of Business and Professional Women's Clubs organized committees and conducted forums. The City Club of New York published an impressive series of bulletins dealing with important topics.

The work of preparation for the convention and the interest of citizens were not by any means confined to civic organizations. Businessmen were interested; chambers of commerce and the Merchants' Association of New York undertook studies of many questions which were not closely connected with their obvious interests. The New York State Automobile Association made an extensive study of the diversion of highway funds and published its results. While this organization may not have been wholly disin-

[23] For examples of the various types of publications mentioned here, see the Third Edition of this volume, pp. 99–100.

terested, it rendered a public service in accordance with the ideal of democracy which accords to every man and group the right to present his case. Other groups, like the State Charities Aid Association, compiled pertinent data on subjects within their range of interest. From these illustrations it is evident that there was widespread interest in the convention and its problems and that a tremendous amount of valuable work was done by citizen groups to insure its success.

Ratification of the Constitution

When all other problems of constitution making have been disposed of, there still remains the question of ratification. The time of the election or the method of fixing it may be set forth in the constitution or determined by the legislature or by the convention. Since a convention has no taxing power and the holding of an election involves expense, it is better for the legislature to assume the responsibility. The size of the vote necessary to insure adoption varies considerably from state to state; unless otherwise provided, such changes take effect immediately upon canvass of the vote, if they have been adopted by the required majority. In some cases where the revision made by the convention has been extensive, there arises a question whether the changes should be submitted as a whole or whether they should be voted upon separately. It is sometimes possible to adopt a combination of these two methods, as when Illinois in 1870 submitted eight proposals separately, besides the question of the approval of the constitution as a whole.[24] New York followed a similar procedure in 1938.

While it is almost the universal practice to ask the voters of a state whether they want a constitutional convention, it is not nearly so universal a practice for conventions to submit their proposals to the people. Thus of thirteen new constitutions adopted from 1890 to 1912, only seven were submitted to the people — Utah, 1895; New York, 1894; Alabama, 1901; Oklahoma, 1907; Michigan, 1908; Arizona, and New Mexico, 1912. In four of these states — Utah, Oklahoma, Arizona, and New Mexico — submission was required by Congressional acts granting statehood. In five states there was no submission — Mississippi, 1890; South Carolina, 1895; Delaware, 1897; Louisiana, 1898; and Virginia, 1902. In Kentucky in 1902 the convention met and altered the constitution after the people had approved it. Promulgation of the Virginia Constitution of 1902 without submission to the voters occurred notwithstanding the fact that the legislation calling the convention directed such submission.

The campaign for ratification is only the final hurdle in a long list of obstacles to be overcome before a new constitution may be adopted and made effective. It takes "a lot of doing" to get a new constitution; careful attention must be given in connection with each step in the procedure to the encouraging of a favorable public reaction. The vital need is to inform the

[24] For a discussion of these questions with illustrations, see Walker, *op. cit.*, pp. 61–63.

people thoroughly on what is wrong with the old constitution, on how the delegates to the convention are chosen and what they are trying to do, and on how the defects of the old constitution are to be remedied in the new.[25]

Experience in New York in 1938. The experience of New York in 1915 and 1938 provides a striking illustration of the wisdom of using the plan followed by Illinois in 1870. New York in 1915 and Illinois in 1919 had conventions that did a splendid job of constitution drafting, but both of them made the mistake of submitting their work to the electorate in its entirety. In both cases it was rejected, not because it was not good, not because it was not generally recognized to be good, but because pressure groups and vested interests were able to unite in their opposition to particular features.

Profiting by the 1915 experience, the New York Convention of 1938 submitted to the voters one omnibus proposal containing forty-nine miscellaneous changes and eight specific proposals. The omnibus proposals were, on the whole, noncontroversial and were generally admitted by representatives of all parties and groups to be desirable. All of the eight specific proposals were highly controversial. These dealt, respectively, with legislative reapportionment, grade crossing elimination, low-rent housing and slum clearance, the creation of a new judicial district, the rights of labor, proportional representation, social security, and the debt limit of the City of New York. Three of these were generally regarded as objectionable by impartial and informed persons, and these three — but only these three — proposals were rejected by the electorate. The proposed legislative reapportionment was of a clearly partisan character; the additional judicial district was not needed; and the proposal to outlaw proportional representation, which had already been approved by the voters of the City of New York and incorporated in their new municipal charter, was uncalled for. The result of the election bore testimony to the wisdom of the convention in choosing this method of submitting its proposals, to the discrimination of the voters in being able to approve the desirable proposals and reject the undesirable, and to the effectiveness of intelligent citizen organization in bringing about this result.

The constructive type of civic influence during the campaign for ratification is illustrated by the work of the New York State Committee of the National Municipal League. As soon as the convention adjourned, the Committee prepared a pamphlet containing a summary of the amendments to be voted on. This summary was prepared by a technical committee, whose statement of the arguments for and against each of the proposals was submitted to interested persons and groups, to insure fairness and accuracy of statement. Ultimately about 25,000 copies of this pamphlet were distributed to key people, leaders of opinion in their respective groups and communities

[25] See Chute, Charlton F., "How to Get a New Constitution," *National Municipal Review*, March 1947, pp. 124–130, presenting a checklist of seventeen ways of securing public support for constitutional revision; see also Keith, John R., *Public Relations Program for a Citizen Committee* (Bureau of Municipal Research, University of Texas, 1950).

throughout the state — teachers, ministers, editors, political leaders, and others. Considering the millions of voters in the state, the number of pamphlets distributed was not large, but the results of the referendum indicated that they had gone to the right people. The work of this Committee was constructive and effective. The Citizens Union through recommendations in its annual *Voters' Directory*, the Merchants Association of New York, and many other groups as well as the press were active in the campaign.[26]

Missouri and New Jersey Campaigns. Campaigns for the adoption of new constitutions were carried on in Missouri and New Jersey in 1944. The Missouri campaign was successful; this particular campaign in New Jersey failed, although a later one, in 1947, was successful. All of these campaigns were well organized and well conducted. In Missouri the Statewide Committee for the Revision of the Missouri Constitution, with the full cooperation of press, radio, and civic associations, did splendid work both before the referendum on the holding of a convention and after the convention had completed its work. A statewide Constitution Day was marked by a radio program broadcast over a state network from the capitol, and leading newspapers issued special editions devoting much space to the discussion of constitutional questions.[27]

In New Jersey, the revision of the state's century-old constitution was begun with a State Commission on Revision of the New Jersey Constitution, which reported to the legislature in 1943. The Joint Legislative Committee to Formulate a Draft of a Proposed Revised Constitution for the State of New Jersey completed its draft in January 1944, and this was approved by the legislature for submission to the electorate in November.

Leadership in the campaign was assumed by the Constitution Foundation, which had the assistance and support of practically all responsible organizations — the State Bar Association, the State League of Women Voters, and many others. "Democratic Discussions," a public forum program operated as a phase of the work of the New Jersey Education Association, put out discussion outlines and held scores of local meetings on the topics, "Should We Revise Our State Constitution?" and "Our State Constitution: How Shall We Vote in November?" The speeches of Governor Edison in favor of revision were published in pamphlet form, while many other radio speeches

[26] National Municipal League, *What's in the Proposed Constitution?* (New York, 1938); and Citizens Union, *Voters' Directory* (New York, October, 1938). See O'Rourke, Vernon A., and Campbell, D. W., *Constitution Making in a Democracy* (Johns Hopkins Press, 1943), and McKinney, Madge M., "Constitutional Amendment in New York State," *Public Opinion Quarterly*, October 1939, pp. 635–645, for discussions of the public opinion aspects of the New York referendum.

[27] On the Missouri effort, see Bradshaw, William L., "Missouri's Proposed New Constitution," *American Political Science Review*, February 1945, pp. 61–65; Sparlin, Estal E., "Missouri Adopts a New Constitution," *Bulletin* of the National Tax Association, March 1945, pp. 185–188; Loeb, Tess, "New Constitution for Missouri," *National Municipal Review*, April 1945, pp. 164–167, 178; Chute, Charlton F., "The New Constitution of Missouri," *State Government*, July 1945, pp. 111–112, 119; and other items cited in the preceding edition of this volume.

were mimeographed for further distribution. The Foundation put out a six-page *Summary of Major Changes Embodied in the Proposed Revised Constitution*, and the full text of the proposed constitution was widely distributed. Neither work nor expense was spared in promoting the new constitution. Defeat came chiefly because the unfounded charges of Boss Hague raised doubts in the minds of many citizens at so late a date that the supporters of the new constitution lacked time sufficiently to publicize the answers to his charges.[28]

Pressure Group Influences. If and when the convention does decide to submit its proposals to the people, the same economic groups whose representatives have been trying to arrive at some kind of agreement in the convention are active in the campaign for and against ratification of the new constitution. According to the nature of the provisions of the proposed instrument, one can list those groups which are in favor and those which are opposed. The California Convention, previously discussed, turned out what was for the time a fairly liberal constitution; therefore it was possible for a San Francisco newspaper to classify as follows the sources of the opposition:

1. Corporations, railroads, et cetera
2. Banks, which had been virtually exempt from taxation
3. Dealers in mining stocks now to be taxed
4. Land monopolies
5. Pro-Chinese aristocrats
6. Newspapers who sell out to the above classes
7. Preachers who serve the above [29]

The making of constitutions is a very human thing, as is shown in any state by a study of the attitudes of important social and economic groups toward constitutional revision.

The antidotes for these pressure group influences are more and more and more public information and more and more and more public discussion. That such objectives are being realized, even in cases where the result of the voting on the new constitution is unfavorable, is evidenced by comparison of past practice with that of the present day. Highway Commissioner Spencer Miller, Jr., President of the New Jersey Constitution Foundation, revealed some interesting facts on this subject in a radio address closing the campaign in New Jersey. He made the statement that "in the last four years, there has been more public discussion of the principles of constitutional government

[28] A blow by blow account of the long effort to revise the New Jersey constitution will be found in the notes in the monthly issues of the *National Municipal Review*. John E. Bebout, leader in the campaign, wrote extensively on the problems involved: "How Can New Jersey Get a New Constitution?" *University of Newark Law Review*, March 1941, pp. 1–69; "New Jersey Commission on Constitutional Revision Reports," *National Municipal Review*, July 1942, pp. 243–245; and *The Making of the New Jersey Constitution* (MacCrellish and Quigley Company, Trenton, 1945); see also Rich, Bennett M., "A New Constitution for New Jersey," *American Political Science Review*, December 1947, pp. 1126–1129.

[29] Swisher, *op. cit.*, p. 102. See also Seabury, Samuel, "Property Representation and the Constitutional Convention," *National Municipal Review*, December 1937, pp. 567–571.

and the structure and substance of a new constitution for New Jersey than ever before in our entire history." In support of this claim, he continues:

> Recently I made some researches into the amount of public discussion which took place in 1844, when a new constitution was adopted by a vote of 20,276 to 3,526. In those days, there was a population of approximately 400,000 people in New Jersey. There was no radio, no motion pictures, and no widely circulated newspapers. The facilities for widespread public discussion were limited. The two leading newspapers at that time were the *Newark Daily Advertiser* and the *State Gazette* of Trenton. Their total circulation was little more than 15,000. The Constitution of 1844, which was drafted by a Constitutional Convention in thirty-seven days, was well reported in the *Newark Daily Advertiser* and the *State Gazette*. It was presented to the people for their adoption at a special election, however, just six weeks after it had been drafted. In these six weeks, for example, there were just $136\frac{1}{2}$ inches of space devoted to the discussion of the new constitution in the *Daily Advertiser*. The constitution itself was printed in full fourteen times.
>
> In contrast, the *Newark Evening News* for today (November 6, 1944) contains no less than $213\frac{1}{2}$ inches of space devoted to the discussion of constitutional revision in news articles, in editorials, in advertising space. This means that in a single day in one issue of one newspaper with a circulation of 215,000, there was nearly twice as much space devoted to the discussion of constitutional revisions as in the whole six-weeks campaign of 1844. During the six weeks prior to the Special Election in 1844, there were but two public meetings reported in the *Newark Daily Advertiser*.
>
> In contrast, there have been thousands of town meetings in this State during the past four years in every county and before every kind of group. The New Jersey Constitution Foundation alone has supplied speakers for hundreds of meetings since the 1944 revision was completed by the legislature. There have been innumerable radio broadcasts; the printed word has been widely circulated; copies of the new constitution have been printed in over 400 newspapers of the State. The State itself has published and distributed 1,100,000 copies of the proposed constitution and 600,000 summaries. The Constitution Foundation and other organizations have distributed hundreds of thousands of summaries and explanations of the new constitution.[30]

SELECTED REFERENCES

Bebout, John E., *The Making of the New Jersey Constitution* (MacCrellish & Quigley, Trenton, 1945). Excellent analysis of constitution-making experience in one state.

Callendar, Clarence N., Carter, Edward W., and Rohlfing, Charles C., Eds., "The State Constitution of the Future," *Annals*, September, 1935, entire volume. Symposium of articles prepared by distinguished authorities on the major problems of constitutional revision.

Dority, Ione E., *General Constitutional Revision in the States: a Selected List of References, Covering the Period 1937–1947* (Bureau of Government, University of Michigan, 1948).

Faust, Martin L., *Organization Manual* (Missouri Constitutional Convention of 1943, Columbia, 1943). Useful handbook prepared for the information and guidance of members of the Missouri Convention.

[30] Note in Bebout, *The Making of the New Jersey Constitution*, p. A.

Hoar, Roger S., *Constitutional Conventions* (Little, Brown, Boston, 1917). Subtitle: Their Nature, Powers, and Limitations.

O'Rourke, Vernon A., and Campbell, D. W., *Constitution Making in a Democracy* (Johns Hopkins Press, 1943). Excellent analysis of the New York experience in the Constitutional Convention of 1938.

Swisher, Carl B., *Motivation and Political Technique in the California Constitutional Convention, 1878–1879* (Pomona College, Claremont, 1930). Valuable study of a much neglected aspect of state constitution making.

Uhl, Raymond, and others, *Constitutional Conventions* (Bureau of Public Administration, University of South Carolina, 1951). Concise coverage of organization, powers, functions and procedures.

Walker, Harvey, *The Legislative Process: Lawmaking in the United States* (Ronald Press, New York, 1948). This recent volume contains several chapters on constitution making.

For additional references, see page 68 at the end of Chapter 2.

PART TWO

Political Parties and Popular Control

Wherever regard for public opinion is a first principle of government, practical reform must be slow and all reform must be full of compromises. For wherever public opinion exists it must rule.

— Woodrow Wilson

4

Parties and Elections

In a volume devoted to the organization and functioning of state government, some attention must be given to the organization of political parties in the states, the relation of this machinery to that in the national and local fields, and finally, the methods and techniques by which political parties manage to maintain control over the people. The general qualifications for the suffrage, and such special problems as Negro suffrage and woman suffrage as well as registration, nominating systems, and the conduct of elections, including campaign methods, ballot forms and voting machines, election officers, election frauds, and the cost of elections will be considered.

The American Party System

Organization. The organization of political parties runs parallel with the structure of the several levels of government. Just as the Federal government is established in Washington with the President, the Cabinet, and the Congress, so in the field of party organization one finds the national chairman, the national committee, and the national convention. Just as the governor, the cabinet, and the legislature function in the state governments, so in the state party organization there are the state chairman, the state committee, and the state convention. In the cities the organization is elaborate but constructed along similar lines: just as the city committee is composed of representatives from the various wards of the city, so the ward committee is composed of representatives from the various election districts or voting precincts, each of which has its own committeeman.

Thus there develops a hierarchy of party leaders, beginning with the smallest local districts and extending to the national organization, as shown in the chart on basic structure of parties.[1] The state party organizations become cogs in the great national political party machinery. In addition, the party may organize itself in special districts, as in Congressional or state senatorial districts, for the purpose of conducting more effectively the party

[1] McKean, Dayton D., *Party and Pressure Politics*, p. 201 (Houghton Mifflin, Boston, 1949). His Chapter 9 on party organization, state and national, gives a very clear picture of the problem of over-all organization.

BASIC STRUCTURE OF PARTIES

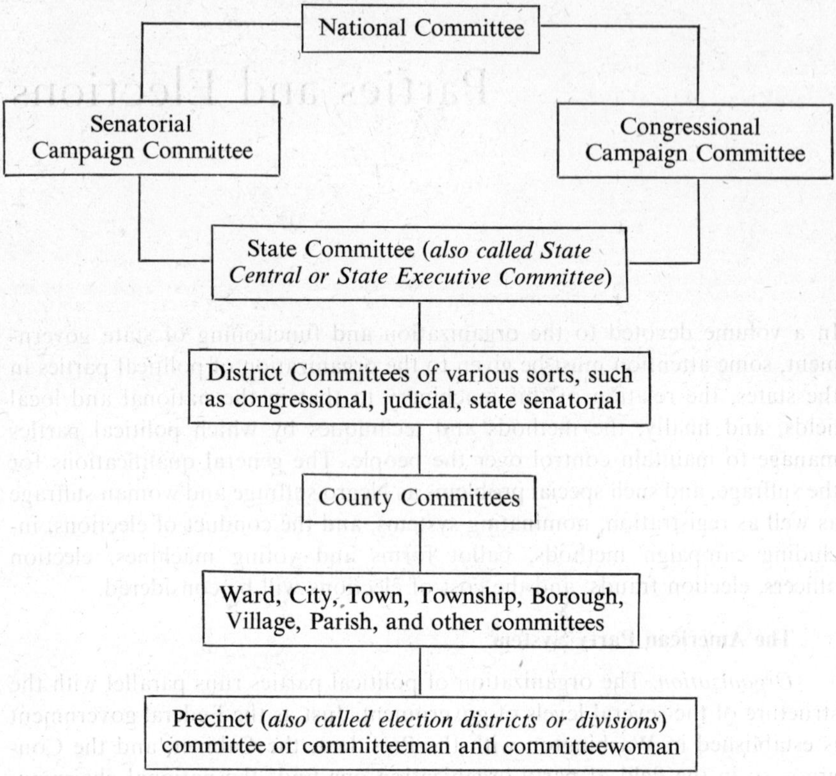

campaigns for legislative offices. Most significant of all is the fact that the party organization in the upper units is unable to function effectively without a strong foundation in the districts where the voters live. It is because of the lack of such organization that reform movements, as Amos Pinchot once said, like a queen bee sting once and die. Many of them do not even sting once. It is impossible to build a party from the top down, for the strength of the party depends upon its strength at the grassroots, in the local communities where the people live.

A strong local organization with a large controlled vote can be used by the party on many occasions. While the connection between national issues and those of the state and local units is relatively slight, local organizations function with equal effectiveness in behalf of the party candidates in all three fields. The techniques and methods by which the organization maintains control over the voters are interesting and important. These controls are exercised more effectively, on the whole, in urban than in rural districts, and decrease in effectiveness in urban districts as the economic and educational status of the people advances. They were far more effective in the past than they are now. Party ties seem to be taken more seriously in the older states along the Atlantic seaboard; their strength is greatly diminished in the Middle West and is apparently nonexistent in the Pacific coast states.

Methods of Control. In the large eastern cities the control of the party organization rests very largely upon two things. In the first place, the division committeeman knows intimately and personally all the people in his district. He calls them by their first names, and they greet him in the same familiar fashion. He knows whether or not a man is married, and if so, how many children he has and what their ages are. He knows whether there are any in-laws residing with the family, or any roomers or boarders. He knows where the man works, what he does, how much he earns, and all the more or less intimate details of the family's affairs. If anyone is ill, the committeeman is solicitous in inquiring for his welfare. If there is a birth, christening, marriage, or death, the committeeman is on hand with congratulations or condolences. He is interested, too, in the group life of the neighborhood. If there is a street carnival, a dance, a baseball game, or a strawberry festival at the church, he always buys a ticket, and if at all possible he attends.

A large number of the party workers are on the public payroll, holding either city or county jobs as a rule, although some of them are able to secure state and Federal positions.[2] Those who are not on the public payroll usually maintain some kind of small business or professional practice. This may be a taproom, a real estate office, an insurance office, a lawyer's office, or an undertaking establishment. The leader may not sell much insurance or much real estate, or practice much law, but he must have some kind of business, for appearance' sake; and more important, he must have some convenient and accessible place in the neighborhood where his constituents may be sure of finding him. A taproom serves this purpose well, since it will enable him to see fairly frequently a considerable portion of his constituents. An undertaking establishment gives him an opportunity to render service to his people at a time when, perhaps, they appreciate it most, while, on the other hand, the fact that he is in politics assists him in the development of his business. One leader in a Philadelphia division runs a small local movie house; in the evening he stands outside to greet and talk with his patrons.

It has long been customary to refer to such political leaders as bosses, and the term has acquired in the minds of many people an unpleasant connotation. Students of government and politics have come to realize that these men are not wholly vicious and that their activities are not without some social justification. Take, for instance, the following comment by Professor William Bennett Munro:

[2] For an able and thorough study of this problem in the Philadelphia Republican organization, see Kurtzman, David H., *Methods of Controlling Votes in Philadelphia* (University of Pennsylvania, 1935). Feldman, Justin N., "How Tammany Holds Power," *National Municipal Review*, July 1950, pp. 330–334, contends that the Democratic machine can smother all opposition because the New York primary laws permit a party to make its own rules.

> For it is the boss who serves, almost single-handed, as the mediator between poverty and power, between the people of the tenements and those who try to be their oppressors. He is the protector of the people against profiteering landlords, avaricious employers, crooked policemen, iron-fisted magistrates, shyster lawyers, and other predatory folks. He is the real friend of the forgotten man. It is to him that the unprivileged go when they are in any kind of trouble. And rarely do they come away empty-handed. To see that they are helped, one and all of them, is what the boss is there for.[3]

This brings us to the second method of control. The leader not only knows his people intimately and personally and identifies himself with the problems of their everyday lives, but he endeavors by every means at his disposal to place them under obligation — financially, if possible — to him. The nature of this obligation depends largely upon the general social and economic status of his constituents, but whatever their status, there is an economic appeal which may be effectively used. In the lower strata of society this may consist in normal times in getting a man a job or getting a clerical position for his son or his daughter, of sending in a ton of coal, a basket of food, or some clothing, or of paying a month's rent. In the upper strata of society, this appeal may be used through influencing the awarding of contracts for supplies and equipment or for public works, by failure to enforce uniformly and fairly the inspection laws, by reducing the assessment on property, by conferring some special privilege not ordinarily enjoyed, or by any one of a hundred other methods. In the former case a family may be counted on for an average of five votes, while in the latter the persons benefited may be influential in the community and therefore able to sway a considerable number of voters at election time.

The Party Worker: The Old Style and the New. In days of old the party worker was at the disposal of his people practically twenty-four hours a day. In addition to rendering service which placed the voter under financial obligation to him, the leader performed other favors of every conceivable sort. If one of his constituents was arrested, he went to the station house to secure his release or a copy of the charge. If a constituent in a foreign district needed a vendor's license from City Hall, he took care of it. If a citizen wanted the street repaired, an additional street light installed or a traffic light at a dangerous intersection, he went to the party worker in his district. If a young man desired to be admitted to law school, he got in touch with his committee-

[3] Munro, William B., *Personality in Politics*, pp. 76–77 (Macmillan, New York, 1934). Significant researches into the organization and methods of municipal bosses and machines were conducted by Zink, Harold, *City Bosses in the United States* (Duke University Press, 1930), and in Chicago by Charles E. Merriam and Harold F. Gosnell; in New York by Roy V. Peel; in Philadelphia by John T. Salter and David H. Kurtzman; in Jersey City by Dayton D. McKean, in Kansas City by Maurice M. Milligan. See Selected References for titles. Professor Peel has edited and provided an introduction for a familiar classic, long out of print: Riordan, William L., *Plunkitt of Tammany Hall* (Knopf, New York, 1948). The writings of some of the leaders themselves are valuable, as, for instance, several volumes by James A. Farley, or Flynn, Edward J., *You're the Boss: My Story of a Life in Practical Politics* (Viking, New York, 1947).

man, who took up the case with someone more influential than himself; if he desired a Senatorial scholarship, he began his negotiations (in states where the competitive examination system is not in use) with the local party worker.

Although people who are not especially familiar with the system may not realize it, the bases or sources of the bosses' power are not necessarily corrupt. Their power rests upon — in addition to financial and personal obligations — personal friendship, sometimes on fear, and very often on the fact that their followers get out to vote in primary and general elections, while the "good" citizens stay at home and moan that "politics are so dirty." Their power rests upon their interest in people and their aptitude for doing the job. It is well to remember that a ward leader is not a good politician because he is a ward leader, but rather that he is ward leader because he is able to carry his ward.

With the passage of time this situation has changed, at least in part. With the establishment of reasonably efficient public employment offices it was no longer necessary for the citizen to go to some party hack to get a job for himself or some member of his family. The growth in the size of the population and the practical elimination of immigration have tended to weaken his power. The extension of civil service has reduced the number of positions at the disposal of members of the organization. Businessmen, made cost-conscious in the depression, became less inclined to pay their cut to support the machine.

The establishment of well-administered systems of public assistance and unemployment compensation relieved the citizen of the need for applying to a local politician for financial assistance. Improvement in the general level of education has made voters somewhat more independent than they were and less inclined to take orders or to seek instructions from the local boss. An enlivened sense of civic responsibility has made possible the public careers of such significant leaders in municipal affairs as Mayors La Guardia of New York, Hoan of Milwaukee, Morrison of New Orleans, Kennelly of Chicago, Seasongood of Cincinnati, and numerous others. All these developments have tended to weaken — although they certainly have not destroyed — the hold of the big city machines upon the voters.

There has been a significant change also in the type of individual who is active in political affairs. This change began to appear after World War I, when Walter Lippmann commented on the passing of the old-fashioned, hard-boiled committeeman, holding forth in the back room of a saloon, and the appearance of a new type of better educated, more polished, and more socially conscious young business and professional man. In the years since, this trend has continued and has become more pronounced. Warren Moscow, able political correspondent for the *New York Times*, after noting that "in general, it is true, all around the country, that the city machines no longer control the vote the way they used to, and that they can no longer elect whom they please, when they please, and how they please," calls attention to the fact that "the boss who sat out on the sidewalk, presiding in tireless and vestless grandeur over a very informal receiving line, has been displaced by the leader — serge-clad, neat, and conscious of issues. His alliances may be with the community's entrenched respectability, rather than the underworld, but he is not necessarily more scrupulous — just more careful and much smoother."[4]

Municipal bosses there have been aplenty over the years, in cities across the land, but there have been relatively few state bosses. Big railroads, mining companies, timber companies, and others have controlled politics in particular states, but there have not been many bosses like Platt in New York, Penrose and Quay in Pennsylvania, Roraback in Connecticut. In fact, they seem to be more numerous now than formerly, and as Moscow points out, "the big bosses are not the men who came up as ward bosses and district leaders. They are businessmen, governors, and United States Senators. Harry F. Byrd's Virginia organization has been called the tightest and best organization in the country today. Harry Byrd, a Senator and member of an old family, is its active leader. In New York and Indiana, to take two states at random, there are powerful Republican organizations of which the active as well as the titular head is the governor."

The conditions favoring the establishment and continuance of such a system have been summarized as follows:

> (1) A constitutional system under which the political center of gravity is very definitely in the legislature; this opens the door to various kinds of special legislation often conceived in the interests of the dominant group; (2) an archaic representative system in which the small towns are vastly over-represented; (3) the persistence of certain aristocratic and deferential traditions which tend to oligarchic government; (4) the absence of machinery by which the voter may make his views felt directly upon the government and the parties; (5) the practical disappearance of an effective legislative minority; (6) the lack of an active opposition press; (7) the fact that the present boss and his lieutenants represent a desirable type of business success and therefore "fit" into their environment successfully; (8) the relatively good government provided by the present system.[5]

Party Discipline. Much caustic criticism has been heaped upon party workers in the large metropolitan areas. It is true that the motives for their good deeds are offensive to many people, but no one who has had an opportunity to observe at close range the functioning of such an organization can believe that any useful purpose will be served by hurling epithets at it or its workers. Until new machinery and administrative techniques were devised

[4] For Lippmann, see summary of his address in the author's *Readings in Public Opinion*, pp. 898–899 (Appleton, New York, 1928), and for Moscow, his article, "Exit the Boss, Enter the Leader," *New York Times Magazine*, June 22, 1947, pp. 16–17, 47–48.

[5] Lancaster, Lane W., "The Background of a State 'Boss' System," *American Journal of Sociology*, March 1930, pp. 783–798. In 1948, it was revealed that thirty-two editors and publishers were kept on the payroll in Illinois. Some of them did some work at the capitol for the more than $300,000 they collected in salaries between 1943 and 1948, but the chief function of many appeared to be "to print canned editorials and news stories lauding the state administration."

to accomplish these purposes, denunciation was idle. Prior to the depression the machine rendered a necessary service in the matter of relief and acted as a buffer between the citizen and the government of which he knew and understood so little.

Party organization was and still is a necessary and inevitable aspect of popular government. It is interesting and perhaps significant that the type of organization here described has been more or less confined to the cities of the East, and that even here it appears to be losing its grip upon the voters. Although there is in each state a branch of the national organization of each of the two major political parties, there is in fact little to bind the local and national organizations together save the desire for victory and a share in the spoils of office. The outstanding issues of a national campaign are not the important issues of a state campaign; the latter are often submerged by the national campaign, although they are important enough to be decided on their own merits. If it be true that the national party labels no longer mean anything, it is doubly true of them as applied to the issues in the various states.

The Suffrage

Much popular misunderstanding exists regarding the nature of the suffrage. It is frequently referred to as a right, using the word "right" in the sense of the natural rights upon which the Founding Fathers laid much emphasis. A "right" is something which belongs to a person by virtue of his status as a human being and a citizen — something the enjoyment of which the government is not at liberty to deny him. Everyone knows that the suffrage is not such a right — that the suffrage may be, and in fact is, withheld from many persons for a wide variety of reasons. It would seem preferable, therefore, to think of the suffrage as a privilege, the exercise of which the state may either grant or withhold, rather than as a right to which one is entitled.

The states enjoy a practically unlimited control in determining qualifications for the exercise of the suffrage. This is clearly shown by reference to certain provisions of the Federal Constitution. In Article I, Section 2, it is stated that the electors for members of the House of Representatives "shall have the qualifications requisite for electors for the more numerous branch of the state legislature," while Section 4 of the same Article continues, "The times, places and manner of holding elections for Senators and Representatives shall be prescribed in each State by the legislature thereof." It thus appears that those persons who are eligible under the provisions of the state law to vote for members of the lower house in the state legislature are by virtue of that fact qualified to vote for members of the lower house of Congress. When in 1917 Amendment XVII was adopted, providing for the direct election of Senators, this idea was extended to electors participating in Senatorial elections. Since the middle of the last century persons possessing such qualifications have been permitted to vote for the members of the

Electoral College. Consequently, the qualifications which the states impose upon voters apply to all voters, usually at all elections, within the respective states.

Three amendments to the Federal Constitution have imposed certain restrictions upon the states in the determination of qualifications. Section 2 of Amendment XIV would, if enforced, reduce the representation in Congress of states withholding the privilege of the suffrage from any considerable number of persons who might normally be considered qualified. This provision is further discussed in connection with the subject of Negro suffrage. Amendment XV provides that "no person shall be denied the right to vote on account of race, color, or previous condition of servitude"; to this, Amendment XIX would add the word "sex." It is important to note that these provisions do not guarantee to anyone, anywhere, at any time, the privilege of voting. Their effect is merely to state that no person shall be denied the suffrage for any one of the four reasons definitely indicated. It is a matter of common knowledge that the states can and do disqualify many persons for a variety of other reasons, and sometimes for these reasons under some other pretext.

In his excellent *History of Suffrage in the United States*, Professor Kirk H. Porter observes that "all of the restrictions and qualifications [on the exercise of the suffrage] can be seen to support one or the other of two fundamental principles: one may be called the 'theory of right' and the other the 'theory of the good of the state.' Every qualification imposed had one of these two principles in view. Either it was established in order to fulfill the right which certain people were supposed to have, or else it was established in order to serve the best interests of the state. It might have been said that a man had the right to vote because he owned property, or because he was a resident or because he paid taxes, or simply because the right to vote was a natural right. . . . Under the theory of the good of the state, men were excluded because they were not church members, because they were criminals, because they had not been residents a long enough time. It is not always possible to classify every restriction definitely, but it may be said that one of these two theories controls every modification of the suffrage." [6]

History of the Suffrage. It has been said, with much justification, that the history of civilization can be traced in the history of the suffrage — in the history of the extension of the privileges of popular participation in government. The evolution of modern government began with an absolute monarchy. In the course of time the monarch was obliged to consult a group of nobles regarding the imposition of taxes and the requirements of military service. The story of the rise of popular government is the story of the slow but steady increase in the size of the group permitted to participate in the making of decisions on public questions. Some considerable portion of this

[6] Porter, Kirk H., *A History of Suffrage in the United States*, pp. 5–6 (University of Chicago Press, 1918).

Voting per State per Population in 1950
United States Bureau of the Census Figures

STATE	POPULATION	POTENTIAL VOTERS	VOTES CAST	PERCENTAGE VOTING
Alabama	3,061,743	1,748,551	152,192	8.7
Arizona	749,587	442,004	177,667	40.2
Arkansas	1,909,511	1,112,872	295,802	26.5
California	10,586,223	7,213,565	3,358,642	46.5
Colorado	1,325,089	844,790	442,892	52.4
Connecticut	2,007,280	1,382,528	860,762	62.3
Delaware	318,085	210,919	129,404	61.4
Florida	2,771,305	1,823,017	253,049	13.9
Georgia	3,444,578	2,008,812	253,108	12.6
Idaho	588,637	349,032	200,084	57.3
Illinois	8,712,176	5,959,188	3,509,836	58.9
Indiana	3,934,224	2,556,680	1,587,298	62.1
Iowa	2,621,073	1,695,155	819,959	48.4
Kansas	1,905,299	1,242,569	606,746	48.8
Kentucky	2,944,806	1,742,931	488,614	28.0
Louisiana	22,683,516	1,587,418	227,095	14.3
Maine	913,774	567,832	237,632	41.8
Maryland	2,343,001	1,527,356	572,937	37.5
Massachusetts	4,690,514	3,206,869	1,947,071	60.7
Michigan	6,371,766	4,107,151	1,904,678	43.9
Minnesota	2,982,483	1,910,633	1,018,267	53.3
Mississippi	2,178,914	1,208,028	87,756	7.3
Missouri	3,954,653	2,643,447	1,250,159	47.3
Montana	591,024	372,417	210,527	56.5
Nebraska	1,325,510	860,291	436,330	50.7
Nevada	160,083	107,174	60,328	56.3
New Hampshire	533,242	352,674	185,247	52.5
New Jersey	4,839,040	3,354,598	1,571,263	46.8
New Mexico	681,187	375,321	173,138	46.1
New York	14,830,192	10,376,277	5,051,897	48.7
North Carolina	4,061,929	2,311,222	522,200	22.6
North Dakota	619,636	366,586	181,369	49.5
Ohio	7,946,627	5,280,602	2,766,706	52.4
Oklahoma	2,233,351	1,382,084	607,786	44.0
Oregon	1,521,341	1,001,690	499,489	49.9
Pennsylvania	10,498,012	6,998,643	3,511,889	50.2
Rhode Island	791,896	538,100	293,400	54.5
South Carolina	2,117,027	1,150,841	50,381	4.4
South Dakota	652,740	401,269	248,426	61.9
Tennessee	3,291,718	1,979,015	262,608	13.3
Texas	7,711,194	4,738,002	360,442	7.6
Utah	688,862	389,855	263,847	67.7
Vermont	377,747	237,550	88,851	37.4
Virginia	3,318,680	2,025,697	211,830	10.5
Washington	2,378,963	1,559,604	723,605	46.4
West Virginia	2,005,552	1,171,860	662,836	56.6
Wisconsin	3,434,575	2,222,525	1,110,192	50.0
Wyoming	290,529	178,582	93,348	52.3
United States	150,697,000	97,416,365	40,429,556	41.5

development had already taken place before our own institutions were established. By long and laborious effort a universal manhood suffrage was attained; as recently as 1919, by the adoption of Amendment XIX, a universal suffrage was achieved.

Those who established the state governments had little confidence in democratic forms. They sought, as has been said, to protect the people from what they feared might be the results of their own folly. They believed in government by the best people; the best people were to be determined by the establishment of tests of religious affiliation and ownership of property. While there was no established church in the several states, as that practice is understood in European countries, it was nevertheless required that voters must be members in good standing, and contributing to the support of, the prevailing religious denomination of the state in which they lived. This same type of qualification was applied, of course, to persons desiring to hold public office. Property-owning and tax-paying qualifications were imposed both upon voters and upon candidates for public office. Some of the states established by law a scale of property qualification for each office, as in Delaware.

In fact, when the Federal Constitutional Convention met in 1787, the ownership of property in specified amounts was a prerequisite to voting in ten of the thirteen original states. In two others, New Hampshire and South Carolina, property ownership was simply one way of qualifying, the other being payment of taxes. These provisions were a survival from colonial times, when it was the theory of the suffrage that property was the foundation of society and that it needed protection by excluding from the vote those floaters, paupers, and apprentices who had no stake in the community. It was feared that a suffrage unrestricted by property and tax tests would threaten vested interests and stable government and would enable the poor to oppose the well-to-do.

In our time religious qualifications have been everywhere abandoned, and property qualifications have disappeared from all but three or four states. During the depression there was some talk of reviving old laws to keep the ballot from recipients of relief, but no such step was taken. Actually, there is little or no connection between the extent of a person's wealth and his or her ability to discharge conscientiously the duties of a citizen. While such qualifications are no longer regarded as in keeping with the spirit of democracy, the Founding Fathers had a logical reason for taking the position which they did. A citizen who owns real estate is apt to have a deeper and more vital concern in the conduct of his local government than is a man who owns no such property. He may be regarded as having roots in the community and as being consequently a more stable citizen. It is possible that this is still true in many cases today, but to enforce such a qualification generally would have the effect of disqualifying those persons who own personal property only or who, like the recipients of public assistance, own neither.

General Qualifications. The qualifications prescribed for voting reflect, at any given time, the judgment of the community as to the things which are important. While some prerequisites have gradually been abolished as no longer pertinent or fair, others have been modified and new ones have been established. Most of the qualifications have been in force for many years and are consequently well known. United States citizenship is a universal requirement, although in times past, during heavy waves of European immigration, there were instances in which states for a time conferred the privilege of the suffrage upon persons who had taken out only their first papers. The age limit of twenty-one years is in effect in every state except Georgia. Residence requirements are everywhere in force. The length of residence required within the state, the county, and the voting district varies greatly from state to state, the length of the period required diminishing from the larger unit to the smaller, as is shown in the table of state voting laws on page 108.

Voting Age. Strong arguments have been presented for reducing the voting age from twenty-one to eighteen, as Georgia did by constitutional amendment in 1943. The prevailing requirement has the support of long-established usage and of conformity with legal age requirements for many other purposes. Under present conditions, however, there is much to be said for the proposal. Young people are far better informed and more mature than they were before the introduction of modern educational methods. In school and college they study social, political, and economic problems and become deeply interested in them, only to be reminded on registration day that they are not old enough to vote. Many resent this, especially when they look at some of the people who are legally entitled to vote. Some lose interest or become absorbed in other matters in the interval between the completion of school and the time at which they become of age. They are left without any effective means of expressing their interest in civic affairs. Most important of all, perhaps, is the fact that young men between the ages of eighteen and twenty-one are especially desirable for military service. If they are old enough to fight and die for their country, they should be considered old enough to vote.

A concession on the voting age might be advantageous both to the community and to thousands of young citizens, but there was, for a time at least, much opposition to the change. Large numbers of bills providing for the change have been introduced each year into the several state legislatures; of these, a few have passed one house, though most have not been acted upon. Some have been defeated. A proposal for a constitutional amendment was introduced in the Seventy-eighth Congress and a hearing was held on it by the House Committee on the Judiciary. The Senate Committee on the Judiciary in the Eighty-second Congress unanimously approved such a proposal in 1952. While only 17 per cent of those questioned in a Gallup poll in 1939 favored the plan, the percentage is now well over 50. Presidential candidates Eisenhower, Harriman, and Kefauver all endorsed the proposal during the 1952 pre-convention campaign. Such a provision was included in the *Model State Constitution* in 1946. Favorable official action may well be taken during the next few years.[7]

Literacy Test. Connecticut in 1855, and Massachusetts in 1857, both by constitutional amendment, adopted literacy tests for voting. The ability to read, or to read and write, is now a constitutional qualification for voting in approximately half of the states. Geographically, one fourth of these states are in the Northeast, one fourth in the West, and one half in the South. The most common literacy requirement, found in the Alabama, California, Delaware, and New York constitutions, specifies that "no person shall be entitled to vote unless such person is also able, except for physical disability, to read and write English."

The New York provision dates from 1923; Dean Crawford, who made a careful study of its working, testifies to its general effectiveness.[8] Basing his judgment largely upon an analysis of its operation over a period of six years, he concludes that the test has been actually enforced, 14.9 per cent having failed to pass in the six years; that there has been a steady increase in the interest of new voters in elections; that the interest in Presidential years is greater than in other elections; that women show a relatively lower percentage of interest than do men; that women are more successful than men in passing the test; and finally, that the test has developed interest in evening schools on the part of the foreign-born.

Poll Tax. Until recently the poll tax was generally thought of as a device for keeping Negroes in certain Southern states from voting. Actually, it grew not out of the Reconstruction movement but out of the Granger movement and the Populist party activity in the last decade of the nineteenth century. The first act containing such a restriction was passed in Florida in 1889. Others followed in rapid succession, until by 1901 eight had been passed in as many states in the southeastern region. Georgia came along last in 1908. The provisions of these laws kept the poor whites as well as the Negroes from voting. They imposed high taxes and required payment many months prior to the holding of the election; and even when the tax had been paid, the colored voter was not permitted to register unless he could present his tax receipt. By setting the amount of the tax high, the assumption was that the colored voter would not have available the amount of money required, or that if he did, he would not be willing to spend it, many months before, for the rather doubtful chance of participating in an election. The tax was cumulative, the

[7] See, for example, Arnall, Ellis G., "Admitting Youth to Citizenship," *State Government*, October 1943, pp. 203–204; Dam, Loring, "Civic Plan to Bridge 18–21 Gap," *National Municipal Review*, January 1945, pp. 10–13, 26; *Editorial Research Reports*, "The Voting Age," issue of September 9, 1944; Johnsen, Julia E., *Lowering the Voting Age* (Wilson, New York, 1944); *Congressional Digest*, "Should the Legal Voting Age Be Reduced to Eighteen Years?" August-September 1944, entire issue.

[8] Crawford, Finla G., "The New York State Literacy Test," *American Political Science Review*, May 1923, pp. 260–263, and November 1925, pp. 788–790; and "Operation of the Literacy Test for Voters in New York," *ibid.*, May 1931, pp. 342–345; Key, Vladimer O., Jr., *Southern Politics in State and Nation*, Chapter 26 (Knopf, New York, 1949).

law requiring that the tax for all preceding years must be paid before the citizen was eligible to vote. This may constitute a financial burden sufficiently serious, especially in lower income families, white as well as Negro, to prevent participation in elections.

The subject has been one of intense controversy in both state and nation for the past several years. Throughout the South, liberals have been trying to abolish the tax. In the six states in which the poll tax still exists in some form as a prerequisite for voting,[9] usually less than 25 per cent of the total voting population have participated in recent Presidential elections, whereas some fifty or more years ago, prior to the enactment of these laws, voting participation in the South compared favorably with that in other sections of the country. The poll tax requirement is undemocratic in its effects and sets apart the states that still retain it. Tennessee tried unsuccessfully to abolish its tax in 1943; Tennessee and South Carolina both succeeded in eliminating it in 1951. Under the able leadership of Governor Ellis Arnall, Georgia abolished its poll tax in 1945. In New England a very similar form of tax is used, the only difference being that, whereas in the South payment of the tax is a prerequisite for voting, in New England the fact that one has voted makes him liable for the payment of the tax.

Since progress in abolishing the poll tax by state action has been so slow and uncertain, the effort has been made to secure Congressional enactment of a measure that would accomplish this purpose in all the states uniformly and simultaneously. A bill for this purpose has been introduced in each session since 1940 and has been the occasion for extended committee hearings, prolonged filibusters on the part of the Southern Senators, propaganda and counterpropaganda, crimination and recrimination. While the argument is advanced that under the Constitutional clause guaranteeing a republican form of government to the states, the Federal government has the power and the duty to pass such an act, there is, in some quarters, grave doubt as to its constitutionality. On the basis of experience up to 1950, it seems unlikely that the measure will be enacted.[10]

Negro Suffrage. The question of Negro suffrage, long of great concern in the Southern states, is of rapidly increasing importance in the Northern cities, where the Negroes now often hold the balance of power. In order to understand the present situation it is necessary to review briefly the circumstances under which it developed. At the close of the Civil War the Radical

[9] These are: Alabama, Arkansas, Mississippi, Rhode Island, Texas, and Virginia. No such tax was levied in the following fifteen states: Arizona, California, Colorado, Idaho, Iowa, Louisiana, Maryland, New Mexico, New York, Ohio, Oregon, South Carolina, Tennessee, Utah, and Wisconsin. In the remaining twenty-seven states such taxes are or may be levied, but payment is not a suffrage requirement. Key, *Southern Politics*, *op. cit.*, devotes Chapters 27 and 28 to the poll tax, variations in form and application, and disfranchising effects. The Tennessee story is told in full, by the Chairman of the Southern Electoral Reform League, in Perry, Jennings, *Democracy Begins at Home* (Lippincott, Philadelphia, 1944). Other discussions of the subject are cited in earlier editions of this volume.

[10] For numerous references on this phase of the poll tax problem, see the preceding edition of this volume, p. 126.

State Voting Laws

Qualifications for Voting in the United States
United States citizenship, and, except in Georgia, age of 21 years.[1]

	RESIDENCE IN—			PERSONS EXCLUDED FROM THE SUFFRAGE—			OTHER—
	STATE	COUNTY	VOTING PRECINCT	CONVICTION OF A FELONY[2]	INSANE, LUNATICS, ETC.	IDIOTS	MISCELLANEOUS[3]
Alabama	2 years	1 year	3 months	x	x	x	3
Arizona	1 year	6 months	30 days	x	x	x	2
Arkansas	1 year	6 months	30 days	x	x	x	1
California	1 year	90 days	40 days	x	x	x	1
Colorado	1 year	90 days	10 days	x			0
Connecticut	1 year	[4]		x	x	x	1
Delaware	1 year	3 months	90 days	x	x	x	1
Florida	1 year	6 months		x	x		0
Georgia	1 year	6 months		x	x	x	0
Idaho	6 months	30 days		x	x	x	1
Illinois	1 year	90 days		x			0
Indiana	6 months	[5]					0
Iowa	6 months	60 days	10 days	x	x	x	0
Kansas	6 months	30 days	30 days	x	x		0
Kentucky	1 year	6 months	60 days	x			1
Louisiana	2 years	1 year	3 months				0
Maine	6 months	3 months	3 months	x			3
Maryland	1 year	6 months	6 months	x			0
Massachusetts	6 months		6 months	x			0
Michigan	6 months	[6]	20 days	x			0
Minnesota	6 months		30 days	x	x		2
Mississippi	2 years	1 year	1 year	x			1
Missouri	1 year	60 days	60 days	x	x		1
Montana	1 year	30 days	30 days	x	x	x	1
Nebraska	6 months	40 days	10 days				
Nevada	6 months	30 days	10 days	x	x	x	1
New Hampshire	6 months		6 months				1
New Jersey	1 year	5 months	30 days	x	x	x	1
New Mexico	1 year	90 days	30 days		x		1
New York	1 year	4 months	30 days	x			2
North Carolina	1 year	4 months	4 months	x	x	x	0
North Dakota	1 year	90 days	30 days	x			1
Ohio	1 year	30 days	20 days	x			2
Oklahoma	1 year	6 months	30 days	x	x	x	2
Oregon	6 months			x	x	x	0
Pennsylvania	1 year		60 days				0
Rhode Island	2 years	[7]	6 months	x			3
South Carolina	2 years	6 months	60 days	x	x	x	1
South Dakota	1 year	90 days	30 days	x	x		2
Tennessee	1 year	6 months		x			1
Texas	1 year	6 months		x	x	x	1
Utah	1 year	4 months	60 days		x	x	2
Vermont	1 year		3 months				0
Virginia	1 year	6 months	30 days	x	x	x	2
Washington	1 year	90 days	30 days	x	x	x	1
West Virginia	1 year	60 days	60 days	x	x		3
Wisconsin	1 year		10 days	x	x		2
Wyoming	1 year	60 days	10 days		x		3
				39	29	20	

Reconstruction leaders in Congress forced through the adoption of Amendment XV, the purpose of which was to guarantee so far as possible the privilege of the suffrage to the newly established group of Negro citizens. The period of reconstruction following the Civil War presents a story of graft and political corruption almost unparalleled in the annals of a civilized community.[11] The carpetbaggers from the North, together with the Southern scalawags, plundered the treasuries of the Southern states in shameless fashion. Personal clothing, food, house furnishings, and the like were purchased in great quantities at public expense for the members of the legislature, their families and friends. These legislatures were composed largely of Negro members. Bars were established in close proximity to legislative chambers, the sessions in which were a riot of confusion and disorder.

In 1877 President Hayes withdrew the last of the troops from the Southern states. From this time on, the white people of the South began a very natural and proper effort to regain control of their governments.[12] It was possible to discourage many colored persons from voting through the activities of the Ku Klux Klan, but the more enlightened Southern leaders well knew that this was neither a suitable nor a permanent solution of their prob-

---

[1] Registration is also generally required, but in Kansas, it is limited to certain cities; in Kentucky, to cities of the first and second class; in Louisiana, to cities of the first, second, third, and fourth classes; in Missouri, to cities of 10,000 and over; in Nebraska, and Wisconsin, to cities of 5,000 and over; in North Dakota, to cities of over 1,500; in Ohio, to cities of 16,000 and over.

[2] Unless pardoned, thereby restoring civil rights (includes prisoners).

[3] Included are paupers and vagrants, 14; illiterates, 8; persons under guardianship, 7; unpaid poll tax and other miscellaneous causes, 5.

[4] Six months residence in the town.

[5] Sixty days residence in township.

[6] Twenty days residence in city or township.

[7] Six months residence in municipality.

---

[11] The essential facts of this era are nowhere more vividly presented than in Fleming, W. L., *Documentary History of Reconstruction*, 2 vols. (A. H. Clark Company, Cleveland, 1906–1907). For later attempts to gloss over the abuses of this period, see Du Bois, W. E. B., *Black Reconstruction* (Harcourt, Brace, New York, 1935), and Allen, James S., *Reconstruction; the Battle for Democracy, 1865–1876* (International Publishers, New York, 1937).

[12] Gosnell, Harold F., *Democracy — the Threshold of Freedom* (Ronald Press, New York, 1948), discusses these problems fully in Chapter 6. He says: "Once the pressure of the Federal troops was gone, the Southern whites employed the harsh political methods that are used by a dominant culture group to subordinate a group that it regards as inferior. Force in the form of tar and feathers, whipping, other forms of torture, and killing, was applied vigorously. In addition, all types of fraud were employed: gerrymandering, inadequate voting facilities, dilatory tactics, withholding of returns, fraudulent election counts, ballot box stuffing, padded lists, and discriminatory enforcement of the election regulations. Social pressure, such as business ostracism, unofficial banishment, and segregation, was used to keep the Negroes from the polls. Finally, bribery in all its forms was employed. Colored voters were paid to stay at home, or, where a poll tax receipt was necessary in order to vote, these receipts were used as admission fees to circuses and other entertainments. With their lack of organization, leadership, education, and economic independence, the Negroes could not withstand these pressures. They were eliminated as effective elements in the electoral process of the Southern States."

lem. They cast about for techniques and methods by which the colored people could be constitutionally and legally barred from exercising the privilege of the suffrage. The first important attempt at the use of legal and constitutional means was made by Mississippi, which, in a new constitution in 1890, imposed numerous restrictions. The voter must have paid all the taxes assessed against him, including a poll tax of two dollars; he must be able either to read any section of the state constitution or to understand it when read to him; the residence requirement was raised from one year to two years. Although there could have been little intention that these provisions would be fairly interpreted as between whites and blacks, the Supreme Court held that they did not contravene the provisions of Amendment XV.[13]

Although these methods spread rapidly through the other Southern states, they did not prove to be as effective as had been anticipated. One writer has observed that this system, although judiciously administered, failed to protect sufficiently the illiterate whites. It remained for South Carolina, in 1895, to introduce one of the most effective devices for this purpose, the grandfather clause. This device also spread rapidly through the South, reducing the size of the electorate in each case by thousands of voters. While the so-called grandfather provisions were temporary in character, they were extremely effective in eliminating from the list of voters the names of colored citizens and in including whites who might otherwise have been eliminated by poll tax, educational provisions, or other tests designed to exclude Negroes. They usually covered two points, providing (1) that persons who had themselves participated in any war in which the United States was a party, or any descendants of such persons, might register to vote; (2) that those persons who were themselves, or whose ancestors had been before them, citizens of any recognized member of the family of nations as of January 1, 1866, might register. The effectiveness of these provisions is not difficult to understand when one recalls that prior to that date Negroes had no standing as citizens of any important country in the world. The attempt of Oklahoma to incorporate provisions of this character permanently in its constitution has been noted in a preceding chapter.

The various technical and more or less devious methods which were employed prior to and along with the grandfather clauses remained in effect long after the latter had passed out of existence. In addition to the imposition of high poll taxes — taxes of three, four, or five dollars — constitution interpretation tests were widely employed. When one considers that lawyers, jurists, and students of political science spend a lifetime studying constitutional law without achieving anything more than a moderate knowledge of it, one wonders how the average layman, who had little time for or interest in such questions, could have been expected to give suitable interpretations of intricate constitutional questions. The fact is, of course, that this was not the purpose of the law. If the applicant for registration did give the right

[13] Williams v. Mississippi, 170 U.S. 213, 1898.

answer, the chances are that the registration officer in most cases would not have recognized it as such. Nobody expected the answers to be correct; the purpose was to enable the registration clerk to say that the white man could register and that the black man could not. Some states required the prospective registrant to have been steadily employed throughout the preceding year, or to list the names and addresses of his employers during a preceding three- or five-year period.

Another device of more recent origin was the white primary. In Texas and other Southern states Negro voters were barred from participation in direct primary elections of the Democratic party by a rule of either the state or local party organization. It took the form, says one authority, of a "declaration by the Democratic party authorities in each state that only white men [are] eligible to membership and permitted to help, in the primary elections, in the nomination of the party candidates." Since the Democratic nomination is equivalent to election in state and local contests in most of these states, debarment from participation in the nominating process is in effect disfranchisement. This result was not achieved without a considerable struggle in the courts. The attempt of the Texas legislature in 1923 to exclude Negroes by specific legislative provision was invalidated by the Supreme Court in Nixon v. Herndon.[14] The Democratic State Executive Committee thereupon adopted a rule permitting "all white Democrats who are qualified . . . and none other" to participate in party primaries. In Nixon v. Condon, in which the plaintiff was the same person who had figured in the earlier case, the Supreme Court ruled this action also invalid, on the ground that it was based upon a discriminatory legislative provision.[15]

In most states a political party is now and has long been regarded as a public body; a legal solution of this problem was possible because in certain Southern states the party was regarded by law as a private organization, which was, therefore, at liberty to make such rules as it saw fit for the management of its own affairs. In 1935, the Supreme Court held, in Grovey v. Townsend,[16] that the State Democratic Convention in Texas was not a mere instrumentality or agency of the state, so as to render its resolution limiting membership in the party to white citizens "state action," within the limitations of Amendments XIV and XV. Nine years later, in 1944, in Smith v. Allwright, the Court completely reversed this decision, the only dissenter being Justice Roberts, who wrote the opinion in the earlier case. The Court

[14] 273 U.S. 536, 1927.

[15] 286 U.S. 73, 1932.

[16] 295 U.S. 45, 1935. O. Douglas Weeks has traced the history of the Texas experience in a series of articles: "The Texas Direct Primary System," *Southwestern Social Science Quarterly*, September 1932, pp. 95–120; "The White Primary," *Mississippi Law Journal*, December 1935, pp. 135–153; "The White Primary: 1944–1948," *American Political Science Review*, June 1948, pp. 500–510; also Strong, Donald S., "The Rise of Negro Voting in Texas," *ibid.*, June 1948, pp. 510–522; Swisher, Carl B., "The Supreme Court and the South," *Journal of Politics*, May 1948, pp. 282–305; and Key, *Southern Politics*, *op. cit.*, Chapter 29.

caused a nationwide sensation by asserting, at long last, that Amendment XV means what it says.[17]

The significance of this decision is well summarized in the Report of the President's Committee on Civil Rights [18]:

> Some states adapted their primary laws to the Supreme Court ruling; others resisted, first, by refusing to open white primaries to Negroes until further litigation made the Texas ruling applicable to them, then by devising other methods of depriving Negroes of the ballot. Today the effort to preserve the pure white electoral system in these states is continuing.
>
> Two states, Louisiana and Texas, repealed white primary provisions immediately after the Supreme Court decision; Florida, Alabama, and Georgia were forced to do so by further court rulings. South Carolina called a special session of the state legislature at which all state laws in any way regulating primaries were repealed. . . . In 1947 the white primary in South Carolina, resting on its new foundation, was held invalid by the United States District Court for the Eastern District of South Carolina in the case of Elmore v. Harris. . . .
>
> Alabama took a different course from South Carolina. Instead of repealing the primary laws it sought to continue disfranchisement by establishing "qualifications" standards under which Negroes could be barred by administrative action. The "Boswell Amendment" adopted by this state in November 1946, set up a provision under which voters would be required "to understand and explain" provisions of the state constitution. Exclusion by this kind of device is a familiar Southern phenomenon.

It is easy for any impartial observer to understand why these things were done but the situation today is greatly changed. Negro education has made considerable progress. Those colored citizens who are able to meet the reasonable qualifications commonly imposed should be permitted to vote. There is a provision in the second section of Amendment XIV which provides that the representation of states in the House of Representatives shall be reduced in proportion to the number of qualified voters who are denied the privilege of the suffrage. This provision has never been enforced, and it seems reasonably safe to predict that it never will be. When, occasionally, a Northern member seeks to invoke the enforcement of this clause, the answer of the Southern members always is that they will correct their election abuses when the Northern cities prove that they can conduct elections without disorder and bloodshed, and show that their elections are reasonably decent and honest. While two wrongs do not make a right, the attitude of these Southern members is easy to understand. Under these circumstances it would be highly desirable if this clause of Amendment XIV might be repealed, for it is unfortunate to retain in the Constitution provisions which are unenforced and unenforceable.

Woman Suffrage. The movement for the adoption of woman suffrage owes its origin to the famous Women's Rights Convention held in Seneca Falls, New York, in 1848. Prior to this time women had enjoyed no rights

[17] 321 U.S. 649, 1944.

[18] Pp. 35–40 (Washington, 1947).

and few privileges; their mission in life was to remain at home and raise a large family. They were not permitted to maintain control over property, secure the benefits of higher education, engage in the practice of professions, appear on the public platform as speakers or musical artists, or participate in any of the other varied activities which now engage their time and attention.[19] A little group of radicals, including Elizabeth Cady Stanton, Lucretia Mott, Martha C. Wright, Mary Ann McClintock, and others, assembled for the purpose of protesting against this situation and of demanding for women opportunities of the types indicated. Although at first they were not greatly concerned with the question of suffrage, this soon became an important item in their program. The question was much debated in Congress, and when the provisions of Amendment XV were under discussion, the attempt was made to add the word "sex" to the three items finally included. When this effort failed, a fifty-year campaign was begun, which culminated in the adoption of Amendment XIX in 1919. As astute an observer as James Bryce predicted in 1888 that nothing would ever come of the movement for at least three decades.[20] Nevertheless, one state after another, as well as a number of territories, adopted woman suffrage provisions operative within its own borders, beginning with the first territorial legislature in Wyoming in 1869 — seventy-five years ago. By the time the amendment was adopted, these were effective in approximately half the states. It was not until 1920 that women were eligible to participate in a Presidential election in all the states.

In the course of the campaign for the amendment, extravagant claims were made by the partisans on both sides. Those who opposed its adoption, including large numbers of women, predicted that the effect of woman suffrage would be calamitous. They foresaw a situation in which women would desert their families and their homes in order to take part in politics. Others thought women were incapable of intelligent participation in public affairs. The supporters of the amendment, on the other hand, painted rosy pictures of the political millennium which might be expected to follow the adoption of woman suffrage. Women, they said, with their greater sensitiveness to moral and ethical considerations, would exercise this power to eliminate graft, corruption, and political connivance. The claims of neither of the partisan groups which participated in the campaign have been substantiated. In general, it may be said that the amendment doubled the number of voters, giving us twice as many intelligent voters as there were before, and twice as many ignorant ones.

[19] See their Declaration of Sentiments, in Anthony, Susan B., *History of Woman Suffrage*, Vol. I, pp. 67–74 (National American Women's Suffrage Association, New York, 1912). These pages also contain the text of the resolutions adopted by the Convention, together with some account of its proceedings. The Association was disbanded in 1947 on the ninety-first birthday of Carrie Chapman Catt, its longtime leader.

[20] Bryce, James, *The American Commonwealth*, First Edition, Vol. III, Chapter 93 (Macmillan, New York, 1888); see also Brooks, Robert C., Ed., *The American Commonwealth: Fiftieth Anniversary*, pp. 61–63 (Macmillan, New York, 1939).

At this date, when women have had an opportunity to vote in all of the states for more than three decades and to participate in several Presidential elections, it is only reasonable to inquire into the effects of this participation.[21] Women accept their responsibility now as a matter of course, having largely overcome their reluctance to participate in public affairs. In general, the interest of women in politics and the effectiveness of their participation have steadily increased. In 1944 — in the midst of war — women outnumbered men on the voting lists for the first time and played their most important role in national politics since they were enfranchised. In a few cases, particularly in local affairs and in matters relating to education and public welfare, broadly defined, it has been demonstrated that the participation of women as voters has had a distinct influence for the improvement of conditions.

While significant changes in the position of women in our society, which some people resent, are taking place, no one will argue that these changes have been due entirely or even chiefly to the participation of women in politics. Politics is but one among a series of factors which brought about this change. On the other hand, there does not seem to be any appreciably greater prevalence of high moral and ethical standards in politics than there was prior to 1919. When one stops to analyze this situation, it seems strange that anyone could have seriously expected that there would be. This view was based on an assumption that male voters would vote deliberately to perpetuate governmental inefficiency and political corruption while their wives, going to the polls from the same homes and from the same social and economic environment, would vote for honesty in public affairs, thereby canceling their husbands' votes. Such an assumption was little short of ridiculous. The political allegiance of individuals does not rest on the basis of sex. People vote for one candidate or against another as they believe doing so will help them to maintain their social and economic position and privileges, if they are well off, or enable them to improve their general status in society if they are not well off. In this important decision the interests of the husband and wife are substantially the same.

Absentee Voting. Absent-voting legislation is not merely a convenience; it is a necessity if, in an age of great social mobility, a large number of persons whose business or professional activity requires them to be much away from home or to travel extensively are not to be virtually disfranchised.

[21] See Thompson, C. Mildred, "A Decade of Woman Suffrage," *Current History*, October 1930, pp. 13–17; "Women Voters Celebrate 25th Birthday," *National Municipal Review*, April 1945, p. 190, and Gosnell, *op. cit.*, Chapter 4, at the conclusion of which he says: "The adoption of woman suffrage did not bring about all the changes hoped for by its advocates. It failed to purify politics, to bring equal rights, and to achieve equal opportunities for men and women. But it did raise the level of politics, bring women a little closer to the ideal of equal rights, and open many new opportunities to women. As women achieve equality in education, their influence on politics will be felt more and more. When one considers the legal and economic position of women a hundred years ago, no one can deny that political agitation and participation has accomplished astounding results."

Initiated for the benefit of soldiers in service, absent voting was first used for a civilian population in Vermont in 1896. After that date the absent-voting privilege was extended until, at the beginning of World War II, there were only six states in which it was not operative, at least to a limited extent. Thirteen states enacted their laws in 1917. Maryland and New Jersey restricted the privilege to voters in the armed forces. Mississippi repealed its law in 1932 and did not replace it; several states lost their laws by adverse court action, but later rewrote and reenacted them. Numerous restrictions and limitations are found in these measures — some geographical, others relating to cause of absence or type of election.

After tremendous agitation, Congress passed the Servicemen's Voting Act in 1944, while a number of states liberalized their laws to facilitate voting by service personnel, only to permit these advances to lapse during the postwar years. A survey made early in 1952 by a committee of the American Political Science Association, appointed at the request of President Truman, showed that more than half of the 2,500,000 Americans then in the armed services and some 200,000 citizens living overseas would lose their right to vote in the 1952 Presidential election unless many changes were made in the laws and regulations then governing absentee voting.[22] Persons resident in New Mexico and South Carolina could not vote under any circumstances because of the lack of any provision for absentee voting in these states. There was no provision for voting by service personnel who were members of the regular military establishment in Texas.

In six states, all voters must register in person within the state, even though members of the armed services. In five states, a special form of ballot application is required, the standardized postcard-ballot application accepted (if at all) only as an application for an application. Although the Department of Defense estimates that a minimum of forty-five days is necessary to deliver the ballots and get them marked and returned, ballots would not be sent out until twenty-one days (or less) before the last date on which they would be received for counting in five states; until thirty days (or less) before the closing date for counting in fifteen states. It thus appeared probable that most of the ballots requested by men from these states would never be counted, even if they had the patience to put up with the intricate system of applying for their ballots.

In thirty states, it is provided that "for purposes of voting, no person shall be deemed to have lost or gained a residence in this state by reason of his absence while employed in the service of the Federal government." Vexatious as is the absentee voting system in many states, as applied to general elections, it is, if anything, even worse in primary elections. Although the President made repeated requests for Congressional action, the Congress adjourned

[22] *Voting in the Armed Forces* (82nd Cong., 2nd Session, House Document No. 407, Washington, March 28, 1952); see also, Reston, James, *New York Times*, March 24, 1952.

before the party conventions without passing any legislation, nor did the states themselves take action to correct the abuses pointed out in the report.

Registration

It has become trite to say that "an honest electoral system lies at the very basis of popular government" — but it is none the less true. The first step in the conduct of such elections is to set the qualifications of voters; these have just been discussed. The next step is for those who are able to meet the qualifications, and are therefore eligible to vote, to establish that fact by the process of registration. The purpose of registration is to compile a list of such persons a sufficient length of time prior to the election, so that the public can have an opportunity to assure itself that none but properly qualified persons are to participate in the approaching election. Of course, if the election is properly conducted, those who have not registered cannot vote, except in those jurisdictions where previously registered voters are permitted to vote on affidavit.

Registration as a means of establishing eligibility to vote is a relatively modern development. In the early days, when the country was predominantly rural and almost every citizen in a community was known to every other, such a process was unnecessary. At present, however, all states except Arkansas and Texas have some form of registration; in a number of states the application of the system is limited to certain cities. Registration by mail is permitted in nineteen states, for Federal employees only in two others — Idaho and Oregon. Twenty-six states do not permit it. Thus, as urbanization has continued, the idea of registration has spread and the methods of registration have been subject to development and change, the primary purpose of preventing election frauds still remaining uppermost. The various types of fraud which it is sought to prevent are: voting the graveyard, voting by persons who have moved away, voting by persons not qualified, voting under fictitious names, repeating, chain voting, and the like.

The first registration law in this country was enacted by Massachusetts in 1800; states outside New England followed slowly, South Carolina adopting such legislation for Columbia in 1819, and Pennsylvania for Philadelphia in 1836. The subject was discussed by the Constitutional Convention in New York in 1821, but it was not until 1840 that an act was passed applicable even to New York City, and this was repealed after a period of two years, apparently without protest by Governor William H. Seward, who had urged its adoption. "The spread of registration laws began about 1860 and continued until about 1910. The first laws were adopted by states with large cities, and registration was required only in those cities. As time went on it was discovered that voting frauds were not confined to the large cities, and the registration provisions were extended to smaller cities and towns, and in some states to rural sections as well." [23] The early measures provided for per-

[23] Harris, *op. cit.*, p. 72.

sonal registration, and there are many jurisdictions in which this type is still used; the present tendency is in the direction of a permanent registration in accordance with such rules as will presently be described. There is too much variation in the history and development of the system in the individual states to attempt a description of any particular one.

Periodic Registration. In the operation of a registration system there are numerous questions and problems, such as the treatment of rural areas and of cities of different size. There is much difference of opinion regarding the first; in New York, for instance, three different systems of registration are in use, according to the size of the cities concerned. Again, there is the question of the relative merits of periodic and permanent registration. There are thirty-six states which use some form of permanent registration, either on a statewide basis or in designated cities and counties. The variations show a total lack of agreement on matters of policy; some states, as Louisiana and Maryland, except their large cities, while others provide for the use of the system in the cities and except the less populous areas, as Wisconsin. Periodic registration, with a frequency varying from one to six years, exists in twelve states. Of the largest cities, New York, Buffalo, and Rochester have an annual system; Los Angeles, San Francisco, Seattle, and Memphis, a biennial system; and St. Louis, Baltimore, Kansas City, and New Orleans a quadrennial one.

Annual registration imposes an unnecessary burden upon the voter, and the lists so compiled are inaccurate within a few months. The biennial and quadrennial forms are less expensive in operation, if administered with a like degree of efficiency, but they are even less accurate than the annual system, and impose some inconvenience upon voters who change their address and are obliged to re-register. All these forms of registration are personal; there exists in some communities an annual nonpersonal registration, which in practice amounts to a permanent registration, since the registry boards meet as prescribed by law and copy the list of the preceding year with but few changes.[24]

Permanent Registration. A survey made by Professor Weeks in 1939 showed that three fourths of the states were using permanent registration, either on a statewide basis or in restricted areas, including the cities of Birmingham, Boston, Chicago, Cincinnati, Cleveland, Denver, Detroit, Louisville, Milwaukee, Minneapolis, Omaha, Portland (Oregon), and St. Paul. These systems may be fitted into two general groups: "(1) those having 'model' or approximately 'model' registration laws of recent date; and (2) those having incomplete or old laws in which most, or at least some of the necessary features of the first group are lacking. Twenty states — Eastern, Middle-western, and Western — fall into the first group; the remaining six-

[24] For a good description of the quadrennial system in Louisiana, see Powell, Alden L., and Asseff, Emmett, *Registration of Voters in Louisiana* (Bureau of Government Research, Louisiana State University, 1951).

teen — Eastern, Southern, and Western — into the second. The first group may be subdivided into two classifications: (a) thirteen with statewide or reasonably extensive systems,[25] and (b) seven which limit the 'model' type to one or a few populous cities or counties.[26] The second general group of states with laws which are not 'model' may in turn be given two subclassifications: (a) five sparsely populated Western states with recent but somewhat rudimentary systems,[27] and (b) five Eastern and seven Southern states with systems clearly of the old-fashioned type." [28]

Under such a system the voter remains registered as long as he continues to reside in the same voting district. The advantages of this are obvious. "It saves the voter the trouble of having to register frequently, and also substantially reduces the cost of registration to the taxpayer . . . and under some permanent systems provision is made for transfers, whereby the voter need register only once as long as he continues to reside in the same city or county." Such a system can be operated in such manner as to have a constantly accurate voting list, if public service companies are required to report new installations and discontinuances of service. Where a discontinuance is reported, the name may be automatically removed from the registry list, whereas an installation normally indicates the arrival of a new tenant and a new voter. An annual check may be made by the police or through the use of return postcards. Mention has already been made of voting on affidavit. This calls to mind the distinction between compulsory and noncompulsory registration systems. In the former, no one may vote who is not registered, while in the latter, unregistered persons may be permitted to "swear in" their votes at the polls. This system is obviously open to abuses.[29]

One of the most serious problems affecting registration, and also the conduct of elections, is the almost total lack of state administrative control over the procedure. The power to appoint local authorities is in some cases placed in the governor; in others, in a state board of elections — in Ohio, in a state supervisor of elections. New York had such an office for many years,

[25] California, Indiana, Kentucky, Michigan, Minnesota, Montana, Nevada, New Jersey, New Mexico, Ohio, Pennsylvania, Washington, and Wisconsin.

[26] Illinois, Iowa, Kansas, Maryland, Missouri, Nebraska, and Oklahoma.

[27] Arizona, Colorado, Idaho, Oregon, and Utah.

[28] Connecticut, Delaware, Maryland, Maine, and Massachusetts; Alabama, Florida, Georgia, Louisiana, Mississippi, North Carolina, and Virginia. Quoted from Weeks, O. Douglas, "Permanent Registration of Voters in the United States," *Temple Law Quarterly*, November 1939, pp. 74–88. See also Horlacker, John P., "The Administration of Permanent Registration in Philadelphia," *American Political Science Review*, October 1943, pp. 829–837; Pollock, James K., *Permanent Registration of Voters in Michigan: An Appraisal* (University of Michigan Bureau of Government, 1937); Legislative Research Commission, *Registration and Purgation Laws of Kentucky* and *Registration and Purgation: An Appraisal of Kentucky Administration* (both, Frankfort, 1951). For the reports of the Joint Legislative Committee to Revise the Election Law on Permanent Personal Registration in New York, see Legislative Documents Nos. 73 (affirmative) and 56 (negative) (Albany, 1951).

[29] Harris, *op. cit.*, pp. 110–112. Even permanent registration can be manipulated; see Lex, William B., "Election Frauds Go Unchecked," *National Municipal Review*, May 1944, pp. 226–228.

but in 1921 abolished it because of inefficiency and expense of operation. In some states the secretary of state exercises some control, but most state officers lack power sufficient to enable them to render any real service. Michigan, however, established a director of elections in 1951.[30] There is a host of problems in the solution of which they might be helpful. In addition to the organization of registration machinery and the selection of personnel, there are such questions as the maintenance of records, the procedure to be followed when registration takes place, the problem of purging registration lists and identifying voters at the polls, and control over the cost of operating the system. Local officials in communities large and small all over the country have abundantly demonstrated their inability to deal with these questions in such manner as to bring about honest elections.

The Committee on Election Administration of the National Municipal League has published and kept up to date a proposed model registration system, which recommends *personal* registration on a *permanent* basis.[31] The system would be statewide and without provision for the swearing in of voters either at the polls or after the close of registration. The administration would be centralized in a single office, with a special office for the more populous cities and counties, under an appointee of the governor or mayor. Individual registration records would be maintained on loose-leaf sheets or cards which can be bound in locked binders for use at the polls; registration would be possible at all times except in the three weeks immediately preceding an election. The correction of the lists would be made from official death notices, and provision would be made for transfers on the basis of a signed request, and for cancellation of the registrations of nonvoters after failure to respond to a written notice. This effort to keep the roll correct would be supplemented by such devices as a police census or a house to house canvass. Identification of the voter at the polls would be made possible through the comparison of a signature made at that time with the signature on the registration card.

Nominating Systems

The Caucus. Three types of nominating machinery have been extensively used in the United States; these are, in the order in which they have served as the prevailing method of nomination: the caucus, the convention, and the direct primary. The caucus may be defined as a meeting of party members for nominating candidates and making decisions regarding party policy on public questions. The legislative caucus, as it exists for both the majority and the minority parties in each legislative chamber, to some extent serves this purpose but is not of major importance at this point. The so-called primary

[30] See Joint Legislative Committee on Reorganization of State Government, Staff Report No. 7, *State Election Administration* (Lansing, January 1951).

[31] National Municipal League, *A Model Registration System*, Third Edition (New York, 1939).

caucus, most important here, has endured for many years in towns and villages throughout the country. The members of the party residing in the local political subdivision concerned assemble at an appointed time and place to perform these duties. Such a caucus as an instrument of party government closely resembles the town meeting in the field of government proper. Both were based on the principle of pure democracy. Just as the male inhabitants of the town came together to decide public questions, so the members of the political party assembled to select their standard-bearers for the ensuing campaign and to determine the attitude of the party on the issues before the people.

The Convention System. Transition from these methods of direct participation to a representative system took place simultaneously in government and in the political party for precisely the same reasons. As society became more complicated and communities increased in size, it was no longer possible for all citizens to assemble at one time and place; this led to the adoption of the representative principle. In government this meant substituting the council and the representative assembly for the town meeting; in the field of party control it meant substituting the convention for the caucus. If the representative principle is sound when applied to governmental institutions, it should be equally sound when applied to party organization in similar geographical areas. The convention as an instrument of party control lost public confidence for two reasons.

Very often, and in many different conventions in different parts of the country, the conventions showed themselves to be responsive to the control of the party boss rather than to the wishes of the people. The late Arnold Bennett Hall used to tell of a caucus that was carried on until far into the night. The irate citizens had come to outvote the organization. As the debate continued, the irate citizens one by one got tired and went home. By 2:00 A.M., when the vote was taken, the organization slate won. Nothing had been done that was wrong. The democratic processes of discussion and debate had been used, but the "good" citizens, as usual, had grown weary of well-doing. Because they would not take the trouble, they came to believe that it was impossible for them to control the convention (or the caucus) as against the party organization.

The second charge — and one that was often justified — against the convention system was that of corruption. The depths to which a convention could descend is well illustrated by an analysis of the personnel of two Cook County conventions held in Chicago in 1885 and 1896; a description of the latter is quoted from Professor Ray:

> Of the other Cook County Convention, held in 1896, a contemporary account runs as follows: "Of the delegates, those who had been on trial for murder numbered 17; sentenced to the penitentiary for murder or manslaughter and served sentence, 7; served terms in the penitentiary for burglary, 36; served terms in the penitentiary for picking pockets, 2; served terms in the penitentiary for arson, 1; ex-Bridewell and jailbirds, identified by detectives, 84; keepers of

gambling-houses, 7; keepers of houses of ill-fame, 2; convicted of mayhem, 3; ex-prize fighters, 11; poolroom proprietors, 2; saloon-keepers, 265; lawyers, 14; physicians, 3; grain dealers, 2; political employees, 148; hatter, 1; stationer, 1; contractors, 4; grocer, 1; sign-painter, 1; plumbers, 4; butcher, 1; druggist, 1; furniture supplies, 1; commission merchants, 2; ex-policemen, 15; dentist, 1; speculators, 2; justices of the peace, 3; ex-constable, 1; farmers, 6; undertakers, 3; no occupation, 71; total delegates, 723." In other words, in this total of 723 delegates, 265 were saloon-keepers, 148 were officeholders, and 128 had served a term either in the house of correction or in the penitentiary.[32]

How many of the conventions were this bad it is impossible to say, but there is no reason to suppose that Chicago and Cook County were any worse than a great many other cities and counties throughout the country.

When the people could no longer endure these conditions, a movement for the adoption of the direct primary system began. This breakdown of the representative principle in party government was accompanied by a similar breakdown in official legislative bodies. The sentiment of the people against representative institutions developed in both fields at the same time and for the same reasons. Consequently, the sentiment for the direct primary was accompanied by a demand for the adoption of the initiative, referendum, and recall as a partial substitute for, or supplement to, the established representative legislative body. A further discussion of this movement will be found in the following chapters.

The convention system is still used in two ways and to a very limited extent. It is used for nominating purposes for statewide offices in five states, and for preprimary purposes in four others. The states in the first group include Connecticut, Indiana, Maryland (for governor only), New York, South Carolina (in the Republican Party only). In South Dakota a state convention nominates in the event that any candidate fails to receive 35 per cent of the party vote for any office. The 1949 legislature in New Mexico adopted a convention system, but the operation of the law was suspended by the Secretary of State when attacked; Rhode Island abandoned the convention system in favor of the primary in 1947.[33] The four preprimary convention states are Alabama, Colorado, Nebraska, and Utah.[34]

Direct Primary. Since the adoption of the first statewide compulsory primary law in Wisconsin in 1903, the system has attained almost universal acceptance. It seems proper, therefore, to note what it is and to attempt an

[32] Ray, P. Orman, *Introduction to Political Parties and Practical Politics*, Third Edition, pp. 71–72 (Scribner's, New York, 1924). This material was printed originally in the *Chicago Tribune*, March 30, 1885, and in Easley, Ralph M., "The Sine Qua Non of Caucus Reform," *Review of Reviews*, September 1897, pp. 322–324.

[33] Cline, Dorothy I., "New Mexico Retains Primary," *National Municipal Review*, May 1950, pp. 233–236, and Childs, Richard S., "Rhode Island Tries Primary," *ibid.*, March 1949, pp. 126–129.

[34] On the latter, see Ballard, Rene N., *The Primary Convention System in Utah* (Institute of Government, University of Utah, 1947). This summary is based primarily on a typewritten report prepared by Samuel H. Still, Jr., Legislative Reference Service, Library of Congress, August 2, 1950.

evaluation of it. A direct primary is an election held within the limits of the membership of a particular political party within a given jurisdiction. Just as the general electorate proceeds to the polls on election day to indicate preferences from among the nominees of the several parties for the several offices to be filled, so in a primary election the members of the party go to

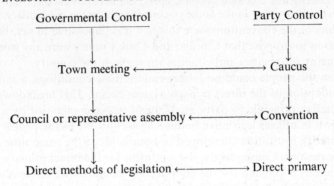

EVOLUTION OF POPULAR CONTROL OF GOVERNMENT AND PARTIES

Governmental Control		Party Control
↓		↓
Town meeting	←→	Caucus
↓		↓
Council or representative assembly	←→	Convention
↓		↓
Direct methods of legislation	←→	Direct primary

the polls on the date of the primary to select the standard-bearers for the party for the ensuing electoral campaign. These selections are made from the slates supported by various factions or groups within the party. Just as the voters in the general election select their officeholders, so the members of the party in the primary select their candidates.

Two types of direct primary are in general use — the open and the closed. Where the closed primary is used, the voter must indicate to the clerk at the time of registration the name of the political party of his preference. When he appears at the polls, his name is read and, subject to challenge, the clerk in charge of ballots is instructed to give him the primary ballot of this party. If voting machines are used, the machine is set for the party indicated. The chief objection to the closed primary is that it violates the principle of the secret ballot. This contention would seem to have little weight in a government operated, as ours is, through political parties. This being the case, none but a supersensitive person should object to indicating that, under normal circumstances, he has a preference for a particular political party.

The open primary used in five states enables the voter to choose, at the time he votes in the primary, the party in the selection of whose candidates he wishes to participate. All the candidates of all parties may appear on the same ballot, the voter utilizing only that portion allotted to the party of his choice; or the ballots of each party may be printed separately. At first thought, this would seem preferable to the closed primary. Experience shows, however, that under the open primary it is possible for a powerful political machine to dominate the selections in the minority as well as in the majority party. Those familiar with party organization in urban communities well know the accuracy with which division committeemen and ward leaders calculate the results of the election the night before it happens. Under such circumstances it is not at all difficult for the organization to apportion a certain number of controlled votes in each ward in excess of the number required to control the result in their own party, to be used to control the result in the minority party as well.

The nonpartisan primary is used in many states for the selection of city and county officers, as well as school and other local officers. In the state field it is frequently used for judicial officers, and in Minnesota since 1913 the members of the legislature have been elected on a nonpartisan ballot. The names of the candidates, which are placed on the ballot by petition, appear with no party designation of any kind. The two persons having the highest number of votes for each office are nominated for that office, and their names appear on the ballot in the general election without party designation. Thus a nonpartisan primary is followed by a nonpartisan election. The final election may be eliminated in some cases by a provision, such as that existing in California, to the effect that a candidate who receives a majority of the votes cast for the office he is seeking shall be declared elected.[35]

Because partisan elections in cities are believed to frustrate united civic action and discourage independents from seeking public office, the use of nonpartisan elections has been spreading much more rapidly than is generally realized.[36] After slow but steady gains, a sudden increase was reported in 1941, when of 2030 cities with a population of over 5000, about 56 per cent had nonpartisan elections. The figure in the 1949 *Municipal Year Book* is 56.9 per cent. This trend toward nonpartisan local elections is significant, both for local government and for its effect on state and national politics.

"Run-off" elections are frequently necessary in ten of the one-party states in the South,[37] all of which require a majority (in Georgia, of county unit

[35] There is also in this state a unique perversion of the partisan primary, known as cross-filing, in effect since 1922, designed to entrench the then majority party in control of most state and local offices. In this, it has been very successful. By encouraging party raiding, it also has the effect of deceiving the voters and at the same time of undermining almost completely any idea of party responsibility; see Binkley, Robert W., Jr., *Double Filing in Primary Elections* (Bureau of Public Administration, University of California, 1945); California State Chamber of Commerce, *Should Cross-Filing in California Be Abolished?* (San Francisco, 1951); Hazen, Evelyn, *Cross-Filing in Primary Elections* (Bureau of Public Administration, University of California, 1951); Johnson, Leroy, "California's Primary Cross-Filing System," *Congressional Record*, daily edition, June 26, 1952, pp. A4222–A4224; McHenry, Dean E., "Invitation to the Masquerade," *National Municipal Review*, May 1950, pp. 228–232 and "Cross-Filing of Political Candidates in California," *Annals*, November 1946, pp. 226–231; and Ogden, Daniel M., Jr., "Parties Survive Cross-Voting," *National Municipal Review*, May 1950, pp. 237–241 (deals with Washington system).

[36] See Bromage, Arthur W., "Partisan Elections in Cities," *National Municipal Review*, May 1951, pp. 250–253, and Childs, Richard S., "500 Non-political Elections," *ibid.*, June 1949, pp. 278–282, 316.

[37] These are: Alabama, Arkansas, Florida, Georgia, Louisiana, Mississippi, North Carolina, Oklahoma, South Carolina, and Texas. Tennessee, likewise a one-party state, does not require a majority to nominate. For a splendid analysis of politics in this group of states, see Key, *Southern Politics*, *op. cit.*, Part I, and on the nominating process, Chapter 19.

votes)[38] to nominate. When there are a number of candidates in the field, in a wide-open race, each with a considerable amount of support, the best that any one of them is likely to do is to win a plurality. Since a majority is required to nominate, the run-off becomes necessary; in this second primary the race is usually limited to the three highest on the list. By this process of elimination the effort is made to discover that candidate most acceptable to a majority of the party members, from among the total number presenting their names for consideration. In all other direct primary states, in which a plurality or the highest number of votes cast is sufficient to nominate, there is no need for a run-off.

Advantages and Disadvantages of the Direct Primary. The supporters of the direct primary promised that it would eliminate, or help to eliminate, political manipulation. This patent political nostrum, it was said, would make it possible for the people to control party affairs in fact as well as in theory. Such has not proved to be the case. As early as 1909 Professor Charles E. Merriam observed that those who supported the primary were wondering why they had done so, while those who had opposed it were engaged in a like speculation.[39] Certain significant defects in the operation of the primary system have been abundantly demonstrated. In the first place, it is exorbitantly expensive. Some good folk have professed to be surprised and horrified, but there is no reason why they should be. The primary system makes necessary the application of practices which are commonplace in merchandising, in which advertising is a very profitable form of economic waste.

There are frequent reports that, even in states of relatively small population and resources, a successful statewide campaign cannot be carried on without expenditures running into five or six figures. This automatically excludes a great number of able men who might be interested in public service but who do not happen to be wealthy. If they obtain the necessary funds from the usual sources, they do so only at the price of their independence in office if nominated and elected. This situation raises some extremely serious ques-

[38] Under this notorious system, established under the Neill Primary Law of 1917, the candidate receiving a plurality or having the highest number of votes in the county receives the full vote of the county on the county unit basis. See Holland, Lynwood M., *The Direct Primary in Georgia* (University of Illinois Press, 1949), and Saye, Albert B., "Georgia's County Unit System of Election," *Journal of Politics*, February 1950, pp. 93–106.

[39] The movement started in California in March 1866, with New York following in April. Wisconsin provided for "primary meetings" in 1891; for the story of Governor La Follette's efforts to improve the system, see his *Autobiography* (Madison, 1913). For some early accounts of its operation, see *Proceedings*, American Political Science Association, 1910: Beard, Charles A., "The Direct Primary Movement in New York," pp. 187–198; Hartwell, E. M., "Primary Elections in Massachusetts," pp. 210–224; Horack, F. E., "Primary Elections in Iowa," pp. 175–186; Jones, W. Clyde, "Primary Elections in Illinois," pp. 138–162; and Loeb, Isidor, "Direct Primaries in Missouri," pp. 163–174. For the claim that the system originated in Crawford County, Pennsylvania, see Booser, James H., "The Origin of the Direct Primary," *National Municipal Review*, April 1935, pp. 222–223. For later surveys, see Salter, John T., Ed., "Direct Primaries," *Annals*, March 1923, entire issue, and Harris, Arthur, and Uhr, Carl, *Direct Primary Elections* (University of California, Bureau of Public Administration, 1941).

tions regarding the compatibility of these financial requirements and the maintenance of a vigorous and sound democracy.

If it could be shown that the caliber of the candidates nominated under the primary system was much better than the caliber of those nominated by conventions, one might reconcile himself to the cost of the system. This, however, cannot be done. Indeed, it is doubtful whether the selections made under the primary are of as high a standard, on the average, as one might reasonably expect of conventions. There are a number of instances in Indiana, Pennsylvania, Wisconsin, and elsewhere where conspicuously able men have been nominated under the primary, but there are also instances, some of them in the same states, in which persons have been nominated for whom almost any party convention would have hesitated to be responsible. In numbers of cases between these two extremes there is no evidence whatever that the voting public has shown any greater ability to select honest, able, and intelligent men than one might expect of a convention.

As a matter of fact, the primary system tends to discourage able men from participation in politics[40]; they do not like the vituperation and the hurly-burly of an electoral campaign. Many of them would, if drafted as candidates by a convention, go through the ordeal once, but they will not enter the primary and then go through the same trying experience a second time and possibly a third, in run-off and electoral campaigns. In his Presidential address to the National Municipal League in 1921, Charles E. Hughes said: "The aversion to a primary contest on the part of men conspicuously well fitted for office is quite apparent. The citizen of ability, well trained and experienced, is a man with a vocation. He is not destitute of public spirit, but he is not in a position and has no inclination to spend time and money trying to get an office he does not want, and which he would take at a considerable sacrifice."

Serious objection to the direct primary may also be registered on the basis that it violates the principle of the short ballot. In general, the purpose of the short ballot is to centralize responsibility and to simplify the task of the voters. The direct primary does not simplify this task; it complicates it by taking the voter to the polls more times and requiring him to make a much larger number of decisions. The short ballot principle is discussed in the fol-

[40] In a case study of the operation of the direct primary for county officers in Iowa, Professor Porter reports an alarming dearth of candidates. "In thirty-four counties, there were no Democratic candidates for nomination for any county office; and in nineteen of these the Republicans presented only one candidate for each office. In fifty-four counties, there was only one candidate for nomination for each office on either the Democratic or the Republican ticket. Thus in more than one-third of the counties of the state, there was no contest for any county office, either in the primary or in the general election. And in well over half of the counties, there was no contest in the primary for any county office. In many of the remaining counties, there were contests for only one or two of the offices available." See Porter, Kirk H., "The Deserted Primary in Iowa," *American Political Science Review*, August 1945, pp. 732–740. This finding supports a widespread impression among students; what is true of the county offices in Iowa is doubtless equally true of other groups of offices in that and other states.

lowing chapter, but it is mentioned here because it is believed that this item, together with the excessive cost of the primary system and its failure to produce a higher quality of candidates, makes imperative a careful reconsideration of our whole system of nominating candidates for public office.

The list of arguments against the direct primary might be extended almost indefinitely. In addition to those mentioned, Professor Harris in a recent article mentions the following[41]:

1. It weakens party leadership and destroys party responsibility.
2. It ignores the necessity for conference and consultation in the selection of candidates and does not provide for the drafting of candidates of high qualifications.
3. It promotes the candidacies of self-advertisers and demagogues and discourages the candidacies of men with the highest qualifications, who will not wage a campaign for nomination.
4. It affords no suitable means for the formulation of party platforms or for the selection of candidates in sympathy with the party program.
5. It entails heavy expense to the candidates because of the necessity of conducting two campaigns.
6. It permits nominations by a plurality vote and contests which are subject to manipulation by the multiplicity of candidates.
7. Since the primary of the dominant party tends to become the decisive election, it is difficult for the minority party to retain its following and to offer effective and salutary opposition. Consequently it tends to weaken and in many states to destroy any real bi-party system.
8. The number of votes cast in the direct primary is usually much smaller than that in the final election, although in some strongly one-party states the opposite is true.

Filing Fees. It happens many times that persons file, either for a primary or as an independent in a general election, who have no chance whatever of winning the election. Some do so for publicity or for bargaining power later, or for other reasons are not bona fide candidates. To discourage this practice, the filing fee system, patterned somewhat after that used in British Parliamentary elections, has been introduced. The candidate posts a specified amount, depending on the importance of the office which he seeks; if he polls a minimum specified percentage of the vote — whether he wins or not — his money is returned to him. This practice prevents cluttering up the ballot with the names of candidates who do not have, or do not think they have, some substantial support. These are sometimes referred to as "name candidates." [42] Although not always effective, it tends to support the principle of the short ballot and is regarded by students as being distinctly preferable to the old-fashioned type of nominating petition.

[41] Harris, Joseph P., "A New Primary System," *State Government*, July 1948, pp. 140–143, 153; Childs, Richard S., "A New Model Primary Law," *National Municipal Review*, May 1950, pp. 225–227, 266; National Municipal League, *A Model Direct Primary Election System* (New York, 1951).

[42] Ramsey, Maurice M., "*Name Candidates*" *in Detroit Elections* (Detroit Bureau of Governmental Research, 1941), and Dorr, Harold M., "Candidates Won't Stay Out," *National Municipal Review*, May 1949, pp. 224–229.

In eleven Southern states candidates merely file written declarations of candidacy, in three cases accompanied by a purely nominal number of signatures. However, in seven of these eleven states they must pay a filing fee which in some instances is a fixed amount running from $1.00 for a minor local office to $100 for a statewide office and in other cases a percentage of the annual salary of the office. Outside the South approximately half of the states have no requirement for the payment of any filing fee for either the primary or the general election ballots, while the remainder fall roughly into three groups. The first consists of seven states which require a fee from primary candidates, but not from independents; seven states in the second group, chiefly Western, require the same fee of candidates independently nominated as is required of primary candidates; while in three states in a third group the candidate for the primary is given an option.[43]

Methods of Improving Nominating Procedures. At this point one may well ask what course is open. Going back to the caucus system or a return to the old-fashioned, boss-ridden type of party convention are both out of the question. There are many who object to continuing with the direct primary in its present form. "More and more," writes Professor Harris, "it is being recognized that normal, healthy, and salutary party life is difficult if not impossible under the existing direct primary system." Actually, there are two possible alternatives available: the local-primary state-convention system, and a pretty thoroughly revised and strengthened direct primary system.

A number of states, as previously noted, continue to use the convention system of nominations for certain offices. New York especially seems to have developed a suitable and workable alternative by retaining the primary for the nomination of candidates for local offices and returning to the state convention for the selection of candidates for state offices and for determining party policy on state questions. The results of this plan, as indicated by the choices of gubernatorial candidates from 1921, when the primary law was repealed, to date are shown in the table on page 128. From this list it is evident that both parties have made use of able and distinguished men. The principle of the short ballot has been, at least in part, preserved. The whole task has been well done at a small fraction of the cost that would have been incurred by a statewide primary for candidates for the state and Federal offices. It is to be hoped that the example of New York may influence the legislation of other states as dissatisfaction with the existing machinery for nominating candidates increases.

The most significant proposal for the revision and strengthening of the direct primary system comes from Professor Harris of the University of California, who proposes that political parties should be authorized to hold preprimary party conferences or conventions, at which they would adopt

[43] The states in these groups are (1) Maryland, Minnesota, Nebraska, North Dakota, Utah, West Virginia, and Wyoming; (2) California, Idaho, Missouri, Montana, Nevada, Ohio, and Washington; (3) Kansas, New Hampshire, and Oregon.

New York State Gubernatorial Candidates

YEAR	DEMOCRATIC	REPUBLICAN
1922	Alfred E. Smith *	Nathan L. Miller
1924	Alfred E. Smith *	Theodore Roosevelt, Jr.
1926	Alfred E. Smith *	Ogden L. Mills
1928	Franklin D. Roosevelt *	Albert Ottinger
1930	Franklin D. Roosevelt *	Charles H. Tuttle
1932	Herbert H. Lehman *	William J. Donovan
1934	Herbert H. Lehman *	Robert Moses
1936	Herbert H. Lehman *	William F. Bleakley
1938 **	Herbert H. Lehman *	Thomas E. Dewey
1942	John J. Bennett, Jr.	Thomas E. Dewey *
1946	James M. Meade	Thomas E. Dewey *
1950	Walter A. Lynch	Thomas E. Dewey *

* Indicates victorious candidate.
** For a term of four years, under constitutional amendment adopted in 1938.

platforms and recommend or nominate to the voters a group of candidates to be voted on at the primary election. Candidates thus nominated should be certified to the officer in charge of printing the ballot, and should be designated on the ballot in a manner to indicate that they were nominated by the party organization, thereby restoring to the political parties their essential functions in a democracy and making them meaningful in state affairs.[44]

The nomination of candidates by petition would be retained, but candidates could run without party endorsement, and contest those so nominated. The names of candidates would be clearly marked to indicate whether they ran with party endorsement or as independents. A single ballot of the office column type would be used in the primaries, voters being permitted to vote for any candidate for each office. A candidate who received a majority of all the votes cast for an office would be declared elected; otherwise the two highest candidates would run in the final election. An official voters' handbook should be published by the state and mailed to each voter for his information, with a copy of the official ballot.

The Conduct of Elections

The conduct of elections presents a large number of difficult problems. It involves the expenditure of "millions of hours of time on the part of voters, electioneers, officials, and watchers." In every state the election law is sufficient to fill a large volume; the enforcement of its provisions requires the expenditure, in the aggregate, of "millions of dollars in materials, advertising, rents, and services." In fact, the cost of elections has become a matter of serious concern to students of government. In the following paragraphs, some of the more important electoral problems will be discussed.

[44] Harris, *op. cit.*, p. 142.

The Campaign. When the candidates have been nominated, by whatever method, when the voters have been registered and the party platforms adopted, the time is ripe for the campaign. Campaign headquarters must be established. It is customary for the party organization to lease one or two floors in a hotel or a large office building. The Republicans in New York in one campaign had "approximately 7032 square feet of floor space [which] was divided off into some twenty offices and waiting rooms. . . . A large office was set up to house the Publicity Division and newspapermen covering state headquarters." This office was equipped with telephones and typewriters for the newspapermen, and every convenience was accorded them for prompt communication with their papers. A staff was set up to assist them in contacting "news sources," to arrange press conferences, and to dig up information. Additional offices were assigned to the Women's Division, the Speaker's Bureau, the United Republican Finance Committee of the State of New York, the Senate and Assembly Legislative Committee, and the Republican State Treasurer. A suite of three rooms was assigned to the Chairman of the State Committee, a suite of two rooms to the Secretary. Quarters were provided for the Chairman of the Executive Committee of the State Committee, of the Veterans' Division, et cetera. "An extensive telephone service has been installed in the new headquarters which permits direct intercommunication with the Republican National Committee, located on the twelfth floor, and with the National Republican Finance Committee in the —— Building. Care has been exercised that ample space for storerooms be reserved, and attractive receptionists have been engaged. . . ."

Many aspects of the ordinary state campaign differ from those of the national campaign chiefly in extent; the methods are essentially the same. There is the usual round of meetings, local and major, with their speeches, debates, and discussions. Headquarters are set up in all centers of population, with posters, banners, and radio or phonograph blaring forth party propaganda to all who care to listen or to those who cannot escape because of the proximity of their homes or their places of business. Printing presses work overtime to turn out copies of the platform and quantities of pamphlets, leaflets, and other printed materials. Campaign buttons and automobile stickers are distributed. Slogans and catch phrases are popularized. Newspapers are filled with accounts of candidates' speeches and of public meetings and with copy sent out from the campaign headquarters. Advertising space is reserved to point with pride or view with alarm, as the case may be. Billboards and other forms of commercial advertising may also be used. While all this is going on, the party workers are busy seeing their people. The coverage is so complete that no citizen can live through the two months before election without being aware of the candidates, the parties, and the issues — whether or not he understands them.[45]

[45] See Gosnell, Harold F., "Does Campaigning Make a Difference?" *Public Opinion Quarterly*, Fall 1950, pp. 413–418, in which it is contended that it definitely does.

There is surprisingly little that is original or different in political campaigns, although "stunts" of various sorts are often featured. Parades are largely a thing of the past; instead, motion pictures are shown on street corners, from automobiles or trucks whose sides are covered with billboards and whose interiors are equipped with amplifying devices emitting raucous sounds. In the rural districts, barbecues, picnics, and outings are common; these are usually organized on the basis of allegiance to some particular leader (who pays all the expenses) or upon a county basis. In either case it is quite an occasion for the party — the members of the party ticket are present, and the program is designed to inform the party workers and inspire them to exert a proper effort in the work of the campaign. Clambakes and outings are always popular with both city and rural workers. There is in the campaign as a whole a vast amount of hokum and showmanship.

Something more specific ought, perhaps, to be said about campaign speaking, both in rallies and by radio. There is usually, as in national campaigns, a speaker's bureau to help arrange the itinerary of the candidates and to handle the assignment of prominent speakers to the more important meetings. The tone of the discussion — indeed, the tone of the whole campaign — rests largely with the candidate at the head of the ticket. If he is a cheap and blatant showman, the campaign as a whole is likely to be of that type; if he is an able and dignified person, the tone is bound to reflect his influence. In spite of occasional unfortunate occurrences, which receive more than their proper share of publicity, it is true that the general tone of political campaigns has been improving during recent years. As will be indicated in another chapter, the governorship has been attracting a higher type of man because the position itself has been dignified by greater power and responsibility. In many states the candidates are outstanding men who discuss seriously, even though with partisan bias, important questions facing the state government. It is in this field that many a state leader develops the skill which later serves him in good stead in national politics.

Radio and television have made an important contribution in elevating the tone of political campaigns. It has made fewer speeches necessary and has indirectly aided in improving the quality of those which are made. Some candidates still visit every county in the state with an automobile entourage, meeting the people and being seen by them, and speaking at every crossroads; but this campaign technique is increasingly a thing of the past. With the radio and television and the use of one powerful station or a network of stations covering a whole state, it is possible for all the important addresses of the candidates to be heard by all who care to listen. With fewer addresses to make, and each of those of greater significance, it is natural that greater care should be exercised in their preparation by the candidate himself and by the ghost writers who assist him. The period of active campaigning has been shortened and the process speeded up. Any important charge can be answered within a few hours or, at the latest, the next day. Radio is expensive to use, television even more so, but there is no doubt of the benefits which these new devices have brought to political campaigning.

Ballots and Voting Machines. When the campaign is over, when the last speech has been made and the last argument presented, the day of reckoning arrives. The first item of interest in the conduct of the election is the ballot. Before considering the ballot forms now in use, the development of the balloting process may be briefly noted. It has often been said that elections are a sort of denatured and humanized warfare — that they are a means of determining the outcome of differences arising between opposing groups by counting heads rather than by breaking them. In early times when the citizen appeared at the polls to vote, he was supposed to state in a loud and clear voice the names of the persons for whom he wished to vote. As the process developed, paper ballots were substituted; to begin with, these were furnished by the party organizations and were of different sizes, shapes, and colors. As more emphasis came to be placed upon the secrecy of the ballot, state laws were enacted requiring that the ballots furnished be of uniform size, shape, and color. The intent of these laws was evaded by the use of different weights of paper and slightly different shades of the same color. At this point government intervened to supervise the preparation and printing of ballots or to furnish them itself.

The Australian ballot was introduced in this country between 1887 and 1900; the term "is generally used to designate an official ballot, printed at public expense, by public officers, containing the names of all candidates duly nominated, and distributed at the polls by the election officers." [46] The original form of the Australian ballot in this country was the Indiana party column type, upon which, by placing a single cross below the party emblem, a voter could vote a straight party ticket. Later the Massachusetts office column type came into general use; this discourages straight ticket voting and makes it necessary for the voter to make a definite choice, or at least a separate cross, for each candidate for whom he wishes to vote. There are numerous variations from these two main types, and various problems with regard to the form and arrangement of ballots. The use of emblems has long been regarded as ridiculous, but organization workers, particularly in cities, have fought for their retention because they made it easier to control an illiterate vote. Sometimes the emblems are confusing even to people who can read.

The practices of the states in this field vary so greatly that broad generalizations are difficult. Such studies as now exist — none of them very recent — indicate that more than half of the states still use the party column ballot, the remainder (with the exception of South Carolina) the office column type. About one fourth offer neither party emblems to guide the voter nor the privilege of voting a straight party ticket by a single mark. In spite of long

[46] Harris, Joseph P., *Election Administration in the United States*, p. 154 (Brookings Institution, Washington, 1934). Chapter 5 of this important study is devoted to the ballot.

years of effort on behalf of the short ballot, the ballots in many states are of tremendous size, the office column type being generally smaller than the party column type. The number of names on the ballot may run into the hundreds, though the ballots in a representative group of states reveal numbers of candidates just below or just above 100. Instructions of some sort — either full or brief — are printed on the ballots of more than three-fourths of the states.

The procedure for getting names on the ballot must be simple and direct; it must effectively restrict the election to really serious contenders; and it must effectively guard against such abuses as unnecessary expense and inconvenience in operation.[47] The necessity of providing a suitable answer to these requirements has been largely responsible for legislation designed to regulate and control the process of nomination and for the spread of the direct primary. Even the order in which the names of the candidates for a given office appear on the ballot is a matter of importance, since it has been conclusively shown that the name which appears first in the list has a distinct advantage in voting strength over other names. Unless the names are rotated on the ballots in the different voting districts, the same candidate enjoys the full benefit of this advantage. Since the two major parties control the government and make the election laws to suit their own advantage, third parties and independent movements often find it difficult if not impossible to qualify for the general election ballots in the various states.[48]

Another problem that has assumed importance in recent years is the use of voting machines. Mechanical voting devices not only eliminate some election frauds and reduce others, but in the long run they save substantial sums of money. They will last a lifetime and can be paid for within a few years out of savings from the printing of paper ballots. In addition, a smaller number of precincts, a smaller number of election officers in each precinct, and, because of the shortening of working hours, a smaller compensation to the precinct officers are all possible. A considerable saving may result from avoiding expensive recounts. Students of election administration are practically unanimous in urging their adoption and use.[49]

The adoption of voting machine legislation has made steady progress since 1892, when the first law authorizing their use was adopted in New York. In 1940 there were only fourteen states in which no such legislation had ever

[47] *Ibid.*, p. 166.

[48] As an illustration, see the summary of the obstacles faced by Henry Wallace and his Progressive Party, as reported in the *New York Times*, January 4, 1948, p. 22.

[49] For arguments for and against voting machines, see Harris, Joseph P., *Election Administration in the United States*, pp. 259–260. See Heavenrich, Max P., Jr., *The Use of Voting Machines in Thirty-five Cities or Counties* (Flint Institute of Research and Planning, 1939); also *The Effect of Division Size upon Voting Conditions in Philadelphia* (Institute of Local and State Government, University of Pennsylvania, 1939); Wisconsin Legislative Reference Library, *The Use of Voting Machines in Wisconsin Municipalities* (Madison, March 1952); and Mayhill, G. Roger, and Britton, E. T., "Taking Politics Out of Politics," *National Municipal Review*, November 1951, pp. 521–523.

been enacted.[50] In 1948, it was reported that there were 3775 cities and towns throughout the country in which voting machines were used. The machines come in four sizes, all of which have nine rows for political parties. The largest, used in California, Illinois, and Indiana, has sixty columns for candidates; the smallest, used in Connecticut and New York, thirty columns. Average preference is for the nine-row, fifty-column machine.

The Conduct of Elections. Those who are now perturbed from time to time by evidences of disorder in the conduct of elections would do well to refresh their memories with regard to conditions in earlier days. In the Pennsylvania Constitutional Convention of 1837, before the registry law was enacted in that state, it was reported that "disturbances, outrages, turbulence, violence, and bloodshed existed in the city [Philadelphia] on election day, even murders being committed." [51] Because of occurrences of this character and of the existence of many types of fraud, the movement for the supervision of elections and returns was initiated. As party spirit increased, "every method was resorted to in order to secure the advantage and election boards did not escape." Important legislation was enacted in Pennsylvania in 1836 and 1839, in New York in 1842, in New Jersey in 1855 and 1877. The general tendency was to create bipartisan boards, chosen on an elective basis; reliance was placed upon this feature and upon publicity in the determination of the applicant's right to vote and in the count of the votes. Professor Logan continues: "The first method presupposes the existence of active parties which will insure that the full quota of their members are in the election boards. The second method requires for its successful operation an electorate divided politically which can be depended upon to make challenges or insure a fair count, or an electorate actively interested in maintaining fair elections. Also the latter method requires a large element of personal acquaintanceship among the voters for its successful operation." [52]

While the framers of these acts may have been justified in expecting their successful operation, it soon became evident that they were inadequate to provide effective control over election machinery. This was notably true in Pennsylvania, where, in 1868, the legislature provided for overseers of elections, to be appointed by the Court of Common Pleas. This was the beginning of a system of multiplying the number of election officers by choosing watchers to watch those who watched the watchers. In recent years rapid progress in the improvement of election law has been made. The states have found ways of doing a better job with a smaller number of election

[50] These were Delaware, Idaho, Louisiana, Mississippi, Missouri, Nevada, New Mexico, North Carolina, North Dakota, South Carolina, South Dakota, Vermont, West Virginia, and Wyoming. Data here presented from Albright, Spencer D., *Ballot Analysis and Ballot Changes since 1930* (Council of State Governments, Chicago, 1940).

[51] Mr. Stevens, in *Debates* of the Constitutional Convention of Pennsylvania, 1837, Vol. III, p. 37. Cited by Logan, Edward B., *Supervision of the Conduct of Elections and Returns*, p. 4 (Lancaster Press, Lancaster, 1927).

[52] Logan, *op. cit.*, p. 7.

officers, chosen by appointment on merit rather than by election, and acting under a more central supervision. Some of the problems in a modern system of election administration will now be considered.

First, there is the election call. Regular elections are provided for by law, but special elections to fill vacancies or to vote upon emergency questions occur through the issuance of a call. A serious question is presented in many jurisdictions by the frequency of such elections. Under the primary system, it is not uncommon for citizens to be asked to go to the polls four or six times in a single year. Small wonder that so many elections bring to the polls only a fraction of the eligible voters! Other questions relate to the size and number of precincts or voting districts, laws regulating voting hours, time off from work for voting, and other similar matters.[53] It is well known that the maintenance of an undue number of precincts tends to increase the cost of operating the election machinery. It is necessary that polling places be accessible to the voter, but this is ordinarily possible in districts of four or five hundred voters. In some of the almost depopulated commercial wards in Philadelphia, on the other hand, there are a number of divisions with only a few dozen voters. There is, again, the question of the kind of polling place that will be used — a private home or office, a store, a garage, a school, a fire house, or other public building, or a portable house. "The ideal qualifications for a polling place include the following: sufficient size to take care of the voters without crowding; well lighted; well ventilated and heated; permanent, so that the voters would not be inconvenienced by changes of location; accessible; suitable surroundings for the conduct of the election; and procurable at a reasonable cost. The polling place greatly influences the conduct of the elections, both from the standpoint of service to the voters and from that of election frauds." Public buildings, such as schools,[54] which are usually conveniently located, best meet these several requirements.

Another question involves the delivery of election equipment and supplies, and their removal at the conclusion of the balloting. A decision must be made, either by the legislature or by election officers, regarding the hours of voting; there is often little or no uniformity even within the same state. The judge of elections or the chairman of the precinct election board, together with his associates, is responsible for the conduct of the election. They are responsible for the enforcement of such rules as are provided for identification of voters, thereby preventing repeating and voting on names of voters who do not appear. There are questions as to the handling of ballots, the assistance of voters, the challenging of voters, the activities of watchers and party workers in the vicinity of the polling place, and finally the impor-

[53] For tabulations of state laws on a number of such questions, see the several volumes of *Constitutional and Statutory Provisions of the States* (Council of State Governments, Chicago, 1940 ff).

[54] Harris, *Election Administration*, pp. 214–215; New York State Conference of Mayors and Other Municipal Officials, *Use of Schools and Other Public Buildings in Cities as Polling Places* (Mimeographed, Albany, 1949).

tant work of counting the ballots. The rendering of assistance has been grossly abused by party workers generally; it should be permitted only in cases of actual physical disability, sworn to by the voter at the time of registration. There are numerous reasons which may justify a challenge: that the voter is not of age, is not registered, has voted before on the same day, is not a naturalized citizen.

With regard to the count, the law is usually quite explicit as to the methods to be followed; the usual procedure is to count all the votes on one ballot before proceeding to the next. Professor Harris believes that it is preferable to proceed with the counting by offices or propositions.[55] While it is the usual practice to determine the final result of an election on the basis of a majority of the votes cast, Georgia uses a vicious county unit system under which the candidate carrying the county gets the unit vote, and the unit vote determines the nomination. Thus Fulton County with well over 400,000 votes has six unit votes; Chattahoochee County with 1,463 population (like several other counties with populations almost as small) has two unit votes. Although such a system appears to be deliberately designed to nullify the will of the majority, several attempts to obtain a review of it by the Supreme Court have been unsuccessful. A lower Federal court upheld the system on the ground that it violates no guarantees of equal rights.[56]

The National Municipal League's Committee on Election Administration, in its model system for election administration,[57] recommended a state board of elections with local control in the hands of the county clerk except in counties with a population of more than 200,000. Precinct workers would be appointed by the officer in charge of elections. An office column ballot of the Massachusetts type, from which the names of Presidential electors are omitted, is recommended, as is rotation of the names of candidates for the same office, for reasons already noted. Each voter would be required to sign his name before receiving his ballot, this signature being compared with the one on his registration card. Absent voting would be authorized. Both in primary and in general elections a candidate would be required to file a petition and deposit a sum of money equal to 5 per cent of the salary of the office which he seeks; this sum would be forfeited only in case the candidate failed to poll 10 per cent of the total vote cast for that office or nomination. A similar provision would be applied to parties which in the last gubernatorial election polled less than 5 per cent of the total vote cast. This deposit is re-

[55] Harris, *op. cit.*, p. 241; see also Eads, James K., "Indiana Experiments with Central Ballot Count," *National Municipal Review*, August 1940, pp. 545–548, 552.

[56] See Saye, Albert B., "Georgia's County Unit System of Election," *Journal of Politics*, February 1950, pp. 93–106; Stone, David O., "Equality of Voting Power as a Constitutional Right: the Georgia County Unit Case," *Syracuse Law Review*, Fall 1950, pp. 73–81; and Talmadge, Herman E., "Georgia's County Unit System, Fountainhead of Democratic Government," *Georgia Review*, Winter 1951, pp. 411–422.

[57] The revised report has not yet been published, but see Childs, *op. cit.*; also Shusterman, Murray H., "Choosing Election Officers," *National Municipal Review*, March 1940, pp. 185–193, 199.

turnable if the vote exceeds 5 per cent. An alternative to the deposit plan is provided in the form of a nomination petition.

The pessimism which is sometimes felt concerning the alertness with which a public votes is occasionally offset by demonstrations of an unusual and intelligent public interest. In passing on the constitutional amendments submitted to New York voters in 1927 (see page 62), and in the mayoralty election in New York City in 1932, when thousands of voters took the trouble to write in the name of an independent candidate, the voters showed their ability to analyze complicated issues and evaluate personalities.[58] That there are considerable numbers of people who are really concerned about their exercise of the suffrage is still further attested by the general interest in absent voting and by the observance by employers of some twenty-five state laws which provide for a period of two hours off from work on election day for purposes of voting.[59]

Election Frauds. The subject of election frauds is unfortunately one to which attention must be periodically directed. Because of a failure to exert a more constant interest in this important aspect of elections, all large cities are obliged to have, from time to time, grand jury or Senatorial investigations of conditions relating to election frauds. There are some indictments, and perhaps some convictions. Things then improve for a time, but before long the whole cycle has to be repeated. Conditions in many rural areas are not much better. It is with no intention of minimizing the importance of such frauds that one points out that elections today are substantially better, in this respect, than those of even a generation ago. The public today will not, in most places, tolerate the brazen and wholesale falsification of election returns that was practiced in earlier decades. This is not to say that the problem has been solved, but that progress has been made, as one might say, from burglary and larceny to petty thievery and peculation. The immediate task is to remove the latter by the development of higher standards of civic responsibility and by the improvement of techniques of supervision and control over election machinery. This has been done, to some extent, by corrupt practices legislation.

It is impossible here to enter into any detailed discussion of election frauds — the subject is still too vast. The Senatorial investigating committee which probed into the Vare-Wilson Senatorial election of 1926 listed and classified the following types of fraud and irregularity: fraudulent returns; failure to tally votes; discrepancies in the records of the persons voting; voting by persons who were not registered or who were registered incorrectly; voting by repeaters; more ballots cast than persons voting — (in 395 out of about 1,400 divisions); padded lists of voters; unfolded ballots in the ballot boxes; a few persons marked many ballots, according to the testimony of a

[58] *New York Herald Tribune*, November 30, 1932.

[59] *Time Off for Voting* (Bulletin No. 138, United States Bureau of Labor Standards, Washington, 1950).

handwriting expert; ballots marked by two persons (by the addition of crosses to 738 ballots at a later time); ballots marked in piles; and ballots unaccounted for (18,954 in 144 election districts).[60] There is scarcely a large city in which from time to time some evidence of this general character is not made public. It sometimes happens that methods and devices intended to bring about an improvement of conditions lead only to the invention of new methods of evasion.

The movement for the adoption of corrupt practices legislation began in 1883, when Massachusetts and New York placed restrictions on soliciting funds from officeholders; today eighteen states have such statutes, and seventeen states make it illegal to treat voters. "Sixteen make it unlawful to solicit funds from candidates; but in Florida, Indiana, Mississippi, and North Carolina, this practice is given legal sanction as 'evidence,' to quote the Mississippi law, 'of the good faith of the candidates and an expense fund of the several political parties.' In thirteen states it is illegal to pay for conveying voters to the polls. Corporations of all kinds are forbidden to make political contributions in twenty-seven states. Nine others confine the prohibition to certain types of corporations, such as public utilities, banks, and insurance companies." Arbitrary maximum expenditures are established by law in one third of the states, percentage limitations in seven, sliding scale limitations in five, miscellaneous restrictions in three. Six states have different limitations for primary and general elections. In eleven states, there are no statutory limitations.[61]

The Cost of Elections. Not the least important aspect of elections is their cost; and students of the subject are generally agreed that this is excessive. One writer has computed the average cost per vote in the larger American cities over a four year period. The highest, $2.13 per vote, was found in Columbus. The following cities had an average of more than $1.00 but less than $2.00: Baltimore, Chicago, Cincinnati, Cleveland, Dayton, Kansas City (Missouri), New York, and San Francisco. In the following cities, the average cost was less than $1.00: Boston, Denver, Detroit, Milwaukee, Minneapolis, Omaha, Salt Lake City, and St. Louis. In Minneapolis and Salt Lake City the cost was 37 cents, the lowest recorded.[62] A like situation exists in the counties of Ohio, where, in 1930, the average cost per vote in

[60] *Senatorial Campaign Expenditures*, 70 Cong., 2 Sess., Senate Report, No. 1858, pp. 30–40, cited by Harris, *op. cit.*, pp. 328–332. Chapter 9 of Harris's book contains an excellent discussion of election frauds. Gosnell reports, *op. cit.*, p. 76, that "the records of the Cook County Court of Illinois show that for the twelve-year period from 1922 to 1934 there were 256 men and only 44 women convicted of violating the election laws. . . ." See also Minault, S. Sydney, *Corrupt Practices Legislation in the Forty-eight States* (Council of State Governments, Chicago, 1942).

[61] Odegard, Peter H., and Helms, E. Allen, *American Politics, A Study in Political Dynamics*, Second Edition, p. 679 (Harpers, New York, 1947) and "State Limitations on Campaign Expenditures," mimeographed memorandum, State Law Section, Library of Congress, May 1, 1947.

[62] Harris, *op. cit.*, pp. 386–387.

twenty-four out of eighty-eight counties was in excess of $1.00.[63] These figures are typical of studies made in various parts of the country.

It may be asked why these costs have become so excessive and why they are permitted to remain so. In the main, the answer is to be found in the fact that the administration has been political rather than professional. Personnel has been added to personnel, until in Michigan this item consumes 50 per cent of the total.[64] The following table indicates the rates of pay in Michigan, the number of cities in the state represented in each salary group being shown[65]:

Rates of Pay of Election Precinct Officials in Michigan

RATE OF PAY	GATE-KEEPERS	INSPECTORS	RATE OF PAY	GATE-KEEPERS	INSPECTORS
$ .30 per hour		1	$ 4.75 per day		1
.40 per hour		1	5.00 per day	2	10
.50 per hour		12	6.00 per day		8
.60 per hour		1	7.00 per day		4
$.62\frac{1}{2}$ per hour		1	7.50 per day		1
2.00 per day	3		8.00 per day		8
3.00 per day	4	8	9.00 per day		1
3.50 per day		2	10.00 per day	1	5
4.00 per day	1	7	12.00 per day	1	5
4.50 per day		1	15.00 per day		3

"There is little relationship between the size of the registered vote and the number of election officials. The greatest variation exists both in the rates of pay and in the number of election officials employed." Professor Harris found that the personnel cost per total vote in the cities noted above varied from 49 cents in New York City to 84 cents in Minneapolis, while the personnel cost per vote cast varied from 24 cents in Salt Lake City to $1.46 in Columbus. He found also that the salaries paid were out of all proportion to the work involved. Since most of these positions go to regular party workers, the full power of the organized local government officials is in each state thrown against any movement for improvement of the system.

The employees used in connection with election administration are of three types: the regular employees, making up the permanent clerical force which handles the registration of voters and performs various election duties; the temporary employees, who assist with the peak loads of work that develop just before and just after elections; and finally, the precinct officers, whose duties are performed on election day and whose compensation consti-

[63] Harris, *op. cit.*, pp. 387–389.

[64] Pollock, James K., "Election Administration in Michigan," supplement to *National Municipal Review*, June 1934, p. 352; also his *County Election Costs in Michigan* (Bureau of Government, University of Michigan, 1935).

[65] Pollock, "Election Administration," p. 354.

tutes the largest item in both the personnel budget and the election budget as a whole. Their cost "depends upon a number of factors, including the number and kind of elections held, the size of the voting precinct, the number of officers used to the precinct, the salary paid, the use of voting machines, and the use of extra counting boards." [66] The whole system is badly organized in most jurisdictions and is most unsatisfactory in practice.

Operating expenses in the conduct of elections include all items other than personnel — the cost of ballots, supplies, printing, rental of polling places, repairs to precinct equipment and portable houses, cartage of such equipment, storage, and advertising.[67] Professor Harris found in his selected list of cities that the ballot cost per vote varied from 1.6 cents in Minneapolis to 14.3 cents in Kansas City. Gross carelessness and waste are frequent occurrences in connection with ballot printing. In his study of election costs in Michigan, Professor Pollock found the greatest variation in the cost of printing the same number of ballots in different counties [68]; also that the number of excess ballots prepared represents an enormous waste — a total of more than 1,600,000 ballots in excess of the number required plus the excess prescribed by law. These figures are illustrative of the manner in which election expenses are, in general, permitted to exceed any necessary or proper limits. He found also that the total election expenditures of counties bore little relation to the population of those counties or to the vote cast.

On the basis of the Michigan survey, Professor Pollock recommends that steps be taken as follows, with a view to reducing the cost and increasing the efficiency of election administration: (1) that contracts for the printing of ballots be awarded only after competitive bidding, to the lowest responsible bidder; (2) that the printing costs of ballots be reduced by eliminating certain unnecessary portions of the ballot; (3) that, because of the high cost of elections, fewer elections be held; (4) that the law be amended to provide more definite restrictions as to the number and pay of precinct election officers; (5) that a greater centralization of power over election matters be concentrated in the hands of the county clerks; (6) that the law be amended to provide a minimum size for precincts and greater discretion be lodged with the local election authorities in prescribing their maximum size; (7) that the system of permanent registration now mandatory for all cities and villages over 5,000 population be made to apply to the entire state; (8) that the secretary of state prepare and send out to every election authority in the state a biennial form of questionnaire which would elicit all information necessary for his guidance in the supervision of state elections; (9) that this officer be required to make an annual report of all relevant data relating to registrations and elections.[69] It may well be that not all of these items will be ap-

[66] Harris, *op. cit.*, p. 428.
[67] For a discussion of all these items, see *ibid.*, pp. 434–439.
[68] Pollock, "Election Administration," p. 351.
[69] *Ibid.*, pp. 357–359.

plicable in other jurisdictions, but their general nature is such that, considering the difficulties known to exist in states in all parts of the country, many of them — perhaps most of them — would in most jurisdictions be useful and beneficial. If anything significant is to be done in reducing the cost of government, it will be by attention to such matters as these — not through any huge and spectacular slashing of governmental expenditures generally.

SELECTED REFERENCES

The parties field is well supplied with texts, among which the better and more recent are the following:

Bone, Hugh A., *American Politics and the Party System* (McGraw-Hill, New York, 1949).

Key, Vladimer O., Jr., *Political Parties and Pressure Groups*, Revised Edition (Crowell, New York, 1947).

McKean, Dayton D., *Party and Pressure Politics* (Houghton Mifflin, Boston, 1949).

Merriam, Charles E., and Gosnell, Harold F., *The American Party System, an Introduction to the Study of Political Parties in the United States*, Fourth Edition (Macmillan, New York, 1949).

Odegard, Peter H., and Helms, E. Allen, *American Politics, a Study in Political Dynamics*, Second Edition (Harpers, New York, 1947).

Sait, Edward M., *American Parties and Elections*, Fifth Edition, by Howard R. Penniman (Appleton-Century-Crofts, New York, 1952).

Baldwin, Raymond E., *Let's Go into Politics* (Macmillan, New York, 1952), and Scott, Hugh D., Jr., *How to Get into Politics* (John Day, New York, 1949). Two successful politicians provide practical and entertaining guides.

Fisher, Marguerite J., and Starratt, Edith E., *Parties and Politics in the Local Community* (National Council of Social Studies, Washington, 1945). Tells how parties operate, how candidates are selected, how bosses influence government, and how invisible government functions.

Gosnell, Harold F., *Boss Platt and His New York Machine* (University of Chicago Press, 1923). A classic, combining biography with keen political analysis; for two significant studies of Chicago politics by the same author, see *Machine Politics, Chicago Model* (University of Chicago Press, 1937), and *Negro Politicians: the Rise of Negro Politics in Chicago* (University of Chicago Press, 1935).

Harris, Joseph P., *Registration of Voters in the United States* and *Election Administration in the United States* (Brookings Institution, Washington, 1929 and 1934, respectively). These volumes, though old, are still the best — if not the only — general treatises on the problems with which they deal.

Kent, Frank R., *The Great Game of Politics* (Doubleday, Page, New York, 1924). Standard journalistic description of the functioning of machine politics in this country. In *Political Behavior* (Morrow, New York, 1938), the same author develops the thesis that the candidate or party spending the most money wins the election.

Key, Vladimer O., Jr., *Southern Politics in State and Nation* (Knopf, New York, 1949). A state by state survey of the realities of Southern politics today, of outstanding merit. Of similar character, see also: Donnelly, Thomas C., Ed., *Rocky Mountain Politics* (University of New Mexico Press, 1940) and Moscow, Warren, *Politics in the Empire State* (Knopf, New York, 1948), a survey of New York politics during the last quarter century.

Kurtzman, David H., *Methods of Controlling Votes in Philadelphia* (University of Pennsylvania, 1935), and Forthal, Sonya, *Cogwheels of Democracy: A Study of the Precinct Captain* (William-Frederick Press, New York, 1946). Two distinctive contributions to our knowledge of machine politics in large cities.

McGovney, Dudley O., *The American Suffrage Medley* (University of Chicago Press, 1949). Urging the need for a uniform national suffrage.

Minault, S. Sydney, *Corrupt Practices Legislation in the Forty-eight States* (Council of State Governments, Chicago, 1942). Valuable compilation and analysis of information on an important aspect of election law.

Porter, Kirk H., *A History of Suffrage in the United States* (University of Chicago Press, 1918). Standard title down to date of publication.

Steffens, Lincoln, *The Autobiography of Lincoln Steffens* (Harcourt, Brace, New York, 1931). A literary classic dealing largely with politics and politicians during the first quarter of the twentieth century.

Wallis, J. H., *The Politician, His Habits, Outcries and Protective Coloring* (Stokes, New York, 1935). A witty and somewhat humorous discourse on the more or less typical politician.

Zink, Harold, *City Bosses in the United States* (Duke University Press, 1930). Part I has thumbnail sketches of twenty famous bosses, Part II an analysis of their characteristics. For excellent accounts of two more recent bosses, see McKean, Dayton D., *The Boss: Machine Politics in Action* (Houghton Mifflin, Boston, 1940) and Milligan, Maurice M., *The Inside Story of the Pendergast Machine by the Man Who Smashed It* (Scribners, New York, 1948). Analyses of the leadership and methods used by bosses in Jersey City and Kansas City.

5

Popular Control of Government

Popular control of government necessarily involves a number of considerations. There are those who for many years relied upon the extension of the suffrage; they believed that if everyone could vote, the ideal of democratic government, of a government popularly controlled, would be realized. Although today nearly everyone can vote if he wants to, government seems to be far from popularly controlled. Still others placed their faith in changes in the mechanism of government, urging the adoption of their favorite prescription, with the assurance that if their advice were taken, our governmental difficulties would be at an end. The initiative and referendum, the short ballot, and proportional representation have been advocated; each has been adopted in numerous jurisdictions, but the political millennium has not come. It is not meant to imply that these devices may not be both useful and desirable — but changes in the machinery will not, *alone*, bring popular control of government. Finally, there is a group which believes that the machinery of government should be improved where possible but that the achievement of popular control is largely dependent upon improved methods of civic organization and civic training. This view prompts a consideration of the development and influence of civic organizations, and of other questions which may be grouped under the heading of popular participation in government.

Direct Legislation

In the preceding chapter, in a discussion of nominating methods, reference was made to the various stages in the development of public sentiment regarding the application of the representative principle in the control of both governmental and party affairs. Mention was made of the spread of direct legislation as a supplement to and a partial substitute for the usual process of legislation through a representative assembly. It is now proposed to inquire more fully into the various procedures to which the term "direct legislation" is applied. These include the initiative, the referendum, the recall, and the recall of judicial decisions.

Prior to the Revolution there had been some conflict between the colonial legislatures and the Royal Governors. The legislatures had defended the interests of the people and had come to be regarded as representative of the popular will. Immediately after the Revolution extensive powers were granted to the legislatures, but over a period of many years these powers were steadily decreased as public confidence in the legislatures declined. This decline was due to legislative inefficiency and to the influence of paid lobbyists and of invisible government. The movement for direct legislation as a remedy for these conditions originated in South Dakota in 1898; twenty states now have a statewide initiative and referendum, while Maryland and New Mexico have the referendum only. All but five of these are west of the Mississippi River, and most of the measures were adopted prior to 1914, many of them under the influence of the Progressive movement.[1] There have been no additions to the list for some time, and in some cases a considerable agitation has developed for the repeal of all or part of the existing provisions.

According to an analysis by Dr. Gosnell, measures involving direct popular participation are of eight kinds [2]:

1. A constitutional amendment originating in the legislature and requiring the approval of the electorate
2. A constitutional amendment initiated by a petition signed by a specified proportion of the electorate and requiring popular approval
3. A law initiated in a similar manner and requiring popular approval
4. A law required by constitutional provision to be submitted to popular vote
5. A law referred by the legislature under a constitutional authorization to a popular vote
6. A law referred to popular vote after a petition has been signed by a specified number of voters
7. A public policy measure which is only advisory to and not mandatory upon the legislature [3]
8. A special election to determine whether an official should be superseded before his term is completed

It may be of interest to inquire about the extent to which these devices have been used. A study made for the New York State Constitutional Convention Committee in 1938 showed that between 1924 and 1935 a total of 1,299 measures were submitted to a popular vote in the various states.[4] Of these, 881 were referred constitutional amendments, 128 were initiated laws, and eighty-four were initiated constitutional amendments. Referenda on laws

[1] "As indicated by the number of articles on the initiative and referendum listed in the *Readers' Guide to Periodical Literature*, popular attention was considerable in 1900, rose with fair constancy to a peak of forty articles in 1911, and dropped thereafter until at the beginning of 1920 little attention was given these measures in the press. The number of states adopting the measures followed approximately the same pattern, maximum legislation for the devices occurring in 1912." The President's Research Committee on Social Trends, *Recent Social Trends*, p. 428 (McGraw-Hill, New York, 1933).

[2] Gosnell, Harold F., *Democracy — the Threshold of Freedom*, pp. 253–254 (Ronald Press, New York, 1948).

[3] See Goldman, Ralph M., "The Advisory Referendum in America," *Public Opinion Quarterly*, Summer 1950, pp. 303–315.

[4] Gosnell, Harold F., and Schmidt, Margaret J., "Popular Law Making in the United States," in *Problems Relating to Legislative Organization and Powers*, being Vol. VII of the Committee's *Report* (Albany, 1938).

required by constitutional provisions numbered seventy-four, on laws by petition seventy, on laws by the legislatures fifty-seven, and on public policy measures five. Most of the measures (974) were on the level of state government; 128 affected counties; ninety-one referred to city government, twenty-seven to school districts, twenty-nine to special districts, and fifty to combinations of levels.

For the use made of these devices in a particular state, see the accompanying table on page 145, relating to California. In Colorado, the experience over a like period of time may be summarized. Proposals for holding a constitutional convention were voted on three times, in 1916, 1922, and 1930. The total number of constitutional amendments and laws voted on between 1912 and 1938, inclusive, was 121. In this period, 73 constitutional amendments were proposed, of which 19 were adopted and 54 rejected. Forty-eight laws were submitted, of which 19 were adopted and 29 defeated. Since 1916, not more than 10 proposals have been submitted in any one year, and the number has usually been considerably less than that.[5]

The Initiative. The idea of the popular plebiscite had long been familiar in this country; as early as 1818, Connecticut had used the referendum in adopting a new constitution. The use of the initiative owes its origin chiefly to the effort to adapt to American conditions a governmental procedure that had long been used successfully in Switzerland.[6] It permits a group of citizens especially desirous of securing enactment of a particular law to bring the subject before the voters of the state at the next general election. There are two forms of the initiative: first, the constitutional initiative under which amendments to the constitution may be proposed and voted upon; second, the statutory initiative, which may be used for ordinary legislation. Some states require a larger petition for constitutional amendments than for ordinary laws, while others make no distinction between them.

The initiative is of two types, direct and indirect. The direct type, used in eleven states, places a proposed measure upon the ballot for submission to the electorate, without legislative action. In the indirect type, used in six states, the initiated measure goes to the legislature, which must act upon it within a reasonable period. If passed unchanged and signed by the governor, it becomes law forthwith, unless a referendum petition is entered. If amended or if not acted upon within the specified period of time, it must be submitted to a referendum. Thus the electorate acts twice, once through the filing of the petition and again through a referendum, should the legislature fail to accept the exact proposition presented by the petition. California, Utah, and Washington have both the direct and indirect initiative.

[5] Colorado Legislative Reference Office, *The Initiative and Referendum in Colorado* (Denver, 1940).

[6] See Lowell, A. Lawrence, *Public Opinion and Popular Government* (Longmans, Green, New York, 1921); Brooks, Robert C., *The Government and Politics of Switzerland* (World Book Company, Yonkers, 1920); and Rappard, William E., *Government of Switzerland* (Van Nostrand, New York, 1936).

Action of Voters on Direct Legislation in California, 1912–1948 *

ELECTION YEAR	INITIATED STATUTES		REFERRED STATUTES		CONSTITUTIONAL AMENDMENTS PROPOSED BY LEGISLATION		CONSTITUTIONAL AMENDMENTS PROPOSED BY INITIATIVE	
	Adopted	*Rejected*	*Adopted*	*Rejected*	*Adopted*	*Rejected*	*Adopted*	*Rejected*
1912	1	0	3	0	2	0	0	2
1914	9	3	4	3	15	7	3	5
1915 **	0	0	2	0	0	9	0	0
1915	0	0	1	0	0	0	1	3
1918	5	1	1	0	9	9	0	1
1919	0	0	0	0	1	0	0	0
1920	3	1	5	2	3	2	2	5
1922	3	2	3	0	7	7	2	6
1924	2	2	0	0	10	4	0	2
1926	3	0	1	0	14	4	1	4
1928	2	0	2	2	14	3	0	0
1930	4	1	0	0	10	10	0	1
1932	3	1	2	1	9	5	1	2
1933 **	0	0	1	1	6	2	0	0
1934	2	0	0	0	6	5	6	2
1935	0	0	0	0	0	3	0	0
1936	1	0	2	0	4	10	0	6
1938	3	1	3	0	6	10	0	3
1939 **	1	0	3	2	0	0	0	1
1940	1	0	0	0	8	8	0	0
1942	2	0	1	1	6	8	0	1
1944	0	0	0	0	6	2	1	2
1946	3	1	0	0	10	3	1	0
1948	3	1	0	0	5	5	1	4
Totals	*51*	*14*	*34*	*12*	*156*	*116*	*19*	*50*

* Data from Crouch, Winston W., and McHenry, Dean E., *California Government, Politics and Administration*, Revised Edition, pp. 22 and 109 (University of California Press, 1949).

** Denotes a special election.

In each case, the law provides for a petition to be signed, usually by 8 or 10 per cent of the electors, on the basis of the vote at the last general election. The data are summarized in the table on page 146. In some cases the signatures must come from two thirds or three fourths of the counties — in order to prevent the presentation of issues which are purely local. The most common requirement with regard to filing with the secretary of state specifies four months before the election. In some states definite provision is made for publicity, although publicity for proposals is a regular feature of the plan.

The pamphlets vary from postcards to pamphlets of substantial size and bulk in which case the expense involved is a not inconsiderable item. But they are an effective means of informing voters on candidates and issues. Certain safeguards are commonly provided, such as (in California) the requirement that the full text of the measure must appear on the petition; that the petition may be signed only by duly qualified electors; that measures must be passed or rejected by the legislature without change; and that they must be accompanied by the affidavit of the persons soliciting the signatures. Supplemental

Signature Requirements for Initiative Petitions

STATE	STATUTES	CONSTITUTIONAL AMENDMENTS
Arizona	10%	15%
Arkansas	8%	10%
California	8%	8%
Colorado	8%	8%
Idaho	10%	Not authorized
Illinois	25% (local) 10% (state)	Not authorized
Iowa	25%	Not authorized
Kentucky	25%	Not authorized
Louisiana	25%	Not authorized
Maine	12,000 signatures	Prohibited
Massachusetts	25,000 signatures	25,000 signatures
Michigan	8%	10%
Mississippi	$\frac{1}{10}$ of electors (local)	Not authorized
Missouri	8%	8%
Montana	8%	Prohibited
Nebraska	7%	10%
Nevada	10%	10%
New Mexico	20% (local)	Not authorized
North Carolina	25% (local)	Not authorized
North Dakota	10,000 signatures	20,000 signatures
Ohio	6%	10%
Oklahoma	8%	15%
Oregon	8%	8%
South Dakota	5%	Prohibited
Utah	10%	Prohibited
Washington	10%	Prohibited
West Virginia	10% (local)	Not authorized
Wyoming	30% (local)	Not authorized

petitions may be permitted. As a rule, no limitation as to subject matter is placed upon initiative proposals, but time limits may be imposed, limiting the frequency with which propositions once defeated may be resubmitted. Measures, when approved, take effect immediately upon approval, upon declaration of the vote, or upon proclamation of the governor, but it is frequently specified that the governor has no veto power.[7]

Criticism of the Initiative in Practice. The proponents of the initiative and referendum argue that these devices are more democratic in character than the ordinary process of legislation, and that they provide a method by which citizens may secure the adoption or rejection of measures concerning which the legislature has failed to follow the popular will. The spread of the movement in the early twentieth century was due in no small part to the leadership of Judson King who, viewing the experience of approximately one third of the American voters in eighteen states over nearly half a century in the use of the initiative and referendum, wrote in a letter to the author that it "constitutes the most vital test of the capacity of a modern people to set up an economic, social and political system for their own well-being, of any experience in human history, as well as of their capacity to repel any kind of exploitation or tyranny by a governing class."

While the theory may be good, it has not operated without the development of serious objections. In the first place, a persistent effort has been made to secure better drafting of the measures enacted into law. An initiative measure may be well drafted, but if this does occur, it is likely to be rather by accident than by design. Second, the argument that this is a means of determining the popular will may be refuted by the fact that so small a percentage of voters express any preference regarding measures submitted in this way. If they are finally adopted, this result is achieved, not through the approval of the majority of citizens nor even by a majority of the voters participating in the election, but by a mere majority of that minority group sufficiently interested in the proposition to vote at all. Another important objection lies in the violation of the short ballot principle, the purpose of which is to simplify the voter's task by reducing the number of choices he must make. If the number of elective offices is reduced and at the same time the ballot is lengthened by adding numerous legislative proposals, the principle of the

[7] See Graves, W. Brooke, and Still, Samuel H., Jr., "Direct Legislation," *Book of the States, 1948–1949*, pp. 155–163. In addition to material cited in previous editions, and books in Selected References, see the following articles: ARIZONA: Kelso, Paul, "Arizona Legislature Invokes Referenda," *National Municipal Review*, June 1952, pp. 305–306. CALIFORNIA: Crouch, Winston W., "Direct Legislation Laboratory," *National Municipal Review*, February 1951, pp. 81–87; Radin, Max, "Popular Legislation in California," *California Law Review*, June 1947, pp. 171–190; and Smith, Alfred F., "Can We Afford the Initiative?" *National Municipal Review*, October 1949, pp. 437–442. OHIO: Fordham, Jefferson B., and Leach, J. Russell, "The Initiative and Referendum in Ohio," *Ohio State Law Journal*, Autumn 1950, pp. 495–532, and Schwartz, Arthur A., "Initiative Held in Reserve," *National Municipal Review*, March 1952, pp. 142–145, 174. OREGON: LaPalombara, Joseph G., and Hagen, Charles B., "Direct Legislation: an Appraisal and a Suggestion," *American Political Science Review*, June 1951, pp. 400–421, and Neuberger, Richard L., "Vox Oregoni," *New York Times Magazine*, October 19, 1947; OKLAHOMA: Ewing, Cortez A. M., "Sufficiency Certification of Initiative Signatures in Oklahoma," *American Political Science Review*, February 1937, pp. 65–70. WASHINGTON: Johnson, Claudius O., "The Initiative and Referendum in Washington," *Pacific Northwest Quarterly*, January 1945, pp. 29–53.

short ballot is more harmed than aided. If the ballot must be long, it had better remain so through the necessity of electing officials rather than through the exercise of choices on legislative proposals. However badly the voters may on occasion perform the first of these tasks, their record in the performance of the second is even more discouraging.

Other criticisms of the initiative process relate to the huge waste of money and energy required to combat unsound proposals, many of which appear on the ballot because some small group can raise sufficient funds to qualify them, and to the necessity of contending against the same unsound proposals year after year, despite their constant rejection by the voters each time they appear. Objection is also raised to the growing practice of "professionalism" in conducting initiative campaigns, which has come to border — in some cases — on racketeering. It is reported that a "mystery man" in California with a unique and extensive organization rounds up signatures for initiative or referendum measures, guaranteeing to get them on the ballot for a mere $100,000. He will get an initiative proposal on the ballot one year, and hire out to the opposition to rig a contrary petition the next. Sometimes both sides must rely upon his organization at the same time although a lawyer (which profession he claims to resemble) cannot act as counsel for both parties to a dispute at the same time.[8] There is also a tendency toward circumventing and restricting the powers of the legislature by advocacy of measures proposing mandatory expenditures and limitations on taxation, while at the same time the legislature, with its hands tied, has full responsibility for finding needed revenues and imposing necessary taxes.

It is true that the states using these devices attempt to inform the voters regarding the merits of the measures proposed, in specially prepared pamphlets. These pamphlets commonly contain a clear and impartial statement of the provisions of each measure, with a summary of the arguments for and against adoption. Organizations interested in any given measure may purchase at cost a limited amount of space in which to set forth their position regarding it. When the voters are asked to pass upon many proposals, the pamphlet becomes a document of formidable size. While every registered voter receives a copy, one may well ponder the extent to which these pamphlets are read and studied prior to the election.[9] If the states had shown the same moderation in the use of these devices which has characterized their use in Switzerland; if they had limited their use to the effort to correct definite abuses; if they had, as Woodrow Wilson once suggested, kept them in reserve as the

[8] Newberger, Richard L., "Government by the People," *Survey*, November 1950, pp. 490–493.

[9] See Lippmann, Walter, *The Phantom Public*, Chapter 2, "The Unattainable Ideal" (Harcourt, Brace, New York, 1925). In this chapter Mr. Lippmann brilliantly portrays one of the chief fallacies of modern democracy in general, and of direct legislation in particular — fallacies which were exemplified in 1948 when California's unwary voters saddled themselves with a prodigious old-age pension plan, only to discover in 1949 that there was no way out except to repeal it, which they did.

settlers of old kept the gun behind the door — rather than regarding them as a method for the general enactment of legislation — there could be little objection to them. Such, however, has not been the case.

Proposals for Modifying Initiative Procedure. Many attempts have been made, more often by the enemies than by the friends of the initiative, to modify the procedure by increasing the percentage of signatures required on the petition, by requiring signatures to petitions to be written in the presence of a public official at some central place such as the county court house, by prohibiting persons circulating petitions from receiving pay for their services, and by excluding such matters as taxation and bond issues from the procedure.[10] While these devices would undoubtedly remedy some abuses, some of them might destroy whatever effectiveness the initiative possesses. There would seem to be no valid objection, however, to a requirement that initiative proposals be required to lie on the table at the next regular session of the legislature. If the legislature should reject them or fail to give them consideration, it would be time enough to go over the heads of the elected representatives directly to the people. Other desirable changes would impose a time limit of perhaps five years on the frequency with which a proposal once rejected by the voters might again be submitted, and would require that, if funds were needed to carry out a new law, provision be made for raising them. There is no good reason why the battle of "ham and eggs" should have to be refought annually or why it should be necessary to adopt a given measure one year and repeal it the next.

The Referendum. Constitutional provisions authorizing the use of the initiative usually authorize the referendum also. Like the initiative, it is of two kinds, constitutional and statutory; it may be invoked by either of two procedures — by petition or by legislation. Constitutional amendments have as a matter of course in most states been submitted to a popular vote. In the case of the statutory referendum, the first method may be employed if the legislature passes an act which is objectionable to a considerable number of citizens. If 5 or 10 per cent of the voters participating in the last general election sign a petition within a specified period of time, the proposal may be brought before the voters at the next election. This use of the referendum does not present any radical departure from established practice in American government — it is merely an extension of the method long employed and generally accepted in the case of constitutional amendments. The second method by which a referendum may be secured is dependent upon action by the legislature. If this body enacts a statute concerning which the members are in considerable doubt or for which they are unwilling to take responsibility, they may provide that it may become law only on condition that it be approved by a majority of the voters at the polls. While no serious objec-

[10] Key, Vladimer O., Jr., and Crouch, Winston W., *The Initiative and Referendum in California*, Chapter 8 (University of California Press, 1939); see also Dow, Edward F., "Portland Limits Initiative," *National Municipal Review*, July 1951, pp. 347–350.

tion can be raised to referenda of the first type, it is certainly true that the second type is a "buck-passing" device which tends further to undermine the prestige of the legislature.

The constitutional and legal rules governing the referendum do not differ greatly from those governing the initiative. The percentage of signatures required for petitions is frequently less, and where a legislative referendum is initiated by the people, the petition must be filed with the secretary of state within ninety days after the close of the legislative session. The same publicity arrangements and the same safeguards apply in one case as in the other. Laws which are necessary for the public health and safety or for the support of the state government are frequently exempted from the operation of the referendum; in some states these are designated as emergency measures. In order to permit the free use of the referendum privilege, many states provide that acts of the legislature shall not take effect until ninety days after the close of the session, except in the case of exempted measures.[11] As in the case of the initiative, the governor has no veto power.

The Recall. The recall has been known in government since the time of the Greeks; its modern development began in Switzerland, where it was applied to local legislatures. Its use in the American states dates from June 1, 1908, when a provision for it was incorporated in the Constitution of Oregon, although the city charter of Los Angeles had provided for it previously. It may be described as a device by which the voters may remove from office, through use of the ballot, persons who have previously been selected by the same means. The principle is applicable to officers in all three departments of the government, although its use in this country has been limited to those in the executive and judicial branches. It has not been used very extensively, having been for the most part restricted to cases of malfeasance in office. There is only one case on record in which the governor of a state has been recalled but several in which mayors or other local officials have been removed.

While there is some variation in the details of procedure, that prescribed in Oregon may be taken as illustrative. In order to recall an officer, it is necessary to present a petition to which are appended the signatures of 25 per cent of the voters of the district which the officer serves. In the case of the governor, it would be 25 per cent of the voters of the state. This petition must also contain a statement of the reasons which, it is claimed, justify the recall. If the officer does not resign within five days, a special election is held within twenty days. On the sample ballot the reasons for the recall must be presented in 200 words; the accused officer is allowed a like number for his defense. In this

[11] But the use of the emergency clause may develop into a habit. In Oklahoma, prior to 1920, the measures including the emergency clause were never more than 62 per cent of the acts passed, while since 1920 this percentage has never fallen below 74. See Ewing, Cortez A. M., "The Emergency Epidemic," State Government, July 1931, pp. 3–4; also Schumacher, Waldo, "The Emergency Clause," *Oregon Law Review*, December 1939, pp. 73–77.

state, the officer subject to recall automatically becomes a candidate for the office at the election which follows. His opponents nominate other candidates; if re-elected, he holds his position; if not, the candidate receiving the most votes takes his place. Any officer must have been in office at least six months before he is subject to recall, an exception being made in the case of senators and representatives in the legislative assembly, where the limit is five days. After one recall election, no additional recall petitions may be circulated against the same officer until the petitioners pay into the public treasury the expenses of the preceding election.[12]

Most of the states that adopted the recall did so by the end of World War I. The table on page 152 shows the states which use this device either on a statewide basis or locally, together with some information as to the petition requirements in each case.[13]

The record shows that recall elections for mayors, councilmen, commissioners, judges, and one governor have been held among these states. Among the charges noted are unfitness, favoritism, carelessness, extravagance, incompetence, inability, no benefit to public, selfishness, neglect of duties, and corruption. A tabulation of twenty-nine cases, scattered over a period of years in the states mentioned, shows seven in which the officials remained in office, seventeen in which they were removed, four upon which there was no vote, and one in which the men resigned and were returned to office in an ensuing election. All except one case involved municipal or county officers. While the number of cases is relatively small, there are numerous instances in which the possibility of recall has been discussed and in which the very fact of the discussion had some influence upon the conduct of the officials in question.

The principle of the recall has rarely been applied to judicial officers. Two members of the minor judiciary were removed with proper cause in San Francisco a number of years ago, but fortunately this device has not been invoked against the members of the higher judicial tribunals. Were this not true, the effect of the recall on the independence of the judiciary might have been serious. If the danger of recall proceedings were in fact great, there are many judges whose concern for the popular will in individual cases and for the security of their positions would be greater than their concern for the administration of justice. This danger was given classic statement by President Taft when in 1911 he vetoed a resolution providing for the admission of Arizona with a constitution containing provisions for the recall. In the course of this message, he said:

[12] Beard, Charles A., and Shulz, Bird E., *Documents on the State-wide Initiative, Referendum, and Recall*, p. 243 (Macmillan, New York, 1912); Barnett, James D., *The Operation of the Initiative, Referendum, and Recall in Oregon*, pp. 192–193 (Macmillan, New York, 1915).

[13] Graves and Still, *op. cit.*, pp. 161–163. See also Illinois Constitutional Convention, *Bulletin* No. 2, "Initiative, Referendum, and Recall," p. 120 (Springfield, 1919); Hannan, William E., *Digest of Constitutions and Laws of the Various States with Respect to Recall of Public Officers* (New York State Library, Albany, 1934).

Where the Recall May Be Used

STATE	YEAR	BASIS	APPLICATION TO ELECTED OFFICERS		PER CENT OF SIGNATURES REQUIRED
			STATE	LOCAL	
Arizona	1911	C	all	all	25
Arkansas	1921	S		cities [1]	35
California	1911	C	all	all	12–25
Colorado	1912	C	all	all	25–40
Idaho	1912	C	all [1]	all [1]	10–35
Illinois	1911	S		cities [1,2]	55
Iowa	1907	S		cities [2]	25
Kansas	1914	C	all [3]	all	10–25
Louisiana	1910	C	all [1]	all [1]	25–33$\frac{1}{3}$
Michigan	1913	C	all [1]	all [1]	25
Minnesota	1941	S		cities	[4]
Mississippi	1918	S		cities	25
Missouri	1919	S		cities	20
Montana	1917	S		cities [2]	25
Nebraska	1911	S		all	25–30
Nevada	1912	C	all	all	25
New Jersey	1915	S		cities [2]	25
New Mexico	1919	S		cities	15
North Carolina	1917	S		cities [2]	25
North Dakota	1920	C	all	all	30
Ohio	1927	C		cities	15
Oregon	1908	C	all [3]	all	Not over 25
South Carolina	1910	S		cities [2]	20–40
South Dakota	1913	S		cities [2]	15
Washington	1912	C	all [1]	all [1]	25–35
West Virginia	1937	S		all	20
Wisconsin	1926	C	all	all	25–33$\frac{1}{3}$
Wyoming	1911	S		all [2]	25
Total			12	28	

[1] Judicial officers excepted.
[2] Restricted to cities under commission form.
[3] Applies to appointive as well as elective officers.
[4] Charter provisions.

> This provision of the Arizona constitution, in its application to county and state judges, seems to me so pernicious in its effect, so destructive of independence in the judiciary, so likely to subject the rights of the individual to the possible tyranny of a popular majority, and, therefore, to be so injurious to the cause of free government that I must disapprove a constitution containing it. . . . [14]

[14] President Taft, August 15, 1911; a special message published as House Document No. 106, 62 Cong., 1 Sess. For other discussions, see list of selected references, especially Brooks, *op. cit.*, Chapter 18. The constitutional provisions in force in California and Missouri, and recommended in the *Model State Constitution*, by which judges run on their record, represents a modified and unobjectionable form of the original recall procedures.

Recall of Judicial Decisions. The most extreme form of direct popular participation in government — the recall of judicial decisions — was advocated by Theodore Roosevelt during the Bull Moose campaign, on the theory that the people at the polls should have it within their power to make effective, by popular vote, a statute which the highest state court had declared unconstitutional. In this way they might in effect amend the constitution without resorting to the prescribed methods. By such a vote they would say, not that the statute in question was constitutional, but that, even though it was unconstitutional, they desired to have it in effect. This proposal seems never to have been taken seriously except in Colorado, where a constitutional amendment was adopted in 1912 prohibiting the lower courts from declaring statutes unconstitutional and providing for the recall of adverse decisions by the Supreme Court, where the question of constitutionality was involved.

A Workable Electoral System

There are three basic principles for the designing of a workable electoral system: (1) the ballot must be short; (2) the officers thereon must be important and significant enough to attract adequate public scrutiny; (3) the districts must be wieldy. All three of these principles are widely violated in American practice. The importance of the first two has been recognized, but surprisingly little has been said about the third.[15]

Manageable Districts. Only in the United States are there any electoral districts of over 100,000 voters or, say, 200,000 population. Representatives to Congress are elected from districts ranging around 300,000 population with, in some instances, representatives at large when the legislature fails to redistrict. In addition, there are great districts used for election at large in most of the big cities, in some populous county elections, and in the statewide elections for United States Senators and state administrative officers. Finally, of course, in the national election the realities override the electoral college device and call for nationwide campaigning.

Such large electoral units are unique among the nations. In contrast, in Great Britain, in the 1948 reapportionment study of parliamentary districts, dividing 482 seats among 28,706,999 electors (or 43,000,000 population) gives an average district electorate of 59,312; then, striving to vary no more than 10,000 on either side of that figure, the result is forty-four districts of 70,000 or more electors (including eight over 80,000), the largest having 87,100. What corrective measures are possible here, given the framework of the American constitutional system, it is difficult to say; but it can nevertheless be recognized that in this respect the unique practice in this country of using election districts of unwieldy size creates a serious problem in the popular control of government.

[15] See chapter in Childs, Richard S., *Short Ballot Principles* (National Short Ballot Organization, New York, 1911). This has long been out of print.

Development of the Long Ballot. Another defect of the American system is the old-fashioned long ballot. With the extension of the powers of government in many fields, the establishment of many new offices was necessary. When these offices were created by statute, it became customary, in keeping with the Jacksonian tradition, to have their incumbents selected by popular vote. Every time a new officer or group of officers was placed on the ballot, three or four times as many names were added in order that each party might present its candidates for that office. So the ballot grew until in many elections in many states it was large enough to cover a fair portion of the side of the wall in an ordinary room. One ballot in New York, some years ago, was fourteen feet long, while ballots in many of our states have been three by five, and five by seven feet in size. A Chicago primary had over 500 names on a single ballot. Needless to say, it is impossible for any human being to know enough about the personalities behind so many names to vote intelligently.

Few important figures in American politics have ever done a greater disservice to the cause of popular government than Andrew Jackson. His assumption was that democracy consisted in voting. If the people voted for a large number of officials, from the governor down to and including the keeper of the dog pound, and did this often enough, their government would be democratic. No ranker nonsense was ever preached, as the evidence through succeeding generations in which this principle has been applied demonstrates abundantly. Democracy does not consist in voting or in the performance of any other single act. The essence of democracy requires that the people shall maintain *control* over their government. Voting is merely one of the ways by which this is done. An excessive amount of voting has many times, in many places, nullified the power of the people to control their government.

Current practice in the states varies all the way between the two extremes. Voters in New Jersey elect only the governor, who appoints all but two of fourteen cabinet members, these two (Institutions and Agencies, and Highways) being selected by boards. In New York and Virginia, the voters select only the governor, lieutenant governor, and attorney general, but in Oklahoma they elect no less than seventeen state administrative officials.

Short Ballot Principles. The short ballot has for many years been advocated as an antidote for that governmental monstrosity known as the long ballot. The principle of the short ballot would in operation restrict the officers chosen by popular election to policy-determining officers. If this principle were applied, our elections could be arranged in four-year cycles in accordance with the plan on page 155. The English elect members of the county Council and of Parliament, at different times, on a ballot even smaller than an ordinary postcard. Under the federal plan it is impossible to achieve this extreme degree of simplicity, but the adoption of the plan suggested above would come as near this as possible.

The short ballot has a number of notable advantages. It would, in the first place, centralize responsibility and do much to insure a more efficient

Proposed Four-Year Election Cycle

First Year	Electors for President and Vice-President, representatives in Congress, and a United States Senator.
Second Year	Governor, representatives in the state legislature, and city councilmen.
Third Year	Representatives in Congress, and, when required, a United States Senator.
Fourth Year	Representatives in the state legislature, and mayor, city councilmen, and county officers.

administration of state government. In states where a number of important department heads must still be selected by popular vote, it is impossible for the governor to exercise proper supervision and insure support of the policies of the administration. If there were no other reasons than this, one would be abundantly justified in urging the adoption of the short ballot principle. In the second place, the principle is in harmony with a sound concept of democracy. It recognizes the fact that popular government does not consist in the mere selection of officials, but rather in the selection of those whose key positions in government enable them to control policy and make them directly responsible to the voting public. Finally, the principle greatly simplifies the voter's task; this problem will be discussed more fully in a later section of this chapter.

In the foregoing chapter, where ballots were discussed as a phase of the conduct of elections, data on the form and arrangement of ballots in the various states were presented. In the conclusions of a study of ballots used in the 1932 and 1934 elections, it is shown that the most complicated local ballots were found, among cities, in Chicago, Cleveland, Denver, Detroit, Omaha, St. Louis, and Salt Lake City; among states, in Colorado, Florida, Georgia, Idaho, Iowa, Kansas, New Mexico, North Dakota, Oregon, Texas, West Virginia, and Wyoming. In each of these states there were approximately twenty local choices on the ballots examined.[16]

In many other cities conditions exist which are highly unsatisfactory and which indicate the need for a further extension of the short-ballot principle. In Philadelphia, for instance, the Bureau of Municipal Research points out a striking contrast between the appointed heads of city departments and the elective county officers:

> Judged by expenditures and number of employees, the elective county offices are rather small jobs. Roll them all into one and the appropriations listed above are not over 15% of the budget of the director of public safety; the number of employees is not over 12%. Why should such offices be permitted to distract attention from the really important ones that the voters must fill?

[16] Albright, Spencer D., *How Does Your Ballot Grow?* (American Legislators' Association, Chicago, 1933), and "General Election Ballots in 1934," *Southwestern Social Science Quarterly*, March 1936, pp. 85–95.

But the county officers of Philadelphia County do not determine policies to any great extent. Even the county commissioners, once a legislative body, lost all of their legislative powers to city council back in 1854.[17]

Illustrations of this type could be drawn from many different states and cities. The need for extending the use of the short ballot is clear. "Students of political science generally agree," concludes Spencer D. Albright, "that precise instructions, absence of Presidential Electors, moderate burden as to positions, names, and propositions, and convenient arrangement of offices and questions are desirable features in a good ballot." On the other hand, huge ballots, excessive reading matter, lengthy voting instructions, long lists of names, great variety of offices as to both character and importance, and numerous propositions are generally condemned. "Short ballot arguments appear even more convincing after an examination of ballots throughout the nation. The handicaps set upon the workings of democracy undoubtedly undermine democratic opportunity." [18]

This proposal has been before the American people for close to half a century, during which time only limited progress in realizing its purposes has been achieved. Ten years ago Professor Pollock stressed the point that the arguments were the same as they were when the proposal was first made, and the situation quite as serious. That is still true today. There are doubtless many factors contributing to this slow progress, such as lack of public interest and understanding, opposition of the political parties, and others. Professor Gaus suggests that another important reason is to be found in the fact that the average governor (or mayor) has found it all but impossible "to combine effectively the tasks both of political and party leadership and of managerial direction." [19] This problem will be discussed in Chapter 9.

Types of Weighted Voting

Faults of District System of Representation. Gross inequalities frequently result from the application of the single member district plan of representation, due in part to the gerrymandering of districts by the legislature and in part to defects inherent in the plan. Although notable increases in the population of a given state may occur, and important shifts in population take place, the legislature frequently fails to enact a reapportionment. Even where the districts are fairly and evenly divided, a large portion of the voting popu-

[17] *Citizens' Business*, June 5, 1934.

[18] Albright, *op. cit.*

[19] See Pollock, James K., "New Thoughts on the Short Ballot," *National Municipal Review*, January 1940, pp. 18–20, 47, and Gaus, John M., "The States Are in the Middle," *State Government*, June 1950, pp. 138–142; also Jones, O. Garfield, "Is the Short Ballot Principle Obsolete?" *National Municipal Review*, April 1943, pp. 185–187, 189, and Childs, Richard S., "We Must Keep the Ballot Short," *ibid.*, July 1949, pp. 328–334. For some of the original comments, see American Political Science Association, *Proceedings*, 1909: Beard, Charles A., "Tendencies Affecting the Size of the Ballot," pp. 93–99; Childs, Richard S., "The Need for Simplification," pp. 65–71; and Ludington, Arthur C., "Proposed Methods of Ballot Simplification," pp. 72–91.

lation is without suitable representation. A majority of one is sufficient to determine the result of an election. While contests are seldom so close, it frequently happens that 30 or 40 per cent of the voters in a district cast their ballots for a candidate other than the one elected. To argue that under the doctrine of majority rule these persons are effectively represented by one for whom they did not vote, and with whose views they do not agree, is to substitute fiction for fact. This considerable percentage of voters in the district concerned are without anyone who can or will express, in any satisfactory manner, their views on controversial issues.

Not only are the results of the single member district plan unsatisfactory within individual districts, but the effect of the plan throughout a state may also be unsatisfactory. Pennsylvania, for instance, has a Congressional delegation of thirty members; for many years it was a rare election in which more than three or four or five members belonged to the minority party. It is true that the majority party in the state long maintained a substantial majority, but it is absurd to suppose that there was any such degree of unanimity of opinion on political questions as would seem to be indicated by the complexion of this delegation in Congress.

These conditions affect a whole state, but the situation is just as bad — perhaps worse — when one turns to a large municipality like New York City, where in eight elections — nearly half of the time — a party with a minority of the votes elected a majority of the members. In more than a fifth of all aldermanic district contests, a minority won at the expense of a divided majority. Forty-two per cent of all the votes cast were wasted on losing candidates. In seven consecutive elections Democratic votes were worth from three to twenty-five times as much as Republican votes in securing representation. In the same seven elections the Socialists polled every time from four to ten times as many votes as the number of Democratic votes for each Democratic member elected, and elected no aldermen at all. It never required as much as one third of the votes cast to elect a majority of the Board of Aldermen for the controlling party. "In short," the author of this study concludes, "our method of trying to secure a representative body has violated every major tenet of American democracy. We have not had majority rule. We have not had fair representation for minorities. We have not even had an approach to equality of voting power." In the 1935 elections the Democrats elected all but three of the sixty-eight members of the Board of Aldermen; in Philadelphia the Democrats, who polled only a few thousand less votes than the Republicans in the mayoralty contest, failed to elect a single one of the twenty-two members of the city council.

Proportional Representation. To correct these abuses, various devices such as proportional representation, commonly called P.R., preferential voting, and cumulative voting, have been advocated. P.R. was first proposed by the son of an obscure English clergyman, named Hare, in 1857. When the plan was published in pamphlet form, it attracted little attention until, some years later, John Stuart Mill incorporated a discussion of it in his volume on *Representative Government*. From that time on, the subject has been regarded as significant; in recent years it has come to have an important practical bearing. The principle of proportional representation has been applied in two different ways: the List system, adopted in Europe; the Hare system, adopted in many communities throughout the United States.

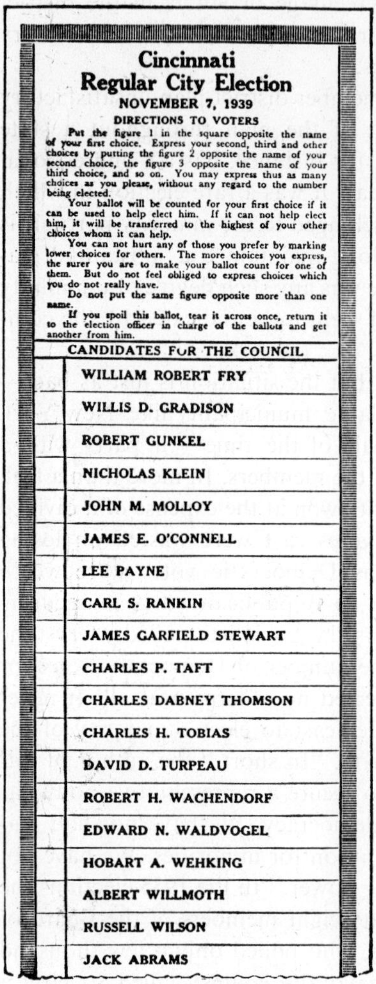

Cincinnati
Regular City Election
NOVEMBER 7, 1939
DIRECTIONS TO VOTERS

Put the figure 1 in the square opposite the name of your first choice. Express your second, third and other choices by putting the figure 2 opposite the name of your second choice, the figure 3 opposite the name of your third choice, and so on. You may express thus as many choices as you please, without any regard to the number being elected.

Your ballot will be counted for your first choice if it can be used to help elect him. If it can not help elect him, it will be transferred to the highest of your other choices whom it can help.

You can not hurt any of those you prefer by marking lower choices for others. The more choices you express, the surer you are to make your ballot count for one of them. But do not feel obliged to express choices which you do not really have.

Do not put the same figure opposite more than one name.

If you spoil this ballot, tear it across once, return it to the election officer in charge of the ballots and get another from him.

	CANDIDATES FOR THE COUNCIL
	WILLIAM ROBERT FRY
	WILLIS D. GRADISON
	ROBERT GUNKEL
	NICHOLAS KLEIN
	JOHN M. MOLLOY
	JAMES E. O'CONNELL
	LEE PAYNE
	CARL S. RANKIN
	JAMES GARFIELD STEWART
	CHARLES P. TAFT
	CHARLES DABNEY THOMSON
	CHARLES H. TOBIAS
	DAVID D. TURPEAU
	ROBERT H. WACHENDORF
	EDWARD N. WALDVOGEL
	HOBART A. WEHKING
	ALBERT WILLMOTH
	RUSSELL WILSON
	JACK ABRAMS

SAMPLE BALLOT

The List system recognizes the existence of political parties and provides specifically for them; under it, each party nominates a slate of candidates, the number of which corresponds exactly to the number of positions to be filled. If we assume this number to be ten, party A, if it polls 40 per cent of the votes, will elect its first four candidates; party B, if it likewise polls 40 per cent of the votes, will elect four candidates; and party C, polling 20 per cent, will elect two. This plan would appear to have considerable merit. While it has been used in Europe, it has not been tried in the United States, and its adoption here has not been widely advocated.[20]

The Hare system uses the principle of the single transferable vote for the purpose of insuring to each important element of the voting population a representation exactly in proportion to its numerical voting strength. In this plan, parties are not directly recognized although they may mobilize their voting strength behind any selection of candidates they may desire. Nominations may be made by petition by any group of sufficient size and interest to secure the required number of signatures. The names of all nominees are printed on the ballot without any descriptive designation. The voter may indicate as many choices as he wishes, voting for one candidate, for a number equivalent to the number of positions to be filled, or for all the candidates whose names appear on the ballot, indicating his choices in the order of his preference. At the con-

[20] See Gosnell, Harold F., "A List System with Single Candidate Preference," *American Political Science Review*, August 1939, pp. 645–650.

clusion of the voting, the ballot boxes are taken under seal and guard to the central counting place, where a group of bank clerks and other persons accustomed to accurate checking are employed to tabulate the results. Until 1936 no voting machine suitable for use in P.R. elections had been perfected, but one based on the punch-card principle has been available since that time.[21]

It has been suggested that one might imagine all the voters in a city gathered together on a certain day and hour in the city park to select office-holders. It is assumed that, under such circumstances, each candidate for each office would have a standard erected, about which his followers might gather. When the signal was given for the citizens to indicate their choices for a particular office, such as member of council, each voter would make his way to the standard of the candidate of his choice, in order that his vote might be counted. If, as he did so, he saw that so many voters were already gathered under this standard that his favorite candidate was already assured of election, he would be foolish to increase further the number of excess votes. As a rational person he would reason that since the candidate of his choice was already assured of election, he might as well lend his support to his second choice. If he should find that his second choice was likewise assured of election, he might then support his third choice, and so on. This is precisely what happens when, in a proportional representation election, the excess votes of an elected candidate are distributed to the later choices indicated on these ballots.

In the counting of the ballots, the rules require as a first step the determination of the quota which represents the minimum number of votes with which a candidate may be declared elected. This number is secured by dividing the total number of valid ballots cast at the election by the number of positions to be filled, plus one. Thus, if 10,000 votes were cast and five candidates were to be elected, it would be necessary to divide 10,000 by six, in which case the quotient would be $1{,}666\frac{2}{3}$. Whether or not the quotient proves to be a whole number, the rules require the use of the next highest whole number as the quota — which, in this case, would be 1,667. The second step is the tabulation of the first choices on the ballots; in this tabulation there are two methods which may be followed. Either all the first choices may be tabulated, regardless of the number which any candidate may receive, or the counters may cease tabulating first choices for any candidate as soon as the full quota has been recorded for him. In the latter case, the second choices from the elected candidate's excess ballots are added to the first choices from the rest of the ballots.[22]

[21] See note in *National Municipal Review*, July 1936, p. 432.

[22] For recent comment, see Gosnell, *Democracy*, *op. cit.*, Chapter 10; Rustow, Dankwart A., "Some Observations on Proportional Representation," *Journal of Politics*, February 1950, pp. 107–127; and Zeller, Belle, and Bone, Hugh A., "The Repeal of P.R. in New York City — Ten Years in Retrospect," *American Political Science Review*, December 1948, pp. 1127–1148.

Preferential Voting. Preferential voting has been defined as "a device whereby a voter in a primary or general election may indicate on his ballot a first and second choice . . . with a view to combining or transferring choices when the votes are counted in such a way as to produce at least a nominal majority in favor of a particular candidate." [23] In other words, it selects the most representative candidate out of any number, eliminating dark horses by a single election. The ballots are not difficult to fill out, and ordinarily they are not hard to count. Between 1907 and 1925 this system was adopted in eleven states, but it has now been abandoned by all except Maryland. The Oklahoma law was declared unconstitutional; the others were repealed. In Idaho, Indiana, Minnesota, North Dakota, Washington, and Wisconsin the plurality system was substituted for it, while in Alabama, Florida, Louisiana, and Oklahoma the run-off primary took its place. The reasons given for repeal were the failure of voters to indicate more than one choice, and the failure of party leaders to educate the voters in the use of a preferential feature. The chief weakness of this system is that a voter's second and other choices are given equal weight with his first choice, if they do not actually work against the election of his first choice.

Cumulative Voting. A system of cumulative voting is one in which a voter, with several votes at his disposal, may use all of them for one candidate if he so desires. Such a system has been in effect in Illinois for years for the choice of members of the lower house in the legislature. Professor Mathews thus describes the system:

> One Senator is elected from each of the fifty-one senatorial districts, and each voter has one vote in voting for a senator; but three representatives are elected from each senatorial district and each voter has three votes which he may "plump" for one candidate or distribute in such manner as he sees fit. This is known as the system of minority representation or cumulative voting provided for in the Constitution of 1870, and is unique among the methods of electing legislative representatives found in the various states.[24]

The Influence of Civic Organizations

During recent years citizens' organizations of various types have assumed an increasingly important role in the guidance of public affairs. Formerly these organizations were composed chiefly of reform elements who were interested in bringing about specific changes in the governmental structure. Little attention was given to the detailed supervision of regular government services, or to the study of routine problems of organization and administration. Interest in social, political, and economic problems, stimulated by the depression and maintained to a considerable extent during the war,

[23] Weeks, O. Douglas, "Summary of the History and Present Status of Preferential Voting in State Direct Primary Systems," *Southwestern Social Science Quarterly*, June 1937, pp. 64–67; Dorr, Harold M., "The Nanson System: A Michigan Experiment in Voting," *Papers* of the Michigan Academy of Science, Arts, and Letters, 1942, pp. 613–621.

[24] Mathews, John M., *American State Government*, Revised Edition, p. 235 (Appleton-Century, New York, 1934).

has continued at a high level in the postwar years. The people have come to realize the necessity for an alert and well-informed citizenry if democracy is to be successful. Many organizations have been developed with this end in view, and colleges and universities, as well as programs of adult education, have laid great emphasis upon public affairs. In the discussion which follows, national organizations which display a real interest in state problems are considered first, followed by important types of statewide organizations and finally by those of a purely local character.

National Municipal League. Probably the oldest organization engaged in this work is the National Municipal League, a nonprofitmaking, nonpartisan corporation founded in 1894.[25] Its former presidents include Charles Evans Hughes, Frank L. Polk, Lawson Purdy, Henry M. Waite, Richard S. Childs, Murray Seasongood, Harold W. Dodds, Clarence A. Dykstra, John G. Winant, and Charles Edison. While the League has confined itself largely to the field of local government, it has maintained a committee on state government, which has kept up to date the Model State Constitution. Since the relationship between state and local government is very close, whatever affects the one is of importance to the other.

The purposes of the League are (1) to create or adapt methods by which local government could be operated more efficiently, less expensively, more responsively; (2) to maintain a clearing house service which covers all phases of local government problems and procedures; (3) to conduct educational activities which seek to crystallize public opinion in support of higher standards and better methods of administration for local government. It is the sole national organization which carries on this type of work. The methods employed and the services rendered include: PUBLICATIONS: *National Municipal Review*, a monthly journal; also the preparation, publication, and distribution of books, pamphlets, and other educational material on government problems. Nearly 400,000 pieces of literature were distributed in 1949. INFORMATION SERVICE: answers inquiries on all phases of city, county, and state government; comprehensive library available to persons seriously interested in government problems. SPEAKERS' BUREAU: speakers and consultants on municipal government and campaign problems supplied at cost. Members of the League staff visit many cities to confer with citizen leaders on the manager plan and citizen organization. CAMPAIGN AID: campaign plans used in other communities are supplied to local groups working for improved government, while literature suitable for educational and campaign use is supplied at cost. CONSULTANT SERVICE: makes administrative and financial surveys of local and county governments, and assists in drafting city charters, reorganizing state governments, revising state constitutions or modernizing county government, at cost. RESEARCH PROJECTS: national committees of the League carry on research and develop solutions to new

[25] See Stewart, Frank M., *A Half Century of Municipal Reform; the History of the National Municipal League* (University of California Press, 1950).

problems in local government. CONFERENCES: national and regional conferences on government are conducted in cooperation with local groups. All of these services are performed by a small staff and on an unbelievably modest budget.

The 1313 Group. Many other types of organizations have demonstrated a keen interest in government problems. Since 1931 a significant group of national organizations interested in various types of governmental activity has been developing in Chicago with headquarters in a single building. The organizations listed below are semiofficial in character; most of them would never have come into existence if there had not been developing, throughout the country, both a public and a professional interest in public administration.

The 1313 Group

ORGANIZATION	FOUNDED	OFFICE IN CHICAGO SINCE
American Public Works Association	1894	1934
International Association of Chiefs of Police	1893	1937
Municipal Finance Officers Association	1906	1932
Civil Service Assembly of the United States and Canada	1906	1935
Governors' Conference	1908	1938
International City Managers' Association	1914	1929
National Association of State Auditors, Comptrollers, and Treasurers	1915	1937
American Municipal Association	1924	1932
American Public Welfare Association	1930	1932
Public Administration Clearing House	1931	1931
Council of State Governments	1933	1933
National Association of Housing Officials	1933	1933
Public Administration Service	1933	1933
National Association of Assessing Officers	1934	1934
American Society of Planning Officials	1934	1935
Federation of Tax Administrators	1937	1937

League of Women Voters. Most important among the women's organizations is the League of Women Voters which grew out of the suffrage groups whose efforts brought about the ratification of Amendment XIX. The League is a national organization, with state and local branches, whose purpose is "to promote political responsibility through informed and active participation of citizens in government." Some 93,000 League members, organized in 739 groups in local communities, are a part of a state League in forty states and two territories. Most local Leagues have from fifty to two hundred members and are in towns and cities of from 5,000 to 50,000 population. There are many small local Leagues in towns and villages under 5,000 population, and twenty local Leagues with from 500 to 1,000 members in the larger cities. There are also nearly fifty "College Leagues." The League is a closely-knit, smooth-functioning organization whose tradition for leadership is outstanding.

The League has from the beginning been a nonpartisan organization which "may take action on governmental measures and policies in the public interest." Its principal activities include its familiar Voters Service and work on a current agenda formulated and adopted annually or biennially, by democratic procedures, for each of the three levels of government. Important items are selected each year so that the efforts of the organization are not dissipated by trying to do too many things at once. It offers unbiased, factual information on the political issues selected, carries on a continuing program of political education, and enables women of all parties and groups to work together toward common objectives. Its program authorizes activities in many different fields, including structure of government, education, social welfare, housing, and economic welfare. In state after state, it has rendered a most significant service in spearheading the drive for constitutional revision.[26]

Other women's organizations include the National Association of Business and Professional Women, the American Association of University Women, and women's city clubs, as well as leagues or federations of women belonging to particular political parties. All of these groups have local organizations in towns and cities of any considerable size, and are showing increasing interest in public affairs.

Commonwealth Club of California. The Commonwealth Club of California was organized in 1903 with five members as a "Public Service Club," "to investigate and discuss problems affecting the welfare of the Commonwealth and to aid in their solution" and "to maintain itself in an impartial position as an open forum for the discussion of disputed questions." It was incorporated and took its present name in 1926. Now, after a life of half a century, it has a membership of over 4000, carefully selected from the business and professional life of all parts of the West. That it has succeeded to a large extent in achieving its objectives is shown by the very high regard in which it is held, not only in the state, but throughout the nation. Its influence stems from the research of its various sections, its published *Transactions*, its meetings, and the personal contact of its members with the body politic.

The Club has organized, and maintains, as many as thirty organized bands of volunteer investigators, known as "Sections," some of them more than one

[26] For facts and figures on the size and growth of the League, see note in *National Municipal Review*, October 1948, p. 507, and two League publications by Kathryn H. Stone, *Twenty-five Years of a Great Idea* and *A History of the League Program* (Washington, 1945 and 1949, respectively). For notes on typical League activities, see Ingersoll, Hugh D., "Wisconsin Women Voters Study State Finance," *National Municipal Review*, April 1950, p. 208; Lindenmayer, Blanche S., "Women Get the Answers," on manager plan in Grinnell, Iowa, *ibid.*, May 1949, pp. 232–235.

hundred strong, engaged in the study of problems concerning the welfare of the Commonwealth of California; and in aid and abatement of the work of those Sections, a Research Service (established in 1926) under the general supervision of an advisory council headed by the presidents and past-presidents of Stanford University and the University of California.

An excellent idea of the nature and scope of the activities of the Club may be obtained by an examination of the annual reports of its executive secretary published in its official journal, *The Commonwealth.* Although the Club holds lecture luncheons, section luncheons, monthly dinners, and social meetings, it is not a luncheon or dinner or social organization. It is today what its founders hoped it would be, a purely investigating and reporting body. General luncheons are held weekly, on Friday, with an average attendance for many years of around 400. The list of speakers constitutes a distinguished group of men recognized as leaders in many phases of national life. Special luncheons, ranging in number up to seven, and in combined attendance as high as eighty-eight a day, are served on Monday, Tuesday, Wednesday, and Thursday noons in adjacent rooms. Thus did twenty-four sections in 1939 hold 373 meetings, in connection with each of which there were either addresses or discussions, or both, on important problems coming within the range of interest of the several sections.

The Club has permanent headquarters in a leading hotel in the central city district, in which it maintains an extensive collection of books and magazines dealing with public questions. There is also a men's chorus and orchestra. The Club carries on various miscellaneous activities including the award of an Annual Literature Medal. Since 1922, postcard votes on topics of current interest have been conducted; in 1939 the subjects of such votes included game management and the Wagner act. The results of these votes receive wide publicity, as do many other Club activities.

The publications of the Club are important. In the course of the years, more than thirty-five volumes of *Transactions* have been published, with ten or twelve numbers per volume, each number presenting the results of a careful study of some question of current interest. Often the numbers are devoted to the same topics upon which postcard votes are taken. A review of all the public questions investigated would show that the Club has more than justified its existence. It has had an influence upon the legislation of the state and has left its imprint on the constitution. It has made studies of such important questions as taxation, judicial procedure, direct legislation, municipal water supplies, public health, public education, public morals, civil service, and various questions of conservation. *The Commonwealth* is published in two parts: Part I supplies members with extracts from Club and section talks, while Part II presents the results of the inquiries noted above.

This extensive program of activity, carried on over a period of years, has resulted in a list of tangible accomplishments of which the Club is justly proud. It is claimed that the Club influence has been directly responsible for important developments in state and local government in California, including, in addition to general questions, improvements in the administration of justice and in the election law. The general items included establishment of an effective budget system and of irrigation districts, extension of civil service, and passage of a driver's license law. A small claims court was established, the office of public defender created, the code of criminal procedure was revised, while provision was made for absentee voting, nonpartisan elections for certain offices, and other matters relating to elections. If this Club in California is able to carry on so effective a piece of work in civic education, and to point to such a fine record of accomplishment, there is no reason why similar methods in other states might not lead to similar results.[27]

Other State Organizations. While the Commonwealth Club is outstanding among state citizen organizations, especially of broad scope, there are in most states a number of statewide citizen organizations that function within the limited fields of their own interests. In most of the states, such organizations exist in the health and welfare fields, along with groups interested in education, conservation, hunting and fishing, parks, corrections and prisons, highways, planning, and other subjects.

In the health and welfare fields, two of the oldest and strongest statewide organizations — whose very names suggest the period of their origin — are the New York State Charities Aid Association and the Public Charities Association of Pennsylvania. The latter, through its Penal Affairs Division, covers legislative matters in the corrections field, while the Pennsylvania Prison Society, oldest organization of its type in the country, concerns itself primarily with the administration of correctional institutions, pardon and parole, and parole supervision. Other organizations in the welfare field include the Missouri Association for Social Welfare and the Ohio Welfare Council. The Iowa Public Health Association, a quarter of a century old, is illustrative of many state groups in the health field. In addition, there is in each state a conference of social work, a professional organization which frequently employs an executive secretary and provides counseling and/or planning service for members and agencies.[28]

The Pennsylvania Parks Association has, under able leadership, done much to influence the development of the fine park system of which the state boasts. The Delaware Citizens Association, founded early in the present century, has concerned itself chiefly with problems in the field of education, gathering and publishing facts, conducting experiments and demonstrations, and helping in emergency situations. In this field also, professional organizations in the form of state education associations exercise a considerable

[27] This comment is based upon material in issues of *The Commonwealth*, supplied by the executive secretary of the Club.

[28] A list of such conferences is obtainable from the headquarters office of the National Conference of Social Work, the United States Public Health Service for state associations in the health field, et cetera.

influence on the course of legislation on educational subjects. Citizens' councils, like the Minnesota Postwar Council, were set up to do a postwar planning job in a number of states.

The postwar crisis in road building has aroused highway users in many states to join good-roads associations to promote road improvements as their fathers did in the early 1900's, when the automobile first became popular. Such groups, which now exist in approximately one third of the states, are illustrative of the manner in which citizen groups spring up at one time, die out at another, in response to fluctuations in the relative importance of the various issues confronting the people.[29]

Nor should one neglect the mention of the impact on state problems of such organizations as the state chambers of commerce, a number of which have excellent research staffs, junior chambers of commerce, and in late years, numerous labor organizations.[30] The Pennsylvania Chamber organizes and conducts in December of alternate years, before legislative sessions, a series of more than a dozen dinner meetings for the discussion of legislative problems, at convenient points throughout the state. Many of these groups issue weekly or monthly publications designed to keep their members informed on current developments on matters within their range of interest.

Taxpayers' Organizations. With the advent of the depression in 1929, organizations of taxpayers sprang up in great numbers in all sections of the United States. These were for the most part born out of the spirit of discontent naturally arising in a period of economic distress. Most of them were devoid of intelligent leadership. Their only concern was to batter down the tax rate. Their leaders had no conception of the duties and responsibilities of government and no regard for the preservation and maintenance of necessary and worthwhile public services. Not content with the demand for all reasonable economies, for the elimination of duplicating and overlapping services and of waste generally, they organized marches on city halls and pilgrimages to state capitols, to awe the members of these bodies into acquiescing to their often unreasonable demands. Most of these organizations, particularly the local ones, motivated by a desire for publicity or organized to further distinctly private purposes, and never having had any constructive program, did not last very long. Others developed along sound lines, and came to function with very beneficial results.

Some, capitalizing on the awakened public interest in governmental problems, organized on a permanent basis and secured the services of a competent staff of research workers; they are conducting scientific and impartial investigations of problems of governmental organization, of revenue,

[29] See "Good-Roads Movement Spreading," *Better Roads*, December 1949, pp. 25–26, and Ashburn, Ike, "The Texas Good Roads Association," *American Highways*, July 1949, pp. 14–15.

[30] For recent comment, see Galatas, S. A., "Good Government and Labor," *National Municipal Review*, February 1950, pp. 79–82, and Kroll, Jack, "Labor's Stake in Civic Affairs," *ibid.*, December 1949, pp. 542–545, 580.

and expenditure.[31] The Pennsylvania Economy League, for instance, set up a field organization for the collection annually of detailed financial data on every subdivision of local government in the state, so that eventually trends may be worked out. By applying a uniform system of classification of items of expenditure, accurate information on the cost and, to a certain extent, the efficiency of individual units may be determined, and fair comparisons made between different units. The League has established numerous county committees with permanent offices and secretaries, and its professional staff is always available for purposes of consultation and advice to local officials. Its legislative committee has formulated a program in each legislative year, prepared carefully drafted bills, and exerted pressure through its legislative representatives to secure their adoption. It has established the Taxpayer's Forum, to publicize the results of the League's investigations, and to carry on a campaign to develop public support for the program. All of this has been done with the purpose in mind to secure "Better Government at Less Cost."

The Indiana Taxpayers' Association undertook similar studies in the field of local government, as well as a valuable study of taxpayers' associations throughout the country. The associations in New Jersey and Tennessee have prepared at regular intervals exhaustive analyses of state government finances. These may be taken as illustrative of the types of useful service which may be rendered by privately supported organizations if they are willing to deal with governmental problems in an honest and impartial manner. Such groups often exert a powerful and beneficial influence on legislation in which they are interested through the use of the usual pressure group methods so familiar in the modern legislative process.[32]

Organizations of Municipalities and Local Officials. The movement for state leagues of municipalities began in Indiana in 1891; in 1951 there were forty such leagues actually functioning in the several states, four of them more than half a century old. It is estimated that 5000 cities belong to these various leagues. While membership is purely voluntary, all but one of the eligible cities in New York are members, and in Michigan 94 per cent of the urban population holds membership. It is unnecessary to discuss here

[31] A careful survey of these organizations, made in 1950, showed the existence of one or more statewide groups in all but ten states: Alabama, Delaware, Georgia, Kansas, Maine, South Carolina, Texas, Vermont, Virginia, and West Virginia. They are normally designated as taxpayers' associations, economy leagues, or public expenditure councils. Of the thirty-eight states in which such groups are in active operation, there were two in each of the following seven states: Illinois, Maryland, Nebraska, New York, Oklahoma, Oregon, and Wisconsin. The Pennsylvania Economy League has its central office in Harrisburg, a State Division in Harrisburg, Southeastern Division in Philadelphia, Western Division in Pittsburgh, and a Northeastern Division in Wilkes-Barre. Practically all of the thirty-eight issue some kind of regular bulletin; some of these, like *The Tax Digest* of the California Taxpayers' Association and the *P. E. L. Newsletters* of the various divisions of the Pennsylvania Economy League, are of high quality.

[32] For an excellent illustration, see Cline, Denzel C., *Executive Control over State Expenditures in New Jersey*, pp. 14–15 (Princeton University Press, 1934).

the numerous functions which these leagues perform, since they are chiefly of interest to the student of municipal government. They do, however, undertake important legislative work. The urban communities of the United States, representing more than half the population of the country, have certain social and political problems and interests which are not readily recognized by state legislatures. The cities, through their state leagues, therefore definitely attempt to express their legitimate interests and points of view both in favor of constructive municipal legislation and against legislation adverse to cities. Among the many legislative accomplishments of these leagues in widely separated states may be mentioned: municipal and home rule laws in Michigan and Wisconsin; zoning enabling acts in Minnesota and New Jersey; city sharing of gas tax revenue in Illinois. The training function of these groups is very important. They conduct formal training courses in various aspects of municipal administration, hold annual meetings, and frequently organize regional conferences throughout the state on legislative problems.[33]

While the influence of state leagues of municipalities is likely to be a constructive one, quite the opposite is often true of other organizations of local government officials. In state after state, these groups range in number from one to a dozen or more, including poor directors, coroners, district attorneys, probation officers, registers of wills, sheriffs, county controllers, township commissioners, township supervisors, magistrates, justices of the peace, school directors, and many others. While they are established for the avowed purpose of discussing questions and subjects relating to their duties and of devising uniform, economical, and efficient methods of administering their affairs, they frequently assume the position of pressure groups interested in maintaining the *status quo*. When any constructive proposal is made for the improvement of local government, one may be sure both of their united opposition and of a great deal of talk about "home rule."[34]

[33] For the best study of these groups, see Smith, Harold D., and Benson, George C. S., "Associations of Cities and of Municipal Officials," in *Urban Government*, Vol. I, pp. 179–245 (National Resources Committee, Washington, 1939); see also Mallory, Earl D., "Origin and Organization of the American Municipal Association," *Texas Municipalities*, April 1947, pp. 78–82. For brief histories of some representative groups, see: ILLINOIS: Drury, James W., "History and Services of the Illinois Municipal League," *Illinois Municipal Review*, September 1940, pp. 174–182. NEW JERSEY: "History of the New Jersey State League of Municipalities," *New Jersey Municipalities*, May 1952, pp. 21–24. SOUTH DAKOTA: Boardman, Norma, *A Study of the League of South Dakota Municipalities* (Governmental Research Bureau, University of South Dakota, 1942), and "South Dakota Municipal League, Its Origin and Growth," *South Dakota Municipalities*, September 1947, pp. 187, 193. TEXAS: Anderson, Lynn F., "A History of the League of Texas Municipalities," *Texas Municipalities*, July 1949, pp. 148–151, and August 1948, pp. 159–165. UTAH: Thorsen, Thomas W., and Iverson, Evan A., *The Utah Municipal League* (Institute of Government, University of Utah, 1949).

[34] See Kurtzman, David H., "Influence of Organizations of Local Government Officials," *Annals*, January 1938, pp. 103–109; also summary of accomplishments of the Pennsylvania State Association of Boroughs, *Borough Bulletin*, June 1940, pp. 54–65; and *An Explanation of the Association's Work* (Hanover, 1942).

Local Citizen Organization. There are many types of local citizen organizations that exert a considerable influence in community affairs. In addition to city clubs, citizen committees, and service clubs, there are groups that devote their efforts to policing elections, to influencing the selection of both appointed and elected officials, et cetera. Others conduct discussion groups and arrange for the broadcast of town meeting discussions of local issues. The city clubs of New York, Boston, Cleveland, Chicago, and other cities, once active and influential, have declined or disappeared altogether. After the City Club of Philadelphia was given up during the depression, its old committee on public affairs continued to function as the Philadelphia Committee on Public Affairs. This group, whose membership is limited to fifty outanding business and professional men, issues carefully prepared statements on public questions, makes recommendations to the governor and the mayor with regard to appointments, and in other ways seeks to influence the course of public affairs in the community.[35] The Rotary, Lions, Kiwanis, and other service clubs frequently have committees that engage in like activities.

One of the best known civic groups in the country is the Citizens Union of the City of New York — founded in 1897 by a group of public-minded citizens including Elihu Root, Nicholas Murray Butler, J. Pierpont Morgan, George Haven Putnam, James Roosevelt, Carl Schurz, Jacob H. Schiff, R. Fulton Cutting, and Charles H. Strong. It has been working systematically ever since as a vigorous and effective nonpartisan representative of citizens' interests. In addition to the executive committee, standing committees are appointed annually on such subjects as legislation, traffic congestion, housing, schools, smoke nuisance, subways, automobile inspection, election rights, and city planning.

Two of its most important activities include the giving of information to the voters through the famous *Voters Directory* and its representation of the public at the city hall and the state capitol:

> Every year at election time the Citizens Union issues a *Voters Directory* containing information and nonpartisan advice on candidates and issues, and maps by which you can tell what Assembly, Senatorial, and Congressional district you are in. Recommendations are based on a thorough study of records and qualifications by a committee which has no axes to grind. Files on all local candidates since 1918 are available to the public and are frequently used by government officials.
>
> The Citizens Union has a representative at City Hall all the time and in Albany every week during the legislative session. It drafts legislation, works with legislative committees, and appears at public hearings. Its bills are frequently passed, its advice is frequently heeded.

The accomplishments of the Union over the years have been significant indeed, the following being among the more important items in a partial list extending over more than half a century:

[35] Graves, W. Brooke, "P. C. P. A. Carries on Thirty-five Year Tradition," *National Municipal Review*, May 1941, pp. 299–301.

1901 — Led fight for the election of Seth Low as the first reform mayor of New York.

1932 — Campaigned for the Seabury Investigation, whose findings were largely responsible for the passing of the old Tammany Hall.

1936 — Led fight for the new City Charter with a city planning commission and the abolition of the useless Board of Aldermen.

1938 — Had a very large part in remaking the New York State Constitution along progressive lines.

1941 — Led campaign for reorganization of county government, saving the City $500,000 annually by the abolition of useless political jobs.

1947 — Spearheaded the transfer of airport development to the Port of New York Authority, coordinating La Guardia, Idlewild, and Newark fields and saving the City's borrowing power for desperately needed schools and hospitals.

Of a somewhat different type is the Committee of Seventy, founded in 1904 in Philadelphia, out of the remains of the old City Party, as "an organization of a permanent character whose purpose shall be to aid in securing good government in Philadelphia." It maintains standing committees on city finances, city government, civil service, elections, legislation, municipal work, and taxation. It is active and aggressive, particularly in all matters relating to registration and the conduct of elections. Specific items covered in the annual report include civil service and city employees, registration and elections, polling places, traffic court, purchase of supplies, city finances, public safety, mayor, gas works, and budget economics. "Through printed matter including pamphlets, digests, calendars and letters; radio broadcasts, newspaper articles and editorials; demonstrations of election and registration procedure; speeches by members of the staff and the Committee, and the giving of information by telephone or in person through the office, the Committee is constantly advocating and working for better local government and attempting to educate the voters."

Effective local organizations have been developed in many cities in support of the city manager plan. Of these, the one in Cincinnati has been notably successful and is perhaps best known.[36] Success in this type of movement is quite as possible in smaller cities and in rural communities as it is in the larger cities. In Yonkers, for instance, the Committee of 100 has given substantial proof of its effectiveness in many different aspects of municipal government. Its purpose is "to acquire information concerning the functioning of the government of the City of Yonkers, to make such information available to the public, to mobilize public opinion and to create an alert body of citizens in the affairs of said City and, in general, to secure a more efficient and economic government for the City."

[36] See *Citizen Organization for Political Activity: the Cincinnati Plan* (National Municipal League, New York, 1944); Frank, Forest, "How Sustain Effort for Good Government," the story of twenty-five years of service by the Cincinnati Charter Committee, *National Municipal Review*, January 1950, pp. 55–57; also Taft, Charles P., *City Management; the Cincinnati Experiment* (Farrar & Rinehart, New York, 1934).

The following are illustrations of significant civic groups in two large midwestern cities:

Cleveland Citizens League — organized in 1925 and patterned roughly after the Citizens Union of New York. It issues reports on candidates at all primary and general elections and publishes a weekly bulletin on the public business.[37]

Woman's City Club of Chicago, organized in 1910 "for an increased sense of social responsibility, for the guarding of the home, the maintenance of good government, and the ennobling of the city." The Club waged a long and finally victorious fight to obtain the use of voting machines in Chicago elections.

Citizen's Association of Chicago, founded in 1874 to insure a more perfect administration of municipal affairs; to protect citizens, so far as possible, against the evils of careless or corrupt legislation; to correct existing abuses, and to prevent their recurrence; and to familiarize citizens with the work of the city council, the activities of its members, and the qualifications of aldermanic candidates.

Civic Federation of Chicago, a citizen agency organized in 1893 for: (1) promoting efficiency and economy in the public business; (2) guarding against wasteful expenditures and excessive taxes; (3) furnishing the public with accurate information concerning governmental revenues and expenditures.

In city after city across the country, there are any number of organizations in specialized fields such as housing, education, health, and welfare. Occasionally, groups like the Philadelphia Committee of Fifteen, created in 1947, spring into existence because of some unusual circumstances (in this case, reports of widespread graft and corruption in the city government); in the same city a citizen's advisory planning commission has rendered useful service on a long-term basis.[38] In Washington, D.C., because of its long unique governmental status, local citizen organizations flourish in such profusion that the newspapers regularly announce meetings of from fifteen to twenty during any normal week.

Research and Citizen Action. The municipal research movement parallels what Professor Munro once called the municipal renaissance in America. In the early years of the present century many such bureaus were established, and some are still functioning. Because of the difficulty of obtaining adequate financial support, others have been consolidated with, or made some working arrangement with, local universities, as in the case of the New York Bureau with Columbia University as the Institute of Public Administration, the Detroit Bureau with Wayne University's School of Public Affairs and Social Work. Although other bureaus have had to restrict their programs or pass out of existence, there is more research work being done in the municipal field than ever before. It is, furthermore, regarded as a necessary basis for any intelligent civic action as a means of helping to resolve the conflict between those who would spend and those who have to pay. The universities,

[37] See Case, George S., Jr., "Playing to Get Touchdowns," *National Municipal Review*, June 1950, pp. 278–282, describing efforts of the League to get action on a costly efficiency report, prepared for the city.

[38] See Phillips, Walter M., "Let the Citizens Play a Part," *National Municipal Review*, November 1948, pp. 529–533.

through their bureaus of municipal research and bureaus of public administration have, in some states, made a very great contribution in this field.

A related type of activity includes the numerous conferences and institutes sponsored by educational institutions, such as the University of Virginia's annual Institute of Public Affairs, the University of Denver's Citizens' Conference on Government Management, the New Hampshire Institute of Public Affairs, and others.

Neither good administration nor high grade research nor conferences and discussion groups will keep a community well governed unless there is cooperation on the part of the press and other channels of public information. William Allen White once said that "research libraries and governmental organizations have shelves filled with tried and proven methods of rendering efficient public service to the people. The great need today is to clear these shelves, to get their treasures of practical guidance into the hands and minds of our citizens." Good public reporting and good public relations on the part of research agencies can do much to bring this about. Most important of all is an active and alert citizenry, effectively organized to make its wants known and to see that they are respected. This has been the key to success in every movement for good government in any American community.[39] In city after city where the city manager plan has been adopted or where improved administration has been secured under existing forms, the change has come because citizens were organized, aroused, and vigilant. The government will stay good so long — and only so long — as they remain organized, aroused, and vigilant.[40] What numerous cities have done, the states can do.

Popular Participation in Government

Popular participation, broadly defined, includes both participation and nonparticipation. One of the more common forms of nonparticipation is nonvoting, the reasons and the remedies for which are to be considered at this point. Much has been said and written about the apathy of a large portion of the population toward government. Many of these articles and speeches are filled with denunciation. It has been said that the fault lies not in the form of government but with the people themselves; that corrupt political machines are able to maintain their control only by reason of the assistance given them by vote shirkers.

The extent of this nonparticipation is a matter of common knowledge. Even in Presidential years, with the tremendous ballyhoo that accompanies a national campaign, not much more than half of the eligible voters go to

[39] See Gill, Norman N., *Municipal Research Bureaus, A Study of the Nation's Leading Citizen-Supported Agencies* (American Council on Public Affairs, Washington, 1944); also Bureau of Governmental Research, *A Quarter-Century of Citizen Concern with Government, 1916–1941* (Detroit, 1941).

[40] For recent illustrations of effective community action, see the files of the *National Municipal Review*.

the polls. In other elections the degree of participation is much less, until in referenda on constitutional amendments and on measures submitted by initiative and referendum petitions, where usually a majority of those voting on the proposition is sufficient to adopt, important provisions are approved by the affirmative vote of small minority groups. So true is this that one distinguished scholar has undertaken to defend the thesis that government by majority rule is a fiction.[41]

Reasons for Nonvoting. There are numerous reasons, many of them more or less obvious, for failure to participate in elections. Some, however, are difficult to determine, because the citizen who failed to vote may not be able to state the real reason or may not be willing to do so even if he is aware of it. Some years ago a careful study of the causes and methods of control of nonvoting was made for some 5000 individuals in Chicago.[42] It was found that, in this number of cases, the percentages by age groups were substantially parallel to the percentages for the same groups for registered voters as a whole. There were approximately twice as many occasional as habitual nonvoters and approximately twice as many women as men. The percentage of nonvoting for the native whites was slightly higher than for the Negroes, but it was more than three times as high for both of these groups as for the foreign-born.

When interviewed by well-trained and carefully selected field workers, nonvoters were asked to explain why they had failed to vote; the reasons which they gave may be grouped under five main headings. One fourth of those who failed to vote were deterred by physical difficulties, such as illness, absence from the city on election day, or being detained by a helpless member of the family. Legal and administrative obstacles accounted for approximately 13 per cent. Under this category came such excuses as insufficient legal residence, fear of the loss of business or wages, congestion at the polling places, and poor voting facilities generally. Still another group — some 18 per cent — was deterred by a disbelief in woman's voting; included in this group were the antisuffragists and those whose husbands objected to their wives' voting. Approximately one fourth of the persons interviewed were "disgusted with politics" or, for other reasons, disbelieved in voting. Some were disgusted with their own party, some had the idea that one vote counts for nothing, while still others would not vote because they believed that the ballot box was corrupted. A small number avowed a disbelief in all political action. Finally, another group — 25 per cent of the whole — failed to vote because of general indifference and inertia. The more specific reasons cited by the members of this group were: indifference to a particular election; the fact that they had intended to vote but had neglected to do so; ignorance

[41] Beard, Charles A., "The Fiction of Majority Rule," *Atlantic Monthly*, December 1927, pp. 831–836.

[42] Merriam, Charles E., and Gosnell, Harold F., *Non-Voting: Causes and Methods of Control* (University of Chicago Press, 1924).

or timidity regarding elections; and the failure of the party workers, for as one committeeman observed, "People don't vote for candidates; they vote for precinct leaders."

A much more recent study by the National Opinion Research Center underscores the importance of education and economic status as factors influencing voting participation. For instance, ten of the thirteen states with the smallest percentage of potential voters who actually cast their ballots in 1940 were among the thirteen states with the lowest educational attainment. Of those who had gone to college 81 per cent cast their ballots in 1940, as compared with 67 per cent whose education ended in or with completion of high school, and with 61 per cent who had not gone beyond grade school. And, similarly, votes were cast by 84 per cent of the upper economic fourth of the population, 68 per cent of the middle economic group (comprising about half of the population), and 53 per cent of the lower fourth. The Center concludes that (1) the educational factor and the closely related economic factor are the strongest determinants of political activity; (2) many Americans need more and better schooling on current social, political, and economic questions.[43]

Quite as important as the nonvoter are the voter and the quality and extent of his participation. While there appears to be a generally upward trend in voting, the reasons for greater interest vary from one community to another. The undermining of political machines in some cities has given voters greater confidence in the electoral process. The development of parties of approximately equal strength in others has made the outcome of an election no longer a foregone conclusion. A higher level of educational attainment is doubtless having its influence. The percentage of eligible voters in the population as a whole appears to be increasing, with the decline of immigration and the progressive elimination of barriers — legal and otherwise — to voting participation.

Compulsory Voting. If these are the facts with regard to voting and nonvoting, what can be done about them? It does little good to draw up a bill of particulars unless at the same time thought is given to the development of suitable remedies. There are in fact several suggested solutions: compulsory voting, the taxing of those who do not, providing incentives,[44] the develop-

[43] See Connelly, Gordon K., and Field, Harry H., "The Non-Voter — Who He Is, What He Thinks," *Public Opinion Quarterly*, Summer 1944, pp. 175–187; and release from the Center, No. 11, April 1948; also Dumas, John N., "Apathy — Our Fifth Column," *National Municipal Review*, October 1947, pp. 494–496, 502; and Bromage, Arthur W., "Fellow Citizens and Taxpayers: a Councilman Discusses Citizen Interest in Municipal Government," *Municipality* (League of Wisconsin Municipalities), July 1950, pp. 141, 154–155.

[44] Short of actual compulsion there are practical methods of vote stimulation which have brought beneficial results; see Myers, Robert C., "A Proposal to Tax Those Who Don't Vote," *New York Times Magazine*, November 6, 1949, pp. 12, 75ff., and Hamilton, Charles H., "Drama Gets Out the Vote," *National Municipal Review*, March 1949, pp. 116–120, 129, in which it is contended that Richmond's Gold Feather Day overcame citizen apathy and brought ten times the usual number of voters to the polls.

ment of a new program of civic education, and the adoption of measures that will to some extent lighten the task now imposed upon the voter.

Many people have urged that compulsory voting legislation should be adopted — that people ought to vote, and if they will not do so voluntarily, they should be compelled to do so by imposing some sort of penalty. If such a law were enforced, hundreds of thousands of citizens in all of our large cities would be caught — 100,000 in Minneapolis, 400,000 in Philadelphia, where in a recent poll 74 per cent opposed the idea of fining nonvoters. There are, however, precedents for the successful operation of the plan in Australia and in several European countries. Against its adoption in the United States must be mentioned the fact that conditions here are different from those existing in the countries referred to, and that the idea of compelling people to discharge their obligation to participate in government seems contrary not only to the temper of the people but to the whole tradition of their history and government. It is, furthermore, exceedingly doubtful whether much would be gained by such a procedure, even if the people would support the enforcement of the legislation. If the functioning of democracy is to be improved, what is needed is not so much a larger number of voters as a larger number of *intelligent* votes. If the present nonvoters are not well enough informed or sufficiently interested to vote under the existing laws it is doubtful whether their votes cast under a system of compulsion would be worth very much.

Simplified Ballot and Electoral Procedure. A second suggestion relates to the extension of the short ballot principle, the simplification of the electoral process, and the lightening of the burden now placed upon the voter. This was discussed in the section on a more workable electoral system. In the days when citizens gathered around the cracker barrel in the corner grocery to discuss public questions, they did so at least in part because of the absence of scores of interests, such as motion pictures, radio, television, the automobile, and dozens of social and fraternal organizations, which compete for the time and attention of the average citizen today. He is actually unable, even if he were theoretically willing, to give the same attention to public questions that his father or grandfather was accustomed to give. There seems to be much justification for believing that many voters are discouraged in the performance of their civic responsibilities by the very complexity of the task imposed upon them. They are asked to register annually in many jurisdictions, and to vote in one or more primaries as well as in general and special elections. Not only must they make repeated trips to the polling place for registration and voting, but they must decide regarding the merits of enormous numbers of candidates with whose names they are unfamiliar and regarding large numbers of issues concerning which they are uninformed, often through no particular fault of their own. It seems reasonable to believe that many voters who now vote unintelligently, and many others who do not vote at all, would participate more willingly and far more effectively if the time and effort required for the performance of their civic duties were made more commensurate with the amount of time and effort they are now able to spend.

Citizen Training for Youth. Until comparatively recently there was no program of citizen training in this country worthy of the name; our efforts were confined to inflicting upon children in the public schools that abomination known as "civics," which consisted largely in memorizing and repeating, with a kind of sacred inattention, the words of the Constitution. Professor Merriam edited the valuable Civic Training Series, contributing to it the significant summary volume on *The Making of Citizens.* The American Political Science Association had a Committee on Civic Training which functioned for a number of years. It made some progress, and its efforts were supplemented by weekly radio broadcasts on a nationwide hook-up over a period of three years.

Developments in the last decade have emphasized the induction of citizens, the training of young voters and of older voters, and programs for community action. In years past, immigrants about to be naturalized were herded into a courtroom and pronounced citizens by the judge, usually a few days before election. The ceremony had no dignity and little significance; later, civic groups did give some attention to the situation, decorating a suitable room and making a dignified public ceremony out of the act of conferring citizenship. No one ever thought that the induction of young voters should be given public notice. Then came the Manitowoc Plan. Under the leadership of the Extension Division of the University of Wisconsin, citizens in Manitowoc County organized in clubs all the young men and women who would come of voting age during the year. These clubs were required to hold a minimum number of meetings for training and discussion, but many of them held several times the minimum specified. On citizenship day public ceremonies were held at the county seat, in which all of the new voters participated. Every band and fife and drum corps in the county took part. Each club prepared a float for the parade, depicting some principle or some event significant in American history. At the mass meeting which followed, addresses were made by the chief justice of the state, the president of the state university, and various local dignitaries. Each new citizen was given a scroll signifying entrance into the status of citizenship.

The plan immediately attracted attention in other counties and in other states, as a result of which Congress passed and the President signed in 1940 a measure providing for Citizenship Week, which should serve in each cooperating jurisdiction as the culmination of the year's work in the education and training of new citizens. In other countries and in other institutions like the church and fraternal groups, extensive use is made of ceremonialism and symbolism; it is anticipated that the cohesive power of these forms of social control will in the years to come be extensively utilized in the United States for purposes of citizen training. Other forms of political organization have managed to tell their story effectively to young people; democracy must do so too if it wishes to survive.[45]

The techniques of "I Am an American Day" and Citizenship Week have been applied in other directions toward the accomplishment of the same end. Many states regularly observe, in addition to the traditional legal holidays, September 17th as Constitution Day, and the week in which that day falls as Constitution Week, celebrating both with appropriate observances. Illinois observes, by proclamation of the governor, Americanism Week between the birthdays of Lincoln and Washington. In December, 1941, on the occasion of the 150th anniversary of the Bill of Rights, a week was observed throughout the country in commemoration of the framing of that instrument. These "days" and "weeks," if appropriately observed, can contribute greatly to the public understanding of and respect for American political institutions.

New York State carried through a novel and interesting experiment in civic training for both young and old when it created its six-car Freedom Train and sent it out on a 7581 mile, year-long trip, including almost every town and city in the state. Since it was designed as a "classroom on wheels," school children were brought to see it on school time. Eight hundred persons an hour could pass through the three specially constructed exhibit cars, which contained eighty-nine of the state's priceless historic documents portraying the foundations and growth of free government in the state from early Dutch times to the present. The exhibits were planned to cover the basic freedoms of religion, press, speech, and representative government; the documents in the collection were said to have a monetary value of $1,000,000 and a humanitarian value that could be measured only in terms of liberty.

In many cases training projects for young people have been operated in the form of boys' states and girls' states, boys' cities and girls' cities, model legislatures, political conventions and constitutional conventions, and youth forums. While there is danger of a model being a "small imitation of the real thing," many of these projects have been well organized and effectively carried out. In some cases high school and college instructors have taken their classes regularly to the city hall or the state legislature and have used the material there discussed as the basis for class work.[46] One of the best

[45] See, in addition to references cited in the previous edition of this volume, Colbert, R. J., "How to Plan for Citizenship Day," *National Municipal Review*, May 1948, pp. 245–247, in which the father of the Manitowoc Plan describes what he regards as an ideal setup. Numerous states have published citizenship training manuals, and the Immigration and Naturalization Service has available leaflets and manuals to assist with the observance of Citizenship Day, as well as general training materials.

[46] See Desmond, Senator Thomas C., "Seedbed for Leadership," *Liberty*, April 1948, and condensed in *Reader's Digest* for the same month; Walker, Robert A., "Citizenship Education and the Colleges," *American Political Science Review*, February 1948, pp. 74–84; Weidner, Edward W., "Boy Legislature Plan Spreading," *National Municipal Review*, June 1944, pp. 283–286, 294, and "Students Investigate Politics," *ibid.*, October 1947, pp. 489–493; and Whitwell, Charles G., "Louisiana Students Hold Constitutional Convention," *ibid.*, April 1948, pp. 219–220.

organized and most successful model student groups is the Pennsylvania Intercollegiate Conference on Government, which has met annually at Harrisburg (with the exception of the war years) since 1934. Attended by some 250 or 300 students from some three or four score of colleges and universities in the state, it has met as a constitutional convention, a conference on interstate cooperation, a national party convention, and several times as a unicameral legislature. Only students participate, and they take an intense interest in the work. They begin their preparation several months prior to the meeting, and most of them are well prepared by the time of the Conference, whose motto is "not to teach, not to preach, but to learn by doing." From these sessions, extending over three days and including both committee work and plenary sessions, they gain an understanding of the realities of politics such as no amount of classroom instruction or work in the library can give them.[47]

Citizen Training for Adults. A number of interesting and important projects in community action for adult citizens have been developed. Ever since the United States Office of Education inaugurated its community forum program on an experimental basis in the early 1930's, the public forum and discussion group idea has spread rapidly in many states and cities throughout the country. "Democratic Discussions," a statewide program carried on for several years under the auspices of the New Jersey Education Association, is an excellent example. In 1943–1944, more than 37,500 persons, located in 152 different communities in the twenty-one counties of the state, participated in this program — 14,000 more than in the preceding year. Any interested individual might organize a group of his friends and neighbors. The office of the Director gives full instructions with regard to the organization and conduct of meetings. Discussion outlines are furnished free on a variety of topics in national, international, state, and local affairs.

In Wisconsin the extension division of the University has organized "citizen-seminars" on various aspects of public affairs. Each has a study kit of materials suitable for use by information discussion groups. In some communities, newspapers have taken the lead in organizing and directing programs of this character; notable examples include the New York *Herald Tribune* Forum, Theodore Granick's (Washington *Evening Star*) National Radio Forum, and, locally, the Yonkers Civil Service Institute. Notable also has been the influence of America's Town Meeting of the Air,[48] the University of Chicago Roundtable, Meet the Press, and other public service features on the radio networks.

Community Action. Any forward movement in a state depends upon

[47] See Webb, Malcolm L., "Collegians Steal Legislators' Fire," *National Municipal Review*, July 1936, pp. 412–416; Gerson, Leonard B., and Zipin, Irving J., "Learning by Doing," *ibid.*, July 1940, pp. 451–458; and "Student Solons Demonstrate Cooperation," *State Government*, June 1938.

[48] See its "*Good Evening Neighbors!" the Story of an American Institution* (Town Hall, Inc., New York, 1950).

leadership. Mark Ethridge recalls the North Carolina situation a quarter of a century ago when "Aycock, the great governor, translated an awakened conscience and consciousness into political action." About the same time there came Gifford Pinchot and his program of progressive legislation for Pennsylvania. Twenty years later there was the Citizens Fact Finding Movement of Georgia, which prepared the way for another great governor, Arnall, who "was able to rewrite the constitution and to initiate half a hundred reforms in short order." Next came Harry W. Schacter and his Committee for Kentucky, which was disbanded at the end of 1949. Kentucky, says its distinguished Louisville editor, "*is* indeed on the march. We do not yet have an Aycock . . . but our Aycock will come, and maybe dollars will get back to normal so that our disposition to be up and doing will reflect itself as we move up in the table of states."[49]

Elsewhere Mr. Ethridge notes that "a governor can do little unless there is pressure from underneath him to do it. Indeed, few public men are so bold as to walk forward faster than their constituencies. Even Mr. Roosevelt liked to hear the voice of the people, and those who dealt with him most astutely sometimes organized the voice so that he could hear it." Brief consideration at this point of the experience of Georgia and Kentucky may help to give an answer to the question: How may the voice be organized?

Tired of hearing their state referred to as "backward," a group of Georgia citizens determined to do something about it. In the summer of 1937 the Citizens Fact Finding Movement of Georgia was established; in its central council were represented about 130 organizations of citizens, many of them statewide and including all types of interests — chambers of commerce, service clubs, manufacturers' groups, labor organizations, agricultural groups, and fraternal orders. This council worked out a plan, according to which one important aspect of the life of the state, such as agriculture, education, and health, should be given intensive study each month for a period of one year. The member groups cooperated by furnishing information and disseminating the results of the study to their own members, after the central office staff had had an opportunity to digest it and write it up.

A survey made at the end of five years of operation disclosed "that 317,000 of the Movement's publications had been distributed, not sent out broadcast, but furnished upon request only. Records showed that they had gone into every incorporated community in the state, to forty-two other states, to the District of Columbia, Canada, England, Alaska, Hawaii, Puerto Rico, Cuba, Argentina, and Brazil."[50] The wide distribution of these

[49] Quotes from Foreword to Schacter, Harry W., *Kentucky on the March* (Harpers, New York, 1949).

[50] Wilkins, Josephine, "Georgians Take Stock," *National Municipal Review*, June, 1943, pp. 337–339; Cohn, David L., "Georgia: These Are the Facts," *Atlantic Monthly*, August 1941, pp. 212–219; Daniels, Jonathan, "Georgians Discover Georgia," *Survey Graphic*, March 1939, pp. 199–203.

publications played no small part in the civic awakening which made possible the election of the able, alert, and progressive Governor Ellis Arnall.

The Committee for Kentucky was organized in 1944 with twenty member organizations; by 1948 it had the support of eighty-eight organizations in agriculture, business, education, labor, the professions, and service—many of them statewide. Together they claimed a total membership of 450,000 citizens. Based on a conviction that the hope of democracy lies in the local community in which the battle for democracy will be won or lost, and that the local community is the training ground for the leaders of America, the Committee fixed as its objectives the strengthening of the communities of the state in a variety of ways. For the accomplishment of these purposes the state was divided into nine areas, in each of which one town was selected to serve as a center of operations for all the towns in the area.

In some respects this program was not unlike the one in Georgia; both worked largely through existing organizations. In order to establish effective contacts, the head of each state organization was asked for a list of the names and addresses of local representatives. As the initial contact in any given community, a set of the Committee's reports was made available to all heads of clubs and organizations and to all college presidents, and each was urged to use these reports as program material for meetings. "Community Weeks" were planned, town meetings held, community needs surveyed, conferences and workshops organized — all with a view to strengthening the community and arousing interest in the over-all program for the state as a whole; this last was publicized also by radio, by newspaper advertisements, and in other ways.

As a result of these efforts it was possible to report in 1949 that Kentucky had started upon a progressive legislative program. "We have a greater awareness of our needs than ever before, and we have more agencies working to do something about them. . . . There are hundreds of evidences that Kentuckians have awakened from their long sleep. For contributing mightily to that, the Committee for Kentucky can take much credit."[51]

Much attention has been given to planning for effective community action in cities, counties, and other local units. The New York State Citizens' Council was organized in 1943 "to stimulate interest in community problems at the grass roots level and to develop citizen understanding of public affairs." Profiting by the experience of social agencies, which have long had central coordinating councils in the larger cities, this state Council through its field service has been helping New York State communities to develop teamwork in their civic affairs. In each community a central planning and coordinating

[51] In addition to the Schacter volume, *op. cit.*, see Committee for Kentucky, *Kentucky on the March*, a descriptive pamphlet, and *Blueprint for a Greater Kentucky*, its final report (Louisville, 1949); also Detzer, Karl, "Kentucky on the March," *Reader's Digest*, October 1949; Reeves, H. Clyde, "Committee for Kentucky," *State Government*, July 1949, pp. 175–176, 182; and note, "Committee for Kentucky Sings Swan Song," *National Municipal Review*, April 1950, p. 207.

council is established, with members from each of the major special-interest groups in the locality. The idea is clearly presented in the chart below.[52]

A Program for the Future. Any program of civic training and citizen

THE COMMUNITY CIRCLE *

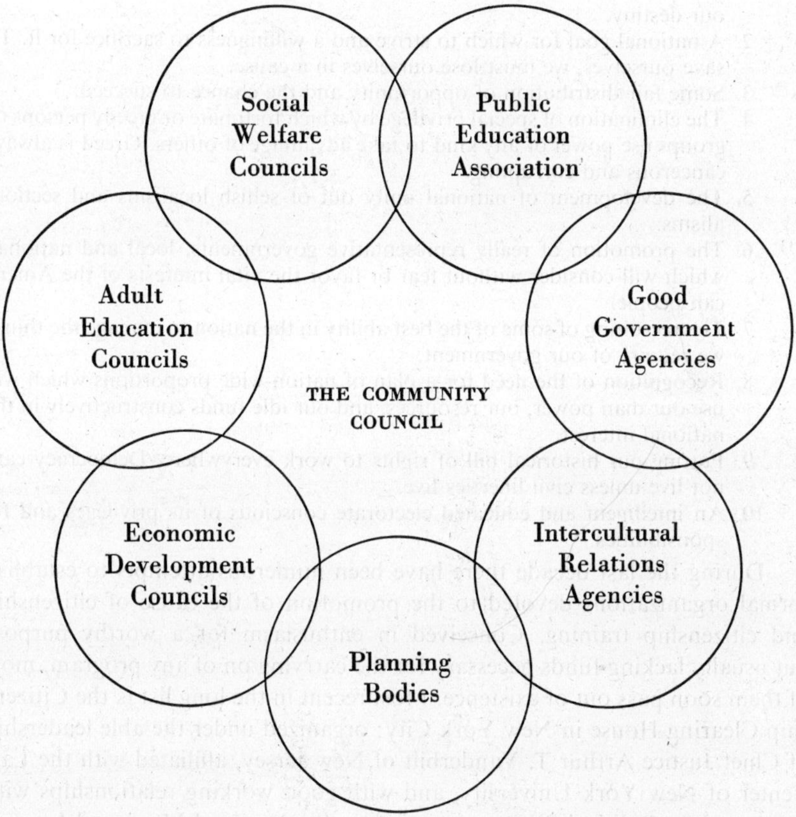

* A complete chart would show antennae going from each type of agency to the related private and official agencies; *e.g.*, planning bodies are related to park boards, sanitation and highway departments, engineering departments, budget offices, and others.

[52] From National Conference on the Community, *Community Building in America*, p. 15 (National Planning Association, Washington, 1947); see also: King, Clarence, *Organizing for Community Action* (Harpers, New York, 1948); Minnesota Postwar Council, *A Program for Community Action* (St. Paul, 1946); Public Administration Service, *Our Rural Communities* (Chicago, 1947); and Chapin, F. Stuart, Jr., "A Plan for Citizen Participation in Community Development," *Social Forces*, March 1947, pp. 313–320. On planning in individual communities, see: Dowagiac Community Plan, *Biennial Report, a Summary of Activities, September 1938 to May 1940* (Dowagiac, 1940); Civic Development Committee, Syracuse-Onondaga County, *Report on Community Organization and Progress* (Syracuse, 1949); Ogden, Jean and Jess, *Small Communities in Action: Stories of Citizen Programs at Work* (Harpers, New York, 1946); Samuels, Gertrude, "Community at Work: a Lesson for Others," *New York Times Magazine*, August 6, 1950, pp. 18–19, 36 ff.

action, if it is to be reasonably successful, must begin with children at an early age and continue through adult life. Too long have Americans taken democracy for granted — too long have they assumed that democracy obviously justifies itself without explanation or effort on their part. The late President Dykstra some years ago outlined an excellent ten-point program:

1. First of all, a faith that our fathers were right, a faith in ourselves and in our destiny.
2. A national goal for which to strive and a willingness to sacrifice for it. To save ourselves, we must lose ourselves in a cause.
3. Some fair distribution of opportunity and the chance to succeed.
4. The elimination of special privilege by which fortunate or greedy persons or groups use power of any kind to take advantage of others. Greed is always cancerous and corrupting.
5. The development of national unity out of selfish localisms and sectionalisms.
6. The promotion of really representative governments, local and national, which will consider without fear or favor the vital interests of the American people.
7. The recruiting of some of the best ability in the nation to manage the things we require of our government.
8. Recognition of the need for a plan of nation-wide proportions which will use our man power, our resources, and our idle funds constructively in the national interest.
9. Putting our historical bill of rights to work everywhere. Democracy cannot live unless civil liberties live.
10. An intelligent and educated electorate conscious of its privileges and responsibilities.[53]

During the last decade there have been numerous attempts to establish formal organizations devoted to the promotion of the cause of citizenship and citizenship training. Conceived in enthusiasm for a worthy purpose but usually lacking funds necessary for the carrying on of any program, most of them soon pass out of existence. Most recent in the long list is the Citizenship Clearing House in New York City; organized under the able leadership of Chief Justice Arthur T. Vanderbilt of New Jersey, affiliated with the Law Center of New York University, and with good working relationships with the American Political Science Association, the National Municipal League, the Association of American Colleges, its prospects are more promising than most. It has conducted a number of regional conferences on citizenship training, and sponsored a significant survey and report on the *Evaluation of Citizenship Training and Incentive in American Colleges and Universities*.[54]

At the planning and policy level the National Citizenship Conference,

[53] Dykstra, Clarence A., "We Thought the Battle Won!" *National Municipal Review*, December 1939, pp. 821–823, 892; also Governmental Research Association, *Citizens in the Dark — Cities in the Red* (Detroit, 1940); and Pollock, James K., "Plea for an Informed Citizenry," *National Municipal Review*, September 1940, pp. 590–592.

[54] By Reed, Thomas H., and Doris D. (New York, 1950); see also its *The Citizen's Participation in Public Affairs*, the proceedings of a conference inaugurating the Citizenship Clearing House (New York, 1948), and Vieg, John A., "The Proposed Citizenship Clearing House," *Western Political Quarterly*, September 1948, pp. 303–310.

sponsored jointly by the National Education Association and the United States Department of Justice, has been bringing together annually since 1946, a thousand civic, professional, business, and school leaders. The program of the Conference has emphasized the duties and responsibilities of citizenship as well as its rights and privileges, and the necessity for world education, including an understanding of the realities of war and of technological advances and a better knowledge of our economic, social, and cultural interdependence.

SELECTED REFERENCES

Bird, Frederick L., and Ryan, Frances M., *The Recall of Public Officers* (Macmillan, New York, 1930). Only existing study of the recall device, now much out of date. See also Zeitlin, Josephine V., *The Recall: a Bibliography* (Haynes Foundation, Los Angeles, 1941).

Gill, Norman N., *Municipal Research Bureaus: a Study of the Nation's Leading Citizen-Supported Agencies* (American Council on Public Affairs, Washington, 1944). Excellent study of an important group of research agencies.

Hermans, Ferdinand A., *Democracy or Anarchy: a Study of Proportional Representation* (University of Notre Dame, 1941). A very critical analysis of P.R. by its leading American opponent.

Hoag, Clarence G., and Hallett, George H., Jr., *Proportional Representation* (Macmillan, New York, 1929). The standard treatise; for a more recent and briefer treatment, see Mr. Hallett's *Proportional Representation* (National Library Foundation, Washington, 1937).

Key, Vladimer O., Jr., and Crouch, Winston W., *The Initiative and Referendum in California* (University of California Press, 1939) and Crouch's *The Initiative and Referendum in California* (Haynes Foundation, Los Angeles, 1943 and 1950); for studies in other states, see Colorado Legislative Reference Office, *The Initiative and Referendum in Colorado* (Denver, 1940); LaPalombara, Joseph G., *The Initiative and Referendum in Oregon: 1938–1948* (Oregon State College Press, 1950); Pelletier, Lawrence L., *The Initiative and Referendum in Maine* (Bowdoin College Bulletin, March 1952); Pollock, James K., *The Initiative and Referendum in Michigan* (Bureau of Government, University of Michigan, 1940); see also Zeitlin, Josephine V., *Initiative and Referendum: a Bibliography* (Haynes Foundation, Los Angeles, 1940).

Merriam, Charles E., and Gosnell, Harold F., *Non-Voting, Causes and Methods of Control* (University of Chicago Press, 1924). One of few existing significant studies of nonvoting.

Reed, Thomas H., and Doris D., *Preparing College Men and Women for Politics* (Citizenship Clearing House, New York University, 1952). Latest of several excellent studies by the same authors of methods of civic training.

Schacter, Harry W., *Kentucky on the March* (Harpers, New York, 1949). A real contribution to the literature on democracy at work.

Stewart, Frank M., *A Half Century of Municipal Reform; the History of the National Municipal League* (University of California Press, 1950). History of an organization that has been an important force in municipal reform in this country since 1894.

Stone, Kathryn H., *Twenty-five Years of a Great Idea*, and *A History of the League Program* (National League of Women Voters, Washington, 1945 and 1949, respectively). Contain excellent material on an important civic organization.

Taft, Charles P., *The City Manager* (Farrar & Rinehart, New York, 1933). An excellent report on the Cincinnati experience, by an active participant, with emphasis on citizen organization.

Tharp, Claude R., *Control of Local Finances Through Taxpayers' Associations and Centralized Administration* (Ford Publishing Company, Indianapolis, 1933). An analysis of the influence of taxpayers' groups, made in the early days of their development.

PART THREE

The Process of Lawmaking

The quality of a legislature, the integrity and capacity of its members, the efficiency of the methods by which it passes laws and supervises the conduct of the executive, must continue to be of significance to a nation's welfare.

—JAMES BRYCE

6

State Legislative Organization

Historical Development

The antecedents of the present state legislatures include the colonial assemblies, the territorial legislatures, and those established under the constitutions adopted early in the present governmental regime. Colonial assemblies existed in the thirteen original colonies, which were in time to become charter members of the Federal Union. Territorial legislatures developed in each of the other jurisdictions ultimately admitted into the Union as states. The early state legislatures immediately succeeded the colonial assemblies and the territorial assemblies of states admitted during the early constitutional period. Since that time the most outstanding group of legislatures which might warrant separate consideration here were those of the Southern states during the period of reconstruction.

Colonial Legislatures. The colonial legislatures were, for the most part, miniature reproductions of the British Parliament. In their history two facts stand out clearly: first, the lower house was almost constantly engaged in serious controversy with the executive; second, in the assembly there developed a form of unofficial party control more important than the organization provided for in the rules.[1] As noted earlier in a quotation from Professor Becker, it was the desire of the colonists to fashion their lives, their thinking, their culture, and their governmental institutions upon the best approved English models. If there was in England a struggle between the Crown and Parliament with regard to taxation and finance, then they in their representative assemblies must wage a struggle with the Royal Governors regarding the same questions. These assemblies also came more and more to reflect accurately the temper of the colonists themselves. Repeated protests against oppressive acts of the British authorities won them the complete confidence of the citizens whose interests they sought to protect.

Territorial Legislatures. By the time independence had been achieved and the new states had come to face the problem of establishing legislative bodies in the territories, the influence of the English tradition had to some

[1] Harlow, Ralph V., *The History of Legislative Methods in the Period before 1825* (Yale University Press, 1927).

extent declined. The controlling influence in modeling the territorial assemblies was that of the older states along the Atlantic seaboard, from which the majority of the settlers in the western country had migrated. Those who are familiar with the thesis of Frederick J. Turner regarding the significance of the frontier in American history will not require any further discussion of this point.[2] Thus Congress apparently found no reason for changing the Wisconsin plan when setting up the legislature for the Territory of Iowa in 1838. This assembly consisted of thirty-nine members, thirteen of whom formed the Council and twenty-six the House of Representatives. With regard to such matters as the qualifications of members, the filling of vacancies, contested elections, term of office, oath, compensation, privileges, and immunities, the territorial legislatures were not substantially different from the state legislatures which followed them.[3] Many of these territorial legislatures were in existence for only a few years.

Early State Legislatures. The organization and powers of the early state legislatures continued much as they had been during the preceding regime — colonial or territorial. Those which came into existence at the time the present institutions of government were established, or soon after, enjoyed to an extraordinary degree the respect and confidence of the people and were consequently intrusted with wide powers. In North Carolina all officers of importance were elected by the legislature, including judges and justices of the peace. The governor had not even the right to call the legislature in special session in time of emergency. In Virginia, one of the gravest defects of the constitution was its grant of disproportionate powers to the legislature, especially to the lower chamber. "The latter alone could originate enactments, and though the Senate could defeat any bill, it could not amend appropriation measures. The two houses elected the principal state officers, including judges, and determined all salaries. The governor was pitifully weak, and could not even call the legislature without his council's consent."[4] These conditions were general, but for reasons that will presently be indicated the legislatures began to forfeit the right to this confidence, and in the course of time drastic limitations were imposed upon their powers.

Reconstruction Legislatures in the South. During the period of reconstruction the legislatures of the Southern states, through the influence of carpetbaggers from the North and scalawags from the South, sank to almost unbelievable depths of degradation. The membership — black and white — was for the most part of the lowest type. Gambling, drunkenness, and vice characterized the private lives of a majority of members; graft, fraud, and

[2] Turner, Frederick J., *The Frontier in American History* (Holt, New York, 1920). The original statement on this thesis was contained in his presidential address delivered before the American Historical Association in 1896.

[3] State histories available in most of the states give some information regarding the territorial and early state legislatures.

[4] Nevins, Allan, *The American States during and after the Revolution, 1775–1789*, pp. 142, 148 (Macmillan, New York, 1924).

corruption, their public life. It is difficult to exaggerate the extent to which these conditions prevailed, and they were common to all the Southern states. Claude G. Bowers vividly describes some of them. The following is typical:

> And even worse was Louisiana. . . . The Legislature we find sitting in Mechanics Hall is typical of the others we have seen in the land of jubilee. . . . The lobbies teem with laughing negroes from the plantations, with whites of the pinch-faced, parasitic type. . . . The abysmally ignorant eschew debate. . . . It is a monkey-house — with guffaws, disgusting interpolations, amendments offered that are too obscene to print, followed by shouts of glee. Bad in the beginning, the travesty grows worse. The vulgarity of the speeches increases; members stagger from the basement bar to their seats. The Speaker in righteous mood sternly forbids the introduction of liquor on the floor. A curious old planter stands in the galleries a moment looking down upon the scene, and with an exclamation, "My God!" he turns and runs, as from a pestilence, into the street. Visitors from the North organize "slumming expeditions" to the Legislature or go as to a zoo. A British member of Parliament, asking if there are any curiosities in the city, is taken forthwith to Mechanics Hall. Corruption is inevitable, and members openly charged with bribery are not offended. . . .[5]

The Legislatures from 1875 to 1925. The decline of public confidence in the legislatures which had begun before the Civil War continued during the War and in the years which immediately followed it. Conditions in the South were abnormal, but there was little about the conduct of the legislatures in other states to inspire confidence. At the outset of the period under consideration there spread through the states a move to impose vigorous constitutional restrictions upon the powers of the legislatures. Half of the state constitutions now in effect were drafted during the last thirty years of the nineteenth century — a period during which public confidence in popularly elected representative assemblies was at an all-time low. States functioning under these constitutions are still suffering from the effects of the unwise limitations then imposed.

The Legislatures from 1925 to Date. The year 1925 marks approximately the beginning of the modern period. All of the legislatures are now well established. As indicated in the table on page 190, the older ones have had a continuous existence extending over more than a century and a half, and those in even the newest states are fifty or more years old. This period has witnessed the organization of the American Legislators' Association (now the Council of State Governments), whose constructive work has produced both a movement to improve the quality of the legislative output and one to restore public confidence in legislative bodies — movements which have already produced significant results.

[5] Bowers, Claude G., *The Tragic Era*, pp. 362–364 (Houghton Mifflin, Boston, 1929). For the most recent treatments, see Coulter, E. Merton, *The South during Reconstruction, 1865–1877* (Louisiana State University Press, 1947), half of which is devoted to the reconstruction governments, with their dismal record of corruption and mismanagement, and Alexander, Thomas B., *Political Reconstruction in Tennessee* (Vanderbilt University Press, 1950).

Interest in the improvement of legislative bodies was accentuated by the spread of dictatorship over Europe in the decade of the thirties and by the realization that dictatorship regularly moved in when representative assemblies were no longer able to function. Interest was further stimulated after the passage of the Federal Legislative Reorganization Act of 1946. The New York legislature established its Joint Legislative Committee on Legislative Methods, Practices, Procedures, and Expenditures, under the chairmanship of Senator Floyd E. Anderson, whose two important reports stand as a monumental contribution in the field. The Council of State Governments set up its Committee on Legislative Practices and Procedures, also under the chairmanship of Senator Anderson, whose report, *Our State Legislatures*, appeared first in 1947 and in revised form in 1948. Many of the legislatures themselves set up committees and commissions looking toward improvements in both organization and procedure and were showing a lively interest in the implementation of legislative controls over finance and a more effective surveillance of the executive. Meantime, the American Political Science Association's Committee on American Legislatures was carrying on a comprehensive study of the problems of the state legislatures, with a view to reporting on the existing situation and making constructive recommendations.

Number of 1951 Legislative Sessions

THIRTEEN ORIGINAL STATES		THIRTEEN NEWEST STATES	
113th	Delaware	20th	Arizona, New Mexico
121st	North Carolina	23rd	Oklahoma
129th	Maryland	29th	Utah
129th	South Carolina	31st	Idaho, Wyoming
138th	Georgia	32nd	Louisiana, Montana, North Dakota, South Dakota, Washington
139th	Pennsylvania		
141st	Connecticut, New Hampshire		
143rd	Virginia	33rd	Florida
164th	Massachusetts	37th	Kansas
172nd	New York		
173rd	New Jersey		
176th	Rhode Island		

Bicameral and Unicameral Systems

For approximately a century the bicameral system of legislative organization enjoyed universal acceptance throughout the United States. This had not always been so, nor is it true today. While the bicameral plan has always been in the ascendancy, there were in the early days a number of cases in which the unicameral form was used. The colonial legislative bodies in Delaware and Pennsylvania were unicameral. When, following the Declaration of Independence, governments were organized in the several states, bicameral systems were established in all but Georgia, Pennsylvania, and Vermont. Georgia changed to a bicameral system in 1789, Pennsylvania in 1790, while in Vermont the change was delayed until 1836.

In 1784 the Committee on the Defects and Alterations of the Constitution in Pennsylvania recommended the change to the bicameral form because (1) there was an insufficient check on the proceedings of a single house, and (2) an uncontrolled power of legislation would enable the legislature to usurp judicial and executive authority. In the conclusions of a study of the unicameral legislature of Vermont during the nearly fifty years of its existence, Professor Carroll sees nothing in the experience of that state which justifies any assumption of the superiority of bicameralism. On the other hand, he believes that the arguments of the leaders who opposed the change appear to be amply justified.[6]

The Nebraska Experiment. In the early years of the twentieth century, there were repeated attempts to secure the adoption of unicameralism. There had been none, however, for more than a decade preceding 1934, the year in which the voters of Nebraska, under the leadership of Senator Norris, voted for it, to be effective as of January 1937. The results have been watched with interest throughout the country; in fact, for several years thereafter numerous proposals of this character were introduced in the state legislatures. The transition from a bicameral to a unicameral system requires considerable time and a great deal of work; in Nebraska, several hundred amendments to existing statutes had to be made to bring the laws of the state into harmony with the new legislative set-up. The constitutional amendment authorized a body of not more than fifty members; the legislature of 1935 divided the state into forty-three districts, and in 1936 the first unicameral body was elected on a nonpartisan ballot for a term of two years. Thirteen of the new legislators were senators, fifteen of them representatives in the last bicameral body. They wisely devoted considerable time to organization, as a result of which a number of important changes were made[7]:

1. Establishment of a legislative council, consisting of fifteen members of the Legislature, to frame a program of legislation between sessions
2. Requirement of public hearings, with five days' advance notice on all bills before passage
3. Reduction of the number of committees from thirty-two in the Senate

[6] These arguments were: (1) that the people were happy and prosperous under the existing system; (2) that the unicameral system was the best feature of the constitution then existing; (3) that the change would increase the cost of government and the tax burden; (4) that the change would lengthen the legislative sessions without giving any compensating benefit; (5) that it would remove the government farther from the people; and (6) that it was unnecessary to have a governmental organization like that of other states. Carroll, Daniel B., *The Unicameral Legislature in Vermont*, p. 75 (Vermont Historical Society, Montpelier, 1933). See also Watt, Irma A., "Why Pennsylvania Abandoned Unicameralism," *State Government*, March 1936, pp. 54–55, and *Massachusetts Law Quarterly*, April 1936, pp. 57–59.

[7] See New York State Constitutional Convention Committee, *Problems Relating to Legislative Organization and Powers*, Chapter 2 (Albany, 1938).

and thirty-six in the House to a total of sixteen, with a regular committee schedule so arranged that no member was on two committees meeting at the same time

4. Publicity for all committee hearings as well as regular sessions
5. Consideration of each bill after its report from the committee and before final passage at three sessions separated by at least three and two days respectively, with careful consideration of its drafting by a Committee on Enrollment and review after each of the first two considerations
6. Requirement that every bill without exception be on the members' desks in final printed form for at least one full day before final passage
7. Abolition of the Committee of the Whole with its *viva voce* votes and establishment of the right of any member to require a record roll call on any motion at any stage of the proceedings
8. Employment for the session of three nonmember counselors to consider the constitutionality of doubtful measures and creation for future sessions of the office of constitutional reviewer, to be appointed by the legislative council, who will give opinions on constitutionality and validity on the request of any member at any stage of the proceedings
9. Establishment of the office of permanent secretary to the Legislature

For purposes of comparison, a statistical summary covering certain essential points in the last bicameral and the first unicameral sessions is presented here:

The Nebraska Legislature

	1935, BICAMERAL	1937, UNICAMERAL
Cost	$202,500	$150,000
Bills introduced	1,056	581
Bills passed	192	226
Vetoes	6	18
Length of session (days)	110	98

It may be customary in other states to speak of the Nebraska "experiment," but the Nebraskans themselves seem well satisfied with their pioneer move and no longer regard it as experimental. The first session, reported Professor Senning, demonstrated an "absence of hasty legislation; a simplified and smoothly working procedure; . . . a better personnel; . . . the liberation of the legislature from the domination of the governor as the titular head of his party, and of the leaders of the political parties; and the general publicity by means of which the unicameral legislature has revived an interest among the people of the state in their lawmaking body." More than a decade later Professor Spencer praised the smooth operation of the single chamber, pointing out that there were fewer bills introduced, more laws passed. He listed five factors that have contributed to the success of the plan: (1) knowledge of what goes on — that is, absence of the uncertainty, so common under bicameral systems, of what another chamber, its standing committees, or committee chairmen or conference committees may do; (2) a bill procedure that is deliberate and democratic; (3) procedure that is clear, understandable, observable, and easily reportable by the newspapers; (4) committee structure that promotes some degree of internal leadership and coordination; (5) a session that is not limited as to duration.[8]

Merits and Defects of Unicameralism. There has been more interest in unicameralism since the Nebraska experiment began, but no other state has as yet adopted it. While it should be given serious consideration, it is not certain that it will accomplish all the things its supporters claim for it, in states whose population is far larger and less homogeneous than that of Nebraska. It does not necessarily touch any of the most pressing problems now confronting our legislatures — organizational, planning, or scientific bill-drafting. It does not accomplish anything that could not be done — indeed, that has not already been done in various states — quite as well under a bicameral system. The size of the legislative bodies and the number and size of committees could be reduced, and the rules of procedure could be modernized. Legislative service agencies can be established; indeed, more than half of the states have already set them up. Adequate bill-drafting services can also be established.

Serious weaknesses, to be sure, have developed in the operation of the bicameral system. In the large cities, the substitution of a small unicameral council for the old-fashioned large, bicameral body has been productive of much good. The experience of the Canadian provinces is also reassuring. While the conditions there differ in many respects from those in the United States, those provinces which formerly operated bicameral systems similar to our own and have substituted single chambers for them have found that the single chambers do better work and maintain public confidence and support better than the old bodies did. The experts who drafted the first Model State Constitution in 1921 recommended this change, and the recommendation has been carried on in each succeeding draft. The opinions of the people who ought to know vary widely; in fact, they are often diametrically opposed. A large majority of political scientists favor unicameralism, while an overwhelming majority of persons with actual legislative experience are opposed to it.

Representative Character

In general, the state legislatures are a good cross section of the American public; if they are not of as high caliber as one might wish, it may be because

[8] Senning, John P., "Nebraska's First Unicameral Legislative Session," *Annals*, January 1938, pp. 159–167. During the first decade the literature on the subject was enormous. The more important items are listed in the preceding edition of this volume; for comments more nearly current, see Senning, "Unicameralism Passes Test," *National Municipal Review*, February 1944, pp. 58–65, and Spencer, Richard C., "Nebraska Idea Fifteen Years Old," *ibid.*, February 1950, pp. 83–86,

they are actually so representative in character. It is significant, too, that this representative character is fairly constant, even in jurisdictions and in periods of great and rapid social change. Professor Hallie Farmer, on the basis of a study of the Alabama legislature over a long period, offers striking proof of this fact.[9] "It is interesting," she says, "to see how little the Alabama Legislature has changed in forty years." She continues:

> For all practical purposes, the Legislature of 1943 is the Legislature of 1903. It is slightly older, it has had a little more schooling, it has a slightly smaller percentage of lawyers and farmers, but there has been no change to affect radically the control of the Legislature. In 1903, the Legislature of Alabama was a white, male, Protestant, provincial Legislature dominated by lawyers. The same sentence could be used to describe the Legislature of 1943. Not an adjective would have to be changed.

Educational Background. It has been said that every degree of education is found in the state legislatures; that in some, the proportion of members who have had a high school, college, or university education is at times considerably greater than that prevailing among the people generally. In a survey of the membership of the Kentucky legislature, made some years ago, the late Professor Jones found:

> In the matter of education, 52 per cent laid claim to some high school training, while the education of 48 per cent was limited to some training in the lower grades. The writer recently had occasion to examine fifty applicants for firemen in a city of 60,000 people. The percentage of high school graduates applying was higher than the legislature's percentage in the same state. There were, however, sixteen graduates of standard colleges, and twenty others claimed to have had some college or other special training in business schools or normal schools; one had attended a theological seminary. Thus, nearly 40 per cent laid claim to some college training. I have no comparable data on legislatures in other states, and am therefore unable to determine whether this is a high, low, or average record for educational qualifications. The fact that it appears to be on about the same level as that of police applicants indicates that, absolutely if not relatively, it is low.[10]

Professional Classification. In late years some attention has been paid to the representative character of the legislatures from the point of view of the business and professional affiliations of their members. Over a period of years one will find in the typical legislature representatives of all the types of business, trades, and professions by which the members of an American community secure their livelihood, as well as persons with every conceivable educational, social, and economic background. In the table on page 196, there is presented a detailed analysis of the membership of the Pennsylvania legislature at intervals from 1927 to 1949. Commenting on this situation, the authors of a standard text on American government observe:

[9] *The Legislative Process in Alabama*, p. 309 (Bureau of Public Administration, University of Alabama, 1949).

[10] Jones, J. Catron, "The Make-up of a State Legislature," *American Political Science Review*, February 1931, pp. 116–119.

> Almost every profession is represented, and almost every conceivable business activity, although lawyers and farmers usually outnumber members following other vocations, and manual laborers are scarce or non-existent. The majority are men in the prime of life, between thirty-five and fifty years of age; although now and then a young man barely a voter, or an octogenarian appears. Every phase and degree of political experience is represented also: "those who have been only voters, those who make politics a business; those who are ardent partisans, and those who are politically torpid; the conservative and the demagogue — all are intermingled in these representative bodies." Even foreign-born citizens have hitherto been well represented. And since woman suffrage became nation-wide a generation or more ago, women legislators have appeared in increasing numbers; in 1949, a total of 214 women served as members of legislatures in a total of thirty-nine states.[11]

The presence of the disproportionately large numbers of lawyers and farmers has a significant bearing upon the character of the work done by the state legislatures.

Lawyers as Legislators. An impartial observer must admit that the lawyer legislators are not, for the most part, the ablest men in their profession. However much one may deplore the fact, the ablest lawyers are usually too busy with a lucrative practice to be able to give the time necessary for legislative work. With the exception of a few whose liking for politics and whose spirit of public service make them willing to undergo a considerable financial sacrifice, and a few able young lawyers not yet established who undertake legislative work for the purpose of developing contacts and acquaintances as a means of professional advancement, one is usually justified in the assumption that most of those members who classify themselves as lawyers are not overburdened by the pressure of professional duties. Even if they were men ranking high in their profession, the effect of their presence would still be a matter of considerable importance. Moreover, most of the *leaders* in legislative work are members of this profession.

The training which an individual undergoes in preparation for the practice of law has a tendency to develop an extreme degree of conservatism. The natural inclination of most lawyers, when confronted by a set of facts, is to see what has been done, to see what the precedents are, rather than to look to the future to see what, in accordance with the existing situation, ought to be done. Many of them see nothing incongruous in setting up against a pressing social or economic need of our own day the decision of a judge in an inferior court handed down twenty-five, fifty, or a hundred years ago.

[11] Ogg, Frederic A., and Ray, P. Orman, *Introduction to American Government*, Tenth Edition, p. 820 (Appleton-Century-Crofts, New York, 1951); Gosnell, Harold F., *Democracy, the Threshold of Freedom*, Chapter 12 (Ronald Press, New York, 1948) on the significance of occupation of representatives. That the representative character of legislatures has not changed much in the last century seems to be indicated by a "List of Senators of the General Assembly of the State of Tennessee, Convened at Nashville on the first Monday in October, 1848 — . . .," compiled by Raymond B. Sloan, who reports that: (1) there were 17 farmers, 7 lawyers, 1 merchant, 1 law student, 2 physicians, 1 printer; (2) 22 were married, 5 single, 1 widower; (3) 17 were born in Tennessee, 6 in Virginia, 1 in Maryland, 1 in New York, 2 in North Carolina, and 1 in Pennsylvania.

Professional Classification, General Assembly of Pennsylvania, 1927, 1935, 1943, and 1949

Profession	1927		1935		1943		1949	
	House	*Senate*	*House*	*Senate*	*House*	*Senate*	*House*	*Senate*
Lawyers	36	17	36	17	38	21	30	17
Merchants	26	5	23	2	15	1	15	1
Clerks	20	..	11	..	5	..	11	..
Manufacturers	13	5	4	7	9	1	4	2
Farmers	10	2	16	2	12	3	15	3
Real Estate and Insurance Men	17	5	15	7	22	4	18	7
Editors, Publishers, and Reporters	5	2	4	2	9	1	6	1
Presidents, Managers, and Superintendents	..	..	6	1	1	..	8	3
Bankers and Brokers	7	3	5	1	6	..	5	..
Teachers	5	..	7	1	7	..	8	2
Contractors, Carpenters, and Machinists	10	1	7	2	14	4	14	..
Railroad Conductors	..	..	9	..	4	2	2	..
Coal Dealers	..	..	3	..	6	..	5	1
Clergymen	2	1	2	..	1	1	1	1
Salesmen	3	..	14	..	8	2	10	4
Retired	..	..	1	1	2	..	2	..
Lumbermen	..	..	2	..	3	..	..	..
Housewives	4	1	..	..	..	..	3	..
Physicians, Dentists, etc.	8	4	10	4	12	4	5	2
Telegraph Operators	..	..	1	..	1	..	..	
Accountants	..	..	4	1	6	..	9	..
Automobile Men	5	..	4	1	8	3	6	1
Pharmacists	..	..	3	..	2	1	..	1
Interior Decorators and Artists	..	..	2	..	..	..	2	0
Miscellaneous	37	4	19	1	17	2	29	4
	208	50	208	50	208	50	208	50

It is not meant to imply that each situation that arises can or should be treated as though it represented an experience new in the development of the race; but the attitude of the legal profession is none the less significant because it so largely explains the difficulty of securing the passage of liberal measures of a social or economic character. The lawyer has a tendency to resist changes in the law because of a feeling of vested right in the law as it is; he resists raising standards for admission to the bar because it would reflect on the training of many present members of the profession; and he resists progressive legislation because it is new and untried.

More important than these considerations are the frequent violations of the public confidence by lawyer legislators. After charges of bribery made on the floor of the California Senate in the 1937 session, an investigation was authorized by the Attorney General of the State and the District Attorney of Sacramento County. The investigators found that several lawyer legislators had solicited and accepted or had been proffered and accepted employment from interests directly concerned with legislation; that after accepting such employment, lawyer legislators had shown a marked tendency to vote for and otherwise act in the interests of their clients, as distinguished from impartial representation of the interests of the public. Other findings dealt with the solicitation of nonlawyer legislators, with corrupt lobbying as distinguished from open legislative representation, and with the marked tendency toward the pre-election influencing of legislators by means of campaign contributions or of tangible, personal favors to prospective members of the legislature. While corruption in legislative halls is not nearly so common as it once was, it is probable that these findings could be paralleled in many other state capitols.[12]

The other side of this question is well stated by a former legislator in a large Eastern state, himself a distinguished member of the bar:

> More or less prejudiced writers have, from the earliest to the present day, sustained an unintelligent critical attack upon the influence of lawyers in legislative bodies. But close study will reveal that few, if any, such writers have either enjoyed the honor or borne the responsibility of membership in a legislative assembly. Only sporadically will there come, by spoken word or pen, an expression of commendation or approval of the public service rendered by the lawyer, in the legislature. Such sentiments, however, are rarely bestowed by other than one who has personally been in the service. Thus, their genuineness and sincerity are questioned if not disbelieved. The Bar, whether through lack of knowledge or want of interest in the practical phases of lawmaking, has remained inarticulate to the criticism not alone of the legislature, but as well of the services of the lawyer-legislator.[13]

It is true here as elsewhere in the public service, that any shortcoming, or even the suspicion thereof, is broadcast while little is said of the conscientious majority.

Urban-Rural Conflict. The members from the rural districts always have constituted a majority in the state legislatures. In the early days when society was predominantly agricultural, this was entirely justified; now one finds the control of the rural members no less complete, although the number who classify themselves as farmers is, for various reasons, much smaller than formerly. This rural control[14] of our legislatures has given rise to what has

[12] See *Legislative Investigative Report*, submitted by H. R. Philbrick, Sacramento, December 28, 1938.

[13] Sterling, Philip, "Some Practical Aspects of Legislation," an address before the Pennsylvania Bar Association, Bedford Springs, June 24, 1932. See also a careful study by a lawyer-political scientist, Rutherford, M. Louise, "Lawyers as Legislators," *Annals*, January 1938, pp. 53–61.

[14] The term "rural" is used here in the sense of nonurban. The line-up is regularly the one or two largest cities against the rest of the state, the small and medium sized cities lining up with the ruralites against the big city, whose influence all fear; see Neuberger, Richard L., "The Country Slicker vs. the City Yokel," *New York Times Magazine*, July 31, 1949, pp. 17, 35 ff., in which it is contended that our farm-dominated legislatures, mistrusting urban ways, tend to slight metropolitan needs.

often been appropriately called the American rotten-borough system. The problem is as old as recorded history; those who have resided in the great open spaces have always regarded their brethren in the cities with suspicion and distrust and have looked upon the cities themselves as dens of iniquity. The Bible tells the stories of Sodom and Gomorrah, of Tyre and Sidon. The psychology of those days and of the intervening years is fundamentally little different from that which prompts the rural member of a modern state legislature to impose, or to attempt to impose, all manner of restrictive regulations upon the life and activities of the cities within his state. This situation is not, however, merely an interesting analogy to conditions existing in other lands and at other times; it is a practical situation which confronts our people and which has a definite effect upon their social and political welfare.

This mistrust of the urban dweller is not only a problem of city-state relations, but one of interrelations at the local level as well. The Board of Supervisors of Tompkins County, New York, for instance, is composed of fourteen members, five from the city of Ithaca and nine from the surrounding rural areas of the county. One member of the Ithaca City Council reports that "the rural members have all the say, the city members none. In welfare, the city contributes 62 per cent of the money, the remainder of the county 38 per cent, but the city has nothing to say as to how it shall be spent." Realizing the practical impossibility of either increasing city representation or reducing rural representation, an effort is being made to solve the seemingly insoluble problem.

The prevalence of this system means, in the first place, that rural members not only can, but must, vote upon many complicated urban problems about which they know little and care less. Members who have rarely seen a subway and who have no knowledge of the rush of traffic in a big city at the beginning and end of a working day must pass upon questions with regard to municipal transportation facilities and complicated problems connected with the financing of such facilities. Without ever having known anything but the agencies of local government, they must pass upon the organization and functioning of governmental machinery for a great metropolitan community. With only such limited knowledge of electoral problems as may be gained in a small community where every inhabitant knows not only the name but the intimate details of the life and business of every other, he must consider and pass upon provisions of an election law to be used in urban communities controlled by powerful and efficient political organizations. In addition to all this, such members frequently seek to impose upon cities all kinds of regulations with regard to Sunday sports, Sunday movies, and other matters in which they constitute themselves the moral protectors of urban dwellers.

This situation is not peculiar to any one state or group of states; it is more or less characteristic of all. It is well illustrated by the facts with regard to Pennsylvania. In this state Philadelphia County sends a delegation of 41 members, and Allegheny County a delegation of 27, representing in the lower house the cities of Philadelphia and Pittsburgh, respectively. Thus these two large urban counties control only 68 out of 208 members, although approximately half the state's total population of more than 10 million people live in the metropolitan areas of which they are the centers. The 140 representatives from the other sixty-five counties have a regular and substantial majority on any question that brings about a division on urban-rural lines; these members commonly stand together against the two largest cities of the state, even though many of them live in and represent cities of the third class.

Although the society of most of our states has definitely changed from an agricultural to an industrial one, there is little likelihood that inequalities in representation will soon be adjusted. The rural districts have always had the majority, and they are not likely to give it up willingly even though the justification for their keeping it can no longer be supported by figures on the distribution of population. Another factor which will no doubt continue to exercise a powerful deterring influence in changing this situation is the existence of a not unjustified suspicion and distrust of the frequently corrupt political machines which urban dwellers have permitted to dominate their affairs in such centers as Philadelphia, New York, and Chicago. Up-state residents in New York and Pennsylvania and down-state residents of Illinois have naturally viewed with great apprehension the possible extension of the control of organizations of this character to the large and important machinery of the state government.

Examples are available in almost every state in any section of the country. In the Connecticut House, Union with a population of 234 and Hartford with a population of 166,326, have equal representation. In Alabama, Dallas County with a population of about 55,000 has three members in the House — the same number as Mobile County with 250,000 population. In Ohio, although there is a state constitutional provision for reapportionment every ten years by an administrative agency, and an additional proviso that the courts may compel such reapportionment, the situation is so bad that the United States Conference of Mayors used Ohio as a "horrible example" in a nationwide drive to remove such inequalities. The fact is that the present system of representation in the states is grossly unfair and inequitable to the urban districts.

Problem of Apportionment. The problem of apportionment is the most serious and, at the same time, one of the most difficult confronting the states, if our democratic system is to be preserved. The practice of allowing sparsely populated districts to be represented by one legislator and more populous districts by several was generally accepted by all states prior to 1820, and many states still follow this practice. In Massachusetts it was optional for a town to send a representative, and at times few of the smaller towns were represented.[15] Although many of the present-day state constitutions affirm the principle that representation should be on the basis of population, and although a considerable number of them call for reapportionment every ten years, a survey made in 1952 showed that reapportionments had been made in only slightly more than one third of the states in the last decade.

This survey also showed that there had been no reapportionment of one or both houses in Connecticut since 1818, in Mississippi since 1890, in Delaware since 1897, in Oklahoma since 1908, in Tennessee since 1905, in Iowa since 1904, in Alabama and Illinois since 1901, in Minnesota since 1913, in Texas since 1920, in Indiana, Kansas, Louisiana, Maryland, Michigan, Montana, and Pennsylvania since 1921, in Arizona, Arkansas, Colorado, Nebraska, North Dakota, Oregon, South Carolina, Utah, Washington, West Virginia, Wisconsin, and Wyoming since the early thirties. In spite of the gross inequalities in representation existing in states throughout the country (see table on page 203), only two or three states have been redistricted since the 1950 census.

Why, one may ask, are reapportionments not made when due? One reason is the struggle for power. Reapportionment means shifts in representation, and shifts in representation mean shifts in power — from one part of the state to another, from rural to urban, from one economic group to another, and perhaps from one political party to another. The rural districts are unlikely — as are these other groups — to relinquish powers that they have held for many, many years, as long as they can hang on to them, no matter what happens to urban dwellers or what professors of political science may write or say. The table on page 201, setting forth the apportionment experience of Indiana, illustrates only too clearly the relationship between the growth of urbanism and the current inability to secure legislative action on apportionment. Reapportionments were made in Indiana, and in other states, fairly frequently and in accordance with the provisions of the constitution as long as a new apportionment meant simply a shift in representation without any shift in control.

When the latter appeared to be a certain result of change, reapportionments virtually ceased. The lengths to which the ruralities will go in this connection is illustrated by the New Jersey experience of 1947. The people of the state were permitted to hold a constitutional convention only at the price of entering into an iron-bound agreement under the terms of which the delegates pledged themselves NOT to tackle the state's most pressing problem — the problem of reapportionment.

Another important obstacle to reapportionment is to be found in the provisions of the state constitutions. The California Constitution states that no county may have more than one senator. So Los Angeles County, with nearly half of the people of the state, has just one of the state's forty senators.

[15] Handlin, Oscar, and Mary F., *Commonwealth, a Study of the Role of Government in the American Economy: Massachusetts, 1774–1861* (New York University Press, 1947).

In New Jersey, as in eighteen other states,[16] each county is entitled to one senator, with the result that Hudson County with a population of 650,000 and Sussex County with a population of slightly less than 30,000 have equal representation. In New York and a number of other states, each county must have at least one assemblyman, regardless of population. The New York law does not permit adjoining counties to have more than half of the total seats in either house. New York City, which cast more than half the total votes for governor in 1946, has less than half of the votes in the legislature. For additional illustrations, see the table on page 203.

State of Indiana Apportionments under Present Constitution (1851) *

YEAR OF APPORTIONMENT	LEGISLATIVE SESSIONS HELD UNDER EACH APPORTIONMENT
1851	1852, 1853, 1855, 1857
1857	1858S, 1859, 1861, 1861S, 1863, 1865, 1865S, 1867
1867	1869, 1869S, 1871, 1872S, 1873
1872S	1875, 1875S, 1877, 1877S, 1879, 1879S
1879	1881, 1881S, 1883, 1885, 1885S
1885	1887, 1889, 1891, 1897
1891 [1]	1893
1893 [2]	Not used
1897	1899, 1901, 1903, 1905
1903 [3]	Not used
1905	1907, 1908S, 1909, 1911, 1913, 1915
1915	1917, 1919, 1920S, 1921, 1921S
1921	1923, 1925, 1927, 1929, 1931, 1932S, 1933, 1935, 1936S, 1937, 1938S, 1939, 1941, 1943, 1944S, 1945, 1947, 1949, 1951

* Prepared by James R. Mock in connection with his work on a forthcoming volume on the government and administration of Indiana.

[1] Held unconstitutional, December 17, 1892.

[2] Held unconstitutional, January 30, 1896 — the Supreme Court held that the 1885 Act was still in effect.

[3] Held unconstitutional, March 9, 1903.

Every one of the forty-eight state constitutions deals in some fashion with the problem of apportionment, stating more or less clearly the basis for representation in each chamber. As Professor Farmer points out, each of them attempts to do four things: (1) to approximate the ideal of equality in representation; (2) to create a geographic unit of representation; (3) to provide flexibility in order to permit adjustment of representation to meet shifts in population; and (4) to assure stability in the legislature. In practice, the requirements of the constitution are often ignored in spirit if not in fact. The basis commonly used is the Federal census or a state census, or both,

[16] These are: Alabama, Arizona, Arkansas, Florida, Georgia, Indiana, Iowa, Kansas, Louisiana, Mississippi, Missouri, New Jersey, New York, North Carolina, Ohio, Pennsylvania, South Carolina, Utah, and Wyoming.

apportionments to take place every five or ten years; but frequently this requirement also is ignored. If the legislature provides no new apportionment, the old continues in effect; the longer it remains in effect, the more inequitable the representation becomes. There is, furthermore, nothing that can be done about it.[17]

A third major obstacle to reapportionment is the influence of politics — a phase of the struggle for power referred to above. While many different currents of political opinion find representation in legislative bodies, those elements in control at any given time are little disposed to do or permit to be done anything that might disturb the *status quo*. If its maintenance requires gerrymandering the districts of the state — or some of them — that will be done. If it requires ignoring a constitutional mandate to redistrict the state at periodic intervals, that too will be done. The urban-rural conflict is reflected here also. There are heavy Democratic majorities in many of the large cities, heavy Republican majorities in the rural districts of many states. Since the representatives of the rural political organizations now hold control, they are not at all disposed to consent to arrangements that will either overturn or imperil that control.

Forty-one states specifically provide in their constitutions that the legislature shall be the apportioning agency, and all but two of these place full responsibility for reapportionment upon the legislature. There is, however, no way of compelling the legislature to act in case it is unwilling to do so or

[17] In addition to references cited in previous editions of this volume, see: Gosnell, Harold F., *Democracy: the Threshold of Freedom*, Chapter 10 (Ronald Press, New York, 1948); Harvey, Lashley G., "Some Problems of Representation in State Legislatures," *Western Political Quarterly*, June 1949, pp. 265–271; and MacNeil, Douglas H., "Urban Representation in State Legislatures," *State Government*, April 1945, pp. 59–61, and on individual states: ALABAMA: Farmer, Hallie, *The Legislative Process in Alabama*, Chapter 2 (Bureau of Public Administration, University of Alabama, 1949) and Alabama Legislative Reference Service, *Reapportionment* (Montgomery, 1950). CALIFORNIA: Greenfield, Margaret, *Legislative Reapportionment* (Bureau of Public Administration, University of California, March 1951) and Assembly Interim Committee on Elections and Reapportionment, *Report* (Sacramento, 1951). ILLINOIS: Christie, Mrs. Ronald, *The Problem of Legislative Reapportionment in Illinois* (Illinois League of Women Voters, Chicago, 1951) and Illinois Legislative Council, *Reapportionment in Illinois* (Springfield, 1945). KENTUCKY: Bureau of Government Research, *Legislative and Congressional Redistricting in Kentucky* (Lexington, 1951). LOUISIANA: Asseff, Emmett, *Legislative Apportionment in Louisiana* (Bureau of Government Research, Louisiana State University, 1950). NEBRASKA: Legislative Council, Subcommittee on Redistricting, *Report* (Lincoln, 1948). NEW JERSEY: Friedelbaum, Stanley H., and Reock, Ernest C., Jr., *Legislative Apportionment in New Jersey* (Bureau of Government Research, Rutgers University, January 1952). NEW YORK: Joint Legislative Committee on Reapportionment, *In the Matter of the Problem of Reapportionment Generally and a Proposed Amendment to Article III of the Constitution* (Legislative Document No. 31, Albany, 1950). OKLAHOMA: Legislative Council, *Legislative Apportionment in Oklahoma*, Constitutional Study No. 10 (Oklahoma City, 1948). PENNSYLVANIA: Bureau of Municipal Research, *Redistribution of State Legislative Representation in Philadelphia* (Philadelphia, 1951). UTAH: Weaver, Ellsworth E., *Legislative Reapportionment in Utah* (Institute of Government, University of Utah, October 1950). WISCONSIN: Legislative Reference Library, *Legislative Apportionment in Wisconsin* (Madison, 1950).

Unequal Representation in State Legislatures *

STATE	COUNTY AND/OR MUNICIPALITY REPRESENTATION
General	*59% of U.S. population is URBAN, elects 25% of representation* *41% of U.S. population is RURAL, elects 75% of representation*
Alabama	Jefferson County (Birmingham) — 140,420 pop., 1 senator Another district — 58,621 pop., 1 senator
Colorado	Denver County (Denver) — 21,500 pop. per representative Basa County — 6,207 pop. per representative
Connecticut	Hartford — 166,000 pop., 2 representatives Colebrook — 547 pop., 2 representatives 8 counties with 60% of pop. have 21% of representatives; remaining 59 counties with 40% of pop. have 79% of representatives.
Delaware	New Castle County (Wilmington) — has 7 out of 17 senators, 15 out of 35 representatives; 67% of pop. has 42% of representation.
Georgia	Fulton County (Atlanta) — 392,000 pop., 3 representatives Echols County — 3,000 pop., 1 representative
Illinois	Cook County (Chicago) — has 19 out of 51 senators, 57 out of 155 representatives; 51% of pop. has 37% of representation.
Iowa	Polk County (Des Moines) — 195,835 pop., 1 senator Mahaska County — 24,485 pop., 1 senator
Maryland	Baltimore County (Baltimore City) — has 6 out of 29 senators, 36 out of 120 representatives; 40% of pop. has 27% of representation.
Michigan	Wayne County (Detroit) — 40% of pop., 27% of representation.
Minnesota	One district with 88,501 pop. has 2 representatives; another with 7,254 pop. has 1 representative.
Missouri	St. Louis County (St. Louis) — 816,000 pop., 18 representatives 18 rural counties — 158,000 pop., 18 representatives
Montana	Silver Bow County (Butte) — 53,207 pop., 1 senator Petroleum County — 1,083 pop., 1 senator
New Jersey	8 urban counties with $\frac{4}{5}$ of pop. have 8 senators; 13 rural counties with $\frac{1}{5}$ of pop. have 13 senators
Ohio	Cuyahoga County (Cleveland) — 16% of pop., 7% of representation
Oklahoma	Oklahoma City — 244,000 pop., 7 representatives 7 rural counties — 57,000 pop., 7 representatives
Oregon	55,406 urban pop. per senator, 9,072 rural pop. per senator 22,202 urban pop. per representative, 5,272 rural pop. per representative
Pennsylvania	Alleghany County (Pittsburgh) — 1,400,000 pop., 27 representatives Philadelphia County — 1,900,000 pop., 41 representatives 36 rural counties — 1,200,000 pop., 36 representatives
Rhode Island	Providence — 36% of pop., 25% of representation
Texas	11 metropolitan centers entitled to $\frac{1}{2}$ of senate representation have slightly over $\frac{1}{3}$.
Wisconsin	67,446 urban pop. per assembly district; 15,827 rural pop. per assembly district

* Based primarily on United States Conference of Mayors, *Government of the People, by the People, for the People* (Washington, 1948).

unable to come to an agreement. The courts treat the matter as a political question, not subject to review. However, if the legislature apportions, a subsequent redistricting can be challenged in the courts on such mandatory requirements as the stipulation that "counties or towns may not be divided" and such discretionary requirements as the rule that "districts shall be equal" and "compact." The courts have shown no great hesitancy in protecting the people from arbitrary and capricious action of districting agencies, whether real or alleged.

The difficulties encountered in obtaining apportionment by legislative action have led to numerous proposals for so-called automatic apportionment, more or less along the lines provided in the Federal Reapportionment Act of 1929. The nearest approach to such a system in the states is the one found in Arizona, in which the Secretary of State is required to certify the number of members of the House to be chosen from each county at the next succeeding election. Under this plan, one member is allotted to a county for each 2500 votes or major fraction thereof which were cast in that county for all candidates at the last general election for the post, subject to the proviso that at no time shall this number be less than that allotted initially upon the effective date of this constitutional amendment in 1930. Thus in Arizona an automatic apportionment occurs every second year upon the basis of the vote cast for governor. In Texas, a board, set up by constitutional amendment to act if the legislature fails, provides at least a partial solution of this chronic problem.[18]

Relations of Members to Their Constituents. In considering the representative character of legislative bodies, attention must be given not only to the professional affiliations of members, the urban-rural conflict, and apportionment, but also to such questions as the place of the members in their respective communities, their relations to their constituents, and the turnover in the membership of legislative bodies.

The members are as a rule persons who are well known in their respective communities, persons who are active in local affairs and in social and fraternal organizations. Some of them are professional "joiners." In the Kentucky legislature already referred to, 80 per cent belonged to some order.

> The Masonic fraternity alone could claim 50 per cent, while some reported membership in as many as five secret orders, the Ku Klux Klan not being mentioned. On the other hand, the Rotarians and Kiwanians were conspicuous by their absence. Only 10 per cent claimed membership in these mid-day oratorical societies. As might be expected, this percentage closely parallels the percentage of so-called business men found in the body.[19]

If one is surprised at the lack of educational qualifications of the members, he may be even more surprised to discover that, as politicians, a great

[18] See McClain, Robert H., Jr., "Compulsory Reapportionment," *National Municipal Review*, June 1951, pp. 305–307, 324.

[19] Jones, *op. cit.*, p. 119; see also Gosnell, *op. cit.*, Chapter 11, and Salter, John T., *The Pattern of Politics*, Chapter 4 (Macmillan, New York, 1940).

many are, as Professor Jones said, "rank amateurs." He found that 65 per cent had never sat in a legislature before; that while 35 per cent had had some legislative experience, more than half of these had had only one term, or, in Kentucky, a total of sixty days. More than 50 per cent had never held any public office prior to their election; most of those who had such experience had occupied minor local positions. There were one ex-Congressman, two circuit court judges, and three county judges. These conclusions can be further supported by a similar analysis of the personnel of the legislature in any other state. In Pennsylvania, for instance, prior to the Democratic overturn in 1934, it had been customary to have sixty or sixty-five new members in each regular session; as a result of this election, the number increased to ninety, or more than 43 per cent. Of approximately 7600 state legislators, 5500 are chosen for terms of one session, and that is all that great numbers of them ever serve. This high turnover greatly impairs the efficiency of our legislative bodies.

Professor Hyneman of Northwestern University has made a number of significant studies of legislative tenure and turnover. If the widespread assumption of a direct correlation between legislative experience and legislative competence is sound, then it is a wonder that the legislatures function as well as they do. Of all the members of both houses in ten legislatures from 1925 to 1935, 35.4 per cent were serving their first term, 22.6 per cent their second, 12.3 per cent their third, and 8.9 per cent their fourth; 16.8 per cent had been there between five and nine terms, and 4 per cent had been there ten terms or more. The average experience in the senate is naturally higher than in the house; if the committee chairmen are men of long service, the lack of experience on the part of members is somewhat less serious. The findings of these studies are well summarized in the following paragraphs:

> If one assumes that the average legislator becomes effective only after he has completed three sessions of service, he will be disappointed to find that in only four of the twenty chambers (California, New Jersey, and New York Senates and the New York House) could as many as 50 percent of the members meet this test. In seven chambers (in lower houses of California, Indiana, Iowa, Maine, New Jersey, Pennsylvania, and Washington), less than a fourth of the members could show three previous sessions of service; to reverse the English, more than 75 percent of the membership of each of these seven bodies fell short of this test. Four other chambers (Minnesota House and Indiana, Iowa, and Maine Senates) bettered this standard by a very slight margin.
>
> If the completion of four sessions be taken as the division point between adequate and inadequate legislative equipment, then the New York House and the Senates of California, Illinois, Minnesota, New Jersey, New York, and Washington are found to be superior bodies, with more than a third of their membership in the select group; by the same measure the lower houses of Indiana, Iowa, and Maine are found to be definitely inferior.[20]

[20] Hyneman, Charles S., "Tenure and Turnover of Legislative Personnel," *Annals*, January 1938, pp. 21–31; also, with others, "Legislative Experience of Illinois Law-

Part of the legislator's task must be performed at the state capitol; the other part involves his relations with his constituents, maintaining his contacts with them in order that he may effectively represent them at the capitol and continue to serve them in future legislative sessions. It would be interesting to have a number of case studies of the relations between members and their constituents, showing who takes the initiative in making such contacts, how citizens make their wants known to their representatives, and other data. How many citizens adopt the "you vote for this bill or else" attitude? What other types of pressure do they attempt to use? How does a legislator feel when angry delegations wait upon him at home, or march on the capitol? The frank answers of a number of experienced legislators to these questions would be illuminating.

The evidence indicates that most of the members are "just plain folks"; their educational background is deficient, little if any better than that of a majority of their constituents. Instead of being the ruthless and successful politicians they are popularly supposed to be, a large part of them are new at the game and, judged by the high turnover, obviously ineffective. These observations are made, not in critical spirit, but as an impartial report of the facts as they exist. The reflection, if there is any, lies not upon the legislators, but upon the electorates which select the members.[21] These members have at least two functions to perform; they serve as agents for the mediation of conflicts which arise between different groups, and they develop among themselves a "we group" morale which enables them to bear up under the criticism and abuse heaped upon elective officials by a none too sympathetic or understanding public.[22]

Women Legislators. During the early years of woman suffrage, the number of women legislators slowly increased until in the decade from 1929 to 1939 it ranged from 130 to 150 members. During the last decade it has further increased, as is shown in the table on page 207, so that it now runs something over 200 in each legislative year. The New England states, in which legislative districts are smaller and campaigning is simpler, have throughout been far in the lead in the number of women members, many of whom are successively re-elected so that they acquire considerable legislative experience. In 1938 Massachusetts had women as presiding officers in both

Makers," *University of Chicago Law Review*, December 1935, pp. 104–118; "Tenure and Turnover in the Indiana General Assembly," *American Political Science Review*, February 1938, pp. 51–67, and April 1938, pp. 311–331; and "Tenure and Turnover of the Iowa Legislature," *Iowa Law Journal*, May 1939, pp. 673–696.

[21] A number of recent studies have shown that a surprising number of members are "slated" at the request of various pressure groups, with the idea that they will serve one or two terms until they obtain passage of some legislation desired by the group to which they owe a primary allegiance.

[22] For an interesting discussion of these functions, see Smith, Thomas V., "Two Functions of the American State Legislator," *Annals*, January 1938, pp. 183–188, and his *The Legislative Way of Life* (University of Chicago Press, 1940); also Gosnell. *op. cit.*, Chapter 13 on the legislature, public interest, and parties.

houses. In 1937 women were serving in thirty-six states; in 1939, in twenty-seven. By 1947 and 1949 larger numbers of women members were serving, in thirty-seven and thirty-nine states, respectively.

Women Members of State Legislatures, 1937–1951

YEAR	SENATE	HOUSE	DEMOCRATIC	REPUBLICAN	OTHER *	TOTAL
1937	13	126	77	55	7	139
1939	13	136	65	78	6	149
1941	8	134	58	78	6	142
1943	12	173	75	102	8	185
1945	16	215	83	137	11	231
1947	18	195	61	141	11	213
1949	19	203	91	131	..	222
1951	23	218	80	159	2	241

* Independent, minor party, or political affiliation unknown.

Bernice T. Van der Vries, able veteran legislator from a suburban Chicago district whose population is larger than that of a number of states, recently made some pertinent comments on "Women in Government."[23] Since political parties are almost exclusively controlled by men, women are not often slated or even encouraged to run for office; but once a woman has been elected and has proved that she has vote-getting ability, she becomes popular with the political organization. Many of the same considerations deter women as deter men from engaging actively in politics. So far, Mrs. Van der Vries believes, women have made a poor showing in the securing of elective positions but a good record in office itself. As a member of a state legislature, she writes, "I can testify that there seems to be no discrimination against women after they are elected and take their places as lawmakers. We are given committee chairmanships, important assignments on committees, and other responsible legislative tasks."

Since there are many women who have the ability, the time, and the means to render useful legislative service, it is to be regretted that more of them have not been willing to make the effort. Their particular interest in and talent for dealing with such problems as health, welfare, and education would enable them to be particularly useful. The legislatures need more women members, elected not out of sympathy but on the basis of their qualifications as individuals. There should be a group of sufficient size so that their presence ceases to be a matter of note or of comment. Under such circumstances — which may come sooner than one might now expect — they would be in a position to render maximum service in legislative bodies.

[23] *State Government*, June 1948, pp. 127–128, 134; see also Gosnell, *op. cit.*, Chapter 4; Young, Louise, *Understanding Politics; a Practical Guide for Women* (Pellegrini & Cudahy, Chicago, 1950); Neuberger, Maurine, "Footnotes on Politics by a Lady Legislator," *New York Times Magazine*, May 27, 1951, p. 18.

Place of the Legislatures in Popular Esteem

The early state legislatures were held in high regard, whereas later ones have been almost universally looked upon with suspicion and distrust. Bryce used vituperative language in describing them, quite in contrast to his usual moderation.[24] It became popular to denounce legislators individually and collectively. When a session is concluded, editors, publishers, and public alike heave a sigh of relief that it is ended, at least for another year. A number of factors have contributed to this unfortunate situation. Over a period of 100 years or more there were land scandals; improper granting of corporate charters; the reconstruction legislatures; the evils of special legislation and the undermining of the credit of many states, sometimes accompanied later by a repudiation of the debt; scandals in connection with the construction of state capitol buildings; and finally, limitations of legislative personnel and improper relations with persons and groups desiring legislation.

The land scandals, once frequent, no longer occur, partly because of higher standards of public morality and partly because there are no more lands open for development. As early as 1810 a flagrant piece of dishonesty committed by the legislature of Georgia fifteen years before brought to the Supreme Court of the United States the interesting case of Fletcher v. Peck.[25] The legislature had granted a large tract of public land under circumstances which the Court agreed were wholly reprehensible; when the facts became known, an incensed electorate returned to office a new legislative personnel pledged to the revocation of the grant. The Supreme Court said in effect that corruption was unfortunate but that the act of a preceding legislature was in the nature of a contract between the state and the persons to whom the grant was made. The rights of those who subsequently purchased portions of this land could not be affected by the fraud. The state could not, therefore, regain control over this land, since doing so would violate the obligation of contract clause in Article I, Section 10. Situations such as this were by no means uncommon.

It is well known that the corporate form of business organization owed its origin to the necessity of securing capital in large amounts for railway construction, beginning in the third decade of the nineteenth century. Gradually this form of organization was extended to other forms of business enterprise. Before the enactment of general incorporation laws, legislatures were accustomed to create corporations by special act. Under the doctrine of the Dartmouth College Case, the privileges and grants of power conferred by these charters endured through all time, without any compensation in

[24] Bryce, James, *The American Commonwealth*, First Edition, Vol. 1, Chapter 40; for a comment on this, see Reinhold, Frances L., in Brooks, Robert C., Ed., *Bryce's "American Commonwealth,"* Chapter 2 (Macmillan, New York, 1939).

[25] 6 Cranch, 87, 1810.

any form coming back to the state. Rights, privileges, and property worth hundreds of thousands — and in some cases millions — of dollars were granted by corrupt legislatures as political favors.

The abuses characteristic of the reconstruction legislatures in the Southern states have already been described. The growing evil of special legislation constituted an additional cause of the declining confidence in which legislative bodies were held. The legislatures expended money and incurred enormous state debts with wanton extravagance; later, when the repayment of these loans became difficult and embarrassing, they were sometimes repudiated. More detailed discussion of this problem is reserved for a later chapter. Throughout the period during which most of the present state capitol buildings were constructed, scarcely a state escaped without evidence of gross fraud and corruption. Some of the buildings were fine, but they regularly cost the taxpayers two or three times as much as they legitimately should. Papier-mâché was substituted for oak paneling, composition materials for costly marbles, furniture was sold by the cubic yard, and inferior grades of goods were supplied at exorbitant prices — all with legislative knowledge and often with legislative connivance.[26] No one of these incidents alone, or no one type of them alone, would have brought about such a decline of public esteem for legislatures as actually occurred; the result was due to the cumulative effect of instances of nearly every type in nearly every state over a long period.

Added to all these factors was the generally inferior caliber of the legislators themselves. Mediocrity was and, in many instances, is common. Not only have many of the members lacked native intelligence and the educational background necessary for effective legislative work, but many of them have been indifferent in the performance of their duties, and not a small number have been actually corrupt. The indifferent ones do not know and do not care what provisions the measures before them contain; they vote for or against them, regardless of their merits, as they have been instructed to do by party leaders or interest groups to whom they are under obligation.

Such was the state of affairs at the turn of the century. In the last two decades there has been a notable improvement, due to increased popular interest in public affairs, to a greater realization of the importance of the

[26] For example, the main building of the Pennsylvania State Capitol was destroyed by fire in 1897; in 1901 the legislature appropriated $4,000,000 for a new building. For the furnishing and decoration, $8,601,922 was expended; the cost of the decorations alone was $7,720,855, while the building cost $3,932,978. The total cost without furniture was $11,653,833. When a new State Treasurer took office in 1906, he discovered a disparity between the cost and amount appropriated. Charges of graft and dishonesty were made and the 1907 legislature authorized an investigation. The net loss to the state through furniture manipulation was about $4,000,000, but the gross loss disclosed at the investigation, plus the trials of the several defendants, was $5,600,000. Apparently the actual contractors received about $1,400,000, the difference going to the conspirators. On the general problem of this section, see Nickerson, Hoffman, "The Twilight of Legislatures," *American Mercury*, February 1930, pp. 129–136.

states, to higher standards of political ethics, and in no small measure to active agencies working for the improvement of legislation. As state governments have been reorganized and improved, men of greater ability and better character have been willing to devote their time and energy to legislative work. Much has been accomplished since 1925, when the American Legislators' Association began its work; since then the legislative council movement has gained momentum, and much thought has been given to the improvement of the legislative process.

Descriptive Features of the Two Houses

Attention may now be given to the descriptive features of the state legislatures — their size, term, compensation, and other related matters. The reader should have available for convenient reference the comparative tables on the legislative branch in the current edition of the Council of State Government's *Book of the States.*

Forty-seven of the forty-eight states have an upper chamber known officially as the Senate. Thirty-nine states call the lower chamber the House of Representatives. Of the remaining nine states, one, Nebraska, has since 1937 had a single chamber called the Legislature. The lower house in California, Nevada, New York, and Wisconsin is called the Assembly; in New Jersey, the General Assembly; and in Maryland, Virginia, and West Virginia, the House of Delegates. Exactly half the states call the two bodies together the Legislature; nineteen use the term General Assembly[27]; Massachusetts and New Hampshire call theirs the General Court; while Montana, North Dakota, and Oregon use the name Legislative Assembly.

Size. The smallest senates are in Delaware and Nevada, with 17 members each; the largest are in Minnesota, with 67, and Montana, with 56. Nine senates have less than 30 members, and only nine have 50 or more. Eighteen have between 30 and 39, twelve between 40 and 49. The smallest lower houses are in Delaware, with 35 members, and Nevada, with 43; the largest in New Hampshire, with 399, and in Connecticut, with 277. The distribution by groups is as follows:

SIZE RANGE OF LOWER HOUSES

50 or less	2 states
51 to 100	22 states
101 to 150	14 states
151 to 200	3 states
201 to 300	5 states
301 to 400	1 state

The largest lower houses are found in the New England states, with relatively small populations and large numbers of districts, each member standing for a small constituency. Delaware and Nevada naturally have the

[27] These are: Arkansas, Colorado, Connecticut, Delaware, Georgia, Illinois, Indiana, Iowa, Kentucky, Maryland, Missouri, North Carolina, Ohio, Pennsylvania, Rhode Island, South Carolina, Tennessee, Vermont, and Virginia.

smallest totals, with 52 and 57, respectively, while Connecticut and New Hampshire have the largest, with 308 and 423, respectively. The total number of legislators shows a slight tendency to decline. In 1951, there were in the country 1,792 senators and 5,683 representatives — 7,475 legislators in all. The average numbers per state — 37,121, and 155, respectively, for the senate, the house, and the legislature as a whole — have remained practically constant for a number of years. In all states except Louisiana and Maine members are elected on the first Tuesday after the first Monday in November.

Qualifications of Members. The constitutions are specific regarding age qualifications for membership in the lower house, stating either that a person shall be twenty-one years old or that he shall be a duly qualified elector. Age qualifications for membership in the upper house differ widely. Alabama, Iowa, Oklahoma, and other states specify twenty-five years; Texas, twenty-six; while others have but one age qualification for members of both houses. In some states these qualifications must be met at the time of election (Alabama, Oklahoma, and Texas), in others at the time of taking office (Iowa and Maine), and in New Jersey one year next before election. The requirement of citizenship is uniform; the constitutions state either that a person must be a citizen to hold a seat in either house or that he must be a duly qualified elector. There is considerable variation with regard to length of citizenship. Maine specifies five years; Alabama and California, three; New Jersey, two; while other states have no such requirement. All the states have residence requirements for membership in either house, either express or implied, ranging from one year to five years. Prospective members must fulfill these requirements "one year next before their election" in Alabama, California, New Jersey, and Ohio; "one year next preceding their election" in Maine and Texas; and at the time of election in Iowa.

The constitutions are also specific in stating conditions which make a person ineligible to membership in the legislature. In Alabama, California, Nevada, Ohio, and Oklahoma, no person who has been convicted of embezzlement or defalcation of public funds, of bribery, perjury, or other infamous crime, or who has been adjudged guilty of a felony, may hold a seat in the legislature. No such restrictions are found, however, in Florida, Iowa, Maine, New Jersey, or Texas. All of the states here mentioned except Alabama enumerate those offices, which, when held, create ineligibility for membership in the legislature. The offices most frequently mentioned include positions under the government of the United States or of any state, and positions as collectors or holders of public moneys, judges of any court or clerk of any court of records, sheriffs, justices of the peace, secretary of state, or attorney general. Service in the armed forces is a disqualification for legislative membership in many states on the ground of dual officeholding.[28]

[28] See Illinois Legislative Council, *Service in the Armed Forces as a Disqualification for Legislative Membership* (Springfield, 1942). In 1940 the California legislature passed a law, which the Attorney General thought might be unconstitutional, providing for a leave of absence for military service.

Length of Term. Members of the senate are elected for a four-year term in thirty-two states; in fifteen states, including all six in New England, they are elected for a two-year term.[29] Nebraska, with its single chamber, elects for two years. Senators serve for one regular session in thirteen states; for two regular sessions in twenty-nine states; and for four regular sessions in five states — California, Colorado, Maryland, New Jersey, and South Carolina. In seven states, the regular session service for which a senator is elected is limited to sixty days. In the lower house, the term is two years in forty-one states. Alabama, Louisiana, Maryland, and Mississippi elect for four years. There are only ten states in which representatives serve in two regular sessions of the legislature, but there are twenty-eight states with four-year senators and two-year representatives. Four Southern states — Alabama, Louisiana, Maryland, and Mississippi — have four-year senators and four-year representatives.

Compensation. The question of the compensation of legislators has long been difficult and troublesome. In the early stages of the development of popular government there was no compensation; the fact that representation was permitted at all was, for many classes and groups, a great victory. It was an honor to serve. Sooner or later, as the newness wore off, those who were elected discovered that it cost money to travel back and forth to the seat of government, to maintain oneself while there, and to be absent for days at a time from one's regular calling. Before any compensation for members was secured, the situation became so serious that none but the wealthy were financially able to serve. Even when compensation was authorized, it was not always paid by the state, local communities being expected to supply stipends when necessary.[30]

In our own time the per diem basis of compensation was first employed. When the public gathered the impression that sessions were unnecessarily prolonged — whether or not this was true — there developed the tendency either to limit the number of days of the session or to adopt lump-sum payments for an unlimited session. At the present time there are still seventeen states on a per diem basis. Some states do not limit the length of session but do limit the number of days for which compensation or full compensation may be drawn. Although public sentiment has long tended to view with disapproval any attempt to increase the salaries or other compensation of legislators, the exigencies of the economic situation during and after World War II have made necessary the liberalization of provisions regarding compensation in many jurisdictions. Sixteen states increased the pay of their legislators in 1949, and others have done so since. The amount of compensation is set by the constitution in all but fifteen states, in which it is subject to legis-

[29] These are: Arizona, Connecticut, Georgia, Idaho, Maine, Massachusetts, Michigan, New Hampshire, New York, North Carolina, Ohio, Rhode Island, South Dakota, Tennessee, and Vermont.

[30] Handlin, *op. cit.*, p. 267.

lative determination. Such a matter should have no place in the constitution.

In very few states may the amount of compensation be considered anything like adequate, even after taking recent increases into account. Members are indeed fortunate if they are even reimbursed for expenses. An Oregon Senator reported in 1947 that he was obliged to hire his own secretary, paying her more than twice as much as he himself received as a member of the Senate. As Henry W. Toll pointed out many years ago:

> State legislators are partially or entirely reimbursed for their living expenses during the session, but almost none of them receive any compensation for their services. In short, the typical law-maker devotes to his legislative work almost his entire time during the weeks of the session, and a great deal of time during the many other months of his term. But he receives nothing for any of this time.[31]

Twenty-five of the thirty-one lump-sum states hold biennial sessions, the amount of compensation ranging from $200 in New Hampshire to $3,000 in Illinois. The other six states hold annual sessions and pay from $1,000 to $5,000 to their legislators each year. Fifteen of these states pay their members $1,000 or less per session. The daily allowances in the per diem states range from $4 to $25; three states pay $5, and seven pay $10. There are only three or four of the seventeen "in which the legislator's entire payment amounts to more than a moderate allowance for living expenses — during the session only." Mileage allowances ranging from five to twenty cents per mile exist in all the states except North Carolina, the usual rate being ten cents. A few states grant allowances for postage.

In addition to having such a ridiculously low compensation in most states, each member must meet the expenses involved in his electoral campaign.[32] It may be that the states cannot offer to able men the same compensation which they could earn in their regular business or profession, but they can and should pay enough so that members will not be obliged to undergo actual financial loss. They should offer enough to make it possible for persons of moderate means but with ability and an interest in public affairs to serve without financial embarrassment to themselves and their families. If, in most states, a drastic reduction in the number of members was made, a considerable increase in compensation per member could be made without additional cost to the state. If in addition the job of legislator were made a full-time job, as it should be at least in the larger states, such states would be justified in offering a compensation sufficient to enable a

[31] Toll, Henry W., "Should We Pay Law-Makers?" *State Government*, February 1931, pp. 10–13.

[32] In 1949, the *New York Times* reported (February 13) a plan of the AFL's League for Political Education to put state legislators on its payroll so that labor sympathizers could afford lawmaking jobs. While this is obviously not the right way to meet what is clearly a public responsibility, many of those who were shocked at the suggestion appeared to forget that labor was only proposing to do what management has been doing, in one form or another, for years.

member to maintain his family at a decent standard, in conformity with living costs in the state or in the section of the country in which the state is located.

Retirement. Since Congress, in the Legislative Reorganization Act of 1946, extended the benefits of the Federal Civil Service Retirement System to its members, sixteen states have extended retirement benefits to legislators, as shown in the table appearing on page 215.[33] With the exception of Illinois and California, which have gone further than other states by providing retirement benefits for legislators through a system designed to meet their peculiar needs, the states have extended benefits to legislators by incorporating them into retirement systems for regular civil service employees. These state contributory systems, originally designed to remove superannuated employees from the state service by the establishment of deferred payments, may tend to offset in part the effects of the very low salaries paid to legislators in most states. The additional security and income derived from a retirement plan appealed to elected administrative officials as well as to civil service employees; the former brought pressure to be included in these systems during the twenties and thirties. State systems were thus gradually extended to include both state and local elected officials.

Legislators in more than one third of the states have, as elected officials, claimed the benefits of state systems in all but seven instances. In Massachusetts, Pennsylvania, Rhode Island, and South Carolina, the term public "employee" has been redefined to include all "persons whose regular compensation is paid" by the state. The New York statute extends the benefits of the state system to legislators specifically, instead of covering them as "elected officials" or "employees." Illinois and California, as noted, have established separate systems for legislators. The provisions of the state systems possess a number of common characteristics:

1. They are optional on the part of the legislator, requiring in most states either an application for membership or, as in Illinois and South Carolina, positive action against becoming a member.
2. Provided they make all back payments or contributions, legislators may in all states except Illinois count all previous public service, legislative or otherwise, toward retirement. South Carolina gives credit for all service as legislators prior to 1945 without cost to the members.
3. There is no compulsory retirement age for legislators, most systems specifically exempting legislators from the compulsory retirement age applying to public employees.
4. In all but five states (Massachusetts, Nevada, and New York at fifty-five, New Mexico at sixty-five, California at sixty-three) sixty is the retirement age, but additional accumulations are permitted beyond that age if the legislator wishes to remain in service.
5. There are minimum service requirements for retirement benefits in many states: Ohio, five years; Massachusetts, six years; Illinois, eight years; Florida,

[33] See Hawaii Legislative Reference Service, *Retirement Systems for Legislators* (Honolulu, 1949), and comment in the report of the American Political Science Association's Committee on American Legislatures, published in 1953.

Montana, and South Carolina, ten years; New Mexico, fifteen years; New York, twenty years; and Georgia, thirty-five years.

6. All plans are contributory, ranging from a low of 3.5 per cent in Montana to 7 per cent in Illinois. State contributions, invariably made by annual state appropriations, range from actuarial needs to a fixed sum as high as 7.2 per cent in California.

7. In all states legislators may withdraw their own contributions, but not those of the state, when they discontinue their legislative service. In all states (except Florida, Georgia, Illinois, Nevada, Rhode Island, in which no interest on contributions may be withdrawn) legislators may receive interest on contributions upon withdrawal. New Jersey, Pennsylvania, and South Carolina allow as much as 4 per cent upon the legislator's contributions.

Retirement Benefits for Legislators

YEAR	STATES
1947	Illinois, Massachusetts, Montana, Nevada, New Mexico, New York, Pennsylvania, Rhode Island
1949	California, Florida, Georgia, Washington
Legislators "covered in" by amendment of previous legislation of:	
1922	New Jersey
1935	Ohio
1943	South Carolina
1945	Maryland

The amount of the annual retirement payments depends upon a number of factors, such as the accumulated fund including interest, years of service, age of the recipient, and age at retirement. Payments are usually distributed according to a previously determined actuarial plan. It is difficult, however, to determine what legislators may expect from these plans in operation. In Illinois a legislator, upon reaching the retirement age of sixty, will receive after ten years' service, 25 per cent of his final salary or $750 (based on present salaries); after twenty years' service, 50 per cent of his final salary or $1,500. After a minimum of six years' service in the legislature, a Massachusetts legislator, on reaching the age of fifty-five, may receive $1,200 per year; after twenty years' public service, which may include nonlegislative service, he may receive $3,000 annually. While these payments may seem sizable in states which pay relatively high annual salaries, retirement benefits in states which follow the practice of per diem payments are of little consequence because of the small opportunity to build an annuity fund. For example, both Florida and Montana extend retirement benefits but legislators do not think it worth the effort to apply for them.

The impact of retirement plans upon the tenure of legislators has not been measured as yet. It is noticeable that legislators serve for longer terms in the states that pay more adequately. Provisions for retirement should act as a further inducement. There are other implications. For example, a study conducted in Illinois in 1948 revealed that of the 204 members of the legislature, 190 elected to join the retirement system. The average age of this group was 54.6, the mean 55. The average service was ten years. In 1948, half of the members of this legislature were eligible for retirement, in terms of length of service, would meet the age requirement within three years, and would be entitled to $750 annually.[34] Will these legislators prefer to retire to their own pursuits on a pension or to continue longer as legislators with the possibility of larger pensions? For obvious reasons, retirement plans may have a different effect upon legislators than upon civil service employees.

Working Conditions. A very serious obstacle to effective legislative work is the absence of suitable working conditions for members. There are elaborate, ornate, and expensive meeting chambers, but there are few offices or conference rooms or facilities for work, except that in about one fourth of the states provision is made for legislative officers and/or committee chairmen. Ordinary members are fortunate if they have lockers in which to leave their coats and hats during sessions. There are caucus rooms and a very small number of committee rooms, but not enough to accommodate a fourth of the standing committees at the same time. The same situation existed in Washington until the House and Senate office buildings were constructed. It may be that few states would be able to provide comparable facilities for their legislators, but some effort should be made to provide suitable working conditions, at least for the officers and for the chairmen of committees. The situation could be improved in most states, without public opposition, by moving the executive departments and agencies into other quarters, leaving the space in the capitol available to the legislature.

The conditions with regard to clerical and secretarial assistance, though improved somewhat during the last decade, are serious because many of the members are accustomed to good offices and secretarial assistance at home. When they are deprived of both at the capitol, their mail must either go unanswered or be taken care of at home on their own time and at their own expense. Most states now furnish clerical and secretarial assistance to all committees, the remainder limiting this service to major committees. One fourth of the legislatures provide members with no secretarial assistance whatever; others maintain a secretarial pool available to all members or provide stenographic, clerical, and typing assistance to legislative leaders only.[35]

Recent progress in the field of communications has raised new questions regarding legislative recording, broadcasting, and televising. Broadcasting of parts of the legislative proceedings appears to be well established in

[34] General Assembly Retirement System of Illinois, *First Annual Statement of the Board of Trustees, June 30, 1948.*

[35] Based on data collected by Herbert L. Wiltsee, Council of State Governments, for the American Political Science Association's Committee on American Legislatures.

Arkansas, Georgia, and Virginia. In the 1951 sessions, the Oklahoma legislature was telecast on a regular schedule, while in West Virginia, the legislature experimented with tape recording. Although the reaction has apparently been favorable in these states, putting legislative proceedings on the air is an innovation, regarding the merits of which there is still much difference of opinion.[36] Speaker Rayburn in the spring of 1952 ruled out newsreel, television, and radio coverage ("live" or tape-recorded) of House committee hearings (although the hearings of the Senate Crime Investigating Committee were telecast).

Privileges and Immunities of Members. A typical statement showing the nature and extent of the privileges and immunities of members of a legislature appears in Section 48 of the Virginia Constitution:

> Members of the General Assembly shall, in all cases, except treason, felony, or breach of the peace, be privileged from arrest during the sessions of their respective houses; and for any speech or debate in either house shall not be questioned in any other place. They shall not be subject to arrest, under any civil process, during the sessions of the General Assembly, or the fifteen days next before the beginning or after the ending of any session.

To these privileges commonly guaranteed by the constitution there may be added numerous others under the provisions of the rules of the house. Members have the right to recognition to speak, subject to such limitations as may have been imposed upon debate, the right of the speaker to decide who is entitled to the floor, and the requirement that they confine their remarks to the subject under discussion; but they may be called to order for transgressing the rules, for the use of offensive language, and for improper conduct. Ordinarily they may not absent themselves from the sessions without a leave of absence voted by their colleagues.

Members are subject during the session to the discipline of the house to which they belong for conduct unbecoming a member.[37] While legislative officers are not subject to impeachment, they may be expelled by a two-thirds vote of the house to which they belong; after expulsion they are subject to indictment and proceedings for any criminal offenses with which they may have been charged. Ordinarily, members will not be denied their seats even if they have a criminal record, if the offenses were committed prior to the date of election. The theory seems to be that if an electorate is stupid enough

[36] See Illinois Legislative Council, *Legislative Broadcasting and Recording* (Springfield, 1952); Day, William L., "Legislative Broadcasting and Recording," *State Government*, October 1952, pp. 225–226, 238; Flannery, William E., "Legislative Tape Recording — West Virginia," *ibid.*, September 1951, pp. 238–239; and Harkey, Paul, "Televising the Legislature in Oklahoma," *ibid.*, October 1951, pp. 249–250, 260.

[37] Determination of what constitutes such conduct often raises interesting questions. In October 1948, the Arizona House expelled two members on the ground that their actions were offensive to other members. It was charged that the pair engaged in "constant personal vilification and impugning of motives of the members of the Legislature" and that they intentionally aroused the "passion and prejudice of groups which are unable to care for themselves, thus trafficking in human misery, to enhance their own personal popularity."

to elect such a person, the legislature has no right to exclude him. Nor do the houses of the legislature have the right to impose qualifications for membership in addition to those prescribed by the constitution. The question of the age of an elected member is seldom raised. Each house is the judge of contests affecting its members.

In all states technical questions arise from time to time in connection with the interpretation of these general rules. While they are fundamentally sound, at least from the long-time point of view, their application sometimes produces strange results, which may incense the public. It is generally true that an individual who has been declared elected and whose election was free from fraud is entitled to his seat.

Officers. Each house has a presiding officer, known in the lower house as the speaker and in the senate as the president, a chief clerk or a secretary, a sergeant at arms, and numerous minor officials. The major officers are chosen by vote of the members, while minor officers are appointed either by the elective officers, or, as in Wisconsin, under civil service rules.

The speaker, or president, must maintain order during sessions and conduct the business of the session both on and off the floor. Upon the advice of his parliamentarian, he decides all points of order, subject to appeal and the possibility of being overruled by the house. He may call upon members to preside in his temporary absence from the chair; in most states he may appoint standing and special committees and act as chairman of the Committee of the Whole. He has control over the journals, papers, and bills of the house. When necessary, he may order the lobby and galleries cleared, assign desks to properly accredited newspaper representatives, and perform any other duties pertaining to his office as are prescribed by law or by rule of the house.

The chief clerk or secretary has charge of all clerical work and of the printing for the house. He must see that the journals, other publications, and records are properly kept; read or allow his assistants to read from the desk such matter as the speaker or the house shall direct; exercise general supervision over all clerks, attachés, and employees, and be responsible for their official acts and their performance of their regular duties. He must perform all duties pertaining to his office as prescribed by law or by rule of the house.

It is the duty of the sergeant at arms to attend all sessions, preserve order, guard the doors when so directed, announce all official messengers, and serve all processes issued by the house and directed by the speaker. He must see that the house chamber and the committee rooms are kept clean, heated and ventilated, and open for the use of members at all necessary times. He has assistants as required, and is responsible for their supervision. He must perform all duties pertaining to his office as prescribed by law or by rule of the house.

Sessions

Regular Sessions. There are four types of sessions — regular, special, split, and adjourned — the first two or all of which may be permissible in any given state. Regular sessions are most frequent and most important; they represent the normal procedure. There are thirty-eight states that hold regular sessions biennially, beginning in January of the odd-numbered years. Ten states — Arizona, California, Colorado, Maryland, Massachusetts, Michigan, New Jersey, New York, Rhode Island, and South Carolina — hold annual sessions. It thus happens that in odd-numbered years nearly all the state legislatures will be in session about the same time. Most of the original state constitutions provided for annual sessions; "gradually, however, biennial sessions were substituted for the annual ones — a trend which was an outgrowth of the distrust of the lawmaking machinery which developed during the nineteenth century and which resulted in the drastic limitations on the length of sessions of the legislature which are found in many states. The theory behind these restrictions seems to have been that since legislatures are necessary evils, they should be allowed as little time as possible in which to do this work. The movement to shift from annual to biennial legislative sessions came to an end in the 1880's"; only two states since then have substituted a session every two years for one every year, and one of these later rescinded its action.[38] The current trend seems definitely to favor a return to annual sessions, several states having recently decided to hold annual rather than biennial sessions.

Special Sessions. In all states the governor is authorized by the constitution to summon the legislature in special session when, in his judgment, the circumstances require it. In seventeen states he has complete control over the number and character of the subjects to be considered in such sessions, by virtue of his authority to include or omit them from the call. Whether the number be one or a dozen, the legislature is prohibited by the constitution from the consideration of bills dealing with other subjects. Eleven states permit the governor to recommend during the special session, by special message, matters in addition to those contained in the proclamation convening the legislature. Only three states — Alabama, Arkansas, and Florida — permit the legislature itself to suggest the consideration of additional business while in special session, and such permission is considered

[38] By constitutional amendment, Georgia made the change in 1924, Massachusetts in 1938, voting a return to an annual session in 1944. Alabama changed from a quadrennial to a biennial session in 1943; see Martin, Roscoe C., "Alabama Falls in Line," *State Government*, March 1940, pp. 43–44, 63, and Pow, Alex S., "Alabama's New Legislative Process in Action," *ibid.*, December 1943, pp. 246–247. See Worrell, Dorothy, *Annual or Biennial Sessions for Massachusetts* (Boston, 1938); Special Commission on Biennial Sessions and Biennial Budgets, *Report* (Massachusetts House Documents, No. 2551, 1938); Wisconsin Legislative Reference Library, *Annual vs. Biennial Legislative Sessions* (Madison, May 1951); and McGeary, M. Nelson, "Changes in Legislative Sessions," *Temple Law Quarterly*, April 1952, pp. 449–459.

upon a two-thirds vote of each house.[39] In some states, to be sure, the courts have given a liberal interpretation of these provisions, thereby authorizing legislation on subjects naturally and closely related to those specifically enumerated.

The number of extra sessions during the decade of the thirties was greatly increased by the repeal of Amendment XVIII, the unemployment and relief situation, and the financial problems resulting therefrom. The study of annual and biennial sessions referred to above attempted to discover the extent to which special sessions were employed in the two types of states. "During the seven and a half year period from January, 1927, to July, 1934, 158 special sessions have been called in the United States. . . . During this period, eighteen of the 158 special sessions were held in the five states having annual sessions. It should be observed, however, that five of the eighteen occurred in New Jersey in the single year 1931. The five states with biennial sessions which may be compared to those having annual sessions found it necessary to call their legislators together on the average of six years out of eight. Annual sessions would have meant for those states a meeting of the legislature in two additional years during this eight year period." The number of special sessions each year rose gradually to forty-three in 1933, thirty-eight in 1934, and forty-six in 1938. From 1927 to 1940 inclusive, Illinois and Texas had nineteen each; Louisiana, fourteen; Ohio, twelve; Arizona and Kentucky, ten each. The remaining forty-two states each had less than ten. Nevada had one, New Jersey nine, with the rest quite evenly distributed in the range from two to eight. The practice of holding frequent special sessions now seems to be firmly established in many states.

Split Sessions. The split session, used for a number of years in California, was adopted in New Mexico in 1940. It was formerly used in West Virginia, and one such session was reported in Georgia. Under this plan the legislature meets for a month for purposes of organization, introduction of bills, et cetera. At the expiration of this period there follows a recess of a month; it was intended that this period would enable the members to study the contents of bills which had been introduced and upon which they would be required to vote at a later date, and to determine the sentiment of their constituencies regarding important legislation. Within the last few years able students of government have made special studies of the operation of this system.[40] Their independent judgments have been that this plan has not

[39] New York State Constitutional Convention Committee, *Problems Relating to Legislative Organization and Powers*, p. 405 (Albany, 1938). Chapter 13 discusses the question, Shall the legislature have the power to convene itself in extraordinary session? and lists the subjects contained in the governor's calls for eighteen special sessions held in New York in the forty-year period from 1898 to 1938. This number of special sessions in an annual-session state is significant. See also Fertig, John H., *Scope of the Legislative Power of the General Assembly* — when convened in special session — (Pennsylvania Legislative Reference Bureau, Harrisburg, 1931).

[40] West, Victor J., "California — the Home of the Split Session," *National Municipal Review*, July 1923, pp. 369–376; Faust, Martin L., "Results of the Split-Session System of

produced legislative accomplishments of a higher order than are to be found in states operating under the usual plan. Professor Barclay points out that in California the operation of the plan since it was adopted by constitutional amendment in 1911 has resulted in the introduction of skeleton bills in considerable number; it has created a pre-recess rush not dissimilar to the familiar rush at the end of the session — which, incidentally, it has not eliminated; and it appears that constituents are in fact rarely consulted. "During the period 1915–1929, post-recess introductions averaged at each session 200 bills for the 120 members." The older and more experienced legislators are practically unanimous in desiring its abolition or modification; numerous proposals toward this end have been introduced, but the necessary majorities to secure their adoption have not been forthcoming.

Adjourned Sessions. Where the device of the split session is used, it is based upon a constitutional provision; the same result can be achieved by action of the legislature itself without any constitutional provision by the use of what is known as the adjourned session. This device has been used in a number of states. "The financial condition of Tennessee presented such a difficult problem [in 1931] that the legislature adjourned on March 20 for recess until May 25, to give the State Investigating Committee time to consider its work." [41] The legislatures of several other states recess for a month or more during sessions; among these are Alabama, Georgia, Ohio, Pennsylvania, and Texas. Recourse to this device in Ohio seems to have been rather frequent. Dean Crawford reports an interesting case, in which, for political reasons, the legislature took a thirty-minute recess — a recess which in fact extended from March 27, 1925, until January 15, 1926, when the members reassembled for a one-day session, after which another recess was taken.

Executive Sessions. The term "executive session" is not concerned with the duration of the meeting or the time at which it is held, but rather with its essential character. Ordinarily, all legislative sessions are open — that is, members of the public are allowed in the chamber as spectators (only former members may go on the floor) as long as there is room and as long as they remain quiet and orderly. An executive session is held behind closed doors for the purpose of considering nominations sent in by the governor for confirmation. There has been a good deal of criticism of this practice on the ground that it violates the principles of democratic government, and at least one state — Michigan — amended its senate rules in 1942 to require a two-thirds vote rather than a simple majority to place that body in executive session.

Weekly Schedule of Meetings. The weekly schedule of meetings is quite

---

the West Virginia Legislature," *American Political Science Review*, February 1928, pp. 109–121; Barclay, Thomas S., "Bifurcation Out West," *State Government*, April 1932, pp. 5–6, and "The Split Session of the California Legislature," *California Law Review*, November 1931, pp. 43–59.

[41] See note in *State Government*, May 1931, pp. 5–6.

different from that prevailing in Congress, where, under ordinary circumstances, daily sessions are held. Practice in the states varies, but it is customary for the state legislatures to convene some time Monday evening for a session which may extend into the early morning hours. By this arrangement members are able to make the trip to the state capitol from their homes during the day. Many arrive at noon or shortly thereafter, devoting the afternoon to conferences and committee appointments. The same use is commonly made of Tuesday and Wednesday forenoons. On these days sessions will begin at eleven or twelve o'clock and continue until late in the afternoon. Evening sessions, similar to the one on Monday, will occur on Tuesday evening and sometimes on Wednesday. The majority of the members have returned to their homes late Wednesday night or Thursday, except in the last week or two of the session, when it may be necessary to continue meetings later in the week. This peculiar schedule is more or less necessary because the work of a legislator is only a part-time job with compensation limited accordingly; it enables members to spend the week end at home, and to exercise some supervision over their business or professional activities — which are usually, during the session, rather seriously neglected. The following paragraphs from a representative in New Hampshire, which has the largest legislature in America, will show how this system works in that state:

> In the first place, New Hampshire is a rather small state geographically, although the largest legislatively. All but a dozen of our members can reach the capitol by eleven o'clock in the forenoon if they leave their homes early in the same morning, and can reach home by evening if they leave the capitol at noon. The state pays all traveling expenses. Even a very busy man, therefore, can afford to serve his turn as a legislator without serious sacrifice in New Hampshire; there is such a short distance to travel that little time is lost, and the state assumes the expenses.
>
> We begin our week's work on Tuesday at 11 A.M. with a short session, which rarely lasts more than an hour. At about 1 P.M. committee hearings begin; they are suspended at 3 P.M. for a second short session of each house after which the hearings are continued until 5 P.M. On Wednesday morning, hearings begin at 9:30 or 10 A.M. and continue until 11 A.M., when a general session is held. On Wednesday afternoon, the Tuesday afternoon schedule is repeated. In cases of extended debate, the 11 o'clock session may be prolonged to as late as 1 P.M. In that event, a recess is taken for lunch until 2 P.M., when the House discussion is again renewed — and the regular 3 o'clock session is delayed until 4 or 5 o'clock. The regular schedule, however, is altered but slightly; the 1 o'clock hearings for that day are simply eliminated. Thursday, the procedure of Wednesday is followed except that the work of the afternoon is advanced to the 11 o'clock session by a suspension of the rules; and that session adjourns at noon. Thus ends the week's work. Our Constitution provides that an adjournment shall not be taken for more than two days at a time. To conform to this provision, there are perfunctory sessions, by general agreement, on Friday morning and Monday evening, but these are usually attended by the clerk, the speaker pro tem, and only a few other members.
>
> In this way our fifteen-week session dwindles to forty-five actual legislative days. As individuals, we devote Tuesdays, Wednesdays, and Thursdays to

the affairs of the State, and Fridays, Saturdays, Sundays, and Mondays to our private interests at home.[42]

Length of Sessions. Many states impose a constitutional limit of sixty days on the length of legislative sessions. In the effort to control the abuses which developed under the system of per diem compensation, the states began to adopt a flat salary compensation for an unlimited session, or if the per diem method of compensation was retained, they limited the length of the session. In eighteen states regular sessions are limited to sixty days, while in twenty-one there is no limitation whatever. The remaining nine have limitations ranging from forty days in Oregon and Wyoming to 150 days in Connecticut.[43] Thirty-three states do not limit the length of special sessions. Six states impose a limit of twenty days, six others a limit of thirty days. Arkansas sets the limit at fifteen days, Indiana at forty, and South Dakota at sixty. A "day" is variously defined by the courts, by custom, or by the constitution as a calendar day, in seventeen states, and as a meeting day, in twelve.

Much criticism has been heaped upon the limited session plan; in practice there is probably little to choose between limited and unlimited sessions. The criticism of the limited session has been based mainly upon the terrific jam which clogs the legislative machinery in the closing days of the session. While there is much justification for this criticism, precisely the same thing happens where the session is limited not by constitutional provision, but by agreement of the leaders. The same dilatory tactics are followed in both cases in the early days of the session. In states with unlimited sessions, members begin to be impatient and to demand an early closing. In the effort to keep them in line, the leaders arbitrarily set a closing date and then struggle to work their way out of a legislative jam just as severe in many cases as that which develops in states with a limited session.

The Committee System

As the number and scope of governmental activities have increased, the task of the legislature has become more and more difficult, and the need for legislative committees has correspondingly increased. Economists talk much about the division of labor in industry; the committee system applies this principle to the process of legislation. The number of subjects with which a legislature must deal is large; the number of bills which it must handle is even greater. It would be a physical impossibility for any one member to familiarize himself with the provisions of all the measures introduced. There is, however, some subject or type of subject in which different members are interested and with regard to which they can express competent judgment.

[42] Duncan, George H., "418 in One House," *State Government*, April 1931, pp. 11–12.

[43] Data from New York State Constitutional Convention Committee, *op. cit.*, p. 396; Alabama and Kansas, fifty days; Indiana, sixty-one days; Tennessee, sixty-five days; Maryland and Minnesota, ninety days.

The committee system affords a member an opportunity to work on legislative subjects in which he is most interested and concerning which he is best informed; it gives the legislature the benefit of such wisdom and experience as its members may have, and it affords citizens and citizens' organizations an opportunity to present their case before legislation is enacted.

A number of important questions with regard to the operation of the committee system suggest themselves. How many committees are there, and on what subjects? How are the members commonly selected? How many members serve on the ordinary committee, and is this number more or less than it should be? How does the system operate, and is its operation reasonably satisfactory? It is difficult, in limited space, to give adequate answers to these questions, but some brief comment regarding them may be made.

Number of Committees; Selection of Members. The table on page 225 shows the number of standing committees in both houses of the legislature in each of the forty-eight states as of 1931, 1941, and 1951. The number of senate committees ranges from ten in Rhode Island to forty-seven in New Jersey, and fifty-four in North Carolina. In the lower house, the range is from eleven in South Carolina (including three joint committees) to fifty-one each in North Carolina and South Dakota, fifty-five in Mississippi, sixty-five in Missouri, seventy-one in Kentucky. Thus the variation in both chambers is wide. In some chambers the number has been purposely raised in order that most of the members of the body may serve as chairman of a committee — in which case most of the work is done by a few important committees, the others being used to placate politically ambitious members who insist on some kind of committee chairmanship.[44] The names of standing committees in any state may be found in the legislative manual; for illustrative purposes the list for Nebraska is included here, together with a proposed standard list (see page 226).

The comparative data in the table on page 225 show a slight tendency for the number of committees in both houses to decrease. If the number of committees is large in one house in a given state, it is usually large in the other also. Using 1931 as a base, the number of house committees had decreased by fifty-nine in 1941, and by another 175 by 1951 — 334 in twenty years. The total had been decreased by thirty when Nebraska changed from a two-chamber to a one-chamber system in 1937. The senate committees, which had decreased by thirty-eight up to 1941, showed a still further decrease of 151 by 1951 — 189 in the twenty-year period. It is significant that the greatest decreases occurred in the larger chambers. On the other hand, substantial increases in the number of house committees were made in Georgia, Kansas,

[44] Senator George Woodward wrote in *The Pennsylvania Legislator*, April 1937: "There are thirty-four committees because there are thirty-four Democratic Senators and each Senator has to be chairman of something. If there ever are fifty Democrats, which God forbid, there will be fifty committees, which seems to prove that simplicity is a work of political genius."

Standing Committees in the State Legislatures

STATE	NUMBER OF MEMBERS	HOUSE * STANDING COMMITTEES			NUMBER OF MEMBERS	SENATE * STANDING COMMITTEES		
	1951	1931	1941	1951	1951	1931	1941	1951
Alabama	106	40	40	15	35	28	30	30
Arizona	72	27	29	21	19	22	22	24
Arkansas	100	41	46	49	35	40	53	39
California	80	58	58	23	40	40	20	23
Colorado	65	37	39	27	35	29	31	20
Connecticut	277	37	34	32	36	37	32	32
Delaware	35	27	27	30	17	23	22	26
Florida	95	69	59	55	38	40	37	40
Georgia	205	51	61	70	54	48	51	44
Idaho	59	39	39	25	44	28	28	22
Illinois	153	32	30	26	51	41	35	28
Indiana	100	58	42	45	50	48	46	41
Iowa	108	48	54	39	50	51	50	38
Kansas	125	37	37	44	40	43	44	30
Kentucky	100	66	75	71	38	39	44	38
Louisiana	100	37	38	38	39	26	39	30
Maine	151	38	45	29	33	38	38	24
Maryland	123	35	37	15	29	29	31	13
Massachusetts	240	30	35	37	40	30	33	35
Michigan	100	62	66	49	32	38	26	22
Minnesota	131	46	44	38	67	40	41	36
Mississippi	140	44	41	55	49	42	37	54
Missouri	154	55	57	65	34	24	36	28
Montana	90	51	52	47	56	39	46	46
Nebraska	—	30	—	—	43	31	15	14
Nevada	43	29	39	26	17	25	25	20
New Hampshire	399	36	37	25	24	28	24	19
New Jersey	60	38	46	59	21	33	31	47
New Mexico	55	31	30	23	24	18	15	18
New York	150	33	37	36	56	27	27	26
North Carolina	120	59	45	51	50	56	51	54
North Dakota	113	42	43	14	49	42	40	14
Ohio	135	36	27	22	33	21	20	11
Oklahoma	118	29	67	27	44	37	52	29
Oregon	60	36	37	25	30	35	36	20
Pennsylvania	208	44	42	35	50	35	26	24
Rhode Island	100	20	20	20	44	17	18	10
South Carolina	124	28	31	11	46	32	33	36
South Dakota	75	59	61	51	35	53	56	51
Tennessee	99	44	45	48	33	34	34	35
Texas	150	38	41	46	31	36	38	42
Utah	60	30	34	37	23	12	15	18
Vermont	246	26	27	29	30	31	31	34
Virginia	100	26	34	39	40	20	24	27
Washington	99	49	50	37	46	51	53	32
West Virginia	94	28	30	28	32	26	29	31
Wisconsin	100	22	23	25	33	9	10	12
Wyoming	56	29	19	21	27	25	21	21
Total	5,683	1,909	1,850	1,675	1,792	1,607	1,569	1,418
Average	121	39.2	39.3	35.6	37	32.8	32.6	29.5

* In 1951, Joint committees, included in the totals for both Senate and House, existed as follows: Arizona and Arkansas, 1 each; Connecticut 33; Delaware 4; Georgia 7; Indiana and Iowa, 2 each; Kansas 1; Maine 22; Massachusetts 31; Michigan 3; Mississippi 5; Missouri 4; New Jersey 16; North Carolina 2; Oklahoma 1; Pennsylvania 2; Rhode Island 5; South Carolina and Texas, 3 each; Utah 2; Vermont 3; Virginia 5; West Virginia and Wyoming, 1 each; Wisconsin 2.

Standing Committees

NEBRASKA *		SUGGESTED
Agriculture	9	Agriculture
Appropriations	11	Education and Labor
Banking, Commerce and Insurance	9	Elections and Apportionment
Claims and Deficiencies	5	Finance, Commerce and Industry
Education	9	Fiscal Policy
Government	9	Government Operations
Judiciary	9	Intergovernmental Relations
Labor and Public Welfare	9	Judiciary
Public Health and Miscellaneous Subjects	5	Local Government
Public Works	9	Military Affairs
Revenue	9	Natural Resources
		Public Utilities
		Public Works
		Rules and Administration
		Social Welfare

* Showing number of members of each committee.

and Missouri; in the number of committees in both houses in Arkansas, Mississippi, New Jersey, and Texas. There was little change in a number of states like Kentucky, New York, South Dakota, and Tennessee — all of which had and still have an excessive number. Along with the general tendency to reduce the number of committees in both houses in a majority of the states, the average size of committees was also reduced. Thus, with fewer committees and smaller committees, the workload of the members was somewhat reduced and, it is hoped, to some extent equalized.

The choice of committee members in the lower house rests with the speaker in two thirds of the states, with the president of the senate in nearly one half of the upper chambers while in the remainder, a variety of methods are used. In more than one fourth of the state senates, the final choice rests with the senate itself, the nominations being made by the lieutenant governor as ex-officio president in three states, by a president elected by the senate in one state, and by a nominating committee or otherwise in eleven states.

Size and Workload of Committees. The size of committees has long been a subject of controversy. In practice most of them are fairly large, while students of legislation have almost unanimously urged that small committees would do more and better work. Senate committees vary in size from an average of two in Connecticut to an average of twenty-three in Illinois; in the lower house the range is from slightly less than five in Nevada to more than thirty-five in Georgia. Professor Farmer makes some pertinent remarks on the way this system works in Alabama, as it relates to both the number and the size of committees [45]:

[45] Farmer, *op. cit.*, p. 152.

> Probably the most significant fact that appears from a study of the tables is that there is gross inequality in the distribution of work among the committees. In the Senate of 1943, ten committees handled 88 per cent of the bills and the fourteen other committees handled the remaining 12 per cent. In the House of Representatives in 1943, ten committees handled almost 77 per cent of the bills introduced, leaving the remaining twenty-four committees to handle some 23 per cent of the bills.
>
> The most overworked committee in both the Senate and the House is the Judiciary Committee. . . . The Committee on Local Legislation comes next. . . . Some committees, on the other hand, do not seem to have justified their existence. . . . On the whole, it would seem that both houses might well consider a reorganization of their whole committee system with a view to relieving the few over-burdened committees and securing a fairer distribution of work.

In Oklahoma in 1947 one member of the House, which had sixty-three committees, served on eighteen, while 108 of the 118 members served on more than five committees each. Forty-eight were on more than ten committees each. In a Senate of forty-four members and with thirty-three committees, only two served on as many as ten committees, and only twenty-five served on more than five committees. This situation is by no means unique; it exists and has existed in other states for years. In Kansas, for instance, there "are in every session two committees that regularly average 30 per cent of the total number of bills referred to committees, and seven committees that handle 61 per cent of the bills." [46] In Nebraska, however, where a somewhat rational committee structure has been established (see list on page 226), the workload of the committees has been very well equalized.[47] In spite of having too many and too large committees and of the uneven distribution of the work assigned to them, they none the less occupy a very important position in the legislative process. Professor Winslow, in his study of legislative committees in Maryland and Pennsylvania, found that the committee action "was really the final action in somewhat more than 92 per cent of instances in the former state, and in 83 per cent in the latter." [48]

Evaluation of the Committee System. Anyone who undertakes to study existing committee arrangements will find them haphazard and unplanned. The author made such a study of senate committees in the forty-eight states in 1937. In most states there were committees that were overlapping and duplicating, while at the same time, in spite of an excessive number of committees, there was none to which bills on certain subjects might be appropriately referred. This was the more surprising because there are certain problems or types of problems that are common to all the states. The lists in some were loaded with "sports." Out of a total of 1,541 senate committees, there were 553, or an average of eleven per state, which existed in no other

[46] Nebraska Legislative Council, *Report of the Subcommittee on Realignment of Legislative Committees*, p. 3 (Subcommittee Report No. 14, Lincoln, 1946).

[47] Kansas Legislative Council, *Expediting Legislative Procedure*, p. 4 (Topeka, 1935).

[48] Winslow, Clinton I., *State Legislative Committees*, Chapter 5 (Johns Hopkins Press, 1931).

state, and this in spite of the fact that every effort was made to group related committees together, regardless of minor differences in terminology. Kansas had only one such committee, but Kentucky, Oklahoma, and Washington had twenty or more each.

The task of developing a model list which might be usable in the several states is not easy. An attempt at such a list is made on page 226, in a second column parallel to the list for Nebraska. It was constructed (1) to simplify the committee structure, eliminating overlapping and duplication; (2) to make a necessary and drastic reduction in the number of committees; (3) to equalize the workload; (4) to provide some committee to which a bill on any ordinary legislative subject might be appropriately referred; (5) to provide some correlation between the committee setup and the structure of the executive branch. The list is a compromise between the ideal and the practical, but since established practice is slow to change, it is unlikely that many states will adopt it.

Professor Winslow in his concluding chapter suggests a number of objective and theoretical tests of the results of committee work. Among the objective tests are the number of repeals and amendments of recent legislation, governors' vetoes, duplicate bills, and the referendum. The committees cannot be blamed for repeals or amendments necessitated by a changed public opinion, although they might be for such technical errors as faulty construction, incorrect references or names, ambiguities, and the like. The vetoes by the governors appear to provide a more reliable index. "A committee system which permits the enactment of from thirty-five to forty-three, or from fifty-three to 104 defective laws (in Maryland in 1927 and 1929) needs attention. It is hardly possible that so many vetoes would be necessary if really 'careful consideration' were given to the bills by the committees receiving them." Duplicate bills — that is, identical bills introduced in both houses and passed by each — were often referred to different committees, except in the case of appropriation bills. Local measures submitted to the referendum in Maryland were frequently rejected by the voters; "a committee system, intended to represent the local communities, should reflect local desires more accurately than is indicated in many cases."

The purposes of these committees are: "(1) to serve as a means of investigating special fields of proposed legislation and collecting information thereon [this function will be discussed in a later chapter]; (2) to deliberate upon (more time being available than in the chamber itself) and give careful consideration to matters referred to it; (3) to permit the application of specialized knowledge so that proposed legislation may be in such form as to accomplish the desired end and that the chamber may benefit by more or less expert advice; (4) finally, to recommend action." The extent to which the existing committee system succeeds in accomplishing these purposes is a matter of personal judgment. Some states do better than others. It is well known that the quality — not to mention the quantity — of work done by any committee depends largely on the ability of the chairman and the amount of time he is willing to spend on it. It often happens that the chairmen of the appropriation committees are the only members who know anything about the appropriation bills, so that the whole responsibility is largely delegated to them.

After a careful study of the system of standing committees in Alabama, Professor Hallie Farmer concludes that[49]:

1. There are too many committees.
2. Many committees are too large.
3. Work is not properly distributed among the committees.
4. The rules of both House and Senate could be revised to provide more effectively for the work of the committees.
5. The committees must have more effective means of acquiring knowledge of the bills upon which they act.

These conclusions with regard to Alabama apply with equal force to the committees in the other states. Some changes could be made to correct these conditions which would be highly beneficial, as has been demonstrated in those jurisdictions in which they have been tried.

The use of joint committees would help. At present separate hearings are scheduled at different times by the two committees considering the same measure. This means that citizens desiring to testify must make two trips to the capitol for the same purpose, at a considerable unnecessary expense, loss of time, and expenditure of energy. All this could be prevented if other states would follow Massachusetts and other New England states in providing for joint standing committees for all the more important subjects. Such joint committees are found in only thirteen states, and they handle the bulk of the work in only three of these — Connecticut, Maine, and Massachusetts. This plan has the additional advantage of making certain that the same data and information are presented to the representatives of both houses; under the present system this can happen only by accident, although it is obviously desirable that both groups be in possession of the same basic information. As Professor Farmer points out, if it is not desired to establish joint committees, it is possible to reduce the total number of committees by abolishing those that have outlived their usefulness, by consolidating those to which few bills are referred, or by establishing a committee setup which corresponds roughly to that of the major executive departments.

It should also be made easier for members to pry bills out of committee. Six states go so far, in one or both houses, as to require the reporting out of all bills referred.[50] While this is not necessary, since it brings to the floor many bills which stand no chance of passage, it should be possible to force

[49] Farmer, *op. cit.*, pp. 161–166; also California Committee on Legislative Organization, *Final Report on Rational Organization of Standing Committees of the Assembly* (Sacramento, 1944), and Illinois Legislative Council, *The Committee System of the Illinois General Assembly* (Springfield, 1940).

[50] In both houses in Massachusetts, North Dakota, Vermont and Wyoming; in the lower houses in Texas and Utah; in the senate in Pennsylvania.

Legislative Committees and Rules of Procedure *

SUBJECT	THE PRESENT OUTMODED LEGISLATURE	THE PROPOSED REORGANIZED LEGISLATURE
Amendments	Amendments not germane to legislation introduced	Amendments not germane to legislation ruled out of order
Committee System	Large, numerous, inefficient committees	Fewer, smaller, more effective committees
Rules of Debate	Lengthy, uncontrolled, filibustering debate	Pertinent, direct, responsible debate
Log-rolling	Log-rolling practices permitted	No log-rolling
Rules of Procedure	Obsolete rules used to defeat and delay legislation	Modern rules to effect prompt enactment of legislation
Adjournment	70-day session	Unlimited session
	Legislation weakened by unsound and unconstitutional provisions	Sound, constitutional legislation

* Adapted from South Carolina General Assembly Joint Committee on Reorganization, *Legislative Reorganization, Findings and Recommendations*, pp. 14–15 (Columbia, 1949).

out of committee any bill which has any appreciable support. In nearly every legislature there are one or more "pickling" committees, which conveniently forget to report out a great many bills. While these bills die in committee, it is often impossible to find out who killed them or why. The situation is the same, whether the bills be freaks, bills favoring some special interest, or important measures in the public interest. Where the rules require the reporting of all bills, the chairman and members of the committee must put themselves on record. Were this the general practice, or were one fifth of the members able to discharge a committee from further consideration of a bill, it is certain that many bills which are now "pickled" would be given such chance of passage as might accompany consideration on the floor. The rules in some states make such action impossible.

Cost of Legislation

Not until the depression did anyone consider seriously the cost of legislation; then, with rising government costs, decreased revenues, and an ever-increasing tax burden, even the cost of making our laws became a matter of some general interest and importance. There has been an impression that the cost was higher than it should be, but such studies as have been made do not support that view. An analysis made in 1945 by the New York State Joint Committee on Legislative Methods, Practices, Procedures and Expenditures shows that with the exception of a few of the larger states the total cost

State Legislative Expenditures, United States, Fiscal Year 1943 *

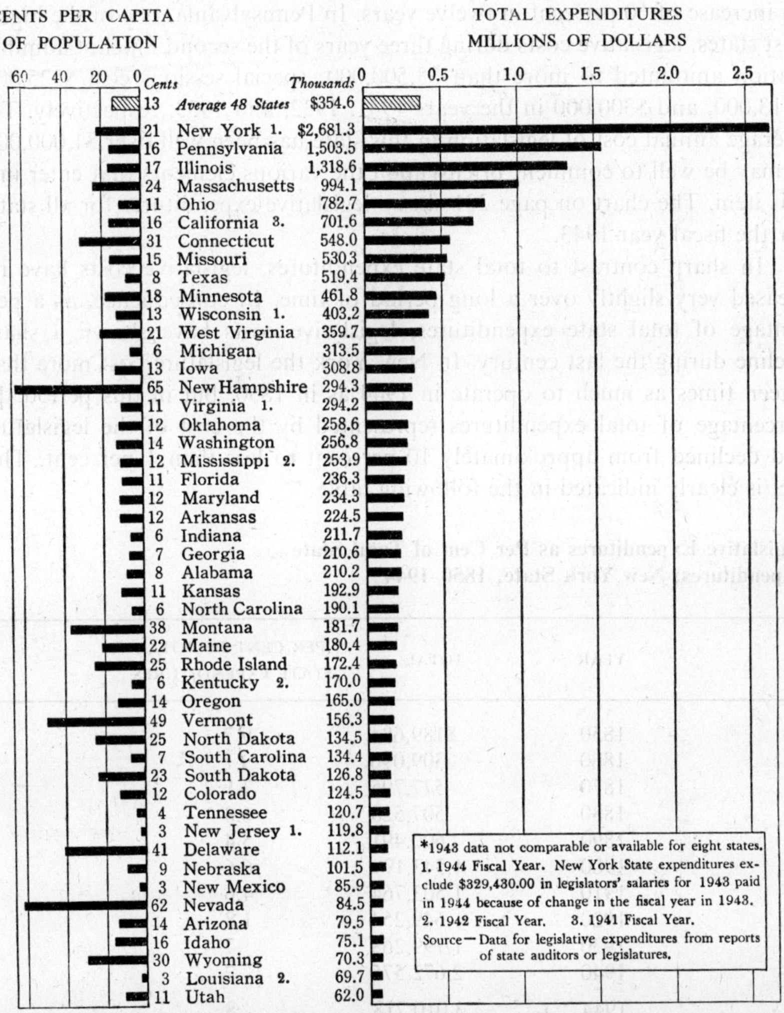

* From New York State Joint Legislative Committee on Legislative Methods, Practices, Procedures and Expenditures, *Interim Report*, p. 23 (Legislative Document, 1945, No. 35); for a more recent partial survey, see Tuttle, Daniel W., Jr., *Legislative Expenditures* (Hawaii Legislative Reference Bureau, Honolulu, 1951).

figures are not impressive and that the per capita expenditures are negligible amounts, ranging from a few cents to amounts nowhere exceeding one dollar. In 1943 the average per capita cost for all of the states was computed at thirteen cents.

A major item in the total cost is the salaries of members, followed by such other items as the salaries of the large group of legislative employees, the cost of legislative printing, and similar items. In Wisconsin, where legislative costs are moderate compared with those in many other states, there has been an increase of 60 per cent in twelve years. In Pennsylvania, one of the higher cost states, legislative costs during three years of the second Pinchot administration amounted to more than $3,500,000; special sessions cost $325,000, $313,000, and $300,000 in the years 1931, 1932, and 1933, respectively. The average annual cost of legislation in this state has been well over $1,000,000. It may be well to comment briefly upon the various elements that enter into this item. The chart on page 231 shows legislative expenditures for all states for the fiscal year 1943.

In sharp contrast to total state expenditures, legislative costs have increased very slightly over a long period of time. In consequence, as a percentage of total state expenditures, legislative costs have shown a sharp decline during the last century. In New York the legislature cost more than fifteen times as much to operate in 1944 as in 1850, but in this period the percentage of total expenditures represented by the cost of the legislature had declined from approximately 10 per cent to less than 1 per cent. This fact is clearly indicated in the following table:

Legislative Expenditures as Per Cent of Total State Expenditures, New York State, 1850–1944 *

YEAR	TOTAL	PER CENT OF TOTAL STATE EXPENDITURES
1850	$189,684	9.7
1860	309,096	9.1
1870	577,795	7.1
1880	507,528	6.8
1890	600,491	5.4
1900	1,343,199	6.6
1910	1,503,764	4.6
1920	1,649,254	1.8
1930	1,799,268	.7
1940	2,672,575	.7
1944	3,010,718	.8

* From New York State Joint Legislative Committee on Legislative Methods, Practices, Procedures and Expenditures, *Interim Report*, p. 26.

Salary Expenditures. In New York, as the survey of its committee shows, less than 20 per cent of the total legislative cost goes for salaries of members. Legislative salaries have been increased somewhat since the war, but with general price increases, the ratio of expense for this and other items has not changed much. The salaries of employees, which constitute the largest single item of expenditure, have shown a marked increase during the past two dec-

Legislative Expenditures, New York State *

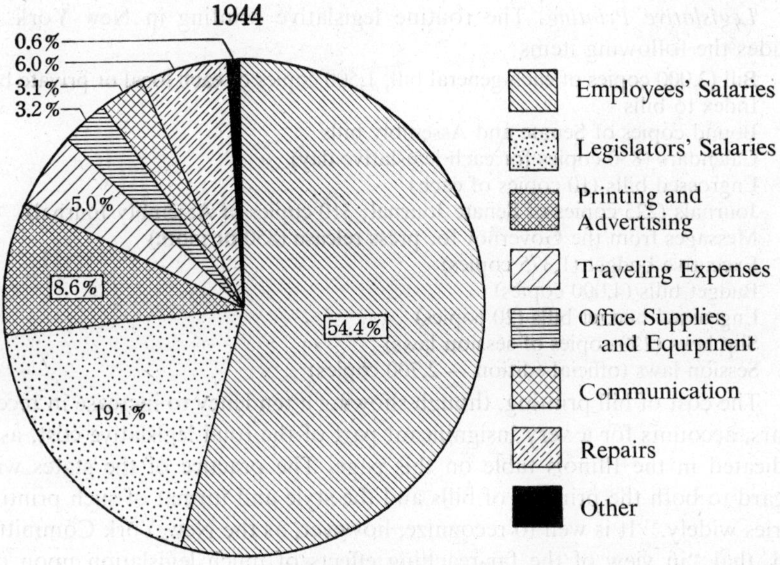

Total — $2,681,288.00

* From New York State Joint Legislative Committee on Legislative Methods, Practices, Procedures and Expenditures, *Interim Report*, p. 28.

ades. Because of the temptation to employ more persons than necessary and to select them on the basis of political favoritism, this item offers considerable possibilities for savings. Both the volume of work and the cost of performing it have steadily increased.

While numerous variable factors preclude the possibility of reducing the cost figures to a common denominator for purposes of comparison, it may be safely stated that the administration of the legislative personnel system is generally unsatisfactory. In the Tennessee session of 1949, it was reported that "the House had 199 employees costing $125,880, the Senate ninety-eight employees costing $69,922. The House had a chief engrossing clerk at $15 a day and 110 assistant engrossing clerks at $10 a day. Only about one third of these did any actual work during the session, the remaining two thirds being friends and relatives of the legislators, who did little more than draw their pay. It was, in fact, the most expensive legislature along this line since 1937." [51] In New York in 1943 the situation had become so bad that a grand jury investigation was necessary. The grand jury recommended that a survey be made to determine how many employees were actually needed by the legislature, and reported that legislative expenses were "channeled through a large number of separate offices, under numerous

[51] Travis, *op. cit.*

grants of authority, and with such a lack of centralized control as to leave loopholes for extravagance and waste."[52]

Legislative Printing. The routine legislative printing in New York includes the following items:

Bill (2,000 copies of each general bill, 1,500 copies of each local or private bill)
Index to bills
Bound copies of Senate and Assembly bills
Calendars (850 copies for each legislative day)
Engrossed bills (10 copies of each)
Journals (225 copies of Senate Journal; 310 copies of Assembly Journal)
Messages from the Governor for press release (850 or more)
Executive budget (1,375 copies)
Budget bills (4,000 copies)
Engrossed budget bills (20 copies)
Slip laws (250 copies of session laws)
Session laws (official edition — 2,700 copies)

The cost of bill printing, though showing a tendency to increase in recent years, accounts for a very insignificant part of the total legislative cost, as is indicated in the Illinois table on this page. The practice of the states with regard to both the printing of bills and the style and format of such printing varies widely.[53] It is well to recognize, however, as the New York Committee did, that "in view of the far-reaching effects of much legislation upon the lives and fortunes of people," the Committee was "reluctant to make any recommendations for economies in printing that would in the slightest degree limit the widespread distribution of bills and reports or hamper the many information services of the Legislature."

State of Illinois
Bill Printing Costs Compared to Total Legislative Costs in Four Regular Sessions, 1943–1949

GENERAL ASSEMBLY	TOTAL LEGISLATIVE COST	BILL PRINTING COSTS			
		Senate	*House*	*Total*	*Per Cent of Total Legislative Costs*
63rd (1943)	$1,318,580	$12,986	$18,208	$31,194	2.4
64th (1945)	1,348,144	14,769	19,380	34,139	2.5
65th (1947)	1,627,569	14,863	23,446	38,311	2.4
66th (1949)	1,827,996	26,096	34,396	60,992	3.3

In addition there are such directories and manuals as are customary in the different jurisdictions. Committees — the important ones, at least —

[52] Quoted by Lederle, John W., "New York's Legislature under the Microscope," *American Political Science Review*, June 1946, pp. 521–527.

[53] See Illinois Legislative Council, *Printing of Legislative Bills* (Springfield, 1949), and table in *Book of the States* on the printing of bills.

may present printed reports; and occasionally the transcript of committee hearings will be mimeographed or printed. The costs of this printing, which are often excessive, are directly influenced by several factors:

1. The uneven volume of bills sent to the printer during the session
2. The legislative printing contract, which may exclude a substantial part of legislative printing
3. The lack of competition for legislative printing
4. Waste in connection with number of copies and with the form of printing, especially of bills [54]

Legislative recording includes senate and house journals, histories of bills, and manuals. "With the exception of Pennsylvania, which prints a full verbatim record (similar to the *Congressional Record*), and of Maine, which prints a condensed verbatim record (including stenographic reports of all debates at the discussion stage of each bill not passed by unanimous consent), no state legislature prints a complete record of its proceedings. Records take the form, varying greatly in detail, of minutes kept by the legislative clerical staff." [55] In many states there is no permanent or adequate record of the evolution of bills enacted into law. No part of a legislative journal could lend itself so easily to standardization of form as the history of bills; yet Professor Bradley found that no part of it is less standardized. The greatest progress has been made in California, New York, Pennsylvania, and Wisconsin, but the histories in some states are woefully inadequate. He suggested that an adequate history of bills might well contain the following data: "(1) the author or introducer of every measure; (2) committee reference; (3) committee action, with the vote of the committee — names included where recorded — on reporting out and names of those appearing before the committee; (4) action on second and third readings — on third reading, votes with the names recorded, including absences and pairs, should be listed; (5) action in other house (in the same detail for each major legislative stage); (6) action on conference; (7) action by governor; (8) subsequent action." This would appear to be the minimum necessary to give a complete record of the activity of the legislature on each item. Considerable attention has been given in recent years to reducing the cost and improving the quality and usefulness of legislative printing.

State manuals or blue books are issued biennially in some form in most states. In addition to the manuals most states issue tiny legislative handbooks, giving the names and addresses of members, and committee assignments for each house. These usually have a very restricted circulation. The manuals themselves vary in size from small handbooks to huge volumes of 1,500 or 1,800 pages, such as are issued in Indiana, Illinois, Louisiana, New

[54] These factors were analyzed in the report of the Moreland Commission, appointed in 1940 to investigate abuses and inefficiency in the purchase of legislative and departmental printing in New York State.

[55] Bradley, Phillips, "Legislative Recording in the United States," *American Political Science Review*, February 1935, pp. 74–83.

York, Pennsylvania, West Virginia, and other states. One who attempts to compare them will be amazed at the diversity of their organization and the variety of their content. The more important items include the constitutions of the United States and of the state; the names of members of the legislature, often with biographical data and individual photographs; a directory of the executive and judicial officers of the state. Many contain detailed election statistics for the state and its political subdivisions, as well as information on the history of the state, its resources, its capitol, flag, bird, flower, song, and the like. The development of a model table of contents for these manuals, which might be a standardizing influence, is badly needed.[56]

Improvements in Organization

The job of the legislator is made needlessly difficult. The term is short. Re-election is uncertain and, very likely, expensive. The working conditions are poor. The compensation, in most states, is woefully inadequate. The expenses connected with the job more than consume the meager salary and allowances. While members of Congress are chosen for full-time service and paid a fair salary, state legislators are asked for only part-time service and scarcely paid for that. As a result, high-grade business and professional men who are willing to serve at all do so only at a personal sacrifice. Many of the legislatures are too large, and the sessions are too short and too infrequent to permit the members to do a good job.

The setup is conducive neither to obtaining competent legislators nor to getting relatively satisfactory performance from those selected. In addition to these external defects, there are others that are internal, as for instance, the failure in many states to do proper legislative planning or to set up a rational committee system. All these conditions should be corrected, and all kinds of remedies have been proposed and tried. Consideration may be given first to the external difficulties. With the beginning of the depression, special sessions became both numerous and frequent. Under unsettled economic conditions it was and is difficult to estimate for one year — much less for two — either the probable yield of existing taxes or those expenditures which fluctuate widely, such as relief.

Some legislators have advocated annual sessions, one in each two-year period to be devoted to general legislation, the other to be devoted exclusively to budgetary and financial problems. Although this proposal has now been

[56] See, in addition to the Bradley article: "State Manuals," a bulletin issued by the American Legislators' Association, July 7, 1934; a discussion of state yearbooks in *State Government*, June 1936, pp. 122–125; Council of State Governments, "Legislative Digests and Indexes," a bulletin issued October 6, 1937; Swisher, I. G., "Election Statistics in the United States," *American Political Science Review*, June 1933, pp. 422–434; and Wilcox, Jerome K., Ed., *Manual on the Use of State Publications* (American Library Association, Chicago, 1940). It is suggested that the reader secure from the secretary of state or from the legislator from his district a copy of the manual of his home state; it will be very helpful to consult it for specific information regarding his own state on many points discussed in this text.

adopted in California and Maryland, it does not meet the need unless it be merely a step in the direction of annual legislative sessions. Financial considerations are so inextricably involved in most questions of public policy that the separation of the two is impossible, and the attempt to separate them highly superficial.

More practical is the suggestion of the committee that framed the Model State Constitution. All the factors contributing to the unsatisfactory organization of the state legislatures led this committee to propose that the legislature be more or less *continuously* in session. Regular sessions would be held quarterly, to receive a report from the governor, and would continue as long as there was business to be transacted. The members of a smaller body, paid adequately, would devote their full time to legislative work.

This proposal is not nearly so fantastic as may at first appear. Ten or fifteen years ago members attended a session and then put legislative matters out of their minds for about a year and a half. Today the officers of the two houses, the chairmen of committees, and even ordinary members make frequent trips to the capitol — often weekly — in connection with legislative work. While their expenses may be paid, they freely give their time, often to the detriment of their personal affairs. The proposal of the Model Constitution would set up machinery suitable for the performance of the duties now imposed upon legislators.

The internal difficulties, many of which relate to procedure, could be handled by the legislators themselves without too much difficulty. Members need legislative reference service, bill-drafting service, and a legislative council for planning and research. These items will be considered in another chapter. But they need also to remodel their committee setup and to modernize their committee procedures. At present there are, in most states, too many committees. They are usually too large, and they are not properly utilized if the legislature is to discharge adequately its responsibility to the citizens of the state.

In 1948, the Council of State Governments issued the revised report of its Committee on Legislative Processes and Procedures. Its recommendations were concerned almost exclusively with questions of organization; it seems appropriate, therefore, to include here for purposes of discussion, the Council's own summary of them.

The Council of State Governments
Committee on Legislative Processes and Procedures

Summary of Recommendations

1. *Legislative Sessions.* Restrictions upon the length of regular sessions should be removed. If legislatures may be called into special session by governors or by a majority of their members without undue restrictions upon the measures to be considered, the question of annual versus biennial sessions is largely resolved.

2. *Legislators — Compensation.* From the viewpoint of good public service the compensation of state legislators is now too low. Annual salaries sufficient to permit competent persons to serve in legislatures without financial sacrifice should be provided by statute. Salaries should not be fixed by constitutional provision.

3. *Legislators — Terms.* In order to strengthen legislatures by increasing continuity of membership the lengthening and staggering of legislative terms should be considered. In representative government frequent elections are necessary. Experienced legislative leadership and smoothly operating legislative machinery likewise contribute to the attainment of democratic objectives.

4. *Legislative Employees.* Skilled and essential full-time legislative employees should be appointed on the basis of merit and competence. The tenure of key legislative personnel should be unaffected by changes in party control, and as far as circumstances permit, the working conditions of legislative employees generally should not be less advantageous than those of employees in the executive and judicial departments.

5. *Legislative Committees — Organization and Procedure.* Committees should be reduced in number wherever practicable and organized with regard to related subject matter, equalization of work, and cooperation between legislative houses.

Committee meetings should be scheduled and announced so as to prevent conflicting duties for committee members, and a permanent and public record of committee action should be kept.

6. *Legislative Committees — Public Hearings.* Provision should be made for public hearings on all major bills, and advance notice of hearings should be published and made readily available, giving time and place of hearing and subject matter of legislation to be heard and, wherever possible, indicating the number and title of bills. Rules of procedure by committees governing hearings should likewise be published and made readily available.

7. *Legislative Councils and Interim Committees.* Provisions for legislative councils or interim committees with adequate clerical and research facilities deserves serious consideration. These facilities can be provided most readily and effectively through a legislative reference bureau.

8. *Reference, Research, Bill Drafting, and Statutory Revision Services.* Legislative reference, research, bill drafting, and statutory revision services should be reviewed in each state, and strengthened wherever necessary by improved organization and more adequate staffing and appropriations.

9. *Introduction and Printing of Legislation.* Consideration should be given to limiting by rule the period during a legislative session when new bills may be introduced. Provision should be made for the drafting, filing, and printing of bills before the opening of the session. All bills and important amendments introduced during a session should be printed promptly after introduction and whenever possible they should be inspected, before printing, by bill drafters or revision clerks. Careful consideration should be given in order to avoid indiscriminate insertion of emergency or immediate-effect clauses in pending legislation.

Publication of manuals covering the form, style, and grammatical construction of bills is suggested.

Adequate provision should be made for printing statutes and making them generally available at the earliest possible time after final enactment.

10. *Legislative Rules.* The rules of legislative houses should be reviewed and revised wherever necessary to expedite legislative procedure, with due regard for adequate deliberation on measures and fairness to minority parties.

Permanent standing committees or a joint committee on legislative organization, rules, and procedure should be established in some form by each legislature.

11. *Legislative Finance.* The legislature should provide for a budget adequate to meet all probable expenditures during a fiscal period. Provision for a fiscal officer responsible for the centralized custody of legislative personnel, pay roll, and expenditure records of each house, and the supervision of legislative expenditures should be considered.

12. *Local and Special Legislation.* Consideration and settlement of claims against the state should be delegated to judicial or administrative agencies, and general, optional, or home rule legislation should provide positive substitutes for special legislation affecting cities, counties, and other political subdivisions of the states, particularly in matters of purely local concern.

SELECTED REFERENCES

Carroll, Daniel B., *The Unicameral Legislature in Vermont* (Vermont Historical Society, Montpelier, 1933). Excellent monograph on sixty years' experience in Vermont, ending in 1836.

Council of State Governments, Committee on Legislative Processes and Procedures, *Our State Legislatures*, Revised Edition (Chicago, 1948). Brief statement of and comment on twelve specific recommendations for the improvement of legislative organization and procedure, with useful appendix.

Farmer, Hallie, *The Legislative Process in Alabama* (Bureau of Public Administration, University of Alabama, 1949). Valuable analysis of all significant phases of the subject in one state, covering the forty-year period from 1903 to 1943.

Graves, W. Brooke, Ed., "Our State Legislators," *Annals*, January 1938, entire volume. Useful symposium by twenty-five authors examines most of the phases of the problem.

Lewis, Henry W., *Legislative Committees in North Carolina* (Institute of Government, University of North Carolina, 1952) and Winslow, Clinton I., *State Legislative Committees: a Study of Procedure* — in Maryland and Pennsylvania (Johns Hopkins Press, 1931). Two excellent studies of committee organization and procedure.

New York State Constitutional Convention Committee, *Problems Relating to Legislative Organization and Powers*, being Vol. VII of the Committee's Report (Albany, 1938). Excellent discussion of problems involved, with special reference to New York.

New York State Joint Legislative Committee on Legislative Methods, Practices, Procedures and Expenditures, *Interim Report* (Legislative Document, 1945, No. 35); *Final Report* (Legislative Document, 1946, No. 31). Best and most comprehensive study of the problems involved now available.

Senning, John P., *The One-House Legislature* (McGraw-Hill, New York, 1937). An ardent proponent of unicameralism presents its case.

Smith, Thomas V., *The Legislative Way of Life* (University of Chicago Press, 1940). A scholar-philosopher with extensive political experience analyzes the problems confronting our legislatures.

Walker, Harvey, *The Legislative Process: Lawmaking in the United States* (Ronald Press, New York, 1948). Most recent and up-to-date treatise on problems of American legislatures.

Willoughby, William F., *Principles of Legislative Organization and Administration*

(Brookings Institution, Washington, 1934). A pioneer student of public administration applies the principles of good organization and management to the problems of the legislature.

Young, Clement C., *The Legislature of California: Its Membership, Procedure and Work* (Commonwealth Club of California, San Francisco, 1943). A former legislator and governor presents a comprehensive analysis of the legislative problems of his own state.

Zeller, Belle, Ed., *Representative Assemblies in the American States*, being the report of the Committee on American Legislatures of the American Political Science Association (Crowell, New York, 1953). Fifteen students of legislative organization and procedure analyze problems in the field, and suggest methods of improvement.

7

Legislative Service Agencies

Between the problem of legislative organization on the one hand and that of legislative procedure on the other, there lies the great and rapidly developing field of legislative services or legislative aids. Legislative organization is concerned with the structural problems discussed in the preceding chapter; legislative procedure is concerned with the actual enactment of legislation, discussed in the chapter which follows. The legislatures perform some of their information-gathering activities themselves, through their committees, but the demands of modern legislative work are so great that they cannot begin to perform all of them. They need assistance, high-grade professional assistance, in the solution of many problems. This assistance is given to both members and committees by legislative service agencies which obtain and analyze information and draft proposals on various subjects which the legislature will, in accordance with the prescribed procedures, enact into law.

These services may be grouped under five major categories — reference and information, research and planning, bill drafting, statutory revision and codification, and budgetary and fiscal analysis. Owing to factors growing out of the historical evolution of the agencies performing these various services — factors which will be considered as the discussion develops — there is little or no relationship between these basic services and the organizational setup responsible for their administration in most of the states. The sections of this chapter are arranged, as nearly as possible, on a functional basis, while in the concluding section, attention is given to the problem of over-all organization. The types of service which have been in process of development for half a century are shown in the table on page 242.

Reference and Information Services

Legislatures have no less than five major sources to any or all of which they may turn for information on legislative subjects, including their own committees — both standing and ad interim, the legislative reference services, bureaus or libraries, the various departments and agencies of the executive

Types of Organized Legislative Service Agencies in the States — 1950 *

STATE	LEGISLATIVE COUNCILS	LEGISLATIVE REFERENCE SERVICES	LEGISLATIVE COUNSELS	STATUTORY AND CODE REVISION	LIBRARIES	ADMINISTRATIVE AND FISCAL OPERATIONS
Alabama	x	x			x	x
Arizona		x				
Arkansas	x			x	x	x
California		x	x			x
Colorado		x				
Connecticut	x	x		x		
Delaware		x				
Florida	x	x		x	x	
Georgia					x	
Idaho			x			
Illinois	x	x				x
Indiana	x	x				
Iowa		x				
Kansas	x			x	x	x
Kentucky	x			x	x	
Louisiana					x	
Maine	x	x				
Maryland	x	x			x	x
Massachusetts		x	x			x
Michigan		x				
Minnesota	x			x	x	
Mississippi					x	
Missouri	x					
Montana		x				
Nebraska	x			x		x
Nevada	x					x
New Hampshire		x				x
New Jersey		x		x		
New Mexico					x	
New York		x		x		x
North Carolina						
North Dakota	x	x			x	
Ohio		x		x		x
Oklahoma	x	x				
Oregon				x	x	
Pennsylvania	x	x			x	
Rhode Island	x [1]	x		x	x	
South Carolina	x			x	x	
South Dakota				x		x
Tennessee		x			x	x
Texas	x	x		x		x
Utah	x					
Vermont		x				
Virginia	x	x		x		
Washington	x		x		x	
West Virginia						
Wisconsin	x	x		x	x	
Wyoming	x		x		x	
Totals	25	28	5	17	20	15

* Compiled by Herbert L. Wiltsee, Council of State Governments.

[1] Inoperative.

branch, and the representatives of the numerous lobbies and pressure groups which infest every capitol.

Standing Committees of the Legislature. The standing committees are often referred to as "little legislatures." It is their responsibility to study carefully the bills referred to them with a view to reporting them out with a recommendation for or against passage. In the performance of this task the committees need assistance, which may be obtained either from the members of their own staffs or by the conduct of open hearings. The states have, however, been very backward in providing competent professional assistance for committees; such staffs are available to only a few of the more important committees in a small number of states. Hearing procedures are likewise very unsatisfactory in many jurisdictions.

When hearings are to be held, the dates should be announced far enough in advance to enable interested parties throughout the state to gather and arrange the data they wish to present, and to enable them to plan to be present when the hearing occurs. In the majority of the states each house maintains a separate committee, each of which schedules its hearings without regard to the corresponding committee from the other house. Thus the citizens who appear are subjected to a double loss of time and a double expense in journeying to the state capitol. This difficulty has been solved in Massachusetts and a few other states by the establishment of joint committees. This device not only saves time and expense but guarantees that the representatives of both houses will be furnished with precisely the same information and opinions at the same time.

There are many cases in which the members of the committee have definitely made up their minds before the hearings are held; in such cases, a hearing is perfunctory and may even be resorted to as a method of procrastination. In some states, where advanced procedures have been adopted, this situation is rare. In Wisconsin, for instance, the law requires that a list of appearances before the various legislative committees be kept. Such a list is shown on page 244; note that in each instance the organization or interest-group for which the witness speaks is recorded. This particular bill, introduced into the senate in the regular session of 1949, dealt with emergency rent controls. A similarly complete record is kept of the deliberations of every committee and conference committee.[1] With such a public record it is possible for any citizen to ascertain exactly what happened to any bill in which he is interested.

[1] Information furnished by Clarence B. Lester, Acting Chief, Legislative Reference Library, February 27, 1950. A similar practice prevails in Minnesota; see "Permanent Rules of the House, 1939," No. 6 in *Legislative Manual*, 1939, p. 122. See also Baker, Roscoe, "The Reference Committee of the Ohio House of Representatives," *American Political Science Review*, April 1940, pp. 306–310.

The Wisconsin Legislature

Bill History

Bill No. 611, S., 1949 Regular Session
Committee on Legislative Procedure

"A bill to repeal and recreate 234.26 of the statutes, relating to the emergency control of rents of and evictions from housing accommodations, and providing a penalty."

May 6 — Referred to Committee on Judiciary

May 18 — Joint hearing of Senate and Assembly Committees on Judiciary held

Present: Senators Buchen, Busby and Kaftan; Assemblymen Thomson, Abraham, Burmaster, Catlin, Duffy, McParland, Marotz, Mockrud, Redford, Squires
Absent: Senators Knowles and Tehan; Assemblyman Finch

Appearances for the bill:
W. H. AuBachon, Madison, representing self
Joseph J. Ott, Milwaukee, representing self and Milwaukee County Property Owners Association
Lewis A. Stocking, Milwaukee, representing Milwaukee Builders Association
Assemblyman Thomas Hickey, Milwaukee
— and eleven other individuals

Appearances against the bill:
Senator William A. Schmidt, Milwaukee
Glenn M. Clarke, Milwaukee, representing Milwaukee County C.I.O.
Robert Gratz, Milwaukee, representing Wisconsin State Council of Machinists, and Trailer Coach Owners Association
Malcolm S. Lloyd, La Crosse
— and eight other individuals

Appearances on the bill in general:
Keith Schwartz, Madison, County Clerk, Dane County

Registrations for the bill:
931 registrations (on file in Senate Judiciary Committee)
Petitions signed by some 4,399 individuals throughout the state
Miscellaneous telegrams, letters, cards, and petitions

Registrations against the bill:
60 registrations (on file in Senate Judiciary Committee)
Miscellaneous telegrams, letters, cards, and petitions

Registrations on the bill in general:
Harvey R. Habeck, Attorney for Evangelical Deaconess Society of Wisconsin — and various others

May 25 — Executive Session

Present: Senators Buchen, Knowles, Busby, Kaftan and Tehan
Absent: None

Moved by Senator Knowles, seconded by Senator Busby, that Amendment No. ——, S., be recommended for adoption.

Ayes: (5) Senators Buchen, Knowles, Busby, Kaftan and Tehan
Noes: (0) None
Absent: (0) None

Motion carried; Adoption recommended

Moved by Senator Knowles, seconded by Senator Busby, that the bill be recommended for passage.
Ayes: (4) Senators Buchen, Knowles, Busby, Kaftan
Noes: (1) Senator Tehan
Absent: (0) None
Motion carried; Passage recommended

ADOPTION OF AMENDMENT NO.——, S. AND PASSAGE RECOMMENDED

(Signed) Pearle B. Erickson
Clerk

Ad Interim Legislative Committees. In addition to the standing committees already discussed, many of the legislatures have established a large but varying number of special or ad hoc committees. In contrast to the standing or regular committees, these special or ad hoc committees usually function in the interval between sessions. Both types have important functions to perform in obtaining and sifting information for the guidance of individual members and of the legislative body as a whole.

The special investigating committee or commission is usually provided for by resolution in one or both houses in the course of the session. It is a temporary agency specifically created to gather information on some designated legislative subject. Appointments are made by the presiding officer or officers of the two houses at the end of the session. The usefulness of this device varies greatly from state to state, and even from time to time in the same state. A professional jokesmith has said that an investigating committee is a group of distinguished persons who individually can do nothing but who collectively decide that nothing can be done. In some states this comes very nearly being true, for ad interim committees are all but worthless as fact-finding bodies. Though a number of such committees may be authorized, they rarely do anything unless there is an insistent public demand for an investigation or unless the chairman is a person of industry and ability who takes the appointment seriously. In many cases the creation of such a committee is merely a device for postponing action.

Interim committees have been used from the earliest days of the state legislatures. They became common in the 1920's and have been widely used during the past two decades. The legislative sessions of 1943 created in the neighborhood of 200 interim committees, directed to explore a wide variety of subjects, in which problems of the war and the postwar period predominated. The states with the largest numbers were; California, forty; Massachusetts, twenty-one; Illinois, nineteen; New York, sixteen; Connecticut,

Oregon, and Texas, thirteen each; and Minnesota, eleven — making a total of 146 for these eight states alone.[2]

Of the forty-four legislatures that met in 1947, all but two created legislative committees or commissions or had permanent legislative councils or research committees. A survey made by the Council of State Governments showed 264 special study groups in thirty-three states — an all-time high. The number in individual states varied widely, ranging from one in Arizona, Colorado, Florida, Maryland, Pennsylvania, and South Dakota, to fourteen each in Illinois and Oregon, eighteen in Michigan, twenty-one in New York, thirty-four in Massachusetts, and fifty-one in California. The appropriations made in support of this work in twenty-three states for which financial data were available totaled $3,287,700, exclusive of allotments to permanent research agencies. The individual states reporting the highest totals were New York, with $990,200; California, $725,000; Washington, $262,000; and Illinois, $254,500.[3]

In 1949 California created sixty-eight interim committees (see table on page 247); Michigan, twenty-nine; New York, thirty-seven. It is to be noted that such committees have been more common in states like these four, which do not have legislative councils. In some of these states, however, special or interim committees have provided a valuable source of information which has later served as the basis for legislation of far-reaching importance. Their greatest weakness is their frequent failure to give attention to a properly trained and qualified research staff. A study made at the University of California some years ago showed that the legislature in that state "had created 352 special committees and commissions during the period 1850–1936, or an average of seven such agencies per session. During the first session there were none, and in the 1883 session only one. Eight sessions of the legislature prior to 1909 established only two each, while three was the number created by each of six legislatures prior to 1917. The 1935 session with its forty-three special committees and commissions established the greatest number of any session to date. A definite trend upward began with the 1923 session."[4] Developments in the next decade were quite as interesting. The number of special committees active in each biennium from 1937 through 1947 steadily

[2] Based on survey made by the Council of State Governments, *State Government*, October 1943, p. 207, and for earlier lists, issues of February 1932, January and November 1937, and on particular states, Farmer, Hallie, *The Legislative Process in Alabama*, Chapter 6 (Bureau of Public Administration, University of Alabama, 1949); Virginia Division of Statutory Research and Drafting, *Legislative Interim Manual, 1944–1946* (Richmond, 1946, and biennially since that date).

[3] *Interim Legislative Study Assignments — 1947* (Chicago, November 1947).

[4] Larsen, Christian L., *The Use of Special Committees and Commissions by the California Legislature* (Bureau of Public Administration, University of California, 1937). See also Chichester, Cassius M., "Interim Activities in Virginia in Aid of Legislation," *State Government*, April 1943, pp. 87, 97–100, and Sikes, Pressly S., "Special Interim Commissions in the Indiana Legislative Process," *American Political Science Review*, October 1942, pp. 906–915.

State of California
Legislative Interim Committees, 1935–1951 *

LEGISLATIVE YEAR	ASSEMBLY	SENATE	JOINT	TOTAL
1935	12	7	0	19
1937	24	10	1	35
1939	17	16	6	39
1941	20	8	9	37
1943	21	23	9	53
1945	34	22	22	78
1947	35 (25) [1]	22 (21) [1]	13	70 (116)
1949	34	34	10	78
1951	23	40	8	71
Total	220	182	78	480

* Based on a report by the Legislative Auditor, *Chronological List of California Legislative Interim Committees and Their Reports, 1937–1951* (Sacramento, November 1951, with annual supplements).

[1] Twenty-five investigating committees created by HR 62, 1947, and twenty-one created by SR 143, 1947, empowered the permanent standing committees of the two houses to act as interim committees until the next regular session.

increased, with some decline in 1949. The table on this page indicates that in the two years 1937 and 1938 there was a total of thirty-five special committees, whereas in the two years 1947 and 1948 this number increased to ninety-three. This latter figure is exclusive of standing committees which act as interim committees until the following regular session, as provided in Senate and House resolutions of 1947. Inclusion of standing committees acting as interim committees would raise the 1947 total to 139.

The figures show New York as another extensive user of the interim committee device. The New York State Commission for the Revision of the Tax Laws, long known as the Mastick Commission, provides a notable illustration. The history of this Commission, which was continued from 1916 to 1938, inclusive, was thus summarized by its clerk:

> During the legislative session of 1915, the Joint Legislative Committee on Taxation was authorized. In 1919, the Special Joint Legislative Committee on Taxation and Retrenchment was created by the adoption of a joint resolution, which provided for an appropriation to make possible the carrying on of the necessary work. The first report of this Committee was made to the Legislature during the session of 1920. The Committee continued to function until it made its report to the Legislature, under date of February 1, 1929, — a report on the various phases of its work, which had been submitted annually to the Legislature from 1920 to 1929, inclusive.
>
> During the legislative session of 1929, a Commission was created to make a study of old age security, and this Commission submitted a report to the Governor and Legislature under date of February 15, 1930. During the session of 1930, a New York State Commission for the Revision of the Tax Laws was created under Chapter 726 of the Laws of 1930.

This Commission was particularly fortunate in having continuously competent leadership and adequate financial support — a regular appropriation ranging from $75,000 to $100,000 a year. Each year the Commission turned its attention to some pressing problem in widely separated fields relating to the establishment of a more equitable revenue system and a more even distribution of the tax burden. Altogether, twenty-nine reports were published, and at the conclusion of the work in 1938 the Commission published a large index volume covering the whole. Embodied in these reports, wrote the Commission at this time, "is the history of the New York tax system, the analysis of the fiscal and administrative problems of state and local government from early statehood to the present time, together with the well-considered conclusions and recommendations of the various commissions and their personnel — composed of persons trained both in the theory and practice of taxation, economics, and government administration." Some of these reports were works of outstanding merit; the one on social security in 1929 is one of the important early studies, while that on local government in 1934 still stands as one of the best state surveys in its field.

In a number of instances the interim committee has been used either as a substitute for or as a step toward a legislative council. The Joint State Government Commission of Pennsylvania is a case in point. This organization is not actually a council, but both its objectives and its methods of operation are similar to those of a council. In Minnesota the House established the Interim Committee on State Administration and Employment in 1943. In 1941, and again in 1943, the House passed a bill for a legislative council, which the Senate failed to approve, so the House went ahead with this substitute, referred to by an eminent political scientist in the state as "a legislative council in embryo." In Missouri provision has been made for a Legislative Research Committee which "is somewhat similar to the legislative councils of other states, although it does not go as far as some in preparing a program prior to the convening of the legislature. The Legislative Committee confines itself largely to maintaining the library and making studies at the request of members of the legislature." [5]

In 1938 the question of the powers of interim commissions was brought before the Supreme Court of California. Can one house of the legislature establish an ad interim committee by single house resolution with power to function after the adjournment of the legislature and of each house thereof sine die? Witnesses summoned before such a committee refused to answer the questions of the chairman. When the committee attempted to secure a court order directing them to testify, they questioned the validity of the committee itself, and were supported in their objection by the decision of the Court in a

[5] Short, Lloyd M., "Minnesota Interim Committee a Legislative Council in Embryo," *National Municipal Review*, May 1944, pp. 251–252, and editorial, pp. 219, 228; letter to the author from Estal E. Sparlin, Legislative Analyst for the Legislative Research Committee in Missouri, May 28, 1945.

five to two decision which relied upon decisions in other states to the same effect, but implied that such a committee could be established by statute. Immediately after this decision the State Controller refused to honor the warrants of any ad interim committee, either of the Assembly or of the Senate. Inasmuch as some cases had drawn a distinction between committees of the Senate and those of the Assembly, an independent action was brought in the Supreme Court directly against the Controller, to require him to honor warrants for expenses incurred by the Senate committees. This was an action for a writ of mandamus directed to the Controller, ordering him to pay the expenses of the committee and thereby putting in issue the validity of the establishment of the committee itself. The Court held in a five to two decision that the Senate could not, by a single-house resolution, or the two houses acting together could not by concurrent resolution, create an ad interim committee with power to function after the adjournment of the legislature sine die.[6] A constitutional amendment authorizing the establishment of such committees was approved by the voters in 1940.

The interim committees, no matter what their number, are not likely to perform as satisfactorily as a council. The selection of subjects is more or less accidental, depending on the interest and influence of the individuals sponsoring resolutions to create such committees. Once they are established, there is no assurance that a carefully planned, comprehensive, and impartial study will be made of those aspects of the subject requiring legislative attention. Other weaknesses of this method of procedure, enumerated by Dr. Perkins,[7] include the fact that each committee created must start *de novo*, thereby wasting much time and effort. The assembling of a competent staff — without which a committee is quite helpless — is difficult, on short notice. In addition, the lack of coordination between committees and the tendency to dump a large number of reports on the desks of members in the early days of the session tend to impair the usefulness of all of them.

Legislative Reference Agencies. Another major source of information is the legislative reference bureau, library, or service. The movement for the establishment of such agencies, inaugurated by the New York State Library in 1890 and the Massachusetts State Library in 1892, and expanded and developed in Wisconsin by Charles McCarthy in 1901, has slowly spread from state to state until in 1950 there was in twenty-eight states a department or agency devoted exclusively to legislative reference work. In addition, state libraries in twenty states were providing some service for legislators. To put the matter in another way, there are twenty states in which members rely

[6] Special Assembly Interim Committee on Public Morals v. Southard, 13 Cal. (2d) 497, 90 Pac. (2d) 304, 1939; Swing v. Riley, 13 Cal. (2d) 513, 90 Pac. 313, 1939; McHenry, Dean E., "The Legislative Power to Investigate on the Anvil: California's Legislature Loses and Regains Investigative Authority," *State Government*, May 1942, pp. 105–106.

[7] Based on Perkins, John A., material prepared for the American Political Science Association's Committee on American Legislatures, *Representative Assemblies in the American States* (Crowell, New York, 1953).

on the legislative reference service for information. In twelve, the state library provides an information service for them. In eight states, as shown in the table on page 242 — Alabama, Florida, Maryland, North Dakota, Pennsylvania, Rhode Island, Tennessee, and Wisconsin — they may obtain information from either legislative reference or the state library. Eight states — Idaho, Missouri, Nebraska, Nevada, North Carolina, South Dakota, Utah, and West Virginia — have no information service for legislators, and three of these — Idaho, North Carolina, and West Virginia — actually provide no services of any description for the members of their legislatures.[8]

There is no uniformity with respect to the organization of this service, the placement of the agency varying widely from state to state. Though it is designed to serve the legislature, in most jurisdictions it is not even under legislative control, having more frequently been assigned to the supervision of the governor than of the legislature. In a few states responsibility for the work is scattered among several different agencies.

The original purpose of legislative reference was twofold: to supply information and to render assistance in the drafting of bills. Some such agencies have been given research and statutory revision functions, although neither of these functions is germane to the purpose of legislative reference, which is an information service primarily for legislators and secondarily for others interested in legislation. As such, it is the responsibility of the legislative reference service, library, or bureau to have on hand, properly classified and filed, up-to-date information on all the important subjects with which the legislature must deal. This information will include newspaper clippings of significant events, articles, speeches and addresses, pamphlets, court decisions, and many other more or less fugitive materials. This material must be immediately accessible, for the bureau staff never knows when some member of the legislature will come rushing in to secure, at the last minute, information regarding a subject which he feels he must talk about on the floor a few minutes hence. The work of the bureau, however, is not confined to collection of general information. In a number of states, of which Wisconsin is a good example, the bureau carries on, through its regular staff members, thorough and detailed investigations of various legislative subjects, always, however, at the request of members.[9] The bureau is furthermore a sort of clearinghouse for information regarding the state government, to which many representatives and private citizens apply. While the bureau attempts to serve all, its duties to the members of the legislature are para-

[8] The Institute of Government at the University of North Carolina and the Bureau for Government Research at West Virginia University do provide some assistance for the legislatures of those states.

[9] See Ohm, Howard F., "Legislative Reference in Wisconsin," *State Government*, December 1948, pp. 240–243, 253, and Toepel, M. G., "The Legislative Reference Library: Serving Wisconsin," *Wisconsin Law Review*, January 1951, pp. 114–124; also Schwartz, Arthur A., "The Ohio Legislative Reference Bureau and Its Place in the Legislative Process," *Ohio State Law Journal*, Autumn 1950, pp. 436–446.

mount. If the members are to make full use of this service, the bureau staff must do two things: it must maintain a position of absolute independence and fairness, and it must avoid any claim to credit for the work which it does. A seeker after publicity has no place on the staff of such a bureau.

The permanent staff of the Wisconsin Legislative Reference Library consists of a dozen persons, including the chief, librarians, and research assistants, stenographers and clerks, and a messenger. During the session it is necessary to make temporary additions to the staff, which is one of the largest in the country. In nine states the permanent staff are civil service employees. The cost of the service in Wisconsin is about $55,000 a year; in other states the annual cost ranges from approximately $75,000 in Illinois and Pennsylvania to $6,000 in Iowa and Colorado. Annual expenditures in thirteen states exceed $25,000.

It is extremely difficult to compare accurately the costs of the service in different states, because in many states no separate appropriation is made for the work. There is the widest diversity in the facilities available for the use of the bureaus in the several states; Wisconsin has a catalogued collection of more than 75,000 items and spends a substantial amount each year on books and subscriptions, while in other states the facilities are severely limited.

Mention should be made of other agencies of this character cooperating with the individual state bureaus. The Legislative Reference Service of the Library of Congress has been functioning since 1914; many of its services are available, indirectly, at least, to state legislators.[10] Shortly after its establishment the American Legislators' Association set up, as an affiliated organization, the Interstate Reference Bureau for the purpose of assisting any legislator or legislative committee or any legislative reference bureau to secure any desired information. This service is now operated by the Joint Reference Library for all the cooperating organizations in the 1313 group. Hundreds of requests for information are answered annually from state legislators, members of Congress, and many other sources. This work has become important not only because of its extent but because of its effort to bring about cooperation and coordination of the state services and to eliminate so far as possible duplication of effort. State bureaus are urged to send copies of all compilations of information on any legislative subject to the Joint Reference Library; these are kept on file and, when copies are available for distribution, are listed in the weekly check list of *Recent Publications on Governmental Problems* distributed by the Public Administration Service.

There are, as previously noted, twenty states in which the state library, law library, or historical library provides information service to legislators, either exclusively, as in twelve states, or parallel with legislative reference

[10] See the author's "Legislative Reference Service for the Congress of the United States," *American Political Science Review*, April 1947, pp. 289–293 — already considerably out of date.

services, as in eight others. In most cases the annual appropriations are small indeed, indicating that the service is very limited. One is reminded of the staff man in one west-central state who reported that the people in his state were surprised that one man should work full time for the legislature the year around, and who wondered what he did and how he spent his time. In one state, legislative reference services are authorized but frankly are not performed. In most instances general reference services are available, spot inquiries are handled, and assistance is provided for committees, both standing and interim.

The Executive Branch. The legislature obtains much useful information from the governor, the budget office, the executive departments and agencies. It may, instead of creating an interim commission, authorize the governor to appoint a special commission to investigate a particular subject, giving it the necessary power and making provision for its expenses. This method has the advantage of bringing more or less outstanding citizens into the picture. On one occasion, the General Assembly of Pennsylvania authorized the governor to appoint a commission to investigate the condition of the blind in the state; the commission was duly appointed with a competent personnel composed of individuals not members of the legislature, who carried on the investigation and made their report. The report outlined a program which it was recommended should be adopted. Among the items in this program was a recommendation for the establishment of a state council for the blind. The report was presented at the next regular session of the legislature, and the council was provided for by legislative action, together with the necessary appropriation. This council has now been in satisfactory operation for a period of approximately twenty-five years.

The legislature may by resolution direct an administrative official or a department to present a report on a designated subject falling within the range of their regular administrative activity. This method of procedure is particularly useful in handling questions which are largely administrative. As has been noted, the representatives of the department should be thoroughly familiar with the existing law and with the administrative problems arising under it. The information is usually supplied promptly, if not willingly, because the agency is dependent on the legislature for its appropriation and hence is anxious to cultivate the good will of the members of that body. When hearings are planned, it is standard procedure to summon the head of the executive department or agency concerned and to give him an opportunity to state the point of view of his agency, and the members of the committee an opportunity to question him regarding any matters relating to the activities of the agency in the field covered by the proposed legislation.

The Lobby. The lobby is an outgrowth of a form of social and economic organization in which special interest groups seek to influence the course of public policy through the agency of paid representatives. The lobby has existed at state capitols for many years. In the early days its methods were crude and often objectionable — so much so, in fact, that the presence of these paid representatives aroused great popular resentment. This was reflected by the enactment of legislation in many states, such as that sponsored by Governor Robert M. La Follette in Wisconsin in 1905, requiring the registration of all such persons. In our own time the number of lobbyists in legislative halls has greatly increased. Edward B. Logan said as far back as 1929 that the lobby "oftentimes outnumbers the membership in the legislature. In one state recently, more than 800 lobbyists or legislative counsel registered during a single legislative session — about half of them being paid; in another state, 140; another state, 124; another 84; and so on."[11]

With this increase in numbers there has been a decided change in type. Many present-day lobbyists are persons of ability and education, gifted with such social graces as may enable them to move in any circle. Many are professionals; they stay in the work year after year, first for one organization and then for another. Their faces become as familiar around the state capitol as the fittings in the legislative halls. When their presence as lobbyists is no longer a secret, much of the supposed evil of the lobbying system vanishes. No legislator can plead ignorance when buttonholed by a member of this energetic and persistent fraternity. The members of this group furnish a great deal of information, biased though it sometimes is. It should be remembered not only that the secrecy of the lobby as an institution has largely passed, but that the efforts of one group very often offset those of another. No important issue is decided in the legislative halls without the presence of the representatives of groups reflecting almost every conceivable position which might be taken on the issue.

Legislative representation by private groups has a threefold aspect — the lobbyist himself, who is the actor in the drama; the legislator, who is the subject upon which he expends his efforts; and the public, which is affected

[11] Logan, Edward B., "Lobbying," *Annals*, supplement, July 1929. The types of lobbying and lobbyists do not change much, but the number appears steadily to increase. There were 170 registered in Ohio in 1924. There were 40 in New York and 77 in Massachusetts in 1928, while 127 were registered in a later California session. There were 164 in New Jersey in 1934 and 1935 (McKean, Dayton D., *Pressures on the Legislature of New Jersey*, Chapter 3. Columbia University Press, 1938). In Connecticut in 1947 only one lobbyist was registered for a racing bill, although 35 were making a systematic approach to all members of the legislature (*New York Times*, January 23, 1947). In Maryland in 1949, James P. Connolly reported that "Swarming Lobbyists Irk Legislature": "There were 152 members of the Assembly and at the last session 126 lobbyists were registered, as required by law. But that is not to say that no more than 126 maneuvered around the meeting. The registration requirement — and, in fact, every other lobby regulation — has been honored more in the breach than in the observance." (*Washington Post*, November 13, 1949). In Wisconsin, "in 1945, according to the records in the Secretary of State's office, $124,742 was spent by lobbying groups. In 1947, that figure was up to $155,000. To date under the new law, there are 137 lobbyists registered for the 1949 session and reports show that $1400 has been spent in a period of approximately one month." Bureau of Community Development, University of Wisconsin, *Community Development Service*, "The Relation of Lobbying to Legislation," September-October 1949, p. 21.

by the outcome. A high-grade lobbyist with a social point of view is interested not merely in getting through a particular bill, but in actually being of assistance to the legislators and reflecting accurately the views of enlightened people. The public-spirited legislator is anxious to see the dependence of the members upon the lobbyist reduced by the development of accurate and impartial sources of information at the capitol readily accessible to the legislator. To the political scientist, whose point of view is to a large extent that of the public, pressure groups hold the key to the future of democratic governmental processes in America. To him it appears that the legislator carries out the public will that is determined and manipulated through channels of mass propaganda, reinforced by the old and tried methods of lobbying.[12]

The most objectionable features of the lobby as it now exists are its corrupting influence — as distinguished from legitimate legislative representation — the secrecy with which it operates in many instances, and its cost. In an earlier chapter mention was made of the findings of a recent investigation in California. An interesting case of this sort in Michigan was reported by Paul H. Todd, former Chairman of the Michigan Public Utilities Commission. A state senator, subsidized by the electric power people, was able to bring about the defeat of three bills providing for the creation of power districts, for the issuance of revenue bonds to pay for hydro-electric or steam power plants, and for facilitating rural electrification in the state.

This same senator received a check for $2,000 from this power company in 1938, and one for $395 for "legal opinions, etc.," in 1939. The case of Senator Thayer in New York in 1934 was similar. Much of this corrupt lobbying is done on a social basis at poker games, drinking parties, and other entertaining carried on in hotel rooms. This revelry often lasts until far into the night; the lobbyist pays the bills. The member knows this, and while there may be no actual bribery, he knows also what is expected of him when he accepts such hospitality. Sometimes the legislator has his room and board at the hotel taken care of by some group which desires his support. Such a system is obviously expensive to operate. In one North Carolina session, $82,006 was reported spent for lobbying services. Of this amount, "sixty-seven registered lobbyists received about $54,000 in fees and expense money or more than half the $102,000 salaries drawn by the 170 members of the Legislature. Forty-nine lobbyists reported that they drew no fees in

[12] *Annals*, January 1938, included excellent articles covering the lobby from three different points of view: that of the lobbyist, Schermerhorn, Gertrude L., pp. 88–94; of the legislator, Parkman, Henry, Jr., pp. 95–102; of the political scientist, Zeller, Belle, pp. 79–87. See also: McKean, *op. cit.*, and "A State Legislature and Group Pressure," *Annals*, May 1935, pp. 124–130; Zeller, Belle, *Pressure Politics in New York* (Prentice-Hall, New York, 1937), "Pressure Groups and Our State Legislators," *State Government*, July 1938, pp. 121–122, 124, and August 1938, pp. 144–147, 155, and "Lawmaker — Legislator or Lobbyist?" *National Municipal Review*, August 1940, pp. 523–532, 544; Ewing, Cortez A. M., "Lobbying in Nebraska's Legislature," *Public Opinion Quarterly*, July 1937, pp. 102–104.

addition to their regular salaries. Forty-six lobbyists reported that they had spent nothing."[13] Much more is spent than ever finds its way into the published reports.

The activities of the lobby are not confined to work for or against the passage of bills. Lobbyists are responsible for the introduction of a great many bills, and they are frequently in contact with administrative officers, for it is often as important for them to influence the interpretation of an act as to get it passed. In fact, this is their last resort, short of court action attacking the measure on grounds of constitutionality or upon the basis of some technicality. Having been unable — for whatever reason — to prevent the passage of an unwanted bill, they must now seek to obtain an administrative determination of its meaning and effect that will produce a minimum of inconvenience or expense to the interests which they represent.

It is possible to control legitimate legislative representation to some extent by laws to regulate lobbying activities, but there is apparently no legal method of preventing the exerting of pressure on legislators through the social lobby and other corrupt methods referred to; certainly the old legislation requiring registration has not succeeded in breaking it up.[14] Nevertheless, twenty-five states[15] and the Federal government have enacted laws requiring the registration of lobbyists and the payment of a small annual fee, penalty for the violation of which ranges from a prison sentence of thirty days to one year in eleven states, to Florida's maximum of twenty years' imprisonment for false swearing. In addition to a fine or prison sentence seven states provide for the disbarment of lobbyists found guilty of violating the act.

Eighteen states and the Federal government require lobbyists to file a statement of disbursements or payments promised in connection with the promotion of legislation. Thirteen of these states require filing of expense

[13] *New York Times*, July 16, 1933.

[14] See Zeller, Belle, *Pressure Politics in New York*, pp. 252–262, for analysis of the application of the New York Law (Prentice-Hall, New York, 1937); also her testimony before the House Select Committee on Lobbying, *Hearings*, Part I (81st Cong. 2nd Sess., 1950), and her discussion in the American Political Science Association's report of the Committee on American Legislatures, *op. cit.;* also Alabama Legislative Reference Service, *The Regulation of Lobbying* (Montgomery, 1949); Collings, Rex A., Jr., "California's New Lobby Control Act," *California Law Review*, August 1950, pp. 478–497; and Gibbs, Clayton R., *State Regulation of Lobbying*, Constitutional and Statutory Provisions of the States, Vol. IX (Council of State Governments, Chicago, 1951).

[15] The number of lobbyists registered in a number of representative states in 1949 was as follows (data from Zeller, *op. cit.*, American Political Science Association report):

California — 461	Maine — 144	North Carolina — 87
Connecticut — 375	Maryland — 126	North Dakota — 130
Florida — 318	Massachusetts — 347	South Dakota — 80
Georgia — 9	Michigan — 265	Texas — 254
Idaho — 5	Mississippi — 9	Vermont — 84
Indiana — 191	Nebraska — 72	Virginia — 111 (1948)
Iowa — 168	New Hampshire — 137	Wisconsin — 356
Kansas — 210	New York — 121	

statements within thirty days of the adjournment of the legislature; as a further check on objectionable lobbying, Wisconsin amended its law in 1945 to require detailed weekly statements of disbursements during the legislative session. Altogether, thirty-eight states provided by law in 1950 for some form of regulation of lobbyists. In one state, lobbyists are limited to making appearances before legislative committees, public addresses, and newspaper publications. The draftsmanship of most of these laws is so poor, their phraseology so vague, the enforcement procedures so inadequate, that they are scarcely worth the paper on which they are printed. They do not reach and, so far as one can see, they cannot reach the type of lobbyist who never goes near the capitol but, well supplied with cash, operates over the telephone and entertains his "friends" in an elaborate suite of hotel rooms.

Under such circumstances the legislation is insufficient to accomplish any effective control.[16] It has become customary to refer to the lobby as the third house of the legislature. It is the element of secrecy that is most objectionable. It has been suggested that this might be eliminated — that the interests represented in this way might be brought out into the open — by giving the lobbyists official standing by some system of functional representation. There are obvious difficulties of considerable magnitude in such a plan, but the idea may be worthy of consideration.

Research and Planning Services

Groping for Effective Planning. Of outstanding importance have been recent efforts at legislative planning. It has become evident to all students of legislation that a considerable part of the difficulty experienced with legislative machinery grows out of the lack of planning which is largely responsible for the rush at the end of the session and for many other legislative abuses. It takes so long to decide what kinds of legislation are needed, and to revise and perfect the necessary bills and get them through the preliminary stages, that, especially in those states which impose a definite limit upon the length of sessions, no adequate opportunity remains for the proper consideration of these measures. It is reasoned that if a plan for the session could be worked out before the legislature convenes, a large part of the time now lost in the early weeks or months of the session could be saved.

A number of schemes aimed jointly at saving session time and at developing a plan for each legislative session have been tried. California and a number of other states experimented with the split session. In 1931, Governor Philip La Follette of Wisconsin sponsored an Executive Council, composed of ten members of the two houses of the legislature together with an equal number of citizens appointed by the Governor. This Council proved to be short-lived. It became increasingly evident that some agency must be found

[16] See, for instance, "Indiana Lobby-Control Found Insufficient," *National Municipal Review*, November 1938, pp. 543–544, 560; also Lowenstein, Karl, "Occupational Representation and the Idea of an Economic Parliament," *Social Science*, October 1937, pp. 420–431.

in which both the legislature and the administration would have confidence, which would have some degree of permanence and responsibility, which could work effectively, and which would not at the same time usurp or be subject to the charge of usurping the prerogatives of the legislature. As Dr. Guild has said:

> Whatever the prevailing idea in the back of individual minds in the respective states, the essential fact is that legislatures were searching for an agency which they could call their own, under their control and direction, whose staff worked solely for the legislature. What they wanted was a legislative service which would provide accurate information, with assurance of careful, comprehensive, impartial analysis of their problems, and adequate and prompt answers to their questions.

The objectives of legislative planning are easier to visualize and to state than to realize. It should be borne in mind, as Dr. Guild has pointed out, that "the Council has no legislative power whatever. Its recommendations must stand on their merits, and Council suggestions are approved not because it was the Council that made them but because they were obviously based upon adequate fact-finding." When the members of the legislature came to realize "that there was no centralization of legislative power in the Council; that the Council was merely another legislative committee whose function was to give preliminary shape to policy formation and to provide adequate factual backgrounds for any points of view; and that all responsibility or power still remained in the hands of the regular standing committees, this critical attitude or fear declined rapidly during the 1937 session."[17]

Kansas Legislative Council. The Kansas Legislative Council, first and most significant representative of its type, was established in 1933. Its membership includes the president of the Senate as chairman, the speaker of the House as vice chairman, and ten members from the Senate and fifteen from the House. It began its work in the special session of 1935, during which it sponsored twenty-eight measures; in the regular session of 1935 it sponsored twenty-six more. These measures were drawn up and printed in the usual form. Its major contribution during its early years, while very great, "did not lie in the policies or bills suggested but merely in providing for all members of the legislature a thoroughly digested background on all major problems" to be considered. The Council emerged from the 1937 session with the reputation of being a successful, fact-finding preparatory body. The research function was recognized as indispensable, weeding out the impossible solutions of problems and sharpening the issue to permit a more concentrated consideration of the more promising solutions. Since new problems are studied only under Council direction, "research" — as Dr. Guild puts it — comes to mean "immediate practical assistance" in the solution of legislative problems, thereby making possible a synthesis of the expert and the legislator.

[17] New York Joint Legislative Committee on Legislative Methods, Practices, Procedures, and Expenditures, *Final Report*, p. 144, and quoted by Hawaii Legislative Reference Bureau, *Legislative Aids*, p. 17 (University of Hawaii, 1948).

A recent progress report of the Council states[18]:

> The Council is a permanent joint committee of the legislature, meeting quarterly at the state capitol and giving advance consideration to problems expected to confront the next legislature. Its purpose is to formulate a program for the next session.
>
> In preparing this program, the Council: (1) acts as a clearing house for ideas on current legislative problems by receiving proposals from any member of the legislature; (2) determines and directs, through its committees and research department, the study and research necessary for proper consideration of all proposals; (3) disseminates advance information on these problems to other legislators and to the general public by means of progress and research reports and through committee activity and discussions at and between council meetings; and (4) reports directly to the legislature, one month in advance of the regular session, making recommendations in the form of bills or otherwise, and summarizing the material prepared for use of the legislature in considering the program.

The results have been extremely encouraging. Although the Council is not particularly interested in how many of its reports are acted upon, a great many of them have been favorably received. The reports grow out of requests from Council members, although the interest may have been inspired by members of the research staff. The reports themselves must be couched in understandable language; if the words are unfamiliar to the member, he is likely to cast the report aside as "theory." The material when completed must belong to the members — the staff must have a "passion for anonymity." As a result of these efforts, the idea has begun to develop among the members, and throughout the state, that preparation for another legislative session should begin promptly after one session has adjourned.

Research reports have been issued on a variety of subjects, such as the sales tax, state police, old age pensions, and institutional problems. Many of these reports have had nationwide circulation and have been used in many states, not only by legislative and administrative officers but by students and research workers. Although the Council is in reality an extension and enlargement of the ad interim committee idea, it has proved to be much more effective than ad interim committees had been in the past; the permanent character of its organization and its adaptability have been important points in its favor. Work of this type cannot be planned far in advance — the important things are done when the opportunity offers, as when some member of the Council drops in for a visit with something on his mind. The research requires a competent director, a trained staff, and months of time.

Spread of the Council Movement. Since 1933 the legislative council idea has spread to more than half the states; some of the details with regard to these bodies are shown in the table on page 259. They range in size from three or four members in South Carolina and Nevada to twenty-seven in Kansas to one hundred and sixty-two in Oklahoma. Ex-officio membership is kept at

[18] Publication No. 156, September 1, 1948.

a minimum; nonlegislative members appear to exist in only one state — South Carolina. The annual budgets for those states that reported this information range from $15,000 to $50,000, with the exception of four states — Kentucky

Legislative Councils and Research Committees *

DATE	STATE	NAME OF AGENCY	SIZE	SENATORS	REPRESENTATIVES	EX OFFICIO
1933	Kansas	Legislative Council	27	10	15	2
1936	Kentucky	Legislative Research Commission	7	3	3	1
	Virginia	Advisory Legislative Council	9	4	5	..
1937	Connecticut	Legislative Council	18	4	8	6
	Illinois	Legislative Council	22	10	10	2
	Nebraska	Legislative Council	43	43	..	..
	Pennsylvania	Joint State Government Commission	24	12	12	2
1939	Maine	Legislative Research Commission	10	3	7	..
	Maryland	Legislative Council	20	6	6	8
	Oklahoma	Legislative Council	162	44	118	2
1941	California	Joint Legislative Budget Committee	10	4	4	2
1943	Missouri	Committee on Legislative Research	20	10	10	..
	Ohio	Program Committee	21	5	5	11
	Wyoming	Legislative Interim Committee	12	6	6	..
1945	Alabama	Legislative Council	12	4	6	2
	Indiana	Legislative Advisory Committee	8	3	3	2
	Nevada	Legislative Counsel Bureau	4	2	2	..
	North Dakota	Legislative Research Committee	11	5	6	..
1947	Arkansas	Legislative Council	22	7	13	3
	Minnesota	Legislative Research Committee	18	9	9	..
	Utah	Legislative Council	13	4	4	5
	Washington	Legislative Council	21	9	10	2
	Wisconsin	Joint Legislative Council	15	5	8	2
1949	Florida	Legislative Council	18	8	8	2
	South Carolina	Legislative Council	3	..	..	3
	Texas	Legislative Council	17	5	10	2
1951	New Hampshire	Legislative Council	48	3	40	5
	New Mexico	Legislative Council	9	3	4	2
	South Dakota	Legislative Research Council	110	35	75	..
1952	Louisiana	Legislative Council	18	8	8	2

* Data from *Book of the States, 1952–1953*, p. 122 (Chicago, 1952).

at $75,000, Kansas and Missouri at $95,000 each, Pennsylvania at $125,000. Eight states spend between $15,000 and $25,000 while nine spend between $30,000 and $50,000. All but two states pay expenses of members incurred in attendance at meetings, and more than half provide a modest per diem. Meetings are held quarterly in six states, quarterly and on call in seven, on call only in eight, while four have miscellaneous provisions.

All of the councils have power to appoint a research staff, and all but two of them — Pennsylvania and Virginia — are authorized to utilize other state agencies, to subpoena witnesses, and to hold hearings. There is surprising uniformity with regard to functions and duties, which include gathering information, preparing research reports, recommending legislation, drafting bills, investigating administrative agencies to effect economy, studying the procedures of the legislature and the financial and personnel needs of the government.

It has often been said that an institution is but the lengthened shadow of a man. The council movement is what it is largely because of the character of Frederic H. Guild, because of his courage and devotion to an idea. He has not only contributed greatly to the success of the Kansas Council, which he helped to establish, but he has had a profound influence upon the development of councils in other states. It has become standard practice for states working on council legislation to send a delegation to visit "the sage of Topeka." In a recent comment on the movement, Dr. Guild said [19]:

> At the time of its initiation in Kansas in 1933, there was no general agreement on a single objective or method of procedure for a legislative council. A combination of objectives, although somewhat different in detail, converged on the central idea of providing the legislature with facilities not available from any previously existing organization. . . .
>
> The research process is frequently a lengthy one. Legislative sessions were short. Legislative committees had to rely upon such materials as had been prepared by other agencies, frequently not for the specific purpose under legislative consideration, such as monograph material, articles in magazines, or other special studies of students in the field, very commonly not applied directly to the particular problem in their state. If these did not cover the particular points involved in current decisions, there was little chance of securing adequate information before adjournment.
>
> Those who were supposed to know could be called in for advice. A frantic effort could be made in the limited time to secure as much additional informa-

[19] "Legislative Councils: Objectives and Accomplishments," *State Government*, September 1949, pp. 217–219, 226. In addition to references in previous editions of this volume, see: Davey, Harold W., *Legislative Councils* (Iowa State College, Ames, 1949); Hawaii Legislative Reference Bureau, *Legislative Aids* (University of Hawaii, 1948); Larsen, Christian L., and Ryan, Miles F., Jr., *Aids for State Legislators* (Bureau of Public Administration, University of South Carolina, 1947); Louisiana Constitution Revision Projet, *The Legislature — The Legislative Council*, Constitutional Problems No. 37 (Louisiana State University, 1947); Miller, William, *The Legislature — The Legislative Council* (Governor's Committee on Preparatory Research for the New Jersey Constitutional Convention, Trenton, 1947); Smith, George D., *Aids for Lawmakers: a Survey of Legislative Reference Services and Legislative Councils* (Bureau of Public Administration, University of Washington, 1946).

tion as possible. Lobbyists and special interests did yeoman service, honestly and liberally in various instances, but often with special motives and to their own advantage in others. One source of information had to be played against the other. The average legislator was confused and bewildered in trying to sift the evidence. There was rarely confidence that the material which the legislature did have was comprehensive and adequate. Hence, the stress on the importance of research and fact-finding on the part of the early created legislative councils, and the immediate recognition of the value of the new service when its results were presented adequately in advance of the session.

Council Relationships with Other Agencies. There are in practice many problems of interrelationships with other governmental agencies which such a council must work out — relations with the governor, the public, and the legislature, and to other agencies such as the judicial council, the legislative reference bureau, the bill-drafting service, and to the state university. Many of these questions were investigated by the Maryland State Planning Commission in a comprehensive report on legislative councils, previously cited. The Kansas Council reports no definite clash with the executive, and apparently few such conflicts have developed in other states. The hostility of the executive in Michigan, however, was one of the factors which brought about the repeal of the act in that state. Public opinion seems to have been favorable except in Michigan and Illinois; in the latter state little attention has been given to the council by the press. In some cases resentment of nonmembers of the council toward members has been reported, although this will probably tend to disappear "as the true purpose and functions of the council become more evident." Members really have little reason to fear that the councils will become superlegislatures.

The problem of relations with other established agencies is more difficult, because the council supplements or supplants their activities. This is true of both standing committees and special committees or commissions of the legislature in so far as their investigating functions are concerned. These functions they are ordinarily not equipped to perform. The council does not in any way infringe upon the prerogative of standing committees in considering and deciding upon the provisions of proposed legislation. The jurisdiction of special committees is limited, while a council has the advantage of being able to investigate any proper subject of legislation. A well-organized council will to some extent overlap the functions of a legislative reference bureau. Both must maintain a library of information on legislative subjects, but the council will normally do more and better work in the field of research than the bureaus have done in the past.

The nature of this interrelationship needs clarification. The council principle is preferable to other forms of organization for legislative service; under it the legislative leaders work out their own program and determine the nature and scope of the research work to be done. In the reference bureau little or no planning is done, and the members are more in the position of having to accept whatever is given them by way of information. There should be no conflict with the bureaus, however, so far as their efforts are devoted to bill drafting, nor should there be any conflict with the legislative counsel in those states where such an officer has been established to give technical assistance to legislators in bill drafting. The job of bill drafting was not within the province of the legislative council as originally conceived but may be an important part of its future program. The councils should seek to avoid, as in practice they have done, any conflict with such agencies as a code commission or a judicial council, whose activities are confined to a definitely restricted field. Close cooperation should be maintained with the state university and other educational institutions.

Legislative Counsels. The office of Legislative Counsel has been created in five states — California, Idaho (inoperative), Massachusetts, Washington, and Wyoming. Nevada has a Legislative Counsel Bureau which functions more in accordance with the legislative council plan. Of the four legislative counsels actually functioning, that of California is most firmly established, has the largest staff (approximately thirty), and does the most effective job. Its annual appropriation runs slightly under $350,000. It is responsible to the legislature, by which body its staff head is selected. It provides all types of legal services for members and committees, including bill drafting, statutory revision, bill and law summaries, research reports, answering spot inquiries, advising and counseling. The Counsel in Massachusetts performs all of the same regular duties except that of preparing research reports.

Bureaus of Governmental Research. In the last decade, bureaus of governmental research and public administration have been established in many institutions. Particularly in the South and West, where these bureaus function in the great state universities, they undertake numerous important research projects — often at the request of members or committees of the legislature — the reports on which are of direct benefit to that body. Some of them, like the Bureau at the University of California, which has a large staff, have developed close working relationships with the legislature. This Bureau, established in 1930, has developed its activities along four lines: (1) *Service* — fact-gathering for California legislators and other public officials; (2) *Library* — building up an extensive library on public affairs; (3) *Training* — preparing young men and women for public service careers; (4) *Research* — conducting useful long-time research projects in public administration. The latter result in legislative bulletins on vital legislative problems of general interest, and in special reports prepared for individual legislators or legislative committees. The Bureau maintains a representative in Sacramento for several days each week during the session, for research and informational assistance to members.[20]

[20] See *Legislative Information Please. . . .* (Bureau of Public Administration, University of California, 1947). Other bureaus of governmental research and public administration at state universities furnishing research service to legislators include: Alabama, Indiana, Kansas, Kentucky, Maryland, Michigan, Mississippi, North Dakota, Oregon, South Carolina, Tennessee, Texas, Virginia, Washington, West Virginia.

Bill-Drafting Services

Evidences of Poor Draftsmanship. The statute books of every state in the Union present indisputable evidence of the failure of legislative bodies to perform the work of draftsmanship in a manner even reasonably satisfactory. Many of the statutes passed cannot have been expected to mean what they say; laws which mean nothing are not uncommon, while others attempt to provide for utterly impossible things. As Professor Holcombe has observed:

> Crude, almost illiterate legislation is constantly coming to light through the proceedings of the state courts; . . . A regulation found in the road law of one state that no one shall operate a political steamroller or band wagon on the highway doubtless was put there in jest, but there is nothing funny about a provision, found in the same state, that proprietors of hotels shall keep the walls and floors of their rooms covered with plaster. In Massachusetts, where things are supposed to be done better, one legislature, in trying to prevent the display of the red flag of anarchy upon the highway, succeeded in forbidding Harvard students from carrying their college banner to the football field.[21]

Best of all, perhaps, was a statute enacted in Kansas some years ago regarding the meeting of railroad trains on a single track; the law provided that in such cases each train should take to a siding, and remain there until the other should have passed. In Ohio in 1913 the legislature provided that the coat of arms should be engraved on the officials of the state. One Pennsylvania member succeeded in getting up to a vote on final passage a bill prohibiting the shearing of hydraulic rams between November 1 and March 31.[22] Governor George H. Hodges of Kansas set forth in an address before the Governors' Conference in 1913 some observations based upon his then recent experiences.

> Notwithstanding the fact my executive clerk and the attorney-general did their best to scrutinize all the bills, Chapters 177 and 178, and Chapters 174 and 175, respectively, are duplicates. Chapter 75 of the laws of 1911 was repealed three times. . . . Chapter 318 of the laws of 1913 was immediately amended by Chapter 319 of the laws of 1913, Chapter 82 of the laws of 1911 was repealed by Section 7 of Chapter 89 of the laws of 1913, and after being repealed was then amended and repealed by Chapter 108 of the laws of 1913.[23]

[21] Holcombe, Arthur N., *State Government in the United States*, Third Edition, pp. 313–314 (Macmillan, New York, 1931).

[22] This kind of material is constantly coming to light; see Seagle, William, "Lunatic Legislation," *Plain Talk*, April 1929, pp. 457–466. Improper punctuation made it illegal for nine years to sleep in a hotel room in North Dakota. A New York senator in 1936 got a pension bill for Private Evael O. W. Tnesba (absent without leave) up to final passage. A jokester in California in 1937 moved along an appropriation bill for over $6,000,000 to dredge "the Pee-Wee River in the County of San Diego, which river flows two and one-fourth inches of water during three days of each year, if and when it rains."

[23] Delivered at Colorado Springs, August 26, 1913. The text of the address may be found in the *Proceedings* of the Governors' Conference or in Ewing, Cortez A. M., and Dangerfield, Royden J., *Documentary Source Book in American Government*, pp. 641–652 (Heath, Boston, 1931).

One should not assume that the lapse of time since 1913 has changed things very much. In 1949 the Legislature of Tennessee, after spending four years and $100,000 preparing a supplement to the State's 1932 code, undertook to enact it into law. The bill that was passed, however, proved to be nothing more than a parenthetical statement saying that a new code was attached. Yet this measure passed both houses, was signed by the presiding officer of each, and by the Governor. It lacked even the elemental requirement of an enacting clause. It was never engrossed or enrolled properly, nor was it ever officially transmitted to the Governor and the Secretary of State.[24]

Upon the basis of a record from which the above illustrations are by no means unusual, there can be little question regarding the incompetence of the legislatures in the drafting of statutes. This difficulty has been due to the absence of adequate bill-drafting services, and to the fact that the legislators introduce large numbers of bills that come, as Woodrow Wilson observed, "out of cubbyholes all over the state." Large numbers of the measures introduced are not drafted by the members who present them but by corporations, groups, and private citizens who have some special privilege which they want conferred by legislative action.

Bill-Drafting Services. The early legislative reference bureaus attempted to combine the information service described above with technical assistance in bill drafting. In later years, when the need for adequate assistance of this type has come to be generally recognized, progress has been made, as is convincingly shown by the improved quality of much of the legislative output. Most of the states now possess some official agency whose business it is to draft, to assist in drafting, or to examine for correction bills submitted by members which have been already drafted by others. A former director of the Legislative Reference Bureau in Wisconsin states that practically all bills introduced in that state have been either drafted or approved as to form by the bill-drafting service. In New York and Pennsylvania competent persons estimate that at least 95 per cent of the bills introduced have been examined by the bill-drafting service. In the latter state the Legislative Reference Bureau often drafts more bills than the total number introduced in the two houses during the session. Of course, many of those drafted are not introduced, while some of those that are introduced were drawn elsewhere than in the Bureau.

There is no uniform plan for the organization of a state bill-drafting service. A survey made early in 1950 by Professor Mona Fletcher for the American Political Science Association's Committee on American Legislatures showed that in eighteen states this service was rendered to members, at least in part, by the attorney general; in fourteen, by the legislative reference service; in eight by the legislative council; in seven by the legislative counsel or comparable officer; in four by the state library or state law library; while in five, no provision is made for such assistance. In Iowa and Pennsyl-

[24] Travis, Fred, "Tennessee Affairs" column, *Chattanooga Times*, November 13, 1949.

State Bill-Drafting Services

ATTORNEY GENERAL	LEGISLATIVE COUNCIL	LEGISLATIVE REFERENCE SERVICE	COUNSEL DIRECTOR REVISOR	STATE LIBRARY	NONE
Arkansas	*Arkansas*	Delaware	Alabama	Arizona	Idaho
Colorado	Maine	*Florida*	California	*Iowa*	Montana
Florida	Missouri	Illinois	Connecticut	*Oklahoma*	Nevada
Georgia	Nebraska	Indiana	Kansas	Rhode Island	West Virginia
Iowa	North Dakota	Kentucky	Massachusetts		Wyoming
Louisiana	South Carolina	*Maryland*	*Minnesota*		
Maryland	*Texas*	Michigan	Virginia		
Minnesota	Utah	New Jersey			
Mississippi		New York			
New Hampshire		Ohio			
New Mexico		*Pennsylvania*			
North Carolina		Tennessee			
Oklahoma		Vermont			
Oregon		Wisconsin			
Pennsylvania					
South Dakota					
Texas					
Washington					
18	8	14	7	4	5

vania, and probably in other states, drafting services are provided in more than one office. The results of the Fletcher survey are shown in the table on this page; names of states using two different methods are in italics.

The Council of State Government's Committee on Legislative Processes and Procedures in its report in 1948 noted that "a number of states have published manuals covering such factors as form, style, and grammatical construction of bills," and recommended that such manuals be made generally available in order to assure greater uniformity and adherence to desirable style and form in the measures introduced into the legislature. A survey made by the Council in 1950 revealed that there were eighteen states having official or unofficial manuals then in use, and six in which such manuals were being planned or were in course of preparation.[25] The remaining half of the states do not appear to have specific bill-drafting manuals, although in most states the rules of the senate and/or house contain certain requirements governing the general form of bills. These do not contain the detailed technical information included in a real bill-drafting manual.

[25] See *State Bill-Drafting Manuals*, Revised (Council of State Governments, Chicago, 1951); Cultice, Robert D., *A List of Selected Publications on the Drafting of Legal and Legislative Instruments* (Ohio State University College of Law, 1951); and Jones, Harry W., "Bill-Drafting Services in Congress and the State Legislatures," *Harvard Law Review*, January 1952, pp. 441–451.

It is difficult for the layman to understand why any reasonably intelligent person should not be able to draft a bill. The truth is, however, that the work is of a highly technical nature — so much so that few lawyers or political scientists are qualified to do it without special training and a period of apprenticeship. Two or three important problems are involved. The draftsman must know, in the first place, the exact nature of the provisions of the existing law; if he does not know this from practical experience, he must be able to use the tools of the lawyer quickly and effectively to secure this information. Secondly, he must know exactly what changes he desires to make. It should be self-evident that he cannot know this if he does not know what the existing provisions are. Finally, he must be able to determine a suitable means of accomplishing these changes, and to express his intention in clear, definite, and understandable language. He should have sufficient imagination to envisage the problems of enforcement which are likely to arise under each of the available methods of treating the subject. As President Wilson once observed, there is nothing easier than to draft an unworkable law, and nothing more difficult than attempting to enforce it.

Certain fundamental principles must be observed in the conduct of a successful drafting service. The bill drafter cannot tell the legislator what ought to go in his bill. He must try to secure a clear understanding of the legislator's purpose and intent and then attempt to write these ideas and principles into a bill which will make their realization possible. He must be concerned with questions of constitutionality, but he cannot pass upon questions relating to the wisdom of the policies proposed. The members must be convinced that they are being given every possible attention and courtesy and that their requests are being handled in the order in which they are received, unless in some particular case there is definite justification for doing otherwise.[26]

Mention should be made here of the work of the Drafting Committee of the Council of State Governments, discussed in Chapter 24, which through interstate cooperation is obtaining better legislation on many subjects of current interest as well as promoting the idea of uniformity in state legislation.[27]

Statutory Revision and Codification

Statutory revision and codification has become a subject of great importance as the total quantity of statutory law has increased. As the years pass, one legislative session after another enacts new measures, repeals old ones, and amends many others. The longer the state goes without a codifi-

[26] See *State Bill-Drafting Manuals*, *op. cit.*, and the manuals themselves for discussions of the technique of bill drafting. In 1937 the General Assembly of Pennsylvania passed a statutory construction act, which answers many questions so far as this state is concerned; see Act of May 28, 1937 (P. L. 282).

[27] See Wilkes, James C., "Better Legislation through Cooperation," *State Government*, January 1949, pp. 16–18, 22.

cation, the more urgent the need for it becomes; the session laws become more bulky, and it becomes increasingly difficult to follow through, with accuracy, the statutory provisions on any given subject.

The table on this page, based on a survey of all the states, shows that provision for continuous revision is made in thirteen states, for periodic revision in nineteen, but that there was no provision at all for revision in sixteen states. There are many different ways in which this work may be done. It may be performed by a public agency, or by a private law publishing firm. However, if the codification is to have the effect of law, it must be approved by the legislature; this requirement tends to encourage the legislatures to assume responsibility for seeing that the work is done. Not only must a distinction be made between periodic and continuous revision — which is mainly a question of timing — but between the different kinds of revision, i.e., comprehensive or bulk revision as contrasted with revision on a topical basis. The two are interrelated. Periodic revision is likely to be comprehensive. Topical revision is likely to be periodic. Comprehensive or bulk revision may be either continuous or periodic.

Provision for Statutory Revisions and Codification

CONTINUOUS	PERIODIC		NONE
California	Alabama	Oregon	Arizona
Connecticut	Arkansas	Pennsylvania	Delaware
Illinois	Colorado	Rhode Island	Florida
Kansas	Idaho	South Dakota	Georgia
Louisiana	Iowa	Tennessee	Indiana
Maine	Missouri	Utah	Kentucky
Massachusetts	Nebraska	Vermont	Maryland
Minnesota	New Hampshire	West Virginia	Michigan
Mississippi	New Mexico	Wyoming	Montana
New Jersey	North Carolina		Nevada
New York			North Dakota
Washington			Ohio
Wisconsin			Oklahoma
			South Carolina
			Texas
			Virginia

Periodic or Bulk Revision. Under a periodic revision plan the task of revision is undertaken at long and often irregular intervals. The resulting code must, very soon, be supplemented by consulting one or more volumes of session laws, if one is to be sure that he has seen all the law pertaining to the subject at hand. In contrast, under a continuous revision plan new enactments are fitted into their proper place in the code structure and given appropriate numbers, thereby keeping the code at all times complete and up to date. It is important, in any case, that the work be done, not only because of the great inconvenience involved in the use of the session laws, particularly by Federal officials and by persons in other states, but because of the impetus which codification gives to the systematic and orderly development of the law.

It is reported that revision in this country dates back to 1776 when Thomas Jefferson was a member of a commission "to revise, alter, amend, or repeal the said laws, to form the same into laws, and report them" to the Virginia legislature. In modern times, it appears that every state has a different conception of the proper composition of a codification commission. A Nevada survey reports [28]:

> When the legislature of the State of Utah authorized the codification of laws in 1941, it provided that the commission was to be composed of the Governor, the Attorney General, and the president of the State Bar. In Ohio, code revision is under the direction of a nine-member commission, composed of three members of the House of Representatives appointed by the Speaker, three members of the Senate appointed by the President pro tem, and three practicing attorneys appointed by the Governor. No more than two of the members in each category are members of the same political party. The Senate and House appointees serve until their successors may be appointed and are qualified, whereas those selected by the Governor serve six-year terms. The law-revision and bill-drafting commission of New Jersey consists of five members, one member from the Senate appointed each year by the President of the Senate, one member from the Assembly appointed each year by the Speaker, and three lawyers of ten years standing appointed by the Governor for a six-year term.

Regardless of the membership of the codification commission, it must have staff assistance for the actual performance of the work. The principal functions of a code-revision program were summarized as follows in the Nevada report: (1) to determine what statutes are in force, to obtain copies of such statutes, and to establish a convenient master file containing true copies of the operative statutory law of the state; (2) to eliminate from the statutes the obsolete, antiquated, unconstitutional, and unnecessary sections; (3) to determine, list, and correct the partially obsolete sections; (4) to bring together, under a logical classification system, those statutes and parts of statutes which, because of similarity of subject matter, properly belong together; (5) to simplify and clarify the statutes by restating them in clear and simple language, and to apply to their reconstruction uniformity of expression, capitalization, spelling, and punctuation; (6) to arrange the statutes relating to each subject in a logical sequence and according to the adopted plan and numbering system; (7) to apply a system of numbers so as to allow a maximum of elasticity for future enactments. The procedure involves the planning of the code, the adoption of a classification and numbering system, and the application thereof in the actual process of revision — a process which may require a great deal of time. New Jersey had a commis-

[28] Nevada Legislative Counsel Bureau, *Survey of Recodification Problems in Nevada*, p. 17 (Carson City, 1950).

sion that worked for twelve years codifying and revising the statutes of that state, reporting in 1937.

Continuous and/or Topical Revision. Where continuous revision is desired, some permanent agency must be established for the purpose, such as the New York State Law Revision Commission, established in 1934. This Commission, appointed by the governor, has made a commendable record. Or the legislature may itself create a commission to carry on the work, as in the case of the California Code Commission, which was established in 1929, prepared the School Code of 1929, and from 1931 to 1937 prepared eleven additional codes. Others are in course of preparation. The codes are printed by the state printer and are available at actual cost.[29] Connecticut has a Statute Revision Commissioner, appointed by the governor for a term of four years, with the advice and consent of the Senate, whose task it is to consolidate and codify all statutes and public acts of the state and to arrange them under chapters and sections. He also has the duty of preparing a cumulative supplement to the statutes after each regular session of the General Assembly.[30]

The New York State Law Revision Commission was created as a legislative aid in the reform and revision of the law. The basic idea of such a group had been presented by Justice Cardozo in an address before the New York City Bar in 1921. It consists of five members appointed by the governor for five-year terms, four of whom must be attorneys and two of whom must be members of the faculties of law schools within the state. This Commission differs from those in other states in that it concerns itself more with private than with public law. It emphasizes also the fact that, generally speaking, the states have been more interested in statutory revision than in codification. The duties of the Commission, as provided by law, are as follows:

1. To examine the common law and statutes of the state and current judicial decisions for the purpose of discovering defects and anachronisms in the law and recommending needed reforms
2. To receive and consider proposed changes in the law recommended by the American Law Institute, the commissioners for the promotion of uniformity of legislation in the United States, any bar association or other learned bodies
3. To receive and consider suggestions from judges, justices, public officials, lawyers, and the public generally as to defects and anachronisms in the law
4. To recommend, from time to time, such changes in the law as it deems necessary to modify or eliminate antiquated and inequitable rules of law,

[29] See biennial reports of the California Code Commission. In other states, either because the legislature fails to provide for a codification or, as in Pennsylvania, because of a constitutional barrier, there is no official code. In such cases, private law publishers may undertake the task. Cf. Purdon's *Pennsylvania Statutes Annotated*, 40 vols. (West Publishing Company, St. Paul). Private companies publish such editions in states which do provide an official code; see McKinney's *Annotated Statutes of the State of New York*, and the more recent Cahill's; or the Smith-Hurd *Revised Statutes of Illinois*.

[30] For a full description of his work, see Armstead, George B., *The State Services of Connecticut*, pp. 24–26 (Hartford, 1946).

and to bring the law of this state, civil and criminal, into harmony with modern conditions

5. To report its proceedings annually to the legislature on or before February first, and if it deems advisable, to accompany its report with proposed bills to carry out any of its recommendations

Some 1600 suggestions for study have been received by the Commission since its creation; its procedure in handling these numerous subjects has developed along the following lines[31]:

1. Presenting bills to the legislature concerning changes in the substantive law, with or without recommendations, but with explanatory notes

2. Presenting bills to the legislature which are revisionary in form with the object of correcting verbal errors, inconsistencies, errors in numbering, and errors in reference

3. Studies made at the suggestion of the governor and referred back to him

In addition to the Commission, New York, like many other states, also has a judicial council. The New York Council, created by statute in 1934, consists largely of attorneys and justices of the state courts, its chief duties being those connected with such studies and recommendations as will expedite the progress of matters before the courts. It is the established agency for instituting procedural reforms relating to the courts. Many of its reports relate to matters of substantive law and are therefore an influence in the direction of correcting and improving existing statutes.

The Wisconsin continuous revision also has worked well. The Office of the Revisor of Statutes was established in 1909. The Revisor is appointed by the justices of the Supreme Court and the Attorney General, his principal work being the continuous revision of the statutes. This includes the clarification of the language and the arrangement of the statutes, the elimination of obsolete and unconstitutional provisions, and the reconciliation of conflicting provisions. The revision work is presented to the judiciary committee of the Senate in "revision bills" which carry full explanation of any proposed changes in the law. The Revisor edits and annotates the *Wisconsin Statutes*, which are issued biennially; these statutes include the permanent general laws of the state then in force.[32]

In the process of continuous revision, bills passed by the legislature must be examined by the staff to determine whether the act is of a permanent and general nature or of a special or temporary nature. If the latter, the fact is noted on the signed copy of the act, and no code number is assigned to it. If, however, the act is of a general and permanent nature, the director assigns

[31] See MacDonald, John W., "The New York State Law Revision Commission: a Legislative Aid," American Bar Association *Journal*, June 1949, pp. 512–513; annual reports of the Commission's Executive Secretary and Director of Research; Illinois Legislative Council, *Law Revision Agencies*, p. 7 (Memorandum File No. 845, January 1949); and Campbell, Willard D., "Continuous Code Revision in Ohio," *Ohio State Law Journal*, Autumn 1950, pp. 553–550.

[32] *Wisconsin Blue Book, 1947*, p. 374, and Platz, William A., "The 1949 Revision of the Wisconsin Code of Criminal Procedure," *Wisconsin Law Review*, January 1950, pp. 28–48, and continued in issues for March and May.

a code section number to each code section in the act (unless the legislature has included such numbers, in which case they must be checked for conformity with the code numbering plan). This number, when assigned, becomes the official number of the section and is so used in the session laws or in any publication of the code.

Process of Codification. The processes of codification are complicated and technical, no two of the available analyses being exactly alike.[33] According to modern standards, a code should have three characteristics differentiating it from ordinary legislation: first, completeness in containing the law in force governing the subject of which it treats; second, a logical, scientific, and convenient arrangement; third, a clear and concise phraseology which avoids prolixity on the one hand and ambiguity on the other.[34] Some branches of the law lend themselves to codification more readily than others. Codes of law are extremely valuable for bringing organization and system into the legal structure; at the same time, they are only relatively permanent, nor can they be made more than relatively simple.

The first step in the codification process is to decide upon a plan which will result in the classification, arrangement, and numbering of all statutory provisions in accordance with some logical plan, and in the revision of such sections of the law as may require it. The framework of such a plan is shown in the table on page 272. A decimal system of numbering secures greater elasticity and provides ample space for new legislation. The following plan, which places at the disposal of the codifiers 1,000,000 section numbers, is used in Ohio [35]:

> The digits to the left of the decimal point indicate the title number. The first and second digits to the right of the decimal designate the chapter number, while the third and fourth digits to the right designate the section number. The first section of the first chapter of the first title is numbered 1.0101. The last section of the last chapter of the last title is numbered 57.4529. [Thus the last section] in the revised code is the twenty-ninth section in the forty-fifth chapter of the fifty-seventh title. In order to allow for the insertion of related new matter, the plan skips a title [several in some states] or chapter number after each title or chapter in the revised code. Because of this procedure, the number of the final title in the revised code is LVII despite the fact that there are only twenty-nine titles. The system will accommodate an unlimited number of new sections by carrying the decimals to additional digits.

Having determined the system of classification and of numbering, all existing sections are assigned to an appropriate chapter, at which time a new

[33] See Nevada study, *op. cit.;* Cullen, Robert K., "Revision of the Oregon Statutes," *Oregon Law Review*, February 1949, pp. 120–127; Heineman, Ben W., "A Law Revision Commission for Illinois," *Illinois Law Review*, January-February 1948, pp. 697–727; and Walker, Harvey, *The Legislative Process: Lawmaking in the United States* (Ronald Press, New York, 1949), as well as a number of references in earlier editions of this volume.

[34] Lobinger, Charles S., *Encyclopedia of the Social Sciences*, Vol. III, pp. 611–612.

[35] Bureau of Code Revision, *Report to the Senate and House of Representatives*, p. 33 (Columbus, 1949), and Campbell, Willard D., "Code Revision in Ohio," *State Government*, July 1947, pp. 195–196.

State of Missouri Code Plan — 1949

Code	Group	Title	Subject
POLITICAL CODE	*Structure of Government*	Title I	Laws and Statutes
		Title II	Sovereignty, Jurisdiction, and Emblems
		Title III	Legislative Branch
		Title IV	Executive Branch
		Title V	Military Affairs and Police
		Title VI	County and Township Government
		Title VII	Cities, Towns, and Villages
		Title VIII	Public Officers, Bonds, and Records
		Title IX	Suffrage and Elections
		Title X	Taxation and Revenue
	Governmental Services	Title XI	Education and Libraries
		Title XII	Public Health and Welfare
		Title XIII	Correctional and Penal Institutions
		Title XIV	Roads and Waterways
		Title XV	Lands, Levees, Drainage, and Public Water Supply
		Title XVI	Conservation, Resources, and Development
		Title XVII	Agriculture and Animals
CIVIL CODE	*Police Power*	Title XVIII	Labor and Industrial Relations
		Title XIX	Motor Vehicles, Watercraft, and Aviation
		Title XX	Alcoholic Beverages
		Title XXI	Public Safety and Morals
		Title XXII	Occupations and Professions
	Corporate Organizations	Title XXIII	Private Corporations and Associations
		Title XXIV	Business and Financial Institutions
		Title XXV	Incorporation and Regulation of Public Utilities
	Commercial Relationships	Title XXVI	Trade and Commerce
		Title XXVII	Debtor-Creditor Relations
		Title XXVIII	Contracts and Contractual Relations
	Property Law	Title XXIX	Ownership and Conveyance of Property
		Title XXX	Domestic Relations
		Title XXXI	Trusts and Estates of Decedents and Persons under Disability
REMEDIAL CODE		Title XXXII	Courts
		Title XXXIII	Evidence, Legal Advertisements, and Juries
		Title XXXIV	Civil Procedure and Limitations
		Title XXXV	Statutory Actions and Torts
PENAL CODE		Title XXXVI	Criminal Procedure [1]
		Title XXXVII	Crimes and Punishment

[1] A proposed revision of the Code of Criminal Procedure in New York in 1939 (Legislative Document No. 76) provided for the following nine titles: (1) Complaint, Arrest, and Examination; (2) Proceedings before Indictment or Information; (3) Indictment, Information, and Bill of Particulars; (4) Proceedings before Trial; (5) The Trial; (6) Proceedings after Judgment; (7) Judgment, Sentence, and Execution; (8) Appeals; (9) General Provisions.

number is substituted for the original one. Cross references should be inserted whenever necessary. A different procedure is established for obsolete or partially obsolete provisions. After the work sheets have been set up and the file of section cards established, the research attorneys can begin their work of examining the various chapters, section by section, for duplication, obsolete material, logical arrangement of material, and other pertinent matters. The chapters, when completed, should normally adhere to some such outline as the following:

ARRANGEMENT OF CODE CHAPTERS

1. Definitions
2. The law or leading principle of the chapter
3. Administration of the law:
    a. Authority to administer
    b. Procedure
4. Exceptional provisions
5. Penalties

When a completed chapter has been cleared with the control clerk, it is ready for typing and filing. If the state makes provision for continuous codification, the steps previously noted in that connection become operative. A definite plan for the order, classification, and arrangement of a code involves the establishment of a master file containing true copies of the operative laws of the state. In setting up such a file, each section of the law is clipped and pasted on a specially prepared card on which space is provided for symbols indicating the determinations of the research attorneys, such as "O" for "obsolete" and "P" for "partially obsolete." An additional sheet is attached to each card indicating the names of the proofreader and of the research attorney, comments relating to the history of the statute, Supreme Court decisions, and other pertinent information. The Nevada report continues:

> During a session of the legislature, this file is kept current with the daily work of the two houses. When a bill affecting a section of the code is introduced in either house, a green signal is placed on the file card containing that particular section. Additional colored signals are affixed to indicate the following legislative actions: blue signal — bill passed by Senate; red signal — bill passed by Assembly; purple signal — bill passed by both houses and signed by the Governor. Bills of a general nature passed by the Legislature and signed by the Governor are noted in the file, and thus a complete and accurate up-to-the-minute "master file," containing all newly enacted laws, can be maintained by the codification commission. The status of each law is readily ascertainable at a moment's notice.

Budgetary and Fiscal Analysis

Over a long period of time, on both sides of the Atlantic, English-speaking peoples fought to establish the right of their elected representatives to control the purse. That fight was won. The principle has now been long established that only the representative assembly can levy taxes and appropriate funds. This principle must be preserved, as one of the essential features of democratic government.

Once won, the problem of legislative control over finances for many years presented no grave problems. In fact, until three or four decades ago, legislative bodies assumed full responsibility for financial planning and policy determination. Government was simple and relatively small. Taxes were very moderate, revenues from an expanding economy were ample, and costs were low. With the development of the executive budget system and the emergence of "big government" in the twentieth century, all this has been changed. The extensive expansion of existing services and the constant addition of new governmental programs has transformed government into "big business." Budgets have become complicated, and call for ever increasing expenditures. Legislators were — and still are — dismayed, torn between the desire on the one hand to keep taxes down, and the necessity on the other of providing funds for a constantly growing number of essential services. In the face of mounting costs and the persistent demand for economy, they are sorely perplexed.

The problem of legislators is aggravated by the fact that they seldom have at their disposal the facts essential to intelligent judgment on budgetary matters. Ever suspicious of the executive, they fear that something is being "put over" on them. Yet, ordinarily, they dare not assume the responsibility for making heavy cuts in the absence of dependable factual data. Since they seldom have such data in a form in which it can be used effectively, the result is that, in session after session, they vote — reluctantly, to be sure — to approve all or most of the items submitted to them in the executive budget.[36]

Faced with this urgent problem, legislators everywhere — at both the national level and in the states — have been groping for help. At the state level, California led off by establishing the office of the Legislative Auditor in 1941, under the supervision of a legislative budget committee composed of five senators and five representatives. This committee employs the Legislative Auditor and a technical staff, the members of which, in addition to performing a good deal of general research for the legislature, have a definite responsibility to furnish assistance in the fiscal field. The staff attends all budget hearings before the Director of Finance and is permitted to question policies and data presented by the agencies as though it were a part of the budget staff. It reviews all audit reports of the agencies. It attends board meetings and conferences with executive agencies. It works closely with the legislative fiscal committees, and with the subcommittees of these committees in the preparation of their budget reports to the full committee, as well as in preparing special reports for them or for the full committee. It prepares

[36] For an illuminating comparison of legislative consideration of the budget in Washington and in Albany, see Mosher, Frederick C., "The Executive Budget, Empire State Style," *Public Administration Review*, Spring 1952, pp. 73–84.

a comprehensive report on the executive budget, line by line, and makes recommendations with regard to each item. At the close of the session, it prepares for the next session, reports on matters which the committees feel require further study.[37] Thus it appears that the Legislative Auditor provides a fairly comprehensive service of fiscal analysis and research for the members and committees of the California legislature. Utah adopted the California plan without modification.

Many other proposals have been made and some have been or are being tried. It has been suggested that the legislature establish a legislative budget bureau, but this proposal has usually been rejected on the ground that it involves duplication of effort and unnecessary expense. In 1947, the Kansas Legislative Council created the position of legislative fiscal officer and appointed a permanent subcommittee of the Council to make continuous study of the state budget. Washington established a similar legislative budget committee in 1951. Maryland in 1947 added a fiscal research bureau to the Legislative Reference Department; this is concerned with matters of local finance, but there is no reason why it might not be expanded to assist the legislature in dealing with the fiscal problems of the state.

Maryland also employs a mechanical engineer, a civil engineer, a farm management adviser, and two budget analysts to assist in getting accurate information. In New York, budget examiners are served by special research units in architecture, engineering, and administrative management. Minnesota has a financial research division. In 1949, a legislative auditor was added to the staff of the Legislative Counsel Bureau in Nevada. Similarly, in the same year, the Nebraska Legislative Council provided for a full time assistant director in charge of accounting and budgetary research. The legislative reference service agencies of a number of states, including Arkansas, Pennsylvania, and Wisconsin, regularly study the state budget.

In still another way, the legislatures are striving to make more effective their control over the purse. As noted in the preceding chapter, there is now a definite trend toward annual sessions in the state legislatures. In some cases, the change from biennial sessions is being made without restriction; in others, it is specified that the regular session in the odd-numbered years will be devoted to ordinary legislative problems, while that in the alternate years will be devoted exclusively to the fiscal problems of the state. If one is prepared to overlook the somewhat naive assumption that fiscal considerations

[37] Based on Post, A. Alan, "Fiscal and Administrative Review for the California Legislature," an address before the Legislative Service Conference, Madison, October 1951; see also California Legislative Auditor, *Analysis of the Budget Bill* (Sacramento, annually) and *Legislative and Executive Action on Budget Act and Special Appropriation Measures Enacted at the 1951 Regular Legislative Session* (Mimeographed Memorandum, Sacramento, July 31, 1951); Illinois Legislative Council, *Appropriation Requests and Enactments, Illinois General Assembly* (Springfield, biennially since 1947); Jones, Victor, *The Legislature and the Budget* (Bureau of Public Administration, University of California, 1941); and Knight, Charles R., *Legislative Budget Facilities* (Mimeographed Memorandum, Montgomery, 1949).

can be segregated from policy matters, so that fiscal problems can be considered in one session, policy matters in another, there is evidence here of an effort on the part of the legislatures (and of the electorates of the states concerned) to function more effectively in the field of fiscal policy.

President Roosevelt made a dramatic statement in 1937 that the President needs help. The legislatures need help also, if they are effectively to discharge their responsibilities in the determination of fiscal policy. The executive has a central budget office, and budget officers in each principal spending agency. It has thoroughly trained and well-qualified experts in each of the fields represented by its many programs. If the legislature is to make intelligent decisions with regard to these matters, it too must have competent staff assistance — engineers, accountants, social workers, agricultural experts, and many more — to assist it in reviewing executive requests for funds. Some of the legislatures are now employing such experts. The development of the executive budget has been a good thing; it is, in fact, essential to good administration. But informed and intelligent legislative review of the financial program is similarly essential to effective operation of the democratic process.

Problem of Over-all Organization

Legislative Service Conference. Although legislative reference work in the United States is now more than half a century old, the development of this and other staff services for legislators, such as bill drafting, research, statutory revision, and library services, has been very slow. Not until the close of World War II did these various services attain any real recognition and something like adequate financial support. In 1946 the Congress included in the Legislative Reorganization Act provisions which have made possible the recent rapid growth of the Legislative Reference Service in the Library of Congress. A rapid increase in the number of state agencies in this general field prompted the Council of State Governments in 1947 to call a conference of professional personnel providing staff services for state legislatures and legislative committees.

This conference authorized the appointment of an organizing committee, whose report was presented and accepted at another similar meeting in 1948. It was at this 1948 meeting that the Legislative Service Conference was formally organized. The 1948 and 1949 meetings were held in Chicago, the 1950 sessions at the Library of Congress in Washington, the 1951 session in Madison, Wisconsin, on the occasion of the fiftieth anniversary of the establishment of the Wisconsin Legislative Reference Library. The sessions now attract approximately 150 official delegates from legislative reference agencies and legislative councils in the states.

The early meetings were devoted largely to instructional talks by some of the ablest and most experienced men in the field, and to the swapping of information regarding work methods and problems, although some attention was given to the problem of exchanging information on research completed or in progress. While this type of thing still finds a place in the program, and probably always will, members of the Conference are beginning to think in terms of help on specific problems and in terms of long-range planning for more effective service in their respective states. Regional conferences of legislative service agencies are also being held, for the discussion of common problems.

Members are interested in obtaining information on significant current problems, so that they may be in a position to give authoritative advice to their legislators at home when these specific problems are presented. In 1950, for instance, the Congress enacted the new Social Security legislation (H. R. 6000), which raised important questions in the field of Federal-state relations. How did the new law affect existing state and municipal retirement systems? Should existing state retirement legislation be repealed? Could this legislation be repealed and then re-enacted? In an effort to secure the best available answers to these questions, a dinner meeting was arranged with selected staff people who had worked with both the Senate and House Committees while the legislation was in course of passage. While, in advance of administrative rules and regulations and of court decisions, final answers could not be given, the Conference members were able to obtain at least the best answers that could be given at the time.

Another important question involves the interchange of information regarding research done or in progress. The Conference, recognizing the waste of time and effort involved in duplication, tackled this problem even before formal organization took place. The Council of State Governments, which serves as secretariat for the Conference, was directed to gather and prepare for distribution among the several state agencies information on research reports received, new research assignments, and progress and status of earlier research assignments previously reported. This instruction resulted in the setting up of the *Legislative Research Checklist* — a forty- or fifty-page mimeographed bulletin appearing several times each year. Members may obtain copies of desired reports when these are available; in other cases they may obtain copies on loan from the Council offices.

A Plan for Over-all Organization. Members of the Conference early became aware of the lack of any orderly pattern of organization for the legislative service agencies in the states, and in 1949 they set up a committee to find out exactly what services were actually being rendered in each state and by whom. At the time of writing, this report had not been completed, but it is known that coverage of the field of essential services is incomplete in many jurisdictions and that every conceivable pattern of organizational arrangements exists. Many of the services are located in the executive branch and are not even under the immediate control of the legislature. The question is: how should these services be organized in order (1) to provide full coverage of essential services — reference and information, research and planning, bill drafting, statutory revision and codification, budgetary and fiscal analysis, and (2) to provide these services with maximum efficiency and at minimum cost?

The existing haphazard organizational arrangements obviously encourage both overlapping and duplication in some areas, and failure to provide service at all in others. There is little or no coordination of the existing services within the individual states. The best proposal for over-all organization that has yet appeared is to be found in the Report of the Joint Committee on Reorganization in the South Carolina General Assembly in 1949, a chart from which, in modified form, is reproduced on this page. It envisions a legislative council of ten members as the central coordinating agency, the council employing a director who would direct, supervise, and coordinate the work in each of the specialized aspects of legislative service work. The

A Proposed Plan of Over-all Organization

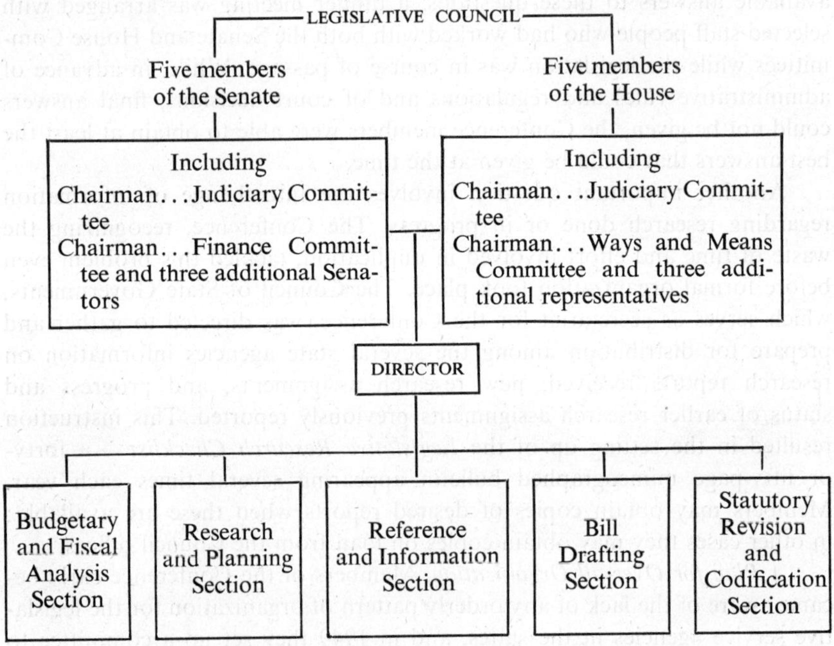

nature of the duties to be performed is indicated by the foregoing discussion and by the organizational setup. The clientele to be served would be primarily the legislative branch, including the individual members and the committees of both houses, and the joint committees, secondarily, the governor and the heads of departments, and private citizens.

A Legislative Institute. In the spring of 1950, Ralph M. Goldman, a student of legislative problems, proposed that a Legislative Institute be established in order to focus attention upon the legislative process as a major problem area of society and government and to provide a means for the scientific study and investigation of the legislative process on an organized and continuing basis. Provision for such institutes has long since been made in other fields which are certainly no more important. This proposal is a worthy one and received some favorable comment in the press. As Mr. Goldman has pointed out, "the need for a permanent, over-all research and service agency concerned with the legislative process is strongly manifest in the growth of certain movements, organizations, and the number of individual statements in recent years in this and closely related fields."

SELECTED REFERENCES

Council of State Governments, *State Bill Drafting Manuals* (Chicago, 1950). Among the better state manuals may be noted: MINNESOTA: Kennedy, Duncan L., *Drafting Bills for the Minnesota Legislature* (West Publishing Company, St. Paul, 1946); NEW JERSEY: New Jersey Law Revision and Bill Drafting Commission, *Manual for Use in Drafting Legislation for Introduction in the New Jersey Legislature* (Trenton, 1948); OKLAHOMA: Cobb, Randall S., *Bill Drafting Manual* (State Legislative Council, Oklahoma City, 1948).

Fitzpatrick, Edward A., *McCarthy of Wisconsin* (Columbia University Press, 1944). Contains chapters on the establishment and early development of the Wisconsin Legislative Reference Library, pioneer in the field.

Hawaii Statehood Commission, State Constitution Committee, *Legislative Aids* (Legislative Reference Bureau, University of Hawaii, 1948), and Davey, Harold W., *Legislative Councils* (Iowa Economic Studies, Iowa State College, Ames, 1949). Two excellent recent analyses of the organization and functioning of legislative service agencies.

Larsen, Christian L., and Ryan, Miles F., Jr., *Aids for State Legislators* (Bureau of Public Administration, University of South Carolina, 1947), and Smith, George D., *Aids for Lawmakers* (Bureau of Public Administration, University of Washington, 1946). Two useful summaries of problems in the field.

Nevada Legislative Council Bureau, *Survey of Recodification Problems in Nevada* (Carson City, 1950). Excellent survey of current practices and developments in the field of statutory revision and codification.

State Legislative Councils, annual or biennial reports. These reports are a mine of information on the nature and scope of the work of the councils, and with regard to the manner in which it is carried on.

8

State Legislative Procedure

In the first chapter on the legislative process the organization and structure of the lawmaking bodies was described, with emphasis on their representative character. In the next, the legislative service function was discussed, as it has developed in recent years. The present chapter is concerned with the powers of the legislature and the limitations on them, with the selection of the subjects to be considered and acted upon, and with actual consideration in committee and on the floor.[1] The formulation of the content of legislation and putting it in proper statutory form was discussed in the preceding chapter. Although the rules prescribe a formal procedure which is normally followed, there are many informal aspects of lawmaking which often have a bearing on the results of the session. These informal aspects, as well as some possible improvements in legislative procedure generally, are discussed in the concluding sections of this chapter.

Lawmaking Powers

The lawmaking powers of the legislatures are restricted by certain provisions of the Federal Constitution, by numerous provisions of the constitutions of the states, and, in some states, by the doctrine of implied limitations applied by the courts. As is shown in Chapter 1 on the nature of the federal system, the state governments are, under the provisions of Amendment X, governments of residuary powers. The legislatures are therefore in general free to act within that scope of governmental authority not definitely assigned to the Federal government in Article I, Section 8, or elsewhere, and not definitely prohibited to the states in Article I, Section 10. Among the acts prohibited are the making of treaties, the granting of letters of marque and reprisal and the passing of bills of attainder, the coining of money, the passing of ex post facto laws, the making of anything but gold or silver legal tender for the payment of debts, the passing of laws impairing the obligation

[1] Holcombe, Arthur N., *State Government in the United States*, Third Edition (Macmillan, New York, 1931), used a different classification of steps, which may still be useful: (1) the selection of the subjects upon which legislation will be considered; (2) the collection of information upon which intelligent legislative action may be based; (3) problems of draftsmanship; (4) actual consideration and enactment of bills.

of contract, the granting of titles of nobility, the levying of tonnage or export duties, and finally, engaging in war or keeping troops or ships of war in time of peace. Even when dealing with a subject which comes within the scope of their constitutional authority, the legislatures are restricted in the exercise of their power by important provisions of Amendment XIV; namely, those clauses which guarantee due process of law, equal protection of the laws, and the privileges and immunities of citizens.

The legislature at all times exercises its powers subject not only to the terms of the Federal Constitution and the constitution of the state, but also subject to such interpretations of the provisions of these instruments as the courts may choose to give them. In New York between 1914 and 1937 the Court of Appeals rendered twenty-six decisions holding legislative enactments unconstitutional. A striking illustration of the havoc that can be created by the abuse of judicial discretion in this connection occurred in Connecticut in 1929, when the State Supreme Court wiped out 1493 laws at a single stroke. By Article IV, Section 12, the Connecticut Constitution requires a law to be signed by the governor within three days of its passage by the legislature in order to become effective. During four preceding administrations governors, bombarded with bills at the end of the session, had studied them and signed them at their leisure. The Court, having to pass on an individual case, ruled by the letter of the law and declared that the act providing for state condemnation of a certain property was unconstitutional because the act was not signed by the governor within three calendar days of its passage. Automatically, as a consequence of this ruling, almost 1500 other laws actually in operation were made legally ineffective. An outstanding example of the resulting confusion was found in a gasoline tax law enacted in 1925, under which at the time more than $11,000,000 had been collected. In such an emergency, of course, a special session of the legislature was required.[2] Recent reports indicate that this practice has not been entirely eliminated.

The legislatures in some states are confronted not only with the normal hazards of judicial review but with the special doctrine of implied limitations which has been designed by the courts to limit legislative powers by narrow interpretations of delegated powers. When this is done, the hands of the legislature are severely tied. Theoretically, the legislature should be entitled to exercise those powers not denied to it by either the Federal or the state

[2] *Philadelphia Record*, July 30, 1929. See also: Fertig, John H., *Scope of the Legislative Power of the General Assembly* (Pennsylvania Legislative Reference Bureau, 1931); Everstine, Carl N., "The Establishment of Legislative Power in Maryland," *Maryland Law Review*, Spring 1951, pp. 99–121. Horack, Frank E., Jr., "The Common Law of Legislation," *Iowa Law Review*, November 1937, pp. 41–56; New York State Constitutional Convention Committee, *Problems Relating to Legislative Organization and Powers*, Chapter 5 (Albany, 1938); Ray, Joseph M., "Procedural Limitations on the Texas Legislature," *Southwestern Social Science Quarterly*, September 1938, pp. 152–160; and "Do Legislators Think Like Judges?" *State Government*, September 1938, pp. 163–164, 177.

constitution. The expressed constitutional restrictions, reinforced by this narrow doctrine of interpretation, tend to place lawmaking bodies in a strait jacket.[3]

Other Types of Legislative Power. A legislative body has executive and judicial powers as well as legislative. Both houses are responsible for exercising a general surveillance over the executive branch of the government, both with regard to its general administrative efficiency and its fiscal operations.[4] The upper house is usually entrusted with power to act on nominations submitted by the governor. If the latter belongs to the same party as a majority of the members of the upper house, there will probably be little difficulty; but if they are of opposite parties or of different factions of the same party, all sorts of obstructive tactics are possible.

The problem of legislative-executive relations is both important and difficult of solution. Under a democratic system of government, it is imperative that it be solved in some manner permitting proper legislative supervision of the executive. This includes, among other things, the power of the legislature, acting through its committees, to investigate any subject, department, or agency as may be necessary for the proper performance of its constitutional duties. As a means of achieving such supervision, Donald Axelrod, staff director of the New York State Joint Committee, whose excellent reports have been previously referred to, has suggested that[5]:

1. Provision be made for the routine forwarding of information from the budget office and other agencies to the fiscal committee on allocation of funds and expenditures
2. Provision be made for the postaudit of fiscal transactions of all executive departments and agencies by an agency of the legislature

[3] The Court of Appeals in New York gave a classic statement of this highly objectionable doctrine more than half a century ago: "When the validity of legislation is brought in question, it is not necessary to show that it falls appropriately within some express written prohibition contained in the constitution. The implied restraints of the constitution upon legislative power may be as effectual for its condemnation as the written words, and such restraints may be either in the language employed or in the evident purpose which was in view and the circumstances and historical events which led to the enactment of the particular provisions as a part of the organic law." Rathbone v. Wirth, 45 N.W. 15, 23 (1896). See also Page v. Allen, 58 Pa. 338 (1868); Mittleton v. Greeson, 106 Ind. 18 (1885); U.S. etc., Co. v. Harris, 142 Ind. 225 (1895); State Board v. Holliday, 150 Ind. 216 (1897); and *American Jurisprudence*, Vol. XI, 1937, Sec. 194, pp. 897–898, and authorities cited therein. See also Benton, Wilbourn E., *Population-Bracket Bills in Texas: A Study in Local and Special Legislation* (Doctoral dissertation, University of Texas, 1948).

[4] For discussion of the methods and scope of such supervision in one state, see Kammerer, Gladys M., "Legislative Oversight of Administration in Kentucky," *Public Administration Review*, Summer 1950, pp. 169–175, and on fiscal controls in another state, Bromage, Arthur W., "Restrictions on Financial Powers of the Legislature in Michigan," *State Government*, May 1947, pp. 141–143, 153.

[5] In material prepared for the American Political Science Association's Committee on American Legislatures, *Representative Assemblies in the American States* (Crowell, New York, 1953); see also Goldmann, Sidney, and Schettino, C. Thomas, *The Legislature — Investigations* (Governor's Committee on Preparatory Research for the New Jersey Constitutional Convention, Trenton, 1947).

3. Legislative leadership be strengthened by giving legislative leaders year-round responsibilities and an adequate staff
4. Working relationships between the legislature and the governor be extended and, in large part, formalized
5. Proposed legislation be examined from the standpoint of administrative feasibility as well as from the standpoint of technical bill-drafting requirements
6. All executive vetoes be reviewed by the legislature
7. Rules promulgated by executive agencies be reviewed by the legislature
8. The legislature extend and improve management controls within the executive departments

On the judicial side, the legislature must constantly make judgments with regard to the constitutionality of measures before it. More strictly judicial in character are the powers of the legislatures in connection with the impeachment process. Only executive or judicial officers are subject to impeachment. As in Congress, the charges are brought in the lower house, while the upper serves as a trial court. The process is cumbersome and time-consuming; it is frequently threatened if not actually used for political purposes, and is in general ineffective for the purpose for which it was intended, namely, relieving the public of the services of public officers who are dishonest or otherwise unfit. Other powers of a judicial or quasi-judicial character are illustrated by the dramatic attempt of Tom Mooney to secure a pardon from the California legislature in 1938 and by investigations of various sorts undertaken in other states. In the same year the General Assembly of Pennsylvania carried on an extensive investigation of charges of graft in the state administration.

Special Legislation. State constitutions establish not only restrictions on legislative power similar to those established by the Federal Constitution, but also many severe additional limitations upon the scope of that power — the result of a loss of public confidence in representative assemblies. Because legislatures in the past frequently sought to deal individually with matters relating to persons and property which should have been adequately covered by general legislation, and because they interfered in an often unintelligent and offensive manner in the regulation of purely local conditions, the restrictions apply particularly to these two types of special legislation. Abundant illustrations of these abuses can be found in the legislative history of any state.

Special or private legislation — i.e., legislation which applies to an individual, association, or corporation as distinguished from general law which applies to the state as a whole — is no new problem in the history of parliamentary bodies. Sir Thomas Smith gives his impressions of the work of an Elizabethan Parliament, specifying that it[6]:

> . . . changeth rights and possession of private men, legitimateth bastards, establisheth forms of religion, altereth weights and measures, giveth form of succession to the Crown, defineth of doubtful rights whereof is no law already

[6] Quoted by Luce, Robert, *Legislative Problems*, p. 621 (Houghton Mifflin, Boston, 1935).

made, appointeth subsidies, tailles, taxes and impositions, giveth most free pardons and absolutions, restoreth in blood and name, as the highest court, condemneth or absolveth them whom the prince will put to trial.

In order to prevent the continuance of practices equally unfortunate, many states have gone to great extremes in their constitutional provisions limiting legislative power, with the twofold purpose of attaining uniformity of laws throughout the state and of preventing the exchange of courtesies between members for the passage of special laws for the benefit of a favored few.[7]

These restrictions, numerous though they are, seem to be of three types: (1) prohibiting special, private, or local laws on any matters and in all situations which can be covered by general law; (2) listing in the constitution subjects which cannot be dealt with by special or local laws; and (3) requiring that all general laws, or laws of a public nature, be uniform in their operation throughout the state. The legislative provisions of all constitutions framed in the reconstruction period were based primarily on distrust of the legislature. The Pennsylvania Constitution of 1873 includes a list of twenty-eight limitations; the California Constitution of 1879, a list of thirty-three. Restrictions on subject matter are found in forty-two states. Some are very short, as in Arkansas and Maine. Delaware has only five restrictions. Others are very long. Alabama has thirty-one; Montana, thirty-six; Wyoming, thirty-four. The following, taken from a list of thirty in the new Missouri Constitution of 1945, are fair samples of this type of restrictive provision, which the reader might well compare with those in the constitution of his own state.[8]

THE MISSOURI CONSTITUTION
PROVISIONS LIMITING LEGISLATIVE POWERS

1. Authorizing the creation, extension, or impairment of liens
2. Granting divorces
3. Changing the venue in civil or criminal cases
5. Summoning or empaneling grand or petit juries
6. For limitation of civil actions
9. Changing the law of descent or succession
10. Giving effect to informal or invalid wills or deeds
12. Authorizing the adoption or legitimation of children
13. Declaring any named person of age
14. Changing the name of persons or places
15. Vacating town plats, roads, streets, or alleys
19. Locating or changing county seats

[7] Follows statement in Hixson v. Burson, et al., 54 Ohio 470, 482 (1896); see also Miller v. El Paso County, 150 S.W. 2d 1000, 1001 (1941); and 25 *Ruling Case Law*, 280, par. 68 ff., and notes.

[8] See Everstine, Carl N., *Local Government: a Comparative Study* (Maryland Legislative Council, 1944), and Biney, Charles C., *Restrictions upon Local and Special Legislation* (Philadelphia, 1894). For a complete compilation of these provisions, see *Popular Government*, February-March, 1949, pp. 58–79; also "Thirty Years of Private, Local and Special Legislation in North Carolina, 1917–1947," *ibid.*, pp. 34–57, in which these enactments are classified under thirty-four subject matter headings.

Even a casual examination of these items indicates that no legislature possessing standards of decency and integrity would deal with them on the basis of special legislation, yet all were at one time or another the subject of special enactments in practically all states. It may, however, be necessary to adopt special acts to meet emergency situations, to free communities from special acts passed years ago, and — in the absence of suitable administrative arrangements for the handling of claims — to make possible the payment of legitimate claims of citizens against the state. Legislatures ought to have power to meet such situations when they arise, and the public ought to have sufficient confidence in them to permit them to do so.

Local Legislation. Local legislation, i.e., legislation which applies to any political subdivision or subdivisions of the state less than the whole — is a distinctive type of special legislation, the often ridiculous character of which is well illustrated by a list of North Carolina statutes cited by Professor Mathews [9]:

To prevent the throwing of sawdust in Big Ivey Creek in Buncombe County
To prevent the sale of malt, near-beer, and beerine in Macon County
Providing that four and one-half feet shall be the lawful height of fences in Perquimans County
To prevent the depredations of turkeys, geese, ducks, and chickens in Catawba County
To prevent the shooting of firecrackers within one mile of the post office at Haw River
To make illegal the keeping of honey bees within 100 yards of the public roads in Pender County

While it is reported that twenty-eight states have granted home rule to cities and that this obnoxious practice of local legislation has been abolished in forty states,[10] it still exists in many more states than these figures might indicate. In these states, municipalities are governed primarily by local laws enacted by their respective state legislatures. In many states, as soon as constitutional restrictions upon such legislation were adopted, the legislature proceeded promptly to set up classes of local units, by the skillful planning and manipulation of which the constitutional restrictions might be partly if not wholly evaded.

In Alabama, Georgia, Nebraska, Tennessee, and Texas — to mention only a few states — the situation is particularly bad. In Alabama, local legislation accounts for approximately one third of the legislative output in regular sessions. A study of the problem in that state, covering the period from 1903 to 1943 inclusive, reveals that the number of local acts sometimes

9 Mathews, John M., *American State Government*, Revised Edition, pp. 247–248 (Appleton-Century, New York, 1934). For a similar list of local laws affecting the cities of New York State, see Wallace, Schuyler C., *Our Governmental Machine*, p. 112 (Knopf, New York, 1924); also Hyman, Dick, *It's the Law* (Knopf, New York, 1936), and Seagle, William, *There Ought to Be a Law* (Macaulay, New York, 1933). The compilation of lists of freak legislation has been a favorite "indoor sport" of magazine writers and feature writers for Sunday supplements.

10 *National Municipal Review*, November, 1947, p. 579.

equaled or exceeded the number of general laws, the average for the forty-year period being 35 per cent. Although exceptions at times interrupt the downward trend, the figures do show a decline from 55.9 per cent in 1903 to 30.1 per cent in 1943. The number of private acts was not large or particularly significant — about 5 per cent for the same period.[11] In Georgia, local measures may account for half of the output while, in addition, the former Constitution was cluttered up with a large number of amendments relating to purely local matters.[12] In Tennessee, where the legislature in 1945 passed approximately 800 bills, most of them local, the situation is acute. The unicameral legislature in Nebraska makes a mockery of classification, thereby disregarding the constitutional prohibition against special legislation for cities.[13]

Classification may be attempted on a subject-matter basis, a geographical basis, or a population basis, or in varying combinations of the three. While a wide range of subjects may be covered, the most popular concern fees, salaries, traveling expenses, and creation of local offices. Where the geographical basis is used, the law may be made applicable to any type of local unit. The Supreme Court of Pennsylvania in 1878 threw out such an act, applying to Crawford County and the City of Titusville, using this rather vigorous language[14]:

> This is classification run mad. Why not say all counties named Crawford, with a population exceeding 60,000, that contain a city called Titusville, with a population over 8,000 and situated twenty-seven miles from the county seat? Or all counties with a population of over 60,000 watered by a certain river or bounded by a certain mountain? There can be no proper classification of cities or counties except by population. The moment we resort to geographical distinctions we enter the domain of special legislation, for the reason that such classification operates upon certain cities or counties to the perpetual exclusion of all others.

The population basis has been widely used, but has apparently been developed to a high state of efficiency in Texas in its "population-bracket bills," which are of infinite variety. Professor Benton found one measure

[11] Farmer, Hallie, *The Legislative Process in Alabama*, p. 229 (Bureau of Public Administration, University of Alabama, 1949).

[12] In the six-year period from 1938 to 1943, the Georgia Constitution was amended more than 160 times. Approximately three-fourths of all amendments applied to a specifically named locality. Other states have not approached Georgia's experience in the use of constitutional amendments as local laws, although the device is not unknown in some states in the South and Southwest.

[13] See Siffin, Catherine F., *Shadow over the City; Special Legislation for Tennessee Municipalities* (University of Tennessee Record, June 1951), and Wasson, Hugh P., "Tennessee's Special Legislation Nuisance," in Seventh Annual Southern Institute of Local Government, *Proceedings, 1948*, pp. 1–4 (University of Tennessee, 1948); also Breckenridge, A. C., "The Mockery of Classification," *National Municipal Review*, November 1947, pp. 571–573, and Maryland Commission on Administrative Organization of the State, *Local Legislation in Maryland* (Baltimore, 1952).

[14] Commonwealth v. Patton, 88 Pa. 258, 259 (1879), and cited by Benton, Wilbourn E., "Population Brackets as a Method of Classification," *Southwestern Social Science Quarterly*, September 1950, pp. 117–135.

which had eleven brackets, under which seventy-four counties would have been included if only the upper and lower figures had been used. Sometimes, he reports, population brackets are mixed in with area or school population, the presence of cities of a certain size, and other factors. In fact, classification may be provided not only by the use of population figures but on the basis of the number of people per square mile, assessed tax valuation, area of local unit expressed in square miles or acres, number of scholastics, votes cast at a previous election, and any number of miscellaneous elements. More than a dozen different combinations of elements were discovered.[15] Thus, while classification was intended to protect local units from unwanted legislation, it often fails to accomplish this purpose. Many legislators are well aware of the defects of the system but are unwilling to support its abolition or modification because of the local prestige it gives them. In fact, it makes their services indispensable to any local unit in their district desiring to obtain new legislation or a change in existing law.

Other protective devices have been tried in other states. In Michigan, for instance, the constitution prohibits the passing of a local or special act in any case where a general act can be made applicable. In 1937 the United States Supreme Court threw out a statute establishing a county board of review of tax assessments applicable only to counties having a population of 500,000 or more, on the ground that it constituted a violation of this provision.[16] In New York, a provision requiring that a special act be accepted by a majority of the voters in the community affected before it could become operative was long in effect; a few years ago, this was changed to permit legislative action only upon the official request of the local unit concerned. A limitation in the Florida Constitution and in nine other states [17] now provides for publication in the community affected at least thirty days prior to passage. Evidence of such publication shall be furnished to the legislature and shall become a part of the official record of the bill in the journals and as filed in the office of the Secretary of State. No publication is required if the measure contains a provision to the effect that it shall not become effective until ratified or approved at a referendum election to be called or held in the territory affected, either under provisions contained in the bill or as provided by general law.

[15] Benton, *Population-Bracket Bills in Texas*, *op. cit.*

[16] Wayne County Board of Review, et al. v. Great Lakes Steel Corporation, 300 U.S. 29, 1937; the clause is in Michigan Constitution, Article V, Section 20.

[17] Article III, Section 21, appearing originally in 1868, and twice since amended, in 1928 and 1938. The nine other states are: Alabama, Georgia, Louisiana, Missouri, New Jersey, North Carolina, Oklahoma, Pennsylvania, Texas. Such a procedural requirement may be provided for by statute as well as by constitutional provision. The New Jersey Constitution, for instance, requires notice and publication, but in addition, there is a statutory restriction to the effect that the author of each private, local, or special act shall be assessed $25. Bills relating to benevolent, religious, charitable, or educational institutions are excepted from this requirement. The money must be paid into the state treasury before the law becomes effective.

In spite of these numerous attempts to curb the abuses of local legislation, the quantity of such legislation continues to constitute a significant portion of the total output in many states. There are, on the other hand, some situations which can be handled only by local laws, which may be good — or at least necessary — as well as bad. Local legislation tends to beget more local legislation, as conditions change and the need for modification arises. The Pennsylvania General Assembly, for instance, repealed in 1933 a section of an 1842 law entitled "An act to appoint commissioners to re-survey and mark that portion of the county line which divides the township of Bristol in the County of Philadelphia from the township of Cheltenham in the county of Montgomery, and for other purposes." Most of the items in the bill dealt with "other purposes," only a partial listing of which is possible here: a road to Dillsburg to be narrowed; four German Reformed congregations authorized to sell land; name of McKean Female Seminary changed to Troy Academy; election in Wysox to be held at the home of George Scott; new ward created in Lewistown; election of constables in Shirleysburg regulated; John Tritle and Jacob Byer authorized to sell real estate in Greencastle; survey of Saltsburg confirmed; three Tioga County townships authorized to elect additional supervisors; killing of birds regulated in Allegheny and Franklin Counties; and so on. This sort of thing, then common, is fortunately no longer possible. It ought not to be necessary for the legislature to repeal

State of Alabama
Bills Introduced and Acts Passed in the Regular Legislative Sessions, 1903–1949 *

YEAR	BILLS INTRODUCED SENATE	HOUSE	TOTAL	ACTS PASSED GENERAL	LOCAL	PRIVATE	TOTAL
1903	911	1298	2209	240	322	14	576
1907	1242	1632	2874	291	309	40	640
1911	799	1084	1883	242	135	9	386
1915	1552	2060	3612	391	239	94	724
1919	1241	1600	2841	455	176	29	660
1923	901	1301	2202	300	181	18	499
1927	1010	1469	2479	316	212	25	553
1931	1164	1536	2700	377	183	53	613
1935	878	1242	2120	316	171	22	509
1939	1061	1297	2358	379	197	25	601
1943	907	1105	2012	356	162	20	538
1945 [1]	328	665	993	226	172	9	407
1947	448	1034	1482	339	236	30	605
1949	658	1137	1795	283	283	26	592

* Compiled from data in Farmer, Hallie, *The Legislative Process in Alabama*, pp. 60 and 229 (Bureau of Public Administration, University of Alabama, 1949). Professor Farmer very kindly supplied the supplementary information to bring the table down to date.

[1] At this point, Alabama changed from a quadrennial to a biennial session plan.

an act of 1859 "relating to billiard saloons et cetera in the counties of Chester and Delaware and extending the same to Lycoming and Clinton Counties" in order to free Lycoming County from undesired restrictions.

Quantity of Legislation. Much comment has been made on the number of laws enacted by state legislatures. In contrast with early British experience, or indeed, with early experience in America, the difference is striking.[18] Americans seem to have retained from Puritan times a naive idea that anything wrong can be corrected by enactment of another statute; this has been particularly evident in the field of legislation affecting public morals. They often forget too that an unenforced and unenforceable statute may do more harm than good. While there has been much ground for criticism of the quantity of legislation, there are extenuating circumstances which prevent the situation from being as bad as it is often pictured. A large number of measures enacted are merely amendments to or modifications of earlier laws or are validations of the acts of public officers who have acted in good faith without proper legal authority. Many others relate to appropriations for various purposes or are classifiable as private bills. In most cases, if the output of a whole session is analyzed and the measures of the types indicated eliminated, the number of new general laws remaining will not be found unreasonable or excessive.[19]

In many states, data on the number of bills and resolutions introduced, the number of bills and resolutions passed, and the number signed and vetoed by the governor have been tabulated over a period of years. A table containing this information for Alabama from 1903 to 1949 appears on page 288; another showing the number of bills introduced in the General Assembly of Illinois at ten-year intervals from 1879 to 1949 appears on page 290. These and tabulations for other states indicate some increases in recent years though in no case anything that might be regarded as startling.

The following analysis of the output for one session in one representative state relates to the measures enacted by the General Assembly of Pennsylvania

18 Luce, Robert, *op. cit.*, comments on the apparently small amount of what we call constructive legislation adopted by the early British Parliament, which "in its first 300 years or more put forth less of new law than American legislatures enact in a single year. All the statutes of the realm up to Charles I fill but five volumes. . . ."

19 Herbert Spencer's piece on "overlegislation," in his *The Man versus the State*, has produced a never-ending curse of the terrible plague of laws, which the statisticians diligently perpetuate. In addition to much special and local legislation, many of the public acts deal with bridges, highways, military affairs, et cetera — measures which impose no personal restraints upon individuals. We suffer much more from the poor quality than from the excessive quantity of legislation. For comment, see the author's article on "Legislation, Quantity of, Federal and State," in *Dictionary of American History* (Scribner's, New York, 1940), and Sullivan, Rodney, "Some Quantitative Aspects of Legislation in Kentucky." *Kentucky Law Journal*, January 1946, pp. 118–137, containing a graph covering the period 1792–1944. An excellent discussion of special legislation will be found in Freund, Ernst, *Legislative Regulation*, Chapter 3 (Commonwealth Fund, New York, 1932); also Mothersead, James G., "The Limitation of Legislation," *Nebraska Law Bulletin*, June 1937, pp. 80–90.

State of Illinois
Bills Introduced at Ten-Year Intervals, 1879–1949*

YEAR	HOUSE	SENATE	TOTAL
1879	913	491	1404
1889	716	401	1117
1899	811	480	1291
1909	740	528	1268
1919	763	580	1343
1929	819	547	1366
1939	1128	631	1759
1949	1133	692	1825

* From Illinois Legislative Council, *Printing of Legislative Bills*, p. 16 (Springfield, 1949).

in 1933; the wonder is, not that there were so many new substantive laws but that there were not more. One may well remember that these eighty-five new laws (most of the rest were temporary measures or amendments to existing law) were the output for a two-year period in a huge state, with a complex social, political, and economic life, and a population of more than 10,000,000 people.

> Historically, the session will be noted for the number of important codes enacted. The number of bills and resolutions exceeded those of any session since the Legislative Reference Bureau was created in 1909, and probably those of any prior session since the Commonwealth was established. The actual number of bills was 2,850. Of these, 781 passed both houses. The governor signed 633. Of the 633 bills signed by the governor, 300 are classified as appropriation laws, and 333 as general laws. These latter may be roughly classified as follows: amendments,171; supplements, 8; repeals, 9; restatements, 6; appropriations, 10; salary laws, 5; temporary laws, 8; local laws, 2; validations, 20; codes, 9; new substantive laws, 85. The bulk of the legislation consists of amendments and codes which are simply corrections, consolidations, revisions, and restatements of existing law. In addition, mention should be made that 731 existing laws were wholly or partially repealed. There has been, as a result of this session, no appreciable growth of legislation.[20]

Selection of Legislative Subjects

It is impossible to obtain a clear idea of the perplexing problems involved in the selection of subjects for legislative action, without first getting a picture of the number of bills introduced over a period of years and the disposition made thereof in one or more typical states. Figures of this type, such as were presented in the preceding section, are impressive for at least two reasons. They indicate, in the first place, a slight tendency toward the reduction of

[20] Statement by John H. Fertig, then Director, Pennsylvania Legislative Reference Bureau.

the number of bills introduced. In the second place, such figures are significant because they indicate the almost staggering complexity of modern government. An analysis of these measures would show that they involve questions relating to almost every conceivable aspect of human life. This is natural when government is called upon to perform countless regulatory duties undreamed of in earlier generations and when the scope of service in existing fields of operation is being extended and new standards of governmental efficiency are everywhere being applied.

Political Considerations. Out of this maze someone must select those subjects on which legislation will be given serious consideration. The roots of legislation in the modern state reach deep into all parts of society. The final selection of subject matter is likely, therefore, to represent a compromise between several different and often conflicting influences, the first of which is the matter of political considerations. Some bills, sponsored by influential members, of course receive attention. The general tendency among politicians — there are exceptions in the cases of particular individuals — is to postpone action on any troublesome question as long as they can do so with impunity. Their philosophy seems to be not to trouble trouble until trouble troubles them, to "sit on the lid," so to speak, hoping that an aroused public sentiment will not blow it off. The tendency is, furthermore, to deal with a problem with palliatives, if they must deal with it at all, until some more thoroughgoing treatment can no longer be postponed.[21]

Public Opinion and Pressure Groups. A second determining factor in the selection of legislative subjects has already been referred to — that of a well-organized and insistent public opinion or of powerful and insistent pressure groups. Unfortunately, well-organized public opinion rarely exists unless the situation has become serious. The public is large, unorganized, and generally incoherent unless it is aroused, in which case it makes its wants clearly and unmistakably known. Pressure groups are vocal because they are organized and have adequate financial support; they know what they want and they know how to get it. They have the additional drive that comes from strong self-interest. It is possible for the methods and techniques of the pressure group to be utilized in the public interest, but they rarely are.

Woodrow Wilson made some interesting observations on this point nearly forty years ago:

> I used to wonder when I was Governor of one of the states of this great country where all the bills came from. Some of them had a very private complexion. I found upon inquiry — it was easy to find — that practically nine-tenths of the bills that were introduced had been handed to the members who introduced them by some constituent of theirs, had been drawn up by some lawyer whom they might or might not know, and were intended to do something that would be beneficial to a particular set of persons. I do not mean,

[21] See Weeks, O. Douglas, "Politics in the Legislatures," *National Municipal Review*, February 1952, pp. 80–86, in which it is contended that in most states, partisanship counts less than blocs and pressure groups.

necessarily, beneficial in a way that would be hurtful to the rest; they may have been perfectly honest, but they came out of cubbyholes all over the state. They did not come out of public places where men had got together and compared views. They were not the products of common counsel, but the products of private counsel, a very necessary process if there is no other, but a process which it would be a very happy thing to dispense with if we could get another. And the only other process is the process of common counsel.[22]

Professor Walker made some studies of the sources of legislation introduced into the Ohio legislature in 1939, the results of which are summarized in the following table[23]:

Ohio Legislature, 1939 Bills Classified by Source

	INTRODUCED		BECAME LAW	
Individual Members	162	24%	30	25%
State Offices	89	13%	28	24%
Local Offices	55	8%	8	7%
Lobby	236	35%	47	37%
No Information on Source	135	20%	8	7%
Total	677		121	

As might be expected, the bills presented by lobbyists came from a wide variety of sources, the strong, well-entrenched business and professional groups with permanent organization being most successful in securing the passage of measures presented. Professor Walker concludes: "The wide range of interests represented is, one may believe, typical of the catholicity of the constituency of the typical modern legislature. It may also constitute an index to the extent of organization among our people. It is a commonplace that legislators no longer have time to consult individual constituents unless they represent an organized vote, that is, conscious groups. Pressures by these groups upon the legislature produce the resultant forces of legislation."

Influence of the Administration. An energetic, forceful, and aggressive governor, assisted by the kind of department heads that such a governor is likely to select, can exercise a profound influence, not only in the selection of subjects of legislation, but on the nature of the provisions enacted regarding them. Such a condition may be regarded as highly desirable. These men are charged with the responsibility for the enforcement of existing laws; they

[22] From an address on cooperation in the business of government, delivered before the United States Chamber of Commerce, February 3, 1915; Wilson, Woodrow, *Papers*, Book II, Vol. III, p. 277 (Harper, New York, 1925).

[23] Walker, Harvey, "Who Writes the Laws?" *State Government*, November 1939, pp. 199–200, 208–209. "Where Does Legislation Originate?" *National Municipal Review*, September 1929, pp. 565–567, and "Well Springs of Our Laws," *ibid.*, October 1939, pp. 689–693.

should be more fully informed regarding the weaknesses and defects of these laws than anyone else, and they should be in a better position to determine the nature of the changes required for the correction of any unsatisfactory conditions that may exist. This influence is, of course, reduced almost to the vanishing point when the governor is of a weak and vacillating disposition — in which case the first two of the factors discussed exercise a controlling influence.

Two interesting studies of the extent of executive influence on legislation were published in 1942. In the first, by Edwin E. Witte, which dealt primarily with the Federal government, it was shown that "the natural result of all of the activities of the administration agencies devoted to legislation is that they have greatly influenced the action of Congress." He felt that the executive influence in the states was much less than in the Federal government, but "in some states, for instance New York, administrative departments seem to play quite as important a role in statute making as in the national government." This conclusion was borne out by a study made of the New York situation, in which it was found that "more than half of all the statutes enacted in 1941 were proposed or sponsored by state and local administrative agencies and officers, and the eighteen state administrative departments proposed more than a quarter of them." In the following year the legislature accepted over three fourths of the program advanced by the administration.[24]

The Passage of Bills

This section is concerned with the formal processes of the enactment of legislation, including questions of organization, rules, and procedure. The procedures now in use have, in general, been followed through a period of many centuries, initially in the British Parliament, later in the American colonies and the early state legislatures. They have thus borne the test of time. Because of that fact, and the fact that they have become so thoroughly familiar, it is most difficult to change them even when new conditions would seem to make change desirable.

Organization. When the session convenes, organization is the first order of business. The clerk calls the roll, and the new members are sworn in. Party caucuses and conferences of the leaders have previously been held, so that candidates can be nominated and elected for the speakership and any other elective offices. The real struggle over the choice of the speaker usually takes place in the caucus of the majority party; the action of the house is merely a formal ratification of the decision reached in the caucus. After the

[24] Witte, Edwin E., "Administrative Agencies and Statute Lawmaking," *Public Administration Review*, Spring 1942, pp. 116–125; Scott, Elizabeth McK., and Zeller, Belle, "State Agencies and Lawmaking," *ibid.*, Summer 1942, pp. 205–220; Scott, Elizabeth McK., "State Executive Departments Play Growing Part in Lawmaking," *National Municipal Review*, November 1943, pp. 529–534. See also Weeks, O. Douglas, "Initiation of Legislation by Administrative Agencies," *Brooklyn Law Review*, January 1940, pp. 117–140.

speaker, the chief clerk, and the chaplain have been elected, the speaker appoints certain members of the staff of house employees, of whom there may be a hundred or more. The nucleus of permanent officers are paid an annual salary, which should be adequate to meet the heavy expenses of weekly travel to and from the capitol and of maintenance while at the capitol. Only in Wisconsin are all legislative employees appointed by the chief clerks and the sergeants at arms of the respective houses from lists of eligibles qualified through civil service examinations. Finally, members draw their "prize packages" containing various essential articles for home and office — a practice which is the cause of a good deal of merriment among outsiders.

Rules. The rules in the colonial legislatures were based upon the English precedents, which continued to exercise a controlling influence until Thomas Jefferson compiled his famous *Manual.* Through all the years since, this manual has continued to be regarded as an authority on questions of parliamentary procedure; Cushing's *Manual* is now used in Massachusetts, as well as in many other states. By custom, each new legislature adopts the rules used in the preceding session, in each house, with little or no modification. As a result, little effort has been made to modernize established practices in either organization or procedure, such as the committee setup or the three-reading system. In some states it is difficult even to obtain copies of the rules — a circumstance that may help to explain the fact that, many times, what happens in practice is not in conformity with the requirements of the rules.

In attempting to give in proper order a comprehensive list of the steps through which a bill must pass in the process of enactment, it must be noted that no two states will follow the same procedure in every detail. In general, the steps are as indicated below. Motions to recommit, to place on the postponed calendar, to pass over in order, et cetera, are commonly in order when a bill is under consideration on the floor. It is also possible to move for a reconsideration of the vote, in accordance with the rules, on a measure that has recently been defeated.

USUAL STEPS IN THE LEGISLATIVE PROCESS

1. Passage of general rules regulating the proceedings of a general assembly
2. Introduction of bills
3. First reading
4. Reference to committees
5. Consideration by committees
6. Reports of committees
7. Action on committee reports
8. Second reading
9. Committee of the whole
10. Third reading and final passage
11. Engrossment
12. Transmission to other house
13. Action by other house

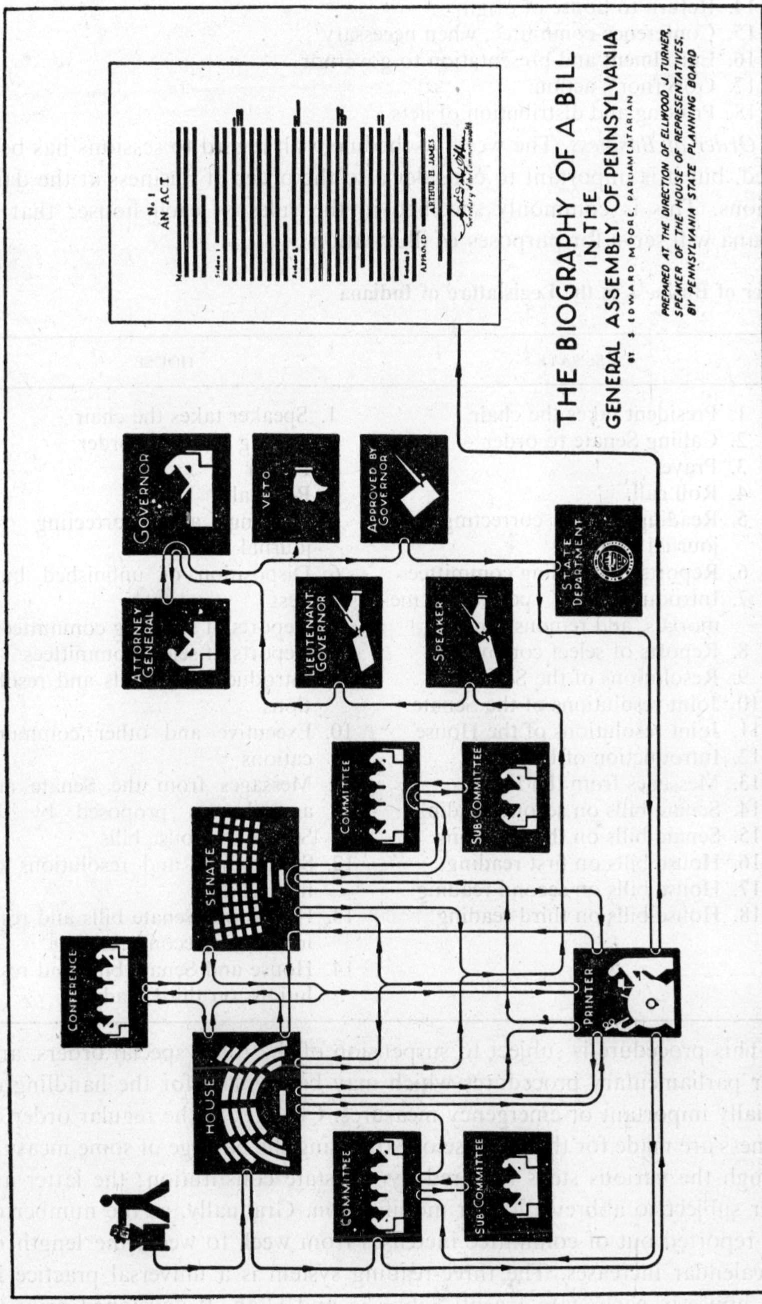
THE BIOGRAPHY OF A BILL
IN THE
GENERAL ASSEMBLY OF PENNSYLVANIA
BY S. EDWARD MOORE, PARLIAMENTARIAN
PREPARED AT THE DIRECTION OF ELLWOOD J TURNER,
SPEAKER OF THE HOUSE OF REPRESENTATIVES,
BY PENNSYLVANIA STATE PLANNING BOARD
No. 1
AN ACT
APPROVED
ARTHUR H JAMES
GOVERNOR
VETO
APPROVED BY GOVERNOR
STATE DEPARTMENT
ATTORNEY GENERAL
LIEUTENANT GOVERNOR
SPEAKER
COMMITTEE
SUB-COMMITTEE
SENATE
CONFERENCE
PRINTER
HOUSE
COMMITTEE
SUB-COMMITTEE

14. Return to house of origin
15. Conference committee, when necessary
16. Enrollment and presentation to governor
17. Governor's action
18. Printing and distribution of acts

Order of Business. The weekly schedule with regard to sessions has been noted, but it is important to consider also the order of business at the daily sessions. This is commonly specified in the rules of each house; that of Indiana will serve for purposes of illustration:

Order of Business in the Legislature of Indiana

SENATE	HOUSE
1. President takes the chair	1. Speaker takes the chair
2. Calling Senate to order	2. Calling House to order
3. Prayer	3. Prayer
4. Roll call	4. Roll call
5. Reading and correcting the journal	5. Reading and correcting the journal
6. Reports of standing committees	6. Disposition of unfinished business
7. Introduction of petitions, memorials, and remonstrances	7. Reports of standing committees
8. Reports of select committees	8. Reports of select committees
9. Resolutions of the Senate	9. Introduction of bills and resolutions
10. Joint resolutions of the Senate	10. Executive and other communications
11. Joint resolutions of the House	11. Messages from the Senate and amendments proposed by the Senate to House bills
12. Introduction of bills	12. Senate bills and resolutions on first reading
13. Messages from the House	13. House and Senate bills and resolutions on second reading.
14. Senate bills on second reading	14. House and Senate bills and resolutions on third reading.
15. Senate bills on third reading	
16. House bills on first reading	
17. House bills on second reading	
18. House bills on third reading	

This procedure is subject to suspension of the rules, special orders, and other parliamentary procedures which may be invoked for the handling of specially important or emergency measures. Changes in the regular order of business are made for the purpose of expediting the passage of some measure through the various steps required by the state constitution; the latter are never subject to abbreviation or modification. Gradually, as the number of bills reported out of committee increases from week to week, the length of the calendar increases. The three-reading system is a universal practice in each house in each state except Nebraska and Utah. It developed prior to the invention of the printing press as a safeguard against the railroading of legislation when those who might be opposed to the measure happened to be absent. After the invention of the printing press the same system was continued, although one and sometimes two of the readings became largely a formality.

Introduction and Reference of Bills. In most cases the first reading is by title only by the clerk at the time of introduction (although the rules may require reading in full). The speaker, hearing the title read, and judging therefrom the nature of the contents of the bill, refers it to the proper committee. Correct reference is aided by the inclusion of interpretative statements — a practice which appears to be spreading, with the sanction and approval of the courts. The bill is ordered printed [25]; in a few states this first printing bears some clearly distinguishing feature, such as the use of pink paper. After the committee has favorably considered the measure and reported it out, it comes out in white, at which time it is placed on the second-reading calendar.

Second Reading. The consideration on second reading is very hurried and is rarely the occasion for extended debate.[26] Measures on second reading are placed on the calendar in the order in which they are reported out by the several committees, but they need not necessarily be considered in this order. A member may call up any such bill when he is in order, or the speaker may postpone consideration of a particular measure until later in the day's session, either on his own initiative or at the request of a member. In some states it is required that such bills shall have been agreed to in committee of the whole. When bills are to be considered on second reading, the speaker announces this fact and presents each measure separately:

"The next bill on the calendar is House Bill No. 1018, Printer's No. 447." [27]

"Is this bill called up?"

"Called up by the gentleman from Cambria, Mr. Andrews. The clerk will read the first section." (The clerk reads rapidly a few words at the beginning of the section.)

"Does the House agree to this section?" (Slight pause.) "Agreed to. The clerk will read the second section." (The clerk mumbles a few words at the beginning of the second section.)

"Does the House agree to this section?" (Slight pause.) "Agreed to. The clerk will read the title."

"An Act Creating a Commission to Make a Study. . ."

"Will the House agree to the bill on second reading?" (Slight pause.) "Agreed to. Will the House agree to having the bill transcribed and placed on the calendar for third reading? Agreed to."

If someone makes a motion to recommit, the speaker says, "The question is on the motion. Those in favor will say, 'Aye,' those opposed, 'No.'

[25] See Illinois Legislative Council, *Printing of Legislative Bills, op. cit.*

[26] Again there is no uniformity of procedure. In Wisconsin the second reading is the stage at which amendments are in order. This is the stage of the most extensive consideration of the bill.

[27] The use of a printer's number is not universal; it is useful, however, as a further means of identifying bills, avoiding errors, and insuring that one has the latest printing of a bill.

The ayes have it. The motion is agreed to." When amendments are offered, they are carried to the desk by one of the page boys and read in full. The speaker then proceeds:

> "Does the House agree to the amendments?" (Slight pause.) "Agreed to. Does the House agree to the section as amended? Agreed to. Does the House agree to the bill as amended? Agreed to."

From this point on, the speaker proceeds as indicated above. There is no roll call. Motions to recommit or to pass over in order are in order with regard to any bill. At the conclusion of this procedure the speaker announces the number of the next bill, continuing the repetition of these steps until all the bills on the second-reading calendar have been disposed of. This procedure can be handled so rapidly that a very long second-reading calendar can be disposed of in less than one hour.

Third Reading. When bills have passed second reading and have been placed on the calendar for third reading and final passage, the speaker announces each bill in similar fashion as follows:

> "This bill has been read three times, at length, on three separate days, considered and agreed to, and is now on its final passage. Agreeably to the provisions of the Constitution, the yeas and nays will be taken. The question is: Shall the bill pass finally?"

Having repeated the words of this liturgy in a loud voice, and in a rapid and almost mechanical fashion, the voice of the speaker booms forth at the conclusion: "The clerk will call the roll." In an increasing number of states where electrical voting equipment is used, the vote may be taken in a few seconds; otherwise the roll must be called. As the session wears on, the clerks have called the roll so many times that they know it from memory; it is seldom necessary for them even to glance at the roll sheets upon which the tally clerks record the votes. Pronouncing the names distinctly but with terrific speed, the voice of the clerk booms forth into the hall of the house: "Andrews, Baker, Baldi, Barnhardt, Bechtel, Beech, Bennett, Bernhard, Blumberg, Boyd, Caputo, Carey, Carson, Chervenak, Cohen, Conner . . . Wood, Woodside, Wright, Yeakel, Yourishin, Zimmerman." If the bill is important and the vote close, the clerk will proceed slowly enough so that each member's voice can be clearly and distinctly heard at the front of the chamber, and his vote recorded by the tally clerks; if the measure is not controversial, the clerk may use the so-called short roll call, racing through the first two or three dozen names at breathless speed, swinging around with a majestic wave of his hand, and concluding with "And Mr. Speaker." The speaker thereupon announces, as soon as the tally sheet reaches him from the clerk's desk, that "On final passage, the yeas were 198, the nays none. The measure is agreed to."

Correction, Verification, Reconsideration. An opportunity is commonly afforded, even on unimportant or noncontroversial measures, for correction of the roll before the result is announced. In such cases a member rises in his place and addresses the chair: "Mr. Speaker" — the speaker then recognizes the gentleman from Cambria, or Lehigh, or Dauphin, whatever the name of the county from which the member comes — "I desire to be recorded as voting 'No' on this measure." The speaker then inquires: "Was the gentleman present within the hall of the House when the roll was called?" to which the usual reply is, "I was, Sir." Thereupon the speaker announces, "The gentleman will be so recorded."

After the completion of a roll call, any member has the privilege of demanding a verification of the roll. Such a verification is commonly requested following the vote on any important measure, particularly if the division is close. Two purposes are served by it. In the first place, it enables each member to assure himself that the tally clerks have correctly recorded his vote; in the second, it affords an opportunity to challenge the vote of any member recorded as voting, but not within the hall of the house at the time the vote was taken. The procedure of the verification involves simply the reading of the list of names of those who are recorded as having voted in the affirmative, followed by an opportunity for correction, after which the same procedure is repeated with regard to the negative roll.

Sometimes the sponsors of a measure which has been defeated on final passage discover that the defeat was caused by a misunderstanding on the part of some members, or that since the vote some members have changed their minds. In such cases it is customary to move for a reconsideration within one, two, or three days after the final vote was taken, as the rules may prescribe. It is also customary for the sponsor of the bill to prepare the motion for reconsideration, which may read as follows: "The undersigned members of the House of Representatives, having voted in the negative on final passage of House Bill No. 684, Printer's No. 783, on March 13, 1952, do hereby move for a reconsideration of the vote on said bill." This motion, signed by two members who voted against the bill, must be presented to the chief clerk, together with two exact copies of the tally sheet on the original vote.[28] If the members of the house agree to the motion to reconsider, the measure may then come up for another vote.

The Senate. The discussion thus far has been concerned with the activities of the House. Generally speaking, the conduct of affairs in the lower branch is much more interesting than in the upper house — quite the opposite of the situation existing in Washington. Measures adopted in the lower house are, of course, sent to the Senate for approval; here they go through substantially the same procedure as in the House. If the second chamber makes amendments to the bill as approved by the first, these changes must be accepted by the house in which the bill originated before it can be sent to the governor. If these changes are objectionable to those who sponsored the bill originally, it is likely that their colleagues will sustain them in refusing to concur in

[28] In some states one signature is sufficient. In Wisconsin, for instance, any member who voted on the losing side can move for reconsideration without formality, but he must do so on the day following the vote.

the amendments, in which case the measure will be sent to conference. Where the bill originated in the House and amendments have been made by the Senate, the speaker may put the question in this form: "Will the House concur in the amendments made by the Senate?" and the vote shall then be taken immediately. The same number of votes is required to concur in the amendments as was necessary for the original passage of the bill. If concurrence is refused, the conference committee will be appointed by the presiding officers of the respective houses, it being customary to select those members most interested and best informed regarding its subject matter. Unless the matter is badly handled, the conferees are usually able to agree on a compromise which is acceptable not only to them, but to their respective chambers.[29]

Other Problems. It is customary for the work to proceed in the manner here described until the end of the session approaches. Gradually the calendar becomes heavier and the speed of the legislative machine materially increases. Much time has been required to iron out differences in committee and to hold public hearings. As the session wears on, the members become more and more impatient to wind up the work and be relieved of their weekly journeys between their homes and the state capitol. The operation of the legislative machinery may be likened to a great locomotive pulling a heavy train of cars out of the railway station. The first movements of the engine come slowly, laboriously, and with a terrific expenditure of effort. As the train gets in motion, it moves forward at great speed with little apparent effort. In similar fashion, the legislative machinery gathers momentum as the end of the session approaches.

This fact is responsible for the employment of various shortcuts. In the course of the session, for instance, a large number of individual appropriation bills will be introduced for schools, hospitals, welfare institutions, and the like. Many of these will be passed by the house in which they originate, as a compliment to the members who introduced them, without any likelihood of their being approved by the other body or by the governor. The chairman of the appropriations committee most influential of the two in the control of policy may take a bill which has passed the other house providing for the appropriation of some specific sum for the biennium to a particular hospital, amend out the name of the hospital and the amount, in fact keeping nothing of the original bill except the number, and insert amendments covering several million dollars to be distributed among several scores of hospitals, the mere printing of the names of which requires several pages. The original appropriation bill thus becomes an omnibus bill by the

[29] In Wisconsin and some other states conference committees are infrequent. Senator Norris has, however, urged the frequent use of the conference committee as one of his chief objections to the bicameral system; see Burdette, Franklin L., "Conference Committees in the Nebraska Legislature," *American Political Science Review*, December 1936, pp. 1114–1116, and "Legislative Conference Committees," *State Government*, June 1938, pp. 103–106, based on Nebraska experience under bicameralism.

terms of which the legislature covers all its appropriations for hospital purposes. This device is significant in two respects. If a deadline for the introduction of new bills has been set, it can be evaded by this means. And frequently this matter of appropriations is not taken up until so late in the session that the passage of an entire new bill would be impossible, a sufficient number of legislative days not being available to permit the bill to come through both houses, even if it did so within the minimum time permitted by the constitution.

An element which contributes greatly to the confusion at the end of the session is the large number of resolutions for recalling bills from the governor. Most frequently this happens when the sponsor of the measure discovers, after it has been approved by both houses and sent to the governor, that it contains some error that needs correction; sometimes this device is used to avoid a promised veto by the governor. These resolutions sometimes come through half a dozen or a dozen at a time. Nearly all of them could be avoided if the attorney general, the secretary of state, and the director of the legislative reference bureau were authorized by law to correct obvious errors in spelling and punctuation, as was provided for in a Pennsylvania statute enacted in 1933.

Another question arises regarding the circumstances under which measures are defeated in course of consideration. From a tabulation covering defeated bills in the 1947 session in Oklahoma which appears on page 302, it appears that nearly half of the measures defeated die in committee. Some died in committee of the whole, while others were permitted to expire by remaining on the calendar without being called up. Other interesting facts are disclosed by the figures in this table.[30]

30 From Oklahoma State Legislative Council, *Strengthening the Legislative Process* (Oklahoma City, 1948); for other useful studies, see: Geary, Thomas C., *Law Making in South Dakota*, Revised (Governmental Research Bureau, University of South Dakota, 1949); Guild, Frederic H., and Snider, Clyde F., *Legislative Procedure in Kansas*, Revised (Governmental Research Series, University of Kansas Publications, 1946); Hawaii Legislative Reference Bureau, *Territorial Legislature: Organization and Procedure* (University of Hawaii, 1949); Hounshell, Charles D., *The Legislative Process in Virginia* (Extension Division, University of Virginia, 1951); Kentucky Legislative Research Commission, *Kentucky's General Assembly, a Working Legislature* (Frankfort, 1952); Lewis, Henry W., *The General Assembly of North Carolina: Guidebook of Organization and Procedure* (Institute of Government, University of North Carolina, 1951); Minnesota League of Women Voters, *Ninety Days of Lawmaking in Minnesota*, Revised (University of Minnesota Press, 1949); New York State Joint Legislative Committee on Legislative Methods, Practices, Procedures and Expenditures, *Interim Report* (Legislative Document No. 35, 1945) and *Final Report* (Legislative Document No. 31, 1946); Plaisted, John W., *Legislative Procedure in the General Court of Massachusetts* (Wright & Potter Printing Company, Boston, 1948); Sinclair, Thornton, *Procedural Limitations on the Legislative Process in the New Jersey Constitution* (Governor's Committee on Preparatory Research for the New Jersey Constitutional Convention, Trenton, 1947); Smith, Rhoten A., *The Life of a Bill* (Bureau of Government Research, University of Kansas, 1946); Still, Rae S., *The Gilmer-Aiken Bills: a Study in the Legislative Process* (Steck Company, Austin, 1950): Washington Legislative Council, *Report of the Subcommittee on Rules, Organization and Procedure of the Legislature* (Olympia, 1948).

State of Oklahoma
Legislative Hazards — 1947

	HOUSE BILLS			SENATE BILLS		
BILLS LOST	*Number*	*% to Bills Lost*	*% to Total House Bills*	*Number*	*% to Bills Lost*	*% to Total Senate Bills*
In committee.........	118	46.8	24.7	76	46.6	24.0
Committee of the whole	42	16.6	8.8	5	3.1	1.6
On calendar..........	23	9.1	4.8	37	22.7	11.7
On passage in house where introduced......	18	7.1	3.8	6	3.7	1.9
Amendment by Senate.	6	2.4	1.3			
Amendment by House.				2	1.2	.6
Between houses.......	3	1.2	.7	2	1.2	.6
In committee of other house...............	12	4.8	2.5	22	13.5	6.9
On calendar of other house...............	18	7.1	3.8	7	4.3	2.2
On passage of other house...............	4	1.6	.8	5	3.1	1.6
Vetoes..............	8	3.2	1.7	1	.61	.32
Total bills lost......	252			163		
Total bills introduced............	478			317		

Informal Aspects of Lawmaking

The business of legislating is infinitely complicated. It is a curious mixture of the formal aspects of procedure considered in the previous section and the personal, informal contacts and behind-the-scenes activities which are invisible to the casual observer and often wholly unknown to him. What this casual observer sees is perplexing to him, and because he does not understand it, it may even seem improper. What he sees is, as it were, the surface phenomena of legislating, while the vital parts of the process — the hours of hearings, conferences during and after the drafting stage, and staff work — do not show. These he often knows nothing about.

The lawmaking process is an intensely human one. The members are politicians, and politicians are interested in people and the problems of people. Otherwise they would not be politicians. They are, for the most part, friendly and approachable. They enjoy being together, telling a story, playing a joke on each other. As a result there is a vast amount of good fellowship and the joy of living in evidence around legislative halls. These things are more or less apparent to the most uninitiated observer, while the work carried on behind the scenes is not. A group of legislators is not, in many respects, greatly different from any other group of men who come together in a lodge, fraternity, or association, except that in many instances they get to know each other better. Working side by side, day after day, session after session, they come to know — and often to play upon — personal peculiarities. There develop among the members close bonds of personal friendship which frequently ignore party lines or other differences.

The Regular Session. These characteristics are in evidence from the very beginning of the session, when the older members play jokes on those elected for the first time, like a group of upperclassmen hazing the freshmen. As the session gets under way, the observer notes a good deal of talking among the members, and milling around, with apparent lack of attention to the proceedings. In this general noise and confusion he wonders how the members can know anything about what is going on; he does not realize that while no member can watch all the bills, some members are watching carefully the progress of every bill. He may see persons who he suspects are lobbyists; he thinks they ought to wear horns or to be in some other manner distinguishable, and he is disappointed because they are not. He may listen to a mediocre debate, wherein one member resorts to the common device of interrogating the sponsor of the bill — not realizing that there are many debates of high caliber in the course of the session. These and many other things perplex him.

Later in the session there are innumerable delays and apparently time-wasting recesses. These things often create a bad impression in his mind. When the session starts late, he does not know that the caucus of the majority party may have been held overtime through inability to come to an agreement. He does not realize that the recesses are called because of the inability of the printer to keep up with the legislature or because of the efforts of a committee to iron out the difficulties relating to some important piece of legislation.

The End of the Session. Then, in due course, comes the end-of-the-session rush, about which so much has been spoken and written. It occurs everywhere, although it is supposed to be worse in the states with a limited session. The leaders and many of the members have put in weeks of grueling hard work. All are tired out. The air is tense with excitement. No man can tell when or how the tension will break and pandemonium be let loose. Anything can happen, and usually does.

In the lull between one outbreak of disorder and another the speaker tries, with some difficulty, to dispose of the remaining items on the calendar. Few questions are asked, and there is little or no discussion. Differences have been all but forgotten, compromises have been agreed to, and deals worked out so that little opportunity for discord remains. The strangest thing of all, perhaps, to a casual observer is the fact that most of the appropriation bills are passed during this general hubbub, sometimes without even a record vote.[31] The explanation is that these bills are, and must be, drafted in committees and in conference with the spending agencies of the government, so that the members are quite unfamiliar with their details and are in no position to raise questions with regard to individual items, even if they were in the mood to do so. Few members venture to raise any questions at all, and these as a rule relate to insignificant items which, nevertheless, make good newspaper publicity.

Many legislatures have developed customs which are regularly observed in the end-of-the-session celebration. There is the dinner for members and for representatives of the press; the mock session in the hall of the House, during which the page boys occupy the seats of the members and carry on proceedings with a fine display of wit, satire, and originality. At intervals, during the recesses, entertainment may be provided by members or by guest artists. Last but by no means least comes the presentation of gifts to the speaker, the clerks, the officers, the pages, and nearly everyone else. A really handsome gift is given to the speaker, and checks to other officers and employees. All manner of inexpensive trinkets are presented to selected members, with great ceremony, usually in reference to some personal characteristic of the member or some interesting incident which has occurred during the session.

Brief periods of work are sandwiched in between these various events, but with the best of planning it is rarely possible to adjourn promptly at the day and hour agreed upon. Final adjournment may be postponed an hour or two, or even a day or two, while a clerk stealthily turns back the hands of the great clock in the rear of the chamber. The final events preceding the adjournment are the adoption of a series of resolutions conferring thanks

[31] Colvin reports that New York, in the 1919 session, passed 400 bills in the last four days, at the rate of 100 a day. In 1929 in the same state they did even better, disposing of 400 bills on the last day. In Ohio in 1935 the House disposed of fifty-one bills in two hours. The prize, however, goes to Kansas, where Governor George A. Hodges reported, quoting from the *Topeka State Journal:*

"The bulk reading of omnibus appropriation bills totaling $1,381,779 was the only vaudeville feature of the day.

"The Speaker announced 'a bulk roll call and a bulk reading of bills'; and, calling a dozen owners of basso voices to the stand, each member was given a bill that carried an appropriation for some state institution or state department. 'Is every one ready?' asked the Speaker. A dozen members, with a dozen bills, answered: 'Aye, aye, sir!' 'One for the money, two for the show, three to make ready — and four, they go!' shouted the presiding officer.

"And the reading members went. They sang, and mumbled and shouted the words on the pages of the typewritten bills — each reading from a different bill, with separate provisions. 'Louder!' shouted the members. 'Louder! Louder!' chorused the gallery visitors, who saw a moment of revelry in an otherwise uneventful day.

"While the bills were being read members pounded their desks and the reading ended in an uproar in which the members, clerks and visitors participated. The roll was called and a deliberative body of lawmakers placed its official approval on measures that called for the expenditure of one and a third million dollars, appropriated in bulk form, in a duration of possibly ten minutes of time." (Quoted from Louisiana Constitution Revision Projet, Constitutional Problems, No. 18, p. 13; Baton Rouge, 1947.)

upon those who have assisted with the work of the session and a series of laudatory speeches in which members of all parties join in paying tribute to the work done by the speaker, both as a fair and impartial presiding officer and as a strategist in guiding and directing the legislative program during the session.

Some Evaluations. The business of the session is normally conducted in an orderly and dignified manner. Many of the debates and discussions are of a high order, showing an understanding of the subject and some knowledge of the problems of statecraft. This the public little seems to realize. Citizens visit the legislature so seldom, and stay so short a time when they do go, that they have little opportunity to acquire an understanding of the serious work that is done there.

The public is far more familiar with the confusion at the end of the session than with any other part of the activities of the legislature. The comments of observers on this have ranged from gentle satire to vigorous and caustic denunciation. As a matter of fact, disorder and confusion in legislative halls is not peculiar either to our country or to our time. Such practices were once far more common than they are now; at present they are confined to the end of the session, and consist for the most part of harmless fun indulged in *after* the serious work of the session has been about completed. Charles Kettleborough, eminent authority on legislative matters, expressed the prevailing view of informed persons when he said, on the basis of experience with eleven sessions in Indiana, that "an average legislature is not only a very able but a very serious body of public servants."

Citizens whose impressions of the legislature are none too favorable would do well to remember that the ordinary legislature has only sixty or ninety legislative days in which to consider from two to five thousand bills and resolutions; that their task of determining the provisions of laws, and enacting them, is made more difficult by the demands which are made upon them by ourselves — their constituents — and by the fact that in many states the governmental machinery is badly out of date; that under these circumstances the average legislator acquires a feeling of utter helplessness and hopelessness. In many cases he is so paralyzed mentally that he sees no alternatives other than to follow the leaders or to oppose everything that comes up. The observer should remember also that the antics and frivolities are largely the work of the newer members, and not of the men who are doing the real work of the session.

The observation made by William B. Belknap many years ago, when he was President of the American Legislators Association, is still true: "The continual shifting of personnel in the legislature along with the outworn machinery is really what brings about the chaos, and it is neither the ignorance nor the stupidity of the legislators that is really responsible." The members are, he continues, "ham-strung and hog-tied by constitutional limitations, precedents, and parliamentary procedures" of such a nature as to make the efficient operation of the legislature impossible. The chaos and confusion — when they do exist — are largelv surface phenomena. The improvement of procedure depends upon an understanding of certain fundamental, underlying problems, to which consideration is given in the concluding section of this chapter.[32]

Professor Shumate, in an excellent reappraisal of state legislatures, notes that their prestige may be regained:

> The low esteem in which the state legislature is now held is not encouraging for the future, but neither is it necessarily fatal. Other political institutions have overcome comparable obstacles and risen to positions of eminence and prestige. Democracy itself was once the most despised form of government. Membership in the United States Supreme Court was so little prized in the early years of the Republic that ambitious men rejected appointments to it in favor of election or appointment to state offices; and service in the British House of Commons was long regarded as an onerous burden, to be avoided whenever possible. Thus, it is not inconceivable that our state assemblies may arise again to positions of honor and trust in our governmental system.
>
> No student of modern American government and politics can be blind to the faults of our state legislatures, but to admit that they have failed comes perilously close to admitting that popular government in the United States has failed. That, in turn, would be to admit that what was once regarded in foreign lands as "the American experiment" has failed, and this we are not prepared to do. If we will but free our legislatures from their constitutional hobbles, pay them decently, organize them so that they can serve adequately, and create a vigilant public opinion which insists upon responsible service of a high caliber (these are not simple reforms, to be sure), there is no inherent reason why they cannot assume the rightful place of representative assemblies in a representative government.[33]

Improvements in Procedure

In the last few years there has been a growing interest in the improvement of legislative organization and procedures. The significant reports of the New York State Joint Legislative Committee on Legislative Methods, Practices, Procedures and Expenditures in 1945 and 1946 and the adoption of the Legislative Reorganization Act of 1946 by the Congress gave great impetus to this development. Special committees were set up in many states to study the subject and make recommendations. In 1947 the Council of State Governments' Committee on Legislative Processes and Procedures submitted its report, which was reissued in revised form in 1948. (For summary of its recommendations, see pages 237–239). Meantime the American Political Science Association reconstituted its Committee on the Organiza-

[32] Letter to the author from William B. Belknap, November 3, 1934; see also Atwood, Albert W., and McGoldrick, Joseph D., "What Is the Matter with the State Legislatures?" in *Legislatures and Legislative Problems*, edited by Thomas H. Reed (University of Chicago Press, 1933).

[33] Shumate, Roger V., "A Reappraisal of State Legislature," *Annals*, January 1938, pp. 189–197.

tion of Congress as a Committee on American Legislatures. This committee, after three years of hard work, published its report in 1953.

It has been said that the two most important developments of recent years affecting the work of legislative bodies are the constant expansion of the volume of work which they are called upon to perform and the increasing complexity and technicality of the subjects with which they have to deal. Obviously, if proper consideration is to be given to a large number of difficult questions, the members should be freed from unnecessarily time-consuming methods of procedure, so that they will have the maximum amount of time to devote to their real work. Some of the more important ways in which these purposes can be realized are briefly indicated in the paragraphs which follow.

Many such suggestions, as a matter of fact, can be gleaned from the three chapters dealing with the legislative branch. A very obvious and very important improvement might result from changes in the committee system, reducing the number and the size of committees, scheduling committee meetings to avoid conflicts, and providing for a public record of committee meetings. The development of an adequate program of legislative aids, with adequate financial support and a competent professional staff, would contribute much. So also would improvement in the position of the members, themselves through longer terms, better salaries, and suitable offices, staffings and facilities for work. The legislatures have, to a large extent, failed to equip themselves to deal with the complex issues of today.

Presession Conferences and Training Institutes. Another device that has been used for purposes of legislative planning and the improvement of procedure is the presession conference on legislative problems and the training institute on legislative procedure. The presession conference idea was begun, on a regional basis, by the American Legislators' Association in the early thirties. Some of these conferences included members from a single state, as the Colorado Conference of 1934; others included a selected group of public officials from several adjacent states, such as the Southern Conference held in Asheville in 1932. The University of Arkansas in 1936 first conducted the Institute of Legislative Procedure, a school for state legislators which has since been conducted biennially.[34]

In Pennsylvania, in 1939, when the late Ellwood J. Turner was Speaker of the House, he conducted a series of weekly conferences or institutes dealing with problems of legislative organization and procedure. These were designed particularly to aid new members and assist them to assume more quickly their full responsibilities as members. Conferences such as these have been largely experimental up to the present time, but where they have been tried they have produced excellent results. Presession conferences have been carried on by the University of Oklahoma for a number of years. In Florida, in 1949, the Institute of Government, under the auspices of the

[34] See Alexander, Henry M., "A School for Legislators," *State Government*, February 1941, pp. 39–40.

House of Representatives and pursuant to a House Resolution of 1947, conducted an orientation course for new members.[35] In 1951, schools and practice sessions were held in Arizona, Massachusetts, and Mississippi.[36] Short courses given a few days before the session for legislative employees may contribute much to smooth functioning when the legislature meets.

Elimination of Three Readings. The three-reading system originated generations ago prior to the invention of the printing press and was universally used to prevent the railroading of legislation. Though still generally retained by constitutional mandate, it is in practice largely a formality, sometimes even a farce, but in either case under modern conditions a serious waste of time. Every member has — or should have — a printed copy of all bills on his desk before final passage. If it were required that such copies should be distributed three days prior to vote on final passage, the members and the public would have the full protection the system was intended to give, and the legislature would be freed from a time-consuming procedure which can no longer be justified. The unicameral legislature in Nebraska eased this requirement by providing for the first two readings by title, with the third a reading in full at the time of final passage (Rule XII, Par. 5).

Improvement through Rule Changes. As noted earlier, the rules of procedure are of ancient origin and have rarely been extensively revised — if, indeed, they have been revised at all. On the basis of a rather extensive study of the rules existing in the two chambers of the several states, Dr. Jack F. Isakoff of the Illinois Legislative Council lists a series of possibilities for legislative improvement through changes and modernization of the rules.[37] His proposals are:

1. Informal introduction of bills rather than time-consuming introduction from the floor, plus checking of bills for proper form by legislative draftsmen
2. Printing all bills upon introduction, and amendments also, as a matter of course, in a form which as nearly as possible would show intended changes in existing law
3. Proper scheduling of committee hearings and adequate notice of committee meetings
4. Adequate committee records
5. Installation of procedures which could routinely minimize opportunities for irregularities in the mechanical handling and reporting of bills
6. At least a minimum impetus to time-saving joint action by the two chambers of the typical bicameral body
7. Daily publication of a calendar which is a meaningful guide to the business actually to be transacted rather than a mere listing of matters which might be taken up

[35] Institute of Government, *Orientation Course for New House Members* (Tallahassee, 1949).

[36] See Fortenberry, Charles N., "Classes for Mississippi Legislators," *State Government*, April 1952, pp. 85, 92–93; Grove, Lawrence R., "Massachusetts School for Legislators," *ibid.*, pp. 84, 92; and note on Arizona practice session, *National Municipal Review*, February 1951, p. 94.

[37] Material prepared for the American Political Science Association's Committee on American Legislatures whose report was published in 1953.

8. Creation of some specific encouragement to tactics which contribute to the common rush of business in the last days of the session

9. Placing responsibility for revision of the standing rules upon some agency likely to act, at least at intervals

Mechanical Voting. In most states the vote is taken by roll call — the time-honored viva voce, or vote by the living voice. In three states — Louisiana, Minnesota, and Virginia — electrical voting machines are used in both houses, and Nebraska uses one in its single chamber. Such machines are used in the lower house in fourteen states.[38] This system, sometimes called flash voting, is a great time-saving device; but it has spread slowly, partly because of adherence to tradition, partly because the companies which sell and install the machines have charged very high prices for them. The installations do require intricate and elaborate wiring systems, but the basic principles involved are well known and are fairly simple. Current figures show the initial cost to range from $18,000 or $20,000 to as much as $50,000 or more, depending to some extent upon the number of members in the chamber.

The machines are very simple in operation. On each desk is a permanently installed device with push buttons or switches to register the member's vote. Each unit is regularly kept locked and can be opened only by a key in the member's possession. When the vote is called by the presiding officer, the member presses the appropriate switch or button — "aye," "nay," or "not voting." Names of all members are listed alphabetically on indicator boards (see illustration on page 311) and are visible from all parts of the chamber. Next to each name on the board are signal lights to designate the vote — usually green for "aye" and red for "nay." A permanent record of the vote is made by a tabulating device which, within five seconds of the vote, electrically punches holes in the aye and nay columns on a tally sheet next to the members' names. At the same time it records the total vote at the top of the tally sheet.

In the Oklahoma House there were 1124 roll calls in 1945 and 1200 in 1947. The number per day is small during the early part of the session, but mounts rapidly as the end of the session approaches, sometimes exceeding 100 in a single day. It is estimated that approximately one third of the entire session of the Oklahoma House is consumed in calling the roll, and the experience in other states substantiates this estimate. An interim committee

[38] *Both Houses:* Louisiana, House, 1922, Senate, 1932; Minnesota, House, 1938, Senate, 1945; Nebraska, House, 1933, and now unicameral; Virginia, House, 1924, Senate, 1930.

Lower House: Alabama, 1945; California, 1935; Florida, 1939; Iowa, 1921; Michigan, 1937; Missouri, 1948; New Jersey, 1950; North Dakota, 1947; Pennsylvania, 1949; Texas, 1922; West Virginia, 1936; Wisconsin, 1917. Arkansas and Mississippi are also reported to be using voting machines.

See note in *National Municipal Review*, April 1950, p. 192, and tables compiled by Dr. Jack A. Rhodes, Oklahoma State Legislative Council, February, 1950; also Illinois Legislative Council, *Electrical Roll-Call, Devices in Legislative Bodies* (Springfield, 1940); see also Kelley, Alice, "Flash Voting in Wisconsin," *State Government*, October 1930, pp. 6–8.

in California, appointed to study legislative procedure and the reduction of legislative expense, made some calculations of the loss of time that had occurred in the session in that state in 1931. From these calculations, which were based upon the Assembly journal, it is possible to get some idea of the magnitude of the waste which commonly occurs at every session in most of our states. There were 2344 roll calls in the course of the session, which consumed more than fifty-nine hours of actual session time. The Committee estimated that these same roll calls could have been taken by an electric system in six and one-half hours. The Report continued[39]:

> During 1931 there were 74 legislative or actual meeting days, totaling 291 hours and 55 minutes. This is an average of 3 hours and 57 minutes per meeting day. Therefore, more than 15 legislative days or three calendar weeks were actually wasted by members answering aye or nay, owing to the absence of a system of electrical voting. It seems incredible that nearly one-fourth of the actual meeting time of the Assembly is being wasted and the session needlessly prolonged more than three weeks at an added expense to the taxpayers.

The Michigan experience tends to support this view; the technician who has looked after the mechanism and kept it in repair since it was installed in 1937, remarked to the author: "It used to take twenty minutes for a roll call in the House; now we take the vote in twenty seconds."

There is no longer any serious question regarding the desirability of installing such equipment; its advantages are obvious. Much time is saved in the routine work of roll call, leaving more available for debate and consideration of issues. A more accurate count and a permanent record of the vote is assured. Independent voting on the part of members is encouraged. Electrical voting requires members to be in their seats, thereby aiding the presiding officer in maintaining order on the floor. The system eliminates the noise and confusion incident to the use of the viva-voce vote and eases the rush at the end of the session, when so many votes must be taken in a short time. And finally, it enables the legislature to complete its business without long night and overtime sessions.

Use of Time. Many of the most serious defects which beset the state legislatures could be partially if not wholly corrected by more effective planning and use of time. Annual sessions of unlimited duration would help, but this remedy — important as it is — would be effective only if the legislatures were to rid themselves of many duties which are wholly unnecessary. Mention has been made of the enormous amounts of time wasted on roll calls. A vast amount of time is also wasted in all the legislatures on matters that are actually no proper concern of the lawmaking body. Some of these conditions could easily be corrected.

In the larger states, volume is a major problem. In New York, there are 4000 or 5000 bills a session, of which 1200 to 1500 are passed. In 1945 the

[39] California Assembly Interim Committee on Legislative Procedure and Reduction of Legislative Expense, *Preliminary Report*, pp. 88–89 (Sacramento, 1932).

Sample Record from an Electrical Voting Machine

VIRGINIA HOUSE OF DELEGATES

NAY	AYE	NOT-VOTING
040	048	011

ROLL-CALL

ON: ______________________ **DATE:** ______________

MEMORANDA: ______________________

NAME	N	A	N-V	NAME	N	A	N-V	NAME	N	A	N-V
ADAMS, A. C.		•		FOWLER		•		POWERS		•	
ADAMS, W. H.	•			FRANCIS		•		PRESSLEY		•	
ALLMAN		•		FREEMAN			•	REASOR		•	
BADER		•		GARY		•		REID			
BAIN			•	GOAD	•			RHODES	•		
BATTLE	•			GREEAR		•		ROBERTS		•	
BEAR			•	HALL	•			RODGERS			•
BEARD	•			HARLESS		•		SCOTT		•	
BIRRELL		•		HARMAN		•		SETTLE		•	
BRAY		•		HARRISON		•		SHRADER		•	
BRENEMAN	•			HICKS	•			SISSON			•
BREWER	•			HILLARD		•		SMITH, H. T.	•		
BROWN				HOBSON	•			SMITH, J. C.			•
BRUCE	•			HUMPHRIES		•		SNEAD	•		
BRYANT		•		JEFFREYS	•			SPANGLER		•	
BUSTARD			•	JONES, E. B.		•		STANLEY		•	
CADMUS		•		JONES, J. P.		•		STEPHENS	•		
CHICHESTER	•			KELLY	•			STUART	•		
CLEVINGER	•			KING	•			TALIAFERRO		•	
COLEMAN, DAN.	•			LAUDERBACK	•			TERRELL		•	
COLEMAN, I. N.		•		LINCOLN	•			TOPPING		•	
COLLINGS		•		MASSENBURG		•		TUCK		•	
COSBY	•			McCAULEY	•			VELLINES	•		
CROWDER	•			McINTYRE		•		VERSER			•
DARDEN		•		McMURRAN			•	WARREN		•	
DAVIS, C. W.		•		MOFFETT			•	WARRINER	•		
DAVIS, L. N.		•		MOORE		•		WATTS		•	
DENNY	•			MORGAN	•			WHITE		•	
DEY	•			MOSS		•		WHITEHEAD	•		
DOVELL		•		NELSON	•			WITCHER	•		
DUFF	•			PAGE		•		WITTEN	•		
EGGLESTON	•			PERRY	•			WRIGHT	•		
EMBREY	•			PORTER		•					
FOLKES			•	PORTERFIELD		•		MR. SPEAKER		•	

Governor had an average of thirty-four bills a day for a thirty-day period, for himself and his Legislative Counsel to pass upon. It is impossible, as Charles D. Breitel pointed out a few years ago while serving as Legislative Counsel to Governor Dewey,[40] to prohibit members from introducing bills — any kind of bills, any number of bills, on any subject. Any citizen has a right to ask his representative to introduce a bill, and many bills are so introduced. It is possible, however, to exclude certain types of bills that are not proper subjects for legislation. To do so would give the legislature

[40] In an address on Improving Legislative Procedure before the Legislative Service Conference, Chicago, January 16, 1947.

more time to consider bills that (1) are important, (2) deal with questions of general policy.

Five types of measures could well be excluded:

1. *Local Bills.* By broadening the powers of home rule of local units, many matters that now come before the legislature could be handled at home. Most of these bills, and there are many of them, could be eliminated if the counties, cities, and other local units were made responsible, under proper state supervision, for the management of their own affairs.

2. *Claims Bills.* Another inconsequential duty upon which much time is wasted is the consideration of bills for the settlement of claims against the state, of which there are great numbers every year. They are of no interest to anyone except the sponsor and his constituent. These bills could be largely eliminated by vesting in administrative officers the power to settle small claims, reporting to the legislature at regular intervals all settlements made under such authorization, as Congress did in Title IV of the Legislative Reorganization Act of 1946. For the settlement of larger claims, the legislatures might establish a court of claims, as a number of them have done.[41]

3. *Changes in Regulations.* Many measures making minor changes in regulations should be entrusted to the appropriate departments. Thus in New York, every year, many measures are passed changing the legal period for fishing for certain kinds of fish or in certain streams. And there are many others, the responsibility for which should be delegated to the executive departments and agencies.

4. *Procedural Matters.* There are many procedural matters that could be dealt with by general law or by extending the rule-making powers of the courts or of the judicial council.

5. *Correction of Errors.* Bills making corrections of obvious errors in existing statutes are numerous; there are various possible solutions of this problem. The power can be delegated to the revisor of statutes, as in Wisconsin, or to a board consisting of the Attorney General, the Director of the Legislative Reference Bureau, and the Secretary of State, as in Pennsylvania.

By divesting themselves of the responsibility for performing routine and insignificant tasks, in so far as they can do so constitutionally, the legislatures might conserve their time and energy for the performance of their vital functions of policy determination, fiscal planning and supervision, and general surveillance of the executive departments and agencies.

Research in the Legislative Process. Research work on the legislative process has been — at least until very recently — much neglected. There is urgent need for work in this field, with much greater emphasis than has been common in the past on objective on-the-spot study of the legislatures in action. As Professor O. Douglas Weeks has pointed out in his effective and persuasive brief for further examination of this subject, there is no need for pessimism regarding the state legislatures and no excuse for regarding them "as something of an obstreperous anachronism, more or less insusceptible to reform, which must be appeased, cajoled, or pressured, but which is in the

[41] See Still, Samuel H., Jr., *Settlement of Claims against the States*, in Constitutional and Statutory Provisions of the States, Vol. VIII (Council of State Governments, Chicago, 1950).

main a meddlesome hindrance to the progress toward a streamlined form of government in which the administrator will play the principal role."[42]

SELECTED REFERENCES

In addition to items listed at the ends of the preceding chapters, the following have a special interest here:

Farmer, Hallie, *The Legislative Process in Alabama* (Bureau of Public Administration, University of Alabama, 1949), and Young, Clement C., *The Legislature of California: Its Membership, Procedure, and Work* (Commonwealth Club of California, San Francisco, 1943). Analysis of all significant phases of the problem in two states.

Guild, Frederic H., and Snider, Clyde F., *Legislative Procedure in Kansas*, Revised (Governmental Research Series, University of Kansas Publications, 1946). For comparable analyses of procedure in other states, see Kettleborough, Charles, *Legislative Procedure in Indiana* (Indiana Legislative Reference Bureau, Indianapolis, 1928); Lewis, Henry W., *The General Assembly of North Carolina: Guidebook of Organization and Procedure* (Institute of Government, University of North Carolina, 1951); and Mason, Paul, *Manual of Legislative Procedure for State Legislatures* (California State Printing Office, Sacramento, 1935).

Horack, Frank E., *Cases and Materials on Legislation* (Callaghan, Chicago, 1940). Of similar type, see Lenhoff, Arthur, *Comments, Cases, and Other Materials on Legislation* (Dennis, Buffalo, 1949), and Read, Horace E., and MacDonald, John W., *Cases and Other Materials on Legislation* (Foundation Press, Brooklyn, 1948).

Illinois Legislative Council, *Scheduling Legislative Workloads* (Springfield, May 1952). After survey of present workloads, consideration is given to procedural devices to lessen congestion, to session patterns, and other matters.

Key, Vladimer O., Jr., *The Problem of Local Legislation in Maryland* (Maryland Legislative Council, 1940, and supplementary report, 1942); see also Kline, Howard M., *Municipal Legislation in Maryland* (Maryland Legislative Council, 1940).

North Carolina Commission on Public, Local and Private Legislation, *Report*, in *Popular Government*, February-March, 1949, entire issue. Excellent historical analysis of North Carolina experience, relation of the problem to city and county home rule, and the constitutional provisions relating thereto.

Still, Rae F., *The Gilmer-Aiken Bills* (Steck Company, Austin, 1950). A significant study in the legislative process, as illustrated by the case histories of a group of bills designed to provide a minimum educational program for Texas.

Weeks, O. Douglas, *Research in the American State Legislative Process* (J. W. Edwards, Ann Arbor, 1947). Subtitle of this important report, prepared for the American Political Science Association's Committee on Research, is: Need, Scope, Methods, Suggested Problems.

[42] *Research in the American State Legislative Process*, p. 2 (J. W. Edwards, Ann Arbor, 1947).

PART FOUR

Executive and Administrative Problems

Administrative questions are not political questions. Although politics sets the tasks for administration, it should not be suffered to manipulate its offices.

— WOODROW WILSON

9

The Governor

History and Development of the Office

The governorship dates back to the beginning of the colonial period. The royal governors in the later portion of this period came to be regarded with suspicion and distrust — as the hated symbols of the power of a foreign oppressor. This fact greatly affected the constitutional provisions on the governorship when new constitutions were framed during and after the period of transition. The early state governors had little power; they were to a large extent figureheads created for the purpose of presiding on ceremonial occasions and making speeches. The changes of the early nineteenth century tended to establish the independence of the governor from the legislature but to weaken his power by diffusion — a condition which continued throughout the century.[1] While there were instances in which conspicuously able men came to the governorship, they were the exception rather than the rule.[2] There was little about the office, save the honor attached to it, to challenge the interest and the creative ability of able men.

Significant changes have occurred during the twentieth century, during the whole of which there has been an increasing tendency to strengthen the governor's powers. This tendency was due in no small measure to the declining public confidence in the legislature; when the people no longer trusted that, they began to look about for some other governmental agency to which its powers might, in part at least, be assigned. Their selection of the governor for this purpose was further encouraged by the appearance in the early years of the century of a number of outstanding leaders in many states, such as Johnson of California, Folk of Missouri, Cummings of Iowa, La Follette of Wisconsin, Hanly and Beveridge of Indiana, Roosevelt and Hughes of

[1] Lipson, Leslie, *The American Governor: From Figurehead to Leader*, Chapter 2 (University of Chicago Press, 1939).

[2] Many of these were in the Civil War period, when Lincoln wrote in a letter to N. F. Dixon, June 28, 1862, "The governors of the northern states are the North. What they decide must be carried out!" See Hesseltine, William B., *Lincoln and the War Governors* (Knopf, New York, 1948).

New York, Wilson of New Jersey, and many others. These leaders capitalized on a wave of democratic sentiment, popular resentment against "bossism," the desire for social legislation, and the general distrust of legislative bodies, thereby giving to the governorship a new popular appeal and a new prestige. Leaders of this type were still, however, in the minority. A study of American governors from 1900 to 1910, made in 1927 by Professor Macdonald,[3] attempted to answer the question, What becomes of our governors? Upon the basis of this study it appeared that nothing much became of them. The governorship was with few exceptions like a road with a dead end; it still led nowhere. There had been no change in the powers of the office corresponding to its changed position in public esteem.

The change in the powers of the office did not take place until 1917 and the years following. In 1917 Governor Frank O. Lowden of Illinois secured the enactment of the first program for state administrative reorganization. This set in motion a series of changes in state government which were to remain in a dominant position in the field for years to come. The influence of these changes has been felt in every state in the Union. Whereas, prior to this movement, the governorship had been a position of some honor and relatively little power, it now became a position of considerable honor and great power. The change in its character brought significant changes in the character of the personnel aspiring to it. It no longer meant that a man would serve a short term and be called "Governor" for the rest of his life; it now offered him the opportunity to develop programs and inaugurate policies of far-reaching importance to the people of his state; to win for himself a reputation for able and constructive leadership upon the basis of which he might advance to important positions in the Federal government either at home or abroad. To mention only one evidence of the change, about one third of the members of the United States Senate are former governors of the states which they represent.[4]

The governorship now offered a challenge to the energy and ability of able men. It brought forth a group of public leaders of whom Smith, Roosevelt, and Lehman of New York, Pinchot of Pennsylvania, and Ritchie of Maryland might be cited as illustrations. This point is supported by a study of "American Governors since 1915," made by Samuel R. Solomon in 1931, the results of which were in marked contrast to those of the Macdonald study previously cited.[5] Of the governors during this period, 113 were Republicans, 115 Democrats. Two were women; 64 per cent had attended college or university; three out of five were native sons; 41 per cent were

[3] Macdonald, Austin F., "American Governors, 1900–1910," *National Municipal Review*, November 1927, pp. 715–719.

[4] See Lehman, Herbert H., "Albany and Washington — a Contrast," *New York Times Magazine*, September 24, 1950, commenting on his experience in shifting from administrator to opinion-maker.

[5] Solomon, Samuel R., "American Governors since 1915," *National Municipal Review*, March 1931, pp. 152–158.

lawyers by profession; practically all were married and had established homes. After their service as governors, 35 per cent either advanced to or tried for Federal offices. Mr. Solomon concluded that "next to the President of the United States, it is the Governor who engaged the interest of the voters."

Several surveys of American governors have been made since 1940; these, without exception, find their leadership still in the ascendancy, with increased administrative power and enhanced political prestige.[6] The percentage of college trained men had greatly increased and approximately one fourth had been elected to Phi Beta Kappa. Of the war governors serving in 1943, the so-called average governor was shown to be:

> . . . a family man, in his early fifties, serving his first term as chief state executive, earning a yearly salary of approximately $8000. His qualifications for his job include previous service in administrative, legislative, or judicial fields of government, and he is drawing from his experience in the nation's armed forces in past wars, or in other capacities connected with those wars, in directing his state's participation in the present victory program.

The war governors were divided exactly evenly between the two major political parties. The oldest was eighty, the youngest thirty-five, with twenty-eight between forty-six and fifty-six. One fourth were born outside the states they were governing. Illinois claimed three, and one was born abroad (Norway). Thirty governors were serving their first terms. Through the death of one governor and the resignation of another, two had acceded to the office through the lieutenant-governorship. Thirteen were serving their second terms, and four — Leverett Saltonstall of Massachusetts, John Moses of North Dakota, John W. Bricker of Ohio, and Prentice Cooper of Tennessee — were serving their third terms. Various combinations of previous governmental experience were reported, but more governors had held administrative posts than had held either legislative or judicial positions.

Conceptions of the Governorship. There are many different ways of viewing the office of the governor. Like the blind men who felt of the elephant, the impression one gets depends to a large extent upon his basic point of view. Those whose approach is legalistic, through the constitutional and statutory provisions regarding the office, have a conception which in many respects is far removed from reality. Great numbers of people regard the governor as the powerful head of the state, responsible for its executive direction and administration; this view fails to take account of the enormous number of

[6] Perkins, John A., "American Governors — 1930–1940," *National Municipal Review*, March 1940, pp. 178–184; White, Leonard D., and Sherman, Harvey, "The Governors March On," *State Government*, October 1940, pp. 195–197, 206; Gurwell, John K., "The Governors of the States," the background and experience of America's forty-eight "War Governors" surveyed, *ibid.*, July 1941, pp. 157–158, 172; a similar article, *ibid.*, July 1943, pp. 154–155; Stokes, Thomas L., "The Governors," *ibid.*, June 1944, pp. 343–345. Leonard D. White made some very bitter criticisms of the governors between the two world wars in *Public Administration Review*, Winter 1944, pp. 68–70; see Frank Bane's reply, *ibid.*, Spring 1944, pp. 153–155. For an excellent study of the Southern governors in the decade from 1938 to 1948, see Ewing, Cortez A. M., "Southern Governors," *Journal of Politics*, May 1948, pp. 385–409.

constitutional and legal restrictions upon his powers.[7] A newer approach centers attention upon what the governor actually does — how he spends his time. Still another emphasizes his responsibilities as popular leader and as leader of his party.

The following discussion is designed to give a well-rounded view of the office. The first section is concerned with its history and development, emphasizing especially the transition from a relatively powerless position to one of great power and influence. After a brief survey of the general characteristics of the office, there are three sections dealing with the executive, legislative, and judicial powers connected with it. While these sections emphasize the constitutional and statutory powers of the governor, and the limitations upon these powers, they also attempt to make clear some of the practical and political problems involved in the exercise of these powers.

A concluding section deals with the actual functioning of the office as it exists today. In some measure, with its analysis of how the governor actually spends his time, it provides an antidote for some of the popular misconceptions of the office. It stresses the importance of the governor as popular leader and leader of his party. It suggests some of the methods of supervision and direction available to the governor and lists some of the obstacles to effective supervision and control. Finally, in line with the concept of executive responsibility to the people, it suggests some of the controls over the governor which prevent him from becoming a "dictator," while at the same time he is prevented from getting too far out of line with the sentiments of the people whom he serves.

General Characteristics of the Office

Before discussing the powers of the governor, it seems desirable to consider briefly the general characteristics of the office — the qualifications, method of nomination and election, length of term, compensation, vacancies, and removals. In a normal election year, governors will be elected in about two thirds of the states; in 1948, there were 100 candidates in thirty-two states, of whom only one — Talmadge of Georgia — was unopposed. Few of the candidates are women; Mrs. Ana Fromiller of Arizona, after twenty-four years as State Auditor, was the only one in 1950. There were none in 1952.

7 Woodrow Wilson once wrote a description of the state executive which is still a valid picture of the office in many states today: "The governor is not the executive; he is but a single piece of the executive. There are other pieces coordinated with him over which he has no direct official control, and which are of less dignity than he only because they have no power to control legislation, as he may do by his veto, and because his position is more representative perhaps of the state government as a whole, of the people of the state as a unit. Indeed, it may be doubted whether the governor and other principal officers of the state can even when taken together be correctly described as *the* executive, since the actual execution of the laws does not rest with them but with the local officers chosen by the towns and counties and bound to the central authorities of the state by no real bonds of responsibility whatever." *State and Federal Governments of the United States*, p. 69.

Qualifications. The early state constitutions prescribed much more rigid qualifications for the governorship than do the present ones. They included religious qualifications, property qualifications, and others which are not now considered necessary or desirable. The age requirement, where specified, is usually thirty years. Maine specifies that only natural-born citizens are eligible. Possession of the status of United States citizenship is sufficient in most states, although a few specify a definite number of years. State citizenship requirements of five or ten years exist in about one fourth of the states, but residence in the state up to as much as seven years is required in most. One fourth of the states require that the governor shall be an elector of the state.

These constitutional qualifications are of little practical significance, relating as they do to conditions that would be readily met by almost any person whose candidacy would receive serious consideration. The tests imposed by practical politics are of far greater significance.[8] No candidate has any chance of receiving the nomination of his party unless he is considered politically available; under this heading are such questions as, In what part of the state does he make his home? This is important because the honors must be passed around from one section of the state to another — in New York, between the city and the up-state districts; in Illinois, between Chicago and down-state; in Pennsylvania, between Pittsburgh, Philadelphia, and the central part of the state.

Again, the candidate must have a political record that is acceptable to the party and to the voters. He must ordinarily be on good terms with the elements of the party exercising control in the state at the time. He must be personally acceptable, and suitable as a potential candidate. His previous business or professional relations must not be of such a nature as to be objectionable to large numbers of voters, or as to make him and the party needlessly vulnerable during the campaign. A candidate might conceivably have the wisdom of Solomon and all the esteemed moral virtues, and yet fail to secure the nomination if he was unable to meet any one or all of these practical tests. Although a large majority of recent candidates have been college or university graduates, the educational qualification is one about which candidates prudently keep silent.

Nomination and Election. It is not necessary to discuss at length the nomination and election of governors. The method of nomination will be that prescribed by the law of the state; in most cases this is the direct primary,

[8] Frank Bane, Executive Director of the Council of State Governments, reports that the chief qualification for the governorship in Virginia used to be that the man look well on a horse. Years ago, when E. Lee Trinkle, a large and heavy man, was governor, there was a big parade which had been carefully planned and organized. It was to be led by the governor and was to start with a salute of guns about which everyone had been informed except Governor Trinkle's horse. The salute was fired, and the Governor went off his horse, high hat and all, at approximately the same time. To this day, no Governor of Virginia has ever been seen on a horse on any public occasion.

but in a few states it is a convention. Methods of campaigning are varied. "Some resort to handshaking, back-slapping, and baby-kissing," observed Governor Prentice Cooper of Tennessee in an address before the Governors' Conference at Hershey, Pennsylvania, on "This Job of Being a Governor," in May 1944. He continued:

> Some rely heavily on a prodigious memory for names and faces; some depend upon pure eloquence to move the heart; some upon ridicule and invective to arouse prejudice; some count solely upon organization and their records to get them by; while still others rely upon music to charm away the senses. If promises are made in whatever type of campaign you are pursuing, it is my belief that the American people of today will require that you keep them. Sometimes the type of campaign is decided by the mere size of the state. No Governor of Texas, I am told, ever campaigns in all of her 254 counties, some of which are as large as the whole State of Rhode Island. Often candidates in Texas are compelled to use the airplane.

Whatever the campaign techniques employed, they are certain in these days to cost plenty of money, and that means that many qualified and public-spirited citizens of moderate means are virtually barred from public life. Time was when a candidate could conduct a successful state-wide campaign on a few thousand dollars put up by himself and his friends. Oswald West, whom Lincoln Steffens described as a "spectacularly progressive" governor of Oregon in 1910, was still living in 1948. Interviewed by Senator Richard L. Neuberger, he said [9]:

> I was elected with $3000. All the money came from my own bank account and that of one friend. Today $3000 would just about buy you half an hour on a state-wide radio hookup. Folks once came from miles around by horse and buckboard to attend a political rally. Now they wait for you to go into their homes by radio and newspaper advertising or direct mail. That takes a lot of money. It makes a candidate reliant on outside financing, unless he happens to be a very rich man. His independence is reduced. He becomes committed to the labor unions or the real estate interests or some other special group.

The election is always a general election, conducted in all but two states on the first Tuesday after the first Monday in November. The question of the timing in relation to the choice of national officers is important. In some states governors are chosen in the years of Presidential elections. Professor Faust reports that "of the twenty-five states which fix a four-year term for the Governor, ten provide that the gubernatorial election and that of most of the other state officials shall coincide with the Presidential election; fifteen of the four-year term group hold their state elections at the intermediate period." [10] The holding of state elections to coincide with national elections is unfortunate because it ordinarily means that little or no serious thought will be given to state problems. Citizens will vote for their preferences in the national offices and will without much consideration

[9] "It Costs Too Much to Run for Office," *New York Times Magazine*, April 11, 1948, pp. 20, 58 ff.

[10] Faust, Martin L., *Manual on the Executive Article*, p. 50 (Missouri Constitutional Convention of 1943, Columbia, 1943).

support the same parties for the state offices, whereas the problems of government in any one of the states are large and significant enough to the well-being of citizens to warrant a decision based upon their own merits. The selection of major state officers should not be merely an incidental aspect of national party contests. It is, of course, to the advantage of the major parties that the existing system be retained; hence the variations from it are few.[11]

Term. By the original constitutions most of the governors served for one year, and none were permitted a term of more than two years. No limits were placed on re-eligibility. At present, twenty-five states have a term of four years, twenty-two have a term of two years. New Jersey until 1948 had a term of three years. It was not until 1920 that the last state — Massachusetts — discontinued the practice of electing a governor annually, although there were in fact in Massachusetts few governors who served for only one year. The current tendency — supported by the weight of informed opinion — is in the direction of the four-year term; "of the twenty-four states operating under constitutions drawn up since 1888, fourteen provide four-year terms for the governors as contrasted to eight which provide two-year terms." [12]

The arguments for the four-year term may be summarized as follows: (1) It permits a more satisfactory development of administrative policies and tends to give a state more efficient government than is possible under a two-year term. (2) It makes possible greater and more consistent economy in administration; it reduces the inevitable extravagance and waste connected with more frequent changes. (3) It is in harmony with the principle of the short ballot, providing as it does for a reduction and simplification of the task which the voter is asked to perform. It is important, therefore, that gubernatorial elections be held at some other time than the Presidential year.

The question of re-eligibility is important. Fortunately the third-term tradition of the Presidency has not affected the governorship in most states. In thirty-two states there is no limit at all: the following restrictions in other states apply to consecutive terms:

Four years (two two-year terms) — New Mexico.
(one four-year term) — Alabama, Florida, Georgia, Indiana, Kentucky, Louisiana, Mississippi, Missouri, North Carolina, Oklahoma, Pennsylvania, and Virginia — twelve states.
Six years (three two-year terms) — Tennessee.
Eight years (two four-year terms) — Delaware and Oregon.

Where the two-year term is used, there are usually no limits on re-eligibility. In New York, for instance, Alfred E. Smith was a candidate in six successive

[11] A tabulation made by William R. Tansill, Legislative Reference Service, Library of Congress, in 1949, shows that in such cases, the vote for governor is always appreciably smaller than that for President.

[12] New York State Constitutional Convention Committee, *Problems Relating to Executive Administration and Powers*, Chapter 1 (Albany, 1938); for more recent studies, see Kallenback, Joseph E., "Constitutional Limitations on Reeligibility of National and State Chief Executives," *American Political Science Review*, June 1952, pp. 438–454, and Ruskowski, Casimir W., *The Constitutional Governor* (Humphries, Boston, 1943).

elections, of which he won all but the second; Herbert H. Lehman and Thomas E. Dewey were successful candidates in four and three elections, respectively. Wilbur L. Cross was a successful candidate four times in Connecticut. George W. P. Hunt of Arizona became governor of that state when it was admitted to the Union in 1912; he was subsequently re-elected six times, and was a candidate in nine elections. In most of the states with a four-year term, a governor is not permitted to succeed himself immediately. In practice this means that few governors are able to secure a second election at all, although there are such exceptions as those of Bibb Graves of Alabama and Robert E. Pattison and Gifford Pinchot of Pennsylvania. A few states have the four-year term without such a restriction, of which group Maryland with its "perpetual governor," the late Albert C. Ritchie, who served four consecutive terms, is illustrative.[13]

If one believes in democratic government, a restriction on re-eligibility seems unjustifiable; the people should have the right to re-elect an executive of whose services they approve, and the opportunity to refuse re-election to one of whose conduct they disapprove. Governor Prentice Cooper of Tennessee well stated this point in his address before the Governors' Conference:

> A governor who is ineligible by law from serving more than one term is in some ways at a disadvantage since he has no certain way of knowing whether he could be re-elected. He is denied the privilege of a vote of confidence by the people, and may lack means of vindication from charges of the opposition that he has done those things that he should not have done, and that he has left undone those things he should have done. [In those states where re-election is permissible] the official mortality rate among governors is unusually high.

Compensation. All the governors receive an annual salary, the amount of which varies from $4,500 in Maryland to $25,000 in California, New York, and Pennsylvania. In 1940, the average was $7,850; in 1945, $8,083; in 1950, $11,314. Michigan pays $22,500; Massachusetts and New Jersey, $20,000; Connecticut, Louisiana, Minnesota, Mississippi, New Mexico, North Carolina, Oklahoma, Rhode Island, Virginia, and Washington, $15,000. As of 1952, half of the states paid between $10,000 and $14,999. One sixth (eight) pay below this range, one third (sixteen) pay $15,000 or above. As is indicated in the table on the next page, there has been a definite trend toward higher salaries for governors.

The compensation is still seriously inadequate in many states; many mayors are paid as much as or more than the governors of their states. In

[13] Many of the states have had governors who served three or more terms. Of the governors between 1900 and 1950, fifty-five had served six years or more, with a total of 414, an average of approximately seven and a half years. In each of three states, Illinois, Montana, and Utah, the terms of four governors had covered thirty-two of this fifty year period. Governor Ritchie of Maryland had the longest tenure of sixteen years; Governor Hunt of Arizona was next with fourteen years. Governors Dewey of New York and Warren of California had each been elected for terms totaling twelve years. See the author's *The Governors of the States, 1900–1950* (Council of State Governments, Chicago, 1948).

Distribution of Governors' Salaries, 1910–1950 *

SALARY	*1910*	*1920*	*1930*	*1940*	*1950*
$ 2,500–$ 4,999	21	12	6	4	1
5,000– 9,999	21	29	31	34	14
10,000– 14,999	5	6	7	7	24
15,000 and over	1	1	4	3	9

* The first three columns are from White, Leonard D., *Trends in Public Administration*, p. 180 (McGraw-Hill, New York, 1933).

addition to the actual salary paid, however, thirty-four states provide housing (two of these rent an executive mansion, but fourteen let their governors select a house themselves), and most states provide allowances for travel, servants, chauffeurs, entertaining of official guests, and other items, so that the actual compensation is considerably in excess of the specified salary. In Maryland, for instance, where the official salary is $4,500, it is estimated that the compensation of the governor is approximately $55,000, of which by legislative act no audit shall be made. He has the use of an executive mansion valued at $231,000, and of a $4,000,000 yacht which the state bought in 1929 from a New York millionaire for a comparatively small sum. This policy was adopted by the legislature some years ago when a man without private income was elected to the office; before that time the office had been, like an ambassadorship, a drain upon the governor's private resources.

The holding of any important public office entails a large volume of personal expenditure, of the nature of which the average citizen is little if at all aware. If one overlooks political assessments and other political contributions, there are still demands for subscriptions to welfare, educational, and civic organizations and projects of every conceivable character. As a matter of political expediency, the governor can afford neither to ignore these appeals nor to give less than might be expected of a person in such a position.

Vacancies and Removals. There are at least six methods by which vacancies, either permanent or temporary, may occur. These include death, resignation, illness or other disability, temporary absence from the state, impeachment, and recall. In the case of temporary absences, the lieutenant-governor acts in those states where the office exists; in other states, provision must be made by law for such emergencies. That provisions with regard to succession are really important is illustrated by the airplane crash in Oregon in 1947, which took the lives of three top officials of the state — the Governor, Secretary of State, and President of the Senate. In this instance, the Speaker of the House became Governor. Provisions regarding succession due to illness and disability are quite as unsatisfactory in the states as in the Federal government, as witness the Horner-Steele controversy in Illinois in 1940, in which the lieutenant governor proclaimed himself acting governor of the state.[14] Few resignations occur; most of these are occasioned by advancement to the Senate or appointment to some other Federal office.

Very unusual situations developed in Missouri in 1941 and in Wisconsin in 1942. In the first instance, Governor Stark stayed on beyond his four-year term, when the legislature attempted to steal the governorship by refusing to seat a duly elected governor who had won by a very small majority but who belonged to the opposition party. In the Wisconsin case, the governor-elect died before the inauguration. The Wisconsin Constitution of 1848, still in force, does not provide clearly for the succession under such circumstances. Consequently the question as to whether the incumbent governor was to hold office beyond his term was presented to the court for determination. The court ruled that he should not, since the constitution was specific on this point. Under these circumstances, the only alternative was to inaugurate the new lieutenant governor, who then became acting governor of the state.[15]

The general vagueness with which the constitutions treat the problem of succession is further illustrated by the exhibition put on in Georgia in late 1946 and early 1947. In the 1946 election, under the county unit system that prevails in Georgia, Eugene Talmadge had been elected to another term as governor. He died a fortnight before he would have been inaugurated for his fourth term. In the absence of any clear mandate in the state's recently revised constitution, the Talmadge forces contended that the legislature was empowered to elect a governor under such circumstances, but their opponents maintained that the regularly elected lieutenant governor should be inaugurated.

The Talmadge faction, in a *coup d'état* which aroused protest throughout the state, seized the governor's office, and for a time conditions were ripe for violence. The opposite party took the matter to the courts, and on January 18 Arnall, the outgoing governor, formally resigned his office in favor of Thompson, the recently elected lieutenant governor. For two months Georgia existed under a dual governorship, each faction refusing to recognize the legality of the acts of the other. Professor Ewing concludes:

> The court held that the function of the legislature was that of canvassing the returns of the election, that its only power to choose a governor came into being when no candidate had received a majority of the popular votes in the general election, that it could not set aside a popular decision and proceed to a choice of its own while performing its canvassing duties, and that it had voted unconstitutionally when it sought to elect Herman Talmadge as governor.[16]

[14] This case is discussed in Snider, Clyde F., "Gubernatorial Disability," *University of Chicago Law Review*, April 1941, pp. 521–529.

[15] See Dilliard, Irving, "Missouri Has No Governor," *Nation*, February 15, 1941, pp. 183–184; and note on "Wisconsin Governorship," *State Government*, February 1943, p. 48.

[16] Thompson v. Talmadge, 201 Ga. 867, 41 S.E. 2d 883, 1947. This account is based on Ewing, *op. cit.*, pp. 404–409; see also comment by Sherwood, Foster H., in "State

Only one removal has been made and relatively few have been attempted through the use of the recall. Governor Frazier of North Dakota was removed from office by this device in 1922. The more common method of making removals, authorized in all the state constitutions except that of Oregon,[17] is through the use of the impeachment process, which operates in the states in a manner similar to that in which it is used in the Federal government. The lower house has the sole power of impeachment, while the trial of the accused on the charges that have been preferred against him is conducted before the senate. If convicted, the accused may be removed from office and may be debarred from holding further office of profit or public trust. Additional punishment, such as fines or imprisonment, may not be inflicted as a result of conviction in impeachment proceedings, although if the charges are such as to involve violations of the criminal law, such punishments may follow conviction in a criminal suit. Although many governors have been impeached, only a few have been convicted.[18]

It was the intent of those who incorporated the impeachment provisions in the state constitutions to establish a method by which the people might be relieved of the services of a chief executive whom, on account of dishonesty or inefficiency, they no longer trusted. In practice, the device has failed to accomplish this purpose. Impeachment proceedings have been instituted, not as a means of protecting the public but as a phase of the political warfare of factions or parties. The results have been determined, not by the merits of the case but by the ability of the accused to muster sufficient voting strength in the senate to retain his position. If he has been able to do this, he has remained in office; otherwise he has been removed. No more conclusive evidence of the political nature of the impeachment proceedings need be asked than the facts relating to its use in Texas and Oklahoma. In Texas, after one legislature had removed Governor Ferguson from office, another legislature removed, so far as possible, the penalties attaching to the conviction. In Oklahoma, a writer who made a study of the impeachment process in that state testifies that down to 1930 there had not been a single governor who had not been either impeached or seriously threatened with impeachment proceedings. When such use is made of this device, it ceases to be a remedy

---

Constitutional Law in 1946–1947," *American Political Science Review*, August 1947, pp. 700–702. Maryland has, since 1910, used a county unit system in primary elections under which, in 1950, Governor Lane obtained a majority of the convention votes (and, therefore, the nomination), although he had about 9,000 popular votes less than his opponent in the primary.

17 The Oregon Constitution, Article VII, Section 6, provides that "incompetency, corruption, malfeasance, or delinquency in office may be tried in the same manner as criminal offenses."

18 Among the convictions are the following: Sulzer of New York, 1913; Ferguson of Texas, 1917; Walton of Oklahoma, 1923; Johnston of Oklahoma, 1927. Long of Louisiana was impeached in 1929, but was not convicted. No case has occurred for a number of years.

for public evils and becomes a political weapon whose use is both ridiculous and deplorable.[19]

Powers of the Governor. Some general idea of the powers of the governor may be gained by examining the appropriate article in any state constitution; the following excerpts are from Article VI of the Constitution of Michigan:

> Sec. 2. The chief executive power is vested in the governor.
>
> Sec. 3. The governor shall take care that the laws be faithfully executed; shall transact all necessary business with the officers of the government; and may require information in writing from all executive and administrative state officers, elective and appointive, upon any subject relating to the duties of their respective offices.
>
> Sec. 4. He shall be commander-in-chief of the military and naval forces, and may call out such forces to execute the laws, to suppress insurrection and to repel invasion.
>
> Sec. 5. He shall communicate by message to the legislature, and at the close of his official term to the incoming legislature, the condition of the state, and recommend such measures as he may deem expedient.
>
> Sec. 6. He shall issue writs of election to fill such vacancies as occur in the senate or house of representatives.
>
> Sec. 7. He may convene the legislature on extraordinary occasions.
>
> Sec. 8. He may convene the legislature at some other place when the seat of government becomes dangerous from disease or a common enemy.
>
> Sec. 9. He may grant reprieves, commutations and pardons after convictions for all offenses, except treason and cases of impeachment. . . .
>
> Sec. 10. Whenever a vacancy shall occur in any of the state offices, the governor shall fill the same by appointment, by and with the advice and consent of the senate, if in session.
>
> Sec. 11. All official acts of the governor, except his approval of the laws, shall be authenticated by the great seal of the state, which shall be kept by the secretary of state.

While, in this case and in the Model State Constitution, the executive power is vested in the governor, it is true in the states generally either that the executive power is dispersed among a number of constitutional officers or that the executive powers that the governor may exercise are enumerated. Either of these devices operates with the effect of limiting his powers quite in contrast to the situation in the Federal government, where both in theory and in fact the executive power is concentrated in the President. Even a casual examination of these provisions of the Michigan constitution reveals that the powers of the governor are of three general types: administrative and executive, legislative, and judicial or quasi-judicial. These three types will now be considered in some detail.

Executive and Administrative Powers

Ministerial and Discretionary Powers. In any discussion of the powers of the executive as the head of the administration, the distinction must be

[19] Stewart, Frank M., "Impeachment in Texas," *American Political Science Review*, August 1930, pp. 652–658; Ewing, Cortez A. M., "Impeachment of Oklahoma Governors," *ibid.*, pp. 648–652; for the most complete account, see Friedman, Jacob A., *The Impeachment of Governor William Sulzer* (Columbia University Press, 1939).

made between ministerial and discretionary powers. Those duties concerning the performance of which the state constitution permits of the exercise of no discretion are regarded as ministerial. The state constitutions, for example, generally provide that the governor must commission all state officers when their election has been properly certified, that he must send to the senate nominations for filling certain other offices, and that he must see that the laws are faithfully executed. When, on the other hand, the decision rests with him regarding the kind of action to be taken, or indeed whether any action at all is required in a given case, the power which he exercises is said to be discretionary. An illustration is found in the provision that he may call out troops for the protection of life and property. In such a case he is the sole judge as to whether or not troops are required and, in the second place, as to the number of troops needed to deal effectively with the existing situation. Another important difference relates to the possible use of mandamus procedure. When a governor, who has taken an oath to "preserve, protect, and defend" the constitution of the state, fails to perform a ministerial act, he may be reached through mandamus proceedings instituted in the courts of the state. On the other hand, it is not possible to mandamus an executive for the purpose of compelling him to exercise his discretion by arriving at some particular decision.

Powers of Administrative Supervision. The governor is the executive head of the state government. Largely as a result of his powers of appointment and removal, of his responsibility in the matter of law enforcement, and of his powers as head of the state's military establishment, he has a general administrative supervision and control over the acts of his subordinates. In thirty-four states the constitution gives him power to require information in writing from the heads of executive departments on any subject relating to their duties, and eight of these states specify that such information shall be given under oath if the governor so requires. In units as large as many of the states, the task of supervision requires an enormous number of conferences and appointments and a careful budgeting of the governor's time. This is the more true when one considers the amount of time necessarily allotted to travel, speechmaking, and ceremonial appearances.

In theory, the acts of administrative subordinates are in many cases the acts of the governor; in practice, since it is a physical impossibility for the governor to pass personally upon any considerable percentage of the total number of decisions made in his behalf by subordinates, they are accustomed to act in all but the most important cases without his knowledge. A good executive will conserve his energy by delegating all the detail work to his subordinates and reserving for his own consideration only those problems which involve decisions on important questions of policy. Where possible there should be consultation before action is taken by subordinates, but in cases in which, for any reason, this is not done the governor always has the power of review. It may happen occasionally also that divergent or conflicting policies will develop in different branches of the service. It is the duty of the governor as chief administrator to review these cases and to make decisions with regard thereto for the purpose of unifying and coordinating the activities of the administration.

It thus happens that all important announcements, whether of appointments or of matters of policy, are given out by the governor's office. The governor performs all those acts which are suggestive of the headship and direction of the administration. He issues executive orders, orders investigations, directs his various department heads and bureau chiefs, and issues proclamations. Even though he may be responsible for the determination of major policies and may take the credit for success as he must accept the blame for failure, he will, if he is a tactful executive, assign to his department heads and other coworkers a large part of the credit for such successes as may come to the administration. He knows that no administration succeeds without able heads of departments and bureau chiefs, and he knows that there is sufficient glory for him in having proved his ability to select such men and to guide and coordinate their activities in such a way as to achieve some degree of administrative success.

Power of Appointment. Of all the important executive and administrative powers exercised by the governor, none is more important than the power of appointment, for the success of an administration rests in no small measure upon wise use of this power. If a governor chooses competent and able persons as advisers and for administrative positions, he can devote his energies to the general supervision of their work and the coordination of their activities. If he chooses weak and incompetent persons, he not only increases the extent of his own burdens as chief executive, but he definitely limits the effectiveness of the work done by the departments concerned and opens his administration to serious danger of fraud, corruption, and incompetence. No governor who has any regard for his reputation and for the success of his administration can afford to take this chance.

The governor not only has the authority to make appointments to many designated offices, but he has as well the duty to see that these positions are kept filled. A department cannot operate properly without a head, nor can a commission of three or five members function properly when vacancies exist in one or more of its positions. Some idea of the extent of the governor's power of appointment may be gained from the tabulation on page 331; not all of these offices exist in every state, and in some cases some means of selection apart from the governor may be used.

Numerous influences operate to restrict the governor's free exercise of the appointing power. He knows that he must make selections such as the senate or council will approve.[20] In Virginia approval by both houses is

[20] Generally speaking, the results of this practice are bad; for a recent study, see Alabama Legislative Reference Service, *Senatorial Confirmation of Appointments* (Montgomery, 1949).

necessary. The law may contain provisions with regard to the bipartisan character of administrative boards and the geographical distribution or technical qualifications of members. There may be ex-officio members or laws fixing definite and overlapping terms; it may be necessary to consider civil service regulations. Then there are political considerations — the pay-

Extent of the Power of the Governor to Appoint Important State Officials

OFFICER	APPOINTED BY GOVERNOR ALONE	APPOINTED BY GOVERNOR WITH CONSENT OF SENATE	GOVERNOR HAS A PART IN SELECTION	GOVERNOR HAS NO PART IN SELECTION	OFFICE OR EQUIVALENT DOES NOT EXIST
Secretary of State	0	7[1]	7	41	0
Comptroller....	2	7	9	12	27
Auditor........	3	3	6	36	6
Treasurer......	1	0	1	47	0
Tax Commission	17	26	43	4	1
Education......	2	12	14	34	0
Attorney General	1	4	5	43	0
Budget Officer ..	16	14	30	1	17
Agriculture.....	10	21	31	16	1
Labor.........	8	32	40	7	1
Health........	13	32	45	3	0
Welfare........	26	22	48	0	0
Public Utilities..	7	21	28	18	2
Securities.......	4	18	22	21	5
Banking.......	12	31	43	5	0
Insurance.......	8	25	33	14	1
Liquor........	9	20	29	10	9
Highways......	17	29	46	2	0
Conservation ...	15	28	43	3	2

[1] In Virginia, with the consent of both houses.

ment of campaign debts, the recognition of different factions of the party, and the wishes of the state leader. Even yet, in some states, the governor is in theory responsible for the state administration, with very little actual authority over it. In New Jersey, where, as Governor Edison expressed it in 1941, the power of the executive had been diluted to an extraordinary degree under the provisions of the Constitution of 1844, only two state officials, the budget commissioner and the finance commissioner, were appointed by the governor, to serve at his pleasure. At least eight were elected by the two houses in joint session, and nine were appointed by the governor with the consent of the senate, usually for a five-year term, whereas the governor's term was three years. In this administrative morass, where millions of dollars are spent annually, not even the nomenclature has been standardized — there are departments, commissions, boards, bureaus, and offices.[21] The New Jersey situation was corrected by the new constitution framed in 1947, but similar conditions still exist in many other states.

The governor is confronted by the question of whether the persons he appoints will be loyal to him and his policies. At the beginning of his second term as Governor of Pennsylvania, Gifford Pinchot required all his appointees to sign a pledge which read as follows: "I will loyally support the policies approved by the people of the Commonwealth in the last election for Governor." This action caused wide comment and created vigorous opposition, for no appointments were forthcoming unless the pledge was signed. It seems like a drastic policy; yet a governor who is responsible for an administration ought to be entitled to the full cooperation and support of those who hold positions by virtue of his appointment. In this instance, Mr. Pinchot was doubtless influenced by his experience during his first term, which began eight years before, when he followed a much more lenient policy and when in numerous cases it was discovered that persons holding office by virtue of his appointment, or continued in office by him, proved disloyal to him and to the policies for which he stood. A governor can scarcely be blamed for resenting the activities of those who bore from within. From the public's point of view, such a policy is certainly dangerous if employed by a governor who is more interested in the spoils of office than in the conduct of an administration devoted to enlightened public service.[22]

As has been suggested, the policy which a governor will pursue in his relations with the party leader and the party organization in his state is a matter of vital concern in the selection of appointees. Generally speaking, there are three possibilities open to him. He may adopt a policy of abject subservience to the state party organization; he may, at the other extreme, defy the organization; or he may adopt the more moderate and more sensible expedient of consulting the party leaders and then using his own judgment. The significance of these attitudes may be illustrated by reference to the policies of a number of well-known governors. A recent governor of a large Eastern state possessed no mind of his own in making decisions with regard to appointments. More than one applicant for a position was definitely told that the state leader would have to be consulted before a decision was made. This governor made no attempt to protect his own reputation in this matter. He might easily have said that he was not ready to make a decision or that there were a number of applicants whose qualifications would

[21] See McKean, Dayton D., *Pressures on the Legislature of New Jersey*, pp. 36–37 (Columbia University Press, 1938).

[22] That such powers of appointment are subject to abuse was strikingly brought out in mid-1949. The Governor of Georgia and the then recent Governor of Illinois were both accused of appointing newspapermen to state positions, presumably as a means of purchasing favorable press comment. The *St. Louis Post-Dispatch* reported that in the latter state, fifty-one editors, executives or other employees of fourteen daily and thirty-three weekly newspapers received state paychecks totaling nearly $480,000 between 1943 and 1949, while they were directly or indirectly associated with their newspapers.

have to be considered, but he failed to use even these simple expedients for avoiding a disclosure of his subservience to the organization.

At the other extreme, the case of Governor Sulzer of New York, who was impeached and removed from office in 1913, may be cited. This man was a professional politician of the type created by the Tammany organization. After being elected, he became impressed with the importance of the office and imbued with a desire to administer it to the best of his ability. This led him to defy the leader of the organization which had placed him in the position. After some futile attempts to persuade him to change his policy, the Democratic leader cooperated with a willing Republican majority in the legislature to divest him of his office.[23]

The third course, not only more moderate but more sensible, is one in which the governor consults the wishes of the party organization and its leaders but makes the final decision himself. Of this type of governor Theodore Roosevelt furnishes an excellent example, as is well shown by the following account of a portion of the Barnes-Roosevelt libel case proceedings:

> Roosevelt testified that, when governor, he habitually consulted Senator Platt, the Republican state boss, before making appointments. In recommending men for appointment to positions allotted to the minority party, the evidence showed that Platt in his turn was accustomed to consider the wishes of Croker, the Democratic boss. When asked why he consulted Platt, Roosevelt answered that he had to, if he wanted to have his nominations confirmed. Question: "That is, you had to be in alliance with the invisible government, so-called, to get the nominations confirmed?" Answer: "To get the nominations confirmed I had to have the support of the Senate, and the Senate was responsive to Mr. Platt's wishes." Ordinarily Roosevelt made no appointments of any kind, even those not dependent upon senatorial confirmation, until he had ascertained that they would not be objectionable to the boss. Yet Roosevelt was not a subservient governor. In Senator Platt's autobiography, published five years before the Barnes-Roosevelt trial, it is stated that "Roosevelt had from the first agreed that he would consult me on all questions of appointments. . . . He religiously fulfilled this pledge, although he frequently did just what he pleased. . . . Roosevelt told me, for instance, that he proposed to remove Lou Payn. I protested, but he was removed, and I was consulted about the appointment of his successor." [24]

Sulzer had the same experience. In an interview shortly after his conviction he told the press [25]:

> I had several talks with Mr. Murphy, and in some of these talks I told him that I was the governor, and that I intended to be governor; that I was not going to be a proxy governor, or a rubber stamp. He laughed at me and rebuked me for this, and said that I might be governor but that he controlled the legislature; that unless I did what he wanted me to regarding legislation and appointments I could not get my nominations confirmed and that he would block everything.

[23] Friedman, *op. cit.*

[24] Holcombe, Arthur N., *State Government in the United States*, Third Edition, pp. 337–338 (Macmillan, New York, 1931).

[25] Friedman, *op. cit.*, p. 249.

While there are theoretically three courses open to the governor, there is only one course open to him if he wants to succeed — and even then he must be a strong man to succeed. It is plain that he cannot deliver himself into the hands of the organization and that he is likely to lose his job if he defies it. His only real choice is to set certain standards of training, ability, and character and then (in the absence of civil service regulations) appoint only those persons acceptable to the organization who meet these qualifications. No one need to be shocked at this suggestion. Ours is a party government and it is likely to continue to be such. There is no justification for assuming that a man who has the backing of the state organization must be either a fool or a rascal; there are large numbers of honest, able, and intelligent men who have associated themselves with the affairs of the major parties. The governor's task is to select men of this type, politically satisfactory to the organization, rather than men of the type all too frequently selected in the past.

Power of Removal. If administration is to be effective and responsible, the chief executive must have not only the power to appoint but the power to investigate and remove for proper cause. An executive officer who must bear the responsibility for the record of his administration must have the power to control his subordinates; he must be in a position to insist not only that their work be well done but that in general the policies which they pursue shall be in harmony with those of the administration as a whole. In other words, if the governor is to be held responsible for the conduct of the administration, he must have sufficient power over it to enable him to conduct an administration for which he is responsible. In recognition of this fact, many states have adopted a policy with regard to removal by the governor in harmony with the principle set forth in Myers v. United States as applying to the President.[26] This rule permits the executive to remove for proper cause, without consent of the Senate, officers for whose appointment the consent of the Senate is required, as well as to remove officers over whose appointment he has the sole power. If the principle of administrative responsibility is to be maintained, this is the only rule which could reasonably be followed.[27] There are, however, certain limitations upon the governor's power of removal, imposed by the constitution and by statute. The governor may not, except in rare instances, remove elective officers; he has no power of removal over judicial officers; and most local officers are beyond his control. He must also be mindful of the fact that, in the majority of cases, the senate must confirm the new man whom he nominates to replace the one

[26] Frank S. Myers v. United States, 272 U. S. 52, 1926.

[27] A few months before the decision in the Myers case, the Supreme Court of Pennsylvania adopted a quite different rule in the case of Commonwealth v. Benn, 284 Pa. 421, 1925. In this case Governor Pinchot sought to remove for cause two members of the Public Service Commission. This doctrine was later modified in Commonwealth v. Stewart, 286 Pa. 511, 1927, and Commonwealth v. King, 312 Pa. 412, 1933.

removed; this provision furnishes a considerable practical restraint upon the exercise of the removal power.

The history of each state will provide illustrations of the type of questions which may arise in connection with attempts on the part of the governor to use his removal power. The more vigorous the governor, the more likely these contests are to arise. Frequently they have taken place in connection with the public service commissions, as attempts have been made by governors in a number of states to make these commissions either more responsive to their wishes (Talmadge of Georgia) or to the public interest (Pinchot of Pennsylvania). Governors Murray of Oklahoma and Johnston of South Carolina fought similar battles for the control of the state highway commissions. Such contests are apt to be largely political in character and can be discouraged by the use of the device of overlapping terms — three members with a six-year term, one membership to expire every two years, or five members with a five-year term, one membership to expire annually.[28]

Power to Enforce the Law. The state constitutions have long provided that the governors should be responsible for the enforcement of the law. Law enforcement is a good, like home and mother. Most governors pledge themselves to "economy" and to "faithful law enforcement." Very often the governor's interest in the latter manifests itself in a "pet" institution, department, or subject-matter field to which he devotes more than a proportionate share of his time and energy. Furthermore, most of the governors have one or two areas of law enforcement in which they propose to administer the law either more rigidly or with more laxity than has been the case previously. It appears, in general, that the governor has a considerable amount of discretion in deciding how many laws and which laws shall be enforced, and to what extent.

The governors, like the President, have also been drawn into the settlement of labor disputes and have been given power, under recent legislation in some states authorizing government seizure of struck properties, to take over the operation of such properties when the continuance of the dispute would imperil the public health or safety. Thus Governor Edge in 1946 seized ten gas and coke plants of the Public Service Electric and Gas Company of New Jersey three hours before the strike deadline, in order to insure uninterrupted household and industrial gas service to 3,500,000 persons throughout the state.[29] Governor Tuck of Virginia used similar powers twice in the fall of 1949. He declared a state of emergency because of the nationwide coal walkout, and put the state in the coal-mining business to "keep Virginia warm." A few weeks later he seized a large motorbus company

[28] See New York State Constitutional Convention Committee, *Problems Relating to Executive Administration and Powers*, Chapter 8, on removal of officers, and Chapter 9, on bribery and corruption of public officers, for an excellent discussion of these problems.

[29] *New York Times*, April 5, 1946.

serving northern Virginia counties adjoining Washington, in order to prevent interruption of service.[30]

In recent years numerous state administrations have assumed active leadership of law observance campaigns, of campaigns for the control and abatement of crime, for highway safety, and for other purposes. The conference of officials and interested citizens has been widely used to develop leadership and to secure publicity; this has been followed by intensive advertising campaigns by means of the press, radio, and billboards. In all such moves the governor plays a leading part.

Legislative Powers of the Governor

The legislative powers of the governor are of two types, constitutional and extra-constitutional. The specific constitutional powers commonly include four things: messages, regular and special; call of special sessions; the veto power; and the power to adjourn the legislature when that body is unable to agree on a date of adjournment (in those states where the session is not of definitely limited duration). The messages include information on the condition of the state and recommendations with regard to legislation. In fact, as was shown in the preceding chapter, a very substantial portion of the legislation passed arises out of the proposals and recommendations of the governor and the executive departments operating under his supervision. The constitutions of thirty-nine states provide that he shall recommend to the legislature matters which he deems it expedient to present for their consideration. The extra-constitutional powers include those acts of leadership by which the governor seeks to enlist popular support for his policies and his legislative program. Each of these powers will be briefly considered.

Reports to the Legislature. Just as the President presents an annual message to the Congress on the state of the Union, so in thirty-nine states the constitution imposes on the governor the duty of reporting to the legislature information on the condition of the state. These messages usually present in outline form the program recommended by the governor and contain definite suggestions for legislative enactments. In many states this message is followed within a short time by the budget message, which is accompanied by a printed document setting forth the recommendations of the administration for the financial program during the ensuing fiscal period. In twenty-two states the governor is required by the constitution to make his reports and recommendations *from time to time*, but in eight of these cases he is required to give such information at every session.[31]

[30] *Washington Post*, September 28, 1949, and October 29, 1949.

[31] Professor Farmer reports that the messages of Alabama governors since 1903 have varied from two pages to 200 pages in length. In general, "earlier messages were longer and more oratorical, more recent messages shorter and less given to eulogy. Earlier messages were usually read by clerks. Later messages usually are read by the governor himself to joint sessions of the two houses. This may explain the reduction in their length." *The Legislative Process in Alabama, op. cit.*, p. 169.

Special messages dealing with important subjects are in order at appropriate times. Those governors who attempt to exert an aggressive leadership usually make frequent use of special messages; before such a message is delivered, the desire of the governor to address the legislature is made known to the leaders. It is then customary for the two houses to adopt concurrent resolutions calling for a joint session at a designated day and hour. It is preferable that these messages be delivered in person, and in practice they usually are.[32] Five constitutions, those of Alabama, Arkansas, Michigan, Missouri, and Nebraska, require governors to report at the close of their terms of office, but many governors in other states do so without such requirement. Such a report gives an outgoing administration a fine opportunity to summarize its accomplishments for the benefit of the people of the state as well as to report to the legislature.

Special Sessions: Adjournment. The governor is the sole judge in all matters pertaining to the calling of special sessions, except in such matters as impeachments. All the state constitutions confer on the governor the power to convene extraordinary sessions, although three — those of Massachusetts, New Hampshire, and North Carolina — provide that he shall exercise this power with the advice of the council. In Louisiana he has not only the power but the duty to convene the legislature when so petitioned by two thirds of the elected members thereof. The governor decides whether a special session is necessary and also the subjects to be considered. These must be specifically mentioned in the call or, in some states, in subsequent messages. In twenty-one states the legislature is without authority to consider subjects not recommended by the governor. In ten states the governor has the power to convene the senate alone in extraordinary session, and fourteen states permit him to call a special session at some place other than the ordinary seat of government if that place is in danger from war, disease, or plague. When a special session looms as a possibility, it always provokes a great deal of discussion because of the public expense involved and the loss of time and the inconvenience to members. The question of special sessions has been considered more at length in the discussion of the legislature.

Eighteen states permit the governor to adjourn the legislature when the two houses are unable to agree on a time of adjournment, but only until the time of the next regular session. Massachusetts and New Hampshire limit the duration of such adjournments to ninety days and permit them only with advice of the council. Delaware limits the duration of such adjournments to three months, Kentucky and Pennsylvania to four months. In practice this power is insignificant and rarely used.

[32] These messages are usually printed in pamphlet form for general distribution. Pressure groups delight to lift paragraphs from them, to show the attitude of the governors on the subject in which they are interested. The successive March issues of *State Government* regularly reprint significant excerpts from these messages.

3 *Veto Power.* Under the Constitution of the United States the President has four alternatives in disposing of the bills submitted to him by Congress. With regard to any given bill, he may sign it; return it to the house in which it originated with a statement of his objections; use what is known as the pocket veto; or permit the bill to become a law without his signature, if, after a ten-day period, Congress is still in session. Before 1789 only two states provided for the veto power over legislation, but — reports Professor Prescott [33] — "distrust of the governor's prerogatives had diminished by 1812 so that no new state except West Virginia has entered the Union without some form of executive disallowance." By 1860 the veto power had become firmly established; North Carolina is the only state in which no type of executive veto is permitted.

The constitutional provisions respecting the exercise of the veto power may be roughly classified as strong, medium, and weak; the characterization of each of these classes is indicated in the table on page 339. Assuming that three or more of the elements in each group are necessary in order to justify assignment of a state to a particular class, the careful analysis of Professor Prescott shows that the governors of twenty-nine states have a strong veto power, fourteen a medium strong power, and four a weak power. As noted, the governor of North Carolina has no veto power at all.

Of the four alternatives open to the President, only the first two are available to the governors of twenty-one states. Veto restrictions during sessions differ from those applying after adjournment. In the former case, three days are allowed in nine states (Indiana, Iowa, Kansas, Minnesota, New Mexico, North Dakota, South Carolina, South Dakota, and Wyoming); six days are allowed in four states (Alabama, Maryland, Rhode Island, and Wisconsin); ten days are allowed in twelve states (California, Colorado, Delaware, Illinois, Kentucky, Louisiana, Michigan, Missouri, New York, Ohio, Pennsylvania, and Texas); while in the remaining twenty-one states, five days are allowed.

In commenting upon the veto power, the distinction between a suspensive and an absolute veto should be noted. The suspensive veto is the one commonly authorized; it is possible for the legislature, if still in session, to pass a measure over the governor's veto by a two-thirds vote where the suspensive veto is used, whereas the absolute veto is final. The vetoes after the legislature has adjourned are in fact, if not in theory, absolute rather than suspensive. Prior to the widespread adoption of budget legislation by the states, the governor was able to accomplish a good deal by way of budgetary

[33] For the best general discussion, see Prescott, Frank W., "The Executive Veto in American States," *Western Political Quarterly*, March 1950, pp. 98–112; see also his "The Executive Veto in the Southern States," *Journal of Politics*, November 1948, pp. 659–675, and "Constitutional Provisions on the Governor's Veto Power," in *Tennessee Papers on Constitutional Revision*, Vol. II, pp. 64–88 (Bureau of Public Administration, University of Tennessee, 1947); Farmer, *op. cit.*, and McGeary, M. Nelson, "The Governor's Veto in Pennsylvania," *American Political Science Review*, October 1947, pp. 941–946.

CHARACTERISTICS OF CONSTITUTIONAL PROVISIONS FOR THE EXECUTIVE VETO

Strong veto provisions:

1. Five or more days for governor's consideration of bills during session
2. Ten or more days for governor's consideration of bills after adjournment
3. Two-thirds of the elected members to override a veto
4. Pocket veto, or bills die after adjournment unless signed
5. Power to veto items of appropriation bills, or parts of all bills
6. Power to reduce items of appropriation bills
7. Governor may submit amendments to bills and return them to the legislature.

Medium veto provisions:

1. Less than five days for consideration of bills during sessions
2. Five days or less to consider bills after adjournment
3. Three-fifths of the elected members or two-thirds of those present necessary to override a veto
4. Bills passed in one session become law unless returned at next session.

Weak veto provisions:

1. Less than five days to consider bills during sessions
2. Less than five days to consider bills after adjournment
3. Majority of elected or present members or three-fifths of those present necessary to override a veto
4. Vetoed bills must be submitted to next session of the legislature or they will become law as if they had been signed by the governor.

control through the use of the item veto, by means of which he could veto certain items in an appropriation bill while approving the measure as a whole. In thirty-nine state constitutions the item veto is now authorized; in the following it is not permitted: Indiana, Iowa, Maine, New Hampshire, Nevada, Rhode Island, Tennessee, and Vermont. While in some states the courts have refused to sanction the practice, the governors of California, Massachusetts, New Jersey, and Pennsylvania have power to reduce individual items. He frequently uses the power when the amounts approved by the legislature exceed the budget recommendations.

The veto power is exercised by the governor for a number of reasons — public policy (by far the most important), economy, and lack of need for the measure submitted. The table on page 340 presents an analysis of all vetoes in all states for the combined years 1945 and 1947, based on a classification used by both Professors Dorr and Prescott; it shows 1209 veto messages, classified according to the principal reason assigned for the veto action, by number and by percentage. In New York, from 1940 to 1950, inclusive, Governor Dewey vetoed 3647 bills of which 1600 were messaged or "vetoed with memorandum" (see table on page 341). Of these, approximately 59 per cent were vetoes on grounds of public policy or expediency, and the remainder for technical reasons. Fully 25 per cent of these vetoed measures were based on administrative memoranda, and an average of 10 per cent of the total bills were disallowed by the Governor with specific objections because of protests from local authorities who strongly advised such action.[34] The veto power, as used in New York, is an instrument by which the governor exerts a tremendous influence in legislative matters.

In general, there has been a strong tendency for increased use of the veto power. While the exercise of this power has varied greatly in the different states and in the course of American legislative history, it has come into its heyday in the twentieth century. It is reported that, in a sampling of states, from one half to three fourths of the total vetoes have occurred since 1900. Some information on the extent of the use of the veto power in particular years from 1915 through 1947 is presented in the table below.

Governors' Reasons for Vetoing Bills, 1945–1947 *

REASON	NUMBER VETOED	PER CENT VETOED
Unconstitutionality	76	6
Defective drafting	84	7
Economy or tax burden	110	9
Public policy or public interest	518	43
Unnecessary	184	15
Duplication or supersedence	95	8
Confused	87	7
Incomplete	30	3
Miscellaneous	25	2
Total	1,209	100

* Prescott, *op. cit.*, p. 109.

Use of the Executive Veto Power, 1915–1947 *

CRITERIA	1915	1923	1937[1]	1947
Number of legislatures	39	44	47	47
Measures introduced	[2]	[2]	66,254	62,304
Measures enacted	16,000	16,500	21,646	24,928
Measures vetoed	1,066	1,120	1,458	1,253
Percentages vetoed	7	7	6.7	5

* Prescott, *op. cit.*, pp. 101–102.

[1] Figures include Kentucky, Louisiana, Mississippi, and Virginia for 1936; Alabama for 1939.

[2] No data available, except for a few states.

The provisions for overriding a veto, which in practice are very little used, show a wide variation. A majority of the members present is sufficient in Connecticut; of the members elected, in Alabama, Arkansas, Indiana, Kentucky, Tennessee, and West Virginia. A three-fifths vote of the members

[34] Prescott, *op. cit.*, p. 110, and Solomon, Samuel R., "The Governor as Legislator," *National Municipal Review*, November 1951, pp. 515–520.

present is sufficient in Rhode Island; a three-fifths vote of the members elected, in Delaware, Maryland, Nebraska, and Ohio. The states of Florida, Idaho, Massachusetts, Montana, New Mexico, Oregon, South Dakota, Texas, Vermont, Washington, and Wisconsin provide for a two-thirds vote of the members present, while the remaining twenty-four states specify a two-thirds vote of the members elected.

Record of Bills in New York, 1940–1950 *

YEAR	INTRODUCED	PASSED AND SENT TO GOVERNOR	VETOED	BECAME LAW
1940	4514	1223	343	877
1941	4381	1335	377	955
1942	4077	1259	308	943
1943	3594	1011	299	712
1944	3792	1079	283	796
1945	4337	1257	346	911
1946	5211	1327	325	1002
1947	5313	1237	329	908
1948	5535	1236	350	876
1949	5782	1243	340	858
1950	6135	1024	347	825

* From New York State *Legislative Manual*, 1950, p. 945.

In twenty-seven states the veto restrictions applying after adjournment require the governor to dispose of all bills submitted to him within from three to thirty days after the expiration of the session; otherwise bills become law. He has three days to dispose of bills in Connecticut and North Dakota; five days in Arkansas, Florida, Montana, and New Jersey; ten days in Colorado, Delaware, Illinois, and Louisiana; and thirty days in New York and Pennsylvania. This is no small task, considering the great mass of legislation passed during the rush at the close of the session. (In 1934 in New York, 750 bills were left on the governor's desk; in 1938 the number was 933.) The measures must all be carefully examined by the staff in the office of the attorney general, whose recommendations are generally accepted by the governor.

In the case of important measures, the signature of the governor is the occasion for much ceremony; a gold pen may be used, to be given afterward to the sponsor of the bill; news photographers may be called in. It is customary for the governor's office to make public announcement of the action taken on measures awaiting his signature; on page 342 appears the text of a typical veto message from the office of the Governor of Illinois, June 30, 1949. Extended announcements and press releases may be made in the case of important measures, whether signed or vetoed.

Four states — Alabama, Maine, Mississippi, and South Carolina — require their governors to return the bills that they wish to veto at the beginning of the next session of the legislature. Five states — Georgia, Kansas, Mississippi, New Hampshire, and Tennessee — prohibit their governors from approving any bills while the legislature is not in session, while pocket vetoes are allowed in the remaining twelve. In four states — California, Delaware, Iowa, and New York — the governors have thirty days during which time bills must be signed and after which, if unsigned, they fail to become law. In two — Missouri and New Jersey — he is allowed forty-five days to consider measures submitted to him. Montana and Oklahoma limit this period to fifteen days, Virginia to ten, Wisconsin to six, Michigan and Vermont to five, and Minnesota to three.

In 1944 the Citizens Union in New York proposed some changes in the governor's legislative powers, especially his use of the veto power. It recommended that he be given more time in which to consider bills passed by the legislature, both during the session and after adjournment. This constitutes a very serious problem in many states — a problem which could be solved by amending the constitution but which is often met by subterfuge.

Use of the Item Veto in the State of Illinois

State of Illinois
Executive Department
Springfield, June 30, 1949

To the Honorable, the Secretary of State:

I herewith file in your office Senate Bill No. 655 entitled "An Act making appropriations for certain additional ordinary, contingent and distributive expenses of State government."

I approved this Bill with the exception of one item therein contained which I hereby veto and from which I withhold my approval.

The adjournment of the General Assembly having prevented the returning of this Bill to the House in which it originated within ten (10) days (Sundays excepted) after its presentation to me, the same is filed in your office with my objections to the said item, which is as follows:

I veto the item appearing in lines five (5) through twelve (12) on page thirteen (13) of said Bill, reading as follows:

"Construction work for a new mental institution in the northern part of the State to relieve the present overcrowded conditions in State welfare institutions, including plans and specifications therefor and all necessary costs and charges in connection therewith.................$1,487,500."

This item is vetoed because under Senate Bill No. 680 the sum of $2,163,000 is appropriated for construction work on a new mental institution in the northern part of the State and since condemnation proceedings for the site have just been initiated, it appears that orderly progress in developing the site and installing utilities will not permit the expenditure in this biennium of more than the amount appropriated by Senate Bill No. 680. Senate Bill No. 680 has been passed and awaits my consideration.

In all other respects I approve Senate Bill No. 655.

Respectfully,
ADLAI E. STEVENSON, *Governor*

In Connecticut the constitutional requirement was ignored for many years, with the result that a difficult problem was created (see page 281). Although Maryland has contrived to give the governor additional time by failing to present bills to him "officially" — that is, by not affixing the Great Seal to the bills — until he is ready to act upon them,[35] the burden that falls upon him at the end of the session is still considerable. Newspaper reports showed that Governor Lane signed seventy-nine bills on one day in 1947 (November 11), seventy-seven bills and nine resolutions in 1948 (June 1, special), sixty-eight in 1949 (March 5).

The second recommendation of the Citizens Union was that the governor's power to veto items of appropriation which he did not himself propose be extended so that he could reduce items which he considered excessive instead of being forced to accept or reject them in their entirety. Professor Weeks has called attention to a third proposal — a practice employed in Alabama, Massachusetts, and Virginia — which deserves wider adoption. The threat of veto by the governor would be less frequently resorted to if compromises between the two branches could be more easily effected ahead of time. Under this plan the governor may return a bill to the legislature with suggested amendments; if these are adopted, as they usually are,[36] the bill as thus amended is returned to the governor, who may act upon it as though it were before him for the first time.

Extra-Constitutional Powers. No governor in modern times who has established a record for constructive leadership has confined his activity in legislative matters to the use of these constitutional powers. In comparison with the extra-constitutional powers, they are relatively unimportant. Most governors have a program of legislation on important matters that they want to get through. Whether or not the governor so indicates in his message, these measures are generally known to the members and to the press and are regarded as administration bills. They are often drafted in the governor's office, are sponsored in each house by prominent administration supporters, and are guided through by the governor's floor leaders. While the members grumble about executive domination, these measures, drawn very often from planks in the party platform, are commonly given preferential treatment. In Alabama something more than half of these bills are enacted into law.

A governor who succeeds in getting his program through the legislature must be in more or less constant contact with the leaders of the two houses. By bargain and compromise, by threatened use of the veto power, by threat of special sessions if the work of the legislature is left uncompleted, he may steadily advance his program. By use of the radio for direct appeals to the

[35] Everstine, Carl N., "The Signing of Legislative Acts in Maryland," a memorandum report (Maryland Legislative Council, 1942).

[36] Such amendments were accepted by the Alabama legislature 207 out of 213 times in the period from 1903 to 1943; see Farmer, *op. cit.*, p. 179, and Prescott, *op. cit.*, p. 105. As a means of budgetary control, the item veto has not been particularly effective.

people and by public addresses to influential groups on legislative subjects, he may build up an insistent public opinion which will demand that members give favorable consideration to measures which he sponsors. By news releases and by frequent conferences with newspapermen the progress of his measures may be still further advanced. By frequent personal appearances before the members of the legislature he can present the case for the administration and for the people whose support he has enlisted for the administration program. The difference between those governors who achieve a national reputation for courageous leadership, and those who do not can be measured largely by the extent to which they succeed in employing these extra-constitutional powers.[37] It is possible, of course, for a governor to carry these tactics too far and arouse such determined opposition that he defeats his own purpose.

The subject of executive leadership in legislation raises several important questions. As the governor's term wears on, it becomes more and more difficult for him to control his legislature. The honeymoon period of this administration fades away, he uses up his patronage, and his power and prestige decline — sometimes to the vanishing point. The large percentage of important bills originating with the governor or with the heads of executive departments raises the question as to the proper function of a representative assembly. It is the popular impression that the legislature makes the laws, but if it be true that most of the important measures originate with the executive, then the legislature really acts as a ratifying body for the proposals submitted to it rather than in the capacity of a body actually "making" the laws which it enacts. This situation illustrates again the case in which the theory of government is at variance with the facts. One may even venture to inquire whether, in the light of the characteristics of legislative bodies already discussed and of the extreme complexity of modern social, political, and economic life, the theory should not be modified so that it might be more strictly in accord with the facts. It is true that the story of the rise of popular government records the prolonged and difficult struggle by which the power to make the laws was gradually transferred from the King to Parliament. At that time, however, there was no responsible executive such as functions under present-day democratic institutions, nor was there the extreme complexity of governmental problems which has grown out of a mechanical and industrial civilization. It may be that these two factors will ultimately be held to justify a partial retracing of some of the steps of that development so that the legislature may again be regarded as a safeguard for the people, passing upon and either approving or rejecting the proposals submitted to it by the executive.

[37] Graves, W. Brooke, *Readings in Public Opinion*, Chapter 29 (Appleton, New York, 1928); see also Fairlie, John A., "The Legislature and the Administration," *American Political Science Review*, April 1936, pp. 241–256, and June 1936, pp. 394–506; Lipson, Leslie, *op. cit.*, and "The Influence of the Governor on Legislation," *Annals*, January 1938, pp. 72–78.

Another significant problem involves the relationship between the executive and legislative branches of the government. A man of moderate ability may be able to achieve some measure of success in dealing with a friendly legislature, but it takes a genius in the art of politics to secure favorable action upon a program at the hands of a hostile legislature, whether that legislature be dominated by the opposing party or by a hostile faction of the party to which the governor belongs. The techniques to be employed in such a situation will vary as the personalities of the governors using them; in general, a policy of conciliation is more likely to be successful than one of violent opposition. As illustrations of the first, there is the success with which Governors Smith, Roosevelt, and Lehman in New York dealt with Republican majorities in the legislature, while of the second, there are the vitriolic attacks with which Governor Pinchot from time to time assailed a hostile Republican legislature in Pennsylvania.

Governor Cooper in the address already referred to observed that, to a large extent, the method a governor chooses in dealing with his legislature, as well as its effectiveness, depends largely on his background and his personal characteristics. A condition so essential to the smooth working of state government as the relations between these two branches ought to rest upon some more substantial basis than the chance variations in the personalities of the men elected to the governorship. Some simple and inexpensive but permanent machinery should be provided by which effective cooperation would be assured. Some progress along this line has been made by the establishment of legislative councils in Kansas and other states. These developments were discussed in Chapter 7.

In the effort to bridge the gap between the executive and legislative branches, it has been suggested that the governor be elected by the legislature. Such a procedure would open the way for development along either of two lines, along either or both of which experimentation might prove to be valuable. An executive so chosen might perform the functions of a manager, opening up a line of development in the states similar to that which has taken place in a large number of cities throughout the country. It is not known, of course, that such a device would operate successfully in the larger unit. The other possibility would be a development in the direction of the parliamentary system, in which the chief executive is chosen by and is responsible to the legislature, and in which he continues to hold his office so long and only so long as he can command a majority in that body. A full parliamentary system would be impossible, of course, as long as the governor was chosen for a stated term; and in view of the failure of parliamentary institutions in Europe to provide competent leadership, this alternative might be less desirable than the first one.

Ordinance and Rule-Making Power. The rule-making power of the governors has developed rapidly and extensively in recent years, largely because of the modification of previous legislative practices. In former days the legislatures tried to foresee and provide for every possible contingency that might arise with regard to a given subject. Acts of excessive length resulted, filled with many details and requiring constant revision. In addition, administrative agencies were frequently hampered in their work, either by the absence of needed provisions or by the fact that those which existed were no longer suitable. More recently, outline legislation has been substituted for detailed legislation; the legislature now attempts to lay down fundamental principles and policies but leaves matters of detail in their application to the governor and the administrative officers. This practice has somewhat reduced the quantity and improved the quality of the legislative output, but it has at the same time increased the power of administrative departments and the difficulty of their task. Most of the supplementary rules, regulations, and ordinances are drafted by the department or by an advisory board; the approval of the governor may or may not be required, although he is in general responsible. Thus it is that only a portion of the law is contained in the statutes, which usually include indirectly much more than appears on the face of the bill enacted by the legislature. "The law is what the citizen meets as the end result of governmental activity — the sum total of statutes and regulations. This means that 'rules and regulations' issued by administrative agencies may actually include more important 'legislation,' in many cases, than the law which the legislature passes." The governor has the power to issue proclamations and executive orders, although the bulk of this legislation comes from the departments and agencies under his supervision. In something over one fourth of the states, both filing and publication are required, while in less than one fourth, filing only is sufficient.[38]

Among the advantages urged for such legislation are economy of legislative time; availability of expert knowledge; absence of partisan conflicts concerning details; flexibility; possibility of drafting under more advantageous circumstances; and completion and clarification of statutory law, with consequent avoidance of unnecessary litigation. Some of the disadvantages that have been urged are that there may be such a scattering of sublegislative functions that inconsistencies in policy will develop; that inadequate publicity may be given either before or after the promulgation of administrative legislation; that the legislature may surrender too many of its legislative powers; and that standards may be improperly or inadequately developed. As circumstances have tended greatly to increase the volume of such legislation, the subject has become more and more a matter of controversy.

[38] For latest available information, see Judicial Council of California, *Report on the Administrative Agencies Survey* (Tenth Biennial Report, Sacramento, 1944); Mindel, Charles, *Filing and Publication of Administrative Rules and Regulations* (Maryland Legislative Council, 1942); *Book of the States, 1948–1949*, pp. 171–175; and the author's *Public Administration in a Democratic Society*, Chapter 30 (Heath, Boston, 1950).

Judicial Powers

Executive Clemency. A governor may occasionally perform duties of a judicial or quasi-judicial nature. Most important of these is the exercise of executive clemency — the pardoning power, the power to parole, and the power to grant reprieves — a duty which may consume at times a great deal of time and energy. It may be in order to note first the meaning of these terms and the differences between them. When a criminal is pardoned, the penalty is remitted; he is permitted to pass without punishment or at least without further punishment than has already been inflicted prior to the date of the pardon. Under a parole, the prisoner is released under certain definite and specific conditions and presumably under the supervision of a parole officer. If the conditions are in any way violated, the parole is forfeited, and the prisoner returns to serve in full the remainder of his unexpired sentence. A reprieve provides merely for a stay of execution, usually in connection with a death sentence. A reprieve is usually good for thirty days, pending the outcome of a motion for appeal or of an investigation by the governor.

The governor also has the power of commutation — that is, of alleviating the penalty, as by changing a death sentence to one of life imprisonment or by reducing the number of years of a sentence. In addition to these various forms of executive clemency, a legislative body may extend amnesty to a group of people who are guilty or alleged to be guilty of neglect or crime against the state, while a court may suspend all punishment prescribed by law. Under this form, which is known as probation, the court gives a convict his liberty under conditions of supervised good behavior.

The power of executive clemency exists in some form in all states, but there is the greatest diversity as to its extent and the method of its exercise. A recent analysis of the provisions governing the pardoning power shows that it is vested in the governor exclusively in nine states; in a board of which the governor is a member in nine states; and in the remainder, in the governor, subject to the advice and consent of some one or more councils, officers, boards, or other advisory agencies. In the second and third categories there is a bewildering variety of restrictive provisions.[39]

In twenty-seven states the pardoning power does not extend to cases of impeachment, and in eight it does not extend to cases of treason. In two states it is limited to criminal cases. In nineteen states advisory pardon boards exist, whose duty it is to investigate and make recommendations. In forty-one states the governor may not pardon until after conviction. The law usually requires that all pardons and commutations of sentence be registered in the office of the secretary of state merely as a matter of record.

[39] Based on Attorney General's *Survey of Release Procedures*, Vol. III, Pardon (Washington, 1939); see also Greene, Lee S., "Restrictions on the Governor's Pardon Power," pp. 89–93, in *Papers on Constitutional Revision*, Vol. II (University of Tennessee Record, Knoxville, 1947).

Only in two states — Kentucky and Texas — are the records of such cases kept elsewhere than in the governor's office. All states except Tennessee and Vermont place at least one constitutional safeguard on the exercise of the pardoning power.

It seems clear from the records in numerous states that the pardoning power has in recent years been used with increasing frequency; the same tendency is shown by parole figures from New York and other states covering the same period. Parole, however, is often regarded as an administrative procedure rather than as a form of executive clemency. The unfortunate men and women who become eligible for such clemency, in whatever form, are in prison for almost every type of act prohibited by the criminal law; a list in a recent report of the Division of Parole of the Executive Department of the State of Maryland lists more than fifty — abduction, abortion, arson, assault of a dozen different types, burglary, bastardy, keeping of a bawdy house, carnal knowledge, carrying weapons, contributing to delinquency of minors, counterfeiting, desertion and nonsupport, embezzlement, false pretense, forgery, gambling, habitually disorderly conduct, incest, offenses against the liquor law, larceny, manslaughter, murder, rape, and vagrancy. Some of the earlier governors made extensive comments upon their emotional reactions in connection with their exercise of this power. Most of them regarded it as "a most difficult and trying task," recognized that their use of it subjected them to much criticism, but contended that they had done the best they knew how. When criminals have been sentenced and their execution is pending, the governor must listen to the appeals for clemency made by distressed relatives. In such cases the governor is apt to be torn by the conflict between a desire to listen to the pleas for mercy, and the duty to see that justice is faithfully administered. In his comments on this matter Governor Smith was more frank and revealing than most [40]:

> I gave a great deal of my time to talking to the relatives of the men in our state prisons. . . . Nothing is so distressing as the attention the governor is compelled to give to applications for executive clemency when the prisoner is to be put to death. It is impossible for a man to escape the thought that no power in the world except himself can prevent a human being from going over the brink of eternity after the Court of Appeals has sustained the verdict of the lower courts. I had very many unhappy nights when executions took place.
>
> The governor is constantly haunted by the terrible question that if anything should develop after the execution to indicate that the prisoner was not guilty, how much of the responsibility would he be compelled to carry personally for the ending of that man's life? I studied and worked very hard, sometimes into the small hours of the morning, on the record and papers, facts and arguments in capital cases. . . .
>
> In their despair the relatives of the condemned appeal to everybody to speak a word to the governor for them. . . . For fear of accident, it has been

[40] Smith, Alfred E., *Up to Now, an Autobiography*, pp. 306–308 (Viking, New York, 1929).

customary for the governor to be in touch with the prison on the night of an execution. . . . In order that I might know exactly to whom I was talking on the telephone, I had arranged a code with the Superintendent of Prisons, who was always at Sing Sing prison on the Thursday night when anybody was to be put to death. . . . Intriguing, sharp individuals might easily impersonate the Superintendent of Prisons, if for no other purpose than to delay the execution.

Mr. Smith then went on to describe incidents of this character, and to show how the governor, in this disturbed state of mind, could easily be made the prey of plausible and unscrupulous attorneys and others pleading for the life of a condemned man. His comments and those of other governors indicate that this task is not only one of the most trying but one of the most time-consuming attached to the office. Governor Lehman reports that "this prerogative particularly weighed upon me; I felt it most keenly in the cases of men condemned to die. I established a rule that prison wardens must call me personally no more than fifteen minutes before an execution, to establish that no new late evidence had turned up. The knowledge that my word could mean life to a condemned man was deeply perturbing. I never learned to take it 'in stride.' "[41]

Numerous governors in the past have confessed to devoting more than half their time to considering applications for executive clemency. In view of his important responsibilities in other areas, the governor should be relieved of this duty by turning it over entirely to a board of pardons — as has been done in many states.[42] In this day and age it is assumed that the governor will be responsible for administration of the affairs of the state; this duty he cannot perform if a major part of his time is to be consumed on pardon cases and other matters entirely extraneous to the business of executive management.

It may be of interest to note some of the more common reasons ascribed

[41] Lehman, *op. cit.*

[42] Grant, Daniel, *The Role of the Governor of Arkansas in Administration*, quotes from an address by Governor Brough delivered before the state bar association in 1917: "The Governor should have an advisory pardon board, one member from each Congressional district, to assist and advise him in the consideration of pardons, for normally the consideration of pardons takes 75 per cent of a governor's time, which could be more profitably spent on questions involving the improvement of finance, taxation, and administration. I realize that a large number of my friends favor the vesting of the pardoning power in the Governor alone, because it fixes responsibility, prevents eight men from playing politics instead of one, and is in harmony with the established precedents of our government. If an advisory pardon board is not created, then definite steps should be taken to place reasonable limitations on the time and strength of the Governor in this heart-breaking and nerve-wracking work. But when I tell you, my friends, that out of the past four nights at least two of them have been devoted to a consideration of pardon petitions, one of them until 1 o'clock in the morning, I am sure that you will bear with the informalities of this modest paper. A pardoning power without an advisory board taxes the very vitality of a Governor. One Governor has been driven to his grave by virtue of this and political complications, and I am very frank to tell you that if a man is consistent and conscientious, it is enough to drive every Governor to his grave." (Doctoral dissertation, Northwestern University, 1948).

for decisions allowing clemency. An examination of a report from almost any pardon board will reveal such reasons as are listed below, occurring over and over again.

REASONS FOR THE EXERCISE OF EXECUTIVE CLEMENCY

Recommended by trial judge	Family in need
Recommended by prominent citizens	Prisoner of weak mind
Ill health of prisoner	Recommended by the injured party
Youth (or advanced age) of prisoner	Accomplices not being punished
Doubt of prisoner's guilt	Prisoner has performed a meritorious deed
Recommended by the members of the trial jury	Good prison record
Ends of justice have been met	To correct court error

Other Judicial Powers. Other powers of a judicial nature include the vetoing for constitutional reasons of bills passed by the legislature; the suspending, on rare occasions, of the writ of habeas corpus; and the making of decisions with regard to requests received from the governors of other states for the extradition of persons charged with crime. The Federal Constitution, in Article IV, requires that the governor shall hand over such persons upon request. The language of the Constitution is clear, but it has been so interpreted by the Supreme Court as to leave the course of action largely at the discretion of a governor of whom the request is made. The legal and constitutional aspect of this topic is discussed more fully in the chapter on interstate relations; it may be appropriate, however, to consider the problem here from the point of view of the burden which it imposes on the governor. With regard to this, former Governor Smith again had an interesting comment:

> One of the largest single drains upon the time of the governor is his necessary attention to extradition proceedings. Every fugitive from justice from any state of the Union apprehended within the state of New York can only be returned under arrest to his own state after the governor signs three sets of papers. Similarly, fugitives from justice from our own state can only be extradited after the governor signs a similar number of papers.
>
> When residents of the state of New York are wanted for crimes in other states and they make a request for a hearing before the governor before he signs the order to extradite, it is difficult, if not impossible, to deny it to them. Much time is taken up in listening to arguments by counsel of both sides as to whether or not extradition papers should be signed. In extradition proceedings the governor is both judge and jury. He passes, in the first instance, upon the law, and then upon the facts. It must be determined whether the prisoner was in the state on or about the time the crime was committed, whether he is the man named in the papers, and then the facts must be studied. In some cases, there are indications of grave miscarriages of justice. . . . Many extradition proceedings are for nonsupport, where a disagreement has arisen between man and wife. . . .[43]

[43] Smith, *op. cit.*, pp. 304–305.

Actual Functioning of the Office

How does the governor's office function? The public — although it pays little attention to administrative qualifications in selecting its candidates for the job — expects the governor to serve as the administrative head of the state government, advising, directing, coordinating the activities of various departments and agencies. The truth of the matter is that this concept is largely a myth.

The governor is the ceremonial head of the state, appearing at all types of functions in that capacity; if the state capitol is located in a large city like Atlanta, he must serve almost in the capacity of mayor of the city as well. He is chief patronage dispenser, speech maker, interviewer, and whatnot else. He must attend the meetings of innumerable boards of which he is ex officio a member. He must guide his program in the legislature. When he does all these things and many more, he has little time or energy left, even if he had the constitutional authority, as he usually does not, to guide and direct the administrative program of the state government.

The situation in this respect has long been bad in most states. It has been improved somewhat where an effective reorganization has taken place, but it appears to be far from satisfactory in any of the states. The powers and duties of the governor are supposed to be defined in the constitution, but what the constitution says these duties are and what the governor is in fact called upon to do may be two very different things. Here is what Governor Cherry of North Carolina said his duties were [44]:

Planning a legislative program
Selecting department heads and staff, often including many minor positions
Preserving the distinctions between the three branches of government
Serving as chairman or member of various boards and commissions [45]
Suspending county officials on proof of proper cause
Exercising the power of pardon, reprieve, and extradition
Countersigning warrants for the disbursement of funds
Serving as commander in chief of the state's national guard
Acting as representative of the state, as before Congressional committees [46]

How the Governor Spends His Time. As far back as 1913 Governor Donaghey of Arkansas, in a very forthright statement, contended that the governor was loaded down with clerical and other details [47]:

[44] Ransone, Coleman B., Jr., *The Office of the Governor in the South* (Bureau of Public Administration, University of Alabama, 1951).

[45] In Florida, most of the key administrative functions are handled by the four constitutional and thirty-four statutory ex-officio boards now in existence; thirty-two of these thirty-eight boards are wholly or partly made up of cabinet officers. The Governor serves on twenty-four of these ex-officio boards, the Secretary of State on fifteen, the Comptroller on nineteen, the Treasurer on twenty-one, the Attorney General on twenty-one, the Commissioner of Agriculture on thirteen, the State Superintendent of Public Instruction on ten (Special Joint Economy and Efficiency Committee, *Report*, p. 22).

[46] Governor Cherry claimed that, up to the time of this interview, he had traveled approximately 16,000 miles within the state, and 5,000 miles outside the state, in connection with official business.

[47] Grant, *op. cit.*

The Governor has but little time or power to bring about the reforms demanded of him by the people. It is generally believed that the office possesses plenary powers to do whatever the people want done. But if it did, the Governor is required to take up so much of his time in detail work that it would be impossible for him to accomplish such results. . . . The Constitution certainly contemplated that he should give the State all of his time in studying the conditions of government and consulting with other departments of the State so that all might work together for its betterment. . . . But through legislative action the Governor has been so overburdened with drudgery that should be done in clerical departments that no man's mental or physical structure is strong enough to meet the requirements.

The idea of putting the Governor on twelve or fifteen different boards, and in one instance expect him to keep up with the price of hay, in another to keep in touch with the mule market, and in another make the purchases of $200,000 worth of meat, dry goods, clothing, boots and shoes; to again demand that he sit in his office and listen to the pleas of attorneys, families and friends of more than a thousand convicts, and then charge him with the full responsibility for the conduct of both the Executive and Legislative departments of the State, is only illustrative of a few of the present demands made upon him.

A few years later, in 1921, Governor Brough described the office as "not only a practical work-house of administration, but a clearing-house for all the ills of the state." Governor Laney's executive secretary illustrated this function of the office by reference to a request of a couple who wanted to adopt a baby and who wished the governor's office to locate one for them. "Usually," he observed, "we get the toughest problems, for people figure the governor's office is a last resort."

The governor, as Professor Grant points out, is required to perform many acts which have no relation to each other except the fact that they constitute a ceremonial representation of the state. Perhaps the best way to define these activities is simply to list a few of them which Governor Laney was called upon to perform:

He broke ground for a new $90,000 plant for the Goldsmith Pickle Company at Atkins. He headed a drive to fill army needs for medical technicians. He served as chairman of the board of the DeSoto Council of the Boy Scouts of America. He threw out the first ball for the opening game of the Little Rock baseball team. He presented Selective Service medals to 1000 members of local draft boards who had given two or more years of continuous service. Innumerable other examples of this ceremonial function could be given, such as the crowning of queens and judging beauty contests, but there is no particular value in making the list all-inclusive.

The government of Arkansas has never been reorganized, but that of Massachusetts has. Even so, the Governor is faced with precisely the same kind of situation — a situation best described by Robert C. Wood in a recent study [48]:

When Dever entered office, the tempo increased. A Democratic Governor, at a State House located in Boston, finds himself in the midst of his most

[48] *The Metropolitan Governor — Three Case Inquiries into the Substance of State Executive Management* (Doctoral dissertation, Harvard University, 1949).

ardent and needy supporters. With politics dictating an "open door policy," the result has been most aptly described as "a mob scene in the Metro-Goldwyn-Mayer tradition." The present Governor averages twenty-five social invitations a day — ranging from the Sons of St. Patrick's banquet to the Treasury Bond Drive; there are two or three functions a night which are considered political necessities. Because all delegations, legislators, administrative heads, politicians, and "anyone from New Bedford" (the Governor's home grounds) have direct access on any problem, most appointments are made on a temporary and amendable basis. A typical week day begins before ten in the morning, goes on until seven in the evening, and is likely to be resumed after public appearances around ten into the night. At least every other Sunday is spent in the State House, working on major problems and answering mail. The resulting average is a 100-hour week.

One may obtain some idea of what the daily schedule of a governor looks like from the data on page 355; no one day would actually be "typical" but this page gives a good idea of major activities during a routine day. From the evidence collected by Grant, one may conclude that 60 per cent of the conferences which occupy much of the governor's working day concern such matters as requests for jobs and special favors, or consist of social calls and visits by representatives of civic, youth, church, and other organizations. Even if this figure were reduced to 50 per cent, and only half of the Governor's conferences were devoted to such matters, they would still be a substantial drain on the time of an individual who is supposedly responsible for the direction of the state's administrative machine.[49]

Dr. Wood, on the basis of an intensive study of the governorship in the New England area, attempted to get at this problem in another way, namely, by studying the major press reports of the activities of the Governor of Massachusetts over a period of a full week. From February 3–9, inclusive, 1949, the following were reported:

Appointment of special review board to hear appeal on removal of reformatory head by Corrections Commissioner
Conference on flood relief
Conference on textile industry
Proclamations and speeches in support of National Heart Week, French Merci Train, Sportsmen's Show
Executive order speeding distribution of state aid to cities and towns
Commutation of three prison sentences

[49] Dr. Grant attempted to classify in major categories the purposes of visits to the governor, with the following results:

Requests for jobs	23%
Requests for special favors	13%
Requests from civic, church, and school organizations	12%
Problems of administrative officials	10%
Criticism of governmental policies and actions	7%
Social calls	6%
Reporting confidential information	5%
Requests for clemency	4%
Requests for extradition	2%
Purposes of visits not known	8%
Other purposes	10%

Appearance at testimonial dinner for Press Secretary
Appointments to Utility Commission, trustee board of Massachusetts College, of Massachusetts Hospital
Four conferences on forthcoming MTA message
Executive order defining Governor's powers regarding suspension of veterans preference in civil service
Washington trip to confer with RFC and President on bankruptcy of the Waltham Watch Company
Approval of extradition papers
Authorization of seven new housing projects
Washington trip to secure additional funds for Massachusetts Employment Service
Boy Scouts reception
Announcement of new highway program

"It is," Dr. Wood concludes, "in this atmosphere of continual concern with almost any activity which is important to the voter, spotlighted by daily press conferences, under pressing ceremonial and statutory obligation, that the Governor operates. Within the limits of time and energy, he seeks to devise ways to effectuate the aims which should assure him continued political success."

The Governor as Popular Leader. With the rise of the governor as popular leader have come responsibilities of two main types: those that pertain to the formulation and sponsoring of policies with the legislature, with the people, and as leader of his political party in the state; and those which go with the occupancy of a position high in the public eye in a democratic society. As a leader in the determination of policy, the governor must interest himself in everything that concerns the welfare of the people of his state; without neglecting the performance of his routine administrative duties, he must keep himself informed regarding the needs and desires of the public.

"I felt strongly moved to use every power inherent in my office to help my fellow citizens . . .," writes former Governor Lehman.[50] "I was, I knew, the only state officer charged with total responsibility for the people of New York." Professor Gaus stresses the same basic point when, referring to the failure of the states to redistrict their legislatures according to population changes, he concludes that this situation "leaves the governorship as almost the sole point on which the political interests of metropolitan populations can center for expression."[51]

Plenty of people who want something will come to see the governor, but if he is to know what the people as a whole are thinking, he must "go places and see things" for himself. He must expect criticism, but he must not let it upset his poise, distort his judgment, or deter him from the pursuit of well-determined policies. He must have a genius for keeping his name on the front page of the newspapers, often with things that seem quite trivial

[50] Lehman, *op. cit.*

[51] Gaus, John M., "The States Are in the Middle," *State Government*, June 1950, pp. 138–142.

COMMONWEALTH OF VIRGINIA
THE GOVERNOR'S DAY *

Time	Activities
8 A.M. to 9:30 A.M.	Reading and answering previously screened correspondence
9:30 A.M. to 10:00 A.M.	Conference with one or more department heads
10:00 A.M. to 10:30 A.M.	Press conference
10:30 A.M. to 12:00 noon	Conferences with public and legislators, the latter particularly when legislature is in session [1]
12:00 noon to 1:30 P.M.	Lunch, during which the Governor welcomes several fraternal, civic, or business groups to the city
1:30 P.M. to 4:00 P.M.	Additional conferences with public, legislators, and department heads
4:00 P.M. to 4:30 P.M.	Press conference
4:30 P.M. to 5:30 P.M., or later	Clears up additional correspondence, makes phone calls, additional conferences
7:00 P.M.	Attends banquet of religious, social, fraternal, civic, or business group, usually making main address, and then shakes hands with 500 to 1500 people
12:00 midnight to 2:00 A.M.	Returns to Executive Mansion

* Interview of Coleman B. Ransone, Jr., with Ben D. Lacey, Administrative Assistant to Governor Tuck, Richmond, Virginia, July 28, 1949.

[1] Daniel Grant kept a record of the purposes of visits to the Governor's Office in Arkansas, for a number of days. The following is an illustrative list:

1. Wanted job with highway construction engineers
2. Wanted liquor permit in spite of Revenue Commissioner's refusal
3. Requested Governor to allow friend to stay on job
4. Wanted section of highway paved in certain section of the State
5. Wanted to keep a State job which he was about to lose
6. Asked to be transferred from a State job in Little Rock to one in his home county
7. Wanted a job as head of one of the State institutions
8. Business not known
9. Reported conditions existing at the Denton unit of the State Hospital
10. Criticized Governor's policy and the employees at a certain State institution
11. Prosecuting attorney brought requisition for extradition to be approved by the Governor
12. Social call
13. Wanted to be reappointed by the Governor to an honorary board
14. Presented long-standing claim for material sold to the State
15. Wanted to keep his job

but which appeal to the imagination of the public. He must entertain distinguished guests, making sure that the fact is reported in the papers.

He must show an interest in Boy Scouts, local anniversaries and celebrations, conventions, business and professional organizations; he may even resort to the creation of Kentucky colonels or Nebraska admirals.[52] He may present packages of candy to several thousand children at an orphans' theater party, or appear in the role of Santa Claus at Christmas time. He may don a wild west outfit, or take part in an anniversary celebration of a society for the detection of horse thieves. He must attend many christenings, weddings, and funerals of the great, the near-great, and the supposed-to-be-great. He must issue proclamations galore, calling upon the people of the state to observe a day or a week devoted to the recognition of some cause — many of them worthy — the promoters of which desire publicity. He must attend numerous commencement exercises and receive honorary degrees from institutions which would never have thought of honoring him before he was elected governor. He must expect to receive and acknowledge graciously many useless gifts, and be properly grateful when someone dedicates to him a book, poem, or musical composition.

He must expect to attend countless dinners and make innumerable public addresses on the radio and in person on holidays, at places of historic interest, and on ceremonial occasions — for the people like to see and hear their governor. Numerous governors have, in recent years, made frequent "fireside chats" to the people of their states, some of them in a regular weekly program, commenting on current public questions and reporting on their stewardship. He will receive countless letters — many of them in response to these addresses — from all kinds of people about all manner of subjects, and he will continue to receive them for many long years after he has left the governorship.

These writers will ask him to do all kinds of things, often assuming, without the slightest conception of the nature of the powers and duties of the office, that he has practically unlimited authority to grant favors, right wrongs, either real or imagined, and in general to remake the universe in any form that the writers might desire.[53] To men of ability, giving attention

[52] "At a public dinner I once said, jokingly, that the constitution of our state should be amended to provide for the election of two governors — one to attend to the business of the state and the other to attend public and social functions not directly connected with the business of the state. I was prompted to make that remark by the enormous volume of invitations, supplemented by personal requests, that come to public men to attend all kinds of functions. Even a slight acquaintance at times leads people to believe that the governor should attend a wedding in the family or a christening. Invitations to attend the laying of cornerstones for private buildings, private charitable enterprises, meetings of trade bodies, anniversary celebrations of all kinds, testimonial dinners, requests for the use of the governor's name for drives for charitable and religious purposes or for donations, all pour into the governor's office. . . . When all is said and done, it seems impossible to divorce the personal equation from politics." Smith, Alfred E., *Up to Now — an Autobiography*, pp. 297–298 (Viking, New York, 1929).

[53] Some of these letters are quite amusing. Former Governor Bricker of Ohio told in a public address of a farmer who wrote to him: "I have your picture on the wall, but so far it ain't done me no good." Wrote another: "My daughter ran away with an old man of forty. What can I do?" Immediately after the 1944 Presidential election, the author had an opportunity to study approximately 600 letters received by former Governor Pinchot, then out of office for nearly ten years. The letters contained requests for gifts of money and of

to these insignificant things is apt to be most distasteful, but the governor must do these things if he wants to maintain his following and his contact with the people, without which popular leadership is all but impossible. These informal contacts may be supplemented by more formal reports to the people at periodic intervals. In late years, numerous governors in Florida, Kentucky, New York, Pennsylvania, and other states, have published, as a permanent record, excellent accounts of their stewardship.[54]

Methods of Supervision and Direction. The executive responsibilities of the governor of a modern state are tremendous. It is reported, for instance, that the Governor of Connecticut is "head of a business which has an inventory of real and personal property exceeding $95,000,000; which owns and operates fifty-four state parks and twenty-five state forests with a total of 132,000 acres; which maintains and reconstructs 2900 miles of state highways; which collects approximately $100,000,000 annually in the form of taxes, licenses, Federal grants, and miscellaneous items, and which expends these sums for the welfare of the citizens of Connecticut."[55] And Connecticut is a relatively small state. The usual constitutional provision that the governor shall see that the laws are faithfully executed is not in itself a specific grant of power to the governor.[56] Dr. Grant, in his analysis of this problem in the office of the Governor of Arkansas, finds no less than six different methods or techniques by which the governor exercises his powers of supervision and direction. These methods, it is believed, are quite as applicable to other states as they are to Arkansas.

1. *Requirement of Information.* Most state constitutions and most state statutes creating executive agencies place upon them a mandate to make annual or biennial reports to the governor. In the case of fiscal officers, more frequent reports of receipts and expenditures may be required — quarterly or monthly, even weekly or daily. Furthermore, the constitution usually gives the governor the power to "require information in writing from the officers of the executive department on any subject relating to the duties of their respective offices." There is no constitutional requirement, however, that the governor exercise this power or that he utilize the reports which agencies are required to submit to him. The possession of the information

War Bonds, expense money, aid in securing old age pensions, relief, blind assistance, new glasses, political support, and many other things. He was asked to get jobs for the writers or their relatives and friends; to get the President to revoke certain War Manpower Commission regulations; to dismiss from the government service individuals whom the writers did not like. A high school boy, in order to win a bet, wanted the Governor to arrange for him to meet the President when the latter came to Philadelphia on his campaign trip.

[54] Examples: *The Administration of Millard F. Caldwell as Governor of Florida, 1945–1949* (Tallahassee, 1949); Johnson, Keen, *Kentucky Government, 1939–1943* (Frankfort, 1943); Willis, Simeon, *Your Kentucky Government, 1943–1947* (Frankfort, 1947); Martin, Edward, *A Record of Achievement, 1943–1945* (Harrisburg, 1946).

[55] Armstead, George B., *State Services in Connecticut*, p. xvi (Hartford, 1946).

[56] See Mathews, John M., *Principles of American State Administration*, p. 95 (Appleton, New York, 1916).

does not give him any additional power to act, but it does provide him with a necessary basis for action under powers conferred upon him, when and if he chooses to use it. The extent to which he acts — or whether he acts at all — depends largely upon the characteristics of the individual governor.

2. *Informal Investigations.* The governor's power to conduct informal inquiries into administrative operations in various departments, agencies, and institutions is probably included in the constitutional provision which requires that he shall see that the laws are faithfully executed. Usually, however, no formal power is granted to him to make investigations, and no money for the financing of such investigations is appropriated to him. Nevertheless he frequently resorts to informal personal investigations in order to correct certain conditions existing within an agency or to resolve a jurisdictional conflict between departments or individuals. While this technique — as Dr. Grant observes — is aimed primarily at obtaining information, the governor can frequently gain compliance with his own policies by means of the publicity which results from an investigation.

3. *Individual and Group Conferences.* Conversations between department and agency officials and the governor constitute the most common means for the governor to make decisions concerning administrative policies and for the agency heads to know what policies the governor desires to have carried out. Such conferences can take several forms, such as between the governor and a single official, between the governor and several officials, and between the governor and all department heads. Any of these types may be held at regular intervals, or they may be nonscheduled conferences which meet on call as problems arise. While individual conferences may make less news copy than group meetings or cabinet meetings, they constitute "the fabric of administrative relationships between the governor and the department heads."

4. *Orders and Directives.* Only in isolated instances, in most states, is there any statutory authorization for the governor to issue orders and directives to the heads of departments and agencies, this power being limited to specific situations when it is granted at all. "So far as the supervision and direction of administration is concerned," concluded Dr. Grant, "formal orders and directives by the governor play a very small part. Both the governor and the department heads seem to arrive at new policies by the process of mutual discussion of the pros and cons of the subject and the compromise of viewpoints when necessary rather than to have them sent down from above in the form of a carefully worded order. The latter resembles too closely the military chain of command."

5. *Approval of Administrative Acts.* Many actions of administrative officials are required by law to receive the approval of the governor before they become valid. Still other acts of department heads are reviewed by the governor even though there is no law requiring or authorizing him to do so, and in such cases the governor depends upon his prestige and the subservience

of his appointed officials to obtain acquiescence to his wishes in the matter. For the most part, the powers of the governor to approve or disapprove the actions of administrative officials is of the latter, extra-legal type. Dr. Grant gives some specific illustrations of both types, based upon his study of the Arkansas situation:

> Illustrative of the first type — the purchasing agent, for instance, must receive the approval of the governor for the contract for rental of a supply warehouse, for sums of money authorized for emergency purchases by institutions, for purchase of fresh produce without open bids, and for purchases of commodities produced by the state institutions themselves. Most of the other power of approval granted to the governor is related to the financial transactions of various state officials. Some other types are specified by law.
>
> In addition to his legal powers to approve certain administrative acts, the governor has been given, as a result of custom and tradition, a more general power of review over administrative acts. The governor has been made, in effect, an administrative court of last resort both for the public and for his administrative officials. Most of the people believe that if their cause is denied by the head of a department, the next logical step is to appeal to the governor for assistance in the form of persuading the department head to modify his decision. There is a wide area of action for heads of departments and agencies in which their duties are entirely ministerial and an appeal to the governor about such matters is usually made to no avail. However, in the area of administrative action which involves discretion on the part of the state official, there is evidence to substantiate the belief that the governor can, and not infrequently does, exercise a power of approval over such action.

6. *Use of Staff Services.* The staff services of the governors have been, until recently, grossly inadequate in all states, and they still are in many. Professor Gaus, who has himself worked in three governors' offices in different parts of the country, believes that "governors' offices are understaffed for the formulation of programs that will rehabilitate the role and importance of the states." [57] It is difficult if not impossible for the governor to supervise and direct effectively the policies and activities of the operating agencies without staff assistance. The purpose of the staff agency is to help the governor in effectuating control by giving him information and advice and rendering service. The staff functions, including finance, personnel, planning, research, and technical assistance on organization and procedure and methods of control, are not always assigned neatly to individuals and independent agencies. While some governments come closer than others to achieving this ideal, no government avoids altogether this discrepancy between theory and practice, for as Dr. Grant points out, "staff functions are frequently assigned to operating agencies, and on occasion, staff agencies are assigned operating functions."

The chief function of the governor, judging by the allocation of time and energy, is to provide public and party leadership. The factors which, to a

[57] Gaus, John M., "Are We Maintaining Our Federal System?" *State Government*, January 1949, supplement, pp. 5–9; see Stace, Homer E., *The Organization of the Executive Office of the Governor* (Institute of Public Administration, New York, 1950) and "The Governor Needs Staff," *National Municipal Review*, October 1951, pp. 462–467, 479.

large extent, control the effectiveness of their efforts are their own character and experience, their program, and their administrative supervision over the executive branch. As Barnard has observed, the administrative organization of the governor's office cannot give him the qualities of vitality and endurance, decisiveness, persuasiveness, responsibility, and intellectual capacity required for leadership,[58] but possessing these qualities, he cannot succeed without it. The organization, however, must be established with a flexibility sufficient to permit each governor to staff his office with men loyal to him, responsive to his particular nature and personality, and capable of bolstering to some degree such weaknesses as may be his.

Obstacles to Supervision and Control. The task of central supervision and control in the states is made needlessly difficult by a number of factors, all of which are perfectly well known and for all of which there are available remedies. One of the most far-reaching is the excessive number of separate agencies. In state after state this number runs from 100 to 200; even where there has been, at some time in the past, an administrative reorganization, there is still the tendency for the addition of new functions and agencies to develop to such an extent that the situation again gets out of control. The second factor is the long list of elective constitutional officers — the long ballot. In addition to the immediate administrative effect of removing these officers and the employees of their departments from the appointing power of the governor, these constitutional provisions exclude them from the governor's cabinet by making them equals rather than subordinates of the governor.

A third basic difficulty arises from the widespread practice of using boards and commissions for administrative purposes. The Arkansas situation, which is no different and no worse than many others, may be taken as illustrative. The executive department of Arkansas consists of approximately 110 administrative agencies and of this number only twelve are headed by single executive officials appointed by the governor. Seven officers are elected by the people, and there remain over ninety administrative agencies which are headed by about eighty-five boards or commissions. Membership on a few of these boards involves full-time employment, but the large majority of them are honorary boards which meet rarely and whose members serve for nominal compensation or for none at all.

Finally, there is the general lack of facilities for supervision, to which reference has already been made. The small staff in the governor's office is frequently fully occupied with the task of handling the governor's correspondence and callers. There is no one under the immediate supervision and control of the governor who is professionally qualified and whose time is available for the performance of the staff work that is urgently necessary if the governor is to perform in any satisfactory manner his duties of super-

[58] Barnard, Chester I., *Organization and Management*, pp. 80–110, on the nature of leadership (Harvard University Press, 1948).

vision and control. In many cases there is no central personnel agency, with the result that all such matters flow into the governor's office, where they consume an undue portion of his time. Without a budget staff and a management staff, the same thing occurs in these fields, thereby accentuating an already bad situation. Under such circumstances the governor must either depend for such assistance upon agencies not actually under his control or go without the help.

Control Over the Governor. Since in a democracy the elected chief executive is responsible to the people and to their elected representatives in the legislature, it is appropriate to consider briefly the nature of the controls which are or may be applied to him. In view of the fact that the subject of controls over administration is discussed later in more detail, it will suffice here simply to enumerate the various types of control — legislative, judicial, popular control, research and planning — any or all of which may be employed.

SELECTED REFERENCES

Friedman, Jacob A., *The Impeachment of Governor William Sulzer* (Columbia University Press, 1939). Excellent monograph on one of the most famous impeachment cases.

Grant, Daniel, *The Role of the Governor of Arkansas in Administration;* Ransone, Coleman B., Jr., *The Office of the Governor in the South;* Wood, Robert C., *The Metropolitan Governor: Three Case Studies into the Substance of State Executive Management* (Doctoral dissertations, 1948 and 1949, at Northwestern University, Harvard University, and Harvard University, respectively). Three new and significant studies of the role of the governor in the modern state.

Jensen, Christian, *The Pardoning Power in the American States* (University of Chicago Press, 1922). General treatise on a little known aspect of the governorship; for a comparable study, restricted to a particular state, see Cheek, Roma S., *The Pardoning Power of the Governor of North Carolina* (Duke University, 1932).

Lipson, Leslie, *The American Governor: From Figurehead to Leader* (University of Chicago Press, 1939). The only authoritative study of the evolution of the governorship.

New York State Constitutional Convention Committee, *Problems Relating to the Executive Administration and Powers*, being Vol. VIII of the Committee's Report (Albany, 1938). Contains much valuable information regarding the governorship in New York and other states.

Perkins, John A., *The Role of the Governor of Michigan in the Enactment of Appropriations* (Bureau of Government, University of Michigan, 1943). An excellent treatment of a very important aspect of the governor's function in a large and important state.

Ruskowski, Casimir W., *The Constitutional Governor* (Humphries, Boston, 1943). A series of tabular analyses of various characteristics of the governor's office.

Scace, Homer E., *The Organization of the Executive Office of the Governor* (Institute of Public Administration, New York, 1950). A valuable compilation of information regarding the organization of the governors' offices, and an analysis of the problems relating thereto.

10

Administrative Organization and Reorganization

The experience of two world wars — and perhaps even a third — within the period of a generation has made everyone keenly aware of the twofold responsibility of government, civil and military. While this distinction between civil and military powers is more obvious in the case of the Federal government, it also applies in the case of the states as well. This chapter will be devoted to the civilian establishment; that which follows, to the military responsibilities of the states.

State Administrative Organization

The administrative organization of the states consists of the governor, the lieutenant governor, the heads of the administrative departments, and the independent boards and commissions. It is the present purpose to sketch in broad outline the structure of this machinery, with some emphasis upon the important changes that have occurred in it in the last quarter of a century.

Position of the Governor. The governor has always been, in theory, the head of the state administrative establishment; in the previous chapter the attempt was made to describe the office of governor and the powers and duties pertaining to it. Prior to the administrative reorganization movement which began in 1917, this theory was largely a fiction. In the first place, the governor had little or no control over the original, constitutional departments whose heads were chosen by popular vote. These officers owed nothing to the governor, for their power was derived from the people directly, as was his. As a rule they showed little disposition to cooperate with him, sometimes for personal reasons and sometimes for fear that they might enhance his political prestige and injure their own. The position of the governor was little better in his relations with the newer services, which had multiplied rapidly and had an almost infinite number of separate boards, commissions, and other independent agencies. The governor was thus in the unfortunate and unfair position of being held responsible for the administration of a governmental machine over which he had very limited control. In New York, for instance, there were at one time 184 administrative agencies. Under such a system, characteristic of all the states, responsible administrative control was impossible; waste, inefficiency, overlapping, and duplication were inevitable.

Professor White admirably summarized this situation in the following paragraph:

> The American state governments until 1910 exhibited almost none of the characteristics associated with the concept of general management. Neither the governor nor any other state officer was in a position to exercise managerial power with reference to state business. The various agencies of administration had no common head and recognized little responsibility to any high executive officer. There was no central planning agency, no unified command, no administrative program, no coordinating agency, no agency to investigate and report except ineffective legislation committees, no fiscal control. American state administration was, in short, atomistic and disorganized to an exceptional degree.[1]

The Governor's Office. The vital importance of proper staffing of the governor's office and the inadequacy of many of the existing arrangements were mentioned in the previous chapter. In considering this question further, it is necessary to know what in fact does exist, and what in the light of existing knowledge of administrative organization and procedure ought to exist. With reference to the question as to what the organization ought to be, Homer E. Scace has suggested certain basic assumptions, to the first of which there are two corollaries: (1) that the staff of the governor's office should be kept small, and (2) that it must be highly flexible [2]:

1. Agencies in the governor's office should do only those things which the governor himself would do if he had unlimited time and capabilities. In practice the best means of limiting the staff to this would seem to be to keep the staff agencies small. Keeping sizable or extraneous agencies out of the governor's office is as important as placing the proper ones directly under the chief executive.
2. If the governor as head of the state government is to personalize to the public a plan of action and a philosophy of government, he should have immediately available to him the means for systematically drawing up a program or plan for the future designed to meet the needs of the residents of the state in a manner in keeping with his own convictions.
3. Furthermore, he should have help, if he needs it, in presenting the program to the public without being left dependent on the efforts of organized pressure groups or his own political party.
4. If the governor is to be held responsible for the quality of state government services, he must have responsive to him the tools of administrative management: program planning, budgeting, personnel policy, and organization and methods analysis.
5. External control is generally periodic in nature rather than continuous

[1] White, Leonard D., *Trends in Public Administration*, p. 176 (McGraw-Hill, New York, 1933). The author traces, pp. 176–180, the various events and published studies which provided the groundwork upon which the Illinois and later reorganizations were based. See also Buck, A. E., *The Reorganization of State Governments in the United States*, pp. 5–10 (Columbia University Press, 1938) and Council of State Governments, *Reorganizing State Government* (Chicago, 1950).

[2] Scace, Homer E., *The Organization of the Executive Office of the Governor*, p. 4 (Institute of Public Administration, New York, 1950).

and current as is scalar control and is dependent for its effectiveness on standards, measurements, and reporting performance and result.

Translating these principles into an actual working organization, the governor's office might look something like that briefly outlined in the chart on page 365. In a report of a nation-wide survey of the governor's office, Scace had replies from the governors of about two thirds of the states. Each governor has a personal secretary, an executive secretary, and such stenographers as are needed. The key personnel are appointed by the governor and serve at his pleasure. The duties of the secretary to the governor are many and varied; he has been described as a "minister with all portfolios." These are among his more important duties: to keep in touch with the progress of the governor's program in the legislature; to act as liaison officer between the governor and his department heads; to investigate pardon cases (in some states); to absorb much of the impact of personal contact which would otherwise strike the governor directly; to devise the governor's itinerary, look after the preparation of his speeches, and handle his correspondence; to supervise the work of the office staff and answer scores of inquiries which come to the governor.

The second function mentioned in the chart is budgeting. The Council of State Governments reports that forty states vest the budgetary responsibility in the governor. While in nineteen the budget officer reports directly to the governor, various degrees of control by the governor over the budget-making process are indicated in their own comments on the subject. The Council notes, furthermore, that "an increasingly popular arrangement, now prevailing in twenty states, puts the budget function in a department of finance or of administration. While this removes the budgetary function one level from the governor, it provides an opportunity for its coordination with other fiscal and administrative controls under an officer who is usually the governor's principal adviser on all administrative matters." [3]

The scope of the governor's power over personnel varies greatly from state to state. More than half have civil service systems covering substantially all state employees. In all but two of these, a commission is appointed by the governor. In nine states, senate confirmation is necessary for appointment, and in two additional states an executive council confirms commission appointments. The executive officer is appointed by the commission in fourteen states. The governor appoints the personnel director in six states, appointment being confirmed by the Senate in Connecticut and being made only after examination in Rhode Island. Merit systems in other states cover at least the employees in Federally aided programs.[4]

The governor's control over planning and research activities in the states is almost nonexistent. In 1936 practically all states had planning commissions;

[3] *Book of the States, 1950–1951*, pp. 172–177, and Council of State Governments, *Administrative Organization of State Government*, pp. 39–55 (Chicago, 1950).

[4] *Administrative Organization of State Government*, *op. cit.*, pp. 64–75.

Brief Outline of the Agencies in the Executive Office of the Governor *

GOVERNOR'S FUNCTION	ORGANIZATION	ORGANIZATION FUNCTIONS
1. Public leadership, legislative relations, party leadership	Office of the Executive Secretary	Keep governor's calendar, screen visitors, act as buffer between governor and public Handle complaints Help governor obtain independent information on political appointees' records Handle press relations for governor and advise on press relations of executive branch Perform other tasks as desired by governor
2. Preparation and presentation of executive budget	Division of the Budget	Preparation of budget estimates Executive control of expenditures Program planning Budgetary information Administrative management studies including organizational planning (sometimes in Division of Research)
3. Concern with quality and performance of state personnel	Division of Personnel	*In states having civil service*, the Department of Civil Service performs routine functions of recruitment, testing, position classification, etc. Division conducts studies and makes recommendations for a constructive, progressive personnel program and conducts post-audits, at irregular intervals, of civil service practices and procedures *In states not having civil service*, the entire personnel function may be carried on by the Division.
4. Long-range planning (resources planning, economic development)	Division of Planning	Outline long-range goals for state development and suggest policies and means for attaining goals Coordinate Federal, state, and local planning Translate technical work into recommendations for action by governor and department heads Coordinate any detailed and specialized planning being done in the departments
5. Legislative program, vetoes (legal aspects)	General Counsel to the Governor	Legal advice to governor on policy-making Bill-drafting necessary to governor's program Reading all bills to be signed by governor for flaws requiring technical veto or return to legislature for correction
6. Administrative coordination and control; gather facts relating to governor's legislative and administrative programs	Division of Research (and Investigation)	Collect technical data on which to base governor's program Investigate administrative practices In some cases, long-range planning, policy advisers to governor, such as specialist in intergovernmental relations, and others
7. Military and Naval Affairs	Office of Military and Naval Affairs	As assigned by law to the state militia

* From Stace, Homer E., *The Organization of the Executive Office of the Governor*, pp. 6–7 (Institute of Public Administration, New York, 1950).

many of these have been abolished or permitted to fall into disuse. The function is now dispersed among numerous agencies when, indeed, it is performed at all. Few of these agencies are under the control of the governor or even available for his use. In 1949 only eighteen planning and development agencies reported that they made special studies at the request of the governor. As a result, the governor obtains such help as he can where he can, from state planning boards, from the departments, legislative councils, legislative commissions, university bureaus of public administration, commissions which he himself appoints, and staff agencies within the executive office.

The governor obtains legal advice on public questions from the attorney general in all but six states — Alabama, Michigan, New Hampshire, New York, Oklahoma, and West Virginia — which give the governor a lawyer on his own staff.[5] The military function is a direct responsibility of the governor but it may or may not be a part of the executive office. In many states there is a separate department of military affairs. The size of the staff varies greatly from state to state, the budget office often accounting for a considerable portion of the total.

The Governor's Council. Maine, Massachusetts, and New Hampshire maintain, by constitutional requirement, an executive council which is a survival of colonial days. These councils are small bodies of five to nine members, popularly selected (except in Maine) for two-year terms from districts. The councils meet almost continuously during legislative sessions, and on a weekly basis at other times. Members receive their expenses and a small salary for the performance of their duties in advising the governor in the executive part of the government. Their duties are numerous and varied, including supervision of state finances and state institutions and concurrence in appointments made by the governor.[6] A somewhat similar purpose is served by the Executive Board in Pennsylvania, established under the Administrative Code of 1923, as amended. This consists of twelve members of the Governor's Cabinet, designated by him, whose duty it is to advise upon administrative matters and to pass upon organizational changes in the various departments and agencies of the state government. A short-lived experiment along this line was begun in Wisconsin in 1931, by Governor Philip La Follette.

The Lieutenant Governor. The office of lieutenant governor, first found

[5] In Michigan the practice regarding legal counsel is rather informal. Sometimes an assistant attorney general is assigned. Professor Dorr reports that sometimes the governor leans heavily upon one of his secretaries, selected because of his legal training. In many cases the governor unofficially takes his legal advice from some prominent attorney who holds no official post. See Akers, Dee A., "The Advisory Opinion Function of the Attorney General," *Kentucky Law Journal*, May 1950, pp. 561–598, and Alabama Legislative Reference Service, *Authority of the Attorney General to Pass upon the Constitutionality of Legislative Acts* (Montgomery, 1950).

[6] Haynes, Evan, *Selection and Tenure of Judges*, pp. 12–16 (National Conference of Judicial Councils, 1944); see also Collins, Paul J., "The Executive Council in State Government," *State Government*, October 1947, pp. 269–274.

in the colonial period, is still retained in nearly three fourths of the states.[7] It has been said that the Vice-President (except in connection with possible succession) is a fifth wheel in the Federal government. If this statement is true of the Vice-President, a similar statement would be doubly true as applied to the lieutenant governor. Under modern conditions it is difficult to discover any useful purpose which the office serves and which could not be served more efficiently and more cheaply in other ways [8]; yet it continues to exist because the people like to elect somebody, because it provides a permanent and impartial presiding officer for the senate without robbing any district of its senator, and because it is in harmony with tradition and precedent. It was created in order to provide a successor to the governor in case of his death, resignation, or disability, but this purpose has not been fulfilled, as will presently be indicated. The occupant of the office is usually required to preside over the senate; occasionally when the governor is temporarily out of the state he functions in his stead. The latter situation has frequently led to breaks in continuity of policy and to squabbles as to whether a vacancy actually existed.

The lieutenant governor has rarely been of much use to the governor either administratively or legislatively, because the two often belong to different factions of their party. Since the ticket must be "balanced," the nomination for lieutenant governor is likely to be given as a consolation prize to the leading rival of the nominee for the governorship. This is almost invariably true where the convention system of nomination is used or where, in connection with the primary system, the party organization designates a slate before the primary is held. Furthermore, the ticket must ordinarily be balanced geographically, and it is extremely unlikely that both candidates will be selected from the same section of the state. Often too the nominees for this office are men of mediocre ability.

Thus the existing plan often fails to provide a suitable successor in case the governorship becomes vacant. In most states the government is so con-

7 See Isom, Warren R., "The Office of Lieutenant Governor in the States," *American Political Science Review*, October 1938, pp. 921–926. There are twelve states in which the office does not exist. In Arkansas, Florida, Maine, Maryland, New Hampshire, New Jersey, Tennessee, and West Virginia the president of the senate serves as substitute governor; in Arizona, Oregon, Utah, and Wyoming the secretary of state so serves. See also Patterson, Robert F., *The Office of Lieutenant Governor in the United States* (University of South Dakota, Governmental Research Bureau, 1944); "The Lieutenant Governor in 1944," *State Government*, June 1944, pp. 348–349, 356; Brewer, Carson, "The Office of Lieutenant Governor," in *Tennessee Papers on Constitutional Revision*, Vol. II, pp. 94–105 (University of Tennessee, 1947), and Crosby, Robert B., "Why I Want to Get Rid of My Job," *State Government*, July 1947, pp. 193–194, 204 — comment by the Lieutenant Governor of Nebraska.

8 The compensation in seventeen states ranges from an annual salary of $900 in Kansas to $8,000 in Pennsylvania, with an average of a little less than $2,700. In six states, reports Isom, the lieutenant governor is paid a salary for each session over which he presides, and in others, a per diem wage. For a good discussion of the office in New York, see New York State Constitutional Convention Committee, *Problems Relating to Executive Administration and Powers*, Chapter 2 (Albany, 1938).

ducted that the lieutenant governor has little opportunity to take part in the development of administrative policies or to acquaint himself with the work of the state government. He is, in fact, seldom consulted with regard to policy and he rarely if ever attends the meetings of the cabinet. On the legislative side, he has power to appoint committees in one third of the states, and where the office exists, he normally acts as presiding officer of the senate. The president pro tempore, who has had actual legislative experience, would probably be more competent as presiding officer, while the question of succession could be settled by suitable constitutional or statutory provision. The lieutenant governor might conceivably be valuable as a liaison officer between the governor and the legislature; this seldom occurs, however, because he is ordinarily opposed to the governor politically. In the lower house the speaker, who is always a member and therefore familiar with legislative procedure, presides more ably than a presiding officer imposed upon the house by the constitution might be expected to do.

The office of lieutenant governor should either be abolished or developed into an important and responsible position. If it were abolished, as it might well be, the salary and maintenance expenses of the office could be saved. If it were not a constitutional office or if it were amended out, the legislature could then make suitable provision for succession, either as other states have done or in a manner similar to that which Congress adopted for Presidential succession by the Act of 1886 (repealed 1947). On the other hand, it might be possible to develop the lieutenant governor into a kind of assistant governor, who could handle many routine duties and thereby ease the strain upon the time and strength of the governor.

The Executive Departments. Next in the administrative setup come the heads of executive departments, of which there are two distinct classes as indicated in the following table:

Heads of State Executive Departments

ORIGINAL OFFICES (*Elective Heads*)	NEWER OFFICES (*Appointed Heads*)	
Secretary of State	Agriculture	Labor
Attorney General	Banking	Mental Health
State Treasurer	Commerce	Mines
State Auditor	Conservation	Property and Supplies
Education (in some states)	Corrections	Public Assistance
Other elective officers	Education (in some states)	Public Utilities
	Health	Reclamation
	Highways	Revenue
	Institutions	State Police
	Insurance	Welfare

An examination of this table reveals a number of interesting facts with regard to the development of state administrative machinery. The heads of the original departments are all elective, as a result of the influence of the Jacksonian tradition. Their departments are provided for in the constitutions, and their duties are confined to what students of public administration call auxiliary services. They are a survival from the day in which the services performed by government were few in number and limited in extent.

The offices listed in the right-hand columns were all established much later, some after the Civil War, some of the most important during the present century. Most of them are provided for by statute rather than by constitutional provisions, and in keeping with the newer trend the heads are appointed by the governor rather than elected. As the reorganization movement has progressed, the heads of some of the older departments have been made appointive. In spite of a large number of state departments and agencies, the heads of departments increasingly find themselves presiding over a group of more or less related activities, in agencies of steadily increasing size.[9]

State Administrative Reorganization

Many writers, including the present one, have in the past taken a too narrow view of the problems of administrative reorganization at the state level, limiting their discussion to one phase of the problem — structural reorganization. While this phase is important, it is only one of four major aspects of state reorganization, all of which have been developed during the first half of the twentieth century. These four aspects are:

Personnel administration: beginning in 1905
Fiscal administration: beginning in 1911
Organizational structure: beginning in 1917
Administrative procedure: beginning in 1937

Because all four of these problems are dealt with at some length either in this or in succeeding chapters, they are dismissed here with a paragraph each, the present purpose being simply to direct attention to their importance, individually and collectively, in the total picture of state reorganization.

Many factors contributed to the awakening of interest in state problems, among them the increase in the number and scope of governmental functions[10] and the public's demand not only for more service but for improvement in the quality. The cost of government, in terms of taxes, once relatively insignificant, was now a matter of serious concern to every citizen and taxpayer. The gradual evolution of a science of administration and its application in business and industry has had its effect upon government. The early changes were usually made within the existing constitutional framework, although recent trends show an increasing tendency to incorporate some of

[9] Monypenny, Phillip, "The Changing Position of the Department Head in State Government," *State Government*, April 1951, pp. 112–114.

[10] See Chatters, Carl H., and Hoover, Marjorie L., *An Inventory of Governmental Activities in the United States* (Municipal Finance Officers Association, Chicago, 1947).

them in the fundamental law either through amendment or through general revision. One of the most important characteristics of this period has been the transformation of the governorship.

Personnel Administration. The spoils system developed a firm hold upon the states in the late eighteenth and early nineteenth centuries, spreading its influence into the Federal government at the beginning of the Jacksonian era. For half a century it held undisputed sway at all levels. Then in 1883 Congress passed the Pendleton Act. In that same year New York passed the first state civil service law, and Massachusetts followed in 1884. For twenty years thereafter no additions to the list were made. The real movement for the improvement of personnel administration at the state level began early in the twentieth century. From 1905 on, when Illinois adopted a civil service law, one state after another has been added to the list, until now approximately half of the states have statewide coverage. The remaining states have partial coverage in those departments and agencies responsible for the administration of Federally aided programs, especially in the social security field. Contemporaneous with the spread of merit system legislation has been the trend toward the improvement in the quality of administration, in connection with which the enthusiasm for reform has been replaced by emphasis on the development and administration of a sound, well-rounded system of personnel management in a government career service.

Fiscal Administration. For generations Americans, living in a land of plenty, were notoriously lax in the management of the financial aspects of the public business. The budget movement, which had made notable progress in governments abroad and in business and industry in this country, obtained its first recognition governmentally when in 1911 California and Wisconsin adopted state budgetary legislation. The subject was being widely discussed at the time in connection with President Taft's Commission on Economy and Efficiency. The time was ripe, and the movement spread with amazing rapidity until by 1926 all states had adopted some kind of budgetary legislation. Not all of it was good, but it represented at least a recognition of basic principles. Much of it has since been rewritten, for there has in fact been steady progress over the years in the development and improvement of budgetary procedures. Interest in budgetary reform, plus an extensive series of administrative surveys in the thirties, led to improvements in other related fields, such as central procurement, accounting and auditing, public reporting, and many more, in each of which substantial progress has been made in both organization and procedure.

Organizational Structure. The weaknesses of the prevailing type of state organization were long recognized. The administrative reorganization movement appears to have begun in Oregon in 1909 or 1910 with a proposal of the People's Power League to concentrate "executive power in the hands of the governor — checked only by an independent auditor, and to establish vital connections between the governor and the legislature." Charles E.

Hughes, in his inaugural address as Governor of New York in 1910 and later in an address at Yale University, likewise urged a concentration of responsibility, with few offices and short ballots. The movement was given further impetus by the report of President Taft's Economy and Efficiency Commission in 1912. Then in 1917 the first code was enacted in Illinois under the leadership of Governor Frank O. Lowden, and a movement that was to hold a position of primary importance in the state field for the next fifteen or twenty years was inaugurated.

Under the Illinois plan, adopted subsequently in Massachusetts, New York, and Virginia by constitutional amendment and in twenty-two other states by statutory provisions, all or most of the existing agencies were abolished by law. The duties which they performed were then carefully classified under a limited number of headings, care being taken to group related services and to eliminate, whenever possible, overlapping and duplication of functions. Each of these groups of activities was then assigned to a newly created department, the head of which was appointed by the governor. It thus became possible for the governor, for the first time in history, to establish a direct line of responsibility through the department heads, bureau chiefs, and heads of sections or divisions down to the minor employees of each department. The governor now became responsible in fact and not merely in theory for the conduct of his administration.

Arthur E. Buck listed many years ago the following standards or principles of reorganization as applied to the executive department:

1. Concentration of authority and responsibility
2. Departmentalization, or functional integration
3. Undesirability of boards for purely administrative work
4. Coordination of the staff services of administration
5. Provision for an independent audit
6. Recognition of a governor's cabinet

These fundamental principles of the reorganization movement represent at the same time benefits to be realized after reorganization takes place. Other advantages may be noted, such as the significant financial savings which are possible through the elimination of waste, inefficiency, and the duplication of services. Second, the reorganization plan provided a much more satisfactory basis for the operation of a budget system. While it is possible to operate a system of financial planning without reorganization, it is much easier to do so under an administrative code. The centralization of control provided in the reorganization plan makes possible a proper supervision of the expenditures of spending agencies during the fiscal period. The centralization of responsibility represents a notable gain from the point of view of administrative structure. Finally, adoption of the plan inevitably results in progress toward a short ballot. It is, in fact, impossible to have any satisfactory reorganization and still retain a large number of elective state officers, for centralization of administrative responsibility cannot be obtained while this condition exists. One of the primary purposes of this plan, as Professor

John M. Mathews once said, is to make the governor the pivotal point around which the whole administration revolves.

Administrative Procedure. With the steadily increasing number of regulatory bodies at all levels of government, there has been a growing concern about observance of the basic requirements of due process in dealing with the rights of citizens. This has been occasioned partly by laxity in the publication of rules and regulations, resulting in ignorance of their requirements, and partly by arbitrary procedures, sometimes real, sometimes alleged. Legislation has been passed in many states designed to correct one or both of these situations. Massachusetts in 1932 was the first state to adopt legislation requiring central filing of rules and regulations; South Carolina in 1937 was the first to require their publication. Numerous states have since adopted legislation requiring either central filing or publication, or both, while four require legislative approval of rules and regulations. On the procedural side, a uniform administrative procedures act has been drafted, and eleven states have adopted either this or acts similar to the Federal law passed in 1946.

Characteristics of Structural Reorganization

Early Reorganizations. Reorganization, developing as it has over a period of more than a generation, in states in every section of the country with varying social, economic, and political backgrounds, has shown little tendency toward uniformity or standardization. This is as it should be, for one of the chief merits of the federal system is found in the opportunity which it offers to member states to adapt their institutions to their own conditions and to the desires and traditions of their people. Buck, a leading authority on the reorganization movement during its early years, found four distinct types: the integrated, the partially integrated, the fiscal-control, and the commission or plural-executive types. The integrated type, which is the one recommended in the Model State Constitution, is found in New York and Virginia, where constitutional changes made it possible.

The partially integrated type was found in the original Illinois plan and also in California, Idaho, Kentucky (1936 plan), Ohio, Pennsylvania, Rhode Island, and Washington. In these states integration was carried as far as possible without those constitutional changes which would be essential if complete integration were to be achieved. In the fiscal-control type the governor is given the authority "to manage the affairs of the state, not through administrative integration, but through financial supervision." This type is found in Connecticut, Maine, North Carolina, South Dakota, and Wisconsin.[11] "Under the commission, or plural-executive type, the governor becomes one of several executives, although usually the dominating one. The constitutional elective officials — a half dozen — are made to share in the administration of many consolidated departments. This type resembles

[11] This analysis follows Buck, *op. cit.*, pp. 28–33.

the commission form of government familiar to our cities." It is found in Indiana, and formerly in Colorado.

Two different procedures have been followed in making these reorganizations effective. The most desirable and the most difficult to use is constitutional amendment or revision. Many of the offices that need to be eliminated or put on an appointive basis are embalmed in the constitution, so that either amendment or revision is often difficult to achieve, in some states well-nigh impossible. In these jurisdictions the only practical alternative is to leave the constitutional offices alone, and by statutory action accomplish as much as can be done within the framework provided by the constitution. It is usually possible to deprive the constitutional officers of any policy-making powers, thereby rendering them more or less innocuous.

If one plots on a map of the United States all the states in which administrative reorganizations have occurred, it is evident that the greatest interest in this subject has been evidenced along the Atlantic seaboard; and second, that the South has shown somewhat less interest in the movement than other sections of the country.

The table on page 374 shows the administrative departments and agencies established in selected states since 1938. The states are arranged in the chronological order in which their respective reorganizations occurred, and the effort has been made to carry across the table, on a single line, the names of those departments or agencies performing identical services. The table reveals, in the first place, that there are a number of fundamental problems of administration for which provision must be made in every state, regardless of variations in the details of its administrative structure. Thus every state has established a Department of Agriculture, a Department of Finance, and a Department of Labor.

In the second place, adoption of the reorganization principle does not, as noted above, require a dead level of uniformity in the administrative structure regardless of the special needs and problems of individual states. In Idaho and Pennsylvania, for instance, there is a Department of Mines. Such an administrative agency may be justified as a separate unit in states where the mining industry constitutes an important element in the economic life of the state; it would be foolish to provide for such a department in a state which had no important mining industry or mineral resources. Similarly Idaho has established a Department of Reclamation, in response to the needs of the people living in that section of the country, but such a department would be of little use in most other states. In some instances the promotion of immigration and development has been dignified by departmental status.

There is, in the third place, a wide variety of terminology applied to the same or similar services. For instance, the department which supervises correctional institutions is variously designated as the Department of Institutions, the Department of Public Institutions, and the Department of Correction. In some states this service is not operated as a separate department but as a bureau or division of the Department of Public Welfare or of the attorney general's department. Similarly the Department of Conservation is designated as a Department of Forests and Waters in one state (where its activities are supplemented by separate commissions for fish and game), as a Department of Natural Resources in another, and as a Department of Conservation and Development in a third. The Department of Labor is variously styled as the Department of Industrial Relations, the Department of Labor and Statistics, and the Department of Labor and Industry. The

Administrative Departments of State Governments Reorganized under Recent Constitutional Revisions

NEW YORK 1938[1]	MISSOURI 1945[1]	GEORGIA 1945[1]	NEW JERSEY[4] 1948[2]
1. Executive	Business and Administration[3]	Comptroller General	....
2. Audit & Control	Audit	Auditing[3]	....
3. Taxation & Finance	Revenue[3]	Revenue	....
4. Law	Law	Law Public Safety[3]	Law & Public Safety
5. State	State	State	State
6. Public Works	Highways	Highways[3]	Highways
7. Conservation	Conservation	Conservation[3]	Conservation & Economic Development
8. Agriculture & Markets	Agriculture	Agriculture	Agriculture
9. Labor	Labor & Industrial Relations[3]	Labor	Labor & Industry
10. Education	Education	Education	Education
11. Health	Health & Welfare[3]	Public Health[3]	Health
12. Mental Hygiene	....	....	....
13. Social Welfare	(Health & Welfare)	Public Welfare[3]	Institutions & Agencies
14. Corrections	Corrections[3]	Corrections[3]	....
15. Public Service	....	....	Public Utilities
16. Banking	....	Banking[3]	Banking & Insurance
17. Insurance	....	....	(Banking & Insurance)
18. Civil Service	....	....	Civil Service
19.	Treasurer	Treasurer	Treasurer
20.	....	Military[3]	Defense
21.	....	Library[3]	....

[1] Constitutional departments
[2] Statutory departments under general constitutional provision
[3] Statutory departments
[4] See *New Jersey State Government: a Summary of the Organization and Functions of the Executive Branch* (Bureau of Government Research, Rutgers University, 1951).

student of public administration must therefore look behind the name assigned to a given administrative agency in order to determine the fundamental administrative problem with which it deals.

Finally, it appears that in the years since the reorganization movement began, there has been a tendency to increase the number of departments provided for by the codes. This may be attributed to two factors. Illinois in 1917 started with nine departments and shortly found it desirable to increase this number by two. Idaho and Nebraska likewise established a minimum number, which came to be regarded as inadequate and as requiring the grouping of unrelated services under the same department. The unwisdom of this procedure was recognized in Maryland, which set up nineteen departments, including several commissions; in New York, Pennsylvania, and Virginia, with eighteen departments each; in Massachusetts with sixteen; and in Minnesota with thirteen. While the centralization of responsibility and control is highly desirable, there is no defense for carrying the principle so far as to require the grouping of unrelated services.

Following the original series of reorganizations which began in 1917 and continued through the twenties, there came in the decade of the thirties an extensive series of broad surveys of state administrative organization and procedure. To a large extent these surveys were made by such outside organizations as the Brookings Institution in Washington, Griffenhagen and Associates in Chicago, and the Institute of Public Administration in New York. While it frequently happened that the recommendations of these surveys were not adopted, they served a number of useful purposes. They strengthened the movement toward the use of the executive budget as the established method in the fiscal field, and toward improved methods of personnel management; they encouraged the system of central procurement; and in general they fostered the trend toward making the governor the general manager and business manager of the state government.

Trends in Recent Constitutional Revisions. Because of the serious difficulty experienced in maintaining an orderly and well-conceived governmental structure on a continuing basis, recent constitutional conventions have given consideration to this problem and have adopted more or less similar plans for meeting it. The old reorganization procedure relied upon a "one shot" treatment, there being no provision for continuing efforts at reorganization as old problems were solved and new ones arose. All of them depended on legislative action, whereas the problems involved were — and are — primarily executive in character. The new reorganization formula thus seeks to accomplish what the old was unable to achieve — namely, a basis for keeping a reorganized government reorganized. The trend during the past decade or more has, without exception, brought added prestige and real responsibility to the chief executive.[12]

[12] Solomon, Samuel R., "U.S. Governors, 1940–1950," *National Municipal Review*, April 1950, pp. 190–197.

The new plan has been evolved out of three things: the pioneering move in New York, Federal reorganization experience,[13] and the recommendations contained in the Model State Constitution (see Article V, Section 506). Under the New York Constitution of 1894, as amended, the number of departments specified was twenty, but in 1938 this number was reduced to eighteen. Under the following provision, however, the legislature was still responsible for keeping the executive house in order:

> Subject to the limitations contained in this constitution, the legislature may from time to time assign by law new powers and functions to departments, officers, boards or commissions, and increase, modify or diminish their powers and functions. No new departments shall be created hereafter, but this shall not prevent the legislature from creating temporary commissions for special purposes and nothing contained in this article shall prevent the legislature from reducing the number of departments as provided for in this article, by consolidation or otherwise. — Article V, Section 3.

While a constitutional establishment of departments with such a limitation tends to prevent the establishment of miscellaneous agencies outside the limits of the reorganization plan, it is inflexible and may in time cause a grouping of unrelated services within departments. There has been a tendency, under this provision, to place all sorts of miscellaneous duties in the Executive Department, apparently because in many cases the legislature did not know what else to do with them. There is, in addition to the staff connected with the executive chamber, the following list of divisions: Budget, Commerce, Military and Naval Affairs, Standards and Purchase, State Police, Parole, Alcoholic Beverage Control, State Planning, and Housing.

Further progress was made in the Missouri Constitution of 1945. In Article IV, Section 12, it is provided that in addition to the Governor and Lieutenant Governor, there shall be fourteen departments. The heads of nine, of which four are popularly elected, are listed specifically (secretary of state, state auditor, attorney general, state treasurer, and departments of revenue, education, highways, conservation, and agriculture, while health and welfare are elsewhere provided for), the sentence concluding: "and such additional departments, not exceeding five in number, as may hereafter be established by law." Under this provision most of the departments are named in the constitution, the discretion of the legislature being limited to four. The governor was given power to assign agencies to departments. Some degree of flexibility in the departmental structure thus became possible.[14]

[13] See the author's *Basic Information on the Reorganization of the Executive Branch of the Government of the United States, 1912–1947* (Public Affairs Bulletin No. 66, Legislative Reference Service, Library of Congress, Washington, 1948).

[14] For comment on the Missouri reorganization, see Faust, Martin L., *Five Years Under the New Missouri Constitution* (Missouri Public Expenditure Council, Jefferson City, 1950), and the following articles: Faust, Martin L., "Reorganization in Missouri," *National Municipal Review*, September 1946, pp. 402–407; Lipson, Leslie, "The Executive Branch in New State Constitutions," *Public Administration Review*, Winter 1949, pp. 11–21; and McCandless, Carl A., "Administrative Reorganization in Missouri," *Southwestern Social Science Quarterly*, March 1948, pp. 334–345.

The Georgia Constitution of 1945 has nothing to contribute on this point. Seven elective officials are specifically listed (Article V, Section 3), but no provision is made for the organization of the executive branch as a whole.

The New Jersey Constitution of 1948 provides much the best answer to this problem yet available. It appears, as a matter of fact, to be almost an ideal answer (Article V, Section 4):

> 1. All executive and administrative officers, departments, and instrumentalities of the State government, including the offices of Secretary of State and Attorney General, and their respective functions, powers and duties, shall be allocated by law among and within not more than twenty principal departments, in such manner as to group the same according to major purposes so far as practicable. Temporary commissions for special purposes may, however, be established by law and such commissions need not be allocated within a principal department.
>
> 2. Each principal department shall be under the supervision of the Governor. The head of each principal department shall be a single executive unless otherwise provided by law. Such single executives shall be nominated and appointed by the Governor, with the advice and consent of the Senate, to serve at the pleasure of the Governor during his term of office and until the appointment and qualification of their successors.

Note the several specific merits of these provisions. The number of executive departments is definitely limited. Departments are headed by a single executive. The heads of departments are appointed by and are responsible to the governor. Only two specific departments are mentioned in the constitution and these two more or less incidentally. The plan is flexible, and subject to change as conditions require. The governor has broad powers of investigation over the conduct of all state departments and agencies. Actually, the only disadvantage is that action by the legislature is required to make changes; it would have been preferable to have left this power with the governor, under executive order or reorganization plan, subject to legislative review, as is the case in the Federal government.

The Little Hoover Commissions. In 1947 the Congress provided for the Commission on Organization of the Executive Branch of the Government of the United States, which soon came to be popularly known as the Hoover Commission. After approximately eighteen months of intense effort, the Commission submitted its series of reports to the Congress, the President, and the American people. The widespread interest which this tremendous undertaking engendered throughout the country prompted the legislatures of many states to authorize administrative surveys of various types in 1949. It was planned that most of these would report at the regular sessions of 1951, although a few were instructed to report at an earlier date. Actually, as of 1952, such surveys had been authorized in approximately three fourths of the states and in the Territory of Puerto Rico. The Council of State Governments found four distinct types, only the first of which bears any close resemblance to the form of organization used by the Hoover Commission.[15]

1. Commissions created specifically for the purpose of developing basic reports and plans for reorganization. Usually these commissions include outstanding citizens, familiar with the problems and obligations of the state government and representing the various major interests, areas, and activities in the state. Frequently also — and especially when extensive legislative action will be required to effectuate the recommendations — leaders in the legislature are included. The reorganization commissions in Connecticut, Delaware, Illinois, Iowa, Massachusetts, Minnesota, New Hampshire, South Carolina, and Puerto Rico are basically of this type.[16]

2. Special interim committees of legislators, created to make an over-all study and to report at the next session. Such committees have been created in Arizona, Idaho, Michigan, and Oregon.

3. Special legislative committees or commissions, re-created each session, for continuing study of administrative organization. The reorganization agencies in California, New York, and Ohio are of this type.

4. Assignment of the reorganization study to general legislative interim research agencies such as legislative councils. In several states, including Nebraska, Nevada, North Dakota, Wisconsin, and Hawaii, the reorganization study has been assigned to the continuing legislative research agency as one of its interim activities.

The successful prosecution of such a program requires adequate facilities for research, including a competent director of research. This, in turn, requires financial support, which ranges from $4,000 in Kentucky to $50,000 appropriated funds in California, Connecticut, and Illinois. In some cases considerable additional amounts have been supplied from such other sources as the governor's contingent funds while, furthermore, full advantage is taken of existing research organizations and facilities. The average ranges from $25,000 to $50,000. The major objectives of such surveys include

[15] Summary of the Conference on State Government Reorganization, Chicago, September 29–30, 1949; this finding is in general in accord with that of Lederle, John W., and Strauss, Dorothee E., "The Little Hoover Commissions," *Michigan Governmental Digest*, November 4, 1949 (Bureau of Government, University of Michigan), and *Michigan Municipal Review*, June 1950, pp. 79–80, 88–90. For the most recent analysis, see Heady, Ferrel, "States Try Reorganization," *ibid.*, July 1952, pp. 334–338, 345.

[16] For comments on several of these, see: IOWA: Porter, Kirk H., "Iowa's 'Little Hoover Commission'," *Iowa Law Review*, Fall 1949, pp. 61–67. ILLINOIS: Watson, George H., "How to Study State Government: the Schaefer Commission Report on Reorganization in Illinois," *Illinois Law Review*, March-April 1951, pp. 19–47. MINNESOTA: Harlow, Leroy F., "A Blueprint for Minnesota," *National Municipal Review*, April 1951, pp. 190–194, 200. NEW HAMPSHIRE: Deming, George H., "The Reorganization of State Government in New Hampshire," *County Officer*, January 1952, pp. 9–11; Langmuir, John E., "New Hampshire Secures Partial Reorganization; State Administrative Setup Revamped after 165 Years," *National Municipal Review*, July 1950, pp. 344–346; and "Reorganization of New Hampshire State Government," *New Hampshire Town and City Notes*, Winter 1950, entire issue. SOUTH CAROLINA: Figg, Robert M., "State Reorganization in South Carolina," *South Carolina Law Quarterly*, December 1950, pp. 133–141. GENERAL: Council of State Governments, *A Progress Report on State Reorganization in 1950* (Chicago, March 1950); and "State Reorganization Studies," *State Government*, September 1950, pp. 200–203, 209–211; and Perkins, John A., "Reflections on State Reorganizations," *American Political Science Review*, June 1951, pp. 507–516.

analysis of the structure and operations of the state government,[17] the development of the commission's recommendations, and obtaining support for these recommendations by the people and the legislature.

The conduct of the survey raises many problems such as the determination of its scope, its time schedule, its budget, its working procedures, and the selection and direction of the staff. Definite arrangements must be made both for enlisting the cooperation of departments and agencies to be surveyed, and of the public. Both are largely problems of public relations. Connecticut attempted to solve the first by having each department designate one person as liaison with the survey staff for continuing contacts and by departmental reviews of its reports before publication. The second may be met by a carefully planned program, including regular press conferences, prepared releases, speaking engagements before interested groups, and radio discussions, as well as other aspects of the usual public relations program. One bad blunder can kill a report, but it takes something spectacular and unusual to sell one.[18]

"The final report should be simple, concise, clear, and sufficiently imaginative to obtain public understanding and support — and enactment." It should be attractively set up, and in order to obtain the maximum press and radio coverage, released in parts or sections. Without effective follow-up, the recommendations are apt to languish and die. The major emphasis should be on achieving an effective and efficient government in which the people can and will have confidence, not on economy. Economies there will be, but they are largely a by-product of good organization and sound administration. Where these conditions prevail and the public has confidence in its government, the demands upon it for new services or the expansion of existing services are likely to consume actual savings and make tax reductions impossible.[19]

Evaluation of the Reorganization Plan. The reorganization movement

[17] In Connecticut the act authorized the Commission to survey "all departments" of the government. This broad authorization, probably unintentional since the state constitution uses the word "departments" in the sense of "branches," nevertheless permitted the Commission to include the legislative and judicial branches of the government as well as the executive, and to come out with a draft of a proposed new constitution for the state. The Connecticut Commission was best organized, best financed, and did the most comprehensive job; see its *Report* (Hartford, 1950), and Sollett, Ralph P., "All the Functions of the State Government," *State Government*, April 1950, pp. 81–85 — a progress report by the executive director of the Commission.

[18] The Hoover Commission found the tanks that were not there, yet were to be reconditioned, purchase orders for small items that cost $10 apiece. In a Maine survey, it was the fish moving up a stream and passing from the jurisdiction of one agency to that of another, and the twenty-one varieties of canned peas found in one institution, one of them imported from France at $.68 a can, and used annually to feed the Board of Viewers, in the hope of increasing the appropriation. In New York City, a survey team found a coat-rack that was bought and paid for seven times, but there was still only one coat-rack.

[19] In addition to the Lederle and Strauss report, see a summary of the panel discussion on state reorganization, *Public Administration Review*, Spring 1949, pp. 138–139, and Gallagher, Hubert R., "State Reorganization Surveys," *ibid.*, October 1949, pp. 252–256.

has seemed so sound that few persons have raised serious question regarding it.[20] Such complaints as have been made relate to the fear of possible abuses of the powers of a strong governor, disapproval of the possibility of changing all key officials every two or four years, the apparent impossibility of achieving in most states a complete administrative integration, and the failure of the plan to do more than one might reasonably expect of it — its failure, in other words, to produce utopia.

The best answer to these arguments is that, where given half a chance, reorganization works. The movement has made progress not only in the states but in the Federal government as well. There are few people, indeed, who would want to turn back the hands of the clock, to restore conditions existing before reorganization. Not all the states have been reorganized, to be sure, but all of them have been affected — to a greater or lesser degree — by the movement. This is not to say that constructive criticism of the plan is undesirable. The administrative problem in the states has not been solved. It has proved difficult to get the states reorganized and equally difficult to keep them so. But significant progress has been made in many jurisdictions.

The most urgent need at the present time is for a series of objective studies made by competent political scientists of the results of reorganization in individual states or groups of states, i.e., New England, the Southern region, and other areas. What progress has been made since reorganization began in Illinois in 1917? Since Coker wrote his critical appraisal of the experience in Ohio in 1922? To what extent has this mechanism strengthened popular control of government, produced efficient and economical government operation? Can it be shown that it has helped to bring a higher caliber of men into the public service? These questions, to be sure, are exceedingly difficult to answer on an objective basis; it may well be that a significant series of volumes now in course of preparation, on government and administration in each of the forty-eight states and four territories, will help to provide the answers.[21]

The reorganization movement serves several different purposes. In addition to making possible greater efficiency in operations and economies — in the sense of the same service for less cost or more service for the same cost — it is a tremendously useful instrument for educating people about their government and inducing them to give serious thought to its problems. By preparing the states to render more and better service, it puts them in a better position to hold their own as members of the American federal

[20] Significant critical comments: Coker, Francis W., "Dogmas of Administrative Reform," *American Political Science Review*, August 1922, pp. 399–411, and Hyneman, Charles S., "Administrative Reorganization: An Adventure into Science and Theology," *Journal of Politics*, February 1939, pp. 62–75 (a review of Buck's book). The literature of dissent is well summarized in Waldo, Dwight, *The Administrative State*, pp. 130–155 (Ronald Press, New York, 1948).

[21] The American Commonwealths Series, of which the author is General Editor, to be published, several volumes a year, by the Thomas Y. Crowell Company, New York, beginning in 1953.

system. The people are constantly demanding increased services, and some unit of government is going to render them — the states and local units, or the Federal government. Unless the states are capable of discharging their responsibilities, the Federal government will be still further expanded at the expense of the states. To put the matter in another way, the contributions of the reorganization movement have been threefold: to enable the states to give better service, to strengthen responsible government, and to make the American system work.

Forms of Control over Administration

Many persons are apt to assume that a governor or department head endowed with proper authority is more or less a free agent in the making of decisions with regard to public questions. This is in practice far from true. Administrative officers are restricted in their freedom of decision by a variety of powerful and often dominating influences, such as public sentiment, pressure groups, political considerations, the possibility of judicial review or of legislative action, the findings of scientific research, reports of the planning staff, and the views of superior officers. These influences are deserving of brief comment.

Administrative Controls. Administrative control over administrative officers is, or should be, an important influence. Every officer and employee should know to whom he is responsible, in what way, and to what extent, in a direct line of administrative responsibility. If he does not abide by the instructions of his superior officer or if he fails to develop his policies in harmony with those of the administration of which he is a part, he may find himself looking for another job. Executive control may extend to independent officers and may even be exercised for the purpose of harassing such officers. Illustrations of this character come to light from time to time in different states. Most of them are as much political as they are administrative in character, but they still serve to indicate the possibilities of the use of the investigatory power of the governor as an instrument of coercion.

Legislative Controls. The legislative influence is manifold. With the exception of such provisions as are incorporated in the constitution, all the powers and duties of an administrative officer, as well as the organization of agencies to perform such activities, are provided for in statutes passed by the legislature. An executive must remember that an unwise or tactless use of the powers entrusted to him may lead to further legislation limiting his powers and making his work more difficult and perhaps less effective. Thus the same governmental authority that created the office and conferred certain powers upon it may, at its discretion, modify those powers or rescind its earlier action, and it may determine the means and methods of supervising the office. The impeachment process is always available, but it does not ordinarily constitute a very feasible method of making the governor accountable for his actions.

The legislature can exercise control over administration through its control over the purse. In fact, there is no more certain way of curtailing administrative activity or of impairing its effectiveness than by reducing the appropriation for a service or striking out the appropriation altogether,[22] or by resorting to an excessive degree of itemization. The greater the degree of itemization, the smaller will be the amount of administrative discretion. It is a proper function of the legislature to exercise a general surveillance over the executive officers and agencies. This control is normally exercised through the review of programs by appropriation committees, by the questioning of officials at committee hearings, by legislative investigations, and through the study of audit reports. A comprehensive audit, made by an independent auditor, has been a traditional means of enforcing the accountability of executive officials, including the governor. Where senate confirmation of appointments is required, this serves as a further control. Ripper legislation is another, the granting or the refusal to grant specific authority requested by the governor still another.

Judicial Controls. The possibility of judicial review of the acts of an administrative officer is ever present. He must be aware that the adoption of procedures which ignore or violate the rights of citizens or groups will lead to judicial proceedings designed to attack either the constitutionality of the law or the legality of his procedure under it. In some cases such a test may be desirable from the administrative point of view for the purpose of clarifying the powers of the officer; in others, it may be unavoidable if the officer is to perform the duties required of him under the statute. Actually the courts interfere very little in the exercise of the governor's powers. They do not attempt to control the governor's discretion in the exercise of his constitutional powers, for there is general agreement among state courts against issuing a mandamus to compel the governor to perform a political act or to control the governor's legal discretion in any way.

Popular Controls. The term popular controls is used here in a very broad sense, to include partisan and pressure group influences as well as those exercised by the general public. The control of the latter may be made effective in any one of several ways — through the influence of public opinion, as expressed through such normal channels as the press, radio, television, or incoming mail; through approval or disapproval of the governor and his party, if he runs for reelection; by means of the recall, in those states where the use of this device is authorized by the constitution. Actually there is only one case on record in which the governor of a state has been removed from office through use of the recall.

An administrative officer must ever be guided in the use of his powers by indications of public sentiment or by reasonable conjectures as to the type of public reaction likely to be elicited by various types of adminis-

[22] See Fairlie, John A., "The Legislature and the Administration," *American Political Science Review*, April 1936, pp. 241–256, and June 1936, pp. 494–506.

trative procedure. A wise executive will refrain from arousing public criticism by the use of one procedure when such criticism might be avoided and the same ends achieved by using another. When the Pennsylvania Liquor Control Board set up the state stores system in 1934, it published a price list. There was an immediate and powerful sentiment that the prices were too high, whereupon the Board undertook immediate steps to meet these objections by reductions and by the listing of less expensive brands. In Iowa in 1930 the Department of Agriculture attempted to enforce a state law providing for the tuberculin testing of dairy cows. The farmers met the veterinarians with clubs and pitchforks because the Department had failed to inform them regarding the program and cultivate a spirit of cooperation among them. An administrative officer must have enough of the sense of the politician to know when and how he can use the powers vested in him effectively without arousing public indignation and resentment.

Pressure groups often exert a powerful influence on administration. Representatives of citizen groups may bring pressure in the public interest, or against it. Professional lobbyists often seek not only to influence the content of legislation while it is under consideration, but to bend the law to suit their purposes after it has been enacted. It is notoriously true that public service commissions are frequently dominated by the very interests they are supposed to regulate and control. Instances are not lacking in which the agents of those subject to regulation have moved in and assumed control of the whole regulatory program. The effective resistance of such pressures by the administrator is not easy; it requires courage and statesmanship of a high order.

The party organization can and often does influence the policies and actions of the governor, and of other administrative officials as well. Party leaders, with a finger on the pulse of public opinion and an eye on the next election, are frequently in a position to exercise a very potent influence on administration. Illustrations are numerous and readily apparent; the actions taken are often in direct conflict with the public interest. Political influence in the assessment of taxes, in police administration, in building inspection and the supervision of work done under government contract, in the enforcement of labor and election laws, and in other fields are familiar to all.

Research and Planning Controls. The results of scientific research and the work of the planning staff exert a growing influence on the processes of administration. In the field of health and safety, for instance, the public tends to accept without protest regulations which are thought to be necessary. Swimming pools may be closed when an epidemic threatens or campaigns of vaccination or immunization may be specified. In such cases the findings of research take precedence over other possible controls which might otherwise influence the course of administrative action. In similar manner, the recommendations of the planning staff may indicate so clearly the proper course of action to be followed in a given situation that the administrator could not reasonably attempt to follow any other.

It is thus clear that an officer faced with a decision on an important policy question must take account of a large number of factors of a practical nature in addition to the constitutional and legal limits of his power as defined by statutes, court decisions, and rulings of the attorney general.[23]

The Problem of Boards and Commissions

Reasons for Their Establishment. In the half century prior to 1917, during which state functions and administrative machinery were both greatly expanded, the commission form of organization prevailed. There were many causes for the creation of boards and commissions, but probably the most common one has been the desire "to keep politics out of the department" and the mistaken idea that this device would accomplish that purpose. Under such circumstances a board is created with overlapping terms for its members, with the hope that it will serve as a "buffer" between the governor and the head of the department.

A second advantage claimed for the board is that of continuity of policy. The collective experience of the board members will be preserved, it is argued, if they have long overlapping terms, whereas policies would shift and fluctuate if a new governor were to come into office every two or four years and appoint a new department head. In order to prevent such removals of department heads and to prevent control by the governor, numerous states have set up large boards with nine members with nine-year overlapping terms.[24] In this way no governor can appoint a majority of its members during the normal two terms of office, except through the filling of such vacancies as may arise. A third argument is that for certain functions a group decision is desirable if not essential. It is contended that the product

[23] A fuller discussion of these controls appears in the author's *Public Administration in a Democratic Society*, Chapter 35 (Heath, Boston, 1950).

[24] This is common in the field of education, but an Arkansas amendment proposed by initiated petition in 1942, and adopted by a narrow margin, had a much wider coverage. This amendment fixes the term of office of members of boards or commissions of the educational, charitable, penal, and correctional institutions at five, seven, or ten years, according to the number of members on the respective boards or commissions. It required the General Assembly to arrange the terms so that only one term of office will expire each year. None of these boards or commissions may be abolished unless the institution is abolished or consolidated with some other state institution. Membership in none of the boards may be increased or decreased. The governor may remove a board member "for cause only, after notice and hearing," and this action is effective only when approved in writing by a majority of the remaining members of the board. Either the governor or the member ordered removed may appeal to the Pulaski Circuit Court. A vacancy occurring before expiration of the term is filled by the governor, subject to the approval of the remaining members of the board. When, however, the senate refuses to confirm the nominees of the outgoing governor, the incoming governor may have an opportunity to make two appointments to a board, instead of one. (Grant, Daniel, *The Role of the Governor of Arkansas in Administration.* Doctoral dissertation, Northwestern University, 1948). If a worse system than this has been devised anywhere, it has not come to the author's attention.

of a council of minds is likely to be better than the judgment of a single person, particularly for such quasi-legislative or quasi-judicial agencies as workmen's compensation or the regulation of public utilities.

It is also contended that a department will serve the people best if it is controlled by a board whose members represent the different groups or sections of the state, and that such a board is likely to formulate policies in the interests of the state as a whole. Another claim is that the best work often comes from private individuals of high caliber who could not be paid enough for full-time employment but who are willing to serve on a board once a month or once a quarter on a voluntary basis. To eliminate such honorary boards — it is contended — would diminish the opportunities for a citizen to take an active part in governmental affairs.

Types of Boards. A discussion of boards in general is of little use, for actually there are many different types — full-time and part-time, with power and without (advisory), elected and appointed (with or without confirmation), elected or appointed and ex-officio. Boards with power to administer may be elected or appointed by the governor. Ex-officio boards whose members are often elected are especially objectionable from an administrative point of view when vested with power, since it is virtually impossible to establish responsibility. Boards without power, i.e., advisory, are usually appointed but can be elected. Such boards probably do little harm and most of them do little good. They are likely to be something of a nuisance, if not actually a hindrance, in the task of administration.

All sorts of devices have been adopted to make sure that the governor has little or no control over board members — or for that matter, over the administration in general. Reference has already been made to the situation in Arkansas. In Colorado in 1919, under the influence of misguided enthusiasts for the merit system, the governor was restricted to the top name on civil service lists in the appointment of heads of departments. In Michigan and Nebraska, board members all have equal authority; under such a plan, whether they are elected or appointed, there can be no fixed responsibility. If such a board appoints an executive officer responsible to it, this officer may be indirectly responsible to the governor if he appoints the members of the board, but not at all if he does not.

Objections to Administrative Boards. The arguments for the boards sound plausible enough but they are all partially if not wholly discredited by the facts of experience. They tend to be irresponsible, to lack initiative, to be unreasonably slow in the handling of routine business, but tradition makes it well-nigh impossible to do away with them. By virtue of their long and overlapping terms they are completely independent, beyond the control of both the people and the governor. The use of this device for administrative purposes has been condemned in practically every survey in state and nation, including at the latter level the President's Committee on Administrative Management in 1937 and the Commission on the Organization of the Executive Branch of the Government in 1949. It is condemned, at least by implication, by the Model State Constitution, and in no uncertain terms by the Connecticut Commission on State Government Organization in 1950. But still the use of boards and commissions continues on a wide scale, if not unabated.

The idea of administrative responsibility makes progress so slowly because the people have been so fearful of the concentration of authority. Whenever a new activity was undertaken, a new board or commission was established to administer it. The board form was used not only because of an inherited and deep-seated fear of a strong executive, but because it seemed appropriate for the performance of duties of a quasi-legislative or quasi-judicial character, involving the exercise of wide discretionary powers. Sometimes it seemed desirable to have a variety of interests represented, or to reduce by this means the influence of party politics in the administration of the service. This practice not only led to the multiplication of administrative agencies, but revealed in time a serious structural weakness in the board or commission as an administrative mechanism.

While the board was effective for purposes of deliberation and in formulation of rules and regulations, it was almost wholly unsuited to the task of administration. Responsibility was not and could not be fixed. Most of the boards were cursed with a generous sprinkling of ex-officio members who lacked either the time or the inclination to give much attention to board work or to devote much energy to it. Usually they sent a substitute, if indeed they were represented at all. With the advent of the reorganization movement, the pendulum swung in the opposite direction. Single commissioners, secretaries, or department heads were substituted for administrative boards and commissions, except in those cases where the latter were established by constitutional provision and had to be retained. This new device was often less satisfactory in the performance of rule-making activities; a single commissioner was not an adequate substitute for a board in matters requiring deliberation.

Working Compromises. Several compromise measures have been adopted by the states to meet the objections to the use of boards and of single commissioners. These are represented by the introduction of advisory boards into the departmental type of organization and the introduction of the executive secretary into the commission type. Under the first plan the department head, instead of depending upon his bureau chiefs as a council of advisers, has the aid of an advisory board or commission attached to the department. For example, the Department of Health in Pennsylvania is a highly centralized administrative agency; yet there is in addition, attached to the Department, an Advisory Health Board, the members of which are appointed by the governor. They serve without compensation for a term of four years and meet quarterly. Actual expenses incurred in attendance at meetings are returned to them. The Board is authorized to adopt rules and regulations on questions pertaining to public health; these are enforced by the Department officials on the same basis as laws enacted by the legislature.

The New Jersey solution has much to commend it. After specifying that "the head of each principal department shall be a single executive unless otherwise provided by law," the Constitution of 1948 goes on to provide for such exceptions:

> Whenever a board, commission or other body shall be the head of a principal department, the members thereof shall be nominated and appointed by the Governor with the advice and consent of the Senate, and may be removed in the manner provided by law. Such a board, commission or other body may appoint a principal executive officer when authorized by law, but the appointment shall be subject to the approval of the Governor. Any principal executive officer so appointed shall be removable by the Governor, upon notice and an opportunity to be heard.

Thus some provision is made for executive control and responsibility.

Another type of organization is illustrated by Wisconsin, which has so far failed to adopt an effective administrative organization, preferring rather to continue with the antiquated structure which still prevails there. This state has, however, had the persistence and ingenuity to make this structure function surprisingly well. Commission control over important functions is still maintained, but each of the boards has hired a competent person to serve during the pleasure of the board as its administrative officer and agent. Thus the Executive Secretary of the State Board of Health performs many of the duties of, and exercises much the same administrative supervision and control as, the Secretary of Health in Pennsylvania or the Commissioner of Health in New York. By the adoption of one or the other of these devices many states have made a definite effort to obtain the benefits of both types of organization without subjecting themselves to the defects most commonly associated with either of them.

Bad as this situation is from the point of view of administrative responsibility, a governor may in practice have more power over the boards and commissions than was intended by the lawmakers who provided for them. This power arises from the fact that a governor can normally make more appointments to such boards than the number provided for in most of the laws, due to Senate approval of two board appointments during a governor's first year, voluntary resignations and the honoring of requests for resignations, abolition of one board and creation of another in its place under a slightly different name, simply to allow the governor to make the appointments. In Arkansas, as Dr. Grant reports, the governor must, under 1947 legislation, be notified at least forty-eight hours in advance of any regular or special board meeting. Either he or a designated representative may attend, and the secretary of the board must furnish him with a certified copy of the minutes within five days after the meeting.

Current Problems and Tendencies

Improvement of Top Level Management. As the movement for administrative reorganization has continued over the years, more and more attention has been given to the problems of over-all organization and management, less and less to the minutiae of the problems of internal management and control. This has been true at the Federal, state, and local levels alike. In reviewing the organization of the executive branch, the Puerto Rico Commission on Reorganization in 1949 made use of eight standards which have stood the test of experience[25]:

1. The chief executive should be equipped with authority adequate to match his responsibility and with sufficient staff to aid him in doing those things which he must do.
2. The subordinates of the chief executive should be accountable to him and, through him, to the legislature and to the people.
3. The responsibilities of the subordinates of the chief executive should be properly located and clearly fixed.
4. The various organization units should be grouped by major purpose so as to minimize conflict, duplication, and overlapping.
5. Each activity of the government should be administered through the form of organization best suited to achieve its stated objectives.
6. Good organization should include adequate provision for planning, coordination, and control.
7. Special provision should be made for continuing attention to efficiency and economy.
8. The executive branch as a whole should be so organized as to manage with maximum effectiveness its relations with the other branches of the Insular Government and with the Federal Government.

The primary purpose of the reorganization movement has been to centralize administrative responsibility, eliminate overlapping and duplication of governmental services, and make possible a better integration of those services. It has often been assumed that the principle of the executive budget was an essential part of the reorganization plan although, as Professor Walker pointed out many years ago, budgeting began before the reorganization movement was started and budgeting is practiced now in all states, including those which have not been structurally reorganized as well as those which have. Where reorganization has been accomplished, financial control has not always been effective. Reorganization has helped, but it has not wholly solved the problem. Consequently, further experiments are now being carried on in a number of states, notably in Kansas, Michigan, Minnesota, Oregon, and Rhode Island.[26]

The Minnesota reorganization act, in force from 1925 to 1939, provided for a Department of Administration and Finance, similar to that under the Massachusetts Act of 1919, headed by three gubernatorial appointees known

[25] *Report on the Reorganization of the Executive Branch of the Government of Puerto Rico*, pp. 3–4 (San Juan, Puerto Rico, 1949).

[26] See Kenyon, Howard A., "Rhode Island's Department of Administration," *State Government*, February 1952, pp. 31–34.

as the State Comptroller, the State Budget Commissioner, and the State Purchasing Agent. Under the leadership of Governor Harold E. Stassen this plan, which had many weaknesses, was abandoned in favor of what has been frequently referred to as a State Manager Plan, the main provisions of which center around the idea of creating a single official responsible for planning and managing the business and financial activities of the state. The Commissioner of Administration has many powers that enable him to keep expenditures under control, to coordinate state activities, and to encourage departmental planning and management.

Important among these, of course, are his powers relating to the preparation and enforcement of the budget. In the latter connection he is responsible for the administration of a system of quarterly allotments, within the limits of a mandatory requirement that expenditures must be kept within revenue receipts. His control extends not only to appropriated funds but to dedicated funds, debt administration, interest payments, and trust fund operations. Only expenditures of the courts, professional licensing boards, and the State University are exempted. The Commissioner has powers sufficient to do the job of managing the state government; in addition to those already mentioned, he is authorized to fix limitations on the number of merit salary raises during the year, approve new positions, approve all contracts (including those for highways), issue regulations relating to official travel, approve departmental reorganization plans, and approve or reject compensation schedules submitted by the Civil Service Board. His staff or overhead activities include[27]:

> . . . the purchasing of all printing supplies and equipment and the usual job of renting and leasing all land, property and equipment; adopting standard specifications for all equipment and supplies; operating a central storeroom, central mimeograph and duplicating service; central mailing service, and central equipment repair shop; and custody of public buildings and assignment of office space to various departments and officials. He supervises the construction, maintenance and operation of all state power, lighting and heating plants, and also keeps a perpetual inventory of all state property and equipment and has the right to transfer or sell all surplus equipment. An architectural engineering division prepares plans for and supervises the building of state buildings as well as all major repair jobs. The division estimates for all repairs, construction and improvements included in the budget to the Legislature.

The experience of Michigan has been more or less parallel with that of Minnesota, and both show some similarity to the recent Federal experience, i.e., the passage of the Federal Property and Administrative Services Act of 1949 and the establishment of the General Services Administration to perform for all Federal operating agencies services comparable to those entrusted to the Commissioner of Administration in Minnesota and the State Con-

[27] Henderson, Harold L., "Seven Years' Experience with the Manager Plan in the State of Minnesota," *GRA Notes and References*, December 1945; for the history of the board, see the volume by Short and Tiller.

troller in Michigan. The Massachusetts Board, established in 1921, provided the pattern for both the Minnesota and the Michigan boards, the latter exercising largely theoretical control until 1948, when under Governor Kim Sigler a Department of Administration was created.

In the reorganization the Board was retained, apparently largely in adherence to tradition but supposedly stripped of its powers. Control over all the "tools of management" except personnel was given to the new Department of Administration, of which the Controller is head. This officer serves as secretary of the Board. The new Department has functioned under very trying circumstances; just after it was established, the governor who sponsored it was defeated at the polls, this defeat serving as a signal for political attacks upon it. The legislature became less friendly, was not too well informed. The new Governor Williams, however, appointed a similarly well-qualified man to the position of Controller, with the result that in a very short period of time considerable progress has been made.

"Greatest accomplishment of the Department of Administration," reports John A. Perkins, the first Controller, "is the integration effected in the work of its own divisions — particularly budgeting, accounting, purchasing, and building. Elimination of duplication, confused responsibility, and conflict between these activities could only be brought about when they were all made parts of one department responsible to a single head. When they were separate agencies with different heads, with no one to coordinate them, there was 'buck-passing' between them and differences in policy. This worked hardships upon the departments and institutions upon which they exerted their separate controls. New procedures and methods introduced by the Department of Administration have proved popular with other operating units of the state government. It is these agencies that are perhaps in the best position to judge the efficiency and effectiveness of centralized service and control activities." [28]

Concept of Continuous Management Planning. One of the most difficult aspects of reorganization heretofore has been to find some way of keeping a reorganized government reorganized. The use of the single shot, once-in-a-generation plan of reorganization leaves much to be desired. It does some good at the time but rarely achieves a completely reorganized and well-integrated governmental structure. And it provides no means of making further adjustments. It is these factors which have finally made us conscious of the fact that reorganization is and should be regarded as a continuous undertaking. Where a society is changing and developing and the government's program of activities is changing in response thereto, it stands to reason that adjustments in the administrative structure should be made at the same time.

[28] Perkins, John A., "State Management Limited," *National Municipal Review*, February 1950, pp. 72–78; Landers, Frank M., "Michigan Seeks Better Government," *State Government*, September 1948, pp. 184–188, 196–197; and Citizens Research Council of Michigan, *A Review of the Department of Administration* (Detroit, n.d.).

The only way to accomplish this purpose is to give the executive continuous authority to study the administrative structure and organization and to prepare proposals for its modification from time to time as need requires. Since reorganization itself is fundamentally much more of an executive than a legislative function, the responsibility for making these proposals should be vested in the governor as chief executive. The actual studies will be made by members of a management planning staff, working under his supervision and a part of his office. Thus there is a Division of Administrative Management in the Bureau of the Budget in the State of New York and in the Federal government in Washington. Virginia claims savings of $1,500,000 a year from its 1950 reorganization, and has created a permanent post to make the improvement process continuous.[29] The task can be attempted by legislative personnel and can be greatly facilitated by legislative action. The proposals made by the executive must, under our system of democratic government, be subject to legislative review. In some jurisdictions, such as California, New York, and Ohio — as has been noted — there exist special legislative committees or commissions, recreated each session, for the continuing study of administrative reorganization.

Improvements in Administrative Procedure. It is well known that government has grown greatly in size and complexity as more and more new functions have been added and old ones expanded. This growth has affected government in many ways, by no means the least important of which has been the growth and development of the system of administrative law and procedure. As the old-fashioned form of detailed legislation was gradually supplanted by the newer type outline legislation, the administrative departments and agencies had an ever-increasing responsibility in the formulation and promulgation of rules and regulations having the force and effect of law. These rules and regulations were of many different types. Some were largely expository and explanatory, telling what the law meant or what the enforcing agency thought it meant. Others supplemented, filled in, and rounded out the provisions of the law with a considerable amount of new material that was itself largely legislative in character. Still others were procedural, indicating simply what was to be done and how. These rules and regulations not only had to be made, they had to be applied and interpreted.

It was inevitable that in the development of a whole new system, difficulties would arise. Some agencies were careless in making known to the public the nature of their rules and regulations, sometimes even of the fact that such rules and regulations existed. This was bad under a legal system which proceeds on the assumption that ignorance of the law is no excuse. Under such circumstances one ought at least to be able to find out what the law is. In some cases there was no sufficient effort to differentiate between the investigatory and prosecuting function on the one hand and the adjudica-

[29] Pinchbeck, Raymond B., "Virginia Reorganizes Again," *National Municipal Review*, July 1950, pp. 339–343.

tory function on the other. Nor were agencies always sufficiently careful in the conduct of hearings, to see that the fundamental rights of citizens were observed.

These same problems arose at both the Federal and the state levels. The Federal Register Act was passed in 1935, and after prolonged discussion and

State Legislation Governing Administrative Procedures *

DATE	REQUIRING FILING OF RULES AND REGULATIONS WITH SECRETARY OF STATE (or other officer)	REQUIRING PUBLICATION OF RULES AND REGULATIONS	REQUIRING LEGISLATIVE APPROVAL OF RULES AND REGULATIONS	ADMINISTRATIVE PROCEDURE ACTS
1932	Massachusetts			.....
1937	.....	South Carolina	.....	.....
1938	South Dakota	.....	.....	.....
1939	Kansas [1]	Wisconsin	.....	North Carolina
	Oregon	.....	.....	.....
1941	California	California	Kansas	North Dakota
	North Dakota [2]	.....	.....	.....
	Ohio	.....	.....	.....
	Tennessee	.....	.....	.....
1942	Kentucky	Kentucky	.....	.....
1943	Indiana	Michigan	.....	Ohio
	Maryland [3]	Ohio	.....	Wisconsin
	Michigan	.....	.....	.....
	North Carolina	.....	.....	.....
1944	New York	New York	.....	Virginia
	.....	Virginia	.....	.....
1945	Connecticut	Connecticut	Connecticut	California
	Minnesota	Indiana	Nebraska	Illinois
	Missouri	Minnesota	.....	Minnesota
	Nebraska	Nebraska	.....	Pennsylvania
	Pennsylvania	Pennsylvania	.....	.....
1946	.....	Missouri	.....	Missouri
1947	.....	.....	Michigan	Indiana
1948	New Jersey [4]	New Jersey [4]		

* Based on Moreland, Carroll C., "State Administrative Rules," in *Book of the States, 1950–1951*, pp. 161–162.

[1] Filed with the Revisor of Statutes.

[2] Filed with the Attorney General.

[3] Filed with the Clerk of the Court of Appeals.

[4] This is the only state establishing a constitutional requirement; see Article V, Section 4: "No rule or regulation made by any department, officer, agency or authority of this State, except such as relates to the organization or internal management of the State government or a part thereof, shall take effect until it is filed either with the Secretary of State or in such other manner as may be provided by law. The Legislature shall provide for the prompt publication of such rules and regulations."

debate the Federal Administrative Procedures Act of 1946. These measures were aimed at (1) the central filing of administrative rules and regulations (except those having to do solely with matters relating to the internal management of the agency) and their publication in some established manner as a condition requisite to their enforcement, and (2) the establishment of standard procedures in the conduct of all administrative proceedings before hearing examiners or boards and commissions.

The same types of legislation were developing in the states during the same period and for precisely the same reasons. The names of the states and the years of adoption for each of these types of legislation are shown in the table which appears on page 392. Twenty states require central filing, fifteen require publication, and four require approval by the legislature. Eleven states have administrative procedures acts patterned more or less exactly after the Model Act.

SELECTED REFERENCES

An exhaustive state-by-state bibliography will be found in Buck, cited below. For more recent titles, see New Jersey Legislative Reference Section, *State Organization and Reorganization: a Bibliography* (State Library, Trenton, January 1948), and Weiner, Grace, *Administrative Reorganization of State Governments: a Bibliography* (Joint Reference Library, Chicago, 1941). This item is brought down to date by Yates, Marianne, and Gilchrist, Martha, *Administrative Reorganization of State Governments: a Bibliography* and *Administrative Reorganization of State Governments, 1948–1952: a Bibliography* (Council of State Governments, Chicago, August 1948 and May 1952, respectively).

Benson, George, C. S., and Litchfield, Edward H., *The State Administrative Board in Michigan* (Bureau of Government, University of Michigan, 1938). For another historical survey of this once popular method of central administrative control of fiscal matters by a plural executive, see Short, Lloyd M., and Tiller, Carl W., *The Minnesota Commission of Administration and Finance, 1925–1939* (University of Minnesota Press, 1942).

Connecticut Commission on State Government Organization, *The Report* (Hartford, 1950), and Puerto Rican Commission for Reorganization, *Report on the Reorganization of the Executive Branch of Government of Puerto Rico* (San Juan, 1949). These are two outstanding reports of the so-called "Little Hoover Commissions."

Council of State Governments, *Reorganizing State Government: A Report on Administrative Management in the States and a Review of Recent Trends in Reorganization* (Chicago, 1950). This excellent study largely supersedes such older works as: Buck, Arthur E., *The Reorganization of State Governments in the United States* (Columbia University Press, 1938) and, for a supplement, bringing the story down to 1947, Bollens, John C., *Administrative Reorganization in the United States Since 1939* (Bureau of Public Administration, University of California, 1947).

Fesler, James W., *The Independence of State Regulatory Agencies* (Public Administration Service, Chicago, 1942). An excellent analysis of the organization and functioning of these agencies.

Freund, Ernst, *Legislative Regulation* (Commonwealth Fund, New York, 1936). Analysis of the problem by a pioneer student of administrative law.

Graves, W. Brooke, *Public Administration in a Democratic Society* (Heath, Boston, 1950). Discusses more fully many of the problems mentioned in this chapter.

Hurt, Elsey, *California State Government: an Outline of Its Administrative Organization from 1850 to 1936* (State Printing Office, Sacramento, 1397–1939). A thorough study of the historical development of administrative organization in an important state over a period of nearly a century.

Michigan Joint Legislative Committee on Reorganization of State Government, *General Management of Michigan State Government* (Report No. 30, Lansing, November 1951). An outstanding report by one of the so-called "Little Hoover Commissions."

Missall, J. Ellsworth, *The Moreland Act: Executive Inquiry in the State of New York* (King's Crown Press, New York, 1946). Analyzes forty years of experience under a statute conferring broad investigatory powers upon the governor.

Scace, Homer E., *The Organization of the Executive Office of the Governor* (Institute of Public Administration, New York, 1950). A valuable compilation of information regarding the organization of the governors' offices, and an analysis of the problems relating thereto.

Symposium, "Administrative Agencies in Missouri," *University of Kansas City Law Review*, Symposium Issue, 1951, entire issue. Excellent survey of the executive branch in a state with a recently revised constitution.

11

The Military Establishment and Civilian Defense

Although it was once assumed that the function of national defense and security was a Federal responsibility, the military responsibilities of the states have come to be very great, in time of peace as well as in time of war. The governor is commander in chief of the National Guard of the state and has the authority to call it out when and if, in his judgment, it is necessary to do so for the protection of life and property. The development of the atom bomb and of other even more destructive weapons, and information that these are in the possession of other nations as well, make it prudent and necessary for the nation, the states, the cities, and the people themselves to give serious attention to civilian defense. Finally, consideration must be given to the great responsibilities of the states to their veterans of recent wars. The important responsibilities of the states in wartime, in cooperation with the Federal government, are considered in Chapter 24.

Military Powers of the Governor

The state constitutions have long provided that the governors should be responsible for enforcing the law and for quelling domestic violence. In New York, for instance, such provision has been in the state constitution since 1777. That first constitution merely carried into the fundamental law what had been a statutory provision since 1665. The major provisions were drawn in 1777, but between that date and 1894 the several sections of the article underwent considerable change. Two of the six sections came in for the first time in 1894, but since that date the article has remained unchanged.[1]

At the same time, there has been throughout our history, and there still is, a strong conviction that the civil authority should be superior to the military, in the states as well as in the nation. Our forefathers did not believe that a country could remain free if the military dominated the civil branch of government. When, for instance, General Charles Lee tried to impose a

[1] New York State Constitutional Convention Committee, *Problems Relating to Executive Administration and Powers*, being Vol. VII of the Committee's Report, pp. 80–81 (Albany, 1938).

loyalty test on the people of New York, Duane, Jay, Alsop, and Morris protested, warning the New York Provincial Convention in 1776 that "there can be no liberty where the military is not subordinate to civil power." [2] This view was expressed in the Constitutional Convention of 1787, and repeatedly since that time. There was a deep distrust of martial law which subsequent experience has done nothing to dispel.

Constitutional Powers. In all forty-eight states, the governor is designated as the commander in chief of the state militia; there are, however, provisions in the constitutions of some states limiting or defining his powers in this capacity. The constitutions of thirty states specify that he shall be commander in chief "except when they [the militia] shall be in the actual service of the United States." Eighteen states have no such limitation. Thirty-five states provide that the governor may call out the militia to repel invasion, execute the laws, and suppress rebellion; only thirteen do not grant this power in the constitution.[3] There are several minor limitations on the powers of the governors. In Kentucky, Maryland, and Vermont the governors are not allowed to command the militia in the field unless so advised by a resolution of the Senate or of the Legislature. In New Hampshire and Maine the governor is forbidden to lead the militia out of the state without the consent of the people or the Legislature. In Alabama and Missouri the constitutions declare that the governor need not command in the field unless so directed by the Legislature.

Preserving the Peace. In so-called normal times the duties of the governor in this connection have not been very exacting; while it has always been possible for him to call out troops and place a troubled area under martial law, it has rarely been necessary for him to do so. Quite the opposite was true in the era of the depression, during which strikes and outbreaks of disorder were frequent. In the decade of the thirties, calling out the troops came to be a common occurrence; the practice was not confined to any one state or section of the country, nor was it attributable to the peculiarities of any particular governor. The United States District Court in Minneapolis, in a decision in 1934, upholding the use of troops by Governor Olson in a labor disturbance, used the following significant words:

> Military rule is preferable under almost any circumstances to mob rule. . . . We are not prepared to find that the Governor's orders have no relation whatever to the necessities of the situation with which he is confronted and fall entirely outside the range of his discretion. While we may personally disagree

[2] New York State Library, *New York State Freedom Train: Official Document Book*, p. 16 (Albany, 1950); Smith, Louis, *American Democracy and Military Power*, Chapter 18 on what he calls "the obsolete role of the states in the restraint of military power" (University of Chicago Press, 1951), and Tansill, William R., *The Concept of Civil Supremacy over the Military in the United States* (Public Affairs Bulletin No. 93, Legislative Reference Service, Library of Congress, Washington, 1951).

[3] These are: Arizona, Connecticut, Delaware, Georgia, Iowa, Kentucky, Maine, New Jersey, New York, Pennsylvania, Rhode Island, Vermont, and Wisconsin. This paragraph is based on the New York report, *op. cit.*, pp. 21–22.

with the Governor as to the manner in which he has handled the entire situation, that will not justify the relief prayed for.

State troops, called out by proclamation of the governor, perform a wide variety of duties in addition to preserving the peace; they protect governors' families, hunt escaped prisoners, patrol summer camps, seek missing persons, and protect public property. There was a time when management was frequently able to bring about their intervention in strike situations. The use of troops when necessary to protect life and property is a legitimate public use; their use to aid an incumbent in office to maintain control or extend his political influence is, to say the least, questionable. In the interval between the two world wars such uses of troops were not uncommon, being made, apparently, without any strong public protest. It is reassuring to note that such incidents have been much less common since World War II, for events in Europe provide abundant proof — if any were required — that the unnecessary and unjustified use of troops is not only unwise but actually dangerous to the liberties of the people.[4]

In the late forties, a number of serious strike situations developed, involving threats to the public peace and calling for the use of troops. In May 1948, Governor Youngdahl of Minnesota was obliged to use the National Guard in connection with a packinghouse strike in St. Paul. At the same time, Governor Blue of Iowa had to use the Guard in connection with the same kind of strike in Waterloo. In August, Governor Herbert of Ohio asked the Adjutant General "to preserve law and order" by sending troops into Dayton in connection with the Univis Lens Company strike, as requested by the Mayor. In August, 1949, Governor Dewey declined, however, to send either state police or the militia to the strike-bound Bell Aircraft Corporation plant in Buffalo.

Disaster Relief. The governors have important responsibilities in the field of disaster relief — fire, blizzards, floods, tornadoes or drought, earthquakes or other natural causes. While such situations may be met in part through utilization of the machinery established for civil defense, they may also require the use of the military powers of the governor, if life and property are to be given adequate protection. The adjutant general's office — along with the state police and numerous other departments and agencies — has a key place in any state-aid plan. Even martial law may be necessary in times of great emergency. In one state, martial law has been in effect as many as seven times in ten years, and during one year it was invoked thirty-two times throughout the country. In many instances, however, a properly organized and equipped disaster relief agency would, in all probability, make the declaration of martial law unnecessary.[5]

[4] See New York report, *op. cit.*, Chapter 4; Sterling, Governor of Texas, et al. v. Constantin, et al., 287 U.S. 378, 1932, and Fairman, Charles, *The Law of Martial Rule*, Second Edition (Callaghan, Chicago, 1943).

[5] See "The States and Disaster Relief," *State Government*, September 1949, pp. 220–221, 228; Cookingham, L. P., "A Plan to Meet Disaster," *National Municipal Review*,

Such plans have become necessary because of the number and frequency of serious catastrophes, and the inability of local agencies to deal with them without assistance. Twenty-seven major disasters have been listed by Federal authorities since 1947, and numerous others occurring prior to that date may readily be recalled. On a somewhat smaller scale, railroad wrecks, tunnel and mine cave-ins, explosions, fires, tidal waves, and storms are frequently so damaging and destructive that local authorities are required to call on state agencies for aid and relief.

The disaster agency provided for in the model bill, based in part on legislation in effect during World War II, calls for the necessary state and local organizations, under the direction of the governor, to deal with such situations when they occur. As in the case of civil defense (see pp. 403–412), provision must be made for advanced planning, for procurement of supplies and equipment, for the planning of training and public information programs, for the emergency use of supplies and equipment, and for the making of mutual aid agreements. In some states the legislation has been put on a stand-by basis, while in others provision is made for a permanent agency to tackle such problems when the need arises.[6]

A very serious problem that arose during World War II seems certain to recur again. When the National Guard units were sworn in as a part of the armed forces of the United States, the states were left without any organization that could be called upon to protect life and property in case of emergency. It was necessary, therefore, for the states to recruit a new force. New York, for instance, organized a substitute Home Guard which, due to manpower shortages, consisted chiefly of older men and of those rejected for service in the armed forces of the United States. In 1950 New York again moved, under existing legislation, to set up an emergency army, a force of some 30,000 state and private highway and public utility workers to clear roads and maintain services in case of bombing attack by an enemy anywhere in the state.[7]

February 1952, pp. 74–79; and Moore, Lyman S., "How Well Are States and Cities Prepared for the Emergency?" *Public Administration Review*, Spring 1951, pp. 81–87; Schubert, Glendon A., Jr., "For Defense or Disaster," *National Municipal Review*, June 1952, pp. 294–299. For a specific example, see *New York Times*, August 27, 1950, containing the story of a forest fire crisis in California where, in the most destructive fire since 1924, 140,000 acres of timberlands and watershed in the national forests of the state were destroyed, at an estimated loss of $4,450,000.

[6] As of March, 1950, disaster preparedness laws were in effect in Hawaii and the Virgin Islands, and in seventeen states: California, Indiana, Maine, Maryland, Montana, Nebraska, New Hampshire, New Jersey, Ohio, Oregon, South Dakota, Vermont. World War II legislation continues in effect in five states: Florida, Idaho, Michigan, Nevada, and Rhode Island. Disaster preparedness plans prepared by executive direction exist in a few other states, as for example, Illinois. See Joint Committee on Atomic Energy, *Hearings on Civil Defense Against Atomic Attack*, Part I, p. 7 (81st Cong. 2nd Sess., 1950).

[7] *New York Times*, July 25, 1950, and August 25, 1950.

The National Guard

In keeping with the tradition of many centuries on both sides of the Atlantic, the states early made provision for the establishment and maintenance of militia. As time passed, the state militia was transformed into the National Guard.[8] The National Guard has, in fact, had the longest continuous history of any military organization in the United States, its origin going back to the 192nd Infantry of Massachusetts, organized in 1636. Another historic regiment, the 176th Infantry of Virginia, goes back to 1652. These and similar units have served with distinction in every major conflict in which the nation has participated.

History and Development. The name "National Guard" appears to have been first employed on August 16, 1824 when, as a compliment to the visiting Lafayette, New York applied it to the units of its state militia. By 1896 only three states still retained the word "militia" in their official designations. With the well-nigh universal use of the term "National Guard," however, it should be remembered that the change in name did not alter the essential characteristics of the Guard as state organizations. On June 30, 1916, also in New York, there occurred the establishment of the first unit of what has now become the Air National Guard.

After the distressing experiences of the American army in Cuba, Secretary of War Elihu Root instituted a general program to reorganize the military establishment, one portion of which called for joint support of the National Guard by the Federal government and the states. With this assistance, the National Guard developed into well-organized and adequately trained regiments. Under the National Defense Act of June 3, 1916, the Guard brought 380,095 men into the Federal service in World War I, two fifths of the Divisions of the AEF being National Guard Divisions. As amended in 1920, this act officially re-established the organized militia as the National Guard, the organization being made to conform to that of the Regular Army. Thus the Guard became a component part of the organized peacetime establishment.

In 1933, under new legislation, the National Guard of the United States was made a component part of the Army. As stated by the Department of Defense, the National Guard of the United States, identical in personnel and organization with the National Guard of the states, "is the designation used to indicate the Guard's Federal mission for the defense and security of the United States." By joint resolution of Congress in 1940, the National

[8] This comment is based largely on a pamphlet, *Welcome to the New National Guard*, from which quotations are taken (National Guard Bureau. Washington, 1950); see also a number of wartime studies of these problems: Beckwith, Edmund R., and others, *Lawful Action of State Military Forces* (Random House, New York, 1944), and "Laws Relating to State Military Power," *State Government*, March 1943, pp. 57–58, 75–77; Colby, Elbridge, and Glass, James F., "The Legal Status of the National Guard," *Virginia Law Review*, May 1943, pp. 839–856; Council of State Governments, "War Powers of Governors," *State Government*, February 1942, pp. 39–40, 46–47.

Guard was ordered into active military service, induction being completed the following year. In the words of Robert P. Patterson, Secretary of War:

> The National Guard took to the field eighteen infantry divisions — 300,000 men. Those state troops doubled the strength of the Army at once, and their presence in the field gave the country a sense that it had passed the lowest ebb of its weakness. . . . Nine of those divisions crossed the Atlantic to Europe and Africa and nine went to the far reaches of the Pacific. The soldiers of the Guard fought in every action in which the Army participated from Bataan to Okinawa. They made a brilliant record on every fighting front. They proved once more the value of the trained citizen-soldier.

Theoretical and Constitutional Basis. The theory of the National Guard was well stated by President George Washington when he told the First Congress that "every citizen who enjoys the protection of a free government owes not only a portion of his property but even of his personal services to the defense of it." In the early period, the colonists believed it to be their right to form these local protective organizations; when the Constitution was framed, protection of this basic right was sought when it was provided in Article I, Section 8:

> The Congress shall have power . . . to provide for calling forth the Militia to execute the Laws of the Union, Suppress Insurrections, and repel invasion;
>
> To provide for organizing, arming and disciplining, the Militia, and for governing such Part of them as may be employed in the Service of the United States, reserving to the States, respectively, the Appointment of the Officers and the Authority of training the Militia according to the discipline prescribed by the Congress.

And a few years later, when the Bill of Rights was added to the Constitution, it was further provided in Amendment II that "A well regulated Militia, being necessary to the security of a free State, the right of the people to keep and bear Arms, shall not be infringed." To this day, in spite of many changes in organization, the National Guard retains many of its original characteristics as a local organization, in the various units of which the states and communities take great pride.

Guard Organization. In all forty-eight states the governor is designated as the commander in chief of the National Guard; there are, however, — as has been noted — constitutional provisions which limit or define his powers. The chief of the state headquarters is the adjutant general, the military adviser to the governor. In most states this officer is appointed by the governor, but in the territories and in the District of Columbia, by the President. Just as the Secretary of Defense and the Secretaries of the three armed services are responsible to the President for the maintenance of the armed forces of the nation, so the adjutant general is responsible to the governor. There is, however, one important difference. In the Federal government there is a time-honored tradition of civilian direction of the military departments, while in the states the position is filled by a high ranking officer.

Under present legislation the National Guard has been allotted a troop basis of 692,000, a strength nearly four times that of the prewar Guard.

Army units of the Guard have an ultimate strength of 635,000 men, Air units, 57,000. This troop basis includes major organizations among the 5,500 Army units for such normal components as infantry, armored, and artillery divisions or groups. In addition there are numerous combat support units, including Field Artillery, Armored Cavalry, Engineer, Quartermaster, Signal Corps, Military Police, and Transportation units. The Air units, on the troop basis, include such major organizations as fighter wings, fighter groups, light bombardment groups, and aircraft control and warning groups. Each Wing is supported by Aviation Engineer, Construction, Maintenance, Communication, Radar, and Service units.

The governor is responsible for the organization and maintenance of the National Guard, as well as for its training and general well-being. The first duty devolves upon him as governor, the second as commander in chief of the armed forces of the state. The military establishment of the states includes arsenals, and material and equipment for many thousands of men. In addition, the state governments are the custodians under Federal law of millions of dollars' worth of supplies and equipment. Few people realize the extensiveness of this organization. In 1949, the Minnesota Guard had 104 Army units and eleven Air units in sixty-six cities and towns — 115 in all. The Department of Military Affairs in Pennsylvania had, even before World War II, custody of approximately $25,000,000 worth of Federal property.

This property was distributed throughout the Commonwealth in some seventy-three separate armories, which served as training headquarters for nearly 150 infantry, cavalry, and other local military units. These armories represent a vast investment and involve large regular expenditures for maintenance. In addition to the extensive assistance of the Federal authorities, the Commonwealth is obliged to make still further investments in order to secure the needed equipment and supplies.

It was estimated in 1949 that the value of the state owned armories and facilities used by the New York Naval Militia alone was $1,800,000, while that of the Federally owned armories and facilities amounted to some $3,000,000. The cost to New York State to maintain these several armories, facilities, full-time personnel, and various military funds runs around $350,000 annually — for this one segment of the whole program.[9] Even before the intense effort to strengthen the nation's defenses was undertaken after the attack on Korea in 1950, the Federal government had been building up the National Guard, enlarging its authorized personnel, and constructing some 1500 new armories at a cost of approximately $600,000,000. The operation and maintenance of these properties alone added considerably to the financial burden of the states for purposes of defense.

A number of states, including New York and Pennsylvania, operate

[9] New York Joint Legislative Committee to Study the Military Law, *Second Interim Report*, pp. 39–40 (Legislative Document No. 58, Albany, 1949).

maritime schools and colleges for the training of officers for the merchant marine. The New York State Maritime College, founded at Fort Schuyler over seventy-five years ago, and a state institution since 1913, is now a full-time professional college in the State University system. The Works Progress Administration rebuilt the old fort at a cost of $4,500,000, with the result that during World War II the college, with an accelerated program, provided the merchant marine with nearly 2000 officers.[10]

A full state military program includes the National Guard, Naval Militia, State Guard, and State Militia. The organization, training, and equipment of many thousands of such troops involves keeping records of drill attendance and of the physical condition of officers and men, making efficiency reports, issuing payroll requisitions, and keeping war records. The department of the adjutant general or of military affairs — whatever it may be called — must account for and preserve Federal military property and stores; it must maintain and repair state armories, operate homes for destitute soldiers and sailors, and perform such other duties as rendering assistance to veterans in presenting claims against the Federal government, administering state funds for the relief of impoverished war veterans, and determining the amount of relief to be paid to guardsmen who are wounded or otherwise disabled while in active service.

In the years after World War II the question of segregation in the National Guard was a hotly debated issue. The practice of excluding Negroes from the Guard in some states, or of accepting them only for service in separate units in others, was of long standing. In 1947 the New Jersey Constitutional Convention incorporated in its draft the following provision, which marked a sharp break with tradition and previous practice:

> No person shall be denied the enjoyment of any civil or military right, nor be discriminated against in the exercise of any civil or military right, nor be segregated in the militia or in the public schools, because of religious principles, race, color, ancestry or national origin. (Article I, Section 6)

New York followed in 1948, with seven more states — California, Connecticut, Illinois, Massachusetts, Minnesota, Pennsylvania, Wisconsin — in 1949. These developments, along with parallel steps taken by the Department of Defense at the Federal level, indicate a definite trend toward the elimination of discrimination in the armed forces based on race or color.

Functions of the Guard. The function of the National Guard in the national defense program as a whole was well stated in the Approved Policies of 1945:

> To provide sufficient organizations in each state so trained and equipped as to enable them to function efficiently at existing strength in the protection of life and property and the preservation of peace, order, and public safety, under competent orders of the state authorities.
>
> To provide a reserve component of the Army and Air Force of the United States, capable of immediate expansion to war strength, able to furnish units

[10] *New York Times*, December 18, 1949.

fit for service anywhere in the world, trained and equipped to defend critical areas of the United States against attack, to assist in covering the mobilization and concentration of the reserve forces, and to participate in all types of operations.

The units of the National Guard, an integral part of the national armed forces, are located throughout the forty-eight states, Alaska, Hawaii, Puerto Rico, and the District of Columbia. In any period of national emergency, as determined by the President or as declared by the Congress — whenever the United States is invaded or in danger of invasion, whenever there is rebellion against the authority of the Federal government, or whenever he is unable to execute the laws of the United States with the regular forces at his command — the President may call the National Guard into the Federal service.

Civilian Defense

An understanding of and a firm belief in the principles of the American system may well be viewed as a prerequisite of any effective civil defense program. In the modern world the job of defense can no longer be regarded as the sole responsibility of the Federal government, for the states, the counties, the cities, and the individual citizen each have a vital part to play. If, in a democratic society, citizens are to cooperate in the common defense, they must know what it is they are defending, and understand why the task is worthy of their best effort.

Definition and Basic Principles. There has been a vast amount of misunderstanding — accompanied in some cases by hysteria, in others by apathy — on the subject of civilian defense. This misunderstanding has related both to what it is and what should be done about it. Whereas, in World War II, civil defense meant, primarily, the protection of one's own family, block, or city from destruction, it means today, according to the *Bulletin of the Atomic Scientists*,[11] "an organized effort of the population as a whole to keep the country as a whole a going concern." The phrase was defined in the Hopley report as encompassing "the entire field of passive defense — as distinguished from active defense, which is the function of the Armed Forces — in saving lives and restoring communities, industrial plants and facilities of all kinds." [12] Two years later the National Security Resources Board stated that civil defense could be defined "as the protection of the home front by civilians acting under civil authority to minimize casualties and war damage and preserve maximum civilian support of the war effort." [13]

In view of the unsettled state of the popular mind, it may be well to consider a program formulated within the framework of four basic principles

[11] Special issue on "Civil Defense Against Atomic Attack," August-September 1950.

[12] Office of Civil Defense Planning, *Civil Defense for National Security*, p. 3 (Washington, 1948).

[13] *United States Civil Defense*, p. 3 (Washington, 1950).

suggested by the Hon. Chet Holifield, Member of the Joint Atomic Energy Commission, who has given serious study to the problem[14]:

> 1. The measures must be practical: we cannot allow ourselves to become panicky and resort to fantastic and impossible schemes.
>
> 2. The major part of the work must be done locally: we want no top-heavy bureaucratic control in Washington imposing orders on everybody.
>
> 3. Civilian defense must be managed by civilians: this job is too far-reaching in its impact, too close to the daily lives of our citizenry, to be delegated to the military.
>
> 4. — and implicit in the three preceding principles — civilian defense must be carried out in the American, democratic way: with the new possibilities of atomic warfare have come new burdens which strain our resources and our institutions to the utmost.

There are additional principles which serve, to a certain extent, as limitations in the planning of a civil defense program. It must utilize existing facilities to the utmost, for a program which costs too much in money and materials would defeat its own purpose, detracting from the defense effort itself urgently needed support. It must rely primarily on civilian help and to a large extent on volunteer service, for to do otherwise would draw off needed manpower from the armed services and the defense effort.

Civil Defense Organization. The Federal government having established a national civil defense plan with accompanying basic policies, the operating responsibility for the program rests with the states. As the National Security Resources Board observes[15]:

> The responsibility of the state government is to provide leadership and supervision in all planning for civil defense, and direction of supporting operations in an emergency. The state is the key operating unit. It is the "field army" of civil defense. Its counties and cities are its "divisions." When one or more divisions are hard hit, the remaining ones are sent in for support — over and above the capabilities of local self-help and mutual aid.

This is a wise policy, in keeping with the basic concepts of the American federal system. Within the states, responsibility rests with the governor, but a full-time civil defense director should be appointed on the governor's staff to head the state organization. "The mission and functions of a state civil defense headquarters," stated the Hopley Report, "are primarily of staff supervisory and technical advisory nature, inasmuch as many of the actual field operations will take place in the local organization. The civil defense headquarters should direct and coordinate all civil defense activities within the state, promulgate methods and techniques in accordance with established policies, and evaluate all civil defense needs within the state in relation to each other." The responsibilities of each level of government are clearly indicated in the chart on page 406. The same report continues:

> A state civil defense organization should be established, which contemplates the full utilization of existing state governmental agencies, such as Office of

[14] "'Tin Hat' Antique in Civilian Defense," *Washington Post*, April 21, 1950, and reprinted in *Congressional Record*, May 22, 1950, pp. A4070–A4071.

[15] *Op. cit.*, p. 5.

State Police, Adjutant General's Department or State Guard, Department of Health, Department of Public Welfare, Office of State Fire Marshal, Department of Highways, Department of Public Works and Buildings, Department of Agriculture, Department of Education, and Office of the Attorney General, insofar as they relate to civil defense operations, supplemented by such additionally created agencies as Communications, Transportation, Administration, Planning, Biological Defense, Chemical Defense, Other Special Weapons Defense, Evacuation, Mutual Aid and Mobile Reserves, Public Information, Training, Warden Services, Fire Services, Police Services, Medical and Health Services, Civilian War Aid, Air Raid Warning and Aircraft Observer, Engineering, and Plant Protection Divisions, as are necessary to carry out effectively the total civil defense mission.

The Director of Civil Defense should be an official of cabinet rank and should head the state civil defense organization as an executive department of the state government. Acting for the governor and subject to his orders, he should have authority to direct state civil defense operations and, in addition, to coordinate all civil defense activities within the state, between his state and other states, and with the appropriate representatives of the Federal civil defense agency. (See New Jersey charts, pp. 407 and 408.)

Both the Hopley and the National Security Resources Board Reports recommend an advisory council with membership representing private citizens and government departments as well as the more important functions or skills required in civil defense planning, such as the following, provided for in the New Jersey setup:

Government	Public Health
Transportation	Medical
Organization and Management	Chemical
Communications	Public Welfare
Public Works	Police
Engineering	Fire

Such a council, though of a purely advisory character, should be of material assistance to the governor and the director of civil defense in the formulation of policy. The two major reports both recommend also that the director be assisted by a number of deputy directors having administrative supervision over such matters as:

All forms of communications and transportation
Plant protection, fire and police services
Medical and health services, chemical defense
Evacuation and civilian war aid
Administration, planning, public information, training

These deputies would serve both to provide leadership for these various groupings of related services and to provide alternate leadership for twenty-four-hour duty at the control centers in emergencies, as well as a succession of command in event of the unavailability of the director or his immediate deputy.

Statutory Basis of Civilian Defense. In order to meet the requirements of the Federal civil defense program, a careful review of existing legislation in

RESPONSIBILITIES FOR CIVIL DEFENSE PLANNING *

Executive Office of the President

National Security Resources Board

1. Coordination of all civil defense planning
2. Transmittal of plans, programs, policies, advice, and assistance to state governments
3. Studies and recommendations on dispersion policies and programs
4. Advice to the President on the status of civil defense planning and recommendations for changes in basic civil defense policies
5. Relation of civil defense requirements to broad aspects of mobilization planning

Other Federal Departments and Agencies
to Whom Civil Defense Duties Are Assigned

Department of Defense	General Services Administration
Atomic Energy Commission	Department of the Interior
Federal Security Agency	Housing and Home Finance Agency
Department of Commerce	Other departments and agencies

State Governments

1. Cooperation with military services on active defense measures which require civilian participation
2. Air raid warnings to local communities
3. Aid, advice, and assistance to local communities on:
   a. Protective measures required before attack
   b. Measures to alleviate and control damage after attack
4. Cooperation with other states on mutual aid

Local Governments

1. Appraisal of community requirements and resources to meet local civil defense needs
2. Development of plans and programs for:
   a. Protective measures required before attack
   b. Measures to alleviate and control damage after attack
3. Recruitment of civilian personnel for participation in active military defense
4. Cooperation with other communities in mutual aid

* Adapted from Atomic Energy Commission, *Civil Defense Against Atomic Attack: Preliminary Data*, p. 7 (Washington, 1950).

the states was necessary, as well as the preparation of far more complete state and local legislation than had ever before been necessary. As has been observed, numerous states had enacted disaster control legislation or statutes to create a planning agency to develop defense plans. Sixteen of the civil defense acts of World War II were still on the statute books. Civil defense, as now conceived, was to a large extent an unknown science when this legislation was enacted. The current legislation is the outgrowth of this earlier experience plus long years of study and investigation; it has been necessary

New Jersey Civil Defense Plan* (1950)

STATE DIRECTOR OF CIVIL DEFENSE

DEPUTY DIRECTOR OF CIVIL DEFENSE

ADMINISTRATIVE OFFICER	SECURITY OFFICER	OPERATIONS OFFICER	SUPPLY OFFICER	WELFARE OFFICER	AIR RAID WARNING OFFICER
Recruiting Records Liaison Army Navy Air Force Coast Guard Government and Civil Agencies Public Administration Press Radio Television Public Education	Police Wardens Chemical Bomb Disposal Traffic Control	Planning Training Fire Organization Road Clearance Rescue Crews Communications Telephone Teletype Television Radio Messenger Emergency Water Supply Civil Defense Battalions	Supplies and Equipment Demolition and Clearance Public Works Gas Electric Power Potable Water Transportation	Evacuation Registration Transportation of People Emergency Welfare Feeding and Housing Public Health Medical Emergency Medical Services Hospitals First Aid Evacuation of Casualties Collection Identification Registration and Burial of the Dead	Organization Training Observation Posts Warning Devices Reporting System

*From State Department of Defense, *Civil Defense Plan* (Trenton, 1950).

New Jersey Civil Defense Plan* (1950)

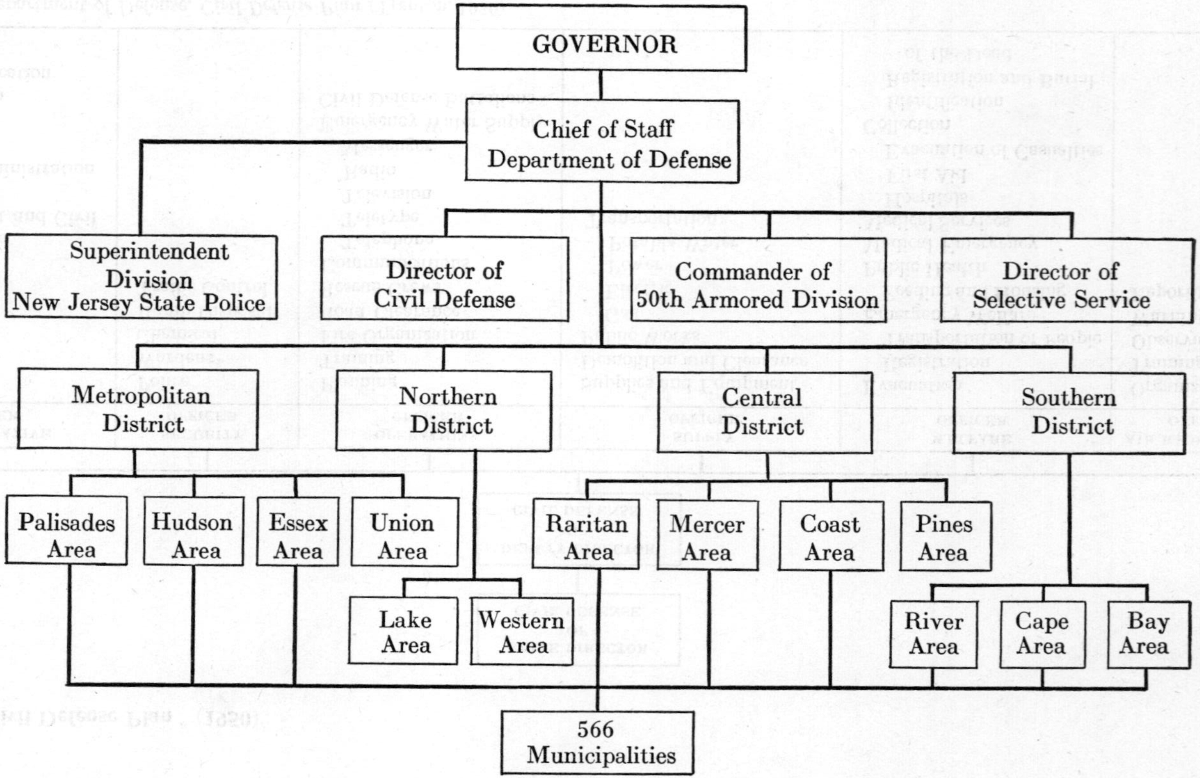

in order to correct the inadequacies and deficiencies of previous legislation.

In 1950, when an intensive drive was undertaken both by the Federal government and by the Council of State Governments at the Tenth Assembly of the States in Chicago in November,[16] there were two major drafts of proposed legislation before the states. The first of these, drawn by the Drafting Committee of the Council of State Governments in 1949, was evolved out of World War II experience; the second was drawn in 1950 by the National Security Resources Board. In most important respects, the two drafts were similar, the major difference between them being with regard to the powers conferred upon the governor. In this respect the NSRB draft went much farther than that prepared by the Drafting Committee of the Council. The Federal authorities contended that these extensive grants of power to the governor were necessary; the legal officers of the states, that the grants were impossible in many jurisdictions under existing constitutional provisions. New legislation on the subject, in general conformity with one pattern or the other, was enacted in virtually all the states by the conclusion of the 1951 legislative sessions.

The nature and scope of the program is indicated in the enumeration of the civil defense powers conferred upon the governor, who in the performance of his duties of general direction and control, is authorized and empowered to:

1. Make, amend, and rescind the necessary orders, rules, and regulations to carry out the provisions of the act
2. Prepare a comprehensive and integrated plan and program for the civil defense of the state
3. Ascertain the requirements of the state or its political subdivisions for food, clothing, or other necessities of life or for medical and surgical equipment and supplies, in the event of attack, and to plan for and procure such supplies
4. Cooperate with the President and the heads of the Armed Forces, and the civil defense agency of the United States, and with the officers and agencies of other states in matters pertaining to the civil defense of the state and nation, including black-outs, screening or extinguishing of lights, warnings and signals for drills or attacks, and many other related matters
5. Take such action and give such directions to state and local law enforcement officers and agencies as may be reasonable and necessary for the purpose of securing compliance with the provisions of the act and with the orders, rules, and regulations made pursuant thereto
6. Employ such measures and give such directions to the state or local boards of health as may be reasonably necessary for the purpose of securing compliance with the provisions of the act
7. Utilize the services and facilities of existing officers and agencies of the state and of the political subdivisions thereof and to direct the cooperation of such officers with other civil defense agencies

16 Three important resolutions on civil defense were adopted: (1) calling for prompt enactment of basic Federal civil defense legislation; (2) calling for similar action by all states; (3) calling for state legislation providing for the indemnification of volunteer personnel who may be injured or killed in the performance of their duties.

8. Establish agencies and offices and to appoint executive, technical, clerical, and other personnel as may be necessary to carry out the provisions of the act

9. Delegate any authority vested in him under the act, and to provide for the subdelegation of such authority

10. On behalf of the state to enter into reciprocal or mutual aid agreements or compacts with other states and the Federal government, either on a statewide basis or local political subdivisions basis or with a neighboring state or province of a foreign country

11. Sponsor and develop mutual aid plans and agreements between the political subdivisions of the state, similar to the mutual aid arrangements with other states referred to above

The emergency powers of the governor are to be invoked only in the case of actual enemy attack. If the states do enact these provisions, martial law will be unnecessary in an emergency period. Included among these powers are the authority to enforce all laws, rules, and regulations relating to civil defense and to assume direct operational control of all civil defense forces and helpers in the state; to seize, take, or condemn property for the protection of the public, and to sell, lend, give, or distribute such property among the inhabitants of the state. Provision is made for the compensation of the owners of property taken under the provisions of this legislation and for the submission of accounts by the governor to the state treasurer covering all transactions taking place under the act.

It cannot be too strongly emphasized that, in the last analysis, civil defense is a civilian matter and it is a local matter. The job must be done in the communities where the people live and in which, it may be assumed, the damage will be done. The Federal government is dependent upon the states, and the states upon the communities, each of which must have its own plan developed on the basis of local conditions. No stereotyped plan can be made for any community at the state level.[17] The Federal act authorizes agreements between states, and between states and the provinces of adjoining countries. In September 1950, the Governors of New York and New Jersey signed the first interstate mutual aid agreement. Many more may be expected in the years ahead.

It would be difficult to overemphasize the importance of the mutual aid principle and of the agreements formulated to make it effective. As James M. Landis has observed, "The central problem of civilian defense is the rapid mobilization of matériel and personnel to the point or points of disaster." Since it is obviously impossible under existing conditions for any community to provide complete protection against possible enemy attack for its entire population, it is vital to the program as a whole that every community be in a position to supply aid promptly in the form of rescue teams, medical aid,

[17] Miller, E. B., "Civil Defense Needs Local Cooperation," *Minnesota Municipalities*, May 1950, pp. 146–148. For a survey of the situation as of the end of 1950, see Hanks, Donah W., Jr., and Blundred, Robert H., *The Status of Civil Defense in American Cities* (American Municipal Association, Chicago, 1950).

and supplies to any stricken neighboring community. Where this involves crossing jurisdictional lines, it is necessary that provision be made in advance for interstate recognition of professional licenses, for the compensation of voluntary personnel injured in course of such rescue work, and for similar matters.[18]

Situation as of July 1952. Early in January 1951, Congress enacted the Federal Civil Defense Act, and the President established the Civil Defense Administration under the leadership of former Governor Millard F. Caldwell of Florida. Every state had enacted civil defense legislation or had established a civil defense organization by executive direction. In sixteen states civil defense statutes enacted during World War II were still presumably in effect. Twenty-one states passed new civil defense laws in 1949 and 1950. In eleven states, civil defense planning was initiated under executive order. In forty states the governor was specifically vested with overall authority for civil defense administration; in seven of those remaining, these responsibilities rested ultimately in civil defense councils or commissions, while in one it was vested in the adjutant general.

Advisory councils of varying composition, but ordinarily appointed by the governor, had been generally established. In most states the director of civil defense, either appointed by the governor or selected by the defense council, is responsible for administration. Approximately twenty states employ their adjutants general as directors of civil defense; the remainder have civilian directors. A well-balanced program requires web defense, mutual aid, and mobile support, and some provision has been made for all three. Most of the states provide for comprehensive mutual aid programs between their political subdivisions, and some are empowered to extend mutual aid not only to their own local units but to communities in other states as well. Mobile support units to supply emergency aid to stricken areas are authorized in about one-third of the states, with indications that the movement is spreading.[19]

Progress in translating legislation into an efficient program capable of providing maximum protection in case of need has been slow and faltering. Although carefully prepared plans, based on European experience during World War II, had been prepared, there was a widespread apathy among the public. The program was admittedly a costly one; states and cities, already under severe financial pressure, professed their inability to finance it without substantial Federal assistance, and Congress seemed strangely unwilling to

[18] See Dreyfuss, Leonard, "Interstate Civil Defense Cooperation," together with the text of the New York-New Jersey Mutual Aid Agreement, *State Government*, November 1950, pp. 246–247, 257.

[19] See "Civil Defense in the States," *State Government*, November 1950, pp. 237–245, 257, for a state-by-state summary of progress up to that time; also a table compiled by the National Security Resources Board and the American Law Section, Legislative Reference Service, Library of Congress, "State Civil Defense Legislation" (Washington, August 15, 1950).

appropriate the funds necessary to finance it. It appeared that, once again, disaster would have to strike before either the public or their elected representatives could be aroused. Then the costs would be far greater and the effort less effective. And it might even be too late.[20]

The States and the Veteran

Although the Federal government has indicated in the terms of the Selective Service Act, the G.I. Bill of Rights, and the Starnes-Scrugham Act of 1945 that it intends to see that all necessary steps are taken to protect the interests of returning veterans, the states also have a responsibility. In recognition thereof, old veteran legislation has been revised in most states and new legislation enacted. New administrative agencies have been created, to the end that the states should be in a position to do everything possible to supplement the Federal effort.

At the end of the war the veteran problem, so far as the states were concerned, involved the community responsibility for giving information, advice, and assistance to the returning serviceman or woman; provision for rehabilitation, including both hospitalization and training or re-training; the problem of employment or re-employment, including the finding of new jobs, reinstatement in old ones, and preference in the state service; and finally, provision for grants, bonuses, and financial assistance, including temporary or emergency relief for the veteran and his family.

In the postwar years these major problems of a temporary and immediate nature have given way to new ones — problems of the long run, in connection with the solution of which the states have enacted a vast amount of legislation dealing with an amazing variety of subject matter. For convenience these scores of enactments may be grouped under some half a dozen headings dealing with such matters as civic recognition of the contribution of the serviceman; veteran organizations; benefits of various sorts, including bonuses and pensions, educational benefits, and health benefits; exemptions and exceptions during and after service, particularly with regard to tax liability; consideration in employment, both public and private; legal considerations

[20] See Prentiss, A. M., *Civil Defense in Modern War* (McGraw-Hill, New York, 1951); Lohr, Lenox R., "Civil Defense in Illinois," *Public Aid in Illinois*, August 1951, pp. 14–15; Heslep, Charter, "Radio's Role in Defense," *Tennessee Planner*, February 1951, pp. 110–119. A good deal of work has been done on civil defense planning in particular fields: HEALTH: symposium in *American Journal of Public Health*, February 1952, pp. 115–133. HIGHWAYS: Holland, Lon E., "Highway Transportation in the National Defense Emergency," *County Officer*, March 1951, pp. 71–73, 80, and Matson, T. M., "Highway Traffic in Civil Defense," *Traffic Quarterly*, July 1951, pp. 272–281. PUBLIC UTILITIES: Feinberg, Benjamin F., "Public Utilities and Civil Defense," *Public Utilities Fortnightly*, November 30, 1950, pp. 727–734. WELFARE: Bevier, Alden E., "Planning the Welfare Services in Civil Defense," *Public Welfare*, December 1950, pp. 222–225, and Craine, Marion K., "Welfare Planning for Civil Defense in Illinois," *Public Aid in Illinois*, December 1951, pp. 3–7.

or benefits; provisions with regard to war records; and provisions for burial or burial assistance.[21]

Administratively there are certain benefits and rights of veterans administered by agencies other than the Veterans Administration, in the attainment of which the state agency provides valuable assistance. From a study of these items, some of which are listed below, it is apparent that such an agency is involved in a wide variety of services necessitating a close working relationship with many other Federal, state, and local agencies.[22]

TYPES OF SERVICES RENDERED BY A STATE VETERANS' AGENCY

Accrued military pay	Selective service records
Benefits for employees	Re-employment rights
Back pay	State vocational rehabilitation
Bonds, lost or destroyed	Emergency army and navy relief
State bonus information	Mustering-out pay
Military decorations	Lost or destroyed personal effects
Lost or destroyed discharges	Gratuity pay
Review of discharges	Travel pay
Headstones and markers	Return of war dead
Missing veterans	Request for military and naval retirement proceedings
Personal problems	
Public records	Review of military and naval retirement
Welfare assistance	
Prisoner of war claims	Social security benefits
Workmen's compensation	

Civic Recognition. It appears to be a universal practice for governments to use their military exploits and successes for the twofold purpose of instilling patriotism in the living and honoring those who have given their lives in the service of their country. A most familiar device for these purposes is to establish by law patriotic holidays dedicated to the commemoration of some significant national hero or event. It appears that there are now approximately 400 state enactments establishing such holidays, commonly celebrated by patriotic parades, speeches, and other observances. All forty-eight states observe Washington's Birthday (February 22), Memorial Day (May 30), Independence Day (July 4), and Armistice Day (November 11).[23]

Other types of legislation may be cited here. There are forty-three state statutes relating to service officers, and forty-one relating to medals and meritorious awards to be presented for service in various wars and expedi-

[21] This analysis is based on Hunter, Carrie E., *State Veterans' Laws* (House Committee Print No. 253, 81st Cong., 2nd Sess., 1950). This 348-page report is an invaluable source of information. State veterans' laws are usually treated as a separate title in the annotated codes of the several states and, for the information of the public, compilations of these laws are often published in pamphlet form.

[22] Virginia Department of Law, Division of War Veterans' Claims, *Report for the Year 1949*, p. 3 (Richmond, 1950).

[23] Others include: Columbus Day (October 12); 41 states; Davis Day (June 3), 9 states; Flag Day (June 14), four states; General Pulaski Memorial Day (October 11), 19 states; Jefferson's Birthday (April 13), three states; Lee's Birthday (January 19), 10 states; Lincoln's Birthday (February 12), 27 states; miscellaneous days, 22 states.

tions, seventeen of which provide for the protection of the uniform. In connection with quite another matter, it may be noted that all forty-eight states authorize absentee voting by military personnel in wartime, and seven by special enactment provide for the exercise of the suffrage by veterans who are inmates of homes and hospitals.

Veterans' Organizations. There are no less than 350 state enactments covering the problems of veterans' organizations, dealing with almost every conceivable aspect of their organization and functioning. Many of these laws — nineteen of them — deal with corporate powers; thirteen provide for the exemption of such groups from license fees for amusements, four from license fees for automobiles, seven from fees and taxes on wrestling and boxing exhibitions. Nineteen states authorize meetings of such groups in armories, fifteen in cities, fourteen in counties, thirteen in memorial buildings, ten in state capitols, six in service centers. Ten states give financial assistance for veterans' meetings. Nine states have legislation conferring parade privileges on veterans' organizations, forty-two for the protection of their insignia, nine protecting the names of such groups, seven authorizing poppy sales.

Financial aid comes both in the form of exemptions from taxes and in direct grants. The former are applied to gifts to veterans' organizations in ten states; to memorial halls, monuments, and the like in seven; and to property, either real or personal, in twenty-eight. Appropriations to such organizations are made for rehabilitation service in fourteen states, for encampments and conventions in thirty-two, for headquarters and operating expenses in fifteen, and for veterans' rest camps in two. Local units of government are authorized by law to make appropriations for the observance of Memorial Day in twenty-one states, and for miscellaneous purposes in six states.

Benefits to Veterans. Even in its early days of financial stringency the United States government strongly felt its responsibility for the welfare of its fighting men, early state records showing that a disabled veterans' program was in effect even before the Revolutionary War was won.[24] Veterans of recent wars receive direct financial benefits from the states — bonus payments, pensions, loans, and such additional aids as educational benefits, state backing for their service agencies and centers, relief and care for the indigent, and care for the sick and disabled.

State bonus legislation is on the books in twenty-one states for World War II; the same number of states paid bonuses to veterans of World War I, not to mention nine further laws of miscellaneous application, chiefly to veterans of the Philippine Insurrection and the Spanish-American War. As of January 1950, it appeared that payments of nearly $2,600,000,000 would go to approximately 8,000,000 veterans. Principal characteristics of the state bonus laws are shown in the table on page 416. About half of the states

[24] "War Veterans' Pensions Paid in 18th Century," *Capitol News*, July 30, 1945 (Pennsylvania clipsheet).

specify a last day for filing. The qualifications are fairly uniform, usually ninety days' service in the armed forces between dates specified in the law, and residence in the state for six months (in some cases, one year) prior to entry into the service. There are thirty-seven enactments providing pensions to veterans and the widows of veterans from previous wars. Most states have undertaken to facilitate loans to veterans, as contemplated under the Federal Servicemen's Readjustment Act; thirty-seven such enactments apply to loans by banks and other financial institutions, forty to veterans who are minors.

There are approximately 112 state laws relating to veterans' education, which may be grouped for convenience as follows:

STATE LAWS ON VETERANS' EDUCATION

General	22
For World War I veterans	8
For World War II veterans	22
Children of veterans killed in action	37
Free tuition	18
Scholarships	5

There are, in addition, fifty-eight enactments on rehabilitation training, twenty-six of which relate to general matters, seventeen to apprenticeship and on-the-job training, others with such specific groups as the veterans of World War II and pardons for certain paroled prisoners. Rehabilitation training is given after physical therapy and vocational training have been completed, as a means of helping the veteran to obtain suitable employment in connection with which he will have an opportunity to use his newly acquired skills.

In the field of relief, the laws are of a widely diversified character. Five states have enacted the Civil Relief Act. Sixty-six enactments relate to veterans' relief agencies — state (forty-four), county (fifteen), local (seven). Sixty-one enactments provide for the relief of indigent veterans, twenty-six of them by the states, ten by the counties, three by towns. In twenty-two states these laws relate, not to political jurisdictions but to the veterans of particular wars. An even larger number of laws (eighty-one) deal with domiciliary homes for all veterans (thirty-three), children and orphans of veterans (thirteen), Civil War veterans (twelve), wives and widows of veterans (twenty-three).

After every war there are many cases requiring psychiatric treatment. Some of these require hospitalization, part of them permanently, part temporarily; much legislation has been enacted for the purpose of aiding such veterans. Some, whose plight is not so serious, can be adequately cared for in mental hygiene clinics and by cooperation with local health and welfare agencies. No less than seventy-six enactments make provision for hospital benefits in state and county hospitals (sixteen), for the care of tuberculars (six), for the care of the insane (ten), and for the transfer or commitment of incompetent veterans to Federal hospitals (forty-four). Thirty-nine juris-

State Bonus Legislation as of July 1, 1952

STATE	DATE APPROVED	AMOUNT PER MONTH AND MAXIMUM	PAYMENT TO NEXT OF KIN	BOND ISSUE AUTHORIZED	TAXES LEVIED
Connecticut	1947	$10 — $300	$300	$50,000,000	General sales and use tax
Delaware	1949	$15 domestic — $225 $20 foreign — $300	300	8,500,000	None
Illinois	1946	$10 domestic $15 foreign	900	385,000,000	Pari-mutuel, cigarette and property taxes
Indiana	1948	$10 domestic $15 foreign	600	....	Bonus not to be paid until funds are collected by taxation
Iowa	1948	$10 domestic — $500 $12.50 foreign — $500	500	85,000,000	Direct annual tax on all taxable property
Louisiana	1948	Graduated on length of service to $250	1000	60,000,000	Tax on beer
Massachusetts	1948	$100 — domestic $200 — foreign	....	....	Corporation, corporation income, liquor, cigarettes
Michigan	1946	$10 domestic $15 foreign	500	270,000,000	None
Minnesota	1948	$10 domestic — $270 $15 foreign — $400	400	84,000,000	Banks, corporations, liquors, severance and property taxes
Montana	1950[1]	$10 domestic $15 foreign	[2]	22,000,000	Tax on cigarettes
New Hampshire	1943	$10 — $100	100	6,000,000	Poll tax of $3 for two years
New York	1949	Graduated on length of service to $250	250	400,000,000	Personal income and cigarette taxes
North Dakota	1948	Graduated on length of service to $250	600	27,000,000	Increase in levy on property
Ohio	1947	$10 domestic — $400 $15 foreign — $400	400	300,000,000	Additional tax on all taxable property
Oregon	1950[1]	$10 domestic — $600 $15 foreign	600	Determined by legislative session in 1951.	
Pennsylvania	1949	$10 domestic — $500 $15 foreign — $500	500	500,000,000	None
Rhode Island	1946	$200	....	19,000,000	None
South Dakota	1948	$15 domestic — $500 $22 foreign — $650	....	30,000,000	Increase in property, sales and use, privilege and excise taxes
Vermont	1941	$10 — $120	120	2,500,000	Appropriated from surplus
Washington	1949	$10 domestic $15 foreign	....	80,000,000	Cigarette taxes
West Virginia	1950	$10 domestic — $300 $15 foreign — $400	....	90,000,000	Cigarette, beer, wine, and liquor taxes

[1] Initiated measure, approved by the electorate November 7, 1950; at the time this table was prepared, its constitutionality was being tested in the courts.

[2] Amount to which the veteran himself would have been entitled.

dictions have adopted the Uniform Guardianship Act, while twenty-four have other legislation relating to the appointment of guardians, supplementing or as a substitute for the Uniform Act. Four states still carry on the books legislation on artificial limbs for Civil War veterans.

Exemptions. The laws of the states contain large numbers of provisions for exemptions and exceptions from normal legal requirements, some applicable to persons in service, others to veterans. In the former group may be mentioned laws preserving unemployment compensation benefits in all but one state, and similarly laws relating to the renewal after war service of motor vehicle operators' licenses (twenty-two); laws providing for exemptions from license fees for paraplegics and amputees (twenty), and with regard to motor vehicles owned by veterans' organizations (five). Sixteen states permit the suspension or substitution of normal requirements regarding fiduciaries and two have legal provisions governing reinstatement of labor union memberships after discharge from military service.

Exemptions applicable to veterans are more numerous and, from a financial point of view, more significant. Two states exempt veterans from jury service, two from National Guard duty. Ten provide for National Guard credit for service in the state militia. Six accept medical certificates by Army and Navy medical officers in connection with applications for marriage licenses. General land settlement benefits are provided in twelve states, in connection with home and land loans in four, preferences for veterans in four. In eight states laws provide for free or reduced fares on common carriers, and twenty authorize the furnishing of motor vehicles to amputees or paraplegics. Three fourths of the states give special consideration to both servicemen and veterans in connection with the issue of hunting and fishing licenses. Three states extend these privileges to all veterans, one to blind veterans, three to Civil War veterans, six to disabled veterans, three to hospitalized veterans. Housing benefits to veterans and their families are provided for all veterans in fifteen states, to veterans of World War II in thirteen states, and to various small groups in a number of other states.

Most significant are the exemptions generally accorded to servicemen and to veterans in the field of taxation. The nature and extent of these benefits are indicated in the table on page 418; that they reach significant proportions for governments, if not for individual veterans, is illustrated by the fact that such relief for California veterans accounted for most of a $78,000,000 increase in the assessed value of tax-exempt property in the state in 1950.

Employment Advantages. Special consideration or advantages are conferred by law on veterans, as regards both public and private employment. In the field of public employment, these advantages may be classified in several different ways. Thirty-nine jurisdictions give preference in appointment — 5 per cent, 10 per cent, or absolute preference. Other credits relate to promotions in eight states, retention rights in five, retirement benefits in

TAX AND LICENSE FEE EXEMPTIONS FOR SERVICE AND EX-SERVICE PERSONNEL

For Military Personnel: (109 enactments)

- Income tax: abatement in case of death, 6 states; military compensation, 26 states; payment or filing deferred, penalties abated, 7 states.
- Poll tax: 11 states
- Professional and occupational licenses: 20 states
- Property tax: payment deferred, penalties abated, 21 states
- Road tax: 2 states
- Tobacco tax: five states

For Veterans: (165 enactments)

- Income tax: pensions, bonus payments, insurance and other benefits, 22 states
- Inheritance tax: as to insurance, compensation, etc., 11 states
- Peddler's licenses: all veterans, 13 states; Civil War veterans only, 4 states; disabled veterans only, 5 states; nominal fee, 1 state.
- Pensions: 12 states
- Poll tax: all veterans, 5 states; certain veterans, 19 states; members of the Armed Forces, 12 states
- Professional and occupational licenses: 18 states
- Property tax: all veterans, 13 states; certain veterans, 12 states; miscellaneous, 4 states
- Special hunting and fishing license: 14 states

thirty-four, special leaves in five; in eight states, preference extends to the wives and widows of veterans.

There are, in practice, as a recent Kentucky survey points out, several different ways in which veterans' preference is granted[25]:

> Eleven states add five points to the passing score after it has been attained by nondisabled veterans.[26] Maryland adds five points regardless of the score attained. New Jersey adds three points; California, Kansas, Michigan, and Pennsylvania add ten points; and Ohio gives the equivalent of 20 per cent of the grade as an addition to the score. All but one of these states which grant five points to nondisabled veterans also grant ten additional points to disabled veterans. Illinois gives five points to both disabled and nondisabled veterans. New Jersey and Pennsylvania grant ten points to disabled veterans, while Ohio confers the same additional 20 per cent of the grade attained upon disabled as nondisabled veterans. California, Kansas, and Michigan give fifteen points to disabled veterans.
>
> The laws of Massachusetts and New Jersey contain an individualistic departure from those of other states in that they waive examination requirements for holders of the Congressional Medal of Honor, Distinguished Service Cross, and Navy Cross. Absolute preference — that is, placing veterans at the top of the eligible lists regardless of standing or exclusion of nonveterans from certain positions — has been adopted in a few states. New Jersey places disabled veterans at the head of every list. A few states require that veterans must be considered before any other eligibles for all state positions.[27] New Jersey

[25] Kentucky Legislative Research Commission, *Merit System Legislation for Kentucky*, pp. 14–15 (Frankfort, 1949).

[26] These are: Alabama, Colorado, Connecticut, Indiana, Maine, Minnesota, Missouri, Oregon, Rhode Island, Tennessee, and Wisconsin.

[27] Massachusetts, New York, and Pennsylvania. New York places time limits on their absolute preference.

requires such absolute veterans' preference only for positions filled by noncompetitive examinations.

Only a few states grant veterans' preference in promotions.[28] Personnel authorities do not recommend this, as it compounds the preference veterans acquire all the way through an organization, defeats competition, and discourages able nonveteran employees. Georgia has no provision for veterans' preference, and Virginia provides for it "so far as is practicable."

General preferences for veterans in public employment exist in forty states, in counties and municipalities in twenty-seven, on public works projects in twenty. Leaves of absence during military service are required by law in thirty-three states, restoration to former positions after war service in forty-one states, while war service credit under retirement systems is likewise provided for in forty-one jurisdictions. Large numbers of persons in professions and occupations commonly subject to licensure are given special consideration under some 100 or more enactments, in connection with renewals after termination of service, as indicated in the table on this page. Attorneys appear to be singled out for preferential treatment in connection with examinations for admission to the bar in approximately one third of the states.

RENEWAL OF PROFESSIONAL AND OCCUPATIONAL LICENSES AFTER TERMINATION OF WAR SERVICE

General	27	Insurance agents	4
Accountants	6	Nurses	1
Architects	5	Optometrists	3
Barbers	7	Pharmacists	5
Beauty culturists	7	Plumbers	2
Chiropodists	1	Real estate agents	4
Cleaners and dyers	1	Social workers	1
Collection agents	1	Teachers and school employees	4
Detectives	1	Undertakers	8
Engineers	11	Watchmakers	2

Legal Considerations. Veterans are given by law various special considerations in connection with legal matters. The laws of forty-four states provide for the free recording of discharge certificates, eleven for free copies thereof, three for copies at reduced fees. Eighteen provide for free notary services, three for notary services at reduced fees. All states but one provide for free copies of public records to be used in connection with veterans' claims, and six for the safekeeping of such records. The statute of limitations is suspended or extended for veterans in five states. Twenty-seven states have laws exempting veterans from execution and other legal processes, and all jurisdictions have special legislation regarding the execution of legal instruments by members of the armed forces. Twenty-eight have such legislation regarding powers of attorney for military personnel. Mention has

[28] California, Illinois, and Pennsylvania. Illinois limits promotion preference points to one promotional examination only and to those veterans who held regular civil service status prior to entering military service.

been made of legislation regarding guardianship. Nineteen states altogether have special legislation on wills of servicemen, including testamentary capacity of minors, admission of wills to probate, and other related matters. More than half of the states have legislation regarding the administration of estates of "missing" military personnel, and on evidence of death or other status of military personnel missing in action.

Death Benefits and Burial. There is a considerable volume of legislation on death benefits, burials, burial assistance, and graves of veterans. Ten states provide that death certificates and burial permits shall include military records. Nine have provisions prohibiting the dissection of the bodies of veterans and governing the removal of bodies to soldiers' plots. There are approximately twenty-five enactments relating to burial grounds for veterans — state, county, municipal, and local. Twenty-seven states have legislation on the burial of veterans, twenty-three on the relatives of veterans, and a few on state aid and the right to a firing squad. About two thirds of the states have legislation on the care and decoration of veterans' graves — nine applying to the states, ten to counties, nine to municipalities, two to townships. Seventeen states require registration of veterans' graves — thirteen by the states themselves, four by counties. Ten states require the securing of United States headstones, and most of the remainder make statutory provision for suitable headstones or markers.

War Records. There are a few state laws on the subject of war records. Four states require compilation of all laws relating to veterans; eighteen provide for the compilation of various types of war records, and, in most instances, for the establishment of a state agency charged with this responsibility. Twenty-five states provide for the preservation of war records, fourteen for the preservation of war relics. In the absence of such legislation, work of this type may be carried on by state and local historical societies; these, of course, are private agencies, and may not be adequately financed for an undertaking of this magnitude.

SELECTED REFERENCES

American Red Cross, *When Disaster Strikes: a Chapter Manual for Disaster Preparedness and Relief* (Washington, 1948).

Beckwith, Edmund R., and others, *Lawful Action of State Military Forces* (Random House, New York, 1944). Valuable treatise on lawful scope of state military action.

Fairman, Charles, *The Law of Martial Rule*, Second Edition (Callaghan, Chicago, 1943), and Rankin, Robert S., *When Civil Law Fails: Martial Law and Its Legal Basis* (Duke University Press, 1939). Significant treatises on a problem of fundamental importance.

Hunter, Carrie E., *State Veterans Laws* (House Committee Print No. 253, 81st Cong., 2nd Sess., 1950). Current edition of a valuable survey of state veteran legislation.

Lasswell, Harold D., *National Security and Individual Freedom* (McGraw-Hill,

New York, 1950). Discussion of the vital problem of maintaining basic freedoms in a world torn by dissension and plagued by a constant threat of war.

United States Office of Civil Defense Planning, *Civil Defense for National Security* (Washington, 1948) — the Hopley Report; and National Security Resources Board, *United States Civil Defense* (Washington, 1950). The two most significant studies of civil defense against atomic attack, emphasizing the responsibilities of the state and local governments.

Wood, Sterling, *Riot Control by the National Guard* (Military Service Publishing Company, Harrisburg, 1940). Deals with the use of troops in peacetime disorders.

12

State Administrative Services

The major types of administrative service — line and staff — are found in the state governments as elsewhere. The line functions, often spoken of as the operating services, include those which come in close contact with the people, such as activities of a regulatory character and those which furnish service or information to citizens. The control of plant and animal diseases, the enforcement of food and drug regulations, blue sky laws, public utility laws, and laws requiring the examination and licensure of practitioners of learned professions and technical trades are all examples of regulatory services. Activities of the service type, called by some writers primary services, include the farm marketing service, those phases of the plant and animal industry service which aid producers in getting a larger output at a minimum investment, public health service, free library programs, and vocational and adult education programs. The United States Bureau of the Census has grouped the services of the states under certain major headings, which are used with modifications in the following table as a basis for classifying the more common activities of the state governments.

The staff services are concerned with the performance of the routine housekeeping activities of government — the collection and disbursement of revenues; the custody and budgeting of the same and the supervision of their expenditure; purchase and maintenance of property, supplies, and equipment; hiring and dismissing, promotion and retirement of personnel; management planning and research. These services are of little direct benefit to the people, yet it would be impossible for the line services to function if these services were not regularly and efficiently maintained. These services relate in the main to the functions of general government provided for in the original constitutional offices.

Reference is made elsewhere to the tremendous increase in the number and scope of governmental services. In a later chapter, this problem will be discussed from the cost angle, and at that time an attempt will be made to indicate some of the reasons for the greatly increased expenditures in the state field. A detailed study of the functional growth of the Michigan government from 1835 through 1949 was recently completed at the University of

Classification of the Functions of State Government
(United States Bureau of the Census classification, as modified by the author)

GENERAL GOVERNMENT	Governor's Office Personnel Military Affairs	State Justice State Police
FINANCIAL MANAGEMENT	Budget Office Taxation and Finance State Treasurer State Comptroller	State Tax Commission Property and Supplies Auditor General
CONTROL OVER BUSINESS AND INDUSTRY	Banking Insurance Labor Mines	Professional Licensure Public Utilities Commerce Weights and Measures
AGRICULTURE AND NATURAL RESOURCES	Agriculture Forests and Waters Fish and Game	Geological Survey Land Planning and Use Public Lands and Parks
TRANSPORTATION	Aviation Motor Vehicles Highways: Use and Safety	Highways: Construction and Maintenance Railways and Canals
HEALTH AND WELFARE	Public Health Mental Health Public Welfare Public Assistance	Social Security Corrections Institutions Recreation
EDUCATION	Libraries Public Instruction	Higher Education Adult Education

Michigan. What happened in that state is typical of the development in others. Starting with a small number of basic functions, the total has grown

State of Michigan
Growth in Number of Administrative Agencies, 1835–1949, inclusive*

DECADE	NUMBER OF NEW AGENCIES	TOTAL	DECADE	NUMBER OF NEW AGENCIES	TOTAL
1835–1839	11		1890–1899	30	106
1840–1849	11	22	1900–1909	24	130
1850–1859	13	35	1910–1919	40	170
1860–1869	9	44	1920–1929	29	199
1870–1879	14	58	1930–1939	51	250
1880–1889	18	76	1940–1949	32	282

* Data from Eckert, Eleanora, *The Growth of Administrative Structure in Michigan* (Unpublished thesis, University of Michigan, 1949).

steadily from decade to decade, though more rapidly in some periods than in others. The number of agencies now totals 282.

General Government

Under general government are grouped the following officers and agencies of the state governments:

OFFICERS	DEPARTMENTS
Governor	Executive
Lieutenant Governor	Executive
Secretary of State	State
Attorney General	Justice
Adjutant General	Military Affairs
Superintendent	State Police
Director	Personnel

Chapter 9 has been devoted to the office of the governor, further mention of which, along with the lieutenant governor, appears in Chapter 10. The military establishment was discussed in the preceding chapter. It remains, therefore, to consider the secretary of state and those services which relate to the protection of persons and property — the department of justice and the state police. Financial administration and personnel management might be regarded as aspects of general government, but because of the size and importance of the problems involved, each of these topics will be considered separately.

The Secretary of State. The office of secretary of state is a very old one, existing in all forty-eight states. The occupant is elected by popular vote in all states except Delaware, Maryland, New Jersey, New York, Pennsylvania, Texas, and Virginia, where he is appointed by the governor by and with the advice and consent of the senate. In Maine, New Hampshire, and Tennessee he is elected by the legislature. He is the custodian of the great seal of the state, carries on correspondence with other states and with the Federal government, and is commonly entrusted with certain duties in connection with legislation and elections. The powers of the office have come to be of such a miscellaneous nature that it may almost be described as a sort of scrap basket of governmental authority. When there has been some new service to be performed that did not logically fit into the duties of any other department, it has been assigned to the secretary of state. On this very ground it is possible to argue both that the office should be retained and that it should be abolished, although the majority of students favor the latter alternative.

The Attorney General. The attorney general is the chief law officer of the state. In those jurisdictions which maintain a department of justice he serves as its head. He may also serve ex officio as a member of various boards and commissions, such as the pardon board and the board of commissioners on uniform state laws. The department furnishes legal advice to the governor and to the administrative departments, boards, commissions, and officers of the state government. Through deputies assigned to the various departments and agencies, who become experts in the law relating to these departments, he conducts their legal business, instituting and conducting court actions when necessary to secure interpretation of the law or to prosecute offenders.

The State Police. The state police system had its origin with the Texas Rangers in the early years of the present century. The organization commonly functions under a superintendent appointed by and responsible to the governor, in the same manner as any other department. The men are carefully selected for physical vigor and mental alertness. They are well trained and disciplined and commonly constitute an efficient force for the protection of life and property throughout the state. Their duties include such general administration of the law as is involved in the preservation of law and order.

Members of the force are often sent to handle large crowds wherever they are congregated for any reason. They usually render service in case of real or threatened riot or disorder or disturbance of the peace. Through their facilities for criminal identification and information they undertake the solution of crimes committed outside of municipalities with a well-organized police force of their own. They are responsible for the enforcement of motor traffic regulations throughout the state, and other duties, such as fire prevention, may be assigned to them.

Control over Business and Industry

The state services which function within the field of business and industry include the departments of banking and insurance, of labor and industry, and of mines, and agencies for the regulation of public service companies, the control of weights and measures and the sale of foods and drugs, and professional licensure.

Department of Banking. Many of the present departments of banking were established in the later decades of the last century — that of New York in 1880, that of Pennsylvania in 1891. The Federal Constitution provides that the states shall not emit bills of credit; the need for departments of banking grew out of the fact that this clause had been evaded. If the states could not issue paper money designed to circulate as currency, they could charter banks, which in turn could issue paper money. During the nineteenth century there was an era of wildcat banking which gave encouragement to the move for regulation. The amount of paper money issued by the state banks became so great as to threaten the position of the Federal currency; this condition prompted Congress to impose a 10 per cent tax upon all such paper money designed to circulate as currency. The tax was sustained in 1869 in the case of Veazie Bank v. Fenno.[1] While this decision took care

[1] 8 Wallace 533, 1869.

of the problem of paper money, the need of regulation for the purpose of controlling other banking activities steadily increased.

At the present time state departments of banking render four important services for the protection of investors: (1) the supervision of banks and trust companies; (2) the supervision of building and loan associations; (3) the supervision of security issues, and the protection of investors through the enforcement of blue sky laws; and (4) the supervision of private bankers, small moneylenders, and steamship ticket agents. For the first two of these purposes the departments maintain forces of public accountants as trained examiners to make periodic examinations of the books and records of the institutions and associations under supervision. In many states it is the practice to levy such fees as will cover the actual costs of examination; in fact, some states exact fees which cover the overhead of the department as well, thereby making the department self-sustaining.

The supervision of security issues may be carried on either as a phase of the work of the department or by a commission, which in turn may be either independent or attached to the department. It is customary to license brokers and salesmen, to pass upon proposed security issues, and to carry on investigational work both before and after issues have been approved. The private bankers are often among the largest financial organizations within the jurisdiction of the state; the small moneylenders and steamship ticket agents, on the other hand, are in a position to prey upon the less fortunate members of the community unless they are subjected to a constant and rigorous supervision.

Department of Insurance. In the early days there existed both widespread distrust of insurance and lack of effective regulation. The establishment of state departments of insurance became necessary when, in the case of Paul v. Virginia, the United States Supreme Court decided that insurance was not commerce and hence not subject to the regulatory power of Congress under the commerce clause. Although this decision was reversed by the Court in 1944, there has been no change in the previously existing method of operation.[2] For many years the work was badly done — when, indeed, it was done at all — and the insurance business took on many of the characteristics of a modern racket. The famous Hughes investigation of insurance companies in New York in 1905 attracted public attention to the existence of the evils, most of which have since been corrected. A well-organized insurance department possesses wide inquisitorial and visitorial powers over the companies under its supervision; it licenses those engaged in the business, both brokers and advisers; and it exercises control over the financial condition of insurers, the forms of policies, rates and premiums, and methods of obtaining business.

[2] 8 Wallace 168, 1868; see also National Fire Insurance Company of Hartford v. Thompson, Superintendent of Insurance Department of Missouri, 281 U.S. 311, 1930; United States v. South Eastern Underwriters Association, 322 U.S. 533, 1944.

For the performance of these duties the department may be organized in accordance with either of two main principles — according to the type of company to be supervised, or according to the type of work to be done. New York State uses the first plan and has separate divisions for life, fire, casualty, marine, and other types of insurance. Pennsylvania uses the second plan and has in its department separate divisions for statements and audits, accounts, agents and brokers, complaints, examinations, liquidations, and actuarial work. The mere listing of these divisions serves to indicate the nature of the several types of work involved in the supervision of insurance companies, both domestic and foreign.

Department of Labor. State departments of labor, or of labor and industry, began thirty or forty years ago as bureaus of factory inspection. In the meantime the departments have grown in the larger industrial states to huge organizations employing many hundreds of persons. The movement for the establishment of such agencies was given impetus in 1895 when the United States Supreme Court in United States v. E. C. Knight Sugar Refining Company established the doctrine that prevailed for approximately half a century, that manufacturing was not commerce — that manufacturing was a change of form, and that commerce was a change of place.[3] The type of organization varies according to the type of state. In the smaller, nonindustrial states the department is neither large nor important. In the principal industrial states the departmental form of organization is used, as in Illinois, New York, and Pennsylvania. There is, however, a third group of states that are still working under an industrial commission; important among these is Wisconsin.

The duties performed by this department are many and important. They include the protection of workers in industry — men, women, and children; the carrying on of extensive inspection services; the administration of the workmen's compensation system; and in cooperation with the Federal government, the administration of the unemployment compensation and public employment services. Other duties lie in the field of industrial relations and industrial standards, or may relate to matters of a miscellaneous character. Under existing court decisions men workers may be protected from excessive hours of labor in industries that are not dangerous as well as in those which are accompanied by unusual occupational hazards. They may be protected from forced labor, and aided by wage collection laws, by laws controlling the method of wage payments and the frequency thereof, by minimum wage laws in some jurisdictions, and by laws requiring payment of wages during time off to vote. All these regulations it is the duty of the department to enforce.

For a great many years women and children enjoyed a preferred position before the law in the matter of protection in industry. Children still do; the effort to protect women workers received a severe setback in a 1923 decision,

[3] 156 U.S. 1, 1895, overruled by Wickard v. Filburn, 317 U.S. 311, 1942.

later reversed by the Supreme Court.[4] The existing legislation relates to such matters as hours of labor, minimum wage, night work, and conditions of labor. It is the business of the department to see that these regulations are enforced. The whole problem has social aspects of very great significance, yet the fact remains that very few of the states have legislation which compares favorably with the minimum standards that have been determined by competent and impartial authorities.

The inspection services represent an exceedingly important part of the work of such a department. Some of these are of a general nature, while others are more highly specialized. The general inspection work includes the inspection of manufacturing and industrial establishments for the joint purposes of enforcing the safety code and of carrying on preventive work with regard to both accidents and occupational diseases. It may be responsible for the enforcement of the fire and panic act in theaters, schools, and other places built for public assemblies. These acts regulate aisle space, seating, exits, fire escapes, emergency lighting systems, and the like. Among the more specialized types of inspection may be mentioned that of buildings, both public and private, for observance of the requirements of the building code; the licensing of motion-picture operators; the inspection and licensing of steam boilers; elevator inspection; and the inspection of mines and quarries, of bedding and upholstery. Upon the honesty and efficiency with which this work is done depends the hourly safety of a large portion of the population of the state — old and young alike.

When an injured employee of an industrial establishment attempted to recover in a court of law, the employer was formerly able, under the common law, to set up the age-old doctrines of the assumption of risk, the fellow-servant rule, or the doctrine of contributory negligence. When these defenses were abolished by statute, a system of employer's liability was tried for a time, followed by the present system of workmen's compensation. There is the greatest diversity in the organization of existing systems of this kind — some are compulsory while others are optional; some are public and some are private; some permit self-insurers while others do not. In the more progressive states there are four different agencies, each of which has a part in the administration of the compensation system. These are: (1) the bureau; (2) the referee; (3) the board; (4) the fund.

The bureau is in general responsible for the enforcement of the law. To it industrial accidents are reported; by it all but a small percentage of the cases are finally settled. It keeps the records of all cases. When it is unable to get the insurer and the insured to agree, the case may be turned over to a referee. (In New York all cases pass through the hands of the referee, although little time is spent on noncontested cases.) If the referee is unable

[4] Adkins v. Children's Hospital, 261 U.S. 525, 1923; reversed by Morehead v. New York ex rel. Tipaldo, 298 U.S. 587, 1936 and West Coast Hotel Company v. Parrish, 300 U.S. 379, 1937.

to effect a settlement, appeal may be had to the board — a quasi-judicial body most of whose decisions are in fact final, although technically appeal may be carried to the courts on points of law. Finally, there is the fund. This is an insurance business operated by the state for the insuring of a particular type of risk; the rates are usually cheaper than those of private companies. In most states insurers are merely required to carry insurance; they may take it with private companies or with the fund, as they prefer.

The department is responsible for the administration of the system of unemployment compensation and for the conduct of the state employment service. Persons out of employment through no fault of their own are entitled to unemployment compensation for a period not to exceed twenty weeks, or as much thereof as may be necessary while they are obtaining new employment. The application of scientific placement procedures in the employment service becomes doubly important in a situation in which prompt placement tends to prevent abuses and to hold down the cost of the unemployment compensation program.

The department is also responsible for the performance of many duties of a somewhat miscellaneous character. A department of labor worthy of the name will find itself offering its good offices in the mediation and arbitration of strikes and industrial disputes; it will, in the effort to cut down the toll of accidents and deaths, carry on experimental work in its laboratories, for the purpose of discovering and perfecting safety devices and procedures. It will cooperate to the fullest possible extent with the Federal government in its industrial rehabilitation program and in the collection of labor statistics. It will cooperate with labor departments in other states and with other departments of the government in its own state. In the field of public relations it will seek to inform the people of the state concerning what is being done and why, and how it will benefit them.

Department of Mines. There is no good reason why the work of a department of mines could not be done just as well in the labor department in connection with its inspection work and its work of enforcing legislation governing hours and conditions of labor, but in some states where mining is important, separate departments are maintained. This may be justified, although even in such cases the department is always a small one. It is responsible for the performance of such duties, prescribed by the mining laws, as the inspection of mines, the investigation of mine accidents, the holding of examinations for mine foremen and mine operators, the issuing of certificates to persons entitled to receive the same, and the compiling and distributing of statistical reports.

Public Service Commissions. By long and laborious effort public service commissions were finally established in each state as a means of regulating and controlling those companies affected with a public interest, supplying to the general public the facilities for heat, light, power, communication, and transportation. Thus some twenty or twenty-five different types of business enterprises come under the control of the commissions. The quality of the work done by most of them has not been very encouraging, but they are none the less about the only force standing, in the interests of the public, between the public and the utilities. Rate-making difficulties experienced under earlier decisions were to some extent cleared up by the decision in Federal Power Commission v. Natural Gas Pipeline Company of America [5] in which the Court said "the Constitution does not bind rate-making bodies to the service of any single formula or combination of formulas. Agencies to whom this power has been delegated are free, within the ambit of their statutory authority, to make the pragmatic adjustments which may be called for by particular circumstances." The public obtains, through the commissions, some assurance of reasonable rates, adequate service, and accuracy of meters through inspection.

The procedure before the commissions is in most cases relatively simple. When the consumer has a grievance, he files with the commission a complaint which is placed on the docket for a hearing. It is not necessary for the complainant to be represented at the hearing by counsel, although of course the utilities are always so represented. In a great many cases the commissions find it possible to settle grievances informally, and this method is encouraged where possible. A typical organization includes a secretary's office; a legal bureau; a bureau of accounts, rates, and statistics; a bureau of public convenience; and a bureau of engineering, in which may be established a standardization laboratory.

The commissions provide a fairly flexible system of regulation and insure a quicker and less costly remedy than court action for minor grievances. Because they are permanent bodies, they are in a favorable position to collect the necessary data for the determination of rates and to maintain standards of service. The utilities are benefited in that they are protected to a considerable extent from a partisan action, and this in turn protects their securities. On the other hand, the commissions have been justly criticised for not representing the public more adequately. The laws require that their members — or part of them — shall be experienced in utility management. Obvious though the purpose of this requirement is, it has in many cases given the commissions the utility point of view. Furthermore, after their appointment the members have a large part of their contacts with the representatives of the utilities, for the public is unorganized and incoherent. The result is that many of the commissions have tended more to favor the utilities than they have to protect the public. They suffer also from the fact that the public is so little informed regarding the nature of their work, and is hence not in a position to avail itself of the service and protection which the commissions otherwise might give.

Professional Examination and Licensure. Few people have any idea of the extent to which the right of persons to engage in professional and busi-

[5] 315 U.S. 575, 1942, in effect overruling Smyth v. Ames, 169 U.S. 466, 1898.

ness activities, or in skilled trades, is subject to state regulation, supervision, and control. The situation is much the same in all the states. In 1929 the Commonwealth Club of California made a preliminary investigation, which included eighteen states. It was estimated then that there were no less than 200 separate professions, callings, and vocations subject in one or more states to examination and licensure. The Council of State Governments made a comprehensive survey in 1952 which shows that the number per state now runs into the hundreds. The tendency has been for the number to increase with each session of the legislature, sometimes because of the demand of the public for protection from quacks and charlatans, at other times because of the demand of those engaged in legitimate business or professional activities for protection from those who resort to unfair competitive practices.[6]

One may obtain a better idea, perhaps, by examining the situation in a particular state. In California, there are (as nearly as one can determine) more than 300 different provisions requiring licensing, registration, permits, and inspection procedures (see table on page 432), all but six or eight of which have been passed since 1900, approximately sixty-five since 1940. The number of new laws per year was small until, in the decade from 1925 to 1935, new licensing provisions came in enormous numbers. Early laws were applicable to the older and established professions, but coverage of these was virtually completed by 1925; since that date, such legislation has been extended to more and more new types of business activity, as the California list for the legislative sessions of 1947 and 1949 well serves to illustrate. The significant fact about this list is not the individual items in it, but the indication it gives of the scope and variety of this type of enactment.

There are more authorizations than there are enactments, since several different types of license may be authorized by a single law. Out of eighty-two specific enactments, twenty-three are administered by the Department of Professional and Vocational Standards; the remainder, provided for in no less than ten different codes, are administered by a variety of departments, agencies, and special-function boards. Fourteen are provided for in

[6] See the author's "Professional and Occupational Restrictions," *Temple Law Quarterly*, April 1939, pp. 234–263, and his *Public Administration in a Democratic Society*, Chapter 31 (Heath, Boston, 1950); Council of State Governments, *Occupational Licensing Legislation in the States* (Chicago, 1952); Marketing Laws Survey, *State Occupational Legislation* (Washington, 1942); and National Education Association, "Statutory Status of Six Professions," *Research Bulletin* (Washington, September 1938, entire issue). For studies in individual states, see: Aumann, Francis R., "The Growth and Regularization of the Licensing Process in Ohio," *University of Cincinnati Law Review*, March 1952, pp. 97–124; De Lancy, Frances P., *The Licensure of Professions in West Virginia* (Foundation Press, Chicago, 1932); Irion, Frederick C., *A Survey of Licensing in New Mexico* (Division of Research, Department of Government, University of New Mexico, 1949); Maryland Tax Survey Commission, *Interim Report: Report on Licenses* (Annapolis, 1950); New York Temporary State Commission on State Activities, *Second Interim Report: Professional Education, Licensure, Registration and Law Enforcement* (Legislative Document No. 63, Albany, 1948); Oklahoma Legislative Council, *The Licensing of Professions in Oklahoma* (Oklahoma City, 1950).

State of California
Growth of Regulatory Legislation, 1900–1950*

YEAR	1900	1910	1920	1930	1940
Before 1900	6	..	..	..	..
First year	0	0	0	1	0
Second year	5	13	4	3	7
Third year	0	0	2	1	0
Fourth year	7	7	8	25	4
Fifth year	0	3	11	0	0
Sixth year	3	6	6	40	15
Seventh year	0	0	0	0	4
Eighth year	2	12	29	11	17
Ninth year	0	0	0	1	0
Tenth year	1	6	39	10	8
Totals	24	47	99	92	55
Grand total					317

* Compiled from data furnished by James A. Arnerich, Director, Department of Professional and Vocational Standards, July 1950.

the Business and Professions Code, ten in the Health and Safety Code, five in the Agriculture Code, while the rest are scattered.

Control over Various Aspects of Commerce. In a well-organized state government agencies are established whose business it is to maintain close supervision over weights and measures and over the sale of food and drugs, milk, and many other types of products where adulteration, misrepresentation, and fraud are possible. Sometimes the agency which supervises weights and measures is independent, while in other states it is a bureau in one of the departments. It is customary for the cities and counties to maintain inspection services, but they are seldom well organized or efficiently administered. The state agency can exercise some supervision over the work of the local agencies, and can do a great deal of testing work of its own. The authority extends to every conceivable kind of weighing and measuring device. The Bureau of Standard Weights and Measures in the Pennsylvania Department of Internal Affairs, in a recent two-year period, made over 3,250,000 inspections, approved almost 3,000,000 weighing and measuring devices, condemned nearly a quarter of a million, and adjusted over 42,000.

Since so many food products are of agricultural origin, it has become common practice to place the regulatory control over the distribution and sale of such products under the department of agriculture. The table on page 433, taken from a Pennsylvania report, will give some idea of the nature and extent of this type of control. Milk control work is sometimes carried on in the department of agriculture and sometimes in the department of health. It involves testing, giving examinations for testers,

State of California
Regulatory Legislation in the Sessions of 1947 and 1949

YEAR	DEPARTMENT	BUREAU	LICENSE, CERTIFICATE, PERMIT, OR REGISTRATION
1947	Agriculture	Entomology	Apiary identification numbers certificate
		Dairy Services	Dairy container brand certificate
			Canneries
			Cold Storage warehouses
			Food processing establishments
			Processors and sellers of milk and milk products
	Board of Equalization	Liquor Control	Club license
	Investment	Corporations	Check seller and cashier license
			Escrow agent license
	Motor Vehicles	.....	Self-insurer permits — financial responsibility
	Professional and Vocational Standards	Board of Registration for Civil and Professional Engineers	Chemical engineer
			Electrical engineer
			Mechanical engineer
			Petroleum engineer
			Structural engineer
			Engineer in Training
		Board of Guide Dogs for the Blind	Guide Dog Trainer
			Guide Dog school
		Board of Pharmacy	Hypodermic license
	Public Health	.....	Establishments for Handicapped Persons license
	Social Welfare	.....	County adoption Agency license
1949	Agriculture	Entomology	Apiary registration certificate
		Chemistry	Agricultural pest control license
			Aircraft pilots pest control certification of qualification
		Dairy Service	Dehydrated milk products permit
			Locker plants
	Professional and Vocational Standards	Cemetery Board	Cemetery broker license
			Cemetery salesman license
		Board of Pharmacy	Hypnotic drug license
	Public Health	.....	Horse meat license (slaughtering, wholesale, importing)

issuing licenses and permits, carrying on investigations, and supervising the work of local inspectors. Milk control boards have been established in order to control the business practices of those who were engaged in retail distribution and sale of milk.

Commonwealth of Pennsylvania
Regulatory Legislation Affecting Food Products*

1876 — State Board of Agriculture established
1805 — Department of Agriculture created

1897 — Adulteration and Coloring of Milk or Cream Law
Vinegar Law
Cheese Law
1901 — Oleomargarine Law
Renovated Butter Law
1905 — Fresh Meat Law
1909 — Eggs Unfit for Food Law
Non-Alcoholic Drink Act
Lard Law
Fertilizer Act
Feeding Stuffs Act
General Food Law
1911 — Sausage Law
Milk and Cream Act
1913 — Tuberculosis Eradication Act
1915 — Coffee and Chicory Law
Meat and Inspection Law
1917 — Insecticide Law
Apple Marketing Law
1919 — Cold Storage Law
Agricultural Marketing Law
Poultry and Egg Marketing Law
Fresh Egg Law
1921 — Apiary Inspection Act
Butter Law
Seed Law
Supplement to Oleomargarine Law
Sanitary Bottling Act
1923 — Ice Cream Law
Filled Milk Law
Supplement to Filled Milk Law
1925 — Fruit Syrup Law
Oyster Law
Milk Container Law
Milk Testing Law
Carbonated Beverage Law
1927 — Plant Pest Act
Nursery Inspection Act
1929 — Grape Marketing Law
Potato Marketing Law
Seed Certification Act
1933 — Bakery Licensing and Inspection Act
1937 — Licensing of produce dealers
Sanitary Container Law
New Plant Pest Act (repealing 1927 Act)
1943 — Apple Marketing Law
Peach Marketing Law
1945 — Regulating and licensing the disposal of dead animals
1947 — New Oleomargarine Act
New Seed Act (repealing 1921 Act)
1949 — Regulating slaughter of equine animals for animal feeding purposes
Barberry Eradication Act
Survey of Nut Trees
Ice Cream Law
Cold Storage Law

* Joint Legislative Committee on Finances, *A Survey of the Government of Pennsylvania*, pp. 17–18 (Harrisburg, 1934), supplemented by data supplied by D. M. Cresswell, Crop Reporting and Information Service, April 28, 1950.

Agriculture and Natural Resources

Under the heading of agriculture and the conservation of natural resources come the state activities carried on by the departments of agriculture, forests and waters, fish and game, mines, geological survey, public lands and parks, and planning activities.

Department of Agriculture. Some administrative agency for the purpose of encouraging and assisting agriculture exists in every state but New Mexico; the function is one of the oldest among the state administrative services. In all but five states — Arizona, Delaware, Kansas, Maryland, and Nevada, where a commission or board is used — the activity is in charge of a department. In twenty-eight states it is called the department of agriculture; in fourteen others it is grouped with industry, labor, immigration, inspection, conservation, and a variety of other things. These departments serve the threefold purpose of protecting the farmer, protecting the consumer, and rendering technical assistance to the farmer in both the production and marketing of his crops. Besides numerous miscellaneous activities, the department carries on a large amount of regulatory work and maintains marketing and crop reporting services.

Important among the various regulatory duties are the several types of quarantine enforced to prevent the spread of both plant and animal diseases and of pests and injurious insects. While some of this work contributes to the public health, the department carries on many activities of which health is the sole aim. Among these are campaigns for the eradication of bovine tuberculosis, Bang's disease, hog cholera, and other diseases that destroy livestock; the inspection of all meats not sold under Federal inspection; and finally, the enforcement of the food law, the milk law, the carbonated beverage law, and many other types of regulatory acts affecting the distribution and sale of food products. A third type of regulatory work is designed chiefly to prevent misrepresentation and fraud: inspection of weights and measures (in some states), and enforcement of standardization and grading laws, seed inspection laws, fertilizer inspection laws, and acts providing for nursery, apiary, and poultry inspection. Finally, there is the very considerable task of enforcing the dog law, the purpose of which is to protect sheep and cattle from stray and marauding dogs.

Just as the bureaus of plant industry and of animal industry, through the regulatory activities just referred to, try to help the farmer to produce more and to get what he pays for when he buys seed, fertilizer, and other products, so the marketing and crop reporting service attempts to assist him in disposing of his products on fair and favorable terms. Toward this end the state department of agriculture, working in cooperation with the Federal department, maintains a market reporting and market analysis service, and supervises and assists in the marketing of hay and grain, fruit and vegetables, poultry and eggs, and other products. Some inspection and supervision is given to roadside markets, and it is only a question of time before all such markets will be licensed annually. In the case of perishable products, the department will usually provide shipping-point inspection and, where needed, maintain a bonded warehouse service for the accommodation and protection of the growers of grain, tobacco, and other crops.

Other services maintained by the department include soil survey work;

reclamation work if necessary; and research and educational work at the state college or university, at the agricultural experiment stations throughout the state, and in its own laboratories. It is responsible for the organization and conduct of the state fair, and for the rendering of guidance and assistance to numerous county and other fairs and exhibitions throughout the state. Of extreme importance is the whole problem of the public relations, for no other department is more dependent for its success upon the skillful handling of its work. The results of research must be put in printed form convenient for distribution, and they must be sufficiently nontechnical for popular understanding without at the same time being inaccurate. Material of current interest to farmers must be brought to them over the radio and through newspapers, pamphlets, and other media. Constitutional problems raised by the work and intergovernmental and interdepartmental relations must receive serious consideration.

Among the newer state developments in agriculture may be mentioned the extensive use of special districts for soil conservation, grazing, weed control, and weed seed extermination, and for other purposes. With regard to these developments, President Renne reports[7]:

> The states, with the encouragement of the Federal government through its Soil Conservation Service, have passed soil conservation laws, permitting farmers to organize soil conservation districts to combat soil erosion and prevent local misuse of agricultural land by cooperative land use regulations. There are now more than 2000 soil conservation districts in the forty-eight states, containing more than a billion acres. This development has occurred within the past decade; the number of districts and the acreage involved has approximately doubled in the past five years.
>
> Many Western states have passed legislation providing for the establishment of grazing districts which are nonprofit, cooperative associations of livestock operators to manage the use of range lands within their boundaries. The first grazing association was established in 1928 in Montana. . . . North and South Dakota, Montana, and Wyoming have had such legislation since 1935. Grazing districts ordinarily may regulate and control the use of district lands and construct improvements for conservation and better land use. . .
>
> Another form of cooperative action to conserve land is the creation of weed control or weed seed extermination districts, authorized by state statutes. After a weed control district has been established, land owners in the district must comply with rules and regulations by the supervisors. If compliance is not affected within a specified time, the supervisors are authorized to destroy and exterminate weeds on the land of noncompliers and assess the costs of such extermination to the owners.

Department of Forests and Waters. The department of conservation in some states has complete charge of all conservation work; in other states there are separate departments and agencies for different types of conservation work. One of the most important is the protection of the forest and water resources of the state. So far as the forests are concerned, the depart-

[7] Renne, Roland R., "State Conservation and Development of Natural Resources," *State Government*, June 1950, pp. 134–137, 143; see also his *Land Economics* (Harpers, New York, 1947).

ment has the twofold task of protecting existing forests and of encouraging reforestation. This involves prevention of forest fires as far as possible, and fighting forest fires where preventive methods have failed; distribution, planting, and supervision of the growth of seedlings; acquisition and management of state lands and parks; and the conduct of forest extension work.

So far as the waters are concerned, the department may be responsible for surveys of the water resources of the state; for the consideration of applications for charters by water companies; for regulation of the sale, franchises, and disposition of the assets of water companies; for the granting of permits for dams and tunnel construction; and for the alteration of the current or the flow of streams. Permits may be granted to municipalities to impound water in, or to convey water over, state forests, and the department may be responsible for the regulation and inspection of freshets, floods, dams, dam sites, and flood control projects.

Protection of Fish and Game. The anglers and hunters of a state often constitute a powerful pressure group. Where they are not well organized, all of the conservation work is under the direction of a single department — as it probably should be. Where they are, they have insisted upon the maintenance of separate agencies for each type of work on the plea that no one person can be adequately informed or equally interested in all the different phases of conservation. In either case problems of protection and of propagation are involved. For protection work it is necessary to have game wardens and fish wardens in sufficient numbers to enforce the law and to provide adequate protection for game refuges and game lands.

The propagation service requires the maintenance of game farms and the construction and operation of fish hatcheries. As a matter of fact, there may be as many as five types of work connected with fish propagation: construction of hatcheries and growing ponds; field service; operation of the hatcheries and other equipment; surveys of lakes, streams, and ponds in order to discover what kind of fish will thrive in each location; and the actual distribution of fish fry from the hatcheries to the waters in which they are to be planted. Bounty systems may be set up to aid in the elimination of animals which constitute a special danger to species which it is desired to protect. In many states the license fees paid by fishermen and hunters are sufficient to make the fish and game work largely if not wholly self-sustaining.

The Geological Survey. At the beginning of the century only about ten states had established permanent full-time officials to make geological surveys and investigations. Now there is a department or bureau of geological survey in sixteen states, with bureaus in the departments of mines, resources, and development or conservation in thirteen more. In twelve states the state university is relied upon, on a part-time basis, for the making of incidental surveys. Seven states have no agency responsible for this work, which consists of surveys, development, and regulation and control of natural resources. Generally it is to a large extent conducted on a cooperative basis with the Federal government. It involves the location of natural resources such as ores, coals, oils, clays, soils, fertilizers, and underground waters for purposes of surveying and mapping. It is beneficial to the agricultural, mining, and metallurgical interests of the state, as well as to the general public.

From time to time deposits of valuable substances may be found in various parts of a state; these are commonly the subject of investigation and report by the geological survey. The survey is also called upon to answer in the course of the year scores of inquiries regarding the identification of mineral substances. Of course, very few of the specimens submitted are of any value, but the fact that the survey exists to give this information saves many people from serious losses at the hands of unscrupulous promoters. The cost of the maintenance of this service is moderate indeed, and its value to the state is much greater than people generally realize.

Planning Activities. Planning represents the attempt of democracy to apply intelligence to the use of natural and human resources for the welfare and happiness of all the people. There was a considerable background of planning in many American cities, but the movement made little headway in the states until, during the depression, financial assistance was given them for the purpose by the National Resources Board. By 1940, planning legislation was or had been in effect in all but seven states. As of that date, when thirty-four laws were in effect, some of the boards were more or less inactive. Nearly all were hampered by inadequate support, which in turn meant an inadequate staff.

Before anything resembling a master plan for the state can be developed, a vast amount of material must be collected through surveys of land and water resources, public works, economic and industrial development, social institutions, and regulation. Analyses must be made of existing data. Out of all these may grow suggestions of new methods, tools, ways of doing things, which may promote a more orderly development and a fuller use of our resources. These are the objectives of planning which, in spite of objections on the part of some, represent a great forward step in the development of democratic processes.

This promising situation has seriously deteriorated during the decade of the forties. Only twelve states now have a real state planning board, and eleven appear to have no planning agency of any description. Sixteen have a resources and development department, board, or commission, in which the emphasis is not on comprehensive planning but on the short-range advantages of industrial and commercial development. Nine are even worse, attaching to their so-called planning agencies names which indicate that the major purpose is to exploit the commercial advantages of the resources of the state, in terms of advertising to attract tourists and new industries.

Transportation Facilities

The department of highways owes its origin, in the early years of the present century, to the desire for better roads that may be traced first to the bicycle and later to the development of the automobile. The present administrative setup places the responsibility for construction and maintenance under the department of highways, and the responsibility for the regulation of the use of the highways under the bureau of motor vehicles and of the state police. State aviation commissioners are responsible for the planning and development of airports and airport facilities.

The Department of Highways. The organization of the department of highways varies greatly from state to state. In three fourths of the states, the work is carried on in a department, usually designated — with the exception of seven jurisdictions [8] — as the department of highways. In the remaining twelve the function is under the control of a commission.[9] All of these departments were created in the period from 1893 to 1917. The twenty-two in existence by 1910 were small but active departments, "busily constructing," in the words of Thomas H. MacDonald,[10] "short sections of road that would bring vociferous demands for more improvements. Only seven had designated a state highway system, but forces were at work that soon would bring rapid change." He continues:

> Less than one-half million motor vehicles were in use in 1910; by 1915 the number was nearly 2.5 million. The vehicles were operated largely in cities, but their owners joined vigorously in the movement for better roads, and particularly for the improvement of roads between cities. . . . Growth of state highway departments to full stature came as a result of the initiation of Federal aid in 1916, . . . by the end of 1917, every state had met this requirement [of matching]. Highway improvement almost ceased during the first World War, but in 1919, Colorado, New Mexico, North Dakota, and Oregon placed a tax on gasoline to provide funds for highways. This proved ideal for the purpose, since it charged for highway use at the time of use, in proportion to weight of vehicle and extent of travel. By 1928, every state was collecting a gasoline tax.
>
> Numbers of motor vehicles grew from less than one-half million in 1910 to more than 9,000,000 in 1920, and they continued the rapid climb thereafter. Highway revenue from registration fees followed a parallel course. Property taxes which had been the principal support of highway improvement soon ceased to be of significance. From 1900 to 1920, then, was a period of improvement and preparation.

[8] In these, highways is combined with other public works activities in a department of public works: California, Idaho, Illinois, Massachusetts, New York, Rhode Island, and Tennessee. For an excellent analysis of the organization of state highway departments, see Council of State Governments, *Highway Safety — Motor Truck Regulation*, pp. 133–137 (Chicago, 1950).

[9] These are: Indiana, Iowa, Maryland, Montana, New Mexico, North Carolina, Oregon, South Dakota, Utah, Virginia, West Virginia, and Wisconsin.

[10] "Fifty Years of Accomplishment on State Highways," *State Government*, June 1950, pp. 124–128.

At first the states undertook to aid the local units in roadbuilding through the subsidy system; when this method proved unsatisfactory the actual process of taking over the roads began. The experience in Pennsylvania has been more or less typical. The first act creating a highway department in that state was passed in 1903; construction work was under a highway commissioner from then until 1911, when the present department was created. At that time the state also took over nearly 9,000 miles of township roads, to which mileage additions have been made through the intervening years, until the state highway system comprises nearly 34,000 miles of road. In 1933 the maintenance of 48,000 more miles was undertaken without actually adding this mileage to the state highway system.

In former times the additions to the state system were made through political influence and "pull"; now additions are made by the legislature upon the basis of careful checks of the volume of traffic made by the highway department. Highways are classified as primary and secondary routes, and the type of construction and the cost are determined accordingly. The tendency in highway construction is toward an almost universal use of concrete. In any state of considerable size the highway department will be organized with a headquarters organization and a field force, the state being divided into engineering districts or divisions. Contiguous counties are grouped together for this purpose, and the counties themselves may serve as subdistricts in such a setup. Both construction and maintenance work are handled through the same organization, although the effort is made to keep the two somewhat separate.

The headquarters office is responsible for financial supervision, for office and engineering supplies, for testing and research, for the planning of signs and safety work, and for the public relations of the department. Here also are handled the legal work, personnel work, contracts, and such forestry work as may be required for roadside planting. In the construction service, plans and specifications for roads and bridges are prepared at the central office, which advertises for bids for contracts. Separate operating units may be set up for designing and drafting highways, designing and drafting bridges, estimates and costs, and the actual work of construction. On the maintenance side, operating units may be set up for equipment; for arrangements with townships and for giving permits for road openings, and the like; for snow removal; and for the actual work of maintenance.

In 1920 the objective was a primary system of two-lane highways connecting cities and serving as main lines for secondary or feeder roads. By prodigious effort this objective was pretty well realized during the twenties and thirties. The number of motor vehicles continued to grow apace — from 25.9 million in 1931 to 34.5 in 1941. Travel on rural roads amounted to 122 billion miles in 1936, the first year for which an estimate is available, whereas it is now well beyond the 200 billion mark. There has always been a wide gap between the needs of the ever-growing volume of traffic and the highways available to serve it. On this point, Commissioner MacDonald says:

> Each state has sought to close the gap by increasing the duties, responsibilities, and financial resources of its highway department. Although established, with few exceptions, to perform construction only, the highway departments soon found themselves with a rapidly increasing burden of highway maintenance. The period from the early twenties to 1933 was the most productive in highway construction of all the years in our history. Between 1923 and 1933, the mileage of designated, primary state-systems grew from 251,611 to 345,751 and that of the surfaced portions of these systems to be maintained from 111,400 to 271,845.

The table on page 442 gives some idea of the remarkable growth in mileage under state highway department care, in income (the states spent virtually every cent they received), and in numbers of vehicles — which in turn necessitated still more highway facilities.

World War II again interrupted new construction as World War I had done and made necessary maintenance exceedingly difficult. The end of the war found the nation with a highway system much of which was worn by heavy wartime traffic and without adequate maintenance, little of which was suitable — even if in good repair — to meet the needs of a postwar era, needs which called for four- or six-lane through-routes avoiding city congestion, and expressways and limited-access highways to accommodate the vast new traffic volume produced by nearly 50,000,000 motor vehicles. Faced with limited revenues whose purchasing power had greatly declined, huge maintenance costs on the old road system, and the unprecedented cost of constructing the new type of highways, the departments of highways were indeed confronted with the solution of exceedingly difficult problems. The cost of a twenty-year program of essential highway construction in New York, led by the State Thruway, was estimated in 1950 in terms of approximately one billion dollars, for roughly one fifth of which the state could count on Federal aid.

Department of Motor Vehicles. As soon as it became apparent that the construction and maintenance of highways would be a large and continuing expense, the states began to impose (1) license fees for the operation of cars and trucks; (2) operators' and chauffeurs' license fees, accompanied by examinations, as a safety measure; and (3) gasoline taxes. Later they made provision for the periodic inspection of motor vehicles, at a nominal fee, also as a safety measure. The fees vary greatly in amount for passenger cars, busses, trucks, trailers, and motorcycles, there being no generally accepted principle upon the basis of which they are computed. Some states have a flat rate for passenger cars, some use horsepower as a basis for computing the amount of the fee, while others use net weight or gross weight. The annual registration fees vary from \$2.50 in Georgia and \$3.00 in Louisiana, Massachusetts, and South Carolina, to amounts ranging from \$22 to \$24 in Iowa, Minnesota, North Dakota, Oklahoma, and Vermont. In addition, property taxes ranging from $5 in Maryland to $40 or more in Kansas and Mississippi make the total cost run high in some jurisdictions.[11] More than 50,000 communities are now entirely dependent on highway transportation for the exchange of farm products and manufactured goods.

It is estimated that 42 per cent of the fresh fruits and vegetables of thirteen large cities is delivered by truck; that 70 per cent of the nation's lumber is so moved, in whole or in part; that seventy-nine metropolitan areas

Growth of the Highway Problem in the States, 1914–1948*

YEAR	MOTOR VEHICLE REGISTRATION	TOTAL STATE HIGHWAY INCOME (IN THOUSANDS)	TOTAL STATE HIGHWAY MILEAGE	TOTAL STATE HIGHWAY SURFACED MILEAGE	TOTAL FEDERAL AID HIGHWAY SYSTEM
1914	1,763,018	$ 75,020	40,000	[1]	[1]
1921	10,493,666	420,485	203,000	84,000	169,000[2]
1931	25,862,038	1,092,637	374,000	258,000	202,000
1941	34,472,145	1,820,280	555,000	456,000	235,000
1944	30,086,189	1,295,724	564,000	473,000	231,000
1948	40,622,264	2,838,943	588,000	506,000	235,000

* Compiled from tables in MacDonald article, *op. cit.*, p. 127.
[1] Data not available. [2] Figure for 1923.

receive their entire milk supply by truck.[12] Although high registration fees are imposed on the ever-increasing number of these monsters of the highway (from 1940 to 1948, while the number of all motor vehicles increased by about 27 per cent, the number of trucks increased by about 57 per cent), it is generally recognized that the fees in most states are in no wise commensurate with the damage which these vehicles do to the highways.

The licensing of operators or drivers involves three operations: (1) examination of applicants in order to enforce a minimum standard of ability; (2) the clerical operation — largely mechanical — of issuing certificates and keeping a record of licenses issued; and (3) driver improvement, i.e., the correction and improvement of the performance of licensed drivers whose records of accidents and violations are serious. The administration of this function appears to be poorly organized and poorly executed in many states.[13] The initial fee varies from $.25 in Missouri to $5.00 in Connecticut, the only

[11] *Highway Safety — Motor Truck Regulation*, *op. cit.*, Chapter 6 and appendix.

[12] Public Roads Administration, *Highway Practice in the United States*, p. 18 (Washington, 1949).

[13] The Council of State Governments report, *op. cit.*, states (p. 30): "In many states, driver licensing is a farce. When licensing is merely a routine, clerical chore, carried on solely for the revenue it produces, it does not serve as a safety measure. Licensing is without value in reducing the number of traffic accidents if anyone who can pay the fee is permitted the use of the highways."

exception being Oklahoma, which charges $8.00 for a chauffeur's license. A moderate fee imposes little hardship upon operators and it may produce a substantial amount of revenue. Licenses are issued for one year in seventeen states, for two years in fifteen states, and for three or four years or for an unlimited time in the remainder. Mandatory revocation of licenses is provided for as follows, upon conviction of:

1. Manslaughter resulting from the operation of a motor vehicle — 43 states
2. Drunken driving — 45 states
3. Any felony in the commission of which a motor vehicle was used — 38 states
4. Successive charges of reckless driving — 35 states
5. Hit-and-run driving — 42 states

Thus registration and licensing provisions serve as a means of keeping unfit and incompetent drivers off the road, and a means of punishing those who are negligent by the revocation of license. In the enforcement of such regulations there is a good deal of reciprocity and cooperation among the states.

The gasoline tax is used in all forty-eight states, its administration belonging not to the highway or motor vehicle department, but to the department of revenue. The rate ranges from two or three cents a gallon in a few states to a maximum rate of nine cents in others. This tax is in addition to the Federal tax collected uniformly in all states. In the past the funds from the gasoline tax and motor license fees were segregated for highway purposes; during the depression there was a tendency to increase the amount of the gasoline tax and to divert portions of the receipts to relief and other purposes — a practice which led to the adoption of a number of anti-diversion amendments to state constitutions.

In many states the law requires either an annual or a semiannual inspection of all motor vehicles, for the purpose of compelling owners to make repairs necessary in the interests of safety, or of eliminating altogether those vehicles found to be in such condition as to constitute a serious highway hazard. In some jurisdictions these inspections are made by stations state-owned and state-operated; in others, privately owned service stations are licensed and authorized to make inspections at a uniform fee. While the administration of the inspection system has not always been as efficient as it should be, the system is of inestimable value in the saving of life and the preventing of damage to property. Some of the more progressive states have title laws for motor vehicles. Without the certificate of title, no vehicle may be sold. This device has been found to be very effective in preventing the disposition of stolen cars.

Responsibility for enforcing the motor vehicle code normally rests with the state highway patrol, the pattern for the administration of which is fairly uniform. In twelve states patrols are administered by the department of public safety, in sixteen by the state police, in sixteen by the state highway department, in two by the motor vehicle department, and in one (Idaho) by the department of law enforcement. In any case constant and vigorous effort is necessary if the highways are to be safe for use. Just as the department of highways is responsible for the construction of roads, so this agency is responsible for seeing that they are, so far as possible, free from drunken and otherwise reckless drivers and safe for the use of the motoring public. The members of this force patrol the highways for the purpose of enforcing the law and, when necessary, rendering assistance to those who are in distress.

Other Forms of Transportation. The state may be responsible for the supervision of types of transportation facilities other than motor highways. A century ago, in the internal improvement era, many of the states embarked on extensive canal-building programs. During this period New York State built the Erie Canal — about the only one that was at all successful. This remains today in the form of the new barge canal, which is operated under the supervision of the Department of Public Works. States along the seacoast, or states bordering on large inland bodies of water, may maintain port or harbor patrols, and may find it necessary to operate patrol boats to aid in the enforcement of various statutes, as for instance, to prevent the bootlegging of gasoline. Several of the states at one time owned and operated railway systems.

Not only do the states own and operate a very large number of cars and trucks, but more than one third of them now own airplanes [14] and some own patrol boats and other vessels. Their responsibilities in the regulation of air traffic are limited by the primarily interstate character of that traffic, but they have an important role in cooperation with the Federal government on the one hand and their own municipalities on the other, in the planning, construction, maintenance, and operation of airport facilities.

Public Health and Social Welfare

This discussion of public health and welfare services will cover, in addition to direct health and welfare service, work done in the fields of mental health, corrections, institutional management, recreational facilities, and the social security program, including public assistance administration, most of which is operated in cooperation with the Federal government for the benefit of the unemployed, the aged, dependent children, and the blind. While, in other words, both terms are broad and to a certain extent overlapping, as used to describe governmental functions, the one has been narrowed to the fields of preventive medicine, sanitation, health education, and regulation in one area, to public assistance, child welfare, and institutional management for the sick, infirm, and prisoners in another.

Department of Public Health. The states began to do a certain amount of public health work soon after the close of the Civil War. As the germ theory became established, as science demonstrated that many diseases are definitely controllable and that "within reasonable limits public health is a purchasable commodity," expenditures showed a steady and consistent

[14] See Barthell, Roger V., "Airplanes for State Governments," *State Government*, June 1941, pp. 136–139, with tables.

increase. By 1900 there were only nine states that had not taken the legislative action necessary to establish a board of health, but where this step had been taken, the agency was in most cases extremely weak. In Illinois, for instance, "the entire staff of the State Board of Health consisted of the executive secretary, four lodging house inspectors, and three clerks." By 1910 all states except two had created boards of health, and these two followed in 1913 and 1919 respectively. Numerous voluntary public health agencies, created in the early years of the present century, succeeded in emphasizing the need for official state services.[15]

The duties of the department are many and varied. They include work in infant and maternity hygiene, control of communicable and social diseases, sanitary engineering, food and drug control, and milk control. They embrace also such other activities as assisting in the solution of local health problems, supervising the work of local health officers, conducting clinics, licensing nurses and midwives, conducting public health laboratories for research and diagnostic purposes, keeping vital statistics records, and carrying on public health education. It is hopelessly inadequate merely to enumerate the duties performed by so large and so important a department of the state government.

Mental Health. Mental health problems have always existed, but only in recent years have they been correctly diagnosed, adequately reported, and properly treated. Persons afflicted with mental illness were regarded as "crazy" and were often thrown into prison with common criminals. Mental illness was regarded as a disgrace to the family. Now all that is changed. While the figures show a great increase in the number of mental cases, due to the nervous strain imposed by the tempo of modern life and the strain of war, the states have developed institutions and facilities for the treatment of such cases. Even more important than curing those who are afflicted is the prevention of as many cases as possible for the future.

This function, important though it is, is still struggling to establish itself in the administrative setup of the states. Only six states — California, Massachusetts, Michigan, New York, Oklahoma, and Virginia — give it the full cabinet status that it probably should have. On a financial basis as well as a professional one, this is well justified. In Pennsylvania the Bureau in the Department of Welfare has jurisdiction over the ten state mental hospitals, and its budget is larger than that of the entire Department of Health. Ten more states give mental health separate status but place it under a council, board, or commission for administrative purposes. Five states — Colorado, Georgia, Idaho, Kansas, and South Dakota — make no provision at all for it in the administrative hierarchy. The remainder have a variety of adminis-

[15] Hoehler, Fred K., "Public Welfare and Health, 1900–1950," *State Government*, June 1950, pp. 129–133, 142, and Willard, William R., "Fifteen Years of Public Health Administration," *Public Administration Review*, Spring 1950, pp. 99–119. This article includes a good bibliography.

trative arrangements.[16] In eleven it is carried on by the state hospital administration, but four place it in a department of institutions — which may include other institutions than mental hospitals. Twelve provide for it a bureau status in the department of health and/or welfare.

Whatever its position in the administrative structure, the agency carries on educational work in the field of mental health, operates clinics and psychiatric hospitals, and supervises privately operated mental homes and hospitals. It is just as important to prevent mental illness as to prevent physical illness. Much illness of both types is unnecessary; both cause great financial loss and much suffering.

Department of Social Welfare. The idea underlying the giving of assistance to those in need has changed very greatly in the last few years. Whereas it was once customary to give alms to paupers and to maintain almshouses, poorhouses, and foundling asylums, clients are now given public assistance, old age pensions and old age assistance, aid to dependent children, and aid to the permanently and totally disabled, every effort being made to avoid commitment to institutions. The old idea looked toward the perpetuation of a permanent class of unprosperous persons; the present system looks toward prompt restoration to a position as self-respecting and self-supporting members of society. The difference may be one of terminology and psychology, but it is not without significance from the point of view of social philosophy.

The location of the department in the state government varies little from state to state, in contrast with the diversity that existed only a few years ago. It is given the status of a department or division in all but three states — North Dakota, Oregon, and Utah — which still cling to the antiquated commission form of organization. Illinois, New Jersey, and a few other states have both a department and an advisory board or commission. Earlier diversity with regard to terminology has all but disappeared, the terms "welfare," "public welfare," or "social welfare," having attained almost universal acceptance. Pennsylvania has both a Department of Welfare and a Department of Public Assistance. The growth and importance of these services, as reflected in state expenditures for them, is clearly shown in the table on page 447.[17] Today's figures would show still larger amounts.

The services rendered by the department include numerous duties which may be classified under the general heading of community work. In connection with child welfare and mother's assistance, the department supervises adoptions; commits dependent children to institutions when necessary, and

[16] Such attempts at classification are rarely made on the same basis, and so seldom agree. This is based on Hoehler, *op. cit.;* for a quite different analysis, see Council of State Governments, *The Mental Health Programs of the Forty-Eight States*, Chapter 4 (Chicago, 1950).

[17] Hoehler, *op. cit.*, p. 132; see also Miles, Arthur P., *An Introduction to Public Welfare* (Heath, Boston 1949); Burns, Eveline M., *The American Social Security System* (Houghton Mifflin, Boston, 1949), and Gagliardo, Dominico, *American Social Insurance* (Harpers, New York, 1950).

State Expenditures for Health and Welfare Purposes, 1902–1948

YEAR	SANITATION AND HEALTH	INSTITUTIONS, WELFARE, CORRECTIONS
1902	$ 3,000,000	$ 53,000,000
1913	6,000,000	87,000,000
1932	26,000,000	328,000,000
1942	54,000,000	830,000,000
1948	712,000,000	1,600,000,000

delinquent children to training schools; administers a system of juvenile probation; has charge of institutions for convalescent and crippled children; and supervises the program of aid to dependent children. It has general supervision also over private welfare institutions, and provides inspection and licensure for maternity hospitals, private nursing homes and hospitals, boarding homes for infants, and private mental hospitals. It licenses persons desiring to solicit funds for charitable purposes, and administers the system of pensions for the blind, in addition to supervising other services for the members of this group. It also administers the old age pension program.

Institutional Management. The management of the state's institutions is, in the larger states, an undertaking of no small proportions. The organization for the handling of the work varies widely. In Pennsylvania there is a Bureau of Institutional Management in the Department of Welfare; New Jersey combines the two types of service in its Department of Institutions and Agencies; California maintains a separate Department of Institutions. Even where, as in these states, there is a separate agency for institutional management, not all of the state institutions may be placed under its control; this is especially apt to be true of correctional institutions. Included are mental hospitals, mental health clinics and psychopathic hospitals, institutions for the feeble-minded, and the colony for epileptics. Louisiana and Pennsylvania make large contributions for the care of the sick-poor, the former operating charity hospitals and the latter owning and operating ten medical and surgical hospitals in addition to making substantial appropriations for the assistance of more than 160 private hospitals throughout the Commonwealth.

There is a good deal of disagreement as to the most desirable form of organization for institutional management. A department of institutions is based upon the theory that all institutions have many managerial problems in common, which is certainly true. The professional staff usually objects to a central management and to the enforcement of uniform policies on the ground that efficiency and economy in management are placed above the welfare of the patients or inmates of the institutions. Conversely, management specialists object to autonomy for individual institutions on the ground that the lack of attention to managerial problems which often results encourages waste and unnecessary expenditures. Controversy still rages over the use of governing boards — whether there should be central control boards or local boards for each institution, or whether, indeed, there should be boards at all. Current thinking tends to the view that advisory boards are a relatively harmless concession to long-established practice and that they may at times be useful in advisory, consulting, and public relations capacities, but that boards with important administrative responsibilities are a serious obstacle to good administration.

Department of Corrections. The functions of charities and corrections were formerly closely associated and were often combined in the same department. The recent tendency has been to regard them as separate functions, setting up a separate bureau, or preferably a separate department, for correctional work. If the bureau is attached to the department of welfare, the human aspects of the problem of corrections are likely to be emphasized; if it is attached to the department of justice, the legal and punitive aspects of the work are likely to receive greater attention. At any rate, some agency in the state government, working on one theory or the other, has to administer the penitentiaries and the homes or reformatories for women and for delinquent boys and girls.

Such an agency should, and in some states does, exercise some supervision over the county jails. These institutions have of late been much improved; they were formerly accustomed to doing everything, in the treatment of prisoners, which science has shown should not be done. There are numerous special problems for the handling of which this agency is responsible — the problem of prison industries and prison labor, the management of a fund for the operation of prison industries, and the problems of recreation and of discipline. In view of the numerous prison riots and disturbances that have occurred in many states, it is clear that these problems are large and of no slight difficulty.

Public Assistance. The function of welfare and assistance was originally regarded as being purely local in character; this belief continued during the early days of the depression. It soon became apparent that the emergency was too great for the resources of private charity, then in turn for local public charity, and finally for the states themselves. When the Federal government began to provide financial assistance through the Federal Emergency Relief Administration, it became necessary for the states to set up a relief organization that was satisfactory to the Federal authorities. In most of the states an entirely new agency was created by the legislature, often with a board to determine policy and an administrator appointed by the governor. In order to reduce, so far as possible, the influence of politics in the distribution of relief, the Federal authorities demanded a highly centralized organization. This meant that the state relief administrations required the setting up of county boards with county administrators responsible to them. Where smaller poor relief districts existed, they were unable to function because they had no money. Most of them have since been abolished. The administration of emergency relief had an enduring influence in centralizing control in the handling of relief problems. There is in Pennsylvania a department of public assistance charged with supervision of the county boards of assistance, but in most states this function is handled as one aspect of the work of the welfare program.

Social Security. The Federal social security program operates on the basis of Federal-state cooperative arrangements, under which the Federal Government reimburses the states for the administrative costs incurred and assists with the financial burden of carrying on the program. Five specific programs are now involved — unemployment compensation, old age pensions, aid for dependent children, aid for the blind, and aid for the permanently and totally disabled. These services may or may not be located in a single department of the state government, but in either case participation on the part of any state is dependent upon meeting certain conditions imposed in connection with the grants-in-aid. It is required that the staff administering the work be selected on a merit basis. In some states this is the only dent the merit system has made in the system of partisan spoils politics.

The funds for the unemployment compensation program are built up from wage deductions, plus equal contributions made by the employer. Old age pensions are designed to prevent suffering on the part of older citizens and to prevent the embarrassment that goes with dependency on relatives. Aid to dependent children, or mother's assistance, is provided for the mothers of small children where the father has died or, because of illness, is unable to support his family. The system of pensions for the blind represents an attempt to provide financial assistance for a relatively small group of citizens who suffer from a very serious affliction. Aid for the permanently and totally disabled was added to the program in 1950.

Recreation. The largest expenditures for public recreation have heretofore been made by the cities rather than by the states; they have been made for public playgrounds, swimming pools and bathhouses, recreation centers, and public parks. The efforts of the states were long largely confined to the establishment of memorial parks at places of historic interest, and of camp sites in state forest lands. Now all but four states have state parks or areas set aside primarily or wholly for recreational use, and all but two have state migratory game and bird refuges, covering over 50 million acres. There were only ten state park agencies at the turn of the century. Even now the total expenditures are not great, in proportion to the total cost of state government, although considerable sums are expended for this purpose in a few states.[18]

[18] See Eppley, Garrett G., "State Government's Role in Recreation," *State Government*, May 1948, pp. 107–109.

Education

Education, like the other older functions of government, was local to begin with, and the local communities have still retained considerable control over it. Through the years state expenditures for this purpose have steadily increased, and the power of the state has been clearly recognized by the courts, although in many cases it has not been used as effectively as it might be. It is still common practice to permit groups of local citizens, functioning as boards of education — well-meaning, to be sure, but totally unqualified — to determine important questions of educational policy.

Elementary and Secondary Schools. Momentous changes have taken place in the nation's public schools during the first half century[19]:

> In 1900 there were 250,000 schools with an enrollment of 15.5 million pupils. Expenditures for them in 1900 were $325 million. Only 50 per cent of the population from five to seventeen years of age attended school and the average child attended for less than seventy-two days a year. Schools were open an average of 144 days a year. The average annual expenditure per pupil was slightly more than $20. Teachers were paid an average monthly salary (twelve months) of $27.12. Only 12 per cent of the children of high school age attended a high school. Less than two persons out of every 100 of the population, twenty-one years of age and over, graduated from college. Some states had not as yet enacted compulsory attendance laws for pupils at any age level. . . .
>
> Consider the situation today, fifty years later. More than 26 million pupils attend schools full time and several million adults are in part-time attendance. Expenditures are more than $4 billion a year. Of the five to seventeen age group, 82 per cent are enrolled in public schools, and the average child attends for 150 days. Schools are kept open for an average of 180 days a year. The expenditure per pupil in average daily attendance is approximately $200. The average teacher's salary on a twelve-month basis is $225. More than 70 per cent of children of high school age are in high school. More than ten persons out of every 100 of the population, twenty-one years of age and over, have graduated from college.

The weak and ineffectual influence of the states over education in 1900 has gradually given way to a greatly increased role in educational developments. The states — at least all but nine of them[20] — have some kind of state board or council of education. These boards range in number of members from three to nineteen, the most common number being seven, the average 8.6. Twenty-two states require membership on the board of one or more professional educators, including the chief state school officer; membership of the boards actually includes more persons engaged in educational work than is required by law. The term of office ranges from two years in two states, to thirteen years in one. In ten states, members serve for four years, in thirteen for six years. In most instances the boards are charged with such duties

[19] Cocking, Walter D., "The Role of the States in Education Since 1900," *State Government*, June 1950, pp. 119–123, 143.

[20] These are: Illinois, Iowa, Maine, Nebraska, North Dakota, Ohio, Rhode Island, South Dakota, and Wisconsin.

as the adoption of rules and regulations, control of teacher certification and of teacher education other than by certification, prescription of minimum standards in specified areas, determination of educational policy and of standards governing the apportionment of state school funds, the adoption of courses of study and of textbooks, as well as the determination of the plan of organization of the state department of education.

The executive head of the state department is elected by popular vote in thirty-one states, appointed by state boards of education in ten, appointed by the governor in seven, with the trend toward the second method. Twenty-six serve for a four-year term, eleven for only two years, but six have an indefinite term. Eight receive a salary of $10,000 or more, but only one of these eight is chosen by popular elections. Nine chief state school officers serve as chairmen of the state boards of education, twenty-two of them as secretaries of such boards. The total number of professional staff members in the departments which serve under them range from 523 in New York to a low of twelve in South Dakota. The size of the staff is influenced by the size of the state and of the school population, and the extent of the services and responsibilities assigned; at the same time, a significant recent survey indicates that state department staffs tend to be too small rather than too large.[21]

The major activities of the department include general supervision of school administration and school finance throughout the state; the carrying on of research work and the compilation of statistical data on the schools of the state; the conduct of the teacher certification work, and supervision of the examining boards for the learned professions; curriculum making and curriculum supervision; the school health program; vocational education; education of the deaf and blind and of other defective groups; and direction of the adult program, the rural school program, and the program for visual education. In addition, the department usually has supervision and control of the state library and the state museum; with this one exception, all the activities here mentioned relate to the supervision of the elementary and secondary schools.

In recent years the financial problems of the public education system have become more and more difficult. The control of the states over the schools has been strengthened in the effort to solve the financial problems of the poorer school districts. For political reasons it was impossible to assist the poor districts without giving assistance to all districts, although progress is being made in school district consolidation. Many different school finance patterns have developed among the several states. Some of these — the Council of State Governments survey concludes — "contribute directly to the attainment of recognized objectives of education; others contribute very little; and some even have a negative effect. It is generally accepted that every state school finance program should: (1) help to assure reasonably

[21] Council of State Governments, *The Forty-eight State School Systems*, Chapter 3 on which this comment is based (Chicago, 1949).

adequate and well-rounded educational opportunities for all children and youth throughout the state and (2) be based on a system of taxation and administration which assures that the burden will be equitably distributed among all types and classes of citizens and taxing units." [22] Through this medium of financial assistance, the states have been able to set standards in many fields, such as teacher training, salaries, length of school term, contents of curriculum, pupil transportation, and other important matters.

Higher Education. In the field of higher education similar financial problems have been met without a corresponding extension of state control. In the states of the West, Middle West, and South, the governments have contributed more or less generously to state universities; in the older states of the East, many of which long sought to meet the problem of providing equal educational opportunities for its youth by state aid to existing private institutions, there has been an extensive movement for the establishment of state universities. States like Connecticut, Massachusetts, and New Jersey have taken over and expanded existing institutions, while in New York authorities are in the process of creating a new state university system, built around the nucleus of the temporary colleges established by the state at the end of World War II for the training of veterans. Pennsylvania, which makes sizable appropriations for the assistance of the four major institutions of higher learning in the state, none of which are state institutions, is about the only state left without a completely state-owned and state-supported university.[23] By 1950, in addition to the state universities, every state had its college of agriculture and mechanical arts, under the land-grant program, and an assortment of technical schools, teachers colleges, other professional schools, and junior or community colleges. The latter are rapidly increasing in number and have already developed into an extensive state-wide system in some jurisdictions.

SELECTED REFERENCES

AGRICULTURE AND NATURAL RESOURCES:

General: Hynning, Clifford J., *State Conservation of Resources* (National Resources Planning Board, Washington, 1939); Renner, George T., *Conservation of Natural Resources; an Educational Approach to the Problem* (Wiley, New York, 1942); Satterfield, Millard H., *Soil and Sky; the Development and Use of Tennessee Valley Resources* (Extension Division, University of Kentucky, 1950); Smith, Guy H., *Conservation of Natural Resources* (Wiley, New York, 1950).

State Studies in Agriculture: Stene, Edwin O., *Kansas State Board of Agriculture* (Bureau of Governmental Research, University of Kansas, 1948); Weiss, Harry B., *History of the New Jersey State Board of Agriculture, 1872–1916*, and *The New*

[22] *Ibid.*, p. 159.

[23] Pennsylvania also appropriates for a dozen other educational institutions in specialized fields, such as medical and industrial schools and the school for the blind. In addition, there is a system of free scholarships, four to each senatorial district, to be awarded on a competitive basis to young men and young women in families most in need of financial assistance to educate their children.

Jersey Department of Agriculture, 1916–1949 (New Jersey Agricultural Society, Trenton, 1949 and 1950); Hedrick, U. P., *A History of Agriculture in the State of New York* (New State Agricultural Society, Albany, 1933).

State Studies in Conservation: Briscoe, Vera, and others, *Safeguarding Kentucky's Natural Resources* (University of Kentucky, 1948); Greene, Lee S., and others, *Rescued Earth, a Study of the Administration of Natural Resources in Tennessee* (University of Tennessee Press, 1948); Larsen, Christian L., *South Carolina's Natural Resources* (University of South Carolina Press, 1947); Ray, Joseph M., and Worley, Lillian, *Alabama's Heritage* (Bureau of Public Administration, University of Alabama, 1947); Wager, Paul W., and Hayman, Donald B., *Resources Management in North Carolina* (Institute for Research in Social Science, University of North Carolina, 1947).

COMMERCE:

Dimock, Marshall E., *Business and Government* (Holt, New York, 1949); Mund, Vernon A., *Government and Business* (Harpers, New York, 1950); Rohlfing, Charles C., and others, *Government and Business*, Fifth Edition (Foundation Press, Brooklyn, 1949); Fesler, James W., *The Independence of State Regulatory Agencies* (Public Administration Service, Chicago, 1942).

EDUCATION:

General: Beach, Fred F., *The Functions of State Departments of Education*, with Gibbs, Andrew H., *The Structure of State Departments of Education*, with Hutchins, Clayton D., *The Financing of State Departments of Education* (Federal Security Agency, Washington, 1950 and 1951); Council of State Governments, *The Forty-eight State School Systems*, and *Higher Education in the Forty-eight States* (Chicago, 1949 and 1952); Keesecker, Ward W., *State Boards of Education and Chief State School Officers* (Federal Security Agency, Washington, 1950); Morphet, Edgar L., and Lindman, Erick L., *Public School Finance Programs of the Forty-eight States* (Federal Security Agency, Washington, 1950); Sears, Jesse B., *The Nature of the Administrative Process, with Special Reference to Public School Administration* (McGraw-Hill, New York, 1950).

Studies in Individual States: Donnelly, Thomas C., *The State Educational System* (Division of Research, Department of Government, University of New Mexico, 1946); Illinois Legislative Council, *School Administration in Illinois* (Springfield, 1948); Regents Inquiry into the Character and Cost of Public Education in New York State (Report in 11 vols., McGraw-Hill, New York, 1939); State Superintendent of Public Instruction, *The Organization, Functions, and Staff of the Office of Education in Oregon* (Salem, 1950); Strayer, George D., *The Administration, Organization and Financial Support of the Public School System, State of California* (State Reconstruction and Reemployment Commission, Sacramento, 1945).

HIGHWAYS AND MOTOR VEHICLES:

General: American Automobile Association, *Digest of Motor Laws* (Washington, annually); Council of State Governments, *Highway Safety — Motor Truck Regulation* (Chicago, 1950); Highway Research Board, *State Highway Administrative Bodies* (Washington, 1952); Labatut, Jean, and Lane, Wheaton J., *Highways in Our National Life* (Princeton University Press, 1950); National Automobile Chamber of Commerce, *Facts and Figures of the Automobile Industry* (New York, annually); Owen, Wilfred, *Automotive Transportation: Trends and Problems* (Brookings Institution, Washington, 1949); Pate, James E., *Highway Administration in the South* (Arnold Foundation, Dallas, 1935); United States Public Roads Administration (now Bureau of Public Roads), *A Bibliography of Highway Planning Reports* and *Highway Practice in the United States of America* (Washington, 1950 and 1949).

Studies in Individual States: Brown, Cecil K., *The State Highway System of North Carolina* (University of North Carolina Press, 1931); Curtiss, William M., *The Development of Highway Administration and Finance in New York* (New York State College of Agriculture, Ithaca, 1937); Goldmann, Sidney, and Graves, Thomas J., *The Organization and Administration of the New Jersey State Highway Department* (Trenton, 1942); National Research Council, *Report of a Study of Highway Laws, Organization and Procedure of Colorado* (Highway Research Board, Washington, 1948); Public Administration Service, *Kentucky Highway Systems and the State Department of Highways* (Kentucky Legislative Research Commission, Frankfort, 1951); Stewart, Frank M., *Highway Administration in Texas* (University of Texas, 1934).

LABOR:

General: Andrews, John B., *Labor Laws in Action* (Harpers, New York, 1938); Cohen, Sanford, *State Labor Legislation, 1937–1947; a Study of State Laws Affecting the Conduct and Organization of Labor Unions* (Bureau of Business Research, Ohio State University, 1948); Graves, W. Brooke, *Fair Employment Practice Legislation in the United States* (Public Affairs Bulletin No. 93, Legislative Reference Service, Library of Congress, Washington, 1951); Killingsworth, Charles C., *State Labor Relations Acts; a Study of Public Policy* (University of Chicago Press, 1948); Riesenfeld, Stefan A., and Maxwell, Richard C., *Modern Social Legislation* (Foundation Press, Brooklyn, 1950); Sanford, Edward F., *Recent State Labor Legislation* (Bureau of Public Administration, University of California, 1949).

Studies in Individual States: Altmeyer, Arthur J., *The Industrial Commission of Wisconsin; a Case Study in Labor Law Administration* (University of Wisconsin Studies in the Social Sciences and History, 1932); Bechner, Earl R., *History of Labor Legislation in Illinois* (Cambridge University Press, New York, 1929); Brown, Virginia H., *The Development of Labor Legislation in Tennessee* (*University of Tennesee Record*, November 1945, entire issue); Newman, Philip C., *The Labor Legislation of New Jersey* (American Council on Public Affairs, Washington, 1943); Ryan, Frederick L., *A History of Labor Legislation in Oklahoma* (University of Oklahoma Press, 1932); Wetherill, Arthur M., Jr., *Virginia Labor Legislation; a Brief Digest* (Bureau of Population and Economic Research, University of Virginia, 1947); Wollman, Nathaniel, *An Appraisal of New Mexico Labor Legislation* (Division of Research, Department of Government, University of New Mexico, 1950).

LAW ENFORCEMENT AND CORRECTIONS:

General: Alabama Legislative Reference Service, *The State Police in the Southern States* (Montgomery, 1950); Barnes, Harry E., and Teeters, Negley K., *New Horizons in Criminology; The American Crime Problem*, Revised Edition (Prentice-Hall, New York, 1950); Reckless, Walter C., *The Crime Problem* (Appleton-Century-Crofts, New York, 1950); Robinson, Louis N., *Jails: Care and Treatment of Misdemeanant Prisoners in the United States* (Winston, Philadelphia, 1944); Smith, Bruce, *Police Systems in the United States*, Revised Edition (Harpers, New York, 1949); Wilson, Orlando W., *Police Administration* (McGraw-Hill, New York, 1950).

Studies in Individual States: Fox, Noel P., *A Survey of the Michigan Correction System* (Lansing, 1949); Habermann, Philip S., *Law Enforcement in Wisconsin; a Study with Suggestions for Improvement* (Legislative Council, Madison, 1949);

Heinberg, John G., and Breckenridge, Adam C., *Law Enforcement in Missouri, 1931–1941* (University of Missouri Studies, 1942); Olander, Oscar G., *Michigan State Police: a Twenty-five Year History* (Michigan Police Journal Press, Lansing, 1942); Moos, Malcolm C., *State Penal Administration in Alabama* (Bureau of Public Administration, University of Alabama, 1942); Rhode Island Public Expenditure Council, *Law Enforcement in Rhode Island* (Providence, 1945); Voigt, Lloyd L., *History of California State Correctional Administration from 1930 to 1948* (San Francisco, 1949); Warp, George A., *Police Administration in Virginia* (Bureau of Public Administration, University of Virginia, 1942).

PUBLIC HEALTH:

General: American Public Health Association, Committee on Administrative Practice, *Keystones of Public Health for Pennsylvania* (New York, 1948); Council of State Governments, *The Mental Health Programs of the Forty-eight States* (Chicago, 1950); Hanlon, John J., *Principles of Public Health Administration* (Mosby, St. Louis, 1950); Hiscock, Ira V., *Community Health Organization* (Commonwealth Fund, New York, 1950); Mountin, Joseph W., *Guide to Health Organization in the United States*, and with Glook, Evelyn, *Distribution of Health Services in the Structure of State Government*, Third Edition (United States Public Health Service, Washington, 1945 and 1943); Mustard, Harry S., *An Introduction to Public Health*, Second Edition (Macmillan, New York, 1944); Smillie, Wilson G., *Public Health Administration in the United States*, Third Edition (Macmillan, New York, 1947); Tobey, James A., *Public Health Law*, Third Edition (Williams & Wilkins, Baltimore, 1947).

Studies in Individual States: Coffey, F. A., and Bratton, Charles A., *Public Health Administration in New York* (New York State College of Agriculture, Ithaca, 1943); Donnelly, Thomas C., *Public Health Administration in New Mexico* (University of New Mexico Bulletin, 1938); Florida State Board of Health, *Life and Death in Florida, 1940–1950* (Jacksonville, n.d.); Illinois Department of Health, *Rise and Fall of Disease in Illinois*, 2 vols. (Springfield, 1922); Kendrick, John F., *Public Health in the State and Counties of Virginia* (State Department of Health, Richmond, 1939); Larsen, Christian L., and Searles, Jeannette, *South Carolina State Board of Health* (Bureau of Public Administration, University of South Carolina, 1949); McIntosh, William F., and Kendrick, John F., *Public Health Administration in North Carolina* (State Board of Health, Raleigh, 1940); South Carolina Research, Planning, and Development Board, *Health Facilities Survey, State of South Carolina* (Columbia, 1947); Texas State Department of Health, *History of Public Health in Texas* (Austin, 1950); Washington Department of Health, *Washington's Health: the Next Fifty Years, 1950–2000* (Seattle, 1950).

PUBLIC WELFARE:

General: Breckenridge, Sophanisba P., *Public Welfare Administration with Special Reference to the Organization of State Departments* (University of Chicago Press, 1934); Burns, Eveline M., *The American Social Security System* (Houghton Mifflin, Boston, 1949); Gagliardo, Dominico, *American Social Insurance* (Harpers, New York, 1950); Hodges, Margaret B., Ed., *Social Work Year Book* (Russell Sage Foundation, New York, annually); Miles, Arthur P., *An Introduction to Public Welfare* (Heath, Boston, 1949); Millspaugh, Arthur C., *Public Welfare Organization* (Brookings Institution, Washington, 1935); White, R. Clyde, *Administration of Social Welfare*, Second Edition (American Book Company, New York, 1950).

Studies in Individual States: Ashcraft, Virginia, *Public Care; a History of Public Welfare Legislation in Tennessee* (University of Tennessee Record, 1947); Buck,

Mildred E., and others, *Public Welfare in Washington; a Statewide Study of Problems of Public Welfare Administration* (State Planning Council, Olympia, 1934); Butler, Amos W., *A Century of Progress; a Study of the Development of Public Charities and Corrections, 1790–1915* (State Board of Charities, Indianapolis, 1916); Cahn, Frances, and Bary, Valeska, *Welfare Activities of Federal, State, and Local Governments in California, 1850–1934* (University of California Press, 1936); Commercial Surveys, Inc., *A Survey of the Florida State Welfare Board* (New York, 1949); D'Agostino, Lorenzo, *The History of Public Welfare in Vermont* (St. Michael's College Press, Winooski Park, 1949); Ellis, Helen H., *Public Welfare Problems of New Mexico* (Division of Research, Department of Government, University of New Mexico, 1948); Harper, Ernest B., and Gibson, Duane L., *Reorganization of Public Welfare in Michigan* (Michigan State College, 1942); James, Arthur W., *The State Becomes a Social Worker* (Garrett & Massie, Richmond, 1942); Lutz, E. A., *Rural Public Welfare Administration and Finance in New York* (New York State College of Agriculture, Ithaca, 1941); North Carolina State Board of Public Welfare, *Public Welfare in North Carolina* (Raleigh, 1949); Schneider, David M., and Deutsch, Albert, *The History of Public Welfare in New York State, 1867–1940* (University of Chicago Press, 1942); Stafford, Paul T., *State Welfare Administration in New Jersey* (State Department of Institutions and Agencies, Trenton, 1934); Wisconsin Department of Public Welfare, *A Half Billion Dollars for Public Welfare in Wisconsin, 1931–1936* (Madison, 1938); Wisner, Elizabeth, *Public Social Services in Louisiana* (Louisiana Conference on Social Welfare, Monroe, 1944).

13

Personnel Management

The governments of the states are so dependent on the intelligent and devoted service of thousands of employees that any general discussion of state government which failed to mention them would be incomplete indeed. Payrolls of state governments reached $212 million in April 1950, compared with $197 million a year earlier and $111 million in 1946. The number of state employees passed the one million mark, rising to 1,033 thousand in April 1950, as compared with 982 thousand a year earlier.

State governments accounted in 1950 for over 16 per cent of the 6360 thousand persons on public payrolls — Federal, state, and local. They had half as many employees as the Federal government and about one third as many as all local governments combined. Of total public payrolls amounting to $1422 million, the states accounted for 15 per cent. The state portion of all public employees and payrolls had increased materially since the end of

State Employees and Pay Rolls: Month of April 1940–1950

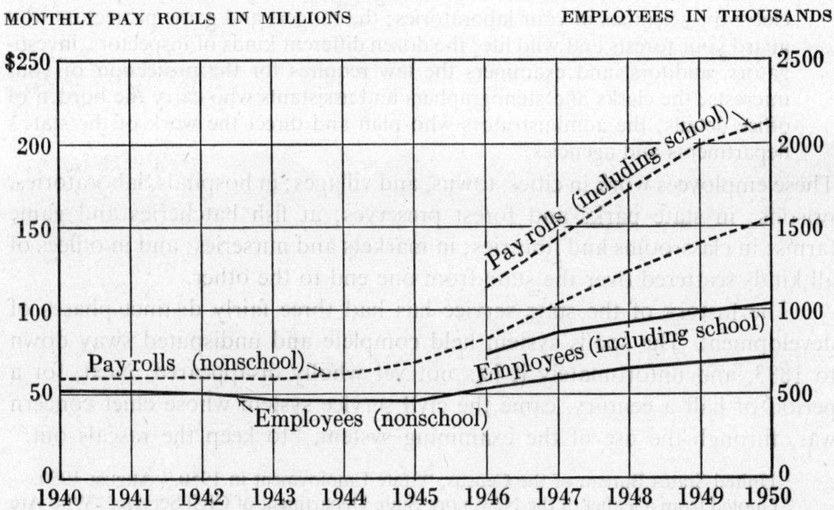

Bureau of the Census

World War II, as has been shown. The trend and the figures on both items are indicated in the graph on page 457.[1]

To illustrate the point in another way, with reference to a specific state, the growth of the service in New York may be noted. The New York State government, which has been growing for 175 years, has expanded most rapidly in recent years. The number of state civil service employees has increased fivefold since 1910 and has more than doubled since 1930.

State of New York
Growth of State Civil Service

YEAR	POPULATION	NUMBER OF EMPLOYEES
1910	9,113,614	13,033
1920	10,385,227	17,470
1930	12,588,066	30,864
1940	13,479,142	51,806
1950	14,743,210	77,861

These state employees in New York and many other states have made government their career, many of them having risen from the lower ranks to positions of great responsibility. Among them are to be found almost every type of skill man has developed, including [2]:

> public health physicians and nurses who care for the sick in your community; the engineers who design and build the highways you travel over every day; the educators who guide your school system, the teachers of the handicapped and the delinquent children; the psychiatrists, nurses, technicians, and attendants devoted to the task of restoring the mentally ill to their place in society; the scientists in your laboratories; the rangers and game protectors who guard your forests and wild life; the dozen different kinds of inspectors, investigators, auditors, and examiners the law requires for the protection of your interests; the clerks and stenographers and assistants who carry the burden of office details; the administrators who plan and direct the work of the state's departments and agencies.

These employees work in cities, towns, and villages; in hospitals, laboratories, prisons; in state parks and forest preserves; at fish hatcheries and game farms; in classrooms and libraries; in markets and nurseries; and in offices of all kinds scattered over the state from one end to the other.

The history of the state service has had three fairly distinct phases of development. The spoils system held complete and undisputed sway down to 1883, and unfortunately it has not yet wholly disappeared. Next, for a period of half a century, came the civil service system whose chief concern was, through the use of the examining system, "to keep the rascals out."

[1] United States Bureau of the Census, "State Employment in 1950," August 1950.

[2] Quoted from a leaflet of the New York State Department of Civil Service, "Who Are Your State Employees? What Do They Do?" (Albany, 1950).

The legal basis for this system first appeared in New York and Massachusetts at the time the Pendleton Act was passed by the Congress, its reform philosophy continuing down to approximately 1935, when the third period began. The publication of the report of the Commission of Inquiry on Public Service Personnel opened the way for emphasis on a career service, based upon merit. Some of the significant differences between the three systems, presently to be discussed, are indicated in the table on page 460.

The Spoils System

Problems of recruiting and organizing the personnel enlisted in performing the functions of government have long been important. In the early days, when the number of services performed by government was small and their extent limited, the number of public employees was small, and their duties were such that they could be performed by any ordinarily intelligent person. Studies in the history of personnel administration indicate that at a very early date such positions as were available were commonly regarded as spoils to be distributed among the party workers who supported the candidates victorious at the polls. In his *Civil Service and the Patronage* the late Professor Carl Russell Fish described in some detail early developments in such states as New York, Pennsylvania, and Massachusetts. In order that the reader may have clearly in mind the nature of the conditions existing at that time, the following excerpts from his book are included[3]:

> *New York*. New York was the first state in which the offices were openly and continuously used for partisan purposes. There the royal appointments had been conspicuously bad, and colonial politics especially active. This experience was probably responsible for the elaborate attempt, made in the first constitution, to limit the appointing power of the executive, and to secure proper recognition for the various geographical sections. The state was divided into four districts, each represented by an equal number of senators. . . .
>
> The conditions which governed the working of this machinery of appointment were complicated and do not readily admit of brief explanation. New York politics had been controlled in the colonial period by family groups or combinations, based largely on land and old manorial privileges. The power of some of these groups was broken by the Revolution, but a large part of the population lacked American political experience and ideals, and were still ready to follow leaders; hence the influence of certain families remained. . . . Although Republican formulas were used, politics continued to be a game played by a number of factions, some aristocratic, some democratic, by bosses and patrons. The political situation reproduced in miniature that of England during the eighteenth century. . . . The spoils system was particularly dangerous in New York because of the enormous extent of the patronage.
>
> *Pennsylvania*. Such was the situation that Thomas McKean found when, in 1799, he was elected governor, first of the *fin de siècle* Republican victors. He accused of combination against him the "officers and expectants of office under the President of the United States, not only in Pennsylvania, but in neighboring states," and he wrote to John Dickinson, "I have been obliged

[3] Fish, Carl Russell, *The Civil Service and the Patronage*, pp. 86–87 (Harvard University Press, 1920).

Three Personnel Systems in Government*

	Under the Patronage System: SPOILS	*Under the Old-style Civil Service System:* REFORM	*Under the Modern Civil Service System:* MERIT
FINDING THE MAN	Local bosses limit applicants to Party Regulars.	Examinations open to Any Individual.	Advertisements, newspapers, radio, schools, attracting Qualified Applicants.
	The test: How Many Votes?	The test: Academic Examination.	The test: evaluation of Education, Experience, Physical Fitness, Intelligence, Personality, etc.
THE MAN ON THE JOB	Politicians interfere. Salaries Used as Bribes.	Department heads lobby. Pay Varies Widely.	Wage and cost of living surveys. Equal Pay for Equal Work.
	No job records.	Inadequate job records.	Scientific job analysis.
	Duties Unknown.	Duties Poorly Defined.	Classification Plan Based on Duties.
KEEPING UP MORALE	Favoritism and insecurity. Good Morale Impossible	"Not our function." Little Constructive Effort.	Not paternalistic but democratic. Employee Organizations, Safety Programs, Medical Care, Credit Unions, etc.
	Political careers only. Job Careers for None.	Careers for a few. Blind Alleys for Most.	In-service training and promotional system. Career Service for All.
REMOVING THE INCOMPETENT	Department heads powerless. Political Protection for Unfit.	Cumbersome. Trial Procedure.	Eliminating the dead wood. Service Ratings.
RETIRING THE SUPERANNUATED	No pension plans: Employees thrown out on Street.	Unsound retirement plans or Retention through Sympathy.	Actuarially sound Pension Plans.

* From Civil Service Assembly of the United States and Canada, *Newsletter*, July 1936.

(though no Hercules) to cleanse the Augean stable." To Jefferson, in July 1810, he outlined his theory of the civil service. "It appears," he said, "that the anti-Republicans, even those in office, are as hostile as ever, though not so insolent. To overcome them they must be shaven, for in their offices (like Samson's hair-locks) their great strength lieth; their disposition for mischief may remain, but their power of doing it will be gone. It is out of the common order of nature, to prefer enemies to friends; the despisers of the people should not be their rulers." The whole tone of this letter indicates that already in Pennsylvania the civil offices were considered as ammunition for political warfare — a fact which Jefferson must have seen clearly when he wrote to McKean, "Some states require a different regimen from others." . . .[4]

Massachusetts. Of the northern states, Massachusetts was perhaps the most exemplary in the conduct of the civil service; yet there, as in Rhode Island, an element existed eager for the spoils. Under the early state government there was practically no complaint as to appointments; but when the Federalists began to condemn Jefferson's removals, their opponents replied by accusing them of excluding all Republicans from office. The best vindication of their administration is found in the conduct of James Sullivan, the first Republican governor. He was a strong, conscientious man, and refused to make any removals. The radicals of the party under the lead of Levi Lincoln controlled the executive council and urged proscription, finally putting on file a protest in which they argued that to make no removals "would be arraigning the wisdom and justice of the national administration, a censure and reproach of its most deliberate acts." Had they been able to add that the conduct of the Federalist governors had been notoriously unfair, Sullivan could hardly have resisted. . . .[5]

The West. The frontier democracy of the West shared the characteristics of both North and South. During this period the people were divided according to personal sympathy and special issues, and consequently party lines were fluctuating. Hence there was no persistent and studied use of patronage to maintain party organization; but offices were none the less used by the leaders to promote the ends of the moment, while the people demanded that all public servants, appointive as well as elective, should be in sympathy with the majority. The conditions of this section are best illustrated by a study of Illinois, for which the career of Ninian Edwards serves as a convenient nucleus. . . .[6]

It has been customary for uninformed persons to blame the advent of the spoils system in the Federal government upon Andrew Jackson. Professor Fish makes it clear that the spoils system originated in the states, that terrific pressure was exerted upon the Presidents preceding Jackson, and that its introduction into the Federal government under Jackson represented simply the fulfillment of an insistent public demand which could not have been resisted much longer by anyone, and which Jackson had no disposition to resist at all. While occasional demands for investigations of conditions in the public service were made in Congress, it does not appear that anything important along this line occurred in the states. Even in the Federal government, the spoils system existed undisturbed for almost fifty years, until in 1883 the Pendleton Act was passed.

Although the supporters of the system have been fighting a slowly losing battle during the last half century or more, the practice of using positions on the public payroll as a reward for political service still prevails in many jurisdictions where political pressures are stronger than the interest in efficient government. Its hold is nowhere complete, however, for all forty-eight states participate in a varying number of Federally aided programs, one of the conditions of which is that the state personnel employed in their

[4] *Ibid.*, pp. 92–93, 94–95.
[5] *Ibid.*, pp. 95–97.
[6] *Ibid.*, p. 99.

administration shall be selected on the basis of merit and fitness and shall be protected in their tenure as long as they competently perform the duties assigned to them.

Effect on State Personnel. In states where the spoils system still prevails, the state service is completely demoralized for some months before and after the inauguration of a new governor. Under such circumstances it is impossible for employees to maintain a high standard of performance. Many employees, taking no chances, spend a great deal of time and energy during this period arranging for private employment in case the need arises. The insecurity of employees during these months is well illustrated by the following quotation from an Arkansas editorial[7]:

> Most statehouse appointees of the present administration, even though Governor-nominee Ben Laney has made no announcement of his plans, are making arrangements to move from capitol hill January 1 if need be. Whether a general turn-over in Statehouse personnel is contemplated by Mr. Laney is anyone's guess, but few of those who owe thanks to Governor Adkins for their jobs have not taken steps to get on another pay roll if necessary.
>
> It has been debated whether Mr. Laney will keep some key men in the major state departments, or whether he will make a clean sweep. Governor Adkins made his replacements in positions gradually, retaining eleven department heads at least six months. . . . But, taking no chances, some employees are arranging for new jobs, many of which no doubt will be more attractive than a political appointment.

The governors of Arkansas have never descended to the tactics of Governor Eugene Talmadge of Georgia, who demonstrated how members of the State Highway Board might be removed. In April 1933, he tried to have certain highway department employees fired and, in order to achieve this end, omitted their names from the quarterly budget which was sent to him for his approval. The chairman of the Board protested this act, and in June 1933, the Governor invoked martial law and removed the chairman and one member of the Board. The remaining member of the Board was placed in charge, and the Governor appointed two other persons to fill the vacancies. The ousted chairman and member of the Board brought suit but were unsuccessful. "The method used by Talmadge was rather high-handed, but it seems that the people approved." [8]

The Civil Service System

Growth of Civil Service. While some agitation for a more suitable system for the selection of public employees had begun before the Civil War, no action had been taken in any of the states. In 1880 the New York Civil Service Reform Association was organized, its name being changed later to the National Civil Service Reform League. It secured its first victory by the passage of the Pendleton Act. A few months later New York established

[7] *Arkansas Gazette*, November 5, 1944, quoted by Grant, Daniel, *The Role of the Governor of Arkansas in Administration* (Doctoral dissertation, Northwestern University, 1948).

[8] Gosnell, Cullen B., *Government and Politics in Georgia*, p. 83 (Nelson, New York, 1936), quoted by Grant, *op. cit.*

a civil service commission, vested with the authority to prepare and administer tests for the selection of persons for the state service. Massachusetts followed in 1884. For more than twenty years these two states served as the sole exponents of something better than the spoils system in state government.

Early in the present century a new era of civil service reform began. In 1905 Illinois and Wisconsin set up civil service commissions and provided for the selection of state employees on a merit basis. Two years later similar action was taken in Colorado and New Jersey; in succeeding years other additions were made, as indicated in the table on page 464, until by 1950 there were state-wide systems covering all departments in operation in eighteen states while in thirteen others, there were one or more departments under some form of merit system, in addition to those with merit system laws under the Social Security Act.

Because of the political opposition incurred in the establishment of a civil service system, it is not an uncommon practice to have such legislation enacted in one session of the legislature and repealed shortly thereafter. This experience occurred in Arkansas (1937 to 1939), and in New Mexico (1939 to 1941). Connecticut adopted a law in 1913, repealed it in 1921, and then after eighteen years of spoils set up its present merit system in 1937. Kansas adopted a statute in 1915 that was continuously inoperative until 1941, when the present constitutional amendment became effective. Arizona adopted a comprehensive civil service act in 1949, only to have it declared unconstitutional by the state supreme court. The Michigan act of 1937, exceptionally well drafted, was seriously weakened by amendments in 1939. This too is not an uncommon practice.

Civil service legislation has been in operation, however, in all of the states for about twelve years, in agencies cooperating with the Federal government under grant-in-aid programs. In Pennsylvania, for instance, the Unemployment Compensation Division of the Department of Labor and Industry and the Department of Public Assistance operate under a civil service system. So also does the State Liquor Control Board, while the Pennsylvania State Police operates under a voluntary merit system. These agencies account for almost half of the total number of state employees. In Florida, however, only 2,500 out of a total of 17,000 are covered. Several states, in addition, have established personnel systems which, while not providing for competitive examinations, perform many of the functions of civil service agencies.[9]

The American public service differs in a number of important respects from that in the European democracies; Arnold Brecht points out four unique features, each technically independent of the other[10]:

[9] The Division of State Merit System Services, Federal Security Agency, issues annually on January 1 a *Directory of State Merit Systems.*

[10] In Morstein Marx, Fritz, *Public Management in the New Democracy*, pp. 107–129 (Harpers, New York, 1940).

Growth of Civil Service Systems in the States

DECADE	NUMBER OF STATES	YEAR OF ADOPTION	STATES
1880–1889	2	1883	New York (1894) [1]
		1884	Massachusetts
1890–1899	0	....	None
1900–1909	4	1905	Illinois, and Wisconsin
		1907	Colorado (1919)
		1908	New Jersey (1947)
1910–1919	2	1913	California (1934), and Ohio (1912)
1920–1929	1	1920	Maryland
1930–1939	7	1937	Connecticut, Maine, Michigan (1940), and Tennessee
		1939	Alabama, Minnesota, and Rhode Island
1940–1949	9	1940	Louisiana (1940), and Oregon
		1941	Indiana, and Kansas (1940)
		1942	Virginia
		1943	Georgia (1945)
		1945	Nebraska, and Missouri (1945)
		1949	North Carolina

[1] Figures in parenthesis indicate constitutional basis in ten states; this provides protection to the system but establishes a rigidity which is highly undesirable. The provision in the Michigan Constitution, for instance, which allows the Commission to increase the salaries and wages of state employees without consulting the legislature or the governor certainly cannot be considered wise.

1. The dichotomy between the merit and the spoils system
2. The specific-job character of the examination given under the merit system
3. The disconnection between public education and recruitment for the civil service
4. The admission of candidates at a late age

Organization. The state civil service commissions consist of three members in ten states, of five members in six states. Maryland has a single commissioner, and Virginia has no commission at all. Ohio has two commissioners, while Indiana and Michigan have four. Missouri has six. Members are appointed by the governor in every instance, in Louisiana from a list of fifteen nominated by university presidents. Confirmation is required by the senate in ten states, by the executive council in two others. The term of office is six years in nine states, but varies from three years in Missouri and Oregon to eight years in Michigan, ten years in California, and indefinite tenure in Connecticut. The terms are overlapping in thirteen states, thus insuring continuity of policy. Only in Maryland, New York, and Ohio can the compensation paid members be considered anything like adequate. Per diem compensation ranges from five to twenty-five dollars, but maximum annual limits prevent members from devoting much time to the job or from regarding it as anything more than an incidental matter.

All commissions are authorized to employ an executive officer and staff. The trend has been to concentrate administrative power and responsibility for directing technical personnel activities in a director, trained and experienced in the field of personnel management and very often selected by means of a special competitive examination. The procedure involves the creation of a committee of experts to design and administer such tests and certify the top three among those who have passed the test. The actual appointment is made either by the governor or by the commission, and special precautions are taken to prevent the removal of the director for political reasons.

The size of the task entrusted to the commissions has already been, to some extent, indicated. In spite of a mounting work load and the basic importance of the work, the expenditures for it are in most states modest if not inadequate. According to some fairly recent figures, four states spent less than $50,000 a year, six between that figure and $100,000. Six spent between $100,000 and $200,000. Michigan and New Jersey spent between $200,000 and $300,000, California more than $500,000, New York more than $700,000.

A study of state personnel administration in Colorado, made in 1949,[11] reveals some very interesting facts regarding the expansion of the personnel program in that state — facts which are probably more or less typical of what has happened in many other jurisdictions. In the decade from 1940 to 1950, appropriations for personal services increased from $17,000 to $80,000 — nearly five times. Costs for maintenance and operation exactly doubled. Capital outlay was two and one-half times as much in 1950 as in 1940. The total costs, including the state's share to the retirement fund, rose from $21,000 to $91,000 — well over four times as much.

In 1947 the California Assembly created an Interim Committee on Governmental Efficiency and Economy; in a report on the Personnel Board and its operation the Committee set forth four basic principles of organization and recommended a plan of organization for the staff of the Board. Both are shown in the table on page 466.

Powers and Duties. The civil service commission or department is the central public personnel agency of the state, whose work covers the whole field of public personnel administration. The duties performed may be governed by as many as three different types of legal authority. Ten states, as already noted, make constitutional provision for a civil service system. The following, from the New York Constitution, is illustrative of the language of these provisions[12]:

[11] Colorado Public Expenditure Council, *State Personnel Administration in Colorado*, p. 7 (Denver, 1949).

[12] Article V, Section 6; see also Cornell, Herbert W., *Civil Service Provisions of State*

STATE OF CALIFORNIA
PROPOSED ORGANIZATION FOR STATE PERSONNEL BOARD

Principles of Organization

1. Clear separation of technical and administrative problems
2. Coordinated supervision of field operations
3. Delegation of functions to branch offices
4. Emphasis upon organization to serve the ends of leadership instead of control

Form of Organization

Top-Level Organization:
1. The Personnel Board
2. The Executive Officer
3. The Assistant Executive Officer
4. The Schedule and Control Unit

Operating Divisions:
1. Administrative Division
   a. Administrative Services — accounting, office management, supplies, publications
   b. Transactions and Records — certification, roster, clerical pool, mail and mimeograph, files
   c. Test Operations — examination arrangements, test scoring, test results, application review, machine processing
2. Classification and Pay Division
   a. Classification Standards and Departmental Relations
   b. Pay Analysis
   c. Classification Surveys
3. Examining Division
   a. Test Construction
   b. Recruiting
   c. Test Services — test pool
4. Training and Utilization Division
5. Field Operations Division
   a. Branch Offices
   b. Field Travel Coordination
   c. Cooperative Services
6. Hearings and Investigation Division

> Appointment and promotions in the civil service of the State, and of all the civil divisions thereof, including cities and villages, shall be made according to merit and fitness, to be ascertained, so far as practicable, by examinations which, so far as practicable, shall be competitive.

Then there are the statutory provisions already mentioned; where there are no constitutional provisions these are the sole basis for the civil service system. Four states restrict the activities of their commissions to the personnel of the state service; others permit a certain amount of supervision or control over their civil subdivisions, though the extent of this supervision

---

Constitutions (Wisconsin Council on Civil Service, Madison, 1940); Faust, Martin L., "The State Constitution and Civil Service," in *Manual on the Executive Article*, pp. 93–103 (Missouri Constitutional Convention of 1943, Columbia, 1943); and Litchfield, Edward W., and McCloskey, Robert G., "Civil Service by Constitution," *National Municipal Review*, January 1945, pp. 14–20, 56.

is not the same in any two states. In Massachusetts the commission handles the recruiting of both municipal and state employees. The New Jersey commission conducts examinations for county and municipal employees, but only in those units that have voted to accept its assistance. New York in 1941 extended the civil service law to all the small units of government in the state. Nothing of this sort had ever been attempted before.[13]

All the merit system states except Maryland and Virginia have a personnel board or civil service commission — a device which has been found useful for three types of administrative duties: (1) handling appeals or quasi-judicial work; (2) rule-making or quasi-legislative work; and (3) review of the work of a single administrator. The Model Civil Service Law makes the commission a rule-making body, an appellate tribunal to which employees may appeal disciplinary actions and dismissals, and an investigatory body. All the commissions have, in fact, made extensive use of their rule-making powers, adopting and publishing a series of rules and regulations governing all civil service matters in the state. Such a series of rules and regulations should, among others, deal with the following subjects:

- Appeals procedure
- Appointments:
  - Labor
  - Permanent
  - Probational
  - Temporary or provisional
- Certification
- Classification
- Counseling
- Demotions
- Discharges
- Disciplinary actions
- Eligible lists
- Employee relations
- Employee services
- Examinations:
  - Competitive
  - Noncompetitive or qualifying
- Grievance procedures
- Health and safety
- Hours of work
- Leaves and holidays
- Notification of candidates
- Performance or merit ratings
- Promotional procedures
- Reductions-in-force
- Retirement
- Suggestion system
- Suspensions
- Training
- Transfers
- Uniform pay plan
- Veterans preference

The Merit System

A merit system is nothing more nor less than a sound system of personnel administration. Whereas civil service, following a negative approach, has been primarily interested in keeping out the unqualified, later in selecting those best qualified, the merit system, utilizing a positive approach, is concerned with the entire personnel management program from the initial recruiting until the final separation of an employee who may have devoted a lifetime to the service of his government. The basic elements of such a

[13] Some states like Kentucky and Mississippi, which have no state-wide merit system, authorize counties and cities to establish civil service standards for the selection of their employees.

program are listed and discussed briefly in the section which follows. Keeping out the unfit was and is necessary, but to make this — in the words of the Connecticut Commission on State Government Organization — "the principal goal of a modern personnel agency is to lose all sense of perspective and proportion."

The present concern is with the development of the basic philosophy of the merit system. There was a growing feeling of dissatisfaction with the existing civil service systems — a feeling that they had not done and probably were not capable of doing the job that needed to be done. Then, in 1934, the Social Science Research Council created the Commission of Inquiry on Public Service Personnel to examine the problems of public personnel within the United States, to outline a program for future action, and to present its findings and recommendations to the American people. After a year's investigation, during which hearings were held in the principal centers of population in the United States and in several foreign capitals, the Commission reported in 1935: "*The time has come in the history of America to adopt an entirely new public policy in the selection and appointment of men and women to carry on the day-to-day work of government.*" This report, probably the most important contribution in the field that has been published in many years, managed to express in concrete terms the basis for the existing dissatisfaction and to propose suitable remedies. It presented a practical, constructive program for improvement.

The report outlined a career service system, presenting certain general recommendations in support thereof; these were followed by a series of twelve recommendations of a more specific nature. Of these twelve, five have a direct bearing upon the personnel problems of the states, although the principles involved in some of the others are equally valid for the state service [14]:

> The extension of the merit system under the supervision of the United States Civil Service Commission, wherever practicable, to the personnel of state and local government agencies receiving or expending Federal funds, as a condition of the grant, with the power to utilize existing local civil service agencies which are able and willing to meet standards set by the United States Civil Service Commission
>
> The amendment of veteran preference laws so that they will adequately recognize the war service experience of veterans without conflicting with merit principles or the efficiency of the public service
>
> The repeal or amendment of all general provisions prescribing residence requirements or geographical apportionment of appointments
>
> The immediate establishment or designation in every governmental department or agency of adequate size, whether Federal, state, or local, of a personnel officer, who should in the larger departments be freed of all other responsibilities
>
> The increase of the appropriations for personnel administration and the

[14] Commission of Inquiry on Public Service Personnel, *Better Government Personnel*, Specific Recommendations Nos. 6, 8, 10, 11, and 12, pp. 8–9 (McGraw-Hill, New York, 1935).

Civil Service Commission in the Federal government and in state and local governments where this is necessary for the adequate maintenance of the merit system, as a step toward the ultimate development of a career service

The report made very clear the urgency of the need for the development of sound personnel policies in the states and in other units of government as well. It urged the development of cooperative relations between the states and their local units,[15] and between both and the United States Civil Service Commission. Professor White, a former member of that Commission, suggested that, among other things, the state and municipal commissions might work with the Federal Commission in establishing joint eligible lists for each of the more common types of position — lists from which Federal, state, or municipal appointing officers might make selections as necessity arose.

Elsewhere in this volume emphasis is laid upon the fact that the states must improve the effectiveness of their administration if they do not wish to lose still further in the struggle for power with the Federal government. Two world wars — perhaps three — and a major depression, along with a variety of other contributing factors, have caused widespread changes in the character of governmental arrangements in this country. Unless the states take prompt and effective steps to strengthen their governmental organization and procedures, "they are almost certainly doomed to be left behind in the race for power which is now going on in this country." There are a good many encouraging signs that the states are aware of this challenge and that they are attempting to meet it. This they cannot do without competent and well-qualified personnel functioning within the framework of a modern system of personnel management.

Experience in Kansas provides some evidence that such a system actually works. The Civil Service Board, in reply to criticisms leveled against it by members of the legislature, presented its reply in its Seventh Annual Report for 1948–1949, showing statistically that departments under civil service are more efficient than those which are not. In the eight years that the civil service law had been in effect, salaries in departments not under the law rose 18 per cent more than those which were under it. Departments under the law showed a decrease in the unit cost of output. Since 1945, out of a total of 7600 employed, 862 had been dismissed with only thirteen requests for hearings and only two reinstatements. This, the Board concluded, showed that civil service in Kansas is not a shelter for the incompetent and mediocre. The Board gave credit for the increased efficiency to the department heads, supervisors, and employees.

In spite of all the elements of superiority of the merit system over the spoils system and the later civil service system, the merit system itself is far from perfect. In many instances, it has, in fact, developed such serious de-

[15] See, for instance, Jamison, Judith N., *Intergovernmental Cooperation in Public Personnel Administration in the Los Angeles Area* (Bureau of Governmental Research, University of California at Los Angeles, 1944).

fects as the retention of unneeded personnel, with unnecessary expense to the taxpayer, and "the placing of a kind of blackmail power in the hands of mediocrity," with resultant inefficiency in the public service. Under the system, the executive is often deprived of the power to control his agency effectively — a power vested in him by law. In a challenging analysis of this situation, Professor Carpenter suggests once again that the amateur bipartisan civil service commission be replaced by a personnel department under the direction of a single commissioner responsible to the chief executive; that there be created by law adequate machinery to solve the problems of employer-employee relationships; and that citizen organizations interested in the promotion and extension of the merit system be strengthened. Only by such devices can the problem of our failure to reconcile the merit system with some method of positive administrative control by the responsible chief executive be solved.[16]

Fundamental Problems in Personnel Administration

It is now generally recognized that there must be some agency in the state government charged with responsibility for handling personnel problems. The idea that the personnel agency must be independent of the operating departments and outside the general administrative plan has been largely abandoned. In modern government one finds this agency accepted and recognized as an integral part of the administrative machinery. It operates in close cooperation with the budget office and with each department and agency of the government. Its interests are identical, in many respects, with those of the operating departments, the legislature, and the people. Its attitude should be one of helpfulness, understanding, and cooperation and it should seek to cultivate and encourage a like attitude on the part of operating officials.

It is the responsibility of the central personnel agency to formulate policies and procedures, within the limits established by constitutional and statutory provisions, relating to each of the following major problems in the personnel field[17]:

1. Recruiting and Examining
2. Appointment and Placement
3. Classification
4. Compensation
5. Training
6. Conditions of Work
7. Employee Relations
8. Health and Safety
9. Changes in Status
10. Separations and Retirement
11. Assistance to Departments and Local Units

The formulation of policies and procedures should be done, not by arbitrary fiat, but in consultation with representatives of the operating agencies. The personnel council, whose membership is restricted to the per-

[16] See Carpenter, William S., *The Unfinished Business of Civil Service Reform* (Princeton University Press, 1952), some portions of which are summarized in "Reformer's Task Never Done," *National Municipal Review*, July 1952, pp. 339–345.

[17] Provision must be made for the administration of payroll and leave records, but this function is not now regarded as a proper responsibility of the personnel office.

Basic Structure for Personnel Management*

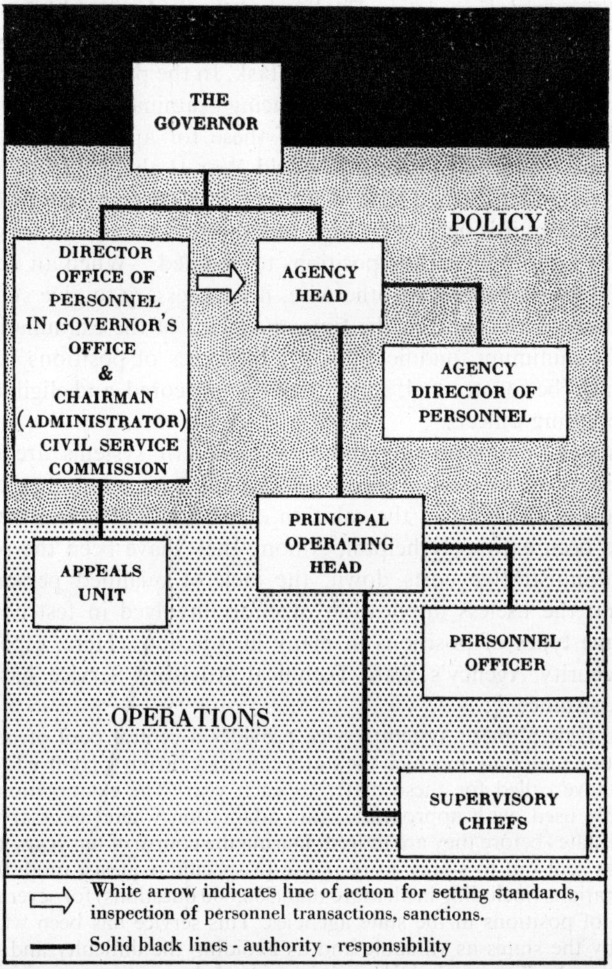

* Adapted from Commission on Organization of the Executive Branch of the Government, *Personnel Management* (Washington, 1949).

sonnel officers of such agencies, has proved to be an effective means of developing such cooperative arrangements. The New York Council is composed of a chairman appointed by the governor, a member suggested by the Department of Civil Service, one suggested by the Division of the Budget, and an official representative designated by each department. Weekly meetings are held by the three members, and monthly meetings by the full Council, which has a small technical and clerical staff. Uniform rules have been established for all departments. The Council functions through committees established to recommend to the Civil Service Commission uniform practices which are acceptable both to the administration and to the employees.[18]

Recruiting and Examining. Finding persons who would be willing to enter the state employ and who have the qualifications for rendering satisfactory service is, in many cases, no easy task. In the past this work was often done in a perfunctory manner by announcing examinations, examining those who applied, and certifying the best of these for appointment. Little real recruiting was undertaken. During World War II the states as well as the Federal government learned that, if well-qualified persons are to be secured for consideration, it is necessary to go out and find them, and very often sell them on the desirability of the positions to be filled.[19] When an examination is to be given, competitive or otherwise, it is necessary to give suitable publicity throughout the state to the time and place of the examination and to indicate the minimum qualifications for the types of positions to be filled. The tests must be constructed, administered, and scored, and eligibles certified to the appointing officers.

The states, and especially those whose merit systems are limited to grant-in-aid programs, have been confronted with a number of difficult administrative problems, in the solution of which the Federal merit system service has been extremely helpful. Among these have been the problem of keeping administrative costs down, the lack of qualified personnel technicians, and the useless duplication of effort involved in test construction for the same types of positions in many jurisdictions. Here, especially, the Federal Security Agency's State Technical Advisory Service has rendered valuable assistance [20]:

> The Federal merit system service provides a central pool of objective examination materials on which the states can draw. From forty-five to forty-eight states have called for these materials each year. The examination items are normally used, with appropriate state adaptation where necessary, in ten to twenty states before they are retired. During the course of ten years, the Federal unit has sent out to states, in response to specific requests, more than 10,000 examinations (including in all more than 500,000 questions) for several thousand classes of positions in the state agencies. This service has been widely recognized by the states as valuable and as avoiding the difficulty and expense of setting up duplicate technical staffs in each of the states.

Positions in the public service are of two types: classified and unclassified. The former, which are under civil service, may be broken down into exempt, noncompetitive, labor, and competitive classes. The table on page

[18] On these councils, see the author's *Public Administration in a Democratic Society*, pp. 252–257 (Heath, Boston, 1950).

[19] On recruiting, see: Civil Service Assembly of the United States and Canada, *Recruiting Applicants for the Public Service* (Chicago, 1942); Graves, W. Brooke, and Herring, James M., "Recruiting Administrative Personnel in the Field," *Public Administration Review*, Autumn 1942, pp. 302–311; Kingsley, J. Donald, "Recruitment, the Quest for Competence," *Public Personnel Review*, January 1941, pp. 28–35; and Graves, *Public Administration in a Democratic Society, op. cit.*, Chapter 7.

[20] Aronson, Albert H., "Merit System Objectives and Realities," *Social Security Bulletin*, April 1950, pp. 1–5.

474 shows this breakdown, indicating for each class the types of positions, method of appointment and civil service jurisdiction, method of layoff when the position is abolished, and method of removal. Where examinations are used, they apply only to positions in the classified service designated as competitive. Positions in noncompetitive or exempt classes are filled merely by certification, on the basis of noncompetitive or qualifying tests. The unclassified and/or exempt positions include both those which are highest

State of New York
Postwar Growth of Examining Function *

YEAR	NUMBER OF EXAMINATIONS	NUMBER OF APPLICANTS	NUMBER OF CANDIDATES ACTUALLY EXAMINED
1947	1,269	56,931	43,823
1948	1,326	50,095	38,594
1949	1,638	80,615	67,153

Examinations Completed and Appointments Made

YEAR	EXAMINATIONS COMPLETED: NUMBER OF EXAMINATIONS COMPLETELY RATED	EXAMINATIONS COMPLETED: NUMBER OF CANDIDATES' PAPERS RATED	NUMBER OF APPOINTMENTS FROM ELIGIBLE LISTS
1947	1,127	44,991	4,114
1948	1,496	56,130	5,530
1949	1,605	67,808	7,261

* From New York State Civil Service Commission, *Civil Service Administration in the Empire State*, p. 12 (Albany, 1950).

in rank and those which are lowest. Both are exempt, the highest because they are policy-determining and therefore political, the lowest, such as common laborer, because no examination is necessary. The tests which are given may be either assembled or unassembled; the former may include short-answer and free-answer questions, practical performance tests, mental and psychological tests, and character tests, as well as an evaluation of the training and experience of the applicant.[21]

The volume of examining work is considerable and is constantly increasing. It has grown from 3000 or 4000 candidates at the turn of the century to twenty times that number at midcentury. It mounted rapidly during the war period when turnover was rapid and when the finding of suitable replacements was exceedingly difficult. For quite different reasons it has

[21] On these and other points, see National Municipal League, *Draft of a State Civil Service Law* (New York, 1946).

State of New York
Framework of the Civil Law *

TOPIC	UNCLASSIFIED SERVICE	CLASSIFIED SERVICE			
		Exempt Class	*Non Competitive Class*	*Labor Class*	*Competitive Class*
Types of Positions	1. Heads of Departments 2. Elected officials 3. Legislative employees 4. Election officers 5. Teachers in public school system (and other positions specifically enumerated in Section 9).	1. Deputies of heads of Departments. 2. Clerks of courts and deputy clerks, if authorized by law. 3. Clerks to judges. 4. Secretaries of boards or commissions authorized by law to appoint a Secretary. 5. In the State and county services, all unskilled laborer positions. 6. All other subordinate positions which cannot be filled by competitive or non-competitive examination.	1. Part-time professional, technical and scientific positions. 2. Such skilled trades positions as it is impracticable to fill by competitive examination.	In the city service, all unskilled and such skilled laborer positions as cannot be filled by competitive or non-competitive examination.	All other employees.
Method of Appointment and Civil Service Jurisdiction	Civil Service Commission has no jurisdiction over these positions.	Appointment made and reported to the Civil Service Commission. There is no inquiry by the Civil Service Com-	Appointing officer nominates person for appointment. Commission determines whether he meets requirements be-	Appointments are made from laborer registers established by the Civil Service Commission. Civil Service Commis-	Appointments are made from eligible lists established as a result of competitive civil service examinations. Civil Service

		mission regarding qualifications of individuals appointed. Civil Service Commission must certify payrolls.	fore appointment becomes effective, also certifies payrolls of such employees.	sion also certifies payrolls of such employees.	Commission certifies payrolls of such employees.
Method of Layoff when Position Abolished	Civil Service Commission has no jurisdiction over these positions.	Employees laid off have no preference for reappointment. However, a veteran or exempt volunteer fireman occupying a subordinate position must be transferred to any position vacant at the time of layoff and which he is qualified to fill. (For exceptions see Sec. 22-1).	Employees laid off have no preference for reappointment except that a veteran or exempt volunteer fireman must be transferred to any position vacant at the time of layoff and which he is qualified to fill.	Employees must be laid off in the following order: 1) Non-veterans; 2) Non-disabled veterans; 3) Disabled veterans. There is no preference for reappointment. A veteran or exempt volunteer fireman must be transferred to any vacant position he is qualified to fill.	Employees must be laid off in the following order: 1) Non-veterans; 2) Non-disabled veterans; 3) Disabled veterans. In each category the lay-off must be in inverse order of original appointment. Employees are entitled to preference in reappointment. A veteran or exempt volunteer fireman must be transferred to any vacant position he is qualified to fill.
Method of Removal	Civil Service Commission has no jurisdiction over these positions.	No charges need be preferred except if employee is a veteran or exempt volunteer fireman and is occupying a subordinate position. (See Section 22-1).	No charges need be preferred except if employee is a veteran or exempt volunteer fireman. (See Section 22-1).	No charges need be preferred except if employee is a veteran or exempt volunteer fireman. (See Section 22-1).	Charges must be preferred in writing and opportunity given for reply. (See Sec. 22-2). In case of a veteran or an exempt volunteer fireman, a hearing must be held in addition. (See Sec. 22-1).

* From New York State Department of Civil Service, *Effective Civil Service*, pp. 8–9 (Albany, 1948).

continued to grow since the war. The table on page 473 shows for New York, our oldest state system, the development of this work in the postwar period.

The number of examinations of all types grows with the service. Note, however, that not only the number but the percentage of positions covered by competitive examinations shows a steady increase, with a corresponding decline in the percentage — but not the number — of noncompetitive examinations. Neither the number nor the percentage of exempt positions has been very great at any time since 1900.

Appointment and Placement. After the examinations have been given, the papers are rated and registers set up. When requisitions are received by the central personnel agency, *i.e.*, the Commission, names are certified to the appointing officer from the top of the register, as required. In most states they operate — as does the Federal government — under the rule of three, which means that the appointing officer has the privilege of selecting one out of three for each vacancy to be filled. Having made his selection, the problem of proper placement rests with the appointing officer.

When the appointments have been made, the individuals assume their duties subject to such conditions of tenure as the laws in their jurisdiction provide — under a civil service system, always for a probationary period. Officials are commissioned by the governor, and hold office as a rule for a definitely stated term, subject to the governor's power of removal; state employees, on the other hand, are not commissioned, and hold their positions at the pleasure of the appointing power or during good behavior.

The problem of preference for veterans presented itself again after World War II, as it has after each major conflict in the past. All states with merit systems make some provision for veterans' preference in appointments to the state service. Eleven states add five points to the passing score attained by a nondisabled veteran. Maryland adds five points regardless of the score attained. New Jersey adds three points, while California, Kansas, Michigan, and Pennsylvania add ten points. Ohio gives the equivalent of 20 per cent of the grade as an addition to the score. All but one of the five-point states — Illinois — as well as most of the others, grant ten additional points to disabled veterans. California, Kansas, and Michigan grant fifteen points to disabled veterans.[22]

Classification. The distinction between officers and employees has often been pointed out. Officers are those who, in positions filled either by election or by appointment, are responsible for the administration of the several departments, boards, and commissions of the government. Certain aspects of their selection and of the organization and functions of their agencies were considered in an earlier chapter. The present concern is with the many types of state employees, all of whom are selected by appointment under a patronage or a civil service or merit system. A distinction should also be

[22] Kentucky Legislative Research Commission, *Merit System Legislation for Kentucky*, pp. 15–16 (Frankfort, 1949).

made between a position and an employee. The position is an amount of work to be done, presumably sufficient to require the full time of an employee during business hours; once created, the position continues to exist, whether or not it is filled. The employee, on the other hand, is the person who fills the position.

The classification of positions can be made only on the basis of a job analysis survey. It is necessary to ascertain and record the duties of all positions in both the classified and the unclassified service, grouping these positions into suitable classes, assigning descriptive titles, and preparing complete written specifications for each class.[23] The result is likely to be a formidable list containing many hundreds of positions. An alphabetical listing of class titles and ranges for the state service of New Jersey in 1950 contained more than 1600 job titles, of which the initial entries, shown in the table on page 478, are typical.

When such an analysis is undertaken, there is always a tendency for employees to try to show that they are indispensable; this difficulty does not occur when the individual enters a service where the classification has already been made. It is of vital importance that this work be done, whether or not the state has a civil service system, because there is no other way in which the principle of equal pay for equal work can be made effective. In a state where no such classification has been made, it is not uncommon to find two workers in different departments doing exactly the same kind of work, one receiving twice as much pay as the other. Obviously there is no defense for such a procedure.

Compensation. Compensation — salary and wage schedules — is closely related to the classification of positions. Very often the provisions on both matters are incorporated in the same legislation. Provision should be made for the local determination of wage schedules. Generally speaking, the levels of compensation in the state service are poor. The top officials — at least in some states — receive good salaries, but the regular employees are poorly paid indeed. This condition became acute during World War II when substantial increases in the cost of living occurred in spite of impressive efforts to prevent inflation. Cost of living increases, which were first regarded as temporary and which later became permanent, merely adjusted for increased costs; they did nothing to correct the general situation with regard to inadequate compensation in the state services. Adequate salary scales exist in a few states; they should be established in others, along with provisions for within-grade increases, meritorious promotions, and cash payments for money-saving suggestions. Such variations exist in the pay plans of the several jurisdictions that it is difficult to generalize about them further than to say

[23] Such classifications are put out from time to time in most jurisdictions. On the principles of classification, see Civil Service Assembly of the United States and Canada, *Position Classification in the Public Service* (Chicago, 1941), and Baruch, Ismar, "Basic Aspects of Position Classification," *Public Personnel Review*, October 1940, pp. 1–17, and *Facts and Fallacies about Position Classification* (Civil Service Assembly, Chicago, 1937).

State of New Jersey
Typical Job Titles and Salary Ranges — 1950

TITLE CODE		TITLE	RANGE	INCREMENT
14	7603	Accountant	$3000–3600	$120
15	7613	Accountant, Utilities	3120–4020	180
18	7647	Accounts Adjuster, Treasury	3660–4560	180
14	8002	Actuarial Assistant	3000–3600	120
34	8024	Actuary	7500–9000	300
3	7332	Addressograph Machine Operator	1680–2280	120
18	9503	Administrative Assistant, I	3660–4560	180
14	9502	Administrative Assistant, II	3000–3600	120
9	9501	Administrative Assistant, III	2400–3000	120
18	6575	Administrative Inspector, Alcoholic Beverages	3660–4560	180

State of New Jersey
Revised Compensation Schedule — 1950

INCREMENT RANGE		RANGE NUMBER	MINI-MUM	INCREMENT STEPS 1st	2nd	3rd	4th	MAXI-MUM
I	$120 (1–14)	1	1440	1560	1680	1800	1920	2040
		7	2160	2280	2400	2520	2640	2760
		14	3000	3120	3240	3360	3480	3600
II	$180 (15–22)	15	3120	3300	3480	3660	3840	4020
		22	4380	4560	4740	4920	5100	5280
III	$240 (23–28)	23	4500	4740	4980	5220	5460	5700
		28	5700	5940	6180	6420	6660	6900
IV	$300 (29–34)	29	6000	6300	6600	6900	7200	7500
		34	7500	7800	8100	8400	8700	9000

that most of them provide for inadequate compensation.[24] The figures in the table above will serve to give an over-all picture of the pay plan of New Jersey — a fairly typical state.

The most progressive and intelligent approach to the pay problem made in the last decade is the sliding scale device developed in Minnesota. As applied in the State Highway Department, it provides for a guaranteed an-

[24] On this point see: California State Employees' Association, *Data Supporting Request for Adjustment of Salaries of State Employees* (Sacramento, 1945); Council of State Government, *Wartime Pay Adjustments for State Employees* (Chicago, 1945); Karlen, Harvey M., "Wage Trends and State Employment, 1929–1944," *State Government*, November 1945, pp. 217–218.

nual income as well as for employment stabilization. The same principle has been applied to the municipal employees of Milwaukee and St. Paul and, as of 1947, fifteen other cities.

An annual adjustment of wages is made in accordance with changes in the cost of living, as revealed by standard indices; under this plan both the civil employees and the taxpayers are assured a fair deal. Under the old system pay increases follow very belatedly increases in living costs and respond rather promptly to decreases in living costs. Under the Minnesota plan, the time lag is largely eliminated.[25]

Training. Training is being gradually recognized as an important aspect of the personnel function. Training takes place in every office or shop every day, whether formally recognized as such or not. The new employee must be inducted into service. The official tells his secretary how he wants a particular job done, or instructs her in handling a new procedure. The foreman tells his men how a new process will affect their work. Instruction may be given either in groups or on an individual basis, ordinarily on agency time.

There are various types of training — pre-induction, orientation, in-service, and on-the-job. Pre-induction training is given before the employee enters on duty. The individual may or may not be actually in the employ of the agency. Orientation training is given at the time of employment for the purpose of explaining to the new worker the organization and functioning of the agency. He must be shown where he works and given instructions necessary for the proper performance of his duties. In-service training is used during the period of employment for the purpose of increasing production, increasing operating efficiency, or in preparation for promotion. On-the-job training is given on a person-to-person basis, in most cases, by the supervisor to the employee, usually at his post of duty, or under conditions simulating those existing at his post of duty.[26]

Training may be carried on either by the central personnel agency or by the departments themselves with the assistance and under the supervision of the personnel agency. The constant need for special training to improve operations in many fields is now widely recognized, although the amount, kind, and method of giving the training will vary with the agency and its problems. Health departments are training their field workers and technicians; in many states members of the state police and state highway patrol

[25] See Leonard, J. M., and Mohaupt, Rosina, *Costs-of-Living Salary Adjustment Plans* (Detroit Bureau of Governmental Research, 1944); Pennebaker, Kenneth C., and Hart, Robert M., "Guaranteed Income and Employment Stabilization Plan for State Highway Employees," *Public Administration Review*, July 1942, pp. 177–189; Koronski, George W., "We Like Our Annual Salary Plan," *Better Roads*, October 1945, pp. 40–42, and December 1945, pp. 29–30; Stover, Robert D., "The Minnesota Cost-of-Living Pay Plan," *Public Personnel Review*, July 1948, pp. 133–137; Turner, Samuel E., Jr., "St. Paul's Adjustable Salary Scale for City Employees," *National Municipal Review*, December 1938, pp. 583–587.

[26] These various types are defined and explained in Civil Service Assembly of the United States and Canada, *Employee Training in the Public Service* (Chicago, 1941).

forces are put through a rigid course of training; departments of education are requiring teachers in the public schools to continue their studies if they are to advance in rank and pay; officials in charge of penal and correctional institutions are trying to help the employees under their supervision to understand better the nature of their work and to improve themselves for the better performance of their duties. Such a list might be extended almost indefinitely.

The State of New York has been carrying on some interesting training programs, including an annual series of public administration internships, a program for the training of administrative analysts and for the orientation and induction of new employees. The Commission says[27]:

> Outstanding students, most of whom have done extensive graduate work, are brought into the state service for one year appointments. Their training and work assignments are planned to develop ability for administrative work. Of twenty-four interns appointed to thirteen agencies in 1947, twelve were later employed by the state in other capacities, and one is employed by a municipal research bureau. A new group of twenty-seven interns was appointed for the 1948–1949 term, which expires June 30, to sixteen state agencies. The scope of the internship program has been broadened in response to requests from appointing officers who want to take advantage of an opportunity to train young people of high ability for future work in their organizations. It is administered by the Training Division under the guidance of the Governor's sponsoring committee.
>
> A new venture was undertaken late in 1948 to seek out hidden talent for a special kind of work. Employees with a natural bent for "methods and procedures" work were wanted. These are the people who can work out ways of getting things done more quickly and efficiently. A group of aptitude tests similar to those used in the "College Series" was given to 951 state employees who wanted a chance in this field. Standards were very high, and only 129 employees qualified in the test, which made them eligible for a full-time two-week program of intensive training under the sponsorship of New York University. Seventeen departments sent ninety-seven employees to classes which were given in New York City in January and in Albany in February. Those who passed the course will have fulfilled requirements for admission to promotion examinations through which they may be appointed to jobs as examiners of methods and procedures.
>
> The training of supervisors who are responsible for the development of other employees, for guiding, encouraging, and correcting them, is important to every department. A training program in the fundamentals of supervision, consisting of sixteen two-hour units, is being developed with assistance from the State School of Labor and Industrial Relations at Cornell University. All new employees need orientation. An induction training program which will probably consist of one full day's instruction is being planned. It will help the new worker to find himself, to see his job in relation to others, and to understand the civil service rules and regulations under which he will work. It is planned also to give new stenographers, typists, and clerks intensive "brush-up" training during their probationary periods to bring their performance up to a high level of efficiency.

[27] New York State Civil Service Commission, *Civil Service Administration in the Empire State*, p. 21 (Albany, 1949).

Conditions of Work. This term covers a large group of matters affecting the employees in the service — such as determining hours of work; checking attendance; handling annual, sick, and special leaves of absence; measuring performance on the job; and effecting transfers from one department or agency to another. On all these matters there should be uniform standards, regulations, and practices throughout the service; they should not be left to the determination of heads of departments, with consequent diversity. These questions must be considered not only with the interests of the taxpayer and the efficiency of the service in mind, but from the point of view of the members of the service as well. These matters may be miscellaneous, but they are of vital importance to the worker and have much to do with the morale of the service.

Employee Relations. The term "employee relations" formerly included both employee relations and employee services; since World War II there has been a general tendency to separate the two. The former term may properly be restricted to the relations of management to its employees and especially to management-labor relations as related to employee unions, collective bargaining, the right to strike, suggestion systems, and grievance procedures. Other aspects of the employee welfare program as formerly conceived include health and welfare activities, credit unions, recreation associations, employee publications, and the counseling program.[28]

It is the purpose of the employee relations program to provide means for the settlement of disputes arising within the agency, and to make possible the correction of conditions creating worker dissatisfaction and tending to increase the turnover rate. The results of exit interviews are analyzed, with a view to eliminating obstacles to good morale within the organization. Probably nothing contributes more to good morale than the operation of a good suggestion system. Such a system provides one more incentive to workers to do their best and indicates to them the interest of management in what they do. Here again, New York State has been doing some pioneering work. After a trial period which proved the value of the plan, the Legislature established the Merit Award Board as a permanent agency in the Civil Service Department in 1948 to administer the program.[29]

> The agencies putting award-winning suggestions into effect estimate that \$110,000 will be saved annually as a result of suggestions adopted in 1948. The cost of running the program for the year, including \$4,510 paid out in cash awards, was \$17,315.
>
> In 1948 a total of 852 suggestions was received. Final action was taken by the Board at forty meetings on 786 suggestions following study and recommendations by committees in the various departments. About half of these had been carried over from the previous year. There were 136 awards of which

[28] See Civil Service Assembly of the United States and Canada, *Employee Relations in the Public Service* (Chicago, 1942), and *Public Administration in a Democratic Society*, *op. cit.*, Chapter 10.

[29] See also Lyser, Herbert S., "California's State Merit Award Program," *Public Personnel Review*, July 1952, pp. 143–145.

ninety-five were in cash, from $10 to $300, and forty-one certificates of merit. Prize-winning suggestions varied from office procedures to equipment for planting trees faster. Some applied to the work of several departments, and in such cases the Board circulated summaries of the suggestions to operating officials.

Health and Safety. As an employer, government has been singularly remiss in making proper provision for the health and safety of its employees. Since a large portion of government work is office work, it is assumed that there are no serious hazards to safety. Numerous accidents with resulting loss of man-hours occur, however, through file drawers left open, materials piled high in insecure positions, telephones lifted across an aisle, and other carelessness. On the health side, free first-aid and dispensary service should be available in every office of any considerable size — not merely out of consideration for the employee, but because prompt attention given to minor illnesses such as colds and sore throats may prevent the spread of infection and save untold numbers of man-hours. By doing all it can to keep its employees safe and well, an agency cuts its operating costs and goes far to insuring the efficient discharge of its responsibilities.

Changes in Status. A phrase commonly used in the Federal service is borrowed here to signify the position of the employee under the Civil Service Act, and the Rules and Regulations. In a given service an employee enjoys "status" in a particular position at a specified grade and salary. If any of these aspects of his position are changed or modified, he is often said to have had "a change of status." Such changes commonly occur through promotion or demotion; other personnel actions involving status are reemployment, reinstatement, or reassignment. Of these there is, perhaps, greatest interest in promotions.

Every well-organized personnel system must make provision for handling the problem of promotions. In a patronage system, promotions, like the original appointments, are likely to be based largely on political influence, but under a merit system the incentive of possible promotion must be held out to those in the service. No such system of promotions is possible without an elaborate system of record keeping — personnel records and statistics and merit ratings, such as are maintained in modern business organizations, both public and private. Not only the responsible administration, but any citizen in the state, as well as the governor and the members of the legislature and the heads of the various departments, ought to be able to learn quickly and accurately the size of the service, the amount of the payroll, the number and causes of additions to and separations from the service, the number and kinds of employees of various types in each department and smaller unit, and a multitude of other significant personnel facts. Such data have rarely been anything like adequate, but without them and without detailed personnel records for each individual in the service, it is impossible to work out promotion policies that are in the best interests of the service as a whole or of the individual members of it.

Separations. Separations may arise from a variety of reasons — death, resignation, transfer to another agency, removal, or retirement on age or disability. Policies must be worked out for handling the various problems which these separations create. The appointing power always has the right to remove for cause — dishonesty, lack of ability or lack of application, lack of ability to cooperate with one's fellow workers, and the like. It is important that everything possible be done to protect the efficient, competent employees and that the protection now inherent in many state procedures for the inefficient and incompetent be withdrawn. The problem of removals would be much easier to handle if appointing officers were more severe in their judgments during the probational period in those jurisdictions operating under a civil service system.

From the point of view of the worker, the last but by no means the least important problem in this series is that relating to retirement. In the operation of such a system it is preferable that there be some security of tenure for members of the service, but states without civil service can and do maintain public employees' retirement systems. State-wide systems are in operation in more than half of the states. The establishment of a retirement system based upon sound actuarial standards and competently administered is a great benefit not only to the employees but to the state as well, through the opportunity which it affords to retire aged and disabled employees and through the improved efficiency and morale in the state service as a whole. The retirement allowances should be on a graduated scale, depending upon the length of service and the age at time of retirement; they should cover all state employees and permit temporary absences without forefeiture of service rights. Benefits may be provided not only for retirement, but also for death, disability, prior service, and minimum service. This activity is usually separately administered.[30] The passage of the Social Security Act Amendments of 1950 created difficult problems of reconciling social security coverage with the already existing retirement systems for public employees.[31]

Assistance to Departments and Local Units. The central personnel agency is — or ought to be — the central service agency of the state with regard to all personnel functions. In this capacity it has several responsibilities. As a staff agency its first duty is the somewhat unpleasant one of policing the operating agencies, to see that there is full compliance with the rules and regu-

[30] See Weinberg, Abraham A., in *Book of the States, 1948–1949* and *1950–1951;* Livingston, Helen, "Public Retirement Systems," *State Government*, February 1952, pp. 39–42, 44; Smith, Charles H., "The Virginia Retirement Plan," *ibid.*, July 1952, pp. 140–142, 159; Wisconsin Legislative Reference Library, *A Comparison of State and Local Public Employee Retirement Systems* (Madison, March 1952), and the author's *Public Administration in a Democratic Society, op. cit.*, Chapter 13, and references contained therein.

[31] See Kuhle, Albert A., "About That Social Security Bill — H. R. 6000, Its Meaning for State and Local Governmental Employees," *Public Aid in Illinois*, April 1950, pp. 7–8, 16, and Shoemaker, Richard E., "Why Not *Both* Social Security *and* the Retirement Act?" *Personnel Administration,* January 1952, pp. 31–33.

lations governing state employment. Its second duty is to assist the operating agencies in the solution of their personnel problems and to help them handle their work with better and smaller personnel. While this is primarily a problem for the operating units themselves, many of them have done the best they could without exhausting the possibilities for improvement. Some central agency familiar with the principles and practices of modern administrative procedure is needed to furnish stimulation, make suggestions, point out ways and means, and help make adjustments when personalities are involved. The personnel agency is the state's formal agency for making personnel and procedure studies and is in a better position than any other to be helpful along these lines.

In a few states the central personnel agency renders valuable assistance to local units of government in the solution of their personnel problems. In New York, for instance, a separate division which has been set up for this purpose, services five counties and assists other local units. The work of this division, like that of the central personnel agency itself, is spread over the whole field of personnel administration. It helps cities, counties, and school districts with the revision and modernization of civil service rules, with classification plans, test construction, salary plans, publications, and other matters.

Technical consultants are available for the assistance of local officials. The personnel manual for local units is another of the important services which may be provided by the state agency. Such a manual, subject to frequent revision, serves as an operating guide to local officials, covering the entire range of problems confronting the local operating official. Special attention may be given to some of the more important problems, such as classification and compensation plans, administrative regulations governing salary advancements, attendance and leave, service ratings, retirement, and forms and instructions with regard to their use.

New York puts out a guide to administration of the merit system in its municipalities, designed to increase the effectiveness of civil service administration in the local units of the state. The plan is to enlarge and expand this guide from time to time, emphasizing other aspects of personnel administration as rapidly as a general acceptance and usage of the tools of the craft are achieved. Three important goals are held out to every local civil service unit: (1) an adequate job description for every job; (2) every job filled by a qualified employee; (3) every job filled by a satisfied employee. The law provides a basis for the first two of these objectives, but the third can be achieved only through leadership, a program of education, and good public relations on the part of the central state personnel agency.

SELECTED REFERENCES

Caldwell, Lynton K., *Personnel Administration in the Public Service: An Outline of Topics and Readings* (Graduate Program in Public Administration, Albany,

1949). Best and most recent bibliography in the personnel field, prepared with special reference to state problems.

Carpenter, William S., *The Unfinished Business of Civil Service Reform* (Princeton University Press, 1952). A challenging discussion of our failure to reconcile the merit system with some method of positive administrative control by the responsible executive.

Civil Service Assembly of the United States and Canada — has published an excellent series of committee reports on fundamental problems in the field of public personnel administration:

Employee Relations in the Public Service (Chicago, 1942)
Employee Training in the Public Service (Chicago, 1941)
Oral Tests in Public Personnel Selection (Chicago, 1943)
Placement and Probation in the Public Service (Chicago, 1946)
Policies and Practices in Public Personnel Administration (Chicago, 1943)
Position Classification in the Public Service (Chicago, 1941)
Public Relations in Public Personnel Agencies (Chicago, 1941)
Readings in Public Personnel Administration (Chicago, 1942)
Recruiting Applicants for the Public Service (Chicago, 1942)

Graham, George A., *Education for Public Administration* (Public Administration Service, Chicago, 1941) and McLean, Joseph E., Ed., *The Public Service and University Education* (Princeton University Press, 1949). Two valuable treatments of the topic of university training for the public service.

Graves, W. Brooke, *Public Administration in a Democratic Society* (Heath, Boston, 1950). Part II contains eight chapters discussing at some length (and including some state material) problems dealt with in the concluding section of this chapter. White, Leonard D., *An Introduction to the Study of Public Administration*, Third Edition (Macmillan, New York, 1948), has excellent chapters on personnel administration.

Mosher, William E., and others, *Public Personnel Administration*, Third Edition (Harpers, New York, 1950) and Torpey, William G., *Public Personnel Management* (Van Nostrand, New York, 1953). Standard texts on the subject.

United States Civil Service Commission, *A Bibliography of Public Personnel Administration Literature* (Washington, 1949). This most comprehensive bibliography has been kept up to date: Supplement No. 1 (Washington, 1950); Supplement No. 2 (Washington, 1951); Supplement No. 3 (Washington, 1952).

14

Financial Management

It may be unconventional to consider the expenditures aspect of the financial problem before dealing with taxation, but there are substantial reasons which may be advanced for doing so. Chapter 10, on administrative organization and reorganization, emphasized the importance of fiscal management as a phase of management at the top level and closed with some discussion of the recent trend toward over-all financial management through an officer functioning in the capacity of a director of administration. It is obvious that no intelligent decision can be made with regard to tax policy until the nature and extent of the spending program have been determined. In other words, government does not simply tax. It taxes in order to meet definite and specific commitments which have been or must be made, and that means financial planning.

This chapter will, therefore, concern itself with problems relating to expenditure, correlation of income and expenditure under a budget system, and methods of fiscal supervision and control. Expenditures, in a sense, are the lifeblood of the public service. The struggle for popular control of the tax power and consequently for the power to appropriate and spend, was one of the striking features of the struggle for popular government. There is no more certain and effective way of eliminating a public service, of impairing its efficiency, or of harassing the officials in charge of it than to withhold necessary funds.

Public expenditures may be classified differently according to the point of view of the individual making the classification. Thus an economist may list ordinary governmental activities, commercial enterprises, carrying and sinking fund charges necessary to discharge the public debt, trust funds and other special public funds, and finally, bookkeeping transactions, or inter-fund transfers. A student of public administration, on the other hand, may set up classifications by funds, by appropriation heads, by organization units, by functions and activities, by character, or by object. Either classification may be used, according to the purpose one has in mind.

The purposes of state expenditures include all the activities and functions of government — executive, legislative, and judicial. The legislature must appropriate for all the departments and agencies whose activities were mentioned in Chapter 10. It must provide also for its own expenses, which, as indicated in Chapter 6, are considerable, and for the salaries and operating expenses of the judicial branch of the government. The increase in the number and scope of governmental services has occurred chiefly in the executive department; the legislatures and the courts spend more than they formerly did, but the increase has not been either proportionately or actually nearly so great as in the executive branch. In Chapter 10 some comment was made on this increase from the point of view of the number and scope of the services rendered; the same problem from the point of view of cost will now be considered.

Financial Administration

In beginning this discussion of fiscal administration, it is well to consider first an over-all view of the fiscal problem in the states, which includes no less than nine or ten separate and more or less distinct operations as indicated in the table on page 488. The operations are listed in the order in which the problems occur, together with the state officer or agency responsible for the administration of each function.

Collection of Revenue. The collection of taxes should be carried on by a single department of revenue, or by a department of taxation and finance to which this duty is assigned by law. It is difficult to give any general description of the state tax collecting agency because the number, size, and importance of the bureaus vary not only according to the size of the state but with its tax pattern. In the organization of this agency provision must be made for each of the major sources of state revenue. The Pennsylvania Department of Revenue, for instance, contains the following bureaus: Administration and Accounts, Investigations and Collections, Corporation Taxes, County Collections, Institutional Collections, and Liquid Fuels Tax. The collection of revenues for motor vehicle registrations and of operators' and chauffeurs' licenses may or may not be under the supervision and control of this department, but it should be.

In some states, where the tax collecting function has not been coordinated, one finds a situation like the following, which existed in Michigan only a few years ago [1]:

> Over half a hundred state departments, boards, and commissions now act as cashiers for the state, accepting money for taxes, licenses, fees, rentals, and other miscellaneous purposes. The collection of the more important state revenues is divided among eleven of these agencies. Miscellaneous licenses and fees are collected by forty-five others.

In some states a portion of the revenues is still derived from the general property tax. It is the practice to maintain a state board of equalization or a state tax commission whose duty it is to supervise the assessment of property.

[1] Michigan Public Expenditure Survey, *Save in the State to Save the Nation*, pp. 3–4 (Lansing, 1944).

Natural History of the State Tax Dollar

FISCAL OPERATION	DEPARTMENT OR AGENCY
Assessment and collection of taxes	Department of Revenue, Taxation and Finance, State Tax Commission, or other agency
Custody of funds (cash and securities)	State Treasurer
Borrowing and debt administration	State Treasurer
Financial planning	Budget Office; finance offices of operating departments
Financial supervision	Budget Office, Board of Administration and/or Finance; Department of Taxation and Finance
Procurement	Department of Administration; Department of Property and Supplies; State Printing Board; Department of Public Works
Property management	Department of Administration; Department of Property and Supplies
Disbursement	State Comptroller; State Treasurer; State Auditor or Auditor General
Financial reporting	State Treasurer; Auditor General
Audit and control	State Comptroller; State Auditor or Auditor General

The purpose is to distribute the burden as fairly as possible, to prevent inequalities and, where necessary, to correct them.

Custody of Funds. The funds brought into the state treasury through the efforts of the tax collecting agency are turned over to the state treasurer, in whose custody they are kept. Usually the state treasurer is a constitutional officer and quite frequently he is elected by popular vote, although, since he is always under bond, there is no special reason why he should be elected rather than appointed. It is his duty to maintain custody of all funds after they are turned over to him by the collecting agency and to pay them out upon proper warrant. His duties "are ministerial in nature. He is controlled in all his actions by the auditor. The treasurer can no more refuse to cash a properly drawn warrant of the auditor than a bank can refuse to cash a properly drawn check." [2]

In connection with the custody of funds the state treasurer has a number of important functions to perform. The receipts bureau or division must keep record of all moneys received, giving an official receipt for them. The bank

[2] Sappenfield, Max M., *Financial Administration in the States of Illinois, Ohio, and Indiana*, p. 7 (University of Illinois, 1934). See also White, *Introduction*, Chapters 16 and 17, and Faust, Martin L., *The Custody of State Funds* (National Institute of Public Administration, New York, 1925), and *The Security of Public Deposits* (Public Administration Service, Chicago, 1936).

and surety division is responsible for the selection of the banks which are used as state depositories, and for the custody of bonds and collateral to secure or indemnify state bank deposits. In the larger states securities representing very substantial amounts are kept in the vaults of the department; the coupons are clipped and the amounts credited to the proper funds. It is the duty of the department to see that the capital and surplus of banks used as depositories are in compliance with the requirement set up by the legislature and that no individual banks are overdeposited.

It often happens that the treasury has on hand funds which cannot be expended for ordinary governmental purposes, such as trust funds or the income from them or from public lands. These cannot be permitted to lie in the vaults for safekeeping; they must be invested in approved securities. Making these investments in accordance with the provisions of law and the decisions of the investment board and with general vigilance over their safety becomes the responsibility of the treasury. When the problem becomes as vast as it is in the larger units of government today, this is no mean responsibility.

Borrowing and Debt Administration. When the recommended or approved expenditures exceed the anticipated revenues, the difference may have to be made up by borrowing, if the budget is to be balanced. In such cases the treasury must prepare the specifications for the bond issue, advertise for bids, and sell the bonds. After these operations are completed, the treasury is again responsible for the administration of the debt, a procedure which involves the supervision and maintenance of the sinking fund (if there is one) or keeping the necessary records for serial bonds — maintenance of records with regard to ownership, accumulation of the funds, and paying off the bonds according to schedule.

Financial Planning. The problem of spending public funds may be considered either from the point of view of management's function of fiscal control or from that of the operating official. The former begins under the governor in the budget office, which is responsible for the formulation of the spending program of the government as a whole and for seeing that the plan is adhered to, within the limits established by the appropriation acts passed by the legislature. The preparation of the budget and the method of making and enforcing allocations and encumbrances for each spending agency for each fiscal period will be considered later. Each state operates on the basis of a fiscal year, a term used to designate the twelve-month period for which a government ordinarily reports on its financial operations. A tabulation made by the United States Bureau of the Census in 1949 showed that forty-two states end their fiscal year on June 30, as does the Federal government.[3]

[3] *Book of the States, 1952–1953*, pp. 166–169. The six states whose fiscal years begin at some time other than July 1 are: New York, Washington, Wyoming, April 1; Pennsylvania, June 1; Texas, September 1; and Alabama, October 1.

Financial Supervision. A financial plan, *i.e.*, a budget, however good, is of little use unless some adequate provision is made for carrying it out. Power and responsibility should be centered in the chief executive. His budget report embodies a plan of action for the future; after enactment into law, it becomes a guide for the present. The process is continuous; one budget is being executed while the next is being prepared. The budget must be comprehensive, taking cognizance of all income and all expenditures and of all financial requirements. Its advantages redound to the executive, the legislature, and the public. The first is obliged to plan ahead; the legislature has a basis for intelligent action; the public is provided with essential information on government operations and proposals.

Other essentials of such a system are a uniform plan for the classification of items of expenditure, a uniform accounting system, and means for preventing overspending or spending so much in the early part of the year that there is not enough left to maintain operations during the latter part. The normal procedures for realizing this purpose involve (1) the allocation of specific sums for specific purposes for a specified period of time and, (2) in connection with the accounting system, the establishment of encumbrances by which funds are set aside to make payment for goods and services when the commitment is made, not when the goods have been received and the bill becomes due.

Procurement. Under a centralized system all spending agencies requisition their needs through the central purchasing agency, which makes all contracts for the state and makes all purchases (except small emergency items and perishable commodities required by state institutions) needed by the several departments of the government. In the decentralized system, on the other hand, there are as many purchasing agencies as there are departments, boards, and commissions in the state government. There are difficulties in centralized purchasing which sometimes arouse criticism in the departments and which have prompted the movement in some states to substitute a system of centralized contracting for centralized purchasing. Although all requisitions would still come through one department, each operating department would be able to draw upon the manufacturer for needed supplies within budgetary limitations. Some states still use a decentralized system in which each spending agency makes its own contracts and goes into the market for the purchase of all needed supplies and equipment. Great waste results through favoritism, lack of knowledge of market conditions, and general absence of good management practices.

Property Management. Efficient management requires that attention be given to the long-neglected subject of property management as applied to both real and personal property. In connection with the former, management is concerned with the construction, leasing or purchase, and maintenance and use of office buildings, warehouses, garages, and other structures required by the various departments and agencies of the government. One of the most difficult aspects of this problem involves the allocation and assignment of space. In connection with the personal property owned by the state — desks, chairs, typewriters, laboratory equipment, and many other things — management is responsible for developing and maintaining a property accounting system, which will enable the state to identify and dispose of property no longer useful or required by any department or agency and will result in the continuous and maximum utilization of that which is retained.

Disbursements. Disbursements are made by the state treasurer, to whose custody the funds of the state are entrusted. The first step in making disbursements is for the operating department or agency to issue a requisition. Payroll requisitions are made out for personal service, while other types are used for payments for construction work and for necessary supplies and equipment, including rent, heat, light, power, printing, postage, and telephone and telegraph service. Payroll requisitions must be prepared well in advance of the due date in order to permit prompt issuance of checks. The procedure involved in making payments for work done under contract and for materials and supplies depends upon the established financial procedure followed in any particular state.

The amount of work involved in this apparently simple operation of disbursing funds has increased tremendously in the years since World War I, owing to such things as expanded road building, relief during the depression, and the social security program. In Pennsylvania the totals of checks written annually by the State Treasurer increased from $385,000 in 1923 to $3,919,000 in 1937 (highest year) and declined to $1,912,000 in 1945. The mere writing of this number of checks required, in addition to the installation of modern office machinery, a very substantial increase in the number of clerks engaged in the work.

Financial Reporting. Financial reporting, though of relatively recent origin, is an important aspect of financial administration. In years past, financial reports were published, to be sure, but they were large and cumbersome, poorly printed, poorly bound, and unattractive in appearance. Little attention was given to the contents, which was often the raw material out of which a good report might possibly have been made. Good financial reporting, on the other hand, is designed to be illuminating. The report does not have to be large; preferably, it should be rather small. It should contain selections of material and summaries of operations so presented that an intelligent citizen can obtain a clear understanding of major programs and policies and how they are working out in practice. The text should be readable and supplemented by charts, graphs, tables, and pictures whenever these devices can be used to advantage. This new type of financial report — neat and attractive in appearance and format, interesting and challenging in content — is rapidly replacing the old.

Audit and Control. The auditing function in public business as in private is intended to insure the accuracy of the records and to make sure that all expenditures have been made in accordance with law and for authorized purposes. The auditing officer is regularly provided for in the constitution and he is commonly elected. There are really three possible methods of choice available: election by the people, election by the legislature, and appointment by the governor. The latter method is not usually regarded with favor since it creates the somewhat anomalous situation of the executive department of the government checking upon the legality of its own expenditures and the correctness of its own records. That this is not a particularly valid objection is shown by experience with the Comptroller General in the Federal government. There is little to be said in favor of election by the legislature even though it is the legislature that provides the state revenues through the operation of its tax measures.

In many states the auditor general is responsible for the performance of a number of different functions. He must examine all invoices and accompanying requisitions before disbursements may be legally made, and he must issue warrants authorizing payment. He must audit the tax collection agency's account of corporations and of others who are subject to the payment of taxes to the state. Finally, he must audit the accounts kept by the departments, boards, and commissions of the state government.

There are, in fact, two main types of audit: the internal or pre-audit and the external or post-audit. The former refers to the checking of revenues and receipts at the time of collection and the examination and approval of claims before payment. This is a function of management and should be done by a financial agency of the administration itself. The post-audit, on the other hand, is made after the transactions have been completed and is a review of what has taken place. To be fully effective the post-audit should be performed by an officer completely independent of the administration.

The need for the post-audit, which is the responsibility of the auditor general, is obvious. There must be some agency legally responsible for the validating of expenditures of state funds, and for examining the accounts of individuals and corporations subject to the payment of taxes. There are so many opportunities for an official to grant unwarranted exemptions and reductions that the state might lose a great deal of money if some such system of audit were not maintained.

When one comes to the auditing of the accounts of the several departments and agencies, numerous problems and difficulties arise. If such audits are not made promptly — and frequently they are not — the reports are of little real value, since they have to be presented to an entirely new administration, which has no responsibility for the details of the fiscal affairs of its predecessors in office and little interest in them. If the auditing officer is of an opposite political party, there may be a lack of cooperation between the members of his staff and the various departments and agencies; if he is of the same political party, there is the possibility of too much cooperation, or at least of cooperation of a not altogether desirable type. A state may rely wholly or partially upon the services of certified public accountants engaged in commercial auditing, but it is possible for a well-organized department to do the work just as well and at far less expense to the state.

The Budget System

Budget procedure has been maturing for some six hundred years — since the fourteenth century, when parliamentary government and civil liberties were being bought from English monarchs at the price of taxes, and the Chancellor of the Checker Table or Exchequer was carrying his estimates of revenues and expenditures into the House of Commons in a little leather bag or "bougette." The budget system in Great Britain, in the modern sense, dates from 1787, the year in which our Federal Constitution was framed, and in France from 1850.

It was not until 1921 that the Federal Budget and Accounting Law was enacted, after years of discussion and countless committee reports and recommendations. No state had a budget system in 1910; in 1926, systems existed in all states. The first legislation was passed in 1911 in California and Wisconsin, the last in Rhode Island in 1926. The table on page 494 shows the states grouped by the years in which their first budget legislation was enacted. When the states are grouped according to five-year periods, it is found that thirty-seven acts were passed between 1915 and 1919. In the twenties, nine states adopted the executive budget in preference to other types previously adopted.

There is a wide variety in the statutes providing for the establishment of these systems, some being executive in character, some of the board or commission type, and one legislative. The preferred form is the executive budget, in which the budget is under the immediate control of the governor and a budget secretary or budget officer such as exists in New Jersey, New York, Pennsylvania, and elsewhere. A board or commission may be constituted in either of two ways: wholly of administrative officers, as in ten states, or by a combination of legislative and administrative officers, as in Wisconsin. The governor is always a member of the budget board. Such a board lacks responsibility, either to the legislature in the formulation of policy or to the executive in the administration of it. The legislative type of budget has all but disappeared. While such a system may be preferable to no budget at all, it falls far short of approved procedure. With any of these methods, a governor who is so authorized may use the item veto in connection with appropriation bills and thereby accomplish a good deal in the way of control.[4]

The Budget as a Plan for Spending. In present-day financial administra-

[4] Fitzpatrick, Edward A., *Budget Making in a Democracy*, Chapter 11 (Macmillan, New York, 1918), and Wells, Roger H., "The Item Veto and State Budget Reform," *American Political Science Review*, November 1924, pp. 782–801.

Enactment of Original Budgetary Legislation *

YEAR	STATES
1911	California and Wisconsin
1913	Arkansas, Oregon, and Ohio
1914	Louisiana
1915	Connecticut, Iowa, Minnesota, Nebraska, North Dakota, and Vermont
1916	Maryland, New Jersey, and Washington
1917	Delaware, Illinois, Kansas, Missouri, New Mexico, South Dakota, Tennessee, and Utah
1918	Georgia, Kentucky, Massachusetts, Mississippi, Virginia, and West Virginia
1919	Alabama, Arizona, Colorado, Idaho, Maine, Michigan, Montana, Nevada, New Hampshire, North Carolina, Oklahoma, South Carolina, Texas, and Wyoming
1921	Florida, Indiana, and New York
1923	Pennsylvania
1926	Rhode Island

* White, Leonard D., *Trends in Public Administration*, p. 189 (McGraw-Hill, New York, 1933). In a table on p. 191 Professor White groups the states according to the type of budget legislation adopted. For a table on current state budgetary procedure, see *Book of the States*.

tion, a budget serves two distinct purposes. In the first place it is a plan for spending. A properly constructed budget will show the financial condition of the government unit concerned at the close of the last fiscal period, its expected condition at the close of the current fiscal period, and finally the recommendations for the ensuing period. It must show the condition of the finances of the government at the end of that period if the anticipated revenues are received and the recommended expenditures are made. Thus it will be possible to view recent trends, to survey the current situation, and to look toward the future; a summary statement with this information should always be included. A budget is like an automobile road map. The tourist who starts out on a long trip can, after he has been on the road for a day or two, spread out his map and follow the route over which he has traveled, observe the point he has reached, and look ahead over the route leading to his destination. In similar manner, a budget serves as a guide to the financial highways over which the state must travel.[5]

[5] On this point Governor Alfred E. Smith is reported to have said: "There are two things that helped me in the Constitutional Convention, that were responsible for any knowledge that I displayed there. First, it was my knowledge of the state government that came from my studies of the appropriation bills. Whatever intimate knowledge I had about the state came from what I knew about how it spent its money, for every item in the appropriation bill tells a story of state problems and state needs, or state extravagance. Secondly, it must be borne in mind that most of the great activities of the state started in 1907, when the Public Service Commission was established, and the Conservation Commis-

In the formulation of such a plan for spending, certain principles governing public expenditures must be observed. Most important of these is the necessity for bringing about ultimately a definite correlation between the total amount of the recommended expenditures and the total amount which careful estimates indicate as probable receipts from existing tax laws during the period in question. If there is no way by which the total amount of recommended expenditures can be brought in harmony with the anticipated revenues, then the budget message should contain definite recommendations to care for this difference. If additional taxes are to be imposed, the message should indicate their nature, explain the necessity for them, and give an estimate of the revenue which may be expected from them. If a probable deficit is to be met through the exercise of the borrowing power, this recommendation should be accompanied by a similar explanation. At all events, the budget must provide for revenues which it is believed will be adequate to meet the program of expenditures.

Formulation of a Budget. The process by which an executive budget is formulated may be briefly outlined. A few months before the opening of the legislative session at which the new budget will be considered, the budget officer submits to the head of each executive department, board, commission, or other spending agency forms upon which estimates for the needs of the department or agency during the coming fiscal period are to be indicated. These forms must be returned by a fixed date. The budget officer then determines the total amount requested by all agencies, well knowing that it will be vastly in excess of the most optimistic estimates of the revenues likely to be received during the period in question. He then returns the budget requests to the spending agencies together with this information so that they may reconsider their estimates with a view to reducing them.

At this point the most difficult work of the budget officer begins. The reduction in the requests of the spending agencies is never sufficient to bring the total in harmony with the anticipated revenues. It now becomes the duty of the budget officer to go over these recommendations in detail with department heads, bureau chiefs, and the responsible officers of other spending agencies, considering the merits of each item and the merits of each item compared with other purposes for which the same funds might be expended. The budget officer is thus placed in the difficult position of having to evaluate and pass judgment upon individual governmental services. He must make decisions, many of them more or less arbitrary, keeping ever in mind his objective that the total amount shall be so expended as to bring the maximum return to the taxpayers. This kind of supervision is productive of substantial savings. Reductions in department requests are possible, how-

---

sion and other important agencies. Being familiar with how they started, I naturally knew something about them when they were discussed in the Constitutional Convention." — In Hapgood, Norman, and Moskowitz, Henry, *Up from the City Streets*, p. 112 (Harcourt, Brace, New York, 1927).

ever, only by careful planning, based on an intimate knowledge of all state functions, by a central agency functioning for that specific purpose.

When this task has been completed, the budget must be printed and prepared for circulation among the members of the legislature and others interested, at some specified date early in the legislative session. This date might well be postponed until March, to give more adequate opportunity for a new governor to familiarize himself with the financial problems of the state and construct the budget in accordance with his plans for the state's work. While all well-prepared budgets contain much the same kind of information, there is wide variation as to details of arrangement. The budget is primarily intended as a technical working tool for the members of the legislature and the officers of administration, but the budget office also has some obligation to provide the public with information about the finances of the government. Most of the published budgets are so technical in character and uninteresting in appearance that few citizens will even try to study them, but this does not have to be so.

Performance Budgeting. Since the publication of the Hoover Commission Report in 1949, much attention has been given to the form of the budget. In the past it has been the practice to set up budgets on the basis of objects of expenditure, showing by department or agency the amounts required for personal service, equipment and supplies, travel, or other purposes. While this plan has much to be said for it, it is difficult to ascertain how much is being spent for any given purpose. Critics assert that this system makes it virtually impossible to study the budget intelligently and know what is in it. One needs to know the actual cost of forest-fire prevention, of the eradication of animal diseases, or of teacher certification, not how much any given department or agency spends for this object of expenditure or that.

It is contended that this problem can be solved if a performance budget is used, *i.e.*, "a budget based upon functions, activities, and projects which would focus attention upon the general character and relative importance of the work to be done, or upon the service to be rendered, rather than upon the things to be acquired, such as personal services, supplies, equipment, etc. The all-important thing in budgeting is the work or the service to be accomplished, and what that work or service will cost." In order to put the conventional type of budget document on a performance basis, it is necessary to do a number of specific things [6]:

1. Extend the use of activity schedules to all appropriations and improve the existing schedules
2. Improve and relocate the explanatory statements, and redirect their emphasis toward program and performance
3. Show a summary of personal services and omit the personal services detail, the detail to be supplied separately upon request in such form as required

[6] Oklahoma Division of the Budget, *Performance Budgeting* (Oklahoma City, 1950), and Stahl, Steve, "The Performance Budget in Oklahoma," *GRA Reporter*, March–April 1950, pp. 1, 6–7.

4. Extend the use of business-type budget statements to show performance for government business enterprises
5. Continue to improve appropriation structure on an activity basis
6. Present information on an "applied cost" basis where applicable, in so far as the accounting system makes this possible

There has been some disposition to regard this performance budget as something new and to present it as a substitute for the existing form. Actually, it is neither. Budgeting began largely on the basis of appropriations for functions and activities. As time passed and budget office activities were geared more closely into the existing accounting classifications and procedures, the emphasis shifted to objects of expenditure. Advocates of performance budgeting want to return to estimates based on functions and activities. They make a valid point, *if* the estimates relating to functions and activities are used to supplement those relating to objects of expenditure. Both types of information are needed; neither one should be regarded as a substitute for the other.

There has been a vast amount of discussion of the problems involved in the adaptation of the performance budgeting idea to the existing budgetary procedures of states and cities. So far, only the state of Oklahoma and the cities of Richmond, Virginia, and San Diego, California, have actually adopted the plan, but it has been recommended for adoption, either by official commissions or by responsible citizen organizations, for the state of Maryland and for the cities of Detroit, New York, and Utica — possibly for others as well.[7]

Consideration of the Budget by the Legislature. Various writers have commented at length upon the consideration of the budget by the legislature; only a few of the more important questions can be mentioned here. In general, it may be said that the legislature ought to approve the budget as submitted. The assumption is that it has been prepared with care; the executive is responsible for it, and should be willing and able to defend it, either before the legislature or, if necessary, before the people. It would be desirable if the governor were given the power to appear before either or both houses of the legislature upon his own initiative; and correspondingly, the legislature should have the power to summon him to appear before it, either in person or through a designated representative, to defend his proposals. The budget office has or should have all necessary information; the legislature does not have it, and it is difficult for that body to secure it.

This raises a question that is of deep concern to the more intelligent legislators. The legislative branch has a real responsibility in connection with the budget; it is difficult for the members to understand the budget, both

[7] For discussion see: Citizens Union of the City of New York, "A Performance Budget for New York City," *The Searchlight*, September 1951, entire issue; Maryland Commission on Administrative Organization of the State, *First Interim Report*, *The Maryland Budget System* (Baltimore, 1951); Cope, Orin K., "Performance Budgeting: San Diego Puts Plan into Effect," *Tax Digest*, December 1950, pp. 415–418; and United States Bureau of the Budget, *Performance Budgeting: Selected References* (Washington, October 1950).

because of its technical nature and because of their lack of information. Especially when the executive and the majority of the legislature are of opposite parties, members may experience difficulty in securing information they need for intelligent action on the general appropriation bill. This has led, in some cases, to suggestions of establishing a separate budget bureau under legislative control for the service of members. This would involve needless duplication; yet the suggestion indicates the seriousness of the problem. The permanent research staff of the legislative council may be the solution. In any event, closer cooperation between the executive and legislative branches of the government than exists in most states would be extremely helpful.

There is abundant evidence that legislators are keenly aware of this problem. In recent legislative sessions, emphasis has been on fiscal research, numerous legislatures taking steps to employ specialists in many technical and highly specialized fields to assist them and their staffs in analyzing budget requests. The objective is to provide the legislature with the facts so that budgets may be reviewed and acted upon intelligently; the methods by which this is being done in an increasing number of states were described in Chapter 7.

It is customary for the budget to be referred to the appropriation committees of the two houses; the report is usually accompanied by a draft of a bill which would, if enacted, carry out the recommendations contained in the report. A joint committee, such as is common in New England, is far preferable to the usual separate committees. Legislative hearings on proposals for expenditure should in all states be an important part of the procedure; the Model State Constitution provides specifically for them in Section 704. Eventually the bill emerges in its final form. There has been much discussion of the relative merits of lump-sum and specific-allotment appropriations. Years ago, before the advent of effective methods of financial supervision, the specific-allotment form was in universal use. At present, with such methods of supervision available and in general use, the lump-sum appropriation provides adequate protection of public funds. The old-fashioned, detailed-appropriation measure is not only no longer necessary; it is an actual obstacle or hindrance to effective administrative control.[8]

Finally, there is the question of the power of the legislature to increase or decrease the amounts recommended in the budget. In all but four states the power of the legislature to change the budget is unlimited; in Maryland, Nevada, New York, and West Virginia, it has the power to strike out or reduce, but not to raise items. Since the executive departments are rarely hesitant about asking for funds, it is a little ridiculous for the legislature to insist that executive departments need more money than has been asked for by the governor. If the three branches of the government are to be retained

[8] For the practice on itemization in thirty-four states, see Jones, Victor, *The Legislature and the Budget*, pp. 20–24 (University of California, Bureau of Public Administration, 1941).

independently, the legislature cannot be denied the right to increase or decrease the amount of its own appropriation as compared with the budget request, although in those states where the governor has power to reduce items, an increase may later be negatived. The same right on the part of the legislature should probably exist with regard to appropriations for the judiciary.[9] If the system of control is well administered, measures providing for either supplementary appropriations or deficiency appropriations should be rare indeed.

Enforcement of the Budget. Making a plan for spending, and securing its enactment, is only part of the function of a budget system; a second major purpose is to see that the plan when made and adopted is faithfully executed — that all expenditures are made in compliance with the appropriation acts. Two devices may be used by the governor, normally acting through the medium of his budget officer, to effect proper control: allotments to govern the rate of expenditure, and encumbrances to prevent commitments not in accordance with the appropriation act and the regulations of the budget office.

As soon as the general appropriation act has been passed and approved by the governor, this agency must undertake the final allocation of funds, according to purposes of expenditure, for each spending agency in the state government. This allocation is concerned not only with purposes of expenditure, but with the items. If the state operates on an annual budget, the appropriation will be broken down into fourths for each department or spending agency; if the state has a biennial budget, half the appropriation for each spending agency must be reserved for the second year, and the yearly allotment be broken down into quarters. This quarterly allotment must then be broken down again, according to the purposes for which the spending agency uses its money.[10] This whole procedure should be under the immediate control of the executive.

An encumbrance reserves a part of an allotment at the time a commit-

[9] White, Leonard D., in his *Introduction to the Study of Public Administration*, Revised Edition (Macmillan, New York, 1939), reports, p. 220, a provision in the Maryland Constitution (Article III, Section 52) as follows: "The governor's estimates for the executive branch cannot be increased, but may be reduced . . . ; the estimates for the courts (prepared by the judges) cannot be reduced, but may be increased; and estimates for the legislative branch may be either increased or reduced."

[10] The following typical classification of the objects of expenditure is that used by Virginia:

11. Personal Service
12. Contractual Service
13. Supplies
14. Materials
15. Equipment
16. Land and Structures
17. Current Charges and Obligations
18. Pensions and Retirement Salaries
19. Rotary Fund

Capital Outlays

25. Equipment
26. Land and Structures

— From *Classifications and Instructions for the Preparation of Budget Estimates* (Richmond, July 1, 1939).

ment is made against it, in order to assure that this amount will be available to provide for payment when the goods are delivered or the service rendered. The accountant must, therefore, maintain his books on an encumbrance basis. Bills for which he has already established an encumbrance will, when presented for payment, be paid out of the encumbered funds. Requisitions, on the other hand, will be charged against the unencumbered balance of the department or agency, for that particular purpose and for that particular quarterly period.

It has been demonstrated by long experience that sound budget procedure, with the accompanying advantages of economical and efficient performance of a well-balanced program of governmental services, involves certain characteristics. Some of these are as follows:

1. The budget should be formulated by the chief executive and should represent his program of work for the fiscal period.
2. It should record all — not part — of the estimated receipts and proposed expenditures of the government.
3. These proposed expenditures should not exceed the estimated revenues.
4. The expenditures should be classified in the budget document by the various "funds" involved, by the specific services to be performed, by the nature of the things to be bought.
5. In the interest of economy, the executive should exercise a large measure of control over the execution of the budget after it is approved by the legislature.

Since no state has yet found the perfect budget system, it is probable that some changes might be made to advantage in order fully to realize these objectives in any one state.

Control of State Expenditures

The term "control of expenditures" may refer to the enforcement of the budget after the appropriation act has been approved by the legislature, as indicated above, or to the attempt to hold within reasonable bounds the amount of the appropriations as related to total income. It is to this second aspect of the problem that attention is now directed. With state expenditures totaling well over eleven billion dollars in 1949, the problem is obviously important.

Increase in Amounts. While the cost of government had increased some before 1900, in the early years of this century conspicuous increases became common. In California an increase of 1,400 per cent occurred in the seventy years from 1860 to 1930. During the first fifty years of this period the rate of increase exceeded only slightly that of the growth of population; from 1910 on, disbursements shot up at an astounding rate. No serious hardship was caused to taxpayers as long as these increases were accompanied by increased income and increases in the total assessed valuation of property. With the advent of the depression, however, the cost of government continued to mount steadily, while such indices of national economic trends as commodity prices, business activity, and factory payrolls declined at a correspondingly alarming rate. Following a slight decline during the depths of the depression, total revenues and expenditures have both continued to rise. In 1939 the California Taxpayers' Association reported a rise of 311 per cent in the preceding fifteen years, of 838 per cent in the preceding twenty years, against a population increase of 92 per cent.

After World War II expenditures again moved upwards at a tremendous rate. State outlays doubled, more than eleven billion reported in 1949 in comparison with six billion in 1946. In 1949, and again in 1950 for the second consecutive year, expenditures exceeded income. "Cost of operation of the California state government during 1947–1948 was $267,545,000, an increase of $59,591,566 over the $207,954,154 expended in 1946–1947, and nearly twice the $135,286,180 spent for relatively the same functions at the state level in 1945–1946." [11] The present state budget for the biennium runs over one billion dollars. Viewed from another angle, this represents an increase of approximately $100 in per capita costs for state government in a period of nearly forty years from 1910 to 1949. The increases at five-year intervals are shown in the table below.

Turning from a representative state on the Pacific coast to another on the Atlantic, one finds interesting figures on the growth of total expenditures in Pennsylvania by biennial periods from 1902 to 1949. These figures are for the General Fund only, and do not, with the exception of highways, include expenditures for purposes financed through special funds.

Changes in Major Purposes. The two tables on pages 502 and 503 present another aspect of the same general situation, showing expenditures classified

State of California
Expenditures of State and Local Governments — 1910–1949 *

YEAR	*Expenditures*		*Per Capita Expenditures*	
	STATE	TOTAL [1]	STATE	TOTAL
1910	$ 8,108,000	$ 84,951,000	$ 3.41	$ 34.78
1915	14,853,000	125,432,000	5.08	42.89
1920	23,856,000	172,710,000	6.96	50.40
1925	38,871,000	356,797,000	8.16	74.91
1930	74,948,000	491,603,000	13.20	86.59
1935	165,241,000	533,438,000	27.40	88.46
1940	214,517,297	738,924,418	31.06	106.98
1945	140,432,970	763,258,702	16.83	91.46
1949	807,775,433	2,158,735,336	80.44	214.96

* From *Tax Digest*, November 1950, pp. 376 and 378.

[1] Includes counties, cities, school districts, special districts, as well as the cost of the state government.

[11] McSweyn, Maxine M., "Three Years of State Costs: Spending Almost Doubles," *Tax Digest*, May 1949, pp. 155–156, 176–179.

Commonwealth of Pennsylvania Expenditures, 1902–1945 *

BIENNIUM	GENERAL FUND	HIGHWAY FUNDS [1]	TOTAL EXPENDITURES
1902–1904	$ 37,362,268	$..........	$ 37,362,268
1912–1914	67,981,590	1,175,000	69,156,590
1923–1925	135,236,493	64,866,964	200,103,457
1933–1935	208,984,164	132,306,138	341,290,302
1935–1937	340,375,072	102,932,637	443,307,709
1937–1939	421,740,717	152,077,822	573,818,539
1939–1941	476,653,696	139,037,452	615,691,148
1941–1943	444,224,718	154,467,942	598,692,660
1943–1945	417,243,914	118,466,724	535,710,639
1945–1947	492,487,750	157,110,641	649,598,392
1947–1949	635,955,823	275,969,840	911,925,663

* These figures do not include Federal contributions, the amounts of which for the last two biennia are indicated below, together with the total expenditures therefor. (Figures supplied by Dr. Edward B. Logan, Budget Secretary)

1945–1947	62,843,231	8,537,017	71,380,248
	555,330,981	165,647,659	720,978,640
1947–1949	88,555,033	40,053,576	128,608,609
	724,510,856	316,023,416	1,040,534,273

[1] The Motor License Fund first operated as a separate fund in the biennium 1918–1920. Expenditures entered in this column prior to that date represent expenditures for highways from the General Fund; subsequent to that date, expenditures are included for the Motor License Fund, the State Bond Road Fund, and the Federal Trust Account, National Industrial Recovery Highway Fund.

State of California
Functional Expenditures for Selected Years — 1935–1949 *

FUNCTION	1935	1940	1945	1949
General Government	$ 34,972,435	$ 43,605,355	$ 57,127,673	$ 179,215,348
Protection to Persons and Property.....	59,834,030	85,124,269	108,122,824	234,000,898
Health and Sanitation	11,225,936	16,785,083	28,094,535	65,114,905
Highways and Bridges	69,430,264	77,202,277	67,419,022	256,187,479
Recreation.........	8,299,610	12,322,044	15,977,335	43,203,725
Charities and Corrections...........	142,829,152	172,040,232	163,593,264	453,414,633
Education.........	141,625,283	191,381,158	232,986,322	518,900,647
Bond Interest and Redemption........	48,547,981	56,562,196	45,411,441	65,587,804
Unemployment Compensation........	....	62,193,575	20,068,433	271,868,634
Miscellaneous.......	16,723,064	21,193,575	24,457,853	71,241,263
Total	533,487,755	738,924,418	763,258,702	2,158,735,336

* From *Tax Digest*, November 1950, p. 381.

according to major purposes, at intervals, for the states of California and Pennsylvania. While there has, in the latter state, been a steady rise in state government costs for many years, the tremendous increases of recent years have been attributable largely to the growth of social welfare functions, to man's quest for economic security. For every dollar spent in Pennsylvania for social welfare purposes in 1929–1931, $82 was spent in 1947–1949. For every dollar spent in subsidizing education, nearly three dollars was spent twenty years later. Custodial care, highways, and other functions of government cost twice as much as they did then. Some of the increased cost is due, of course, to the decline in the purchasing power of the dollar, although it can

Commonwealth of Pennsylvania
Expenditures (in millions), 1929–1931 and 1947–1949 *

1929–1931	MAJOR FUNCTION	1947–1949
$ 6.6	Social Welfare	$ 492.5
92.4	Education	257.4
43.5	Custodial Care	95.1
138.9	Highways	288.2
70.8	All Other	167.9
352.2	Total	1301.1

* The 1947–1949 column contains expenditures for Unemployment Compensation and for operations of the Liquor Control Board, not usually shown in state financial statements.

be shown that the rise in the cost of government, percentage-wise, is less than this shrinkage. For example, the basic salary of $960 in 1929–1931 was only $1,572 in 1947–1949, and the percentage increase in salaries in the upper bracket employees has been even less.[12]

The truth of the matter is that two world wars, the economic spree of the twenties, the awful depression of the thirties, and the postwar ideological struggle with Russia have bewildered us. "The manifestations of our search for security," notes William A. Sponsler, "are to be found in the various forms of social assistance, in cash payments to the aged, to the blind, to mothers, to the unemployed, and to the unemployable; government controls of business; guaranteed incomes to farm and laboring groups; the rise in the power of labor unions; demand for private pensions and health insurance; and international economic aid to other peoples." In this welter of unaccustomed activity the state governments have already been very greatly affected and the outlook for the future is not bright. Existing contractual commitments will require the Pennsylvania legislature to raise an additional

[12] Data from Sponsler, William A., "Government in Pennsylvania at Mid-Century," a paper presented at the Annual Meeting of the Pennsylvania Political Science and Public Administration Association, Harrisburg, April 15, 1950.

minimum of $107,000,000 for the biennium 1951–1953; additional commitments will very likely increase this amount to $150,000,000 or $200,000,000. This is a sizable increase in a two-year period, even in a large, populous, and wealthy state.

Adjusted Figures on Government Costs. The report of the Joint Legislative Committee on Finances in Pennsylvania in 1934 discussed the problem of adjusted figures, as related to the cost of government in that state. Except for the abnormal period of the depression, governmental expenditures when adjusted for purchasing power have increased less rapidly — much less rapidly — than the figures in actual dollars would indicate. Thus from 1912–1914 to 1927–1929, actual expenditures increased about four times, whereas expenditures measured in 1913 dollars increased less than threefold.

The $350,000,000 spent in this state in 1931–1933 had a purchasing power of over $500,000,000 in terms of 1926 dollars, and much more than that in terms of the 1913 dollar. Comparisons of this type give a better picture of governmental costs than the use of per capita figures, which are frequently employed. While only slight variations in percentages occur from one biennium to another, the change over a period of twenty or thirty years is striking. Commenting on this matter, the Budget Secretary said:

> Such a comparison as this shows only the relative financial rank of the general functions. It does not show growth of individual functions. For example, out of the six functions four have the same financial rank now as they had twenty years ago. Highways, with third rank in 1913–1914, have taken first place, while Health and Welfare, of first rank in 1912–1914, are now in third place. This does not mean that the State has ignored Health and Welfare in favor of Highways. The fact is that expenditures for Health and Welfare have grown but Highway expenditures have grown faster.[13]

The causes of these increased costs are to be found not alone in increased populations and declining purchasing power of the dollar; developments in science and the arts and concurrent changes in our concepts of social and governmental responsibility have been important factors. Scientific developments have made necessary new and previously unheard of forms of regulation and control, while new concepts have been responsible not only for the establishment of new services but for the extension of old ones. In addition, higher standards of administrative efficiency have been developed — people expect more and better service from their government than they did a few years ago. Nor can one ignore the fact that the unplanned and unsystematic development of government services prior to the inauguration of the reorganization movement led to much overlapping, duplication, and wasteful and inefficient management. These factors are gradually being reduced.

Control of Amounts Expended. In the interests of over-all financial management, a number of techniques and methods have been used to control the amount of public expenditures. Among the more desirable are good

[13] Logan, Edward B., "Costs, Trends, and Predictions Relating to Governmental Expenditures Other than Education," Schoolmen's Week *Proceedings*, p. 37 (University of Pennsylvania, 1932).

executive management and the independent audit, both of which have been considered earlier. Legislative controls are exercised not only in the periodic review of activities that precedes the passage of appropriation acts but through investigations carried on by legislative committees — regular and special. Members of the legislature soon find out, from their mail and from personal contacts with constituents, when a department or agency is not doing its job well. The legislature's general surveillance of administration is one of its more important obligations, and one that has a very close relationship to the control of expenditures.

Among the less desirable methods of control may be mentioned tight and arbitrary limitations on tax rates and the power to incur debt, and public outcries against "overlapping, duplication, and waste." As regards the former, it may be noted that some states have constitutional limitations on both tax rates and the power to incur debt. It often develops that the people want more and better service but that they do not want to pay for it. There are instances on record in which the voters have approved at the same time a measure which would inevitably increase the need for revenue and one which would impose additional limitations upon the possibility of raising it. The trouble with attempts to control public spending by such methods is that the limits established are arbitrary and inelastic; they do not represent, even at the time of adoption, any reasoned judgment with regard to the fiscal policies and needs of the state.

Crusades for "economy" break out every once in so often. These usually call for the appointment of an economy committee or commission to carry on an investigation for the elimination of unnecessary and useless services, but when an effort is made to discover what these services are, it is generally found that they relate to some subject that is of no concern to the group entering the complaint. Since a service which seems unnecessary and useless to one group is a matter of vital concern to another, little can be saved by this method unless the legislature and administration are willing to engage in reckless and wholesale slashing of essential services. It is obviously desirable to eliminate overlapping, duplication, and waste, but the truth of the matter is that these investigations have been made so often, in state after state, that only minor savings can be expected to result. Furthermore, the increasing emphasis on the practice of good administration that has been in evidence in recent years has tended further to restrict the opportunities for spectacular savings.

Popular Fallacies. It has frequently been assumed that these great increases in the cost of government were largely unjustified and a proof of waste and extravagance. This explanation, although indicating a contributing cause, fails to account for important factors that have justifiably increased the expenditures of state government. In the first place, the population is much larger now than it was in 1900 or 1910; if the same services had been continued without change and other factors had remained constant, a considerable increase in expenditures would have been justified on this basis alone. When, however, it is argued that the cost of government has increased much more rapidly than population, it should be remembered that this period was also one of rising prices; in other words, of a steady decline in the purchasing power of the dollar. Indeed it is surprising that the increase in government expenditure has not been greater.

Among the popular fallacies long widely accepted was the assumption that money spent by government was less beneficial to trade and commerce than money spent by private agencies. It is difficult to understand the basis for this belief, since a large part of such expenditures goes into salaries and wages and for the purchase of supplies, materials, and equipment, as do the expenditures of private concerns. Furthermore, such spending may be productive of greater social values than like amounts spent in the construction of new factories. Again, it is urged that government is something apart from the people and "that every increase of the power and the activity of the government is a burden and an oppression to the people." The fallacy of this argument should be apparent to anyone. Every one of the services and activities of government is carried on either because some group demanded it for its own protection or because the public interest required it.

Though modern government is more a servant than a ruler, there are still complaints from many quarters that the government has gone into business, into social service, and even into the supervision of the homes of citizens. It is true that government is doing more in all these fields than ever before — and it is likely to do still more in years to come. All of the scientific developments of modern life contributing to the raising of the general standard of living create demands for new services, new problems of regulation and control, the demand for all of which comes from every class and stratum of the population — farmers, labor, industry, home owners, and practically every organized group. As the character of our civilization changes, the needs for government and the responsibilities of government must, of necessity, change with it.

Finally, there is the oft-repeated charge that there is wastefulness and graft in public expenditures. The assumption seems to be that the government does not receive as much in goods or service for the dollar which it spends as do private individuals. To say that, in general, government receives much more is not to deny that there are occasional instances both of wastefulness and graft. "Let any man go out and buy an education for his children, instead of sending them to public school. Or let him try to buy roads or any other thing. The idea is so silly that it, of course, does not merit further discussion. The public has asked the government to do many things for it just because the private citizen could not get a fair and economical deal in any other way." In addition, there is the fact that government, through the exercise of the taxing power, can distribute the burden of the cost of services more equitably than would otherwise be possible. Furthermore, before public expenditures are made, they must be provided for in the budget; this gives an annual opportunity for their reconsideration.[14]

The Borrowing Power

History of State Borrowing. There have been four periods in the history of the states when their borrowing power has been used more extensively than is usual in ordinary times: first, the period of the Revolution; second, the period of rapid internal expansion following the War of 1812, during which there was an extensive development of public works; third, the reconstruction period following the Civil War; and finally, the period of the depression which began in 1929, during which there was large borrowing for relief. The loans obtained during the first period either were paid back by the states that secured them or were assumed by the Federal government and paid off in full. They occurred so far back in our history that no extended discussion of them here is necessary. The large loans of the second period, for internal improvements, were recklessly spent on post roads, canals, and railways. In the 1840's serious difficulty arose in the payment of these obligations and many were canceled. The fact that many of them were held by foreign bondholders led to international complications, the echoes of which have only recently died away.[15] In some of the older states the remains of some of the canals built with this money may still be seen — grim reminders of wastefulness and bad judgment, and ultimately of bad faith. A second period of default, between 1848 and 1860, was one in which the states involved were widely separated and the causes varied. Texas defaulted on the payment of a debt incurred in connection with the Mexican War, and California on a debt incurred during the inflation days of the Forty-Niners. Minnesota defaulted as a result of an ill-advised venture into state banking.[16]

The loans made after the Civil War gave rise to a third period of defaults in the late seventies and early eighties; all the Southern states that had comprised the Confederacy were involved. Like many of the earlier debts, these were incurred in other sections of the country upon the basis of optimistic tales about the future of the American states, in a "setting of apparently inevitable financial stringency, followed in turn by acrimonious debates between creditors and debtors, and finally the default by some debtors unable to adjust income to expenditures." [17] Most of the debts which were repudiated

[14] These three paragraphs are based on an article by William Anderson, "The Other Side of the Tax Problem," *Oklahoma Municipal Review*, April 1932, pp. 80–83.

[15] See Monaco v. Mississippi, 292 U.S. 313, 1934.

[16] No defaults have occurred in the following states: Arizona, Colorado, Connecticut, Delaware, Idaho, Iowa, Kansas, Kentucky, Maine, Massachusetts, Montana, Nebraska, Nevada, New Hampshire, New Jersey, New Mexico, New York, North Dakota, Ohio, Oklahoma, Oregon, Rhode Island, South Dakota, Utah, Vermont, Washington, Wisconsin, and Wyoming.

[17] See McGrane, Reginald C., *Foreign Bondholders and American State Debts* (Macmillan, New York, 1935). Each group of debts in the second and third periods is analyzed

were created during the second period of borrowing. This process of repudiation — total or partial through the scaling down process — occurred mainly between 1842 and 1892; many states used the latter method, but some used both. Only the major defaults are included, but the total amount involved — long before huge figures became commonplace during the two World Wars and the depression — reached the substantial total of approximately $161,-000,000.

The loans made during the depression which began in 1929, except those for casual deficiencies or those made on a short-term basis, have not yet come due. It seems unlikely that any considerable number will be defaulted. So far there has, with a single exception, been no move on the part of the states to escape their just payments, heavy though the burden is in some cases. The exception is Arkansas, which in 1933 practically forced the holders of its bonds paying from 4 to 5 per cent to exchange for 3 per cent bonds at par by refusing to continue interest payments on the former issues. This action actually constituted partial repudiation. In 1941 these new bonds were bought by the Reconstruction Finance Corporation in a deal which may yet prove to be of great significance in the field of state finance.[18] Even with the heavy increases in indebtedness during the depression period, the states were unable in most cases to meet the extensive demands upon them without substantial assistance from the Federal government.

Constitutional Limitations on State Debt. Because, during the depression, extensive use of the borrowing power was necessary, the constitutional restrictions on it were of particular interest. They are numerous, some of them are drastic, but the record clearly shows that they have not been effective in holding down the total amount of state debt. Several studies have been made of these provisions of the state constitutions.[19] Twenty-eight states have fixed sum limitations upon the amount of outstanding debt, while in nine states the limitation is based upon a percentage of the assessed valuation of taxable property. Fifteen states provide an exemption in case the proposed bond issue is ratified by popular referendum; this method of restriction has proved to be most ineffective, for there is always a tendency on the part of voters to think that someone else will have to pay most of the bills. On this point, Paul Studensky says: "The time seems ripe to abolish the requirements of referenda for the issuance of bonds by the states, and to vest the legislature with power to issue bonds without the approval of the people. The abuses of the state credit by legislatures ninety years ago should not be held

by states, with emphasis upon the origins and action by the state governments with regard to them. See also, by the same author, "Some Aspects of American State Debts in the Forties," *American Historical Review*, July 1933, pp. 673–686.

[18] See Ratchford, B. U., *American State Debts*, Chapter 15, on Arkansas, a state that borrowed too much (Duke University Press, 1941), and note in *National Municipal Review*, April 1941, pp. 238–240.

[19] In addition to references cited in previous editions, see Ratchford, *op. cit.*, Chapters 17–19, and Tax Foundation, a compilation of *Provisions in State Constitutions Controlling Debt* (New York, 1945).

against the legislatures of today."[20] If these referenda are not necessary today, they are further objectionable in that they violate the principle of the short ballot.

In sixteen states borrowing for general purposes is prohibited unless authorized by the legislature and a popular referendum; borrowing is prohibited in nineteen states unless the specific purpose is authorized in the constitution, and in four states unless the loan is authorized by a vote of two thirds or three fourths of the legislature. The specific purposes for which the constitutions authorize the making of loans include the suppression of insurrection and the repelling of invasion in forty states; assistance in the defense of the United States in five states; casual deficiencies, usually to the extent of definitely specified amounts, in twenty-three states; and payment or refund of existing debts in fifteen states. Among what might be called the miscellaneous provisions affecting the borrowing power the following are the most common: prohibition upon the lending of credit to individuals or corporations in forty-one states; a maximum number of years for the maturity of state bonds in nineteen states; and the requirement that a tax to provide for the payment of interest and principal must accompany the issue in twenty-six states. In addition to the usual ease with which many of these requirements are evaded, the exigencies of the depression were responsible for many studied attempts to evade them in order to secure funds necessary for relief. Furthermore, an easy provision for amending the constitution tends to nullify any debt limitations it may contain.

Growth of State Debts. There has been through the years, without regard to the four periods mentioned above, a steady increase in the gross debts incurred by the states, the extent of which, over the last seventy years, is indicated in the table on page 510. During this period there has been a notable increase not only in the totals, but in the per capita amounts of debt outstanding — from $5.48 in 1880 to $16.35 in 1930, and $35 in 1950.

The gross debt of California from 1910 to 1949, inclusive, as shown on page 511, illustrates what this increase has meant in the case of one representative state. On June 30, 1910, the gross bonded debt of this state was $4,881,500. At no time during the preceding sixty years of statehood had the debt exceeded $5,500,000. As of 1920, the total was up to almost $50,000,000; by 1930, it was over $120,000,000; by 1940, over $171,000,000; by 1950, over $263,000,000. That these figures are by no means unusual among the states is well shown by the table on page 512 covering state debts for all states at ten-year intervals from 1902 to 1950.

These debts were contracted for a variety of purposes, among which permanent improvements have been a most important one, others being park developments, public welfare, hospitals, corrections, schools, agriculture, and general purposes of government. More than half of the indebtedness incurred during the twenties was for purposes of highway construction.

[20] Studensky, Paul, *Public Borrowing* (National Municipal League, New York, 1930).

Debt of State Governments *
(Amounts expressed in thousands)

	Gross Debt		*Sinking Fund Assets*	*Gross Debt Less Total Sinking Fund Assets*	
YEAR	TOTAL	FUNDED OR FIXED [1]		AMOUNT	PER CAPITA
1880	$ 306,017	$ 286,819	$ 31,271	$ 274,746	$ 5.48
1890	258,195	238,283	46,985	211,210	3.37
1900	265,133	253,332	29,821	235,454 [2]	3.10
1910	322,949	311,093	66,814	256,143 [3]	2.78
1919	693,623	588,606	146,677	546,946	5.20
1930	2,444,122	2,238,606	449,910	1,994,212	16.35
1931	2,666,070	2,426,302	496,293	2,169,777	17.61
1932	2,907,495	2,502,665	520,577	2,386,918	19.27
1937 [4]	3,275,677	3,023,103	659,848	2,615,829	20.39
1938 [4]	3,300,648	3,116,526	664,531	2,636,117	20.47
1940	3,643,000		718,000	2,925,000	
1943	2,946,000	2,686,000	533,491	2,326,000	22.12
1945	2,526,000	2,300,000	632,165	1,838,971	19.26
1948	3,629,220	3,522,709	576,073	2,946,636	24.74
1950	5,246,276	5,128,502	854,072	4,392,204	35.00

* Source: United States Bureau of the Census, *Wealth, Debt, and Taxation*, 1913, Vol. I, p. 38, for data for years prior to 1915; *Financial Statistics of States* (annual studies) for data for 1915 and subsequent years.

[1] Revised to include special debt obligations to trust funds, and to agree with figures as published in state reports.

[2] Sinking fund assets exceed debt by $142,000 in one state.

[3] Sinking fund assets exceed debt by $8,000 in one state.

[4] Exclusive of public service enterprises.

Soldiers' bonuses were an important reason for borrowing in the early twenties and the late forties, as was relief in the decade of the thirties. More than a third of the debt now has to do with the financing of publicly owned enterprises. With increased tax receipts and little opportunity for spending during the defense period and during World War II, little new borrowing took place and substantial reductions were made in the amount of existing debt. It seems highly probable that these questions relating to surpluses accumulated under force of circumstances may again be upon us during the early fifties.

Postwar Trends. From its low point in 1946 the trend of state debts in the postwar years again started upward. The total state debt in 1950 was more than twice the amount outstanding in 1946, and barring a third all-out war effort, further increases are to be expected. Borrowings have been undertaken for the financing of highways, institutional construction, and other public works; to meet the requirements of enlarged programs of state

State of California
Bonded Indebtedness — 1910–1949

YEAR	STATE	STATE AND LOCAL
1910	$ 4,881,500	$..........
1915	25,511,500	205,412,706
1920	49,724,500	287,975,608
1925	98,607,500	608,754,728
1930	120,213,500	838,511,367
1935	180,958,500	933,310,810
1940	171,404,000	932,004,676
1945	110,093,000	727,724,329
1949	176,098,000	1,208,404,038

aid and of social legislation; and for veterans' benefits of one type or another.[21] The states came out of World War II in a much stronger financial position than they were when they went in. In view of increasing demands, higher costs, and limited sources of revenue, it now appears practically certain that they are not going to be able to retain these gains. In view also of the excessive and sometimes unwise use of the borrowing power in some jurisdictions in the past, by issuing bonds that equaled or exceeded the life of the improvement, the borrowing power of the states should be protected by exempting debt service from tax limitation provisions of state constitutions. In at least two states, Alabama and North Carolina, this has not been done. From the point of view of the prospective purchaser, it is preferable not only that the states pledge "full faith and credit," but that the constitutions provide unlimited taxation for debt service.

Some Current Problems. The rapid growth of non-guaranteed obligations — both state and local — presents a serious fiscal problem. For some time there has been a question regarding the responsibility of states for the indebtedness of their political subdivisions. There seems to be no basis upon which the states can be compelled to make good on the defaults of their municipalities and other local subdivisions, but the states should be expected so to supervise the finances of these subdivisions as to prevent defalcations. This the states in the past have not done, but the movement for state supervision of the finances of cities and other local units has been making such progress that effective supervision of this character can be expected in most states in the near future.

The states are now resorting to the same device. From 1937 to 1949, non-guaranteed state debt increased from 1 per cent to 16 per cent of total

[21] Note, for instance, the record borrowing for a veterans' bonus program, authorized by the voters of Pennsylvania in 1949. The sale of $375,000,000 in bonds out of the $500,000,000 authorized, constituted the largest issue ever sold by a state in a single block, and established a new record for borrowing by a unit other than the Federal government.

Growth of State Debt
(Totals expressed in thousands)

STATE	GROSS DEBT LESS SINKING FUND ASSETS					
	1950	1942	1932	1922	1912	1902
Alabama	$ 40,945	$ 74,739	$ 82,342	$ 15,233	$13,132	$12,727
Arizona	3,109	3,134	3,676	2,740	3,065	3,099
Arkansas	125,102	154,558	164,424	2,722	1,236	1,101
California	114,489	219,436	145,723	85,267	10,223	2,955
Colorado	12,901	24,099	6,747	12,019	3,174	3,797
Connecticut	79,848	30,213	108	6,088	7,111	1,678
Delaware	75,000	5,174	2,072	5,834	763	762
Florida	14,995		391	869	619	1,032
Georgia	2,403	22,967	12,488	5,419	6,934	7,876
Idaho	808	2,689	6,961	7,673	2,143	324
Illinois	412,066	149,252	221,404	13,880	2,273	2,155
Indiana	11,044	7,923	4,730	2,325	1,350	2,914
Iowa	35,440	2,038	16,495	1,457	357	50
Kansas	4,145	15,522	21,810	78	243	632
Kentucky	8,730	9,053	16,224	7,745	4,441	2,291
Louisiana	217,052	182,112	83,743	14,829	13,546	13,593
Maine	8,684	26,323	27,219	12,906	1,255	2,785
Maryland	95,841	57,965	31,198	22,129	7,334	4,942
Massachusetts	203,971	111,187	62,856	76,996	79,551	65,964
Michigan	237,654	41,094	60,582	50,934	7,089	6,566
Minnesota	119,918	105,221	40,156	20,308	1,345	1,755
Mississippi	66,353	82,998	36,320	14,864	4,461	2,877
Missouri	37,198	87,907	103,302	30,456	4,671	4,366
Montana	20,994	13,509	9,316	7,579	1,513	1,204
Nebraska	608	947	929	1,038	374	2,005
Nevada	740	431	1,370	1,751	608	624
New Hampshire	8,610	17,912	6,505	3,018	1,956	1,551
New Jersey	104,852	105,906	62,198	16,355	642	....
New Mexico	26,811	27,242	11,407	4,954	1,218	999
New York	516,347	703,412	463,068	186,542	86,205	8,187
North Carolina	138,503	135,445	177,210	34,713	8,059	6,755
North Dakota	21,352	29,971	5,005	5,913	820	968
Ohio	190,800	12,062	7,696	30,143	5,142	4,685
Oklahoma	92,435	40,159	11,438	4,797	6,931	510
Oregon	10,598	31,225	33,388	39,983	31	236
Pennsylvania	709,260	288,784	75,858	49,968		389
Rhode Island	46,953	29,333	16,807	9,338	5,127	2,620
South Carolina	91,021	86,537	77,984	8,729	6,190	6,730
South Dakota	22,048	32,056	15,510	15,431	370	457
Tennessee	97,435	94,394	94,032	19,142	11,812	17,984
Texas	49,676	18,169	10,317	6,145	4,656	3,993
Utah	158	2,019	5,694	9,819	1,430	974
Vermont	6,263	6,850	9,545	2,112	570	363
Virginia	23,949	25,716	25,983	21,756	22,043	23,546
Washington	89,497	16,262	8,257	13,191	1,556	1,271
West Virginia	70,815	79,695	86,394	24,181		......
Wisconsin	4,075	1,184	1,184	2,164	2,251	2,278
Wyoming	2,934	3,240	5,568	4,011	122	301

State Debt — Fiscal Years 1941–1950
Postwar Trend in Millions of Dollars*

YEAR	SHORT TERM DEBT	SINKING FUND OFFSETS	NET LONG TERM DEBT	GROSS DEBT
1941	211	617	2638	3466
1942	163	544	2553	3259
1943	21	615	2301	2937
1944	8	680	2097	2785
1945	3	630	1893	2526
1946	25	608	1734	2367
1947	84	604	2269	2956
1948	108	657	2827	3592
1949	16	735	3330	4080
1950	117	854	5128	5246

* From Tax Foundation, *Postwar Trend in State Debt: A State by State Analysis*, chart opposite p. 1 (New York, 1950), and United States Bureau of the Census, "Governmental Debt in 1950."

Per Capita Gross Debt, by States and Selected Distribution — Fiscal Year 1950*

PER CAPITA GROSS DEBT	NUMBER 1949	NUMBER 1950	STATES
$100 and over	1	1	Delaware
$80–$100	1	1	Louisiana
$60–$80	2	5	Arkansas, Connecticut, North Dakota, Pennsylvania, Rhode Island
$40–$60	7	11	Illinois, Maryland, Massachusetts, Minnesota, Montana, New Hampshire, New York, North Carolina, Oklahoma, South Carolina, South Dakota
$20–$40	13	11	California, Michigan, Mississippi, Missouri, New Jersey, New Mexico, Ohio, Oregon, Tennessee, Washington, West Virginia
Less than $20	24	19	Alabama, Arizona, Colorado, Florida, Georgia, Idaho, Indiana, Iowa, Kansas, Kentucky, Maine, Nebraska, Nevada, Texas, Utah, Vermont, Virginia, Wisconsin, Wyoming

* *Postwar Trend in State Debt*, *op. cit.*, p. 15, and "Governmental Debt in 1950," *op. cit.*

state long-term debt, more than half of which consists of bonds for such enterprises as toll bridges, toll roads, university dormitories, water and power projects. The remainder is classified as debt for general government activities. In the forty-one states in which more than $500,000,000 has been incurred, the distinguishing feature seems to be that it is not backed by the full faith and credit of the states.[22]

[22] Smith, Gordon P., "Who Owes State Debt?" *Tax Review*, August 1950, pp. 29–32.

Another difficulty, affecting both states and their subdivisions, has to do with the relations of the unit of government with the bankers. There is an old maxim to the effect that he who pays the piper calls the tune; this has been all too true in the field of government. Bankers and combinations of bankers have frequently insisted upon dictating policies of government as the price of their assistance. The sounder the credit of the unit, the more independent it can afford to be. In some cases, rather than submit to the dictates of private bankers, administrations have gone directly to the banks of the state and sold their issues in that way.

SELECTED REFERENCES

Benson, George C. S., and Litchfield, Edward H., *The State Administrative Board in Michigan* (Bureau of Government, University of Michigan, 1938). For another historical survey of this once popular method of commission control of fiscal matters, see Short, Lloyd M., and Tiller, Carl W., *The Minnesota Commission of Administration and Finance, 1925–1939* (University of Minnesota Press, 1942).

Durfee, Waite D., Jr., *Intergovernmental Fiscal Relations* (University of Minnesota Press, 1950); see also Council of State Governments, *Federal Grants-in-Aid* (Chicago, 1949), and Reed, Thomas H., *Federal-State-Local Fiscal Relations* (Municipal Finance Officers Association, Chicago, 1942).

Graves, W. Brooke, *Public Administration in a Democratic Society* (Heath, Boston, 1950). Contains two chapters on budgeting, and several on various other phases of the problem of fiscal management.

Jones, Victor, *The Legislature and the Budget* (Bureau of Public Administration, University of California, 1941). A study of a very difficult and very important aspect of the budgetary process; for a significant study of the same problem, with emphasis on the executive, see Perkins, John A., *The Role of the Governor of Michigan in the Enactment of Appropriations* (Bureau of Government, University of Michigan, 1943)

Ratchford, B. U., *American State Debts* (Duke University Press, 1941). Standard title on the subject.

Tannery, Fladger F., *State Accounting Procedures* (Public Administration Service, Chicago, 1943). Only available treatment of governmental accounting problems gauged at the state level.

Tax Foundation, *Rising State Expenditures* (New York, 1946) and *Recent Trends in State Expenditures, 1942–1947* (New York, 1948). Two excellent postwar surveys of expenditure trends.

——, *Recent Trends in State Debt, 1941–1947* (New York, 1948) and *Postwar Trend in State Debt: a State by State Analysis* (New York, 1950). Significant analyses of trends in postwar debt at the state level.

15

The Revenue System

Representative government owes its origin to financial necessities. As William B. Munro has observed, when the medieval kings needed money, they summoned representatives of the people to parliaments. Problems of public finance, once simple, are now complex, but they are still among the chief problems of the executive and legislative branches of government. These problems may be considered under three headings: those aspects of budgeting which have to do with financial planning — the formulation and adoption of the budget; the problems of expenditure and expenditure control — enforcement of the budget; and finally, the raising of the necessary funds either through taxation or through borrowing. The present chapter is concerned with the problem of raising revenues.

Sources of State Income

Taxation. If one were to make a careful and detailed study of the tax system in the states, he would find almost every conceivable combination of the forms of taxation known to students of public finance. Some of these forms are not used frequently enough to justify including them in a general discussion, but there are certain major forms each of which is used in all or nearly all the states. Among these are the general property tax, corporation and business taxes, income taxes, consumption and sales taxes, excise taxes such as those on alcoholic beverages, tobacco, and gasoline, and inheritance and estate taxes. The states raise only 25 per cent of their revenues by direct taxes, whereas the Federal and local governments raise about half of theirs in this way.

The revenue sources used by the states can be grouped for convenience under the six major headings which are used for section headings in this chapter:

General property — now mainly a local source
Corporation and business taxes, including licenses and fees
General sales, use, or gross receipts taxes
Excise taxes, as on alcoholic beverages, gasoline, and tobacco
Income taxes, individual and corporate
Inheritance and estate taxes

State Tax Collections by Major Source: Selected Years, 1923–1948 *
(in millions)

TAX SOURCE	1923 POST-WAR I PERIOD	1928 BOOM PERIOD	1933 GREAT DEPRESSION	1938 THE LATE THIRTIES	1943 WORLD WAR II	1948 POST-WAR II PERIOD
Total tax collections:						
Including unemployment compensation..........	[1]	[1]	[1]	$3,834	$5,132	$7,791
Excluding unemployment compensation..........	$1,020	$1,756	$1,724	3,312	3,961	6,732
General sales, use, or gross receipts..................	.....	.....	16	447	671	1,479
Motor vehicle fuel sales.....	39	305	518	777	776	1,260
Tobacco products sales......	.....	.....	20	55	141	339
Alcoholic beverage sales and licenses................	.....	.....	10	227	335	426
Motor vehicle and operators licenses................	189	323	303	359	414	593
Individual income..........	[2]	[2]	64	218	293	499
Corporation income........	[2]	[2]	57	165	340	585
Property..................	353	381	285	244	259	279
Death and gift.............	75	128	127	142	109	[3]
Severance.................	.....	.....	14	58	75	[3]
Unemployment compensation	[1]	[1]	[1]	702	1,172	1,059
Other....................	272	436	311	440	547	343

* From United States Bureau of the Census, "Historical Review of State and Local Government Finances," p. 20 (Washington, June 1948) and *Compendium of State Government Finances in 1948*, p. 6 (Washington, 1949).

[1] There was no unemployment compensation tax prior to 1936.

[2] Breakdown not available.

[3] Included in "other" below.

Social security taxes should perhaps be included, but they are so definitely earmarked for a specific purpose that they do not contribute in any way to general fund revenues. In addition to these major tax sources, the states collect considerable sums from miscellaneous sources. The growth in revenue receipts for all the states is indicated, at five-year intervals since 1923, in the table shown above. In 1950 the Bureau of the Census reported that, for the seventeenth consecutive year, state tax revenues had increased.[1] Michigan and Pennsylvania may be taken as illustrative of what has happened gen-

[1] For statistical data and analysis, see Council of State Governments, *Sources of State Tax Revenue*, 1940–1949 (Chicago, 1950), and Tax Foundation, *Major State Taxes*, 1939 and 1950 (New York, 1951).

Commonwealth of Pennsylvania
Income (in millions), 1929–1931, and 1947–1949 *

1929–1931	SOURCE	1947–1949
$ 72.6	Sales Taxes (Beer, cigarettes, soft drinks, liquor, and gasoline)	$ 430.7
.....	Corporate Net Income	152.8
228.1	Basic Taxes of 1929 (Capital stock, franchises, loans, inheritances, and licenses, including motor vehicles)	299.2
16.4	Federal Aids (Public assistance, unemployment compensation, education, and highways)	336.2
32.3	All Other	73.6
$349.4	Total	$1,292.5

* The 1947–1949 column contains receipts from the Federal government for unemployment compensation grants and administration rather than total taxes collected in Pennsylvania and forwarded to the Federal government. It also contains State Liquor Store profits in gross amount before operating expenses are deducted. State Liquor Board operating expenses are shown under expenditures (see p. 503). To this extent, these figures deviate from the usual state financial statements.

erally; the chart on page 518 shows the growth of tax revenues in the former from 1920 through 1947, by major sources.

In Pennsylvania, for every dollar of state income raised in 1929–1931, four dollars were raised in 1947–1949. The historic tax structure, developed over a period of 100 years or more, has been retained with only slight modifications. It yields today only the modest increase that might be expected, but the yield of the sales tax has been multiplied by six — and this state has no general sales tax. The corporate net income tax has been added, to yield $150 million, and grants from the Federal government have increased to the extent of about $23.00 for every dollar received in 1929–1931. This situation is indicated in the above table.[2]

During the depression years when the receipts from the major sources declined sharply, the states engaged in a widespread search for new revenue sources; they continued, nevertheless, to relinquish the general property tax for state purposes. During World War II there were few instances of tax reductions or of the repeal of tax laws, although, with treasuries overflowing with revenues derived from the boom of industry, there were no new taxes. These surplus funds were used to balance current budgets, retire debt, and create reserves for postwar needs. In the postwar era expenditures

[2] See Sponsler, William A., "Government in Pennsylvania at Mid-Century," a paper presented at the Annual Meeting of the Pennsylvania Political Science and Public Administration Association, Harrisburg, April 15, 1950.

increased so rapidly that the so-called surpluses were soon dissipated, and additional revenues had to be obtained.

In 1947 all the legislatures except one were in session, and almost all of them adopted increased budgets. Most of the new or increased levies were on sales, cigarettes, gasoline, and liquor, to finance pay raises, increased state aid, highways and institutional construction, and generally higher costs. While few new levies were adopted in 1949, more revenue was sought in many states through increased rates on existing taxes. In 1950, state expenditures were exceeding revenues for the second consecutive year.

State of Michigan Tax Revenues — 1920–1947

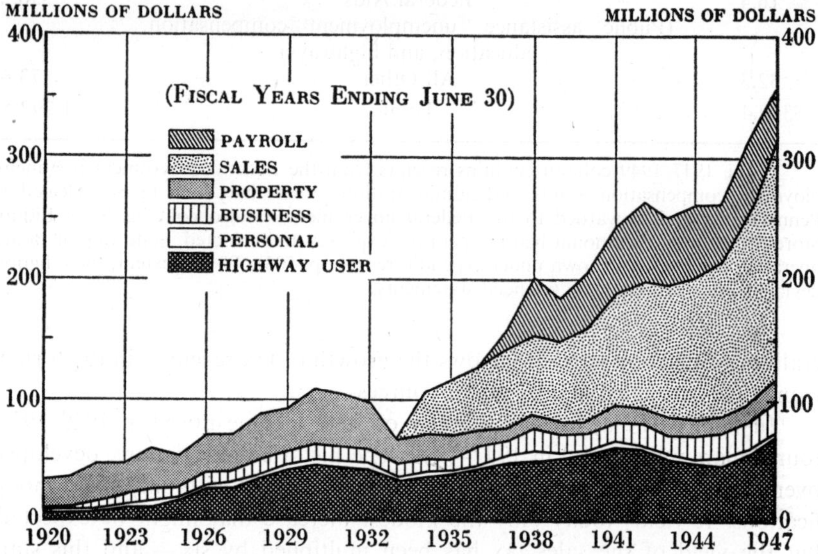

Sources Other Than Taxation. Contrary to a widely held but mistaken belief, the states obtain receipts in very considerable amounts from sources other than taxation. The importance of these varies greatly from state to state. In a list of such sources one thinks first of the receipts derived from the state's borrowing power; such receipts are definitely outside the revenue classification, even though they become funds in the state treasury, subject to appropriation by the legislature and to requisition and payment at the time, and for the purpose for which, the loan was made. The loan, of course, becomes a fixed charge upon the revenues of the state until the obligation has been met. During the depression many states made extensive use of the borrowing power, some of them to the extent of impairing their credit. The retirement of much of this debt was possible during the boom of the war years.

The states derive some income from the public domain, although in most cases the amount is not large. Portions of this domain may be sold as authorized; mineral rights may be sold or leased; and revenues may be derived from the rental or leasing of camp sites. The conservation and forestry movement is now old enough so that some states are able to derive some annual income from the sale of timber. This is, in fact, necessary in the interests of real conservation and good forest management, but it is a difficult policy to execute because of a general misunderstanding of the meaning of conservation.

If a state maintains and operates any kind of business, any income derived therefrom is classifiable as commercial revenue. In most such cases the goods or services produced are offered to the public at cost. Illustrations include the production and sale of seedlings in order to encourage the reforestation of wastelands, and the management of public service enterprises or of a state insurance fund in connection with the enforcement of the workmen's compensation law. Since the adoption of Amendment XXI, sixteen states have entered the wholesale and retail liquor business; here the effort has been made to establish prices low enough to discourage bootlegging and high enough to enable the state to make a reasonable profit — often earmarked for relief or other purposes. The profits from this source were often less than was anticipated but still reached substantial amounts.

The United States Bureau of the Census reported that in 1944 — the last year for which figures have been published — twenty-nine of the states owned forty-eight public service enterprises. These consisted of sixteen alcoholic beverage monopoly systems,[3] mentioned above, and of thirty-two utility and other commercial enterprises in twenty-four states, as indicated in the table below.

TYPES OF STATE ENTERPRISES — 1944

Alcoholic beverage monopoly systems	16
Toll bridges	10
Port facilities	5
Ferries	2
Water conservation and irrigation works	2
Electric power systems	2
Canals	2
Airports	3
Other	6

Administrative revenues, collected through the sale of licenses and the imposition of fees, constitute a fourth source of income. It is a universal practice to require licenses of hunters and fishermen, operators of motor vehicles, and persons desiring to practice one of the learned professions or skilled trades. There appears to be a growing tendency to impose fees designed to cover the cost of inspection and regulation of various types of business. Thus it is customary to assess banks not only with the actual cost

[3] In addition, Wyoming engaged in the liquor business, wholesale only. In North Carolina, liquor stores are county owned and exist only in those counties voting for them.

incurred by the banking department in making examinations but for their prorated portion of the overhead cost of the operation of the department. The same procedure is often applied to building and loan associations, to the inspection of buildings and the approval of plans for their construction, to the inspection of elevators, steam boilers, bedding and upholstery, and many other things. As the states have gradually expanded in the number of services rendered to the public, receipts from departmental earnings, as from other sources, have substantially increased. The Bureau of the Census reported $182,000,000 from this source in 1937 in the forty-eight states, $508,374,000 in 1948.

Yet another source of nontax revenue is found in bookkeeping revenues, or interfund transfers. These do not represent new income, but they do provide additional funds which may be appropriated against, or spent by, the agency to which they have been transferred. Thus in Pennsylvania in 1933 the Joint Legislative Committee on Finances recommended that $500,000 be transferred from the Prison Labor Fund to the General Fund. This amount represented the total appropriation made by the General Assembly for the purchase of equipment and materials for the establishment of prison industries in the state penitentiaries. The industries had been established, were in a fairly prosperous condition, and had earned profits of more than a quarter of a million dollars. The Committee felt that this amount was sufficient to meet their needs. Thus half a million dollars might become a revenue for the General Fund, which the legislature would be free to appropriate in a period of emergency.

Last in this list are the funds received from the Federal government under the subsidy or grant-in-aid system. Such grants have normally been made under two conditions: first, that the states match the Federal grant dollar for dollar or in some other specified proportion; and second, that the total amount be expended in accordance with the conditions under which the grant is made. This system has been applied in many different fields, as indicated in an earlier chapter, under approximately sixty different programs. The receipt of these funds is dependent upon action by the state legislatures, but the states have seldom failed to avail themselves of these offers. The amounts of money expended by the Federal government, and therefore received by the states from this source, have increased rapidly since World War I, until they now total more than $2,000,000,000 a year. Although the amount of such aid has now become a sizable item, even in a total budget of sixty or seventy billion, there has never been any attempt to survey the grant-in-aid program as a whole or to evaluate it either in its individual segments or in relation to the spending program of the Federal government as a whole.

In addition to these major nontax sources, there are such miscellaneous ones as special assessments, court fines, forfeits and escheats, donations, pension assessments, highway privileges, rents on investment properties, interest, and other items. A steady increase in the amount of these receipts is accounted for chiefly by public service enterprises, which the Bureau of the Census classifies as a miscellaneous source. Special assessments are really taxes levied against property owners affected by improvements or against individuals or corporations by reason of services performed. Court fines or forfeits are amounts charged for violation of criminal statutes and moneys received from forfeited bail. Escheats include debt obligations canceled after being long overdue, as well as receipts from private trust funds or accounts of which no owner could be located. Donations and gifts are self-explanatory. Pension assessments include dues or contributions from salaries of state employees for the establishment and maintenance of pension funds. Highway privilege taxes, receipts from which have greatly increased in recent years, include payments from various types of public service companies for the use of the public highways. They differ from rents, which give the payer the exclusive control and use of the property rented. The states may receive rents from properties held by them for investment purposes or otherwise, and interest on invested capital in sinking funds, public trust funds, and investment funds.

Some Fundamental Aspects of the Tax Problem

It is difficult to overemphasize the importance of the tax power; it is impossible to exercise the other powers of government without a prior exercise of the tax power, since funds are required to maintain any governmental service. In each legislative year several thousand tax bills are put into the mill, and ordinarily about one fourth of these are enacted into law. In the exercise of this power, however, the state is subject to the restrictions imposed both by the Federal Constitution and by the constitutions of the states. The due process clause of Amendment XIV, applying as it does to the states, restricts them from any confiscatory levies. The state constitutions contain similar clauses and, in addition, usually include a statement in the clause on eminent domain which prevents the taking of private property for public use without just compensation.

Some Requirements of a Sound Tax System. Each of the states has combined the various possible forms of taxation into a pattern peculiar to itself. There are, nevertheless, certain tests and fundamental requirements by which students of public finance attempt to measure the soundness of tax systems. The first test is fiscal adequacy: does the tax system yield sufficient revenue to meet the expenditure program necessary for the governmental unit concerned? This test is the simplest and much the easiest to meet. In the second place, any given tax should be reasonably economical in administration; the cost of collection should not consume a considerable portion of the amount collected. A tax or a tax system which violates this requirement is bad because it removes money from the pockets of citizens without giving any return. Thus a state gasoline tax collected from retailers violates this principle, because of the number of accounts which must be carried and the overhead expense entailed. A similar tax can be collected from refiners and wholesalers much more thoroughly and at much less expense.

A third test requires that the burdens of taxation shall fall equitably upon the various classes in the community. A tax system which levies heavy burdens upon one group and permits another with equal ability to pay to escape its proper share is unfair. Graded taxes on income and inheritance were developed to meet this test. A fourth test relates to the ease with which the tax system may be adjusted to either an increased or decreased need for revenue; in other words, to the elasticity or flexibility of the system. It is obviously necessary that a tax system be capable of adjustment to changed conditions, supplying additional revenue by the application of higher rates when needed, or reducing the burden by imposing lower rates when such rates will yield the amount of revenue required. Fifth, the tax system as a whole and the individual acts of which it is composed should be as simple and comprehensible to the ordinary citizen as they can be made. Some income tax laws, particularly the Federal law, are flagrant offenders against this principle. The burden should not be regressive, and it is preferable that it bear much more heavily upon income than upon capital.

Finally, it is desirable that the tax system should have such diversity as will tend to stabilize the yield, regardless of general economic and business conditions. It is easy to devise systems for raising adequate revenue in prosperous times, but government must function in bad times as well as in good. In periods of depression many additional burdens are imposed on government. If it is to be prepared to meet these responsibilities, the tax program must be so designed as to bring in receipts from such a wide variety of sources that the collapse of one will not upset the entire program.

Distribution of the Tax Burden. In the effort to develop a system which would come near to meeting all these requirements simultaneously, the theory of taxation has passed through a number of different stages. Perhaps the earliest principle to be widely adopted was the equality principle, which is illustrated by such forms as the poll tax, head tax, or capitation tax. When it became evident that the distribution of the burden under this principle was inequitable, the states turned to the benefit principle, in accordance with which it was assumed that each individual should contribute in proportion to the benefit which he received. This principle was particularly applicable to public improvements and is still retained in modified form where special assessments are used to raise a portion of the cost of such improvements. Applied to the maintenance of public schools or to police and fire protection, this principle becomes ridiculous; it is not altogether fair as applied to streets and highways, which are used by the general public perhaps more than by abutting and adjacent property owners.

It was next concluded that the weight of the tax burden should be distributed in accordance with ability to pay. This theory has been applied in two forms, the first known as the proportionate application of the principle. Under this plan all properties were assessed and a uniform rate applied to all, regardless of their size. The same principle was followed in the early income taxes. Although the rate in a given case might not be high, it was soon apparent that the application of this rate to a small assessment or a small income imposed upon the individual paying such a tax a far greater burden than that imposed upon the owner of extensive properties or the recipient of a large income. In the effort to eliminate this inequality, the progressive application of the ability to pay principle was next tried. This principle is now incorporated in all Federal and state laws which impose a graded tax upon income, inheritances, or estates. It is doubtless true that there is no such thing as an ideal or a perfect tax system, but serious efforts have been made to improve existing tax systems and to make them more equitable.

A number of problems have arisen in this connection. Advocates of the single tax have argued that an equitable distribution was possible only through the use of the single tax method. Very practical problems have grown out of double, treble, and other forms of multiple taxation. After some hesitation the Supreme Court is at present willing to sustain multiple state taxation of intangible personal property. It is obvious, moreover, that such taxes are unwise from the point of view of public policy, and that they result in an unfair distribution of the tax burden.

Of the possible methods of tax avoidance, part are legal, part illegal. First of the legal methods is the shifting of the tax burden, a phenomenon which is referred to technically as the incidence of taxation. By this is meant the tendency for those who pay the tax to pass on to others as much of the actual burden as they can. Thus in normal times the landlord includes the taxes on a property in his computation of the rental; he is responsible to the tax-collecting authorities for the payment of the tax, but he passes on to his tenant the actual financial burden. Secondly, it is often possible to escape taxation by availing oneself of technicalities in the law. In the third place, many tax laws include definite exemptions; in income tax laws, for instance, it is customary to exempt persons in the lower income brackets. Finally, many persons succeed in evading all or part of their proper tax burden by illegal and unethical methods. Such tax dodgers are subject to prosecution, since they are seeking to evade a duty and responsibility which all governments place upon their citizens.

Tax Provisions in State Constitutions. Among the more common constitutional provisions governing the use of the tax power are those requiring uniformity and/or equality in the imposition of taxes, and full value assessment.[4] The clause in the Pennsylvania Constitution is typical: "All taxes

[4] See Illinois State's Attorneys Association, *The Full-Value Assessment Program* (Springfield, 1946); and Troupis, Christ T., "Full Fair Value Assessment in Illinois," *Illinois Law Review*, May–June 1949, pp. 160–180.

shall be uniform, upon the same class of subjects, within the territorial limits of the authority levying the tax, and shall be levied and collected under general laws" (Article IX, Section 1). The leading cases on this subject indicate that uniformity is the important thing, not full value. In some instances, the courts have interpreted these clauses as prohibiting the use of graded taxes, thereby necessitating either the abandonment of the sound grading principle or the amending of the constitution. It is to be hoped that in future constitutional revisions these clauses will be omitted.[5]

> Another of the usual provisions is that similar to the New York Constitution (Article III, Section 24) to the effect that no tax shall be levied except in pursuance of law and every law imposing a tax shall state distinctly the object of the tax. Some provide in effect that "no moneys arising from a tax levied for one purpose shall be used for any other purpose." Another quite common feature is the provision that "the power of taxation shall never be surrendered, suspended or contracted away;" . . . in others the applicability of such provision is limited to corporations. Many of the constitutions contain rate limitations at which property may be taxed and make provision for the exemption of certain property from taxation or authorize the legislative bodies to make such exemptions.[6]

These latter provisions will be considered later in connection with the general property tax.

Many of the constitutions provide that taxes may be levied only for a public purpose. What is a public purpose? To say that it is to be contrasted with a private purpose is not enough; at the same time it is difficult to present an adequate definition, since the courts have followed in this instance their usual practice of deciding each case on its merits. The point that taxation for a "private purpose" constitutes an invasion of the constitutional rights of the taxpayer was clarified and illustrated by the case of Loan Association v. Topeka.[7]

The practice prevailing in many municipalities of offering free factory sites and the promise of tax exemption for a specified number of years to firms willing to locate within the city is familiar. The City Council of Topeka went much further; it made a direct appropriation to a manufacturing company as an inducement to locate its plant within the city limits, the assumption being that the value of the plant to the city was sufficient to justify such a use of public funds. The Court decided that the city, which

[5] See Girard, Richard A., *The Scope for Uniformity in State Tax Systems* (New York State Tax Commission, Albany, 1935); Mathews, William L., Jr., The Function of Constitutional Provisions Requiring Uniformity in Taxation," in four parts, *Kentucky Law Journal*, November 1949 — May 1950; White, Charles P., "Revision of the Taxation Uniformity Clause in the State Constitutions," in *Papers on Constitutional Revision — 1947*, pp. 79–86 (Bureau of Public Administration, University of Tennessee, 1948).

[6] Saxe, Martin, "Tax Provisions in State Constitutions," *Bulletin of the National Tax Association*, February 1938; Hawaii Legislative Reference Bureau, *Fiscal Provisions of State Constitutions* (Honolulu, 1947), and Neeld, Aaron K., *Taxation — the Tax Clause* (Governor's Committee on Preparatory Research for the New Jersey Constitutional Convention, Trenton, 1947).

[7] 21 Wallace 655, 1874.

was the agent of the State of Kansas, was not justified in making such an appropriation — that the benefit to the manufacturing company was greater than that accruing to the community from the location of the plant within its boundaries.

In some form or other this is the question which the courts usually have to answer. There is, of course, no question about public buildings, highways, expenditures for salaries of public employees, and the purchase of property and supplies. Most of the questions that are brought to the courts involve borderline cases, and judgments with regard to these vary with different courts and different sections of the country, with the passage of time, and with the presence or absence of emergencies. Purposes which would never be classified as public under ordinary circumstances may, in an emergency, become such. In general, it is also true that the courts will not sanction the use of public funds for purposes which are normally served adequately through the employment of private capital and by private initiative.

General Property Tax — Real and Personal

The general property tax is applied to realty and to personalty or to both. It is the oldest form of taxation used in this country, and it still serves as an important source of revenue — increasingly important in the local units, declining considerably in relative importance in the states. As originally employed in Colonial America and in the early national period, the general property tax as applied to real estate was reasonable and just, as well as simple and inexpensive in administration. It was easy to designate at the town meeting some citizen to visit the landowners in the community for the purpose of noting the number of acres of cleared land held by each and assessing this at so much an acre. In modern times, however, assessment has become difficult and highly complicated.

Tax on Real Estate. A number of specific steps occur in the administration of the tax on real estate. There is, first, the problem of assessment. When the assessors have completed their task, opportunity must be given for the filing of complaints and for hearings on the complaints before local boards of review. These agencies have not been effective in the correction of inequalities or abuses. In those states, however, where a state tax commission or a state board of equalization exists, there has been some influence toward the development of uniform and equitable assessments. Finally, after the taxing power has adopted its budget for the ensuing fiscal period and determined the rate, there is the task of collecting. The collecting agencies vary in organization and efficiency of operation all the way from the medieval system of farming out the taxes under a fee system, as in Pennsylvania, to a centralized county collection system such as is now used in more than three fourths of the states.

In this brief outline certain weaknesses of this tax have been indicated. Perhaps the most serious is the lack of uniformity. All but a few constitutions require, but few states practice, assessment at full value. Studies of the administration of this tax in state after state show variations between adjoining counties in average rates of assessments running as high as 100 per cent. If property is assessed in one county at 45 per cent of market value and in an adjoining county at 90 per cent, and the same rate of taxation is then applied to the total assessed valuation of both counties, it is evident that the one with the 90 per cent assessment is paying actually twice as high a tax as the neighboring county with the assessment half as high.

This situation is not quite so important where collections are made for local purposes only, but the same lack of uniformity still exists between the smaller local units, and between individual taxpayers within those units.[8] It will be impossible to secure a uniform application of the general property tax until a policy of assessment at full valuation, or at some agreed fraction, is uniformly adopted and enforced. The requirement of full value assessment is almost universally ignored for a variety of reasons, disclosed in a canvass of assessors in New York in 1942. The more important of these were: belief that high assessment means high taxes, desire to minimize the share of state and county taxes paid by the area assessed, political considerations, the assessor's desire for re-election, and difficulty in determining full value with fair accuracy.

A second major defect in administration lies in untrained or incompetent personnel. In the vast majority of communities, urban and rural alike, the assessor is a hanger-on, whose political connection constitutes his only qualification. Early experiments in scientific assessment were conducted in New York City and Cleveland, while more recent work has been done in Pittsburgh, Detroit, Richmond, and other cities, as well as in some counties — all of which prove that it is possible to develop and enforce definite rules for making assessments and to secure trained and competent personnel.

In a modern assessment system the property must first be listed and described. The descriptions are often complicated and follow the legal description of the property. Each property is located on block and lot maps and on land value maps. On the former, each unit is numbered, and this number is used in all official real estate records. The land value maps show the front foot value of all land in the city. Each unit is written up on a separate card or sheet suitable for loose-leaf filing, showing the entire tax history of the property. Entries are made for sales, leases, rents, foreclosures, alterations, repairs, and demolitions, so that each assessor or deputy has full information with regard to all properties assigned to him. These data are

[8] The New Jersey Taxpayers' Association, in its study of the *Tax Exemption Policy in New Jersey*, shows the ratio of assessed valuation to true value in various cities throughout the state; in each city, from 300 to 700 property sales were compared with the assessed valuations to secure the data. The figures represent the percentage of true value assessed: Clifton, 44.0; Elizabeth, 54.0; Atlantic City, 66.0; Jersey City, 67.4; Camden, 65.5; Trenton, 60.0; Newark, 58.7; Bayonne, 45.5; Kearny, 50.8. In many rural taxing districts the assessed valuation is less than 40 per cent of true value (p. 11).

a matter of public record and are widely used by real estate men and others. A complete assessment manual gives the deputy the statutory and administrative rules which are to be followed in his work. The value of the land as though unimproved and the improvements on the land are separately determined, and added to indicate the total assessment. In a progressive system property is classified, depending upon the class of property, which will determine the percentage of full and true value to be used in determining valuation. Finally, the assessment roll is prepared; this is a copy of the annual record made up after valuations have been corrected.[9]

Many other criticisms have been directed against this tax. Two definite alternatives seem to be available. One is to abolish the tax, at least for state purposes; the other is to reform its administration. Some of the elements necessary for such reform have already been indicated. They include the development of a competent and adequately trained personnel; the development of workable rules that can be applied with uniform results; supervision of local assessments through a state tax commission or board of equalization; and separation of state and local revenue sources. Because of lack of adequate appropriations and competent staff, this work is rarely well done.

Tax Exemption. The policy of exempting certain kinds of property from taxation has been the subject of much discussion. It has been claimed, on the one hand, that such exemptions make the taxes higher for other people, and on the other, that such a policy is essential to the encouragement of many worthy purposes — religious, charitable, educational, and the like — and that the strengthening of these agencies reacts to enhance the value of other classes of property in the community. At any rate, the policy of such exemptions is well established. Most state constitutions require the uniform taxation of all property whether owned by individuals or by corporations. There are at least four major types of exceptions to this universal rule: (1) government property; (2) homesteads and personal property used in connection with one's trade or vocation, up to a specified limit; (3) property owned and used by educational, religious, and charitable institutions; and (4) veterans' exemptions.[10]

[9] For general discussion, see Noonan, Albert W., "Some Essentials to Good Assessment Practice," published in 1948 in various journals of the state leagues of municipalities, and for studies of particular states, in addition to those listed in previous editions of this volume: Arnold, James A., Jr., "General Property Tax Assessment in New Jersey," *New Jersey Municipalities*, May 1948, and "New Jersey General Property Tax in 1949," *ibid.*, November 1949; Henry County Council on Intergovernmental Relations, *Assessment of Property in Henry County, Indiana* (New Castle, 1946); J. L. Jacobs & Company, *J. L. Jacobs Looks at the Assessment Problem* (Kentucky Department of Revenue, Frankfort, 1948); Muehlenkamp, George, "Remedies for Disproportionate Tax Assessment in Kentucky," *Kentucky Law Journal*, May 1948, pp. 401–419; Kentucky Legislative Research Commission, *The Assessment Problem and School Equalization Aid* (Frankfort, 1949); Pennsylvania Economy League, *Real Estate Assessment Procedures in Northampton County* (Easton, 1948); Tracy, Truman G., *Valuation of Illinois Oil Producing Properties for Tax Assessment* (Illinois Department of Revenue, Springfield, 1947).

[10] For some typical comments, see: Borden, Mary G., "Extent of Exemption from

These constitute a group that has been called "the tax untouchables." Many additional exemptions may be provided by statute; a careful listing of those provided in the General Tax Act in New Jersey shows a total of twenty-five, some with as many as ten subdivisions. Others may be provided in specific tax acts, such as income and sales. The Constitution and the statutes in California provide specific exemptions for sixteen types, the value of which was almost $600 million in 1949.[11] The Wisconsin Taxpayers Alliance has worked out an interesting classification of tax-exempt property by ownership, purpose, and type, as is shown below. The effect of all these exemptions upon the revenues of the taxing unit is tremendous. A summary of the exempt property in the City of New York covering the years 1947–1948 showed government exemptions — Federal, state, and local — plus the usual miscellaneous ones totaling approximately $5.5 billion. The figures are summarized in the table below.

TYPES OF TAX EXEMPT PROPERTY IN WISCONSIN *

1. Public Ownership Property — owned by Federal, state, county, city, and political subdivisions
2. Quasi-Public Ownership — Agricultural and historical societies, fair associations, fire companies, libraries, cemetery associations, national guard armories, community centers, veterans housing authorities
3. Non-Profit Ownership — (a) Religious, charitable, and educational (b) Fraternal, other societies and organizations

* *Wisconsin Taxpayer*, August 1948, pp. 60–61.

City of New York
Tax Exempt Property — 1947–1948

BY TYPE	AMOUNT	BY BOROUGH	AMOUNT
United States Government.	$ 325,777,300	Manhattan..	$2,844,532,275
New York State..........	119,935,975	Bronx......	585,200,296
New York City...........	4,146,721,455	Brooklyn....	1,313,182,795
Miscellaneous............	933,181,546	Queens.....	610,492,075
		Richmond...	172,208,835
Total..................	$5,525,616,276	Total.....	$5,525,616,276

Taxation of Charitable Institutions under the Kentucky Constitution," *Kentucky Law Journal*, February 1947, pp. 151–155; Chudy, M. M., and Leedecker, Charles F., "Tax Exempt Property in Cities of the Third Class," *The League of Cities of the Third Class in Pennsylvania*, July–August 1949, pp. 4–13; Crockett, Earl C., "The Problem of Tax Exempt Property in Colorado," *Rocky Mountain Law Review*, December 1946, pp. 22–48.

[11] Holland, J. Roy, "California Tax System," *Tax Digest*, November 1949, pp. 365–368, 385–395; Flanagan, Charles W., "Tax Exemptions Top $400 Million," *ibid.*, December 1947, pp. 408–411. State Board of Equalization release, September 6, 1949, showed that the total went up to $500 million in 1948, $600 million in 1949. See Winter, Richard, "Tax Exempt Property: 1949–1950 Total Up 15 Percent," *Tax Digest*, February 1950, pp. 43–44, 68–71, and Senate Interim Committee on State and Local Taxation, *A Legal History of Property Taxation in California* (Sacramento, January 1951).

4. Private Ownership — (a) Intangibles, including pensions from the United States, moneys and debts, stocks and bonds (b) Productive goods, including growing crops, tools of mechanics (c) Consumption goods, including wearing apparel, furniture (d) Property otherwise taxed, such as automobiles, forest land crops, public utilities

In spite of the opposition of students of public finance to tax exemptions, the policy has continued to spread. Once established, there is always the plea for their extension into new areas or for the enlargement of existing exemptions. During the depression, pressure groups worked for homestead exemption and exemption of manufacturing establishments and other sources. Further extensions have continued since, until the total is now a matter of very serious concern to governmental units. The National Association of Assessing Officers reported in 1947 that nearly one fifth of the total assessed valuation of real estate in the United States consisted of tax-exempt real property owned by governmental units and tax-exempt institutions such as churches, schools, and charitable organizations. The limitations imposed on homestead exemptions apply to value and to area; the former range from $500 to as high as $8000 and several states provide no limitation at all. Area limitations run from forty to 320 acres.[12] Added to these losses in valuation are those resulting from exemptions extended to veterans — very extensive exemptions, in some states. Government-owned property takes another large slice out of total taxable valuations, although in this case fairly substantial in-lieu payments are made by the Federal government and by sixteen states to the local units affected.[13] During recent years this type of property has shown an enormous increase. All of these exemptions which narrow the property tax base tend to undermine the financial structure of local government.

Tax Delinquency. Governments, like businesses, have bad debts. Uncle Sam collects his. Businessmen collect theirs — or write them off as uncollectible. Local governments, generally speaking, allow them to pile up. And thereby hangs a harrowing tale. The Western Division of the Pennsylvania Economy League reported in March 1945:

[12] See Alabama Legislative Reference Service, *Alabama's Homestead Exemption: Should It Be Enlarged?* (Montgomery, 1948); Hatfield, Roland F., and Sulerud, Allen C., "Homestead Preference in the Minnesota Property Tax System," *Bulletin* of the National Tax Association, March 1947, pp. 162–170; and Hunter, Carrie E., "Homestead Exemptions" (Legislative Reference Service, Library of Congress, report, May 15, 1946).

[13] On Federal property in Pennsylvania, see Alderfer, Harold F., "Federal Property Exempt from Local Taxes," Department of Internal Affairs *Bulletin*, November 1945, pp. 28–31; "Federal Contributions to State and Local Governmental Units with Respect to Federally Owned Real Estate," *Hearings* before a Subcommittee of the Senate Committee on Public Lands and Surveys, (79th Cong., 2nd Sess., 1946), and "Contributions to Local Governments on Account of Nontaxable Federal Lands," Senate Report No. 270 (80th Cong., 1st Sess., 1947). On the situation as regards state property, see Joint State Government Commission, *Commonwealth-Owned, Tax-Exempt Real Property* (Harrisburg, 1949), and American Municipal Association, *Taxation of Publicly-Owned Real Estate* (Chicago, 1950).

> Right now, neglectful, forgetful, or indifferent taxpayers owe more than $45,000,000 to fifty-two governments in Allegheny County — the County, the City, the Pittsburgh School District, and forty-nine boroughs and townships, comprising altogether 87 per cent of the population and 90 per cent of total real estate assessments.
>
> Year after year, these delinquents are carried by people who pay their taxes. And if the debt were collected, the faithful taxpayers would enjoy a Roman holiday. $45,000,000 is equal to 27½ mills on the total assessments and would finance both the City and County governments for a year.

Tax delinquency reached acute proportions in many communities during the depression. The inability of many taxpayers to pay and the inability of collecting officials to collect the taxes on their rolls brought many governmental units to the verge of financial ruin. Often hundreds of properties would be listed for a single sheriff's sale. There were widespread demands for relief, and much legislation was enacted, such as laws authorizing installment payments, discounts, lien laws staying sheriff's sales, and lengthening the period and easing the conditions under which property might be bought back. As one abatement act was piled upon another, the seriousness of the revenue problem of the local units increased. Many home owners were unaware of the changes made in the law and very often the only taxpayers who took advantage of the ameliorative legislation were the hotels and mid-city office buildings, most of which were perfectly able to pay their taxes without such assistance. Because of this legislation and steadily improving economic conditions through the defense boom and the war and the post-war periods, the trend of tax delinquency has continuously declined since 1933. A study made in 1947, covering 150 cities with a population of over 50,000, showed that the percentage of delinquency had declined from 26.35 in 1933, to 11.3 in 1937, to 3.2 in 1946.[14]

Tax Limitation. Tax limitation, which will be referred to again in Chapter 21 on state-local relations, owed its widespread popularity largely to the popular psychology, fostered by taxpayers' associations, that led to taxpayers' marches on city halls and state capitols in the days of the depression. It was based upon the unthinking emotional reaction of people in a difficult financial situation, inspired by leaders who knew little and cared less about the functions and services of government. In the more prosperous years which have followed, rising governmental costs have led to a number of new proposals in the states.[15] The limitations adopted have been of a number of different types:

[14] Bird, Frederick L., *Trend in Tax Delinquency, 1930–1946* (Dun & Bradstreet, New York, 1947), and in addition to the studies in particular states listed in previous editions of this volume, the following: Housing Authority of the County of Cook, Illinois, "*Dead*" *Land: a Study of Chronic Tax Delinquency and Abandonment* (Chicago, 1949): Michigan Planning Commission, *A Study of Tax Reverted Lands in Michigan* (Lansing, 1941); and Stace, Arthur W., *What Are We Going to Do . . . With 2,208,975 Added Acres?* (Michigan Department of Conservation, Lansing, 1947).

[15] Extensive references by states are given in previous editions of this book; on recent proposals, see: Faist, Carl J., *The 15-Mill Amendment*, Second Edition (Seemann & Peters,

1. Tax limits which state a fixed maximum rate of tax
   a. Blanket-rate limitations on the aggregate levy on each $100 value
   b. Maximum-rate limitations for each governmental unit
   c. Maximum-rate limitations for various purposes or funds
2. Limitations which restrict the amount of levy to a stated percentage of the amount of some previous year, or average of certain years
3. Limitations which restrict the amount of revenue to be raised to a fixed amount per capita
4. Limitations which give the maximum levy permitted in terms of dollars
5. Limitations which fix the ratio between revenues from general property taxes and revenues from other sources

Of these types some states consistently use one, whereas others use two or more jointly. In some cases one is applied to some units of government and another to other units. The maximum-rate limitations for various purposes or funds are the oldest and most widely used type; they are usually provided for in the state constitution and, generally speaking, are unobjectionable. The limitations restricting the levy to a stated percentage of a previous year or years are of more recent origin, are often provided for by statute, and illustrate the type of limitation to which there is serious objection. From 1932 to 1937 nine states adopted over-all rate limits, six of them by constitutional amendment. These are shown in the table on page 532.[16] Twenty-six states are limited either by statute or by the constitution as to the amount of the state rate imposed on property, and forty states limit the amount minor civil divisions may raise by such levies.

It is urged that these laws do reduce property taxes and prevent increases, that they do force economy, efficiency, and a broadening of the tax base; but in practice they have proved to be a dangerous device that not only has been disastrous to local government but has failed to achieve its avowed purpose. The limitations are often evaded; in many cases, taxes were not actually lowered. Ways were found by which it was legally possible to tax outside the levy or to impose additional taxes on other sources in order to make up the deficit.

Declining Importance of Realty Tax. In twenty-one states — Arizona, Arkansas, California, Connecticut, Delaware, Florida, Illinois, Iowa,

Saginaw, 1947) — which discusses what it is, how it operates, and the results of the first twelve years of its operation in one typical Michigan city; Michigan State Tax Commission, *Coordinated Analysis of the Provisions of the Property Tax Limitation Act* (Lansing, 1948); Newark Bureau of Municipal Research, *Local Revenues II — Property Tax Limitations* (Newark, September 1949); Oregon Tax Study Commission, *Summary of Opinions of the Oregon Supreme Court and Attorney General Relative to the Constitutional 6 Percent Limitation* (Memo, Salem, 1946); Syracuse Governmental Research Bureau, *Proposed Real Estate Tax Limit Amendment to the New York State Constitution* (Memo, Syracuse, 1949); and Thompson, James H., "Effects of Property Tax Limitation in West Virginia," *National Tax Journal*, June 1951, pp. 129–138.

16 Hillhouse, A. Miller, and Welch, Ronald B., *Tax Limits Appraised*, p. 2 (Public Administration Service, Chicago, 1937); for an excellent study of the effects in a particular state, see Shamberger, Harold J., and Thompson, James H., *The Operation of the Tax Limitation Amendment in West Virginia* (Bureau of Business Research and Bureau of Government Research, West Virginia University, 1950).

Michigan, New Hampshire, New York, North Carolina, Ohio, Oklahoma, Oregon, Pennsylvania, Rhode Island, South Carolina, South Dakota, Vermont, and Virginia — the realty tax is not used for state purposes, and in many cases has not been used for many years. The list of states abandoning this source or reducing their dependence upon it might vary slightly, according to one's basis for classification. In 1947 only seven states relied

Digest of Over-all Tax Limitation Laws in Nine States

STATE	CONSTITUTIONAL OR STATUTORY	BASIC RATES *Urban Per Cent*	BASIC RATES *Rural Per Cent*	ADDITIONAL RATES *Requiring No Special Authorization*	ADDITIONAL RATES *Requiring Special Authorization*
Indiana	S	1.5	1.0	Prior debt service	Unlimited
Michigan	C	1.5[1]	1.5	Prior debt service	3.5%
Nevada	C	5.0	5.0	None	None
New Mexico	C	2.0	2.0	All debt service	None[2]
Ohio	C	1.0[1]	1.0	None	Unlimited
Oklahoma	C	1.7[3]	1.7[3]	Prior debt service	School districts, 1%
Rhode Island	S	2.5	2.5	All debt service	Unlimited
Washington	S	2.0[4]	1.25[4]	Prior debt service	Unlimited
West Virginia	C	1.5 to 2.0	0.5 to 1.5	Prior debt service	50% of basic rates

[1] Not all incorporated cities or villages are subject to this limit.

[2] The constitution permits unlimited additional rates upon approval of a majority of voters, provided legislation to this effect is enacted.

[3] Out of this total, 0.2 per cent is reserved for counties for separate schools for whites and Negroes.

[4] Actual statutory rates are 4% and 2.5%, but property is assessable by law at only 50% of full value.

on the property tax for as much as 10 per cent of total tax revenues, as compared with twenty-one states in 1941. Nebraska and Nevada were the only states which still derived more than 20 per cent of their total state tax revenue from this source. The property tax in 1947 accounted for only 4.5 per cent of the total state tax revenues, as compared with 7.4 per cent in 1941.[17] In New Jersey 90 per cent of the property tax levy is returned to

[17] Data from Tax Foundation, *Recent Trends in Major State Taxes, 1941–1947*, p. 31 (New York, 1948), and *Major State Taxes, op. cit.* While state dependence on the property tax was declining, local revenues from this source increased from $4224 million in 1941 to $4904 million in 1946. For studies in particular states, in addition to those listed in previous editions of this volume, see: Anderson, Lynn F., *The State Property Tax in Taxes* (Bureau of Municipal Research, University of Texas, 1948); Brooks, Robert P., *The Georgia Property Tax: History and Administrative Problems* (University of Georgia Bulletin, 1950); California State Board of Equalization, *California Property Taxes, 1937–1938 to 1948–1949* (Sacramento, 1949); Crockett, Earl C., *The Colorado Property Tax* (University of Colorado, 1947); Kendrick, M. Slade, *The Property Tax as a Fiscal Instrument in New York State* (Staff Study No. 7, Fiscal Policy for Public Education in New York State, New York, 1947); Oregon Tax Study Commission, *Problems of Property Taxation in Oregon* (Salem, 1945).

the localities for school support, while in Wisconsin the .2 mill levy is for the purpose of conservation and forestry development.

There are a number of factors responsible for this development. There has been widespread criticism of the disproportionate tax burden borne by real estate. There has also been a mounting pressure from the cities and other local units for revenues with which to discharge their responsibilities; many states have surrendered this field wholly or partially to them, turning to other sources to meet increasing state costs and increased grants-in-aid to the local units. Tax limitation provisions have reduced, to some extent, the amount that either states or local units could obtain from this source, and the trend has been away from special assessments as a means of financing important improvements. Improved methods in property tax administration have, however, tended to raise the percentage of collection wherever this tax form was used.

Tax on Personal Property. The tax on personal property is almost as old as the tax on real estate. In its early forms it was applied to such possessions as cattle and livestock; in modern times its application is much broader, including both tangible and intangible property. In general, three types of tangible property are now subjected to taxation in a number of states. In the Southern states particularly, personal items such as jewelry and household possessions ranging from the lawnmower to the family silverware are assessed. Although the blanks used for the reporting of this tax are long, complicated, and all-inclusive, the usual practice is to make a very moderate lump sum estimate, as determined by the general character and location of the residence. Motor vehicles constitute the second type. In fifteen states their original status under the general property tax has not been materially altered; in eight others, in which the tax has been retained, the law requires that a person licensing a motor vehicle give satisfactory evidence (usually a tax receipt) of payment of a property tax thereon. Seven states have abandoned the ad-valorem base, but special taxes, licenses, and fees may be assessed. In the eighteen remaining states motor vehicles are not ordinarily subject to either general or special property taxes.[18] The third type includes manufacturing plants and machinery. In half the states these are subject to property taxes on the same terms and conditions as other tangible property. Temporary exemption for newly located or newly constructed plants is provided in sixteen states, while in the remainder such property is classified in a number of different ways.[19]

18 Kansas Legislative Council, *Personal Property Taxation in Kansas*, Part III, Motor Vehicles (Topeka, July 1940); National Association of Assessing Officers, *Property Taxation of Motor Vehicles* (Chicago, 1938); Tremper, Charles W., *Assessment of Motor Vehicles* (Mimeographed, Institute of Public Service, University of Connecticut, July 1947); Walker, William P., *The Assessment and Collection of Motor Vehicle Property Taxes in Maryland* (Agricultural Experiment Station, University of Maryland, February 1936).

19 National Association of Assessing Officers, *Exemption of Manufacturing Plants and Machinery from Property Taxation* (Chicago, 1938).

In practice, the tax on intangibles presents quite a different problem. As early as 1871 an investigating committee in New York declared that it was "a tax on ignorance, honesty, and helplessness." It was then and it is now almost wholly unsatisfactory, but in 1949 it was still in use in all but sixteen states. There are several different methods of taxing intangibles.[20]

The arguments against the tax on intangibles have been summarized under five points: it is extremely difficult to find such property; interest and dividend yields have been adjusted to the expectation that intangibles would not be taxed; great encouragement is given to the concentration of owners of intangibles in low-rate "tax-colonies"; owners of intangibles probably receive fewer direct benefits from local government than owners of real and tangible personal property; and double taxation is likely to result whenever representative intangibles and tangibles are taxed.

It is one of the time-honored canons of taxation that no tax should be imposed upon items which can be hidden or otherwise withheld from the knowledge of the taxing authority. It is a matter of common knowledge that there has been, since the development of the corporate form of business organization, a steady and rapid increase in the volume of intangibles held by our citizens. In spite of this fact, however, and in spite of steady increases in the tax rate applied to such holdings, the gross receipts from taxes of this character show a steady and persistent decline. This is a striking commentary on the honesty of the ordinary citizen in his tax-paying capacity. It indicates that the tax imposes a financial penalty upon those citizens who are honest enough to make a correct statement of the nature and extent of their holdings. Such a tax is obviously an undesirable source of revenue from the point of view of public policy.

From another point of view this tax has shown itself to be equally objectionable. It is difficult to collect, and tax officers have frequently made no serious effort to collect it. Where such a law exists, the collections under it represent only a fractional part of the revenues due the state. The collections are "spotty," because of the varied intensity of the efforts of various collection officers. There is little or no disagreement among students of public finance on this point — in general, property taxes as applied to personalty, especially intangibles, should be eliminated in favor of taxes that are more equitable, which provide less incentive for dishonesty, and which are less difficult in administration.

Corporation and Business Taxes

The rapid growth of corporations in number and size has made it necessary, for purposes of regulation and equitable taxation, that specific taxes under the administration of some central authority be levied on this type of

[20] National Association of Assessing Officers, *Property Taxation of Intangibles* (Chicago, 1938); and Governmental Research Institute, *The Taxation of Intangibles in Missouri and Other States* (St. Louis, 1944); Thatcher, George W., "Taxation of Intangible Personal Property in Ohio," *National Tax Journal*, December 1951, pp. 351–360.

business organization. Professor Groves has classified the taxes affecting business in two groups, general and special, as follows:

TAXES AFFECTING BUSINESS [21]

General	*Special*
Sales Taxes	Occupational Taxes
Property Taxes	Incorporation Fees
Excess-Profits Taxes	Capital Stock Taxes
Corporate Net Income Tax	Corporate Excess Taxes
Gross Income Taxes	

The general taxes are considered elsewhere in this chapter, under appropriate headings. The present discussion will be confined to those special taxes affecting corporations, although business taxes can be and in some jurisdictions are levied upon unincorporated businesses as well as upon corporations.

> Fees and licenses which are required from corporations in many states are theoretically payments for certain services rendered by the state to corporations, or for the privilege on the part of the corporation to exercise certain rights, which without a license would be illegal; practically in many states the fees and licenses are either excise or franchise taxes on the corporation for the purpose of producing revenue for the state. Taxes on corporations are now collected as franchise taxes, license taxes, income taxes, excise taxes, corporate excess taxes, registration fees, license fees, none of which has any well defined meaning. The term franchise tax is applied to a tax on net income in New York, the actual value of the capital stock in Ohio, the authorized capital stock in Texas, the nominal value of capital stock in Illinois, and the value of assets in the State of Maryland.
>
> In a majority of the states public utilities are taxed differently from private corporations. . . . While regulation may be accomplished through taxation, the two need in no way be considered inseparable, and it is evident that the whole system of corporate taxation in many states needs to be overhauled in order that there be a more equitable distribution of the tax burden, between the public and private corporations and between corporations as a group and individuals.[22]

The New York State corporation tax law may be taken as illustrative of legislation of this character in a large industrial state. All companies pay the filing fee and organization tax when they start in business, and annually thereafter they pay that one of the franchise taxes which is applicable to the type of business in which they are engaged. Different assessment formulae are provided by law for such different types of corporations as real estate, including joint stock companies and associations; transportation and transmission corporations and associations; cooperatives; water, gas, electric, or steam heating, lighting, and power companies; insurance corporations; and holding corporations.[23]

[21] Groves, Harold M., *Financing Government*, Third Edition (Holt, New York, 1950).

[22] Bureau of Business Research, Indiana University, *Taxation of Corporations*, pp. 1–2 (Bloomington, 1934).

[23] In New York, as in the majority of states, substantially the same rates are applied

Franchise Taxes. A franchise tax is a payment to the state for the privilege of doing business as a corporation instead of as an individual or as a partnership. The corporation thus continues to pay for the right to exercise the powers granted to it by the state, paid for originally by the filing fee and the organization tax. Because of the differences existing in the size of companies and in the extent of their resources, a flat rate would be inequitable and unfair. The franchise tax is, therefore, a graduated license fee, the size of which is measured by a rule prescribed by law, depending upon the size and resources of the company. There are many different types of franchises and many different bases for the measurement of the tax — capital stock, gross earnings, net earnings, stock transfer, and corporate excess, as is clearly shown in the classification of franchises used in California.[24]

FRANCHISE TAXES COLLECTED IN CALIFORNIA

1. Agriculture
2. Amusements
3. Building and Loan
4. Business and Professional Services
5. Construction
6. Gas and Electric
7. Highway Transportation
8. Manufacturing
9. Mining
10. Miscellaneous Financial
11. Motion Picture Production
12. National Banks
13. Oil Production
14. Other Utilities
15. Personal Services
16. Railroads
17. Real Estate and Investment
18. Retail Trade
19. State Banks
20. Telephone and Telegraph
21. Utilities under Public Utilities Act
22. Water Supply
23. Wholesale Trade

Bank Taxes. Because of the peculiar nature of their business, special taxes have been devised applicable to banks. In 1864 Congress placed a narrow limitation on state taxation of national banks, but under present Federal legislation four methods of taxing national banks are possible. The underlying principle is that they shall not be taxed at a rate higher than other capital in competition with them. In New York, banks were subject to a franchise tax until 1921, when the State Supreme Court declared the act unconstitutional. After experimenting with a tax on moneyed capital, also declared unconstitutional, the present levy on net income was adopted.

Chain Store Taxes. All the states derive a substantial revenue from corporation taxes. While most of this comes from domestic corporations, the states sometimes seek to evade the principle of equality of treatment set up for the protection of foreign corporations by imposing cleverly devised

to foreign as to domestic corporations, although the base may be different, in order to reach only that portion of the corporation's assets employed, or business transacted within the state. The Supreme Court has established the principle that foreign corporations may not be discriminated against; they may be kept out of the state if they desire to transact only local business, but having once been admitted, they are on the same basis before the law as domestic corporations within the state engaged in the same or similar business. See Western Union Telegraph Company v. Kansas, 216 U.S. 1, 1909.

[24] Franchise Tax Commissioner, *Annual Report, 1951* (Sacramento, 1952).

levies particularly applicable to the latter, most of which are interstate in character. Among these is the chain stores tax, which had an amazing development during the thirties. Many of the laws were fostered by independent merchants and therefore intended to be discriminatory; this consideration was often more important than the revenue produced.[25] As of 1948 such laws were in existence in nineteen states,[26] most of which follow a graduated license or bracket rate schedule. Under this plan the tax is graduated as the number of stores increases. A few states use the numerical license or totality rate schedule, under which the tax is determined either by the number of stores within the state or by the number of stores within and without the state. The yield has never been very large, Florida being the only state that obtains more than $1,000,000 in annual revenue from this source. The table on page 538 shows the manner in which this tax operates in a typical state — Iowa.

Severance Taxes. Severance taxes are not corporation taxes, but they are business taxes. Some states impose such taxes, in lieu of or in addition to property taxes, on coal, crude oil or petroleum, mine products, natural gas, salt, sulphur, stone, sand and gravel, timber or lumber cut, turpentine, fish, oysters, clams, shells, and shrimp. Severance taxes may be general, applying to all natural products extracted from the soil, or selective, applying to a limited number of such products. Taxes of the general type exist in Arkansas and Louisiana; taxes of the selective type are in force in seventeen other states.[27] Texas reported the largest amount of revenue from this source, followed by Oklahoma, both of which states tax the production of oil, natural gas, and ores. Louisiana was the third state to adopt this tax method, with a general law covering many products at varying rates. In 1937, nineteen states collected $44 million from this source.

Taxes on Pari-mutuel Betting. In recent years, horse racing has become

[25] See, for instance, Liggett v. Baldridge, Attorney General of Pennsylvania, 278 U.S. 105, 1928, and Liggett, et al. v. Amos, 287 U.S. 600, 1932.

[26] Several states formerly having these laws have repealed them or permitted them to expire. A graduated tax based on the volume of sales has been adopted in a number of states, but the state supreme courts of Kentucky and Pennsylvania have declared legislation of this type unconstitutional: Kentucky Tax Commission, et al. v. Great A. & P. Tea Company, 278 Ky. 367, 1939; American Stores Company v. Boardman, Secretary of Revenue, 336 Pa. 36, 1939; and Reeves, Commissioner of Revenue v. Adam Hat Stores, 303 Ky. 633, 1946.

[27] In addition to references cited in earlier editions of this volume, see: Besley, Lowell, *Taxation of Forest Lands in West Virginia* (Agricultural Experiment Station, West Virginia University, 1948); Marquis, Ralph W., *Forest Yield Taxes* (United States Department of Agriculture, Washington, April 1952) and "Severance Taxes on Forest Products and Their Relation to Forestry," *Land Economics*, August 1949, pp. 315–319; Nebraska Legislative Council, *Regulation and Taxation of the Production of Oil and Natural Gas* (Lincoln, 1950); Roberts, Warren A., *State Taxation of Metallic Deposits* (Harvard University Press, 1944); United States Forest Service, *State Forest Tax Law Digest of 1945* (Washington, 1945); Virginia Commission to Study the Taxation of Natural Resources, *Taxation of Natural Resources in Virginia* (Richmond, 1951); Walker, William P., and DeVault, S. H., *Forest Taxation in Maryland* (Agricultural Experiment Station, University of Maryland, 1947).

State of Iowa
Application of the Chain Store Tax Law *

NUMBER OF STORES	TAX ON EACH	GROUPS EXEMPT FROM TAX
1–10	$ 5.00	1. Cooperative associations not for profit
11–20	15.00	2. Gardeners or farmers selling own produce
21–30	35.00	3. Retailers of coal, ice, lumber, grain, feed, seeds, twine, fertilizer, building materials
31–40	65.00	
41–50	105.00	4. State liquor stores
51–	155.00	5. Hotels and rooming houses including cafes and dining rooms operated in connection therewith

Operation of the Chain Store Tax *

YEAR	CONCERNS REPORTING	STORES OPERATED	AMOUNT PAID
1936	473	2,464	$ 44,650.10
1940	384	3,391	711,022.81[1]
1945	722	2,798	31,791.47
1949	658	2,641	28,346.56

* From Scott, David C., *Iowa State Tax Commission*, pp. 58–60 (State Historical Society of Iowa, Iowa City, 1950).

[1] $576,165 of this amount was collected from fourteen major oil companies through Consent Decree in respect to unit tax on bulk stations after suit had been pending in the Federal District Court.

big business. Out of twenty-five states authorizing betting on this sport, Nebraska was the only one not imposing a tax on pari-mutuel wagers. The postwar era has seen not only new tax laws enacted but amendments to old laws raising the rates. New York receives more than $30,000,000 annually from this source and California more than $8,000,000, while nine more collect from $1,000,000 or more to $4,000,000 or more. The Tax Foundation puts the matter in another way: the major portion of pari-mutuel tax revenues accrue to a very few states. Four states — California, Florida, Massachusetts, and New York — collected two thirds of the total pari-mutuel tax receipts in 1947; eight states — Illinois, Maryland, New Jersey, Rhode Island, and the four above — accounted for 90 per cent of the aggregate collections. That this tax is lucrative in these few states, however, is evidenced by the fact that it produced in excess of $110,000,000 in 1947.[28]

[28] *Recent Trends in Major State Taxes*, *op. cit.*, p. 47; see also Shain, Isaiah J., *State Income from Horse Racing* (Bureau of Public Administration, University of California, 1947).

Business and State Tax Differentials. In the large industrial states the discussion about business enterprises being driven out by the burden of taxes still continues. For many years there was a migration of industry from the Northern to the Southern states, where both taxes and wages were lower. The passage of the Federal Wages and Hours Act and the spread of unionization in the South have now tended to equalize wage rates, and taxes too have risen. The tax differential, however, tended to be less important when the scarcity of skilled labor in the South and the nearness to markets in the North were considered. The problem is by no means a new one — the records show that it was seriously discussed in the Pennsylvania General Assembly in 1885. It is customary for states to advertise for new industries on the basis of claims of low taxes and various kinds of services offered to business and industry. Claims of low taxes are difficult to substantiate. If state taxes are low, local taxes may be high. If direct taxes are low, indirect taxes may be high. It takes money to run a government, and the money has to be raised by taxes which somebody has to pay. No very wide differential is likely to exist for very long, for all the states need all the revenue they can raise to maintain existing programs — to say nothing of future expansion. In the keen competition between the states for new industries and new plants, some amusing situations arise.[29]

[29] In 1948, after the publication of the Tax Foundation study of recent tax trends, previously cited, the Pennsylvania Department of Commerce put out a pamphlet based thereon, boasting:

STATE TAXES HAVE INCREASED *LESS* IN PENNSYLVANIA THAN IN ANY OTHER STATE. Following a long series of more specific claims, the pamphlet concluded that "all this means a great competitive advantage for companies which have plants in Pennsylvania." Full two-page advertisements were taken in national periodicals to tell the joyous news. This was in the early part of 1948, following the publication of the report; in October of the same year, the State Chamber of Commerce put out a pamphlet called "Pennsylvania's Legislature Can Erase This Tax Question," likewise very attractive in appearance, but stressing throughout that the state's tax system is a strong deterring factor to the development and growth of business and industry within the state. This type of claim and counterclaim in state after state serves simply to prove that government everywhere costs money, and that business, which is a major tax source, always feels that it is being called upon to bear an undue burden.

For some of the more recent studies in this field, see Burkhead, Jesse, and Steele, Donald C., "The Effect of State Taxation on the Migration of Industry," *Journal of Business*, July 1950, pp. 167–172; Martin, James W., and Morrow, Glenn D., *Taxation of Manufacturing in the South* (Bureau of Public Administration, University of Alabama, 1948): Martin, James W., and others, *Southern Manufacturer's Tax Bill* — a symposium covering seven states (Bureau of Business Research, University of Kentucky, 1947); and for individual states: Connecticut Development Commission, *Taxes to Be Paid by a Manufacturing Corporation in Connecticut* (Hartford, 1949); Massachusetts Special Commission on Taxation, *Report*, Part IV, The Comparative Impact of Corporate Taxes in Massachusetts (Boston, June 1951); Ohio Department of Taxation, *A Study of the Tax Burden in Ohio in Comparison with Other States* (Columbus, 1946); Hanning, Irene, *How North Dakota Taxes Industry* (North Dakota Research Foundation, Bismarck, 1947); Marsh, Charles F., "Industrial Taxation in Virginia: the Relative Load," *Bulletin* of the National Tax Association, June 1947, pp. 260–268; Knight W. D., *Subsidization of Industry in Forty Selected Cities in Wisconsin, 1930–1946* (Bureau of Business Research and Science, University of Wisconsin, 1947).

General Sales, Use, and Gross Receipts Taxes

In the decade of the thirties, while the sales tax was spreading so rapidly from state to state, it was calmly assumed that it represented a new form of taxation. As a matter of fact, it was more than a century old in the United States and has been used in every state in the Union in some form for many years. Pennsylvania levied a general tax upon wholesale and retail transactions which has been collected since 1821. The wholesale license tax provides for an annual license fee of $5.00 plus a tax of 5 per cent on the gross annual turnover, while the retail license tax provides for an annual fee of $2.00 plus 1 per cent on the entire volume of the year's business. Virginia likewise had an early law. The Delaware gross receipts tax dates back to 1906. In 1909 Missouri authorized its municipalities to collect turnover taxes. Since 1921 Connecticut has collected a gross income tax from unincorporated manufacturing and mercantile establishments, and in the same year West Virginia adopted its gross sales tax. Georgia and Mississippi — the Mississippi law was much discussed — followed in 1929. In the thirties, eleven states adopted and later repealed such legislation.

The term "sales tax" is used rather loosely to apply to a number of different types of tax; on this basis, general sales, use, and gross receipts taxes existed in twenty-seven states as of 1949. These were of two main types — taxes on general sales and taxes on the privilege of engaging in business. Twenty-one states had a use tax, intended to tap the rich field of sales made in interstate commerce, while half a dozen others had similar taxes under other names. These laws took several different forms, such as taxes on retail sales, general sales, gross receipts, and gross income. With the exception of the early laws mentioned above, all were adopted between 1933 and 1937.[30] The rates are 3 per cent in seven states, 2 per cent in nineteen.

The selective sales tax differs from the general type and is somewhat older; it has been defined as "a tax upon and measured by the receipts from the sale of a particular article." Every state in the Union uses at least two taxes of this type — that on gasoline and that on liquor. In addition, taxes on nonintoxicating beer and on nonalcoholic beverages and commodities entering into the manufacture thereof exist in many states. Selective sales taxes on other commodites had been adopted in 1950 as follows: public amusements, not including business licenses or inspection fees, in thirty-

[30] The best source of current information on such matters is the latest edition of *Tax Systems*. In addition to references listed in earlier editions of this volume, see Blakey, Roy G. and Gladys C., *Sales Taxes and Other Excises* (Public Administration Service, Chicago, 1944); Ford, Robert S., and Shepard, E. Fenton, *The Michigan Retail Sales and Use Taxes* (University of Michigan Press, 1941); Institute of Distribution, *Retailers Manual of Taxes and Regulations* (New York, annually since 1935); League of Virginia Counties, *Virginia Needs a Sales Tax: The Operation of State Sales Taxes in the United States* (Charlottesville, 1948); Nevada Legislative Counsel Bureau, *Survey of Sales Taxes Applicable to Nevada* (Carson City, 1948); Waters, Lawrence L., *Use Taxes and Their Legal and Economic Background* (Bureau of Business Research, University of Kansas, 1940).

three states; cigarettes and tobacco, in thirty-nine states; oleomargarine, in thirty states; severance taxes, in twenty-four states; pari-mutuel betting, in twenty-one states; and on electricity, per kilowatt hours generated, in four states. Following the depression there was a marked increase in the number of states in each of these groups and in the rates imposed. There are, in addition, a great many other miscellaneous types of excises, royalties, and licenses.[31]

The problem of exemptions is important here, as in the case of the general property tax. Most states exempt commodities already taxed under other laws, such as gasoline, cigarettes, insurance companies, and banks. Some exempt certain transactions, such as sales to the state or its subdivisions. Some formerly exempted foodstuffs or made lump-sum exemptions from the tax base, but these forms of exemption have about disappeared.[32] This problem, however, leads directly to the fundamental question of the merits of the sales tax principle. This tax form stands in the peculiar position of having scarcely a friend or defender among students of public finance, and yet of having spread rapidly from state to state.

Against all the arguments of the tax experts have been weighed two facts, in the light of the urgent need of the states for additional revenues during the depression years when nearly all the laws were adopted: the sales tax does produce revenue in sizable amounts, and it produces it quickly. In some states it is, in fact, the largest single source of state revenue. Receipts shot upward during the defense period and declined somewhat with restrictions in the supply of civilian goods during World War II. No one denies that the tax is burdensome to the low-income group or that it is regressive, probably to a greater extent than any other tax now in common use. While it is to be hoped that for these reasons it may gradually be abandoned, this is scarcely to be expected.

Excise Taxes

It is difficult to classify taxes. Writers use the existing terminology in many different ways. Very often the terms themselves are not mutually exclusive. In the discussion of sales taxes mention has been made of special levies on alcoholic beverages, gasoline, and tobacco. These levies are usually in the form of sales taxes, but they are also excises. Both the general sales tax and these special sales taxes or excises may be classified as consumption taxes. There are other excises in addition to these three, but these constitute such an important part of the state revenue picture that it is deemed proper to deal with them specifically.

Alcoholic Beverage Taxes. The states may derive revenue from the alcoholic beverage industry in either or both of two ways. They may, as

[31] See tables in *Tax Systems*.
[32] Illinois Legislative Council, *Exemption of Food Under Sales Tax Statutes* (Springfield, 1940).

State and Local Revenues from Alcoholic Beverages — 1951 *

	32 LICENSE STATES	16 MONOPOLY STATES	TOTAL
Total state sales	$..........	$ 930,283,242	$ 930,283,242
State license fees	55,778,280	24,858,291	80,636,572
State ABC taxes	337,048,869	111,618,360	448,667,229
Miscellaneous State ABC income	4,794,159	3,951,145	8,745,305
Gross state receipts	397,621,309	1,070,711,040	1,468,332,350
Cost of ABC administration and collections	13,891,924	15,126,634	29,018,559
Cost of goods sold	....	688,511,456	688,511,456
Cost of sales operations	....	41,408,833	41,408,833
Total state ABC costs	13,891,924	745,046,924	758,938,849
Net state ABC revenue	383,729,385	325,664,115	709,393,501
General sales tax	47,455,592	12,923,927	60,379,519
Local ABC revenues	62,310,683	12,478,413	74,789,097
Total state and local revenues	493,495,661	351,066,456	844,562,118

* Distilled Spirits Institute, *Public Revenues from Alcoholic Beverages*, pp. 12–13 (Washington, 1952).

sixteen states do, engage in the wholesale distribution of wines and hard liquor, realizing a substantial profit from the operation of the business. Or they may, through a central licensing agency, issue licenses or permits to taprooms, eating places, and night clubs, for the retail sale, for consumption on the premises, of wine, beers, and liquors. In all states the licensing of liquor dispensers is required as a police measure, but in some the licenses

Gallonage Tax on Distilled Spirits — 1950*

DOLLARS PER GALLON	NUMBER OF STATES	STATES
$ .75–$1.00	11	California, Connecticut, Delaware, Georgia, Illinois, Kansas, Missouri, Nebraska, Nevada, Rhode Island, South Dakota
1.01– 1.50	7	Arizona, Kentucky, Maryland, New Jersey, New Mexico, New York, Texas
1.51– 2.00	4	Colorado, Louisiana, Tennessee, Wisconsin
2.01– 2.50	4	Florida, Indiana, Massachusetts, North Dakota
2.51– 2.75	19	All states not mentioned above

* Council of State Governments, *Sources of State Tax Revenue, 1940–1949* (Chicago, 1950).

are issued locally by the county, municipality, or other civil subdivision within which they carry on their business. In either case the practice is pretty well established of turning over to the local units all or part of the revenue derived from the issuance of such licenses.

The table on page 542 shows the state and local revenues from alcoholic beverages for 1951 for both license and monopoly states, as well as the costs incurred in the administration of the alcoholic beverage commissions. The total revenue derived from this source is considerable. The monopoly system is not only a better means of controlling the traffic, but is productive of substantially greater revenues than the license system. The license states are twice as numerous as the monopoly states, but they collect only one and one half times as much revenue. During the war period the receipts from this source increased sharply, in spite of decreased supply due partly to increased demand and partly to increased tax rates.

Gasoline Taxes. The first gasoline tax law was enacted in Oregon in 1919; the rate was one cent a gallon. Colorado, New Mexico, and North Dakota followed in the same year. By the close of the legislative sessions of 1925 such legislation was in effect in all but four states, and they soon succumbed. The tax was not adopted in Illinois and New Jersey until 1927, in Massachusetts until 1928, and in New York until 1929. The rates began gently enough, at one or two cents, and increased steadily through the depression period to a range of from three to five cents, with a few states collecting as much as nine cents a gallon. The State of Wisconsin, to use one state as an illustration, collected $779,838 from the gasoline tax in 1925; $15,626,032 in 1935; $16,527,594 and $28,284,000 in 1945 and 1948, respectively. The total highway users' taxes amount to $50,000,000 a year in this one state alone.[33] To the state rate must be added the two cents a gallon collected for the Federal government.

The liquid fuels tax (for the base has been broadened to include liquid fuels in general), along with motor license and operators' license fees, raises in acute form the question of special or designated funds. Every special group that pays a tax or an administrative license fee wants the receipts earmarked, and their expenditure restricted to purposes beneficial to the group paying the tax. The motor car, truck, and bus owners constitute a numerous and powerful group, and have generally been successful in preventing the diversion of liquid fuels and motor license revenues to purposes other than highways. The psychology of these interest groups is readily understandable, but administratively there is little or no justification for the establishment and operation of special funds. All tax receipts belong to the state as a whole, not to any individual group of taxpayers. They should go into the general fund to be used as the financial needs of the state require.

[33] See *Wisconsin Taxpayer*, July 1949, entire issue, and Tennessee State Planning Commission, *The Gasoline Tax in Tennessee, a Review of Its Present and Proposed Distribution* (Nashville, 1946).

Gallonage Tax on Gasoline — 1950 *

CENTS PER GALLON	NUMBER OF STATES	STATES
9	1	Louisiana
7	7	Florida, Georgia, Kentucky, Mississippi, New Mexico, North Carolina, Tennessee
$6\frac{1}{2}$	3	Arkansas, Oklahoma, Washington
6	9	Alabama, Colorado, Idaho, Maine, Montana, Nebraska, Oregon, South Carolina, Virginia
5	8	Arizona, Delaware, Kansas, Maryland, Minnesota, Pennsylvania, Vermont, West Virginia
$4\frac{1}{2}$	2	California, Nevada
4	13	Connecticut, Indiana, Iowa, New Hampshire, New York, North Dakota, Ohio, Rhode Island, South Dakota, Texas, Utah, Wisconsin, Wyoming
3	4	Illinois, Massachusetts, Michigan, New Jersey
2	1	Missouri

* Council of State Governments, *Sources of State Tax Revenue, 1940–1949* (Chicago, 1950).

Cigarette and Tobacco Taxes. State laws taxing the sale and consumption of tobacco are of two types, from the standpoint of the objects taxed: those applying to tobacco products as a group, and those applicable only in certain specified forms of manufactured tobacco, such as cigars and cigarettes. Only one state, South Carolina, taxes all forms of tobacco products, but more than half of the states impose special tobacco taxes of various kinds. Every state levying such taxes requires that all or some dealers be licensed to do business. In addition, many states levy a commodity tax upon the tobacco itself as a base. Cigarette smoking has become so common a practice among all ages and both sexes throughout the country that the cigarette tax, originally confined to a small number of tobacco-producing states, is now found in all but seven states. The rates as of 1950 are shown in the table on page 545.

Income Taxes

Mention has been made of the development of the theory of taxation, from one basic principle to another, in the effort to find means of distributing the tax burden more equitably. In the opinion of tax experts, the income tax meets the ability-to-pay test better than any other. State income tax legislation began in 1911, when the Wisconsin act was passed.[34] Massachusetts, Missouri, Montana, and New York had adopted such taxes by 1917,

[34] See Slater, Harry, "Wisconsin's Income Tax Act on Its Thirtieth Birthday," *Tax Magazine*, January 1942, pp. 27–33, and February 1942, pp. 95–101.

Cigarette Taxes — 1950 *

CENTS PER PACK	NUMBER OF STATES	STATES
8	1	Louisiana
5	4	Georgia, Massachusetts, North Dakota, Oklahoma
4	9	Arkansas, Florida, Maine, Minnesota, Mississippi, New Mexico, Pennsylvania, Texas, Vermont
3	16	Alabama, Connecticut, Idaho, Illinois, Indiana, Kansas, Michigan, Nebraska, Nevada, New Jersey, New York, Rhode Island, South Carolina, South Dakota, Tennessee, Wisconsin
$2\frac{1}{2}$	1	New Hampshire
2	9	Arizona, Delaware, Iowa, Kentucky, Maryland, Montana, Ohio, Utah, Washington
1	1	West Virginia
0	7	California, Colorado, Missouri, North Carolina, Oregon, Virginia, Wyoming

* Council of State Governments, *Sources of State Tax Revenue, 1940–1949* (Chicago 1950).

when Delaware joined the income tax states. In the meantime Amendment XVI to the Federal Constitution had made possible the Federal Act of 1913. From this time on the income tax became more and more firmly established in the tax thinking of the country. By 1918 such laws existed in twelve states; in 1923, in fourteen; in 1933, in twenty-seven, with the present total standing at thirty-one.

With the decline of revenue from the general property taxes and other sources during the depression, it is not surprising that there was a general extension of income tax legislation, which may be applied to either persons or corporations or both. The financial stress and strain to which state governments were subjected during the depression necessitated the securing of as much revenue from as many sources as possible and led many states to adopt some form of income taxation. Modern industrial development has produced conditions which indicate to many the advisability of giving a larger scope to state income taxation.[35]

In the first place, sharp differences have developed between the distribution of property, on the one hand, and of income on the other. Some groups have property, but no income; some have income, but no taxable property;

[35] Ferguson, Vaughn B., and Davisson, Malcolm M., *Personal Income Tax* (Bureau of Public Administration, University of California, 1934); for other studies, in addition to those listed in previous editions of this volume, see Back, Kenneth C., *The Indiana Gross Income Tax* (University of Kentucky, 1950); Brandt, Louis K., *Mississippi: Corporate Fees and Taxes* (Bureau of Public Administration, University of Mississippi, 1948); Northrup, Arthur H., "Indiana Gross Income Tax," *Indiana Law Journal*, Winter 1950, pp. 148–167; and Tax Institute, Inc., *How Should Corporations Be Taxed?* (New York, 1947).

some have both. A tax on property largely exempts one group, a tax on income exempts the other. It would therefore seem logical that a tax system distributed in some rational relationship would rest on both groups and be fairer to all concerned.

Secondly, an income tax falls upon those who at least have some income, rather than those who have none, as is the case of many property holders. Such a tax would then be based on the taxpayer's ability to pay rather than upon the benefits received from the governmental unit.

In the third place, with taxes as high as they now are and likely to continue for some time, it is highly important to know who are paying the taxes levied. We know that property taxes can be, and are, shifted with such results that no one has ever been able to say just where they finally rested. One reason for a larger development of income taxation is that we can know, approximately at least, where the tax is going to rest and can form some judgment as to what its import and effects are likely to be.

In view of these considerations, the use made of the income tax becomes an important matter. As of 1949 there were thirty-one states having personal net income taxes in some form. From another approach, twenty-four states taxed the income of both corporations and individuals. Of the thirty-one states taxing income in some form, seventeen had adopted their laws since 1930. The twenty states with general sales or gross income tax laws had, with one exception, adopted them since 1930; thirteen of them in 1933. Sixteen states which had a sales or gross income tax also had a net income tax. Some of the items in this classification, to be sure, overlap with certain types of the sales tax group discussed earlier. Only ten states had neither a sales or gross income tax nor a net income tax. Some of the populous and wealthy states, such as New York and Massachusetts, are among those having a net income tax; on the other hand, Illinois, Michigan, and New Jersey have no income tax legislation. Ohio has no general personal income tax. Delaware, South Dakota, and West Virginia repealed their income tax laws during World War II, and a number of states made substantial reductions in rates.

Personal Income Taxes. Personal income taxes were in effect in thirty-one states in 1949. The rates on personal net incomes begin at 1 per cent in a majority of states, and reach a maximum of 10 per cent in Colorado and Minnesota. The amount of income of single persons which is exempt from tax varies from \$500 in Vermont to \$3000 in California, eleven states permitting \$1000. Seven states allow amounts between \$500 and \$1000. Exemptions for married persons range from \$1000 in Vermont to \$4500 in California, with six states permitting \$2500; six states, \$2000. In the five states which allow deductions after the tax has been computed, the amounts range from \$17.50 to \$50.00. All states allow deductions for dependents, ranging from \$200 to \$500.[36]

These exemptions operate in such manner that a man, his wife, and three dependents pay no tax on an income of \$2000; a single man pays from \$10

[36] *Wisconsin Taxpayer*, April 1949, p. 28.

to $100. On an income of $5000 a man with the family indicated may pay from $50 to $250, while the limits for a single man are the same, although in most instances the tax is somewhat higher. For an income of $25,000 the limits extend from $500 to $2,500. The state tax commission or commissioner is commonly designated as the administrative officer for this tax. After expenses of collection, which average 2 or 3 per cent, have been deducted, the money is used for refunding or for the general fund, although remainders may be assigned to schools, local governments, charities and relief, or casual deficiencies. The revenues derived from the tax represent very considerable sums, particularly in the larger industrial and commercial states, and are usually turned to general fund purposes.

The National Tax Association has proposed a Model Personal Income Tax Act based upon certain principles which the Association believes are essential to the successful imposition of such a tax. They contend that such a tax should be levied upon persons in respect to their entire net incomes from all sources, and should be collected only from persons and at the places where they are domiciled; that it should be levied on net income — operating expenses and interest on indebtedness to be deducted; that small incomes should be exempted; and that the rate should be the same for all kinds of income, the rate not being affected by the source. The rates should be progressive; the administration of the tax should be placed in the hands of state officials under a state tax commissioner; and the tax should be collected from the taxpayers upon the basis of strictly enforced and controlled returns, and without any attempt to collect at the source. The taxpayer, it is claimed, should be made to realize that *he* is paying the tax.

Certain trends have become evident in the recent application of this tax; the first is lower exemptions than were formerly customary — a trend which students of tax problems almost unanimously consider desirable. "A second significant development, based on the pioneer experiment in Wisconsin, is the practice of providing for personal exemptions by a tax offset rather than by excepting certain taxable incomes. This newer plan has the merit of giving no larger exemptions for persons receiving large incomes than are available for those receiving small ones. A still more constructive development is the recent enactment in certain states of statutes which make the maximum rate effective at a relatively low income level. This practice means steep graduation so that the maximum rate, though moderate, is attained on upper middle class incomes." The experience of the depression showed that the productivity of the tax was better sustained and more satisfactory than many had anticipated. Finally, the practice of requiring a filing fee, which materially reduces the administrative expense, has shown a slight gain.

Corporate Income Taxes. Extensive use is made of taxes on corporate income in nearly three fourths of the states.[37] The table on page 548 shows

[37] See Goode, Richard, *The Corporation Income Tax* (Wiley, New York, 1951).

something of the diversity of rates applied in the different states. Uniform rates vary from 2 to 8 per cent, while six states (Arizona, Arkansas, Idaho, Mississippi, North Dakota, and Wisconsin) use graduated rates ranging from 1 to 5, 1 to 6, 1 to 8, 2 to 6, or 3 to 6 per cent. Alternative minimum rates are provided for in six states, and Wisconsin has a surtax formula which calls for an amount equal to the normal tax less $75 divided by 6.

Corporate Income Tax Rates — 1950 *

RATE IN PER CENT	NUMBER OF STATES	STATES
8	2	Idaho, Oregon
6	5	Massachusetts, Minnesota, Mississippi, North Dakota, Wisconsin
5	6	Arizona, Arkansas, Colorado, New York, South Carolina, Virginia
4	9	California, Kentucky, Louisiana, Maryland, Oklahoma, Pennsylvania, Rhode Island, Tennessee, Vermont
3	5	Alabama, Connecticut, Montana, South Dakota, Utah
2	4	Iowa, Kansas, Missouri, New Mexico

* Council of State Governments, *Sources of State Tax Revenue, 1940–1949* (Chicago, 1950).

Inheritance and Estate Taxes

The inheritance tax is one of the oldest forms of tax, not only in the United States, but in the world at large. "Congress first levied a death duty in 1797; Pennsylvania in 1820 enacted the first state inheritance tax law; Louisiana and Virginia followed with laws in 1826 and 1844, respectively; and California utilized this source in 1893." [38] The right of states to levy taxes upon the transfer of property is therefore well established by custom and usage; the main problem now is to secure a substantial yield from this source without undue hardship to the persons concerned or disruptive effect upon the organization and operation of productive enterprise.

Neither the estate nor the inheritance tax is a tax upon property; both are taxes upon a privilege, the first levied upon the entire net amount of wealth possessed by the decedent at death, the second upon a computation of the value of the individual share of each beneficiary. The first is a tax upon the right to bequeath an estate, the second on the right to receive an

[38] For a history and chronology of inheritance tax legislation in Virginia, see *Inheritance and Gift Taxes* (Virginia Department of Taxation, Richmond, 1947), and for an extensive study of the law in another state, Kentucky Department of Revenue, *Inheritance and Estate Taxes in Kentucky* (Frankfort, 1947). Ohio enacted the first progressive inheritance tax law in 1894, but it was declared unconstitutional.

inheritance. Rodman Sullivan, in the Kentucky study referred to, explains that:

> The rates employed under either form may be proportional, that is, at the same rate regardless of the size of the estate or beneficial share, or progressive, which means increasing the rate as the size of the estate or beneficial share increases. The progression also may be based upon the degree of relationship existing between the heir and the decedent, the more distant the kinship, the higher the rate. Today a majority of states have progressive inheritance taxes on both direct and collateral heirs. The Federal government levies a progressive estate tax, but the progression is only on the size of the estate and not on the beneficial shares; hence it is not affected by the degree of relationship to the deceased.

As of January 1, 1934 — and since — forty-seven states have had some form of death duty in force, leaving only Nevada without such a tax. One and a half years previously (on July 1, 1932) fourteen states had had an inheritance tax only, twenty-seven had had inheritance and estate taxes, and six states had estate taxes only. The great change in so short a period was due to the pressure of the Federal government through the amendment in 1932 of the credit provision in the act of 1926. A survey in 1948 showed that nine states levy estate taxes only; five, inheritance taxes only; one imposes both inheritance and gift taxes; twenty-one levy inheritance and estate taxes; and eleven impose all three types. Despite their broad coverage, these taxes are relatively minor revenue producers. Revenues from them amounted to less than 3 per cent of the total state tax collections in 1947, New Jersey deriving a greater percentage of total tax revenues from this source than any other state. Even in this case they amounted to less than 10 per cent.

In its survey of recent trends of major state taxes, covering the years 1941 to 1947, the Tax Foundation reported a gain in revenues from this source of 41 per cent, as against an average gain of 58 per cent in total tax collections. Collections in those states having rates unchanged during the period covered by the survey ranged from increased revenues of nearly 450 per cent in Indiana to a decline of more than 30 per cent in Georgia — thereby indicating the unstable yield of these taxes. In many states the total amount derived from this source is so small that the settlement of one or two large estates in one year causes a great fluctuation and percentage fluctuation in revenues. The most spectacular change during this period occurred in New Mexico where two changes were made in the law, as a result of which there was a 498 per cent increase in collections.

Some Current Tax Problems

Tax Pattern of the States. At the conclusion of this discussion of the various types of taxes relied upon as chief sources of revenue by the states, it may be of interest to examine the tax patterns of the states — the patterns in which the several states combine these different tax forms for the purpose of securing necessary revenues. That these patterns are complicated is well illustrated by the record in California, where it was reported in 1936 that there were 101 levies in effect, adopted from 1850 to date. In 1850 the state property tax (discontinued in 1910), the poll tax, military commutation tax, foreign miner's license tax, and the auctioneer's license tax were adopted; in 1935 the legislature approved legislation for a personal income tax, a use tax, and a distilled liquor tax. In nearly every intervening legislative session one or more such acts were added to the list.

STATE TAX SOURCES — 1949 *

1. Corporate Organization and Qualification Fees	48
2. Corporate Franchise Tax	
General	45
Annual Corporation Report	22
Miscellaneous	2
3. Income Tax	
Individual	31
Corporate Franchise	11
Corporate Miscellaneous	18 [1]
4. Property Tax	
General	48
Intangibles	17
Financial Institutions	23
Grain	10
Miscellaneous	38 [2]
5. Business Licenses	11
6. Alcoholic Beverage Taxes	48
7. Motor Fuel Tax	
Gasoline	48
Fuel Use Tax	22
Miscellaneous	3
8. Severance or Production Taxes	
General	24
Miscellaneous	23 [3]
9. Motor Vehicle and Aircraft	
General	48
Motor Carrier Fees	38
Miscellaneous	6
10. Chain Store Tax	19
11. Admissions and Amusements Tax	33
12. Luxury Excise Tax	
Cigarettes and Tobacco	41
Oleomargarine	19
Miscellaneous	19 [4]
13. Documentary and Stock Transfer Tax	14
14. Sales Tax	
General	27
Use Tax (compensating)	19
Miscellaneous	7
15. Public Utilities Tax	
General	22
Railroad	11
Gas and/or Electric	11
Express	19
Telephone, Telegraph and Cable	13
Private Car	12
Miscellaneous	31 [5]
16. Insurance Company Taxes	48
17. Inheritance — Succession Tax	
General	39
Estate	33
Gift	12
18. Poll Tax	10
19. Pari-mutuel Taxes	21
20. Unemployment Compensation	48

* Based on Lester, William M., *A Summary Comparison of State Revenue Systems* (Georgia Tax Revision Committee, Atlanta, 1949), and United States Bureau of the Census, *Sources of State Revenue in 1949* (Washington, 1950).

[1] Direct income, 3; personal income, 9; unincorporated business, 3; and miscellaneous, 3.

[2] Capital stock, 4; public utilities, 7; private car companies, 4; motor vehicles, 2; vessels, 5; mines, 4; forest lands, 8; miscellaneous, 4.

[3] Oil, 7; gas, 2; coal, 2; carbon black, 2; other ores and stones, 2; timber, 6; miscellaneous, 2.

[4] Soft drinks, 4; malt extracts, 6; playing cards, 2; carbonic acid gas, 2; automobiles, 3; miscellaneous, 2.

[5] Street railroad, 5; water, 2; hydro-electric, 4; heat and/or steam, 5; transportation, 5; bus, 2; steamship, 4; miscellaneous, 5.

No two states have tax patterns exactly alike. Certain major sources of revenue are utilized by all, others by nearly all, as will be seen by reference to the table on page 550. Although the urgent need for more revenue creates a strong tendency toward uniformity, there is still a large group of miscellaneous taxes, each utilized by only a few states. In many cases, the receipts from particular taxes are used for both state and local purposes. In some instances the receipts are used entirely by the state, in others by the local units, while in still others they are used by both. Some of these overlapping taxes are state-collected, locally shared, while for others duplicate collecting agencies exist.[39]

Broadening the Tax Base. In recent years there has been great dissatisfaction with the real estate tax. During the depression many property owners were unable to pay their taxes at all, while others did so with great difficulty. This situation gave rise not only to widespread delinquency, but to all sorts of measures — tax limitation, homestead exemption, and others — designed to lessen the burden. As has been shown, these devices have not solved the problem; they have provided a modicum of temporary relief and have engendered new difficulties as great as those they were intended to relieve. In the face of this situation, many have argued a reconstruction of the whole tax program with a view to broadening the tax base. In such a program the state assumes additional responsibility for financing essential services formerly supported locally by real estate levies; to raise this money the state imposes new taxes of various sorts (often sales and income) and enlarges its grant-in-aid program so that the local units can offset this by reduced rates on real estate. The purpose is not to raise more money but to distribute the burden more equitably.

Such a program has been adopted in a number of states, including California, Colorado, Illinois, Iowa, Kansas, Michigan, New York, Ohio, and Pennsylvania; it has been discussed in many more. The results have been beneficial, but the anticipated reductions in real estate taxes have not always been realized, at least to the extent that was expected. In an era of expanding government services and increasing costs, all or part of the increased revenue intended for schools, roads, and health work has gone into public assistance, public works, social security, and other new state activities. As a result, chambers of commerce and taxpayers' associations have developed a vigorous opposition to proposals to broaden the tax base.[40]

Community Property. The concept of community property, which may be defined as that marital property which is not the separate property of either the husband or the wife, has in recent years, because of its bearing on Federal income tax liability, come to have a widespread interest and signifi-

[39] See Colm, Gerhard, and Wald, Haskell P., "Some Comments on Tax Burden Comparisons," *National Tax Journal*, March 1952, pp. 1–14.

[40] See, for instance, New Jersey State Chamber of Commerce, *Do New Taxes Relieve the Tax Burden on Real Estate? — the Experience of Nine States* (Trenton, 1939).

cance. This legal concept, of French and Spanish origin, has spread to nine states — Arizona, California, Idaho, Louisiana, Nevada, New Mexico, Oklahoma, Texas, and Washington — in some cases by inheritance, in others by voluntary adoption. Oregon in 1945 repealed a community property statute adopted in 1943. Agitation for such legislation arose in many jurisdictions, due to the advantage formerly enjoyed by married Federal income taxpayers living in community property states.

This advantage derives from the assumption underlying the community property concept that income accruing after marriage is the product of the joint endeavors of the husband and wife. Dr. Norman J. Small has thus summarized the effect of this theory[41]:

> By this theory the salary of the husband, who may be the sole producer of the income, becomes the common property of the wife and her husband, each having a vested one-half interest therein. Accordingly, in meeting Federal income tax requirements, the husband need report only one-half of his total income, which for the purposes of this illustration, represents salary only, and the wife may file a return reporting the other half. Each is entitled to all the privileges granted to income taxpayers, i.e., the same deductions, the same accounting methods for computing gains and losses, and the rates applicable to the net income disclosed in the return. . . .

Because this arrangement tended to reduce Federal collections of income and other taxes, and because it appeared to provide an unfair legal advantage to taxpayers in a few states as compared with those in the remainder, the Federal government extended to married couples, beginning in 1948, the privilege of filing joint returns. Taxpayers widely availed themselves of this privilege, and the agitation for the further adoption of community property legislation for the time being subsided.

Double and Overlapping Taxation. For more than a century after the establishment of the present system of government in this country, there was a segregation of sources of revenue among the various units of government — national, state, and local — in order to avoid double and multiple taxation. Thus customs and excise duties were regarded as sources of Federal revenue, while the general property tax, inheritance taxes, and corporation taxes were regarded as sources of state revenue. The local units depended almost wholly upon the general property tax; this was the only instance of major dependence of two units upon the same source, in the whole system. When the Federal government levied the estate tax, it established a reciprocal arrangement under which the unfortunate effects of a double tax on inheritance have been largely avoided.

Then began the unfortunate series of events by which these distinctions were broken down, particularly during the mad scramble for new revenues

[41] "Memorandum on Community Property," Legislative Reference Service, Library of Congress, April 28, 1947; see also Clark, Robert E., "Transmutations in New Mexico Community Property Law," *Rocky Mountain Law Review*, April 1952, pp. 273–300, and Daggett, Harriet S., *The Community Property System of Louisiana* (Louisiana State University Press, 1945).

during the depression. By the provisions of Amendment XVI, the states turned over to the Federal government the right to use the income tax; later, being short of funds, they began to use this form themselves, and have continued to do so until more than half of them now depend upon this form for a substantial portion of their revenues. Then came the tobacco taxes — at first only a few, then more, until now they exist in more than three fourths of the states. These were state invasions of Federal fields; it was only a question of time before the Federal government would begin its invasion of the state fields. This occurred in 1932, when Secretary of the Treasury Mills proposed and Congress adopted a tax of one cent a gallon (now two cents) on gasoline. He said he did not approve of the states' taxing tobacco, but if they were going to do that, then the Federal government might as well tax gasoline. In other words, if the tax situation was already becoming chaotic, the Federal government might as well step in and do what it could to make it worse.

It is improbable that it will ever again be possible to segregate individual tax sources to the several units of government, and unlikely that an equitable distribution of the tax burden could be achieved in that way, either economically or governmentally. Recent decisions of the Supreme Court have shown a marked tendency to modify — if not to abandon altogether — previously accepted doctrines of intergovernmental immunity.[42] At the same time it seems obvious that the existing chaotic system, in which each unit taxes everything in sight without regard to the policies of other units, cannot continue indefinitely. The available alternatives that seem workable are a system of federally collected, state-shared taxes on the one hand, and some system by which the Federal government and the states each continue to collect their own taxes but make some reciprocal arrangement with regard to the distribution of the revenues therefrom. At the present time it is impossible to say which of these two plans should or will be adopted. Each has certain advantages, and each has important supporters among the authorities in the tax field.

On the basis of logic alone one would be at first disposed to favor the

[42] See Helvering v. Gerhardt, 304 U.S. 405, 1938, and Graves v. New York ex rel. O'Keefe, 306 U.S. 466, 1939, which makes a double repudiation of ". . . an implied constitutional immunity from income taxation of the salaries of officers or employees of a national or a state government." In Adkinson, et al., v. State Tax Commission of Oregon, et al., 303 U.S. 20, 1938, a state personal income tax imposed on an individual engaged in work on the Bonneville Dam did not involve any interference with the carrying out of the Federal project. In the Gerhardt case the Court upheld a Federal levy on the salaries of the employees of the New York Port Authority. In Allen v. Regents of the University of Georgia, 304 U.S. 439, 1938, it was held that the Federal amusements tax could be collected on the receipts from football games; this did not differ greatly from the doctrine of the earlier South Carolina v. United States, 199 U.S. 437, 1905.

The literature is voluminous. In addition to the references cited in previous editions of this volume, see Graves, W. Brooke, "What Is Happening to Our Federal System?" *State Government*, November 1949, pp. 255–259, 270; Division of Tax Research, *Federal-State Tax Coordination* (Treasury Department, Washington, 1948); symposium on Federal-State-Local tax relations, *State Government*, November 1947, entire issue.

system of federally collected, state-shared taxes. By this is meant that the collection of all or of certain designated taxes would be centralized in the Federal government, with the understanding that there would be turned over to the states certain agreed portions of the receipts. This would simplify the process of collection and would probably insure the maximum degree of efficiency. In the case of gasoline, it would be much simpler and cheaper to collect all the tax due at the refineries — or, in the case of imported gasoline, at the ports of entry — than to leave the task to forty-eight different state governments. So with the income tax, it would be much simpler and more logical to have the Federal government make the entire collection in those states which desire to use this tax form, and turn over to the state governments the portion due them; but in both cases there are serious drawbacks.

In the first place, many states feel that if they surrender the power to collect their own taxes, even though they cannot do the work as efficiently or as cheaply as the Federal government, they will be surrendering a power so vital as to undermine the states in the federal system and reduce them to mere administrative units of the Federal government. There are those who say that this is what ought to be done. In the second place — and this is probably much more important — if the states accept this proposal, there is no assurance whatever that the Federal government will continue to hand over to the states, without restriction, their just share of the taxes collected. As early as 1934, in the famous Hayden-Cartwright Act, Congress attempted to prevent the further diversion of state highway funds, by providing for the withholding of one third of the Federal aid that might otherwise be allowed in those states where the policy of diversion was practiced. If the independence of the states is worth saving, this is too big a chance to take.

The second alternative — by which each state continues to collect its own revenues, but with an agreement regarding the distribution of the revenues collected — is, generally speaking, strong where the first method is weak and weak where the first method is strong. It will cost a little more to duplicate, to a certain extent, the collection facilities; it will be a little less efficient; but it will insure the continued independence of the states under the federal system, and it will make sure that they have their revenues without further restrictions imposed upon them by the Federal authorities. Those who, including the author, believe that the states are worth preserving are inclined to favor this method, viewing its weaknesses as a price which must be paid for the successful operation of a federal system.

SELECTED REFERENCES

Commerce Clearing House, *Tax Systems: A Reference Book of Legislative and Statutory Information for All of the United States and for Numerous Other Countries and Jurisdictions*, Twelfth Edition (Chicago, 1950). An indispensable working tool for the student of tax and fiscal policy.

Council of State Governments, *Sources of State Tax Revenue, 1940–1949* (Chicago, 1950). An excellent summary of state tax rates and yields in the last decade. See also the Council's *Postwar State Taxation and Finance* (Chicago, 1947), and Tax Foundation, *Recent Trends in Major State Taxes, 1941–1947* (New York, 1948).

Graves, W. Brooke, *Public Administration in a Democratic Society* (Heath, Boston, 1950). Chapter 13 deals with problems of assessment and tax administration.

Hansen, Alvin H., and Perloff, Harvey S., *State and Local Finance in the National Economy* (Norton, New York, 1944). A standard treatise of fairly recent date.

Lester, William M., *A Summary Comparison of State Revenue Systems* (Georgia Tax Revision Committee, Atlanta, 1949), and California Senate Interim Committee on State and Local Taxation, *Report*, Part III, *State and Local Taxes in California; a Comparative Analysis* (Sacramento, April 1951). Two useful compilations of comparative data prepared for state tax study committees.

New York State Constitutional Convention Committee, *Problems Relating to Taxation and Finance*, being Vol. X of the Committee's *Report* (Albany, 1938). Valuable compilation covering the prewar decade of the thirties.

New York State Department of Taxation and Finance, *The New York State and Local Tax System* (Albany, annually). An excellent analysis of the history of the New York tax system, and of the state and local taxes imposed.

Sunderland, J. Wilner, and Mushkin, S. J., *The Measurement of State and Local Tax Effort* (Bureau of Research and Statistics, Social Security Board, Washington, 1944). Data on an important, basic problem, in connection with grants-in-aid.

Tompkins, Dorothy C., *State and Local Finance and Taxation: a Bibliography of Materials Published in 1941–1946* (Bureau of Public Administration, University of California, 1946). Covers publications of the war and early postwar period.

United States Bureau of the Census, *Compendium of State Government Finances* (Washington, annually). Authoritative figures on state revenues and expenditures.

PART FIVE

Judicial and Legal Problems

The success of our institutions lies in the respect which is inspired by these contacts [with the courts] and the impression that the average man and woman in the country has that justice is really sought and measurably obtained in our courts of justice.

—CHARLES EVANS HUGHES

16

The Legal Systems of the States

The legal systems of the states include the whole body of constitutional law, common law, and statutory law under which the governments themselves and their agencies are organized, under which they function, and which it becomes their duty to enforce throughout their respective jurisdictions. In discussing the place of the states in the Federal Union, the obligation of the states to observe and enforce those portions of the Federal Constitution which are applicable to them was noted. While the observance of these clauses constitutes a primary responsibility, the clauses are not numerous and do not require the consideration of state officers as frequently as do the provisions of the state constitutions. Just as the Federal Constitution is of paramount importance to the Federal government, its officers and agencies, so the state constitutions are paramount for the officers and agencies of the state governments except in that relatively small number of cases where provisions of the Federal Constitution apply.

In similar fashion, the states provide a fundamental law for their municipalities in the form of charters issued to or framed by them individually, the provisions of these charters being supplemented by a body of municipal law applicable to all cities or to those in a given class throughout the state. A similar practice has been adopted in some states with regard to counties, townships, boroughs, and other local subdivisions.

Next in the legal system of a state comes the great body of common law, the statutory enactments, and the decisions of the courts. The significance and importance of each of these elements will be discussed in later sections of this chapter. The origin and development of the common law and of equity and the place of each in the legal system will be considered, as will also statutory law, which includes the body of public law providing for the organization and outlining the powers and duties of the various agencies of state government and the subdivisions thereof; the great mass of private law, which governs the ordinary, everyday relationships of individuals; the criminal law, which defines the different types of offenses against the state and provides for the punishment of offenders; and finally, such law as the state has developed with regard to military affairs. The chapter ends with a discussion of the nature of the judicial process, and of the doctrine of judicial review.

The Common Law

The Supreme Court has on several occasions put the question: "What is the common law?" The answer has uniformly been in words quoted from Kent's *Commentaries:* "The common law includes those principles and security of persons and property, which do not rest for their authority upon any express and positive declaration of the will of the legislature." Others have defined the term as that body of common or customary law developed in England down to the date of the settlement at Jamestown, the date of the American independence, or some other date arbitrarily fixed, and since that time in each of the American states.[1] Developed on English soil and inherited by the American colonies, the common law forms the basis of the legal institutions of all the states except Louisiana, whose legal system was based originally upon the Napoleonic Code. Even in this instance the law of the state has been deeply influenced by the common law tradition of the surrounding states.

Before considering the development of the common law in England and America, it may be well briefly to note what is meant by saying that the system of law in the states is based upon the common law. This system has some important characteristics that distinguish it from the Roman law, the only other legal system widely used in the western world. The principles of the common law govern the procedure of the courts, which function with a single judge in a trial court; guarantee to the individual the right to indictment by a grand jury in criminal cases, the right of complaint in civil cases, and the right of trial by jury; assure him that he has the presumption of innocence until proved guilty, in proceedings regularly conducted in open court; and provide access to equity procedures when necessary in order to obtain substantial justice.

Under the American system of court procedure the judge is the impartial arbiter between contending parties, while under the Roman law he represents the sovereignty of the state and actively conducts the trial. Likewise, under the Roman law, the defendant is not presumed to be either innocent or guilty. Roman law makes no provision for indictment as it is understood by English-speaking countries, nor for the use of equity procedures. Since juries are not used, cases are tried by the court, but the court consists, not of one judge, but of a number of judges sitting in banc.[2] This

[1] There is no uniformity on this matter; Virginia uses the first date, Florida and Georgia the second. New York uses April 1775. Nevertheless, the prevailing view in both East and West favors 1607. Lawyers well know that the question has practical aspects which cannot be ignored; see Pope, Herbert, "The English Common Law in the United States," *Harvard Law Review*, November 1910, pp. 6–30.

[2] On the relation of these two legal systems, see Buckland, W. W., and McNair, Arnold D., *Roman Law and Common Law* (Macmillan, New York, 1936); Radin, Max,

system is not without significance in the development of English law, since the Romans occupied England for a period of some 400 years; but considering the length of their occupation, the Roman system made remarkably little imprint on either the thinking or the legal practices of the British people.

In the United States, the courts originally held that the common law belonged to the states, and not to the Federal government. In 1842 Mr. Justice Story, in Swift v. Tyson,[3] enunciated the doctrine of a Federal common law in matters relating to commerce. This was extended to matters of general jurisdiction, but not to the field of crime. Consistently, the Federal courts took cognizance of, and usually abided by, the rules of the common law when they were applicable to the question before them. Then in 1938, after ninety-six years, the Court reversed the Swift case, in Erie Railroad v. Tompkins.[4]

History and Development in England. The origin of the rules of the common law is found in the customs and practices of the people of England in Anglo-Saxon times, the present rules having developed through succeeding generations of English and American life. It is easy to reconstruct in imagination something of the process by which these rules developed. They were observed by the people, not because observance was required by the king or by any powerful external force, but because the rules represented the conception of the common man as to what was fair and reasonable and just. The longer they were used, the more strongly were they able to enlist the support that comes from custom and tradition. To illustrate, let it be assumed that in the early days, while civilization was still in a crude and rudimentary state of development, a dispute arose between two neighbors over the ownership of some cattle or over the point at which the line should be drawn separating their respective properties. A few generations earlier such a dispute would have been proper justification for a trial of physical strength, but civilization had now developed to such an extent that the parties to this dispute were willing to have it settled by counting heads, rather than by

---

Roman Law (West Publishing Company, St. Paul, 1927); Dorsey, Roscoe J. C., "Roman Sources of Some English Principles of Equity and Common Law Rules," *American Law School Review*, May 1938, pp. 1233–1243; Kirchberger, Hans, "The Significance of Roman Law for the Americas and Its Importance to Inter-American Relations," *Wisconsin Law Review*, July 1944, pp. 249–273; and Schiller, A. Arthur, "Roman Interpretation and Anglo-American Interpretation and Construction," *Virginia Law Review*, April 1941, pp. 733–768.

[3] 16 Peters 1, 1842; see Waterman, J. S., "The Nationalism of Swift v. Tyson," *North Carolina Law Review*, February 1933, pp. 125–139.

[4] 304 U.S. 64, 1938; this decision brought forth numerous comments, such as: Cushman, Robert E., in *American Political Science Review*, April 1939, pp. 246–248; and other articles cited in previous editions of this volume. For the most recent discussion, see Wendell, Mitchell, *Relations Between Federal and State Courts* (Columbia University Press, 1949); Broh-Kahn, Lawrence E., "Uniformity Run Riot — Extension of the Erie Case," *Kentucky Law Journal*, January 1943, pp. 99–121; Farinholt, L. W., Jr., "Angel v. Bullington: Twilight of Diversity Jurisdiction?" *North Carolina Law Review*, December 1947, pp. 29–50; Frierson, William L., "A Revolutionary Decision — Erie v. Tompkins," *George Washington Law Review*, June 1940, pp. 1221–1229.

breaking them. Courts, as now conceived, were still in a primitive stage of development. Since the parties were unable to agree upon a solution of their problem, they resolved to take the case to one of the numerous courts for settlement. Here the facts and the arguments on both sides were heard, and decision rendered in favor of some particular solution. The parties accepted the decision, which thus became an influence in the future development of the common law.[5]

Let it be further assumed that some years later a similar dispute developed between other inhabitants of the same community. They likewise resolved to have their difficulty settled by one of the numerous local courts. Someone present remembered the earlier case, and observed that the rule there adopted seemed applicable to the case at hand. This point of view was accepted, and the rule became still more deeply entrenched in the life and practice of the people. It may be imagined that instances of this sort occurred at various times over a period of many years with regard to most of the important subjects coming within the range of the common law, in communities scattered all over England. By this process individual rules of law developed in separate communities over hundreds of years. As the process continued without the intervention of any unifying force, it is easy to understand the diversity which developed in the common law rules covering essential subjects, and to appreciate the need for some systematizing and unifying force.

This force was supplied over a period of years by a group of great writers including Coke, Bracton, Glanville, Blackstone, and others, who undertook the tremendous task of surveying the practices which had developed in England in the handling of various legal subjects, and of writing comments in which they pointed out prevailing tendencies. This work has been, down to the present day, an invaluable source of information to lawyers and laymen alike, interested in the history and development of the common law. "This unwritten or Common Law," wrote Blackstone, "is properly distinguishable into three kinds: (1) General customs, which are the universal rule of the whole Kingdom, and form the Common Law, in its stricter and more usual signification. (2) Particular customs, which for the most part affect only the inhabitants of particular districts. (3) Certain particular laws, which by custom are adopted and used by some particular courts of pretty general and extensive jurisdiction."[6] Blackstone, whose influence in America was the greatest, was accorded little recognition in

[5] Holdsworth, W. S., in *A History of English Law*, Vol. I (Methuen, London, 1921), discusses at length the practice in the communal courts, county courts, and other types of courts. Many different types existed side by side without any system or organization; as a matter of fact, it took nearly 400 years to bring all these together into an organized judicial system. At one time all citizens were obliged to attend these numerous courts — a duty which became very burdensome.

[6] Blackstone, William, *Commentaries*, pp. 67–68; on the subject of these paragraphs, see Plucknett, Theodore F. T., *A Concise History of the Common Law* (Lawyers Coöperative Publishing Company, Rochester, 1929).

England, where his work was regarded as elementary; it has seldom been cited by an English court.

It is exceedingly difficult to give in brief space any adequate idea of the influences and agencies that contributed to the development of the common law. Plucknett takes more than 400 pages for his *Concise History;* under the general heading of the Crown and the State, he deals successively with the various periods of English history during which significant developments in the common law took place. These begin with the Anglo-Saxon period, with its emphasis on race and religion, and end with the eighteenth century and the Industrial Revolution, with such intervening topics as the period from the Conquest to Henry II, which included the beginnings of administration; the period of the Great Charters, during which law was separated from administration; the period extending from Edward I to Richard II, marked by the development of statutes and the conduct of a social revolution; the fifteenth century, with its problems of law enforcement; the Tudor period, including the Renaissance and the Reformation; and the Stuart period, with the struggle for the supremacy of law.

When the development of the common law began, such law as there was, was purely local in character and the system was dominated by the church. With the passage of centuries all this was changed. The numerous types of local courts — communal, seignioral, manorial, central, et cetera — were slowly and gradually replaced by the courts of the Crown. Meantime the jury system developed, as did the profession and literature of the law. External forces made their significant contributions to the development of the system — the civil law of Rome, the canon law of the church, the law merchant, and the system of equity. Progress was made, because of the flexibility of custom, and through the development of forms of action and of legislation and the establishment of the principle of precedent in matters of interpretation. One might also undertake the study of the history of the common law from the point of view of the development of the legal status of real property or of contractual relations. In the first instance, he would be concerned with such matters as the feudal system, the development of inheritance, fee simple, and the rise of entail, common law estates, uses and trusts, conveyances, et cetera.

Development in America. The majority of the American colonies were either predominantly English at the time of their establishment, or came subsequently under the influence and control of the English. The practice with regard to social institutions — legal and otherwise — was precisely in accordance with the practice of other great colonizing powers before and since. Colonists brought with them and established in the colonies here, in modified form, the system of the common law under which they had been born and under which a majority of them had lived before their departure for America. Here the development of the rules of the common law continued under new circumstances and under conditions heretofore unknown.

Pound has admirably summarized this development in the following paragraph:

> Legal theory has it that the colonists brought the common law of England with them to America. But for a long time the colonists had no need of so advanced and technical a body of precepts as the seventeenth century English law. It was not until the eighteenth century that there was a need for courts manned by lawyers and for trained lawyers to advise litigants and assist the courts. Before the American Revolution two circumstances made for a reception of the English common law in the colonies. One was economic. Expanding commerce, acquisition of wealth and the rise of a more complex social structure called for tribunals of another type from those which sufficed for the beginnings of the colonies. About 1700 colonial legislation began definitely to run an independent course, but economic growth became too rapid for legislation to meet its demands. The other circumstance was political. The conditions which later led to the Revolution caused the colonists to insist on the common law as a birthright, protecting them against the Crown, the royal governors and even Parliament. . . .The very events which were separating them from England politically tended to make for a reception of the common law.[7]

For a considerable time after the Revolution a number of causes operated to hold back an immediate and complete acceptance of the English law; chief among these was the suspicion, even the hostility, with which for a time all things English were regarded. Ohio, for instance, had on its statute books for many years an enactment which prohibited the citation of English cases in its courts.[8] Even more important was the religious influence; the Scriptures were regarded from an early date as a subsidiary law, especially in New England. As time passed, many colonists were quite unfamiliar with the common law. There were no persons trained in the law; the judges were no exception. The proceedings of all of the colonial courts were popular and informal. In many colonies evidence was taken in writing — a practice utterly abhorrent to common law actions, but not to minds to which the evidence was the most important part of the case.[9]

Pound observes that Kent's *Commentaries* (1826–1830) "and above all, the writings of Story between 1832 and 1845 started a current of law writing on the basis of English legal institutions which insured that the common law should be the basis of the law in all but one of the United States." This development has continued without interruption down to the present time. However, just as, before the work of Blackstone, the common law developed in England independently in a large number of communities without any coordinating or unifying force, so in the United States the

[7] Pound, Roscoe, on the Common Law, in *Encyclopaedia of the Social Sciences*, Vol. IV, p. 52 (Macmillan, New York, 1931–1935); see also his *The Spirit of the Common Law* (Marshall Jones, Boston, 1921).

[8] Long before the Revolution some of the colonies declared the common law of England subsidiary in cases not controlled by colonial legislation; this was true in Maryland, Virginia, and the Carolinas (American Law Schools Association, *Select Essays in Anglo-American Legal History*, Vol. I, p. 410. Boston, 1907).

[9] *Ibid.*

same situation has existed within these forty-seven states. This fact became a matter of concern to an increasing number of people interested in the growth of our legal institutions. The work undertaken by the American Law Institute in 1925, and in progress since, will very likely prove to have supplied, for the clarification of the rules of the common law among the states, the same kind of influence that Blackstone supplied centuries ago with regard to the rules of the common law as developed in England up to that time.

Besides the restatements of the common law, the Institute has undertaken the formulation of the *Model Code of Criminal Procedure*, published in 1930. Because of widespread interest this Code has already had a significant influence on the laws of the states. This effort has been extended to include a restatement of the whole substantive criminal law. A *Model Code of Evidence*, as well as other work in the field of criminal justice, has been completed. There has been no more important or helpful influence in American law than that of this Institute.[10]

Relation of the Common Law and the Statutes. When there is no statute applicable to determine the merits of a controversy between adverse parties, the common law still affords in the American states a rule and a guide. It covers the whole range of law not included in the constitutions and statutes. The term "common law" in this country is understood to mean the unwritten law of England so far as it is not inconsistent with the constitutions and statutes; it consists of broad and comprehensive principles inspired by reason and a sense of justice and receives its binding force from common consent and immemorial usage "whence the mind of man runneth not to the contrary." Therefore it may be said to have its beginning in so remote an antiquity that its source cannot be exactly traced. It is the product of evolution and not legislation, but those who presided as judges in the remote past and who rendered judicial decisions assumed there was a law not made by legislatures and that it was part of the life and custom of the people.[11]

A statute, on the other hand, is a formal utterance of a legislative body — an enactment in accordance with the terms of the constitution. In this discussion it remains to note the relationship between the common law and the growing body of statutory law. In the early days, when relations between individuals were less complicated than they are today and when life itself was simple, practically all these relationships were governed by rules of the common law. With the passage of centuries, during which have occurred tremendous developments in the field of natural science, resulting in equally significant changes in the field of human relations, it has been necessary with increasing frequency to supplement or to modify the rules of the common law. This has been done by statute, as in the law governing the rights of

[10] For a fuller discussion of the work of the Institute, see *The Restatement in the Courts*, Fourth Edition (American Law Institute Publishers, St. Paul, 1945), and the reports of the annual meeting in the *American Bar Association Journal*.

[11] Follows statement of Dean Robert E. Lee, Wake Forest University School of Law.

injured employees, in which the three time-honored defenses of the employer under the common law have been abolished and an intricate set of workmen's compensation statutes substituted therefor. Similarly, in most states married women have been permitted to contract and to hold property to the same extent as though unmarried — a thing which they were formerly unable to do.

In other cases the statutes have declared and put in more definite terms parts of the common law in order to establish more firmly the intent of the latter; this is known as codification. The Negotiable Instruments Act, for example, is largely a codification of the law on a subject that had for centuries been developing in the decisions of common law. Legislative bodies have the power to pass statutes modifying or suspending the common law, but until they do so, the principles of the common law as defined by the courts are as binding upon the citizens of a state as though passed by a legislative body. So, in one field after another, either a statute has been enacted to cover a modern situation to which the rules of the common law do not apply, or the common law rule has been modified when that rule seemed no longer applicable to the changed conditions of modern life. The common law must therefore be regarded more and more as a foundation upon which our legal system has been built, and less and less as a body of rules suitable for the regulation of present-day problems. Americans find themselves governed more and more by legislative enactments.

The Important Writs. One writer has observed that in its widest aspect a writ is a written command in the name of the sovereign, addressed to an official or more rarely a private person, often but not always relating to the administration of justice. It is also said that the regular use of writs implies a centralized government which by this means keeps close control over a large number of distant agents. As soon as it became apparent that most forms of writ could be constantly repeated in similar circumstances in accordance with a regular routine, the regular administration of justice was simplified. The writs which have survived under the influence of the common law include: (1) the original prerogative writs, which are in very general use; (2) certain judicial writs, especially writs of execution; and (3) some of the old administrative writs.[12] No attempt will be made here to describe in detail the enormous number of different types of writs used in the ordinary course of legal proceedings. There are, however, a number of these writs some knowledge of which is important to the student of government, since they relate not only to technical matters in the law but to problems which frequently arise in the conduct of government. Habeas corpus, mandamus, injunction, quo warranto, error, certiorari, procedendo, prohibition, and summons will be discussed here.

Most important is the writ of habeas corpus — a writ named from the

[12] See Plucknett, Theodore F. T., on Writs, *Encyclopaedia of the Social Sciences*, Vol. XV, pp. 503–504.

Latin phrase which means "you may have the body." This writ has for its object the bringing of a party before a court or a judge, especially to inquire into the cause of the person's detention by another, with a view to the protection of the right of personal liberty. William F. Willoughby says concerning this important writ[13]:

> A power of the court which is of special importance is that of compelling the production in court of anyone under arrest, or deprived of his liberty through imprisonment, confinement in an institution for the insane, or in any other way, for the purpose of determining whether he is legally held. This power is exercised through what is known as a "writ of habeas corpus," which is an order addressed by the court to the officer or other person having custody of the person confined, directing him to produce such person in court and to show cause why he should not be given his liberty. It need hardly be said that the power to issue and enforce such writs constitutes one of the greatest guarantees of individual liberty to be found in our political system.

The writ of mandamus is an order issued by a court commanding an officer, a corporation, or a court to perform some legal, ministerial duty, or a duty not involving discretion. Most familiar, perhaps, is the attempt made in the famous case of Marbury v. Madison to get the Supreme Court of the United States to issue such a writ commanding Madison, the new Secretary of State, to deliver a commission to Marbury, as a judge in a court in the District of Columbia. A decision of the same court in 1931 stresses the fact that the writ will issue only where the duty to be performed is ministerial and the obligation to act peremptory and plainly defined.[14] In the case of United States v. Wilbur, Secretary of the Interior, the Secretary had refused to lease certain lands to the plaintiff, although an act of Congress gave him power to grant prospecting permits under such necessary rules as he might prescribe, and to lease lands upon the establishment of satisfactory proof of the discovery of valuable oil and gas deposits. Under the terms of the act it was compulsory for him to issue such leases; the plaintiff therefore had a proper case for the issuance of a writ of mandamus. The Supreme Court rendered judgment in favor of the Secretary of the Interior, holding that the duty to grant permits and issue leases was entirely discretionary. In the course of the opinion the following significant statement occurs:

> Under established rules, the writ of mandamus cannot be made to serve the purpose of an ordinary suit. It will issue only where the duty to be performed is ministerial and the obligation to act peremptory and plainly defined. The law must not only authorize the demanded action, but must require it; the duty must be clear and indisputable.

A writ of injunction is a writ or process granted by a court of equity, and in some cases, under statute, by a court of law, whereby a party is required to do or to refrain from doing certain acts, according to the exigency of the writ. While a writ of mandamus is a positive writ, a writ of injunction

[13] *Principles of Judicial Administration*, p. 225 (Brookings Institution, Washington, 1929).

[14] United States ex rel. McLennan v. Wilbur, Secretary of the Interior, 283 U.S. 414, 1931. The citation of Marbury v. Madison is 1 Cranch 137, 1803.

is more often negative in character, being used as a preventive rather than as a restorative process, although it is by no means confined to this use. In those cases where the writ of injunction is positive, it is known as a mandatory injunction; where it is negative, it is called a prohibitory injunction. The writ of injunction has been used most frequently in connection with labor disputes, for the purpose of protecting property of the employer subject to possible damage at the hands of the strikers. There has, in fact, been much criticism of "government by injunction" — of the readiness with which many judges have issued such injunctions before any damage occurred, and sometimes when none was contemplated.

A writ of quo warranto was originally, in the English common law, a writ brought before the proper tribunal to inquire by what warrant a person or a corporation acted, or exercised certain powers. It is still used in that sense in the states today to test the validity of incorporations, but it is more commonly used in connection with contested elections. In such cases the contestant brings suit against the one who has been declared to have received the majority of the votes, before a final settlement of the contest, demanding that he show by what warrant he occupies the office, exercising the powers and performing the duties thereof.

The writ of error was originally the only means of reviewing decisions of law made by the central courts, but it was useful only for reversing errors on the record of the court below; this tended to make many material matters not reversible because they did not, in fact, appear in the record. In present-day practice the writ of error has been defined as an original writ, which lies after judgment in an action at law, in a court of record, to correct some alleged error in the proceedings or in the judgment of the court. The mistake may relate to matters of law or of fact. It has come to be a common method of appeal from a court of original jurisdiction to a higher court.

There are many other types of writs in common use. A writ of certiorari is a court order addressed to a public officer or inferior judicial tribunal, directing that he or it send up the papers or record in a specified case so that the court may take action in respect to it, or review the action already taken. A writ of procedendo may be used to secure an effect contrary to that of a writ of certiorari; it is defined as a writ by which a cause which has been removed on insufficient grounds from an inferior to a superior court by certiorari, or otherwise, may be sent down again to the same court. A writ of prohibition may be issued by a superior court to an inferior one, prohibiting the latter from proceeding; it is generally issued to protect the jurisdiction of the higher court. Certain other writs are employed in the effort of the creditor to get possession of property to which he has some claim.

A writ of execution is an order to the sheriff to seize and sell the property of the defendant for the satisfaction of a judgment, while a writ of ejectment orders the same officer, forcibly if necessary, to eject the defendant from the real estate which he holds, but which the court finds should belong to the complainant. It thus becomes actually a means of trying the title to real estate. The writ of summons has been defined as a warning to appear in court at a specified time for the purpose of answering the plaintiff appearing as a witness. It is a written notification signed by the proper officer, and is commonly served in person. Many other writs might be added to this list; it has not been intended here to attempt anything like a complete description of the various kinds of writs or orders that may be issued by courts. The aim has been merely to make clear the power of courts, by this means, to enforce the law and their decisions.

Equity

In order to understand the growth of our legal institutions, it is necessary to know something of the nature of equity, although this type of procedure is used less and less in the settlement of disputes. The term "equity" has two meanings, one professional, the other popular. When lawyers speak of equity they are thinking of that part of the law of England which is derived not from the custom of the realm nor the enactments of Parliament but from the decisions of the old courts of chancery. In this sense, equity may be defined as a system of rules originated by the King's Chancellor and the Court of Chancery to supplement the English common law, which had very early become too rigid. On the other hand, when the man in the street talks of equity, he is thinking of local justice which is not regulated by the law and may even be contrary to it. The popular meaning of equity is that which it originally bore in the Court of Chancery.[15]

> *History and Development.* In early times the administration of the law was not altogether free from abuses of the grossest kind. The king's officers were sometimes corrupt or partial, and for a considerable period the king's courts stood in awe of unscrupulous and powerful nobles. In extreme cases the poor subject had to seek redress of his wrongs by petition to the king, who, in theory, was the ultimate fountain of justice. Originally, these petitions were heard by the sovereign himself; later, however, they were referred to the king's council. The foremost figure in this body was the chancellor. This official was the secretary to the king, head of the king's chaplains, and keeper of the royal seal. In the early days the office was always in the hands of an ecclesiastic, because of the literary qualifications demanded. In time he became the chief law member of the council as well as the most powerful executive officer of state next to the king. He was learned in the canon and moral law. He has commonly been spoken of as the "keeper of the king's conscience." It was, therefore, an easy development that after the middle of the fourteenth century all "matters of grace" were addressed directly to the chancellor; and in no long time this practice led to the establishment of a new tribunal in England which received the name of Court of Chancery.

[15] Lee, Robert E., *Introduction to the Study of Law* (Mimeographed, 1935). On these points, see Plucknett, *Concise History*, Part III, Chapter 4; Cook, Walter W., *Encyclopaedia of the Social Sciences*, Vol. V, pp. 582–588. The following quotation is from Lee's *Introduction to the Study of Law.*

By gradual stages there grew up a jurisdiction in chancery to grant relief in situations where the application to particular cases of rigid and general legal rules resulted in hardship or injustice. The rules applied by chancery in the exercise of this jurisdiction became known as "equity," whereas those administered by the previously established courts were designated as "common law." Three circumstances concurred to increase the jurisdiction of the chancery courts: first, the tendency of the common law rules to hardness and rigidity by reason of the deference paid to precedents; secondly, the refusal of the common law to adopt that part of the Roman law which may be called equitable, as distinguished from that which is merely *stricti juris;* and, finally, the desire to increase the dignity and importance of the office of chancellor.

For generations equity consisted of whatever the chancellor thought best in any particular case. No attention was paid to precedent or to principle; even in the time of the Stuarts, nobody thought a knowledge of law necessary for a chancellor. Sir Thomas More was the first professional lawyer chancellor. His successors were sometimes lawyers, sometimes priests, and sometimes laymen. A change, however, was impending. Young practitioners in the chancery had begun to report the court's decisions. As soon as this took place the old practitioners began to cite to the chancellor all the decisions of previous chancellors which favored the decision they desired. When the facts were identical, the chancellor felt bound, as a rule, to follow the decisions of his predecessors. As lawyers became the only chancellors, the practice grew. Soon equity hardened into a set of principles as unalterable by subsequent decision as those of the common law.

Many rights not recognized in the common law were created and enforced in equity. For example, no right existed in the common law by which a defective instrument could be reformed, a fraudulent conveyance set aside, a mistake or accident effectually relieved against, or a contract could be specifically enforced. Thus, equity became an important liberalizing agency in our legal system. Some of the things equity has jurisdiction over are: accident, mistake, fraud, mortgages, trusts, assignments, receiverships, specific performance, and injunctions. These doctrines can be better understood by considering them in connection with the various topics which form the subject matter of a law course.

For centuries law and equity were administered in England by two separate and distinct sets of courts, each applying exclusively its own system of jurisprudence, and following its own system of procedure. This dual system was abolished by the Judicature Act of 1873. By this statute the courts which had sat so many centuries at Westminster Hall were consolidated into one supreme court of which chancery became simply a division, and it was provided in substance that equitable relief should in a proper case be administered concurrently with law in each division and that in case of conflict the principles of equity should prevail over those of the common law.

Another writer, Plucknett, comments as follows on the variety of theories that have been proposed to account for the origins of Chancery jurisdiction; the result of the most recent research, he says, has been to establish an old theory first put forward by Palgrave[16]:

According to this view the Chancellor's jurisdiction was not by virtue of

[16] Palgrave, Sir Francis, *Original Authority of the King's Council* (London, 1834); Baldwin, James F., *The King's Council*, pp. 236–261 (London, 1913). Quotation from Plucknett, *op. cit.*, pp. 138–139.

his office; still less had it anything to do with his supposed position of keeper of the King's conscience. At a later date, it is true, Chancery became a court of conscience, with a jurisprudence deliberately based upon this idea, but this was a later development, and will not account for the earliest period of Chancery history. It now seems clear that the Chancellor's position was originally that of a delegate of the Council. Overburdened with work of every description, the Council delegated particular matters to the Chancellor, who of all the officials was the one who was most constantly in attendance. Another advantage of this arrangement was that the Chancellor already had a well organized staff, and for a long time had exercised the power of issuing writs, both judicial and administrative, to all the King's officials, central and local. The Chancellor, therefore, commanded the machinery which sooner or later would have to be set in motion in order to give redress to the petitioners, and so nothing could be simpler than for the Council to transmit the petitions addressed to it to the Chancellor, sometimes (but not always) endorsing them with a brief instruction what to do.

It is obvious that two competing legal systems could not long endure in a well-ordered country. After years of struggle it was finally possible to work out a solution; in one sense, equity lost a great deal, while in another it gained, as it has continued to do down to the present day. It lost in the sense that its identity as a separate judicial system declined from that date on. Where there had been, originally, separate judges for the courts at law and the courts in equity, it became customary to choose judges who would at different times consider cases under both sets of rules. The extent of this development is well stated, so far as this country is concerned, by Dean Lee:

> In the United States, courts of equity fall into three distinct classes: (1) In Alabama, Arkansas, Delaware, Mississippi, Tennessee, and Vermont there are still separate courts of common law and of equity with separate rules of procedure. (2) In the Federal courts and in Florida, Illinois, Maine, Maryland, Massachusetts, Michigan, New Hampshire, Oregon, Pennsylvania, Rhode Island, Virginia, and West Virginia the same court administers both common law and equity, but the procedure is kept distinct. (3) In all the states which have not been mentioned, common law and equity are administered by the same court under the same system of procedure. Changes made from time to time in certain jurisdictions from one system of administration to another, and minor departures from the typical systems, render any such classification as this often misleading. Each jurisdiction presents its own peculiar history.[17]

It is evident therefore that separate courts of equity have disappeared from many jurisdictions; on the other hand, the influence of the principles of equity has, in the opinion of competent lawyers, steadily increased, until today they are being applied more and more in the settlement of cases coming before the courts of law.

Distinction between Law and Equity. It thus becomes important to know something of the nature of equity jurisdiction, and some of the more im-

[17] Lee, *op. cit.* See also 21 *Corpus Juris* 24; Bispham, George T., *Principles of Equity*, p. 27 (Bankers Law Publishing Company, New York, 1926); and Emmerglick, Leonard J., "The Legal Adoption of Equitable Principles," *New Jersey Law Review*, January 1936, pp. 53–63.

portant characteristics which distinguish it from law. Since it was, and is, the primary objective of equity to right a wrong, to achieve substantial justice, it was always said that it was necessary for the parties to an equity proceeding to come into the court "with clean hands." In another form: "He who seeks equity must do equity." It is essential in all legal proceedings that the parties thereto shall tell the truth, but the very nature of equity proceedings makes it essential that they do more than that. In the conduct of equity proceedings there is no jury, since there is no oral argument; all evidence and arguments are submitted to the court in the form of briefs. Since there is no jury, the judge decides the case.

Still another difference between the two systems is to be found in the outcome of the proceedings. Suits at law terminate in judgments, while suits in equity result in decrees which may be positive demands to do or to refrain from doing certain things. Thus in a business relationship in which one of the parties to a contract has failed to do as he agreed, the injured party may in some instances either bring suit for damages, which is an action at law, or he may institute an equity proceeding. In the first instance, the amount of damages requested will represent his estimate of the loss he has suffered through the failure of the defendant to perform under the contract as he agreed. If the suit is successful, he may get the judgment which states that he is entitled to collect a specified amount. The remedy is uncertain because the defendant may not have the amount specified, or may by some means succeed in evading payment. In the equity proceedings, on the other hand, the injured party may, if successful, secure a court decree calling for specific performance under the terms of the original contract. The violation of such a decree constitutes contempt of court and is punishable by fine or imprisonment. The selection of the method by which redress will be sought in any given case will depend upon the nature of the case, and upon the advice of the plaintiff's attorney.

Civil Law

Civil law is a term used technically to designate the Roman jurisprudence; in another and more common sense, it is applied to that portion of the great body of municipal law which is enforced by the ordinary civil courts and which governs the great bulk of the relationships of one individual with another. In this sense it is to be distinguished from criminal law on the one hand and military law on the other. It applies to persons and to property. The body of civil law in force in the states today is based upon the heritage of the common law, supplemented by the enactments of the British Parliament prior to 1607, 1776, or some other specified date, and by the enactments of the legislatures of the states in the years subsequent to that time. The percentage of the total volume of law represented by the statutes was, until recently, very small. As the nature of the American civilization has changed, it has been necessary to modify more and more rules of the common law through the enactment of statutes, which thereafter served as a substitute for the original rules handed down through generations and often through centuries.

The term "civil law" has been used in various ways; generally, it designates all the rules of law governing the members of a given political state. In this sense, it governs the relations of men in civil society and becomes practically synonymous with the concept of law itself. In the Middle Ages the term came to mean to Europeans private law — that is, the law governing the ordinary relations of private individuals. Its origin and basis were fundamentally Roman, but it came to include many other elements, derived from the canon law, Teutonic laws, and feudal laws. The term also has common law as well as statutory phases, but to the common law lawyer it means simply the Romanized system of Continental law in contradistinction to the system of common law which developed in England. He rarely uses the term "civil law" in the sense of private law.[18]

Public Law and Private Law. A clear distinction must be drawn between public law and private law; this dualistic division is a historical product of a definite state of sociological development. The degree and scope of this technical differentiation is determined according to the unlimited discretion and the usage of the society concerned. In general, a law which applies to a class of persons, and not to individuals as such, or which, though for the benefit of individuals, includes provisions of general legislation, is a public law. On the other hand, a law for the relief of one or several specified persons, corporations, or institutions is known as a private law. It is limited in its application and its benefits, whereas a public law relates to public matters and deals with individuals by classes only. In the past, the legislatures have often passed excessive amounts of private legislation; lately there has been a tendency to discourage this method of handling such problems, and to substitute therefor statutes of general application.

This important distinction is but one of many that have developed in our legal system. The modern legal orders, as they are called, have become divided, in the course of their historical development, into various legal branches which are determined by the character of their social functions. Constitutional law, administrative law, and criminal and canon law have long been regarded as branches of public law, while civil law and commercial law are regarded as private. Certain other branches, such as labor law and social law, have not been so definitely classified. The law of procedure has come to be regarded as public, as has also international law. Many of these classifications hold only within a given legal system, and even there they may be subject to modification with the change of time and circumstances.[19]

[18] Based on Declareuil, J., *Encyclopaedia of the Social Sciences*, Vol. III, pp. 502–508.

[19] Based on Walz, Gustav A., *Encyclopaedia of the Social Sciences*, Vol. XII, pp. 657–659.

Substantive and Adjective Law. Another important distinction in the field of civil law involves the differences between substantive and adjective law. The former has been defined as including those rules which give recognition to rights and duties, which rules are the very foundation and substance of the law. These are static, immobile, and lifeless until set in motion by generic remedial rules embodied in adjective law. Substantive law includes all statutes of a generic nature, i.e., all except those regulating administrative and court procedure, as well as the greater part of case law — all except those decisions interpreting administrative regulations, codes of procedure, and court rules. Adjective law includes those rules which provide remedies for infringement of rights and failure to perform duties. While there is no clear line of division between the two, the one creates rights and obligations, while the other provides a method of enforcing and protecting them. In other words, adjective law is the law of procedure. Contracts, negotiable instruments, sales, bailments, partnerships, corporations, for example, are subjects dealt with in substantive law. Adjective law defines the nature and powers of judicial tribunals, and prescribes their methods and procedure.

Written and Unwritten Law. Statutes are frequently referred to as the "written law," in contradistinction to the common law, which is called the "unwritten law." In the beginning the decisions of the courts were not reduced to writing; hence they were called unwritten law to distinguish them from the acts of Parliament, which were always set down in writing. In course of time, these decisions were collected and published in book form, but this publication did not make the common law "written law." Being originally unwritten, it continued to be so regarded.[20]

Criminal Law

Since some state constitutions outlaw prosecution for crimes under the common law, those states have been obliged to enact and others have voluntarily enacted statutory definitions of the principal crimes. With the multiplicity of laws resulting therefrom, they have later been compelled to codify their criminal law. The statutory definitions in general follow those that have come down from the common law. These codes, in addition to defining criminal acts, make provision for the trial of those who are accused of committing the acts prohibited and, so far as possible, insure that the machinery for the conviction and punishment of violators moves swiftly and certainly. A criminal code under which criminals, after having served their sentences, are more detrimental to society than they were before they were sentenced is in serious need of overhauling. The codes in force in this country are perilously near the point where such a charge may be properly made. The prime consideration in such a code is the protection of society from the wrongful acts of individuals, rather than the reformation of the criminals; yet this latter consideration must ever be an important one.

[20] Lee, *op. cit.*

Definition of Offenses. The various types of offenses that are prohibited in a penal code may be classified in a number of ways. There are those acts which are regarded by common consent as being wrong in and of themselves: these are technically described as *malum in se*. Other acts, not necessarily coming within this group, are regarded as being contrary to public policy or otherwise undesirable; these are commonly known as *malum prohibitum*. All the more serious offenses against persons and property come within the first group.

The various types of criminal offenses are classified according to their seriousness as treason, felonies, and misdemeanors. Treason, which is the only crime defined in the Federal Constitution, is declared to consist in levying war against the United States, or adhering to their enemies, giving them aid and comfort. The same definition appears in the constitutions of many states; the crime is everywhere regarded as a fundamental attack upon the existence of the state itself, and it is for this reason that it is put in a separate category. The death penalty is provided for treason in Michigan; the same is true in other states. The famous case of John Brown at Harper's Ferry, Virginia, is perhaps the only case on record in which the extreme penalty has been inflicted for treason against a state.

A felony at common law has been defined as "any crime which occasioned a forfeiture of lands and goods, and to which might be superadded capital or other punishment." Forfeiture of lands and goods as a punishment for crime has been abolished in both England and the United States, so that the term no longer has its original meaning. "Today the term has no very definite or precise meaning, except in those states where it is defined by statute. Under these statutes, a felony is any crime punishable by death or imprisonment in a state prison. Some thirty odd states have this statutory definition of felony." [21] The crimes of murder, manslaughter, arson, burglary, larceny, and robbery are commonly classified as felonies, while the following were misdemeanors under the English common law: conspiracy, assault and battery, false imprisonment, common nuisance, forgery and uttering, breach of the peace, unlawful assembly and riot, and libel. All these crimes are subject to severe punishment. In some states some of them have been classified as felonies, and in all states additional offenses have been added to the lists of both felonies and misdemeanors. The legal classification of these offenses is not particularly important, however, since some misdemeanors carry a heavier penalty than some felonies.

From another point of view, the various offenses prohibited by law may be classified as offenses against persons, offenses against property, and offenses against public order. The following classification is a combination of several lists [22]:

[21] 16 *Corpus Juris* 55, and Wharton's *Criminal Law*, 3 vols., Twelfth Edition (Baker, Voorhis, New York, 1932).

[22] Judicial Council of Massachusetts, *Sixth Report*, last page (Public Document No.

CLASSIFICATION OF CRIMINAL OFFENSES

A. *Offenses against the person*

1. Assault
2. Duels
3. Felonious assault
4. Homicide
5. Kidnapping
6. Libel
7. Maiming
8. Manslaughter
9. Murder
10. Rape
11. Robbery
12. Suicide
13. Other offenses against the person

B. *Offenses against property*

14. Arson
15. Breaking and entering
16. Burglary
17. Destruction of ships and vessels
18. Destruction of insured property
19. Extortion
20. False personation
21. Forgery
22. Frauds in selling tickets
23. Frauds in documents of title
24. Insolvency of individuals
25. Insolvency of corporations and other frauds of management
26. Larceny, embezzlement
27. Larceny of automobile
28. Malicious mischief
29. Receiving stolen goods
30. Trespass
31. Weights and measures
32. Other offenses against property

C. *Offenses against public order*

33. Perjury
34. Forgery
35. Carrying weapons
36. Sex offenses, except rape
37. Nonsupport
38. Violating drug laws
39. Violating liquor laws
40. Driving while intoxicated
41. Drunkenness
42. Disorderly conduct
43. Gambling
44. Violating Lord's Day
45. Violating food or health laws
46. Violating fish and game laws
47. Vagrancy
48. Violating traffic or motor vehicle laws
49. Violating municipal ordinances
50. Other offenses against public order

D. *Offenses against the state and its administration*

51. Treason
52. Anarchy and seditious utterances
53. Riots, unlawful assemblies and societies
54. Offenses against the flag
55. Offenses against the military establishment
56. Offenses against the electoral franchise
57. Offenses affecting the public officers and official duty

The general nature of most of these offenses is sufficiently well known so that extended discussion of any of them would seem, for the present purpose, to be unnecessary. Murder may be defined as the unlawful killing of a human being with malice aforethought. Since this is unlawful, it must be distinguished from executions ordered by the state. Because murders

144, Boston, 1930), and Commission on the Administration of Justice in New York State, *A Proposal for the Reclassification of Crimes*, p. 17 — Legislative Document (1934) No. 50 (R).

differ with regard to the degree of premeditation with which they are committed, most jurisdictions have established by law a distinction between first and second degree murder. In those states which still use capital punishment, this is usually the penalty for first degree murder[23]; the penalty for second degree murder is a long term of imprisonment, usually life. Murder must also be distinguished from homicide, which is a more general term applying to any killing of one human being by another. Homicide may be of three kinds: justifiable, when the killing is performed in the exercise of a right or the performance of a duty; excusable, as when done, not as a duty or a right, yet without culpable or criminal intent; and felonious, involving what the law terms malice. The latter may be either manslaughter or murder.

Manslaughter is sometimes defined as unlawful homicide; a distinction is made between voluntary and involuntary types. The former is intentional, committed in a sudden passion caused by adequate provocation, but without malice aforethought; the latter is applied to an unlawful killing, either in negligence or incidentally to the commission of an unlawful act, but without specific malice. The legal definition of rape is "sexual connection with a woman without her consent." An assault is an apparently violent attempt, or willful offer with force or violence, to do hurt to another; an attempt or offer to beat another, accompanied by a degree of violence, but without touching his person, as by lifting the fist or a cane in a threatening manner, or by striking at him and missing him. If the blow takes effect, it is battery. The distinction and the connection between assault and battery is well stated by one writer in the following words[24]:

> Assault is the threat of force or violence to do corporeal hurt to another. Battery is the unlawful touching of the person of another by the aggressor or by some substance put in motion by him. An assault may not result in battery, but every battery necessarily includes an assault. Thus, for example, to shoot or strike at another and to miss him is assault but not battery. To shoot or strike a person is assault and battery.

Of the offenses against property, arson is mentioned first. The definition of this crime, which at common law meant the willful and malicious burning of the dwelling house or outhouse of another, is varied by the statutes of different countries and states. The English law has been considerably modified in the United States; in some states it has been materially enlarged, while in others various degrees of arson have been established with corresponding punishment. Robbery is the felonious and forcible taking of goods or money

[23] The Legislative Reference Service, Library of Congress, checked the session laws of the states early in 1949 and found that capital punishment had been abolished in the following states: Maine, Michigan, Minnesota, North Dakota, Rhode Island, South Dakota, and Wisconsin. In certain instances four of these states allow capital punishment: Maine, for murder committed in prison; Michigan, for treason; North Dakota and Rhode Island, for murderous attacks on prison guards. In Washington, the jury decides as between life imprisonment and hanging.

[24] Kimball, Everett, *State and Municipal Government in the United States*, pp. 254–255 (Ginn, Boston, 1922).

from the person or presence of another by violence or putting in fear, while, at common law, burglary is the breaking and entering of the dwelling house of another at night with intent to commit a felony therein. Breaking and entering is itself an offense, defined as the removal or setting aside with violence and a felonious intent of any part of a house or of the fastenings provided to secure it. Larceny is the taking and carrying away of the *personal* property of another, with intent to steal; robbery is an aggravated form of larceny, but is treated as a distinctive crime. With the widespread use of the automobile, the offense of larceny of automobile has come to be classified separately. The receiving of stolen goods is an offense if the recipient knows the goods are stolen; the seriousness of this offense varies in the several states.

It is impossible to mention all the crimes against property or to consider any of them at length; a few more may, however, be noted. Malicious mischief is the term applied to wicked or malicious injury done to the property of another, while trespass is a tort or wrong committed against property by force. A tort is a civil wrong or an injury — a wrongful act — not involving a breach of contract, for which an action will lie. In some parts of the country it is a term applied to a form of action for a wrong or an injury. All in all, the offenses against public order are numerous; while many of these would be found in a list compiled for any one of the forty-eight states, there are numerous others which might be found in a few states but not in the rest.

Enforcement of Criminal Law. While the problem of enforcement is administrative, the quality of the enforcement work done affects not only the crime rate but, in time, the provisions of the law itself. The administering of punishment to those convicted of crime has through the years become more humane. In England at one time there were well over one hundred offenses for which the death penalty was inflicted; in the United States today, there are not over four types of crime for which this extreme penalty is commonly used — first degree murder, arson, burglary, and rape. For the last named, the death penalty is used chiefly in the Southern states. In Georgia, train robbery is so punished — probably as a result of public indignation at some particular offense. Horse stealing was generally a capital offense in the Western states at one time, and still is in some of them. As a result of the Lindbergh case, kidnapping was made a capital offense in a number of states. Some of the most important crimes in connection with which this punishment is used are not defined at all by statute in many states, the definitions of the common law still being relied upon.

On the other hand, there are now eight states in which capital punishment has been wholly or partially abolished. While not a punishment for a crime, imprisonment for debt was a common occurrence; this penalty, in many of the older states, was abolished nearly a century ago. The development of civilization has brought a gradual shift of emphasis in the administering of punishment from the old *lex talionis*, or law of retaliation, to the desire and effort to assist the offender to readjust himself and return to society as a law-abiding, self-supporting, and self-respecting member of the community. "Dean Pound has told how Sir Edward Coke, in the dawn of the seventeenth century, bewailing the savagery of the criminal law and procedure of his time, made an impassioned plea for a preventive instead of a punitive justice and invoked the blessing of God upon him 'that layeth the first stone of this building.' The first stone is being laid."[25]

It is not meant to imply that this change has become completely effective. There is a more or less constant conflict between those who are anxious to exact of every offender the full measure of punishment permitted under the law, and those who tend to support the more lenient views advocated by modern criminologists and sociologists. After World War I, when there developed the so-called "crime wave," New York answered with its famous Baumes Law, the principle of which was shortly adopted in a number of other states. This was popularly known as the fourth offenders law, and provided that those convicted a fourth time should be thereafter kept in prison. While there were certain elements of reasonableness about such a measure, its rigidity proved to be a serious obstacle to the fair treatment of some prisoners and their dependents. Its effects came to be generally regarded as unfortunate.

The function of the courts should be to determine the innocence or guilt of the accused; it is clear from modern criminology that members of the bench are seldom qualified by training or temperament to impose sentence. This should be done by trained technicians — psychologists, psychiatrists, and criminologists — after careful examination of the convict and study of his case record. The indeterminate sentence is preferred to the fixed sentence previously used. First offenders should be segregated and accorded a different treatment from that used in the case of hardened criminals. All persons under sentence should be under the supervision of persons with adequate technical training; parole should be more widely used in deserving cases, but with a larger staff of parole supervisors, adequate to give careful supervision to all parolees. These are only a few of the more important recommendations of this group; there is much justification for the belief that the essential facts in the treatment of prisoners are just now being discovered.

Students of criminology now believe that speedy apprehension, arrest, trial, and conviction of guilty persons have a much more important effect as a deterrent upon crime than the severity of the sentence. In the effort to improve the functioning of the machinery for the administration of justice, and thus make speedy convictions possible, many reforms are now under way in the various states. Among these are the movement to establish state bureaus of criminal identification; the influence of the United States Department of Justice in bringing about cooperation and coordination of the

[25] Kirchwey, George W., *Encyclopaedia of the Social Sciences*, Vol. IV, p. 578; see also Radin, Max, "Pretense and Reality in Our Criminal Law," *Oregon State Bar Bulletin*, June 1939, pp. 134–152.

police forces of the nation; the move to establish state departments of justice and improve and expedite judicial procedure.

Other Types of Law

A survey of the various types of law under which the people in our states live must cover not only the older forms of the common law and equity and the present-day distinctions between civil law and criminal law, but also certain miscellaneous forms of more limited application, so far as the states are concerned: international law and treaties; constitutional law, involving the Federal Constitution and the acts of Congress; and finally, martial law. In Chapter I, in a section devoted to the relations of the states with foreign nations, it was pointed out that the former are forbidden by the Federal Constitution to make treaties, and that such relations as they have with foreign powers are incidental and accidental — although they may be troublesome. Since this chapter is confined to the legal system of the states, there seems to be no good reason for going into the subject of international law, even though the activities of the Federal government in that field are a matter of vital concern to every citizen of every state.

Constitutional law is more relevant to the present discussion; yet even here the law of the Federal Constitution belongs primarily to the Federal government — not to the states. Certain aspects of the subject are discussed, however, in subsequent chapters, notably those dealing with constitutional protections and the police power. The constitutions of the states are dealt with at length in an earlier part of the book. With regard to American constitutional law in general, it may be said, as Ernst Freund has done, that it represents political action through judicial methods, dependent for success upon the ignoring, by common consent, of the political nature of the process." He continues:

> . . . To judge the performance of the courts by purely legal standards is to misjudge it. The uncertainty of standards, which is a legal defect, is the salvation of the doctrine of judicial power. How much the exercise of the power has added to the stability of American institutions must be a matter of speculation. It is not even possible to speak of its effect upon the sanctity of vested rights with any assurance. . . . A comparison between American and foreign legislation in this respect would yield no definite results. The American doctrine of freedom of contract does not impress foreigners as a gain to genuine liberty. . . .
>
> It is, on the other hand, a strong tribute to American constitutional law that it has been found possible to conduct government for a century and a half in war as well as in peace without recourse to "acts of state" or to emergency powers to suspend the constitution. While occasionally the judicial nullification of statutes has caused popular resentment, there has been substantial acquiescence in the exercise of the power and there is no disposition to doubt the soundness of the structure of which it is the corner stone.[26]

Martial Law. Martial law may, in emergency situations, become of importance in any state. Although variously defined, martial law is a legal

[26] Freund, Ernst, *Encyclopaedia of the Social Sciences*, Vol. IV, p. 254.

concept by which the Anglo-American civil courts have sought in times of disorder to define the limits of the executive in military control over citizens in domestic territory. It has been said that it is regarded as the substitution of the will of the executive or the military commander for the process of the courts. "Its justification is necessity and its existence is a question of fact, the most usual test of which is to determine whether or not the courts are open."[27] Thus, when disorder or violence occurs in a given state, the proclamation of martial law by the governor does not establish, but only proclaims, the fact of its existence. Such a proclamation means in theory that the disorder is such that no court can remain open. Practically everything that can be done under martial law can also be done by troops, in aid of the civil authorities.

Since the term "martial law" is not used except to describe the suspension of the ordinary protective maxims and the procedure of domestic courts, it is not difficult to make formal distinctions between it and such concepts as "the laws and customs of war" and "military law and military government." The laws and customs of war are the rules of international law, derived from usage and international agreements, while the latter is the law applied to troops in peace as well as in war. Military government is a descriptive term which applies to any form of government by an army, with or without the aid of civil authorities. Theoretically, says Thurman Arnold, it cannot be established over citizens in domestic territory unless a revolt has become sufficiently serious to justify the recognition of the rebels as belligerents, as that term is commonly understood in connection with the laws of war. A system of martial law may be set up in enemy or alien territory, in war, or in pursuance of treaty rights, or for the protection of the lives or property of nationals. Fortunately, the need for such use of the system of martial law seldom arises among the states.

The Nature of the Judicial Process

Before discussing the organization and procedure of the state courts, it may be well to consider briefly the nature of judicial power and of the judicial process. Judicial power has been defined as that power pertaining to the judicial department in any given case or circumstance, requisite for the attainment of the constitutional objective — justice. This great object is stated in the preambles of the Federal and state constitutions in the phrase "to establish justice" or in some similar form; its realization has been one of man's chief purposes in organized society. The existence of judicial process gives assurance to the individual that he cannot be deprived of life, liberty, or property unless a specific violation of the law is proved against him under regular procedure in open court.

Strange as it may seem, the courts which are responsible for the ad-

[27] Arnold, Thurman W., *Encyclopaedia of the Social Sciences*, Vol. X, pp. 162–166; much of this comment is based on Professor Arnold's article.

ministration of the judicial process and largely responsible for the achievement of the ends of justice, are without any power except the confidence of the public in their integrity and the strength of public opinion to enforce their judgments[28]:

> The court does not possess the purse, neither does it brandish the sword; it is in material strength the weakest of the departments of government. It is utterly dependent for subsistence and brawn upon others. Its only power is the wisdom, if any, of its thought and the logical justice of its words. It may command, but it cannot compel obedience, when resisted by those in charge of armed force. It may seek and commission aids, but it cannot itself pay for the services rendered it. In finality, its judgments are suggestive and its planning is advisory only.

In a brilliant work on the nature of the judicial process the late Justice Cardozo raised some questions which he thought an intelligent layman might like to have answered for him by a member of the bench[29]:

> What is it that I do when I decide a case? To what sources of information do I appeal for guidance? In what proportions do I permit them to contribute to the result? In what proportions ought they to contribute? If a precedent is applicable, when do I refuse to follow it? If no precedent is applicable, how do I reach the rule that will make a precedent for the future? If I am seeking logical consistency, the symmetry of the legal structure, how far shall I seek it? At what point shall the quest be halted by some discrepant custom, by some consideration of the social welfare, by my own or the common standards of justice and morals?

Justice Cardozo concludes that the directive force which guides a jurist in providing logical and reasonable answers to these questions and in the determination of his opinions may be derived from a number of sources. This force may, in the first place, be exerted along the line of logical progression, which he refers to as the rule of analogy or the method of philosophy; it may be exerted along the line of historical development, which he calls the method of evolution; along the line of the customs of the community, which he calls the method of tradition; or along the lines of justice, morals, and social welfare, the *mores* of the day, which he refers to as the method of sociology.

By the method of philosophy is meant the method of logical development. It has sometimes been said that a case is only an authority for what it actually decides, and that the law is not always logical. But, says Justice Cardozo, "logical consistency does not cease to be a good because it is not the supreme good," nor is logic to be ignored when experience is silent. "I am not to mar the symmetry of the legal structure by the introduction of inconsistencies and irrelevances and artificial exceptions unless for some sufficient reason, which will commonly be some consideration of history or custom or policy or justice. Lacking such a reason, I must be logical, just

[28] Riley, Fletcher, "Powers of Courts and Vitalization of Judicial Powers in Oklahoma," *Journal* of the American Judicature Society, June 1934, pp. 8–13.

[29] Cardozo, Benjamin N., *The Nature of the Judicial Process*, p. 10 (Yale University Press, 1925).

as I must be impartial, and upon like grounds. It will not do to decide the same question one way between one set of litigants and the opposite way between another. 'If a group of cases involves the same point, the parties expect the same decision. It would be a gross injustice to decide alternate cases on opposite principles. If a case was decided against me yesterday when I was defendant, I shall look for the same judgment today if I am plaintiff. To decide differently would raise a feeling of resentment and wrong in my breast; it would be an infringement, material and moral, of my rights.'"[30]

With regard to historical development as a directive force, it may be observed that the whole history of the law represents a continuous attempt to adapt existing legal principles to changed situations. At one point Justice Cardozo observes that "for every tendency, one seems to see a counter-tendency; for every rule its antinomy. Nothing is stable. Nothing absolute. All is fluid and changeable. There is an endless 'becoming.'" Elsewhere, he observes, quite in the manner of Justice Holmes, that "the great generalities of the Constitution have a content and a significance that vary from age to age."

If philosophy and history do not serve to fix the direction of a principle, custom may step in, although, "undoubtedly the creative energy of custom in the development of common law is less today than it was in bygone times. Even in bygone times its energy was very likely exaggerated by Blackstone and his followers. 'Today we recognize,' in the words of Pound,[31] 'that the custom is a custom of judicial decision, not of popular action.' It is 'doubtful,' says Gray, 'whether at all stages of legal history, rules laid down by judges have not generated custom, rather than custom generated the rules.' In these days, at all events, we look to custom, not so much for the creation of new rules, but for the tests and standards that are to determine how established rules shall be applied. When custom seeks to do more than this, there is a growing tendency in the law to leave development to legislation."[32]

"From history and philosophy and custom, we pass, therefore, to the force which in our day and generation is becoming the greatest of them all, the power of social justice which finds its outlet and expression in the method of sociology. The final cause of law is the welfare of society. The rule that misses its aim cannot permanently justify its existence. 'Ethical considerations can no more be excluded from the administration of justice which is the end and purpose of all civil laws than one can exclude the vital air from his room and live.'[33] Logic and custom and history have their place.

[30] *Ibid.*, pp. 32–34; quotation from Holmes, Oliver Wendell, *The Common Law*, p. 1 (Little, Brown, Boston, 1881).

[31] Pound, Roscoe, "Common Law and Legislation," *Harvard Law Review*, April 1908, pp. 383–406.

[32] Cardozo, *op. cit.*, pp. 59–60.

[33] Dillon, John F., *Laws and Jurisprudence of England and America*, p. 18 (Little, Brown, Boston, 1894), quoted by Pound, Roscoe, in a note in *Harvard Law Review*, May 1914, pp. 731–735.

We will shape the law to conform to them when we may; but only within bounds. The end which the law serves will dominate them all. . . . I mean that when they [the judges] are called upon to say how far existing rules are to be extended or restricted, they must let the welfare of society fix the path, its direction and its distance."[34]

Justice Cardozo considers at length such questions as judge-made law and the proper influence and weight of precedent in the determination of judicial opinions. With regard to the first of these questions much has been said and written. It has apparently been assumed by some that there was something inherently improper or wrong in what these critics delight in denouncing as judge-made law. Mr. Cardozo shows clearly that it is an inevitable part of the whole system of the adjudication of cases and the interpretation of laws by judicial officers. If the facts of the case are clear, and the provisions of the constitution or of the statutes specific, the task of the judge is easy. Often this is not the case. The judge is then obliged to consider the purpose and intent of the legislature, so far as it is ascertainable from the statute, and to guide himself accordingly. In such case, he is faced with the possibility of selecting one among two or more possible alternatives. No matter which he selects, he must of necessity "make law." His opinion can have no other effect than to guide or direct the current of legal development. Many of the cases with which a jurist is confronted revolve around points with regard to which the lawmaking body has made no provision, and which very often the lawmaking body did not even consider when the act was passed. In these cases his power as a lawmaker is much greater.

Likewise a great deal has been written on the doctrine of *stare decisis*, which means the decision of present cases on the basis of past precedents. Whether one likes it or not, this doctrine is "the everyday working rule" of the law in the English-speaking countries. Against the use of this principle, it is argued that it exerts an unduly conservative influence upon the development of the law, that it looks backward to see what has been rather than ahead to see what ought to be. Thus current difficulties are often resolved upon the basis of decisions which are irrelevant to the facts of the current situation. In defense of the principle, it may be noted that it is first of all a time-saving and a labor-saving factor in a busy world.

One can ill afford to ignore or disregard the experience of the race, beginning with each case *de novo*, as though it represented a new development in the history of mankind. The dockets of the courts would be far more crowded than they are if such a procedure were to be adopted. Decision based upon precedent is largely a time-saving device but it is an important factor in the development of a reasonable continuity in the rules and principles of the law. The influence of this doctrine is not as strong in the United States as in England, and it is much weaker in the United States today than it was a few decades ago. Justice Cardozo takes the very reasonable attitude,

[34] Cardozo, *op. cit.*, pp. 65–67.

characteristic of the more liberal jurists, that the doctrine of *stare decisis* is a guide which may properly be followed in the absence of new factors or conditions which so change the situation as to make the following of precedent clearly indefensible. The adherence of American courts to this doctrine does not mean, therefore, that decisions once made may not be reversed; they may be, and they are.[35]

The Doctrine of Judicial Review

The doctrine of judicial review has been one of the most controversial in the whole field of American government. The courts have been attacked on the one hand for having "usurped" the power to nullify the action of an equal and coordinate branch of the government, and have been praised on the other as having some peculiar qualifications for determining what is right and what is wrong. Neither claim is justified, and the attempt to make a moral issue out of a clear question of governmental policy and procedure is unfortunate.

In every organization, public or private, there has to be someone in authority — some one person or some group of persons whose decision is final and from whom there is no immediate appeal. In government there are three possible agencies to which this power of final determination may be entrusted. In the monarchies of old and in the recent dictatorships this power rested with the executive — a solution of the problem which has little appeal in a democratic society. In a parliamentary government, such as that of Great Britain, it is vested in the legislature. There may be practical limits to the power of the British Parliament, but there are no legal limits. This solution has worked in a satisfactory manner in England, but governmental institutions in America did not happen to develop along this line. The third possibility is, obviously, to entrust the power to the courts, and this solution, as will presently be indicated, has its roots deep in the history and practice of American government.

Early Origins of Judicial Review. The idea of judicial review did not suddenly spring into existence in the early nineteenth century, when John Marshall handed down his famous opinion in Marbury v. Madison. This was, in fact, a crystallization of long years of practice, a strikingly clear statement of ideas long familiar and apparently generally accepted by the people in the colonies. If one refrains from citing some of the very early cases as precedents (on the ground, as Professor Corwin points out, that they were unknown to those who were responsible for the adoption of judicial review), it still appears "that the courts of the colonies, reasoning by analogy from the powers of the Privy Council, believed that in the usual

[35] See also Shartel, Burke, "*Stare Decisis* — A Practical View," *Journal* of the American Judicature Society, June 1933, pp. 6–7; Kocourek, Albert, and Koven, Harold, "Renovation of the Common Law through *Stare Decisis*," *Illinois Law Review*, April 1935, pp. 971–999; Pound, Roscoe, "What of *Stare Decisis?*", *Fordham Law Review*, January 1941, pp. 1–13.

and necessary procedure when cases were brought before them involving acts alleged to be beyond the provisions of their charters and laws they might refuse to give effect to such acts. Precedents which substantiate this belief are indeed rare, but the few recorded show unmistakably the notion that colonial courts did not hesitate to refuse to give effect to an order of the King or to resist an act of Parliament deemed contrary to their rights as English subjects."[36]

Although some of the cases date back more than a century earlier, as for instance, Frost v. Leighton in the Superior Court of Judicature of Massachusetts in 1738–1739, their number increased rapidly in the latter part of the eighteenth century. The first *recorded* case appears to be Holmes v. Walton, decided in 1780 by the Supreme Court of New Jersey. Here the Court assumed the role of interpreting and enforcing upon members of the legislature the terms prescribed in their oath of office, and asserted the right to determine what constituted trial by jury according to the terms of the constitution. Some writers have ascribed to this decision great influence upon the Federal Convention; at any rate, three members of the New Jersey delegation were prominently connected with the case and were favorable to judicial control. A decade and a half later, in 1795, as many years after the Federal Convention as Holmes v. Walton preceded it, Justice Paterson in the Federal Circuit Court for the Pennsylvania district wrote these significant words[37]:

> I take it to be a clear position that if a legislative act impugns a constitutional principle, the former must give way, and be rejected on the score of repugnance. I hold it to be a position equally clear and sound, that, in such case, it will be the duty of the court to adhere to the Constitution, and to declare the act null and void. The Constitution is the basis of legislative authority; it lies at the foundation of all law, and is a rule and commission by which both legislator and judges are to proceed. It is an important principle, which, in the discussion of questions of the present kind, ought never to be lost sight of, that the judiciary in this country is not a subordinate, but a coordinate branch of the government.

By 1803, the date of the Marbury case, the following states had either been definitely committed to the doctrine of judicial review by judicial decision or practically so by judicial dicta: North Carolina, 1787; New Hampshire, 1791; South Carolina, 1792; Virginia, 1788, 1793; Pennsylvania, 1793, 1799; New Jersey, 1796; Kentucky, 1801; Maryland, 1802. The Kentucky Constitu-

[36] Haines, Charles G., *The American Doctrine of Judicial Supremacy*, Revised Edition, p. 67 (University of California Press, 1932), and Corwin, Edward S., *The Establishment of Judicial Review* (Princeton University Press, 1930).

[37] Vanhorne's Lessee v. Dorrance, 2 Dallas 310. Other significant statements of similar import: Caton v. Commonwealth of Virginia, 1782; Wilson, James, in *Works*, Vol. I, pp. 415–417 (Ed., Andrews, James D.); Hamilton, Alexander, in *Federalist* No. LXXVII. Among the more useful titles are: Bizzell, William B., *Judicial Interpretation of Political Theory* (Putnam's, New York, 1914); Corwin, Edward S., *The Doctrine of Judicial Review* (Princeton University Press, 1914); McLaughlin, Andrew C., *The Courts, The Constitution, and Parties* (University of Chicago Press, 1912); McLaughlin, Andrew C., and others, Eds., *Source Problems in United States History* (Harper, New York, 1918).

tion of 1792, for instance, provided: "All laws contrary . . . to this Constitution shall be void."[38]

Present Significance. So, through decade after decade, the idea of judicial review grew and developed. The power was seldom specifically conferred upon the courts; it grew out of peculiar American concepts of a written constitution, and while not without its critics, was exercised by the courts by common consent. It was not "usurped" by the courts; it was not necessary for them to "usurp" power the right to the exercise of which was generally conceded. This historical record is clear.

The question of the wisdom of the policy is quite another matter. All power conferred on governmental officers and agencies is subject to possible abuse; the power of judicial review is no exception. On occasion it has been

Classification of Unconstitutional Statutes in Illinois and New York

NATURE OF SUBJECT MATTER	ILLINOIS 1870–1941		NEW YORK 1914–1937	
Constitutional Protections	45		26	
Under Federal Constitution		..		7
State and Federal Due Process		..		13
Bill of Rights		45		..
Suffrage; Indictment and Trial by Jury		..		6
Distribution of Powers	4		..	
Civil Service	..		7	
Legislative Department	48		19	
Legislative Power Vested in Legislature		5		8
Senatorial Apportionment		1		..
General Rules for Legislature		1		..
Style and Passage of Laws		12		..
Public Moneys and Appropriations		5		..
Special Legislation		24		11
Judicial Department	9		5	
Education	2		..	
Revenue Article	31		14	
Uniformity, Exemptions, Further Taxation		12		..
Release from Taxation Forbidden		1		..
Local Improvements and Taxation		17		14
Limitation of Municipal Indebtedness		1		..
Miscellaneous	5		5	
Totals	144		76	

abused, but it is normally exercised with sufficient moderation and restraint to avoid serious popular criticism. Several interesting studies of the use of the power in Illinois, New York, and Virginia have been made.[39] In Illinois,

[38] Article XII: list from Corwin, *The Doctrine of Judicial Review*, p. 75.

[39] New York State Constitutional Convention Committee, *Problems Relating to Legislative Organization and Powers*, Chapter 5, "Judicial Restraint on Legislation, the Statistics,

144 statutes were declared unconstitutional in seventy-one years, while in New York, the number was seventy-six in a period of twenty-three years. In this state, in addition, the court decided thirteen cases in which the constitutionality of certain statutes was discussed but in which there were no direct rulings on validity. The lower courts decided twenty-one cases, which were not appealed to the Court of Appeals, in which laws were held to violate constitutional restraints, and the attorney general wrote seven opinions in which he ruled that legislative enactments were invalid. In this period the Court of Appeals ruled on the validity of approximately 232 statutes, holding that no provisions of the constitution were violated. Thus three statutes were upheld by the highest court for every one that was declared unconstitutional. The seventy-six decisions in New York and the 144 in Illinois were grouped in eight categories, as indicated in the table on page 587.

Another view of the same problem may be obtained by study of a series of tables of Supreme Court decisions declaring state laws and other actions unconstitutional, appearing in the successive volumes of the *Book of the States*. In the two years, 1948–1949,[40] there were, for instance, only two enactments declared unconstitutional, and neither of these was, strictly speaking, a state law. One was a Chicago city ordinance, the other the District of Columbia Emergency Rent Act. There were twenty-one cases in which "actions" of state judicial, executive, or administrative agencies were declared to be contrary to provisions of the Federal Constitution.

SELECTED REFERENCES

Cardozo, Benjamin N., *The Nature of the Judicial Process* (Yale University Press, 1925). A distinguished jurist analyzes in nontechnical language the considerations which enter into the determining of judicial opinions.

Chafee, Zechariah, Jr., *Some Problems of Equity* (University of Michigan Law School, 1950). Deals with a number of basic concepts, such as the clean-hands maxim, and the precept that equity follows the law.

Corwin, Edward S., *Court over Constitution: a Study of Judicial Review as an Instrument of Popular Government* (Peter Smith, New York, 1950). An eminent authority in the field gives a fresh interpretation of an old, important and much debated problem.

Field, Oliver P., *Judicial Review of Legislation in Ten Selected States* (Bureau of Government Research, Indiana University, 1943); Nelson, Margaret W., *A Study of Judicial Review in Virginia, 1789–1929* (Columbia University Press, 1947); and Smith, Franklin A., *Judicial Review of Legislation in New York, 1906–1938* (Columbia University Press, 1952). Useful studies of the actual functioning of judicial review in selected states.

Holmes, Oliver W., Jr., *The Common Law* (Little, Brown, Boston, 1938) and O'Sullivan, Richard, *The Inheritance of the Common Law* (Stevens & Son,

---

1914–1937" (Albany, 1930); Illinois Legislative Council, *Problems of Constitutional Revision in Illinois*, p. 31 (Springfield, 1941); Nelson, Margaret V., *A Study of Judicial Review in Virginia*, 1789–1928 (Columbia University Press, 1946).

[40] 1950–1951, pp. 144–146.

Ltd., London, 1950). A reprint of a classic work, along with an excellent newer work, dealing not with the technicalities of the law but with its sources and fundamental principles.

Hurst, James W., *The Growth of American Law: the Law Makers* (Little, Brown, Boston, 1950); for analysis of the trends of change, see: Aumann, Frances R., *The Changing American Legal System* (Ohio State University Press, 1940) and Ribble, F. D. G., Ed., *Significant Developments in the Law During the War Years* (Practicing Law Institute, New York, 1946).

Kinnane, Charles H., *A First Book on Anglo-American Law*, Second Edition (Bobbs-Merrill, Indianapolis, 1952). An introduction to the study of the Anglo-American legal system.

Pound, Roscoe, *Social Control Through Law* (Yale University Press, 1942); *The Province and Function of Law* (Harvard University Press, 1950); and *The Task of Law* (Franklin and Marshall College, Lancaster, 1944). Three recent discussions of the nature and purpose of law by one of the nation's most distinguished legal scholars.

Reuschlein, Harold G., Ed., *Jurisprudence; Its American Prophets* (Bobbs-Merrill, Indianapolis, 1951). Contains statements by leading American scholars on the source, nature, and efficacy of law and legal institutions.

Rutledge, Wiley, *A Declaration of Legal Faith* (University of Kansas Press, 1947). A challenging statement by a recent Justice of the Supreme Court.

17

State Courts: Organization and Jurisdiction

It has long been regarded as one of the most important functions of government to adjudicate controversies between individuals, between individuals and officers or agencies of the government, and cases involving criminal prosecution. This function is performed by the judiciary, which is composed of various types of courts. A court may be defined as a tribunal established by the state for the administration of justice according to law. For the student of American government, the situation is complicated by the fact that there are two separate and distinct judicial systems, one for the Federal government and one for the state, exercising simultaneously jurisdiction over the same persons and within the same territory. Because the system by which the powers of government are allocated between the Federal government and the states has proved to be fairly successful, these two judicial systems are able to operate without any very serious conflicts of jurisdiction.

The state courts were organized and in operation before the Federal Constitution was framed and the Federal government established. When the Constitutional Convention met in Philadelphia in 1787, there was much discusssion as to what should be done about the judiciary. The possibility of abandoning the state courts in favor of a federal system was not even considered. There was, in fact, doubt as to whether a federal system was needed, but this was finally resolved, for a number of reasons, in favor of the establishment of Federal courts. It was thought that they would be necessary in order to secure a uniform interpretation of the Federal Constitution and Federal laws. Again, it was feared that without such a system the various state courts would do what in practice the Federal courts have done; namely, interpret the Constitution and the laws in their own favor. If the state courts had been permitted to do this, the powers of the Federal government would have been greatly curtailed; as it is, it has been the powers of the states that have been limited in favor of the Federal government. Finally, there was the question of diverse citizenship. Where controversies arose between citizens of different states, it was feared that neither of them would want to leave the determination of the case to the courts of the state in which his opponent lived. In order to meet this situation, it was decided that a separate system of courts, organized on a national basis and impartial so far as the states were concerned, would be needed.

Historical Development of the State Courts

It is well known that the law and legal system of the states had their origin in the legal system of England. Because of the supervision of the colonies by the English authorities, colonial law was kept in line with English law, as least so far as fundamental principles were concerned. Professor Clarence N. Callender points out that the evolution of the colonial judiciary proceeded along similar lines:

> . . . The charters prescribed the general character of court organization and, subsequently, acts of Parliament, royal decrees, or acts of the provincial legislatures, dominated by English governors or councils of state, established the courts themselves. In England the highest court of appeals was the House of Lords; in America for a long time the English precedent was followed, and the colonial legislatures exercised the appellate jurisdiction. In many instances similar names were used to designate the courts. The justice of the peace in America was in many respects the counterpart of the justice of the peace in England. The grand and petit juries, ancient institutions in English judicial procedure, became integral parts of the legal system in America. The system of equity jurisprudence was likewise derived from the same source. . . .
>
> The intervention of the Revolution brought into existence the American states, and with them came many changes in the governmental organization, including some important modifications in the court system. In the first place, the appellate jurisdiction of the Privy Council disappeared, with the result that the provincial legislatures became the courts of last resort. This, however, was changed when the state constitutions were adopted. In them the theory of the separation of governmental powers between the executive, legislative, and judicial branches was introduced. Supreme courts and courts of errors and appeals supplanted the legislatures as the highest appellate bodies in all types of litigation except in certain matters of a semipolitical character, such as of legislative election contests, impeachment trials, and the like. In some instances the lower courts were established by constitutional provision; in others, the authority to establish inferior courts was delegated to the legislatures. The colonial judiciary provided the framework for the new state system. Many old courts were reëstablished, with their jurisdictions substantially the same as before. The change from the old to the new order produced few changes in the main body of the substantive law. The common law of England became in general the common law in each of the states and so, in a measure, it continues to be today.
>
> A century and a half of development has produced many changes in American institutions, but it is still remarkable how much there is in the field of law and in the organization and procedure of the courts that is similar in most essential respects to that of the English system. . . .[1]

[1] Callender, Clarence N., *American Courts: Their Organization and Procedure*, pp. 18–19 (McGraw-Hill, New York, 1927). See also Williams, Nathan B., "Independent Judiciary Born in Colonial Virginia," *Journal* of the American Judicature Society, December 1940, pp. 124–127.

Another student of the American judiciary notes that while the French influence was strong during the formative period, it had relatively little effect upon the courts. In a discussion of English origins and early development, he finds that judges were to proceed according to established rules so far as such rules might exist; that they were to proceed in analogy to established rules as to points which no established rule might cover; that they were to look to the common law and political institutions of England to determine what rules were established as to points not covered by local usage or legislation; that local usage or legislation might within certain limits depart from the common law and even from the political institutions of England, but that there were limits to such a departure, as it might be subject to review by a higher political or judicial authority.[2]

Growth of the New York Court System.[3] New York, if not a representative state, is one of the most important. Its courts have a history extending back over approximately three centuries, during which time two major trends may be observed: (1) the progressive reorganization of the judiciary in the direction of integration and coordination; (2) the growth of special judicial and administrative agencies for the adjudication of particular types of questions — a development particularly noticeable in the last fifty years. The courts of New York, as of others of the older states, are the result of a gradual evolution extending back into the colonial period when the administration of justice was highly localized. In this field there was no sharp line of distinction between state and local responsibility, nor had the courts been as yet completely divorced from the influence of the executive.

The transition from the status of a royal province to that of statehood, accomplished by the work of the Constitutional Convention of 1777, retained the colonial judicial system without substantial change. This first state constitution did not contain a separate judiciary article. Judges were appointive, and continued to be until 1846. They held office during good behavior or until they reached the age of sixty. Control of judicial procedure was still in the hands of the judges. The Constitutional Convention of 1821 made few changes in the existing system.

The reorganization of the judiciary began with the Constitutional Convention of 1846, and since that time has been a matter of almost continuous concern. Provision was made for the popular election of judges and for legislative control over rules of procedure. The Court of Chancery was abolished and its jurisdiction transferred to the Supreme Court which became the

[2] Baldwin, Simeon E., *The American Judiciary*, pp. 16–17 (Century, New York, 1920).

[3] Based on New York State Constitutional Convention Committee, *Report*, Vol. IX, Problems Relating to Judicial Administration and Organization (Albany, 1938), and Caldwell, Lynton K., *Government and Administration in New York State*, Chapter 6 (in American Commonwealths Series, Crowell, New York, 1953); see also Amer, Francis J., *The Development of the Judicial System of Ohio from* 1787 *to* 1932 (Johns Hopkins Press, 1932), and Wennerstrum, Charles F., "Historical Development of the Judicial System of Iowa," reprinted from *Iowa Code Annotated* (West Publishing Company, St. Paul, 1950).

"great state-wide court of unlimited original jurisdiction at law and in equity." (New Jersey was the last state to accomplish this change in 1947 — just about a century later.) An effort to abolish the county courts was unsuccessful though their jurisdiction was materially reduced. In order to establish an intermediate level of appeal from decisions of the Supreme Court (sitting in divisions and replacing the numerous independent local courts previously existing) the Convention provided for General Terms of the Supreme Court to be held in each of the eight judicial districts into which the state was divided. This, observes Professor Caldwell, clearly anticipated the present Appellate Divisions of the Supreme Court.

This system, with a few modifications and perfecting changes, endured for more than half a century. No important changes were made by the Constitutional Convention of 1869; the Constitutional Convention of 1894 found the structure basically sound, but deficient in methods of coordination and administrative supervision. A recent rapid growth of the state prompted this Convention to enlarge the jurisdiction of the Supreme Court, increase the number of its justices, establish the Appellate Divisions with certain powers of administrative supervision over the Supreme Court, and reduce the number of review cases then overwhelming the Court of Appeals. The county courts were made the primary courts of local jurisdiction (though other local courts of jurisdiction no greater than that of the county courts might be established by the legislature). Since in 1873 the people had voted to retain the elective judiciary, the Convention thought it desirable to establish minimum qualifications for judicial office.

Numerous comprehensive studies of judicial organization and administration have been undertaken during the present century — notably by the Constitutional Conventions of 1915 and 1938, and by the Judicial Convention of 1921, some of whose recommendations were embodied in a revision of the Judicial Article adopted in 1925, and by the Commission on the Administration of Justice in New York State, established by the legislature in 1931. In 1942, Robert M. Benjamin's significant report on *Administrative Adjudication in New York State* was filed. Several important changes have been made as a result of all these studies, notably the establishment of the Judicial Council in 1934 (for discussion of this movement, see pages 619–625), the establishment of the Law Revision Commission in 1934, and the Court on the Judiciary by Constitutional Amendment in 1947, to handle cases involving the retirement or removal of judges. The rapid growth of administrative adjudication since 1900 and the tendency to limit judicial appeals from their actions to questions of law, along with the establishment of the Court of Claims in 1897, the Workmens Compensation Board in 1913, and the children's courts and courts of domestic relations in 1921, have all tended to remove certain types of cases from the general courts and to lighten their burden.

This tendency has to some extent modified another significant trend —

that of consolidation and integration of the state judiciary. Some progress has been made in central supervision, however, through the requirement of regular reports, assignment of judges, or power to appoint additional judges to clear overloaded dockets, and in other ways. At the present time, the judiciary of New York may be divided into two dissimilar parts: (1) the general state-wide judicial system consisting of the Supreme Court, the Appellate Divisions of the Supreme Court, and the Court of Appeals; (2) all other judicial courts. These courts, both constitutional and statutory, have jurisdiction limited either to special types of controversies or to local geographic areas. In no sense do they constitute an integrated judiciary.

State Court Organization

Courts may be classified in many ways: from the point of view of their fundamental character (administrative or judicial); of the type of law which they enforce (law or equity, civil or criminal); or of the geographical area within which they have jurisdiction (as for instance, county courts). These attempts at classification are not mutually exclusive. There is a judiciary article in each of the state constitutions describing in more or less detail the structure of the court system for the state.[4] In spite of wide variation in the number of courts and in the nomenclature applied to them, there is none the less a skeleton organization to which all the state court systems in a general way conform. This organization is suggested by the diagram on the following page, which will be used as the basis for discussion of certain important features of the judicial system of the states. The diagram attempts to show the successive types of courts through which appeals may be taken. The discussion begins with the lower courts, because it is in them that the proceedings in the great majority of cases are instituted and finally disposed of. Thus the quality of justice which the majority of the people in a given state receive is determined by the quality of justice dispensed by the lower courts. If these courts do their work badly, the people may become dissatisfied and lose faith in the judiciary, no matter how high the quality of the work performed by the higher courts. It is more important, so far as a majority of the people are concerned, that the lower courts be run honestly and efficiently than that the higher courts be so run. It is unlikely, however, that the lower courts will be better run than the higher ones in any state, for experience shows that it is a far more difficult job to provide an effective administration of justice in the smaller local units than it is to provide an honest and efficient service in the appellate courts.

In Rural Areas — the Justice of the Peace. The office of justice of the peace as it still exists in the United States can be traced to origins developing in medieval England when transportation was slow, difficult, and expensive.

[4] The power of the states to establish their courts and to determine their jurisdiction within the limits of state power in such manner as they see fit was considered in Broderick, Superintendent of Banks, v. Rosner, et al., 294 U.S. 629, 1935.

It was also a part of the system of government by landed families. When the office was introduced in America, the positions were usually filled by appointment, but in the Middle Period, as a result of the spread of the Jacksonian ideas of democracy, the elective system was extended, and has since been used. As the centralization of power developed in England, the justices were taken over as a part of the national system for the administra-

STATE COURT ORGANIZATION

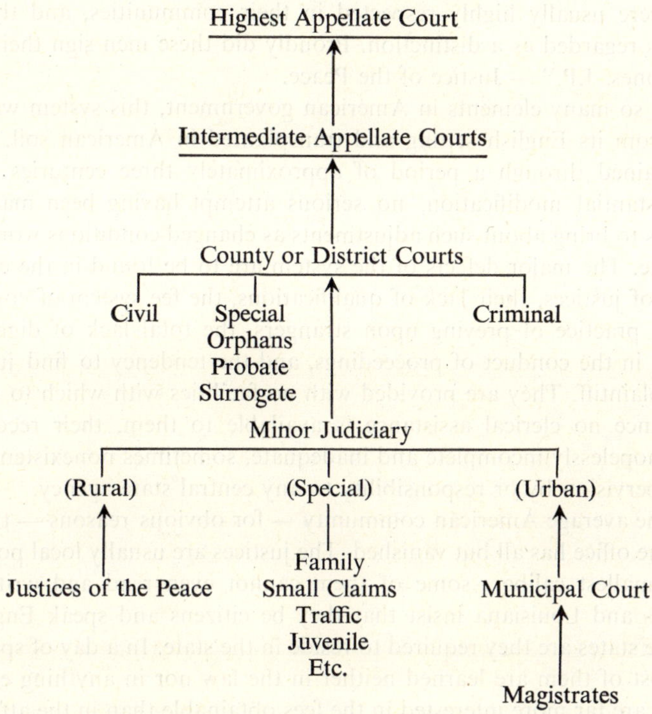

tion of justice.[5] These courts had then, and to a certain extent still have, several useful purposes. They were set up to decide local disputes that otherwise would go to a county court which might be two days' journey away by carriage, with the expense and loss of time involved — which would, in fact, have denied him an opportunity for the judicial settlement of his difficulties. Furthermore, there are many minor disputes — little squabbles

[5] Webb, Sidney and Beatrice, in their *English Local Government from the Revolution to the Municipal Corporation Act*, Vol. I (Longmans, Green, London, 1908), comment at length upon the development of the early English judicial institutions. For instance (p. 18), they say: "When it was held that the Court Baron was of private, not public nature, those words were used in a sense very different from that nowadays given to them. All that the lawyers meant was that the Court Baron was not a Court of the King, to be held only by his authority or subject to his will. . . ." In course of time, as noted, these private courts were taken over as a part of the judicial system of the realm.

between neighbors, reprimanding unlicensed hunters, and disposing of numerous petty claims without the delay and expense of an ordinary court, for the settlement of which intelligence, human sympathy, and common sense are more essential than a detailed knowledge of the intricacies of the law. Upon this basis, it was possible to make use of leading citizens in each community; these persons, who came to be known as justices of the peace, were vested with the necessary authority for the adjudication of minor disputes. For many years the system worked well. The men who held the offices were usually highly respected in their communities, and the office itself was regarded as a distinction. Proudly did these men sign their names "John Jones, J.P." — Justice of the Peace.

Like so many elements in American government, this system was lifted bodily from its English setting and transplanted in American soil. Here it has remained through a period of approximately three centuries without any substantial modification, no serious attempt having been made until late years to bring about such adjustments as changed conditions would seem to require. The major defects of the system are to be found in the excessive number of justices, their lack of qualifications, the fee system of compensation, the practice of preying upon strangers, the total lack of dignity and decorum in the conduct of proceedings, and the tendency to find judgment for the plaintiff. They are provided with no facilities with which to do their work; since no clerical assistance is available to them, their records are usually hopelessly incomplete and inadequate, sometimes nonexistent. There is no supervision by or responsibility to any central state agency.

In the average American community — for obvious reasons — the prestige of the office has all but vanished. The justices are usually local politicians of the smallest caliber; some of them cannot even read and write. Only Arkansas and Louisiana insist that they be citizens and speak English. In only nine states are they required to reside in the state. In a day of specialization, most of them are learned neither in the law nor in anything else. The majority are far more interested in the fees obtainable than in the attainment of justice. The fact that most justices are compensated on a fee basis rather than by salary constitutes one of the most serious defects in the system. So much is this so that the initials "J.P." have often been jocularly translated as "judgment for the plaintiff" — since only through finding judgment for the plaintiff can the justice be sure of his fees. Large numbers of them have entered into dishonest arrangements with constables and other local functionaries, establishing "speed traps" for the purpose of harassing motorists. Strangers in the community are their particular targets, for these people are without political influence and are usually willing to pay their fines in order to avoid further delay. There are, of course, a few who honestly and conscientiously seek to perform the duties of their office, but the percentage of the total number who do this is pitifully small.[6]

[6] These major defects are discussed at some length in Morris, Gail M., *Justice of the*

While these comments constitute a serious indictment of the whole system, they represent the deliberate judgment of practically every person who has taken the trouble to investigate the functioning of the office. The American Bar Association's report on traffic courts and justices of the peace, published in 1940, stated that "The justice of the peace system is outmoded and its plan of organization ineffective for good . . . law enforcement." Numerous studies of the office by political scientists all point to the same conclusions. "The recommendation that the present justice of the peace system should either be eliminated or greatly improved epitomizes all recommendations of every study made of that system."

The occupational background of the justices, in the majority of cases, as Bruce Smith observes, "provides no guaranty, nor even expectation, that their experience prior to ascending the local bench would offer any degree of special qualification." The Pennsylvania Bar Association in 1942 reported[7]:

> Occupations of 3225 justices in sixty-four counties were taken from county registration records. These occupations vary with the county, depending on the dominant occupational pattern of the county: in rural counties most of the justices were farmers, and in the urban counties most of the justices were skilled and unskilled laborers. Many justices listed their occupations as "justice of the peace," indicating that their judicial duties were their only gainful occupations. A very few were lawyers, and only a small number had any experience that would be of value in judicial work.
>
> Nearly every occupation was represented: there were doctors, blacksmiths, reporters, bartenders, students, morticians, W.P.A. workers, and many others. The most numerous occupation listed was justice of the peace — 669 or 21 per cent of the total. Seventeen per cent or 552 were laborers and unskilled laborers; 12 per cent were farmers; 11 per cent were skilled laborers; 61 per cent of the justices and aldermen surveyed were in these four occupations.

A survey made in Hamilton County, Ohio, some years earlier, reveals some interesting facts with regard to both the income of justices and their dockets.

> The average annual income of justices (from all fees of whatever nature) was $415.75 . . . with yearly income ranging from $4.30 to $2557.06. Twenty-six per cent of them earned less than $200, and sixty-eight per cent less than $300. Only eight per cent of the justices earned more than $1000. . . . The correct concept to form of the squire is that of a judge, poorly paid and subsidized, to whom the state farms out its work in the administration of justice in the counties and townships upon the consideration that he shall collect occasionally some civil fees. If the desire for economy in local government

---

Peace Courts in Indiana (Bureau of Government Research, Indiana University, 1942); see also Judicial Council of Indiana, *Fourth Annual Report* (1939), pp. 11–137 (Indianapolis, 1940).

[7] Litke, William W., *Survey of the Minor Judiciary in Pennsylvania*, p. 27 (Pennsylvania Municipal Publications Service, State College, 1942). See also: Smith, Bruce, *Rural Crime Control*, pp. 247–248 (Institute of Public Administration, Columbia University, 1933). Similar results were obtained from occupational studies of justices in New Jersey and New York (p. 248). Chapter 7 of this volume contains a very able discussion of the office of the justice; see also Callender, *op. cit.*, Chapter 4.

> led to the development of the present system, arithmetic proves that the desire apparently has been realized.[8]

In a few cases found in Erie County, New York, salaries ranging from $2500 to $5000 are paid, but this is unusual; in Pennsylvania, out of 1194 justices interrogated in an earlier survey, only five were on an exclusively salaried basis.

Under such circumstances, it is small wonder that the work is usually done badly. The Hamilton County survey reported that "the docket entries were made whenever the squire or his family have a few spare minutes. Wives and children do a considerable amount of clerical work. The report continues[9]:

> . . . A few magistrates permit their cases to accumulate until something happens to force them to bring their records up to date. On one occasion a justice sat up all night to make his entries and have them ready for the perusal of an interested party the next morning. The call of the state examiner for the records stimulates a few judges to feverish clerical activity. As a consequence of the dilatory manner of keeping official records, the dockets frequently have cases [arranged in fantastic sequence]. One squire delighted in finding blank pages in old dockets and entering his cases. He achieved such serial order as June 10, December 6, June 12. [Although some of the justices employed systematic filing methods] one squire filed the papers of each case in the docket book. Three kept the papers in desk drawers, being sometimes able to locate the proper documents and sometimes not. In three cases the papers could not be located. In two cases papers transferred from squires to their successors were completely lost. . . . A few dockets were either lost or could not be located for examination.

There are 50,000 justices of the peace in the United States, approximately one tenth of them in Pennsylvania. A survey made in Michigan illustrates again the excessive number of these officials. The state constitution requires that there shall be elected in each organized township not more than four justices of the peace. This provided a total of 290 justices in six counties studied, but — and this is a tribute to the good sense of the people — all of the judicial business in these counties, outside of the cities, was handled by twenty-one justices, leaving 269 having no judicial business whatever. Many of these, though elected, never bothered to qualify and never heard a case. In its general conclusions, the report condemned both the township and the smaller municipalities as units for the administration of justice, on the grounds that this is a state function. "The township," said the report, "is not a suitable unit to be charged with the performance of any judicial duties whatever, and the Justice of the Peace, as a township officer, is wholly out of place in a modern judicial system." [10]

[8] Douglass, Paul F., *The Justice of the Peace Courts of Hamilton County, Ohio*, p. 70, and quoted by Smith, *op. cit.*, p. 241.

[9] *Ibid.*, pp. 61, 66.

[10] This comment is based entirely upon Sunderland, Edson R., "The Efficiency of Justices' Courts in Michigan," published as Appendix D, *Report* on Organization and Cost of County and Township Government, by the Michigan Commission of Inquiry, 1933; reprinted in *Fourth Report* of the Judicial Council of Michigan, May 1934, Appendix, pp.

At long last, a few things are beginning to happen, looking toward the improvement of this situation. Three solutions are available: abolish the justices of the peace, improve the administration, educate the justices. Missouri and New Jersey have abolished the system, under their new constitutions. This is the best answer, involving, of course, the organizational changes required in order to provide substitute machinery for handling the judicial business formerly entrusted to the justices. Virginia has adopted a trial justice system, Maryland a somewhat similar trial magistrate. These plans represent probably the most constructive move yet made to do something about the justice of the peace system. The Virginia plan provides for a new type of commissioner or magistrate who is given the title of "trial justice." Herbert Harley, for many years Secretary of the American Judicature Society, thus describes this notable attempt to administer justice in small cases expertly and economically throughout both urban and rural communities[11]:

> The Virginia system is this: in counties in which the supervisors have voted to dispense with justices of the peace the circuit judge (equivalent to district judge), if he agrees, shall appoint an assistant to serve for a term of four years. This assistant of course will be a lawyer. He will take such classes of cases as may be assigned to him from time to time by his superior officer. His will be a mobile court, prepared at all times to convene court at the place most convenient to those concerned. The Virginia law provides that such an assistant judge may be appointed for any of the larger cities that realize the need. In thinly populated areas one assistant judge may serve two counties, or there may be half-time service.

After outlining various advantages of this system in operation, he continues:

> Perhaps most important of all is the obvious fact that this system creates a body of experienced, well tested, competent lawyers from which future judges are likely to be chosen. The Virginia system creates a school for judges, but the novitiates must already have met all educational requirements for the practice of law and must have spent some time at least in the service of clients. By assisting a judge of full trial jurisdiction, they round out their training and have much to offer the public in either capacity, as lawyer or as judge.

Several states, including California, Iowa, Michigan, Oregon, Tennessee, Texas, and Washington, are now carefully reexamining this whole problem with a view to replacing the justice courts with state-wide, supervised personnel. Where the justice courts are still retained, their functioning can be improved by imposing and enforcing minimum qualifications for the office, furnishing justices with clerical assistance and with proper facilities, requiring

---

169–172; see also his later articles, "Qualifications and Compensation of Minor Court Judges," *Journal* of the American Judicature Society, December 1945, pp. 111–116, and "Territorial Jurisdiction of Minor Courts," *ibid.*, December 1946, pp. 147–155; Arkansas Legislative Council, *Survey of Minor Court Systems*, Part I, of Arkansas, Part II, of Other States (Little Rock, 1950).

[11] *Journal*, August 1942, p. 26, and Kingdon, Arthur F., "The Trial Justice System of Virginia," *ibid.*, April 1940, pp. 216–221; see also Abbuhl, Forest E., "Maryland Modernizes Its Justices of the Peace System," *County Officer*, March 1951, pp. 77–78, 81; and McKenna, William J., "Justice in the Minor Courts," *Temple Law Quarterly*, April 1952, pp. 436–448.

them to keep satisfactory records and to submit reports at frequent and regular intervals, and by seeing to it that they are subject to proper state supervision by a central agency such as a chief justice, administrative officer, or judicial council.

Concurrently with this movement for reorganization, there has been a growing effort to improve the personnel through the educational process. The American Bar Association has encouraged the formation of the American Association of Trial Courts of Limited Jurisdiction, the first meeting of which was held in 1947. Manuals of forms and procedures for justices and constables have been prepared in California, Mississippi, Nebraska, Oregon, and other states. New Hampshire, New York, and Pennsylvania have been running training courses for justices. In the latter state, the Public Service Institute (organized to administer programs under the George-Deen Act) has conducted several sessions of the Minor Judiciary School. The work is divided into courses in civil and criminal law, both of which are conducted in twenty-four three-hour sessions meeting once each week, and for both of which instruction guides have been prepared. Such activities have improved the functioning of local courts and should continue to do so.[12]

In Urban Areas — the Magistrate. The justice of the peace functions in the rural districts; his urban counterpart is the magistrate, police magistrate, or alderman. If it be true that a satisfactory administration of justice in the rural districts is impossible until the justice of the peace system is either abolished or extensively modified, it is doubly true that anything approximating substantial justice in urban communities is impossible unless or until the magistrate system is abolished. If it be true that the justices of the peace are usually inefficient and often dishonest, it may be said that the record of the magistrates is very much worse — they are rarely efficient and rarely honest. In the magistrates' courts, commonly held in a police station or in a small, stuffy office, there is no dignity to the proceedings, and usually little justice results from them. Indeed, it may be said that the innocence or guilt of those who are arraigned before the magistrate has little or nothing to do with the disposition which he makes of the cases. The decisions are determined either in a back room before the hearing takes place, or by whispered conversations carried on between the magistrate and some local politician while the hearing is in progress. Thus it is that an individual, no matter how innocent, may be held on bail or sent to jail if he is unfortunate enough to be unable to bring some political pressure to bear in his behalf, while another individual, no matter how guilty, may get off absolutely free if he is able to summon the assistance of the proper political influence.[13]

[12] Vanderbilt, Arthur T., Ed., *Minimum Standards of Judicial Administration*, pp. 306–316 (Law Center of New York University, 1949); see also Howerton, Huey B., and McIntire, Helen D., *A Guidebook of the Justice of the Peace* (Bureau of Public Administration, University of Mississippi, 1950).

[13] This comment, which one friend of the author thought "a little too strong," is certainly true as applied to New York City, Philadelphia, Pittsburgh, and many other large

These conclusions with regard to the office of the magistrate are supported by a large number of studies made by competent persons. Such a study of the magistrates' courts of Philadelphia was made by Spencer Ervin in 1931; he found that these courts were notable for the lack of any adequate reporting system — even the annual report of the chief magistrate is utterly inadequate and confused. The dockets and records of many of the individual magistrates have been kept in a "disgraceful condition," since these officers are without guidance as to the character of entries that should be made in different classes of cases. This situation has been pointed out repeatedly — in 1926 by the Law Association's Crimes Survey Committee; in 1927 by District Attorney Charles Edwin Fox; in 1928 by the famous grand jury investigation; in 1935 by the Criminal Justice Association, and by the investigation conducted by the State Department of Justice. It has also been shown repeatedly that many of the magistrates fail to make prompt return of cases to the clerk of the court of quarter sessions and to the district attorney, and that they are delinquent in making certain returns to the city controller and the city treasurer.

It is a familiar subject of comment by observers at the hearings conducted by many of the magistrates that there is a total lack of order in the room, and a lack of dignity and tact on the part of the bench. "Lateness at the hearing, conduct unbecoming a judicial officer during the hearing, and improper disposition of cases are common complaints," but unfortunately the basis of complaint does not stop here. Short shrift is often made of civil cases, and in criminal cases there are frequent and well-supported charges of intimidation and oppression, bail irregularities of every conceivable type, political influence in the determining of decisions, et cetera. Clearly justice is not administered "according to law."[14] In many cases the whole magistrate system is a veritable stench in the nostrils of decent people. In 1935 the situation in Philadelphia became so bad that at one time twenty-seven of the twenty-eight magistrates in the city were under indictment for various types of irregularities. While more than half these courts were formerly under the direction of ward leaders and committeemen, a legislative act of 1937 prohibits political activity on the part of magistrates. Philadelphia

---

cities. "Rotten as they are," this commentator continued, "they are the appropriate thing in a considerable proportion of cases." It may be admitted with regard to the magistrates, as with the justices of the peace, that they can and do settle many minor disputes, and that they do, where the political influence is not too strong, render useful service in "holding for court."

The late Chief Justice Hughes told of a police magistrate who came up to speak to him after an address, saying: "I represent the lowest form of judicial life." "Well," replied Mr. Hughes, "in certain respects far more important than mine," because for every one who may be a litigant in the Supreme Court of the United States, there are thousands who go through the magistrates' courts. (Remarks before Judicial Circuit Conference, Washington, D.C., May 24, 1940).

[14] Ervin, Spencer, *The Magistrates' Courts of Philadelphia* (Thomas Skelton Harrison Foundation, Philadelphia, 1931).

is by no means unique, for similar conditions are found whenever an investigation is made in any large city which still uses the magistrate system. Few persons have forgotten the sensational disclosures of corruption in New York City made by the Seabury Investigation.[15]

Municipal Courts. In the larger cities, where the volume of judicial business is sufficient to justify such a course, the legislatures have provided for the establishment of municipal courts, which serve in the dual capacity of courts of first instance for large numbers of cases involving small amounts of money and minor infractions of the law, and as appellate courts for cases previously heard by magistrates. In Chicago, Detroit, New York, and Philadelphia these courts have been organized into divisions, set up either geographically or on a functional basis. Other specialized municipal courts have been established in Atlanta, Buffalo, Cincinnati, Cleveland, Kansas City, Milwaukee, and Pittsburgh.

In this development, Chicago led the way in 1906. The jurisdiction of some fifty-four justices and police magistrates was conferred upon thirty-six associate justices and a chief justice who presides at meetings, assigns justices to the different specialized divisions, and prepares court calendars. Criminal jurisdiction extends to misdemeanor cases, and to examination and holding for trial in felony cases, while civil jurisdiction depends on the amount of money involved in the controversy. Specialized divisions, set up on the functional basis, have been added to the unified court from time to time, including domestic relations, traffic, small claims, morals, and juvenile. Professor Bromage reports that three principal objectives have been achieved by this court: (1) independent justices of the peace and magistrates were abolished in favor of a unified court; (2) the chief justice was given supervisory authority over other justices; (3) special divisions were developed.[16]

In New York, the geographical system of organization is used, the Municipal Court having jurisdiction over civil actions in which the amount involved is not more than $1000 (except in summary proceedings over which it has unlimited jurisdiction). Appeals from its judgments and orders are made to the Appellate Term of the Supreme Court, First and Second Departments. The Court is intended to be a self-governing body with control vested in its Board of Justices, with the President-Justice as the administra-

[15] Moley, Raymond, *Tribunes of the People: the Past and Future of the New York Magistrates' Courts* (Yale University Press, 1932); for other cities, see: CINCINNATI: Porter, Charles O., "Defects in the Administration of Justice in Hamilton County, Ohio," *Journal* of the American Judicature Society, June 1948, pp. 14–22. DETROIT: University of Michigan *Survey of Metropolitan Courts: Detroit Area* (Ann Arbor, 1950), summarized in "Administration of Justice in Metropolitan Areas Is Studied in New Survey of Detroit Area Courts," *Journal* of the American Judicature Society, December 1950, pp. 111–116. ST. LOUIS: Bar Association of St. Louis, *Magistrate Courts in St Louis* (Governmental Research Institute, St. Louis, 1948).

[16] Bromage, Arthur W., *Municipal Government and Administration*, p. 671 (Appleton-Century-Crofts, New York, 1950); see also Sawyer, Leonard, *Municipal Courts of New Hampshire* (Bureau of Government Research, University of New Hampshire, 1949).

tive head. Structurally, it is an aggregation of twenty-eight district courts scattered among the five boroughs of the Greater City of New York — ten in Manhattan, two in the Bronx, eight in Brooklyn, six in Queens, and two in Richmond — and a Century Jury Part in Manhattan.

In Philadelphia, as in Chicago, the functional basis of organization is used. The Municipal Court functions under an act passed in 1913, providing for five divisions, each of which handles cases involving a particular branch of the law, as follows:

Civil Division: For trial of cases up to $2500.

Juvenile Division: For the hearings of boys and girls under sixteen years.

There is a probation department, petition bureau, labor bureau, and house of detention for children.

Criminal Division: All criminal actions, except crimes of the most grave nature. There is a probation department for men and for women.

Domestic Relations Division: Exercises exclusive jurisdiction in all cases on nonsupport and desertion, and in all proceedings for the custody of children. There is a probation department, as well as a petition bureau and a labor bureau.

Misdemeanant's Division: For trial of incorrigibles over sixteen years. There are separate departments for women, and for men and boys, and a house of detention for women offenders.

This court handles approximately 50,000 cases a year; from 1914 through 1946, it had dealt with 1,584,668, an average of more than 48,000 a year. It has a President Judge (its first President Judge served continuously for more than a quarter of a century), eleven associate judges (one for each 200,000 population), and a staff of approximately 2500. The employees, except those assigned to the various divisions of the court proper, are organized in six main groups, as follows: executive office, court hearing and court proceedings, probation department, medical department, statistical department, and equipment and maintenance. Among the more important activities reported on are adoptions; the conciliation, small claims, and legal division; the medical department, with its visiting nurse staff, nursery, and laboratory; the statistical department; and the department of support accounts.

In these cities and in others in many parts of the country, much progress has been made in judicial administration; the municipal court system has fully demonstrated its merit. It is possible to secure for judges in these courts lawyers of greater ability and higher ethical standards, and men with higher standards of civic responsibility, than can normally be secured for the magistrates' courts. It is clear that the line of progress in the development of city courts lies in the direction of the extension of this system. There is no reason why it cannot be introduced in cities where it has not yet been tried, nor why it cannot be extended in others by enlarging the existing set-up, thereby making possible the elimination of the magistrates. Many experiments have been tried with separate divorce courts, family courts, children's courts, small claims courts, people's courts, "poor man's courts," traffic courts, "cafeteria courts" for traffic violators, and other types.[17]

The People's Court of Baltimore City handles approximately 65,000 small claims cases a year, with four judges. Cases filed are scheduled for trial according to category, of which there are five: (1) suits sounding in contract; (2) summary ejectment suits for non-payment of rent; (3) suits against tenants holding over after notice to quit; (4) suits by Baltimore City for unpaid taxes; and (5) suits sounding in tort. Suits come up for trial on a day fixed at the time the suit is filed. Each category is scheduled for a particular time and court room, but since all court rooms are on a single floor, it is possible for the clerk of a judge whose assignment has been completed to go to an adjoining room and pick up any cases ready for trial and for which the parties and witnesses are awaiting their turn. As a consequence, litigants who appear in court for trial are ordinarily out in an hour or less.[18]

County or District Courts. The county or district courts are definitely state courts rather than local, and are, with the exception of the municipal courts, the lowest courts of record in the state judicial system. Their jurisdiction extends to both civil and criminal cases, and is both original and appellate. In some New England states the county is, in fact, merely a judicial district, the officers of which are state officers, chosen and paid by the state. In densely populated states, courts of this type have been set up in each county, although occasionally, even in these states, it has been found necessary to group a number of sparsely settled counties into a single district. In these states the name "county court" is most commonly used, while in the states with smaller population and a large number of counties, where a system of districting has to be used, they are commonly referred to as district courts, or in some cases, as circuit courts. New York has nine districts, Illinois seventeen, while Pennsylvania has fifty-seven — only ten less than the number of counties.[19] In any case these courts function in the state judicial system in much the same way.

[17] In addition to titles cited in previous editions of this volume, see the following on juvenile courts: Administrative Office of the United States Courts, *Federal Probation*, September 1949, a special issue commemorating the fiftieth anniversary of the juvenile court; Juvenile Court of Cook County, *Fiftieth Anniversary Report* (Chicago, 1949); Reinemann, John O., "Fifty Years of the Juvenile Court Movement in the United States," *Mental Hygiene*, July 1950, pp. 391–399; Sanders, Wiley B., *The Juvenile Courts of North Carolina* (University of North Carolina Press, 1948); Texas Juvenile Court Research Project, 8 vols. (State Department of Welfare, Austin, 1950), covering such subjects as *Adoption of Children in Texas*, *Juvenile Court Statistics and Related Services for Texas Children*, and *Texas Statutes Governing Court Proceedings in Children's Cases;* Winnet, Nochem S., "Fifty Years of the Juvenile Court: an Evaluation," American Bar Association *Journal*, May 1950, pp. 363–366; also "Eight Standards for a Progressive Juvenile Court," *ibid.*, August 1951, p. 51.

[18] Rhynhart, Allen W., "Baltimore People's Court Saves Time of Litigants," *Journal* of the American Judicature Society, June 1950, pp. 24–25; see also Fisher, Edward C., *People's Court* (Northwestern University Traffic Institute, 1947) — the story of the Lincoln, Nebraska, people's court which is concerned with traffic matters.

[19] See Illinois Legislative Council, *Circuit Court Redistricting in Illinois* (Springfield,

In many states the same judges sitting in the same court handle cases in both civil and criminal law, as well as equity proceedings. In other states, as in Pennsylvania, separate courts have been established for civil and criminal cases, although the same judges sit in both courts. In this state the civil courts are known as courts of common pleas, which name is also used in several other states. The criminal courts are known as courts of oyer and terminer when considering the more serious offenses, and as courts of quarter sessions when hearing lesser charges. As late as 1938 Massachusetts still had part-time judges in its district courts, although this practice is now both unjustified and unusual. The jurisdiction of these county and district courts also varies from state to state with regard to their power to handle certain special types of cases, such as, for instance, those involving the settlement of decedents' estates. In some states these cases are a part of the general jurisdiction of these courts, while in many states separate courts, variously designated as probate courts, orphans courts, or surrogates courts, have been established to handle them.

Two other problems in connection with the operation of county courts deserve mention. One involves taking care of the state's judicial business, most of which originates at the capital. If these cases are thrown into the county court of the county in which the capital is located, they are handled by judges, elected by the voters of that county, without any special qualifications for this state work. It has been proposed, therefore, that a special tribunal with state-wide jurisdiction be established, the members of which are elected for this special court by all the voters of the state. This would provide more competent service, probably at no greater cost than is involved in contributing to the support of a particular county court. Appeals from such a court would be taken directly to the state supreme court. It has also been proposed that separate labor courts be established, similar to labor courts abroad and to the court established by the ill-fated Kansas Industrial Disputes Act.

The other problem relates to the criminal work of the county court, especially in populous centers. The Behavior Clinic of the Allegheny County, Pennsylvania, courts provides an excellent illustration of effective work in this field. This Clinic was established in 1936 for the purpose of making available to the judges, and indirectly to the defendants, all the resources of modern science in the handling of criminals. The staff of the Clinic includes social workers, sociologists, criminologists, psychologists, psychiatrists, and others in a position to make a contribution to the case study of the defendants brought before the court. The record of each defendant and the findings of the staff, together with their recommendations, are given to the judge

1938); although the state constitution requires that the districts be as compact as possible, with due regard to territory and population, they vary, like legislative districts, from 155,000 to 396,000 in population, outside of Chicago. On Massachusetts, see *Report* by the House Committee on the Judiciary of its investigation and study of the district court system (House No. 1719, 1938).

before he imposes sentence. From a normal case load of 500, the Clinic's Annual Reports for 1948–1949 and 1949–1950 showed totals of 735 and 783, all but about fifty of whom were, in each case, men. Approximately two thirds of the charges involve sex offenses. Similar procedures have long been followed in progressive municipal courts.[20]

Appellate Courts. Next in the organization of the state judicial system, in about one third of the states, are those courts which may be classified as intermediate appellate courts; these are the courts which stand as a buffer between the county or district courts on the one hand and the highest court of appeal on the other. The number, size, and jurisdiction of these courts will depend, in any given state, largely upon the volume of judicial business, which is in turn largely dependent upon the size of the population. In many cases there is only one of these intermediate courts, which may be designated either as a superior court or as a court of appeals. In a state like New York, with its large population and its great industrial and commercial interests, there is a Supreme Court, with trial and appellate divisions. While the bulk of the work performed by these courts is in original jurisdiction, there are many cases heard on appeal by the court sitting in banc. The Supreme Court is the only court exercising general jurisdiction in law and equity. As an additional protection to the highest court of appeal, this court is given final jurisdiction in handling several types of cases.

Finally, one comes to the capstone of the state judicial system, the highest appellate court. The most common designation applied to this court is "supreme court" although, to refer again to New York, one finds the anomalous situation of a supreme court that is not supreme, the final appellate jurisdiction resting in the Court of Appeals. Texas has two supreme courts, one for civil matters, and another for criminal. These courts range in size from three to nine members. Fourteen states have five members, eighteen states have seven. The jurisdiction of the highest court is chiefly appellate in character, sometimes accompanied by a rule-making power, and sometimes enlarged by grants of original jurisdiction made in the constitution of the state.[21] This is usually confined to the issuance of original writs — a power which in fact is seldom used. It would be extremely interesting, if space permitted, to inquire into a number of important questions relating to the organization and functioning of the highest appellate courts — questions such as the growth of these courts in number of judges, the character of the personnel, the use of commissioners and of divisional organization, et cetera. A study of judicial influence made in 1936, showing the combined

[20] Data from a letter to the author from the late Judge Ralph H. Smith, Allegheny County Court of Common Pleas, July 10, 1939. For a record of nearly a quarter of a century of this work in Detroit, see Selling, Lowell S., "The Psychopathic Clinic in a Criminal Court, Its Uses and Possibilities," *Journal* of the American Judicature Society, April 1945, pp. 169–173.

[21] See "A Study of the Illinois Supreme Court," *University of Chicago Law Review*, Autumn 1947, pp. 107–176.

prestige rating of these courts in the order of rank, put New York first, with the next eight as follows: Massachusetts, Illinois, New Jersey, California, Pennsylvania, Michigan, Minnesota, and Wisconsin. Some of these questions will be referred to later.[22]

Over-all Organization. The National Conference of Judicial Councils, in its important survey of the extent to which the standards of the American Bar Association for improving the administration of justice have been accepted throughout the country, classifies the state court systems in four groups, as indicated in the table on page 608. Of the states in the second group, seven have either a constitutional or statutory mandate providing that the supreme court shall have general superintendence over all courts of inferior jurisdiction. In practice, this appears to mean very little. Five states have provision for a form of control "falling between strict external control and strict internal control." The other five utilize a minimum number of controls of any kind.[23]

Considerable attention is now being given to problems of over-all organization, and greater progress should be in evidence in the next few years. While constitutional conventions, as in Georgia, Missouri, New Jersey, and New York, provide an excellent opportunity to survey the existing court organization, efforts at improvement need not be limited to such occasions. New Jersey, to be sure, has had a complete judicial reorganization as a result of the provisions of its new Constitution. State reorganization commissions, whose powers are sufficiently broad, may include the judicial system in their surveys of state governments; the Connecticut Commission did this, coming out with recommendations for a complete reorganization along the lines of the new structure in New Jersey. The judicial councils, and occasionally the legislative councils, have done their part. State legislative committees and commissions in many states have been studying problems of judicial organization and procedure. State bar associations, goaded on by the American Bar Association, are giving serious attention to these problems, and pressing for the adoption of new and improved methods of court organization, selection of judges, and other matters. This section, with the exception of the discussion of the minor judiciary, has been concerned primarily with existing structure; the nature of the proposed changes will be considered later.

Conference of Chief Justices. In a historic meeting full of import for the advancement of the judicial systems of the states, sponsored jointly by the Council of State Governments and the American Bar Association, the chief justices of the states gathered in St. Louis in 1949, to organize the Conference

[22] See Mott, Rodney L., "Judicial Influence," *American Political Science Review*, April 1936, pp. 295–315; and other references, cited in earlier editions of this volume. The reader should not pass over this discussion without consulting the legislative manual of his own state, or some other convenient source, in order to get clearly in mind the details of the specific organization provided for by the constitution and the laws of that state.

[23] Vanderbilt, *op. cit.*, pp. 39–43; the data in the table are from the same source.

Effective Judicial Administration

DEGREE OF CONTROL	STATES
1. "Substantially no measure of external control is exercised over any part of the state judicial system."	11 states — Arizona, Arkansas, Colorado, Delaware, Georgia, Indiana, Mississippi, Nevada, Vermont, Wisconsin, Wyoming
2. States having "minimum number of elements of external control."	17 states — Florida, Iowa, Kansas, Kentucky, Minnesota, Montana, Nebraska, New Hampshire, New Mexico, North Dakota, Oklahoma, Rhode Island, South Carolina, South Dakota, Tennessee, Utah, Washington
3. States having "provision for some effective external control of one or more sets of courts, but not for all of them."	16 states — Alabama, Connecticut, Idaho, Illinois, Louisiana, Maine, Massachusetts, Michigan, New York, North Carolina, Ohio, Oregon, Pennsylvania, Texas, Virginia, West Virginia
4. "A substantial degree of control exercised over all or almost all of the courts."	4 states — California, Maryland, Missouri, New Jersey

of Chief Justices. This Conference — said the Council, which serves as secretariat — "epitomized the conviction of the justices that by pooling information on state judicial problems, impressive improvements could be effected in the organization and administration of justice on a nationwide basis." It further symbolized the intent of the judicial branch of state government to keep pace with the executive and legislative branches — which have profited so much from interstate consultation and cooperation — in scrutinizing and improving its processes and procedures. Two major problems were given special consideration at the first annual meeting, court organization and administration and the various aspects of court procedure and the writing of opinions.

The American Bar Association has high hopes for the future usefulness of the Conference, stating in its 1949 *Handbook*[24]:

> The Conference will provide not only a medium for the exchange of information and views of the chief officers of the judicial systems of each of the forty-eight states, but it can also do much to promote unanimity of judicial decisions and the adoption throughout the country of uniformly needed improvements in the business practices of the courts and in their administration and procedure. As a counterpart on the state level of the Federal conference

[24] See "The Conference of Chief Justices," *State Government*, December 1949, pp. 276–277 and December 1951, pp. 297–299, 307; "Conference of Chief Justices Is Organized in St. Louis," *Journal* of the American Judicature Society, October 1949, pp. 70–73; and a two-page spread in *Life*, September 19, 1949, pp. 56–57.

of chief justices of the United States courts of appeals, it may bring to the state courts a degree of efficiency and a correlation of judicial viewpoints that may well make its organization a memorable milestone in the annals of judicial administration.

The Selection of Judges

No aspect of the organization and functioning of courts is more vital than the methods used in the selection of judges. In colonial times the members of the judiciary were appointed by the Crown for life, during good behavior. When the new constitutions were framed after the independence of the colonies had been achieved, the system of selection by appointment, and usually the same conditions of tenure, were retained. The great change came in the Middle Period, when the wave of democratic sentiment swept over the country, causing a widespread substitution of popular election for appointment, and also a drastic reduction in tenure. Although few states now appoint their judges, much attention has been given to the relative merits of the two systems and to the consideration of other devices which might be used for the purpose of improving the caliber of our judges.

Appointment. It was natural that the original form of selection should have been by appointment, for the judicial function was an offshoot from the executive branch of the government. It is of the utmost importance to every individual that the independence of the judiciary be maintained, and that every effort be made to secure as jurists men of the highest character and ability. It was generally believed then, and is still believed by students, that these objectives can be much better achieved by appointment by the governor than by popular election. In an earlier chapter, it was noted that the increased powers and responsibilities of our state executives have generally served to attract men of a higher type than those who formerly served. This fact provides an additional assurance that the power of appointment will not be used for partisan and political purposes.

Popular Election. When popular election was adopted, it was believed that this was more democratic, and that it would bring to the bench men who were more concerned with the public good and more responsive to the popular will. It is a matter of record that the first of these hopes has not been realized and that the effect of the second, so far as it has been realized, has been to undermine, to a considerable extent, the independence of the judiciary. The majority of those who have studied the problem are convinced that the electoral method attracts less able men than might be secured by appointment. Men of ability and high attainments are often reluctant to enter a political campaign, particularly in states where the campaign for election must be preceded by one or more bitter primary fights. It is, furthermore, somewhat unusual to find in the same individual the qualities that are essential for a good judge and for a good candidate. Since the primary interest of the party is in winning the election, the party organization is likely to support the good candidate, regardless of his ability, qualifications, and training. Thus, under the electoral system, judges are more likely to be chosen on the basis of a friendly and engaging personality, a flair for politics, and ability as a campaign speaker, than on the basis of intellectual qualifications and general fitness for the bench.

Fantastic situations in judicial elections are not uncommon. In 1947, it was reported that more than 100 Staten Island lawyers, comprising about 50 per cent of the Richmond County Bar Association, were seeking the party designations for City Court Justice. Stuart H. Perry thus describes another rush of candidates occurring in Detroit and Wayne County some years earlier[25]:

> In the party primaries for the eighteen circuit judgeships there were 220 candidates; in the non-partisan primaries there were forty for the recorder's bench and forty-eight for the court of common pleas — a total of 308 candidates for judicial offices. More than one lawyer out of every ten in Detroit wanted to be judge. Nominations were also to be made for three non-judicial offices, which brought up the total of all primary candidates in Wayne County to about 400. . . .
>
> The number of candidates and the size of the electorate made impossible anything like an intelligent popular selection. The majority of Wayne County's 543,000 voters could not name half of the eighteen judges actually on the bench. Hardly anyone outside of the bar could name them all. Tens of thousands could barely recognize the names of a few judges, without being sure which court they belonged to, and without understanding the difference between the circuit, recorder's, and common pleas courts. An intelligent selection therefore would have been impossible even if there had been but two candidates for each position. With 220 candidates for the circuit bench and eighty-eight for other benches, the situation was fantastic.

Mr. Perry then goes on to describe the huge display advertising campaign that was carried on by candidates, the humiliating and sometimes degrading methods of campaigning that were used by them, their slogans, and their campaign pledges — some impossible to keep and some obviously ridiculous. The Polish bloc was able to exercise a disproportionate influence in the selections, getting eight out of the eighteen positions on the Democratic ticket. Among other things, he concludes that when the electorate is large, and especially when there are numerous candidates, it is impossible for most voters to appraise the judicial fitness of candidates.

Two practices have developed in some jurisdictions that tend to minimize the unfortunate effects of popular elections on the regular party ballot. Used in approximately half of the states, either of them could be developed in any state. The first is the practice of re-electing sitting judges: under this plan any judge who comes to the end of his term and who desires to continue in office automatically becomes a candidate for re-election with the support of both political parties. Without partisan opposition, no campaigning is

[25] Perry, Stuart H., "Shall We Appoint Our Judges," *Annals*, September 1935, pp. 97–108, at 99.

Methods of Choosing Judges of Higher Courts *

POPULAR ELECTION			APPOINTMENT
PARTISAN BALLOT	PARTISAN BALLOT [1]	NONPARTISAN BALLOT	APPOINTMENT OR OTHERWISE [2]
10 STATES	10 STATES	16 STATES	12 STATES
Alabama	Colorado	Arizona	California
Arkansas	Illinois	Idaho	Connecticut
Florida	Indiana	Michigan	Delaware
Georgia	Iowa	Minnesota	Maine
Louisiana	Kansas	Montana	Massachusetts
Mississippi	Kentucky	Nebraska	Missouri
New Mexico	Maryland	Nevada	New Hampshire
North Carolina	New York	North Dakota	New Jersey
Pennsylvania	Oklahoma	Ohio	Rhode Island
West Virginia	Texas	Oregon	South Carolina
		South Dakota	Vermont
		Tennessee	Virginia
		Utah	
		Washington	
		Wisconsin	
		Wyoming	

* From Council of State Governments, *State Court Systems*, Table IV (Chicago, 1951); see also Haynes, Evan, *Selection and Tenure of Judges* (National Conference of Judicial Councils, n.p., 1944), and *Book of the States, 1950–1951*.

[1] With independent ticket allowed.

[2] For more detailed information, see Footnote 27, p. 612.

necessary. The second factor is due to the fact that most judges do seek re-election. There are consequently few of what might be called original vacancies; those vacancies which do occur arise by reason of the death or resignation of a judge in the middle of the term for which he was elected. Under these circumstances, the governor usually has the power to appoint until the next election. The temporary appointee thus becomes a sitting judge, and automatically a candidate for election. Thus, in fact, most of the judges may actually be selected by appointment, even though they are elected. A study of the Common Pleas Court of Philadelphia in 1937 showed this to be true over a period of more than sixty years. Of sixty-three who served in that Court from 1873 to 1937 only eleven were originally elected; fifty-two were originally appointed. Of the twenty-one serving in the latter year only four were originally elected. The Orphans Court had had twenty judges during its existence, only the original three of whom were elected; of the six then serving all were originally appointed.[26]

Other Methods of Selection. It is unfortunate that in the minds of the

[26] *Philadelphia Record*, October 26, 1937.

general public the idea of popular election should be so deeply entrenched. In some states the mere mention of appointive judges is enough to defeat a proposal for constitutional revision. If, however, the method of election must be retained, then the election ought to be conducted on a nonpartisan ballot and at a time when the voters are not concerned with selections for important political offices. This method was used in 1951 in sixteen states. Election by the legislature is another possible method of selection used in four states. In a summary prepared by the Council of State Governments, judges were found to be nominated by party convention in six states, by party primary in twenty-one states, and by nonpartisan primary in thirteen. To summarize the practice with regard to method of selection: the governor has a part in the procedure in eight states; the legislature makes the choice in four; twenty states use the party ballot; and sixteen states use the nonpartisan ballot.[27]

Some states are making progress in working out and securing the adoption of new plans for the selection of judges. California did a pioneering job when in 1934 it adopted a constitutional amendment providing

> that vacancies in judicial office shall be filled by appointment of the governor, subject to approval by a majority of a commission consisting of the chief justice of the state, the presiding justice of the appellate court of the district involved and the attorney general. The appointments are for moderate terms, superior court six years, appellate and supreme courts twelve years. On approaching the end of his term any judge may declare his candidacy and his name will be put on the ballot at the ensuing election with no opposing candidate's name.

In the event that a judge does not so declare himself, or in the event of the need for an ad-interim appointment, the governor, with the requisite approval of a special Commission on Qualification, makes the necessary appointment or nomination. Thus appellate court judges are elected on their records, *i.e.*, on a nonpartisan ballot, the electorate deciding whether or not the incumbent judge is to be retained in office.

In 1940, Missouri adopted by constitutional amendment a somewhat similar plan, approved in 1937 by the American Bar Association, and advocated for adoption in all states not having an appointed judiciary. This

[27] California — Appointed by Governor from panel furnished by Commission
Connecticut — By General Assembly on nomination by Governor
Delaware — Appointed by Governor with advice and consent of Senate
Maine — Appointed by Governor with advice and consent of Council
Massachusetts — Appointed by Governor with advice and consent of Council
Missouri — Appointed by Governor from panel furnished by Commission
New Hampshire — Appointed by Governor with confirmation of Council
New Jersey — Appointed by Governor with advice and consent of Senate
Rhode Island — Elected by both houses of the legislature in grand committee
South Carolina — Elected by General Assembly, and by partisan ballot
Vermont — Elected by legislature, and by partisan ballot
Virginia — Elected by joint vote of both houses of General Assembly; all inferior court judges except in municipal courts (appointed by Governor) are elected by the people

plan, approved a second time in a referendum in 1942, was carried over into the new Constitution in 1943. It provides for appointment to vacancies on the bench by the governor or other elected official or officials, such appointment being restricted to a list proposed by a specially constituted commission or board representative of the bench, the bar, and the public. The appointee at the end of a certain term, and all other incumbents at the expiration of their terms, must then stand for election on a ballot in which the only vote possible is on the question of whether the judge should be retained in office.

Thus, while appointment to judicial office rests with the executive originally, his discretion is limited — which is the major difference from the California plan — and the appointee at the end of a certain term may be retained or discharged by the people.[28] The governor may select a member of his own party from the panel of names submitted, but this method insures that the individual will be qualified. Experience in Missouri has demonstrated a significant improvement in the caliber of higher court judges.

The Model State Constitution (Article VI, Section 602) provides for the election of the chief justice, and vests in him the power to "appoint justices of the supreme court department and of the other departments of the general court of justice from an eligible list, containing three names for each vacancy, which shall be presented to him by the judicial council." It continues with provisions for the electorate to vote at the next regular election, on a separate ballot, on the question whether the newly appointed judge shall remain in office or be removed. If the vote is affirmative, the judge remains to serve out his term; if not, the chief justice makes a new appointment, subject to the same type of recall.

The term of office is twelve years, at the end of the first four of which, the judge's name again appears on the ballot for a similar popular referendum on his record. Herbert Harley, long-time secretary of the American Judicature Society, describes this plan as "The best system of choosing judges and of determining how long they shall serve that has been worked out during the thirty-five years since the recall of judges movement gave the country a great scare. . . . Instead of all the judges being bedevilled every four or six years with political campaigns to save their lives, there will be only the referendum every four years, which can harm no worthy incumbent, and then eight more years of the twelve year term."

Influence of Organized Bar in Selecting Judges. Whatever the final method of selection, it seems clear that the bar associations should be per-

[28] Vanderbilt, *op. cit.*, pp. 3–4. The Missouri Plan continues to receive wide publicity: Douglas, James M., "Judicial Selection and Tenure: Missouri Plan Works Well in Actual Results," American Bar Association *Journal*, December 1947, pp. 1169–1172; Hyde, Lawrence M., "Choosing Judges in Missouri," *National Municipal Review*, November 1949, pp. 481–493, 503, and "Judges: Their Selection and Tenure," *New York University Law Quarterly Review*, July 1947, pp. 389–400; "Forty Lawyers Appraise Operation of California and Missouri Methods of Selecting Judges," *Journal* of the American Judicature Society, April 1948, pp. 176–184; Kenworthy, Charles E., "The Pennsylvania Plan to Divorce Judges from Politics," *Temple Law Quarterly*, April 1952, pp. 400–419.

mitted to exercise some influence somewhere in the process. It is fairly obvious that under ordinary circumstances the qualifications of a business or professional man and the quality of his work can best be judged by those who are engaged in the same profession or in the same line of work. It follows, therefore, that the members of the bar in a given state or in a given judicial district are in a better position to judge the qualifications of those who aspire to the bench than are ordinary laymen. If the final method of selection is to be by appointment, then the governor's choice should be made from a list certified to him by a specially constituted commission on qualifications, as under the Missouri Plan — or failing that, by the bar association itself — containing the names of those who are regarded by their professional colleagues as possessing the qualities of mind and character desired in a judge. If the final method of selection is by popular vote, then a poll may be taken of the members of the bar in the governmental unit concerned, the result of this poll being made available to all through the press and the other usual avenues of communication. Although experiments along this line were conducted in a number of jurisdictions a couple of decades ago, it now appears that this function can be better performed through the medium of the standing committees of the organized bar.[29]

Characteristics of the Judicial Office

Qualifications: Politics. In the numerous studies that have been made of the courts, court procedure, and judicial personnel, little attention has been given to the formal qualifications required of judges — constitutional, professional, or otherwise. There are no constitutional or statutory requirements for Federal judges, and the same condition exists in most states. "Formal educational and professional requirements are not of too great importance," says the American Municipal Association, whose report continues: "This is especially true where there is a growing tendency to appoint or elect men as judges who are endorsed by local practicing attorneys as being reasonably capable of performing their duties." [30]

As in the case of other public positions, the unwritten and informal qualifications are likely to be more important than those specified. Many efforts have been made to divorce the judges from politics, yet in many jurisdictions, it is impossible for a lawyer to get the support necessary to be elected unless he is active politically. After he becomes a judge, his political

[29] See Wilkin, Robert N., "The Judicial Function and the Need of Professional Selection of Judges," *Journal* of the American Judicature Society, December 1945, pp. 107–110; Winters, Glenn R., "A Better Way to Select Judges," *ibid.*, April 1951, pp. 166–173 and "The New Mexico Judicial Selection Campaign, a Case History," *ibid.*, April 1952, pp. 166–176.

[30] American Municipal Association, *Formal Professional Qualifications Required of Judges* (Chicago, 1938); see also Council of State Governments, *op. cit.*, and Cunningham, Warren, "The Judiciary in Ohio," *University of Cincinnati Law Review*, March 1951, pp. 239–264.

activity becomes an even more serious problem. The American Bar Association has taken a strong stand to require judges seeking political office to resign from the bench. Most of these candidates do resign; in 1938 Judge Charles Poletti promptly resigned his judicial position when he was nominated for Lieutenant-Governor of New York. On the other hand, Arthur H. James, a member of the Superior Court of Pennsylvania nominated for Governor in the same year, refused to resign, continued to draw his salary ($18,000 a year), and carried on his campaign for election while his colleagues faced a docket of 199 cases. When he was inaugurated, Judge James handed his resignation to Governor James. Fortunately, such violations of judicial ethics are not common.

Tenure. Members of the bench in colonial times and under the original state constitutions had a life tenure during good behavior. The democratic movement which brought about a change in the method of selection also brought about a great decrease in the length of term. In some jurisdictions this movement went so far as to reduce the term of some judges to two years. In one state where this occurred nearly every lawyer is called "judge," for there were few lawyers who had not at some time or other had an opportunity to serve on the bench. The tendency has been of late to increase somewhat the length of term. This is a wholesome sign, for if the office is to be nonpolitical in fact as well as in theory, if it does not exercise any important influence in the determination of public policy, there is certainly no justification for such very limited tenure. It is customary to provide longer terms for justices in the higher courts. A tabulation made in 1945 of the terms of supreme court justices showed a range from two years in one state to indefinite tenure in three states. Nineteen states provided a term of six years, nine states a term of eight years, six states a term of ten years, four states a term of twelve years, and the remainder, terms of various lengths.[31]

A curious situation developed in Pennsylvania, where the term for the members of the Supreme Court is twenty-one years. This would seem to be reasonable enough, since it would ordinarily provide life tenure — that is to say, a man who was old enough to aspire to this office and of sufficient standing in his profession to enable him to secure it would ordinarily, in a term of twenty-one years, serve during the remainder of his active life. A chief justice who had been elected at an early age claimed that this provision was unfair, because he was not ready to retire, and he had no group of clients to whom he might look for employment. He argued, furthermore, that long years of service on the bench had developed in his mind impartial habits of thought which actually disqualified him from pleading the cause of a particular client. It is unlikely that such a situation would arise often.

While moderately long tenure is not only desirable but necessary for the proper conduct of judicial business, there is a widespread popular

[31] See Swancara, Frank, "Short Terms as Deliberators of the American Judiciary," *Rocky Mountain Law Review*, June 1939, pp. 217–232.

prejudice against it. Albert Kales, eminent Chicago attorney, made a wise comment on this attitude some years ago when he wrote:

> It is a grave mistake to suppose that judges exercise their judicial power in a distasteful and arbitrary manner merely because they hold for life or during good behavior. An arbitrary or disagreeable course of action by a judge arises principally from the fact that he is subject to no authority which can receive complaints against him and act upon those complaints by way of private or public criticism and correction of the judge. The best protection against arbitrary and disagreeable actions by judges is a duly constituted body of fellow judges who hold a position of superior power and authority and to whom complaints as to the conduct of judges may be brought and who may investigate those complaints and exercise a corrective influence. When a considerable number of judges in a metropolitan district are provided with a chief justice and organized for the efficient handling of a great volume of business, the means of securing the exercise of a corrective influence over their conduct at once appears.[32]

Compensation. The compensation paid to judges has in most cases been fairly adequate. It is true that it is not generally as high as able members of the profession can earn in private practice, but there is some question as to the extent to which government should try to compete with private practice in the matter of compensation. There are connected with public positions a prestige value, an opportunity for public service, and in many jurisdictions a relative permanence of tenure through possibility of re-election, which go far to make up for the difference in income. In addition, the work is pleasant and agreeable, and often not so burdensome as private practice.

The salaries of judges in the various states, like those of other officials, have shown a marked upward trend since World War II. Whereas, in 1945, there were only four states paying $15,000 or more to members of their highest appellate courts, there were fourteen in 1952.[33] New York pays $28,000; New Jersey, $24,000; and Pennsylvania, $23,000. Other states in this upper bracket include California, Connecticut, Delaware, Illinois, Louisiana, Maryland, Massachusetts, Michigan, Ohio, Rhode Island, and Texas. Five states pay $10,000 but fourteen more pay between $11,000 and $14,400. Fourteen pay less than $10,000, the actual range being from $7,200 in South Dakota to $9,500 in three states. The amount of compensation should be determined by statutory provision, rather than by the constitution as is done in a few states. In addition to the specified salary, there are in numerous states provisions for allowances, expenses, and supplementary compensation.

[32] Kales, Albert, "Methods of Selecting and Retiring Judges in a Metropolitan District," *Annals*, March 1914, pp. 1–12. This subject has been one of the most widely discussed in American government; see, for instance, "Rufus Choate on Judicial Tenure," an address delivered in the Constitutional Convention of 1853, in *Journal* of the American Judicature Society, July 1933, pp. 10–20.

[33] For current information on judicial salaries, see table in latest edition of the *Book of the States*.

The salaries of judges in inferior courts are fair, but with the exception of New York, are substantially less than is paid to members of the highest court. Salaries in intermediate appellate courts in eleven states range from $8,000 or $9,000 in Georgia and Alabama to $15,000 in California. New York pays $30,000. The range in other courts — circuit, district, superior, probate, county, and municipal — is so wide that useful generalizations are impossible. Members of these courts are well paid in such states as California, New York, Michigan, North Carolina, and Pennsylvania, very poorly paid in others. In probate courts, fees and per-diem arrangements still exist in a few states.

Retirement and Removal. There are no less than seven different methods by which judges may be removed from active service; these are: death, resignation, retirement, impeachment, recall, by concurrent resolution of the legislature, or removal by action of the supreme court. Not all of these methods of removal are operative in any one state, and some of them are of such a nature as to require no comment here. There are relatively few resignations, but because the majority of the men elected or appointed are middle-aged or older, there are numerous retirements, due either to advanced age or to ill health. As has been noted in an earlier chapter, the impeachment process is effective only in theory in removing from public office those who have demonstrated their unfitness. During the entire history of the State of New York, there have been but seven proceedings for the impeachment or removal of judicial officers in the higher courts, and only two of these resulted in a judgment of removal from office. These cases all occurred between 1865 and 1939.[34]

No matter how strong the case against the accused, removal by impeachment is in practice a political proceeding. The recall is used in only about one third of the states, and in a much smaller number as applied to the judiciary. Furthermore, there are serious objections to its use in connection with judges; nowhere have these objections been better stated than in the veto message of President Taft to the resolution providing for the admission of Arizona into the Union in 1911.[35] A few states permit removal by legislative address or by the action of the supreme court.[36]

The truth of the matter is that, with the exception of those who die in office or retire from service under the provisions of a retirement law, there are few vacancies. All of the states now provide some kind of retirement system for their judges. Many of the laws are relatively new, but the provisions of some of the older ones have been liberalized. As in many other fields, these laws show the widest range of diversity with regard to such essential provisions as minimum age, minimum number of years of service, amount

[34] Edelman, Alber J., *Removal of Judges*, p. 3 (City Club of New York, 1941).

[35] See discussion, *supra*, Chapter IV, Section 1.

[36] See Frothingham, Louis A., "The Removal of Judges by Legislative Address in Massachusetts," *American Political Science Review*, May 1914, pp. 216–221.

of annuity, judges to whom applicable, and contributory provisions. Nor are the rules governing any given point uniform for all judges in the same state.[37]

The minimum age for retirement of judges in most states is sixty-five or seventy, optional in some, compulsory in others. Louisiana requires a minimum age of eighty. In some states, failure to retire at the specified age results in the loss of all retirement benefits. Ten years of service is a minimum requirement in eleven states, although four have a lower minimum and seven prescribe no minimum. Different minimal periods of service up to twenty-five years vary with the age of the judge and the rank of his court in the judicial hierarchy. Only three states follow the Federal plan of allowing full pay upon retirement. Approximately one fourth of the states allow one-half salary, four allow two thirds, four three fourths. Others specify amounts ranging from $1,200 to $4,500, the amount in some cases being determined in part by length of service. Few states attempt to run the system on an actuarial basis. Only about one third of the states having retirement systems require contributions from the judges themselves; these range from 2 per cent to 6 per cent, with most making deductions ranging from $2\frac{1}{2}$ to 5 per cent. Even these rates, noticeably lower than those applying to employees under other public retirement systems, do not apply to judges in two thirds of the states maintaining retirement systems applicable to judges.

Powers of Judges. The official powers and duties of judges vary considerably according to the type of court to which they belong. Trial judges conduct judicial proceedings in open court, and render decisions in the cases tried. In criminal proceedings their duties may also include the imposing of sentence, if the accused is convicted. Judges of appellate courts, sitting either in banc or in divisions, listen to the arguments of opposing counsel, possibly interrupting from time to time to ask questions. Oral argument is followed by a further study of the record, and discussion of the points raised. After the attitude of the court has been agreed upon in a given case, one of the justices is assigned the task of preparing the opinion of the court.

There is always a great temptation to impose upon judges responsibility for the performance of nonjudicial duties. In some cases, they become responsible for the management and administration of sizable properties and business enterprises, although they are not necessarily qualified to perform such duties. More often, they are called upon to exercise the appointing power. Because jurists are intelligent, educated, and supposedly nonpolitical, they are frequently required to select members of school boards, tax boards, park commissioners, boards of city trusts, et cetera.

[37] For analytical tables, see *State Court Systems*, *op. cit.*, Table VII, or the current edition of the *Book of the States;* for discussion of one state plan, Diehl, John, and Minkin, Noah, "A Retirement System for Judges and Justices in Wisconsin," *Wisconsin Law Review*, July 1950, pp. 662–676.

Judges in Philadelphia, for instance, appoint the members of eight governmental agencies handling millions upon millions of dollars of public moneys and employing thousands of workers. Generally speaking, this is bad practice, although there are cases in which this method of selection has worked well. As a matter of principle, judges should not be required by the constitution or by statute to engage in the performance of nonjudicial duties.

The Judicial Council Movement

The judicial council movement is one of the most important developments which has taken place during the first half of the twentieth century, for the improvement of judicial organization and administration. Like most apparent innovations in government, it developed in part out of experience, in part out of "theory." The first ancestor, so to speak, of the modern council was formed in Wisconsin in 1913 when twenty-five circuit judges met and organized a Board of Circuit Judges which met annually for twenty years to discuss problems related to the administration of justice. Similar bodies were established in New Jersey in 1915, later in Pennsylvania. More conference than council, these agencies indicated a groping in the direction of the council idea, first proposed in the Model State Constitution in 1921.

The judicial council of today, in the judgment of some students, "is directly traceable to the Massachusetts Judicature Commission of 1919 created by the legislature to investigate the judicature of the Commonwealth, to ascertain whether any or what changes in the organization, rules and methods of procedure and practice of the several courts, the number and jurisdiction thereof, the number and powers of the judges and officers connected therewith, would insure a more prompt, economical and just dispatch of judicial business." The first adoption of the plan in its present form occurred in Ohio in 1923. By 1949, it had spread to three fourths of the states, as indicated in the table on page 620.[38] Among the more significant councils are those of eight states — California, Connecticut, Kansas, Massachusetts, Michigan, New York, Ohio, and Texas. The growth of this movement has been due to a constantly increasing realization of the need for improvement in the methods of administering justice; more specifically, the causes have been stated in classic form by Roscoe Pound[39]:

[38] National Conference of Judicial Councils, *Handbook* (Newark, annually). The *Journal* of the American Judicature Society reports on current developments, and bibliographies appear in the Conference' *Handbook*. In addition to items cited in previous editions of this volume, see Vanderbilt, *op. cit.*, pp. 64–74; Kentucky Legislative Research Commission, *Judicial Councils* (Frankfort, 1949); Merican, Harry B., "A Checklist of State Judicial Council Reports from Their Beginnings Through 1947," *Law Library Journal*, May 1948, pp. 135–144; Nims, Harry D., "The Judicial Council: A Quarter Century of Progress," American Bar Association *Journal*, October 1949, pp. 817–820; Winters, Glenn R., "Silver Anniversary of the Judicial Council Movement," *Journal* of the American Judicature Society, August 1949, pp. 43–49, and October 1949, pp. 79–84.

[39] "The Crisis in American Law," *Journal* of the American Judicature Society, June 1926, pp. 5–11.

In the substantive law there has been steady growth. But growth by judicial decision, through experience of the operation of legal precepts in their application to litigated cases, is too halting to meet the needs of business in an era of rapid development of business methods. . . . Here the main difficulty is that it is no one's business to study the law functionally, to perceive how and where it falls short, and why; to discover leaks in our apparatus of precepts and doctrines and find out how to stop them. Fifty years ago the judiciary committees of the houses of the legislature were equal to the small amounts of investigation of this sort that was required for the efficient functioning of the law. Later committees of law reform in bar associations have been able to do part of this task. But today the task has become too great for these agencies. They are not continuously at work. They have no means of surveying the whole field. They can give but a fraction of their time. *We must find some agency which is always in operation, which works under conditions of permanence, independence, and assured impartiality, in which, therefore, the public may repose confidence. . . .*

The judicial councils have to a large extent met this need in those states in which they have been established.

Judicial Councils — 1949 *
Showing Date of Enactment of Original Law

1. State having no judicial council or similar body (12)

Colorado	Idaho — 1929[1]	Montana	Oregon — 1923
Delaware	Illinois — 1929	Nevada	South Carolina
Florida	Louisiana	New Mexico — 1933	Wyoming

2. Judicial councils now defunct, inactive, or unable to function (10)

Arizona — 1936	Iowa — 1936	Mississippi	Utah — 1931
Arkansas — 1941	Maine — 1932	Pennsylvania — 1937	
District of Columbia	Maryland — 1929	Rhode Island — 1939	

3. Judicial councils of judges without representation of bar and legislatures (12)

California — 1926	Massachusetts — 1924	Missouri — 1934	Vermont — 1945
Connecticut — 1927	Michigan — 1929	New Hampshire 1945	Virginia — 1926
Kentucky — 1928	Minnesota — 1937	North Dakota — 1927	West Virginia — 1933

4. Judicial councils with rounded representation recommended by the American Bar Association (15)

Alabama — 1945	Nebraska — 1939	Ohio — 1923	Texas — 1929
Georgia — 1945	New Jersey — 1930	Oklahoma — 1933	Washington — 1925
Indiana — 1935	New York — 1934	South Dakota — 1933	Wisconsin — 1929
Kansas — 1927	North Carolina — 1931	Tennessee — 1943	

* Vanderbilt, *op. cit.*
[1] In process of restoration.

Professor Sunderland, who was intimately connected with the movement at its inception, and for many years thereafter, developed in more detail the existing defects, indicating thereby the opportunities for service by the councils[40]:

> If the administration of justice is to meet the needs of the public, a thorough testing and overhauling of the organization and operation of courts, commissions, and other cognate agencies must take place. New methods must be devised and old methods reformed or applied to new uses. Venue must be made more convenient, service of process simplified, ex parte pleadings must surrender their dominant position in ligitation, greater use must be made of discovery before trial, of judicial framing of issues, and of proof by affidavit and by admissions of parties, procedural rules must be directory, not mandatory, actual prejudice must be the indispensable basis for all procedural objections, rules of evidence must be radically revised, calendars must be arranged in a way to avoid the shocking waste of time on the part of judges, lawyers, and witnesses which has become familiar practice, better coöperation between judge and jury must be reëstablished, a much more comprehensive system of references and auxiliary administrative machinery must be developed, the economic waste and legal risks of new trials must be reduced, the mechanism for the review of judgments must be enormously simplified and cheapened, courts must be unified and judicial personnel be subject to mobilization wherever needed, and better methods must be devised for the selection and retirement of judges.

Organization. The organization of the councils has been simple. They vary in size from five or six in Vermont and Rhode Island to twenty or more in New York, North Dakota, and Tennessee. Kentucky has fifty-four. In twelve states, including five of those whose councils are rated as most significant, the size ranges from nine to twelve. The purpose is to give representation to laymen and to various types of lawyers — practicing lawyers, judges, professors of law, chairmen of the judiciary committees in the legislature, and the attorney general. George M. Morris, former President of the American Bar Association, has made some interesting observations on this point[41]:

> Where either lawyers or judges serve alone they seem to lack the energy for sustained attack. Where judges and lawyers serve together, each group seems to have a diffidence about imposing its views upon the other, which stultifies action. Where, however, laymen are included, their presence seems to act as an "icebreaker" and to stir activity among the professional members of the council. Laymen's criticisms are sharper.

The Kansas statute provides that the Council shall be composed of one justice of the Supreme Court; two judges of different judicial districts, each of whom shall have served in such capacity four years previous to his appointment; four resident lawyers, each of whom shall have been admitted to practice for not less than ten years previous to his appointment; the

[40] Sunderland, Edson R., "The Function and Organization of a Judicial Council," *Indiana Law Journal*, May 1934, pp. 479–497, at 484–486.

[41] "The Judicial Councils of the States," American Bar Association *Journal*, July 1943, pp. 366–368, and quoted by Winters, Glenn R., Silver Anniversary article, *op. cit.*

chairman of the Judiciary Committee of the House of Representatives; and the chairman of the Judiciary Committee of the Senate. The Council in Texas is larger, but the personnel is designated in accordance with the same underlying principles[42]:

> The Chief Justice of the Supreme Court, who shall be president and chief executive officer of the Council.
> An Associate Justice of the Supreme Court to be selected by that Court.
> The Chief Justice of each of the Courts of Civil Appeals.
> The presiding judge in each of the administrative judicial districts.
> The Attorney General.
> Two members of the Legislature who shall be chairmen, respectively, of the Senate and House committees on civil jurisprudence.
> Four practicing attorneys of the state to be selected, two by the State Bar Association and two by the Supreme Court.
> One member of the faculty of the State University Law School to be selected by the President of the State University.
> Three laymen, citizens of this State, one of whom shall be by profession a journalist, and all of whom shall be appointed by the Governor.

Powers and Duties. The powers and duties of the councils have been variously enumerated and classified; it seems appropriate, for the present purpose, to group these powers under three general headings: (1) general administrative supervision; (2) rule-making power; (3) research and investigation. Before considering the exact nature of the work performed under these powers, it is important to emphasize the fact that, legally, the judicial council stands in a unique position. It is not a legislative body; it enacts no laws, although it may recommend legislative policies, and may draft acts for the consideration of the legislature. It is not a judicial body; it decides nothing, although it is deeply concerned with the procedure under which cases are moved through the courts, ultimately to the determination of the questions which they raise. Nor is it actually an executive or administrative body, although its powers of this type are more extensive than in the legislative and judicial fields. It is primarily an advisory and investigating body, so constituted that in most cases its recommendations are more effective and more likely to be translated into action than are those of most other bodies.

(1) *General Administrative Supervision.* Under its power of general administrative supervision of the judicial business of the state, the council is responsible for the collection of statistics and other information showing the condition of the dockets at all times in every civil and criminal court in the state, and for the annual publication of these records. Seventeen states will make no provision for, or do not require the collection and compilation of judicial statistics. Fourteen states do so only in isolated instances or in a sporadic way. In thirteen of the remaining states — Alabama, Connecticut, Kansas, Kentucky, Michigan, Minnesota, North Carolina, North Dakota,

[42] Kansas *Laws of 1927*, Chapter 187, Sec. 1, and Texas *Laws of 1929*, Chapter 309, Sec. 2.

Ohio, Pennsylvania, Texas, Virginia, and Washington — handling the collection of statistics is the work of the judicial council, while in the remaining four — California, Massachusetts, New Jersey, New York, — and also in the District of Columbia, the judicial council also collects judicial statistics, but on a more complete and comprehensive basis than in other jurisdictions.[43]

Prior to the establishment of the councils — and even now in many states — data of this type were rarely if ever available, even to the judges themselves. Upon the basis of this information, it becomes the duty of the council, when authorized by law, to transfer judges from districts in which the dockets are clear, to others in which there are long calendars of cases awaiting trial. This practice is based upon the important principle that the state should at all times have the right to the service of its entire judicial force. This objective has been in part achieved in some states without judicial councils, but the assignment of judges may itself lead to abuses unless proper safeguards are established. In most states the councils can and should exercise the right to make suggestions to judges, for the more efficient handling of the work of their courts.

(2) *Rule Making.* The second power usually exercised by the councils is that of rule making. On this subject the American Judicature Society urged, as far back as October 1928:

> . . . We should place rule making power first, as the power which dovetails with administrative direction, and which in every way is better vested in a representative board of judges, than in a supreme court. The only yielding on this point is to say that if the supreme court has complete rule making power, as in Washington, then the judicial council should take the initiative, do all the work of gathering data, drafting rules, discussing proposals with the bar, and finally pass them up to the court for adoption. All these steps are ordinarily required in drafting rules and it is not to be presumed that any supreme court will have the time and patience to devote to them. . . .

Statutes have authorized the establishment of judicial councils or advisory committees to aid in the study of procedure for the formulation of rules in more than half the states — twenty-six in 1949, to be exact. In nineteen states, the courts have expressly maintained that the rule-making power of the courts is inherent, and have acted on that principle. Miscellaneous arrangements exist in the three remaining states. Because judicial councils have an advisory function and courts have actual rule-making power in many states, it should not be assumed that this power is exclusive or that the legislatures have withdrawn from the field. Their importance in rule making is certainly declining, but they still play an active role in many jurisdictions.[44]

(3) *Investigation and Research.* The research may consist of making

[43] See Pound, Roscoe, "Judicial Councils and Judicial Statistics," American Bar Association *Journal*, February 1942, pp. 98–105; and Vanderbilt, *op. cit.*, pp. 74–87.

[44] Vanderbilt, *op. cit.*, Chapter 3, especially pp. 128–136, and Sunderland, Edson R., "Implementing the Rule Making Power," *New York University Law Review*, January 1950, pp. 27–41.

reports on special subjects from time to time, with recommendations to the legislature or to the governor, and of drafting acts to carry out such recommendations as an aid to the legislature. Even if the council has the rule-making power, there will be some matters that can be properly handled only by statute. The subjects under consideration are likely to be numerous and of a widely varied nature; the New York Council, set up and financed on a bigger scale than any other, has a most impressive list of accomplishments. The *Fourteenth Annual Report* for 1948, following a uniform pattern of previous volumes, lists two pages of current recommendations, six new ones having to do with review of tax assessments, abolishing tender after suit, removal of statutory limitations on counterclaims in matrimonial actions, proposed improvements in the handling of trust cases, small abandoned court deposits, and removal of existing age limitations on certain official referees; and twenty-two renewed recommendations, some of them of several years' standing. Two more pages list thirty-two subjects under consideration; research on many of these is now under way. The Council reviews its own activity through the years as follows:

> From 1934 to 1941, the Judicial Council concentrated principally on the problem of eliminating undue delay in the courts of civil jurisdiction. . . . This problem of delay, which had loomed very large in 1934, appeared to have been substantially solved by 1941. Accordingly, from 1941 to 1947 the Council concentrated on the simplification of procedure, practice and administration in the courts and the reduction of uncertainties and expenses of litigation. However, since 1945, delays in tort jury cases have been manifest in some counties of the Supreme Court [due to] the large increase in Supreme Court litigation. . . . In order to prevent a continuing deterioration of the condition of the calendars, the Council has reinstated the problem of delay in its primary concern.

The National Conference of Judicial Councils meets annually in connection with the American Bar Association, for the purpose of coordinating the work of all the judicial councils and of facilitating the exchange of information derived from the investigations and research of each. Its aim is to serve as a great clearing house of information and experience on all questions relating to judicial organization and administration. The significance of the work done in this field is such that some years ago, former Dean Pound observed that "No one can be sure that he is in a position to speak with assurance upon or draft a statute or rule with respect to any important question until he has looked through the reports of the judicial councils." [45]

In 1931, Professor Sunderland summarized the possibilities of the judicial council movement when he said: "A judicial council organized with not too large a personnel, with authority to require reports from the clerks of courts, with adequate research facilities available, and with the support derived from the confidence of the public, will find unlimited pos-

[45] Address to Boston Bar Association, 13 *Boston Bar Bulletin* 77, and quoted by Nims, *op. cit.*

sibilities for improving and developing the administration of justice." This statement, true when it was written, is equally true nearly a quarter of a century later.

Problems of Administrative Reorganization

Many administrative problems connected with state court organization await some remedial or corrective action. While it is impossible to discuss any of them at length here, the nature of some can be suggested. There is, in the first place, the problem of the selection of clerks, bailiffs, tipstaves, and other court officers. There is the problem of reorganizing the units of judicial administration, and the desirability of eliminating justices of the peace, thereby making it possible to entrust the administration of justice in rural areas to one or more competent, full-time county judges. The urban magistrates constitute an obstacle to the administration of justice which could be remedied either by establishing well-organized municipal courts in the larger cities, or by transferring the function to a county unit in the case of the smaller ones. The administration of justice is hampered by intricate and too technical rules of procedure, by unsound practices with regard to the conduct of trials and the filing of appeals, and in many other ways.

Necessary Constitutional Changes. The first and most obvious need in many states is to simplify the constitutional provisions which provide for the establishment of the judicial system. Many of these are not only needlessly long and complicated, but they freeze into the constitution a particular judicial organization which, although suitable at the time the constitution was adopted, is not adapted to modern conditions. Oftentimes the entire judicial structure is included, even to the justices of the peace and the magistrates. It avails little to say that such provisions can be changed to bring them in line with present-day needs, if the amending process is as unworkable as that provided in many state constitutions. The states might well take a leaf from the experience of the Federal government, and follow the recommendation contained in the Model State Constitution.

The Federal Constitution provides in the opening sentence of Article III that "The Judicial power of the United States shall be vested in one Supreme Court, and in such inferior courts as Congress may from time to time ordain and establish." The Model State Constitution puts the idea in these words: "The judicial power of the state shall be vested in a general court of justice. . . ." The problem of correcting defects in the organization of the state courts would be a relatively simple matter if the state constitutions, in similar manner, were to provide that the judicial power of the state should be vested in a supreme court and such inferior courts as the legislature might from time to time ordain and establish.

Unified Court System. In recent years there has been much discussion of the need for a uniform system of state courts. The prevailing practice sets up a number of different types and kinds of courts, each independent and each exercising particular types of jurisdiction, usually within definitely specified areas. In the words of Presiding Justice Peck of the Appellate Division in New York, "our trouble is that we have too many courts separated into narrow compartments by arbitrary jurisdictional lines or boundaries with no means of moving either judges or cases across the boundaries."

The proposal is to make all courts THE COURT, in the belief that there is no reason why any judge should not hear any cause of action. This recommendation finds precedent in the provisions of the English Judicature Acts which effected important changes in the organization of the English courts. The Court of Appeals supplanted the several intermediate appellate courts which had existed before its creation; the High Court replaced the Courts of King's Bench, Common Pleas, Exchequer, Chancery, Admiralty, et cetera, and from it are drawn the Justices of Assize, who go on circuit to try criminal cases. The conditions in the states may not be quite as serious as those which had developed in England, but in many jurisdictions they are bad enough. In addition, it is urged that this highly centralized court organization gives an elasticity to the machinery for the administration of justice that is impossible where an elaborate court structure is provided for in the constitution.

The plans for unification have been numerous, but there seems to be a general agreement upon certain fundamentals in the structure of the state court system, including[46]:

1. Establishment of a general court of judicature for the state.
2. Abolition of justice of the peace and magistrates courts, with provision for the changes necessary to handle cases formerly handled by them.
3. Establishment of several main divisions of the court, as supreme, district, and county.
4. Establishment of a judicial council.
5. Provision for adequate central administrative supervision and control.

A proposal for complete unification is contained in Article VI of the Model State Constitution, and has long been vigorously advocated by the American Judicature Society.

Not until 1948 was it possible to point to a single state in which a comprehensive judicial reorganization had been effected, although administrative controls over the courts existed in California, Maryland, and Missouri. The New Jersey Constitution of 1947 transformed — in the words of Glenn R. Winters, Editor of the *Journal* of the American Judicature Society and Secretary of the Society — "America's worst court system into America's best." The Constitution provided for a Supreme Court, a Superior Court, and a County Court; the nature of these provisions is indicated in the chart on page 628. It did not abolish the inferior courts, but left their establishment, alteration, or abolition within the province of the legislature. The

[46] See *Journal* of the American Judicature Society, issue of April 1940, especially article by Roscoe Pound, "Principles and Outline of a Modern Unified Court Organization."

legislature promptly abolished them, and provided for — in the words of Governor Driscoll's Inaugural Address of 1950 — "a state-wide system of county district courts and municipal courts to replace police courts, recorders' courts, family courts, magistrate courts, justice of the peace courts, city district courts, and small claims courts. The new courts are an integral part of the State Judicial System, under the supervision of the Chief Justice of the Supreme Court." The new system is achieving its objective and appears to be working well.[47]

The report of the Commission on State Government Organization in Connecticut, issued in 1950, called for a unified court functioning in five divisions, namely, the Supreme Court of Errors, the Superior Court Division, Common Pleas Division, Family Court Division, and Probate Division. It also called for a "coordinated administrative authority and facilities and a rule making power." The former responsibility would be given to the Chief Justice who would be assisted by an Office of Judicial Services, comparable to the Administrative Office of the United States Courts. The Supreme Court would be vested with rule-making powers.

It is the contention of Roscoe Pound that "unification of the courts would go far to enable the judiciary to do adequately much which we have been committing to administrative boards and commissions." The controlling principle, he points out, must be not specialized courts, but specialized judges. He would achieve this objective through unification, flexibility, conservation of judicial power, and responsibility. "Unification is called for in order to concentrate the machinery of justice upon its tasks, flexibility in order to enable it to meet speedily and efficiently the continually varying demands made upon it, responsibility in ordering that someone may always be held, and clearly stand out as the official to be held, if the judicial organization is not functioning the most efficiently that the law and the nature of its tasks permit."

An Administrative Officer. One of the most urgent needs of the state courts is the establishment of some plan for an administrative officer. As one state supreme court justice has said, "It must be admitted that the legal machinery we have was designed for heavy duty and long wear, rather than for speedy and economical action." The Model State Constitution recommends, in Article VI, Section 603, that this power be vested in the chief justice. Some states have made some progress toward the solution of this problem — a problem which should not be too difficult now, with the very satisfactory Federal experience to serve as a guide. In 1948, the National Conference of Commissioners on Uniform State Laws put out a model act to provide for an administrator for the state courts, whose duty it would be to:

[47] See Woelper, Willard G., "Jersey Justice Streamlined," *National Municipal Review*, June 1952, pp. 283–287, 315; also Habermann, Philip S., "Strengthening Wisconsin's Judicial System," *State Government*, May 1952, pp. 104, 114–115.

New Jersey's Court System under the Constitution of 1947 *

ARTICLE	COURT	COMPOSITION	SUMMARY OF PROVISIONS
Art. VI Sec. i, ii	Supreme	Chief Justice and six Associates	With broad powers of administration over all courts in the state. Jurisdiction: final appeals in all important and selected cases. First term, seven years. Tenure on reappointment, retirement at seventy.
Art. VI Sec. iii, v	Superior	Minimum of twenty-four judges	Functions in three divisions: Law, Chancery, and Appellate. Latter decides appeals from other divisions and county courts, and as may be provided by law. Term, tenure and retirement same as Supreme Court.
Art. VI Sec. vi	County	Minimum of one county judge in each county	Jurisdiction same as that of all five old county courts, with equity powers when required for complete determination of case. Jurisdiction subject to change by law.
Art. VI Sec. i	Inferior — including country traffic; district; police, recorder and family; juvenile and domestic relations; surrogate; criminal district; small cause, and justice of the peace.		Not abolished by revision but may be established, altered or abolished by law. Appeals therefrom as provided by law.
Art. VI Sec. vi			All judges appointed by Governor with approval of Senate, except municipal judges and surrogates.

* Prepared for the New Jersey Committee for Constitutional Revision, by Joseph Harrison, and reproduced in *Journal* of the American Judicature Society, February 1948, p. 143.

1. Examine the administrative methods and systems employed in the offices of the clerks of the several courts.

2. Examine the state of the dockets of the courts and determine the need for assistance by any court.

3. Make recommendations to the Chief Justice relating to the assignment of judges.

4. Collect and compile statistical and other data and make reports of the business transacted by the courts.

5. Prepare and submit budget estimates of state appropriations necessary for the maintenance and operation of the judicial system.

6. Draw all requisitions for the payment of state moneys appropriated for the maintenance and operation of the judicial system.

7. Collect statistical and other data and make reports relating to the expenditure of public moneys, state and local, for the maintenance and operation of the judicial system.

8. Obtain reports from clerks of court in accordance with law or rules adopted by the court of last resort on cases and other judicial business.

9. Act as secretary of the judicial council and perform such other duties as may be assigned by the council.

10. Formulate and submit to the court of last resort recommendations of policies for the improvement of the judicial system.

11. Attend to such other matters as may be assigned by the court of last resort.

In Iowa, as in many other states, the Constitution provides that "the Supreme Court shall . . . exercise a supervisory control over all inferior judicial tribunals throughout the state," and sixteen other states have a more or less similar requirement. As noted earlier, these provisions have little practical significance or affect. Missouri and New Jersey under their new constitutions make provision for a real system of judicial administration, and some other states have gone part way. Connecticut has established by law an executive secretary to the judicial department, with duties similar to those provided in the Model Act, while other states are thinking and moving in this direction.

The plan for an administrative judge has its basis in the development of the English system. It has been used in the municipal courts of Cleveland and Detroit, and in the state courts of Massachusetts. In the former state the jurisdiction of the Chief Justice of the Superior Court is statewide; in the latter, the Chief Justice of the Circuit Court possesses similar jurisdiction, while an administrative judge, known as the Presiding Judge, serves in the Circuit Court of Wayne County. In Ohio there is no Chief Justice of the Court of Common Pleas with statewide jurisdiction, but there is a Chief Justice of the Court of Common Pleas of Cuyahoga County.

In all these instances the adoption of the plan has brought a decided improvement both in the quality of judicial performance and in the calendar situation. In Detroit the improved calendar situation is explained by an increase in the number of juries waived and by improved executive management of the court's business, as well as by the addition of a number of judges. As applied in a state court situation, it is argued that the adoption of the plan would make possible (without a unified court) the assignment of judges to the more congested courts, the reduction of the number of jury trials, the development of a conciliation or settlement calendar, and improved administration of the business of the courts. The bar associations have generally approved the plan, but there has been a natural reluctance on the part of the judiciary to accept it.

Improvements in the Appellate Courts. The proposal to simplify the constitutional basis of the state courts (and for a unified court system) affects the whole judicial system of a state. The proposal for an administrative judge would affect mainly the lower courts. It is now proposed to present briefly some suggestions for the improvement of the operation of the courts of review. Perhaps the best study of this subject is the one made for the Judicial Council of Michigan.[48] This report discusses ten specific proposals, the first of which is the enlargement of the membership of the court to increase its operating capacity. A tabulation of the number of regular judges

[48] Curran, Edward O., and Sunderland, Edson R., "The Organization and Operation of Courts of Review," in *Third Report* of the Judicial Council of Michigan, 1933, pp. 50–246.

of the courts of last resort for the forty-eight states shows that most of these courts began with three or five judges, and that they have since been increased to seven or, in a few cases, to nine judges. These increases have been helpful, but without accompanying improvements in the procedure of these courts they are not of sufficient importance to solve the problem. The second proposal is the use of commissioners; this device has been resorted to for brief periods in many states since 1875, but it is nowhere regarded as anything more than a measure of temporary relief for congested calendars.

A third proposal is the temporary use of lower court judges. Virginia was the pioneer in this movement as early as 1789. Many arguments have been advanced for and against this solution, the most important of which is, perhaps, the fact that it tends to lower the prestige of the higher courts. This defect might be avoided by the creation of appellate departments of trial courts. The fourth suggestion, a more practical one for increasing the capacity of reviewing courts, calls for the setting up of a divisional organization. This method is now used in Alabama, Arkansas, Colorado, Florida, Georgia, Iowa, Kentucky, Mississippi, Missouri, Nebraska, Oregon, Texas, and Washington; it has been used at some time, for a limited period, in California, Illinois, Kansas, Louisiana, New York, Ohio, and Oklahoma. Two or three divisions are commonly used, with either a fixed or a rotating personnel. For the more important cases the court sits as a whole.[49]

The fifth suggestion is to provide judges with trained assistants, usually referred to as law clerks; this device has been used in California, Illinois, Oklahoma, and Pennsylvania, and for certain judges in Massachusetts, New Jersey, and New York. The sixth proposal is for the use of intermediate appellate courts; such courts have long been in use in the larger and more populous states, and are functioning now in about one third of the states, including Alabama, California, Georgia, Illinois, Indiana, Louisiana, Missouri, New Jersey, New York, Ohio, Pennsylvania, Tennessee, and Texas. This is one of the most important of the many proposals submitted. The seventh would impose restrictions upon the right of review. This has been done in some form in all the states, but it is obviously easier in those states which have an intermediate court of review.

The eighth proposal is concerned with the methods of dealing with the problem of written opinions; it has been popularly expected and usually required by law that there would be a written opinion in every case heard by a court of review, but there is in fact little reason why such opinions should be prepared, with the consequent expenditure of time and effort, unless there is involved in the case some fundamental legal or constitutional question. This occurs in only a relatively small percentage of the cases brought before a court of review. These courts have therefore, in many jurisdictions, resorted to the use of mere orders, in some instances with

[49] In addition to Chapter 5 of the Curran and Sunderland study, see Sharp, Susie M., "Supreme Courts Sitting in Divisions," *North Carolina Law Review*, June 1932, pp. 351–365.

— and in others without — an accompanying brief statement of reasons. This device is an enormous time saver for the members of the court, and has not aroused the popular resentment that might have been expected. Other proposals relate to the more effective use of briefs and oral arguments, and to the problem of rehearing.

Relations of State and Federal Courts

There are in the United States two parallel judicial systems, each exercising jurisdiction simultaneously within its own field over the same persons without any serious conflict. There are in practice a number of cases in which jurisdiction of the Federal and state courts is concurrent. In the field of criminal jurisdiction, situations arose, during the life of the prohibition amendment, in which the same individual could be prosecuted, tried, convicted, and sentenced for the same acts, separately and independently, in both the state and the Federal courts. In such cases it became a matter of practice for the Federal government to take precedence over the state, although if the Federal government failed to secure a conviction, it was still possible for the state concerned to attempt to do so. The control over citizenship provides an illustration of concurrent jurisdiction in the civil field.[50] The Federal law provides that citizenship may be granted, either by the Federal courts or by a state court of record. Although the Federal government has always possessed full power to control this subject, the greatest diversity is permitted with regard to the conditions under which citizenship is conferred.

Another important aspect of the relation of the state and Federal courts involves the attitude of the latter toward state legislation. Since the Federal courts must interpret state law when the parties are of diverse citizenship, it has been necessary for them to develop some consistent policy with regard to such interpretation. This policy has been for the Federal courts to accept, save in exceptional cases, the interpretation of the state statute which has been adopted by the highest state court. Thus the Federal courts have properly assumed that the highest court of the state was in a better position to judge the purpose and intent of the legislature in its own jurisdiction than the Federal courts could possibly be. The question upon which the Federal court passes in cases of this sort is not, therefore, whether the state act, as they read it, is constitutional, but whether the state act as understood and interpreted by the state court is within the limits of state power, so far as the provisions of the Federal Constitution are concerned. There have been a number of cases before the Supreme Court involving various aspects of this main question.[51] In over a century and a half, the Court has declared

[50] On the dual system and concurrent jurisdiction, see Wendell, Mitchell, *Relations Between the Federal and State Courts*, Chapters 1 and 2 and Part V (Columbia University Press, 1949), and Talbott, Forrest, *Intergovernmental Relations and the Courts*, with special reference to Minnesota (University of Minnesota Press, 1950).

[51] The United States Supreme Court will interfere with a decision of a state court only

unconstitutional upwards of 400 state laws, under the commerce clause, Amendment XIV, impairment of the obligation of contract, and for miscellaneous reasons. Eight state supreme courts had always avoided reversals on points of constitutionality — those of Connecticut, Delaware, Idaho, New Mexico, Oregon, Rhode Island, Vermont, and Wyoming.

Finally, there are the questions of the relations of the state and Federal courts, of rules, and of the conditions upon which appeals may lie from the state courts to the Federal. The dual system assumes cooperation; although the Federal courts have not been particularly cooperative in dealing with state courts, at least one state — Florida — has authorized and empowered its supreme court to provide, by rule of court, for the receiving and answering of certificates, as to state law, from the appellate courts of the United States, or of other states.[52] Although there are obvious advantages in a uniform system of rules in the two sets of courts, considerable diversity actually exists. It has been proposed that the states should adopt the Federal rules, and it is claimed that such adoption would not result in serious disruption of existing procedure in the substantial majority of states which now have a so-called code procedure. A comparison with the varying state rules shows that, quite apart from considerations of uniformity, the merits of a given situation are largely in favor of the Federal rules.[53] Whenever a Federal court — even a District Court — acquires jurisdiction in a case by virtue of Federal questions, such court has power to determine all questions in the case, local as well as Federal.[54]

Appeals from state courts may be taken only from the highest state court to the highest Federal court. The reasons for this are obvious. There would be no purpose in the Federal courts' considering an appeal on a case properly within the jurisdiction of the state courts until the highest court in the state had had an opportunity to pass upon it. To have a case taken from the state court to any Federal court other than the Supreme Court

---

when, in the judgment, the state ruling amounts to mere arbitrary or capricious exercise of power, or is in clear conflict with those fundamental principles which have been established for the protection and enforcement of private rights; see Jacobson, J. Mark, "Federal Interpretation of State Law," *University of Pennsylvania Law Review*, February 1938, pp. 335–369; and a series of reports on this subject, prepared by the State Law Section, Library of Congress, while current information appears in each edition of the *Book of the States*.

[52] *Laws of 1945*, Chapter 23098; see also Lewis, James R., "Comity in Relations Between Governments of the Several States and the National Government as Affected by Federal Judicial Review," *Kentucky Law Journal*, January 1947, pp. 129–142.

[53] See Wendell, *op. cit.*, Parts II and III, in which are discussed Swift v. Tyson, 16 Peters 1, 1842, and Erie Railroad Company v. Tompkins, 304 U.S. 64, 1938; Talbott, *op. cit.;* Gavit, Bernard C., "The New Federal Rules and State Procedure," American Bar Association *Journal*, May 1939, pp. 367–374, 435; and "Federal Conformity to State Rules on Presumptions and the Burden of Persuasion," *Illinois Law Review*, May 1938, pp. 101–104.

[54] Railroad Commission of California, et al., v. Pacific Gas and Electric Company, 302 U.S. 388, 1937.

would be an affront to that more or less mythical thing known as the sovereignty of the states.

There are several conditions upon which such appeals may be made. In the first place, the United States Supreme Court will receive on appeal a case in which the state court has declared a Federal law invalid. For obvious reasons there are few such cases, but the desirability of having a final review of them when they do arise, by the highest Federal court, is equally obvious. Any other procedure would open the way for numerous state court decisions invalidating Federal laws, thereby destroying the uniformity which is one of the virtues of Federal control, and thereby making possible a diminution of the Federal power by a series of decisions which might gradually whittle it away. In the second place, the Federal Supreme Court will review cases in which the constitutionality of a state statute has been questioned under the provisions of the Federal Constitution, and in which the highest state court has upheld the validity of the state law. If any other policy were followed, the provisions of the Federal Constitution applying to the states would soon cease to have an effective restraining power. Again, under a Federal law adopted in 1914, it is possible to transfer cases from state to Federal courts by certiorari.

With regard to all these problems, evidence has accumulated through the years that where a dispute arises between the state and Federal courts, the latter almost invariably win their point. Professor Field has pointed out that the Federal courts may release a party who is in the custody of a state officer, if proper showings justifying issuance of the writ of habeas corpus are made.[55] The state courts may not interfere by habeas corpus with the work of Federal officers or courts.[56] The Federal courts are careful to say that they will interfere only upon great provocation, but the fact remains that they do interfere in a manner not permitted to the states to interfere with Federal officers. Federal officers may surrender a person in their custody to the state courts if they wish to do so, but such a surrender is a matter of comity, and not one of legal obligation.[57]

"The Federal courts may enjoin state courts from proceedings with a case, and have done so occasionally,[58] but the state courts are not permitted to enjoin the Federal courts in their work."[59] Federal courts constantly interfere with state administrative officers by injunction, particularly in the field of public utility regulation and in taxation, but how often do the state courts step in to call a halt to any Federal administrative action? Con-

[55] Moore v. Dempsey, 261 U.S. 86, 1923. The constitutionality of the Federal statute permitting this was sustained in Frank v. Mangum, 237 U.S. 209, 1914.

[56] Tarble's Case, 13 Wallace 397, 1872; state courts may not issue the writ to a Federal military officer to test legality of enlistment.

[57] Pomi v. Fessenden, 258 U.S. 254, 1922.

[58] United States Code (1926), Title 28, Section 379, forbids such injunctions to issue except in bankruptcy cases.

[59] Rigg v. Johnson County, 6 Wallace 166, 1867.

gressional attempts to curtail Federal injunctive interference with state administration have been so restricted in application by the courts that they have been relatively ineffective.[60]

Diversity of citizenship cases may be removed from state to Federal courts under the provisions of a Congressional statute, and removals of this kind are legion because of the broad construction given this statute.[61] State attempts to curb removals by corporations in diversity cases have met with Supreme Court rebuffs and have proved futile.[62] Federal statutes also provide for the removal of criminal prosecutions against Federal officers in the state courts to the Federal courts; such removals have been held to be constitutional.[63]

> . . . The only consolation left to the states in the relations between the two judicial systems is that arising from the permission granted them by Congressional statute to try cases involving Federal questions, and that they not only decide questions arising under the Constitution of the United States in some instances, but may decide them as matters of first impression if no Federal precedent exists, and may even ignore such precedent when it exists, and evade compliance with the known rule of law for several years at a time.[64] But of course Supreme Court review substantially restricts the states in the long view, because of Congressional statutes permitting that Court to override state decisions upon Federal constitutional questions.[65] But here also, such questions are commonly brought to the Supreme Court at the initiative of the aggrieved individual rather than at the instance of the governments involved.[66]

SELECTED REFERENCES

Council of State Governments, *State Court Systems*, Revised Edition (Chicago, September 1951). Best current statistical data on state court systems.

Haynes, Evan, *The Selection and Tenure of Judges* (National Conference of Judicial Councils, n.p., 1944). This is the standard title on the subject, but see also Illinois Legislative Council, *Selection of Judges* (Springfield, 1948).

[60] See the fate of the "Three Judge Rule" of United States Code (1926), Title 28, Sections 380–389, as described in *Yale Law Journal*, May 1929, pp. 955–983.

[61] An important case on removal is Gaines v. Fuentes, 92 U.S. 10, 1875. The technical law on removal, mostly district court law in fact, is in hopeless confusion.

[62] Terral v. Burke Construction Company, 257 U.S. 529, 1922.

[63] Tennessee v. Davis, 100 U.S. 257, 1879. See a later case stating rules of pleading on such a removal, Colorado v. Symes, 286 U.S. 510, 1932.

[64] It often takes several years before state practice is really changed to conform to Supreme Court decisions on state powers, partly because a decision that a statute of one state is invalid does not automatically or immediately strike down similar statutes in other states.

[65] It seems commonly to be overlooked that statute now provides for the appellate jurisdiction of the Supreme Court, and that a repeal of the statute would leave to the state courts final jurisdiction over questions of Federal constitutional law arising in the state courts and not removed under the removal statutes. Appellate jurisdiction on this head is subject to "regulation" by Congress. Important early cases: Cohens v. Virginia, 6 Wheaton 264, 1821; Martin v. Hunter's Lessee, 1 Wheaton 304, 1816.

[66] Quotations from Field, Oliver P., "State versus Nation, and the Supreme Court," *American Political Science Review*, April 1934, pp. 233–245.

Kentucky Legislative Research Commission, *Judicial Councils* (Frankfort, 1949). An excellent report on an important development affecting the judiciary; see also National Conference of Judicial Councils, *Handbook* (Newark, annually since 1939).

New York State Constitutional Convention Committee, *Problems Relating to Judicial Administration and Organization*, being Vol. IX of the Committee's Report (Albany, 1938). Contains much valuable material on the problems of state courts.

Pound, Roscoe, *Organization of Courts* (Little, Brown, Boston, 1940). Most recent treatise on the subject by a recognized authority.

Sanders, Wiley B., *The Juvenile Courts of North Carolina* (University of North Carolina Press, 1948), and Warren, George, *Traffic Courts* (Little, Brown, Boston, 1942). Two excellent studies of specialized types of local courts.

Talbott, Forrest, *Intergovernmental Relations and the Courts* (University of Minnesota Press, 1950), and Wendell, Mitchell, *Relations Between the Federal and State Courts* (Columbia University Press, 1949). Two significant studies of intergovernmental relations in the judicial branch of government.

Vanderbilt, Arthur T., Ed., *Minimum Standards of Judicial Administration* (Law Center of New York University, 1949). A survey of the extent to which the standards of the American Bar Association for improving the administration of justice have been accepted throughout the country, and containing an enormous amount of specific information nowhere else available in convenient form.

18

State Courts: Procedure

The American courts, in spite of much criticism and of widely recognized defects, have occupied a unique position in public esteem. They have been generally admired and respected by the people, who have regarded them as the guardians of the Constitution, the custodians of the great heritage of the common law, and the protectors of their rights. While particular jurists or courts have sometimes been severely criticized, while particular decisions have been regarded with deep disapproval, the people have nevertheless cherished their judicial institutions and granted their judges more extensive powers and a deeper respect than have the people in any other major country.

The Powers and Duties of Courts

The powers of courts may be determined by constitutional or statutory provisions, or by both. Regardless of the type of court or of the nature of its jurisdiction, certain constitutional limitations are imposed upon it. From the Federal Constitution comes the limitation found in the supreme law clause of Article VI, which imposes upon the state judicial officers the duty of enforcing the Federal Constitution as well as that of the state. Due process and equal protection clauses binding upon the state courts are found in the War Amendments to the Federal Constitution and in the constitutions of all the states. In addition, the latter include, chiefly within their bills of rights, a large number of guarantees which may on occasion limit the jurisdiction of the state courts.

Some states have placed in their constitutions detailed provisions regarding the organization, powers, and duties of the courts.[1] Whatever the method of their determination, the powers state courts regularly exercise are of two types: inherent and jurisdictional. The inherent powers belong to the courts by virtue of the fact that they are courts, by reason of their function to determine judicially the settlement of cases brought before them.

[1] On the unwisdom of this practice, see Callender, Clarence N., "The Shackled Judiciary," *Annals*, September 1935, pp. 109–114, reprinted in *Journal* of the American Judicature Society, December 1935, pp. 101–104.

Among these are the right to preserve order within the courtroom, to punish for contempt, to employ officers, and by appropriate methods to require the enforcement of their decisions. The exercise of these powers is indispensable if the courts are to perform their duties.

There are a number of types of jurisdictional powers — original, appellate, concurrent, final, and exclusive. Original jurisdiction is exercised by courts of first instance, usually lower courts, although the constitution or the legislature may confer such jurisdiction upon the higher courts in particular types of cases. The phrase "appellate jurisdiction" is almost self-explanatory. No appeal is permitted where a court has final jurisdiction; while supreme courts commonly exercise this type of jurisdiction, the legislature can and sometimes does confer it upon other courts in particular types of cases. Many instances of concurrent jurisdiction between different courts may be found. Some cases, for instance, might be taken before a magistrate, a municipal court, or a county or district court. The selection of the proper court is a problem in procedure to be decided largely by the attorney handling the case. There are a few instances in which exclusive jurisdiction has been conferred upon some particular court in a particular type of case.

The functions of the state courts may be classified in various ways. The eminent jurist, Judge John J. Parker, in an article on the judicial office in the United States, lists three [2]:

1. The administration of justice
2. To declare the law; just as the duty of applying the law in the administration of justice is primarily the function of the trial judge, that of declaring the law is primarily the function of the appellate judge
3. To uphold the Constitution of the country, as the supreme law of the land

The performance of these functions entails many different kinds of work, as Dr. William F. Willoughby pointed out many years ago [3]:

1. The investigation and determination of facts, which function must be clearly distinguished from the work done in interpreting and applying the law to these facts
2. The application of the law to the facts as thus determined
3. The determination and construction of the law, resulting in the preparation of written opinions [4]

[2] *New York University Law Quarterly Review*, April 1948, pp. 225–238.

[3] *Principles of Judicial Administration*, Chapter 16 (Brookings Institution, Washington, 1929).

[4] These opinions, in addition to being published in separate series for each of the states, can be found in the different units of the National Reporter System, a uniform series of reports covering the courts of last resort of all the states as well as the Federal Government. Arranged geographically, the several series are as follows: (1) *Atlantic Reporter*, 1885 to date, covering Connecticut, Delaware, Maine, Maryland, New Hampshire, New Jersey, Pennsylvania, Rhode Island, and Vermont. (2) *Northeastern Reporter*, 1885 to date, covering Illinois, Indiana, Massachusetts, New York, and Ohio. (3) *New York Supplement*, 1888 to date, covering all intermediate and lower courts of record of New York. (4) *Southeastern Reporter*, 1887 to date, covering Georgia, North Carolina, South Carolina,

4. The prevention of infractions of law and the violations of rights, through the issuance of restraining orders and injunctions
5. Advising the legislature and the executive branches of the government in respect to the law[5]
6. Acting as public administrative agencies
7. The administration of property, in connection with the settlement of decedents' estates, bankruptcies, receiverships, et cetera
8. Acting as agencies for the enforcement of judicial decisions, through the compelling of the attendance of witnesses, the execution of process, et cetera
9. The determination of the rules of judicial procedure, except in those jurisdictions in which the laws provide for legislative determination

Volume of Judicial Business. It is not only the duty of courts to perform these functions; it is equally important that they should be able to handle promptly and efficiently such cases as may be brought before them. The inevitable effect of serious congestion in the courts is to deny justice to citizens. The volume of judicial business tends to fluctuate somewhat, but the general tendency in late years has been downward. The Judicial Council of New Jersey in its 1932 report showed a heavy increase up to that time — 935 per cent since 1900, as compared with a 27 per cent increase in the number of judges. But, as of 1948, the volume of judicial business in the highest appellate court in the same state, as shown in the table on page 640, has declined to one half of what it was in 1900 and to one third of what

---

Virginia, and West Virginia. (5) *Southern Reporter*, 1887 to date, covering Alabama, Florida, Louisiana, and Mississippi. (6) *Northwestern Reporter*, 1879 to date, covering Iowa, Michigan, Minnesota, Nebraska, North Dakota, South Dakota, and Wisconsin. (7) *Southwestern Reporter*, 1886 to date, covering Arkansas, Kentucky, Missouri, Tennessee, and Texas. (8) *Pacific Reporter*, 1883 to date, covering Arizona, California, Colorado, Idaho, Kansas, Montana, Nevada, New Mexico, Oklahoma, Oregon, Utah, Washington, and Wyoming. On the distinction between "opinions" and "decisions," see Rogers v. Hill, 289 U.S. 582, 1933; the terms are not equivalent, the court's *decision* of a case being its judgment thereon, and its *opinion* being the statement of reasons on which the judgment rests.

[5] Advisory opinions are common, especially in the New England states. Massachusetts adopted a constitutional provision in 1780; New Hampshire, Maine, Rhode Island, Florida, Colorado, and South Dakota followed. Alabama and Delaware provided for advisory opinions by statute, and Vermont permits the governor to make inquiries concerning the rectitude of his official acts. Comprehensive statutes have been repealed in Minnesota, Missouri, and Vermont. The system has fallen into disuse in Nebraska, New York, North Carolina, Oklahoma, and Pennsylvania, the courts of these states now expressly denying their power to render advisory opinions: see New York State Constitutional Convention Committee, *Problems Relating to Legislative Organization and Powers*, Chapter 6 (Albany, 1938). While the opinions of the Massachusetts court are frequently cited, they have no binding authority; in Colorado, advisory opinions have the same legal effect as opinions handed down in settlement of actual cases considered by the court. It has been urged that this device be more widely adopted as a means of preventing the passing and enforcement of statutes later declared unconstitutional. The soundness of this argument is open to question. For recent comment, see Edsall, Preston W., "The Advisory Opinion in North Carolina," *North Carolina Law Review*, April 1949, pp. 297–344; Field, Oliver P., "The Advisory Opinion — an Analysis," *Indiana Law Journal*, Winter 1949, pp. 203–230; and Sands, C. Dallas, "Government by Judiciary Advisory Opinions in Alabama," *Alabama Law Review*, Fall 1951, pp. 1–43.

it was in 1930. A companion table showing the volume of work in the Supreme Court of Illinois shows a slight decrease in that state during the postwar period.

Not only are there changes in the volume of litigation, but there were significant changes in the major types of suits filed. Albert Smith Faught of the Philadelphia Bar studied the types of cases in the courts in 1736, 1836, and 1936. In the latter years, he used the supreme court reports; since the jurisdiction of these courts is largely appellate, the cases which they considered may be taken as a fair sample of the types handled by the lower Federal and state courts. In the comparison of 1836 and 1936 he found notable decreases in cases in business law, real estate law, and probate law and the elimination of slave cases. Torts, security law, and tax law showed the largest increases, but increases were also found in government law, criminal law, bankruptcy, family law, admiralty, and natural resources law.[6]

Current reports from judicial councils show pretty clearly that the volume of judicial business is now declining. The measures taken to deal with the congested court calendars of a few years ago — establishment of more courts, enlarging their size, changes in procedure designed to expedite business, and adoption of substitute procedures — appear to have been generally successful. The considerable increase in the number of divorce actions has tended to offset in part the decline in other types of civil actions. The number of jury trials has dropped to a small fractional part of the figure of two decades ago.

Procedure in Civil Cases

In the discussion of the legal system of the states, mention was made of the various aspects of civil law, including that governing property — real and personal; torts — against persons, against property, and against persons and property; contracts and matters relating to the conduct of business, including partnerships and corporations; domestic relations, including marriage and divorce, and the status of women and children, et cetera. It now remains to consider the steps through which a civil action must normally pass. Civil actions are of two types, those at law and those in equity.

Pretrial Conferences. Much attention has been given in the last decade to the development and extension of the use of pretrial procedures, a device which originated in Wayne County, Michigan, in 1929.[7] Under these procedures, the court may in its discretion direct the attorneys for the parties to appear before it for a conference to consider such questions as (1) the simplification of the issues; (2) amendments to the pleadings; (3) admissions of

[6] Faught, Albert S., "Three Centuries of American Litigation," *Temple Law Quarterly*, July 1939, pp. 488–504.

[7] New Jersey claims to have had pretrial procedure since 1910, and points out that the English "summons for direction" had long pointed the way toward modern pretrial. See "New Jersey Had Pretrial Procedure Thirty-five Years Ago," *Journal* of the American Judicature Society, June 1947, pp. 25–26.

State of Illinois
Volume of Work in the Supreme Court *

	1943–44	1944–45	1945–46	1946–47
Opinions Published	264	258	245	248
Petitions for Rehearings	138	113	110	88
Petitions for Leave to Appeal	74	157	96	103
Allowed	14	31	22	23
Denied or Dismissed	60	126	74	80
Petitions for Writs of Error in Compensation Cases	14	24	38	30
Allowed	6	11	18	13
Denied or Dismissed	8	13	20	17

* From "A Study of the Illinois Supreme Court," *University of Chicago Law Review*, Autumn 1947, pp. 107–176, at 166.

State of New Jersey
Volume of Work in Appellate Courts, 1900–1948 *

COURT OF ERRORS AND APPEALS		NEW JERSEY SUPREME COURT TOTAL CASES LISTED			
YEAR	ALL CAUSES REVIEWED	PART I	PART II	PART III	TOTAL
1900	232	201	221	99	521
1905	348	205	204	119	528
1910	491	233	203	231	667
1915	410	198	254	235	687
1920	240	198	102	139	439
1925	398	272	236	219	727
1930	310	306	276	212	794
1935	365	83	211	167	461
1940	257	51	254	110	415
1945	181	45	172	59	276
1948	143	34	185	29	248

* From Administrative Office of the Courts, *Annual Report of the Administrative Director of the Courts, 1948–1949*, pp. 108–122 (Trenton, 1950).

fact and documents which will avoid unnecessary proof; (4) limitation of the number of witnesses; (5) advisability of preliminary reference of issues to a master for findings to be used as evidence when the trial is to be by jury; and (6) such other matters as may aid in the disposition of the action. These procedures all look toward pretrial settlement if possible or, if that is not possible, to a clarification of the issues and a shortening of the trial.[8]

[8] For recent comment, see Anggelis, John C., "Procedure — Pretrial Conference," *Kentucky Law Journal*, January 1950, pp. 302-316; Black, George K., "Interrogatories as

Prior to 1940 the movement had not progressed very far beyond the discussion stage; in 1949, pretrial conference procedures, modeled for the most part on the Federal practice under Rule 16, were authorized either by rule or by statute in twenty-nine states.[9] They are employed in some of the courts of a number of large cities, in a few instances by court order in jurisdictions not using pretrial conferences on a state-wide basis. In four states, Massachusetts, Michigan, Ohio, and Pennsylvania, such conferences are used only in metropolitan areas.

In Courts of Law. The great majority of civil actions at law — and the great bulk of litigation is confined to the civil trial courts — are heard before a magistrate or a justice of the peace; in these courts of the minor judiciary, the parties appear in person and tell their story. The "judge" decides the case. It is not necessary for attorneys to appear for the litigants, although they may do so. In more important cases, which originate in municipal, county, or district courts, the plaintiff goes to his attorney, discusses with him all the facts of the complaint, and arranges for the steps preliminary to the filing of the papers. The sequence of steps in civil actions, which are more or less standardized, is indicated in the table below; the preliminary steps are well described in nontechnical language by Professor Johnson:

SEQUENCE OF STEPS IN CIVIL ACTIONS

1. Commencement of Action
2. General Rules
3. Pleadings
4. Complaint Declaration or Petition
5. Summons and Service
6. Parties
7. Motions
8. Answer or Demurrer
9. Reply
10. Counterclaims and Cross-claims
11. Third Party Service
12. Amended and Supplemental Pleadings
13. Service of Pleading
14. Time
15. Preparation for Trial; Discovery, Interrogatories
16. Depositions, Examination of Persons or Things
17. Pretrial Conference
18. Trial
19. Judgments
20. New Trial
21. Specific Remedies
22. Contempts
23. Appeals in Civil Cases

> The attorney directs the clerk of the court which has jurisdiction to issue a writ of summons. This writ summons the defendant to appear in court

Pretrial Discovery in Massachusetts," *Massachusetts Law Quarterly*, April 1948, pp. 9–27; Johnson, Warren C., "Pretrial Procedure; Formulating Issues," *Nebraska Law Review*, November 1946, pp. 110–116; Laws, Bolitha, "Pretrial Procedure — A Modern Method of Improving Trials of Law Suits," *New York University Law Review*, January 1950, pp. 16–26; note on "Pretrial Procedure in Indiana," *Indiana Law Journal*, April 1947, pp. 279–288; Paschal, J. Francis, "Pretrial in North Carolina: the First Eight Months," *North Carolina Law Review*, June 1950, pp. 375–380.

[9] These states are: Arizona, Arkansas, Colorado, Connecticut, Delaware, Florida, Illinois, Indiana, Iowa, Massachusetts, Michigan, Missouri, Montana, Nebraska, New Hampshire, New Jersey, New Mexico, North Carolina, North Dakota, Ohio, Oregon, Pennsylvania, South Dakota, Texas, Utah, Vermont, Washington, West Virginia, and Wisconsin. Data from Vanderbilt, Arthur T., Ed., *Minimum Standards of Judicial Administration*, pp. 208–218 (Law Center of New York University, New York, 1949).

at a specified time to answer the plaintiff. It is given to the sheriff, whose duty it is to find the defendant or his attorney and serve the writ. Ordinarily, the action cannot proceed until actual service has been made; but in certain cases, for example, divorce actions, where the defendant is outside the jurisdiction or residing in parts unknown, publication in newspapers is deemed sufficient. If the defendant has not already engaged a lawyer, he should do so at once; for failure to enter appearance in connection with the suit will mean that judgment will be entered against him by default. It is quite likely that he will find a lawyer, who will take the necessary steps to defend the case. This attorney "files an appearance" for his client with the clerk of the court. He then notifies the attorney for the plaintiff that the appearance has been filed, and the two attorneys thereafter notifiy each other of all the subsequent steps taken in the case.[10]

After these preliminary developments comes the filing of the declaration by the plaintiff (sometimes called the complaint or petition), and the answer of the defendant. Professor Johnson continues:

The declaration must be very carefully drawn, for it must show a cause of action sufficient in law to warrant a judgment for the plaintiff. It is filed with the clerk of the court, and a copy of it is served on the defendant, together with a notice that he shall file an answer to the declaration within a certain date. The defendant, acting through his attorney, of course, may file a demurrer; that is, he may admit the facts as set forth by the plaintiff, but deny their legal sufficiency. In common parlance a demurrer is, "Yes, but what of it?" This passes the question of the sufficiency of the declaration to the judge. If he adjudges it legally sufficient, he "overrules" the demurrer and the plaintiff wins his case, unless the court, as it generally does, allows the defendant to file an answer to the declaration. If the demurrer is sustained, the defendant wins this point and would have judgment in his favor but for the fact that the court then generally permits the plaintiff to remedy his declaration by amendment. Assume, now, that the defendant answers the declaration of the opposing party. This answer or plea may admit certain allegations of the plaintiff and deny others. The points on which the declaration and answer differ are the points which will be in issue at the trial. The nature of the defendant's answer may be such as to warrant a response by the plaintiff, and in a number of states this replication (or reply) is permitted in order that all the points may be brought out clearly. It often happens that the defendant's answer does not constitute a sufficient defense. It is now the plaintiff's privilege to demur, which he does by asking the court to enter judgment for him "for want of sufficient answer," from the defendant.

As these proceedings continue, it may be possible for the attorneys to arrive at a settlement out of court of the differences between their respective clients or that they be settled at pretrial conferences; this is always preferable if possible, for court actions are expensive, time consuming, nerve racking, and often unsatisfactory in their results. Judge Baldwin stated dogmatically that most lawsuits never get to trial, either because the defendant has no defense and is well aware of the fact or because the plaintiff does not care to press for a judgment, knowing that if he had it, he could not collect.

[10] Johnson, Claudius O., *Government in the United States*, Third Edition, pp. 445–446 (Crowell, New York, 1945). See also Callender, Clarence N., *American Courts*, Chapter 6 (McGraw-Hill, New York, 1927).

This may make him the more willing to enter into any reasonable compromise, even though he may be certain that he has a good case.[11]

If the case goes to trial, the trial may be either by jury or by judge. As will be noted more fully later, the tendency is to diminish the number of civil trials by jury. If jury trial is used, the panel must be called, the members of the jury selected and sworn. The judge may then order the attorneys to proceed with the case. The counsel for the plaintiff opens the argument by informing the court and the jury of the facts in the plaintiff's case, the nature of the evidence he will offer in proof of these contentions, and the damages or redress he demands. Naturally, he "does his best to create a favorable impression with the jury for his client. His case may be won or lost by this initial effort. In some courts, this statement is immediately followed by the opening statement of the defendant's attorney; but in others, this may be delayed until the evidence for the plaintiff has been offered. In any case, the opening statement for the defendant has the same general purpose as that delivered by the plaintiff." [12]

After these opening statements, witnesses may be called, first for the plaintiff, later for the defendant. The witnesses of each party are subject to cross-examination by the attorneys for the other. Much of a lawyer's success in court depends upon the skill with which he is able, by adroit questioning, to bring out the points he desires to emphasize, and to secure admissions damaging to the case of his opponent. The examination of witnesses often makes a good "show" in court, but if the attorney is not considerate in his treatment of witnesses, he may turn the jury against his client's case. "During the examination of witnesses, one attorney may 'object' to questions asked by the other, and the judge overrules or sustains the objection. In either case, one of the lawyers is ruled against and he may 'take an exception' to the judge's ruling. These exceptions often constitute grounds for appealing the case." [13]

At the conclusion of these proceedings the attorneys are given an opportunity to summarize the case before it goes to the jury. The presiding judge, in his charge to the jury, is supposed to give an impartial statement of the law governing the case; he will point out clearly the nature of the verdict they should return in accordance with each of the possible findings as to the facts. Many judges acquire great skill in indicating to the jury the nature of the decision which is expected of them, by inflection, emphasis, et cetera, but without anything appearing in the record that would seem unduly to influence the jurors. Professor Johnson reports that in a number of Western states the judges' charge precedes the arguments of the attorneys;

[11] Baldwin, Simeon E., *The American Judiciary*, p. 201 (Century, New York, 1905); Chapter 14 of this volume is devoted to trial courts for civil causes. See also Callender, *American Courts*, Chapter 7.

[12] Johnson, *op. cit.*, pp. 441–442.

[13] *Ibid.*, p. 448; see also Curran, Henry H., "What Makes up the Juror's Mind," *New York Times Magazine*, November 27, 1949, pp. 17, 66 ff.

this procedure has been properly criticized for leaving as a last impression in the minds of the jurors the eloquence of the attorneys rather than the statement of the law made by the judge. Sooner or later the jury arrives at a verdict, which will probably be unsatisfactory to one of the litigants, and may be to both of them. Either may file a motion for a new trial, which must then be argued before the judge who presided at the trial. If the new trial is allowed, the appellate court may or may not sustain the findings of the lower court.[14]

Quantity of the Law. Judicial opinions are much too long and much too numerous, with the result that "the lawyer ceases to reason and becomes a mere digger in the dustheap of decisions." Back in 1915, a justice of the Wisconsin Supreme Court wrote an article on "The Courts and the Papermills," in which he quoted a remark of one practicing lawyer that he would "rather be a dog and chew rags for a papermill than have your job" (that of a Supreme Court Justice).[15] Various arguments have been advanced to explain, if not to justify, the number and the extensiveness of the arguments in the published decisions. It is said that cases are much more likely to be decided correctly on the law, if such opinions are written; that the writing of opinions increases respect for the courts by convincing all parties concerned that cases are carefully considered and rightly decided; that the law is more certain and better known if opinions are written.[16] Whatever the justifications, the result of this tremendous output has, in any event, been little short of a calamity.

Growth in the Volume of Reported Case Law

PERIOD	NUMBER OF DECISIONS	CUMULATIVE TOTAL
1790–1840	50,000	....
1840–1890	450,000	500,000
1890–1940	1,250,000	1,750,000
1940–1990	2,000,000 (est.)	3,750,000 (est.)

[14] On new trials and appeals, see Callender, *American Courts*, Chapter 6, and Willoughby, *op. cit.*, Chapter 37; Stone, Ferdinand F., *The Scope of Review and Record on Appeal* (American Bar Association, monograph of Committee on Improving the Administration of Justice, Chicago, 1942).

[15] Winslow, John B., *Illinois Law Review*, October 1915, pp. 157–160, reprinted in *Journal* of the American Judicature Society, December 1942, pp. 124–127.

[16] See King, Archibald, "The Number and Length of Judicial Opinions," *Journal* of the American Judicature Society, December 1949, pp. 108–111; Pollack, Ervin H., and Leach, J. Russell, "Ohio's Reported Decisions — an Integrated Survey," *Ohio State Law Journal*, Autumn 1950, pp. 413–435; Wall, Mary K., "What the Courts Are Doing to Improve Judicial Opinions," *ibid.*, February 1949, pp. 134–151; Winters, Glenn R., "Reducing the Volume of Published Opinions," *ibid.*, August 1946, pp. 45–51.

In 1942, a Chicago lawyer made a study of the reported decisions, Federal and state, to date, put the figures on a graph, and projected the curve into the future to 1990.[17] The results are shown in the table on page 644. If the present rate of growth in the "output" of the law continues, it will become increasingly difficult as the years go by to "find" the law on any given subject, unless drastic changes are made in present methods of deciding and reporting cases.

The laws of the states regarding the publication of opinions follow no set pattern. In Missouri and New Mexico a commission determines which written opinions shall be published. Arkansas, California, Delaware, Florida, Illinois, Iowa, Kansas, Maine, New York, Texas, and Virginia leave the matter of selection of opinions for publication to the discretion of the court whence they issued, or to the discretion of the reporter with whose choice the court must concur. Still other states — Alabama, Mississippi, Nebraska, Rhode Island, and Utah — prescribe by statute in which cases the court must issue a written opinion, and then require the publication of all written opinions. The balance of the states require either that every opinion be published or a report of some type be published in every case.[18]

Equity Procedure. The origin and development of equity has already been discussed, as well as the distinction between law and equity. In an equity case the plaintiff or complainant files a bill in which he states the nature of his grievance and prays for the aid of the chancellor in securing relief. The bill is filed with the clerk of court, and a copy is served on the defendant in the mode prescribed by statute or by the rules of court; proof of service must appear in the records of the case. The defendant may plead in his defense in the form of a demurrer, as in common law, or in the form of an answer. The plaintiff may take advantage of defects in the answer of the defendant, by an exception. The case finally goes to court on the points at issue, as shown by the bill and answer. If the defendant fails to file an answer, or files one admitting the allegations of the plaintiff, the latter may have judgment by default, as at common law.

Hearings and proof constitute the next step in the proceedings; the more common methods of proof include depositions, reference to special examiners, hearings before the court, and jury trial. The judge may refer any particularly complicated question involved in the case to an examiner or master in chancery, who will investigate and report to the court. This procedure is especially common in divorce and bankruptcy cases. Jury trial is possible but uncommon in equity proceedings. In general, these proceed-

[17] Lavery, Urban A., "The 'Findability' of the Law," *Journal* of the American Judicature Society, June 1943, pp. 25–28.

[18] Based on Mahady, Jane O., "Regulation of Opinion Writing and Publication," a report prepared in the State Law Section, Legislative Reference Service, Library of Congress, May 1947; see also Whitehair, Francis P., "Some Suggestions for the Elimination or Reduction of Publication of Unnecessary Opinions," address before the Fifth Circuit Judicial Conference, New Orleans, May 23, 1947.

ings move more rapidly than those at law. Equity has declined as a separate type of procedure, but as has already been suggested, the principles of equity have come to be more and more important in the consideration of all legal matters.[19]

Procedure in Criminal Cases

The various steps that occur in a criminal proceeding and the significance of each will now be considered, in the order in which they normally occur. When a criminal offense has been committed and the identity of the offender is known, a warrant will be issued for his arrest, and the arrest will be made as soon as his whereabouts can be determined. If the identity of the offender is unknown, in some jurisdictions a John Doe warrant may be issued, authorizing officers of the law to take into custody persons whom, for one reason or another, they suspect. In the Federal procedure, and in that of many states, the citizen desiring to swear out a warrant must be able to describe the individual to be arrested with sufficient accuracy so that he may be identified, even though his name may not be known. Multiple arrests, in which persons are held on suspicion, occur in practice, but have no basis in law. They are not permitted in Great Britain. Persons may be held without formal charge only so long as it takes an attorney to secure a writ of habeas corpus — usually twenty-four to forty-eight hours. This requirement is sometimes evaded by holding the individual on another charge. False arrests are not uncommon here, but they are in Great Britain, where a heavy penalty attaches to them. There investigation is made first and arrest afterward.

Preliminary Hearing: Bail. As the second step, the defendant will be brought up for a preliminary hearing, which must be held promptly and without prior resort to third-degree methods.[20] These courts of preliminary hearing play an important role in the administration of justice:

> They hear the evidence, usually only that of the state, and determine whether or not there is reasonable cause to believe that a crime has been committed, and that the accused committed it. If such cause is shown the accused is confined or released on bond if the offense is a bailable one, to answer any charge which may be lodged against him by the prosecutor or grand jury. If no charge is filed before the first day of the next regular term of the circuit or other court having jurisdiction, he is entitled to be released if in confinement, or to be discharged on his bond if at liberty on bail.[21]

In other words, if, as a result of this preliminary hearing, the charges against the accused appear to be unfounded, he may be discharged by the magistrate

[19] This comment is based primarily on Callender, *American Courts*, Chapter 10, pp. 147–148.

[20] The police lock-ups and temporary detention facilities are often a disgrace to a civilized community; on the physical aspects of such lock-ups, especially in Chicago in 1947–1948, see Zemans, Eugene S., *Held Without Bail* (John Howard Association, Chicago, 1949).

[21] *Missouri Crime Survey*, p. 164 (Macmillan, New York, 1926).

or the justice of the peace; if there appears to be some foundation for the charges, he may be held over for the grand jury. If the defendant is known to be a responsible person, he may be let out on his own recognizance; if not, he will probably be retained in custody, awaiting the action of the grand jury. If he has sufficient political influence, he may be able to get out on bail anyway, in which case the amount will be determined by the magistrate who conducted the preliminary hearing. All offenses except first degree murder are or may be bailable; the abuse is found, not in the types of offenses for which bail is accepted, but rather in the kind of bail furnished and accepted.

In most states the right to bail is a constitutional right,[22] which in itself is evidence of the importance commonly attached to the right. Unfortunately, in the administration of the system, serious defects have developed in many jurisdictions. Too frequently, bail bonds are accepted in felony cases. Often there is no one responsible for compelling bondsmen to keep their qualification sheets up to date, or for a prompt and vigorous follow-up on forfeited bonds. There are few large cities in which, at one time or another, investigations have not clearly demonstrated the abuses committed by professional bondsmen. One case cited by the Missouri Crime Survey will serve to illustrate: a man whose real estate was valued at $24,100 with a mortgage of $31,500, was permitted to become surety in one year on bonds aggregating $670,295. In all probability his compensation was not less than $33,000, and it is estimated that it may have been as high as $100,000.[23] An investigation in Philadelphia in 1938 showed a widespread failure on the part of magistrates to comply with the provisions of the bail law, and a total of $250,000 in worthless bail bonds accepted during the preceding six years. A magistrate in New York was ousted in 1939, after over eleven years' service, for "co-operation" in a bail bond scandal. Such instances could be multiplied indefinitely.

Indictment. Let it be assumed that the defendant has been held in order that his case may be considered by the grand jury. The institution of the grand jury is a part of the heritage of the English common law; its function is not to try the case, but to decide whether there is sufficient evidence against the accused to justify holding him for trial. The grand jury has been defined as a body of persons chosen to inquire into offenses against the state and the conduct and management of public institutions and officers. In England, in early times, the commission of a crime was looked upon as a personal matter between the author of the crime and the person injured; gradually, however, the idea developed that crime is an offense against the peace and security of the state and that it is to the interest of the state to proceed against the offender.[24]

[22] According to the *Missouri Crime Survey*, p. 190, there are only nine states in which bail is not a constitutional right: Alabama, Georgia, Maryland, Massachusetts, New Hampshire, New York, North Carolina, Virginia, and West Virginia.

[23] *Ibid.*, pp. 211–212; the whole Part V of this *Survey*, by Raymond Moley, deals with bail bonds. See also Willoughby, *op. cit.*, Chapter 39.

[24] Willoughby, *op. cit.*, pp. 174–175; Chapter 14 is devoted to the grand jury; see also

Maitland describes how, under the Assize of Clarendon, royal justices were sent throughout England "to inquire by the oaths of the neighbors of all robberies and other violent misdeeds."[25] This machinery, which the king kept in his own hands, thereby making it necessary for those who were accused of crime to be brought before his justices, was in full force at the time of the founding of the American colonies and was introduced in them as an important feature of the common law. As in the case of the petty jury, the grand jury was regarded by the colonists as one of the bulwarks of their liberties, and it was retained in force after independence was achieved.

If the grand jury believes there is sufficient evidence against the accused, the foreman will bring in what is known as a true bill, in which the name of the accused must be stated with absolute accuracy, as well as the exact nature of the charges under which he is held. It must also contain a statement to the effect that the crime charged is prohibited by law. In the American states the grand jury varies in size from six men to twenty-four, plus a foreman; Michigan experimented for thirty-two years with a one-man grand jury, abolished it in 1949 under pressure of a United States Supreme Court decision, only to reestablish it again in modified form in 1951.[26] There has been much controversy in some states regarding the right of women to serve on grand juries, but their right to serve is gradually being recognized. The theory was that this body would conduct an investigation of the charges against the accused, and determine for itself whether or not he should be held for trial. Practice has come to be widely at variance with this theory. The grand jury, except in rare and exceptional instances, conducts no investigation, but confines itself to the consideration of evidence presented by the prosecuting attorney, whose recommendations are commonly followed.

This procedure is followed, not by logic, but by tradition; it is slow, cumbersome, expensive, and inefficient. There has been recently a movement in the Western states to abolish the grand jury and substitute indictment by information, a method which has shown itself to be quick, inexpensive, and efficient. Under this system the district attorney simply makes a presentment, which serves to bring the case to court. This method obtains substantially the same results, without the loss of time and the expense involved in the consideration of routine cases by the grand jury. This does not mean that the grand jury as an institution should be abolished, but simply that in routine matters it would not be used. It would still be possible to have grand

---

Arizona State Legislative Bureau, "Grand and Petit Juries in the United States," *Legislative Briefs*, February 15, 1940.

[25] Maitland, Frederic W., *Constitutional History*, pp. 109–110 (Cambridge University Press, 1920).

[26] See Waite, John B., "Michigan's One-Man Grand Jury Before the Supreme Court," *Journal* of the American Judicature Society, April 1948, pp. 184–186. The Supreme Court held in In re Oliver that this system was incompatible with due process (333 U.S. 257, 1948).

jury investigations of particular cases or situations in which such a procedure would be in the public interest.[27]

Much has been written on the question whether the intervention of a body of laymen to pass upon the action of a trained and technically qualified officer, acting under a permanent responsibility, serves any useful purpose. Dr. Willoughby cited many authorities who believe that it does not, summarizing their objections as follows:

> The objections to the grand jury, from the standpoint of the prosecution, are: that it is in the nature of a fifth wheel; that real responsibility for the bringing of criminal charges is in fact exercised by the prosecuting attorney, the grand jury doing little or nothing more than follow suggestions; that it complicates by just so much the machinery of criminal administration; that it entails delay which is an evil in itself; that it renders prosecution more difficult through important witnesses getting beyond the jurisdiction of the court, or through memory of facts becoming weakened by lapse of time; that it entails unnecessary expense to the government; and that it imposes a great burden upon the citizens called upon to render jury service.[28]

It is not enough, however, to show that the grand jury is not an aid to the prosecution, or even that it is a positive drag and a source of avoidable expense and delay, to establish a case for its abolition. "It must also be shown that it does not render a desirable service from the standpoint of the protection of persons from being unjustifiably forced to defend themselves in court against charges of which they are innocent." This, however, can also be done,[29] not only by the production of specific data based upon studies of the operation of the system, but by reference to the fact that the grand jury is not considered an essential feature of judicial administration in any country whose judicial system is derived from sources other than the common law of England.

Arraignment in Court. After indictment has been obtained, either by grand jury or by information, the case is placed on the docket awaiting trial. The court opens with the usual formalities — the "Oyez, Oyez, Oyez" of the court crier, and the prayer by the chaplain.[30] The trial may result in the conviction of the accused or in his exoneration. It is important to note the difference of attitude toward the accused in the United States and in the countries of Continental Europe and elsewhere whose legal systems are based upon the principles of the Roman law. In the English-speaking countries there is what is known as the accusatorial system, under which it is

[27] For further discussion of this proposal, see Moley, Raymond, "The Use of the Information in Criminal Cases," American Bar Association *Journal*, May 1931, pp. 292–294.

[28] Willoughby, *op. cit.*, pp. 180–186; quoted are Judge Olsen of the Chicago Municipal Court, who believes that in 95 per cent of the felony cases the grand jury cannot do any good whatever; Shaw, A. Vere, "The Grand Jury — Use It or Lose It," *Journal* of the American Judicature Society, June 1948, pp. 6–9.

[29] On this point, see Baldwin, *op. cit.*, pp. 238–239, quoted by Willoughby, *op. cit.*, pp. 184–185.

[30] Baldwin, *op. cit.*, Chapter 13, discusses the formalities of judicial procedure.

assumed that the accused is innocent until proved guilty, whereas under the inquisitorial system, which developed under the Roman law, no assumption is made regarding the guilt or innocence of the accused. This difference in attitude toward the accused is responsible for more fundamental differences in the matter of procedure. Under our system, a large number of people who may be detained for questioning can be arrested and held pending further investigation of the case, while under the system governed by the Roman law, the work of investigation has to be carried much further before charges are lodged against anyone.[31]

While it has been customary to try all criminal cases with a jury, certain problems in connection with jury trial discussed in the following section suggest the desirability of waiver of jury trial, at least in felony cases. If the accused is convicted as a result of this trial, he will either at the conclusion of the trial or some days later be brought before the court for sentence. Some consideration may be given to his attorney, if it is decided to prepare a motion for the appeal of the case. When sentence has been pronounced, the prisoner will ordinarily be moved from the city or county jail in which he has been confined during the trial, to a state penitentiary or other correctional institution. The chart of criminal procedures on page 651 clearly indicates the sequence of steps involved in a criminal proceeding.

The Jury System

There is no aspect of the administration of justice that has come in for greater censure, by lawyers and laymen alike, than the operation of the jury system. Trial by jury has been preserved inviolate in the state constitutions as it existed when the states achieved their independence. The constitutional guarantees, therefore, apply mainly to the essential factors of jury trial as developed in England. The United States Supreme Court has held that these were three: a jury of precisely twelve persons, a unanimous verdict, and trial before a qualified judge with power to direct the trial and instruct the jury as to the law and the evidence.[32]

History and Development. The jury system developed in medieval England on the theory that the citizen who had a grievance against his neighbor, or a person accused of crime, would be more likely to receive fair treatment at the hands of the law if the facts in his case were weighed and decision rendered by a group of his neighbors. At this time two qualifications were emphasized in selecting persons for jury duty. The juror was supposed to be acquainted with the parties to the case, or, in a criminal case, with the accused. It was assumed that a knowledge of the character and personal life of the individual would be of value in considering the legal situation in which he was involved. If the case was a civil one involving some

[31] For full discussion, see Willoughby, *op. cit.*, Chapter 15; the criminal courts are discussed at length in Callender, *American Courts*, Chapters 12 and 13.

[32] For discussion of the position of the judge, see pp. 658–659.

Chart of Criminal Procedures *

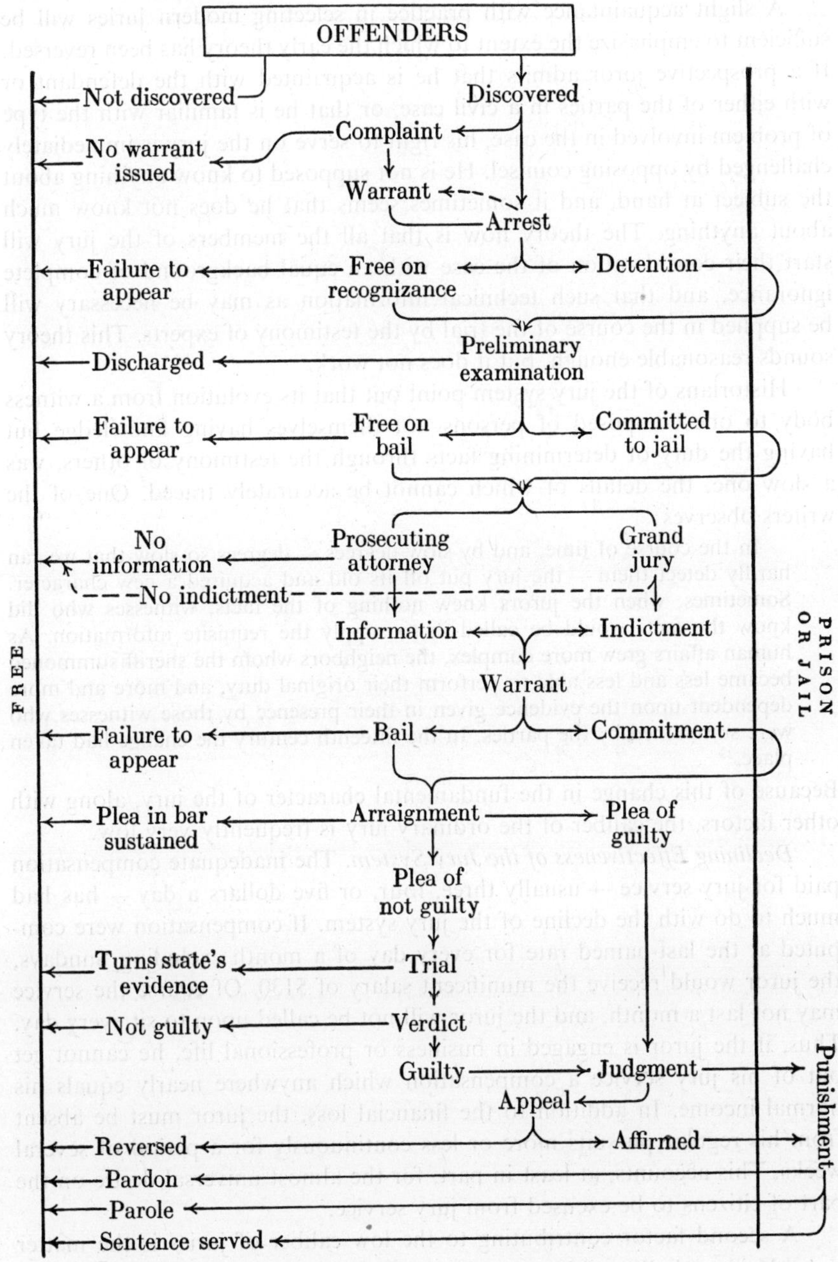

* From Bureau of Government Research, University of Kansas, *Your Government*, December 15, 1949, p. 4.

type of business relationship, the jury was selected to include persons who had an intimate and first-hand knowledge of the subject matter involved.

A slight acquaintance with practice in selecting modern juries will be sufficient to emphasize the extent to which the early theory has been reversed. If a prospective juror admits that he is acquainted with the defendant or with either of the parties in a civil case, or that he is familiar with the type of problem involved in the case, his right to serve on the jury is immediately challenged by opposing counsel. He is not supposed to know anything about the subject at hand, and it sometimes seems that he does not know much about anything. The theory now is that all the members of the jury will start their consideration of the case with an equal background of complete ignorance, and that such technical information as may be necessary will be supplied in the course of the trial by the testimony of experts. This theory sounds reasonable enough, but it does not work.

Historians of the jury system point out that its evolution from a witness body to one composed of persons not themselves having knowledge but having the duty of determining facts through the testimony of others, was a slow one, the details of which cannot be accurately traced. One of the writers observes:

> In the course of time, and by slow degrees — degrees so slow that we can hardly detect them — the jury put off its old and acquired a new character. Sometimes, when the jurors knew nothing of the facts, witnesses who did know the facts would be called in to supply the requisite information. As human affairs grew more complex, the neighbors whom the sheriff summoned became less and less able to perform their original duty, and more and more dependent upon the evidence given in their presence by those witnesses who were summoned by the parties. In the fifteenth century the change had taken place.[33]

Because of this change in the fundamental character of the jury, along with other factors, the caliber of the ordinary jury is frequently very low.

Declining Effectiveness of the Jury System. The inadequate compensation paid for jury service — usually three, four, or five dollars a day — has had much to do with the decline of the jury system. If compensation were computed at the last-named rate for every day of a month excluding Sundays, the juror would receive the munificent salary of $130. Of course the service may not last a month, and the juror will not be called upon to sit every day. Thus, if the juror is engaged in business or professional life, he cannot get out of his jury service a compensation which anywhere nearly equals his normal income. In addition to the financial loss, the juror must be absent from his regular pursuits more or less continuously for a period of several weeks. This accounts, at least in part, for the almost universal desire on the part of citizens to be excused from jury service.

A second factor contributing to the low caliber of juries is the matter

[33] Maitland, F. W., and Montague, Francis C., *Sketch of English Legal History*, p. 57 (Putnam's, New York, 1915); quoted by Willoughby, *op. cit.*, p. 485; see the whole of Chapter 36 in this work.

of exemptions. In most jurisdictions the law provides for the exemption of teachers and others whose professional activities are of such a character as to make their interruption inadvisable.[34] In addition, the majority of those called for service attempt to bring political pressure to bear in order to be excused. This is due partly to the financial reasons already noted and partly to other causes. The result is that the higher types of citizens are either exempted by law or excused from service by the judge.

There are undoubtedly many citizens whose sense of civic responsibility would be strong enough to induce them to serve in spite of financial losses and absence from their accustomed activities, if it were not that the delays of the law and the frequent miscarriages of justice have developed in their minds a sense of futility with regard to the whole undertaking. They have seen criminals set free because of some trifling inaccuracy in the indictment. They have seen weeks of labor and thousands of dollars of expense cast aside as of no account, when for some petty technical reason a new trial has been granted. They have seen juries render decisions which could not be explained by reference to the facts or to any rules of logic, juries made up of individuals who never possessed a hundred dollars, passing upon complicated business questions involving thousands of dollars of other people's money. They have seen juries "hung" by the stubbornness of a single individual, and they have seen others rush through important cases to an ill-considered decision, in order that one of the men might catch the five-fifteen train or that one of the women might keep an appointment with her hairdresser. Under such circumstances, it is not surprising that many conscientious and intelligent citizens have thrown up their hands in despair, and exclaimed, "What's the use!"

Should the Jury System Be Abolished? In view of the serious objections to the jury system as it now operates, there have been numerous proposals for its abolition. The proper adjudication of controversies requires the exercise of a very special faculty, usually described as judicial temperament. It is often contended that persons intrusted with determining individual rights should be required to perform their duties under a system of continuing responsibility; that the work of adjudication should be performed with dispatch, involve the minimum of technicalities, and entail a minimum of expense for both government and litigants. "No one of these requirements is met, even in measurable degree, by the jury system"; it would, on the other hand, "be difficult to devise a system that would be more productive of trouble, expense, and delay." [35]

"Technically considered, therefore, the jury system is defective, and all the arguments from this standpoint are in favor of the alternative system where complete responsibility for the determination of matters both of fact and the law and the rendering of the decision is vested in a permanent

[34] On exemptions, see p. 657, and Rawlins v. Georgia, 201 U.S. 638, 1906.
[35] Willoughby, *op. cit.*, pp. 490–491.

trained bench." This indictment applies not only to the use of the jury in civil cases, but to its use in criminal cases as well. In each of the numerous surveys of the administration of justice in individual states, the recommendation has been made that the waiver of a jury be permitted either in all but capital cases or in all cases. A study of the attitude of bench and bar in Ohio some years ago showed that 80 per cent or more favored waiver, approximately half of them very strongly. The possibility of waiver has been in existence for years in Maryland, Ohio, and other states.[36]

Although the jury system is not without its defenders, there is a wide area of agreement to the effect that, unless it is to be abolished or its use drastically curtailed, there must be significant improvements in the quality of the personnel and the functioning of the system. Charles A. Boston well states the argument for a better trained and more competent personnel:

> We train recruits to bear arms, we license lawyers, physicians, dentists, midwives, veterinarians, horseshoers, and chauffeurs, but so long as a man speaks any sort of English, can hear, is on the jury list and has not formed an opinion, he is deemed a competent man to decide disputes in a court of justice. He would not be accepted to run a street car, nor to perform any number of ordinary duties for a private employer, but he is legally a fit juryman if he has these qualifications. . . .[37]

Reconstruction of the Jury System. The defects of the jury system are widely recognized. It is important not only to consider the various points in the indictment, but to lay even greater emphasis upon the possible remedies. As a first step, the abolition of jury trials in all or at least a majority of civil cases and trial by judge rather than by jury in criminal cases where the parties agree to this procedure might well be provided by law. In addition, everything that properly can be done to encourage the use of these alternatives should be done. In England, where the jury system originated, such steps were taken long ago; similar steps have now been taken in many states.

The second type of remedial action involves the use of substitute procedures, such as quasi-judicial boards and commissions for particular types of cases, and the development of self-government in industry for the settlement of civil cases. The prevailing practice in the enforcement of workmen's compensation legislation well illustrates the first. In former times, when the three common law defenses might be invoked by the employer in injury cases, and under the employer's liability system which followed, all cases involving recovery for industrial accidents were thrown into the courts and decided by juries. When, in 1915 and thereabouts, these earlier systems were superseded by workmen's compensation legislation, an administrative bureau was placed in charge of enforcement work. Where the bureau was unable to bring the parties to an agreement, the case would be

[36] Martin, Kenneth J., *The Waiver of Jury Trials in Criminal Cases with Special Reference to Ohio* (Johns Hopkins Press, 1933).

[37] Boston, Charles A., "Some Practical Remedies for Existing Defects in the Administration of Justice," *University of Pennsylvania Law Review*, November 1912, pp. 1–32; quoted by Willoughby, *op. cit.*, p. 491.

assigned to a compensation referee, from whose decision still further appeal might be had to a workmen's compensation board. Thus an enormous block of cases was lifted out of the courts by a single piece of legislation. Technically, appeals might be carried from the board to an appellate court, but in practice the number of such appeals was small.

Another huge block of cases has been lifted out of the jurisdiction of the courts and removed from consideration by juries by the movement for self-government in industry, under which trade associations established mediation and arbitration facilities for the settlement of differences between their members. Following World War I, most of these trade associations adopted codes of ethics and standards of correct practice, the latter containing exact definitions of important trade terms. These statements represented the highest ideals of the business group and serve as guides to mediators and arbitrators in the settlement of disputes. The more business can be encouraged to regulate itself, the less regulation it will need by government. Likewise, the more disputes it can settle through machinery it has established and administers itself, the smaller will be the burden placed upon the courts.

These first two remedies were designed to remove large numbers of cases from consideration by juries, either by statute or by substituting private means of settlement. For the number which remains, drastic changes in the jury system itself are proposed — changes designed to modernize and improve it and adapt it to present-day needs. The common law jury has twelve members; there is no reason why a statutory jury of six or eight members cannot be used. This expedient was adopted many years ago in Utah, and was upheld by the Supreme Court except in cases where its use might be considered ex post facto.[38] The proposal has been brought up from time to time in other states; in Kansas, for instance, in 1935 the Judicial Council suggested legislation establishing juries of six, unless twelve were requested.[39] In some states, in courts of record, the parties by agreement in open court may stipulate a smaller jury than the traditional twelve. A system of carefully selected, adequately trained and compensated professional jurymen has also been suggested.

Nor is there any good reason why the requirement of a unanimous verdict from the jury should be continued.[40] Unanimity does not carry with it any magical assurance that the case will be considered wisely and well. It rather tends to encourage either hasty and superficial consideration of cases in order to get through, or prolonged disagreements, or "hung"

[38] Thompson v. Utah, 170 U.S. 343, 1898.

[39] Kansas Judicial Council, *Bulletin*, April 1935, pp. 17–18.

[40] Those who agree with this view argue that the law is not a sacred thing above the people, but an attempt to write the mores of the people into legal sanctions. The theory is that, if twelve men selected at random unanimously agree that the accused has not outraged the mores of the community, he ought to be turned loose. He should not be subjected to punishment if there is such ground for reasonable doubt as will prompt one (or more) of these twelve men to believe him innocent.

juries, or new trials. The unanimous verdict in civil cases has not been required in California since 1879. In 1949 there were twenty-six states which permitted a verdict, in civil cases in courts of record, of a number less than the total number of jurors. Any majority is sufficient in three states, two thirds in three others. Ten states specify five sixths, fourteen three fourths. In addition, five permit majority verdicts in certain criminal cases.[41]

The Selection of Jurors. The adoption of some of the suggestions here discussed would almost automatically bring about the selection of a higher type of juror. There should, however, be a planned attempt to bring this about through improvement in the methods by which the selections are made and in their administration. The generally prevailing process of selection was described some years ago by Judge Baldwin of Connecticut[42]:

> The selection of jurors is a long process. The general plan is to commit to some local authorities in each city, town, or county the choice of a considerable number out of the inhabitants whom they may think suitable to serve in that capacity; then to have that list revised by some higher officials or persons specially appointed by the courts for the purpose, who must strike out a large part of the names; and finally to have those who are to be summoned to attend any particular term of court for jury duty chosen by drawing from the remaining names by lot. In many states special qualifications as to age, education, and intelligence are required. Out of the jurors thus summoned to attend the court, there is a further choice by lot of those to try each particular case, subject to objections made by either party to any thus drawn, for proper cause.

The National Conference of Judicial Councils survey of 1949 dealt at length with the various aspects of the selection and service of jurors. The table shown below lists twelve qualifications commonly imposed, in the order of their frequency, thereby illustrating both elements of similarity and of difference in the requirements. As the survey report notes, this classification indicates only the general spheres in which there is regulation, but

COMMON QUALIFICATIONS AND DISQUALIFICATIONS FOR JURORS

	States
Minimum and maximum age limits	48
Character, morals, criminal record	48
Residence in the locality	46
Education and native intelligence	34
Prior service as a juror	29
General health (9), ability to see and hear (20)	29
Eligibility as a voter	27
Citizenship	18
Ownership of property (11), or payment of taxes (4)	15
Ability to speak and understand English	14
Membership in a specified group or class (as lawyers)	13
Request for jury service	10

[41] Winters, Glenn R., "Majority Verdicts in the United States," *Journal* of the American Judicature Society, October 1942, pp. 87–92. There is a table covering all the states and territories using this system, in each successive edition of the *Book of the States.*

[42] Baldwin, *op. cit.*, pp. 192–193.

does not — and cannot — create a true picture of the complicated variations of these requirements among the states.[43]

There are no less than seven major types of exemptions commonly authorized by law: (1) persons practicing certain professions considered vital or valuable to the public, including teachers, druggists, physicians, lawyers, undertakers, and many others; (2) persons engaged in certain businesses or trades where private or public interest require they should not be taken from their employment, such as printers, millers, ferry boat men, and bank tellers; (3) specified governmental officials and employees in government departments of particular public interest, such as post office employees, firemen, policemen, and the like; (4) women, who are barred in twelve states, compelled to serve in twenty states, and subject to voluntary service in sixteen states; (5) persons of certain ages; (6) persons who have served once already within a certain period; (7) particular named classes because of special private hardship, such as students, persons having physical disabilities, conscientious objectors to jury service, et cetera. Persons may also be excused temporarily because of emergencies of one sort or another causing particular hardship at the time.[44]

In thirty-four states the selection is made by jury commissioners appointed by the courts, in certain areas of sixteen states by elected county officers, or in eight by municipal officers, and in nine by the judges themselves. Selections are made in eighteen states more or less at random from the assessor's roll or tax list, the poll list or voter's registry, the telephone and city directories, and other lists such as census reports, care being taken to get names that are representative geographically and of the various callings, but to omit persons belonging to legally exempted classes. Before the names are placed on the final jury list or in a jury wheel, an investigation is made in twenty jurisdictions to determine whether the prospective juror meets the statutory qualifications, whether he is exempt, and whether in addition to meeting the statutory qualifications he possesses the personal qualities of education, experience, and intelligence that would make him a satisfactory juror.[45]

The names, when chosen, are placed on individual slips in the jury wheel, in which they are indiscriminately mixed. Every precaution is taken to prevent tampering with the jury wheel and to prevent favoritism in the final selections. When a judge needs a jury for his court, he issues a writ of venire, directing the sheriff or other officer in charge to draw at random the requisite number of names from the wheel and to summon the persons whose names are drawn for service at the designated time. Out of this panel

[43] Vanderbilt, *op. cit.*, pp. 162–171.

[44] Based on Vanderbilt, *op. cit.*, pp. 171–181, which gives full statutory citations for each category.

[45] *Ibid.*, pp. 181–205. The Supreme Court held that a New York special or "blue ribbon" jury, the members of which are more carefully selected, resulted in no denial of due process or equal protection. Fay v. New York, 67 Sup. Ct. 1613, 1947.

it is hoped to secure a number sufficient to constitute a trial jury, after excuses and challenges. The period of service varies from one to three weeks, being in the majority of cases two weeks. In some jurisdictions, prospective jurors are allowed to select the months during which they prefer to serve. Compensation is normally three dollars a day, although in Chicago five dollars is paid. Summons may be by personal service, although registered mail is usually used.

After the enfranchisement of women, women jurors, when occasionally one appeared, were regarded with a good deal of curiosity. Gradually, the woman juror came to be less of a novelty. During the war, with so many men away in service, and others engaged in important war work, women jurors were in the majority in almost every case, both civil and criminal. It was not at all unusual to have an all-woman jury. The fitness of women for jury service ceased to be questioned.

Improving Judicial Procedure

For years there has been great dissatisfaction with the prevailing methods of administering justice in the United States. One of the earliest discussions of this situation is contained in an address delivered in 1906 by Roscoe Pound, later Dean of the Harvard Law School.[46] Mr. Taft, while President and throughout the remainder of his life, called attention time and again to the necessity for improving and modernizing the machinery and procedure. The American Bar Association has for many years had committees at work on various aspects of the problem. The American Law Institute, organized in 1923, was a result of the culmination of these influences. This organization has carried forward an intensive program of work which is certain to have a profound effect upon the development of American law — restatements of the law on various subjects in the field of civil law, and the development of a model code of criminal procedure. Judicial reforms at the Federal level, which have included the establishment of improved rules of procedure, the establishment of pretrial procedures, and the creation of administrative services to enable the courts to function more effectively, have likewise had a profound influence on developments in the states.

The Position of the Judge. There is a sharp contrast between the position of the judge in an American and in a European court. In Europe it is customary for the judge to conduct the trial. He guides the proceedings, taking an active part in them, with the objective of revealing the essential facts and making more certain the proper and speedy disposition of the case. In the United States the judge presides but cannot be said by any stretch of the

[46] "The Causes of Popular Dissatisfaction with the Administration of Justice," 29 American Bar Association *Reports* 395, 1906. The snail's progress of law reform in the United States over the last forty years is illustrated by the similarity of Justice Vanderbilt's criticisms of judicial administration in 1949 to those of Dean Pound in 1906; see his *Men and Measures in the Law* (Knopf, New York, 1949).

imagination to conduct the case. The attorneys do that — all too often with neither dignity nor dispatch, nor, so far as one can determine, with any sincere desire to see that justice is administered. The judge is reduced to the position of referee between a couple of sparring partners, whose rounds are fought with arguments and torrents of legal verbiage, rather than with boxing gloves. Rules for this game have been agreed upon and established, and it is the business of the judge to see that neither party strikes a foul.

The American Bar Association makes three specific recommendations with regard to this matter:

1. That the common law concept of the function and authority of the judge be uniformly restored in the states which have departed therefrom
2. That after the evidence has been closed and counsel have concluded their arguments to the jury, the trial judge should instruct the jury orally as to the law of the case and should have power to advise them as to the facts by summarizing and analyzing the evidence and commenting upon the weight and credibility of the evidence or upon any part of it, always leaving the final decision on questions of fact to the jury
3. That the trial judge should be at all times the governor of the trial in the sense of activity, and firmly when necessary, requiring that the proceedings be conducted with dignity, decorum, and the avoidance of waste of time

The National Conference of Judicial Councils' survey found that the states are almost evenly split on the question of summing up the evidence, twenty-seven states permitting, twenty states prohibiting, and one — Iowa — making such summarization compulsory. In only one fourth of the states is the trial judge permitted to comment on the weight of the evidence. In a large majority of the states the trial judge is required to instruct the jury as to the law applicable to all issues in the case. In nearly half of the states the law requires the charge to the jury to be in writing, but oral instruction to the jury seems to be the rule in many jurisdictions.[47]

The Attitude of the Bar. It is not likely that substantial progress in the improvement of judicial procedure in either civil or criminal cases will be made until the judge is given authority to conduct the proceedings and until members of the bar have a deeper concern for the impartial administration of justice than for the winning of cases. Years ago, when the American Bar Association held its annual meeting in London, the members were interested in a murder case which developed just before they landed. The unidentified body of a young woman was discovered by the seashore late in June; there seemed to be no clues by which the mystery could be solved. By the second of August the victim had been identified, motives for the murder established, the guilty party apprehended, arrested, indicted, tried, convicted, sentenced, and executed, having had every opportunity for appeal and having enjoyed every protection to which the law of England entitled him. In this country, such a speedy and certain execution of the law is rarely achieved unless there develops a case so horrible that public sentiment is aroused to demand

[47] Vanderbilt, *op. cit.*, Chapter 6.

immediate action. In this, there is danger of the conviction and punishment of an innocent person, or of punishment as a form of vengeance.

Observers of the English courts bring back similarly striking illustrations of the manner in which the attitude of the English barrister differs from that of great numbers of American lawyers. In one case, an English prisoner had been convicted and was standing before the bar of the court awaiting sentence. The judge had in his hand a record of the previous offenses and convictions of the prisoner. As he was about to pronounce sentence, he was addressed by the attorney *for the defense:* "Your Honor, I desire to call your attention to the fact that in one particular, this record is incomplete." He then proceeded to inform the judge that at a certain date his client had been convicted of another offense, not listed on the record. Not only have few American lawyers taken so seriously their obligation as officers of the court to see that justice is administered, but recent revelations have shown many cases in which members of the bar have worked with lawbreakers, not merely to defend them before the court (as they have every right to do), but to connive with them for the purpose of preventing their detection and of enabling them to break the law with impunity. Until the bar associations succeed in expelling from their ranks this kind of attorney, judicial administration will continue to be unsatisfactory.[48]

The Integrated Bar. Until a few years ago bar organization was either voluntary or federated. In 1921 Alabama and North Dakota set up an integrated bar, which means giving all of the lawyers of the state the organization necessary to enable them to function effectively as a group. Integration involves not the state bar association but the state bar, which is a different entity, already in existence and with a well defined membership, but incapable of action or expression of any kind without organization. "Whether the voluntary and selective state bar association is continued or discontinued after the bar is integrated is up to its members. If it is continued, as it has been in a few states, it is separate from, independent of, and without control over the integrated bar." Integration means that the state bar, in addition to achieving an effective organization, which is self-governing in character, becomes a legally recognized part of the machinery for the administration of justice.[49]

[48] To some extent, this is a problem of public relations: Iowa State Bar Association, Committee on Public Relations, *Lay Opinion of Iowa Lawyers, Courts and Laws* (Des Moines, 1949), and article by Riley, William F., in *Journal* of the American Judicature Society, August 1949, pp. 38–42; Blashfield, Albert E., "A State Bar Public Relations Program," *ibid.*, February 1947, pp. 162–166 (Michigan); Cary, Robert W., "Ethical and Social Problems of the American Lawyer," *ibid.*, December 1947, pp. 120–122; Laws, Bolitha J., "Participation of Judges and Laymen in Improving the Administration of Justice," *Virginia Law Review*, December 1945, pp. 89–94; Winters, Glenn R., "Bar Association Activities; Suggestions for Bar Association Executives," American Bar Association *Journal*, July 1950, pp. 546–549, 602–605.

[49] See Brand, George E., "Bar Organization and Judicial Administration — A New Horizon," *Journal* of the American Judicature Society, August 1950, pp. 38–45, and editorial in the same journal, December 1950, pp. 100–101.

By 1949 the number of jurisdictions with an integrated bar had passed the half-way mark. In thirteen states the system is established by statute, and in seven jointly by statute and court rule. One state provides for integration by constitutional amendment and court rule, and four by court rule alone.[50] Actually, the bar has little choice in the matter. There is much dissatisfaction among progressive lawyers and laymen alike over the failure of the bar in the past properly to discharge its responsibility. The profession must either adopt integration and give effective service to the state, on the one hand, or resign itself to the establishment of some form of "socialized law" on the other.[51]

Certain desirable results of an integrated organization have been demonstrated in many states. The state association becomes able to speak for the bar as a whole, every practitioner having a voice in the decisions made. The organization has better financial support and is thus able to carry on its work more effectively. It is able to raise standards for admission to the bar and to improve bar discipline. Integration brings about a decided increase in interest and participation by lawyers in the business of the association, and, finally, local associations are so strengthened that they are able to render better service to their members. All told, integration can scarcely fail to bring about closer relationships between the bar and the legislature, the bar and the judiciary, and to improve the administration of justice generally.

The Cost of Litigation. In 1919 Reginald Heber Smith completed a study of the denial of justice to the poor, and of the agencies making more equal their position before the law.[52] He discussed three important defects in the existing system — delay, court costs and fees, and the expense of counsel. Two of these are important factors in the cost of litigation. Wrote Mr. Smith:

> The actual expenses in a trial court exclusive of witness fees, may be reduced to the writ or summons, the service of process, entry fee, calendar fee, trial fee, entry of judgment, and issuance of execution. It is proper to eliminate the jury fee, for so long as a trial by a judge is possible, no denial of justice can fairly be alleged. For similar reason, fees for attachment of garnishment are excluded. Each court uses a different combination of these items. In some, one or two payments cover everything; in others, the charges are made separatcly. Since our inquiry is only to determine the actual expense, all the various

[50] These states are: *by statute:* Alabama, Arizona, California, Idaho, Mississippi, Nevada, New Mexico, North Carolina, North Dakota, Oregon, South Dakota, Utah, and Washington. *By statute and court rule:* Kentucky, Louisiana, Michigan, Texas, Virginia, West Virginia, and Wyoming. *By constitutional amendment and court rule:* Arkansas. *By court rule only:* Florida, Missouri, Nebraska, and Oklahoma.

[51] See Behle, Calvin A., "Twenty Years of the Utah State Bar," *Journal* of the American Judicature Society, December 1951, pp. 117–119; Burney, Cecil E., "Texas Lawyers Take Time for Leadership," *ibid.*, June 1952, pp. 13–21; Stephens, Charles B., "Public Responsibility of Bar Associations," *ibid.*, October 1951, pp. 67–68; and Webb, Frederick W. C., "Whole Bar Organization — A Necessity," *ibid.*, August 1945, pp. 38–48, with bibliography.

[52] Smith, Reginald H., *Justice and the Poor*, Third Edition (Carnegie Foundation for the Advancement of Teaching, New York, 1924).

items may be rolled into one total. The figures given are not absolute; they may be varied by the distance traveled for service, by the number of motions or interlocutory proceedings, and by other factors; but they fairly represent the minimum cost in an ordinary case.[53]

These figures, which range from fifty-two cents in the Small Claims Courts of Cleveland to $15.51 in the Superior Court of Hartford, show an average cost of two to three dollars. They would be much higher if it were not for the advent of the municipal courts, which have done much to reduce costs; in a few instances it is provided that costs, exclusive of witness fees, shall not exceed two dollars.

In 1932 the Institute of Law of Johns Hopkins University published a survey of the cost of civil litigation in New York, made for the year 1930. The total cost for courts of all types was put at $11,000,000 a year; it was found that each inhabitant of New York City paid eight cents a year to help litigants get justice in the Municipal Court, the "poor man's court," whereas he paid fifty cents annually so that the man of larger affairs might have his disputes settled in the Supreme Court. Litigants in the Municipal Court paid 71.7 per cent of what it cost the city to dispense justice in that court, while those who made use of the City and Supreme Courts, handling claims involving much larger amounts, defrayed respectively only 7.4 per cent and 12.8 per cent of what it cost the taxpayers to operate these courts. These costs have continued steadily to increase, year by year. It is abundantly clear that the cost of securing justice at the hands of the courts is as much as or more than the poor man can afford to pay, and that those who are least able to pay contribute a larger percentage of the total cost.

Legal Aid. The second major item in the cost of litigation is counsel fees. To many who have a real grievance and who are therefore entitled to legal redress, this item is so great as to prevent their turning to the courts at all for the enforcement of their rights. In a variety of ways, through agencies both public and private, the effort has been made to provide free, to such persons, the service of counsel. In the field of civil law one finds public agencies such as the Office of the Friend of the Court in Wayne County, Michigan, and private agencies such as the Legal Aid Society of New York, which was incorporated in 1876. The Legal Aid Bureau of Philadelphia, for a few years operated as a public agency, is now private. The number of such agencies increased from fifty-five in 1923 to eighty-five in 1939. By 1950 New Jersey had legal aid societies in every county in the state, thus becoming the first in the Union to provide free legal assistance to every citizen who cannot afford to pay for the services of a lawyer.[54]

Professor Bradway divides the history of the movement into three

[53] *Ibid.*, pp. 24–25; for current data on court costs and fees, see Brand, George E., "The Impact of the Increased Cost of Litigation," *Journal* of the American Judicature Society, December 1951, pp. 102–109.

[54] Bell, Robert K., "Legal Aid in New Jersey: the Answer to a Socialized Legal Profession," American Bar Association *Journal*, May 1950, pp. 355–358.

periods: 1911–1923, 1923–1934, and 1934 to date. The first was the formative period, which preceded the formation of the National Association of Legal Aid Organizations in 1923. The ultimate goal is that every man, woman, and child shall receive, and none shall be denied, protection in every legal right, and redress for every legal wrong. In the field of criminal law one finds the propcsal for a public defender and, in many communities, voluntary defenders' committees. In either case the purpose is to provide counsel for those defendants who are financially unable to pay counsel fees. This may, of course, be done by the long-established practice of the assignment of counsel.

The uninformed person is apt to underestimate the value of free legal aid. He reads in his paper a summary of the annual report of the agency, observes that several hundred or several thousand persons were assisted, and then observes that only a few thousand dollars were collected. He thereupon concludes either that the service is unimportant or that the staff is inefficient, whereas the truth is that the service is tremendously important and that in all probability it is being efficiently conducted. The amounts collected for individual clients are small, but this very fact enhances the economic and social significance of their collection. A large percentage of the cases involves wage claims — a few dollars to a washerwoman or a laboring man, to whom the loss of even a small amount is a vital concern. In many cases it means the difference between being fed and being hungry, or between paying the rent and being dispossessed. It may be that few types of social service are productive of greater benefits than this.

A voluminous literature has grown up on the subject of legal aid.[55] The National Association of Legal Aid Organizations has formulated a statement of the essential characteristics of the private legal aid agency; it is, they say, "a law office, which deals with all kinds of legal problems where the client cannot afford to pay a fee and where the case is one for which a fee cannot be secured. There is a close relationship between the work of the ordinary law office and the work of this special type of law office. . . . The quality of service in a legal aid organization should be equal to that in a private law office, or the principle of equal protection of the laws means nothing in a practical sense. The legal aid organization should and does act as an observation post from which information may be made available showing how the law and the machinery for its administration are succeeding in their ultimate task of providing equal and exact justice."[56]

[55] See, among the numerous writings of John S. Bradway on this subject: "Frontiers of Legal Aid Work," *Annals*, September 1939; *Legal Aid Work and the Organization of the Bar* (Duke University, 1939); "Legal Service for the Indigent," *Journal* of the American Judicature Society, December 1942, pp. 117–122; and by Smith, Reginald H., in addition to his standard title, *Justice and the Poor*, *op. cit.*, the following: *Legal Service Offices for Persons of Moderate Means* (The Author, Boston, 1947); article by the same title, *Journal* of the American Judicature Society, August 1947, pp. 37–47; and Brownell, Emery A., *Legal Aid in the United States* (Lawyers Cooperative Publishing Company, Rochester, 1951).

[56] Bradway, John S., *Legal Aid Bureaus*, pp. 2–3.

A legal aid organization may provide aid in criminal as well as civil cases, where there is no statute providing for the assignment of counsel or for a public defender; provide for the investigation and handling of workmen's compensation and other special types of cases; establish contacts with the organizations which act as contacts and serve as the sources of legal aid cases; work for the establishment of small claims courts, domestic relations courts, and other specialized types of courts. The obstacles to the development of legal aid work include the general impression that individual lawyers are rendering free assistance to indigent persons (just as physicians give their services freely to charity patients) and the hostility of some lawyers who regard legal aid as organized competition. The cost of operation is another difficulty; this varies with local conditions. The form of organization varies, but there seem to be four fundamental elements: a definite place at which to meet clients; a definite time, exact office hours; a definite personnel to carry on the work, the same person to be assigned to a case until it has been concluded; and an active advisory group.[57]

The Office of the Friend of the Court, established in 1918 in Wayne County, Michigan, is a public agency rendering a service similar to that more frequently supplied by a legal aid society. Organized by an overburdened metropolitan court to expedite the collection of alimony, the Office has developed into an important administration agency, performing a variety of functions and available for new uses as new needs arise. A year later the legislature authorized by law the appointment of a friend of the court in every county, for the purpose of enforcing alimony decrees for the benefit of minor children. Over the years the functions of the Office have been extended to include service to clients in matters relating to land contracts and mortgage foreclosures, to services as fiduciary, to bastardy proceedings, to cooperation with the Juvenile Court, and with other social agencies. In addition, the Office has succeeded in developing and maintaining a high degree of respect and confidence among the members of the bar.[58]

Experiments with new types of assistance to persons of moderate means have been conducted during recent years. Eleven neighborhood law offices were inaugurated in Philadelphia in 1938 under the auspices of the National Lawyers Guild, and the number has since increased. Similar forms and routines were worked out by a supervisory committee whose members had no financial interest in the offices, in which $1.00 was charged for a half-hour consultation. Later charges to those who find it necessary to come back average $5.00 or less in 87 per cent of the cases. After eleven years it was found that 80 per cent of the clients had never consulted a lawyer before; of these, six out of every ten cases dealt with domestic relations, contracts, landlord and tenant, real estate, collections, and wills.

[57] *Ibid.*, pp. 10–12.

[58] Pokorny, Edward, "Friend of Court Aids Detroit Judges in Divorce Cases," *Journal* of the American Judicature Society, April 1946, pp. 166–170.

With similar purpose the American Bar Association has sponsored the lawyer reference plan, in 1950 in operation in twenty-nine cities. The individual feeling the need for such service may go to the bar association headquarters in his city, pay a registration fee of $1.00, and sit down with an able and experienced lawyer to talk over his problem. This lawyer refers the client to one of the attorneys on the bar association's reference list. Here also, 80 per cent of the clients have never consulted an attorney before, but 86 per cent of those who have legal problems are able to get them cleared up without litigation, by following the advice of the attorney to whom they have been referred.[59]

Assistance in the field of criminal law may be rendered by the usual legal aid bureau. Where this is not done, it may be given by a private organization of voluntary defenders or by a public defender. Although the theory of the public defender has been widely accepted, little progress has been made in securing necessary legislation. Voluntary defenders committees exist in many cities; while in some ways they resemble other legal aid agencies, their activities are confined to the field of criminal law. The Voluntary Defenders Committee in New York, which was organized in 1917, is a good illustration; in all these years the Committee has handled thousands of cases, many of which are dismissed before trial, owing to its efforts. Because of the careful and impartial nature of their service, the lawyers of the Committee are held in high esteem by the courts. "The social service adjunct of the Committee is an asset which could not be eliminated, and through its efforts it affords defendants a far more comprehensive study than their cases would ordinarily receive, their problems being referred and directed to the proper channels. . . . No work among charitable endeavors is more worthy of support than that which helps him who is in difficulties and without the proper legal advice.[60]

In a few jurisdictions this type of service is provided for indigent persons under criminal charges by a public defender. Although the law of Spain as early as the year 1496 provided for a public defender, it was not until 1913 that the office was first established in the United States, in Los Angeles County. The public defender system is now functioning in six counties and several cities in California, has been established in all eight counties in

[59] See Abrahams, Robert D., "The Neighborhood Law Office Experiment," *University of Chicago Law Review*, April 1942, pp. 406–426, and "The Neighborhood Law Office Plan," *Wisconsin Law Review*, July 1949, pp. 634–647; Gallagher, Harold J., "The Lawyer Reference Plan: Legal Service for Persons of Moderate Means," American Bar Association *Journal*, January 1950, pp. 24–26; and Porter, Charles O., *Lawyer Reference Plan: A Manual for Local Bar Associations* (American Bar Association, Chicago, 1949).

[60] Tighe, Edward T., "Voluntary Defenders Committee Does Excellent Work," *The Panel*, January–February 1935, pp. 4–5; see also Brownell, *op. cit.*, Chapter 6; Goldman, Mayer C., "Public Defenders in Criminal Cases," *Annals*, September 1939, pp. 16–23; Pollock, Herman I., "The Voluntary Defender as Counsel for the Defense," *Journal* of the American Judicature Society, April 1949, pp. 174–177, on the Philadelphia situation; and "The Public Defender," *Virginia Law Review*, January 1940, pp. 275–283.

Connecticut, and in at least twelve major cities in eight states, in some instances by state law, in others by local ordinance. In all, it exists in twenty-eight jurisdictions, although only in Connecticut and Rhode Island is there effective statewide coverage and responsible state direction of the program. There are two other means by which counsel may be provided for needy persons charged with crime — assigned, unpaid counsel, serving as a matter of public duty, and assigned, paid counsel, with compensation determined either by law or fixed by the court.[61]

Move to Modernize Procedure. The law is notoriously conservative, but progress is being made in the effort to modernize court procedures. The new Federal rules went into effect in 1937, but five states — Arkansas, Connecticut, Illinois, Michigan, and Utah — must be credited with modernized procedures adopted prior to that date. Arizona, Colorado, South Dakota, West Virginia, and Wisconsin all have new codes adopted since 1937, and conforming substantially with the Federal rules. With the reorganization of its judicial system, New Jersey completely revised and modernized its rules in 1948. Quite a number of states have codes completed and awaiting adoption or have a program for amending existing rules without adopting a code. In all of this work the state bar associations have a prominent part. In the remaining states efforts are being made to stimulate interest in a revision of the rules.

Woodrow Wilson once said that "the speediness of justice, the inexpensiveness of justice, the ready action of justice, is the greater part of justice itself." It was these considerations that Professor Sunderland had in mind when he summarized all the needed changes under three headings. Many of the rules of law which control the action of courts are uncertain and difficult to ascertain, and are often poorly adapted to contemporary conditions. The machinery by which the rules are applied has been criticized because it is too slow, too uncertain, and too expensive. All these objections are justified — and all could be corrected. Finally, the personnel engaged in the administration of justice consists primarily of the members of the bench and the bar; "to establish and maintain this personnel upon a high level of ability and ethical conduct requires adequate methods for admission to and exclusion from the bar, and for election to and retirement from the bench. These are problems of the most critical importance, and of the most baffling difficulty."[62]

[61] See Brownell, *op. cit.*, Chapter 6, and Freeman, Donald, "The Public Defender System," *Journal* of the American Judicature Society, October 1948, pp. 74–78, and references therein cited; Bennett, James V., "To Secure the Right to Counsel," *ibid.*, April 1949, pp. 177–181; Stewart, William S., "The Public Defender System Is Unsound in Principle," *ibid.*, December 1948, pp. 115–118.

[62] Parker, John J., "Improving Appellate Methods," *New York University Law Review*, January 1950, pp. 1–15; Sunderland, Edson R., "Progress Toward a Better Administration of Justice," *Journal* of the American Judicature Society, August 1933, pp. 49–55; Winters, Glenn R., "A Century of Progress in Judicial Administration," *ibid.*, June 1946, pp. 22–30.

SELECTED REFERENCES

American Bar Association, Section of Judicial Administration, *A Handbook on the Improvement of the Administration of Justice* (Chicago, 1949). Contains the recommendations of the professional group most directly concerned.

Frank, Jerome, *Courts on Trial: Myth and Reality in American Justice* (Princeton University Press, 1949). A critical appraisal of the current situation.

Keeney, Barnaby C., *Judgment by Peers* (Harvard University Press, 1949). Most recent analysis of the operation of the jury system.

New Jersey Supreme Court, *Rules Governing the Courts of the State of New Jersey* (Soney & Sage, Newark, 1948). Rules adopted under new state constitution which completely reorganized and modernized the state's judicial system.

Nims, Harry D., *Pre-Trial* (Baker, Voorhis, New York, 1950). A lawyer's treatise on pretrial procedures by one of their strongest supporters.

Orfield, Lester B., *Criminal Procedure from Arrest to Appeal* (New York University Press, 1947). Best available work on the subject.

Pirsig, Maynard E., *Cases and Materials on Judicial Administration* (West Publishing Company, St. Paul, 1946). A standard casebook; for a survey of the problems in a particular state, see Rhode Island Public Expenditure Council, *Judicial Administration in Rhode Island* (Providence, 1945).

Pound, Roscoe, *Appellate Procedure in Civil Cases* (Little, Brown, Boston, 1941), and Orfield, Lester B., *Criminal Appeals in America* (Little, Brown, Boston, 1939). Significant treatises on the appeals problem in the two major branches of the law.

Smith, Reginald H., *Justice and the Poor* (Carnegie Foundation for the Advancement of Teaching, New York, 1919), and Brownell, Emery A., *Legal Aid in the United States* (Lawyers Cooperative Publishing Company, Rochester, 1951). Here are the original edition of a classic work which formed the basis for the whole legal aid system, and a recent authoritative compilation on the subject, prepared by The Survey of the Legal Profession, under the auspices of the American Bar Association.

19

Constitutional Protections

The bill of rights is one of the most important parts of any constitution; it is essential, in any state operating under a written constitution, that both persons and citizens be protected by written guarantees from infringements of their rights by the government and its officers. Thus in the Federal Constitution the citizen is guaranteed certain fundamental personal and civil rights by the first ten amendments, commonly referred to as the Bill of Rights. Similar guarantees are included in the state constitutions. Clauses intended to protect persons and citizens in the enjoyment of some of these rights as against possible infringement by the states were added to the Federal Constitution by the War Amendments. Thus the fundamental rights are guaranteed, so far as the action of the Federal government is concerned, by the Federal Constitution, and so far as the state governments are concerned, by both the state and Federal constitutions.

The War Amendments

Thirteenth Amendment. Amendments XIII, XIV, and XV were adopted in 1865, 1868, and 1870, respectively. They were framed and adopted solely for the purpose of protecting and improving the condition of the Negro, even though in later years they have been applied to the protection of almost everything and everybody except the Negro. Since these amendments include the only provisions of the Federal Constitution with regard to the duty of states to observe and protect the fundamental rights of persons, it is necessary to consider briefly the history and the wording of these guarantees.

Amendment XIII provides that "neither slavery nor involuntary servitude, except as a punishment for crime whereof the party shall have been duly convicted, shall exist within the United States, or any place subject to their jurisdiction." The history of this phraseology carries one back to the early years of the nation's history. It was a part of the Northwest Ordinance of 1787. In the years during which the controversy over slavery was being waged in Congress, it appeared again and again in the resolutions introduced, and sometimes passed, through the influence of the antislavery members. One finds it in the famous Creole Resolutions introduced by

Representative Joshua R. Giddings of Ohio in 1842; in the provisions of the Wilmot Proviso of 1846; in the Act of 1850 abolishing slavery in the District of Columbia. It is not strange, therefore, to find that it eventually becomes incorporated in the fundamental law. It is interesting to note, however, that in the closing days of the Buchanan Administration a resolution proposing a thirteenth amendment with provisions which were the exact opposite of those finally adopted was introduced in Congress, designed to effect a compromise and preserve peace.

As the Constitution now stands, since the repeal of Amendment XVIII, this amendment is the only one which bears directly upon or which attempts to regulate and control in any way the conduct of individuals in their relations with each other. All other provisions relate either to the organization and the powers and duties of government, or to restraints placed upon government for the purpose of protecting the rights of persons and property. Two or three interesting questions have arisen with regard to the application of this amendment. One of these involves contracts for personal service. Strange as it may at first seem to one who recalls the original purpose and intent of the amendment, the courts have used it to prevent orders for specific performance under such contracts. Suppose, for instance, that a baseball player who has already signed a contract with one club subsequently finds that he could make more advantageous arrangements with another. While the courts are willing to enjoin him to prevent his performing under the second contract, they have regularly refused to compel specific performance under the first, on the theory that to do so would be to require an involuntary servitude as prohibited in the terms of this amendment. Similar rulings are on record with regard to sculptors, painters, musicians, and others rendering personal service of a highly specialized and technical nature.

Perhaps the most important problem arising under Amendment XIII is its application to the peonage laws enacted in a number of the Southern states at the close of the Civil War. To understand this situation, it is necessary to refer briefly to certain historical facts. The colored people who were freed from slavery by this amendment were wholly unprepared to assume the duties and responsibilities of free members of society. In the majority of cases — in some instances through several generations — these people had assumed no responsibility for their own welfare. Under the plantation system, their cabins and food were provided for them by the owner of the plantation, and clothing suitable to the season was distributed to them in the fall and spring. When the amendment was adopted, many of the plantation owners gave the former slaves their homes, but they were obliged to provide their own food and clothing. Under the new regime, freedom to most Negroes seems to have meant absence from work. Many of them took to wandering through the country, getting food when and where they could. Because of this wave of vagabondage the landowners of the South found themselves suffering from considerable losses of food crops. They also found it impossible to hire dependable help to cultivate their fields.

To meet this situation, the Congress in 1867 enacted a drastic anti-peonage law. It resulted from practices then prevailing in the Territory of New Mexico and inherited from the days of Spanish rule but, as former Attorney General Biddle pointed out, it "went beyond the particular evil involved and prohibited the holding of anyone in involuntary servitude anywhere in the United States."[1] This measure, still in effect, tends to eliminate "the various indirect methods by which many persons of low income status in many of the states have been forced to labor for a particular employer against their will."

Numerous states adopted similar laws. An important test case, Bailey v. Alabama,[2] was decided by the Supreme Court in 1911. Under the A'abama law it was possible for employers to hold their help by a system of indenture. The employee was forced to purchase goods, often in considerable amounts and beyond his needs, in return for which he pledged himself to work out the debt in service. Severe penalties were provided for attempts to escape. The employers so managed that the worker was constantly heavily in debt and thus unable to change his employment or to move elsewhere. The Court decided that this system was unconstitutional, inasmuch as it required the performance of an involuntary servitude within the limits set up by Amendment XIII. The Court said with reference to the Federal statute that "Congress thus raised both a shield and a sword against forced labor because of debt."

Fourteenth Amendment. Amendment XIV contains four sections, together with the customary enforcing clause. Section 1 contains provisions which are as important as any in the whole Constitution, while Sections 2, 3, and 4 are interesting chiefly from the point of view of the student of history. In the first section there are four important clauses, which are quoted verbatim here and numbered for convenience of discussion:

1. All persons born or naturalized in the United States, and subject to the jurisdiction thereof, are citizens of the United States and of the State wherein they reside.
2. No State shall make or enforce any law which shall abridge the privileges or immunities of citizens of the United States[3];
3. nor shall any State deprive any person of life, liberty, or property, without due process of law;
4. nor deny to any person within its jurisdiction the equal protection of the laws.

[1] *Safeguarding Civil Liberty Today*, p. 119 (Edward L. Bernays Lectures of 1944, Cornell University Press, 1945); see also his *The Fear of Freedom* (Doubleday & Company, Garden City, N.Y., 1951).

[2] 219 U.S. 219, 1911; see Wilson, Walter, *Forced Labor in the United States* (International Publishers, New York, 1933). For more recent cases, see Taylor v. Georgia, 315 U.S. 25, 1942, and Pollock v. Williams, 322 U.S. 4, 1944.

[3] Interpreted in Colgate v. Harvey, 296 U.S. 404, 1935; see comment by Cushman, Robert E., in *American Political Science Review*, April 1938, pp. 296–298.

Careful reading of these provisions indicates that those who framed the amendment, and those who voted for its adoption, were attempting to confer upon the recently freed Negroes a state of citizenship, and to guarantee to them, so far as possible, the rights, privileges and immunities pertaining to that status. The definition clarified the only reference to the subject of citizenship contained in the original Constitution (Article IV, Section 3); since the control over citizenship rests largely with the Federal government, no further discussion of the subject will be included here. The provisions with regard to due process and equal protection are so fundamental that they will be discussed in later sections of this chapter.

The second section of this amendment contains the much disputed provisions on the suffrage discussed in Chapter 4. It provided for a reduction in the representation of any state in the Federal House of Representatives, in proportion to the number of inhabitants in such state, "being twenty-one years of age and a citizen of the United States," who should be denied the privilege of the suffrage for any reason other than participation in a rebellion or other crime. This provision has never been enforced, and so far as one can foresee, it is not likely to be enforced, for reasons earlier discussed.

The third section disqualified from membership in Congress, and from any other office of profit or public trust under the government of the United States, any person who, having previously taken an oath to support the Constitution and government of the United States, had "engaged in insurrection or rebellion . . . or given aid or comfort to the enemies" of the United States. Congress was authorized by a vote of two thirds of each house to remove such disability. While no persons are now living to whom this provision might apply, it is not difficult to understand the psychology which prompted its adoption. Those who remember the intensity of the hatred of Germany which existed at the close of World War I can understand the apprehension with which the majority of the members of Congress viewed the appearance of a man like Alexander H. Stephens demanding admission to the Senate as the representative of one of the Southern states. While this attitude may not now seem to have been justified, it was none the less human and understandable.

The fourth section affirmed that "the validity of the public debt of the United States, authorized by law, including debts incurred for payment of pensions and bounties for services in suppressing insurrection or rebellion, shall not be questioned." This section further provided that neither the United States nor any state should assume or pay any debt or obligation incurred in aid of insurrection or rebellion against the United States, or any claim for the loss or emancipation of any slave, all such debts, obligations, and claims being illegal and void. No one had questioned the public debt of the United States, but the Radical Reconstructionists in Congress did not want to take any chances. The second provision was intended to inform all and sundry that, from the financial point of view, insurrection and rebellion against the duly constituted authority of the United States was not a paying proposition. The clause with regard to claims for the loss or emancipation of slaves served in the spirit of the time, as a reminder to the South that President Lincoln had offered them a plan of compensated emancipation which they had refused. Now it was too late.

Fifteenth Amendment. This amendment provides that "the right of citizens of the United States to vote shall not be denied or abridged by the United States or by any State on account of race, color, or previous condition of servitude." These provisions were considered in Chapter 4, in the discussion of the suffrage. The series of three amendments of which this is the last constitutes, for all practical purposes, a single change in the fundamental law. Amendment XIII made the Negro free; Amendment XIV defined his status as a citizen and attempted to secure for him the enjoyment of his rights as a citizen; Amendment XV attempted to insure him the privilege of the suffrage. There is in these three amendments a logical progression of ideas, the three key words for which are: free, citizen, vote.[4]

Due Process of Law

There are two due process clauses in the Federal Constitution, found in Amendments V and XIV, respectively. The clause in Amendment V provides that "no person shall be deprived of life, liberty, and property without due process of law"; the provision in Amendment XIV appears in precisely the same words. There is thus an apparent repetition; but none exists in fact because the Bill of Rights, of which Amendment V is a part, applies solely to the Federal government. This was made clear in the decision in Barron v. Mayor and City Council of Baltimore in 1833.[5] Baltimore had undertaken a program of harbor improvement. In executing this program, certain dredging was done which so deflected currents in the vicinity of a wharf owned by one Barron as to cause a heavy deposition of sand and silt, thereby impairing the value of the property. There was no question as to the fact of the damage or, under the theory of the common law, as to the right of Barron to recover. When, however, he based his contention on that clause of Article V which prohibits the taking of property without due process of law, the Court held that this provision (and, by implication, all of the Bill of Rights) applied only to the Federal government. The provisions of the War Amendments, on the other hand, apply exclusively to the governments of the states. It would thus appear that there are two kinds of due process of law — Federal and state.

It is not difficult to define Federal due process, because the elements of which it is composed are clearly and definitely enumerated in the Bill of

[4] For an account of the enactment of Amendment XV, see Braxton, A. Caperton, *The Fifteenth Amendment* (J. P. Bell Company, Lynchburg, 1934).

[5] 7 Peters 243, 1833.

Rights, especially in Amendments IV and V. When, on the other hand, one undertakes to define state due process, he finds himself faced with almost insuperable difficulties. Instead of dealing with a single unit of government possessing a written constitution in which the essential elements of due process are clearly stated, he must deal with forty-eight governments, each with its own constitution, set of statutes, and doctrines of judicial interpretation. It is unlikely that the student could find any two states in which precisely the same definition of due process would apply. So it is that an individual who had received due process at the hands of the government of one state might not have had due process if his case had been handled in precisely the same way in any other state. One might almost despair of finding any common elements in the various definitions of due process, had not the presence of the due process clause in Amendment XIV brought a number of cases involving its interpretation before the Supreme Court. From these decisions, and from the various treatises on the subject, it is possible to discover certain elements which are essential to due process in any one of the forty-eight states. These are:

1. Due notice
2. A hearing
3. Hearing before a competent tribunal
4. A trial free from irregularities of procedure
5. Freedom from arbitrary legislative action

The first three items rest upon the decision in Twining v. New Jersey,[6] which in turn rests in part on the decision in the earlier case of Den ex dem. Murray v. Hoboken Land and Improvement Company.[7] The remaining items are based on the writings of students of constitutional law.[8]

The element of notice is required in order that the accused may be informed of the nature of the charges that have been preferred against him and have some opportunity to prepare his defense; he must be permitted to secure witnesses in his behalf and to arrange for their attendance at the trial; still more important, perhaps, he must have opportunity to employ counsel, which in turn must have some chance to prepare the defense. If this safeguard were not enforced, it would be possible for officers of the law to seize persons without warning, and to take them immediately before the bar of the court. Under such circumstances, innocent persons would be easily railroaded to a conviction. While trial by jury was commonly considered essential to due process, it has always been required that there must at least be a regular trial before some judicial body, unless, as in the case of hearings in connection with the administration of the assessment of taxes, the enforcement of such a requirement would block the operation of the whole governmental machine.[9]

[6] 211 U.S. 78, 1908.
[7] 18 Howard 272, 1855.
[8] Mott, Rodney L., *Due Process of Law* (Bobbs-Merrill, Indianapolis, 1926).
[9] On the subject of notice and hearing, see *ibid.*, Chapter 13.

The requirements regarding hearing are quite as important as those regarding notice. By the right of the accused to a hearing is meant, as noted above, the right to trial by jury — the right to one's day in court, to an opportunity to be heard and to present one's defense through one's attorney, through witnesses, and by personal testimony. Important as is the hearing itself, it is equally necessary that it be conducted before a tribunal of competent jurisdiction. If this guarantee were not enforced, it would be possible to wear out the accused by successive trials conducted before tribunals which had no authority to adjudicate the case.

The fourth requirement involves, from the point of view of judicial procedure, the right to a trial free from irregularities of procedure — a trial, in other words, conducted in accordance with the requirements of the statutes and the rules of the court. Professor Mott writes on this aspect of due process under the heading of settled usage. At any rate, the rules governing the submission of evidence must be observed, no rule must be enforced against the defendant that might be considered ex post facto, the accused must not be required to testify against himself, etc.

On the legislative side, the individual, whether a natural person or a corporation, has a right, in both civil and criminal law, to freedom from the enforcement of arbitrary and unreasonable regulations. This protection may extend to regulations which are so indefinite that the individual is unable to ascertain, even with the advice of counsel, the exact nature and extent of his rights or his duties. This principle is illustrated in the case of Connelly v. General Construction Company,[10] in which the Supreme Court declared invalid an Oklahoma statute which required contractors engaged in state work to pay a rate of wages equaling the pay given for similar types of work in the communities in which the contractor was engaged, and for which an eight-hour day was also provided. The General Construction Company was engaged in constructing bridges for the state, but was hiring laborers on the basis of an eight-hour day and paying them $3.20, whereas the State Commissioner of Labor contended that the current rate paid in that locality for similar labor was $3.60. The Supreme Court found the requirement so vague and ambiguous as to be unenforceable, and therefore unconstitutional. The argument was similar to that in the case of the United States v. A. Cohen Grocery Company.[11] The Court found it difficult to determine the meaning of "the current rate of wages"; it was a variable depending upon a great many factors such as the efficiency of the workmen, the kind of work done, and the conditions under which the work was done. The phrase "current rate" might be construed as meaning either the lowest rate or

[10] 269 U.S. 385, 1925; see also Mott, *op. cit.*, Chapter 12.

[11] 255 U.S. 81, 1921. On the affirmative side, the Court has upheld statutes as being sufficiently certain when: (1) they employed words or phrases having a technical or other special meaning; (2) the terms had a well-settled common law meaning; (3) for reasons found to result either from the text of the statutes involved or the subjects with which they dealt, a standard of some sort was afforded.

the highest rate. Likewise, it is difficult to define concretely the word "locality." In holding the act unconstitutional, the Court held that "the constitutional guarantee of due process cannot be allowed to rest upon a support so equivocal."

Charles A. Beard observed on one occasion that Amendment XIV had become the Magna Charta of American business. This statement is true — so much so that one could prophesy with almost unerring accuracy that any regulatory measure would be tested in the courts on the grounds of a violation of due process. Walton Hamilton well expressed the current point of view when he wrote:

> In the era of constitutional law that flickers to a close, no doctrine has enjoyed greater prestige than "due process." It has come to be the symbol habitually invoked by private right, the barrier that guards the frontiers of business against the interference of the state, a sanction by which the judiciary reviews the work of the legislature. It has woven itself into the folkways of an industrial culture and called into being an august corpus of the law. . . . A novelist who made ideas his characters would not — for fear of provoking disbelief — have dared to allow his imagination to contrive such a series of events [as that by which this doctrine rose to its position of eminence in American law].[12]

This curious development of law has by no means been confined to business; it has been applied in education and many other fields.[13]

That the amendment was adopted for the protection of individuals has already been emphasized, yet for more than half a century the Court has insisted that it applies to corporations as well as to persons. In 1938 Justice Black, in a very significant dissenting opinion, challenged this interpretation and called upon the Court to reverse its earlier decisions, so that the amendment might in fact mean what those who framed it and the states that adopted it intended that it should mean.[14] Commenting on this dissent, Professor Lerner expressed the fear that it might be nothing but a courageous gesture, after the elapse of more than fifty years. "Nor is it merely the time that has elapsed; it is the fact that the personality of the corporation has become an integral part of our constitutional law — right or wrong. The second is that his opinion would have been more complete if he had taken account of the fact that where 'person' has been used previously in the language of the law of lawyers, it has also been construed to include the

[12] Hamilton, Walton H., "The Path of Due Process of Law," in Read, Conyers, Ed., *The Constitution Reconsidered*, pp. 167–190 (Columbia University Press, 1938).

[13] J. P. Waugh v. Board of Trustees of the University of Mississippi, 237 U.S. 589, 1915; for an interpretation of "liberty" under the due process clause, in relation to compulsory drill in a state university, see Hamilton v. Regents of the University of California, 293 U.S. 245, 1934, and comment of Cushman, Robert E., in *American Political Science Review*, February 1936, pp. 79–80. For other interpretations, see Mooney v. Holshan, Warden of San Quentin Penitentiary, 294 U.S. 103, 1935, and Snyder v. Commonwealth of Massachusetts, 291 U.S. 97, 1934.

[14] Connecticut General Life Insurance Company v. Johnson, Treasurer of California, 303 U.S. 77, 1938; see comment in Lerner, Max, "Justice Black, Dissenting," *New Republic*, March 5, 1938.

corporation. The third is that the more strategic line of attack on the abuse of power by the courts would have been to insist that 'due process' should be interpreted only to mean procedural safeguards and not substantive determinations of social policy."

The circumstances under which test cases arise are many and varied. The Constitution, however, offers no definition of due process, nor has the Supreme Court defined the term with precision. Many decades ago Cooley wrote a definition which has been accorded wide acceptance:

> Due process of law in each particular case means such an exercise of the powers of the government as the settled maxims of law permit and sanction, and under such safeguards for the protection of individual rights as those maxims prescribe for the class of case to which the one in question belongs.

Equal Protection of the Law

The concept of equal protection of the law must not be confused with due process. It was once defined by the late Dean Burdick of the Cornell Law School by a transposition of the words in the original phrase as it appears in the Constitution. Equal protection of the law, he said, means for all practical purposes the right of the individual to the protection of reasonably equal law. The courts have repeatedly made it clear that the phrase requires that all persons who are similarly situated shall be treated alike; or conversely, that there shall be no discrimination in the treatment of persons in like circumstances. It forbids all invidious discrimination but does not require identical treatment for all persons without recognition of differences in relevant circumstances. It requires

> that equal protection and security should be given to all under like circumstances in the enjoyment of their personal and civil rights; that all persons should be equally entitled to pursue their happiness and acquire and enjoy property; that they should have like access to the courts of the country for the protection of their persons and property, the prevention and redress of wrongs, and the enforcement of contracts; that no impediment should be interposed to the pursuits of anyone except as applied to the same pursuits by others under like circumstances; that no greater burdens should be laid upon one than are laid upon others in the same calling and condition, and that in the administration of criminal justice no different or higher punishment should be imposed upon one than such as is prescribed to all for like offenses.[15]

The Amendment was not

> designed to interfere with the power of the state, sometimes termed its police power, to prescribe regulations to promote the health, peace, morals, education, and good order of the people, and to legislate so as to increase the industries of the state, develop its resources, and add to its wealth and prosperity. From the very necessities of society, legislation of a special character, having these objects in view, must often be had in certain districts, such as for draining marshes and irrigating arid plains. Special burdens are often necessary for general benefits — for supplying water, preventing fires, lighting

[15] Barbier v. Connelly, 113 U.S. 27, 31 (1885).

districts, cleaning streets, opening parks, and many other objects. Regulations for these purposes may press with more or less weight upon one than upon another, but they are designed, not to impose unequal or unnecessary restrictions upon anyone, but to promote, with as little individual inconvenience as possible, the general good. Though in many respects necessarily special in their character, they do not furnish just ground of complaint if they operate alike upon all persons and property under the same circumstances and conditions.

One of the most frequent causes of litigation under this clause are acts involving "class legislation." In one sense, most legislation is class legislation, for there are relatively few enactments of legislative bodies which are of equal application and importance to all. In the more common and popular usage, however, the phrase implies the presence of an unfair advantage accorded to one group, or the presence of discriminatory provisions with regard to another. As the Supreme Court said in Barbier v. Connelly:

> Class legislation, discriminating against some and favoring others, is prohibited; but legislation which, in carrying out a public purpose, is limited in its application if within the sphere of its operation it affects alike all persons similarly situated, is not within the amendment.

The fact of discrimination is all that is necessary — it makes no difference whether it exists by reason of legislative provisions or through improper administrative procedures. In Connolly v. Union Sewer Pipe Company[16] the Court held invalid an Illinois antitrust law which forbade combinations among producers to restrict competition, but which especially exempted farmers from the provisions of the law and thereby afforded them an advantage not given to other classes of producers. In 1940, in Tigner v. Texas, the Court held this principle no longer controlling.[17] In both of these cases the objection was to the legislation itself, but in Yick Wo v. Hopkins[18] the discrimination resulted from unfair and unjust administrative policies. San Francisco provided by ordinance that no laundries should be operated in frame dwellings without a permit or certificate from the city inspector. The apparent purpose was to reduce the fire hazard; in practice, it appeared to be to reduce the number of Chinese laundries, for permits were denied to all Chinese and were given without question to others. Thus an ordinance which was fair on its face and impartial in appearance was so

[16] 184 U.S. 540, 1902.

[17] 313 U.S. 635, 1940; holding that a Texas antitrust law imposing penalties upon various forms of combination and monopoly in restraint of trade may exclude activities of agriculture and still not contravene the constitutional provision requiring equal protection of the laws.

[18] 118 U.S. 356, 1885; on the question of classification, see Morf v. Bingaman, Commissioner of Revenue for New Mexico, 298 U.S. 407, 1936. The act taxed the privilege of dealers to bring in motor vehicles for sale, on their own wheels, imposing a flat fee without regard to mileage. Said the Court: "If a state taxing provision, of whatever form its words, results in the application of the tax to a class which may be separately taxed without denial of equal protection, those within the taxed class may not complain because the class might have been more aptly defined by the statute or because others not of that class might have been taxed."

applied and administered as clearly to violate the equal protection clause of Amendment XIV. The Court warned that unless these administrative practices were corrected, it might become necessary to invalidate the ordinance.

The question of the relation of due process and equal protection has, in the words of Professor Mott, "proved one of the enigmas of constitutional law." Many authorities have held to the view that equality in application — equal protection, in other words — is an element in due process. "Even before the passage of the amendment, the state courts had worked out a fairly intensive, although far from comprehensive, body of law covering arbitrary classification. By the time of the Civil War a number of states had definitely linked this with due process of law," and this practice continued after the adoption of the amendment. The inferior Federal courts, in passing upon diverse citizenship cases, had frequently had occasion to deal with the same problem, and had adopted a somewhat similar practice. Dean Burdick, after careful examination of all the evidence, concluded that "the conception of due process does exclude legislation which inflicts inequality of burden which is clearly arbitrary and without any basis in reason." [19]

Chief Justice Taft, in Truax v. Corrigan,[20] admitted that "the equality clause of the Fourteenth Amendment does not apply to congressional but only to state action." He took the position that the due process and equal protection clauses overlap but that the spheres of protection they offer are not coterminous, the former tending "to secure equality of law in the sense that it makes a required minimum of protection for everyone's right to life, liberty, and property, which the Congress or the legislature may not withhold," while the latter "was aimed at undue favor and individual or class privilege, on the one hand, and at hostile discrimination or the oppression of inequality, on the other."

Constitutional Protections of Personal Rights

Of the several basic rights of citizens protected by constitutional provisions, freedom of speech and of the press and religious liberty will be briefly considered. Some questions arise, however, that cut across these more or less arbitrary categories. For instance, does a state statute requiring a special license with graduated fees for any parade or procession on the public streets abridge freedom of speech, press, religion, or assembly? In Cox v. New Hampshire,[21] the Supreme Court held that it did not.

The appellants, members of the Jehovah's Witnesses sect, marched through a city street without obtaining a license, in groups of twenty in

[19] Quoted in Mott, *op. cit.*, p. 284.

[20] 257 U.S. 312, 332–333 (1921); see Dowling, Noel T., "Equal Protection of the Laws," *Annals*, January 1938, Supplement, pp. 65–78.

[21] 312 U.S. 569, 1941.

single file, carrying placards to advertise a meeting. They alleged that the statute violated the fundamental civil liberties guaranteed by Amendment XIV, that it gave the licensing authorities unlimited, arbitrary, and discriminatory power, and that it was fatally vague and indefinite. The Court unanimously rejected all of these contentions, emphasizing that the state had the right to make reasonable police regulations with respect to the orderly use of the streets; that the state court's interpretation of the act did not give "arbitrary or unfettered discretion" to the licensing board; and that the fee was a reasonable charge to cover the cost of the extra police service necessary.

Freedom of Speech. There has been much popular misunderstanding with regard to the nature and extent of the liberty which may properly be enjoyed by the individual under the constitutional guarantee of freedom of speech. The right of the individual is relative, not absolute. Paradoxically enough, it is circumscribed by many restrictions which society has found it necessary to impose upon a theoretically complete freedom, in order that the individual might in fact enjoy freedom worthy of the name. In the first place, one's freedom of speech is limited by the consequences of his action. To shout loudly "Fire!" or "Murder!" in a crowded theater or railway station might cause injury and distress too horrible to contemplate, while to do the same in open fields would be quite harmless. Furthermore, one is bound to observe the customs and conventions of society — he may not, at least in public, resort to the use of obscene, profane, or abusive language. He is bound by the law of libel — he has no right to injure or defame the reputation of another, without adequate cause and proof. He is responsible for what he says, in the sense that he may not make serious charges against another and hide behind the cloak of anonymity. If he wants to expose something, he must be willing to stand in public and defend the charges. Again, while he may theoretically have the right to say anything he likes about any subject, at any time, and in any place, his own good judgment and a sense of the fitness of things ought to indicate to him that in fact he is not at liberty to discuss all subjects at all times and with all types of audiences. Thus freedom of speech is actually limited by many different considerations.[22]

Among important recent cases, attention will be confined to three problems: the right of an individual to make rabble-rousing speeches, the right to utilize sound amplifying equipment, and the right to regulate labor unions. Mention may be made of the possibility of encroachment on personal rights through the use of television in official investigations, but there are as yet no cases dealing with this problem. Two decisions of far-reaching importance have been handed down involving the use of strong and even

[22] See Niemayer, Gerhart, "A Reappraisal of the Doctrine of Free Speech," *Thought*, June 1950, pp. 251–274, and Pennock, J. Roland, "The Free Speech Doctrine: Some Doubts Resolved?" *Western Political Quarterly*, December 1950, pp. 566–573.

abusive language. In Chaplinsky v. New Hampshire,[23] the plaintiff, a Jehovah's Witness, used abusive language tending to cause a public disturbance, in violation of state law. The Court said that the "English language has a number of words and expressions which by general consent are 'fighting words' when said without a disarming smile. . . . Such words, as ordinary men know, are likely to cause a fight." They are not protected by the constitutional guarantee of freedom of speech. The Court did not find the state statute under which the case arose so vague and indefinite in its definition of crime as to render a conviction under it a denial of due process.

The Terminiello case[24] involved the conviction of a truculent rabble-rouser for disorderly conduct in violation of a city ordinance prohibiting the making of or assisting in a breach of the peace. His language was so violent and intemperate that only the presence of the Chicago police made it possible for him to make his speech and depart uninjured. On ample evidence, he was convicted and fined $100. Although his language might come within the concept of "fighting words" referred to in the Chaplinsky case, a sharply divided Court reversed the conviction, in part on the basis of the judge's charge to the jury (which was far from impartial), and in part on the theory of absolutism in freedom of expression. Though disavowing that free speech is absolute, the Court agreed that it is protected against censorship or punishment "unless shown likely to produce a clear and present danger of a serious substantive evil that rises far above public inconvenience, annoyance or unrest."

Similarly, there have been two cases on the use of sound trucks and sound amplifying equipment. The Saia case[25] involved a Lockport ordinance forbidding the use of sound amplifiers except with permission of the chief of police, but prescribed no standards for the exercise of his discretion. Five Justices held this ordinance unconstitutional on its face, as establishing a previous restraint on the right of free speech. The following year, however, and less than four months before the Terminiello case, the Court took some of the absolutism from the concept of freedom of speech, upholding a Trenton ordinance prohibiting the operation on the streets of any sound truck or amplifier, or any instrument emitting loud and raucous noises if attached to a vehicle.

Justice Reed, speaking for the Court,[26] held that "loud and raucous"

[23] 315 U.S. 568, 1942; for a parallel New York case, see People v. Feiner, 300 N.Y. 391, 91 N.E. 2d 316, 1950. In this and succeeding comments on Supreme Court cases, the author has made extensive use of the annual reviews by Cushman, Harris, Fellman, and others, published in the *American Political Science Review*.

[24] Terminiello v. Chicago, 337 U.S. 1, 1949; see Rosenwein, Samuel, "The Supreme Court and Freedom of Speech — Terminiello v. City of Chicago," *Lawyers Guild Review*, Spring 1949, pp. 70–77, and Latham, Earl G., "The Theory of the Judicial Concept of Freedom of Speech," *Journal of Politics*, November 1950, pp. 637–651.

[25] Saia v. New York, 334 U.S. 558, 1948.

[26] Kovacs v. Cooper, 336 U.S. 77, 1949; see note, "Constitutionality of the Municipal Regulation of Sound Amplifying Equipment," *Rutgers Law Review*, June 1949, pp. 250–266.

was not so vague and indefinite as to deny due process of law, nor was the ordinance an interference with free speech since the devices could be used elsewhere. The case differed from Saia v. New York in that the Trenton ordinance, unlike that in Lockport, did not vest uncontrolled discretion in the chief of police. The Court held that speech in the streets is not beyond all control and suggested that the "preferred position" of free speech "does not require legislators to be insensible to claims of citizens to comfort and convenience."

Several cases have been concerned with efforts of the states to regulate labor unions and the activities of their members. Laws forbidding peaceful picketing have twice been held an abridgment of freedom of speech and of the press,[27] and likewise, laws prohibiting the posting of bulletins and speeches by company officers advocating a company union.[28] Texas, along with a number of Southern states, had passed a law designed to regulate labor unions. This statute, enacted in 1943, required all labor unions operating in the state to secure from the Secretary of State an organizer's card before soliciting members. Applicants were to give their names and union affiliations and to show credentials. The Secretary of State had no discretion to refuse to register such an organizer if his application was properly made. Thomas, who did not apply for a card, addressed a meeting and solicited members, for the purpose of testing the statute. Prior to the meeting, a restraining order had been served on him, as a result of which he was cited for contempt. Five Justices produced three opinions holding the Texas statute invalid as an unreasonable interference with freedom of speech.[29]

Freedom of the Press. Many of the limitations which apply to freedom of speech apply with equal force to freedom of the press. The Court has for many years diligently protected the latter. In 1931, in Near v. Minnesota,[30] it was called upon to consider the attempt of the state legislature to prevent the growth of the blackmailing industry; although the Court divided sharply on the issue, the majority held "that while a malicious, defamatory publication rendered its publisher liable in damages *after* issue, any law which provided for the stopping or prevention of publication *before* issue was an interference with liberty, particularly when the publication discussed the conduct of public officers and their duty in the suppression of crime."

27 Thornhill v. Alabama, 310 U.S. 88, 1940, and Carlson v. California, 310 U.S. 106, 1940; in Giboney v. Empire Storage and Ice Company, 336 U.S. 490, 1949, the Court modified somewhat the doctrine of the Thornhill case when it sustained an injunction issued under a Missouri antitrust law restraining the picketing of an ice plant because it refused to agree not to sell ice to non-union peddlers, no issue of freedom of speech being involved. See Aaron, Benjamin, *Protecting Civil Liberties of Members of Trade Unions* (Institute of Industrial Relations, University of California at Los Angeles, 1950), and Fraenkel, Osmond K., "Peaceful Picketing — Constitutionally Protected?" *University of Pennsylvania Law Review*, October 1950.

28 National Labor Relations Board v. Virginia Electric and Power Company, 314 U.S. 480, 1941.

29 Thomas v. Collins, 323 U.S. 516, 1945.

30 283 U.S. 697, 1931.

Between 1937 and 1947, the Court restricted the power to punish for contempt in a number of cases, in at least three of which the issue of freedom of the press was squarely raised.[31] In each instance, matter had been published which either sought to influence the court in the disposition of pending litigation or accused the court of misconduct. The convictions for contempt were set aside as invalid restrictions on the freedom of the press. Such attacks upon or advice to the court can be punished as contempt only when they constitute a "clear and present danger" to the administration of justice. The Court found no such danger in any of these cases and expressed the belief that a judge worthy of his office should be immune to the influence of such publications.

The Court has dealt with a number of questions more or less closely related to freedom of the press. It has held repeatedly, for instance, that this freedom includes the right to distribute propagandist literature on the public streets,[32] but this right does not extend to commercial advertising.[33] It has even held invalid a city ordinance making it unlawful to ring doorbells or knock on doors in order to summon the occupant of a residence to the door so as to give him handbills, circulars, or other advertisements.[34] In its decision in this case, the Court emphasized the fact that such door-to-door distribution had long been an accepted method of communication and held that to forbid it altogether, as in this ordinance, is to violate the freedom of speech and of the press protected by the Constitution.

In another case, Marsh v. Alabama,[35] a Jehovah's Witness was distributing pamphlets on the sidewalk in a company-owned town in Alabama. Warned by a police officer that she could not do so without a permit, and requested to leave the premises, she refused and was arrested under a state statute which makes it unlawful to remain on the premises of another after having been warned not to do so. Over objections that the statute would abridge the freedom of religion and press, she was convicted in the Alabama courts. The Supreme Court went to lengths which it has rarely reached, saying in effect — to use the words of one commentator — "Let my people go."

A novel question was presented to the Court when it was called upon to consider a New York statute prohibiting the printing, selling, or distribution of any publication "principally made up of criminal news, police reports, or accounts of criminal deeds, or pictures, or stories of deeds of bloodshed, lust, or crime." The New York Court of Appeals interpreted the statute as forbidding these publications as "indecent or obscene" in the sense that materials dealing with bloodshed or lust "can be so massed as to

[31] Bridges v. California, 314 U.S. 252, 1941; Pennekamp v. Florida, 328 U.S. 331, 1946; Craig v. Harney, 331 U.S. 367, 1947.

[32] Jamison v. Texas, 318 U.S. 413, 1943.

[33] Valentine v. Christensen, 316 U.S. 52, 1942.

[34] Martin v. Struthers, 319 U.S. 141, 1943.

[35] 326 U.S. 501, 1946; in Tucker v. Texas, 326 U.S. 517, 1946, the result was the same.

become vehicles for inciting violent and depraved crimes against the person." A majority of six, in Winters v. New York,[36] held that this statute, even as interpreted by the state court, was in conflict with the principle of a free press, because it was too vague and indefinite to satisfy the standards of certainty necessary for criminal prosecutions. It rejected the contention that the constitutional protection of a free press applies only to the exposition of ideas, for

> The line between the informing and the entertaining is too elusive. . . . Though we can see nothing of any possible value in these magazines, they are as much entitled to the protection of free speech as the best literature. Whether the statute satisfies the standards of certainty depends upon whether men of ordinary intelligence must guess at its meaning. While some terms in the criminal law, such as obscene, lewd, lascivious, filthy, indecent, or disgusting, are well understood through long use in the criminal law, the words used in the present statute, even as interpreted, do not give effective notice of what is forbidden.

Freedom of Religion. The Court has in recent years given almost unfailing support to freedom of conscience. Cases involving such freedom arise in a surprising number of ways. Reversing an earlier decision,[37] the Court in West Virginia State Board of Education v. Barnette[38] held that to compel "conscientiously scrupulous children" (Jehovah's Witnesses, in this instance) to salute the flag deprives them of the freedom of religion guaranteed by the due process clause of Amendment XIV. The refusal to salute the flag does not involve any "collision with rights asserted by any other individual, nor was it accompanied by any conduct which was not peaceful and orderly. It is now commonplace that censorship or suppression of opinion is tolerated by our Constitution only when the expression presents a clear and present danger of action of a kind the state is empowered to prevent and punish." No one claims that the refusal by school children to salute the flag creates any such "clear and present danger."

In Taylor v. Mississippi,[39] the Court unanimously set aside the conviction of three Jehovah's Witnesses under a statute which made it a felony to teach or preach orally any principles or to distribute any printed matter calculated to encourage violence, sabotage, or disloyalty to the state or nation, to advocate the cause of our enemies, to disclose military information or secrets, to utter or distribute material which would "incite any sort of racial distrust, disorder, prejudices or hatreds, or which reasonably tends to create an attitude of stubborn refusal to salute, honor or respect the flag or government of the United States, or of the State of Mississippi." While one of the appellants appeared to have announced that it is wrong to fight the nation's enemies and that its soldiers were being shot to no purpose, the prosecutions were in the main focused on the activities of all

[36] 333 U.S. 507, 1948.
[37] Minersville School District v. Gobitis, 310 U.S. 586, 1940.
[38] 319 U.S. 624, 1943.
[39] 319 U.S. 583, 1943.

three in condemning on religious grounds the salute of the flag, thereby violating Amendment XIV. "It punishes them although what they communicated is not claimed or shown to have been done with an evil or sinister purpose. . . ."

The Jehovah's Witnesses have been a prolific source of important test cases in the field of civil rights; for their contribution toward the clarification of many disputed points, all may be grateful. Reference has already been made to their successful attack upon a Dallas ordinance restricting the right to distribute propagandist literature on the public streets. In dealing with a similar type of question — namely, the licensing of persons peddling religious tracts — the Court handed down an affirmative decision one year and reversed itself the next.[40]

In the latter case, Murdock v. Pennsylvania, the Court was called upon to decide whether religious liberty is violated by imposing on the sale of religious books and tracts a nondiscriminatory license tax designed to raise revenue and required of all who engage in canvassing or soliciting for the sale of books or merchandise of any kind. The City of Jeannette imposed substantial fees for the privilege of such canvassing. Justice Douglas, speaking for a majority of the Court, argued that a tax laid on the free exercise of religion, as protected by Amendments I and XIV, is unconstitutional. The circulation and sale of religious literature by Murdock was an exercise of religion. The ordinance placed a tax upon that circulation and sale, and therefore the ordinance was void. The activities of Murdock and other Jehovah's Witnesses here involved constituted an exercise of religion and not a commercial enterprise. They were, said the Court, engaged in a kind of religious evangelism which is "age-old."

Perhaps the sole important exception to the Court's support of the concept of freedom of conscience in late years is to be found in In re Summers,[41] in which it sustained the right of Illinois to exclude a conscientious objector from admission to the bar. The law examiners of Illinois did not dispute the good character and professional fitness of Summers, but excluded him solely because his religious scruple against bearing arms "seems inconsistent with the obligations of an attorney at law." They contended that Summers could not in good faith take the oath to support the state constitution, which contains a peculiar militia clause. He was willing to take the prescribed oath but was not permitted to do so. Five Justices, through Justice Reed, held that Summers had not been denied due process

[40] Jones v. Opelika, 316 U.S. 584, 1942, reversed by Murdock v. Pennsylvania, 319 U.S. 105, 1943. The following year, in Follette v. Town of McCormick, 321 U.S. 573, 1944, a unanimous Court, following the doctrine of the Murdock case, adhered to this doctrine even though the facts showed that Follette, a Jehovah's Witness, earned his living in his home town by the sale of such literature. See Barber, Hollis W., "Religious Liberty vs. Police Power: Jehovah's Witnesses," *American Political Science Review*, April 1947, pp. 226–247.

[41] 325 U.S. 561, 1945.

by state infringement of the freedom of religion protected by Amendment I. The Court granted that the state could not exclude members of a particular religious sect but denied that there was such religious discrimination in this case. It relied largely on the Schwimmer and Macintosh cases, the situation in which was roughly parallel to that of Summers, and in which conscientious objectors were denied citizenship.[42]

Two very significant cases which reached the Court involved religious considerations in the public schools. The case of Everson v. Board of Education [43] arose under a New Jersey statute which authorizes local school districts to make rules and contracts for the transportation of children to and from schools. The Board of Education of the town of Ewing authorized reimbursement of parents for the cost of transportation of their children on regular busses operated by the public transportation system. Catholic parents were reimbursed in this way for the cost of having their children ride by public bus to and from parochial schools. These parochial schools give their students, in addition to secular education, regular religious instruction. Their superintendent is a Catholic priest. Everson brought a taxpayer's action to restrain this reimbursement of Catholic parents, alleging that it was a violation of due process of law to use money raised by taxation for the benefit of private individuals, and that the payments amounted to state support of schools maintained by the Catholic Church.

The opinion of the Court was written by Justice Black, who rejected the contention that private property was taken through taxation and devoted to a private purpose. The New Jersey legislature had decided that paying for the transportation of school children to and from their schools, whether public or private, was a public purpose by which the public interest would be served. If it is supporting a private interest to transport children to a parochial school, it would be equally so to transport them to any other nonpublic school. "It is much too late to argue that legislation intended to facilitate the opportunity of children to get a secular education serves no public purpose."

The crucial issue was the second one, whether the New Jersey statute can be attacked as a "law respecting the establishment of religion." The Court, admitting that the prohibition of Amendment I is binding upon the states through the operation of Amendment XIV, reviewed at length the history of this clause, concluding: "We cannot say that the First Amendment prohibits New Jersey from spending tax-raised funds to pay the bus fares of parochial school pupils as a part of a general program under which it pays the fares of pupils attending public and other schools." While this policy does indirectly aid Catholic priests and parochial schools, this is only

[42] United States v. Rosika Schwimmer, 279 U.S. 644, 1929, and United States v. Macintosh, 283 U.S. 636, 1931.

[43] 330 U.S. 1, 1947; see note in *New York University Law Quarterly Review*, April 1947, pp. 331–337.

its indirect result. Amendment I requires a state to be "a neutral in its relations with groups of religious believers and non-believers; it does not require the state to be their adversary. State power is no more to be used so as to handicap religions than it is to favor them." In Pierce v. Sisters of the Holy Name, the Supreme Court had itself recognized the constitutional right of parents to send their children to private and parochial rather than to public schools.[44]

In Illinois ex rel. McCollum v. Board of Education,[45] eight Justices agreed that the "released time" plan of religious education in the public schools of Champaign was inconsistent with the principle of separation of church and state, and therefore under the ban of Amendment XIV. The issues caused great disagreement among the members of the Court — as, indeed, they have done wherever seriously considered. Under the plan, religious teachers employed by private religious groups were permitted to come into the school buildings weekly, during school hours, for thirty to forty-five minutes of religious teaching. This was given only to those pupils whose parents had consented in writing. The religious instructors were not paid but were subject to the supervision and control of the school superintendent. Pupils not enrolled in the religious classes went on with their regular secular studies.

Current Trends. Americans have, through all the years, prided themselves on their devotion to the ideals and principles of democracy, a democracy built on freedom for the individual and respect for the rights of the individual. That there is a keen and healthy interest in many quarters in the protection and preservation of the fundamental civil rights, none will deny. The past decade has seen, not only many legislative enactments adopted with this end in view, but numerous decisions of our highest court, some of which have been cited here. Yet there are numerous evidences of contrary tendencies so strong that one cannot help wondering how secure these rights really are.

The superpatriots seem to be having a heyday. It is supposed to be defending Americanism for the legislature to enact all sorts of restrictive laws, most of them without merit, most of them legislative declarations against civil liberties. "We the people" are largely to blame, for our representatives generally reflect the state of mind of their constituents. What is that state of mind? It is fear. "We are afraid," says Professor Johnson, "more afraid than any other people. . . . Being frightened," he continues,[46]

[44] 268 U.S. 510, 1925; see Cushman, Robert F., "Public Support of Religious Education in American Constitutional Law," *Illinois Law Review*, July–August 1950, pp. 333–356; Lardner, Lynford A., "How Far Does the Constitution Separate Church and State?" *American Political Science Review*, March 1951, pp. 110–132.

[45] 333 U.S. 203, 1948; see McCollum, Vashti C., *One Woman's Fight* (Doubleday, New York, 1951).

[46] Johnson, Claudius O., "Civil Liberties: the Citizen's Business," *Western Political Quarterly*, December 1950, pp. 501–511.

we do what frightened people usually do — we do foolish things. We act like people in a panic when a house is afire. We carry a pillow dowstairs and throw a clock out of the window. Anyhow, we must do something. And so we decide that children shall be compelled to salute the flag, their teachers to take an oath, and that people must be prevented from joining certain organizations.

These excesses in the field of legislation give rise to many other things which no sane person wants to encourage. They give to many groups, official and unofficial — Federal, state, and local — courage and strength to proceed in complete and utter disregard of the basic rights of citizens and of established principles of investigatory procedure. These occurrences stimulate a popular belief that the American people live in a turmoil of spying and counterspying, of espionage and counterespionage. They literally strike terror into the government service. The threat of investigation, often by questionable methods, not once but time after time, of misrepresentation and misinterpretation of harmless and innocent facts, prompts those who are not in the service to stay out and those who are in to get out.

A certain element of the public is no longer satisfied with the exercise of the unquestioned right of Americans to make constructive criticisms of public officials and their actions, or with the exercise of the questionable right to make destructive criticisms. Instead, they find it necessary to engage in character assassination and in persecution, ruthlessly maligning the character and motives of loyal fellow citizens who happen to hold public office, until they are, in many cases, broken in health and forced to retire. Such conduct, its perpetrators boast, is defending American institutions and the American way of life against attack by subversive elements. Actually, it is a serious threat to the American way of life — a threat which, if carried on long enough and carried far enough, might ultimately destroy it completely.

These tactics are threatening freedom of speech, freedom of the press, freedom of assembly, freedom of thought, and civil liberties generally, everywhere. Many dare not even speak frankly, unless they are thoroughly sure of the person to whom they speak. One of the nation's leading state universities makes the headlines, week after week and month after month, in a sorry controversy over a teacher's oath law. Academic freedom is being challenged, not only in California, but elsewhere throughout the country. Authors of standard textbooks widely used in schools and colleges are being hauled up for "un-Americanism." Indeed, one may cynically wonder if it is any longer safe to have an idea, let alone to express it, or if it is any longer safe to have ever had an idea which might be dug up by the professional snoopers and made to appear subversive.[47]

[47] See Alabama Legislative Reference Service, *State Anti-Communist Legislation* (Montgomery, 1950); MacWilliams, Carey, *Witch Hunt: the Revival of Heresy* (Little, Brown, Boston, 1950); Pates, Gordon, "California: the Oath Epidemic," *Reporter*, December 26, 1950, pp. 29–31; Prendergast, William B., "State Legislatures and Communism: the Current Scene," *American Political Science Review*, September 1950, pp. 556–574;

There is an element of conflict, of course, arising in many situations involving civil rights, a conflict between two basic principles, both of which may be generally accepted by the community as desirable. Most striking, perhaps, is the conflict between freedom and security. But there are many others. Both freedom and security are necessary, but neither hysteria nor blindness to Communist intrigue can guard liberty. If security is given preference, freedom may suffer. If freedom is given priority, this may mean a certain amount of danger from a security standpoint. There are conflicts, too, between freedom and the right of the public to peace and quiet. Should the police power be used to regulate and control the use of sound trucks? Which is more important, the right of a candidate for public office to tell his story to the voters or the right of the voters to protection from unwelcome noises, to an invasion of the right of privacy? Should public funds be used to transport pupils to private or parochial schools, or school time in the public schools be released for purposes of religious education? In these instances, which is more important, the aid to religion, on the one hand, or the strict observance of the principle of the separation of church and state, on the other? What weight should be given to the right of parents to determine what type of religious instruction their children should have, or whether they should have any at all? However these questions are decided, other basic considerations are bound to suffer.[48]

Statutory Protection of Personal Rights

Civil Rights Legislation. Both the Federal and state constitutions protect citizens from infringements of their rights by the government and its officers. They do not, however, cover infringements of the rights of persons or attacks upon their property by other persons. This does not mean that persons who suffer such violations of personal or property rights are left without means of redress. The point is that the basis of their redress is to be found in the statutes as interpreted by the courts, and not in the provisions of the Constitution. In Chapter 16 on the legal systems of the states, mention was made of some of the more common types of conduct which infringe upon individual and property rights. Many of these are purely personal and are protected by ordinary statutes and by recourse to judicial process; others

---

Stewart, George R., *The Year of the Oath: the Fight for Academic Freedom at the University of California* (Doubleday, New York, 1950); Wood, Fred B., "The Permissible Scope of State Statutory Regulations Concerning Subversive Activities, Considered in the Light of Applicable Limitations of the State and Federal Constitutions" (mimeographed address, Sacramento, 1948); and the studies prepared at Cornell University in the project under the direction of Professor Robert E. Cushman, on the control of subversive activities in California, New York, Washington, and other states.

[48] See the author's *Developments in the Field of Civil Rights*, 1945–1950 (Legislative Reference Service, Library of Congress, 1951), and the following: Barth, Alan, *The Loyalty of Free Men* (Viking, New York, 1950); Gellhorn, Walter, *Security, Loyalty and Science* (Cornell University Press, 1950); and Lasswell, Harold D., *National Security and Individual Freedom* (McGraw-Hill, New York, 1950).

involve violations of fundamental rights on the part of government. It is now proposed to consider the attempts that have been made by injured parties to invoke the protection of the Constitution, and to observe the results of such attempts.

The Negroes are probably the group that has suffered most from the inability to enjoy rights and privileges exercised without question by other groups in the community. For many years after the adoption of Amendment XIV, the effort was made by the Radical Reconstructionists in Congress to pass legislation assuring the Negro a large measure of social equality. In the Senate this movement was led by Charles Sumner of Massachusetts; because of constitutional difficulties, obvious to anyone familiar with constitutional law, he was unable to secure a favorable vote. After his death, however, the Senate waived its scruples with regard to constitutionality, and adopted, largely as a tribute to a departed friend and colleague, the Civil Rights Act of 1881.

Two years later, this act was declared unconstitutional by the Supreme Court in the famous Civil Rights Cases,[49] in which it was held that it was not the intent or purpose of those who proposed and adopted Amendment XIV to place in the Constitution a guarantee of the personal rights of individuals as against invasion by other individuals, no matter how important their enjoyment might be to the happiness of the injured parties. In this case, various Negroes had been denied by the proprietors of hotels, theaters, and railway companies the full enjoyment of accommodations, for reasons other than those excepted by the statute, the most important section of which provided as follows:

> Section 1. That all persons within the jurisdiction of the United States shall be entitled to the full and equal enjoyment of the accommodations, advantages, facilities, and privileges of inns, public conveyances on land or water, theaters, and other places of public amusement; subject only to the conditions and limitations established by law, and applicable alike to citizens of every race and color, regardless of any previous condition of servitude.

The proprietors had been indicted and sued for the penalty prescribed by the act — the forfeit of a sum of $500 for each offense to the person aggrieved, and conviction of a misdemeanor.

In its opinion the Court pointed out that "it is state action of a particular character that is prohibited" by the amendment; later, at greater length, it said that "until some state law has been passed, or some state action through its officers or agents has been taken, adverse to the rights of citizens sought to be protected by the Fourteenth Amendment, no legislation of the United States under said amendment, nor any proceeding under such legislation, can be called into activity, for the prohibitions of the amendment are

[49] 109 U.S. 3, 1883; for excellent discussions of constitutional rights, see Biddle, Francis, "Civil Rights and the Federal Law," in *Safeguarding Civil Liberty Today, op. cit.*, and Konvitz, Milton R., *The Constitution and Civil Rights* (Columbia University Press, 1947).

against state laws and acts done under state authority." It is thus clear that if legislative action is to be taken for the purpose of protecting the civil rights of this portion of the population, it must originate in the states.

Surveys made in the late forties showed the states divided into three groups of approximately equal size, so far as the statutory protection of civil rights is concerned. Sixteen had laws requiring segregation, eighteen had laws prohibiting it, while the remainder apparently had no statutory provisions on the subject. In the sixteen states requiring segregation, fourteen laws apply to common carriers, fourteen to schools. Five require the segregation of prisoners, two of the audience in tent shows. Segregation is required in individual states under a variety of circumstances as follows: at the races, in library reading rooms, in parks and recreation areas, in cotton textile factories, and in cities and towns. The antisegregation and antidiscrimination laws apply in hotels, restaurants, theaters, and shops.

It is a serious mistake to assume that the problem of discrimination is confined to any one group or section of the country. It varies considerably, as the author has pointed out elsewhere,[50] from one section of the country to another, but is everywhere present in some form. "It varies because the composition of the minority group varies from place to place. There really is no standardized minority group in America. In New York, which has representatives of all such groups, the Jews are especially numerous, as they are in fact, in all large urban centers. The Negroes, formerly a minority group only in the South, now exist in appreciable numbers in all large urban centers — New York, Philadelphia, Chicago, Detroit, St. Louis, and many more."

> While the Jews and the Negroes are the most numerous, minority groups in wide variety exist in sections, states, and cities throughout the country. All are the victims of local prejudice, oftentimes of actual discrimination. In southern New Jersey, it is the Italians; in Pennsylvania, Nebraska, and Wisconsin, the Germans; in Minnesota and the Dakotas, the Scandinavians; in the New England mill villages, the French-Canadians, and in Boston, the Irish; in Chicago and Detroit, the Poles; in Texas and the Southwest, the Mexicans; on the Pacific Coast, the Orientals.

Public Accommodation. One third of the states still require segregation of the races in many areas. Even in those jurisdictions with civil rights laws designed to insure equality of treatment in places of public accommodation, the members of minority groups have been subjected to all manner of discriminatory practices by the proprietors of such establishments. Resort to the courts has provided little relief, since the courts have — at least until very recently — been guided by two considerations: (1) the assumption that segregation did not imply anything with regard to the superiority or inferiority of either race; (2) the parallel assumption that, where segregation

[50] Graves, W. Brooke, *Fair Employment Practice Legislation in the United States — Federal, State, Municipal*, p. 16 (Public Affairs Bulletin No. 93, Legislative Reference Service, Library of Congress, 1951); for additional titles, see Selected References.

was required by law, the facilities provided for each race would be equal in quality and adequate in quantity.[51] Rare indeed was the case in which either of these assumptions was realized in practice.

During the last decade, the Supreme Court has — as previously noted — given a new emphasis to, and has taken a more liberal attitude with regard to civil rights problems generally. It has been gradually abandoning the doctrine of equal and adequate service and in a number of cases has taken a positive stand in favor of nondiscrimination. True, the Court held in 1914 that Pullman accommodations could not be denied to Negroes if they were available to white persons, but it was not until the decade of the forties that it consistently refused to tolerate discriminatory practices in this area.[52]

In Mitchell v. United States[53] it was made clear that the Court would insist that, in spite of Southern segregation laws, Negroes receive accommodations and treatment substantially equal to those given whites. The test of equality is not met by giving Negroes with first class tickets accommodations equal to those enjoyed by white persons traveling second class, nor by allowing such Negro passengers to buy drawing room space if available. The Court held that a Virginia statute requiring the segregation of Negroes and whites on interstate busses unduly burdened interstate commerce.[54] Eighteen states, the Court noted, prohibit racial segregation on public carriers while ten require it on motor carriers. The enforcement of these state laws against carriers engaged in such commerce produces cumulative inconveniences and burdens, among which are the repeated shifting of seats upon reaching state lines, as well as the difficulty of applying the various definitions used to identify white and colored passengers. Desiring a simple, uniform rule to promote and protect national travel, the Court held the Virginia statute invalid. It is to be noted that the protection given members of minority groups in this case came under the commerce clause of the Constitution, not under the Bill of Rights.

Still later, in 1950, the Supreme Court banned segregation in railway dining cars.[55] One Elmer W. Henderson had been refused service on a Southern Railway diner in 1942 because there were no empty seats at tables

[51] The classic statement of this doctrine is found in Plessy v. Ferguson, 163 U.S. 537, 1896; see also Groves, Harry E., "Separate but Equal — the Doctrine of Plessy v. Ferguson," *Phylon*, First Quarter 1951, pp. 66–72, and Ransmeir, Joseph S., "The Fourteenth Amendment and the Separate but Equal Doctrine," *Michigan Law Review*, December 1951, pp. 203–260.

[52] McCabe v. Atcheson, Topeka & Santa Fe Railroad Company, 235 U.S. 151, 1914; see also Pethia, Theodore J., and Thomas, George J., "The Beginning of the End of the 'Separate but Equal' Doctrine," *Catholic University of America Law Review*, January 1951, pp. 70–74.

[53] 313 U.S. 80, 1941; Mr. Mitchell was a Negro Congressman from Chicago. The case arose under Arkansas law.

[54] Morgan v. Virginia, 328 U.S. 373, 1946.

[55] Henderson v. United States, 339 U.S. 816, 1950.

reserved for Negroes, although there were seats at tables for whites. Speaking for the Court, Justice Burton said:

> Where a dining car is available to passengers holding tickets entitling them to use it, each such passenger is equally entitled to its facilities in accordance with reasonable regulations. The denial of dining service to any such passenger by the rules before us subjects him to a prohibited disadvantage.

The Supreme Court has also ruled that a state can forbid racial discrimination on an excursion boat, even though the boat goes into foreign waters. By a 7–2 decision, it upheld the conviction of the Bob-Lo Excursion Company of Detroit for putting a Negro high school girl off one of its boats. The Company was found guilty of violating the Michigan civil rights statute and fined $25.[56]

Discrimination in Education. Actually all three branches of government have been moving toward the removal of discriminatory practices. The Southern states, seeking an effective means of controlling the Ku-Klux Klan, have been rewriting legislation prohibiting the wearing of masks or hoods on the public streets and highways, without regard to the purpose for which such covering is worn.[57] Governor Chester Bowles of Connecticut, in 1949, took the lead in opposition to the establishment of a "Jim Crow" unit in the state National Guard to take care of Negro enlistments. New Jersey, in its new constitution, framed and ratified in 1947, included the following provision (Art. I, Sec. 5):

> No person shall be denied the enjoyment of any civil or military right, nor be discriminated against in the exercise of any civil or military right, nor be segregated in the militia or in the public schools, because of religious principles, race, color, ancestry, or national origin.

The principle that "separate but equal" facilities satisfy constitutional requirements has not been reversed, but in the words of Milton R. Konvitz, it is beginning to crumble in the field of education, as elsewhere.[58] The Court has, in recent years, been increasingly inclined to view more critically the facts of cases brought before it to ascertain whether equality has in fact been offered. This has been especially true in the field of education.

In Missouri ex rel. Gaines v. Canada,[59] the Court held that the state was denying equal protection of the law in failing to provide a legal education within the state for Negroes comparable to that afforded white students. Missouri maintains a separate university for Negroes which does not provide legal instruction; a statute authorizes the board of curators to arrange for scholarships to the university of any adjacent state for taking any course provided at the University of Missouri but not taught at the Negro university. The petitioner refused to avail himself of the scholarship and brought

[56] Bob-Lo Excursion Company v. Michigan, 333 U.S. 28, 1948; see also Hall v. DeCuir, 95 U.S. 495, 1878, in which a state law forbidding steamboats on the Mississippi to segregate passengers according to race was held unconstitutional under the commerce clause.

[57] Graves, *Developments in the Field of Civil Rights*, *op. cit.*

[58] "The Courts Deal a Blow to Segregation," *Commentary*, February 1951, pp. 158–166; see also Pethia and Thomas, *op. cit.*

[59] 305 U.S. 580, 1938.

mandamus to compel his admission to the state university law school. The State Supreme Court refused the writ. Reversing the decision, the United States Supreme Court held that the out-of-state scholarship plan was insufficient and in contravention of the equal protection clause of Amendment XIV. The obligation of the state to afford the protection of equal law can be performed only where its laws operate, that is to say, within its own jurisdiction. It is there that equality of rights must be maintained.

A decade later, in the Sipuel case, the Court held that Oklahoma was obliged to provide legal education for a qualified Negro applicant as soon as it did for applicants of any other group.[60] A young Negro woman who was admittedly qualified to receive professional legal education applied for admission to the University Law School, the only institution for legal education supported and maintained by the taxpayers of Oklahoma. The Court held that the petitioner was entitled to secure legal education afforded by a state institution and that "the state must provide it for her in conformity with the equal protection clause of the Fourteenth Amendment and provide it as soon as it does for applicants of any other group." The case was remanded to the State Supreme Court "for proceedings not inconsistent with this opinion."

To comply with this mandate, the State court entered an order requiring in the alternative the admission of a Negro to the state-maintained law school or nonenrollment of any other applicant until a separate school with equal educational facilities could be provided for Negroes. Over the objection of two Justices, the Supreme Court held that this order did not depart from its mandate.[61] Having been effectively rebuffed in its effort to maintain segregation by means of separate institutions, Oklahoma next sought to maintain it by another device. A Negro student, after being admitted to the Graduate School, was required to sit apart at a designated desk in an anteroom adjoining the classroom; to sit at a designated desk on the mezzanine floor at the library; and to sit at a designated table and eat at a different time from the other students in the cafeteria. The lower court held that these conditions did not violate the provisions of Amendment XIV.

During the interval between the decision of the lower court and the hearing in the Supreme Court, the treatment afforded the appellant was modified, he having been assigned a seat in the classroom in a row reserved for colored students, assigned a table in the library on the main floor, and permitted to eat at the same time in the cafeteria although he was assigned to a special table. The Supreme Court reversed the decision below and held that "State-imposed restrictions which produce such inequalities cannot be sustained."[62] The Court said further:

[60] Sipuel v. Oklahoma, 332 U.S. 631, 1948.
[61] Fisher v. Hurst, 333 U.S. 147, 1948. Mrs. Fisher was the former Miss Sipuel.
[62] McLaurin v. Oklahoma, 339 U.S. 637, 1950.

> The Fourteenth Amendment precludes differences in treatment by the state based upon race. Appellant, having been admitted to a state-supported graduate school, must receive the same treatment at the hands of the state as students of other races. . . .

In 1950, a unanimous Supreme Court addressed itself to the question: to what extent does Amendment XIV limit a state's power to distinguish between students of different races in professional and graduate education at a state university? Continuing its opposition to racial segregation in the graduate and professional schools of state universities, the Court held that the exclusion of a Negro applicant from the University of Texas Law School was a denial of equal protection in the face of arguments that a separate law school for Negroes provided equal facilities.[63] The facts resembled those in Missouri v. Canada, referred to on pages 692–693.

The Chief Justice, speaking for the Court, drew pointed contrasts between the two law schools, with respect to size and prestige of their faculties, the size of the respective student bodies and libraries, the presence of the Order of the Coif at the state university and its absence at the Negro school, the existence of a law review at the University and its lack at the Negro school, the positions of distinction occupied by the alumni of the University Law School in private practice and public life in contrast to that of the solitary and lonely alumnus of the Negro Law school, and the accredited standing of the University Law School. In addition to these items, the Court pointed to the greater variety of courses and opportunity for specialization at the University Law School, a combination of factors producing "those qualities which are incapable of objective measurement but which make for greatness in a law school." Said the Court: "The Equal Protection clause of the Fourteenth Amendment requires that petitioner be admitted to the University of Texas Law School. . . ." Although refusing to re-examine the equal and separate facilities doctrine of Plessy v. Ferguson, the Court effectively undermined it by laying down criteria which render application of it impossible and which in effect require identical facilities, if the humane demands of equal protection are to be satisfied.

Three specific influences appear to be cracking the color line in institutions of higher learning in the South: (1) the constant pressure of the Supreme Court for the observance of the basic constitutional protections; (2) the huge and unjustified financial burden of maintaining two separate sets of professional schools at state expense; (3) a changing public opinion on matters of race relations in the Southern region. Evidences of change are apparent on every hand. In 1948, the University of Arkansas announced that qualified Negroes would be accepted in its graduate schools, thereby becoming the first Southern state voluntarily to take this position. The

[63] Sweatt v. Painter, 339 U.S. 629, 1950; on these cases, see DeMay, John A., "Segregation in Law and Graduate Schools," *University of Pittsburgh Law Review*, Winter 1951, pp. 261–269.

Connecticut Interracial Commission made a study of discrimination against members of minority groups in admission to colleges and universities within the state, and drew up recommendations.[64]

In 1948, the University of Delaware lifted its ban on Negroes, claiming also that it was "the first such action taken by a Southern university." The Kentucky legislature in 1950 amended its 1904 school segregation law to permit Negroes to attend any white institution of higher learning, public or private, under two conditions — if the institution's governing body approves and if comparable courses are not available at the State's Negro college.[65] In the same year, the president of the University of Maryland announced the determination of that state to maintain duplicate facilities, but at the same time requested $3,500,000 to expand the University's Negro branch. In 1948, the board of curators of the University of Missouri recommended limited enrollment of Negroes at all state-supported institutions of higher learning. In the same year, Governor Dewey of New York requested and the legislature passed a drastic measure to prevent colleges from turning down prospective students because of race or religious beliefs. In 1951, the trustees of the University of North Carolina authorized the admission of qualified Negroes to the graduate schools of the University, with the exception of the Law School.

Procedural Rights. During the last few years, the Supreme Court has been called upon to review a number of cases in the field of procedural rights. In Screws v. United States,[66] the Court sustained a portion of the Federal Civil Rights Act as well as the conviction of Screws and his associates, who had beaten to death a Georgia Negro whom they had arrested. The Court held that they had willfully deprived the victim of the privileges and immunities guaranteed by the Constitution in Amendment XIV, and of rights protected by due process of law. The Court has, as a matter of fact, for well over a decade, rather consistently applied its rule laid down in the Brown and Chambers cases,[67] that coerced confessions and third degree methods are a denial of due process of law, on the ground that they are contrary to civilized standards of justice. Such a rule is not always easy to apply.[68]

Whether a denial of the right of counsel amounts to a denial of due process depends upon the circumstances of the denial and its effect upon

[64] Stetler, Henry G., *College Admission Practices with Respect to Race, Religion, and National Origin* (Hartford, 1949).

[65] Kentucky Laws 1950, Chapter 155.

[66] 325 U.S. 91, 1945.

[67] Brown v. Mississippi, 297 U.S. 278, 1936, and Chambers v. Florida, 309 U.S. 227, 1940.

[68] The ruling that the character of a confession is to be determined by a conclusion as to whether the accused at the time of confession possessed the "mental freedom" to confess or deny a crime (Lyons v. Oklahoma, 322 U.S. 596, 1944) was not satisfactory to those judges who would incorporate the whole of the Bill of Rights into the due process clause.

the essential fairness with which the accused is treated.[69] At any rate, due process does not require the state to furnish counsel in all cases in which the accused is unable to provide it.[70] Since this case, the Court has on a number of occasions proclaimed the right to counsel fundamental to any material steps in a proceeding after indictment or other similar charge or arraignment.[71]

Many questions have arisen regarding the composition of grand juries and juries. The Court has repeatedly held that a Negro is constitutionally entitled to be indicted and tried by juries from which Negroes have not been excluded because of their race.[72] In Smith v. Texas, the Court reversed the conviction of Smith for rape, on the ground that he had been indicted by a grand jury from which Negroes had been excluded because of their race.[73] The evidence of such discrimination was persuasive when in a county having a Negro population of over 20 per cent, only five out of 384 grand jurors serving over a period of eight years were Negroes. Two years later, in another Texas case,[74] the Court again reversed a conviction on the basis of statistics showing that for at least sixteen years, no Negroes had been called for grand jury service in the county and that there were hundreds of Negroes whose education would presumably qualify them for such service.

It is thus well established that the exclusion of Negroes from either a grand or petit jury because of their race deprives a defendant brought before it of the equal protection of the laws. The Supreme Court has stressed the invalidity either of excluding Negroes from grand juries or of limiting their numbers because of their race.[75] While failure of a community ever to call Negroes for jury duty over a long period of time, when there are many qualified for such duty, constitutes an evidence of discrimination, it has been held that a Negro was not denied equal protection on this ground when indicted by a grand jury on which only one Negro served.[76] But a unanimous Court set aside the conviction of a Mississippi Negro by an all-white jury after indictment by an all-white grand jury.[77]

The same type of question has been raised where it appeared that women

[69] Canizio v. New York, 327 U.S. 82, 1946; Foster v. Illinois, 332 U.S. 134, 1947, and other cases decided during the same term.

[70] Betts v. Brady, 316 U.S. 455, 1942, and subsequent cases: Uveges v. Pennsylvania, 335 U.S. 437, 1948, Gibbs v. Burke, 337 U.S. 773, 1949, and Quicksall v. Michigan, 339 U.S. 660, 1950; see also Kerrigan, John W., "Limitations on an Accused's Right to Counsel," *Journal of Criminal Law and Criminology*, November-December 1947, pp. 375–379.

[71] Hawk v. Olson, 326 U.S. 271, 1945, and other cases decided during the same term.

[72] Strander v. West Virginia, 100 U.S. 303, 1880; see Gillespie, John R., "The Constitution and the All-White Jury," *Kentucky Law Journal*, November 1950, pp. 65–78.

[73] 311 U.S. 128, 1940, following the doctrine of the Strander case and of Norris v. Alabama, 294 U.S. 587, 1935.

[74] Hill v. Texas, 316 U.S. 400, 1942.

[75] Cassell v. Texas, 339 U.S. 282, 1950.

[76] Akins v. Texas, 325 U.S. 398, 1945.

[77] Patton v. Mississippi, 332 U.S. 463, 1947, and for an earlier case, Hale v. Kentucky, 303 U.S. 613, 1938; also Mangum, Charles S., Jr., *The Legal Status of the Negro* (University of North Carolina Press, 1940).

or wage earners had been systematically excluded, or where, as in the case of blue-ribbon juries, all except persons possessing superior qualifications had been excluded. In the recent Thiel case,[78] the Court held that the systematic exclusion of wage earners from a Federal jury violated the jury trial requirement of the Bill of Rights, emphasizing the point that the American tradition of jury trial "contemplates an impartial jury drawn from a cross section of the community." The same principle applies to trial by a jury from which women have been systematically excluded, even though such exclusion takes place under a Federal law providing that jurors in a Federal court shall have the same qualifications as those of the highest court of law in the state.[79]

In 1947 and 1948, the Court was asked to declare the New York special or blue-ribbon jury unconstitutional.[80] In the latter instance, two Negroes were convicted of first degree murder by such a jury, and it was admitted that in the jury panel of fifty names, there were no Negroes. The Court once more refused to declare the New York law unconstitutional, holding that there was no proof in the record that Negroes were intentionally and systematically excluded. Justice Murphy wrote a vigorous dissenting opinion in which he took the position that the exclusion of any particular group was immaterial. "The vice," he said, "lies in the very concept of a jury consisting only of the 'best' people."

Questions regarding self-incrimination arise frequently. In Taylor v. Alabama,[81] the plaintiff, just prior to his scheduled execution, petitioned the Alabama Supreme Court for an order granting him the right to file a petition in the Circuit Court of his county, where he had been tried, for a writ of error. He alleged for the first time that the confessions used in his trial had been induced by threats and physical violence. A divided Court held that, on the record, the denial of permission to file the petition was not in itself wanting in due process, since the new petition did not present such a prima-facie case as to require an overruling of the state court's conclusion. The Court has, of late, resolutely followed the policy of protecting defendants from the overzealous efforts of law enforcement officers to establish a record for themselves, even at the price of the brutal treatment of suspects.

Protection of Property Rights

Obligation of Contract. In Article I, Section 10, the Federal Constitution imposes upon the state a restriction that "no state shall impair the obli-

[78] Thiel v. Southern Pacific Company, 328 U.S. 217, 1946.

[79] Ballard v. United States, 329 U.S. 187, 1946.

[80] Fay v. New York, 332 U.S. 261, 1947, and Moore v. New York, 333 U.S. 565, 1948; see Ketler, David W., "The Constitutionality of Blue Ribbon Juries," *Journal of Criminal Law and Criminology*, November-December 1947, pp. 369–375.

[81] 335 U.S. 252, 1948; for recent related cases, see Watts v. Indiana, 338 U.S. 49, 1949; Turner v. Pennsylvania, 338 U.S. 62, 1949; Harris v. South Carolina, 338 U.S. 68, 1949; also Inbau, Fred E., *Self-Incrimination: What Can an Accused Person Be Compelled to Do?* (Charles C. Thomas, Publisher, Springfield, Ill., 1951).

gation of contract." This restriction was regarded by the framers of the Constitution, and has been regarded by lawyers since, as of the utmost importance in the protection of the rights of the individual. It is true that the enforcement of such a rule makes for stability in the business and economic life of the nation, but it also raises some important questions. During the depression which began in 1929, wholesale execution of mortgage foreclosures took place, affecting the homes of citizens in urban communities and the farm properties which were both the homes and the means of livelihood of citizens in rural communities. Honest but helpless people were moved into the streets, so that many people wondered which society valued more — the sacredness of human life or the sacredness of the obligation of contract. A fetish was made of a legal doctrine, the observance of which under normal conditions is admittedly for the general good. Some states went so far as to translate some of these doubts into mortgage moratorium statutes, designed to aid the debtor under the terrific strain of the depression. The Supreme Court, in its decision in the Minnesota Mortgage Moratorium Case,[82] upheld the validity of such emergency legislation.

Some of the most serious difficulties with regard to this subject have grown out of the famous decision of the Supreme Court handed down by John Marshall in the Dartmouth College Case in 1819.[83] Not many years after this decision was made, changes were under way in our economic life, leading to a widespread substitution of the corporate form of business organization for the individual enterpreneur and the partnership. In the early days of the corporate form, every corporate charter was conferred by a separate legislative action. Under the terms of this decision, every one of these charters became an irrevocable, unmodifiable contract between the state and the persons to whom it was granted. If the legislatures had always been careful and honest in the granting of charters, the situation would have been bad enough. Unfortunately, they were often neither careful nor honest. Vast portions of the public domain were given away in connection with these charters, without any consideration whatever coming to the state, then or in the future. Rights and privileges of incalculable value were conferred for all time without restriction and without any compensation to the state therefor. The situation thus created was indeed critical.

This decision has never been officially modified or reversed, and in all probability it is now so deeply intrenched in our legal system that this is impossible. In a significant dissenting opinion, however, Justice Black, in Indiana ex rel. Anderson v. Brand, in 1937,[84] vigorously urged that this ancient wrong be corrected, that a fluid system of legislative supremacy be substituted for the plan by which property institutions have in effect frozen

[82] Home Building and Loan Association v. Blaisdell, et al., 290 U.S. 398, 1934; W. B. Worthen Company v. Kavanaugh, 295 U.S. 56, 1935; and Palitz, Max, "Legislative Relief of the Mortgage Debtor," *Temple Law Quarterly*, April 1937, pp. 404–409.

[83] 4 Wheaton 518, 1819.

[84] 302 U.S. 678, 1937.

the economic order for more than a century. Under the circumstances, the states have been forced to invent methods of evading and circumventing the Dartmouth decision in order to bring about a control over corporations which should have been theirs without question. They have been obliged to insert in corporate charters, as a condition of their adoption, some limitation upon the life of the charter, and they have likewise inserted clauses reserving the right to modify or to abrogate the charter as the public interest may require. By such roundabout methods the states have succeeded in regaining a limited measure of control over the corporations which they themselves have created. It seems strange indeed that a decision the consequences of which have been so widely detrimental to the best interests of the states should still be regarded by many people as one of the great landmarks of our constitutional history. If the decision was great, it was so in the sense of being a great mistake, from the point of view of public policy and from the point of view of the states.

Right to Work. "The right to work is a property right." So said the Supreme Court of Massachusetts in 1916.[85] About the same time, Chief Justice Hughes had delivered an opinion for an all but unanimous Court (Justice McReynolds dissenting) in which he said, "It requires no argument to show that the right to work for a living in the common occupations of the community is of the very essence of the personal freedom and opportunity that it was the purpose of the [Fourteenth] Amendment to secure." [86]

Over a period of three quarters of a century, the states have adopted laws designed to protect the right to work by forbidding discrimination in employment in many different fields. The total number of adoptions of which the Legislative Reference Service, Library of Congress, had record in 1950 was 152, relating to no less than two dozen different callings and occupations. One hundred and six enactments fall into six groups, as indicated in the table on page 700. Illinois seems to have adopted the largest number of such provisions, having altogether a total of sixteen.

Greatly increased interest in antidiscriminatory legislation during the past decade has led to many new enactments, the characteristics of which differ in two important respects from earlier legislation. One new tendency has been to broaden the coverage of such legislation sufficiently to include all forms of discrimination in relation to all types of employment — not merely race and color, but religion, national origins, and ancestry as well. The other tendency has been to shift from a type of wishful thinking, now-won't-you-please statute to a new type with some legal sanctions behind it. This evolutionary process, of course, is by no means new; it is rather one which may be illustrated by reference to the development of other types of regulatory legislation.

New York State provides an excellent illustration of this process of

85 Bogni v. Perotti, 224 Mass. 162, 1916.
86 Truax v. Raich, 239 U.S. 33, 41, 1915.

State Legislation Prohibiting Discrimination in Six Important Phases of Employment — 1950

TYPE OF DISCRIMINATION PROHIBITED	EARLIEST LAW —		NUMBER OF LAWS
In civil service employment	Massachusetts	1884	28
In the selection of public officers and employees	Pennsylvania	1941	26
Inquiry as to religious affiliations and beliefs of candidates for teaching positions in the public schools	Colorado	1876	19
In employment in public works	California, Illinois, Indiana, New Jersey	1933	11
Conditioning membership in labor unions on considerations of race or religion	Pennsylvania	1937	18
In work on defense and war contracts	Illinois, New York	1941	4

growth and development. Prior to 1945, when the Ives-Quinn Act was passed, New York had six specific antidiscrimination statutes on the books: (1) providing equal rights, privileges, and treatment in places of public accommodation — 1895; (2) forbidding teachers' employment agencies and school officials to inquire about the religion of any applicant for appointment — 1932; (3) making it a misdemeanor for any public utility to refuse to employ a person because of his race, color, or religion — 1933; (4) prohibiting discrimination in the hiring of employees working under state public works contracts — 1935; (5) forbidding discrimination by labor unions in membership requirements or in designating members to employers for placement — 1940; (6) prohibiting discrimination in any industries performing work under defense contracts — 1942. In 1948, another law prohibited racial and religious discrimination in admissions to institutions of higher learning.

The Ives-Quinn Act is broad, prohibiting "practices of discrimination in employment or otherwise against persons because of race, creed, color, or national origin." It is significant because in it, for the first time, all of these different bases of discrimination were gathered together and listed in one statute, applicable to all employment situations. The act provides for the creation in the Executive Department of a state commission of five members, appointed by the governor, defining their functions, powers, and duties, and providing for the appointment and compensation of officers and employees. Stated in simplest terms, the act prohibits discrimination with regard to: (1) hiring and firing; (2) upgrading and promotion; (3) conditions of work; (4) application form; (5) employment agencies; (6) membership in labor union; (7) discrimination by fellow employees.

By the end of 1952 there were eleven state acts of generally similar char-

acter and purpose, some thirty or more municipal ordinances. In general, the statutes are of two types, viewed from the point of view of their enforcement provisions. The first group includes the laws of Connecticut, Massachusetts, New Jersey, and New York, which undertake to define unfair employment practices, grant extensive powers to the enforcing agency, and provide penalties for noncompliance. The second type of law, in effect in Indiana and Wisconsin, carries no provision for the issuance of enforcement orders, the administering agency acting in an advisory, not in a regulatory, capacity.[87]

The growing strength of labor unions in recent years has been responsible for the development of another problem. Closed shop agreements, insisted upon by the unions in many of their contracts, have made it well-nigh impossible for many workers, not members of unions, to obtain employment. Believing that, in a free country, workers have a right to choose whether or not they will join a union, without being discriminated against in either case, the legislatures of many states have considered, and some have enacted, legislation outlawing the closed shop. The Indiana act, for instance, declares the right of employees to organize and bargain collectively but outlaws contracts which condition employment on membership or nonmembership in a union. The Massachusetts act makes it unlawful to exclude persons from employment because of nonmembership in a labor organization.

The Supreme Court in 1949 upheld the validity of three such provisions. It rejected the contention that an Arizona constitutional amendment prohibiting the closed shop denied equal protection in that it failed to protect union as well as nonunion workers against discrimination, finding adequate protection for union members in other Arizona laws. Only Justice Murphy dissented.[88] A unanimous Court sustained a Nebraska constitutional amendment and a North Carolina statute prohibiting closed shop contracts and forbidding employers to discriminate against nonunion workers. The two cases were combined.[89] In citing the changed character of due process, Justice Black concluded that the clause did not put Congress or the state legislatures "in a strait jacket when they attempt to suppress business and industrial conditions which they regard as offensive to the public welfare." And thus, observes one commentator, "the cup that had once been passed to property was now passed to labor."

Restrictive Covenants. For many years it was a common practice for real estate developers to offer their clients an assurance that their property would be protected from the entry of representatives of unwanted groups

[87] Comment based on the author's *Fair Employment Practice Legislation in the United States*, *op. cit.;* see also Shumate, Roger V., *Report of the Committee on Unfair Employment Practices* (Nebraska Legislative Council, Lincoln, 1950).

[88] American Federation of Labor v. American Sash and Door Company, 335 U.S. 538, 1949.

[89] Lincoln Federal Labor Union v. Northeastern Iron and Metal Company, 335 U.S. 25, 1949.

in the neighborhood by the device of the restrictive covenant running with the land, and enforceable in the courts. In 1948, however, in Shelley v. Kraemer,[90] the Supreme Court ruled that it is a violation of Amendment XIV for a state court to enforce a restrictive covenant barring the sale or transfer of real estate to Negroes. "It cannot be doubted," the Chief Justice declared, "that among the civil rights intended to be protected from discriminatory state action by the Fourteenth Amendment are the right to acquire, enjoy, own, and dispose of property." At another point, he says: "It is clear that but for the intervention of the state courts, supported by the full panoply of state power, petitioner would have been free to occupy the properties in question without restraint." This was not a case in which the state had merely abstained from action; on the contrary, the state had made available to individuals "the full coercive power of government" to deny persons the enjoyment of property rights on the grounds of race or color. The contention that the state courts stand ready to enforce restrictive covenants against white persons was brushed aside with the observation that "equal protection of the laws is not achieved through indiscriminate imposition of inequalities."

The restrictive covenant device was designed to prevent certain elements in the population from acquiring residential property in certain neighborhoods. Related in principle but much more drastic in its application was the California alien land law, which was designed to prevent aliens from acquiring ownership of agricultural land within the state. Specifically, the law forbade aliens ineligible for American citizenship (Orientals) to acquire, own, occupy, lease, or transfer agricultural land, and provided that property acquired in violation of this statute escheats to the state.

One Oyama, a Japanese citizen not eligible for naturalization, paid the purchase price for a piece of land, with title in the name of his son, a minor and an American citizen. Six Justices agreed to reverse the judgment of the state court upholding the validity of the statute, but were unable to agree on a rationale for their decision.[91] In the same term, the Court likewise found inconsistent with the equal protection clause a California law prohibiting the issuance of commercial fishing licenses to such aliens, finding no "special public interest" or "ownership" rights of California justifying exclusion of aliens who are lawful residents from fishing within the three-mile belt of water along the shore.[92]

Eminent Domain. The right of eminent domain has been defined as that superior dominion of the sovereign power over all the property within the state, including that previously granted by itself, which authorizes it to appropriate any part thereof to a necessary public use, reasonable com-

[90] 334 U.S. 1, 1948; also Hurd v. Hodge, 334 U.S. 24, 1948, and Uricola v. Hodge, 334 U.S. 24, 1948, the District of Columbia cases, and McGhee v. Sipes, 334 U.S. 1, 1948.

[91] Oyama v. California, 332 U.S. 633, 1948.

[92] Takahashi v. California Fish and Game Commission, 334 U.S. 410, 1948.

pensation being made therefor. The Federal Constitution and all the state constitutions except those of Kansas, New Hampshire, and North Carolina now contain express prohibitions against the taking of private property for public use without compensation. In Kansas, corporations are also prohibited in the same way.[93] In these three states, substantially the same result has been reached by holding that the due process of law clause covers the matter.[94] Not only do nearly all states prohibit a taking without compensation, but a large number require compensation for property damaged or injured for public use; a case in point is that of the Tidewater Railway Company v. Shartzer, in which the Supreme Court of Virginia held the railway liable, under the damage clause of the Virginia Constitution, for annoyance from smoke, noise, dust, cinders, and danger from fire resulting to lands no part of which was taken.[95]

Like the power to tax, the power of eminent domain may be exercised only for a public purpose; generally speaking, those purposes which have been judged to be public for purposes of taxation are also public when considered in connection with the exercise of the power of eminent domain. While this power is not to be confused with the power of taxation, such a policy is reasonable and just, for both involve the taking of property, in one case to a limited extent, with a return in the form of services rendered by government, in the other, completely, with such financial return as the owner of the property may be judged to be entitled to. To state the same matter in another way, one may observe, as Professor Mott has done, that "logically, it would seem that what is a public purpose for one power of government should be also public in another, inasmuch as the publicity of the enterprise depends upon the legal privileges and obligations which have been given it."[96]

The same authority points out that the use of the power of eminent domain in aid of public service corporations did not become important before the development of railroads as a means of transportation. He continues:

> . . . The power had frequently been used in aid of privately controlled turnpikes, bridges, ferries, and canals, and its constitutionality was generally taken for granted. In a few cases it was contended that the power could not be used for enterprises of this nature, but the contention was uniformly rejected by the courts. There was at first a great popular prejudice against the steam railroads and consequently the cases involving grants of public powers to them were more stubbornly fought. It was in this connection that due process of law first became an important factor in eminent domain cases.

93 The final clause in Amendment V to the Federal Constitution reads: "nor shall private property be taken for public use, without just compensation." The state constitutions usually follow this wording exactly.

94 Buckwalter v. School District, 65 Kan. 603, 1902; Opinion of Justices, 66 N. H. 629, 1891; Staton v. Norfolk and Carolina Railway, 111 N. C. 278, 1892.

95 107 Va. 562, 1907.

96 Mott, *op. cit.*, p. 471; Chapter 22 deals at length with the question of public purpose.

Thus in addition to uses in connection with public buildings and other public works, the power came to be used, in behalf of the government, by private corporations such as are commonly regarded as being affected with a public interest. Even so, the power of eminent domain has been regarded as a right inherent in government, and so essential to the performance of its necessary functions that it may not be contracted away, or the right to its exercise otherwise impaired.[97]

Most authorities have found it difficult to state exactly what constitutes a public purpose; many such purposes have been established by long lines of judicial opinions, but many borderline cases still arise. Such a case was that of the Mount Vernon-Woodberry Cotton Duck Company v. Alabama Interstate Power Company, the opinion in which was written in 1916 by Justice Holmes.[98] The power company sought to condemn private land, water, and water rights, in order to manufacture and sell to the public power produced by water. In answer to the owner's argument that the purpose of the company was not a public one, Justice Holmes said:

> In the organic relations of modern society it may sometimes be hard to draw the line that is supposed to limit the authority of the legislature to exercise or delegate the power of eminent domain. But to gather the streams from waste and to draw from them energy, labor without brains, and so to save mankind from toil that it can be spared, is to supply what, next to intellect, is the very foundation of all achievements and all our welfare. If that purpose is not public we should be at a loss to say what is.

It would be encouraging indeed to be able to feel that the courts would always take a similarly enlightened point of view.

One further point remains to be considered — the process by which the property of individuals may be taken, either by the government, or by a corporation authorized by it to exercise this power, in connection with a development of general public interest. The decision to take one's property once having been made, the individual has no recourse, for it has long been held that the right of the public to take — with just compensation — property which it needs is paramount over the right of a single individual or a corporation. The usual procedure is to appraise the value of such portion of the property as may be required by the public, and make an offer to the owner. This he may either accept or reject. It seems to be characteristic of individuals to value their property very highly when condemnation proceedings are in prospect, and to complain of overvaluation in connection with assessments. If the government or the corporation exercising the power of eminent domain is unable to arrive at a satisfactory agreement with the owner by conference, the owner may appeal to the courts, where a jury will decide what he may receive, and what he must accept, by way of compensation.[99] Most property owners are reluctant to carry a case this far,

[97] See, for instance, Pennsylvania Hospital v. Philadelphia, 245 U.S. 20, 1917.
[98] 240 U.S. 30, 1916.
[99] Rather comprehensive studies have been made of this procedure in at least two

because of the expense and the uncertainties attendant upon the consideration of such a matter by a jury. It might also be added that many jurisdictions permit what is known as excess condemnation when the portion of the property that remains would be of little or no value to the owner, or when a failure to take all of it might in some way impair the value of the development for which the power was exercised.[100]

SELECTED REFERENCES

Alabama Legislative Reference Service, *State Anti-Communist Legislation* (Montgomery, 1950); on the same general subject, see Wood, Fred B., "The Permissible Scope of State Statutory Regulations Concerning Subversive Activities" (Mimeographed address, Sacramento, 1948).

Becker, Carl L., *Freedom and Responsibility in the American Way of Life* (Knopf, New York, 1945). Five lectures on the American political tradition, freedom of speech and press, freedom of learning and teaching, constitutional government, private economic enterprise.

Berger, Morroe, *Equality by Statute: Legislative Controls over Group Discrimination* (Columbia University Press, 1952). An evaluation of Federal and state laws protecting minority rights and of the effectiveness of law as a means of social change.

Corwin, Edward S., Ed., *Constitution of the United States, Annotated*, Third Edition (Government Printing Office, Washington, 1953). A monumental work by a recognized authority on problems of constitutional interpretation.

Graves, W. Brooke, *Fair Employment Practice Legislation in the United States — Federal, State, Municipal* (Public Affairs Bulletin No. 93, Legislative Reference Service, Library of Congress, Washington, 1951), and Senate Committee on Labor and Public Welfare, *Federal Equality of Opportunity in Employment Act* (82nd Cong., 2nd Sess., Senate Report No. 2080, Washington, 1952). Surveys of an important recent development in American law; both contain a state by state summary of existing legislation.

——, *Developments in the Field of Civil Rights, 1945–1950* (Legislative Reference Service, Library of Congress, Washington, 1951). A survey of developments during the postwar period, covering executive, legislative, and judicial actions at all three levels of government.

Konvitz, Milton R., *The Constitution and Civil Rights* (Columbia University Press, 1947). Legal analysis of the rights enumerated in the Federal Civil Rights Act of 1875.

Lasswell, Harold D., *National Security and Individual Freedom* (McGraw-Hill, New York, 1950). Discusses crisis of defense as it affects four principles of a free society: civilian supremacy, freedom of information, civil liberties, a free economy. See also Barth, Alan, *The Loyalty of Free Men* (Viking, New York, 1951); Biddle, Francis, *The Fear of Freedom* (Doubleday, Garden City, 1951); and Commager, Henry S., and others, *Civil Liberties under Attack* (University of Pennsylvania Press, 1951).

---

states: Corrick, Franklin, "A Synopsis of the Kansas Supreme Court Decisions Relating to Eminent Domain and Condemnation Procedure," Kansas Judicial Council *Bulletin*, July 1933, entire issue; and Emory, Richard W., *Highway Condemnation* (Maryland Legislative Council, Baltimore, 1940).

[100] The standard work on this subject is by Cushman, Robert E., *Excess Condemnation* (Appleton, New York, 1917).

Mangum, Charles S., Jr., *The Legal Status of the Negro* (University of North Carolina Press, 1940); see also Nelson, Bernard H., *The Fourteenth Amendment and the Negro Since 1920* (Catholic University of America, 1946).

Murray, Pauli, Comp. and Ed., *States' Laws on Race and Color, and Appendices* (Woman's Division of Christian Service of the Methodist Church, 1950); and Wisconsin Legislative Reference Library, *A Study of State and Local Legislative and Administrative Acts Designed to Meet Problems of Human Rights* (Madison, January 1952). Analytical discussions with complete text of pertinent state laws, and in the case of the latter, municipal ordinances.

President's Committee on Civil Rights, *To Secure These Rights* (Washington, 1947); and for comment and interpretation, Carr, Robert K., *Federal Protection of Civil Rights — Quest for a Sword* (Cornell University Press, 1947).

Wood, Virginia, *Due Process of Law, 1932–1949* (Louisiana State University Press, 1951). An analytical survey of the Supreme Court and its powers of judicial review, as related to due process.

20

State Police Power

The police power has come to occupy a position of such importance that no study of state government could fail to consider it. The police power belongs to the states alone. While the phrase is frequently used in connection with the Federal government, one should not forget that this power has never been recognized by the Supreme Court as one of the powers or attributes of the Federal government. In using the phrase in this connection, therefore, one is taking a certain liberty with the accepted interpretation of the Court — a liberty justified only by the fact that the Court has on many occasions sanctioned the exercise of Federal powers so similar to the police power of the states that the effort to separate the two has seemed to be an effort to maintain a distinction where there was no difference.

Origin of State Police Power. While the state police power was known before the important decision of the Supreme Court in the Slaughter House Cases,[1] its extensive use in modern times dates from this decision. The case arose through the efforts of the City Council in New Orleans to remedy unsanitary conditions such as existed in many American cities at that time. The business of slaughtering animals for food was carried on by a large number of small independent dealers, each of whom maintained his own slaughter house. These establishments were scattered over the city. In the effort to rid the city of what would now be considered a public nuisance, the City Council enacted an ordinance providing for the abolition of these independent slaughter houses, and for the construction of a large municipally owned and operated abattoir in which butchers might rent time and space in accordance with their needs.

It was natural that these businessmen should seek to prevent this action, which they conceived to be an interference with the rights of private property. They instituted proceedings in the courts, which were carried by successive appeals to the Supreme Court of the United States. The attorneys for the butchers argued that the ordinance was unconstitutional inasmuch as Amendment XIV had transferred from the states (and therefore from their creatures, the municipalities) to the Federal government the power to make

[1] 16 Wallace 36, 1873.

and enforce regulations of this character. The Supreme Court was thus presented with the opportunity of selecting one of two diametrically opposed views with regard to the interpretation of Amendment XIV. One was the view presented by the attorneys for the butchers; the other was the view which the Court accepted in one of the most important decisions in its history: namely, the view that Amendment XIV was proposed for the purpose of protecting the rights of the newly created group of colored citizens and that it was adopted by the states with this understanding. The Court stated that there was no intention on the part of those who framed the amendment, or of the Congress which proposed it, or of the state legislatures which ratified it that it should be so construed as to disturb the long-established principles governing the allocation of powers between the Federal government and the states. It is scarcely possible to overemphasize the significance of this decision. If the Court had chosen to adopt the alternative point of view, the whole nature of our Federal system would have been fundamentally changed. It is upon this decision that the whole doctrine of the police power rests.

Definition of the Police Power. The field in which the police power has been applied has been expanded to such an extent that it is difficult to define the power in definite and concise terms. Probably the first inclination of the layman is to define it by reference to the authority of the patrolman who stands at the corner. Such a conception of the police power is correct as far as it goes; the officers of the law are an evidence of the power and duty of the state to protect life and property, to maintain peace and order, and to prevent domestic violence or disturbance of any sort. But there is another aspect of the police power, which in modern times has assumed a position of equal importance; this relates to the right of the state to impose regulations or restrictions upon our use of our property or our exercise of our personal civil rights when such use interferes with the fundamental rights or privileges of our neighbors. In practice, this doctrine means that the state has in many important respects regulated or restricted individuals and corporations in the enjoyment of the rights of both person and property. The attempts to exercise this power, whether successful or unsuccessful, can be classified under the following headings:

1. Protection of the public health
2. Protection of the public safety
3. Protection of the public convenience
4. Protection of the public morals
5. Prevention of fraud
6. Suppression of a public nuisance

Each of these will be discussed below, with appropriate illustrations and references to Supreme Court decisions. There are few, if any, attempts at the exercise of the police power which cannot be reasonably and properly classified under one of these headings or under a combination of them.

In commenting on the legitimate objects of the exercise of the police power, the United States Supreme Court on one occasion used the following words:

> Another vital principle is that, except as restrained by its own fundamental law, or by the Supreme Law of the Land, a state possesses all legislative power consistent with a republican form of government; therefore each state, when not thus restrained and so far as this court is concerned, may, by legislation, provide not only for the health, morals, and safety of its people, but for the common good, as involved in the well being, peace, happiness, and prosperity of the people.[2]

A word of caution with regard to the definition of police power is perhaps necessary. It is primarily a legislative power, although in conformity with present-day legislative practice it tends frequently to be exercised by administrative officers under legislative authorization. Its application is very broad, but it is not unlimited. Justice Holmes, in Noble State Bank v. Haskell,[3] made the statement that the police power extends to all great public needs. This is, however, quite different from saying, as some careless commentators have done, that the police power may be exercised in the interests of the public welfare. This phrase is so broad and expansive in its application that, if it were accepted, there would be virtually no limits to the application of the police power. Such eminent constitutional authorities as Willoughby and Burdick have taken special pains to warn students of this misinterpretation.

The scope of the police power is great, and the serious consequences of its exercise are never to be underestimated. This point was well illustrated in Asbury Hospital v. Cass County,[4] in which the Supreme Court held valid a North Dakota statute of 1933 providing that corporations, both domestic and foreign, which own lands used or salable for farming or agricultural purposes, except such as are reasonably necessary to the conduct of their business, should dispose of them within ten years. Upon their failure to do so, the county in which such lands were located was required to sell them at public auction and pay the proceeds, less the expense of the sale, to the corporate owner. Asbury Hospital, owning lands in Cass County, acquired by the foreclosure of a mortgage, attacked the constitutionality of this act in a suit for a declaratory judgment. Its lands were leased to farmers, but efforts to sell them at a price sufficient to cover the original mortgage debt had failed. The Court alluded to the well-established doctrine that Amendment XIV does not deny to a state the power to bar foreign corporations from doing business or acquiring or holding property within the state. This power does not end as soon as a corporation has entered the state lawfully and acquired property therein. Such a corporation continues to hold property in the state on sufferance, and may, without denial

[2] Halter v. Nebraska, 205 U.S. 40, 1907.
[3] 219 U.S. 104, 1911.
[4] 326 U.S. 207, 1945.

of due process, be required to sell it. Nor does due process require that the corporation recapture the cost of the land.

The police power is not by any means an emergency power, although it is often invoked after some disaster which causes serious loss of life or property damage which might have been prevented if proper precautions had been taken. A public, shaken from its lethargy, may then take drastic action. Instances in point include the famous Triangle shirtwaist factory fire in New York in 1911,[5] the Ward's Island Fire, the insurance scandals of 1905, and the panic of 1907. A state report pointed out many years later that the first of these was responsible for a complete reorganization of the system of factory inspection; that the second had the immediate effect of securing the adoption of a $50,000,000 bond issue for state welfare institutions in 1923; while the last two called attention to the necessity for changes in the regulatory system. This list of catastrophes might be extended almost indefinitely.

Protection of the Public Health

Regulations designed to protect the public health commonly affect property rights more than personal rights. There have, of course, been some restrictions upon the conduct of persons, such as quarantine regulations or the universal rule prohibiting expectorating in public places; but illustrations of restrictions on the use of property are much more numerous. These regulations cover a wide variety of subjects: they include regulations governing the sale of food and drug products, sanitary measures to prevent the spread of contagious diseases, regulations affecting the disposition of wastes of all types. Under food and drug control, one finds such measures as those requiring the inspection and licensing of eating houses, soda fountains, soft drink establishments, and market places. These regulations are concerned not merely with the cleanliness of the premises but with "the easements of light, and air, and access."

Protection of Food and Drug Supplies. The conditions under which food products are kept and displayed and the freedom from contagious or communicable diseases of those who handle such products are most important to the public health. The rigid regulations imposed upon the production, transportation, processing, and sale of milk and milk products provide further illustrations. These include the extensive program of tuberculosis eradication which has been carried on at great expense over a period of

[5] The Triangle Fire is a milestone in I. L. G. W. U. history. Garment makers once customarily kept their workers locked in like prisoners. On the evening of March 25, 1911, fire swept through the workroom of the Triangle Waist Company in a building near Washington Square in New York City. Trapped by locked doors, 146 employees died, many by leaping to the sidewalk. Their fate shocked the nation, led to many reforms, inspired I. L. G. W. U. to fight harder than ever. Union members still make yearly pilgrimages to their graves. From *Life*, August 1, 1938, p. 23; see also a novel based on the story of this fire by Sholem Asch, *East River* (Putnam's, New York, 1946).

many years; the enforcement of requirements regarding the cleanliness of barns and the care of the fluid milk before, during, and after shipment; the inspection and supervision of the pasteurizing and bottling plants; the regulation, or in some jurisdictions the prohibition, of the sale of milk in bulk. Similar laws apply to meat and meat food products. Although many regulations affecting foods and drugs had been adopted in the states before the passage of the Federal act of June 30, 1906, as revised and rewritten in 1938, a great body of new legislation in support of the Federal act has grown up since. These laws cover such matters as correct labeling, net weight, claims of manufacturers with regard to curative properties, and other matters.

New York ex rel. Lieberman v. Van de Carr, decided by the Supreme Court in 1905, illustrates the manner in which such regulations come before the courts.[6] Lieberman was arrested for violating Section 66 of the sanitary code of New York City, which provided that no milk should be received, held, kept, either for sale or delivery, in the city, "without a permit in writing from the board of health, and subject to the conditions thereof. . . ." The violation of this code was made a misdemeanor. Lieberman's writ of habeas corpus was dismissed by the State Supreme Court, and this judgment was affirmed by the Appellate Division and by the Court of Appeals, from which it went to the Supreme Court of the United States, where the objections to the section on Federal grounds were: first, that it conferred upon the board of health absolute and despotic powers to grant or withhold permits to milk dealers, and was not, therefore, due process of law; and second, that singling out the milk business for regulation was a denial of the equal protection of the laws to the people engaged therein. After citing an extensive list of authorities, the Court concluded:

> These cases leave in no doubt the proposition that the conferring of discretionary power upon administrative boards to grant or withhold permission to carry on a trade or business which is the proper subject of regulation within the police power of the state is not violative of rights secured by the Fourteenth Amendment. There is no presumption that the power will be arbitrarily exercised, and when it is shown to be thus exercised against the individual, under sanction of state authority, this court has not hesitated to interfere for his protection, when the case has come before it in such manner as to authorize the interference of a Federal court. Yick Wo v. Hopkins, 118 U.S. 356, 1885.
>
> There is nothing to show upon what ground the action of the board was taken. For aught that appears, he may have been conducting his business in such wise, or with such surroundings and means, as to render it dangerous to the health of the community; or his manner of selling or delivering the milk may have been objectionable. There is nothing in the record to show that the action against him was arbitrary or oppressive and without a fair and reasonable exercise of that discretion which the law reposed in the board of health. We have, then, an ordinance which, as construed in the highest court

[6] 199 U.S. 552, 1905.

> of the state, authorizes the exercise of a legal discretion in the granting or withholding of permits to transact a business which, unless controlled, may be highly dangerous to the health of the community, and no affirmative showing that the power has been exerted in so arbitrary and oppressive a manner as to deprive the appellant of his property or liberty without due process of law.
>
> In such cases it is the settled doctrine of this Court that no Federal right is invaded, and no authority exists for declaring a law unconstitutional, duly passed by the legislative authority, and approved by the highest court of the state.

The tremendous growth of the frozen foods industry has imposed new responsibilities upon the states. The laws commonly define cold storage warehouses as establishments in which articles of food are placed or held for thirty days or more. Licenses from the state department of health are required for the operation of establishments handling meat, fish, poultry, eggs, milk, fruit, and vegetables. The cold storage law gives the department power to inspect and supervise every cold storage warehouse, and to make such inspection of articles therein as may be necessary to secure the proper enforcement of the law. No articles intended for human consumption shall be placed, received, or kept in a cold storage warehouse if diseased, tainted, or so deteriorated in any other way as to injure its keeping qualities.[7]

Eating and Drinking Establishments; Hotels and Lodging Houses. Public eating and drinking establishments are regulated and inspected by state and local authorities to insure the observance of minimum standards of cleanliness and sanitation in the maintenance of the premises, the sterilization of utensils and equipment (or the use of paper receptacles), the preparation and handling of food, and the cleanliness of the employees themselves. A model ordinance and code regulating such establishments, prepared by the United States Public Health Service, has been adopted in many jurisdictions.[8] This type of regulation assumes a growing importance both to individuals and to the community, in a day of great mobility of population, when so large a number of people, especially in urban communities, are accustomed to frequent public restaurants, lunchrooms, soda fountains, bars, taprooms, and cocktail lounges.

Many sanitary measures concern public utility companies and other businesses affected with a public interest. The keepers of hotels, inns, and lodging houses, for instance, are required to use cotton sheets of sufficient length to prevent blankets and bed coverings from coming in direct contact with successive guests, while other regulations require the laundering of sheets, pillow cases, and towels. Because such regulations are now universally

[7] Scofield, Walter W., "Frozen Food Storage," New Jersey *Public Health News*, February 1948, pp. 50–55.

[8] *Ordinance and Code Regulating Eating and Drinking Establishments* (Washington, 1940); see also Kettleborough, Charles, "Inspection of Hotels and Public Lodging Houses," *American Political Science Review*, February 1913, pp. 93–96. The progress that has been made in the last few years is illustrated by the fact that, as late as 1932, the Supreme Court of Utah declared that a board of health had exceeded its power in requiring sterilization of receptacles, or the use of paper receptacles.

observed, no one should assume that such has always been the case. Railways and other common carriers are prohibited from using common drinking cups and the old-fashioned roller towels in their cars and stations. Similar regulations apply to common drinking cups in rest rooms of theaters, clubs, and other public places. Barber shops and beauty shops are also subject to sanitary regulations. All these measures are designed to prevent the spread of contagious diseases by reducing to a minimum the known causes of their transmission.

Domestic Sewage and Industrial Wastes. Similarly, individuals and corporations, both public and private, are regulated in the disposition of wastes of every character which might conceivably affect the public health. Local ordinances require citizens to place garbage in covered containers, accessible to the collectors at regular intervals. Corporations are strictly regulated in most states with regard to the disposition of mine wastes, industrial wastes, et cetera, with the idea of preventing the pollution of water supplies, and in some cases for the protection of fish. Individuals are regulated and supervised in the construction of cesspools and in the use of other methods for the disposition of sewage in localities where no public sewage system exists. In cases where such systems have been constructed, the state often requires the submission of the plans, and usually inspects the system and regulates the methods of disposal.

In California Reduction Company v. Sanitary Reduction Works, the Court upheld a San Francisco ordinance requiring all garbage and refuse to be delivered in closed wagons at the works of the Sanitary Company, there to be cremated at the expense of the person conveying it. The Sanitary Company sought by injunction against householders and a rival reduction works to compel compliance with this ordinance, it having a fifty-year monopoly on this cremation at twenty cents a load. That the case has a relation to the use of the police power for the suppression of a public nuisance as well is clearly indicated in the following excerpt from the opinion:

> . . . The garbage and refuse matter were all together, on the same premises, and, as a whole or in the mass, they constituted a nuisance which the public could abate or require to be abated, and to the continuance of which the community was not bound to submit. And when the obnoxious garbage and refuse was removed from the place of their origin, and put in covered wagons to be carried away, the municipal authorities might well have doubted whether the substances that were per se dangerous or worthless would be separated from such as could be utilized, and whether the former would be deposited by the scavenger at some place that would not endanger the public health. They might well have thought that the safety of the community could not be assured unless the entire mass of garbage and refuse constituting the nuisance, from which the danger came, was carried to a crematory, where it could be promptly destroyed by fire, and thus minimize the danger to the public health.[9]

Compulsory Vaccination. A number of states have passed compulsory vaccination laws; these have not gone without challenge on the part of

[9] 199 U.S. 306, 1905.

the ignorant or the careless. The leading case on this subject, Jacobson v. Massachusetts, was considered by the Supreme Court in 1905.[10] The Massachusetts statute authorized local boards of health, whenever in their opinion it was necessary for protection of the public health, to require the vaccination of all inhabitants of their city or town, except such children as might present medical certificates to the effect that they were unfit subjects for vaccination. Jacobson was convicted in the Superior Court of Middlesex County of refusing to comply with such an order of the Cambridge Board of Health. The trial court declined his offer to prove that vaccination was useless to prevent smallpox and that it was often dangerous. The State Supreme Court confirmed the conviction, and appeal was taken to the Supreme Court of the United States, which likewise affirmed the judgment. As usual in police power cases, the decision of the Court hinged upon the reasonableness of the regulation.

> The legislature assumed that some children, by reason of their condition at the time, might not be fit subjects of vaccination; and it is suggested — and we will not say without reason — that such is the case with some adults. But the defendant did not offer to prove that, by reason of his then condition, he was in fact not a fit subject of vaccination at the time he was informed of the requirement of the regulation adopted by the board of health. . . . Until otherwise informed by the highest court of Massachusetts, we are not inclined to hold that the statute establishes the absolute rule that an adult must be vaccinated if it be apparent or can be shown with reasonable certainty that he is not at the time a fit subject of vaccination, or that vaccination, by reason of his then condition, would seriously impair his health, or probably cause his death. No such case is here presented. It is the case of an adult who, for aught that appears, was himself in perfect health and a fit subject of vaccination, and yet, while remaining in the community, refused to obey the statute and the regulation adopted in execution of its provisions for the protection of the public health and the public safety, confessedly endangered by the presence of a dangerous disease.

Premarital and Prenatal Examinations. For several years there was a growing disapproval of the hasty marriages encouraged by the "Gretna Greens" which were permitted to operate in a number of states. The result was the adoption of legislation in more than half of the states, calling for a waiting period of one to five days between the application for and the receipt of a marriage license, often with exceptions for service personnel on short leaves.[11]

[10] 197 U.S. 11, 1905.

[11] See tables in *Journal of Social Hygiene*, November 1948, and "Summary of Premarital Examination Laws in the United States," *California's Health*, April 30, 1949, and May 15, 1949. The waiting periods required are as follows, although in many states judges are empowered to waive the waiting period altogether or in part:

One day: Illinois

Three days: California, Kentucky, Missouri, New Jersey, New York, Oregon, Pennsylvania, Tennessee, Washington, West Virginia

Four days: Delaware

Five days: Connecticut, Maine, Massachusetts, Michigan, Minnesota, Mississippi, New Hampshire, Ohio, Rhode Island, Vermont, Wisconsin

Other states have gone much farther, requiring, in addition to a waiting period, a premarital health examination. Since 1935, when the first legislation of this character was adopted in Connecticut, thirty-six states have passed both premarital and prenatal examination laws, thus helping to protect the contracting parties and babies in these states from venereal disease — and, incidentally, setting an amazing record for lawmaking speed and activity. Only a few states have failed to enact either type of legislation;

Status of State Premarital and Prenatal Examination Laws — 1951

PREMARITAL ONLY	PRENATAL ONLY	NO LEGISLATION	BOTH
Alabama Tennessee Wisconsin	Arizona Arkansas Nevada New Mexico South Carolina Washington	Maryland Minnesota Mississippi	All Other States [1]
3	6	3	36

[1] Louisiana and Texas require premarital blood tests for males only.

the status of such enactments as of 1951 is shown in the table above. Thirty-eight states and the Territory of Hawaii require examination by a physician of both bride and groom, including a blood test. Twelve states, mostly in the South and Southwest, grant marriage licenses without regard to venereal disease infection.

Medical records show that if syphilis is discovered early enough in pregnancy cases, and adequate treatment is given, the baby has a 95 per cent chance to be born free from this infection. Accordingly, more than three fourths of the states, beginning with New York in 1938, now seek to protect the health of babies by requiring that physicians and midwives see that a serological test for syphilis is included as a part of the examination of every expectant mother seeking medical care. The use of premarital and prenatal examinations is part of a long-term plan for stamping out venereal disease, attacking the problem where the results are the most tragic — in marriage and in the family. While it is still too early to assess definitely the effectiveness of this type of legislation, the present indications are that the law is successfully accomplishing its original objective.[12]

Protection of the Public Safety

Police power regulations designed for the protection of the public safety include numerous types of measures which affect the daily lives of

[12] Paper in *American Journal of Syphilis, Gonorrhea and Venereal Disease*, summarized in *California's Health*, December 31, 1947; for a number of earlier studies of these types of legislation, see the Third Edition of this volume.

all, such as crime control measures and the rules and regulations for the police and other law-enforcing machinery for the protection of life and property; provision for factory inspectors and regulation of industrial safety; the regulation of common carriers, including grade crossing elimination; fireworks and firearms restrictions; building codes; and the provisions of the motor vehicle codes — to mention only a few.

Motor Vehicle Regulation. The motor vehicle codes are one of the most important evidences of the exercise of the police power in the field of public safety. They provide in most jurisdictions for the examination and licensing of motor vehicle operators, for the periodic inspection of motor vehicles to insure their road-worthiness, and for the rules of the road — all of which are designed to protect the lives and property of both motorists and pedestrians. Many questions have arisen and many cases have been decided regarding the right of the states to enforce these measures. In 1941, for instance, in Reitz v. Mealey, the Supreme Court decided that the New York statute which authorizes the suspension of a driver's license if judgment is rendered against him for personal injuries caused by operation of an automobile, and the judgment is not satisfied or discharged otherwise than by bankruptcy, is not obnoxious to the due process clause of Amendment XIV.[13]

Building Inspection. Police power regulations of tenements and lodging houses relate quite as often to safety as to health. In 1940, a four-story lodging house which complied with all existing applicable laws, was erected on the Bowery in New York City. In 1944, the New York Multiple Dwelling Law was amended to require that, among other things, all lodging houses of nonfireproof construction existing prior to the enactment of the amendment should meet certain new requirements, including the installation of an "automatic wet pipe sprinkler system." In Queenside Hills Realty Company v. Saxl,[14] a suit for a declaratory judgment, the Supreme Court held that the lodging house owner was not denied due process by the requirement of the sprinkler system. "It is for the legislature to decide what regulations are needed to reduce fire hazards to a minimum." The police power is not being exercised arbitrarily under such circumstances. One cannot prove discrimination by prophesying inequalities which may come into existence in the future, but which do not at the time exist.

The truth of the matter is that America suffers annually a staggering loss of life, property, and natural resources destroyed by preventable fires. Reference has already been made to our characteristic failure to take effective action designed to prevent the constantly recurring disasters, of which the following are a few of the more significant during recent years:

Knickerbocker Theater collapse, Washington, D.C., 1922.
Hotel fire in Lansing, Michigan, 1934, in which seven legislators lost their lives.
Dance club fire in Natchez, Mississippi, 1940 (216 lost their lives).

[13] 314 U.S. 33, 1941.
[14] 328 U.S. 80, 1946.

Cocoanut Grove fire in Boston, 1942 (489 lost their lives).
Ringling Brothers circus fire, Hartford, 1944 (107 lost their lives).
LaSalle Hotel fire, Chicago, 1946 (61 lost their lives).
Canfield Hotel fire, Dubuque, Iowa, 1946 (19 lost their lives).
Winecoff Hotel fire, Atlanta, 1946 (122 lost their lives).
Empire Building collapse, Washington, D.C., 1947.
Holland Tunnel chemical fire, New York and New Jersey, 1949.

At least 200 persons were killed in hotel fires during the last half of 1946, more than one fourth of the total of 789 hotel fire deaths in both the United States and Canada since 1858. The loss of property has reached in late years the enormous total of $2,000,000 a day, approximately $750,000,000 a year.[15]

Factory Regulations. Another important type of regulation involves the inspection work of a state department of labor. In addition to many regulations designed to protect the health of workers, there are many others to insure safety of life and limb. These regulations require the caging of moving belts and dangerous machinery. They apply to the inspection of mines with regard to such matters as ventilation and the handling of explosive gases, inspection of electrical apparatus, inspection of hoists, shafts, and other necessary operating equipment. Such regulations need not be confined to matters affecting labor; they may apply as well to recreational activities. Examples are the regulation of amusement parks, the restrictions on the sale of fireworks for Fourth of July celebrations, and the closing of certain streets to traffic after a snowstorm, to permit coasting, or in the summertime, to permit their use as play areas.

Regulations affecting industry may be imposed for the protection of property as well as of life. Georgia v. Tennessee Copper Company, decided by the Supreme Court in 1907, raises important questions with regard to the protection of both.[16] Georgia had filed a bill in equity, in pursuance of a resolution of the legislature and by direction of the governor, to enjoin the defendant copper companies from discharging noxious gas from their works in Tennessee over the territory of Georgia. It was alleged that in consequence of such discharge there was a wholesale destruction of forests, orchards, and crops, and that other injuries were either done or threatened in five counties of the state. A preliminary injunction had been denied, but the Supreme Court ordered the injunction to issue. The case is the more interesting and the more conclusive because of the interstate feature involved, Georgia already having made application in vain to Tennessee for relief.

15 National Fire Protection Association, *The Cocoanut Grove Night Club Fire*, Boston, November 28, 1942 (Boston, 1943); Greeley, W. R., "Massachusetts Considers a New Safety Code," *State Government*, May 1943, pp. 119–120, 126–127; McElroy, James K., *The LaSalle and Canfield Hotel Fires*, and *The Winecoff Hotel Disaster* (National Fire Protection Association, Boston, 1946 and 1947); Cook County Inspection Bureau, *Report on Hotel LaSalle Fire* (Chicago, 1946); National Board of Fire Underwriters, *The Holland Tunnel Chemical Fire* (New York, 1949). See also Kartman, Ben, and Brown, Leonard, Eds., *Disaster!* (Pellagrini & Cudahy, New York, 1949) giving the stories of forty-six disasters that made yesterday's headlines.

16 206 U.S. 230, 1907.

Regulation of Common Carriers. The cases in the field of railway regulation are an interesting group. A New York statute forbade the use of coal stoves for the heating of passenger cars[17]; an Indiana statute required the use of headlights with 1,500 candle power on all locomotives hauling trains within the state[18]; and a Pennsylvania statute required the use of safety couplers on trains operated within the limits of that Commonwealth.[19] In an Alabama case the court upheld the validity of an act requiring all engineers to pass an eye examination in order to secure a license as locomotive engineers from the state board of examiners.[20] In upholding the power of the states to regulate and control commerce, the Court even went so far as to sustain a Mississippi statute making injuries inflicted by the running of locomotives or cars prima-facie evidence of negligence on the part of railroads, and an Ohio statute permitting the Public Utilities Commission to prescribe a route for a motor common carrier even when such carrier was engaged in interstate commerce.[21]

An equal number of statutes and decisions on the other side can easily be cited. The Supreme Court rejected another Pennsylvania law which sought to regulate the size, end-rails, steps, etc., of the last cars on trains operated within the state.[22] In another case the Court declared unconstitutional a Texas statute forbidding any person from acting as conductor on a railroad train within the state without having previously served for two years as a brakeman or conductor on a freight train.[23] In still another, Georgia sought to impose exceedingly unreasonable restrictions upon the operation of trains as to speed at grade crossings, blowing the whistle as a warning, etc.[24]

Grade Crossing Elimination. Millions of dollars have been devoted to grade crossing elimination with the sole aim of reducing the terrific toll of human life resulting from railway crossing accidents. There are many other regulations imposed upon the intrastate traffic of railways, trolley and bus companies, and other common carriers. These regulations cover the service-

[17] New York, New Haven and Hartford Railroad v. New York, 165 U.S. 628, 1897.

[18] Vandalia Railroad Company v. Indiana, 242 U.S. 255, 1916; the Court held that, since the regulation was a reasonable one designed to protect the public safety, it might be enforced with regard to locomotives hauling interstate trains, as well as with regard to those hauling intrastate trains. This was contingent upon the fact that Congress had not acted. See also Atlantic Coast Line Railroad Company v. State of Georgia, 234 U.S. 280, 1914.

[19] Pennsylvania Railroad Company v. Ewing, 241 Pa. St. 581, 1913.

[20] Smith v. Alabama, 124 U.S. 465, 1888.

[21] Mobile, Jackson and Kansas City Railroad Company v. Turnispeed, 219 U.S. 35, 1910, and Bradley v. Public Utilities Commission of Ohio, 289 U.S. 92, 1933.

[22] Pennsylvania Railroad Company v. Pennsylvania, 250 U.S. 566, 1919; in this case the Federal government had acted. The Federal Safety Appliance Act and the Post Office Department both regulated the end cars on certain interstate trains.

[23] Smith v. Texas, 233 U.S. 630, 1914.

[24] Seaboard Airline Railroad v. Elizabeth Blackwell, 244 U.S. 310, 1917.

ability of equipment, adequacy of equipment for fires and for first aid, speed, distance between cars and trains, and many similar matters.

Fireworks Regulations. After the Fourth of July celebration in 1938, the *New York Times* reported 358 dead as the holiday toll. While many of these deaths were due to traffic accidents, fireworks played their part. In 1937 there were 1180 persons in the New York area injured through carelessness and accidents due to fireworks; as a result of a safety campaign, this number was cut in 1938 to 466. While most of the injuries were minor ones, many were not. Philadelphia in 1921 adopted a ban on the sale of fireworks within the city limits, but in spite of this, in the next seventeen years sixteen persons were killed and 1072 were injured. In 1938, 314 persons were injured in the city, and the number who lost their lives celebrating was the highest since 1910. Although there was an interruption in the sale of fireworks during World War II, the problem is clearly of sufficient importance to justify the exercise of the state's police power.

A survey completed in 1940 showed that there were still six Southern and Western states with no legislation, while regulatory measures of some type had been adopted in thirty-three states. Nine states had practically prohibited fireworks to the ordinary user — Delaware, Indiana, Iowa, Michigan, New Jersey, Pennsylvania, Rhode Island, Utah, and West Virginia. The regulatory laws were of five general types: (1) laws making it the duty of some state administrative officials to make and enforce regulations governing the sale and use of fireworks; (2) laws granting local units permission to treat the problem as they see fit — this is the most common type; (3) laws regulating the type or content or the size of fireworks; (4) laws limiting the time or place, or both, at which firecrackers may be sold or exploded; and (5) laws providing in detail for the manufacture, storage, and sale of explosives. In some instances these laws are designed to prevent industrial fires and explosions, in which case they apply only indirectly to the problem under consideration.[25]

Firearms Legislation. Problems affecting the public safety are very numerous. As an aid in the control of criminal activities, many states have adopted firearms legislation, under the terms of which sales of firearms are reported and owners must register with a state authority. These regulations, which apply especially to small firearms, do not violate the guarantee of the Federal Constitution, found in the Bill of Rights. As in many other fields, the practices of the states in dealing with this matter vary widely. All forty-eight states have statutes in one form or another forbidding the carrying of concealed weapons.

Thirty-one states have licensing requirements governing the ownership and possession of small, concealable firearms. Eight require license to

[25] Everstine, Carl N., *Regulation of Fireworks*, and *Supplementary Report on Regulation of Fireworks* (Maryland Legislative Council, Baltimore, 1940); also *Model State Fireworks Law* (National Fire Prevention Association, Boston, 1938).

purchase under some or all circumstances, six to own or possess. In most cases, a license to carry on the person is necessary only when the weapon is concealed. Fifteen require a license to carry such weapons in motor vehicles, but eighteen grant exceptions when weapons are carried in a fixed place of business or abode. In the seventeen states where licensing is not required, the attempt to control concealable firearms adheres to what may be called the traditional approach. This involves punishment, as a criminal offense, of acts stated to be in violation of the law. Such prohibitions include, in practically every instance, at least the carrying of firearms concealed on the person. Permissible acts involving the carrying, possession, or sale of firearms are generally not set forth, nor do these penal statutes ordinarily include careful definitions of the various classes of firearms that are being regulated.[26]

Crime Control. Modern conditions have made it impossible for states to deal effectively with many problems affecting the public safety. The Federal government has recognized the interstate character of the white slave traffic, of the traffic in stolen motor vehicles and other forms of stolen property, and of kidnapping, racketeering, and other offenses, and has given assistance in dealing with them, in the form of the Federal Crime Laws of 1934 and the cooperation of Federal law-enforcing officers.[27]

Oklahoma enacted a statute providing for the sterilization of "habitual criminals," i.e., persons thrice convicted for felonies involving moral turpitude. Although it set up elaborate procedural requirements, including jury trial of the question whether "the criminal may be rendered sexually sterile without detriment to his or her general health," it contained exemptions so arbitrary as to constitute — in the judgment of the Supreme Court — a denial of equal protection of the laws.[28] These exemptions included "offenses arising out of the violation of the prohibitory laws, revenue acts, embezzlement or political offenses" which were not to be considered within the terms of the act. Skinner was convicted in 1926 of stealing chickens, in 1929 of robbery, and in 1934 of robbery again; an order for his sterilization was issued.

Under Oklahoma law, grand larceny is a felony when the property taken exceeds $20 in value. The embezzlement of property worth $20 or more is also a felony. "A clerk who appropriates over $20 from his employer's till and a stranger who steals the same amount are thus both guilty of felonies. If the latter repeats his act and is convicted three times, he may

[26] See Blair, James C., "Carrying a Concealed Weapon — Nature of the Offense in Kentucky," *Kentucky Law Journal*, January 1950, pp. 275–282; Illinois Legislative Council, *State Regulation of Firearms*, pp. 10 and 18 (Springfield, 1946); and for an earlier study, International Association of Chiefs of Police, *Study of State Legislation Regulating Sale and Possession of Firearms* (Chicago, 1940).

[27] For a discussion of this legislation, see Graves, W. Brooke, "Federal Leadership in State Legislation," *Temple Law Quarterly*, July 1936, pp. 385–405, and Corwin, Edward S., *Court over Constitution* (Princeton University Press, 1938).

[28] Skinner v. Oklahoma, 316 U.S. 535, 1942.

be sterilized. But the clerk is not subject to the pains and penalties of the act, no matter how large his embezzlement or how frequent his convictions." The Court found this discrimination so arbitrary as to deny the equal protection of the laws guaranteed by Amendment XIV.

Rainmaking. While there are tremendous possibilities in the newly discovered means of weather modification, they abound in opportunity for disaster if left without public controls in the hands of incompetent or irresponsible parties. The general view of the courts has been that any hazardous enterprise, however valuable to society as a whole, must pay its way and be responsible for damages that it may cause. Until such time as an accurate determination may be made in physical terms of the nature and extent of the possible benefit and/or damage resulting from the use of the power to control precipitation, formulation of adequate legislation and rules and regulations will be difficult if not impossible.[29]

Protection of the Public Convenience

Questions involving the use of the police power for the protection of the public convenience are relatively few, and usually involve reasonableness of rates or adequacy of service by public utility companies. Among such questions are the number of trains or cars to be operated on a given line, the number of stops they will be required to make and the points at which they will be made, and the schedule upon which service will be maintained. Illustrative of these points are such cases as the Lake Shore and Michigan Southern Railway v. Ohio[30]; Cleveland, Cincinnati, Chicago and St. Louis Railway v. Illinois[31]; and Atlantic Coast Line v. Railway Commissioners of South Carolina.[32] According to the first of these decisions, railroads may be required to furnish adequate transportation facilities at each station, and if this is not done through the service of local trains, the deficiency must be met by a sufficient number of interstate trains. It was held that an Ohio act requiring railways to stop three trains daily each way at towns on their line of 3000 population or more was reasonable; since the act did not specify interstate trains, the companies could avoid slowing down the running time of interstate trains by providing sufficient service by local trains. Such a solution would certainly be appropriate in the service of suburban communities, such as Lakewood, outside of Cleveland, in connection with which the case arose.

In the Cleveland, Cincinnati, Chicago and St. Louis Railway case, Illinois had attempted to require the stopping of all trains at county seats; this rule applied, therefore, to both interstate and intrastate trains. If, as in the case of Hillsboro, the community already had adequate service, the

[29] California State Chamber of Commerce, *Scientific, Economic and Legal Aspects of Weather Modification* (San Francisco, 1951).

[30] 173 U.S. 285, 1899.

[31] 177 U.S. 514, 1900.

[32] 207 U.S. 328, 1907.

state could not constitutionally require a fast interstate train, running between St. Louis and New York in competition with similar trains on other roads, to stop at this town, with consequent loss of time and slowing down of schedule. "In determining what is reasonable, the Court examines the number of trains already stopping at a given point, the population to be served, and the amount of traffic." This point is well illustrated by the Atlantic Coast Line case, in which the Railroad Commission of South Carolina had attempted to require a through train between New York and Tampa to stop at a hamlet of 453 persons which already had adequate service. These considerations are not necessarily effective if a train runs entirely within a state, even though it carries both mail and interstate passengers.[33]

A regulation of quite a different type considered by the Court as in the interests of the public convenience was dealt with in the case of Williams v. Arkansas, in 1910.[34] The constitutionality of an Arkansas statute forbidding the solicitation for certain kinds of business upon trains in the state was upheld; in the course of the opinion, this significant paragraph was included:

> The legislature clearly has the power to make regulations for the convenience and comfort of travelers on railroads, and this appears to be a reasonable regulation for their benefit. It prevents annoyance from the importunities of drummers. It is suggested in the argument that the statute was especially aimed at the protection of travelers to the city of Hot Springs. If this be so, we can readily see additional reason why the regulation is a wholesome one. A large percentage of those travelers are persons from distant states, who are mostly complete strangers here, and many are sick. Drummers who swarm through the trains soliciting for physicians, bath houses, hotels, et cetera, make a burden to those who are subjected to their repeated solicitations. It is true that the traveler may turn a deaf ear to these importunities, but this does not render it any the less unpleasant and annoying. The drummer may keep within the law against disorderly conduct, and still render himself a source of annoyance to travelers by his beseeching to be allowed to lead the way to a doctor or a hotel. . . .
>
> This statute is not an unreasonable restriction upon the privilege one should enjoy to solicit for his lawful business, which, it is rightly urged, is an incident to any business. It does not prevent anyone from advertising his business, or from soliciting patronage, except upon trains, et cetera. This privilege is denied him for the public good. It is a principle which underlies every reasonable exercise of the police power, that private rights must yield to the common welfare.

Rent Controls. It is not easy to decide what aspect of police power regulation is predominant in rent control legislation. Looked at from the point of view of overcrowding and the use of unsuitable accommodations, it might be a health matter. If one regards only the unreasonable rentals which some landlords would charge — often for inferior accommodations — in the absence of restraints, there is almost an element of fraud involved. In

[33] See Gladsen v. Minnesota, 166 U.S. 427, 1897; for a helpful note on this subject, see Hall, James P., *Cases on Constitutional Law*, p. 1187.

[34] 217 U.S. 79, 1910.

general, however, the enforcement of rent control legislation resembles more closely the rules governing reasonableness of rates in relation to the quantity and quality of service associated with police power regulation in the interests of the public convenience.

Attempts at rent control were made in New York and the District of Columbia during World War I. As a result of this experience, the principle was established that government might properly undertake such regulation to protect the public in periods of emergency.[35] Federal legislation of nation-wide application was adopted in World War II, as a part of the general price control program administered by the Office of Price Administration. In the postwar years, it was annually extended, with a growing number of exceptions and restrictions. There were, in fact, no less than six different ways in which the operation of this legislation might be suspended for particular states, rental areas, types of property, or for the country as a whole.

During this long period of uncertainty regarding the continuance of Federal legislation, many states adopted so-called stand-by legislation which would become effective only at such time as Federal controls might be discontinued. No less than eleven states have had stand-by legislation rent control laws, now expired.[36] All Federal controls expired September 30, 1952[37]; leaving only two states — New York and Wisconsin — able to operate under a substitute system of state rent controls for housing accommodations. The Wisconsin stand-by law expired and its permanent law became effective in 1949 when the state was decontrolled by the Federal Housing Expediter. In 1950, the New York Legislature enacted a statute which became effective May 1, and under which state controls replaced existing national and city controls. The constitutionality of the act was upheld by the state Court of Appeals in July of the same year.[38] Local communities are authorized to maintain rent controls, but few are in a position to enforce them.

[35] Block v. Hirsh, 256 U.S. 135, 1916; Marcus Brown Holding Company v. Feldman, Schwartz, et al., 256 U.S. 170, 1921.

[36] These states, with the expiration dates of their stand-by legislation, are: 1946: Michigan; 1948: Lousiana, Missouri, New Jersey, Rhode Island; 1949: Connecticut, Illinois, Minnesota, Wisconsin; 1950: Virginia; 1951: Maryland.

[37] Of the seven states not under Federal controls in 1950, only Wisconsin and New York had state rent control laws in operation. Nebraska and Texas had been decontrolled by the Federal Housing Expediter, following action by their legislatures declaring Federal controls no longer necessary. Alabama, Arizona, and Utah had been completely decontrolled, partly by action of municipalities in passing decontrol resolutions and partly by the Federal Housing Expediter on his own initiative.

[38] Two studies, on which this comment is based, have been made in the Legislative Reference Service, Library of Congress: Hunter, Carrie E., *State Rent Control Laws* (Public Affairs Bulletin No. 62, 1948), and Still, Samuel H., Jr., *The Rent Control Situation as of January 1, 1950* (Manuscript report, 1950); see also Geller, Morton and Betty R., "New York State Rent Control — 1950," *New York Certified Public Accountant*, June 1950, pp. 1–10.

Protection of the Public Morals

Police power regulations designed to protect the public morals affect both the rights of persons and the rights of property. In the first category, one finds prohibited by law such acts as indecent exposure, solicitation by prostitutes, procurers, bookmakers, dope peddlers,[39] distribution and sale of obscene or immoral literature, contraceptive devices, etc. On the property side, one finds prohibitions upon the maintenance of gambling dens, disorderly houses, and dope establishments, and stringent regulation of public dance halls and the licensing and sale of wines, beer, and liquors. The theory of such regulations, of course, is that the right of the public as a whole to be protected from the influence of conditions quite generally regarded as immoral is paramount over the right of any individual in the exercise of his personal rights, or over the right of any individual to make such use of his property as he sees fit. In general, the right of government to exercise the police power for the purposes indicated is so well established as to be no longer open to serious question.

Liquor Control. There are, however, occasional cases of a borderline nature particularly involving the use of property. In one of these, Mugler v. Kansas,[40] the principle was established that where individuals or corporations choose to invest their money in businesses the propriety of which is open to question, they have no redress if the public decides that the discontinuance of the business is desirable. Kansas had passed an act in 1881 which forbade the manufacture or sale, except for medicinal purposes, of all intoxicating liquors. Mugler was convicted, under this act, of selling beer. His attorneys argued that, since he had invested his money in a brewing business, and had done so under the sanction and with the authority of the state, he could not now be denied the right to continue the operation of his business. To require such discontinuance was, they said, to deprive him of his property contrary to the guarantee of Amendment XIV. The Court refused to accept this position. This principle of law would seem to apply similarly to such businesses as the conduct of public dance halls, the operation of a race track betting system, or the use of lotteries for charitable or other purposes.

The sale of intoxicating liquors has long been recognized as a privilege subject to regulation, rather than an inherent right. Sometimes, however, local option in matters of police regulation leads to amusing or ridiculous situations; thus in a certain New Jersey community it is illegal on Sunday to sit on the right-hand side of a particular theater. Similarly, local option laws on the sale of liquor have sometimes given rise to situations in which

[39] See Hughes, James E., "Dope: State Narcotic Laws and the Need for the Uniform Narcotic Drug Act," *State Government*, September 1933, pp. 11–14; Council of State Governments, *Radio Symposium on Marihuana — the Killer Drug* (Chicago, 1937).

[40] 123 U.S. 623, 1887; see also Bartenmeyer v. Iowa, 18 Wallace 129, 1873.

the bar was removed from one side of a hotel building to the other, according to the way the vote went.

The liquor business has been subject not only to licensure, but to regulations of other types, as illustrated by the case of Crowley v. Christensen, decided by the Supreme Court in 1890.[41] In this instance the Court sustained the conviction of the defendant for violating a San Francisco ordinance forbidding the issuance of liquor licenses except to persons who obtained the written consent of a majority of the city board of police commissioners, or twelve citizens owning real estate in the block where the business was to be conducted. As the liquor business is one "attended with danger to the community, it may be entirely prohibited, or be permitted under such conditions as will limit to the utmost its evils. The manner and extent of regulation rest in the discretion of the governing authority. That authority may vest in such officers as it may deem proper the passing upon applications for permission to carry it on, and to issue licenses for that purpose. It is a matter of legislative will only."[42]

Laws against Prostitution. The American Social Hygiene Association reports that, as early as 1909, some states saw the need to protect family and community from the moral and health hazards of commercialized prostitution. Pressure of this problem during World War I and the years following spurred widespread legislative action, so that by 1929 all states had some type of law to combat this evil. The report of the Association continues:

> Existence of these laws and improvement in community conditions made necessary comparatively little new legislation from 1925 to 1941, but mobilization — both military and industrial — in the national defense effort of 1939–1941, and the plunge into World War II, with a great increase in prostitution activities around strategic communities, again stimulated a drive for better laws. As of November 1, 1944, twenty-nine states and the District of Columbia had acceptable laws with only two states having laws considered inadequate.

These laws have been used during the war period to clean up conditions in many communities, but good laws are needed more than ever in these restless postwar years. In its classification of the laws existing in the several states, the Association reports that nineteen states have adequate laws against most aspects of prostitution, and that ten more have adequate laws, with the exception of their coverage of the activities of the customers of prostitutes. Of the remaining nineteen states, all but two have laws against some activities of prostitutes and their exploiters. These two have some legislation, but it is regarded by the Association as quite inadequate.[43]

[41] 137 U.S. 86, 1890.

[42] For a good discussion of the regulation of public morals, see Callcott, Mary S., *Principles of Social Legislation*, Chapter 7 (Macmillan, New York, 1932).

[43] See Gould, George, "Laws Against Prostitution and Their Use," *Journal of Social Hygiene*, October 1941, and Special Committee on Enforcement of the National Advisory Police Committee, a series of recommendations in "Techniques for Repressing Unorganized Prostitution," supplement to *Police Chiefs Newsletter*, November–December 1942.

Lotteries. Lotteries have been banned by statute in this country for so long that many have assumed that they are wrong in and of themselves. Actually, they "are not, in the legal acceptation of the term, *mala in se*, . . . but may properly be made *mala prohibita*."[44] In the early history of the country, Congress and the state legislatures felt no compunction whatever in resorting to lotteries as a means of obtaining revenue. In the twelve-year period from 1796 to 1808, seventy-eight different lotteries were authorized in Pennsylvania, the proceeds being used to finance churches, canals, and many other public improvements. In the thirty-eight years from 1782 to 1820, Virginia authorized no less than seventy different lotteries to raise money for a variety of educational purposes, for waterways, highways, counties, towns, churches, private societies, and even to assist individuals in the completion of various worthy projects.

The last lotteries in actual operation were those in Mississippi under an act of 1867, Louisiana under an act of 1868. In 1892, Louisiana became the last state to ban lotteries; contemporaneously, the transmission of lottery tickets through the mails was prohibited by Congress. There has been no relaxation of any of these prohibitions since, although, with legalized lotteries existing in many other countries, there have been numerous proposals for their use for charitable and other purposes here. This interesting bit of historical background serves merely to illustrate the fact that the states may exercise their police powers in their own discretion, either by permitting, prohibiting, or regulating gambling, bingo, and other games of chance.[45]

Pari-Mutuel Betting. For many years, betting on horse racing in the form of book making, pool selling, et cetera, was generally frowned upon in this country, and was in most jurisdictions prohibited by law. This did not by any means stop the practice, which was frequently carried on in barber shops, tobacco shops, and pool rooms. Gambling and lotteries, operated by the government or under close government supervision, had long been common in Europe; with the advent of the depression, there were numerous proposals to legalize these methods of raising funds for welfare and charitable purposes. Public opinion gradually changed to the point where pari-mutuel betting on horse racing is permitted in approximately

[44] Stone v. Mississippi, 101 U.S. 814, 1879; this comment is based on Treadway, W. E., "Lottery Laws in Early America," American Bar Association *Journal*, May 1949, pp. 385–388.

[45] Treadway points out that local sentiment may operate to produce opposite decisions as to what constitutes a lottery. In Kentucky, betting on horses by a pari-mutuel system was held not to constitute a lottery (Commonwealth v. Kentucky Jockey Club, 238 Ky. 739, 38 S.W. 2d 987), while in Nebraska such a system was originally held to be a lottery and therefore unlawful (State v. Ak-Sar-Ben Exposition Company, 118 Neb. 851, 226 N.W. 705, and 121 Neb. 248, 236 N.W. 736. For current comment, see McKean, Dayton D., "Who Gets the Billion Graft?" *National Municipal Review*, December 1949, pp. 546–550, 570, and Peterson, Virgil W., *Gambling: Should It Be Legalized?* (Charles C. Thomas, Publisher, Springfield, Ill., 1951); Ploscowe, Morris, and Lukas, Edwin J., Eds., "Gambling," *Annals*, May 1950, entire issue.

half the states. A joint legislative committee in New York, investigating the first year of operation under the law in that state, thus describes the operation of the system[46]:

> Under the Pari-Mutuel System of Betting, the racing associations operate the System under regulations. The patrons purchase the tickets at windows, at varying amounts, the basic tickets costing two dollars ($2.00). Tickets may be bought for a horse to "win," "place" (place second) or may be bought for a horse to "show" (place third), and any number of tickets may be purchased on any number of horses in a race to finish in all or any of the three successful positions. All of the money bet on horses to "win," less deductions for the State and racing associations, is pro-rated among the persons holding tickets on the winning horse, and all the money for second or "place," and third or "show," are similarly divided, among those holding tickets on horses which finish second or third.
>
> When a patron purchases a ticket, the seller presses a button which automatically releases the ticket. The same impulse records, on an electrically operated machine known as a "Totalizator," the amount of the bet, the number of the horse selected, and whether the ticket is for "win" or "place" or "show." The Totalizator adds the money bet on each horse in a race, in the three separate pools and accumulates the totals for each pool. All such statistics, and the odds for the different horses in the winning pool, are projected on a larger indicator in the infield in view of the public.
>
> The most important feature of the Pari-Mutuel System, proven by experience, is that it makes for temperance in betting. This moderation stimulates a sense of enjoyment into the sport of horse racing, and limits its use as an instrument of gambling.

Motion Picture Censorship. Seven states — Kansas, Maryland, Massachusetts, New Jersey, New York, Ohio, Virginia — and the District of Columbia, not to mention some 200 cities, review films to decide whether they may be shown. New York licenses everything except newsreels, and the license is denied to films which are "obscene, indecent, immoral, inhuman, sacrilegious, or . . . of such a character that [their] exhibition would tend to corrupt morals or incite to crime." New Jersey and Pennsylvania censor every film brought into the state to be sure it is "moral and proper." Kansas bans, among other things, "ridicule of any religious sect or peculiar characteristics of any race of people," "prolonged and passionate scenes suggestive of immorality," and "evil suggestion in the dress of comedy characters."

Although officials would not dare to preview newspapers or radio programs, in jurisdictions within which live a sizable portion of the nation's population, they regularly preview and censor motion picture films, clipping away in accordance with their several predilections as to what is good for

[46] Joint Legislative Committee for the Study of the Pari-Mutuel System, *Report*, pp. 15 and 49–132, for detailed analysis of the laws of twenty-four states (Legislative Document, 1941, No. 69); Illinois Legislative Council, *Taxation of Pari-Mutuel Wagering at Horse Races* (Springfield, 1940); MacLeod, William C., "The Truth about Lotteries in American History," *South Atlantic Quarterly*, April 1936, pp. 201–211; and Library of Congress, Division of Bibliography, *Lotteries in the United States and Foreign Countries*, a list of recent references (Washington, 1942).

the public to see. In these jurisdictions, there is no such thing as freedom of the films. The public, dimly aware of the censors' existence, has no conception of the nature and extent of their operations. Pictures banned in one jurisdiction may be freely shown in another. The censorship is active and aggressive. No one has ever made a compilation of the total score over the years, but in Massachusetts alone, in a single year, almost 200 reels of film were censored either in whole or in part. Five were banned entirely in Maryland in the same period, and 219 others were cut. These are merely random illustrations of the kind of thing that goes on in states and cities throughout the country.

The Prevention of Fraud

Blue Sky Laws. The state may exercise the police power for the purpose of protecting its citizens from fraud. Illustrations are to be found in Blue Sky legislation, usury laws, and laws designed to insure honest weights and measures and honest labeling of food and drug products. Blue Sky laws have been enacted in many states to prevent the sale of fraudulent securities; under their provisions, brokers and their salesmen must be registered with the state enforcing agency. Securities may not be offered for sale until the enforcing agency has been given full and complete information regarding the financial condition of the company, its credit rating, the purposes for which the funds are to be used, and other related matters. It is difficult to overestimate the importance of this type of legislation; for years the people have been "fleeced" of millions of dollars annually by fly-by-night salesmen offering them fabulous returns from oil wells in which there was no oil, gold mines in which there was no gold, and copper mines in which there was no copper. When sensible people had become suspicious of proposals of this character, these disreputable promoters organized fictitious companies for all sorts of other purposes. They were able to ply their trade often among supposedly intelligent people because of the almost universal human desire to get something for nothing. Many were credulous enough to believe that it could be done, but usually ended by losing the full amount of their investment.[47]

Regulation of Small Loan Companies. Another common type of fraud against which the police power has been invoked is that practiced by small

[47] In Hall v. Geiger-Jones Company, 242 U.S. 539, 1917, the Court upheld the constitutionality of an Ohio statute forbidding any dealer to sell corporate securities in the state unless first licensed therein, even as applied to securities sent in from other states to be sold. The state's power to regulate is not to be determined by a discussion of the place of making or executing a contract, but by its consequences: Hoopeston Canning Company v. Cullen, 318 U.S. 313, 1943. So the Court sustained a provision of the Virginia Blue Sky law which requires sellers of insurance and securities in the state to obtain a permit and agree to the filing of suits against them by service on the secretary of state, even though applied to a small health insurance agency conducting all of its activities in Nebraska, and doing a mail order business in Virginia through its members acting as unpaid solicitors: Travelers Health Association v. Virginia, 339 U.S. 643, 1950.

loan companies. These companies advertise through the newspapers, by radio, and through the mails, presenting the benefits of their so-called service in the most glowing terms. This service was often a necessity for many small homeowners with taxes to pay or with some unusual expenses such as those incurred for illness, funerals, or other causes. When these small loan companies once had an unsuspecting borrower within their grasp, he soon found himself beset by exorbitant interest charges and every conceivable kind of sharp practice. In most states, this evil has now been brought under control.

The problem is age-old, and the need for regulation was early recognized in the United States; early attempts at control and the period of experimentation extended from 1884 to 1910. This was followed by a period of coordination and finally, in 1917, by the Uniform Small Loan Law, which has been in force in an increasing number of states since that date. Small loan legislation in some form now exists in all but five states (Kansas, Montana, North Dakota, South Carolina, South Dakota), but there are no maximums in three states. The laws of the Uniform Small Loan type exist in thirty-six states, laws of other types in seven. These acts commonly provide for licensing of loan companies, and regulation by a public official or commission. Their application is limited to loans of not more than $300 in twenty-nine states, $500 in eight states. In Wyoming, the maximum is $150; in Ohio, $1000. Interest rates are regulated, but the maximum rates vary widely from state to state; the absolute sale of wages has in most acts been prohibited. Certain exemptions to the operation of the laws have been provided, but it is quite possible to draft them in such ways as to insure their constitutionality.[48]

Control of Ticket Scalpers. A number of states have enacted legislation designed to control ticket racketeering by making it impossible for scalpers to move from one community to another in order to avoid local ordinances. State-wide licensing of ticket brokers is authorized through local authorities. Resale premiums are limited to one half of the price on the face of the ticket, plus taxes. All forms of entertainment are covered, including theatrical performances, concerts, movies, and athletic events. First offenders are fined $100, while second offenses may be punished as misdemeanors with maximum fines of $1000.

Among the numerous court cases that have arisen, two may be mentioned. In Indiana, a defendant who was not a ticket broker challenged the constitutionality of the state statute. He had been convicted of selling tickets

[48] See Foster, LeBaron R., *Small Loan Laws of the United States*, Fifth Edition (Pollock Foundation, Newton, Mass., 1943) and the following articles: Bogart, George G., "The Future of Small Loan Legislation," *University of Chicago Law Review*, December 1944, pp. 1–25; Ewart, P. J., "California Leads the Way in Small Loan Legislation," *Southern California Law Review*, February 1947, pp. 172–210; and Kelso, R. W., "Social Implications of the Small Loan Laws of the United States," *Modern Law Review*, April 1948, pp. 143–149.

to a state basketball tournament at a price in excess of that printed on the face of the ticket. While recognizing that a state may, under its police power, fix the prices of certain commodities, the state supreme court, relying on the Tyson case, held the act invalid.[49] A California case dealt with a quite different subject matter. The statute in question regulated the business of agents who sell "transportation over the public highways of the state." Each such agent must secure a license, pay a fee of $1 and file a bond of $1000 as a guarantee of the faithful performance of the transportation contracts which he negotiates. The Supreme Court, reversing an earlier decision, found that Congress had passed no laws on the subject, and that the act did not obstruct or burden interstate commerce.[50] Purchasers "are peculiarly unable to protect themselves from fraud and overreaching of those engaged in a business notoriously subject to those abuses."

Heart-Balm Legislation. Conceived in a rash of newspaper publicity and ballyhoo, heart-balm legislation had its inception a decade and a half ago when in 1935 Indiana passed the first such act. The years since have seen the number of such enactments increased to fourteen.[51] In 1946, the Illinois supreme court declared the heart-balm act of that state unconstitutional.[52] In general, these acts fall into one or the other of two categories: those directed at eliminating the actions of breach of promise to marry, alienation of affections, criminal conversation and seduction, and those directed only at the abolition of actions for breach of promise to marry. All but three of the state laws — Maine, Massachusetts, and New Hampshire — are of the broader coverage falling in the first category.[53]

Weights and Measures. Mention has been made of the effort to prevent fraud in the sale of merchandise. The establishing and enforcing of standard weights and measures by city, state, and nation is an evidence of this type of police power regulation. A case involving constitutional questions arose in North Dakota a few years ago.[54] In 1911 the state legislature had enacted a law which provided that lard must be sold in containers holding one, three, or five pounds, respectively, or multiples of these numbers, unless the lard was sold in bulk at wholesale. In 1917 this act was amended to provide that retail sales of lard must be labeled with the quantity in the container. This change was made because practice showed that dealers were

[49] Kirtley v. State, 84 N.E. 2d 712 (Ind. 1949), based on Tyson & Brothers v. Banton, 273 U.S. 418, 1927.

[50] California v. Thompson, 313 U.S. 109, 1941, overruling Di Santo v. Pennsylvania, 273 U.S. 34, 1927.

[51] These are: Alabama, California, Colorado, Illinois, Indiana, Maine, Massachusetts, Michigan, Nevada, New Hampshire, New Jersey, New York, Pennsylvania, Wyoming.

[52] Heck v. Schupp, 394 Ill. 296, 68 N.E. 2d 464, 1946.

[53] See note in *Virginia Law Review*, May 1947, pp. 314–322.

[54] Armour and Company v. North Dakota, 240 U.S. 510, 1916; also Schmidlinge v. Chicago, 226 U.S. 578, 1912, upholding a weight law for loaves of bread offered for sale, and Hauge v. Chicago, 299 U.S. 387, 1937, which held that even an apparently repetitious and unreasonable weighing was constitutional.

accustomed to include the weight of the container in making sales of lard. The State Food Commissioner bought a three-pound pail of lard that had been packed by Armour and Company; upon examination, he found that he acquired two pounds six ounces of lard and ten ounces of tin. Accordingly, he imposed a fine of $100 for violation of the law. In its defense in court the company contended that the act operated with the effect of depriving the company of its property without due process of law; that it represented an interference with interstate commerce; that it represented an interference with the Federal Pure Food and Drug Act; and finally, that the state had no authority to require the sale of commodities in packages of certain sizes only. The decision of the Court — that the state could fix the quantity of retail sales if the purpose was to prevent fraud — turned largely on this last point in the defense. The Court assumed that when a purchaser asked for three pounds of lard, he wanted that amount, and not a lesser amount of lard and a considerable amount of tin. It was pointed out further that the company could not be serious in its objections to the provisions of the law, since it had for many years been furnishing a grocery company in New York City with lard in containers of the sizes specified.

Misrepresentation of Merchandise. A much older case, involving a milder form of misrepresentation, Frost v. Chicago, was decided by the Supreme Court of Illinois in 1899.[55] The plaintiff in error had been found guilty in the court below of violating an ordinance of the city of Chicago, and fined fifteen dollars and costs. The ordinance provided:

> Sec. 1000. Colored Netting for Covering. It shall be and is hereby made unlawful to cover any box, basket, or any other package or parcel of fruit, berries or vegetables of any kind, with any colored netting, or any other material which has a tendency to conceal the true color or quality of any such goods which may be sold, offered for sale, or had in possession for the purpose of being sold or offered for sale. Any person who shall violate the provisions of this section shall, upon conviction, be fined not less than $10 or more than $25 for such offense.

The opinion states that testimony tended to show that the defendant sold peaches in baskets covered with red tarlatan — a perforated cloth — and that these baskets had been shipped to him from Michigan put up in the same manner in which he sold them. There was some evidence that this colored netting tended to conceal the "true color or quality" of the fruit, and some to the contrary. This appeared to have been a common trade practice, preventing pilfering and loss from other causes and giving ventilation. The Court reached the conclusion that the ordinance was "a vexatious and unreasonable interference with and restriction upon the rights of dealers in certain articles of trade and commerce," and accordingly reversed the judgment of the lower court.

At the close of the nineteenth century and the beginning of the twentieth, the agricultural interests of the country were able to secure the passage of

[55] 178 Ill. 250, 1899.

legislation to restrict the distribution and sale of oleomargarine. The product was harmless enough — more wholesome, no doubt, than much of the butter then offered for sale — but it provided competition which the farmers considered dangerous. There was, of course, the possibility that unscrupulous dealers might sell oleomargarine, artificially colored to resemble butter, as a substitute therefor, thus greatly increasing their profits. It was upon the idea of preventing this possible fraud that most of the statutes were built; the Supreme Court held that they might be enforced by the states, even as applied to the sale of goods brought in from other states.[56] These laws did not usually attempt to prevent the sale of oleomargarine, but only its sale in such manner as involved fraud; the Constitution did not secure to anyone the right to commit a fraud in the sale of merchandise, whether or not the goods were shipped in interstate commerce. A Pennsylvania statute which did forbid the "manufacture, sale, or the keeping with intent to sell" of oleomargarine was upheld by both state and Federal courts,[57] but this type of act was not enforceable as applied to a product brought into the state in interstate commerce.[58]

The Suppression of Public Nuisances

The police power may be exercised, either by the state itself or by its political subdivisions, for the suppression of nuisances. Such nuisances may develop either from the inconsiderate exercise of personal rights or from a similar use of property. The Federal and state constitutions guarantee to the citizen the enjoyment of certain fundamental rights. No one is permitted, however, to make such use of these rights as will annoy his neighbors. An individual has a right to freedom of religious belief and worship, but if a person, as an act of worship, were to arise at two A.M. nightly and blow a trumpet from his window, he would clearly be exceeding his rights. Similarly, people have the right to enjoy music and to entertain guests in their homes; they have no right, however, to keep a radio blaring far into the night, nor to conduct their festivities in such a boisterous fashion as to keep all the people in the apartment house in which they live awake. Individuals have the right to maintain cats or dogs as pets, but when these animals are permitted to roam unrestrained over the property of their neighbors, the pets become a nuisance. Likewise, the dwellers in the neighborhood are under no obligation to permit frequent nocturnal cat fights, nor the continual barking of a dog through the hours of the night.

Nuisances involving the use of property may develop from a wide variety of causes, some of them deliberately conceived with the intention of annoying one's neighbors. Such a case was Rideout v. Knox, decided many years ago by the Supreme Judicial Court of Massachusetts, the opinion

[56] Plumley v. Massachusetts, 155 U.S. 461, 1895.
[57] Powell v. Pennsylvania, 127 U.S. 678, 1887.
[58] Schollenberger v. Pennsylvania, 171 U.S. 1, 1898.

being written by the late Oliver Wendell Holmes when he was a member of that tribunal.[59] The Court upheld a statute making the malicious erection of a so-called "spite fence" over six feet high, for the purpose of annoying adjoining occupants, a private nuisance. Justice Holmes commented upon the limited application of the act, and observed that it would be hard to imagine a more insignificant curtailment of the rights of property; his comment on the rules of the common law applicable to such cases is significant:

> It is plain that the right to use one's property for the sole purpose of injuring others is not one of the immediate rights of ownership. It is not a right for the sake of which property is recognized by the law, but is only a more or less necessary incident of rights which are established for very different ends. It has been thought by respectable authorities that even at common law the extent of a man's rights in cases like the present might depend upon the motive with which he acted. . . . We do not so understand the common law . . . but it does not follow that the rule is the same for a boundary fence unnecessarily built more than six feet high. It may be said that the difference is only one of degree. Most differences are, when nicely analyzed.

The rules of law have so developed that the existence of a nuisance in any given instance will depend largely upon the character of the neighborhood. A machine shop or a boiler factory is a natural and legitimate part of an industrial district, but when such an establishment is set up in a residential district, where the noises emanating therefrom disturb the peace of the community and annoy the inhabitants, it becomes a public nuisance. Such nuisances may result also from the presence of disagreeable and offensive odors such as emanate from a fish glue factory or a fertilizer plant. The smoke that belches forth from the chimneys of great factories may be taken for granted (although it is no longer necessary) in an industrial district, when it would constitute a public nuisance in the commercial or residential section of the city.[60] Property may also be used in such manner as to constitute a public nuisance on moral grounds. If an individual permits the use of his premises for any one of the familiar forms of vice and crime, he may subject himself to nuisance proceedings as well as the possibility of criminal prosecution.

Classification of Nuisances. The Supreme Court of Illinois, in Laugel v. City of Bushnell, classified nuisances as follows:

> . . . . First, those which in their nature are nuisances per se or are so denounced by the common law or by statute; second, those which in their nature are not nuisances, but may become so by reason of their locality, surroundings, or the manner in which they may be conducted, managed, et cetera; third, those which in their nature may be nuisances, but as to which there may be honest differences of opinion in impartial minds. The power granted by the

[59] 148 Mass. 368, 1889.

[60] A smoke abatement ordinance was upheld in Northwest Laundry v. Des Moines, 239 U.S. 486, 1916; an act forbidding the conducting of a livery stable within a designated area, in Reinman v. Little Rock, 237 U.S. 171, 1914. See also: Barkley, J. E., *Some Fundamentals of Smoke Abatement* (Information Circular, United States Department of the Interior, 1939), and St. Louis Committee on Elimination of Smoke, *Report* (St. Louis, February 24, 1940).

statute to the governing bodies of municipal corporations to declare what shall be nuisances, and to abate the same, et cetera, authorizes such bodies to conclusively denounce those things falling within the first and third of these classes to be nuisances, but as to those things falling within the second class, the power possessed is only to declare such of them to be nuisances as are in fact so.[61]

It is not only difficult but probably unnecessary to cite specific court cases to illustrate the first type — nuisances per se — since the definition of many of them has come down through the rules of the common law. The common law nuisance was usually a nuisance to the sense of smell or a danger to life, such as an unsanitary building or drain.[62] Noise in extreme form was often considered a nuisance, and it is even more so in the modern city. In England, interference with the easements of light, air, and access constituted a nuisance. As far back as 1910 one writer reported a rapid increase in police power legislation of this general type. "Legislation is now eagerly desired in many states of this country," he said, "to make in certain cases that which is a nuisance to the sense of sight also a legal nuisance, as, for instance, the posting of offensive bills on the fences, or the erection of huge advertising signs in parks or on public highways. . . . There is some legislation against the blowing of steam whistles by locomotives, although I believe none against the morning whistle of factories, and some against the emission of black smoke in specified durations and quantities."[63]

It is not particularly difficult to determine whether or not a given situation is of such a character as to constitute a public nuisance. It is, however, sometimes difficult to secure the abatement of a nuisance, particularly in some of the larger cities, if the persons responsible for it have considerable political influence. In such a case, the law is clearly on the side of the plaintiff, and usually a little persistence will enable him to secure abatement. The courts have fortunately taken the position that the existence of a nuisance is sufficient to enable one to secure relief — it makes no difference whether the plaintiff moves in where the nuisance is already established or whether it is the nuisance which moves in. These nuisances are of the second type mentioned above — those which become nuisances by reason of their locality, surroundings, or the manner in which they are conducted. An interesting case in point is that of the Northwestern Fertilizer Company v.

[61] 197 Ill. 20, 1902.

[62] The following are among the more common types of nuisances: filth, garbage, ashes, slops, cesspools, drains, dumps, weeds, dead animals, pollution of water, offensive odors, noise, smoke, and dust. See Peacock, Robert, "What Is a Public Health Nuisance and What Evidence Shall Be Brought into Court to Prove Its Existence?" New Jersey *Public Health News*, August 1950, pp. 247–251, and de Funiak, William I., "Equitable Relief Against Nuisances," *Kentucky Law Journal*, January 1950, pp. 223–235.

[63] Stimson, Frederic J., *Popular Lawmaking*, Chapter 7 (Scribner's, New York, 1910); for a recent study see Bureau of Governmental Research and Services, *Nuisances: Their Control and Abatement in the State of Washington* (University of Washington, 1949); also note in *Rutgers Law Review*, "Constitutionality of the Municipal Regulation of Sound Amplifying Equipment," June 1949, pp. 250–266.

Hyde Park.[64] Hyde Park was then an exclusive suburban residential district adjacent to Chicago. A $15,000 rendering plant, with the growth of population, came to be entirely surrounded by residences; the Supreme Court sustained a decision of the highest state court compelling its abandonment as an offensive nuisance, even though plants engaged in other businesses were allowed to remain.

In 1855 the Supreme Court of New Hampshire upheld a statute which delegated the regulation of "quasi-nuisances" to municipalities, under which one of the cities of the state prohibited bowling alleys within twenty rods of any dwelling, store, shop, or church; bowling alleys conducted within that distance were to be considered nuisances.[65] A quasi-nuisance was defined as one which might become a nuisance by the manner in which it was conducted; the fact of a nuisance, it was pointed out, depended upon when, where, and how the alleys were conducted. This doctrine is one which applies to dance halls, night clubs, or tap rooms.

The third type of nuisance includes those which in their nature may be nuisances, but with regard to which there may be honest difference of opinion. This type is best illustrated, perhaps, by the numerous cases growing out of attempts to enforce billboard regulations and zoning ordinances. The early decisions on billboards were apt to be adverse to such regulations,[66] but later decisions have been more favorable. A leading case was decided by the Supreme Court in 1917. Chicago had provided by ordinance that if a billboard were to be erected, the advertising company must first secure the consent of a majority of the property frontage on both sides of the street in the block in which the billboard was to be erected. In Thomas Cusack Company v. Chicago, the Court held that such billboards might be dangerous to the safety and decency of the district, and that the ordinance was a reasonable regulation, and therefore constitutional.[67]

Zoning. In the state courts, zoning regulations likewise met with difficulties in the early days. In 1911 the Supreme Court of California, in Ex parte

[64] 97 U.S. 650, 1878; in this connection see the somewhat similar brickyard case, J. C. Hadacheck v. C. E. Sebastian, Chief of Police of the City of Los Angeles, 239 U.S. 394, 1915, but an airport, landing field, or flying school is not a nuisance per se, and can be regarded as such only if it is operated in such a manner as to interfere with the comfort of adjoining property owners; see Batcheller et al. v. Commonwealth *ex rel.* University of Virginia, 10 S. E. (2nd) 529 (Virginia, 1940). The following types of business have frequently been held to be offensive trades:

Rendering works	Fish handling plants	Tanneries
Soap works	Glue works	Varnish works
Slaughter houses	Gas works	Rubber works
Oil refineries	Breweries and distilleries	Smelters

[65] State v. Noyes, 30 N. H. 279, 1855, cited by Mott, Rodney L., *Due Process of Law*, pp. 315 and 571.

[66] See, for instance, City of Passaic v. Patterson Bill Posting, Advertising and Sign Painting Company, 72 N. J. Law, 285, 1905.

[67] 242 U.S. 526, 1917; in 1943, the billboard decision of the Vermont Supreme Court has been described as making history in billboard control. See Kelbro, Inc., v. Myrick, Secretary of State, *et al.*, 30 Atl. Rpts. (2), 527, 1943.

Quong Wo,[68] discharged an application for a writ of habeas corpus entered by one Quong Wo. Los Angeles had by ordinance established seven industrial districts, and declared the rest of the city to be a residential area. In the residential district, it was forbidden to maintain any stone crusher, rolling mill, carpet-beating establishment, fireworks or soap factory; or any factory using mechanical power; or any hay barn, wood or lumber yard, public laundry or washhouse; or to establish anew any hospital, asylum for feeble-minded, wine or brandy manufactory, or blacksmith shop (existing ones being unaffected). Quong Wo had continued to operate a laundry, his lease upon which, at the time of his arrest, had two years to run. By 1925 the Supreme Court of Illinois, in the City of Aurora v. Burns,[69] was willing to affirm the decree of a lower court, enforcing a zoning ordinance adopted by Aurora, under the Illinois general zoning law. The defendant, Burns, was enjoined from erecting and maintaining a grocery store in a part of Aurora zoned as B residential district by the local ordinance.

Since 1909 the Supreme Court has upheld a number of acts of this character, in important decisions. In Welch v. Swasey et al.[70] it was held that regulations with respect to the height of buildings and their mode of construction in cities, made by legislative enactment for the safety, comfort, or convenience of the people, and for the benefit of property owners generally, are valid if the height and conditions provided for can be plainly seen not to be unreasonable or inappropriate. Later, in 1926, in the Village of Euclid, Ohio, et al. v. Ambler Realty Company,[71] the Court said that the power to forbid the erection of particular buildings or of buildings for particular use is to be determined not by abstract considerations of buildings or use, but by considerations in connection with circumstances and locality. If the validity of the legislative classification for zoning purposes is debatable, the legislative judgment must be allowed to control; the fact that the ordinance has the effect of diverting industrial development along other lines than it might have been expected to follow does not render it invalid. To be declared unconstitutional, the ordinance must be clearly arbitrary and without substantial relation to the public health, safety, morals, et cetera. Unless such conditions exist, a zoning ordinance does not violate the due process clause, or the equal protection clause of Amendment XIV, or similar provisions to be found in the constitutions of the states.

Zoning is not, or need not be, solely a matter of concern to municipalities. Nearly twenty years ago, Wisconsin county boards of supervisors pioneered a new and significant development in the regulation and control of

[68] 161 Cal. 220, 1911.

[69] 319 Ill. 84, 1925; see Babcock, Richard F., "The Illinois Supreme Court and Zoning: a Study in Uncertainty," *University of Chicago Law Review*, Autumn 1947, pp. 87–105.

[70] 214 U.S. 91, 1909; for a recent discussion of this problem, see Sayre, Paul, "Aesthetics and Property Values: Does Zoning Promote the Public Welfare?" American Bar Association *Journal*, June 1949, pp. 471–472, 529 ff.

[71] 272 U.S. 365, 1926.

rural land in the sparsely settled sections of the state. The program requires careful land classification, full public discussion and understanding, but as a result, the rural zoning ordinances adopted provide a means of reducing local government expenditures, guiding and directing new settlers to good farm lands, making the best use of all the land, and developing new sources of taxable wealth. Costs are kept down by avoiding construction and maintenance of unnecessary roads, avoiding either small one-room schools or excessive school bus transportation costs, and in other ways. Here, with fullest participation of local residents, is a kind of Resettlement Administration.[72]

Advertising Billboards. Thirty years ago, the billboard problem did not exist. There were very few well-paved rural highways and a relatively small number of motor vehicles in use. Roadside advertising became profitable only with the growth of a vast network of hard surfaced roads. Its volume now totals more than $50,000,000 and its growth is greater than that of any other form of advertising, including radio. In Alleghany County, Pennsylvania, one advertising company alone owns 3,000 standard size billboards. On U.S. Route 1 north of Philadelphia, a motorist traveling at fifty miles per hour passes signs at the rate of one a second. There are 1,800 signs in a sixteen-mile stretch on U.S. Route 1 just east of New York, or 112 per mile. Going south on Route 1, a motorist on the 28.5 miles of the Baltimore-Washington Boulevard passes 2,450 billboards and signs. On 300 miles of Route 1 in Florida, outside of towns, there are more than 1,000 billboards, 6,000 signboards, and 14,000 signs on trees and business places. These figures show a 100 per cent increase within a six-year period.[73] For many years, the use of the police power for aesthetic purposes was usually frowned upon by the courts, on the ground that such interests had no substantial relation to the public welfare. Where other grounds existed, such regulations were upheld even though they were in part motivated by aesthetic considerations. That beauty might have some part in public welfare was first recognized in eminent domain proceedings, and more recently in cases arising out of zoning regulations. The ground for a more liberal and progressive attitude toward such attempts at the exercise of the police power was broken by the Supreme Court in Packer Corporation v. State of Utah,[74] which upheld the constitutionality of a Utah statute prohibiting the advertising of tobacco in any form on billboards, street car signs, or placards. While other questions were involved in this case, and while it cannot be denied that a moral consideration may have weighed heavily in the minds of the members of the legislature, the aesthetic aspects of the measure cannot be denied.

[72] See, for a good account, Rowlands, W. A., "Zoning Is Shaping the Destiny of Wisconsin's Undeveloped Areas," *Better Roads*, November 1949, pp. 23–26.

[73] Survey conducted by the National Roadside Council of New York, and cited by Thompson, Arthur H., *Billboards and Zoning* (Pennsylvania State Planning Board, Harrisburg, 1950).

[74] 285 U.S. 105, 1932.

In 1935 the Supreme Court of Massachusetts decided the famous Massachusetts billboard cases after nearly ten years of litigation.[75] This decision then became "not only the leading billboard case in the country, but also the leading case on the protection of public amenity under the police power." The important aspects of this case may be summarized as follows:

> Fifteen cases were decided, involving the general restrictions of the State Department of Public Works, somewhat more onerous restrictions of the town of Concord, and the refusal of the Department to renew the permit for the conspicuous Chevrolet roof-sign which overlooks and disfigures Boston Common and the State House, the latter refusal being based wholly on considerations of "taste and fitness." The regulations and the public authorities are sustained in every particular.
>
> In barest outline the decision covers the following points, among others: (1) The billboard companies may be compelled to relocate their boards in accordance with the regulations, in spite of the expense, without compensation. (2) The billboard business is in a class by itself and may be regulated as such under the police power. (3) One basis for its regulation is the safety of travelers. There is danger both from obstruction of view and distraction of attention. Inattention causes accidents. Billboards cause inattention. (4) The regulations are also legal in that they are designed to protect travelers from the annoyance of commercial propaganda. The traveler has a right "to a peaceful and unannoyed journey." (5) Scenic beauty contributes a highly important factor to the welfare of the state; "to preserve such landscape from defacement promotes the public welfare and is a public purpose." To this end advertising on private property within public view may be controlled. . . . (6) In a town of the character of Concord the restrictions may legitimately include and apply to business districts as well as to the others, without special exceptions or special concessions to the billboard business in business districts. (7) The sign overlooking Boston Common may be refused a permit upon the sole ground that it is "an inappropriate and obnoxious intrusion into that locality," without regard to considerations of safety, health, or morals. Considerations of "taste and fitness" are sufficient to exclude. (8) The effect of the 1918 amendment to the Massachusetts Constitution was to overrule a decision of the Supreme Court in 1905 limiting the police power of the State in its control over outdoor advertising. The police power over this subject is now complete. (9) The regulations in question are also wholly in accord with the Federal Constitution.[76]

Billboard laws of one sort or another have been enacted in nearly half of the states, aimed both at safety and at aesthetic considerations. Twenty-one states regulate outdoor advertising to some extent. Twenty prohibit posting of signs without the permission of the owner — which offers little determent to their erection. Eight impose curbs on untrue or misleading claims in such advertising, while others have miscellaneous regulations. Twelve appear to have no legislation whatever on the subject.

[75] General Outdoor Advertising Company, Inc., et al., v. Department of Public Works, 193 N. E. 799, 1935. See also the Vermont case, cited above, and for an excellent study, the Illinois Legislative Council, *Billboard Control* (Springfield, 1944).

[76] Bard, Albert S., "Massachusetts Supreme Court Protects Public Amenities in Billboard Decision," *National Municipal Review*, February 1935, p. 117, and later, "Courts Expand Scope of Police Power Regulation," *ibid.*, May 1942, pp. 280–281.

In California, for instance, regulations of the Department of Public Works, issued in accordance with the provisions of the motor vehicle code, prohibit display advertising within any right of way, or near a right of way when it might either be mistaken for a traffic direction sign or otherwise distract or confuse the motorist. Illuminated displays may not be placed on a building or on the same parcel of land occupied by a business, nor in an incorporated village, town, or business district. Flashing lights and displays containing reflector units or reflecting elements are likewise prohibited.[77]

These laws, which usually regulate the size of billboards and provide for setbacks from the highways varying from 50 to 200 feet, according to their size, have not accomplished the purposes for which they were intended. Every billboard is licensed for a small fee, varying from $1 to $4. These small fees, based on cost of administration rather than the production of revenue, tend to discourage the erection of small signs but have no effect upon the large ones. Although there would appear to be no legal barrier to setting the fees high enough to discourage the erection of the larger signs,[78] the most effective method of clearing the highways of billboards would be to zone all the highways.

SELECTED REFERENCES

Bowden, Aneta, and Gould, George, *Summary of State Legislation Requiring Premarital and Prenatal Examinations for Syphilis*, Second Edition (American Social Hygiene Association, New York, 1944), and Gould, George, *Laws Against Prostitution and Their Use* (American Social Hygiene Association, New York, 1942).

Everstine, Carl N., *Regulation of Fireworks*, and Supplement (Maryland Legislative Council, Baltimore, 1940).

Illinois Legislative Council, *Billboard Control* and *State Regulation of Firearms* (Springfield, 1944 and 1946, respectively); and Thompson, Arthur H., *Billboards and Zoning* (Pennsylvania State Planning Board, Harrisburg, n.d.).

New York State Joint Legislative Committee for the Study of the Pari-Mutuel System, *Report* (Legislative Document No. 69, Albany, 1941).

Ploscowe, Morris, and Lukas, Edwin J., Eds., "Gambling," *Annals*, May 1950, entire volume.

Rhyne, Charles S., *Municipal Control of Noise: Sound Trucks, Sound Advertising, Aircraft, Unnecessary Noises, Model Ordinance Annotated* (National Institute of Municipal Law Officers, Washington, 1948).

[77] These regulations are printed in full in *California Highways and Public Works*, May–June 1947, p. 17.

[78] See St. Louis Poster Advertising Company v. St. Louis, 249 U.S. 269, 39 S. C. 274, 63 L. E. 599, 1919, cited by Thompson, *op. cit.*, on whose conclusions this paragraph is based; also "Billboards — a Nation-Wide Problem," *Better Roads*, January 1951, pp. 33–35, 42.

PART SIX

Intergovernmental Relations

The Federal system was created with the intention of combining the different advantages which result from the magnitude and the littleness of nations; and a glance at the United States of America discovers the advantages which they have derived from its adoption. . . . The Federal system rests upon a theory which is complicated, at the best, and which demands the daily exercise of a considerable share of discretion on the part of those it governs.

— ALEXIS DE TOCQUEVILLE

21

Local Government

Until very recently, in every period of American politics there was at least one unit of government which functioned badly and the study of which was largely neglected. For some years following the Civil War — indeed until after the beginning of the present century — the states were in somewhat this position; the reconstruction of these units did not begin until 1917. In 1887, when Bryce published the first edition of his *American Commonwealth*, he made the statement that the government of our cities represented the one conspicuous failure in the American governmental system. This judgment was supported in the early years of the present century by the literature of the muckrakers, of which Lincoln Steffens's *The Shame of the Cities* is perhaps best known. The reflections which these writers cast upon American municipal government were well deserved; since then, however, enormous progress has been made both in research in municipal government and in the improvement of municipal administration. In fact, this progress has been so great that there need be no hesitancy in asserting that, if there are still within the United States municipalities whose governments are dishonest and inefficient, these cities have such governments because they do not want any other kind. Our knowledge of the problems of municipal government and administration is sufficient to enable us to provide honest and efficient government for any city that wants it.

In 1917 Henry S. Gilbertson published a volume on American county government, the subtitle of which was "The Dark Continent of American Politics."[1] This indictment was also well deserved; it is only in the recent past that any serious study has been made of the problems of county government, or any serious effort by county officers to improve the standards of administration. There is now a steady stream of surveys and research studies issuing from the press, and political scientists are beginning to give the subject the attention it deserves. While some improvements have resulted from these efforts, much work still remains to be done. The judgment which Mr. Gilbertson applied to counties may still be applied with perfect accuracy to the

[1] Gilbertson, Henry S., *The County* (National Short Ballot Organization, New York, 1917).

smaller units of rural local government, the towns and townships, villages, boroughs, and districts.

History of American Local Government

Before undertaking an analysis of the various forms of organization of local government, one must be familiar with certain essential facts concerning the origin and development of local institutions. It is well known that the town originated in, and became characteristic of, the New England area. There were a number of definite and rather obvious reasons for this fact. The country was for the most part rocky, if not mountainous; the soil was thin and poor; the climate severe. In addition, the land was densely wooded, which constituted a serious hindrance to agriculture as well as a source of danger from Indians and wild animals. Taken together, these conditions present abundant justification for the small and compact forms of settlement which characterized the New England region, and for the town meeting form of government which developed in them. At a later date, the continued concentration of population in small and compact communities was further encouraged by the development of manufacturing.[2]

Just as the town, with its town meeting, came to be the prevailing form of local government in New England, so the county form came to predominate in the South. Again, there were definite reasons to account for this development. The South was from the beginning an agricultural area; the crops which early achieved a position of importance — cotton, indigo, rice, and tobacco — were all of a type requiring the cultivation of large areas of land. Under these circumstances the plantation system developed, in sharp contrast to the densely populated communities in the North. In addition, the southern settlers had, except for the five tribes in the Far South, no serious danger from the Indians at any time. Under these circumstances, therefore, a broader and more extensive unit of local government was both natural and necessary. The county, in which a number of plantations were grouped together into a single unit for purposes of government, came to be the dominating type. In the West, where settlement was sparse, the same form became prevalent.[3]

Interesting questions present themselves in those areas in which these two types came in conflict, or at least in contact. In general it may be said that the importance of each of these units varies directly in proportion to

[2] This classification is based on Porter, Kirk H., *County and Township Government in the United States*, Chapter 4 (Macmillan, New York, 1922). Only the six New England states are included in this first group. For a good brief summary, see Tooke, Charles W., "Progress of Local Government, 1836–1936," in *Law: A Century of Progress*, Vol. II, pp. 105–143 (New York University Press, 1937).

[3] Porter, *op. cit.* The states in the South and Far West group follow (townships exist in those states whose names appear in italics, but they are merely justice of the peace districts and do not possess the characteristic township organization): Alabama, Arizona, *California*, Colorado, Delaware, Florida, Georgia, Idaho, Kentucky, Louisiana, Maryland, Mississippi, *Montana*, *Nevada*, New Mexico, *North Carolina*, Oregon, *South Carolina*, Tennessee, Texas, Utah, Virginia, Washington, West Virginia, and Wyoming.

the distance from the area of its origin. That is to say, the county form steadily diminishes in importance as one travels north along the Atlantic coast; conversely, the town diminishes in importance as one travels south along this coast. The contact of these two major forms has resulted in the development of two interesting hybrid forms in New York and Pennsylvania. In these states both the town and the county exist, and in both of them both types of unit are important. In New York, however, the town is more important than the county, while in Pennsylvania the county is more important than the township.[4]

It is important to note the results of the contact of these various forms of local government with the settlement of the western country. In general, these forms were carried due west with little or no modification. The settlers in the western country invariably set up the same general type of local government to which they had previously become accustomed. This is, of course, in harmony with the thesis of the late Professor Turner with regard to the significance of the frontier in American history.[5] At the same time no one should assume that these forms developed without themselves being influenced by the frontier. As early as 1787, when the Northwest Ordinance was passed, the practice was begun of laying out the land in a very artificial way (for land in the West was more extensive and in general more level) in township units six miles square. This practice was continued under the present government, beginning with the admission of Ohio in 1803. Each township consisted of thirty-six sections, one mile square; from the beginning, one of these — and later two — was reserved for school purposes. When there developed within one of these townships a settlement of 500 or more persons, it might be incorporated as a village; a settlement of 1000 or more might be incorporated as a city. In the course of time multitudes of special districts for roads, schools, fire, water, sanitation, lighting, drainage and sewage, and utilities were set up. School and road districts were the earliest to be established.

The Units of Local Government

Until about two decades ago, nobody knew how many units of local government there were in the United States. The Division of Governments, United States Bureau of the Census, made the first survey in 1932, reporting a total of 182,651 units. Professor William Anderson in 1934 found approximately 181,000 units of all types. Subsequent surveys have shown a consistent decline; summary figures for surveys at ten-year intervals are shown in a

[4] *Ibid.* The North Central group includes Illinois, Michigan, Nebraska, New Jersey, New York, and Wisconsin, while the South Central group includes Arkansas, Indiana, Iowa, Kansas, Minnesota, Missouri, North Dakota, Ohio, Oklahoma, Pennsylvania, and South Dakota.

[5] See Goodman, A. Bristol, "Westward Movement of Local Government," *Journal of Land and Public Utility Economics*, February 1944, pp. 20–34, and succeeding articles in this series.

table below, while in the table on page 749, the distribution of the various types of units by states for the 1951 survey is also shown.[6]

Minor discrepancies in the findings of different surveys may be explained by the fact that there are no generally accepted criteria for determining what is and what is not a unit of government. As Professor Anderson pointed out,

Governmental Units in the United States, 1932, 1942, and 1951 *

TYPE	1932	1942	1951
United States Government	1	1	1
States	48	48	48
Counties	3,062	3,050	3,049
Municipalities	16,442	16,220	16,677
Townships	19,978	18,919	17,338
School districts	128,548	108,579	70,452
Special districts	14,572	8,299	11,900
Totals	182,651	155,116	119,465

* United States Bureau of the Census, *Governmental Units in the United States, 1932, 1942, 1951.*

State of Illinois — Number of Governmental Units, 1932, 1942, and 1951

TYPE	1932	1942	1951
States	1	1	1
Counties	102	102	102
Townships and towns	1,444	1,434	1,152
Cities and villages	1,129	1,137	1,418
School districts	11,993	12,138	4,580
Special districts	1,673	1,042	1,341
Totals	16,342	15,854	8,594

the concept of a "unit of government" had nowhere been legally or officially defined. After listing and discussing a series of seven essential characteristics, he suggests, as a summary of these characteristics, the following:

> A unit of government may be defined as a resident population occupying a defined area that has a legally authorized organization and governing body, a separate legal identity, the power to provide certain public or governmental services, and a substantial degree of autonomy including legal and actual power to raise at least a part of its own revenue.

The Original Units. The most important local units are the counties and cities, whose organization and administration are considered briefly in the

[6] United States Bureau of the Census, *Governmental Units in the United States, 1932, 1942, 1951*; see also Anderson, William, *The Units of Government in the United States* (Public Administration Service, Chicago, 1934; revised, 1945).

chapter which follows. The smaller units include the towns, townships, villages, boroughs, and special districts for schools, highways, and a wide variety of other purposes. Most of the states have, obviously, far too many separate and independent units. Illinois is (except for its excessive number of school districts, which is now in process of being reduced) typical of the midwestern states; the table on page 746 contains a breakdown of the figures for that state for the same three years. The special districts are for roads, parks, sanitary purposes, forest preserves, fire protection, mosquito abatement, and public health.

It is not necessary for the present purpose to engage in a detailed discussion of the organization and functioning of these various local units. It is appropriate, however, that some mention be made of the states in which these forms exist, and the purposes for which they are employed. Most important is the township, which exists generally in Indiana, Iowa, Kansas, Michigan, Minnesota, New Jersey, New York, Ohio, Pennsylvania, and Wisconsin. There appears below an organization chart of town government in New York; it may be noted that the town in New York corresponds to the township in other states and has a similar structure. Officials appointed by the town board in addition to the health officer may include constables, election officials, and a welfare officer.

Organization of Town Government in New York *

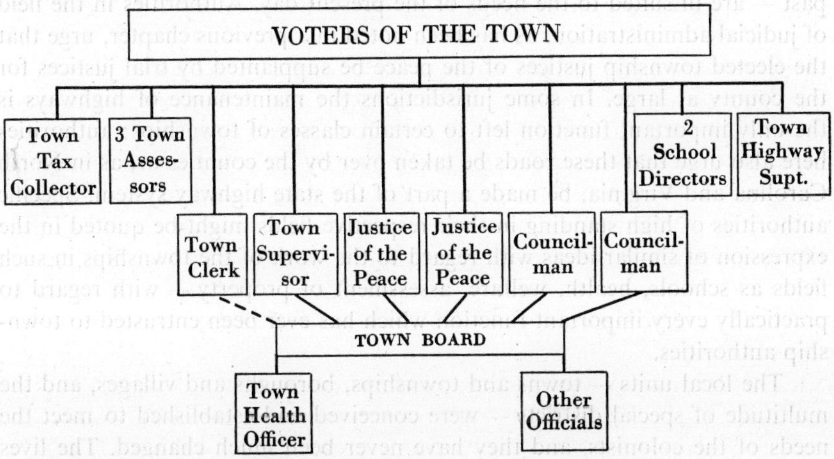

* From Catherwood, M. P., and others, *Rural Government in New York*, revised by A. E. Lutz (New York State College of Agriculture, Ithaca, 1947).

In another group of states township organization is spotty. In Illinois there are sixteen counties in the southern part of the state which have no townships; in Missouri less than one fourth and in Nebraska less than one third of the counties have township organization. In North and South Dakota some townships have been organized for school purposes; in Oklahoma townships exist in less than half of the counties. In a third group of states the township exists in name, but it does not possess political organization analogous to that of the typical midwestern township. In Arkansas, townships serve primarily as judicial districts; in California they are called judicial townships; in North Carolina they are used for purposes of assessment. Similar conditions exist in Montana, Nevada, and South Carolina.

The fourth group of states includes those in which the township generally does not exist at all; here the primary districts of government are known by other names, as follows:

Beats — Mississippi
Civil districts — Tennessee
Election precincts — Alabama, Colorado, Florida, Idaho, Maryland, New Mexico, Oregon, Utah, Washington, and Wyoming
Election precincts, Justices' precincts, and School districts — Arizona
Justices' precincts, and Commissioners' precincts — Texas
Militia districts — Georgia
Police jury wards — Louisiana
Representative districts — Delaware

In a fifth and final group are found the states in which the New England town is still preserved — Connecticut, Massachusetts, Rhode Island, and, except for certain localities, the other three New England states.[7]

Need for Consolidation. There is a substantially unanimous agreement among students of government that these tiny units — relics of an age long past — are ill suited to the needs of the present day. Authorities in the field of judicial administration, as has been noted in a previous chapter, urge that the elected township justices of the peace be supplanted by trial justices for the county at large. In some jurisdictions the maintenance of highways is the only important function left to certain classes of townships; authorities here also urge that these roads be taken over by the counties or, as in North Carolina and Virginia, be made a part of the state highway system. Specific authorities of high standing in their respective fields might be quoted in the expression of similar ideas with regard to the work of the townships in such fields as schools, health, welfare, assessment of property — with regard to practically every important function which has ever been entrusted to township authorities.

The local units — towns and townships, boroughs and villages, and the multitude of special districts — were conceived and established to meet the needs of the colonists, and they have never been much changed. The lives of the people, owing to developments in science and in the useful arts, have

[7] New Hampshire, except Carroll County with two locations, and Coos County with eight grants, six purchases, six townships, and three locations; Vermont, except several unorganized townships and divisions known as grants and gores; Maine, except a number of plantations, townships, grants, gores, surpluses, and tracts. By some accident, a single town exists in Pennsylvania. See *Town Management in New England*, which gives the experience of nearly fifty towns (National Municipal League, New York, 1940); Citizens' Committee Survey, *Town Government; Organization and Administration* (Greenwich, Connecticut, June 1951).

Number of Governmental Units, by State: 1951

STATE	ALL GOVERNMENTAL UNITS[1]	LOCAL GOVERNMENTS EXCEPT SCHOOL DISTRICTS					SCHOOL DISTRICTS[3]
		Total	*Counties*[2]	*Municipalities*	*Townships and towns*	*Special districts*	
United States..	119,465	48,964	3,049	16,677	17,338	11,900	70,452
Alabama........	531	422	67	300	.....	55	108
Arizona.........	379	107	14	44	.....	49	271
Arkansas	1,156	733	75	380	.....	278	422
California	3,774	1,666	57	304	.....	1,305	2,107
Colorado	1,948	597	62	243	.....	292	1,350
Connecticut	363	359	8	33	152	166	3
Delaware	70	54	3	50	.....	1	15
Dist. of Columbia	2	2	....	1	.....	1	.....
Florida	619	551	67	284	.....	200	67
Georgia.........	905	717	159	478	.....	80	187
Idaho	912	599	44	187	.....	368	312
Illinois	8,594	4,013	102	1,152	1,418	1,341	4,580
Indiana	3,061	1,945	92	528	1,010	315	1,115
Iowa	5,810	1,156	99	933	.....	124	4,653
Kansas	7,398	2,961	105	604	1,530	722	4,436
Kentucky	762	528	120	289	.....	119	233
Louisiana	488	420	62	206	.....	152	67
Maine	642	637	16	21	494	106	4
Maryland	259	258	23	150	.....	85	.....
Massachusetts ..	585	584	12	39	312	221	.....
Michigan	6,752	1,914	83	488	1,264	79	4,837
Minnesota	9,309	2,829	87	787	1,883	72	6,479
Mississippi	699	605	82	267	.....	256	93
Missouri	7,117	2,179	114	799	329	937	4,937
Montana	1,609	321	56	120	.....	145	1,287
Nebraska	8,318	1,627	93	531	476	527	6,690
Nevada	251	83	17	15		51	167
New Hampshire .	548	319	10	12	220	77	228
New Jersey......	1,155	672	21	331	237	83	482
New Mexico	294	185	32	72		81	108
New York	4,583	2,487	57	612	932	886	2,095
North Carolina .	643	642	100	425	.....	117	.....
North Dakota ..	3,960	1,893	53	346	1,399	95	2,066
Ohio	4,002	2,499	88	898	1,359	154	1,502
Oklahoma	2,781	667	77	503		87	2,113
Oregon	1,709	637	36	210		391	1,071
Pennsylvania	5,178	2,658	66	989	1,573	30	2,519
Rhode Island....	90	89	....	7	32	50	.....
South Carolina ..	1,976	379	46	236	2	95	1,596
South Dakota ...	4,956	1,557	64	303	1,138	52	3,398
Tennessee	406	402	95	230	.....	77	3
Texas	4,031	1,538	254	713	.....	571	2,492
Utah	353	312	29	207		76	40
Vermont	415	394	14	71	239	70	20
Virginia	355	354	100	216	.....	38	.....
Washington	1,540	991	39	236	68	648	548
West Virginia	348	292	55	212		25	55
Wisconsin	7,299	1,923	71	529	1,271	52	5,375
Wyoming	529	207	23	86		98	321

[1] Includes Federal Government and the 48 States.

[2] Number of county governments excludes 54 areas corresponding to counties but having no organized county government.

[3] These figures include only those school systems which are independent of the city and county governments in their respective areas.

changed in almost every conceivable way. Small units, once necessary if government was to be accessible and convenient to citizens, have become, under modern conditions of transportation and communication, obstacles to the efficient administration of the public services. Larger units have become a practical necessity; at the same time, there must be a reallocation of the functions of government between the Federal government and the states as well as between the states and their political subdivisions. Experience has demonstrated that functions that once had to be carried on locally if they were to be performed at all cannot now be efficiently administered in such restricted areas. It is impossible to secure the services of competent, full-time salaried personnel under such conditions.

Special Districts. Evidence of the uselessness of some of these units is now being demonstrated in a novel manner. As efforts are made to organize new activities of such a nature that they must be administered locally — such activities as soil conservation, irrigation, mosquito abatement — the existence of the old units is repeatedly ignored. This ever increasing demand for governmental services, in addition to a population growth which did not always correspond to the boundaries of existing units, led to the creation of wholly new districts with different boundaries. In New York, county fire districts were established in 1880; now there are thirty different types of special districts, with a total of approximately 2,500 of them.

In California, it is estimated that more than 4,000 special districts have been organized under 100 different laws and carrying on more than thirty separate functions; these may be grouped into four major classes, based on type of function, scale of operations, and relationships with other governments, as follows[8]:

1. Agricultural Districts, for irrigation, reclamation, drainage, soil conservation, and water conservation
2. School Districts, most important both in number and in volume of expenditures
3. Quasi-Municipal Districts, to furnish municipal services to small, unincorporated communities
4. Metropolitan Districts, carrying on large-scale operations in sanitation, utilities, water, bridge and highway, parks, ports and harbors, and airports, all of which cross over numerous local government boundaries

A further illustration is to be found in the steady growth in the number of "authorities" for housing, port development, and other purposes. Truly, local government institutions are in the midst of an important period of transition.

Local Authorities. During the depression, when many governmental units had already exhausted their borrowing capacity, the special authority

[8] Scott, Stanley, and Bollens, John C., *Special Districts in California Local Government* (Bureau of Public Administration, University of California, 1949), summarized in "Special Districts in California Local Government," *Western Political Quarterly*, June 1950, pp. 233–243, and on the use of these devices in lieu of consolidation, Bollens, John C., "When Services Get Too Big," *National Municipal Review*, November 1949, pp. 498–503.

was devised for the dual purposes of evading constitutional and statutory debt limitations and of making available funds necessary to carry on capital improvements. Such an authority is a special public corporation, usually organized for a single purpose and deriving its revenues solely from receipts from the activity in which it is engaged. Its bonds are self-liquidating and tax-exempt. It has no power to tax or to levy special assessments. It is not a governmental unit in the usual sense; although it performs a governmental function, it lacks many of the powers of a municipal government. Such authorities are administered by governing boards appointed by the local units creating them.

Fairly extensive use has been made of this device in many jurisdictions. The serious financial plight of the cities in the postwar years suggests the desirability of exploring the possibility of developing self-liquidating projects at the municipal level, by this or other means. The extent to which this device has been employed in one California county in the last twenty years is shown in the table on page 752. A municipal authorities act was passed in Pennsylvania in 1935. As of January 1, 1948, there had been 128 authorities created under it; because some of these were still in the planning stage, sixty-nine were in actual operation, classifiable by type as follows:

Water — original construction, 9; acquisition, 43
Sewage — 10
Miscellaneous — 7

Data covering 1949 show that thirty-seven new ones were created during that calendar year. The device has been used by all types of units — cities, counties, townships, and boroughs — for all types of public purposes. In addition to work on water systems and sewers and sewage disposal plants, one built a combined theater and municipal building, one purchased a factory building, and another constructed a gymnasium. It is apparent that this device can be adapted to meet almost any need for a substantial public improvement in any community.[9]

General Summary. The use of special districts and local authorities developed on an extensive scale because of widespread dissatisfaction with the existing local units for general government. Many of the original units appear to be dying out. Professor Bromage reports that the town is dying in Michigan, and a similar report on the Minnesota town comes from Professor Weidner. The second-class township is dying out in Pennsylvania. The same kind of thing is doubtless true elsewhere.[10]

There were three main reasons why, in comparison, the new units seemed

[9] See Pennsylvania Joint State Government Commission, *Municipal Authorities* (Harrisburg, 1945); and Weintraub, Tina V., and Patterson, James D., *The Authority in Pennsylvania: Pro and Con* (Bureau of Municipal Research, Philadelphia, 1949).

[10] See Snider, Clyde F., "The Twilight of the Township," *National Municipal Review*, September 1952, pp. 390–396, and Spencer, Richard C., "Iowa Townships Still Here?" *ibid.*, pp. 397–399. These authors contend that these small units have outlived their usefulness, that the Bureau of the Census has dropped them, that their functions have been transferred to the counties, yet — in Iowa, at least — they continue to function.

LOS ANGELES COUNTY, CALIFORNIA

Comparison of Number of Units of Local Government in Selected Years *

Type of Unit	1932	1940	1950
School Districts (Elementary, High School, Junior College, and Unified)	160	144	119
Incorporated Cities	45	45	45
Acquisition and Improvement Districts	294	42	1
Cemetery Districts	3	3	3
Drainage Districts	11	1	None
Fire Protection Districts	28	30	21
Flood Control Districts	1	1	1
County Library Districts	1	1	1
Lighting Districts	65	64	77
Lighting Maintenance Districts	32	29	30
Mosquito Abatement Districts	None	1	2
Park, Recreation and Parkway Districts	None	2	5
Road Districts (with bonds outstanding)	91	9	None
Sanitation Districts	5	8	14
Sewer Maintenance Districts (Health and Safety Code)	39 (both)	29 (both)	30
Sewer Maintenance Districts (Streets and Highways Code)			48
Supervisorial Road Districts	5	5	5
County Water Districts	3	9	10
Metropolitan Water Districts	1	1	1
Waterworks Districts	8	12	9
County Improvement Districts (lights, water, and other)	982	368	315
Opening and Widening Districts	38	19	6
City and County Improvement Districts	5	5	48
Districts Organized Under Act of 1915	4	2	None
Garbage Disposal Districts	None	3	14
Irrigation Districts	None	6	6
Assessment Bond Refunding Districts	None	4	11
Refunding Bond Assessment Districts (Act of 1935)	None	2	3
Library Districts	None	2	2
Public Utility District	None	None	1
Total Number of Districts in County	1821	847	828

* Morosco, A. H., "Government Within Government," *Tax Digest*, February 1932, p. 42, and Holland, J. Roy, "Taxing Units in Los Angeles," *ibid.*, November 1940, p. 372; for a survey of the situation in the state as a whole, see Scott and Bollens, *op. cit.*

attractive. Although some of them use county and city boundaries, it was generally believed that none of the existing units were suitable for the purpose at hand. The second reason — the financial one, involving the effort to escape from or to evade existing constitutional or statutory tax or debt limits — has already been mentioned. The third reason was to secure better admin-

istration and to "free the service from politics." But in special districts, as well as in units of general government, some are and some are not free from politics. The special district has no magic charm for dispelling politics, as the Henry-Kerwin study of special school districts well demonstrates.

New districts and authorities have been created in many cases in a more or less haphazard manner, without regard to future consequences, and without any effort to establish guiding principles or standards. In 1943, however, in vetoing a bill to create a parking authority in New Rochelle, Governor Dewey applied four tests which appear to be generally applicable [11]:

1. Does the service to be performed require such new techniques and methods that it is beyond the scope of the conventional agencies of government?
2. Can the service be made self-supporting?
3. Does the area to be served extend beyond the boundaries of the governmental unit which otherwise might provide the service?
4. Do constitutional debt limitations stand in the way of providing the service proposed?

Professor Fesler has suggested that the cycle has been about completed. Although some of the older units have been abandoned, new ones have frequently been substituted for them; these new units are now proving to be as bad as or worse than the evils they were created to avoid. If one wanted to return to the original units, what assurance is there — asks Professor Fesler — that they are now better able to perform their duties than they were when the special-district movement began?

Almost without exception these special districts start as single-purpose units, but they often acquire additional functions, as in the case of Montgomery County, Maryland, water, sewage, and refuse collection, and the now numerous programs and projects of the Port of New York Authority. Many of them acquire half a dozen or more functions. They might hold promise if they could acquire sufficient functions to become units of general government, but such a development seems most improbable. As things stand, the units of general government have fairly adequate powers but are administratively weak; the special districts with new functions and special projects in which there is a good deal of public interest, have only fragments of authority. Hence the lack of coordination of local government services is just as great now as it was before. Only the organizational pattern has been changed.

Original Functions of Local Government

The functions of local government — and the functions of the different units are sufficiently alike so that they may be discussed in general — are of two fairly distinct types. There are the original functions which local agencies have traditionally been expected to perform,[12] while in a second

[11] Cited by Caldwell, Lynton K., *New York Government and Administration* (Crowell, New York, 1953, in American Commonwealths Series).

[12] This list was originally based upon Porter, *op. cit.*, Chapter 6, but has been extensively modified since.

group, to be considered later, there are an increasing number of newer functions growing out of the concept of the service state.

1. *Protection of Life and Property.* Maintenance of the peace has throughout our history been regarded as a function of local government. The colonial governments never maintained a police force, the Federal government has never maintained one, and until recently only a limited number of the states have done so. At the present time all cities maintain police forces of their own, while in the rural districts the practice of maintaining such forces is increasing. Some experiments have been made with the county constabulary plan. In the more backward districts the enforcement of the law still rests largely in the hands of the sheriff, the constable, and the coroner, antiquated and unsatisfactory though this arrangement is.[13] The character of modern crime and racketeering is making it increasingly urgent that problems of law enforcement be handled by larger units with better and more adequately trained personnel. Thus greater effort is being made by the states in crime control, and the Federal government has developed facilities for the handling of crime problems of an interstate character. This development is in line with long established practice in European countries, where crime control is regarded as a national rather than a local function.

2. *Judicial Functions.* The administration of justice has always been, and is still, a major function of local government. In fact, the origin of county government in some states is to be attributed largely to this function; all of the original constitutional county officers had duties relating to it. The quality of justice received by the minor offenders against the criminal law and by the small claims litigant under the civil law is, in fact, the kind of justice which the majority of the people receive. These cases must be handled locally. If the parties to them receive a square deal, it is evident that a large percentage of those who become involved in court proceedings at all are receiving a square deal. It is also obvious that if the intermediate and appellate courts are of the very highest quality, they can deal with only a very small percentage of the total number of cases in which proceedings are instituted.

[13] See Palmer, Ben W., "The Vestigial Sheriff: the Shrunken Giant of the Present Day," American Bar Association *Journal*, May 1950, pp. 367–369. Governor Tom J. Terrel of Arkansas favored the abolition of the game and fish commission and the transference of law enforcement duties to the sheriffs and constables. He denied any intention of relaxing the enforcement of these laws in a rather humorous statement to the legislature, contained in his Inaugural Address, January 14, 1925:

> I would not relax at all the laws now on our statute books for the protection of either our fish or our game. I would rather strengthen those laws. But I see no reason why there should be a special set of officers to enforce these fish and game laws. Are the laws that prohibit the killing of fish and game at certain seasons more important than the laws that prohibit the killing of human beings? We have no commission or special wardens to enforce the laws against murder. Are the lives of the fox-squirrels, the jack-rabbits and the goggle-eyed perch of more importance to the State than the lives of the people themselves? Why cannot our sheriffs and their deputies and our constables and their deputies be depended upon to enforce our fish and game laws just as they are depended upon to enforce the laws for the protection of the lives of

Not only must the quality of the work be good, but it is essential that the courts be convenient and easily accessible to all citizens. The whole theory of the common law, with its minor courts and its jury system, is based upon the belief that the citizen can and should have his disputes adjudicated in a fair and equitable manner, with the aid of his neighbors. In more than 300 years of national history Americans have not departed from this belief, and it seems unlikely that they will. This does not mean that the size of the local units may not be enlarged, nor a more adequate supervision of their work be established; in fact, it seems highly desirable that both of these things be done.

In all states the settlement of estates is administered as a local function by such officers as the register of wills, the probate judge, the surrogate, or the judges of the Orphans' Court. The purpose is twofold: to see that the property of deceased persons is disposed of in accordance with provisions of the will, where such exists; and to see that in the case of estates of persons who die intestate, the property and resources are disposed in accordance with the provisions of the law of inheritance. In connection with this work there are such additional problems as the administration of trusts and the handling of the property of minors and other persons not in the enjoyment of full legal rights.

3. *Collection of Taxes.* Tax collection always has been considered a function of local government. In recent years the authorities engaged in this work have come under supervision by state departments and agencies. There have, however, been relatively few attempts at the collection by state agencies of revenues intended for purely local use. The local assessors are subject to supervision by the state tax board or board of equalization; the local collecting officers are under bond in accordance with state law, their accounts in many cases being audited by state officials, and the form in which they shall be kept being prescribed by uniform accounting acts. It is only within the last few years, during which the states have come to rely less on the general property tax for state purposes and more upon business taxes, income taxes, inheritance taxes, motor vehicle and gasoline taxes, and the like, that the function of collecting large amounts of revenue destined for local use has been transferred from the local agencies to the states.

In some of the older states taxes are still collected on a fee basis; this procedure dates back to a time when, in the large number of units of local government and special districts which were created for a variety of purposes, it was customary to confer the taxing power upon each and to provide for a tax collecting officer. Since so many of the districts were small and the collection of taxes therefore only a part-time or temporary job, those who performed the work were paid on a fee basis rather than by salary. The conditions which have developed under this practice have been very objectionable and

our people? (Quoted by Grant, Daniel, *The Role of the Governor of Arkansas in Administration*, unpublished dissertation, Northwestern University, 1948).

have constituted a strong argument for the reorganization of local government. In one instance in Pennsylvania a few years ago a county treasurer received $34,000 for no greater exertion than receiving a check and turning it over to the State Department of Revenue. This represented the fee on the tax due on a very large inheritance; it is an extreme case, but it indicates what may happen under the fee system.

4. *Education.* Except in a few states, in which control over the school system is highly centralized, the public schools have from the very beginning been regarded as a subject of local concern. The United States Commissioner of Education pointed out in an address some years ago that there were 143,445 separate one-room schoolhouses in the several states. The number of separate school districts was almost as great, Illinois having the largest number, 12,138 in all; Kansas stood second with 8,632, Missouri third with 8,613, and New York fourth with 6,064. Ohio has only 1,655; Pennsylvania, 2,546, as of 1942.

Since World War II substantial progress has been made in bringing some semblance of order out of this chaotic situation. In 1946 the National Education Association created a National Commission on School District Reorganization, whose report, *Your School District*, was published two years later. Late that year state activity in this field had been so stimulated that, it was reported,[14] twenty-seven states were actively engaged in programs to reduce the number of districts, and fifteen had already enacted school district reorganization acts. The NEA, in a burst of enthusiasm, exclaimed that "the little red schoolhouse joins the town meetinghouse as the end of an era approaches." In 1950 the work was still in progress in many jurisdictions, it then being impossible to state exactly how much had been accomplished or what the final outcome might be.

The normal procedure involves three steps: (1) state enactment of a reorganization law; (2) a state survey to obtain the facts and develop an overall plan [15]; (3) local campaigns to arouse and inform the public, followed by a referendum to obtain popular approval before any change in the existing arrangements is made. On the basis of such procedures the number of school districts in Arkansas was cut by two thirds, thereby achieving not only greater efficiency but higher standards.[16] The California Commission on School Dis-

[14] Wochner, R. E., "School District Reorganization Activity in the United States," *School Board Journal*, September 1948, pp. 25–26.

[15] Illustrative surveys: California Commission on School Districts, *Findings and Recommendations* (Sacramento, 1949), and subsequent progress reports; Illinois State Advisory Commission on School Reorganization, *Report* (Springfield, 1949); Joint Legislative Committee on the State Education System, *Master Plan for School District Reorganization in New York State* (Albany, 1947); Virginia Advisory Legislative Council, *Special School Districts* (Richmond, 1949; California Commission on School Districts, *A Brief Survey of School District Reorganization in the State of Washington* (Sacramento, 1949). In Pennsylvania — possibly also in other states — an excellent guide was prepared for the use of local communities: Department of Public Instruction, *A Guide to School Reorganization in Pennsylvania* (Harrisburg, 1948).

[16] Benton, E. Maxwell, "Better Schooling, Less Cost," *National Municipal Review*,

tricts reported in 1949 that in the three-year period, 1946–1949, proposals for change affecting 836 districts had been made — 754 elementary, seventy-eight high school, and four unified districts. For instance, 112 districts (all elementary except nine) had been consolidated to form nine new unified districts. In Illinois — one of the worst offenders under the old system — 217 community unit districts had been approved by the electorates concerned under the new state law. The State of Washington, whose efforts at consolidation long antedate the current effort in other states, had reduced its total number of school districts from 1,609 in 1937 to 548 in 1951. These are but a few random illustrations of changes that are taking place throughout the country.

Originally the financing of the schools was entirely a local matter; in recent years the practice of assisting the local districts with subsidy grants has been gradually extended, and this has been accompanied by an extension of state control. Nevertheless it is generally recognized that people in the communities take greater interest in the schools than they do in the other activities of local government. Rightly or wrongly they have insisted upon choosing by popular vote the members of the local school board or board of school directors; they have joined parent-teacher associations and have in other ways given evidence of a deep concern over the problems of the local schools. One of the present major problems is to find methods of developing more efficient supervision of the schools without antagonizing the people in the local districts and without causing them to lose their interest.

5. *Highway Construction and Maintenance.* The construction and maintenance of highways were originally regarded as purely a function of local government. Streets — when they were paved at all — were paved by cities, towns, and boroughs. Later the counties undertook to construct roads connecting centers of population and the county seats; and when this proved to be inadequate for the development of a well-planned system of highways, the task was undertaken by the states or by the states with the assistance of the Federal government. The construction and maintenance of the more important highway routes have therefore been transferred to the states in order to reduce the cost, secure greater efficiency, and eliminate jurisdictional disputes between local units. While there has been a definite tendency to increase the mileage in the state highway systems, there remain in most states, considerable numbers of miles of road still under the supervision of counties, boroughs, and townships. In some states there are units of local government for whose continued existence there would be no need if the road-building and maintenance function were taken over by the state highway department. Thus the local importance of this function, though originally great, has been steadily declining.

6. *Administration of Elections.* The administration of elections has been

November 1949, pp. 494–497; and Chisholm, Leslie L., "School District Reorganization Today," *State Government*, September 1952, pp. 197–199, 216.

regarded in all sections of the country as a function of local government. Where the town is the prevailing form of local government, the town has supervised elections; where the county is the prevailing form, control over elections has been entrusted to the board of county commissioners. In most states the state government possesses very limited powers of supervision over elections. The local authorities are responsible for the printing and distribution of the ballots, the determination of the number and the size of the voting districts, and the reporting of the returns after the close of the polls. In most cases the judges of election and other election officials, as well as the watchers and other functionaries, are under the control of the local party organization. Where this control is complete and effective, conditions such as those existing in the so-called "Zero Wards" in New York, Philadelphia, and other large cities develop, illustrations of which were presented in an earlier chapter.

7. *Clerical and Recording Functions.* From time immemorial the clerical and recording function has been a major responsibility of local government, performed either by the town clerk or by the county clerk. The duties of the latter include reports to state officers on various subjects such as marriage licenses issued and certificates returned, assessment rolls, and tax levies. He is the official record keeper of the county with regard to a variety of matters, and the custodian of all kinds of papers and records. A variety of miscellaneous duties may be imposed upon him. In addition to the county clerk, there are the clerks of the various courts, the clerk of the county board, and other clerical functionaries.

The recording of land titles was originally performed by the smaller local units but is now commonly a function of one of the county officers, either of the recorder of deeds, the abstracter of titles, or even the county clerk. The importance of having an accurate record of all transfers of land is obvious. No prudent person will purchase real estate without having a search made of the title, to make certain that the property is free from encumbrances and that the present owner is in a position to give a "clear title." These same officers may record deeds, mortgages, liens, attachments, and other instruments affecting title, and may be charged with the responsibility for maintaining a current system of indexes and abstracts thereof so that information may be readily available to citizens, businessmen, and attorneys who have need for it.

8. *Military Organization.* Students of American history are familiar with the organization and drilling of local militia units in the colonies; they recall also how, in the Revolutionary period, the armies were made up by a consolidation of these local units. Tradition has maintained a deep interest in and a strong attachment for local military units. Many people who are unfamiliar with the elaborate organization and the extensive properties held by a state for military purposes underestimate the present-day importance of military matters in the organization and conduct of local government (see Chapter 11). The attachment which the people of the communities feel

for these various military units was well illustrated by the acclaim with which they were regarded during World Wars I and II.

9. *Units for Administrative Purposes.* Just as the Federal government frequently uses the states and sometimes the counties as units in the administration of many of its activities, so the states make use of the counties and other local units for administrative purposes. This is done largely as a matter of convenience; no one would seriously contend that these local units are well adapted to this purpose, but they are in existence and it is frequently easier to use them than to undertake the task of laying out new districts which might be more suitable. Since the machinery in these units is already established, the use of it may, in an emergency, make possible a considerable saving of time, as is illustrated by experiences with relief administration during the depression. This is apt to be true of some of the newer activities of government, which, as Professor Porter observes, the local areas do not and ought not to claim as being part of their functions.

Newer Functions of Local Government

1. *Agriculture.* The promotion of agriculture was originally performed privately by local agricultural societies; later it became a state and Federal function. It is now carried on locally by the county agricultural agent, who is employed jointly by the State College of Agriculture, the United States Department of Agriculture, and the several county boards of commissioners or supervisors, and who is in charge of all extension activities carried on within the county. He works under the direction of state leaders of major phases of the program, and is administratively responsible to the extension division of the State College of Agriculture.

The duties of the county agent relate to the conservation of the soil and other natural resources, work with 4-H clubs, the securing of better livestock and crops, the marketing of farm produce, organization of groups of young farm people, control of disease and pests affecting crops and livestock, poultry raising, feed production, and assistance to the home program. The number of these agents and the exact nature of their work vary somewhat according to the needs of the state in which they serve. In Michigan, in 1941, there were seventy-three agents employed for the eighty-three counties. Of these, seven served two counties and one served four. In addition five assistant agents were employed jointly by the Bureau of Agricultural Economics and the Division of Extension Work at the State College of Agriculture.[17]

Some counties have promoted agricultural interests through feed and seed loans to farmers, the purchase and operation of terracing machinery, and the establishment and maintenance of agricultural marketing centers.

[17] Tharp, Claude R., *A Manual of County Administrative Organization in Michigan*, pp. 226–227 (University of Michigan, Bureau of Government, 1944). This is an excellent study of the organization, powers, and duties of all of the county government officers in a representative state. See also Baker, Gladys, *The County Agent* (University of Chicago Press, 1939).

An analysis of the agricultural aids provided for by the laws of one midwestern state reveals the following items: operation of limestone quarries for agricultural uses in counties where there are no privately owned quarries in operation; the mandatory appointment of a county weed commissioner; financial assistance for farm aid associations organized for the purpose of improving and advancing agricultural, domestic science, animal husbandry, horticulture, and the marketing of farm products; aid for county and district fairs for agricultural exhibits under certain conditions; and small appropriations for various other purposes such as the growing of experimental crops on county-owned lands and for the eradication of bee diseases, of bovine tuberculosis, and of Bang's disease.[18]

2. *Public Welfare.* From the earliest times poor relief was regarded as a distinctly local function. It was assumed that poverty was inevitable, and relief was provided in the form of almsgiving, as it was called, or by commitment to almshouses, poorhouses, or poor farms. In New England every town had its town poor farm. In late years there have been fundamental changes in the theory of public welfare work, the effort being made to restore needy persons to a position as self-supporting and self-respecting members of the community. County institutions and state institutions have replaced those formerly operated by the smaller units of local government, and there has been a steady increase in the amount of outdoor relief, based upon the theory that it is more satisfactory to the individual and more defensible from a social point of view to help the needy to maintain themselves in their own homes wherever possible. This is the theory of mothers' assistance, old age pensions, and other modern forms of relief. In the administration of these forms both the states and the Federal government have, since 1933, assumed a very important role. Even under such conditions it is inconceivable that the functions or the responsibility of the local units in this work can ever be eliminated.

The Social Security Act of 1935, by providing grants-in-aid for a wide variety of welfare activities, has had the two-fold effect of reducing greatly the responsibility of the local units in the whole field and of reducing the number of almshouses, while at the same time local welfare machinery has been strengthened and made uniform within the states and more or less uniform throughout the country. County departments of welfare have been established and staffed with competent, trained personnel to replace the overseers and superintendents of the poor.

The late Professor Satterfield reported that in Alabama, for example, it was found that 63 per cent of the inhabitants of county almshouses were eligible for old-age assistance. Steps were taken to find suitable homes for these residents, and by the end of 1939 the number of almshouses had been

[18] Zenor, Dean, *A Handbook for County Supervisors*, pp. 31–33 (Institute of Public Affairs, State University of Iowa, 1950); for a general discussion, see Satterfield, Millard H., "The Growth of County Functions Since 1930," *Journal of Politics*, February 1941, pp. 76–88.

reduced from sixty-three to eleven. Similar progress has been made in many other states toward closing such institutions.

3. *Public Health Work.* There are many public health functions for the performance of which local units are at least in part responsible. The fact that they frequently fail to perform these duties well does not lessen their responsibility. These are the units which must take action for the elimination of public nuisances affecting health conditions, for the collection and disposition of refuse, for the enforcement of quarantine regulations, for the keeping of vital statistics and records of the prevalence of contagious diseases. The local units are responsible, under state supervision and with the aid of one or more public health nurses, for the administration of child health and school health programs. The authority of the state departments of health has been extended so that they may intervene in, or if necessary assume complete control of, health matters in communities where the local authorities fail to function effectively.[19]

As in the public welfare field, and for the same reasons, local activities in health have increased greatly in recent years. Although Federal aid for rural health work began in 1917, the amounts were small before 1935. The increased grants since that time have resulted in a rapid increase both in the number of local health units and in the number of major health programs. In the first five years under the new legislation the number of full-time county health units grew from 594 to 1,577 — or 165.5 per cent — and growth has continued since along similar lines. Grant-in-aid programs cover tuberculosis, venereal diseases, maternal and child health, and mental health, not to mention the hospital survey and construction program. It has long been known that in each community of 5,000 population or more there should be at least one general hospital, centrally located and adequately equipped and staffed to handle emergency cases as well as routine hospital work. It appears that the Hospital Survey and Construction Act will make possible the realization of that objective.

4. *Recreation Program.* On the welfare side the increased leisure of workers means that the local units have the duty of developing recreational facilities and a program for their use, in order to assist them in making both a pleasant and profitable use of this time. The local units must extend their programs for the construction and maintenance of well-equipped playgrounds and parks within easy access of congested centers of population. School properties should be developed as community centers, being kept open and providing facilities for the use of adult groups. Such programs, of course, are expensive but much less so than is the attempt to get along without them. Engaged as it is in an effort to reduce the amount of crime, the public can scarcely afford to fail to provide pleasant, enjoyable, and socially defensible

[19] See Illinois Legislative Council, *County Health Departments* (Springfield, 1943), and Stoner, John E., and Field, Oliver P., *Public Health Services in an Indiana Defense Community* (Indiana University, Bureau of Government Research, 1942).

opportunities for the use of leisure. If such a program is neglected, there need be no surprise if many persons use this time for purposes which are socially objectionable or if they become involved in crime.

The problem of the use of leisure time involves much more than merely having fun in a city park, playground, or recreation center. It may include camping, fishing, swimming, or mountain climbing in a state park or forest, or, from a more serious angle, reading programs in a public library, study courses, or discussion groups.

5. *Library Services.* The shorter work day and work week now required for normal business and industrial activities imposes upon local authorities the responsibility for providing adult education programs under competent instructors. Such courses need not be confined to the conventional academic subjects but may include current literature, drama, art, and music appreciation; courses designed to develop an understanding of current social, economic, and political questions; and courses on technical and scientific subjects. A program of this character will certainly require larger expenditures for library purposes. As the years pass, an increasing percentage of the population will have had the opportunity for high school and college training. One of the major purposes of their formal education will have been to cultivate intellectual interests and to stimulate intellectual curiosity.

County library work was begun around 1900 but progress was slow. Availability of state and Federal funds has brought about a great extension of such services in rural areas in recent years. From 1938 to 1940 they were organized in 150 new counties, making a total of 447 at that time. In several states the state library is taking the lead in furnishing library service on a regional basis. In Vermont, for example, four regional library centers serve fourteen counties. The Tidewater Regional Library in Virginia serves ten counties. Other states in which regional library service is being rendered include Alabama, Iowa, Kentucky, New York, North Carolina, and Tennessee. Many local units, particularly in the Southern and Western states, are carrying books to the people with Bookmobile service.[20]

6. *Planning and Zoning.* Planning and zoning had their origins in the cities and spread from there to counties and rural areas, where they received great impetus from the state planning boards and during its lifetime from the National Resources Planning Board. Although county planning legislation exists in nearly half of the states, there are relatively few active over-all planning commissions. Most of those which do exist are located in California, Colorado, Florida, Idaho, Missouri, Montana, New York, North Dakota, Oregon, Tennessee, Virginia, Washington, and Wisconsin.

With many of the planning commissions, zoning is a primary interest.[21]

[20] United States Department of Agriculture, *Rural Library Service*, Farmers Bulletin No. 1847, Revised Edition (Washington, 1949).

[21] See Solberg, Erling D., *Rural Zoning in the United States* (Bureau of Agricultural Economics, Department of Agriculture, Washington, January 1952).

In California, county planning commissions have been particularly active in the control of suburban and roadside developments. For example, in San Mateo County — the California county most active in zoning — there are over 1000 miles of zoned highways where business is restricted and billboards prohibited except in established towns. Los Angeles, Marin, Santa Clara, and Santa Cruz are other California counties active in highway zoning. Other states which contain counties that have embarked on urban and highway zoning programs include Colorado, Georgia, Illinois, Maryland, Missouri, New York, and Virginia.

The control of land use in rural areas through zoning has made considerable progress in Maine, Michigan, Minnesota, and Wisconsin, while legislation authorizing zoning has been enacted in Colorado, Georgia, Indiana, Pennsylvania, Tennessee, Virginia, and Washington. In Wisconsin, which pioneered this movement in 1933, such ordinances are in effect in twenty-four counties, most of which are in cut-over regions in the northern part of the state. The purpose has been to direct agricultural settlement into the more suitable farming areas and to reduce the need for and the cost of public services in the less productive areas. Under these ordinances the counties are divided into three use-types or districts: agriculture, forestry, and recreation. By a program of public education public cooperation is enlisted in the administration of a series of little "resettlement administrations." More than 5,000,000 acres are zoned against agricultural use in these twenty-four Wisconsin counties. Similar developments have taken place in Maine, Michigan, and Minnesota.

7. *Conservation of Resources.* The beginning of the conservation movement in the states dates from the Governors' Conference called by President Roosevelt at the White House in 1908. Since then it has spread from the Federal government and the states into the local units, where land-use planning and soil conservation work are carried on under programs sponsored by the United States Department of Agriculture. The Bureau of Agricultural Economics is responsible for the land-use work in the local units, in which there are three stages: (1) organizing county agricultural committees and acquainting them with the scope and objectives of land-use planning; (2) mapping and classifying the land within the county, in order to formulate immediate and long-term plans; (3) developing a program translating the plans into action.

The adoption of state laws authorizing the creation of soil conservation districts is another of the significant developments of the last few years. Enabling legislation, first adopted in 1937, now exists in all the states. Many of these laws follow the standard act developed under the leadership of the United States Department of Agriculture and provide for the creation of soil conservation districts with power (1) to establish and administer erosion control projects, and (2) to prescribe land-use regulations for the prevention and control of soil erosion. Under these laws, regulations may be adopted requiring the retirement of highly erosive areas from cultivation and requiring the construction of terraces, check dams, dikes, ponds, ditches, and other engineering operations. Landowners may be required to observe particular methods of cultivation such as contour furrowing, strip cropping, reforestation, and similar practices. Under this legislation, 314 soil conservation districts, comprising nearly 200,000,000 acres, had been created in thirty-four states by 1941, and 1,889 districts by 1947.

The development of parks and forests may be regarded either as a phase of conservation work or as a separate function. As a result of Federal work programs during the depression era, by 1940 there were 174 county park systems in twenty-five states. While there was only one such system in Montana, in Nevada, in New Hampshire, in Ohio, in Virginia, and in Wyoming, there were twenty-one in California, thirty-six in Michigan, and thirty in Wisconsin. Other states in which counties are authorized by law to establish county park systems are Colorado, Louisiana, Mississippi, South Carolina, South Dakota, and Tennessee.

In addition to the established park systems, many counties maintain forest reservations which may be used for recreation purposes. In the survey by Professor Satterfield, already referred to, it is reported that Hancock County, West Virginia, has a forest park of about 2,400 acres. The five Illinois counties with forest preserves ranging in size from eighty-one to 33,000 acres furnish recreation facilities essentially the same as those of county parks. In New York there are over 400 county and community forests comprising nearly 200,000 acres.

8. *Rural Housing.* Long years of insufficient new construction and of depreciation of existing housing accommodations, a growing population, the lengthening of the average life-span, and the development of higher standards have brought the country face to face with an acute housing shortage. President Roosevelt, in a well-remembered phrase, noted that one third of the nation was ill-housed, ill-clothed, and ill-fed. Conditions in the rural areas are often quite as bad as those in the cities. By 1940 twenty states had passed legislation authorizing counties to undertake rural housing, under which 208 county housing authorities had been established in twelve states. In the Southern states, where rural housing conditions have been particularly inadequate, there were twenty-eight such authorities in Arkansas, 109 in Georgia, thirty-two in Mississippi.

9. *Public Utility Services.* Time was, not so long ago, when rural units had no concern with public utility services; now, like their urban counterparts, they operate water, gas, and electric services and sewage disposal plants. In Virginia, for example, such semi-urban counties as Arlington, Henrico, Washington, and others, are vested with the same powers and authority as cities and towns. They are authorized to establish and maintain water, electric, and sewer systems and to provide fire protection, garbage removal, and other services.

The electrification of rural areas, stimulated to a large extent in the Tennessee Valley by the Tennessee Valley Authority, and elsewhere by the Rural Electrification Administration and other Federal programs, has proceeded at a rapid rate in recent years. By 1940 approximately 25 per cent of all farms in the United States were wired for electric service furnished to a large extent by rural cooperatives, power districts, and municipalities. In a few states legislation has been enacted authorizing counties to acquire and operate electric distribution systems.

In order to take advantage of the surplus power available from the Tennessee Valley Authority, Mississippi in 1934 authorized counties to construct or to acquire and operate electric light and power plants, transmission lines, and such other properties necessary for the generation and distribution of electricity. Similar legislation was passed in 1935 in Alabama and Tennessee. Three Tennessee counties — Benton, Carroll, and Weakley — purchased distribution systems within their boundaries and contracted with the Tennessee Valley Authority for the purchase and resale of power. Crisp County, Georgia, acting under an amendment to the Georgia Constitution, constructed a hydroelectric dam and power plant. The system was put in operation in 1930 and now serves over 2,000 customers. Greenwood County, South Carolina, operates its own electric distribution system. Through a loan from the Rural Electrification Administration, the county constructed 193 miles of lines and in 1939 was serving 917 customers.

10. *Other Local Functions.* There are other functions, more or less miscellaneous in character, which have been developed in some jurisdictions; they serve, in a way, to illustrate the constantly expanding scope of governmental activity. Federal aid for construction projects has helped many rural communities and counties not only to obtain much needed hospital facilities but to acquire airports which in quite a few cases are jointly owned and operated by city and county.

States and cities — likewise some counties — are making sizable expenditures for advertising and publicity designed to attract tourists, vacationers, permanent settlers, and new industries. Some rural units have engaged in a number of regulatory, inspectional, and licensing activities. County boards of supervisors are usually authorized to regulate or prohibit "any kind of traveling show, rodeo, or other public display of any kind"; they inspect and certify weights and measures, license dogs, and carry on many other activities. There are county liquor stores under the North Carolina law, while tourist camps, amusement parks, and various other undertakings are now regulated by many units of rural local government.

SELECTED REFERENCES

General surveys of the units of government:

Anderson, William, *The Units of Local Government in the United States* (Public Administration Service, Chicago, 1934; revised, 1945).

Division of Governments, United States Bureau of the Census, *Governmental Units in the United States* (Washington, 1932, 1942, 1951).

Illustrative of the studies of local units that have been made in individual states:

Alabama: Reid, Joseph W., *The Units of Government in Alabama* (Bureau of Public Administration, University of Alabama, 1946).

Mississippi: Highsaw, Robert B., and Mullican, Carl D., Jr., *The Units of Government in Mississippi* (Bureau of Public Administration, University of Mississippi, 1948).

Oregon: Bureau of Municipal Research and Service, *The Units of Government in Oregon — 1941* (University of Oregon, 1943).

Texas: MacCorkle, Stuart A., *Units of Local Government in Texas* (University of Texas Press, 1941).

Useful treatises dealing with local government in general:

Lancaster, Lane W., *Government in Rural America*, Revised Edition (Van Nostrand, New York, 1952).

Porter, Kirk H., *County and Township Government in the United States* (Macmillan, New York, 1922).

Wells, Roger H., *American Local Government* (McGraw-Hill, New York, 1939).

For comprehensive studies of local government in individual states:

California: Bollens, John C., and Scott, Stanley, *Local Government in California* (University of California Press, 1951).

New York: New York State Constitutional Convention Committee, *Problems Relating to Home Rule and Local Government*, and *State and Local Government in New York*, being Vols. XI and IV, respectively, of the Committee's Report (Albany, 1938).

22

County and Municipal Government

County Government

There are in the United States more than 3000 counties; this type of governmental organization is found in every state except Rhode Island, in which counties are not organized as local governments. The number of counties varies from three in the tiny state of Delaware to 254 in Texas. Approximately half of the states have less than sixty, half more than that number. Eight have less than twenty; eight others have more than 100. In the majority of cases the number seems to bear some relation to the size of the state and to population, although there are states in which it is well known that the number is much too large. The table on page 768 gives some idea of the ranking of the states as regards the average size of their counties in square miles and the average population of their counties in thousands.

Prevailing Organization. The organization of county government has remained substantially in its original form since the days of the founding. In the western states these same county institutions were established by settlers from the East. While there are minor differences in the structure of county government in different states, the major characteristics have been much alike. In some states all counties maintain the same type of governmental organization, as in Mississippi; in others, the county law provides for the classification of counties according to population, as in Pennsylvania. In the larger counties the "row offices" are filled by full-time, salaried officials; in the smaller ones, by part-time officers paid on a fee basis. At the top of the governmental structure is found, irrespective of these differences, a county board, designated officially either as the board of county commissioners or as the board of county supervisors. In the South, where the county form originated, the former exists, consisting of three or five members who are elected by direct vote, either at large or from districts.

In the North, where the influence of the town form predominates, one finds the larger board of supervisors, the members of which are chosen by the electors, one from each town within the county. In Illinois, Michigan, New York, and Wisconsin the township serves as the unit of representation

Average Size and Average Population of the American County — 1952

AREA IN SQUARE MILES	STATES	POPULATION IN THOUSANDS	STATES
300	Georgia, Indiana, Kentucky, New Jersey	Below 10,000	Nevada, South Dakota
400	Maryland, North Carolina, Ohio, Tennessee, Virginia, West Virginia	10,000	Idaho, Kansas, Montana, Nebraska, North Dakota, Wyoming
500	Illinois, Iowa, Massachusetts, Mississippi	20,000	Arkansas, Colorado, Iowa, Kentucky, Mississippi, New Mexico, Oklahoma, Utah, Vermont
600	Connecticut, Delaware, Michigan, Missouri, Pennsylvania, South Carolina, Vermont	30,000	Minnesota, Missouri, Tennessee, Texas, Virginia, West Virginia
700	Alabama, Arkansas, Louisiana, New York, Wisconsin	40,000	Alabama, Florida, Indiana, Louisiana, North Carolina, Oregon, South Carolina, Wisconsin
800	Florida, Kansas, Nebraska	50,000	Arizona, Maine, New Hampshire
900	Minnesota, New Hampshire, Oklahoma	60,000	Washington
1,000	Texas	70,000	Michigan
1,100	South Dakota	80,000	Illinois
1,300	North Dakota	90,000	Ohio
1,600	Colorado	100,000	Delaware, Maryland
1,700	Washington	150,000	Pennsylvania, Rhode Island
1,800	Idaho, Maine	180,000	California
1,900	California	200,000	Georgia
2,600	Montana, Oregon	230,000	New Jersey, New York
2,800	Utah	250,000	Connecticut
3,900	New Mexico	330,000	Massachusetts
4,200	Wyoming		
6,500	Nevada		
8,100	Arizona		

on the county board. Where the number of towns is considerable or where there are one or more large cities, the board of supervisors may be a large, cumbersome, and unwieldy body. A large county in western New York has such a large board, constituted as indicated in the table below; Westchester County has a board with forty-seven members, Albany County one with thirty-nine.

STATE OF NEW YORK
ERIE COUNTY BOARD OF SUPERVISORS

City of Buffalo (1 from each ward)	27 members
City of Lackawanna	1 member
City of Tonawanda	1 member
Towns (1 from each town)	25 members
Total	54 members

The board in Wayne County, Michigan, has 149 members. These bodies are certainly not representative, and the duties and compensation of the members as county officers are secondary to those pertaining to their status as town officials.[1] These boards perform administrative as well as legislative functions except in those counties which employ a county manager or other type of executive officer.

In addition to the county board — however constituted — there is the long list of "row offices," including county clerk, treasurer, auditor, receiver of taxes, the board of assessors; the legal officers, including the public prosecutor, district attorney, or state's attorney, and the public defender, if such exists; the sheriff, coroner, clerks of court, recorder of deeds, superintendent of schools, health officer, and the engineer or surveyor, and an almost indeterminable number of boards.[2] All of these officers and many of the board members are still chosen, in most of the states, by direct vote of the people, as indicated in the chart on page 770 illustrating the prevailing form of county organization. The duties of these several officers are somewhat familiar; no attempt will be made here to describe the duties of the individual officers as they relate to the several functions of local government previously outlined.

Reorganization of County Government. In the last few years many studies have been made of the organization and functioning of county government, the findings of which indicate clearly that some thorough overhauling of the existing machinery is imperative. While most students have come to this conclusion, there is a considerable difference of opinion with regard to the manner in which these necessary changes should be made. Without any extensive discussion of the merits and defects of the several plans, the plans themselves are outlined here.

1. *Making the Prevailing System Work Better.* The first possibility is to leave the machinery in substantially its present form, illustrated by the chart on page 770, relying upon the selection of a better type of county officeholder and upon the stimulation of a more active and intelligent interest on the part of citizens in their county government to bring about the desired results. This seems to be far from the most desirable of the alternatives available, but it is much better than nothing and there are a few cases in which it has actually been made to work. Thus in New Castle County, Delaware, the county officers have for some time been of a higher type and the work has been done in a very creditable fashion. Reports issued by some of the officers in this county are better prepared than those issued by many state departments.

[1] New York State Commission for the Revision of the Tax Laws, *Report* on local government, pp. 67–70, Legislative Document (1935) No. 63. The reader may well study the more detailed facts of the setup of county government in his home state in their relation to the data here presented; these may usually be found in the legislative manual.

[2] See Weidner, Edward W., *The American County — Patchwork of Boards* (National Municipal League, New York, 1946).

State of New York — Typical County

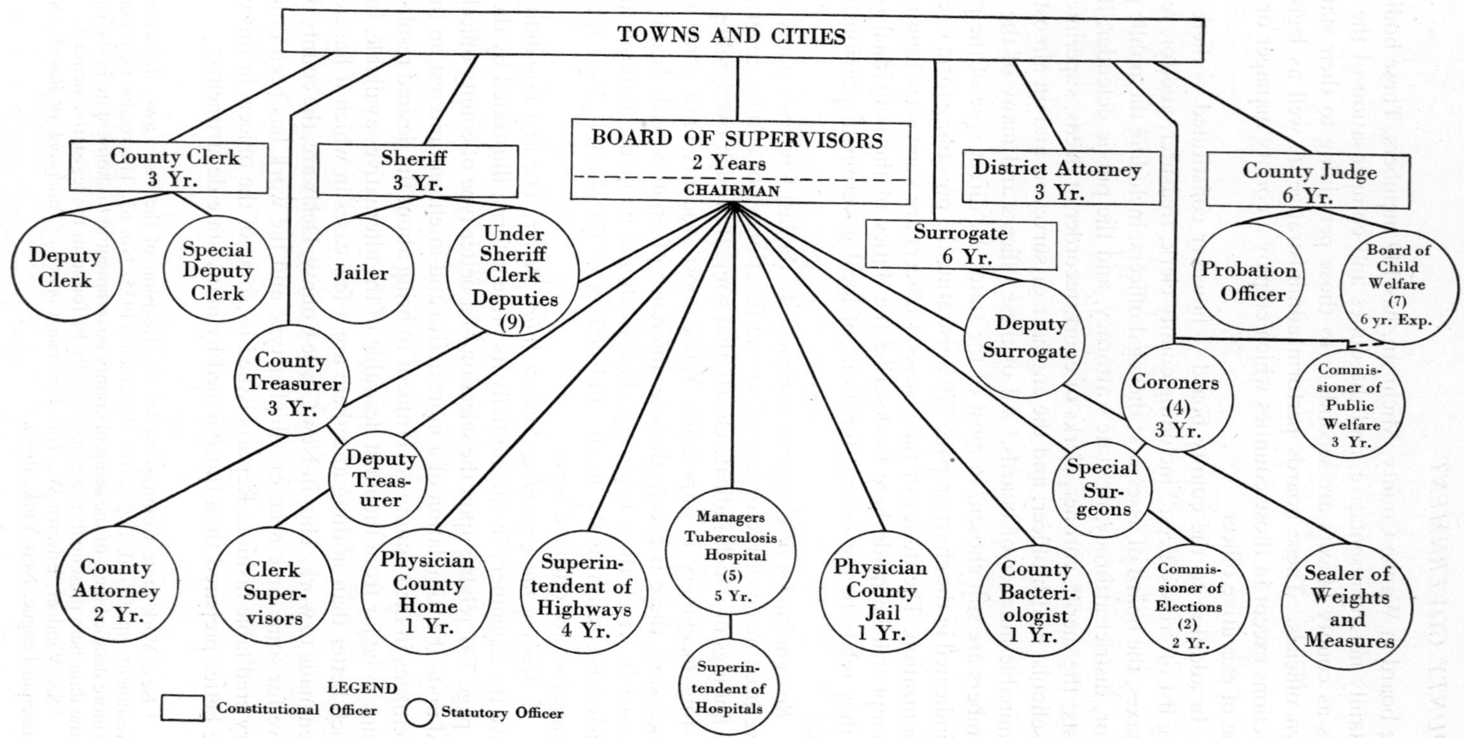
TOWNS AND CITIES
County Clerk 3 Yr.
Sheriff 3 Yr.
BOARD OF SUPERVISORS 2 Years
CHAIRMAN
District Attorney 3 Yr.
County Judge 6 Yr.
Surrogate 6 Yr.
Deputy Clerk
Special Deputy Clerk
Jailer
Under Sheriff Clerk Deputies (9)
Probation Officer
Board of Child Welfare (7) 6 yr. Exp.
Deputy Surrogate
County Treasurer 3 Yr.
Coroners (4) 3 Yr.
Commis-sioner of Public Welfare 3 Yr.
Deputy Treas-urer
Special Sur-geons
County Attorney 2 Yr.
Clerk Super-visors
Physician County Home 1 Yr.
Superin-tendent of Highways 4 Yr.
Managers Tuberculosis Hospital (5) 5 Yr.
Physician County Jail 1 Yr.
County Bacteri-ologist 1 Yr.
Commis-sioner of Elections (2) 2 Yr.
Sealer of Weights and Measures
Superin-tendent of Hospitals
LEGEND
Constitutional Officer
Statutory Officer

2. *The County Manager.* Most students of municipal government have a high regard for the city manager plan. If this is the best method of organization for the machinery of municipal government — and the problems of counties are in many respects similar to those of cities — then it follows that the county manager form may be the most desirable form of county government organization. In the operation of this plan the citizens of the county would elect a board of county commissioners, who in turn would select a properly trained and properly qualified individual, preferably from outside, to serve in the capacity of county manager. The established offices in the county government need to be somewhat revised, but when this has been done the manager will be authorized to select the heads of the several administrative agencies thus created. The proponents of this plan argue for it that it is more efficient and more businesslike and that it will more completely eliminate partisan politics from county government than a county president or other form of county executive. The manager form is illustrated in the chart below.

This form has made relatively slow progress. In 1940 there were only seven real county manager counties; by 1945 this number had increased to eleven, distributed in six states; by 1950, to fifteen in eight states. In addition

County Organization — County Manager Plan

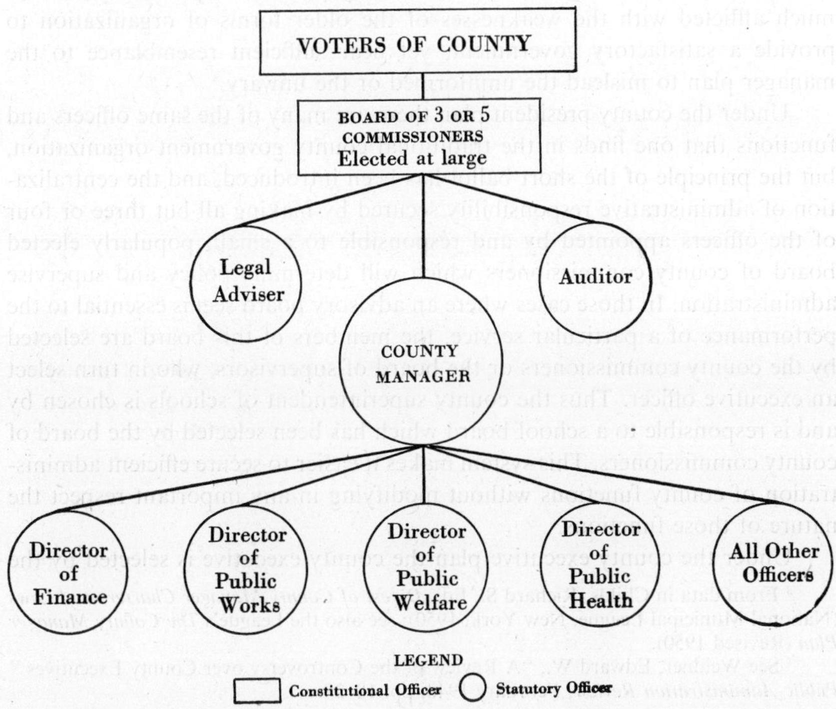

there were six appointive executives in as many counties in five states. The distribution of both types is shown in the table below.[3]

County Managers and County Executives — 1950

STATE	COUNTY MANAGERS	COUNTY EXECUTIVES
California	Sacramento, San Mateo, Santa Clara	Los Angeles, San Diego
Georgia	Fulton	——
Maryland	Anne Arundel, Montgomery	——
Montana	Petroleum	——
New York	Monroe	
North Carolina	Durham, Guilford	Robeson
South Carolina	——	Charleston
Tennessee	McMinn	Hamilton
Virginia	Albemarle, Arlington, Henrico, Warwick	Fairfax

3. *Modified Manager Government.* For those who do not understand the basic principles of manager government, or for those timid souls who, while understanding it, are torn between dissatisfaction with the old and fear of the new, there are available some hybrid forms of organization. Usually spoken of as the county executive or county president forms, they are too much afflicted with the weaknesses of the older forms of organization to provide a satisfactory government, yet bear sufficient resemblance to the manager plan to mislead the uninformed or the unwary.[4]

Under the county president plan there are many of the same officers and functions that one finds in the traditional county government organization, but the principle of the short ballot has been introduced, and the centralization of administrative responsibility secured by making all but three or four of the officers appointed by and responsible to a small, popularly elected board of county commissioners which will determine policy and supervise administration. In those cases where an advisory board seems essential to the performance of a particular service, the members of this board are selected by the county commissioners or the board of supervisors, who in turn select an executive officer. Thus the county superintendent of schools is chosen by and is responsible to a school board which has been selected by the board of county commissioners. This system makes it easier to secure efficient administration of county functions without modifying in any important respect the nature of those functions.

Under the county executive plan the county executive is selected by the

[3] From data in Childs, Richard S., Ed., *Digest of County Manager Charters and Laws* (National Municipal League, New York, 1950); see also the League's *The County Manager Plan* (Revised 1950).

[4] See Weidner, Edward W., "A Review of the Controversy over County Executives," *Public Administration Review*, February 1948, pp. 18–28.

board of supervisors and holds office during its pleasure. Like the manager under the county manager type of organization, he selects the officers who serve as heads of the various departments; and like the manager, he is responsible for their performance of their duties. This type of county organization differs from the county president type in that the county executive is selected by the board of supervisors, whereas the county president is chairman of the board. It differs from manager government in much the same way that the mayor and council form of municipal government — which it resembles — differs from a city manager. Nevertheless it has found acceptance in a number of counties in North Carolina and Virginia — two states that have made a good deal of progress in the improvement of county government.

County Consolidation. There is accumulating evidence of the fact that there are too many counties; that many of those now existing are too small in either area or wealth or population to serve effectively as administrative units under modern conditions. Some would go so far as to abolish them, creating in their place new and larger districts which would be used as administrative areas. Such proposals have been made from various sources in various states from time to time — in Michigan, New Jersey, Oregon, Pennsylvania, to mention only a few. A New Hampshire editor has been carrying on a one-man crusade to abolish the counties in that state, on the ground that there is no longer anything for them to do.

County consolidation offers a more realistic, more reasonable, and more desirable solution of the problem, although the movement has made little progress to date. Tennessee has had some success with consolidation, and in 1944 two counties in South Dakota were combined by legislative act. In sparsely settled areas some counties have found it best to revert to an unorganized status and have the state or adjoining counties administer the few necessary services. Obtaining agreement on such proposals is always difficult and is especially so in the South, where the sentimental attachment to the county is even stronger than it is to the state. Often, also, there are age-old rivalries between adjoining counties — which are obviously the only ones that could be consolidated.

The cost factor is sometimes strong enough to compel cooperative effort between counties, if not consolidation. While no recent surveys of the per capita costs of county government are available, it appears that costs are highest in the smallest counties and in the largest ones — naturally for quite different reasons — and smallest in those of medium size. Unreasonably low per capita costs, which usually indicate low standards of service, are no more to be desired than costs that are excessively high. It appears that a minimum population of at least 30,000 to 35,000 is needed for maximum service at minimum cost. Three fourths of the counties in the United States fail to meet this standard; thus consolidation may help to solve the problems of many counties.

Progress in County Structural Reorganization *
Summary of Constitutional Amendments and Statutes

STATE	HOME RULE AMENDMENT	PERMITS COUNTIES TO PROPOSE NEW CHARTERS	REQUIRING LEGISLATION FOR OPTIONAL PLANS
California	1911	1936	—
Georgia	—	1922	1945
Louisiana	—	—	1921 1924
Maryland	1913	—	—
Minnesota	—	[1]	—
Missouri	1945		—
Montana	—	1922	1931
New York	—	—	1921 [2] 1935 [3] 1936 1937
North Carolina	—	1927	—
North Dakota	—	1940 1941	—
Ohio	1923	1933	—
Oklahoma	—	[1]	—
Oregon	—	1944 1945	—
Pennsylvania	1923 [4]	—	—
Tennessee	—	[1]	—
Texas	1933	1933	—
Virginia	—	1928 1930 [5] 1932	—
Washington	1948	—	—

* From Childs, Richard S., Ed., *Digest of County Manager Charters and Laws, op. cit.* In twenty-five states, county government provisions imbedded in the constitution prevent legislation that would make county manager government available.

[1] Legislature has full powers to authorize county manager government.
[2] Limited to Nassau and Westchester Counties.
[3] Amendment adopted and legislature proposed optional forms in same year.
[4] Subject to legislative implementation, which has never been provided.
[5] Limited to Albemarle County.

Municipal Government

Importance and Growth of Cities. For centuries cities have been the centers of learning and culture. Every great advance in the arts and sciences has come from cities — in fact, it is no exaggeration to say that the greatness of a nation may be measured by the number, the size, and the development of its municipalities. The growth of cities in the United States during the last century and a half has been phenomenal. In 1790 Philadelphia was the largest in the country, with a population of less than 60,000. By the census of 1950, New York, our largest city, had a population of nearly 8,000,000. So great has been the trend of urban development that since 1920, according to Census Bureau classifications, considerably more than half of our people have lived in urban communities.

In 1790 there were only six places in the United States with populations of 8,000 or over, and only two with 25,000 or more. The entire urban population, comprising all persons living in cities and incorporated villages of 2,500 or more, formed 5.1 per cent of the total population. By 1850 there were sixty-two places of 10,000 or more inhabitants, containing 11.3 per cent of the total population. By 1900 this percentage had risen to 31.7 per cent of the total population; by 1950, to 59 per cent, distributed according to a United States Bureau of the Census classification as indicated in the following table:

Classification of Cities According to Size — 1952

GROUP	POPULATION RANGE	NUMBER OF CITIES
I	Over 1,000,000	5
II	From 500,000 to 1,000,000.........	13
III	From 250,000 to 500,000.........	24
IV	From 100,000 to 250,000.........	67
V	From 50,000 to 100,000.........	125
VI	From 25,000 to 50,000.........	243
	Total	477

In 1952, there were 1,231 communities with a population of 10,000 or more, 2,318 with a population of 5,000 or over. While many may not regard a community of this size as a city, the Bureau of the Census classifies as urban, communities of 2,500 or more. Such places may still serve as a center of a large and important trading and business area. The returns from the 1940 and 1950 censuses showed a trend away from the big cities, with the exception of New York, but a continuance of the trend toward urbanism. People were moving before the war and have been moving since, both from the country and from the large cities, to small towns and cities, to satellite cities and suburban communities. Nearly half of the people now live in or on the edge of cities of 50,000 or more population. Lewis Mumford, in an address before the annual convention of the American Institute of Architects in 1950, declared that the age of the big city is over[5]:

> The metropolitan regime has fallen by its own weight, although the monuments to its folly and arrogance may long remain in existence, provided we do not, as a final act of madness, bring on a war which will wipe out its inhabitants and leave it a waste of radioactive cinders and dust. But if the small,

[5] *New York Times*, May 14, 1950, p. 110; see also Gulick, Luther H., "Future of an Oversize City" (New York), *National Municipal Review*, July 1950, pp. 324–329.

> bio-technic city is to come into its own as the agent of a new civilization, it will have to learn the arts of regional planning, regional culture and regional design, and create a life more highly organized and more purposeful and far more widely cultivated than that of the outmoded metropolis.

Mr. Mumford advised the convention that the development of such balanced communities — limited in size, area, and density and keeping close contact with the open country — was the best hope for sound urban growth in the future. Regional authorities would serve to guide the growth and destiny of neighborhoods; already ripe for such development, he contended, are the Columbia River Valley, the San Bernardino Valley, and the Tennessee Valley.

There are a number of important reasons for this extensive development of urban communities. Not the least significant reason has been those developments in the science of agriculture which have made possible the large-scale production of necessary commodities. Without these developments, without the introduction of agricultural machinery on a large scale, a considerable percentage of those who now dwell in urban districts would be required on farms to produce necessary articles of food and clothing. In this country about 30 per cent of the people produce the nation's food supply, and there is still a large surplus to be disposed of by export or otherwise. As an emergency measure, the Agricultural Adjustment Administration found it necessary during the depression to adopt artificial methods of crop reduction. While these methods had to be abandoned, because of adverse court decisions, others of similar purpose have taken their place.

Another important factor in the growth of cities is to be found in the industrial changes growing out of the Industrial Revolution. Manufactured goods are no longer produced by hand at home for sale in the immediate community; they are produced by machinery in factories for distribution in a market often worldwide. Industry has located in those places where there was an adequate supply of labor and of power. It has settled in the cities because there it could secure better transportation, a more elastic labor supply, and large markets close at hand. The development of methods of transportation has encouraged commerce, to which nearly every great city owes its eminence. For the most part, urban workers have been able to secure a higher rate of compensation than has been possible in rural districts.

The attractiveness of urban life has also contributed greatly to urban growth. Man is a gregarious animal; there are, in addition, many ways in which urban life offers opportunities which have, until recently at least, been denied to the residents of rural districts. Among these are opportunities for recreation, education, medical and hospital care, and the many comforts enjoyed by residents of urban homes and apartments — electric lights, electric refrigeration, and sanitary equipment. It is of course true that the rural home is by no means as uncomfortable or as isolated as it was a few years ago. The extension of electric power lines and of the telephone, the construction of modern highways, the distribution of automobiles, labor-saving machinery for the home, and radio and television have changed all this and may in the future accentuate the present trend away from the larger cities.

Charter Drafting and Revision. Whatever the form of municipal government adopted, it rests upon a charter which serves as the city's fundamental law. Charters, like constitutions, become out of date and have to be revised or rewritten. This is a necessary step if important changes in the form and structure of the government are to be made, as in a shift from mayor and council government to a city manager. When the movement for charter revision becomes strong enough, it is customary either to obtain a new charter from the legislature or, in a home rule state, to submit the question to the electorate. It is often provided that the members of the charter commission shall be selected, preferably on a nonpartisan ballot, at the same time, their service being dependent upon an affirmative vote on the basic question of revision.

The charter commission makes a study of the provisions of the existing charter, of the problems and needs of the city, and of the experience of other comparable cities. Committees will be appointed, and hearings will be held on various important questions, in order to get the views of citizens and the opinions of experts.[6] With proper staff assistance, the commission may after a few months come up with the draft of a new charter which will be submitted to the voters for their approval or rejection. If approved, it will become effective, usually on a date specified in the charter itself.

Forms of Municipal Government. The weak mayor and council form of municipal organization was the original and, prior to 1900, the universally accepted form of organization in the United States. There was a mayor, but he had little real power, his duties being largely of a ceremonial nature. All important municipal functions were performed by departments and agencies whose heads were elected or chosen independently of the authority of the mayor; very often they were administered by independent boards and commissions. The legislative branch consisted of two chambers, a common council and a select council. In Philadelphia, for instance, the select council consisted of fifty members, while the common council had 150. Someone has observed that the common council was common in more than one sense of the word. At any rate, here was a legislative body for a single municipality, containing approximately 200 members. In addition there was, of course, the judicial system, which in many communities has not been substantially changed down to the present time. It was this form of municipal government which existed throughout the country at the time Bryce penned his memorable indictment. It was under this form that there developed the famous Tweed Ring in New York, the Gas Ring in Philadelphia, and similar rings of one sort or another in cities throughout the country.

This form of municipal organization has been gradually disappearing.

[6] See Anderson, William, *A Guide for Charter Commissions* (National Municipal League, New York, 1947).

It represented an attempt to adapt the complicated machinery of the Federal government to the governmental needs of small, compact, densely populated areas. The effort was a total failure. The form of the Federal government was devised for the purpose of controlling the public affairs of a people widely scattered over a considerable area; when the attempt was made to adapt it to the needs of even a large population in a small and compact area, the powers of government were divided into so many small segments and distributed among so many people that it became an utter impossibility for even the most conscientious and well-intentioned citizen to keep track of them.

1. *Mayor and Council Form.* Out of the indictment of American municipal institutions contained in the writings of the muckrakers and the studies of an earnest group which began to analyze scientifically the problems of municipal government and administration, there gradually developed a demand for the improvement of the generally prevailing conditions in city government. The first attempts at reorganization took the form of what was long known as the strong mayor and council type. It is the only type of mayor and council government now in general use,[7] and it is rapidly giving way to the far superior form of manager government. Under it the mayor became something more than a figurehead. He was authorized to appoint the heads of the administrative departments, who constituted an advisory board frequently called the cabinet. Since the members of this board were directly responsible to the mayor, it became possible for him to be in fact as well as in theory the head of the administration; whether he has been able in practice to perform the job expected of him, however, is open to serious question.[8] The job cannot be done without a competent staff, but in most cases there is no provision for staff and no realization that one is needed.

The changes made in the legislative branch of the city government were quite as important. The old cumbersome bicameral council was abolished and a small compact unicameral chamber substituted. These new councils often had seven, nine, or eleven members; the larger ones now existing include those of Chicago with fifty aldermen, Cleveland with thirty-three, Minneapolis with twenty-six, Milwaukee with twenty-seven, and Boston and Philadelphia with twenty-two each. For years New York City had the largest

[7] But there are exceptions, such an Ann Arbor, in which officials under a weak-mayor strong-council charter need personality, perseverance, and practice to make things go; see Bromage, Arthur W., "Running a City the Hard Way," *National Municipal Review*, June 1950, pp. 283–287.

[8] John E. Bebout, on the basis of extensive observation in the offices of the National Municipal League, writes (letter to the author, June 20, 1950): "Outside of a few large cities, most mayor-council governments are still essentially weak mayor jobs fairly well typified by Ann Arbor as described by Professor Bromage. In most cases where the mayor has a strong position charterwise, he does not perform the job contemplated largely because he hasn't the remotest idea what the job is, and he doesn't have a staff to tell him or to help him, even if he does have a glimmering idea of it." This same problem arises with regard to the governor; see Chapter 9.

Mayor — Council Form*

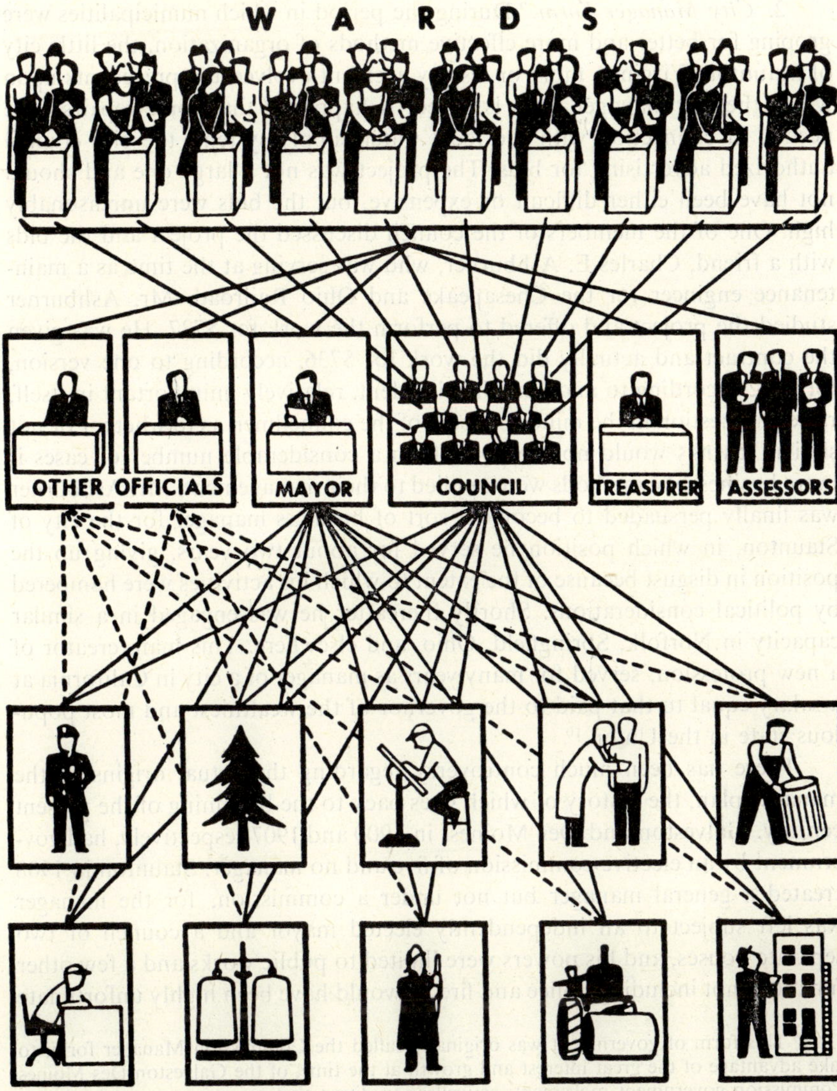

* From *The Story of the Council-Manager Plan,* Revised Edition, p. 6 (National Municipal League, New York, 1949).

board of aldermen, with seventy-two members, but by the 1937 charter, this number was reduced to twenty-five. The judicial branch of the government remained unchanged, at least so far as this particular form of reorganization was concerned. Where the mayor and council form of municipal organization is still in use, it is the form here discussed, for the old weak mayor and council form has practically passed out of existence.

2. *City Manager Form.*[9] During the period in which municipalities were groping for better and more effective methods of organization, the little city of Staunton, Virginia, more or less by accident evolved the precedents upon which the city manager form is based. It happened that some repairs were needed in connection with the local water supply system; the city council authorized advertising for bids. The project was not a large one and should not have been either difficult or expensive, but the bids were unreasonably high. One of the members of the council discussed the project and the bids with a friend, Charles E. Ashburner, who was serving at the time as a maintenance engineer for the Chesapeake and Ohio Railroad. Mr. Ashburner studied the project and offered to perform the work for $737. He was given the contract and actually did the work for $736, according to one version, for $712 according to another. This incident, relatively unimportant in itself, raised a question in the minds of some of the councilmen as to whether or not similar savings would not be possible in a considerable number of cases if more businesslike methods were applied to their management. Mr. Ashburner was finally persuaded to become a sort of business manager for the city of Staunton, in which position he served for about two years, giving up the position in disgust because of the extent to which his activities were hampered by political considerations. Shortly thereafter he was engaged in a similar capacity in Norfolk, Springfield, Ohio, and elsewhere. This man, creator of a new profession, served for many years as manager of a city in California at a salary equal to that paid to the governor of the wealthiest and most populous state in the Union.[10]

There has been much controversy regarding the actual origins of the manager plan, the history of which goes back to the beginning of the present century. Galveston and Des Moines, in 1900 and 1907 respectively, had government by an elective commission of five and no manager. Staunton in 1908 created a general manager but not under a commission, for the manager was left subject to an independently elected mayor and a council of two separate houses, and his powers were limited to public works and a few other functions not including police and fire. It would have been highly unfortunate

[9] This form of government was originally called the Commission Manager form, to take advantage of the great interest and growth at the time, of the Galveston-Des Moines Commission government movement, as well as to divert that movement toward a better structure. Much of the information presented here was obtained from Richard S. Childs, pioneer advocate of manager government, and one of its principal architects.

[10] White, Leonard D., *The City Manager*, pp. 90–97 (University of Chicago Press, 1927); Bromage, Arthur W., *Introduction to Municipal Government and Administration*, Chapters 18 and 19 (Appleton-Century-Crofts, New York, 1950). The Committee on Public Administration of the Social Science Research Council completed in 1940 an extensive survey of a quarter century of city manager government (see Selected References); for more recent comment, see National Municipal League, *The Story of the Council-Manager Plan* (New York, 1949).

if the original Staunton form had been copied by other cities, but it never was, and Staunton itself changed to a real manager about 1920.

In 1909 Richard S. Childs and H. S. Gilbertson, both connected with the New York State Short Ballot Organization, devised a manager plan for submission to the New York legislature. This plan received consideration in Lockport, New York, and in Sumter, South Carolina, by which it was first adopted. Woodrow Wilson, while touring in the West, picked up the idea and used it in some of his speeches. Sumter's first manager — a nonresident — was hired in 1913; the city still carries on its letterhead the legend: "The First Council-Manager Municipal Government," while Staunton characterizes itself in a somewhat misleading fashion as "The Birthplace of the City Manager Form of Government." Actually, Staunton was the first government to employ a city manager — which, as has been shown — is something quite different. For many years the Des Moines Commission form, which came to be regarded as a standard form of municipal organization, enjoyed some degree of popularity. While commission governments still remain in New Orleans, Trenton, and a few other cities, this form is rapidly giving way to manager government. Des Moines itself, after a bitter battle, made the change in 1949.[11]

Two cities, Morganton and Hickory in North Carolina, adopted the plan in 1913; and when Dayton and Springfield, Ohio, adopted it in 1914, the movement was well under way. The Board of Freeholders in Dayton, set up in 1913, had as its chairman a farsighted and public-spirited citizen by the name of James M. Cox. The members of the Board took a trip to Staunton to study the organization and the functioning of the new plan; they returned to their homes to prepare a charter providing for a city manager for Dayton, the first sizable community in which the plan was tried. The spread of this new idea was extremely rapid, city manager governments being set up in cities and towns in all sections of the United States within a short time. The extension of the movement has continued until there are at present more than 1000 cities, towns, and boroughs living under this form. It has been adapted to the needs of counties, and a number of states have made its adoption by these units optional. New adoptions come now at the rate of about eighty a year; manager government seems likely to become the prevailing form of municipal government in the United States by 1960.[12]

The spread of the city manager plan indicates an increasing realization on the part of the public of the need for trained, professional service in gov-

[11] Stroud, Katherine R., "Des Moines Drops Own Plan," *National Municipal Review*, June 1949, pp. 269–272, 277, and for an account of its preceding form, *The Des Moines Plan of Commission Government* (City of Des Moines, 1939).

[12] It has had considerable acceptance abroad also; the list includes four cities in Ireland, where the twenty-six counties have the plan, and thirty-six cities in Canada. Thirty-six American cities have adopted the plan and discontinued it by vote of the people; some of them have since readopted it. See Bromage, Arthur W., *Manager Plan Abandonments* (National Municipal League, New York, 1949).

ernment. Authorities in municipal government have estimated that more than 90 per cent of the work of a municipal executive consists in the performance of duties similar to those of executives in private business: the letting of contracts for goods and equipment and for construction work, the inspection and acceptance of goods received and of work done under contracts, the keeping of proper records, and the hiring, promoting, dismissing, and retirement of personnel. When an executive is chosen in private business, it is customary to select someone whose training and experience give some reasonable basis for hoping that he will be able to do the work successfully.

The city manager plan is an attempt to apply this same principle in the conduct of the public business. Under this plan it is possible to select a municipal executive on the basis of his qualifications and experience, rather than, as has been customary in this country, upon the basis of his ability to secure votes — his ability to call people by their first names, to smile pleasantly, to shake hands in a friendly fashion, to notice babies, and to make more or less ambiguous speeches. Where the city manager plan works best, the occupant of this office is a man who has made a special study of public administration and who, beginning with positions of minor importance, has gradually been promoted to more responsible positions as his experience and ability warranted. He is preferably a man from outside and therefore free from entanglement in the local political disputes of the past. His is a profession requiring personal qualifications of a high order. He is neither a dictator nor a boss; if successful, he must have courage, poise, and tact in dealing with people. The criticism that the city manager plan is undemocratic has developed chiefly in communities where the manager was deficient in these essential qualifications.

Municipal Administration

In the preceding chapter, the functions of local government — both the older and the newer functions — were outlined. The emphasis there was on the counties and on rural local government generally. While many of the basic functions are the same in either case, the problems of administration are somewhat different in cities from what they are in the country. Furthermore, the major administrative problems of the cities are much different now from what they were even a few years ago. While Federal laws permitted unrestricted immigration, the cities had the difficult problem of assimilating the foreign-born. Now, after a number of years of either restricted immigration or no immigration at all (with the exception of a limited number of displaced persons), the problem has become more a question of providing clean, attractive, and sanitary housing facilities to replace the poorly built, congested, and unsanitary tenements which breed disease, increase fire hazards, and menace the physical and moral well-being of their inhabitants.

Staff Services. The problems of municipal administration may, as in the case of the state and Federal governments, be divided into two major categories — line and staff. The latter includes here, as elsewhere, the basic

Council — Manager Form*

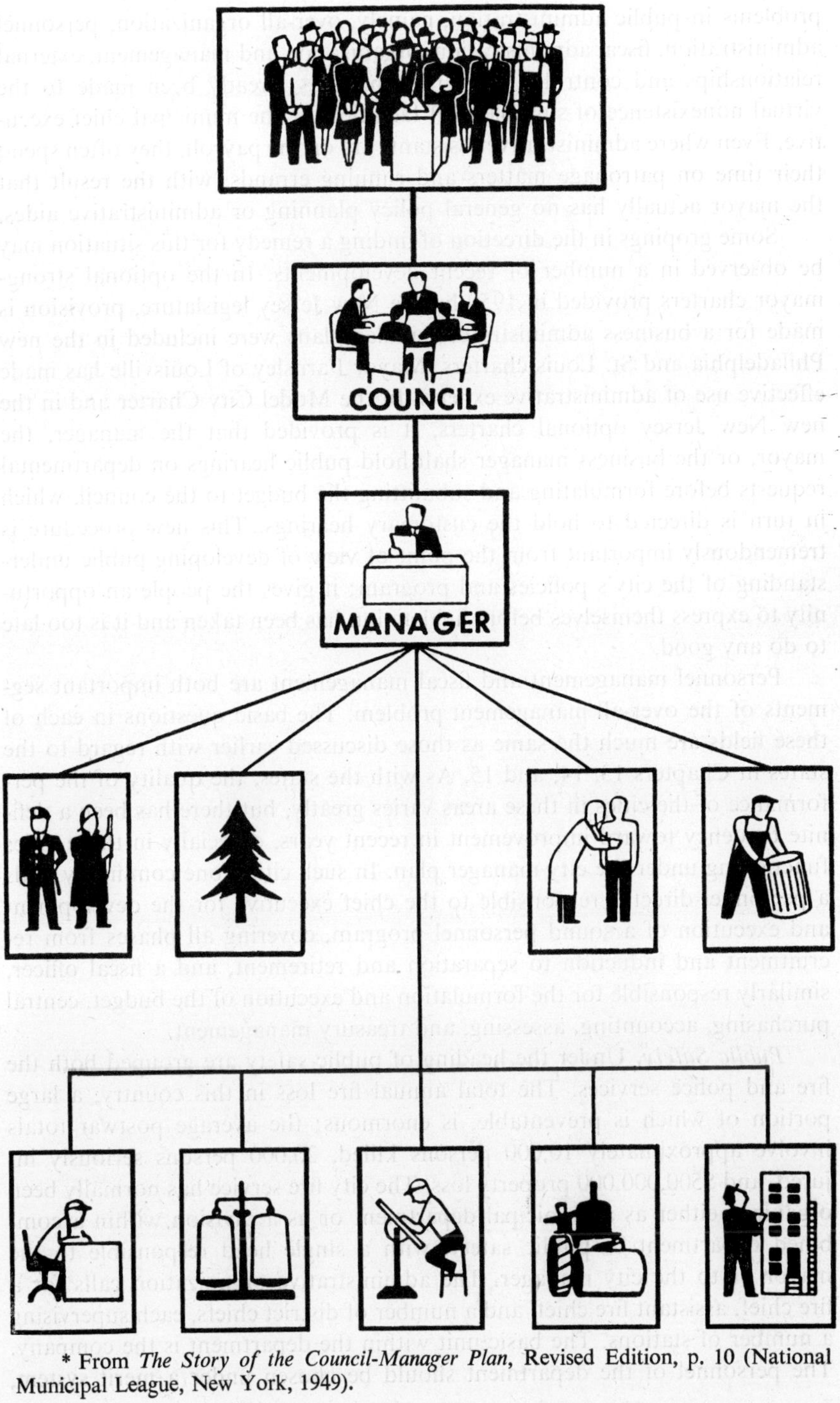

* From *The Story of the Council-Manager Plan*, Revised Edition, p. 10 (National Municipal League, New York, 1949).

problems in public administration, namely, over-all organization, personnel administration, fiscal administration, organization and management, external relationships and controls. Some reference has already been made to the virtual nonexistence of suitable staff facilities for the municipal chief executive. Even where administrative assistants are on the payroll, they often spend their time on patronage matters and running errands, with the result that the mayor actually has no general policy planning or administrative aides.

Some gropings in the direction of finding a remedy for this situation may be observed in a number of recent developments. In the optional strong-mayor charters provided in 1950 by the New Jersey legislature, provision is made for a business administrator; similar plans were included in the new Philadelphia and St. Louis charters. Mayor Farnsley of Louisville has made effective use of administrative experts. In the Model City Charter and in the new New Jersey optional charters, it is provided that the manager, the mayor, or the business manager shall hold public hearings on departmental requests before formulating and submitting the budget to the council, which in turn is directed to hold the customary hearings. This new procedure is tremendously important from the point of view of developing public understanding of the city's policies and program; it gives the people an opportunity to express themselves before final action has been taken and it is too late to do any good.

Personnel management and fiscal management are both important segments of the over-all management problem. The basic questions in each of these fields are much the same as those discussed earlier with regard to the states in Chapters 13, 14, and 15. As with the states, the quality of the performance of the cities in these areas varies greatly, but there has been a definite tendency toward improvement in recent years, especially in those cities functioning under the city manager plan. In such cities, one commonly finds a personnel director responsible to the chief executive for the development and execution of a sound personnel program, covering all phases from recruitment and induction to separation and retirement, and a fiscal officer, similarly responsible for the formulation and execution of the budget, central purchasing, accounting, assessing, and treasury management.

Public Safety. Under the heading of public safety are grouped both the fire and police services. The total annual fire loss in this country, a large portion of which is preventable, is enormous; the average postwar totals involve approximately 10,000 persons killed, 20,000 persons seriously injured, and $500,000,000 property loss. The city fire service has normally been organized either as a municipal department or as a division within a combined department of public safety, with a single head responsible to the mayor or to the city manager. The administrative organization calls for a fire chief, assistant fire chief, and a number of district chiefs, each supervising a number of stations. The basic unit within the department is the company. The personnel of the department should be chosen under a merit system, promotions, discipline, and dismissals being made under a sound system of personnel administration.

The apparatus of a department includes the pumper (with pump, water tank, and hose) and ladder trucks for lifesaving and fire fighting, for use in industrial and business areas; and for use in residential areas, combination pumper-ladder trucks. This equipment is housed in central stations and substations so situated as to distribute the equipment and companies in such a manner as to provide adequate protection for all sections of the city. Since cities and city populations are constantly changing, frequent adjustments are necessary. The department has two important functions to perform: (1) to fight fires when they occur, and (2) by means of education and through the location and elimination of fire hazards, to do the best fire prevention job possible.

There are several ways of organizing a police department, in its relation to the chief executive, as Professor Bromage points out.[13] The police chief may: (1) serve directly under the chief executive; (2) serve under a police commissioner who serves under the chief executive; (3) serve under a police board which serves under the chief executive; (4) serve, along with the fire chief, under a director of public safety, who serves under the chief executive. Whatever the type of top level organization in any particular instance, the basic internal organization of the department must be constructed in such manner as to provide for each of the eight major types of police activity, as listed by Bruce Smith, noted authority in the field of police administration[14]: (1) patrol; (2) traffic; (3) criminal investigation; (4) records; (5) property, including communications; (6) personnel management; (7) crime prevention; and (8) morals regulation.

As in the case of the fire service, the police force must be deployed so that protection will be provided for life and property in all parts of the city at all times. This requires careful planning and an elaborate organization. The usual pattern provides for police districts and platoons. Police inspectors, serving under the police chief, each supervise a number of district captains who in turn supervise three platoons. The platoon system is used in both fire and police services as a means of providing twenty-four hour protection.

Public Health and Welfare. Municipal public health authorities perform a great many services which in less densely populated districts are performed either directly by state authorities, or by the local authorities under a closer supervision by the state than is commonly exercised over municipalities. The density of population so increases the danger of contagion that in cities individuals cannot be left to handle their own health problems. Thus there is an infinite variety of inspections for medical and sanitary purposes, quar-

[13] *Op. cit.*, p. 516.

[14] *Police Systems in the United States*, pp. 253–265 (Harper, New York, 1940); for a briefer discussion of these problems, see Bromage, *op. cit.*, Chapter 25. For a current survey in a typical state, see Larsen, Christian L., and Mester, Edmund C., *Maryland Municipal Police Systems* (Bureau of Public Administration, University of Maryland, 1950).

antines, and sanitary requirements. Such scientific knowledge and administrative techniques in public health are now available as to make many communicable diseases definitely controllable; epidemics of these diseases are inexcusable.

The United States Public Health Service has indicated that it takes a population of at least 50,000 to support an adequate local health program. The organization varies greatly according to the adequacy of the program and the size of the city. The health officer may serve under the chief executive or under a board of health which serves under the chief executive. In a fair sized city, the various activities of the department may be grouped under five major divisions, as follows: (1) administration, including vital statistics, health education, and other matters; (2) sanitation, including food and milk inspection [15]; (3) laboratory division; (4) communicable diseases, including among others, the tuberculosis and venereal disease programs; (5) child hygiene. Because of the existence of a large number of Federal grants and the interest and responsibility of the states in this field, there are numerous interlevel and interjurisdictional relationships in the public health field.

In some cities health, hospitals, and welfare are grouped together in the same department. In such instances, there will normally be separate boards for each, serving under the chief executive, with a health officer, a superintendent of hospitals, and a director of welfare. It is probably preferable to have separate departments for health and welfare, with hospital administration under the former. When such is the case, the organization for the department of welfare, in its place in the governmental structure, will be parallel with that for health.

Generally speaking, the public welfare responsibilities of the cities were small prior to 1930, rose to major importance during the depression, and have since declined, particularly since the establishment of the Federal Social Security program in 1935, under which the major responsibility for administration is divided between the Federal government, the states, and local units, usually the counties. Thus it is that many cities no longer have any real responsibility in this field. Some cities administer general relief but have no responsibility in connection with Federal-state programs. Some of the larger ones take part in both, especially where they are administered on a joint city-county basis.

Public Utilities. The problems of cities in the field of public utilities are of two sorts: ownership and operation, and regulation. Activity in the former has shown a steady increase over the years. In 1948, of 2033 cities of more than 5000 population, 1296 or 68.2 per cent reported municipal ownership of water supply and distribution systems. Although cities have gone into the water business on a conspicuously large scale, they have been active in other

[15] For a discussion of inspectional services in this field, with special reference to San Francisco, see the author's *Public Administration in a Democratic Society*, Chapter 32 (Heath, Boston, 1950).

fields as well. In the same year and in the same group of cities, some 267 or 13.1 per cent reported municipal ownership of electric generation and distribution systems. An additional 168 cities or 8.3 per cent had municipally owned distribution systems. Only forty-five cities or 2.2 per cent reported municipally owned gas manufacturing and distribution, together with forty-two or 2.1 per cent in the business of gas distribution only. Bus or trolley-bus systems were owned by forty cities or 2 per cent, and eleven cities had municipally owned street railway systems. But approximately half of the cities had municipally owned sewage treatment plants — 964 or 47.4 per cent. 357 cities or 17.7 per cent reported municipal ownership of airports; 375 or 18.4 per cent, a municipally owned auditorium.[16]

For the administration of these business-type functions, several types or patterns of organization are found. A corporate structure may be established in the form of an "authority"; several different utilities may be set up as divisions of a department, under a board, commission, or a single executive head; or each operating utility may be set up in a separate department. In some instances, where a municipality owns a gas works or a transit facility, it is leased on a long-term basis to an operating company, usually under the pressure of business interests which still object to government ownership and operation. Regulatory activities such as rate making and inspection are relatively unimportant at the municipal level, most such problems falling within the jurisdiction of the state regulatory bodies.

The problem of transportation has been and still is of outstanding importance. In the past the chief concern was with the provision and operation of transit facilities which would carry people quickly and cheaply to and from their homes in the residential districts and the suburbs and their offices and places of business. If in the process of rebuilding cities, their industrial and commercial life is to some extent decentralized, the problem of transportation may be somewhat different. The peak loads which now exist in the morning and evening hours may diminish. People would be able to walk to their places of employment, and traffic would be more evenly distributed throughout the day.[17]

Public Works. The department of public works, like other municipal departments, functions under a head who is responsible to the chief executive. The major divisions of the department, in addition to administration, are engineering, motor equipment, and property management, while the major functions to be performed include construction and maintenance of streets and highways; collection and disposal of garbage, ashes, and other refuse; and operation of the sewer system and sewage disposal plant. All or some of the work may be done by the department's own force, which is ordinarily a large one, or it may be done by private firms under contract.

[16] Statistical data from Bromage, *op. cit.*, pp. 578–579.

[17] Bauer, John, *Postwar Planning for Metropolitan Utilities* (National Municipal League, New York, 1945), urges a regional basis.

Construction and maintenance of streets, as in the past, is not enough; the modern city requires elevated highways, expressways, through routes, and limited access highways around and through congested areas. Provision of parking facilities to relieve traffic congestion — off-street as well as on — presents a major problem. The department establishes and enforces regulations and procedures governing street openings (or "pavement cuts"). Many operations such as street cleaning and snow removal can now be performed to a large extent by mechanical equipment. Street lighting, which might seem to be a fairly simple matter, is yet a matter of great importance, both from the point of view of traffic control and from that of police protection to citizens and their property.

However common it may once have been to "burn the trash," the fire hazards attending such an operation have compelled cities everywhere to forbid the practice, leaving to the municipality the responsibility for collecting "refuse," by which is meant all solid wastes — garbage, ashes, rubbish of all types, whether or not it is combustible. While the best solution is municipal collection and disposal, two other alternatives are available: letting the job out on contract, or permitting private collectors, paid by individual householders, to make the collections.

The time-honored practice of dumping raw sewage, industrial wastes, and ground water run-off into rivers, lakes, and harbors is no longer sanctioned. This practice is obviously unsanitary and may even constitute a serious health hazard to the community itself and to thousands of other people elsewhere. It is also destructive of plant and aquatic life in any form. The alternative is the construction and operation of domestic and storm sewers, and sewage disposal plants. Industrial plants can remove serious impurities from waste before discharging it. These are expensive but necessary requirements of modern urban life.

Schools and Library Administration. In some communities the administration of schools is separate from the rest of the city government, being placed under the direction of an independent board of education in order to "keep the schools out of politics." It is by no means certain, however, that this separation represents sound public policy or that it prevents or minimizes politics in school administration.[18] Whatever the type of administrative control, the city is responsible for the maintenance of the public school system. It must provide suitable buildings, keep them heated, lighted, ventilated, in a sanitary condition, and in repair; it must employ and pay a qualified staff of teachers; it must purchase supplies, equipment, books, and other necessary working materials — all of this at a very great financial cost, most

[18] For a significant study of this problem, see Henry, Nelson B., and Kerwin, Jerome G., *Schools and City Government* (University of Chicago Press, 1938), and more recently, McLaughlin, Frederick C., *Fiscal and Administrative Control of City School Systems, New York State* (Public Education Association of New York City, 1949), and New York Citizens Budget Commission, *Should New York City Adopt Fiscal Independence for Education?* (New York, 1950).

of which is met by the school tax upon real estate. But the responsibility of the community does not stop there.

An adequate program of adult education requires study courses, special instruction, books and equipment, vocational training. The Library is an indispensable part of any such program.[19] In many cities the public library has developed within the framework of municipal administration in a semi-independent position and with a close interrelationship with the local school district. In the larger cities branch libraries are conveniently located in different parts of the city. On the whole, financial support has never been adequate but has shown some tendency to improve in the postwar years.

Parks and Recreation. The need for recreation facilities has grown out of the increased leisure of the average employed person and out of the terrific congestion that came to characterize cities which had been permitted to grow without planning and without restriction on real estate promoters who covered every available square foot with some kind of "improvement." Only by clearing and reserving some open space can some of these cities be made livable. The more common types of facilities provided in a modern recreation program include play lots, neighborhood playgrounds, playfields, large parks, reservations, specialized areas such as golf courses, swimming pools, and bathing beaches, and other miscellaneous areas such as squares and neighborhood parks reserved for the public and available for organized sports.

Minimum standards for play areas and for equipment for each of the usual types of sport have been developed, based on population size. The administration of the function is now usually assigned to a separate municipal department (the movement in this direction has developed rapidly since 1940), which has divisions in charge of administration, recreational activities and program services, special recreation facilities, and construction and maintenance.[20]

SELECTED REFERENCES

COUNTY GOVERNMENT AND ADMINISTRATION

Baker, Gladys, *The County Agent* (University of Chicago Press, 1939). This is a valuable study of cooperative relations in agricultural administration, centering around the county agent.

Bosworth, Karl A., *Black Belt County; Rural Government in the Cotton Country of Alabama* and *Tennessee Valley County; Rural Government in the Hill Country of Alabama* (both — Bureau of Public Administration, University of Alabama,

[19] New York Public Library, *After One Hundred Years*, 1848–1948 (New York, 1948).

[20] For a general treatise, see Butler, George D., *Playgrounds: Their Administration and Operation*, Revised Edition, prepared for the National Recreation Association (A. S. Barnes & Company, New York, 1950), and as an example of a good city guide, Love, Gilbert, *Recreation Guide to the Pittsburgh Region* (Recreation, Conservation, and Park Council of the Alleghany Conference on Community Development, Pittsburgh, 1950).

1941). Two notable case studies of Alabama county government in representative counties.

Gilbertson, Henry S., *The County, the Dark Continent of American Politics* (National Short Ballot Organization, New York, 1917). A pioneer and greatly influential study in this field.

Satterfield, Millard H., *County Government and Administration in the Tennessee Valley States* (Tennessee Valley Authority, Knoxville, 1940). An excellent regional study.

Wager, Paul W., Ed., *County Government Across the Nation* (University of North Carolina Press, 1950). Describes the organization and operations of one county in each state in a valuable compilation that goes far beyond the generalizations to which a textbook must of necessity be confined.

Weidner, Edward W., *The American County — Patchwork of Boards* (National Municipal League, New York, 1946). A good analysis of some of the major defects characteristic of American county government.

For studies of county government in some representative states, see:

Arkansas: Brannan, C. O., *Characteristics and Costs of County Government in Arkansas* (Agricultural Experiment Station, Fayetteville, January 1937).

California: Bollens, John C., and others, *County Government Organization in California* (Bureau of Public Administration, University of California, 1947).

Connecticut: Faeth, Henry J., *The Connecticut County; a Description of Its Organization, Function and Relationship with Other Governmental Units* (Institute of Public Service, University of Connecticut, January 1949).

Georgia: Hughes, M. Clyde, *County Government in Georgia* (University of Georgia Press, 1944).

Illinois: Snider, Clyde F., *County Government in Illinois* (Illinois Tax Commission, Springfield, 1943).

Kentucky: Manning, John W., *Government in Kentucky Counties* (Bureau of Governmental Research, University of Kentucky, 1937).

Michigan: Tharp, Claude R., *A Manual of County Administrative Organization in Michigan* (University of Michigan Press, 1944).

Nebraska: Shumate, Roger V., *Reorganization of County Government* (Nebraska Legislative Council, Lincoln, 1950).

Nevada: Legislative Counsel Bureau, *County Consolidation and Reorganization in Nevada* (Carson City, 1948).

South Carolina: Andrews, Columbus, *Administrative County Government in South Carolina* (University of North Carolina Press, 1933).

Texas: Murphy, Wallace C., *County Government and Administration in Texas* (University of Texas, 1933).

Virginia: Spicer, George W., *Fifteen Years of County Government in Virginia* (Division of Extension, University of Virginia, 1952).

Washington: Campbell, Ernest H., and Legg, Herbert H., Jr., *County Government in the State of Washington* (Bureau of Gcvernmental Research, University of Washington, 1948).

Wisconsin: Wisconsin Historical Records Survey, *County Government in Wisconsin*, 3 vols. (Madison, 1941).

All of the available textbooks in county government are quite old:

Bromage, Arthur W., *American County Government* (Sears, New York, 1933).

Fairlie, John A., and Kneier, Charles M., *County Government and Administration* (Century, New York, 1930).

Porter, Kirk H., *County and Township Government in the United States* (Macmillan, New York, 1922).

MUNICIPAL GOVERNMENT AND ADMINISTRATION

Griffith, Ernest S., *History of American City Government*, 2 vols. (Oxford University Press, 1938).

Jones, Victor, *Metropolitan Government* (University of Chicago Press, 1942); and for an earlier study, Stukenski, Paul, *The Government of Metropolitan Areas* (National Municipal League, New York, 1930).

Mott, Rodney L., *Home Rule for America's Cities* (American Municipal Association, Chicago, 1949).

Mumford, Lewis, *The Culture of Cities* (Harcourt, Brace, New York, 1938). An outstanding sociological study.

Pfiffner, John M., *Municipal Administration* (Ronald Press, New York, 1940) and Reed, Thomas H., *Municipal Management* (McGraw-Hill, New York, 1941). Two out of several approximately contemporaneous treatises in this field.

Social Science Research Council, Committee on Public Administration.
City Manager Government in the United States
City Manager Government in Nine Cities
City Manager Government in Seven Cities
(all, Public Administration Service, Chicago, 1940). Together, these volumes present a fairly comprehensive survey of experience with manager government in cities of various sizes, over a period of a quarter of a century.

For studies of progressive government in two different cities, see:

Hoan, Daniel W., *City Government: the Record of the Milwaukee Experiment* (Harcourt, Brace, New York, 1936).

Taft, Charles P., *City Management: the Cincinnati Experiment* (Farrar & Rinehart, New York, 1934).

For studies of municipal government in individual states, see:

Alabama: Cooper, Weldon, *Municipal Government and Administration in Alabama* (Bureau of Public Administration, University of Alabama, 1940).

Florida: Grobman, Hulda, Ed., *Municipal Government Problems of Interest to Florida Municipalities* (Public Administration Clearing Service, University of Florida, 1950).

Georgia: Raisty, Lloyd B., *Municipal Government and Administration in Georgia* (University of Georgia Press, 1941).

Iowa: Shambaugh, Benjamin F., Ed., *Municipal Government and Administration in Iowa*, 2 vols. (Iowa State Historical Society, Iowa City, 1930).

Mississippi: Satterfield, Millard H., and Urban, Hugh W., *Municipal Government and Administration in Mississippi* (Mississippi State Planning Commission, Jackson, 1940).

Tennessee: Abbott, Lyndon E., and Greene, Lee S., *Municipal Government and Administration in Tennessee* (University of Tennessee Extension Series, 1939).

Of the numerous available textbooks in the field, the following are among the more recent:

Anderson, William, and Weidner, Edward W., *American City Government*, Revised Edition (Holt, New York, 1950).

Bromage, Arthur W., *Introduction to Municipal Government and Administration* (Appleton-Century-Crofts, New York, 1950).

Kneier, Charles M., *City Government in the United States*, Revised Edition (Harpers, New York, 1947).

MacCorkle, Stuart A., *American Municipal Government and Administration* (Heath, Boston, 1948).

Schulz, Ernst B., *American City Government, Its Machinery and Processes* (Stackpole & Heck, Inc., New York, 1949).

Zink, Harold, *Government of Cities in the United States*, Revised Edition (Macmillan, New York, 1948).

23

State-Local Relations

The tendency to centralize authority through the shifting of power from the smaller to the larger units of government is one of the striking trends of modern government. In discussions of American national government it is customary to devote some attention to Federal centralization, noting how under the influence of the subsidy system the Federal government has extended its control over such subjects as agriculture, conservation, education, health, highways, and labor — all of which had been regarded, under the doctrine of residuary powers, as belonging exclusively to the states. Similar extensions have occurred under the Federal police power, the commerce power, the tax power, and the postal power. Simultaneously with this shift of power from the states to the Federal government there has come a shift of power from the local agencies to the states. In many cases where no actual diminution of the powers of the local agencies occurred, the states have extended their authority by establishing and enforcing standards. This has resulted in state supervision of local units in many of the same administrative fields in which power has been transferred from the localities to the state and from the states to the Federal government.

Reasons for State Centralization

The reasons for this concentration of power in successively larger units of government are not difficult to discover. The development of machinery and large-scale production in industry and agriculture has made possible the growth of metropolitan areas, each with a tremendous population. Modern methods of transportation and communication have created mobility of population and channels for cheap and expeditious transmission of ideas. Under these new conditions it has become impossible to administer governmental services effectively in administrative units conceived in and suitable for the day of the oxcart, the stagecoach, and the messenger galloping on horseback.

The discovery of this fact by large numbers of people during the last few years has apparently occasioned great surprise, though there is no reason why it should. A study of the development of state administration in Michigan made in 1948 showed that in a period of a little more than a century from 1835 to 1949, under three constitutions, more than 260 agencies were created. There were twenty-two between 1835 and 1849, eighty-four between 1850 and 1899, and 162 between 1900 and 1948.[1] The list covering the years from 1945 on shows twenty-one new agencies and is typical of the entries in a list which takes approximately seven typewritten pages.

STATE OF MICHIGAN
GROWTH OF ADMINISTRATIVE AGENCIES, 1945–1948

1945	1. Michigan Public School Employees' Retirement Fund Board
	2. Board of Hearing Examiners
	3. State Tax Commission
	4. License Appeal Board
	5. Department of Aeronautics, and State Aeronautics Commission
	6. Michigan Agricultural Marketing Council
	7. Michigan Tourist Council
	8. Department of Mental Health, and State Mental Health Commission
	9. State Office Building Commission
1947	1. Commission on Agriculture
	2. Michigan Cherry Commission
	3. Department of Insurance
	4. State Department of Corrections, and State Advisory Council for Corrections
	5. Workmen's Compensation Commission
	6. Department of Economic Development, and State Economic Development Commission
	7. Soo Locks Celebration Commission
	8. Michigan State Highways Commission
	9. Office of Hospital Surveys and Construction
1948	1. Department of Administration, and State Controller
	2. State Building Commission

One gets another view of the same problem from the table which appears on page 795, arranged from data compiled by the Henry County Council of Intergovernmental Relations in 1945. According to this tabulation, the people of one typical American county were receiving no less than 245 governmental services from the various units of government. There are many significant factors, to be sure, of which such a tabulation takes no account, namely, growth of population, territorial expansion, changes in transportation and communication, shift in concept of governmental role, and interrelations of one governmental unit with another.

The growth of state services by additions and by transfers from the local agencies is not to be explained wholly on the basis of developments in natural science. It has long been evident that, to use the words of the late President F. D. Roosevelt, Americans are living under too many "layers of government." There are counties — three, four, five, six, perhaps as many as eight

[1] Data from Eckert, Eleanora, *The Growth of Administration in Michigan* (unpublished thesis, University of Michigan, 1949).

Growth of Governmental Services and Functions, Henry County, Indiana, 1787–1945

PERIOD	FEDERAL	STATE	COUNTY	TOWN & CITY
1787–1806	18	0	0	0
1807–1826	1	6	0	10
1827–1846	1	2	2	2
1847–1866	2	3	1	0
1867–1886	6	3	0	2
1887–1906	11	15	5	6
1907–1926	19	33	5	4
1927–1945	45	30	3	10
Total	103	92	16	34

classes of them; cities of the first, second, third, or more classes; boroughs; towns and townships of two or more classes; villages; and administrative districts of every imaginable variety for every conceivable administrative purpose. Most of these agencies have, and use, the taxing power and the borrowing power. There are increasing numbers of government corporations and, of late, a great many "authorities" which are to a large extent exempt both from normal regulation and taxation. It has become apparent that there can be no logical justification for such a multiplicity of overlapping governmental units.

In the preceding chapter mention was made of the number — very often the excessive number — of counties. The situation with regard to school districts — to use one type of special purpose area as an example — is even worse. In New York there are more than 9,000 school districts. In Pennsylvania there were 2,582 in 1934, of which almost half were districts with a population under 1,000. By 1941 the number had been reduced only thirty-three, the total of 2,549 being distributed among the various classes as follows: first class, two; second class, twenty; third class, 258; and fourth class, 2,269. The total number of separate governmental units in this state is 5,635 — and Pennsylvania is no worse than most of the other states. A striking illustration of the extent to which special purpose districts have been permitted to multiply is shown by the table for Los Angeles County, California, on page 752. That progress has been made in the last few years is apparent by comparing the figures in the second column with those in the first, but the number is still far too large.

Local government has frequently broken down because, from one point of view there was too much of it, and from another point of view, too little of it. The units are so numerous and so small that individually they cannot do what needs to be done, and their efforts are so uncoordinated that they cannot function effectively as a group or on a cooperative basis. Many studies of this situation have been made. In 1945 it was shown, for instance, that there were 188 local governments in St. Louis County. The result is that the public does not receive the service that it should and that, on the basis of the taxes it pays, it has a right to expect.

It has often been said that nature never permits a vacuum. Likewise, in the field of government a governmental vacuum, a kind of governmental no man's land, does not long continue. If the local units break down, the states must either attempt to do the job themselves or establish and enforce upon the local units minimum requirements for the performance of the function. The reasons why and the methods by which the power and influence of the states increase in the state-local relationship are substantially the same as those which account for the growth of Federal power in the Federal-state relationship.

Still another reason for the shift of power from the localities to the states is to be found in the fact that our people are becoming accustomed to higher standards of administrative efficiency. They expect more adequate and prompt service from their government. Service of this improved character the local units have rarely been able to give them, since they are staffed by untrained and/or part-time employees, many of whom are inadequately paid. Illustrations in support of this general thesis will be cited under appropriate headings in the paragraphs below, in which will be indicated the more important fields of government in which centralization has occurred, and the nature of and the reason for the transfer of power or the extension of supervision in each case.

State Relations with Local Governments

The states are supposed, under the American system of government, to assume a very considerable degree of responsibility for the organization and conduct of their political subdivisions. In truth it may be said that, generally speaking, they have discharged this responsibility in a very indifferent manner. Frequently they have failed to perform it at all. One important reason for their shortcoming is to be found in their failure to provide suitable procedures and machinery either for their own use or for that of their local units. These needs might be met by the establishment of departments of local government at the state level and by the provision of workable procedures for home rule for local units.

Executive Controls: the Governor. The governors of the states should have — and some of them do have — the power to remove local officers for proper cause and to supervise the officers and agencies of local government. In most states this power is very limited, if it exists at all, because of the reverence with which the principle of local self-government has been regarded — reverence so great as to justify, in the eyes of many, the failure of the state to interfere in the case of inefficiency on the part of local officers. It has been assumed that democratic government requires local control of local affairs, even at the price of excessive cost and inefficiency in operation. Consequently the state police have been kept out of cities, and local communities have been permitted — as earlier noted — to exercise an almost exclusive control over school, health, and welfare problems, and have been allowed almost a free hand in the collection of taxes.

In New York the governor may remove district attorneys and sheriffs; in Wisconsin, district attorneys and coroners — provided in each case that a copy of the charges is furnished and an opportunity for a hearing is given. In Nebraska, Oklahoma, Tennessee, and Wyoming the governor may direct the attorney general or the county prosecuting officers to institute proceedings for the removal of county officers; and in Nebraska and Wyoming he may suspend such officers pending trial. In Minnesota, New York, and Wisconsin he may remove a sheriff; and in Illinois, Kansas, Michigan, and Ohio he may do so under such circumstances as the legislature may prescribe. In Maine, Maryland, and New Hampshire the governor may appoint coroners with the consent of the council or the senate, and in Massachusetts and Rhode Island, the medical examiner. Officers under the governor in some states appoint local enforcement officers. In Alabama the governor may appoint a special force of inspectors to assist him in enforcing the laws of the state, and in Nebraska he may call to his assistance and appoint any number of persons necessary to enforce the provisions of such laws. Many other illustrations might be cited.[2]

In the realm of local finance, reports Professor Grant,[3] the governor of Arkansas has some degree of supervisory power by virtue of the authority vested in the state comptroller, who serves at the pleasure of the governor. The comptroller has the power to prescribe uniform sets of accounts for all county and township officers. He is director of county audits and is required to make a complete audit of the books and accounts of county and township officers in each county annually. If the comptroller detects a shortage or other liability on the part of a local officer, he must certify such information to the state attorney general or to the prosecuting attorney of that circuit. If no action is taken, the comptroller can, upon written approval of the governor, employ special counsel and sue to recover the shortage or liability.

Department of Local Government. Every province in Canada has a department of local government; strange as it may seem, few states have taken steps to provide such governmental machinery for their use. Notable exceptions are to be found in at least four states: New Jersey, which has a Division of Local Government in its Department of Taxation and Finance; New York, which has a similar division in its Department of Audit and Control; North

[2] Based on Fairlie, John A., and Kneier, Charles M., *County Government and Administration*, pp. 242–245 (Appleton-Century, New York, 1930). The Florida Constitution authorizes the governor to suspend from office county officials who have been, in his opinion, guilty of certain offenses. This is an extraordinary power and one which, in the opinion of former Governor Caldwell, is of somewhat doubtful value. "It may be good in theory but practically, its exercise has accomplished little of value."

[3] Grant, Daniel, *The Role of the Governor of Arkansas in Administration* (unpublished doctoral dissertation, Northwestern University, 1948).

Carolina, which has a Local Government Commission; Pennsylvania, which has a Bureau of Municipalities in its Department of Internal Affairs, and a permanent Local Government Commission, the oldest existing interim commission of the Pennsylvania legislature.[4]

The North Carolina Local Government Commission, consisting of nine members, including the State Treasurer, the State Auditor, the Secretary of State, the Secretary of Revenue, and five members appointed by the Governor, was established in 1931. The four state officials are members ex officio and comprise the executive committee. It is specified that of those appointed by the Governor one shall have had experience as an executive officer of a municipality and one shall have had experience as a member of the governing board of a county at the time of their appointment. The State Treasurer is chairman of the Commission and is also ex officio Director of Local Government. All actions required or permitted to be taken by the Commission may be taken by the Executive Committee, but the Committee shall not overrule or reverse any action of the Commission as a whole. Appeal may be taken to the whole Commission from action of the Executive Committee. The Commission is required to meet quarterly and may hold special meetings. The members are allowed expenses for attending meetings but receive no compensation for their services.

It is the duty of the Commission to approve the issuance of all bonds and notes of local units of government and to keep record of all such bonds and notes that are issued in order that it may notify each unit thirty days in advance of the maturity of principal and interest of its bonds and notes, as is required by law. All contracts or agreements of local units made with any person or persons for the preparation of proceedings and forms incident to the issuance of bonds and notes, except when such agreements are made with licensed attorneys, must be approved. The Commission must furnish each local unit thirty days in advance of the annual levy of taxes an itemized statement showing the amount of principal and interest maturing in the fiscal year for which such levy is made. It shall also require of local units a report of remittances for the payment of principal and interest on bonds and notes on a form prescribed by them. It has the power to determine whether the sinking funds of local units are being adequately maintained and to approve all proposed investments of such funds; to supervise bank deposits of local units, to approve all agreements between such units and certified public accountants with respect to audits. It may appoint an administrator to conduct the affairs of a local unit which has defaulted in the payment of principal and interest on its indebtedness.

The New Jersey setup is similar in many respects, consisting of the office

[4] See, as a sample of their annual reports, Livengood, William S., Jr., "My Report to the People on Local Government," Pennsylvania Department of Internal Affairs *Bulletin*, June 1950, pp. 3–9, and Mahany, Rowland, "The Local Government Commission," *League of Third Class Cities* monthly bulletin, November–December 1949, pp. 3–5.

of the director of local government, and of the local government board. The latter administers the laws pertaining to finance; it acts as Municipal Finance Commission, directing the finances of localities in an unsound financial condition, and as the State Funding Commission which directs refunding operations of local governments. It is authorized to assume controlling power of a municipality if it (1) defaults on debt principal or interest; (2) does not make tax payments due to the state or other government; (3) carries a budget deficit for two years in excess of 5 per cent of the tax levy; (4) has excessive floating debt, based on a per cent ratio of the budget; (5) has excessive tax delinquency, measured by a percentage of total taxes levied.

The division keeps localities informed of the amounts needed for current debt service and provides post audits to determine the adequacy of disbursements for debt service, with the power to enforce local levies to reduce deficits. It prescribes a uniform accounting system for local governments and supervises annual audits for the larger cities, semi-annual audits for the smaller ones. Annual financial reports on state-prepared forms are required, and fiscal statistics are computed and published. In short, the division is responsible for the administration of the laws pertaining to local finance. All points considered, the New Jersey system is one of the strongest for state supervision in this field.

Home Rule. In Chapter 8 mention was made of the extent to which cities were originally under the domination of the state legislatures. The cities owed their existence to legislative enactments and were therefore subject to the legislative will with regard to even the most minute details of their administration. As the size and complexity of municipal problems increased, it was obviously impossible for the legislatures to perform these duties well. The size of the undertaking was appalling, even if the legislators had always been, as they were not, free from the desire to gain political advantage at the expense of the cities. These conditions led to a widespread discontent and to the organization of a movement for the establishment of municipal home rule.

The movement for home rule evolved gradually through a series of experimental stages. The first of these was the amendment to the Constitution of Ohio adopted in 1897, requiring that the legislature group the cities of the state into not more than seven classes on the basis of population. This provision proved to be quite inadequate, for the number of classes permitted was so large that the legislature was able to adjust the population limits in such manner as to include only one city in each of the first five classes, the remainder of the cities being grouped in classes six and seven. It was thus possible for the legislature to continue its domination of local affairs in all the larger communities. One act, for instance, provided for the paving of certain blocks of "Euclid Avenue in all cities of the first class." This classification plan, with a smaller number of classes, is now in effect in the majority of states having any considerable number of urban communities.

New York adopted another plan which was quite effective in operation from the point of view of protecting the right of communities to control their own affairs, but it was not, strangely enough, copied in other jurisdictions. This plan provided that in those cases where the legislature adopted provisions purely local in character, the provisions should not, even though properly passed by both houses and signed by the governor, be effective in the cities to which they applied unless, within a period of thirty days thereafter, the mayor of the city affected should have given his consent. This plan was changed in 1938 to one requiring a petition from the local unit affected, specifically requesting the legislature to pass a particular measure.

The next step in the development of the movement for home rule also originated in New York. This was the optional charter plan, under which the legislature drew up model charters for each of the more common types of municipal government. Communities which were dissatisfied with their existing system were authorized to vote on the question of charter revision and to choose a board of freeholders which would study the problems of the municipal government and select one of the optional charters contained in the act to be submitted to the electorate with its recommendation for adoption. Thus the communities were permitted to determine, in a general way, the form and the structure of their local government organization.

By 1915 the movement for municipal home rule had developed to the point where fifteen states had adopted constitutional amendments providing for home rule, as shown in a careful study by Professor Howard L. McBain. It was evidently his belief, as it certainly was that of many others, that this movement for constitutional home rule would spread rapidly through the remainder of the states, so that in the future the right of cities to determine the form of the government under which they lived would no longer be questioned. In 1933 Joseph D. McGoldrick brought the story down to 1930. During this period of fifteen years only one additional state had adopted a home rule amendment,[5] and only two have done so since, as shown in the table on page 801. Some of these provisions require legislative implementation, as in Pennsylvania, where it has never been provided; others, as in Ohio, are self-executing, granting authority to municipalities to exercise all powers of local self-government and to adopt and enforce within their limits such local police, sanitary, and other regulations as are not in conflict with general law. Even in such cases the cities often find themselves restricted by unwise court decisions.[6]

[5] McBain, Howard L., *Law and Practice of Municipal Home Rule* (Columbia University Press, 1916); McGoldrick, Joseph D., *Law and Practice of Municipal Home Rule, 1916–1930* (Columbia University Press, 1933).

[6] See Bromage, Arthur W., *Introduction to Municipal Government and Administration*, Chapter 8 (Appleton-Century-Crofts, New York, 1950); Keith, John P., *City and County Home Rule in Texas* (Institute of Public Affairs, University of Texas, 1951); Mott, Rodney L., *Home Rule for America's Cities* (American Municipal Association, Chicago, 1949); and the following articles: Keith, John P., "County Home Rule for Michigan," *County Officer*, August 1952, pp. 234–240, 245, 252; Kenney, David T., "County Home Rule Today," *ibid.*, March 1951, pp. 74–76, 81; Perkins, John A., "State Responsibility and Home Rule,"

Home Rule States — 1952

STATES	CITIES	COUNTIES	STATES	CITIES	COUNTIES
Arizona	1912		New York	1923	1935
California	1879	1911	Ohio	1912	1933
Colorado	1902		Oklahoma	1908	
Connecticut	1951		Oregon	1906	
Georgia	1951		Pennsylvania	1923	
Illinois	1951		Rhode Island	1951	
Maryland	1915 & 1951	1915	Texas	1912	1933
Michigan	1908		Utah	1932	
Minnesota	1896		Washington	1889	1948
Missouri	1875	1945	West Virginia	1936	
Nebraska	1912		Wisconsin	1924	
New Jersey	1950				
			Total	23	7

The home rule movement, sharply arrested for a number of years, has now been revived. Both cities and counties, long hampered by restrictive constitutional and statutory provisions, have been clamoring for broader powers of self government. Their demands have been actively supported by such national organizations as the National Municipal League and the American Municipal Association. The latter clearly stated the case for the kind of strong and self-reliant local government, so basic to the Anglo-Saxon tradition, when in its National Municipal Policy Statement for 1950, it said that local government "should be autonomous so far as practical and consistent with public welfare. While the Federal government and governments of the several states may invoke their broad powers and great financial resources to make possible some local government services, still these powers and finances should be delegated for the purpose of administration to the municipal authorities, in a manner consistent with responsible local self-government." This philosophy is basic in the American system of government.

There are several conditions essential to the realization of any real home rule for American local units. They must be accorded an opportunity to use productive tax sources sufficient to meet the costs of education, city streets, traffic control, social services, and all the other important (and often costly) services which the people demand. This they cannot do as long as the Federal government and the states continue to monopolize virtually all of the pro-

---

State Government, February 1949, pp. 32–35; Shoup, Earl L., "Constitutional Problems of County Home Rule in Ohio," *Western Reserve Law Review*, December 1949, pp. 111–132; Walker, Harvey, "Let Cities Manage Themselves," *National Municipal Review*, December 1947, pp. 625–630; White, Thomas R., "Constitutional Changes in Matters of Home Rule and Municipal Government," *Temple Law Quarterly*, April 1952, pp. 428–435.

ductive sources of revenue; recent legislation in New York and Pennsylvania indicates a possibility that this practice may be modified.

At the same time the cities must begin to think in terms of new tax patterns whose returns will be adequate to meet the requirements of their new responsibilities. One fact is plain: the cities must have more money. There has been a great deal of propaganda, promoted chiefly by the real estate people, on the overtaxing of real property. At one time it may have been that real estate was carrying more than its fair share of the burden, but one has yet to be convinced that under present conditions, with mounting taxes in so many other fields, real estate cannot properly yield at least as much as it has been paying. But in addition, the cities must have access to sales taxes, income taxes, gasoline taxes, cigarette and tobacco taxes, amusement or admissions taxes, hotel taxes, liquor taxes, utility taxes, and various other forms.

As noted later in the discussion of Federal-municipal relations, the Federal government must continue to provide financial assistance in connection with emergency needs, even after such adjustments as are recommended have been made. The local units themselves may well explore and develop further the possibilities of self-liquidating projects. But most important of all, they must be freed from unreasonable restrictions and restraints, constitutional and statutory. Some of these are financial, applying to tax sources, tax rates, debt limitations, and the like; others arise from the grossly discriminatory provisions in the laws of most states with regard to apportionment. While these provisions continue in effect, it must continue to be true, as the late Professor Merriam said long ago, that the states seem to be unwilling either to govern the cities or to permit them to govern themselves; they have given the cities too much power without supervision, and not enough with wise and temperate supervision.

The home rule policies used in connection with cities are quite as applicable to counties. A general law providing for a certain amount of local autonomy, as recommended in the *Model State Constitution*, might be supplemented by an optional charter plan or by authorization to frame their own charters. There are so many barriers, constitutional, statutory, and judicial, standing in the way of county government reform that the people and the legislature would do well to concentrate on clearing some of them away, as a preparatory step toward greater home rule and a more economical and efficient administration of county functions.

State Supervision of Local Finances

There is no phase of public administration of more vital concern to the average citizen than control over finances. In nearly a dozen different aspects of financial administration the states have extended their authority over local agencies. These include supervision of assessments; supervision of tax collection; limitation of tax rates; control over budgets and expenditures; limitation of debt incurrence and supervision of debt retirement; financial aid to local governments in the form of shared taxes or grants-in-aid; supervision of accounts, audits, and reporting; as well as control of receiverships and credit facilities, and control over the selection of the personnel engaged in the work.[7]

Control over local finance, as Professor Kilpatrick points out, is not a very precise term. In any given case it may mean all of these things or any combination of two or more of these types of supervision. One difficulty has been that supervision has rarely been on the basis of complete coverage of the whole fiscal process in the local units concerned. Each state has regulated certain phases of the process, but few have attempted to control all phases. Those left unsupervised provided opportunities for financial leaks and for the use of unsatisfactory practices.

The scope of the supervisory function involves the setting of standards, instruction of local officials as to their meaning and observance, and finally, inspection to ascertain that they have been observed. Several methods of making supervision effective are available: constitutional, which is highly rigid; legislative, which is moderately elastic; administrative, which is most elastic; and judicial. The character of the supervision which may be employed is likewise subject to wide variation. It may involve actual control of a local process or transaction. It may involve cooperation on the part of state and local officials in some part of the fiscal process. It may involve the rendering of a state service for a fee, as in auditing, where the actual costs are frequently assessed against the unit or service audited. Or it may be merely an advisory service to local officials, or even a nominal, perfunctory, and more or less sterile examination of their financial records after the transactions have been completed and it is too late to do any good.

State Supervision of Local Assessments. In Chapter 15 the inequities characterizing the assessment of real estate were discussed, as well as the causes and the methods of improving such practices. Of necessity, all of the states (except Delaware and Pennsylvania) have felt obliged to establish state supervision of this activity. The supervisory agencies in seven states (Connecticut, Florida, Oklahoma, Rhode Island, Texas, Vermont, and Virginia) have limited power; the other thirty-nine have a relatively greater degree of authority. Alabama, Louisiana, Maryland, and Ohio have some of the strongest legislation. In the latter, all taxable property is assessed by the state. The State Tax Commission, which has wide authority with respect to real estate assessment, must approve all tax exemptions and has the power to control personnel in all county assessing offices. It may issue rules and regulations with respect to assessment principles and methods. Even in Virginia,

7 For a tabular summary of state laws covering all of the various types of supervision of local finance, and the administrative provisions for such supervision, see Kilpatrick, Wylie, *State Supervision of Local Finance* (Public Administration Service, Chicago, 1941), and reproduced in Council of State Governments, *State-Local Relations*, pp. 32–33 (Chicago, 1946).

the state tax commissioner may withhold the salaries of local commissioners for neglect of duty or failure to make the required reports, and he may report to the circuit court any incapacity, misconduct, or neglect of duty on the part of local commissioners and thereby institute ouster proceedings against such officers. The supervisory powers of these agencies are varied and cover a wide field, as is indicated in the table below.[8]

Supervisory Powers of State Agencies over Local Assessments

POWER	NUMBER OF STATES
General supervision	33
Advising local assessors	36
Instituting procedures to remove assessors	26
To call meetings of assessors	25
Interpret tax laws	8
Require reports	33
Visit offices of local assessors	25
Investigate complaints regarding assessments	27
Issue rules and regulations	24
Prescribe assessment forms	45
Enforce penalties against taxpayers	32
Assess properties omitted by local officers	18
Order or make reassessments	22
Order local boards of review to convene to correct inequities	9

State Control of Local Tax Sources and Rates. Recent developments of far-reaching importance have taken place with respect to this aspect of state-local fiscal relations. In the past, severe restrictions were placed on the scope of the taxing powers of local units by limiting both sources and rates. In Pennsylvania, for instance, the Sterling Act of 1925 forbids the city of Philadelphia to levy on sources taxed by the state; the law applies regardless of which tax measure may have been first enacted. There is also the possibility that taxes imposed by local units may be thrown out by the courts on constitutional grounds. Assuming, however, that the source is available to the local unit and that the act is drawn in a manner acceptable to the courts, laws regulating rates have long been common. In the decade of the thirties, tax rate limitation laws were widely adopted, often without much consideration and largely as a result of an almost hysterical desire to reduce the tax burden. These were discussed in Chapter 15.

Gradually the state leaders realized that it was impossible to continue on this basis. The local units needed more revenue, but under existing conditions it was impossible for them to raise it in amounts adequate for their needs. As a result there was a constant and growing pressure for more and more state aid. The states, with pressing needs of their own, did not have the

[8] *State-Local Relations, op. cit.*, pp. 36–37, and titles in Selected References.

money to give to the local units, and they did not want to assume the responsibility for imposing heavy additional taxes. The alternative was to tell the local units, in substance, if they needed the money, to raise it themselves. In one sense this was a good thing, for it put responsibility on the spending unit to impose the taxes necessary to support its program. Significant experiments in this direction were initiated in New York and Pennsylvania.

In 1947, under Public Act No. 481, Pennsylvania suddenly shifted from one extreme to the other, granting to its local governments the broadest taxing authority of any state in the country. Under this act all local jurisdictions other than rural townships and the City of Philadelphia (which already had broad taxing powers) were given authority to impose taxes upon "any and all subjects of taxation" not already levied upon by the state; such taxes might be levied on persons, transactions, occupations, privileges, subjects, and property within the limits of the unit imposing the levy. The Act obviously went too far; the local units produced an array of new taxes that would stagger the imagination. Amendments adopted in the 1949 session for the purpose of correcting inequities and abuses arising under the original Act, imposed some limitations, but the basic principles remained unchanged. The people in the state claim that it is working well.[9]

As of the end of 1949 some 1,067 taxes had been levied under this permissive legislation — sixty-six by cities, 271 by boroughs, twenty by townships, and 710 by school districts. Amusement taxes had been imposed by 184 jurisdictions, income taxes by 185, per capita taxes by 288, severance or related privilege taxes by 181, mercantile or business privilege taxes by thirty-nine. In general, most of the large municipalities levied broad-based taxes such as those on amusements, mercantile business, and income.

New York, under its famous Moore Plan, known officially as the General Local Government Assistance Plan, attacked the same problem in a little different manner and with considerably more restraint. Legislation adopted in 1947 and 1948 permits all counties and cities having a population in excess of 25,000, to levy certain specified taxes. Cities, however, may levy only to the extent of the rate not used by the counties. The list follows:

[9] There is a considerable literature on this Act: Hobart, Marielle, Comp., *Taxes Levied Under Act 481: Types — Rates — Receipts* (Department of Internal Affairs, Harrisburg, April 1952); Joint State Government Commission, *Report on the Pennsylvania Tax System*, Part II (Harrisburg, 1949); Sigafoos, Robert A., *The Pennsylvania Local Tax Law; an Analysis of Pennsylvania Act No. 481* (Bureau of Business Research, Pennsylvania State College, 1950); Smedley, Elizabeth, *Legal Problems Involving Act 481*, Second Edition (Department of Internal Affairs, Harrisburg, 1952); and the following articles: Alderfer, Harold F., and others, "Act 481: Its First Two Years of Operation," Department of Internal Affairs *Bulletin*, February 1949, pp. 17–27; and "Pennsylvania's Local Taxes," *State Government*, July 1948, pp. 144–145, 154; Boran, Joseph B., "School District Tax Changes, Act 481," Department of Internal Affairs *Bulletin*, July 1949, pp. 24–32; Spaulding, Richard C., "Pennsylvania Amends Permissive Local Tax Law," *National Tax Journal*, September 1949, pp. 272–277, and "Loosening the Purse Strings," *National Municipal Review*, January 1950, pp. 14–16; Stout, Randall S., and Myers, Eugene A., "The Development of Permissive Local Taxation since 1945," *Current Economic Comment*, August 1951, pp. 20–35.

STATE OF NEW YORK
AUTHORIZED LEVIES UNDER GENERAL LOCAL GOVERNMENT
ASSISTANCE PLAN

2% tax on retail sales and use
3% on restaurant meals if the charge is $1 or more
3% tax on utility bills
Annual tax on privilege of selling alcoholic beverages at retail, not in excess of 25% of the annual state license fees
5% tax on admissions
$25 per annum tax for each coin-operated amusement device
$5 per annum tax on the use of passenger cars weighing not more than 3,500 pounds, and $10 on passenger cars in excess of that weight, and on all commercial vehicles
Gross receipts tax on businesses or professions at rates of $\frac{3}{10}$ of 1%, $\frac{3}{5}$ of 1% on gross income of financial business
5% tax on occupancy of hotel rooms

In interesting contrast with the Pennsylvania law, which — as noted above — has been extensively used, the New York law has been used scarcely at all. Only two counties — Erie and Monroe — and five cities — Syracuse, Troy, Poughkeepsie, Binghamton, and Newburgh — have used the law. In California, 122 cities were levying sales taxes in 1949, and sixty-five cities throughout the country had city income or wage taxes.[10]

State Supervision of Tax Collection. In most jurisdictions there is little state supervision over the collection of property taxes. Taxes are "received" by the treasurer, tax collector, or receiver of taxes for each local unit, such supervision as exists commonly being of the legislative variety. The law prescribes who shall collect taxes, and how, and sets up without any provision for the supervision of the process the procedure to be followed in the collection of delinquent taxes and the disposition of tax delinquent properties. In a few states, as in Pennsylvania, the counties collect certain types of taxes for the state; in these instances an extensive supervision is exercised by the state revenue collecting agency.

State Control over Local Budgets. The fourth type of state financial supervision over the local units involves control over local budgets. Forty-one states require the preparation of budgets by some or all of their local units. Thirty-seven states require budgets for counties, and twenty-eight for municipalities. Other local governments, not counting school districts, must prepare budgets in twenty-two states.[11] Originally, budgeting was required with re-

[10] On these problems, see: Blank, David M., "Reform of State-Local Fiscal Relations in New York," *National Tax Journal*, December 1950, pp. 326–347 and March 1951, pp. 77–91; California State Board of Equalization, *City Sales Taxes in California* (Sacramento, 1948, and supplement, 1949); Egger, Rowland A., "The Pattern of State-Municipal Financial Relations," *Virginia Municipal Review*, October 1950, pp. 221–227; Grodzins, Morton, "State-Municipal Fiscal Relations: a Critical Summary," *National Tax Journal*, March 1950, pp. 1–17; and New Jersey Commission on State Tax Policy, *Taxation and Public Policy in New Jersey* (Fifth Report, Trenton, 1950).

[11] Kilpatrick, *op. cit.*, pp. 23–24, and Council of State Governments, *State-Local Relations*, pp. 30–33. The states without such a requirement are: Delaware, Georgia, Mary-

spect to current operations only; gradually, budget requirements have become more inclusive, covering both capital outlays and debt transactions as well. Budget forms for all or some local units are prepared in thirty-one states, but only twenty-five states issue forms for all local units from which budgets are required. Thirty states make some kind of periodic audit to check adherence to the budget.

There are, as a matter of fact, two types of budgetary control: first, the checking of the form of local budgets to insure their compliance with state laws; second, the exercise of discretionary powers over the purpose and amount of the various items contained in the budget. The former is used in most states where regulation exists, Indiana, Massachusetts, and North Carolina, among others, having devised budget forms for use in the localities. Massachusetts, New Jersey, New Mexico, and other states check budgets to insure compliance with state laws. There is wide diversity among the states regarding the official responsible for supervision. This duty naturally belongs to the unit supervising local government, if there is one; in the majority of cases, otherwise, it is assigned to the comptroller or the auditor.

Professor Kilpatrick believes that the states should be responsible for laying down the budget procedure of their localities and for supervising its enforcement, and in this connection he sets forth four primary duties of the state: (1) by statute and administrative ruling to prescribe the procedure through which localities administer budgets; (2) to create and adequately staff supervisory agencies to interpret and to enforce the law and assist local units; (3) to insure the enforcement of minimum budget and fiscal standards applicable to all local units; and (4) to assume promptly direct budgetary and fiscal control for the duration and correction of the breakdown in any individual units where chaotic conditions impel state intervention and temporary control.[12]

State Control of Local Indebtedness. In this fifth method of state control of local finances, nearly all states impose more or less inflexible constitutional and/or statutory limits on the powers of their local units to incur debt; these laws, which regulate the purposes, amounts,[13] terms, and forms of local debt, are supplemented by several different types of administrative supervision. Thirty-six state constitutions, in fact, limit local debts, and forty-four states

land, Michigan, Rhode Island, South Carolina, and Vermont. In certain other states, such as Illinois, Tennessee, and Wisconsin, supervision is limited to relatively few localities.

[12] Kilpatrick, Wylie, *State Supervision of Local Budgeting* (National Municipal League, New York, 1939); Morrow, Glenn D., "Supervision of County Debts in Kentucky," *Public Administration Review*, Autumn 1943, pp. 335–352.

[13] Some of these limitations are based on percentages of the total annual assessments for short periods of time; Professor Karl Scholz has shown that if Philadelphia, which uses a five-year average, had introduced a nine-year moving average, as the base, the debt margin would have varied inversely with the business cycle. The boom period would have found the city unable to borrow, while there would have been an enlarged borrowing capacity in the depression period. See his *Municipal Borrowing Power, Debts, and Unemployment* (Pennsylvania State Planning Board, Harrisburg, 1937).

limit the terms of local bonds. Nearly all the limits are defined in terms of a percentage of the assessed valuation of all property in the municipality concerned; with the defects in the system of assessments already indicated, it is clear that this is a most inaccurate measure of the borrowing capacity of the various units.

The study by the Council of State Governments classifies the various types of administrative controls under four headings, as follows[14]:

1. Reporting of local bond issues to a state office in thirty-eight states
2. State examination of the amount and purposes of new local borrowing in five states (Indiana, Kentucky, Louisiana, Michigan, and North Carolina)
3. State assumption of control of some or all aspects of the fiscal operations of defaulting localities in fifteen states, among them Alabama, Maine, Massachusetts, New Hampshire, New Jersey, and North Carolina. Where defaulting localities are not subject to state administrative receiverships, they may come under court-appointed receivers, as in Minnesota and Texas for all units, and in Arkansas, California, Florida, Idaho, New Mexico, Tennessee, and West Virginia for special districts
4. State extension of credit facilities to local units in a few states

In some states, supervision occurs *only* when a question of indebtedness is involved; in others, the law confers discretionary power upon the authorities, under which they may pass upon questions of policy and procedure, such as the necessity for the improvement for which bonds are to be issued. Massachusetts, New Jersey, and Pennsylvania use the former method, while Indiana and Iowa employ the latter. In Pennsylvania, the Bureau of Municipalities has been able to maintain a fairly effective supervision over the financial affairs of those cities which have applied for permission to borrow money, checking the legality of the issues and examining the financial records of the cities concerned, except in the case of special assessment bonds.

North Carolina has one of the most drastic laws for the control of local bond issues. Since 1927 every county has been required to appoint an accountant and to operate on a budget basis. A few years later, in 1931, the legislature created the Local Government Commission, whose organization and duties were discussed previously. Under the provisions of this act, no note or bond of any municipality, county, or other political subdivision is valid unless approved by the Commission. The notes or bonds are sold by the Commissioner of Revenue at Raleigh. The securities are delivered to the purchaser by the State Treasurer, who receives the proceeds and remits them to the proper local authorities. In case any local unit defaults in payment of its debt obligations, the Commissioner may appoint an Administrator of Finance to collect all taxes and disburse all funds.

Financial Aid to Local Governments. Local units receive financial assistance from the states in the form of grants-in-aid, shared taxes, and — most recently — direct grants. The movement for financial aid, stimulated originally by the desire on the part of the states to extend control over local units

[14] *State-Local Relations, op. cit.*, pp. 31–35.

whose financial management had too often been characterized by waste, extravagance, and incompetence, was later accelerated by the financial distress of large numbers of local units during the depression. Rapidly mounting costs and severely restricted revenue sources have still further increased local pressures for aid since World War II.

Grants-in-aid and shared taxes are two separate kinds of payments, yet they are not too clearly distinguishable. Generally speaking, shared taxes go back to the governmental unit in which the revenue was collected, while grants-in-aid are distributed for a particular activity, in accordance with some prescribed formula, regardless of the origin of the funds. Very often there is a matching requirement, and there are normally supervisory controls. A number of states, including New York and Pennsylvania, have used grants as a part of a positive program to encourage consolidation of ineffective local units. The growth of the grant-in-aid system is shown in the table below, which indicates also the major purposes for which aid is given.

The development of the subsidy system in the states has been generally parallel to its growth in the Federal government. The most important single purpose of state aid has been education — to secure buildings and equipment, standards of teacher training, and adequacy of curriculum. Other purposes of long standing include health and sanitation, highways, and conservation. State aid for poor relief for orphans, the aged, and the blind has in late years been supplemented by aid for unemployment relief. The system of state grants has developed under similar group pressures and with the same planlessness which has characterized the Federal grants; the same need exists in the states for some effort to see the picture as a whole, to determine in each state what portion of the total revenues are to be so expended, and how this sum shall be apportioned among the various purposes for which aid is granted.

State Aid by Purpose: Selected Years, 1925–1949
(Amounts in millions)

YEAR	TOTAL	SCHOOLS	PUBLIC ASSISTANCE	HIGHWAYS	OTHER SPECIFIED PURPOSES	UNSPECIFIED
1949	$3,544.2	$1,727.5	$641.8	$562.6	$161.6	$450.7
1941	1,697.8	735.4	407.0	341.7	22.6	191.1
1939	1,537.0	676.5	371.8	298.4	19.5	170.8
1937	1,368.5	642.6	220.5	302.0	23.4	180.0
1932	758.6	397.4	42.1	229.0	16.2	73.9
1925	535.8	254.1	3.9	150.2	19.5	108.1

The shared-tax device has been used most frequently with liquor, gasoline, and motor license levies, but occurs occasionally in other fields as well.

A tabulation made in 1944 showed that some portion of the receipts from state liquor taxes was allocated to municipalities in nine states, while receipts from state liquor monopolies were allocated in five more. Liquor license receipts were allocated in seventeen states. Property tax exemptions by in-lieu payments were authorized in twenty-three states. Some portion of the motor fund revenues from the liquid fuels tax, registration fees, operators' license fees, and other similar levies are allocated in all of the states.[15]

The financial, political, and social implications of these forms of financial aid to local units are clearly outlined in the following list, compiled by Carl H. Chatters [16]:

1. A central government, national or state, uses financial aid to promote social and economic programs which it considers desirable.
2. Grants-in-aid are effective devices for assisting hard pressed areas. Great difficulties are experienced in making payments to them without giving some money also to all other governmental units of the same kind at the same level, regardless of need.
3. State aid and Federal aid take taxes from one area and spend them in another, thus becoming a kind of "share the wealth" program.
4. The centralization of government cannot be separated from the consideration of state and Federal aids. The two go hand in hand. "State aid implies dependency and in the end invites regulation. This is inevitable, logical, and generally fair." But this dependency status of the local government may exist because something was taken away from it.
5. The larger the proportion of the expense of a particular activity paid from grants or shared taxes, the greater is likely to be the degree of control exercised.
6. Grants-in-aid may be used to raise the standard of performance of a particular activity at the local government level.
7. The temptation to use grants-in-aid for political purposes is very great. A specific project may be granted or withheld as a political club to get votes. Or, the members of a legislative body may urge large and unwarranted grants to show how well they serve their constitutents.

In an effort to escape these defects of the older forms of financial aid, stabilize the financial situation in the local units and enable them to do a better job of budget planning, and put the finances of the state itself on a better basis by making its future commitments definite and specific, the State of New York adopted the Moore Plan to which reference has been made. This Plan, now generally regarded as a notable development in the history of state-local fiscal relations, has two main features and a number of secondary provisions, as indicated in the listing below. Note that the first feature of the Plan called for direct grants to local units under a definite formula but with "no strings attached." Thus responsibility for a wise and proper use of the money is placed where, theoretically at least, it should be.

[15] See Woodworth, Leo D., *Shared Taxes* (American Municipal Association, Chicago, 1944); also Kansas Legislative Council, *State-Collected Locally-Shared Revenues in Kansas*, 1937–1950 (Topeka, November 1950).

[16] Municipal Finance Officers Association, *Grants-in-Aid and Shared Taxes* (special bulletin, Chicago, March 1945). For other titles on grants-in-aid, see Selected References.

STATE OF NEW YORK
ESSENTIAL PROVISIONS OF THE GENERAL LOCAL
GOVERNMENT ASSISTANCE (MOORE) PLAN

1. Virtually the entire complicated scheme of shared taxes is replaced by simple per capita grants, at the rate of $6.75 per capita for cities, $3.55 for towns, and $3.00 for villages.

2. The local share of relief expenditures is reduced and stabilized at 20 per cent, the state assuming 80 per cent of these costs (a portion of which is supplied by Federal grants). Thus the local responsibility for relief was substantially reduced.

3. State aid for education, which had recently been increased, is continued as a separate assistance to local governments.

4. Counties (outside of New York City) continue to receive their current proportion of motor license fees and motor fuel taxes.

5. Counties and towns continue to receive current aid for highways.

6. The state program in public health (largely for counties) is continued on the current basis.

7. The state assumes the entire cost of snow removal on state highways.

State Supervision of Accounts. Another form of state financial supervision provides for the auditing of local accounts and indeed for the supervision and control of the whole accounting system. Massachusetts and New Jersey did pioneer work in this field, and during recent years most of the states have undertaken supervision of this character. New York since 1932 has required the State Comptroller to supervise the accounts of its local units through a field force of state examiners. These men, all trained accountants, examine the records of the local agencies in a manner somewhat similar to that in which bank examiners examine the records of banking institutions under their supervision and control, or in which building and loan examiners inspect the records of the building and loan associations of the state.

The New York law further provides for uniform local accounting systems, which must be used by each of the several types of local government agencies. Systems involving the uniform classification of the objects of expenditure are provided for cities, counties, towns, and villages. At the end of each year these several units are required to submit a detailed statement of their fiscal operations on forms which are provided by, and which must be returned to, the State Comptroller. With the introduction of such a system, it becomes possible for the first time to compare the expenditures of communities of the same size for a particular administrative purpose. Unless the items of expenditure are classified in the same way, such figures are worthless. Under such circumstances an inquirer has no way of telling whether different totals are due to a different classification of items or whether there exist actual differences in the administrative problems confronting the communities in question sufficient to explain the variation in expenditures.

A tabulation of the states supervising the accounting of local units shows that thirty-seven supervise their counties, twenty their municipalities, and thirteen supervise districts or other local units. Local accounting is state supervised for both counties and municipalities in seventeen states, and for all local units in thirteen states. The states may, for this purpose, be grouped in three general categories: first, those with complete control[17]; second, those with partial control; and finally, those with no control at all.[18] About 50 per cent of the states fall in the middle group; approximately one fourth have complete control, while the remaining fourth have little or no control at all. Forty states supervise one or all classes of local government.

One writer has pointed out the need for intelligent and adequate accounts and reporting, and listed four fundamental qualities which must be present in any adequate system of governmental accounting.[19] First, "the accounts must be classified by funds in such a way that all of the resources and obligations of each fund are clearly set out from all other accounts, and the surplus or deficit of each fund clearly shown at all times. Second, a clear separation should be maintained between the accounts of current operations and those of a capital nature. The current assets and liabilities of each fund should be clearly separated from the fixed assets and bond obligations of that fund. Third, the accounts must provide for an adequate system of budgetary control. It is not sufficient merely to record the receipts and disbursements or the income and expenditures. Fourth, the system must be operated on an income and expenditure basis and not merely on a cash receipts and disbursements basis." In all such systems some recognition must be given to the different activities of local government.

State Auditing of Local Units. In Chapter 14 mention was made of the distinction between the different types of audit — internal or operating, and postaudits. In the field of local government the responsibility for operating audits rests clearly with the local officials, while that for postaudits is or should be a state concern, the purpose being to verify the accounts and discover any irregularities that may exist, as well as any violations of statutory requirements or accepted standards. Professor Kilpatrick thus describes the coverage of the auditing process, which varies greatly among the states.[20]

> Of the forty-five states with supervisory audits, Delaware and Georgia restrict their audits to school districts, leaving municipal and county records untouched. Four restrict their examinations to records of the collection of taxes and other receivables due the state. Here the question is whether the state is getting its "due," not whether local transactions are honest, legal, and efficient. In Maryland, Texas, and Utah, the state audit is confined to county finances, chiefly the county treasurers. In Pennsylvania, the examina-

[17] Complete control exists in Indiana, Iowa, Mississippi, Montana, Nebraska, New Mexico, New York, North Carolina, Ohio, Washington, and West Virginia.

[18] The states having no control are California, Delaware, Georgia, Illinois, Nebraska, North Dakota, Pennsylvania, and Utah. Five states have very limited control — Louisiana, Minnesota, Rhode Island, Tennessee, and Vermont. See Kilpatrick, *State Supervision of Local Accounting*, p. 55, and *State Supervision of Local Finance*, p. 8.

[19] Morey, Lloyd, "Uniform Accounting for Local Governments," *National Municipal Review*, July 1934, pp. 377–379, and June 1938, pp. 309–313.

[20] Kilpatrick, *State Supervision of Local Finance*, p. 13.

tion extends to any municipal officers collecting state funds. One of the largest state auditing staffs in the country is necessary for the Pennsylvania audit.

Including these six states, the most extensive state service is for the auditing of counties in forty states. Over half, or twenty-nine of the states, make auditing services available to municipalities, or supervise private accountants who examine municipal books. Half the states audit districts, rural townships and other units. The emphasis upon counties, attributable to the county function of collecting state revenue, results in fourteen states disregarding municipalities and limiting examinations exclusively to counties. Only in the two New England states of Vermont and Rhode Island, where the county is an unimportant "shell," is state auditing exclusively for municipalities. Despite these variations in practice, twenty-one states make auditing services available to all their local governments. Even in this group, the states do not recurrently examine all local units, because local officials in some states may choose state or private examinations.

In Massachusetts the law requires the state supervisory agency to audit the accounts of local units once every two years, and they may do so annually at the request of the local units, many of which have requested an audit as often as possible. In Oklahoma the state must audit the books of county treasurers at least twice a year, but there is no requirement for the auditing of the books of cities, towns, or school districts, except upon request. The treasurers were at first hostile and uncooperative, but now most of them have their books in good shape in anticipation of the audit. Most shortcomings are not criminal in character but may be corrected by giving proper assistance and advice to the treasurer.

Supervision of Local Government Reporting. It should be emphasized that budgeting, accounting, auditing, and reporting are not separate but closely interrelated processes. Any exaggeration of the importance of one to the neglect of the others will prevent the attaining of the major goal of efficient financial administration. Uniform reporting is really a by-product of uniform budgeting and accounting, and is easily and inexpensively accomplished if these first two steps have been properly done. Reporting is but the collecting of information concerning local financial transactions and the furnishing of this information to the state and to the public.[21] About one fourth of the states publish comprehensive annual reports; eight publish no report.[22] The remainder publish either comprehensive reports for selected topics or units only, or reports restricted in scope.

Good reporting is essential for any comparison of the costs of governmental service in different governmental units. If — and only if — the figures are established on the basis of the same classification of items of expenditure,

[21] See Dickerson, Milton B., *State Supervision of Local Taxation and Finance in Michigan*, Chapter 6 (Michigan State College, Lansing, 1944); and Miller, Loren B., *Local Finance and Procedure* (Report to the Michigan Commission of Inquiry into County, Township and School District Government, Detroit, 1933).

[22] Kilpatrick, *op. cit.*, p. 19. Comprehensive report states: California, Indiana, Iowa, Maryland, Massachusetts, New Hampshire, New Jersey, New Mexico, New York, Ohio, and Oklahoma. States with no published reports: Alabama, Delaware, Georgia, Illinois, Nevada, Rhode Island, Pennsylvania, and Texas.

comparisons may be made revealing significant facts regarding the relative efficiency and economy of the spending agencies. Such data provide a sound basis for legislative action. In fact, any supervision or control, either by law or by a state agency, must be built on these local reports, which in addition serve to inform the taxpayer what he is getting for his money, in much the same way as the financial statement of a corporation informs the investor what is being done with his money.

Control over Personnel. No system of control can be effective unless it be administered by competent personnel; in this connection a few states have gone so far as to provide for the appointment of local assessing officers by state agencies and for the supervision of the choice of other local fiscal officers. For more than a quarter of a century this practice has been followed in a number of states, as reported by Professors Fairlie and Kneier:

> In Maryland, the state tax commission appoints a supervisor of taxes for each county from a list proposed by the county commissioners. In West Virginia, all local boards of review are appointed by the state board of public works. In Louisiana, one member of each parish board of equalization is appointed by the state tax commission. . . . In addition to the direct state appointment of county officials, there are also significant cases of state supervision over the selection of county officers and other local functionaries. . . .
>
> Direct state appointment to any large extent will involve a radical change from traditional methods, though it would seem to be justified in the case of some officials whose functions are most clearly those of agents of the state government. But there should be less objection to the extension, to officials whose duties call for special qualifications, of definite requirements as to such qualifications, and of state examinations for testing them or of state approval of local appointments. Such methods may well be applied further, not only in the fields of education and of health and highway administration, but also in the selection of prosecuting attorneys, sheriffs, assessors, auditors, and others.[23]

Conclusions. Although any conclusions to be drawn from such a survey must of necessity be expressed in the broadest and most general terms, the following are suggested [24]: (1) The problem is one of insuring to citizens the opportunity of intimate participation in their own public affairs on the one hand, and of providing a government capable of rendering efficient service on the other. (2) The frequent incompetence of local government, as well as the excesses of state centralization, have seriously obstructed progress to this goal. (3) A certain measure of state supervision is not only inevitable, but essential to the general welfare. (4) Minimum standards of fiscal procedure and functional performance should be set and maintained by the state, with the opportunity on the part of local units to exceed these standards, and with responsibility on the local officials for results. (5) Every effort should be made to improve local administration from within. (6) Efficient and responsible local administration is more important than state centralization. If democ-

[23] *Op. cit.*, pp. 103–104.

[24] Spicer, George W., "Fiscal Aspects of State-Local Relations," *Annals*, January 1940, pp. 151–160.

racy is to work at the apex of our governmental pyramid, it must first be made to work at the base. (7) A single central agency to serve primarily as a liaison between the state and local governments should be established. (8) Finally, there can be no arbitrary separation of state and local responsibility for providing and supporting public services. They must cooperate, or both will suffer.

State Supervision of School Administration

In all the states except Delaware, local control over the public schools has become an established tradition. In colonial days the early settlers built a little log schoolhouse, which in the course of time was replaced by the old-fashioned one-room country school. The people have been exceedingly reluctant to relinquish local control over their schools, even though they have often been unable, either financially or by technical training, to maintain them in a manner satisfactory from the educational viewpoint. Delaware alone has kept complete control over its schools, but there has been in the other states, particularly in North Carolina and West Virginia, a steady and gradual extension of the state powers of supervision and control. Since it was impossible to proceed directly toward this end, much of the extension of state authority has taken place by such indirect means as the subsidy.

The reorganizations in North Carolina and West Virginia were both an outgrowth of the depression. The former guarantees a basic school program of eight months from state funds. Its 1933 law establishing this support dissolved all of the previously existing 1200 school districts and established county units headed by boards of education. State agencies prescribe and supply textbooks, allocate teachers on a uniform basis, require teachers to hold state certificates, pass upon county school budgets, and control pupil transportation. At the same time West Virginia substituted fifty-five county units for 450 old units and conferred upon the State Board of School Finance broad powers similar to those provided for in the North Carolina Act.

State Subsidies to Education. State subsidies to school districts have been an important means of equalizing educational opportunity and of centralizing control over the schools. Subsidies were originally offered in an attempt to equalize the tax burden for educational purposes and to assist those districts which were financially unable to bear the cost of maintaining their own public school systems. All of the states award funds to the local districts under certain conditions and for certain purposes. Most of them regulate school age, the attendance of pupils, the training and qualifications of teachers, and the ratio of pupils to teachers; some give funds on conditions regulating the use of textbooks and the types and condition of the school buildings to be used. Four fifths of them require regular written reports to be submitted to the state authorities.

Every state now gives some financial assistance to localities for public education, and the proportion of total school costs paid by the states has increased in virtually every state during recent years. Delaware and New Mexico pay a larger share of school costs than other states, contributing 86.4 and 87.5 per cent, respectively. Louisiana and South Carolina provide approximately 61 per cent; Arkansas, 63; West Virginia, 64; North Carolina, 66; and Alabama, 73. The average percentage is highest in the group of southern and south-central states, in all of which the state pays half or more of the bill. At the other end of the scale, only one state — Nebraska at 5.5 per cent — provides less than 10 per cent of the total cost of its public day schools.[25]

It is difficult to determine the exact basis upon which these funds are allocated, because so many laws have been passed that it becomes difficult to determine which ones are now effective.[26] There are about twenty bases used by the different states in the distribution of such funds, including population, average daily attendance, number of teaching units, and such other factors as number of pupils enrolled, salaries paid to teachers, and number of school days per year. Nor is there any clear cut pattern by which the funds appropriated are allocated to the various school levels — elementary, secondary, and junior colleges. Some appropriate for general school purposes, making little or no distinction between any school grades in the matter of school support; others make a distinction, particularly regarding the state's part of such support.

The United States Office of Education made a study of this problem in 1943.[27] They found three major plans or procedures followed among the states in the distribution of funds for education. Some make one apportionment to all grades, on a formula which has no provision for measuring the amount distributed for high schools and for the elementary schools separately. All of the states provide specifically for vocational education in high school, but in seven states — Arkansas, Kansas, Kentucky, Louisiana, Oregon, South Dakota, and Virginia — no other specific reference to secondary education is made in the allocation of state school funds. Approximately half of the states provide specifically for their high schools or for special high school purposes. In some cases such funds are for general expenses of high schools; in others they are for special projects or purposes in connection therewith, while in still others they are provided for equalizing costs of specialized high school education throughout the state.

Publicly controlled and supported junior colleges, ordinarily offering two years beyond the four-year high school, have been established in many communities throughout the country, in some thirty-five states. In a number

[25] United States Office of Education, Statistical Circular No. 270 (Washington, 1950).

[26] In one large eastern state, a new head of the State Department of Education found certain allocations of subsidy funds on his desk when he took office. He tried figuring these himself by every conceivable principle that he thought might have been used, but was unable by any of these methods to arrive at the results obtained by his predecessor.

[27] Covert, Timon, *State Aid for Secondary Education*, Circular No. 225 (Washington, 1943), and other references cited in the previous edition of this volume.

of states these schools are considered a part of the local secondary school system. In seven states the only publicly controlled junior colleges are operated by the state; in nineteen states the only publicly controlled ones are operated by local school districts as parts of local public school systems. The report continues:

> State support for local junior colleges is not commonly provided to the extent that it is for high schools. Seven of the nineteen states — Arizona, California, Colorado, Mississippi, Missouri, Texas, and Washington — in which these junior colleges are maintained by local districts appear to provide 12 to 35 per cent of the funds used by the colleges. A few of the others provide some aid, but the amounts appear to be comparatively small, with the possible exception of the State of Utah.

General State Supervision. There are very few aspects of elementary or secondary education which do not somewhere or somehow come under state control. This control is obtained in a wide variety of ways. Under their powers of general supervision, more than half the states permit state educational authorities to require reports, and to prescribe the forms in which these reports shall be submitted and the forms in which the records of the several school districts shall be kept. In eighteen states the state is given power of ordinance making within the limits set up by the state constitution and the statutes. In about the same number of states all controversies arising under local school laws are subject to state adjudication.

In 1912, it is reported, high schools were accredited by state departments in fourteen states; in 1922, forty-one state departments carried on this function, while in 1940 the number was forty-four (all states except California, Colorado, Michigan, and Wisconsin).[28] Early inspection grew largely out of the concern of midwestern universities (especially Michigan, Indiana, and Wisconsin) over the caliber of the secondary schools from which their students came. At first, state supervisory officers were principally concerned with accrediting programs, and this is still a function of first importance. State supervision has tended more and more, however, to emphasize an adequate educational program for all high school students, including the non-college group. There has been a growing emphasis on the content of high school courses and on the methods of teaching. Even accrediting has taken the form of emphasizing continuous improvement of schools as well as attainment of established standards necessary for an approved rating.

Teacher Certification. By the use of the system of grants-in-aid it is possible for the state to exercise an extensive control over the personnel engaged in public school work, including such matters as training and salaries. In the matter of salary control, the locality is obliged to pay its teachers at the rate prescribed by law, or lose its appropriation. In five states, at least,

[28] In California, Colorado, and Michigan, the state universities issue lists of accredited schools; Wisconsin, while it issues no accredited list, must approve high schools before they receive state grants, and this list of state-assisted schools is commonly accepted as an accredited list. Every state has established one or more agencies to certify schools for veterans.

this method was used to raise teachers' salaries, with the hope of attracting teachers of a higher type and with better qualifications. In seven states it was used for the definite purpose of raising the educational attainments of teachers, and in eleven states to secure an adequate staff to carry the teaching load. The qualifications of teachers are controlled by regulations requiring certification for permanent teaching positions in the state school system. In forty-four states examinations for teachers are administered by the state, and certificates are issued upon the passing of these examinations. In twenty-four states the supervising authorities have power to set up standards for admission to the teaching profession.[29] Suspension or removal has been placed under the control of the supervising authorities in eleven states, removal being usually accomplished by the revocation of license.

State Control over the Curriculum. All forty-eight states to a greater or lesser degree exercise some supervision over public school instruction. State staffs concerned with such problems have increased fourfold in the last forty years. Definite courses of study have been established in many states. For a great many years New York, whose controls are now less rigid than they once were, was the outstanding example of central control over local schools. The State Department of Education not only prescribed the subjects which should be taught, specifying the number of weeks and the number of hours per week, but it outlined in detail, in a series of syllabi, the exact nature of the subject matter to be presented in each course of study.

State supervisory agencies are concerned with curriculum revision and either prepare prescribed courses of study or issue suggested guides and outlines. In some states — the Council of State Governments reports — curriculum planning is the basic factor of the supervision program. This is true in Virginia. In many states, as in Michigan, activity in curriculum development includes cooperation with educational associations, teachers, and local administrators. Almost every state supervisory body uses the technique of demonstration classes, and in some states (Arkansas, Oklahoma, Wisconsin) model or "key" schools are maintained for demonstration purposes.

State Control over Textbooks. At least two thirds of the states have established control over the choice of textbooks used in the public schools, under their ordinance-making power. In some cases this regulation has taken the form of prescribing certain books for certain courses of study, while in others a list of books acceptable to the state department is prepared and distributed to the localities. From these lists, individual selections may be made. In a few cases the state has undertaken to publish its own texts for many of the courses required.

[29] Almost 1,200 institutions of collegiate grade are engaged in the training of public school teachers, 65 per cent of them privately or denominationally controlled. Among them, teacher training is state supervised directly through state accrediting practices or indirectly through prescribing certain courses that must be taught if graduates are to receive teaching certificates. Accrediting of teacher-training schools is carried on by all but a few states.

State Control over School Buildings. Many states supervise school buildings, from the point of view of exits, emergency lighting systems for auditoriums, and safety from fire hazards generally. Such buildings are usually under the control of the state administrative agency charged with building inspection and the enforcement of fire and panic regulations. Some states, however, have undertaken to pass upon building plans for schools with regard to their suitability and architectural design. In Pennsylvania, for instance, where such supervision is in effect, the Department of Public Instruction is able to assist any community in the state with the planning of a public school building of any type required. Complete blueprints of many types of buildings, which have been inspected and approved by the State Art Commission as well as construction experts, are on file.

Supervision of school buildings may become a very real and effective method of control. Some years ago, in a small town in central New York, the high school building was a dilapidated structure that had been condemned for years as unsafe and unsuitable for school purposes. The local authorities had paid no attention to the repeated pleas of the State Department of Education for the construction of a new building. In the meantime the state law was amended, giving the Department greater authority with regard to school buildings. As a result of this enactment the Department was able to tell the local authorities that their state funds would be withheld unless they undertook immediately to plan for the new building. Needless to say, the local authorities lost no time in selecting plans, making financial arrangements, and advertising for contracts for the new building.

Thus, by the use of these several devices, most of them incidental to the distribution of state funds to the local school districts, the states have steadily extended their authority over the public school system, usually at the expense of the power of the local units. In a few instances, however, legislative acts have provided for definite transfers of authority.[30]

State Supervision over Public Health

While public health administration is one of the oldest and most important of the administrative services of modern government, it is still of rather recent origin. Students of history are familiar with the accounts of epidemics and plagues which swept over cities, taking a heavy toll of human life. Prior to the discoveries of modern science, events of this character were regarded as acts of God. They were considered inevitable, and it was generally believed that there was nothing that man could do about them. Consideration of sanitary conditions was an idea that had yet to penetrate the mind of man. Medieval cities have been described by Frederic Harrison [31] and other writers

[30] For an excellent summary, see White, *op. cit.*, Chapter 6.

[31] Harrison, Frederic, *The Meaning of History*, pp. 232–239 (Macmillan, London, 1894).

as literally reeking with filth and squalor. The sanitary conditions in early American cities were not much better. In the absence of facilities for the proper disposal of refuse, sewage, and other wastes, all of these were thrown into the back yard or into the streets. An individual walking down a street in an early American city never knew when refuse might be dumped from a window or door just ahead or behind.

With the discovery of the germ theory and the knowledge that diseases are communicable and that dirt and filth breed sickness, some attention came to be paid to conditions of this character. Most of the early supervision was entirely local. As further progress was made in science, it became evident that the local communities were badly in need of assistance. Individual communities were still more or less isolated, but the state health commissions attempted to assist them by furnishing scientific information which would enable them to cope more successfully with local conditions. This type of commission is well illustrated by that established in Massachusetts. A little later, the Indiana board was vested with powers not only to advise and assist the local authorities in the performance of their duties, but to direct their work and to remove them from office for inefficiency, negligence, or disregard of instructions received from the state board.

Reference has already been made to the changes which the development of modern science has wrought in the field of government. It may have seemed reasonable to permit local communities, under the guise of home rule, to disregard known principles of public health and sanitation, if they chose to do so, when the evil effects of that disregard were isolated in that single community. When, however, the development of railroads, steamships, the automobile, and the airplane produced a mobility of population in which such a community might serve as a point of origin affecting a whole state or region, this kind of local self-government ceased to be practical. Certain aspects of these problems have become of national significance.

The Department's Local Relationships. The administration of health in the local units is well illustrated by the arrangements existing in Pennsylvania. In this state there are ten district medical officers and 155 sanitarians, acting as a field force. The sanitarians work under the district medical health officers or under county medical directors in the local areas. The arrangements between the State Department of Health and the 754 subordinate health jurisdictions in the state are as follows:

1. In the forty-nine cities of the state the local boards of health and health officers administer health functions generally without state aid. Only when the city health authorities request assistance, or when a health emergency exists, does the State Department of Health or its officers enter into the picture.

2. In 648 boroughs and fifty-seven townships of the first-class there are three distinct types of arrangements:

a. Where the municipality handles the local health administration through its own board of health or health officer, who are appointed by the local council or board of commissioners, and where all costs are borne by the local unit. About 800 of the 1,000 boroughs and townships operate under this arrangement. While the Department of Health stands normally in a supervisory relationship to these municipalities, actually the county medical officers and Department sanitarians located in the area are often consulted by the local authorities and render assistance upon request.

b. Where the Department of Health takes direct charge of the local health administration under the terms of the basic board of health act of the state, which gives the Secretary of Health power to take over when he finds conditions to be such as to constitute a health menace to persons living outside the boundary of the municipalities or if it be known to him that any borough or first-class township is without an existing or efficient board of health. Under this arrangement, the Department of Health is paid by the local units for its specific services.

c. Where boroughs and townships of the first-class voluntarily surrender the administration of their health functions to the State Department of Health. In such cases all expenses incident thereto are carried by the Department of Health.

3. In all second-class townships, health administration is handled directly by district or county medical officers and their staffs employed by the State Department of Health. There are no local health officers in second-class townships.[32]

State Control over Personnel. Important among the ways in which the authority of the states over public health matters has been extended is the control over the personnel engaged in the work; this can be administered by collecting and tabulating data from reports furnished to the state department by each municipality or local subdivision. In twenty-three states the local health officers may be removed for failure to perform their duties, and in forty-two states failure of local officers to enforce properly rules and regulations pertaining to health matters may result in the state taking over control of these local activities. Some states go so far as to control local appointments. In twenty-five states the local registrars of vital statistics are appointed by the state. This state supervision of vital statistics is but a result of the efforts of the United States Bureau of the Census to develop complete and uniform reporting of vital statistics in the Birth Registration Area and the Death Registration Area. About eight states provide for the state appointment of regular health officers, and in two states all local health authorities must be approved by the state administrative authorities.

Maryland has developed over a period of years extending from 1930 an excellent system of cooperation in health matters between state and county. In the beginning a careful study was made of each county to determine its needs and conditions. After a program had been developed, a local organization was set up to sell it to the county and to the board of county commissioners. As a result of this preliminary work Maryland claims to be the only state with a trained, full-time county health officer and staff in every county

[32] See Dodson, George W., "State Health Department's Local Relationships," *Bulletin* of the Department of Internal Affairs, April 1943, pp. 9–16, and other articles in this series of four on local health administration in Pennsylvania; "Health Jurisdictions in Pennsylvania," *Pennsylvania's Health*, December 1947, pp. 6–7.

in the state. The program is supported 49 per cent by the county, 51 per cent by the state, thereby insuring state control.

The personnel aspects of this program are very important. The county commissioners of each county are required by law to sit once a month as a county board of health. One of their duties is to appoint a county health officer. The state law also requires the State Department of Health to appoint a deputy in each Senatorial District (i.e., each of the thirty-three counties of the state). In practice, the head of the State Department goes to each board of county commissioners and agrees on a man, adequately trained and carefully selected, who is then appointed to do the job. This is important, because the legislator judges the health work by what he observes in his own county.

There appears to be a serious shortage of the qualified and licensed personnel in the public health field whose services are so essential to adequate local health administration. In 1950 a Committee on Local Health Administration appointed by Governor Driscoll of New Jersey reported that there were seven counties in that state without full-time health officers, that 14 per cent of the population had only the services of a part-time health officer, and that most municipalities had no licensed health officials at all.[33] Only 51 per cent of the people had full-time help. It this is the situation in New Jersey, conditions must be much worse in many other states.

Venereal Disease Control Work. In many states venereal disease control work is carried on very largely as a state function; in others this is not the case, although there are many communities that are not financially able to set up and maintain a satisfactory program in this field. To meet the needs of these communities, the State Department of Health in Illinois arranged several years ago to assist financially in the establishment and maintenance of clinics which serve as one phase of a well-rounded program of community social hygiene. While the Department has no intention of establishing clinics of its own, it encourages the cities to do so through subsidy grants, insisting, however, upon high standards of service in each such state-aided clinic. Otherwise the administration of the clinic is strictly a local affair.

Control over Health Ordinances. State control over health ordinances is another method of centralization. In eighteen states all local health ordinances must be submitted to the state authorities for approval. In nine of these states such approval is limited to quarantine regulations; in all others all ordinances must be so approved. Ordinances of the state boards supersede those of municipalities and other local agencies. In some cases where local health departments have been taken over by the state because of their inefficiency or the existence of an emergency, the state ordinances are paramount.[34]

Control over General Sanitary Conditions. Though the state boards of health were originally advisory groups, their control has extended into many

[33] "Health Officers Held Jersey Need," *New York Times*, June 25, 1950.

[34] Wallace, *op. cit.*, p. 122; centralization in public health administration is discussed in White, *op. cit.*, Chapter 7.

fields. The control over general sanitary conditions has been accomplished in a number of ways. In forty-four states all sorts of health and sanitary statistics are collected. These statistics inform the state department regarding health matters throughout the state and provide a means by which the department can measure the effectiveness of the work done by the various local officers. The mere fact that the states have the authority to collect this information gives them a certain amount of control over the local officers, since the departments have authority to prescribe the nature and extent of the data to be furnished and the form in which they shall be presented, and since they have the power to compel local officers to comply with the request.

Inspection of local conditions by the state authorities is another method of control. In Florida the state agents may at any time visit any city for the purpose of investigating the sanitary conditions therein. Still another method of state control is maintained by the dissemination of health information through the use of the various channels of publicity, such as distribution of printed materials, radio and lecture engagements, conferences, motion pictures, and correspondence. These methods are almost universally employed. Again, the state may extend its control over general sanitary conditions through the use of its ordinance-making power, which is granted to the health authorities in forty-seven states. Illustrative of this type of control is the Pennsylvania Advisory Health Board, a nonsalaried board which holds quarterly meetings for the purpose of considering and approving sanitary and health regulations. These rulings commonly deal with matters of detail not covered in the general health laws, the provisions of which they serve to supplement and clarify.

In one other respect the states can and some of them do exercise an important control over general sanitary conditions. Many American rivers, once clear streams, have for years been little less than open sewers, loaded with mine wastes, industrial wastes, and sewage. New legislation and administrative action have sought to accomplish a purification of streams in many states. One phase of this program involves state pressure upon communities to provide proper sewage treatment works to the end that dumping sewage into streams may be eliminated and the streams purified. In Pennsylvania, for instance, the Department of Justice, working in cooperation with the Sanitary Water Board, carried on during 1944 and 1945 an aggressive campaign to prevent cities and townships from dumping sewage into the Schuylkill River and its tributaries.

Control over Sanitary Engineering Projects. Many states have established an extensive supervision over sanitary engineering projects in the various cities and other local units. These include particularly control over municipal water supplies and sewage systems; the methods used with regard to water supplies differ considerably in the various states. In twelve states reports are required, and in about forty states central inspection is maintained. State approval of all construction plans is necessary in thirty-one states, while the operation and maintenance of these plants are subject to state approval in twenty-two states. In thirty-three states power to issue specific orders for operation has been given to the state authorities, as has the ordinance-making power in twenty-six states.

Control over sewage systems includes both construction and maintenance. In six states municipalities are required to submit reports, while in thirty-eight states the power of inspection has been given to the state. In two states, Indiana and Wyoming, the complaint must originate with the citizens of municipalities. In most states approval by the state authorities is necessary for construction and operation. Approval of plans is required in many states before any construction work is undertaken.

In many states legislation has been enacted extending the regulatory and supervisory powers of the sanitary engineers to a wide variety of subjects, such as bottling plants for mineral water and soft drinks, the inspection of public bathing places, the abatement of nuisances, housing inspection, inspection of cemeteries and mausoleums, care of environmental sanitation, and many other things.

State Supervision of Public Welfare

State centralization has been extended to the field of charity and public welfare work; this tendency was much in evidence prior to the depression and has been greatly accentuated by the developments since 1929. "For centuries we have had prisons, almshouses, hospitals, and outdoor relief administered by public officials. The nineteenth century added children's institutions, parole, and probation. The twentieth century has given us mother's pensions, juvenile courts, workmen's compensation, employment bureaus, housing commissions, public playgrounds and social centers, psychiatric clinics, and visiting nurses." [35]

The history of the states in the field of public welfare supervision and administration may be divided into three periods.[36] The period between 1863 and 1900 is known as the disorganized one, during which each state institution was under a separate board charged with full responsibility for its administration. In New England the town was the center of charity administration, although in Massachusetts the state took direct responsibility for this work at the beginning of the period under consideration. In New Jersey, New York, Pennsylvania, and some of the western states responsibility was divided between county and town; in the southern states the county was the center of welfare administration.

Between 1900 and 1917 state boards of control were organized; these consisted of a small group of people appointed by the governor, exercising

[35] Warner, Amos G., Queen, Stuart A., and Harper, Ernest B., *American Charities and Social Work*, p. 531, Fourth Edition (Crowell, New York, 1930).

[36] National Conference of Social Work, *Proceedings, 1929*, pp. 523–530. See also: Breckinridge, Sophonisba P., *Public Welfare Administration in the United States, Select Documents* (University of Chicago Press, 1927).

both administrative and executive control of state institutions and agencies. The first centralized board of welfare was established in Massachusetts in 1863. This was followed by the establishment of similar boards in New York and Ohio in 1867; in Illinois, North Carolina, Pennsylvania, and Rhode Island in 1869; in Michigan and Wisconsin in 1871; and in Connecticut and Kansas in 1873. All these states had unpaid boards with supervisory powers but with no centralization of authority. The authority was transferred from one board to another. In Massachusetts the Act of 1863 provided for a Board of State Charities; in 1869 a State Board of Health was established, followed in 1879 by the Prison Commission. Finally, in 1919, when the state government was departmentalized, there were set up separate departments of health, correction, public welfare, and mental hygiene. The same process of development occurred in Illinois and New York.

The latter part of this development falls within the third period — from 1917 to date — which is characterized by: (1) the centralization of management and control of public charities in a single individual who serves as a member of the governor's cabinet; (2) the development of the social security program. Thus began a new era in welfare administration, in which efforts were made to secure cooperation between departments and at the same time to centralize authority in the states so that they might control or even take over welfare institutions formerly operated by counties and cities. With the advent of the depression, emergency relief boards were established in many states; later to be established on a permanent basis as departments of public assistance, leaving to the departments of welfare chiefly the functions of institutional management. In the following paragraphs illustrative types of departmental organization are described, and the techniques by which the states have extended their control over welfare problems previously regarded as purely local are emphasized.

The adoption of the Social Security Act in 1935 gave tremendous impetus to the development and improvement of the public welfare programs of the states. Actually it was not one act, but three acts in one — public assistance, social insurance, and health and welfare measures. Four major risks are covered in the social security aspects of these programs: (1) the risks of loss or interruption of income due to old age; (2) short period unemployment; (3) sickness; and (4) death of the principal bread winner. All of these, of course, require local relationships and local administration, for service must be provided in the local communities where the people live.[37]

Illustrative Types of State Organization. In 1917 North Carolina enacted a law requiring the State Board of Charities and Welfare to appoint a local board of three unpaid members for each county. It was specified that the

[37] See Miles, Arthur P., *An Introduction to Public Welfare* (Heath, Boston, 1949); Burns, Eveline M., *The American Social Security System*, pp. 52–59 (Houghton Mifflin, Boston, 1949); and Gagliardo, Dominico, *American Social Insurance* (Harpers, New York, 1950).

duties of these boards should be to assist the State Board in the work of the county and to act in a general advisory capacity to the county and municipal authorities in questions relating to delinquency, dependency, and social conditions generally. This law also provided for the consolidation of municipal and county welfare departments.

The New Jersey organization for welfare administration, established in 1918 and retained in the reorganization of 1948, is regarded by many experts as more satisfactory than that of any other state. The governor appoints an unpaid board of eight members, which chooses a commissioner; this board is authorized to create divisions of education, medicine, labor, statistics and research, agriculture, et cetera. It also appoints boards of managers for each state institution and for noninstitutional agencies caring for the insane, feeble-minded, and other dependents. The state board supervises the county, municipal, and private agencies to which state aid is given.

In Massachusetts the work is divided among four departments: namely, the Department of Public Welfare, the Department of Mental Diseases, the Department of Correction, and the Commission on Probation, at the head of each of which is a commissioner appointed by the governor. The Department of Public Welfare has authority to supervise state institutions, to inspect county and municipal institutions, as well as private agencies, and to administer the public assistance program.

This centralization program has been carried on very successfully. In 1949, there was not a single state without a central state department or agency in the welfare field. In thirty-five states it was designated as either the department of public welfare or the department of social welfare — usually the former. Five states had a state board or commission of welfare (Delaware, Florida, North Dakota, Oregon, Utah). Another group of states had a department of public assistance (Idaho, Nebraska, West Virginia), a department of health and welfare (Maine, Missouri), a department of social security (South Dakota, Washington), while New Jersey has its Department of Institutions and Agencies. Pennsylvania, as noted, has both a Department of Welfare and a Department of Public Assistance.[38]

Illustrations of the Extension of State Control. From the numerous forms of assistance administered by state and local authorities, the Mothers' Assistance movement may be taken as illustrative. This movement started in 1909 at a White House Conference on Child Welfare called by President Theodore Roosevelt. The Conference stressed the importance of home life for children. The movement itself was not new, since a limited number of states had already made some provision for the assistance of orphaned children. These acts were not of statewide application. The first statewide Mothers' Aid Acts were adopted in Illinois in 1911 and in Colorado in 1912. Missouri enacted similar legislation in 1911, but limited its application to Jackson County. By 1913 the number of such laws had increased to eighteen,

[38] On the historical development of welfare organization, see Miles, *op. cit.*

while by 1931 there were forty-four — in all states except Alabama, Georgia, New Mexico, and South Carolina. The provisions of these acts varied considerably from state to state. Some granted aid to deserted mothers and to mothers whose husbands were incapacitated or in penal institutions or in institutions for the insane or feeble-minded. Some went so far as to grant aid to divorced mothers and to unmarried mothers. In six states aid was also given to expectant mothers. With the adoption of the Federal Social Security program, of which mothers' aid is a part and in which all of the states are cooperating, the problem assumed its present-day aspects.

This summary indicates the extent to which an administrative agency reached down into the communities to provide relief for persons who would formerly have been subjects of local charity. In twenty-one states such state control over mothers' aid was maintained, usually by the department of welfare. In Arizona and New Hampshire the state paid the full amount, while in twelve states the state shared the cost with the local communities, either on a fifty-fifty basis or in some other proportion. These provisions for the administration of mothers' aid are the more significant when one considers that the methods used here have been employed in somewhat similar fashion in all the newer phases of public welfare administration, notably during the depression, beginning in 1929, in the handling of emergency relief and, in some cases, programs of public works.

State Supervision of Highways

In tracing the growth of state centralization, illustrations may be drawn from practically any field of administration. The function of road building, now to be considered, was to begin with, purely a local function. In the era of internal improvements, to be sure, the Federal government undertook the construction or the giving of assistance in the construction of turnpikes, but this was later discontinued. The modern era of highway construction begins with the widespread use of the bicycle and later of the automobile. Highways within the cities and towns were first improved; then the counties undertook to connect the various centers of population with each other and with the county seats. It soon became apparent that such a multiplicity of governmental units would be unable to develop any comprehensive system of highways. At this point the states began to enter the field of highway construction.

New Jersey appears to have originated the system of state aid for public highways by legislation enacted in 1891; this act provided for the raising of money by local authorities to build and improve roads, for which the state undertook to pay one third of the cost. In 1893 Massachusetts passed an act which provided for a State Highway Commission consisting of three men appointed by the governor with the consent of Council. The Commission was required to make investigations and to advise the counties with regard to construction, alteration, and the maintenance of roads. It was also authorized to hold a public meeting in each county at least once a year for the purpose of discussing matters relating to roads. At approximately the same time Vermont adopted a similar method of state highway administration. By 1910 seven states had passed laws authorizing aid to the counties for highways; by 1917 legislation of this character had been enacted by every state.

By 1935 there were four states in which the highway function had been completely centralized — outside of the cities (Delaware in 1935, North Carolina in 1931, Virginia in 1932, and West Virginia in 1933). No others have since been added to the list; when North Carolina inaugurated its program, it took over 45,000 miles of road previously controlled by counties and townships. In the other forty-four states, there is some degree of local participation in highway administration, though in many of them there is a definite tendency for the state to assume a steadily greater responsibility. In 1946 twenty-seven states distributed authority between the state and its counties, and in four states the once prevalent state-township division still existed. Several states have established state-aid divisions in their highway departments for the purpose of coordinating and supervising the state-aid system of county roads. More complex three-unit systems involving states, counties, and townships existed in thirteen states.[39]

The process by which control over road building passed gradually from the local units to the states is significant. As has been noted, the original state expenditures for highways were administered on the grants-in-aid basis; the roads still remained under the control of the local units, although the state authorities exercised some supervisory control over those highways for which state money was used in construction or maintenance. When it became evident that this method was inadequate, the states began to take over certain highways connecting important centers of population and county seats. These were designated as state highways. Acts of this character were adopted in many states around 1910. From that date on, the records show additions to the several state highway systems made at each successive legislative session as the financial inadequacy of the individual units and their failure to attract capable highway administrators became more and more apparent. Pennsylvania, for instance, began its state highways system by an act passed in 1911, taking over 8,835 miles of road. Minor additions were made at intervals until 1931, when 20,000 miles of rural road were added to the state highway system, making a total of 33,989 miles. In the session of 1933 the General Assembly took over the maintenance of 48,500 miles of additional rural roads. This policy was abandoned for a time but was later resumed. In 1948 the total state highway system consisted of nearly 41,000 miles, or more than all the state highways in ten other northeastern states. "There was a total of about 100,000 miles of public roads in Pennsylvania of which city, county, borough and first class township streets and roads comprised about 14 per

[39] Figures from United States Bureau of Public Roads, and from *State-Local Relations*, *op. cit.*, pp. 25–26; see also Hebden, Norman, and Smith, Wilbur S., *City-State Relationships in Highway Affairs* (Yale University Press, 1950).

cent. The remainder was equally divided between state highway and second class township (45,000) mileage." [40]

The taking over of roads, or the assumption of responsibility for their maintenance and repair, raises some difficult problems. When the state controls a piece of highway, the local residents expect a very high standard of construction and maintenance, whereas if this highway is a local responsibility, almost anything will do. With an increasing percentage of the annual receipts of the Motor License Fund absorbed in maintenance costs and with urgent needs for new construction, the department is much less anxious than formerly to assume new responsibilities.

The alternative to taking the roads over is to give financial assistance in such form and such amounts as will enable the local units properly to discharge the responsibility themselves. The allocation formula is prescribed by law. In some instances it is extremely complicated and may result in gross inequalities as between different local units. This has been the case in Michigan, where the Tax Study Advisory Committee reported in 1945 variations in the per capita apportionment of highway funds ranging all the way from $.80 in one county to $7.19 in another. Five other counties received less than $1.00 per capita, and thirty received less than $2.00. Thirty-four received between $2.00 and $3.00, with seventeen receiving more than $3.00.

To correct this situation, the Committee proposed a new allocation formula under which all three units of government — the state, the municipalities, and the counties — would share proportionately on a fixed percentage basis in any increase or decrease in highway-user taxes and which would eliminate much of the existing friction between county and municipal officers. Their proposal was that all revenues from liquid fuel and motor vehicle taxes should "be commingled in one fund and then divided into three parts in the following proportions: 40 per cent to the state highway department, 35 per cent to be distributed to the counties, and 25 per cent to be distributed to incorporated cities and villages." [41]

Up to the mid-thirties, attention was largely concentrated on the centralization of highway management. Since that time, emphasis has been on the broadening of Federal-state-local relationships. The Federal highway legislation of 1944 authorized funds to be expended only in urban areas, but did not disturb the existing system of channeling funds through the state highway departments. This enlarged responsibility called for the development of a new and enlarged system of state-city relations, a system that would provide better coordination and improved relationships with the cities. For a

[40] Tanger, Alderfer, and McGeary, *Pennsylvania Government: State and Local*, p. 308 (Penns Valley Press, State College, 1950).

[41] Michigan Tax Study Advisory Committee, *Preliminary Report*, pp. 35–41 (Lansing, 1945); see also Colorado Municipal League, *The Cities' Share of Gasoline Tax Revenues in Colorado* (Boulder, 1940); Pennsylvania Joint State Government Commission, *Liquid Fuels Tax* (Harrisburg, 1945); and *State Aid from Gasoline Taxes on Texas County and Road District Bonds and Warrants* (Ranson-Davidson Company, San Antonio, 1942).

number of reasons the state highway departments are in a better position to evolve suitable solutions of these problems than are the city engineers, who must supervise a variety of services in addition to the building and maintenance of streets and highways. What is involved here is, of course, but one more phase of the problem of cooperative federalism, later to be discussed more fully.

General Conclusions

Having now observed the extent to which and the means by which the states have extended controls over local units in important fields of activity, it may be appropriate to consider briefly some of the important questions which these developments raise. What are the most effective types of control? What steps are necessary at the state level? At the local level? What effect has the growth of state power had upon the strength of local institutions?

With regard to the first question, it may be said that there are at least a half dozen important types of control. Where standards are to be established or where an emergency situation arises, orders may be issued; otherwise cooperation and persuasion are normally much more effective. And, in general, they are effective, especially if the supervisory agency is known to have greater powers or authority than under ordinary conditions it chooses to exercise. Since so much of the success of any program depends on the character and the caliber of the personnel that administers it, the states have a powerful control device in setting minimum qualifications for personnel, in certifying individual applicants or appointees, or in exercising a veto power over appointments. Since local administration is often so inadequate, more direct supervision may be necessary after appointment than would otherwise be the case.

Well planned training programs for workers in specific fields can be organized and given to the appropriate groups of employees throughout the state on a county or regional basis. The state, being a larger unit and having greater resources in funds and staff, may exercise great influence at the local level by providing technical assistance to local officials and by cooperating with them in important undertakings. Finally, if grants-in-aid are provided, the state agency has available for its use all the control techniques normally attaching to that system.

If supervision in any field is to be effective, the administrative organization and procedures of both the supervisory agency and the local units to be supervised must be set up in a manner appropriate for the performance of their respective responsibilities. A prerequisite of sound administrative supervision in any field is the establishment of good legislative relationships with both the administrative personnel and the local units. The state supervisory personnel must be competent and well qualified. All of the supervisory activities relating to a given function must be drawn together in one place and should function under a single head. As in administration within a department or agency, there must be clear channels for communication between the supervisory agency and the units supervised, so that information and instructions may be passed down, information from the field and reports of operations may be passed up. It is helpful to all concerned if all legislation pertinent to the undertaking is drawn together as in a code and arranged for convenient use.

Supervisory relationships of this type are not basically different from supervisory relationships elsewhere. Success depends to a large extent on giving the local officers the maximum opportunity for the exercise of initiative, in restraint on the part of the supervising agency so that local officers will not feel that they are being completely dominated. It is a sound principle that confidence and self-reliance be developed in the local units, that they be encouraged to do themselves everything that can be done economically and efficiently at the local level. If these principles are observed, local government will not be undermined but will rather be strengthened as a result of good cooperative relationships.

SELECTED REFERENCES

Betters, Paul V., *State Centralization in North Carolina* (Brookings Institution, Washington, 1932), and McPheron, E. B., *A Summary of Indiana Centralization* (Bureau of Government Research, Indiana University, 1938).

Bitterman, Henry J., *State and Federal Grants-in-Aid* (Mentzer, Bush, Chicago, 1938). Latest general treatise; for more detailed studies in particular states, see:

California: Crouch, Winston W., *State Aid to Local Government in California* (University of California Press, 1939).

Illinois: Illinois Legislative Council, *Financial Aid to Local Governments* (Springfield, 1948).

Michigan: Tharp, Claude R., *State Aid in Michigan* (Bureau of Government, University of Michigan, 1942), and Wiledau, Paul H., *State Aid and Local Finance in Selected Michigan Counties* (Bureau of Government, University of Michigan, 1942 and 1949).

Minnesota: Institute of Governmental Research, *The Problem of State Aids in Minnesota* (St. Paul, 1947).

New York: Hinkley, Russell J., *State Grants-in-Aid* (New York State Tax Commission, Albany, 1935).

Pennsylvania: Stout, Randall S., *State Grants-in-Aid in Pennsylvania* and *Recent Trends in State Grants-in-Aid and Shared Taxes* (Bureau of Business Research, Pennsylvania State College, 1945 and 1948); also Municipal and Local Finance Officers of Pennsylvania, *Proceedings of the Fifteenth Annual Meeting*, devoted entirely to state grants to local governments (Institute of Local Government, Pennsylvania State College, 1950).

Virginia: Snavely, Tipton R., and others, *State Grants-in-Aid in Virginia* (Century, New York, 1933).

Carpenter, William S., *Problems in Service Levels* (Princeton University Press, 1940). A standard title in this field.

Council of State Governments, *State-Local Relations* (Chicago, 1946). Best available general survey; for studies in individual states, see:

Pennsylvania: Pennsylvania Economy League, State Division, *State-Local Relationships in the State of New York* (Harrisburg, 1946).

Rhode Island: Public Expenditure Council, *A Study of State and Local Relationships* (Providence, 1948).

Graves, W. Brooke, Ed., "Intergovernmental Relations in the United States," *Annals*, January 1940, entire volume. Symposium covering all phases of intergovernmental relations, including state-local.

Hansen, Alvin H., and Perloff, Harvey S., *State and Local Finance in the American Economy* (Norton, New York, 1944); see also Reed, Thomas H., *Federal-State-Local Fiscal Relations* (Municipal Finance Officers Association, Chicago, 1942).

Hebden, Norman, and Smith, Wilbur S., *State-City Relationships in Highway Affairs* (Yale University Press, 1950), and Hebden, Norman, *Effective Administration in State-City Highway Activity* (Yale Bureau of Highway Traffic, 1950). Two notable studies in the highway field.

Hutchinson, Ruth G., *335 State-Administered Locally-Shared Taxes* (Columbia University Press, 1931); see also Kansas Legislative Council, *State-Collected Locally-Shared Revenues in Kansas, 1937–1950* (Topeka, November 1950); Merlin, Sydney, *American Taxes Shared and Allocated, 1938* (American Municipal Association, Chicago, 1939), and Woodworth, Leo D., *Shared Taxes* (American Municipal Association, Chicago, 1939 and 1944).

Institute of Local and State Government, *City-State Relations* (University of Pennsylvania, 1937); see also MacCorkle, Stuart A., *State Financial Control over Cities in Texas* (Arnold Foundation, Dallas, 1937), and Wallace, Schuyler C., *State Administrative Supervision over Cities in the United States* (Columbia University Press, 1928).

Kilpatrick, Wylie, *State Supervision of Local Budgeting* (National Municipal League, New York, 1939); for studies of other fiscal processes, see:

Accounting: Scheps, Clarence, *Central Control of Municipal Accounts in Louisiana* (Bureau of Government Research, Louisiana State University, 1941).

Assessments: Pardue, Beulah L., *State Supervision of Property Tax Assessment in Kentucky* (Bureau of Business Research, University of Kentucky, 1948) and Waldby, Hubert O., *Recent Trends in State Supervision of General Property Assessments* (Bureau of Government Research, University of Oklahoma, February 1951).

Borrowing: Ford, Robert S., and Goodrich, Kenneth S., *State Supervision of Local Borrowing* (Bureau of Government, University of Michigan, 1942).

Kilpatrick, Wylie, *State Supervision of Local Finance* (Public Administration Service, Chicago, 1941). In addition to this excellent general treatise, see the following relating to particular states:

California: Vanderlip, Loren C., *State-Local Fiscal Relations in California* (State Chamber of Commerce, San Francisco, 1946).

Georgia: Brooks, Robert P., *State Supervision of Local Fiscal Affairs in Georgia* (Institute for the Study of Georgia Problems, University of Georgia, 1948).

Illinois: Leland, Simeon E., *State-Local Fiscal Relations in Illinois* (University of Chicago Press, 1941).

Kentucky: Legislative Research Commission, *State-Local Fiscal Relations* (Frankfort, 1952).

Louisiana: Asseff, Emmett, and others, *State Supervision of Local Finance in Louisiana* (Bureau of Government Research, Louisiana State University, 1951).

uniform administrative policies enforced by cooperation among the states, or, finally, by the development of uniform principles of judicial interpretation.

Since only the general question of interstate relations is being considered here, it is unnecessary to dwell on uniformity achieved — at least in peacetime — through Federal centralization by amendment of the Federal Constitution, or through the influence of such factors as concurrent powers, the grant-in-aid system, or the leadership of Federal administrative agencies in developing uniform practices and policies among the states. Nor is it necessary to dwell upon such obvious influences toward uniformity as are provided by the provisions of the Federal Constitution or of Congressional legislation. During the defense period and the early part of the second world war, some of these obstacles to the free flow of interstate trade had a serious effect on the war effort. Corrective measures were adopted, in some cases by the states themselves and in others by the exercise of the war powers of the Federal government, as for instance, when the Office of Defense Transportation took over full control of trucking operations.

The primary concern here is with those influences which have originated in the states and which are organized and maintained by them for the purpose of developing uniform policies. One of these influences, interstate compacts and agreements, has already been briefly referred to; the other, involving movements for the adoption of uniform laws and for the development of uniformity, cooperation, and reciprocity among administrative officers in different states, will now be considered.[16] Since there has been so little actual accomplishment in the field of judicial uniformity, no further discussion of that topic will be included here.[17]

Interstate Compacts and Agreements

The efforts of the Council of State Governments, which has diligently promoted the idea of the compact device, have produced encouraging results. These may be classified on the basis of subject matter or, from another point of view, as National (crime control, oil), regional (education, river development, fisheries), and local (apportionment of waters, public works). Significant examples of each of these types are described below. In very general terms, these agreements may be said to fall into three different classes, as regards their legal origin: compacts and agreements ratified by legislative action of the signatory states and approved by Congress; reciprocal legislation; and executive agreements and contracts.

Interstate Parole and Probation Compact. The Interstate Parole and Probation Compact, which in 1951 had been adopted in all forty-eight states, has achieved virtually complete uniformity in interstate cooperation in parole and probation supervision. It provides a simple, businesslike, legal, and

16 Graves, *op. cit.*, Chapter 2, and in greater detail in succeeding chapters.

17 *Ibid.*, Chapter 18, and Hargest, William M., "Keeping the Uniform State Laws Uniform," *University of Pennsylvania Law Review*, December 1927, pp. 178–184.

constitutional method of granting probationers and parolees the privilege of moving outside of the state in which they were sentenced and into other jurisdictions where they may have better opportunities for adjustment, with full protection to society. Prior to the drafting of this Compact and the passage of its enabling legislation by the states, some 10,000 parolees were living outside of the states of their offenses without control or supervision. Now, when a state enters into the Compact, the governor appoints an official administrator whose duty it is to administer the Compact for that state and to provide, by conference with his fellow administrators in other compacting states, rules and regulations for carrying out its provisions.[18]

Interstate Oil Compact Commission. The Interstate Oil Compact Commission, eighteen years old in 1953, is a notable example of the success and practicability of the compact method in the solution of the perplexing interstate problems in oil and gas affecting nearly half of the states in the Nation. The sole purpose of this organization for the conservation of oil and gas by the prevention of waste from any cause, through established state agencies, had grown in 1952 to include twenty-two widely scattered states. The Commission is the administrative agency organized to carry out the functions of the Compact; it consists of one representative from each member state. Under most of the state enabling statutes, the governor is named official representative with authority to appoint a substitute or assistant representative. In others, the governor appoints or designates the official representative. One state designated the director of the State Department of Conservation as its representative.

The Commission holds quarterly meetings, the proceedings of which appear in a substantial quarterly bulletin. Studies are made of methods and practices for prevention of physical waste in oil and gas production and for the discussion of questions affecting oil and gas conservation. These meetings are widely attended by state officials, industry representatives, and other interested persons. A formal program and open forum discussions are features of the sessions. Outstanding engineers, lawyers, economists, and technicians are brought to the Commission's roundtable, where the results of their studies and experiments are presented for the information of the entire petroleum and natural gas industry. This body has succeeded in instilling in the minds of the public and of the various branches of the state and Federal governments, confidence in its aims and objectives, and general approval of the voluntary collaboration method of reconciling divergent views and opinions.[19]

[18] See Council of State Governments, *The Handbook on Interstate Crime Control*, Revised Edition, Chapter 4 (Chicago, 1949); see also Ellis, William J., "Interstate Parole and Probation Compact: an Appraisal After Ten Years of Operation," *State Government*, March 1945, pp. 40–42.

[19] See the Commission's *Summary of the Background, Organization, Purposes and Functions of the Interstate Compact to Conserve Oil and Gas; Saving Your Oil: Accomplishments in Oil and Gas Conservation; Utilized and Cooperative Projects in the United States*

Regional Education Compacts. The Southern Regional Education Compact which was before Congress for approval in 1949,[20] along with the Western Regional Education Compact, are interesting examples of regional agreements. The former provides for a Board of Control consisting of the governor and three members from each participating state. Planned originally to include fifteen Southern states, nine governors signed; there were in 1952, fourteen signatories to this compact which provides the foundation for a regional system of higher education. There was some suggestion at the time that it was a neat trick to circumvent the decision of the Supreme Court in the Sipuel case [21] and to perpetuate the system of segregation in higher education by establishing, through the pooled resources of a number of states, professional schools for Negroes who have been excluded by law from the tax-supported institutions of the cooperating states. If this was ever contemplated as one of the purposes of the plan, it was actually a minor consideration, as subsequent developments in the South and West have clearly shown. The Southern Region has for years been losing large numbers of its most able young people who went North or West for professional training — and remained there. No region can prosper if its most promising leadership is continuously siphoned off.

Many of the states in the South and West are not in a position economically to provide high grade professional training in all fields, for all eligible applicants, either white or Negro. The plan, as former Governor Caldwell of Florida pointed out on numerous occasions, closely parallels the action of three or four farmers who contribute to the purchase of an expensive piece of machinery for their joint use. Institutions offering training in the fields of medicine, dentistry, and veterinary medicine had been caught between rapidly rising costs and relatively fixed tuition rates. More and more of the funds of these institutions had to be devoted to professional offerings, while at the same time, demands for persons trained in these fields were constantly increasing. Against this background, the Board in 1948 helped to execute contracts between states and institutions under which the states pay

---

(Oklahoma City, 1947, 1950, and 1950); Dow, Hiram M., "The Oil Compact as an Impetus to Sound Conservation Practice," *Rocky Mountain Law Review*, February 1952, pp. 154–162; Murphy, Blakely M., "The Administrative Mechanism of the Interstate Oil Compact to Conserve Oil and Gas: the Interstate Compact Commission, 1935–1949," *Tulane Law Review*, March 1949, pp. 394–402; Webb, Wilfred D., "The Interstate Oil Compact — Theory and Practice," *Southwestern Social Science Quarterly*, March 1941, pp. 293–301.

[20] For comment, see Dunbar, Leslie, "Interstate Compacts and Congressional Consent," *Virginia Law Review*, October 1950, pp. 753–763; Ferguson, Jo M., "The Legal Basis for a Southern University — Interstate Agreements Without Congressional Assent," *Kentucky Law Journal*, March 1950, pp. 347–359; Zimmerman, Frederick L., and Wendell, Mitchell, "Congressional Consent to the States," *State Government*, April 1949, pp. 116–119, 125–127. The latter gives some instances of constitutional interpretation and the development of cooperative federalism.

[21] Sipuel v. University of Oklahoma, 332 U.S. 631, 1948 (68 Sup. Ct. 299).

the institutions for the costs of training the students which they admit under the program. The cooperating institutions agree to admit qualified graduate students from other states on the same basis as residents of their own. If Florida, for instance, sends its medical students to Tulane University, it pays $1500 for each student; it pays a similar amount for dental students, and $1000 for each student in veterinary medicine. Under these contracts, several hundred students and in the neighborhood of $1,000,000 are now channeled across state lines each year.

In 1950, in an extension of the plan, topflight graduate programs were contemplated in agriculture, social work, engineering, forestry, and other fields. Recognizing both the small number of institutions in the region offering work for the doctorate, and the urgent need of the region for such trained personnel, conferences of university presidents and faculty members were held to determine which fields should first be developed, and where, so that funds to support the plan might be sought in the 1951 legislative sessions. The larger number of students which this cooperative plan provides, together with the reimbursement feature, under which each state pays for the number of students it contributes, makes possible the maintenance of the highest scholastic standards in the cooperating institutions.[22]

In 1948, the governors of the Western states made a beginning in the development of a similar program in their region, for the same purposes and for the same reasons. Twelve states and the Territory of Alaska have developed a regional compact; in 1953, six states had given their approval and seven more ratifications were expected. In February 1950, the Wyoming legislature authorized its state university to contract with out-of-state schools for the training of Wyoming students in certain health service fields — medicine, dentistry, veterinary medicine, and nursing. Under the enabling legislation, the University of Wyoming negotiated a contract with the University of Colorado School of Medicine.

> Under the terms of the contract, Colorado agreed to accept a specified number of qualified medical students who are Wyoming residents, and Wyoming agreed to pay Colorado the full cost of their training. Wyoming, in turn, can require each student to shoulder a portion of the cost as "tuition." Thus, from one point of view, the University of Wyoming has added a school of medicine "away from home." Colorado, on the other hand, can expand its staff and equipment, thus strengthening the training program for all its students at no additional cost to Colorado taxpayers. This simple bilateral ar-

[22] See Board of Control for Southern Regional Education, *The Second Step in Regional Education* (Atlanta, 1951), and the following articles; Caldwell, Millard F., "Regional Education Planning Makes Progress in the South," *State Government*, May 1948, pp. 100–101; Gant, George F., "The Southern Regional Education Program," *Public Administration Review*, Spring 1952, pp. 106–111; Ivey, John E., Jr., "An Emerging Regional Program in Higher Education," *The Educational Record*, April 1952, pp. 2–24, "Regional Education: It Is Working in the South," *State Government*, December 1949, pp. 278–280, and "Southern Regional Education — a Progress Report," *ibid.*, September 1952, pp. 207–210; Robb, Felix C., "The South and Its Regional Education Program," *Harvard Educational Review*, Winter 1951, pp. 26–48, including bibliography.

rangement points the way toward a solution of the West's perplexing dilemma in the field of higher education.[23]

Once cooperative relations are established, there is an encouraging tendency for them to be developed and expanded. Techniques that are applicable in one field may often be adapted to another. In the West, a regional cooperative program for institutional care is being developed,[24] while in the South, the Southern Regional Training Program in Public Administration, involving several Southern state universities and the Tennessee Valley Authority, has been in operation for a number of years. Quite separate and distinct from the Southern Regional Education Compact, there was set up in the spring of 1952 a Committee on Government Research and Training in the South. This Committee was charged with making a study and recommendations regarding the status, needs and opportunities for research and training in the field of government in Southern universities.

River Basin Development. Early in the Roosevelt era, the Congress created, under the leadership of the President and Senator Norris, the Tennessee Valley Authority for flood control and for the development of the hydroelectric power and other resources of the Tennessee Valley. This agency has been well administered and has been notably successful in the accomplishment of the purposes for which it was created. Numerous proposals have been made for the establishment in similar manner of other authorities to cover the major watersheds of the country, particularly those of the Missouri and Columbia Rivers.

In spite of the success of the TVA and of the care which its officials have exercised in dealing with the states affected and their subdivisions, this program represents a kind of compulsory regionalism. In contrast with this, voluntary forms of interstate cooperation have already demonstrated their usefulness in dealing with a great many of the problems which are too large for any one state to handle alone. Their greatest limitation arises in connection with the development of power, which is, perhaps, the most important problem of all. Most of the rivers, like the Tennessee, possess considerable possibilities for the development of large quantities of cheap electric power, but the initial cost of the construction of dams and the building of hydroelectric plants is enormous. So far, no region has solved this problem on a cooperative basis.

This is not to say that it cannot be solved, but until it is, voluntary regionalism will be at a serious disadvantage in competition with compulsory regionalism of the TVA type. A number of solutions are possible. Where there

[23] Council of State Governments, *Western Regional Cooperation in Higher Education, a Proposed Program* (Chicago, 1951); Alphin, A. Ray, "Educational Cooperation in the Western States" and Humphrey, George D., "Regional Cooperation in Education in the West," addresses before the Land-Grant Association of College Presidents, Houston, November 12, 1951; Condon, Mary M., "Western Regional Education," *State Government*, December 1951, pp. 293–294, 307.

[24] See Macfarlane, Grant, "The West Looks to Regional (Institutional) Care," *State Government*, May 1948, pp. 102–104, 110.

Interstate River Basin Development*

RIVER BASIN AND ENFORCING AGENCY	LENGTH OF RIVER (MILES)	AREA OF WATERSHED (SQUARE MILES)	POPULATION OF WATERSHED	STATES INCLUDED [1]	PRINCIPAL PROBLEMS [2]
Arkansas *Arkansas River Compact Administration (1949)*	1,450	160,375	....	(2) 5, 14	c, 1
Canadian *Canadian River Commission (1952)*	906	47,615	300,000	(3) 29, 34, 41	1
Colorado *Colorado River Basin States Committee (1938)*	980	242,000 (in U.S.)	900,000	(7) 2, 4, 5, 26, 29, 42, 48	c, g, 1
Upper Colorado *Upper Colorado River Compact Commission*	430	107,900	....	(5) 2, 5, 29, 42, 48	1
Columbia *Northwest States Development Association (1943)*	750	220,000	2,000,000	(4) 10, 24, 35, 45	c, e, g, 1
Connecticut *New England Interstate Flood Control Committee (1945)*	292	11,320	1,500,000	(4) 6, 19, 27, 43	b, c, f, g, 1
Delaware *Interstate Commission on the Delaware River Basin (1936)*	275	13,000	5,000,000	(4) 7, 28, 30, 36	a, b, e, f, g, h, i, j, k, 1
Lower Mississippi *Mississippi River Commission (established by Congress, 1880)*	900	63,000	4,000,000	(6) 3, 15, 16, 22, 23, 40	b, e
Missouri *Missouri River Committee and Missouri River Inter-Agency Basin Committee*	3,000	530,000	15,000,000	(10) 5, 13, 14, 21, 23, 24, 25, 32, 39, 48	b, c, e, g, h, k, m

Ohio	967	203,900	20,000,000	(8) 11, 12, 15, 30, 33, 36, 44, 46	b, d, e, f, g, h, i, k, l
Ohio River Valley Sanitation Commission (1948)					
Pecos	735	33,200	150,000	(2) 29, 41	l
Pecos River Commission (1949)					
Potomac	390	14,500	2,000,000	(5) D.C., 18, 36, 44, 46	f
Interstate Commission on the Potomac River Basin (1941)					
Red	310	93,450	1,900,900	(3) 21, 32, 39	l
Tri-State Waters Commission (1938)					
Savannah	314	10,579	200,000	(3) 9, 31, 38	e, g, h, j
None					
Snake	1,038	108,750	....	(2) 10, 48	l
Snake River Compact Commission (1949)					
Tennessee	652	40,611	2,000,000	(7) 1, 9, 15, 22, 31, 40, 44	l
Tennessee Valley Authority (established by Congress, 1933)					
Yellowstone	671	70,400	....	(3) 24, 32, 48	l
Yellowstone River Compact Commission (1951)					

* Based originally on articles in *State Government*, July 1946, and *Interstate River Basin Development*, a report of the Committee on Water Resources of the Council of State Governments, January 1947, with additions and corrections to 1952.

[1] Numbers conform with alphabetical listing of the states from Alabama, 1, to Wyoming, 48.

[2] Letters conform with the following key:

a — Agriculture
b — Flood control
c — Irrigation
d — Low flow control
e — Navigation
f — Pollution control
g — Power
h — Recreation
i — Reforestation
j — Salinity control
k — Soil conservation
l — Water supply
m — Wild life protection

is a formal interstate organization, there is no reason why it should not be authorized to issue bonds for power development. A second possibility, though perhaps less practical, is that the cooperating states should appropriate or borrow, in amounts agreed upon, to provide the necessary capital. Finally, there is no reason why the Federal government could not provide the money as it did for TVA, either as a loan to an interstate corporation (like the Port of New York Authority) or for use in a revolving fund. This would be possible through the regular operations of the Reconstruction Finance Corporation or by act of Congress.

The extent to which the major rivers of the country have been covered by these voluntary interstate organizations is clearly indicated by the table on pages 848–849. Illustrative groups selected for brief comment are the Ohio River Valley Water Sanitation Commission, the Interstate Commission on the Delaware River Basin (Incodel), and the Interstate Commission on the Potomac River Basin (Incopot), all of which had made significant contributions to the solution of the problems of the drainage basins affected. Problems of pollution control and sanitation are among the more important — though they are not the only — problems dealt with by these groups.[25]

The Ohio River Valley Water Sanitation Compact owes its origin to the fact that the Director of Health in Ohio discovered shortly after World War I that the water supplies of several Ohio communities were being impaired by the discharge of untreated waste from by-product coke ovens. The Director succeeded, in 1924, in entering into an agreement with the Pennsylvania and West Virginia Departments of Health, known as the Ohio River Interstate Stream Conservation Agreement. This agreement was extended to include eleven of the fourteen states in the Ohio River drainage basin. The sanitary engineers in these states developed a high degree of cooperation, whereby all downstream areas are notified promptly of any condition which might affect the taste, odor, or purity of their water supplies, regardless of the state or states in which these communities may happen to be located.

Since 1948 eight member states function under the compact as the Ohio River Valley Water Sanitation Commission, the third organization established during a quarter of a century of effort. The operations of the Commission are carried on under the direction of a board of twenty-seven members, of whom three are appointed by the governor of each signatory state, and three representatives of the Federal government, appointed by the President of the United States. Since the members of the Commission provide representation of many related fields, it enjoys, in the formulation of policy, a wide variety of viewpoints. Administration of Commission activities is carried on by a salaried staff of seven, legal counsel and accounting services being secured through appointment and contract. The chairman and vice-

[25] For an "Analysis of Stream Pollution Legislation in the United States — 1948," see *Report* of the Special Committee on Pollution Abatement of the Joint Legislative Committee on Interstate Cooperation, 1949, Appendix A, pp. 71–74 (Albany, Legislative Document [1949] No. 51).

chairman are elected by the members of the Commission for a term of one year; twelve committees have been established to deal with various phases of the Commission's work.[26]

The Interstate Commission on the Delaware River Basin is the joint governmental agency which was created in 1936 by the states of New York, New Jersey, Pennsylvania, and Delaware for the purpose of formulating, adopting, and executing wise and constructive policies for the most appropriate development and utilization of the natural resources of the Delaware River basin and its tributaries. Each of the member states has a commission on interstate cooperation. These agencies have jointly organized Incodel, which through its technical advisory committees on Quantity of Water, Quality of Water, Research and Information, and Planning, and the staff, is developing practical programs for the use of the natural resources of the basin. The Commission, about fifteen years old, has a notable record of accomplishment in many different fields — abatement of stream pollution; soil, water, and forest conservation; oyster, fish, and wild life resources; flood control; recreation; highway and transportation facilities — all directed toward a unified river-basin development.[27] It now has under way a $150,000,000 basin-wide project to clean up the Delaware and its tributaries, carried out by the states, municipalities, and industries of the region.

Four states — Maryland, Pennsylvania, Virginia, West Virginia — and the District of Columbia entered into a compact in 1941, creating the Potomac Valley Conservancy District. Under the terms of the compact the signatories mutually agree to faithful cooperation in the abatement and control of pollution in the streams of the District; to the enactment of adequate and, so far as practical, uniform legislation for the abatement and control of such pollution; and to the appropriation of funds to finance the operations of the coordinating agency. This agency consists of three members from each signatory body and three appointed by the President of the United States.

[26] In addition to the annual reports of the Commission, see Biery, Hudson, "Intergovernmental Plans for Pollution Control: Ohio River Valley," *State Government*, October 1948, pp. 210–213, 220; Cleary, Edward J., "Interstate Commission Tackles Pollution Problem in Ohio River Valley," *Civil Engineering*, August 1950, pp. 32–34; Duffy, John, "Ohio Participation in Interstate Compacts," *Ohio State Law Journal*, Autumn 1950, pp. 552–556. In State ex rel. Dyer v. Sims, 58 S.E. 2d. 766, 1950, the West Virginia Supreme Court held the participation of that state in the Compact unconstitutional on the grounds that: (1) one legislature cannot bind a succeeding one, and (2) the act of ratification in 1939 resulted in an unconstitutional delegation of police powers. This very narrow and legalistic decision was reversed by the United States Supreme Court in State ex rel. Dyer v. Sims, 341 U.S. 22, 1951; see Zimmerman, Frederick L., and Wendell, Mitchell, "The Interstate Compact and Dyer v. Sims," *Columbia Law Review*, December 1951, pp. 931–950, and Bogart, George G. "Decision of the Supreme Court in the West Virginia Compact Case," *State Government*, June 1951, pp. 162–164.

[27] In addition to its numerous reports and publications, see Robinson, David W., "Voluntary Regionalism in the Control of Water Resources," *Annals*, January 1940, pp. 116–123; *Incodel, A Report on Its Activities and Accomplishments* (Philadelphia, annually); and Allen, James H., "The Delaware River Basin: a Home Rule Program for the Development of Its Resources," *Journal* of the American Waterworks Association, January 1944.

A successful stream pollution control program must recognize the interrelation of all water resources of the entire basin regardless of state boundaries, for there are complex administrative, planning, legal, engineering, and financial problems to be solved. The Commission has no control over water resources and does not supersede any existing governmental authority. Rather, it serves all such authorities by determining the status and effects of stream pollution, and by assisting in the promulgation, adoption, and operations of a unified pollution control program in conformity with plans for the judicious development of the basin's resources. It seeks to accomplish its objectives through an informed public opinion that demands protection of these vital resources.[28]

Protection of Fisheries. In the past decade, after long years of effort, three important fisheries compacts have been accepted and agreed to by the states and approved by the Congress. The Atlantic States Marine Fisheries Commission was organized in 1942 and now has fifteen signatory coastal states extending from Maine to Florida. The Pacific Marine Fisheries Commission, organized in similar fashion, was approved in 1947, with California, Oregon, and Washington as members. The Gulf States Marine Fisheries Commission was likewise organized in 1947, with Alabama, Florida, Louisiana, and Texas as members. Each was established for the two-fold purpose of promoting better utilization of marine, shell, and anadromous fisheries and of creating an interstate commission as a policy determining and enforcement agency.

In the Atlantic Commission each state is represented by three commissioners, including the administrator of fisheries, a member of the legislature appointed by the commission on interstate cooperation, and a citizen appointed by the governor "having a knowledge of or an interest in the marine fisheries problem." During the first few years of its existence (a prior organization functioned from 1941), the Commission developed panels on particular species — eight in all. Later it supplemented them and finally replaced them with four sections covering specific portions of the Atlantic Coast — North, Middle, South, and Chesapeake Bay. These proved much more effective and have helped to produce a greater degree of teamwork among the states.

[28] In addition to the Commission's numerous publications, including a biennial report, see Kittrell, F. W., "Pollution Control in the Potomac," *State Government*, April 1942, pp. 79–80, 90; also Caldwell, Lynton K., "Interstate Cooperation in River Basin Development," *Iowa Law Review*, January 1947, pp. 232–243, and Friedrich, Julius M., "The Settlement of Disputes Between States Concerning Rights to the Waters of Interstate Streams," *ibid.* pp. 244–282; Hess, Seth G., "Interstate Action to Control Pollution," *State Government*, September 1950, pp. 204–207. On the Colorado, see Houghton, Neal D., "Problems of the Colorado River as Reflected in Arizona Politics," *Western Political Quarterly*, December 1951, pp. 634–643, and Stone, Clifford H., "Interstate Water Compacts," *Rocky Mountain Law Review*, February 1952, pp. 141–153. On the situation in New England, see New England Interstate Water Pollution Control Commission, annual reports and *Industrial Wastes in the New England Interstate Water Pollution Control Compact Area* (Boston, December 1951), and Smith, Lincoln, "The Proposed Development Authority Compact for New England," *Political Science Quarterly*, March 1951, pp. 37–64.

Uniform acts have been generally adopted relative to a number of different species, and other types of cooperative arrangements have been made effective.[29]

Interstate Sanitation District. Limitations of space permit reference to only a few of the new compacts of a more or less local nature. In 1936 Connecticut, New Jersey, and New York entered into the Tri-State Compact establishing the Interstate Sanitation District and the Interstate Sanitation Commission. The preamble to the compact recites the growth in population and development of the New York metropolitan area, the serious nature of the health hazards created by the pollution of adjacent waters, and the belief that these problems can best be solved through the cooperation of the interested states, "by and through a joint or common agency." The Pecos River Compact between New Mexico and Texas was agreed to in 1949 after nearly a quarter of a century of effort; its major purposes are "to provide for the equitable division and apportionment of the waters of the Pecos River; to promote interstate comity; to remove causes of present and future controversies; to make secure and protect present development within the states; to facilitate the construction of works for (a) the salvage of water, (b) the more efficient use of water, and (c) the protection of life and property from floods." [30]

Port of New York Authority. The Port of New York Authority was created in 1921 by compact, ratified by Congress, between the states of New York and New Jersey. This unique corporate municipal instrumentality, which was necessary because of the unusual nature of certain geographical and other factors, provides a medium through which the two states combine their efforts in promoting the commercial development of the Port of New York, with particular regard to the improvement of terminal and transportation facilities. The states authorized it to exercise certain corporate powers within the Port District which, roughly speaking, embraces the area within a radius of twenty miles of the Statue of Liberty. Originally it was provided that the Port Authority should be administered by six commissioners, three from each state, appointed by the governors with the advice and consent of the respective senates.

In 1930, when the Port Authority was reconstituted through merger with the Holland Tunnel Commission, the membership was increased to twelve — six from each state, appointed in the same manner. The commissioners serve for a term of six years, without pay, in a manner similar to that of a board

[29] See accounts by Wayne D. Heydecker, Secretary-Treasurer, in *Book of the States, 1943–1944*, and succeeding editions; Zimmerman, Frederick L., "Atlantic States Marine Fisheries Compact," *State Government*, April 1941, pp. 81–83, 95; and "Interstate Cooperation and Fisheries," *ibid.*, August 1942, pp. 159–162, 166; and Heydecker, Wayne D., "Exploratory Intercoastal Fisheries Conference," *ibid.*, October 1946, pp. 260–264.

[30] See *Pecos River Compact* (Senate Document No. 109, 81st Cong., 1st Sess., 1949); also National Resources Planning Committee, *Interstate Water Compacts, 1785 to 1941* (Washington, 1942).

of directors of a private corporation. They hold regular and frequent meetings. A favorable vote by a majority is necessary before any action is official, and every action must have the approval of at least three commissioners from each state. The Authority has direct responsibility for the administration of its various projects; the corporate form of organization was provided for so as to enable it to finance self-liquidating public improvements upon its own credit, thus avoiding additional taxes or assessments.

The success of the Authority has been notable. The expansion, begun in 1930, has continued through the years until today it operates the following long list of important projects, with a staff of several thousand employees [31]:

PROJECTS OPERATED BY THE
PORT OF NEW YORK AUTHORITY

Bayonne Bridge	Manhattan Union Motor Truck Terminal
Columbia Street (Brooklyn) Piers	Newark Airport
George Washington Bridge	Newark Seaport
Goethals Bridge	Newark Union Motor Truck Terminal
Holland Tunnel	New York International Airport
La Guardia Airport	Outerbridge Crossing
Lincoln Tunnel	Port Authority Grain Terminal
Manhattan Union Bus Terminal	

Also in New York, the Triborough Bridge and Tunnel Authority, a similar type of organization — not interstate in character, to be sure — operates the following eight projects: Battery Park Garage, Brooklyn-Battery Tunnel, Cross Bay Parkway Bridge, Henry Hudson Bridge, Marine Parkway Bridge, Queens Midtown Tunnel, Triborough Bridge, and Whitestone Bridge. The legislatures of New Jersey and Pennsylvania have ratified an interstate compact creating a Delaware River Port Authority to improve the river, develop the business of the port of Philadelphia-Camden, and provide transportation and river-crossing facilities in the port district, including a high speed transit system in South Jersey. The port district is defined as Delaware and Philadelphia counties on the Pennsylvania side and eight counties in New Jersey, starting at a line a little south of Trenton and running generally eastward to the Atlantic Ocean.

Legislative Uniformity

National Conference of Commissioners on Uniform State Laws. New York pioneered in the effort to secure uniform legislative provisions on subjects of general interest to the states, some consideration being given to this question as early as 1857. No really significant action was taken, however, until 1889, when, due at least in part to the suggestion contained in a resolu-

[31] In addition to the Authority's annual reports, and its numerous other publications, see Bard, Erwin W., *The Port of New York Authority* (Columbia University Press, 1941), and Bird, Frederick L., *A Study of the Port of New York Authority* (Dun & Bradstreet, New York, 1948). *State Government*, September 1947, was devoted to a description of port authorities and similar state agencies in eight states; see also Crothers, J. A., "Port of Boston Authority," *ibid.*, April 1948, pp. 91–93.

tion adopted by the legislature of this state, the American Bar Association summoned a conference on the subject. Nine states were represented in this first conference; since 1912 all the states, territories, and the District of Columbia have been officially represented. The Conference is composed of three commissioners from each state, chosen usually by the governor from the legal profession to serve without compensation. They have developed an elaborate organization of regular and special committees, concerned with the drafting of uniform acts relating to a wide variety of subjects coming within the jurisdiction of the state governments.

Two tables are shown on page 856 for the purpose of indicating in a general way the scope and nature of the subject matter considered by the Conference. In the first table are listed the major types of laws proposed by the Conference, the number of uniform acts proposed by it as of 1949, and the number of adoptions of these acts as of 1934, 1939, and 1949, respectively. In the second table are listed the nine acts which had received twenty or more adoptions in 1934, with the number of adoptions as of 1939 and 1949. In the latter year there were, not sixteen but twenty-two acts with twenty or more adoptions each. In addition to the fifty-two uniform laws with their 996 adoptions there were fifteen model acts with thirty adoptions. Altogether there were in 1949 sixty-seven acts before the states, with a total of 1026 adoptions.

From the data presented in the tables it appears that the uniform acts relating to commerce, civil procedure, and property have been most successful in securing the approval of the state legislatures. The Uniform Negotiable Instruments Act is in force in all states, some territories, and some Latin American countries. Likewise, the Uniform Warehouse Receipts Act, which makes warehouse receipts generally acceptable in business transactions, and the Uniform Stock Transfer Tax Act, each in fifty-one jurisdictions; and the Uniform Sales Act, which concerns the transfer of title to personal property, in thirty-seven jurisdictions. In 1953 the Conference, in cooperation with the American Law Institute, completed the draft of a new and comprehensive uniform commercial code containing 389 sections arranged in ten articles. The theory is that the existing uniform laws, many of which are old and out of date, do not cover, either adequately or comprehensively, all of the important aspects of commercial law.[32]

A number of interesting questions arise with regard to the geographical distribution of adoptions of uniform acts. According to 1949 data Georgia, Mississippi, Oklahoma, and Texas had adopted ten or less, while twelve states had adopted twenty-five or more. Wisconsin had adopted thirty-one;

[32] For views, for and against, see: Schnader, William A., "The New Commercial Code: Modernizing Our Uniform Commercial Acts," American Bar Association *Journal*, March 1950, pp. 179–182, 252–254; Williston, Samuel, "The Law of Sales in the Proposed Uniform Commercial Code," *Harvard Law Review*, February 1950, pp. 561–588; and symposia containing discussions of the code in *Law and Contemporary Problems*, Winter Issue, 1951, and *Wisconsin Law Review*, March 1952.

National Conference of Commissioners on Uniform State Laws Acts Proposed and Adopted, 1934, 1939, 1949

TYPE OF ACT	PROPOSED 1949	TOTAL ADOPTIONS 1934	1939	1949
Commercial	6	188	201	202
Property	13	99	123	191
Public	5	95	126	79
Social Welfare	4	35	115	86
Corporations	2	4	6	63
Courts and Criminal	3	38	78	45
Civil Procedure	19	154	151	211
Totals	52	613	800	877

Adoptions of Leading Acts, 1934, 1939, 1949

NAME OF ACT	TOTAL ADOPTIONS 1934	1939	1949
Bills of Lading Act	29	29	33
Limited Partnership Act	20	22	32
Sales Act	34	35	37
Warehouse Receipts Act	48	48	51
Negotiable Instruments Act	53	53	53
Stock Transfer Act	24	27	51
Aeronautics Act	22	22	..
Proof of Statutes Act	23	25	30
Veterans' Guardianship Act	33	35	41
Total	286	296	328

Maryland, thirty-three; and South Dakota, thirty-seven. Approximately half the states were in the eleven to twenty zone, as they had been ten years earlier. The figures show a substantial increase, however, over the totals for earlier years. When these data are plotted on an outline map of the United States, it is impossible to present any conclusions with regard to sectionalism, since one finds in each section states with a notably large number of adoptions and states with a very small number. The uniform laws before the states for adoption at the end of more than half a century of activity relate to approximately fifty subjects, nearly every law has been adopted by at least one state, and at least three have been approved in fifty or more jurisdictions.

Uniform Vehicle Code. The Uniform Vehicle Code was originally drafted in 1925–1926 by the National Conference on Street and Highway Safety, in cooperation with the National Conference of Commissioners on Uniform State Laws, to serve as a basis for uniform traffic laws throughout the United

States. During the years since, the Code has been reviewed and revised periodically by the original committee, and in 1947–1948 by the reorganized National Committee on Uniform Traffic Laws and Ordinances. "It is today," says the Council of State Governments, which actively supports its adoption, "the most practical aid yet devised for greater highway safety." [33]

There are, in all, five acts, fifty articles, and 408 sections of the Code, which should be regarded, not as a strait jacket, but as minimum basic standards essential to the safety of motorists and pedestrians. The component parts of the Code, and the number of adoptions of each, to a total of 136, as of 1952, are shown in the table below. Thirteen states have enacted the code in its entirety [34] and seven others have enacted as many as three acts.

Uniform Vehicle Code — 1952

ACT	TITLE	ADOPTIONS
I	Uniform Motor Vehicle Administration, Registration, Certificate of Title, and Antitheft Act	18
II	Uniform Motor Vehicle Operators' and Chauffeurs' License Act	29
III	Uniform Motor Vehicle Civil Liability Act	[1]
IV	Uniform Motor Vehicle Safety Responsibility Act	45
V	Uniform Act Regulating Traffic on Highways	26

[1] Although a substantial number of states have enacted some of the provisions of Act III, the laws of some twenty states still do not provide adequately for owners' liability in accident cases.

Uniform Reciprocal Support Act. The speed with which the spread of uniform legislation is now possible is well illustrated by the Uniform Reciprocal Support Act. During 1948 and 1949, a small number of states, led by New York, embarked upon this experiment in the field of family relations. It was designed to provide a workable method of securing support for dependent wives and children when the person legally responsible therefor had removed himself to another state. This attempt to control "skippers" resulted in the development of reciprocal legislation known as the Uniform Reciprocal Support of Dependents Act, adopted by mid-1952 in three territories and all but five states. Thirty-two of these laws follow the provisions of the Uniform Act, which confers civil jurisdiction only, while eleven are patterned after the original New York approach.[35]

[33] *Highway Safety — Motor Truck Regulation,* Chapter 1 (Chicago, 1950).

[34] Excluding Act III which presents special problems: Arkansas, California, Delaware, Idaho, Maryland, Michigan, New Mexico, North Dakota, Ohio, Pennsylvania, Tennessee, Utah, and Washington.

[35] See Council of State Governments, *Reciprocal State Legislation to Enforce the Support of Dependents* (Chicago, August 1951) and the following articles: Allison, Junius L., "The 'Skippers' Act of 1949," *Public Aid in Illinois,* May 1951, pp. 1–3, 9; Brockelbank, W. J., "Is the Uniform Reciprocal Enforcement of Support Act Constitutional?" *Missouri*

Drafting Committee of the Council of State Governments. The National Conference of Commissioners on Uniform State Laws has ceased to be the only important agency working for the adoption of uniform legislation. In 1940, a new cooperative arrangement involving the Conference, the Council of State Governments, and the United States Department of Justice was worked out and put in operation.[36] Undertaken as a means of meeting an emergency situation, these arrangements have been continued in peacetime and have proved to be enormously useful in extending the benefits of uniformity into many new fields. The machinery is as simple as it is effective. The Council receives from state officials or from special state committees, proposals for state legislative consideration, having a Federal effect and requiring Federal administrative cooperation. These proposals are transmitted to the Assistant Solicitor General's Office of the Department of Justice for reference to appropriate Federal agencies. Similarly, the Assistant Solicitor General's Office receives proposals which Federal agencies wish to call to the attention of the states. With respect to both types, the Office consults with affected Federal agencies, assists in the coordination of views and the resolution of conflicts, and acts in a liaison capacity with the Council.

The Council's drafting committee is composed of state Attorneys General, Commissioners on Uniform State Laws, and Commissioners on Interstate Cooperation. The proposals are discussed by representatives of the Federal agencies and with members of the Committee. Federal and state views are integrated and, where appropriate, representatives of local governments and of nongovernmental organizations are brought in for consultation. Drafts of acts, to be included in the Federal-state program, are developed through interdepartmental, and at times intergovernmental conferences, and are then sent for advance study to the Council's drafting committee, together, in each case, with an Interpretative Statement, designed to make clear the outlines of the problem, the suggested solution, and any particular sponsorships or endorsements.

After final clearances which include the affected Federal agencies and the Board of Managers of the Council, the Acts and Interpretative Statements are sent as "Suggested State Legislation" to the governors of the states, the state attorneys general, the commissioners on interstate cooperation, and other state officials interested in particular proposals. The commissioners on interstate cooperation assume responsibility for the study of the proposals and their introduction, where appropriate, in the state legislatures. These proposals, while drafted in act form, represent basically no more than statements of legislative principles which the states are expected to adopt to meet their own particular needs and requirements.

Law Review, January 1952, pp. 1–15; Seaman, Grace C., "Making the Reciprocal Support Law Work," *State Government*, June 1952, pp. 132–135.

[36] Andrews, John W., "New Mechanics of Federal-State Cooperation," *Federal Bar Journal*, October 1945, pp. 42–54.

During the past ten years, upwards of 150 proposals of special importance have been processed through this mechanism. The 1952 program contained four new acts or amendments to acts from the drafting committee, ten new uniform laws, together with statements and recommendations on a number of other matters. The following items are illustrative of the measures proposed:

Act Concerning Trial of Court Martial Cases
Narcotic Drug Act Amendment Concerning Marihuana
Divorce Recognition Act
Marriage License Application Act
Photographic Copies of Business and Public Records as Evidence Act
Enforcement of Foreign Judgments Act
Prenatal Blood Test Act
Model Small Estates Act

American Law Institute. Realization of the need for a closer and more effective cooperation between the states developed in many quarters after World War I. In 1923, there met in Washington a conference called the Preliminary Committee for the Establishment of a Permanent Organization for the Improvement of the Law, set up by the American Bar Association the preceding year, with Elihu Root as chairman. The Institute, which grew out of this conference, was incorporated under the laws of the District of Columbia for the purpose of promoting "the clarification and simplification of the law, and its better adaptation to social needs, to secure the better administration of justice and to encourage and carry on scholarly and scientific legal work." In carrying on its task of "the improvement of the law," the Institute has had the fullest cooperation of scores if not hundreds of the leading lawyers and judges from every state in the Union. It has had such distinguished presidents as Elihu Root (honorary), George W. Wickersham, and George Wharton Pepper. William Draper Lewis served as its Director for a quarter of a century, being succeeded by Judge Herbert F. Goodrich of the Third United States Circuit Court, its present Director.

The Institute early undertook the monumental task of preparing its Restatement in an "attempt to give orderly expression to the common law," by restating in modern form, upon the basis of exhaustive study and research by the ablest legal scholars in the country, the principles of the law. The first published result of this project was the *Restatement of the Law of Contracts*, published in 1932; others followed, in due course, at the rate of one or two volumes a year until 1947, when the task was completed. In addition to contracts, the following subjects are covered: trusts, judgments, property (five volumes), restitution, agency (two volumes), security,[37] torts (four volumes), conflict of laws, and history of the Restatement. There are twenty volumes in all, including index volume and 1949 supplement.

It was planned to parallel the volumes of the Restatement with annotations on each subject, for each state. While this ambitious program has not been completed, annotations have been completed and published on agency

37 Including pledges of personal property, suretyship, et cetera.

in nineteen states, on trusts in thirty-three states, on conflict of laws in twenty-seven states, on contracts in twenty-eight states. Some annotations on other subjects have been published, while numerous others were in course of preparation in 1950.

The effect of this program is comparable to that of Blackstone on the common law of England. It not only clarifies and simplifies the tangled and conflicting legal rules and doctrines which had developed in this country on common law subjects over many years, but it provides a powerful stimulus toward a more uniform application and interpretation of the principles of the common law among the several states. Its influence has already been considerable, and it appears to be growing very much as its original promoters had hoped. A study of the decisions of the Pennsylvania Supreme Court from 1938 to 1949 reveals only one instance in which the court cited a section of the Restatement without following it. Up to April 1, 1950, paragraphs of the Restatements had been cited by American courts 18,000 times (state, 14,401; Federal, 3,550). The number appears to grow at the rate of approximately 1,500 citations a year. The late Judge O'Connell put the matter this way in a paper written shortly before his death [38]:

> When we find ourselves citing with confidence a paragraph of the Restatement in addition to, if not instead of, a dictum from an earlier opinion, I think we shall be making substantial progress toward solving the problem. . . for, with ever-increasing necessity of case-hunting on every question presented to them, lawyers may find it more expedient to build their libraries around such splendid resources as the Restatements, and to establish group libraries for the casebooks.

The Model Code of Criminal Procedure, another major project of the Institute carried on by methods similar to those followed in the Restatements, was published in 1930. Because of the widespread interest in criminal law and procedure, this code has already had a significant influence on the laws of the states. This effort has been extended to include a restatement of the whole substantive criminal law. A *Model Code of Evidence* was prepared; and model statutes dealing with the arrest, trial, conviction, and treatment of youth between sixteen and twenty-one have been published, the first of these in 1940 as the Youth Correction Authority Act, which relates to the treatment of convicted youths,[39] adopted — as of 1950 — in five states (California, Massachusetts, Minnesota, Texas, and Wisconsin).

Model Laws. Many organizations have drafted and submitted to the states for adoption, model laws relating to subjects in various fields. Although

[38] "A Dissertation on Judicial Opinions," *Temple Law Quarterly*, July 1949, pp. 13–19; this quotation and other data from the 1950 Annual Report of the Director of the American Law Institute.

[39] *See The Restatement in the Courts*, Fifth Edition (American Law Institute, St. Paul, 1945), and two articles on the Youth Act, American Bar Association *Journal*, May 1942: Lewis, William D., for, pp. 322–324, and Hall, Jerome, against, pp. 317–321; also note, "Youth Correction — the Model Act in Operation," *University of Chicago Law Review*, Summer 1950, pp. 683–697.

a major purpose of these measures is to attain uniformity of legislation among the states, such models should not be confused with the uniform laws proposed by the National Conference of Commissioners on Uniform State Laws. Illustrative of the former type is a group of public laws sponsored by the National Municipal League and listed in the table on page 862. A number of model laws have been submitted in the field of aviation: Model State Aeronautics Commission or Department Act, by the National Association of State Aviation Officials, and adopted in approximately half of the states; Model Airport Condemnation Act, Model Airport Zoning Act, Model Flight Strip and Highway Act, and others.[40]

Tremendous progress has been made in securing the adoption of uniform crime control legislation and/or compacts. As of 1952, model acts recommended by the Interstate Commission on Crime or the National Conference of Commissioners on Uniform State Laws were in effect in four major areas as follows [41]:

Interstate Crime Control Legislation — 1952

ACT	ADOPTIONS
Interstate Fresh Pursuit Act I	36
Interstate Fresh Pursuit Act II	5
Extradition Act	34
Out-of-State Witness Act	46
Interstate Crime Compact	48

Significance of the Movement. A very large number of organizations have, at one time or another, concerned themselves with the development of uniform statutory provisions on a wide variety of subjects. Indeed it may be said that there are few national organizations concerned with the provisions of the laws of the several states affecting subjects within their range of interest which have not at some time or other advanced the adoption of uniform measures. While in many cases they have prepared the drafts of model statutes, they have rarely had the financial resources or the extensive organization necessary for the successful promotion of these acts.[42]

There has been a good deal of discussion as to the usefulness of uniform legislation. There is no denying the fact that the Conference and the Council as governmental agencies concerned with reducing interstate friction, preparing and urging the adoption of uniform acts, have made a real contribution to the cause of better government. President Dodds of Princeton commends both the progress made and the effect of this uniform legislation. "It would be difficult," he wrote in 1944, "to measure the full extent of the influ-

[40] For a good discussion, see Legislative Reference Service, Library of Congress, *Current Ideas in State Legislatures, 1944–1945*, pp. 93–97 (Washington, 1947).

[41] These are fully discussed in *Handbook on Interstate Crime Control, op. cit.*

[42] Many are cited in Graves, *op. cit.*, Chapter 4.

questions of the day. During four decades the governors have developed a new and effective instrument for perfecting the union of the states. At the Hershey Conference in 1944, and in succeeding conferences, vital questions relating to the war effort and to postwar development were freely discussed. At the 1950 meeting major topics considered included administrative reorganization, water resources, and truck regulation. At these gatherings the governors showed a disposition, not merely to talk about states rights, but to do something about them. The obvious thing to do is to make the states such efficient instruments for the rendering of essential services that there will be no need for and no temptation to "run to Washington" in order to get things done.[45]

In addition to the national Governors' Conferences, held annually, there are many sectional or regional meetings of state governors, some of them held annually, some occasionally for the consideration of a single subject, in various parts of the country. It is not unusual to find really constructive measures undertaken as a result of meetings of this character. In 1925 the New England Council was created at the suggestion of the governors of the six New England states. The governors have continued their meetings for the discussion of common problems, but the Council, with its permanent secretariat, has been able to devote a steady and persistent effort toward the advancement of the common interests of the member states. The southeastern states have established a somewhat similar council with the cooperation of the governors in that section of the country. The Western Conference of Governors has held more or less regular meetings. As illustrative of the occasional meetings, one might mention the Interstate Commission on Unemployment Insurance, which grew out of a conference of seven governors of industrial states called by Governor Roosevelt of New York in 1931; a conference of the governors of the Middle Atlantic states for the discussion of problems of state and local government called by Governor Moore of New Jersey in 1933; and the conferences of the agricultural states in the Middle West held on a number of occasions during the period of the depression. Many such conferences of governors were held during World War II.

Organizations of Department Officials. Reference has been made to the extensive organization of the heads of the various types of administrative service represented by the usual administrative departments in our state governments. A few illustrations of the work of these organizations may be in order. In agriculture, a whole series of organizations has been developed, corresponding to each of the units of government, from the largest to the smallest. Thus, in the administration of the food and drug laws, one finds the Association of Dairy, Food, and Drug Officials of the United States, seven

[45] Graves, *op. cit.*, Chapter 5. The proceedings of the Conference are published annually by the Council of State Governments, and brief summaries of the sessions appear regularly in *State Government* in the August issue. See also: "Governors' Conference, 1909–1946," *ibid.*, July 1946, pp. 184–189, and Nixon, H. Clarence, "The Southern Governors' Conference as a Pressure Group," *Journal of Politics*, August 1944, pp. 338–345.

organizations of officials in the same field organized on a sectional basis, supplemented in turn by small regional conferences of administrators. It thus becomes possible, either through the adoption of policies by the National Association or through the influence of the United States Food and Drug Administration, to secure the uniform enforcement of rules and regulations applying to food and drug products. A similar elaborate organization of enforcement officials is to be found among those engaged in milk inspection work.[46]

The National Association of Supervisors of State Banking, the National Convention of Insurance Commissioners, and the National Conference on Weights and Measures are all organized on a similar basis for the purpose of securing the enforcement of uniform practices and the development of cooperative and reciprocal relations among the state officials engaged in supervising these phases of business activity. There are national organizations of highway officials and of motor vehicle administrators, but the latter have been more concerned with and more successful in the development of a high degree of interstate cooperation. The National Conference on Street and Highway Safety, organized and maintained under the supervision of the United States Department of Commerce, has been instrumental in developing considerable uniformity out of the previously chaotic situation with regard to the law governing the operation of motor vehicles. The American Conference of Motor Vehicle Administrators, which grew out of the Eastern Conference, has exerted a considerable influence in the direction of a uniform enforcement of this legislation. Further illustration could be cited in practically every important administrative field.

Prior to World War II, as the rate of the gasoline tax was increased in many jurisdictions, there has been an added incentive to engage in the illegal distribution of gasoline in order to evade the tax. In some jurisdictions the extent to which this bootlegging is carried on is sufficient to affect appreciably the receipts from the tax. In order to check these losses, Pennsylvania and Ohio entered into an agreement whereby a border patrol is maintained twenty-four hours a day at each of the points at which a main highway crosses the boundary line. A full and detailed record is kept of every tank car of gasoline that crosses this state line. This agreement was later extended to include New York and New Jersey. The latter states already maintained patrol boats in New York Harbor and in the Delaware River.

The Council of State Governments

In 1925, under the able leadership of Senator Henry W. Toll of Colorado, the American Legislators' Association was organized. Its headquarters, first located in Denver, were later moved to Chicago. In 1935 the Council of State Governments, long projected, came into being. Under the direction of Senator

[46] Graves, *op. cit.*, Chapter 6; also Routt, Garland C., "Interstate Compacts and Administrative Cooperation," *Annals*, January 1940, pp. 93–102.

Toll and the late Governor John G. Winant, it held its first meeting in Washington in the spring of 1935.

What the Council Is.[47] The Council is a joint governmental agency established by the states for service to the states and supported by them. It serves as: (1) a central clearing house for information and research; (2) a medium for improving legislative and administrative practices of state governments; (3) an instrumentality for encouraging full cooperation among the states in the solution of interstate problems, both regional and national; (4) a means of facilitating and improving Federal-state relations. The Council is composed of Commissions of Interstate Cooperation established in each of the forty-eight states. The typical commission consists of ten members of the legislature — five from each house — and five administrative officials. Legislation establishing these commissions provides that "The Council of State Governments is hereby declared to be a joint governmental agency of this state and of the other states which cooperate through it."

The Council serves as secretariat for the Governors' Conference and four other national associations of state government officials, as noted below. Its central office is located in Chicago,[48] with regional offices in New York and San Francisco. A contact office for the Federal government charged specifically with "facilitating and improving Federal-state relations" and with keeping the states currently informed of activities of the Federal government of interest to them, is maintained in Washington. Regional representatives of the Council work closely with state legislators and officials and assist the states not only with respect to national and regional programs of the Council but also in the solution of problems arising in individual states.

What the Council Does. The Council serves the following organizations of state officials:

American Legislators' Association, organization of the nation's 7500 state legislators

Governors' Conference, national organization of the chief executives of the states

Legislative Service Conference

National Association of Attorneys General

National Association of Secretaries of State

National Association of State Budget Officers

National Association of State Purchasing Agents

The Council and the state commissions on interstate cooperation also cooperate, as has been noted, with the legislative program of the National Conference of Commissioners on Uniform State Laws. In addition to serving these specific organizations, the Council's staff provides research and technical assistance to all elective and appointive officials of the states. In addition to maintaining an inquiry and information service available to all the states,

[47] This analysis follows rather closely a published brochure of the Council.

[48] At 1313 East 60th Street, Chicago 37; see p. 162.

and extensively used by them, it undertakes research projects at the request of state legislators and state officials. It conducts an extensive publications program designed to provide full information on state government to all interested persons.[49] It assists the states in the establishment of nationwide and regional compacts and commissions. In late years, particularly in time of war, it has acted as the agent of the states in organizing nationwide programs requiring joint Federal-state action, and it has increasingly served as a means for facilitating and improving Federal-state relations.

What the Council Has Accomplished. The services of the Council may be grouped into four major categories: (1) common interstate problems; (2) Federal-state relations; (3) national interstate problems; and (4) regional interstate problems. In connection with the first of these it may be noted that each state is faced with common or similar problems in such matters as public finance, employment, veterans' affairs, legislative practices and procedures, and state-local relations. The Council, acting through committees of state legislators and state officials, studies these problems and develops programs for the consideration of the states. Suggestions by recent committees on Tax and Fiscal Policy, Postwar Reconstruction and Development, and Legislative Processes and Procedures — to cite only a few — have achieved significant results.

The Council is a channel through which Federal-state cooperative programs are organized and put into effect. During World War II, for instance, the Council, at the request of the Federal government and in cooperation with the states, set up a nationwide program of civilian defense. State programs were also established for selective service, rationing, conservation and salvage, soldier-sailor voting, motor transport regulation, and a number of related matters.

For more than a decade the states have worked through the Council to prevent or eliminate interstate trade barriers. The Council has also pioneered in the establishment of uniform criminal legislation; all but three states have passed uniform statutes relating to parolees and probationers, and many states have passed additional uniform laws with respect to pursuit, extradition, out-of-state witnesses, and narcotic drugs. The Council's program, in cooperation with the National Conference of Commissioners on Uniform State Laws, includes measures in the fields of commercial, property, trust,

[49] Chief items in its publications program are:

The Book of the States, biennially, with frequent supplements.
State Government, monthly magazine of state affairs.
Washington Legislative Bulletin, with news of Congressional activity and administrative actions of interest to the states.
Weekly Digest of Opinions of Attorneys General.
Current Legislative Sessions, a weekly checklist of meetings and adjournments.
Proceedings of the annual meetings of the Governors' Conference, and of the National Association of Attorneys General.
A wide variety of special reports and research studies, list of which the Council will supply, on request.

tax, and administrative law, evidence, veterans' affairs, and other topics. Other nationwide programs fostered by the Council relate to aviation, insurance, control and use of water resources, and legislative policies and procedures.

The Council promotes a wide variety of agreements for the solution of regional problems, some of which have been discussed in the preceding pages. Through efforts of the Commissions on Interstate Cooperation, a number of interstate boundary disputes have been settled. The Council has acted on behalf of the states on the International Board of Inquiry for the Great Lakes Fisheries, which recommended the establishment of international management of fisheries on the Great Lakes.

How the Council Does Its Work. As an instrumentality of the states, the Council is governed and controlled by the states. As at present organized, it is governed by a Board of Managers, composed of forty-nine delegate members representing the forty-eight states and Alaska, sixteen ex-officio members, and ten members-at-large. A state-delegate member is chosen by each state. Ex-officio managers are the nine members of the Executive Committee of the Governors' Conference and the presidents of the several associations for which the Council serves as secretariat and provides service. To provide continuity of membership, the Board of Managers itself elects ten managers-at-large who serve staggered five-year terms. Two managers-at-large are elected each year.

The Executive Committee of the Board is composed of the President (who is a governor), the First Vice-President (who is a legislator and who serves as Board Chairman), two additional Vice-Presidents, an Auditor (who is a state fiscal officer), the Honorary President of the Council, and the Executive Director. The Board of Managers meets annually and at special call to consider general matters of Council policy. The Executive Committee meets more frequently throughout the year, working with the Executive Director in the solution of day-to-day problems. The Executive Director is appointed by the Executive Committee, subject to the approval of the Board of Managers. All members of the staff are selected by the Executive Director and operate under his direction and supervision.

The Council sponsors a biennial General Assembly of the States which is composed of three official representatives of each state — one from each house of the legislature and one representing the governor. It provides a common meeting place for all state legislators and officials and is a forum for the consideration and discussion of problems common to the states. Each of the associations of state officials for which the Council serves as secretariat, has an annual meeting of its own. At these conferences problems of importance to the specific group are discussed and policies determined. An interchange of ideas is facilitated by these meetings, and the machinery of interstate cooperation is strengthened. Regional meetings of Commissions on Interstate Cooperation are held several times throughout the year to consider current problems requiring joint state action and to review plans and formulate policies for more effective interstate cooperation.

State Commissions on Interstate Cooperation. Attempts at interstate cooperation are not new, but formerly they were not as effective as they might have been. There was no person or group of persons in any state government whose business it was continuously to try to solve interstate problems. The first such agency was the New Jersey Commission on Interstate Cooperation, created in April, 1935. From that time on, the movement spread rapidly — more rapidly than civil service, legislative councils, judicial councils, or any other movement except that for the creation of budget agencies. By 1945 all forty-eight states had become members of the Council of State Governments by establishing commissions patterned after the model bill drafted by the Council.[50] Hubert R. Gallagher, who was intimately connected with the movement for many years, thus described the organization of these commissions:

> The commissions, with few exceptions, consist of fifteen members, including ten legislators and five administrative officials. Five of the legislative members constitute the senate standing committee on interstate cooperation, and five make up the house standing committee on interstate cooperation. These committees are appointed as are other committees of the legislatures. In most cases, the speaker appoints the house members, the president of the senate appoints the senate members, and the governor names the administrative committee, usually from the members of his cabinet.

Not only does the personnel of the commission consist of a majority of legislators, but it frequently includes the legislative leaders. This means, in practice, that when legislation is required, the commissions have someone in each house in a position to take charge of the necessary bills. Financial support is necessary, to employ an executive secretary and in some instances a research staff. In general, those commissions that have had the best financial support have been the most effective. The states have shown an increasing willingness to accept the idea of cooperation, and to provide the funds necessary to make it work. The commissions have tackled whatever problems were at hand, depending somewhat upon the section of the country. While these have come from a wide variety of fields, those that have been most frequently recurring can be grouped under the following headings:

Business and Industry: banking and securities, migration of industry, interstate trade barriers
Conservation: oil, fisheries, stream pollution, flood control, and water management
Highways: highway safety, motor truck regulation
Law Enforcement: crime, probation and parole, liquor control
Welfare: unemployment compensation, transients, marriage law

[50] On this movement, see Gallagher, Hubert R., "The Development of Interstate Government," *National Municipal Review*, July 1937, pp. 345–351, and "Work of Commissions on Interstate Cooperation," *Annals*, January 1940, pp. 103–110; also successive editions of the *Book of the States*. For the text of a California court decision upholding the

In commenting upon their work, Mr. Gallagher concludes that they "are daily demonstrating that they can deal with these complicated problems of interstate and Federal-state relationships in a constructive manner."

Other Organizations. The efforts of the Council and of the organizations connected with it are from time to time supplemented by those of groups set up, usually on a temporary basis, sometimes nationally, sometimes regionally. In 1940 there were six such groups functioning on a national basis — the Interstate Commission on Conflicting Taxation, the Interstate Commission on Crime (which is now much stronger and more active than at that time), the Interstate Commission on Social Security (which has now, with the new Social Security Act of 1950, served its purpose), the Interstate Commission on Council Development, the Interlevel Commission, and the Tax Revision Council. All of these were composed of representatives of the cooperating states, and consequently they had a distinct advantage over the older associations of state administrative officials, whose rapid turnover permitted but short periods of service. Private citizens may be appointed, while many of the official members are in positions of relatively secure tenure, which gives them an opportunity to make some real contribution. The work is not showy; it cannot be done rapidly. It requires prolonged conference and discussion, research, earnestness, and application. On this basis, these commissions have made substantial progress.

Others function on what may be called the basis of the occasional conference, the best illustration of which is, perhaps, the National Conference on Interstate Trade Barriers held in Chicago, in April 1939. The problem which confronted this gathering has been previously outlined. Careful preparation and planning of such a conference is necessary. Months were spent in research, resulting in a series of bulletins clearly indicating the facts. Some 400 delegates registered, including a number of governors and many other officials. Although the conference listened to speeches and adopted resolutions, its influence did not stop there. Careful preparation had been made for nationwide publicity over the radio and through newspapers and magazines. Thousands of citizens who had never heard of a trade barrier before now became interested and to some extent informed. The public became "trade barrier conscious." The result was that "the drive to erect additional trade barriers in the forty-four legislatures meeting in 1939 was stopped in its tracks." Legislators who attended went home to kill bills of this character in committee, governors to use their influence against them or to exercise their veto power if the bills were passed.[51] This Conference, like most of the others, was organized by the Council of State Governments, which has, for instance, recently conducted a number of conferences between Members of the Con-

---

state commission on interstate cooperation, and discussion thereof, see *State Government*, August 1941, pp. 198–200, 207.

[51] National Conference on Interstate Trade Barriers, *Proceedings* (Council of State Governments, Chicago, 1939).

gress and of the Governors' Conference, for the purpose of ironing out some of the tax conflicts currently existing between the Federal government and the states.

Uniformity as a Possible Substitute for Centralization

There has of late been much discussion with regard not only to the extension of the functions of the Federal government, but to the transfer to the Federal government of functions formerly regarded as belonging to the states. Many have expressed fears that the Federal government would become too large and unwieldy, that the people might become weighed down by bureaucracy, and that the states might become mere subdivisions in a great Federal administrative machine. These protests have come from responsible leaders in both of the major political parties. In these developments it has been notable that the Democrats, who were traditionally the exponents of the states' rights theory, have, under Presidents Wilson, Roosevelt, and Truman, vastly extended the Federal power, while the Republicans, who have traditionally favored a strong central government, have of late assumed the role of spokesmen for the states' rights idea.

To the student of government it seems obvious not only that the changes which have taken place in the allocation of powers between the states and the Federal government will remain relatively permanent, but that there will be additional changes of a similar nature. These changes are but natural when one considers the extent to which scientific developments have reduced the older limitations of time and space. Government must function in larger units if it is to be reasonably efficient under modern conditions. This, together with the fact that government is expected to do more and that higher standards of performance for government service have been established, explains to some extent the reasons for these shifts in the allocation of power. It is noteworthy, however, that in all the changes which have thus far occurred, the states have not lost a single power of which they were making effective use; they have lost power only when they were either unable or unwilling to perform effectively governmental functions which the people demanded.

If these changes had taken place without justification, there might possibly have been some reason for the fears which have frequently been expressed. When, however, they present simply a part of that continuous process of adjustment of governmental institutions to the needs of a people living in a rapidly changing social and economic order, there would seem to be little reason for alarm. The state governments are larger, more powerful, and engaged in performing more necessary services than they have ever been in the past. This is due in part to the public demand for additional governmental services, to the demand for more adequate service in fields where the states are already active, and to the tendency to shift power from the local units to states, which was discussed in the preceding chapter.

Even though the reasons for these changes in Federal-state relationships are known and recognized, most students of government will agree that the states ought to retain just as large a portion of the powers which they now have as they can use effectively. The whole of the preceding discussion of uniformity and of the relation of the states to the Federal government has been predicated upon the assumption that the states can maintain all the powers which they now have, if they will further develop and use known methods and techniques for cooperation among themselves and for the development of uniform policies. The need for uniform rules and regulations in many fields of state government activity has already been emphasized. In each of these fields, uniformity will sooner or later be attained. Unless the states work out among themselves suitable methods for making uniform laws and enforcing these by uniform and cooperative administrative policies, there will be no alternative but to develop still further existing tendencies toward Federal centralization.

SELECTED REFERENCES

Bard, Erwin W., *The Port of New York Authority* (Columbia University Press, 1941), and Bird, Frederick L., *A Study of the Port of New York Authority* (Dun & Bradstreet, New York, 1948). Two excellent studies of a unique experiment in interstate cooperation.

Committee on Intergovernmental Fiscal Relations, *Intergovernmental Fiscal Relations* (Treasury Department, Washington, 1943). This Newcomer-Gulick report is an outstanding analysis of the problems in this field.

Graves, W. Brooke, *Uniform State Action, a Possible Substitute for Centralization* (University of North Carolina Press, 1934). Comprehensive survey, now much out of date, of developments in interstate cooperation.

——, Ed., "Intergovernmental Relations in the United States," *Annals*, January 1940, entire volume. Symposium by twenty-five specialists in the field, including coverage of interstate relations.

Kleinsorge, Paul L., *The Boulder Canyon Project: History and Economic Aspects* (Stanford University Press, 1941). A study of one of the earliest and most famous interstate compacts in the field of water resources.

Marketing Laws Survey, *Bibliography of Barriers to Trade Between the States* (Department of Commerce, Washington, 1942). This bibliography and the series of monographs prepared by the Survey contain valuable information on interstate relations.

Melder, F. Eugene, *State and Local Barriers to Interstate Commerce in the United States: a Study in Economic Sectionalism* (University of Maine Studies, 1937). Best monograph available on the subject; see also National Conference on Interstate Trade Barriers, *Proceedings* (Council of State Governments, Chicago, 1939), and the working papers prepared by the Council for this Conference.

Purcell, Margaret R., *Interstate Barriers to Truck Transportation* (Bureau of Agricultural Economics, United States Department of Agriculture, Washington, December 1950). History and current status of regulations regarding size and weight, taxes affecting trucking.

Stone, Clifford H., Ed., *Interstate Cooperation: a Compilation of Articles from*

Various Sources (Colorado Water Conservation Board, Denver, 1946). Extremely valuable collection of papers, mostly from law journals and other widely scattered sources.

Thursby, Vincent V., *Interstate Cooperation; A Study of the Interstate Compact* (Public Affairs Press, Washington, 1953). A thorough study and appraisal of the interstate compact as a device for resisting the extremes of centralization.

Zimmerman, Frederick L., and Wendell, Mitchell, *The Interstate Compact Since 1925* (Council of State Governments, Chicago, 1951). The first comprehensive treatment in many years of the constantly growing number of interstate compacts.

25

Cooperative Federalism[1]

Some Historical Considerations

In any consideration of the future of the American states, it is desirable at the outset to recall the circumstances of their development and of their entry into the Union. When the present Constitution was framed and adopted, the states were more than a century and a half old. Their origins were traceable, not to the date of independence, but to the granting of the letters patent to individuals and groups of individuals for the establishment of colonies in America; they had existed as colonies down to the date of independence, and had at that time, or soon after, been transformed into states. For many years after, it was the states to which the people gave their primary allegiance. Under the Articles of Confederation the strength of the states was so great that it was impossible for the central government to function with any degree of effectiveness. It has been argued that during this period the states usurped the sovereignty of the *people of the nation*, and that in order to establish an effective government, it was necessary for the *people* to reassert their sovereign power.[2] When the Constitution was framed, the people were still greatly concerned about "states' rights," those in the smaller states contending that only by the preservation of these rights would it be possible to secure the rights of the individual.

There is much evidence to indicate that the people regarded the new central government with fear and viewed the possible extension of its powers with great apprehension. It had been possible to secure the ratification of the new Constitution only on the basis of a pledge that the government to be organized under it would immediately submit to the states for adoption a series of amendments designed to protect the rights of the individual. This was done, resulting in the Bill of Rights as it is now known. Not long there-

[1] The author is indebted to the editors of the following journals for permission to reprint those portions of this chapter which appeared in their respective publications: *American Political Science Review*, "The Future of the American States," February 1936, pp. 24–50; *State Government*, "What Is Happening to Our Federal System?" November 1949, pp. 255–259, 279.

[2] Burgess, John W., "The American Commonwealth," *Political Science Quarterly*, March 1886, pp. 9–35.

after, the Supreme Court, in the case of Chisholm v. Georgia,[3] ruled that a state might be sued in the courts of the United States without its consent; this created such a furor that Amendment XI was promptly proposed and ratified. It was inconceivable to the people of that day that a sovereign state should be subjected to the indignity of being brought into court like an ordinary citizen. Throughout the period of controversy on the slavery question this question of states' rights was ever in the foreground.

The states were in the beginning, and they continued for many years to be, the chief interest and concern and the chief object of the governmental allegiance of the people. In the formative period the fear was not that the central government would become too large and too powerful, but that it would be unable to get power and prestige enough to enable it to survive. In view of the difficulties that had been experienced by the colonists before and during the Revolution, this attitude is not surprising. When the debate on the subject of ratification was in progress, the authors of the Federalist papers argued that the powers of the central government could not become oppressive, because, they said, it was the tendency of the divisional governments to enlarge and enhance their powers at the expense of any central agency that might be created. At the time everything seemed to indicate that they were right.[4]

The priority of the states in the Federal system continued through the nineteenth century, down to the period of the Civil War. While there were signs of an impending change, in the form of added restrictions upon the legislative power, both the executive and the judiciary were gaining in power. In the earliest constitutions framed after 1789 "the governor was restored in large degree to powers lost during the period of the Revolution," and during the first three or four decades of the nineteenth century "he seemed to hold his own." "His independence of the legislature was worked out through the constitutional developments between 1789 and 1840, and has been preserved as a permanent principle, and a longer term has been accorded him." By the fifth decade of the century the tendency to limit his administrative discretion, to hedge in his pardoning power, to narrow the scope of his power to appoint and dismiss by making many officers elective by the voters, "and to place him under the surveillance of a cabinet of elective officers, not necessarily in political accord with him, whose duty it is to record his acts and report the same to the legislature," was clearly in evidence. Despite these tendencies, the governor continued in the states generally to be an important personage down to 1861.[5]

In the closing decades of the nineteenth century state government in the

[3] 2 Dallas 419, 1793.

[4] *The Federalist*, Nos. XVII and XXXI, both of which were written by Hamilton. The present author has elsewhere discussed this question; see *Uniform State Action*, Chapter 19 (University of North Carolina Press, 1934).

[5] This paragraph is based upon Burgess, *op. cit.*, from which source quotations are taken.

United States sank to its lowest depths. In the era of reconstruction in the Southern states there developed an orgy of graft, corruption, and inefficiency that is quite without parallel. In the other states interest in the state governments lagged and they suffered greatly in efficiency by reason of a poor personnel and an inadequate and unsatisfactory organization. In a thirty-year period of intense activity in constitution making at the close of the nineteenth century an appalling number of restrictions and limitations were placed upon the powers of the legislatures, which during this period were at their lowest point in public confidence. The restrictions upon the executive were further developed. The judiciary suffered greatly from a reduced tenure, from choice by election rather than by appointment, from an inferior quality of personnel, and from a consequent loss of dignity and influence. All these unfortunate characteristics of state government of the period were reflected in the constitutions currently framed — constitutions which still constitute approximately half of the total number now in effect.

The Indictment of the States

Thus for many years, the states were the hub around which the wheel of the governmental universe in America revolved; during this period the states seem to have performed fairly satisfactorily the services required of them, and it appears therefore that there was little if any serious criticism of them. When, in the latter decades of the nineteenth century, the states slumped into a long period of decline in both prestige and efficiency, there began to appear from time to time ringing indictments of the whole state system. Criticism of the states was fostered also by the fact that, unfortunately for them, their decline took place at a time when increasing demands were being made upon them and at a time when people were in a position to give more thought and attention to their structure and functioning. In the days of exploration and settlement government was and could be simple, for little was needed, or at least little was expected of it; with the advent of a new economic and industrial era, more government was needed, more was expected of it, and its shortcomings were more obvious.

Expressions of apprehension regarding the course of events appeared from time to time, as in the following comment written by John Fiske, historian and author, in 1888, in his *Critical Period of American History:*

> Our Federal government has indeed shown a strong tendency to encroach upon the provinces of the State government, especially since our late Civil War. Too much centralization is our danger today, as the weakness of the Federal tie was our danger a century ago. . . .
>
> If the day should ever arrive (which God forbid) when the people of the different parts of our country shall allow our local affairs to be administered by the prefect sent from Washington, . . . on that date the political career of the American people will have been robbed of its most interesting and valuable features, and the usefulness of this nation will be lamentably impaired.

The subject of Federal-state relations was one of great general interest then, as it had been 100 years before and as it is today. What appears to have been the first serious public criticism of the inadequacies of the states appeared at approximately the same time, near the close of the nineteenth century, from what may now be regarded as the older school of political scientists. In 1886 Professor John W. Burgess of Columbia University, writing in the first issue of the *Political Science Quarterly*, commented at length upon the various evidences of the decline of the states and the causes of this decline; it was his contention that:

> The two natural elements in our system are now the Community and the Nation. The former is the point of real local self-government; the latter that of general self-government; and in the adjustments of the future these are the forces which will carry with them the determining power. The commonwealth government is now but a sort of middle instance, beginning to be regarded as a meddlesome intruder in both spheres — the tool of the strongest interest, the oppressor of the individual. This has been its history in other lands and other times; and the mere fact that it professes to be popular here, while it has been princely or aristocratic elsewhere, will not save it from the same fate.[6]

About the same time another great American scholar was arriving at similar conclusions; Professor Simon N. Patton of the University of Pennsylvania, in 1890, writing in the *Annals* of the American Academy of Political and Social Science, also in the first issue, comments at length upon the lack of intelligence displayed in setting up the state boundary lines:

> The old colonies grew up having common bonds of religion or of descent holding together their inhabitants. . . . The western states have no such origin. They were laid out before they were inhabited, and have rivers, lakes, or even worse, lines of latitude and longtitude for their boundaries. Of course, such a method is an easy way to divide up a new country, but no worse way could be devised for making states. Rivers and lakes are the natural means of transit and should be the center of states. Nothing could be more arbitrary than to make the Ohio and Mississippi rivers state boundaries. The two slopes of these rivers have a similar climate. Their inhabitants have the same centers of trade, and migrating from the same states have similar ideas as to education and government. The same facts are true of the regions about the lakes. And yet our forefathers disregarded all these considerations and threw together the most discordant elements into one state. . . . What can be expected but that these states should be merely inharmonious units out of which can grow none of those common feelings which are needed to give vitality to state institutions?[7]

Like Burgess, Patton regarded the states as an obstacle to the growth of real local government, as being too small to serve the purposes of administrative districts, and too large and too heterogeneous in composition to serve satisfactorily as units of local government. He blamed the state system for the widespread prevalence of political corruption:

[6] Burgess, *op. cit.*, pp. 33–34.

[7] Patton, Simon N., "Decay of State and Local Governments," *Annals*, July 1890, pp. 26–42; quotation from p. 30.

> It is therefore the absoluteness of our boundary lines and the unchangeableness of the territorial extent of our states, that are the sources of the present degenerate tendencies in our politics and a cause of the subordination of the individual to party power. Instead of regarding the boundaries of our states as fixed and unchangeable, we should recognize that we are only beginning to get the data upon which to decide where the boundaries of states can be properly located.[8]

Interest in the states and in government generally was greatly stimulated in the United States by the publication in 1887 of the first edition of Bryce's *American Commonwealth*.[9] While it is true that no specific attempts were made to put in practice the recommendations of these distinguished scholars, it is also true that the states did begin to make some progress in the early years of the present century. There arose in many of the states, particularly in the Middle West, a group of able and aggressive leaders who were able to rally extensive popular support and who in the governor's office were able to arouse a new interest in state government and to bring a new vitality and efficiency to the conduct of its affairs. In 1917 the administrative reorganization movement began in Illinois, and from this date on, the progress of the states has been rapid.

A period of depression and two World Wars subjected the states to new burdens and to great new responsibilities — neither of which they were always able to discharge adequately. Their most conspicuous failures during the last half century occurred during the depression, when they were subjected to a new series of indictments and attacks, often at the hands of very distinguished political scientists. These attacks were often vigorous, sometimes intemperate, and wholly unjustified if not untrue, as for instance[10]:

> Is the state the appropriate instrumentality for the discharge of these sovereign functions? The answer is not a matter of conjecture or delicate appraisal. It is a matter of brutal record. The American state is finished. I do not predict that the states will go, but affirm that they have gone.

Like the famous report of the death of Mark Twain, this announcement of the demise of the states was somewhat premature. Not only are the states still here in a reasonably live and vigorous condition a quarter of a century after these lines were written, but they are likely to be here long after both the author and the readers of these pages have passed to their reward.

The criticisms leveled against the states through the years have, in general, centered around the fact that their boundaries were not determined in accordance with any guiding principle, that they were often unreasonable and illogical, being determined in some cases by obvious geographical considerations, in others by bargain and compromise, and in still others by the arbitrary fiat of the courts. Probably no one will deny that if the task were

[8] *Ibid.*, pp. 39–40.

[9] For an appraisal of the influence of this work, see Brooks, Robert C., Ed., *Bryce's "American Commonwealth": Fiftieth Anniversary*, especially Chapter 2 by Frances L. Reinhold (Macmillan, New York, 1939).

[10] These indictments are discussed at some length and documented in previous editions of this book; in Third Edition (1946), pp. 939–944.

being undertaken at the present time, the problem would be solved quite differently. The development of modern methods of communication and transportation has made the existing arrangements seem to many people highly unsatisfactory.

The claim has been made that the states constitute an obstacle to effective local government, and the charge that they have often failed to deal adequately with many of the pressing responsibilities with which they have been confronted. The failure of the states to render efficient service and to coordinate their activities with the Federal government on the one hand and the local units on the other has brought about a number of definite tendencies in American government. In some cases the breakdown of state control has been reflected in the drift toward Federal centralization, and in the extension of the Federal subsidy system. Controversies have developed over taxation and other important subjects.

Federal-State Relations in Emergency Periods

During the past three decades the states — like the nation as a whole — have passed through three great emergency periods of war and depression. Prior to the twenties, the scope of state functions was relatively limited. In the second place, their administrative structure was often poor, and their efforts generally ineffective when, throughout the fifty years following the Civil War, they did bestir themselves in an attempt to deal with a rising tide of important governmental problems. This charge became less and less true in the years following 1917. Third, the states failed in many respects to keep up with the changes that had been taking place in modern life.

The States in the Depression. In the depression period there were numerous influences that tended to diminish the prestige if not the power of the states. There was a great increase in the influence of Congress and of the Federal departments and agencies in directing the course of state legislation concerning subjects of interest to them. In relief, the Federal government not only dictated the policies but further undermined state control over the relief situation by carrying on negotiations and making agreements directly with municipalities. Finally, the development of the metropolitan area raised the old problem of the urban-rural conflict in a new and acute form.

Even a casual observer of American government in the thirties could not fail to notice the greater Federal influence on state legislation in many different fields. Nearly all the agencies, to be sure, denied any intention of exerting pressure on the legislatures to secure the adoption of desired legislation; the only exceptions in a survey made at the time were the Department of Labor, the Bureau of Narcotics, and the Bureau of Public Roads. Without question, these activities were undertaken with the best of motives and the legislation so sponsored was generally of a desirable character. Yet there were some pertinent questions which presented themselves regarding the effect of this practice upon the established system of American government, the ethics of the Federal government's using tax moneys for the support of propaganda, and of its carrying on pressure group activities at the state capitols.[11]

An inquiry into this general subject during legislative sessions in the depression years indicated that the number of Federal departments and agencies attempting to exert such influence was much greater than had previously been the case and that they were better organized, knew better what they wanted, and were more insistent about getting it than in previous years. The National Recovery Administration, in 1935, through its State Relations Division, approached the appropriate state officials and the state party leaders in and out of the legislature in the hope of advancing its model act designed to insure the cooperation of the states with the NRA. In the utility field, the Federal Power Commission sought supporting legislation from the states, which makes it possible for the Commission to designate the state commissions as its agents in certain aspects of utility control. There has been for years an extensive amount of cooperation between the Interstate Commerce Commission and the state commissions in the matter of railroad regulation.[12] The Federal Housing Administration sought and obtained legislation permitting all lending and savings institutions to make loans, where they were insured by FHA or where FHA issued the obligation.

The Bureau of Criminal Identification and the Bureau of Prisons in the Department of Justice both extended their activities in this field, sponsoring Congressional legislation, state legislation, and administrative policies, all designed to bring both greater unity in organization and greater uniformity in policy to the task of enforcing the criminal law and the administration of justice. California and several other states adopted legislation designed to insure a maximum amount of cooperation on the part of the state with the Agricultural Adjustment Administration, and this organization sought to encourage the adoption of such legislation elsewhere. The Federal Deposit Insurance Corporation was concerned not merely with supporting legislation in the states, but with the possible modification of existing provisions of state constitutions where such provisions have interfered with the work of the Corporation; the Reconstruction Finance Corporation in some instances encountered similar problems. The Home Owners Loan Corporation drafted and advanced by such means as were at its disposal supporting legislation in the states; the most helpful thing that the states could do would be to

[11] Graves, W. Brooke, "Stroke Oar," *State Government*, December 1934, pp. 259–262; "Federal Leadership in State Legislation," *Temple Law Quarterly*, July 1936, pp. 385–405; and "Influence of Congressional Legislation on Legislation in the States," *Iowa Law Review*, May 1938, pp. 519–538.

[12] Lindahl, Martin L., "Coöperation between the Interstate Commerce Commission and the State Commissions in Railroad Regulation," *Michigan Law Review*, January 1935, pp. 338–397; Kauper, Paul G., "Utilization of State Commissioners in the Administration of the Federal Motor Carrier Act," *Michigan Law Review*, November 1935, pp. 37–84; Collins, John L., "Fellowship Between Federal and State Commissions," *Public Utility Fortnightly*, February 28, 1935, pp. 243–248; and Fesler, James W., *The Independence of State Regulatory Agencies* (Public Administration Service, Chicago, 1942).

defense, and other wartime needs. Civilian defense included, in addition to protective services, other services in the field of medicine, public utilities, and transportation, not to mention an elaborate warning system to be used in case of air raid or attack.[19]

Civilian defense had a national organization and a strong state organization in every state, but much of the responsibility for its administration devolved upon the local communities. Similarly, the cities had an important role to play in providing recreational facilities for men and women in the armed forces, in bond drives, blood donor service, drives for the salvage of scrap metal and waste paper, and in a multitude of other activities familiar to all during the war period.

Financially the cities fared well during the war, as did the states. Receipts from taxes were high, and grants in substantial amounts continued to come in for various purposes related to the war effort — defense housing, vocational training, and many other things. Direct Federal-city relations were largely an experiment born of the depression; the Lanham Act, with its reliance on loans and grants, and Federal-local relationships to provide public works, followed in the pattern made familiar during the depression.

The Cities in the Postwar Era. The war over and wartime "surpluses" soon expended, the cities quickly found themselves in an extremely serious financial plight. They were ground, as it were, between the upper and the nether millstones. Faced with the responsibility for furnishing more and more costly services than they had ever been asked to supply before, for a constantly increasing population, they were — and they still are — bedeviled by a multiplicity of disturbing factors in the field of finance. They were saddled with the same problems of inflation that have confronted everyone else. Many of them were strangled by obsolete constitutional and statutory provisions imposing inflexible limitations on tax rates, tax sources, and the power to incur debt. They were saddled, in other words, with an antiquated system of raising revenues, a system developed over generations and centuries, based largely on a general property tax whose assessments are still tied to prewar standards.

In many different ways the Federal government has been helping the cities in meeting this critical situation. In housing, airport development, hospital construction, highway improvement, and other phases of public works, substantial assistance has been provided. Since 1947 the Housing and Home Finance Agency has functioned as the single permanent agency responsible for Federal housing activities. Those functions affecting cities — and most of its functions do — have included disposition of Federal public war housing and the administration of Federal contracts with local housing authorities

[19] See American Municipal Association, *Cities and the National Defense Program* (Chicago, 1941); Gill, Corrington, "Federal-State-City Cooperation in Congested Production Areas," *Public Administration Review*, Winter 1945, pp. 28–33; and other references cited in the previous edition of this volume.

in the field of low-rent housing and slum clearance. The Housing Act passed by the 81st Congress in 1949 contained important new provisions on urban redevelopment.

The construction and maintenance of large municipal airports is an exceedingly costly undertaking. Civic pride seems to require that each city have its own airport, and Federal aid has been made available for this purpose. The Federal Airport Act of 1946 authorized appropriations up to $500,000,000 for airport aid over a seven-year period. Applications for new airport projects or certain expenditures on existing facilities might be made directly to the Civil Aeronautics Administration except in those states which required by law that such requests be channeled through the appropriate state agency. Aid was fixed at 50 per cent of the allowable costs of construction for small airports, with variable percentages up to or, with the approval of Congress, even exceeding 50 per cent for the larger ones. The Civil Aeronautics Administration not only administers this program but develops and fosters the coordination of a national system of airports.

The Federal Highway Act of 1944 provided funds for cities and other local units in the construction of expressways and through thoroughfares, thereby taking cognizance of the very serious problems of traffic congestion existing in all major cities. The Federal Hospital Survey and Construction Act of 1949 provided $150,000,000 annually until 1955 in order to help communities build needed hospitals and hospital facilities. This program, begun in 1946, has now reached impressive proportions. The United States Public Health Service, which is responsible for the administration of this Act, reported as of January 1, 1950, that allotment of Federal money to hospital construction involving municipal hospitals and health centers had passed the $20,000,000 mark, these city and city-county hospitals being located in 117 municipalities. More than 1000 projects had been approved for funds in all the several categories of non-Federal hospitals.

Similarly, the Public Health Service Act of 1944 authorized a broadening of the Federal-state-local relationship in cooperative health programs. It contemplated a national tuberculosis control program patterned after the venereal disease control program begun in 1938. The Federal government has for years given assistance to municipalities faced with disaster, and to prevent the recurrence of disaster, as by the construction of floodwalls. It will doubtless continue to render assistance in the solution of major problems, whether or not they are the result of a natural catastrophe. These are only a few examples of the increasing number and scope of Federal-municipal programs and relationships.[20]

Aid may be given to the cities in other ways. Various Federal laws al-

[20] See Senate Committee on Expenditures in the Executive Departments, *Intergovernmental Relationships Between the United States and the States and Municipalities* (82nd Cong., 1st Sess., Senate Report No. 94, 1951) which reviews Federal grant-in-aid programs for fiscal 1950. Current information on the progress of these various programs may be obtained from the annual reports of the Federal departments and agencies charged with their ad-

ready provide for numerous exemptions from Federal taxes applicable to municipalities, exemptions ranging from 5 or 7 per cent to as much as 25 per cent of the cost of specified purchases. But it should do something about in-lieu payments on the vast amount of nontaxable Federal lands and other property. A tremendous increase in the number of such properties occurred during the war period; many of them are still in government possession. If they cannot be turned back into private hands, the least the Federal government should do is to provide in-lieu payments which would offset in part the loss of revenue resulting from the withdrawal of valuable properties from the tax rolls.

Regionalism: Sub-National and Metropolitan

A review of the historical background of the states shows that they have often failed in the past and that they are ill-suited to many of the needs of modern government. Whether or not one agrees with the extreme demands of those who see no solution for the shortcomings of the states except their abolition, anyone must admit that some modification of existing practices must be made, unless, as Elihu Root predicted about fifty years ago, they are to lose their power. The possible alternatives are two. If the states are to be abolished, there must be set up in their place some system of zones or regions to serve for those administrative purposes which require a unit smaller than the central government and larger than the local units. If the state organization is to be retained, a remedy will have to be provided for the more serious defects in the existing system.

Proposals for Sub-National Regionalism. The idea of the use of regions for administrative purposes is not new either in Europe or in America. In Europe it has been common for at least a hundred years — in Great Britain, France, Spain, Russia, and elsewhere. Historically, it is much older, having existed in Italy under the Romans, in Manchuria under the Chinese, and in Crimea under the Russians. In the United States the problem of sectionalism was long one of great concern and is still a favored subject for historical study and investigation. It has commonly been regarded with disapproval because of its supposed detrimental effect upon national unity. It is therefore important to distinguish between sectionalism and regionalism. Professor Odum has said of the latter that it "envisions the nation first, making the total national culture the final arbiter, while sectionalism seeks the region first, and the nation afterward." Only recently has regionalism been advanced by serious students as an end to be fostered and encouraged. This may be merely a characteristic of a larger movement which has found expression in various countries.

One of the most convincing plans for the reconstruction of the states and the development of regions came from Professor Leland:

ministration, as the annual reports of the Civil Aeronautics Administration on the Federal Airport Act.

. . . Rural government should be turned over to the state, with suitable rural administrative areas taking the place of existing counties. The states, in turn, should be divested of their legislative functions and be made administrative area of the Federal government with flexible boundaries. The anomaly of having forty-eight legislatures to solve similar problems in forty-eight different ways would be ended. Legislative chaos would be replaced by national uniformity in codes, technique, and quality of administration. The states long ago demonstrated their inability to regulate railroads, trade, commerce, or corporation finances. Conferences, conventions, and uniform law commissions have failed to solve these problems or bring order out of legal chaos. The alternative remedy of changing our form of government so as to make possible the intelligent solution of these problems has received little or no consideration. At a time when security of private banking and the revival of industrial prosperity so clearly call for unified national action, the follies of maintaining the traditional governmental set-up with its forty-eight independent states should be strikingly demonstrated. If, then, to the Federal government were transferred those problems of more than local concern, if the states met the rural needs and if the cities were given complete jurisdiction over urban problems, our major economic, social, and fiscal dilemmas would be near solution. Complete fiscal coordination would then be easily attained.[21]

The Progress of Regionalism to Date. No one can read the proposals for the establishment of regional government in the United States without being impressed by the lack of agreement among the authors either as to the number of regions or as to the basis upon which they should be set up. This in itself might tend to some extent to discredit the proposals. While the Federal government has used the states for many administrative purposes as a matter of convenience, there are many purposes for which zones have been established which disregard state boundary lines. There are literally dozens of Federal activities and services in the conduct of which a zone or regional system of administration has been in use for years. States have been employed as administrative districts in the older services and also in many created for emergency purposes.

In the last two decades, during the emergencies of depression and of war, state units or directors were widely employed by Federal agencies. In the depression, in the temporary agencies set up for the administration of the agricultural, public works, and emergency relief programs, the states were used as administrative units. They were so used in the National Youth Administration, the National Resources Board, and many others. Among the war agencies, the states were used as administrative units, at first in the Office of Price Administration and the War Production Board, later being combined into regions. The Department of the Army, although it employs larger units also, has always made use of the states as units for certain administrative purposes.

A significant study of regionalism in the United States was made in 1935

[21] Leland, Simeon E., "The Coordination of Federal, State, and Local Fiscal Systems," *Municipal Finance*, August 1933, pp. 35–46.

by the National Resources Committee.[22] This covered the evidences of the problem, some attempts at solution, geographical factors and criteria, and finally, the integration of administrative and geographical factors in regional planning. The interstate compact and interstate cooperation were considered, along with Federal departmental procedure, as possible solutions. In the latter connection it was found that seventy-four Federal agencies of bureau status or higher had designed sets of regions and that there were 108 separate regional schemes in operation, with numbers of regions ranging from one to 307. Eighty-two regional schemes had 1300 regional offices, in 195 cities. When these were plotted on a map of the country, it was found that eight metropolitan centers led by a substantial margin in the frequency of choice by Federal agencies. Thirteen cities are regional centers for twenty or more regional schemes. The Board showed various plans for establishing multi-purpose regions, ranging in number from eight to twenty, each based upon a different principle, such as metropolitan influence or administrative convenience.[23]

The Merits of the Regional Plan. It is clear that the idea of regional or zone administration is not new in the United States; the current proposals would merely extend the principle and introduce it as at least a partial substitute for other administrative devices now in use. There is nothing revolutionary about it; the important questions center rather about such considerations as its wisdom and its practicability. To the present writer, there seems to be little indeed to commend the plan for the regionalization of the United States, if by this is meant the virtual abolition of the present states and the establishment of new administrative districts in lieu thereof. So drastic a plan is not required to remedy the admitted weaknesses of the present system; even if it were, there seems to be little likelihood that its adoption could be brought about at any time in the near future.

There has developed within the states a civic cohesion, a sense of attachment, a love of locality, which cannot easily be broken down. The longer the states remain as states, the stronger this attachment becomes. To say that

[22] National Resources Committee, *Regional Factors in National Planning* (Washington, 1935); Odum, Howard E., and Moore, Harry E., *American Regionalism* (Holt, New York, 1938); Jensen, Merrill, Ed., *Regionalism in America* (University of Wisconsin Press, 1951); "A Symposium on Regional Planning," *Iowa Law Review*, January 1947, entire issue; Hart, Henry C., "Legislative Abdication in Regional Development," *Journal of Politics*, August 1951, pp. 393–417; and Manvel, Allen D., "State Government and Regional Trends in Economic Growth," *State Government*, June 1952, pp. 125–127, 136. For further references, see Culver, Dorothy C., "A Bibliography of Intergovernmental Relations in the United States," *Annals*, January 1940, pp. 210–218, and extensive references in the previous edition of this volume.

[23] This was followed by Wilk, Kurt, *Decentralizing Governmental Work* (Institute for Public Administration, New York, 1942), and with special reference to the effects of the defense program and war mobilization on Federal field services: Legislative Reference Service, Library of Congress, *Federal Field Offices*, A Letter from the Director to Senator Carl Hayden (78th Cong., 1st Sess., Senate Document No. 22, 1943); see also the author's *Public Administration in a Democratic Society*, Chapters 5 and 6 (Heath, Boston, 1950).

it is illogical and sentimental is to beg the issue — although it is both. There is a devotion to the soil, to the life and history and institutions of the state, to the land of one's fathers, which no one can deny who has ever come in contact with natives of California, Indiana, Maryland, Massachusetts, New York, Pennsylvania, Virginia, or any other state. In some instances, it may be noted, there is an attachment to the county, particularly in the South, that is as strong as or stronger than the attachment to the state.

Against such emotional attachments the considerations of pure logic are ineffective indeed. This "persistence of the states is due to many historic facts; to the real differences in character, customs, and loyalties which obtain in colonial days; to the use of constitutional arguments by men like Taylor, Roane, and Calhoun, who were actually defending not state, but sectional interests; to geographic isolation as in California, or cultural homogeneity as in Louisiana; and to the accumulative psychological force of state pride, with its separate institutions, leaders, histories, songs, mottoes, battle-flags, and relics. And, in addition to all these forces, the state has persisted in America because it has been looked upon, even by party leaders with widely divergent views as the natural bulwark of local self-government."

Even if one were to grant that the establishment of such a system was theoretically desirable, there is nothing in the record to indicate that it could be accomplished much before the coming of the millennium. Zones have been used by the Federal government for a wide variety of purposes, but in nearly every case the number of zones has been different. In those few instances in which the same number of zones was set up for two or more different purposes (as in the twelve districts for the Federal Reserve Banks and for the Federal Land Banks) the boundaries of the zones have been different. This is not a criticism of what has been done; it is simply an observation upon an inevitable and inescapable fact. No one who possessed anything less than the intellect of an Aristotle, the wisdom of a Solomon, and the political acumen of a Roosevelt could possibly hope to devise and secure the adoption of a regional plan for the United States which would reconcile all the conflicting requirements of an extensive number of different administrative purposes. There is little evidence at hand to indicate that there is any possible grouping of states that would be uniformly satisfactory.

Metropolitan Regions: Proposals for City-States. A metropolitan region or area is not necessarily, at least, a political unit but rather an area including all the thickly populated territory in and around a city or group of cities. The Bureau of the Census has set up for its use a metropolitan district in connection with each city of 50,000 or more inhabitants, two or more such cities sometimes being in one district. On this basis there were in 1950 approximately 84,500,000 people, or approximately half of the total population, living in 168 metropolitan areas.

The larger centers of population have continued to grow, not only without regard to the geographical boundaries of the minor political subdivisions within the states, but without regard to county, city, borough, township, or even the boundary lines of the states themselves. These cities and the suburban areas which surround them have problems quite distinct from the rural districts of the states, which still maintain their control of the legislative bodies. Neither group shows much understanding of or concern for the social and economic problems of the other.

The Council of State Governments notes that "a complex welter of local governments serves the 140 [now 168] metropolitan regions. The total number in 1940 was 15,827 units. These include 1,741 municipalities, 272 counties, 895 townships, 11,822 school districts, and 1,097 special districts. In the New York Area, for example, responsibility for public affairs is divided among 1,038 governments, including fourteen counties, seventy-eight townships, 286 municipalities, 520 school districts, and 141 special districts."[24] The need for coordination of the essential services maintained by these different units of government has become more and more obvious. Where such coordination is lacking, as it often is, everyone suffers loss and inconvenience. Under these circumstances many of the larger cities have undertaken extensive programs of metropolitan or regional planning, in which, regardless of political boundaries, the economic and social interests of the area have been considered as a whole.

If progress was to be made in the solution of problems of transportation, light, power, gas, water, police, highways, and sewage disposal, it was necessary that these political barriers should be broken down or at least prevented from serious interference with service. Professor Munro in 1923 pointed out four specific ways in which this might be done: by the creation of a municipal federalism; by the outright annexation of encircling municipalities; by a compromise between these two methods, such as was developed in the city of Greater New York with its five boroughs; and by the development of cooperation between the various political units.[25] Progress has been made in many cities along one or another of these lines.

Professor Merriam suggested, as a solution of this problem, the establishment of city-states, the boundaries of which would completely ignore existing political subdivisions. Thus the city of New York would be completely separated from the up-state region and would include as well the southwestern portion of Connecticut and the northern counties of New Jersey. The Philadelphia unit would include not only the six counties in southeastern Pennsylvania but certain portions of southern New Jersey, including the city

[24] *State-Local Relations*, pp. 187–188 (Chicago, 1946).

[25] Munro, William Bennett, *Municipal Government and Administration*, Vol. I, p. 438 (Macmillan, New York, 1923). See also: Jones, Victor, *Metropolitan Government* (University of Chicago Press, 1942); Rutherford, Geddes W., *Administrative Problems in a Metropolitan Area: the National Capital Region* (Public Administration Service, Chicago, 1951); Tableman, Betty, *Governmental Organization in Metropolitan Areas* (Bureau of Government, University of Michigan, 1951); Gist, Noel P., "Developing Patterns of Urban Decentralization," *Social Forces*, July 1952, pp. 257–267; and Tableman, Betty, "How Cities Can Lick the Fringe Problem," *Public Management*, March 1952, pp. 50–54.

of Camden and its surrounding territory, and all or part of Delaware, including the city of Wilmington. The relentless logic of this proposal is inescapable; if there were no existing machinery for purposes of local government, it is not unlikely that some such plan would be adopted. Under the existing circumstances, however, it does not seem likely that much progress will be made in securing the important constitutional changes that would be necessary in order to make this proposal effective, nor does it seem likely that the inhabitants of the several states concerned would consent to such sweeping changes in the governmental system. They may be distrustful and suspicious of the representatives from the cities, but they will not voluntarily relinquish the substantial portion of the state revenues which the urban areas provide.

Professor Merriam, who urged the adoption of this city-state plan on many occasions, visualized units comparable to those existing in several European countries, which would provide an answer to many of the problems now confronting American local government. They would have an autonomous government, divorced from state control, transcending state boundaries, and having their own legislative, administrative, and judicial bodies. In every state containing large metropolitan areas — California, Michigan, New York, and Pennsylvania, for example — a divergence of interests exists between those areas and the rest of the state. Constant friction arises between representatives of the rural and the urban populations in state legislatures; in many instances this has developed into a bitter hostility. Elsewhere he observed:

> . . . In the Chicago region, for example, which we construe as fifty miles from State and Madison streets, there are not less than 1500 independent governing agencies undertaking to carry on the governmental functions incidental to the life of a community of three and a half million people. Metropolitan Chicago extends into four different states, Illinois, Wisconsin, Indiana, and a corner of Michigan; it includes fifteen counties and an innumerable array of cities, villages, towns, townships, school districts, park districts, drainage districts. . . It is conservatively estimated that the population of the Chicago area in 1950 will approach eight million. Problems of regional organization are presented not only in American cities such as Boston, Philadelphia, Pittsburgh, Cincinnati, San Francisco, but in the great cities all over the world.[26]

This situation makes it difficult to carry on efficiently in almost the whole range of public activities. Meanwhile, the emigration from the central urban areas continues: "There are more Bostonians outside of Boston than inside the corporate limits, in the ratio of 750,000 in, to 1,000,024 out. There are 205,000 Cincinnatians outside the city and 400,000 inside. There are over 600,000 Pittsburghers outside the city. . . . Chicago has half a million Chicagoans who are not in the city and three million who are." There are as many New Yorkers outside the five boroughs as in them, and the city supplies facilities for all of them — a situation which prompts one writer to suggest

[26] Merriam, Charles E., "Metropolitan Regions," an address in *University of Chicago Record*, April 1928, and in *Introductory General Course in the Social Sciences*, pp. 427–440, at 428 (University of Chicago Bookstore, 1933).

that "the suburbs are strangling the city." [27] The financial implications of this situation are quite as evident in other areas as they are in New York.

So little has actually been accomplished by these various methods that some attention has been given to the possibility of finding others. If consolidation or annexation cannot be accomplished, city-county separation may be a possibility. Virginia has tried this, apparently with some success. The state might take over many of the services now performed by the cities; this would relieve the cities of the financial burden involved and would be in accordance with recent tendencies to administer many functions through larger units of government. Functional consolidation among the units themselves is also a possibility. Some degree of control over the administration of certain services might be maintained by the use of state subsidies or by a system of state-collected, locally shared taxes. At present it seems more likely that progress in the field of city-state relations will be made by these means than by those earlier attempted.[28]

The Emerging Pattern of Intergovernmental Relations

The problems of federalism are peculiar neither to our country nor to our time. They have beset every federal government that has ever existed. They were among the most hotly contested issues in the Constitutional Convention of 1787 and have been a matter of continuous concern from that day to this — more acutely at some times, to be sure, than at others. They have never been more important than they are today.

Significant Trends. In the last half century tremendous changes in our Federal system have occurred. They have all taken place within the original framework of the Constitution, whose provisions with regard to such matters were never very full or explicit. They have occurred so gradually, almost imperceptibly, that few have been aware they were happening at all.[29] Transfers

[27] See Lass, William, in *New York Times Magazine*, June 18, 1950, pp. 22, 52 ff; Sawyer, Robert K., "Commuters Aid City Comeback" (by means of the Philadelphia wage tax), *National Municipal Review*, June 1950, pp. 273–277, 287.

[28] For recent comment, see Anderson, R. T., "Income Tax Aids Annexation," (in Toledo), *National Municipal Review*, October 1949, pp. 443–447; Bollens, John C., "They All Want to Stay Out," (in San Francisco), *ibid.*, June 1948, pp. 309–314; Bromage, Arthur W., "Fringe Dwellers Present Governmental Puzzle," *ibid.*, November 1947, pp. 574–575; Fryer, Robert E., *Analysis of Annexation in Michigan, Together with a Comparison of Annexation in Other States* (Bureau of Government, University of Michigan, 1951) and "Annexation Procedures in Michigan," *Michigan Governmental Digest*, April 2, 1948; Hartman, Fred, "Three Oil Towns Become One," *National Municipal Review*, April 1948, pp. 201–205; Moore, Lee C., "Annexations by Pennsylvania Municipalities, 1940–1948," Department of Internal Affairs *Bulletin*, May-June 1951, pp. 22–32; Spain, August O., "Recent Municipal Annexation in Texas," *Southwestern Social Science Quarterly*, June 1949, pp. 299–310; Spencer, Richard C., "29 Cities Within Cities," *National Municipal Review*, May 1945, pp. 256–258; Willmott, John F., "City-County Consolidation," *GRA Notes and References*, September 1948 (Governmental Research Association, New York).

[29] See the author's "What Is Happening to Our Federal System?" *State Government*, November 1949, pp. 255–259, 270, and symposium at the General Assembly of the States in Detroit, December 1948, by Messrs. Bricker, Drummond, Gaus, and Lane, in Supplement to *State Government*, January 1949.

of authority from local units to the states, from the states to the Federal government, were never complete and were rarely clear cut. The transfers have, in fact, resulted in a fragmentation of authority, a distribution of it among two or more levels or units of government, without any clear definition of responsibility. In this way the situation has become confused, all three levels of government developing programs within the same fields and without any over-all plan or central coordinating influence. Overlapping, duplication, and waste have resulted.

One of the initial steps was the adoption of the Federal income tax amendment in 1913. This brought extensive new revenues to the Federal government and opened the way for the growth of the subsidy system and a consequent shift in the relative fiscal importance of the various units of government. The Federal subsidy program began gently enough. Grants were made in small amounts for only a few programs. Now they are made in amounts not so small for more than half a hundred different programs. Grants which totaled only a few hundred thousand dollars in the war period have increased to well over $2,000,000,000 a year since the war. And the end is not yet, for demands for new and/or higher grants are constantly being made. Huge commitments in increasing but undetermined amounts, for a host of different programs, make proper budgeting impossible. Nor is there any rhyme or reason to the allocation of funds. The proponents of each type of grant are competing with all the rest for all they can get, and under prevailing pressure group methods "the wheel that squeaks the loudest gets the grease."

The faults of the system lie not with its purposes, which are laudable and good, but with the effects of its operation. It tends to stifle the initiative of the states and make them dependent upon Federal "handouts." [30] It "skews" their spending programs by encouraging them to spend, not for what they need most but for what will give the maximum benefits in grant-in-aid dollars. It tends to make them careless in handling funds; they apparently feel accountable for the moneys they raise themselves by taxation, but not similarly accountable for budgeting and supervision of grant-in-aid funds which often are regarded as "manna from heaven." [31]

The unfortunate effects and consequences of this plan, as it now operates, are by no means confined to the states. The Federal government is affected, but in a different way. It is called upon to assist in the support of various and sundry programs in the states — perfectly worthy, but often for things which the states could and would support themselves if adequate sources of revenue

[30] For an excellent discussion of the shortcomings of the grants, with suggestions for remedial action, see Studenski, Paul, and Baikie, E. J., "Federal Grants-in-Aid," *National Tax Journal*, September 1949, pp. 193–214.

[31] Some take the opposite view; in his speech at the dedication of the Friendship International Airport in Baltimore, June 24, 1950, President Truman said, in relation to Federal grants for airports: "As in all our grant-in-aid programs, local government has been strengthened and given new responsibilities by virtue of the Federal interest."

were available to them. There is no plan for these expenditures; nobody knows how many there will be, how long they will run, how much they will cost. At the state-local level, much the same kind of thing occurs.

GRANTS-IN-AID FOR CONTINUING ACTIVITIES
BY YEAR SINCE 1944

1944 expenditures	$ 579,500,146
1945 expenditures	676,089,112
1946 expenditures	737,226,172
1947 expenditures	1,174,917,749
1948 expenditures	1,592,515,224
1949 expenditures	1,854,789,515
1950 expenditures	2,234,699,542

FEDERAL, STATE, AND LOCAL TAX COLLECTIONS, 1932 AND 1947
ON THE BASIS OF PERCENTAGES

	1932	*1947*
Federal	24.0	74.7
State	22.6	13.6
Cities	24.7	5.7
Others	28.7	6.0
Total	100.0	100.0

ON THE BASIS OF DOLLARS COLLECTED

	1932	*1947*
Federal	$1,790,000,000	$35,117,000,000
State	1,890,000,000	5,776,000,000
All Other Taxes	4,468,000,000	5,795,000,000
Total	$8,148,000,000	$46,688,000,000

Much has been written on the subject of tax competition between the various units and levels of government. Actually, there is only one source of revenue for which the Federal government and the states are not competing: the general property tax, which the states themselves are abandoning to the local units. The Federal government collects more money every year from specialized sales taxes than all the states collect from theirs. It imposed its gasoline tax as an emergency levy to pay for relief in the depression era, but the tax is continued year after year on the basis of the mistaken belief that it has something to do with Federal aid to roads. The income tax provides another illustration. Adopted in 1913 by amendment of the Federal Constitution, it subsequently spread to nearly two thirds of the states and to nearly 300 local units. Now there are also more than sixty wage-tax ordinances in cities — and the number is growing rapidly.

In addition to this unfortunate element of competition there has been over the past decade and a half an enormous shift in distribution of tax receipts among the levels of government. As the accompanying table shows, the Federal government collected only one fourth of the government revenues fifteen years ago, and collects three fourths of them now. The states, which collected one fourth then, collect only a little over one eighth now. The decline of the cities has been even greater. In terms of dollars the figures are still more striking. The figure for the Federal government for 1947 was approximately eighteen times that of 1932; at the state level, the increase is only a little more than threefold. The amount of the increase is important, but the vital question is the significance of these changes upon the nature of our governmental system.

The prolonged controversy over the tidelands provides another illustration of the uncertain conditions existing in American federalism today. Time was when the right of the states to control such lands would not have been seriously questioned. "The several states have always felt secure in their title to tidelands, marginal seas, and navigable waters and have asserted undisputed title to such areas from the founding of the Republic," — wrote the Executive Committee of the Interstate Oil Compact Commission in 1947. Actually, the state titles have not only been questioned, but the Supreme Court has ruled in three different cases that these lands rightfully belong to the Federal government.[32]

From the moment the ruling in the California case was handed down, the states have been protesting it, and they have cooperated with one another in an effort to find ways and means of overturning or circumventing it. The struggle is not so much for political control as it is for economic control. Thus one is confronted with a very difficult choice between alternatives, neither of which provides a satisfactory solution. If the theory of Federal title to the tidelands is accepted, it can be done only at the expense of clearly established rights of the states. If, on the other hand, the existing decisions are overturned, it opens the way — so the public fears and the big oil companies hope — to the exploitation of these resources with a minimum of governmental interference. The only other consideration is that of the necessity of national control over the supply of petroleum as a critical item, from the point of view of the national security.[33]

Groping toward a Solution. It is one of the essential principles of government under the Anglo-Saxon tradition that the basic functions of government be kept as closely at home as possible. That principle Americans seem to have forgotten, at least temporarily. Control over great numbers of important functions has passed from local units to states, from states to the Federal government. The era of centralization has been in its heyday. Thinking people have, however, begun to question the wisdom of this development,

[32] United States v. California, 332 U.S. 19, 67 S. Ct., 1658, 1947; United States v. Louisiana, 339 U.S. 699, 1950; and United States v. Texas, 339 U.S. 707, 1950.

[33] Out of a considerable literature, perhaps the best articles are: Bartley, Ernest R., "The Tidelands Oil Controversy," *Western Political Quarterly*, March 1949, pp. 135–153; Goldstein, Nathaniel L., "Judicial Encroachment on States' Rights," *Bulletin* of the New York State Bar Association, December 1947, pp. 219–222; and Harder, Marvin A., *The Tidelands Controversy* (University of Wichita Bulletin, November 1949).

not because they fear or distrust either the Federal government or the states, but because they have been concerned with the tendency to transfer to higher levels functions which could be quite competently performed at home and because they know that there is apt to be a greater sense of public responsibility when the bill is paid by taxpayers in the community being served.

Such persons have been confused and perplexed. They know full well that it is impossible to turn back the hands of the clock, that a government that has become complex cannot again return to the simplicity of former times. They have been groping for concepts which might make possible the application of the age-old principle of local control and responsibility within the limits set by conditions which appear to be an inescapable part of a modern urban-industrial civilization.

Experience in depression and in war has shown that the scope of state authority has become less a question of constitutional law than one of governmental policy. Arguments over constitutional authority seem pretty sterile and purposeless in the face of urgent needs for public service. The solution may be found in what Professor William Anderson has called a "functional federalism," based upon a cooperative relationship between all units and levels of government. This new functional federalism would displace a legal federalism based on a division of functions into non-communicating compartments, with an assumed hostility between the center and the parts. He believes that a greater degree of decentralization from Washington is required to make national administration as efficient as it should be, but that to increase the efficiency of national administration without correspondingly improving state government will contribute to a still further weakening of the states.

This question of state power has become a very practical one, the answer to which is incident — as Walter F. Dodd has said — to the form of government that will in the long run best function in this country, and the form of which will in the future be largely determined at the polls — not in the courts. At this time the nation stands at a crossroads. Contending forces struggle to control the direction of future development.

Exponents of the old constitutionalism point to the dangers of a "too big" central government, to the administrative failures of prohibition and NRA, to the waste of WPA, to the uneven quality of administration attained by OPA and other war agencies. Exponents of the new functionalism point to the urgent social and economic needs of our time — the extension of the Federal social security program, full employment, and legislation relating to the regulation and control of both business and labor. In this struggle functionalism seems definitely in the ascendency, as new patterns of federalism are shaped to meet the problems of the future and the challenge of a new industrial age.[34]

[34] See Anderson, William, "Federalism — Then and Now," *State Government*, May 1943, pp. 107–112, and comments thereon by Oswald D. Heck, Harold W. Dodds, and

In this process of adjustment the states have a new and increasingly important role to play. While they have lost powers to the Federal government, they have gained new powers and expanded old ones through (1) the increase in the number and scope of governmental services; (2) the transfer of functions at one time performed locally; (3) responsibility for the discharge of new duties growing out of grant-in-aid programs and other duties involved in the new pattern of cooperative federalism. Indeed, the fact is that — as Professor Merriam has so well expressed it — "if we did not have states, it would be necessary to create them, with the fundamental purpose that is now our goal, of maintaining the balance between liberty and authority, between central and local, and with an adequate division of functions and responsibilities. We need not apologize for our American states." [35]

TYPES OF INTERGOVERNMENTAL RELATIONS *

By informal cooperation:	
Police	Federal-state-local cooperation in apprehension and arrest of law violators.
Narcotics Control	State-local cooperation with Federal officials in enforcing narcotic drug laws.
By agreements and contracts:	
Agricultural Economics	Federal Bureau in 1937 had over 400 agreements between its divisions and state bureaus.
Veterans' Training	Veterans Administration-state contracts relating to on-the-job training for veterans.
	Veterans Administration-state university contracts relating to tuition costs under G. I. Bill of Rights.
Indian Service	Department of the Interior-state contracts for health and educational services for Indians.
By cooperative use of personnel:	
Elections	Federal government uses state election officials in elections in which Federal officials are chosen.
Naturalization	State Courts act as Federal agencies in naturalization.
Health	United States Public Health Service may detail personnel to state health and mental health authorities to assist them, on request.
Conservation	Federal forest officers often serve as state fish and game wardens.
Agricultural Extension	County agent is selected by, paid by, and governed by the policies of all three levels of government.

* Compiled from data, thoroughly documented, in Clark, Jane P., *The Rise of a New Federalism* (Columbia University Press, 1938), and Dowell, E. Foster, *Federal-State Relations and Oklahoma's Constitution* (Oklahoma State Legislative Council, Oklahoma City, 1948).

William L. Chenery, *ibid.*, June 1943, pp. 141–144; and Dodd, Walter F., "The Decreasing Importance of State Lines," American Bar Association *Journal*, February 1941, pp. 78–84.

[35] Merriam, Charles E., "State Government at Mid-Century," *State Government*, June 1950, pp. 114–118; this is one of a series of excellent articles on "The Government of Our States at Mid-Century," to which this issue is devoted. See also another symposium, "Are We Maintaining Our Federal System?" *ibid.*, January 1949, supplement, and the author's "What Is Happening to Our Federal System?" *op. cit.*

By interdependent law and administration:

Power Development	Federal authorities require observance of relevant state laws before granting licenses for power developments.
Air Pilots	State authorities require Federal license to operate aircraft within their borders.
Conservation	Wild game killed in violation of state laws may not be shipped in interstate commerce.
Counterfeiting	State laws make it a crime to counterfeit coin, or postage stamps, or to injure or damage Federal property.
Custody of Prisoners	Federal prisoners may be housed in approved state or local jails, under agreement with the Federal government for payment.
Indian Lands	County courts may act as Federal agents in approving under Federal law deeds of adult full-blooded Indians conveying their inherited lands.
Bank Examinations	State banking officials may accept Federal Deposit Insurance Corporation examinations of state banks in lieu of their own.
Postal Inspection	Post Office Department will, on request, aid states in enforcement of inspection and quarantine regulations, as applied to packages in the mails.
Flood Control	Army Engineers will employ Federal condemnation power, under certain conditions, to enable states to acquire land for flood control projects.

By grants-in-aid and other fiscal relationships[36]*:*

Land Grants	Federal grants to states for education, public improvements, and other purposes.
Money Grants	Federal grants to states and cities for a variety of purposes.
Tax Credit	Federal, in inheritance tax field to prevent competition.
Tax Credit and Grant-in-Aid	Used by Federal government in unemployment compensation, to induce nation-wide acceptance of plan.
Shared Revenues	Used in various situations, as when 75 per cent of Federal revenues derived from leasing lands acquired for flood control purposes go to states for schools and roads in counties with such lands.
Cooperative Agreements	Federal contracts with states for performance of Federal services, such as flood control; may impose conditions similar to those in grants-in-aid.
Direct Disbursement	Federal, to state personnel, in connection with National Guard program.
Emergency Grants	Federal, as for disaster relief, or in periods of National emergency, as under the Lanham Act.

The war effort provided an excellent demonstration of the manner in which the total resources of the nation, public and private, might be geared together for the accomplishment of a national goal of supreme importance.

[36] See discussion of grants-in-aid, pp. 25–26; also Council of State Governments, *Federal Grants-in-Aid* (Chicago, 1949), as well as Dowell, *op. cit.*

The work of the President's Committee for Congested Production Areas [37] operated as a coordinating agency with definitive authority that was resorted to very infrequently. Its activities presented additional evidence of the problems of central office-field office relationships and demonstrated that quick action can be obtained despite the complexity of Federal procedures and regulations and in addition providing interesting material on cooperation between the executive and legislative branches of the government.

In still another way, in peacetime activities, the new cooperative federalism is being demonstrated in connection with programs like hospital construction and airport construction, essentially local in character, in which the Federal government provides financial assistance and sets standards. In these and other areas surveys are made and state plans developed. Such plans are given wide publicity with a view to general public discussion and understanding, following which a project construction schedule is established, based on priorities determined on the basis of need. Specified standards of construction and equipment are enforced through inspection procedures. A plan for construction payments is worked out, as well as plans for the establishment and maintenance of a merit system of personnel administration and for fiscal controls and accounting. In all these steps, all three levels of government are involved, each in a different way.[38]

PACBIR. The development of the Pacific Coast Board of Intergovernmental Relations is a striking example of the successful effort to coordinate the activities of all three levels of government in a given area; initiated for the accomplishment of certain wartime purposes, it has proven to be quite as useful for the purposes of peacetime. What began in 1945 on an experimental basis in the closing days of World War II, for a limited time by representatives of California, Oregon, and Washington, has now become established on a permanent basis for the serious discussion of the problems of government, by officials at all levels. A grant was obtained from one of the foundations for a small staff and incidental expenses. Its purposes are stated as follows in its "Principles of Organization":

> This Board is created purely on a voluntary cooperative basis for the purpose of mutual discussion and cooperation in administrative efforts to solve problems affecting people, and most especially such problems as are the responsibility of governments during the postwar readjustment period. Such mutual discussion and cooperation will strive for the elimination of duplication in the execution of local, state, and Federal laws and regulations, the pooling of facts regarding economic and social conditions, especially those due to industrialization, and the planning of local, state, and Federal governments for dealing with these matters constructively.

[37] See Gill, Corrington, "Federal-State City Cooperation in Congested Production Areas," *Public Administration Review*, Winter 1945, pp. 28–33. The Committee was established by Executive Order of the President on April 7, 1943, and continued by Congressional appropriation through December 31, 1944.

[38] Vermont Hospital Survey and Construction Commission, *The State Plan for the Construction of Hospitals and Health Centers*, pp. 56–60 (Montpelier, 1948); similar plans were published in each of the states.

Membership on a purely voluntary basis is confined to representatives of local, state, and Federal governments, as follows:

From each state the membership shall be the Governor of the State, the Chairman of the State Commission on Interstate Cooperation, an official representative of the League or Association of Cities or Municipalities, and an official representative of the State Association of County Supervisors or Commissioners.

From the Federal government membership shall be Field Chiefs of Federal agencies, as selected by the Pacific Coast Federal Regional Council, and shall be less in number than the combined total of representatives of the other jurisdictions.

The meetings of the Board are held quarterly, alternating between California, Oregon, and Washington. The governor of the host state serves as host and as general chairman of the session. At the close of the war much attention was given to helping states and local units obtain surplus war materials useful in their departments and institutions. Later, at a meeting in mid-1950, the two principal items on the agenda included the "Community Job Creation Programs" in each of the three states, and the discussion of the problem of organized crime, with a view to bringing the members up to date as to the success of inter-city cooperation, as well as to give an indication of the range and extent of the total problem confronting the Pacific coast area. Although the conclusions of the Board are purely advisory, participants report that in these meetings ways and means have been developed for cutting through red tape and getting difficult assignments done through the cooperative efforts of all levels of government.[39]

Another interesting proposal, developed in the same region but having no connection with PACBIR, calls for a government center in which space would be provided for all departments and agencies of all levels of government functioning within Santa Clara County. This recommendation of the Council on Intergovernmental Relations was based on a comprehensive survey of space requirements, made in 1947. It was generally agreed by city and county officials and by representatives of the public that the existing government buildings were inadequate, obsolescent, and in many cases dangerous and that corrective measures must soon be taken. The Council believed that this situation presented an ideal opportunity for a government center which would include city, county, state, and Federal offices; it recommended that such a center be constructed on a scale large enough to provide for all the needs of government in the area.[40]

Proposal for a Comprehensive Survey. For at least a decade, leading

[39] See *Annual Report 1949;* Appendix III contains the Board's "Principles of Organization." There is a regular mimeographed report of the proceedings of the quarterly meetings. The author is indebted to J. W. Rupley, Chief Field Representative, United States Bureau of the Budget, in San Francisco, and to Professor Samuel C. May, University of California, for information. For an early account, see Rohrer, Miriam, "Coast States Try Cooperation," *National Municipal Review*, November 1945, pp. 484–487.

[40] See *A Practical Basis for Developing Better Intergovernmental Relations* (Santa Clara, 1947).

scholars in the field of intergovernmental relations in this country have been urging the need for a broad and comprehensive survey of the entire field, covering Federal-state, interstate, state-local, and Federal-local relations. Regarded at first as a somewhat theoretical proposal, it has now come to

Interrelationships in American Government

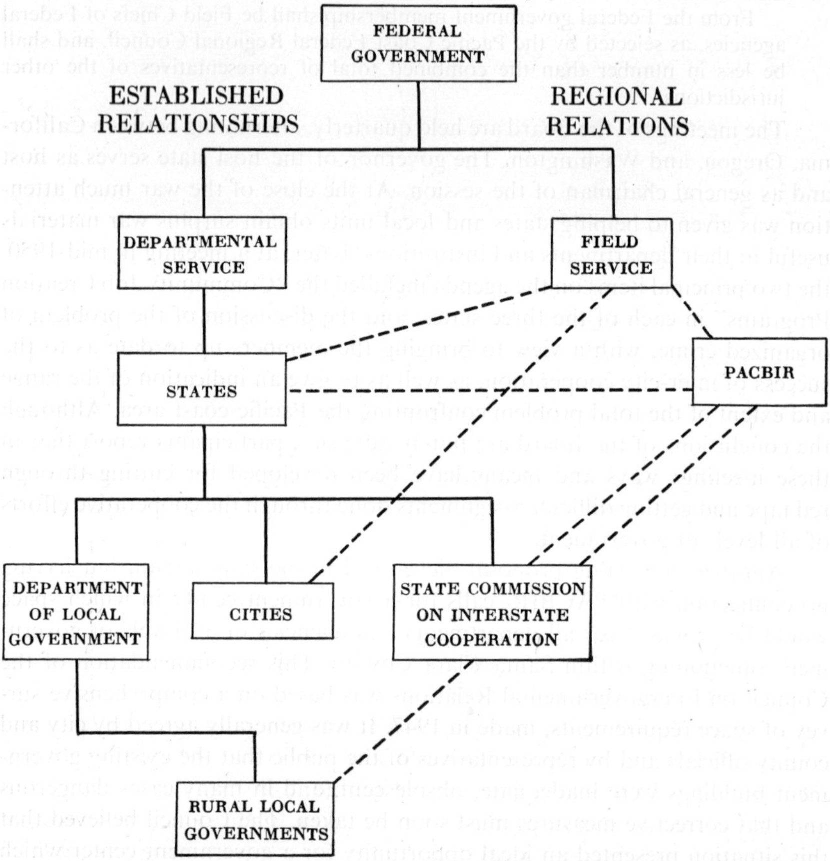

have a wide acceptance among so-called practical people. The Commission on the Organization of the Executive Branch of the Government, popularly known as the Hoover Commission, came out for the establishment of a permanent agency. Recommendation No. 5 of its Report on Federal-State Relations says:

> We recommend, in order to accomplish all of these things in an adequate and orderly manner, that a continuing agency on Federal-state relations be created with primary responsibility for study, information, and guidance in the field of Federal-state relations.

Important as this is, before any permanent agency is established there should be a temporary nonpartisan study commission in which all three levels of government would be represented, to explore this whole area and to make recommendations.

These are some of the questions to which answers should be found: In connection with every major governmental service, all three levels of government are involved; but how much is each of them involved and how much should each be involved to get the most adequate and efficient service at minimum cost? Large units are necessary for the administration of some functions, perhaps for some aspects of most functions, but it does not follow that the largest unit is best for the administration of all phases of all functions. Just what functions is each unit of government performing, and what part should each unit have in the performance of each major function?

There was introduced in both Houses of the 81st Congress in 1949 a bill providing for exactly such a commission. There were four co-sponsors of the original bill in the House (H. R. 2389), and eight in the Senate (S. 810). The bill was revised in the Senate Committee on Expenditures and was reported out in a somewhat mutilated form as S. 1946, this time, however, with thirty-three co-sponsors. Although placed on the consent calendar, it was not called up. A substitute draft, subsequently prepared, again had more than one third of the members of the Senate as co-sponsors, but no action was taken upon it. This bill passed the Senate during the First Session of the 82nd Congress, but was recalled.

The American Municipal Association in its 1950 National Municipal Policy Statement urged its adoption in these words:

> The National Commission on Intergovernmental Relations, proposed as S. 1946, should be enacted at the earliest possible date. Clarification of the difficult questions arising between Federal and local governments can be accomplished best by such a commission. Few activities are more urgent or more important as a means of proving that a democratic federal government can work effectively and harmoniously. The Commission must have direct representation by municipal officials.

In 1952, the Council of State Governments again strongly recommended that Congress enact legislation to create such an agency. The Eleventh General Assembly of the States, meeting in Chicago, urged that the Commission "study and make recommendations with respect to the administration and operation of functions performed by, and the tax responsibilities of each level of government," pledging the enthusiastic cooperation of the Council in the work of the Commission. Although these two groups, the National County Officers Association, and many other organizations support the proposal, and although the need for favorable action upon it daily grows more urgent, no action has as yet been taken.

Working Tools for Cooperation. Such a commission would not solve all the Nation's problems in this area, but it should provide a series of fundamental principles, a sort of blueprint, which might serve as a guide in bringing some measure of order out of a situation that now approaches chaos. It would also make available, in convenient form, the basic factual data which are so much needed. Such a study would be of limited permanent value unless provision were made to carry out its recommendations through an indefinite future. The necessary working tools for intergovernmental cooperation at all levels would seem to be two in number: (1) a permanent staff agency in the Federal government; (2) a permanent central agency — presumably Federal — to collect and analyze current information relating to all aspects of the subject.

During the past decade there has been a significant development of staff services for the President of the United States. To the corps of staff assistants already provided for, there should be added a staff coordinator in the field of intergovernmental relations. It is probably impractical to bring the administration of all of these activities, cutting across so many subject matter fields, together in one office, but it is certainly a proper responsibility of the Chief Executive to see that these relationships are carried on in accordance with some consistent pattern, legislatively and administratively. No such agency now exists, and little effort in this direction has ever been made. All of the states have established state commissions on interstate and intergovernmental cooperation, with which agencies a Federal coordinator might work on the development of over-all policies acceptable to all three levels of government — national, state, and local — not to mention the growing number of organized regional groups of states.

At the time of writing, the task of record keeping and reporting — when, indeed, it is done at all — is scattered all over Washington. Some records are kept in the Division of Governments, Bureau of the Census, some in the American Law Section, Legislative Reference Service, Library of Congress, some in the Department of Agriculture, some in the Federal Security Agency. Most of these agencies have been strangled by grossly inadequate financial support. The job needs to be done — it urgently needs to be done. Congress should provide for some central agency — presumably in the Library of Congress — whose business it would be to collect and analyze information on all phases of state and local government, on a service basis, for Federal departments and agencies, and to the state and local units which supply much of the information.

After all, this *is* a federal system, and the component parts thereof have neither the technical staff nor the resources to do this job independently forty-eight different times. Nor, in a federal system, should they be expected to perform services essential to all which can be most effectively and economically performed by the central government. But what the states do in this area should be made freely available to other states, as New York so generously did with the reports of the Constitutional Convention Committee in 1938. Not all of the states have done this.

The Future of the States. The situation which now confronts us is nobody's fault. The blame cannot be pinned on the President or Congress, on the Federal government or the states, on the Republicans or the Democrats. It is a responsibility which all share. To a large extent it results from the unguided extension of practices and procedures that are as old as the nation itself. Used with moderation and restraint, the grant-in-aid system would not create any very serious problem. The difficulty has arisen because, in the anxiety to accomplish quick results, the people have not given adequate consideration to the methods used or to their effects.

What can be done now to remedy the current situation? That question involves asking another question: what kind of government do the people in these United States want? A completely centralized system in which all taxes are levied, all funds appropriated, and all policies determined at the national capital? If that is what they want, they are well on the way to achieving it. Or do they want to try, to the fullest extent possible under prevailing conditions, to preserve their ancient heritage of local control over all problems which can be handled effectively and economically in the smaller units of government? If they do, they must take prompt and decisive action before it is too late.

The suggestion that the latter course should be pursued is not based on any idle fears of the Federal government. It is *our* government, too, as are those of the states and cities. It renders many services important to all citizens, and it performs them well. The ancient controversy over states rights and centralization is, as Professor Gaus has said, "either a sham battle or a diversion of energy and feeling from significant tasks." The real issue is that, in the vast expansion of governmental services, the Federal government has been asked to do too much. The remedy lies in limiting its activities to those things which state and local units cannot do, and at the same time revitalizing and strengthening the state and local units so that they can do more things and do them better. This involves a readjustment of our tax patterns so that they will have financial resources adequate for the demands upon them, and it presupposes a serious effort on the part of the states to put their houses in order.

The states must put their financial affairs in a sound condition, streamline their administrative procedures so that they will be efficient enough to handle any problem that may arise. They must develop a real career service that will attract a reasonable share of the able young men and women trained in their universities. They must improve the organization and procedures of their legislatures. They must review the whole problem of their relationships with other units, particularly with their local units. They must make up their minds to oppose all moves to remove operating controls from the people, and do all within their power to encourage effective citizen participation in government. Above all, they must concentrate on selling and reselling the idea of the climate of democratic government.

All this is based upon the assumption that, during the second half of the century as during the first, the states will continue to perform their long-established functions; that they will continue to be responsible for the organization, assistance, and supervision of their political subdivisions; that their responsibilities as intermediate units of government will continue to expand while at the same time their place in the Federal system continues to change.[41]

It is no exaggeration to say that this problem of maintaining and strengthening the American system of self-government is the most important governmental problem in the United States today. What is going to be done about it? Neither the responsibility for the preservation of heritage from the past can be avoided nor responsibility for the kind of heritage which is left for future generations. As Elihu Root said more than forty years ago in an address before the New York State Legislature on the occasion of his acceptance of the senatorship, "If the powers of the states are to be preserved and their authority is to be continued, the states must exercise their powers. The only way to maintain the powers of government is to govern."

SELECTED REFERENCES

Ball, Carleton R., *Federal, State and Local Administrative Relationships in Agriculture*, 2 vols. (University of California Press, 1938). See also, in this same field, Baker, Gladys, *The County Agent* (University of Chicago Press, 1939).

Clark, Jane P., *The Rise of a New Federalism: Federal-State Cooperation in the United States* (Columbia University Press, 1938). A very able study, related largely to the field of social security.

Council of State Governments, *Federal Grants-in-Aid* (Chicago, 1949), and their report prepared for the Hoover Commission, *Federal-State Relations* (Senate Document No. 81, 81st Cong., 1st Sess., 1949). Taken together, these two items give a comprehensive survey of the whole Federal-state relationship.

Fesler, James W., *Area and Administration* (University of Alabama Press, 1949). An excellent series of lectures on the problem of area in administration.

Graves, W. Brooke, Ed., "Intergovernmental Relations in the United States, *Annals*, January 1940, entire volume. A symposium in which about twenty-five authors deal with various aspects of the subject.

Jamison, Judith N., *Intergovernmental Cooperation in Public Personnel Administration in the Los Angeles Area* (Bureau of Governmental Research, University of California at Los Angeles, 1944). This was one of the first of a series of significant studies of interlevel and interjurisdictional relationships in the Los Angeles area.

Jensen, Merrill, Ed., *Regionalism in America* (University of Wisconsin Press, 1951) and "A Symposium on Regional Planning," *Iowa Law Review*, January 1947, entire issue. Two excellent — and fairly current — collections of material on regionalism in this country.

Jones, Victor, *Metropolitan Government* (University of Chicago Press, 1942) and Tableman, Betty, *Governmental Organization in Metropolitan Areas* (Bureau of Government, University of Michigan, 1951). In addition to these two general treatises, see for the National Capital Region: Rutherford, Geddes W., *Administrative Problems in a Metropolitan Area* (Public Administration Service, Chicago, 1951).

Kallenback, Joseph E., *Federal Cooperation with the States under the Commerce*

[41] For an excellent comment, see Gaus, John M., "The States Are in the Middle," *State Government*, June 1950, pp. 138–142.

Clause (University of Michigan Press, 1942), and Ribble, Frederick D. G., *State and National Power over Commerce* (Columbia University Press, 1937). Two studies of one important source of the expansion of Federal power.

Peel, Roy V., *State Government Today* (University of New Mexico Press, 1948). An interesting and provocative comment on the question: What is happening to our Federal system?

Turner, Frederick J., *The Frontier in American History* (Holt, New York, 1920), and *The Significance of Sections in American History* (Holt, New York, 1932). An eminent historian considers influences in American life that are important also to the student of government.

INDEX

Absentee voting, 114–116
Accounts: as phase of fiscal process, 492; supervision of local, 811-812
Ad interim committees, as fact-finding agencies, 245-249
Adjective law, and substantive law, distinguished, 574
Adjourned sessions, 221
Adkins, Governor Homer M. (Ark.), and spoils system, 462
Administration: legislative influence of, 336–346; forms of control over, 381-384; financial, 487-513; departments of, 388–390; judicial, 627–629
Administrative organization: position of governor in, 362–366, 371; executive departments in, 368–369; reorganization of, 369–381; boards and commissions in, 384–387; current problems in, 388–393
Administrative procedure, movement for improvement of, 372, 391–393
Administrative revenues, 519–520
Administrative services, 422–452; classification of, 423; for general government, 423–425; for control of business and industry, 425–434; for agriculture and natural resources, 434–438; for transportation, 439–444; for public health and welfare, 444–449; for education, 450–452
Advisory opinions, history and use of, 638
Agriculture: powers and duties of department of, 435–436; references on, 452–453; as a local function, 759–760
ALABAMA: constitutional conventions in, 69, 86; adoption of constitution of, 70; voting population of, 103; use of literacy test in, 106; voting laws of, 108, 160; primary elections in, 112, 160; convention system in, 121; representative character of legislature of, 194, 211; apportionment in, 199, 200, 201, 203; legislative term in, 212; legislative sessions in, 219, 221; legislative committees in, 225, 229; cost of legislation in, 231; legislative service agencies in, 242, 250, 259, 265, 266, 267; restrictions on legislative powers in, 284; local legislation in, 285–286, 287; quantity of legislation in, 289; Governor Graves in, 324; governors' messages in, 336, 337; veto power in, 338, 340, 342, 343; administration measures in, 343; functions of attorney general in, 366; powers of governor in, 359, 396, 797; civil service law of, 464; adopts budget law, 494; public debt of, 511, 512, 513; liquor taxes in, 542; gasoline tax in, 544, 545; income tax in, 548; inheritance tax in, 549; equity system in, 571; judicial administration in, 608, 630; selection of judges in, 611; salaries of judges in, 616; judicial council in, 620, 622; advisory opinions in, 638; publication of judicial opinions in, 645; integrated bar in, 660; peonage case in, 670; freedom of the press case in, 682; self incrimination in, 697; pre-marital examinations in, 715; safety legislation in, 718; local government in, 748, 749, 768; county welfare work in, 760–761; local library services in, 762; rural power distribution in, 765; property assessment in, 803; control over local debts in, 808; supervision of schools in, 816; mothers' aid in, 827; interstate compacts in, 839, 849, 852
Alaska: proposed admission of, 35; National Guard in, 403; in Western Regional Education Compact, 846; in Council of State Governments, 868
Albright, Spencer D., on characteristics of a good ballot, 156
Alcoholic beverages: taxes on, 516, 540, 541–543, 550; monopoly systems for, 519; regulation of, under police power, 724–725
Alleghany County, Pennsylvania: tax delinquency in, 530; criminal court work in, 605; billboard nuisance in, 737
Allocations, budgetary, use of, 499–500
Altgeld, Governor John P. (Ill.), in Pullman strike, 20
Amending process: of Federal Constitution, 21–24; influence of, in expansion of Federal power, 30; of state constitutions, 52–64
American Bar Association: activities of, on minor judiciary, 597, 600; standards of,

for administration of justice, 607; sponsors Conference of Chief Justices, 607, 608; and National Conference of Judicial Councils, 624; on judicial procedure, 658; on position of the judge, 659; legal aid work of, 665; sponsors movement for uniform laws, 854–855; sponsors American Law Institute, 859
American Conference of Motor Vehicle Administrators, sponsors uniform laws, 865
American Judicature Society: on Virginia trial justice system, 599; on selection of judges, 613; on judicial rule making, 623; on unified court system, 626
American Law Institute: organization and work of, 658, 859–860; uniform commercial code of, 855
American Legislators' Association, organization of, 865
American Municipal Association: on qualifications of judges, 614; supports home rule, 801; supports survey of intergovernmental relations, 907
American Political Science Association: report of, on absentee voting, 115; committee of, on civic training, 176; and Citizenship Clearing House, 182; on legislative service, 264–265, 306–307
American Social Hygiene Association, report of, on prostitution, 725
Anderson, Senator Floyd E. (N.Y.), heads committees to study legislative organization and procedure, 190
Anderson, William: on fallacies on public spending, 505–507; on local government units, 745–746; on cooperative federalism, 901
Animal industry, bureau of, 435
Appellate courts: in state court system, 606–607; improvement of, 629–631; Federal-state relations of, 631–634
Appointment: governor's powers of, 330–334; and placement, in state service, 476–477
Apportionment: for representation in Congress, 19–20; judicial, in New York, 87; urban-rural conflict in, 197–199; problem of, in states, 199–204
ARIZONA: use of amending procedure in, 60; adoption of constitution of, 70; constitutional convention procedure in, 86; voting population of, 103; voting laws of, 108; initiative in, 146; President Taft vetoes admission of, 151–152, 617; recall in, 152; legislative sessions in, 190, 219, 220; apportionment in, 200, 201, 204; expulsion of members in, 217; legislative committees in, 225, 246; cost of legislation in, 231; legislative service agencies in, 242, 265, 267; Ana Fromiller runs for governor in, 320; Governor Hunt of, 324; administrative reorganization in, 378; agricultural commission in, 435; experience of, with civil service, 463; adopts budget law, 494; growth of debt in, 512, 513; general property tax in, 531; liquor taxes in, 542; gasoline tax in, 544; cigarette tax in, 545; income tax in, 548; inheritance tax in, 549; community property law in, 552; equity system in, 571; judicial administration in, 608, 666; selection of judges in, 611; judicial council in, 620; closed shop legislation in, 701; prenatal examinations in, 715; local government in, 748, 749, 768; home rule in, 801; state school aid in, 817; public welfare administration in, 827; interstate compacts in, 839, 848
ARKANSAS: procedure for constitutional amendment in, 56, 60; adoption of constitution of, 70; voting population of, 103; voting laws of, 108, 116; initiative in, 146; recall in, 152; apportionment in, 200, 201; broadcasting legislative proceedings in, 217; legislative sessions in, 219, 223; legislative committees in, 225, 226, 245; cost of legislation in, 231; legislative service agencies in, 242, 259, 265, 267, 275; restrictions on legislative powers in, 284; presession training in, 307; governors' messages in, 337; veto power in, 340, 341; executive clemency in, 349; powers of governor in, 351–352, 355, 797; boards and commissions in, 384, 385, 387; operation of spoils system in, 462; experience of, with civil service, 463; adopts budget law, 494; public debt of, 508, 512, 513; liquor taxes in, 542; gasoline tax in, 544; cigarette tax in, 545; income tax in, 548; inheritance tax in, 549; equity system in, 571; justice of the peace in, 596; judicial administration in, 608, 630, 666; selection of judges in, 611; judicial council in, 620; publication of judicial opinions in, 645; teacher's oath law in, 687; racial discrimination in, 694; prenatal examinations in, 715; solicitation on trains in, 722; local government in, 748, 749, 768, 772; law enforcement in, 754–755; school consolidation in, 756; rural housing in, 764; control over local debts in, 808; supervision of schools in, 816; vocational education in, 816; demonstration classes in, 818; interstate compacts in, 839, 848
Arkansas River Compact, 848
Armour & Company v. North Dakota (240 U.S. 510, 1916), 730–731
Arnall, Governor Ellis G. (Ga.): on constitutional revision, 58; leads fight to abolish poll tax, 107; leadership of, 180; in gubernatorial controversy, 326; in interstate rendition case, 835
Arraignment, in court, 649–650
Asbury Hospital v. Cass County (326 U.S. 207, 1945), 709
Ashburner, Charles E., first city manager, 780
Ashton v. Cameron County Water Improvement District (299 U.S. 619, 1936), 888
Assembly, freedom of, 678, 687

Assessment: of general property tax, 526–527; state control over, 803–804
Association of Dairy, Food and Drug Officials, organization and work of, 864–865
Atlantic Coast Line v. Railway Commissioners of South Carolina (207 U.S. 328, 1907), 721, 722
Atlantic States Marine Fisheries Compact, 852
Attainder, bills of, defined, 32
Attorney general: and legal advice to governor, 366; powers and duties of, 424–425
Audit: as phase of fiscal process, 491–493; state supervision of, 812–813
Authorities, local, 750–753
Axelrod, Donald, on executive-legislative relations, 282–283
Aycock, Governor Charles B. (N.C.), leadership of, 179

Bail, in criminal cases, 646–647
Bailey v. Alabama (219 U.S. 219, 1911), 670
Baldwin, Governor Simeon E. (Conn.): on evolution of state courts, 592; on trial of civil cases, 642–643; on selection of jurors, 656
Ballot: history of, 131; Australian, 131; party column and office column, 131–132; getting names on, 132; and voting machines, 132–133; long, development of, 153–154; short, principles and use of, 154–156; P.R., illustrated, 158; simplified, and electoral procedure, 175–176
Baltimore: quadrennial registration in, 117; cost of elections in, 137; People's Court in, 604; Barron case in, 672
Banking: powers and duties of department of, 425–426; institutions, control state fiscal policy, 514; administrative revenues of department of, 520
Bar: influence of, in selection of judges, 613–614; attitude of, toward justice, 659–660; integrated, 660–661
Barbier v. Connelly (113 U.S. 27, 1885), 676–677
Barclay, Thomas S., on split sessions in California, 221
Barnard, Chester I., on executive leadership in administration, 360
Barron v. Mayor and City Council of Baltimore (7 Peters 243, 1833), 672
Barter Theater, of Virginia, 10
Beard, Charles A., on Amendment XIV, 675
Bebout, John E., on staff work for mayors, 778
Becker, Carl L., on popular government, 47
Belknap, William B., on legislative procedure, 305–306
Benson, George C. S., on federalism, 17–18
Benton, Wilbourn E., on local legislation in Texas, 286–287
Beveridge, Governor Albert J. (Ind.), as progressive leader, 317
Biddle, Francis, on civil rights, 670
Bill of Rights: in state constitutions, 50–51; application of, in Federal Constitution, 672
Billboard regulation, 737–738
Bills: printing of, 238; drafting of, 238, 263–266; passage of, 293–302; biography of (chart), 295; recall of, from governor, 301; of credit, issuance of, 425–426
Bird, Frederick L., on tax delinquency, 530
Black, Justice Hugo L.: on Amendment XIV, 675; on school bus issue, 685–686; on contract clause, 698–699; on closed shop legislation, 701
Blind: Pennsylvania Commission for, 252; aid for, 449
Blue, Governor Robert D. (Ia.), use of troops by, in labor dispute, 397
Blue sky laws: enforcement of, 426; under police power, 728
Boards and commissions: reasons for establishment of, 384–385; types of, 385; objections to, for administration, 385–386; working compromises on, 386–387
Bob-Lo Excursion Company v. Michigan (333 U.S. 28, 1948), 692
Bonus laws, for World War II veterans, 414–417, 510, 511
Bookkeeping revenues, 520
Borrowing: and debt administration, 489; history of, 507–508; constitutional limitations on, 508–509; growth of, 509–510; postwar trends in, 510–511; current problems in, 511–514; as a source of revenue, 518
Boss rule, in Connecticut, 100
Boston: cost of elections in, 137; City Club of, 169; billboard cases in, 737–738; city council in, 778; metropolitan area of, 896
Boston, Charles A., on jury personnel, 654
Boundaries: interstate compacts on, 839; disputes over, 841–842
Bowers, Claude G., on Reconstruction legislature in Louisiana, 189
Bowles, Governor Chester (Conn.), bans racial discrimination in National Guard, 692
Bradley, Phillips, on legislative recording, 235
Bradway, John S., on history of legal aid, 662–663
Brandeis, Justice Louis D., on states as laboratories, 6–8
Brecht, Arnold, on features of American civil service, 463–464
Breitel, Charles D., on excluding certain types of bills from consideration, 311–312
Bremen incident, 40
Bricker, Governor John W. (Ohio): length of service of, 319; letters received by, from constituents, 356
Bridges v. California (314 U.S. 252, 1941), 682
Bromage, Arthur W.: on municipal courts, 602; on town government, 751; on municipal government, 778; on police department organization, 785; on Federal-municipal relations, 887, 888

Brookings Institution, state surveys made by, 375
Brough, Governor Charles H. (Ark.): on role of governor in executive clemency, 349; on work of governor's office, 352
Buck, Arthur E., on principles of administrative reorganization, 371, 372
Budget system: analysis of, for legislature, 274; as staff function, 364; improvements in, in Minnesota, 389; as plan for spending, 493–495; formulation of budget document in, 495–496; performance budgeting in, 496–497; function of legislature in, 497–499; enforcement of, 499–500; expenditure control in, 500–507; local, state control over, 806–807
Building and loan associations, supervision of, 426
Building inspection, 716–717
Burdick, Charles K.: on equal protection, 676; on privileges and immunities, 835–836
Burgess, John W., on weaknesses of the states, 877
Burton, Justice Harold H., on racial discrimination, 692
Business: and industry, regulation and control of, 425–434; revenues derived from, 519; taxes affecting, 539; self-government in, 655; interstate cooperation in, 869
Byrd, Governor Harry F. (Va.): on constitutional revision in Virginia, 58, 72; as party boss in Virginia, 100

Caldwell, Governor Millard F. (Fla.): heads Civil Defense Administration, 411; on power of governor over local officers, 797; on Southern Regional Education Compact, 845
CALIFORNIA: disability insurance in, 10; school case in, 39–40; case on effect of United Nations Charter in, 41–42; length of constitution of, 46; constitutional revision commissions in, 58; constitutional initiative in, 59; use of amending procedure in, 59, 60, 61; need for constitutional revision in, 64; adoption of constitution of, 70; Constitutional Convention of 1878 in, 84, 89; voting population of, 103; voting laws of, 106, 108; use of voting machines in, 133; use of direct legislation in, 144–145, 146, 148, 152; Commonwealth Club of, 163–165; legislative abuses in, 196–197; apportionment in, 200–201; legislative turnover in, 205; legislature of, 211, 212; legislative retirement in, 214, 215; legislative sessions in, 219, 220–221, 237; legislative committees in, 225, 246–247, 248–249; cost of legislation in, 231, 235; legislative service agencies in, 242, 259, 262, 265, 267, 269, 274–275; abuses of lobby in, 254; legislative auditor in, 274–275; pardoning power in, 283; restrictions on legislative powers in, 284; legislative time wasted on roll calls in, 310; Governor Johnson of, 317; salary of governor in, 324; veto power in, 338, 339, 342; passes early budget law, 370; administrative reorganization in, 372, 378, 391; administrative procedure legislation in, 393; forest fires in, 398; nonsegregation policy in, 402; veterans' benefits in, 417; veterans' preference in, 418, 476; professional licensing in, 431–432, 433; department of mental health in, 445; management of institutions in, 447; civil service law of, 464; expenditures of, for civil service, 465; organization for personnel administration in, 465–466; adopts first budget act, 493, 494; increase in expenditures of, 500–502; debt default in, 507; growth of gross debt in, 509, 511, 512, 513; general property tax in, 528, 531, 551; franchise taxes in, 536; pari-mutuel taxes in, 538; liquor taxes in, 542; gasoline tax in, 544; cigarette tax in, 545; income tax in, 546, 548; inheritance tax in, 548, 549; community property law in, 552; equity system in, 571; study of justice courts in, 599, 600; appellate courts in, 607; judicial administration in, 608, 626, 630; selection of judges in, 611, 612, 613; salaries of judges in, 616; judicial council in, 619, 620, 623; publication of judicial opinions in, 645; jury system in, 656; public defenders in, 665; discrimination in employment banned in, 700; discrimination in land ownership in, 702; use of blood tests in, 715; control of ticket brokers in, 730; planning and zoning regulations in, 736, 762, 763; billboard regulation in, 739; local government in, 748, 749, 750, 751, 752, 768, 774, 780; school consolidation in, 756–757; county park systems in, 764; home rule in, 801; city sales taxes in, 806; control over local debts in, 808; state school aid in, 817; school accreditation in, 817; interstate compacts in, 839, 848, 852; Youth Authority Act in, 860; urban-rural conflict in, 896; member of PACBIR, 904
California Reduction Company v. Sanitary Reduction Works (199 U.S. 306, 1905), 713
Callendar, Clarence N.: on evolution of state courts, 591; on equity proceedings, 645–646
Campaigns: political, 129–131; law observance, 336
Capital punishment, extent of use of, 577
Capitol buildings, scandals in construction of, 209
Cardozo, Justice Benjamin N.: on purpose of state constitutions, 54; proposes law revision commission, 269; on nature of judicial process, 582–585
Carpenter, William S., on organization for personnel administration, 470
Carroll, Daniel R., on unicameralism in Vermont, 191
Caucus, for nominating candidates, 119–120

equity system in, 571; court reorganization proposed in, 607; judicial administration in, 608, 666; selection of judges in, 611, 612; salaries of judges in, 616; judicial council in, 619, 620, 622; supreme court of, 632; public defender system in, 666; racial discrimination banned in, 692, 695, 701; first blood test law in, 715; local government in, 748, 749, 768; home rule in, 801; public welfare administration in, 825; interstate compacts in, 839, 848, 853
Connelly v. General Construction Company (269 U.S. 385, 1925), 674
Connolly v. Union Sewer Pipe Company (184 U.S. 540, 1902), 677
Conservation: of forests and waters, 436–437; of fish and game, 437; work of geological survey in, 437–438; planning activities in, 438; references on, 452–453; interstate compacts on, 839, 844
Consolidation: need of, in local government, 748–750; of school districts, 756–757; of counties, 895–896
Constitution, Federal: Tenth Amendment to, 16–17; amendment of, 21–24; amendment of, in expansion of Federal power, 30; limitations of, on state power, 31–34; draftsmanship in, 79–81; provisions of, affecting suffrage, 102, 671; reasons for judicial provisions of, 590–591; protections under, 668–706; provisions of, affecting interstate relations, 834–840
Constitutional protections: in War Amendments, 668–672; due process of law in, 672–676; equal protection of the law in, 676–678; of personal rights, 678–688; of property rights, 697–705; references on, 705–706
Constitutions, state: effect of United Nations Charter on, 41–42; history and characteristics of, 43–49; comparison of early and present day, 46–49; essential elements of, 49–54; amendment of, 52–64; contents of, 54; current needs for revision of, 65–68; dates of adoption of existing, 69; trends of types of changes in, 82–83, 375–379; ratification of, 86–90; limitations of, on debt, 508–509; tax provisions in, 523–525; needed changes in judicial provisions of, 625
Contract: Dartmouth College case on, 32, 37, 208, 698–699; restatement of the law on, 859
Conventions, constitutional: use of, for proposing amendments, 57–58; vs. commission procedure, 58; calling and composition of, 70–71; place of meeting of, 72; size of, 72–73; method of choosing members of, 73; preparation for, 73–76; powers of, 77–78; work of, 78–79; problems of draftsmanship in, 79–81; serve to spotlight major issues, 81–82; motivation and control of, 83–86
Conventions, party, 120–121, 127–128
Cook County, Illinois: powers of, under constitution, 80–81; party conventions in, 120–121; election frauds in, 137
Cooper, Governor Prentice (Tenn.): length of service of, 319; on campaign techniques of governors, 322; on reeligibility for governors, 324; on leadership by governor, 345
Cornwall, Governor John J. (W.Va.), in mine strike, 20
Corporation and business taxes, 515, 516, 535, 550; franchise, 536; bank, 536; chain store, 536–537; severance, 537; pari-mutuel, 537–538; tax differentials on, 539
Corrections: of errors in legislation, 301, 312; organization, powers and duties of department of, 448; references on, 454–455
Corrupt practices legislation, 137
Corwin, Edward S.: on American and Canadian federalism, 19; on judicial review, 585
Cost of government: in legislatures, 230–236; increase in, 500–504; in judiciary, 661–662
Council of State Governments: prepares program of suggested legislation, 41, 858–859; services of, in legislative improvement, 189–190, 237–239, 306; survey of ad interim committees by, 246; on legislative manuals, 265; Drafting Committee of, 266, 858–859; sponsors Legislative Service Conference, 276–277; analyzes types of reorganization commissions, 377–378; urges passage of civil defense legislation, 409; conducts study of professional licensing, 431; on motor vehicle operators' licenses, 442; survey of state school systems by, 451–452; sponsors Conference of Chief Justices, 607; on state court systems, 611, 612; on state controls over local debt, 808; on curriculum planning, 818; as secretariat for Governors' Conference, 863, 866; organization and work of, 865–871; wartime leadership of, 883; on welter of local governments, 895; supports survey of intergovernmental relations, 907
Counties: cost of elections in, 137–138; courts of, 604–606; number of, by states, 749; functions of, in agriculture, 759–760; organization of, 767–769; reorganization of, 769–773; consolidation of, 773–774; references on, 789–791; manager form for, 771–772
Courts: historical development of, 590–594; organization of, 594–609; selection of judges for, 609–614; office of judge in, 614–619; judicial councils in, 619–625; administrative reorganization of, 625–631; relations of state and Federal, 631–634; references on, 634–635, 666; powers and duties of, 636–639, 754–755; procedure, in civil cases, 639–648, in criminal cases, 648–650; jury system in, 650–658; improving procedure of, 658–666

Cox, Governor James M. (Ohio), leads city manager movement in Dayton, 781
Cox v. New Hampshire (312 U.S. 569, 1941), 678–679
Coyle v. Smith (221 U.S. 559, 1911), 36
Craig v. Harvey (331 U.S. 367, 1947), 682
Crawford, Finla G.: on New York literacy test, 106; on adjourned session in Ohio, 221
Criminal law, 574; offenses under, defined, 575, classified, 576–578; enforcement of, 578–580, 720–721; courts for, 605–606; court procedure under, 646–651; interstate compacts on, 839, 840, 843–844; interstate legislation in, 861; informal cooperation in, 902
Cross, Governor Wilbur L. (Conn.), successful candidacies of, 324
Crowley v. Christensen (137 U.S. 86, 1890), 725
Cummings, Governor Albert B. (Ia.), as progressive leader, 317
Cumulative voting, in Illinois, 160
Curriculum, state control over, 818

Dartmouth College v. Woodward (4 Wheaton 518, 1819), 32, 37, 208, 698–699
Daugherty, Harry M., proposes method of enforcing treaty obligations, 41
Dayton: cost of elections in, 137; city manager government in, 781
Debt: administration of, 489; history of, 507–508; constitutional limitations on, 508–509; growth of, 509–510; postwar trends in, 510–511; current problems in, 511–514; state control over local, 807–808
DELAWARE: early chief executive in, 44; constitutional amendment procedure in, 55, 61; adoption of constitution in, 70; constitutional convention procedure in, 72, 86; voting population of, 103; voting laws of, 106, 108; statewide civic groups in, 165; legislative sessions in, 190, 210; apportionment in, 200, 203; legislative committees in, 225; cost of legislation in, 231; legislative service agencies in, 242, 265, 267; restrictions on legislative powers in, 284; legislative adjournment in, 337; veto power in, 338, 341, 342; administrative reorganization in, 378; bonus legislation in, 416; secretary of state in, 424; agricultural commission in, 435; adopts budget law, 494; growth of debt in, 512, 513; general property tax in, 531, 803; gross receipts tax in, 540; liquor taxes in, 542; gasoline tax in, 544; cigarette tax in, 545; income tax in, 545, 546; inheritance tax in, 549; equity system in, 571; judicial administration in, 608; selection of judges in, 611, 612; salaries of judges in, 616; judicial council in, 620; supreme court of, 632; advisory opinions in, 638; publication of judicial opinions in, 645; racial discrimination in, 695; blood tests in, 715; sale of fireworks banned in, 719; local government in, 748, 749, 767, 768; audit supervision in, 812; supervision of schools in, 815, 816; public welfare administration in, 826; highway administration in, 828; interstate compacts in, 839, 848, 851; boundary dispute with New Jersey in, 841
Delaware River Port Authority, 854
Denver: cost of elections in, 137; long ballot in, 155; American Legislators Association originates in, 865
Detroit: cost of elections in, 137; long ballot in, 155; performance budgeting proposed in, 497; assessment procedure in, 526; municipal court in, 602; judicial primary in, 610; judicial administration in, 629; legal aid in, 664
Dever, Governor Paul A. (Mass.), work of the office of, 352–354
Dewey, Governor Thomas E. (N.Y.): handling of bills by, at end of session, 310–312; successful candidacies of, 128, 324; exercise of veto power by, 339–340; refuses to use troops, in labor dispute, 397; on creation of special authorities, 753
Direct legislation: 142–153; constitutionality of, 21; use of, in constitutional amendment, 58–59; initiative, 144–149; referendum, 149–150; recall, 150–152; recall of judicial decisions, 153
Direct primary: exclusion of Negroes from, 111–112; defined, 121–122; open and closed, 122–123; nonpartisan, 123; "run-off" elections in, 123–124; advantages and disadvantages of, 124–126; filing fees under, 126–127; methods for improving, 127–128
Disaster relief, in states and cities, 397–398
Disbursements, as phase of fiscal process, 491
District of Columbia: civic organizations in, 171; National Guard in, 403; building collapses in, 716–717; rent control in, 723; motion picture censorship in, 727; boundary dispute of, with Virginia, 841–842
District, or county, courts, 604–606
Divorce, full faith and credit in, 836–838
Dodd, Walter F., on state power, 901
Dodds, Harold W.: President of National Municipal League, 161; on value of uniform laws, 861–862
Dodson, George W., on state-local health relations, 820–821
Domestic violence, duty of states regarding, 20, 335–336
Donaghey, Governor George W. (Ark.), on duties of the governor, 351–352
Dorr, Harold M.: on public attitude toward constitutional conventions, 83–84; on veto power, 339; on functions of attorney general, 366
Double and overlapping taxation, 552–553
Drafting: in constitutional conventions, 79–81; of statutes, 263–266
Driscoll, Governor Alfred E. (N.J.): on judicial reorganization, 627; appoints

tive powers in, 284; qualifications for governor in, 321; veto power in, 339, 342; governor's council in, 366; administrative reorganization in, 372; military powers of governor in, 396; secretary of state in, 424; civil service law in, 464; adopts budget law, 494; growth of debt in, 512, 513; liquor taxes in, 542; gasoline tax in, 544; cigarette tax in, 545; inheritance tax in, 549; equity system in, 571; judicial administration in, 608; selection of judges in, 611, 612; judicial council in, 620; advisory opinions in, 638; publication of judicial opinions in, 645; blood tests in, 715; heart-balm legislation in, 730; local government in, 748, 749, 768; rural zoning in, 763; power of governor over local officers in, 797; control over local debts in, 808; public welfare administration, 826; interstate compacts in, 839, 852

Management: improvement at top level, 388–390; continuous planning for improvement of, 390–391

Mandamus, writ of, defined, 567

Manitowoc Plan, for civic training of youth, 176–177

Marbury v. Madison (1 Cranch 137, 1803), 567, 585, 586

Marsh v. Alabama (326 U.S. 501, 1946), 682

Marshall, John: on purpose of a constitution, 52; on judicial review, 585, 586; and Dartmouth College Case, 698

Martial law: in disaster-struck areas, 397–398; defined and discussed, 580–581

MARYLAND: increasing length of constitution of, 46–47; adoption of constitution of, 70; voting population of, 103; voting laws of, 108, 115; convention system in, 118; referendum authorized in, 143; use of preferential voting in, 160; legislative sessions in, 190, 210, 219, 237; apportionment in, 200, 203; legislative term in, 212; legislative retirement in, 215; legislative committees in, 225, 228, 246; cost of legislation in, 231; legislative service agencies in, 242, 250, 259, 260, 265, 267, 275; Governor Ritchie of, 318, 324; salary of governor in, 324, 325; nomination of Governor Lane in, 327; veto power in, 338, 341, 343; executive clemency in, 348; administrative reorganization in, 375; administrative procedure legislation in, 393; military powers of governor in, 396; veterans' preference in, 418, 476; secretary of state in, 424; agricultural commission in, 435; motor vehicle property taxes in, 442; civil service law in, 464, 467; adopts budget law, 494; performance budgeting proposed in, 497; power of legislature over budget in, 498, 499; growth of debt in, 512, 513; corporation taxes in, 535; pari-mutuel taxes in, 538; liquor taxes in, 542; gasoline tax in, 544; cigarette tax in, 545; income tax in, 548; inheritance tax in, 549; equity system in, 571; judicial review in, 586; trial magistrate in, 599; judicial administration in, 608, 626; selection of judges in, 611; salaries of judges in, 616; judicial council in, 620; segregation in education in, 695; blood tests in, 715; motion picture censorship in, 727–728; billboard nuisance in, 737; local government in, 748, 749, 768, 772, 774; highway zoning in, 763; power of governor over local officers in, 797; home rule in, 801; property assessment in, 802; audit supervision in, 812; state-local health relations in, 821–822; interstate compacts in, 839, 849, 851–852; oyster war of, with Virginia, 841; boundary dispute of, with Pennsylvania, 841; uniform state laws in, 855

Mason, George, drafts first state bill of rights, in Virginia, 50

MASSACHUSETTS: a commonwealth, 15; partition of, to form Maine, 38; early legislative election of governor in, 44; retains provisional government, 46; initiative requirements in, 59; efforts to revise constitution of, 64; effect of 1919 constitutional revision in, 69; adoption of constitution of, 70; voting population of, 103; early literacy test act in, 106; voting laws of, 108, 116, 135; corrupt practices legislation in, 137; initiative in, 146; league of municipalities in, 167; legislative sessions in, 190, 210, 219, 337; early apportionment practices in, 199–200; legislative retirement in, 214, 215; legislative committees in, 225, 243, 245, 246; cost of legislation in, 231; legislative service agencies in, 242, 249, 262, 263, 265, 267; rules of legislative procedure in, 294; Governor Saltonstall of, 319; gubernatorial tenure in, 323; salary of governor in, 324; adjournment of legislature in, 337; veto power in, 339, 341, 343; duties of the governor in, 352–354; governor's council in, 366; early civil service law in, 370; administrative reorganization in, 371, 375, 378; requirement of central filing of rules in, 372; management improvement in, 388, 390; administrative procedure legislation in, 393; history of National Guard in, 399; non-segregation policy in, 402; bonus legislation in, 416; veterans' preference in, 418; motor vehicle registration fees in, 441; department of mental health in, 445; establishes state university, 452; civil service law in, 459, 463, 464; origins of spoils system in, 461; civil service administration in, 467; adopts budget law, 494; growth of debt in, 512, 513; pari-mutuel taxes in, 538; liquor taxes in, 542; gasoline tax in, 543, 544; income taxes in, 544, 546, 548; cigarette tax in, 545; inheritance tax in, 549; equity system in, 571; early judicial review in, 586; district courts in, 605; appellate courts in, 607; judicial administration in, 608, 629; selection of judges in, 611, 612; salaries of judges in, 616; judicial council in, 619, 620, 623; advisory opinions in, 638; discrimination in employment banned in, 700, 701; closed shop legislation in, 701; compulsory vaccination in, 714; blood tests in, 715; motion picture censorship in, 727–728; heart-balm legislation in, 730; billboard case in, 738; local government in, 748, 749, 768; power of governor over local officers in, 797; control of local budgets in, 807; control over local debts in, 808; supervision of accounts in, 811; audit supervision in, 813; public health administration in, 820; early public welfare administration in, 824, 825, 826; highway administration in, 827; interstate compacts in, 839, 848; Youth Authority act in, 860

Mathews, John M.: on cumulative voting in Illinois, 160; on local legislation in North Carolina, 285; on purpose of administrative reorganization, 371–372

Mayor-council, form of city government, 778–780

Mechanical voting: in elections, 132–133; in legislatures, 309–310

Mental health, organization, powers, and duties of department of, 445–446

Merit system: in Colorado, 385; in the states generally, 467–470

Merriam, Charles E.: edits Civic Training Series, 176; on city-state relations, 802; proposes city-states, 895–896; on importance of the states, 902

Messages, of governors, regular and special, 336–337

Metropolitan areas: in California, 750; proposals of city-states for, 894–895

MICHIGAN: constitutional revision commissions in, 58; adoption of constitution of, 70; constitutional convention procedure in, 72, 78, 79, 86; voting population of, 103; voting laws of, 108; election costs in, 138–140; initiative in, 146; recall in, 152; home rule legislation in, 168; apportionment in, 200, 203; legislative sessions in, 219, 221; legislative committees in, 224, 225, 246; cost of legislation in, 231; legislative service agencies in, 242, 261, 265, 267; abuses of lobby in, 254; local legislation in, 287; mechanical voting in legislature of, 310; salary of governor in, 324; powers of the governor in, 328; governor's messages in, 337; veto power in, 338, 342; functions of attorney general in, 366; administrative reorganization in, 378; boards and commissions in, 385; management improvement in, 388, 389, 390; administrative procedure legislation in, 393; bonus legislation in, 416; veterans' preference in, 418, 476; growth of administrative services in, 422–424; department of mental health in, 445; experience of, with civil service, 463, 464; expenditures of, for civil service, 465; revenue collection in, 487; adopts budget law, 494; growth of debt in, 512, 513; tax sources in, 518; general property tax in, 532, 551; liquor taxes in, 542; gasoline tax in, 544; cigarette tax in, 545; income tax in, 546; inheritance tax in, 549; equity system in, 571; justice of the peace system in, 598, 599; appellate courts in, 607; judicial administration in, 608; selection of judges in, 611; salaries of judges in, 616; judicial council in, 619, 620, 622, 629–631; one man grand jury in, 648; modern court procedure in, 666; blood tests in, 715; sale of fireworks banned in, 719; local government in, 747, 749, 767, 768, 773; rural zoning in, 763; county park systems in, 764; growth of state services in, 793–794; power of governor over local officers in, 797; home rule in, 801; control over local debts in, 808; school accreditation in, 817; curriculum development in, 818; public welfare administration in, 825; highway administration in, 829; interstate compacts in, 839; urban-rural conflict in, 896

Military affairs: powers of governor, 395–398; local organization for, 758–759

Milk, regulation of the sale of, 432–433

Miller, Spencer, Jr., on New Jersey campaigns for ratification of constitutions, 89–90

Mines, powers and duties of the department of, 429

MINNESOTA: tries to tax Federal land grants, 37; highway system described in constitution of, 66; adoption of constitution of, 70; voting population of, 103; voting laws of, 108, 160; recall in, 152; statewide civic groups in, 165; zoning legislation in, 168; apportionment in, 200, 203; legislative turnover in, 205; legislature of, 210; legislative committees in, 225, 246, 248; cost of legislation in, 231; legislative service agencies in, 242, 259, 265, 267; mechanical voting in legislature of, 309; salary of governor in, 324; veto power in, 338, 342; administrative reorganization in, 375, 378; management improvement in, 388–389, 390; administrative procedure legislation in, 393; use of troops in labor dispute in, 396–397; organization of National Guard in, 401; non-segregation policy in, 402; bonus legislation in, 416; motor vehicle registration fees in, 441; civil service law in, 464; sliding pay scale in, 478–479; adopts budget law, 494; debt default in, 507; growth of debt in, 512, 513; liquor taxes in, 542; gasoline tax in, 544; cigarette tax in, 545; income tax in, 546, 548; inheritance tax in, 549; equity system in, 571; appellate courts in, 607; judicial administration in, 608; selection of judges in, 611; judicial council in, 620,

622; advisory opinions in, 638; freedom of the press case in, 681; blood tests in, 715; local government in, 747, 749, 768, 774; rural zoning in, 763; power of governor over local officers in, 797; home rule in, 801; control over local debts in, 808; interstate compacts in, 839, 848, 849; Youth Authority act in, 860

MISSISSIPPI: test case on defalcation of, 39; procedure for constitutional amendment in, 56; adoption of constitution of, 70; constitutional convention procedure in, 86; voting population of, 103; voting laws of, 108, 110, 115; corrupt practices legislation in, 137; initiative in, 146; recall in, 152; apportionment in, 200, 201; legislative term in, 212; legislative committees in, 224, 225, 226; cost of legislation in, 231; legislative service agencies in, 242, 265, 267; code plan of, 272; salary of governor in, 324; veto power in, 342; motor vehicle property taxes in, 442; adopts budget law, 494; growth of debt in, 512, 513; sales tax in, 540; liquor taxes in, 542; gasoline tax in, 544; cigarette tax in, 545; income tax in, 548; inheritance tax in, 549; equity system in, 571; justice courts in, 600; judicial administration in, 608, 630; selection of judges in, 611; judicial council in, 620; publication of judicial opinions in, 645; subversive acts and material prohibited in, 683; blood tests in, 715; safety legislation in, 718; lotteries in, 726; local government in, 748, 749, 767, 768; county park systems in, 764; rural housing in, 764; rural power distribution in, 765; state school aid in, 817; interstate compacts in, 839, 848, 849; uniform state laws in, 855

Mississippi River Commission, 848

MISSOURI: initiative requirements in, 59; adoption of constitution in, 70; preparation for constitutional convention in, 74–75; campaign in, for ratification of constitution, 88; voting population of, 103; voting laws of, 108; initiative in, 146; recall in, 152; state-wide civic groups in, 165; apportionment in, 201, 203; legislative committees in, 224, 225, 226, 248; cost of legislation in, 231; legislative service agencies in, 242, 250, 259, 260, 265, 267; restrictions on legislative powers in, 284; Governor Folk in, 317; gubernatorial succession controversy in, 326; governors' messages in, 337; veto power in, 338, 342; administrative reorganization in, 374, 376; administrative procedure legislation in, 393; military powers of governor in, 396; motor vehicle operators' licenses in, 442; civil service law in, 464; adopts budget law, 494; growth of debt in, 512, 513; turnover taxes in, 540; liquor taxes in, 542; gasoline tax in, 544; income taxes in, 544, 548; cigarette taxes in, 545; inheritance tax in, 549; equity system in, 571; abolishes justices of the peace, 599; court reorganization in, 607; judicial administration in, 608, 626, 629, 630; selection of judges in, 611, 612–613, 614; judicial council in, 620; advisory opinions in, 638; publication of judicial opinions in, 645; racial discrimination in, 692–693, 695; blood tests in, 715; local government in, 747, 749, 768, 774; school districts in, 756; county planning and zoning in, 762, 763; home rule in, 801; state school aid in, 817; public welfare administration in, 826; interstate compacts in, 839, 848

Missouri ex rel. Gaines v. Canada (305 U.S. 580, 1938), 692–693

Missouri v. Holland (252 U.S. 416, 1920), 30–31

Missouri River: Committee, 848; Inter-Agency Basin Committee, 848

Mitchell v. United States (313 U.S. 80, 1941), 691

Model City Charter, provisions of, 784

Model Civil Service Law, basic provisions of, 467

Model laws, 860–861

Model Personal Income Tax Act, 547

Model State Constitution, 68, 161; amending procedure in, 53–54; on eighteen year voting age, 105–106; on unicameralism, 193; on annual legislative sessions, 237; powers of governor in, 328; uses integrated form of reorganization, 372, 376; position of, on administrative boards, 386; provides for joint budget hearings, 498; on selection of judges, 613; proposes judicial council, 619; on judicial organization, 625, 626, 627; on state-local relations, 802

Monaco v. Mississippi (292 U.S. 313, 1934), 39

MONTANA: adoption of constitution of, 70; voting population of, 103; voting laws of, 108; initiative in, 146; recall in, 152; legislative sessions in, 190, 210; apportionment in, 200, 203; legislative retirement in, 215; legislative committees in, 225; cost of legislation in, 231; legislative service agencies in, 242, 265, 267; restrictions on legislative powers in, 284; veto power in, 341, 342; bonus legislation in, 416; grazing districts in, 436; adopts budget law, 494; growth of debt in, 512, 513; liquor taxes in, 542; gasoline tax in, 544; income taxes in, 544, 548; cigarette tax in, 545; inheritance tax in, 549; equity system in, 571; judicial administration in, 608; selection of judges in, 611; judicial council in, 620; blood tests in, 715; has no small loan legislation, 729; local government in, 748, 749, 768, 772, 774; county planning in, 762; county park systems in, 763; interstate compacts in, 839, 848, 849

Moore, Governor A. Harry (N.J.), calls governors' conference, 864

Morey, Lloyd, on local government accounting, 812
Morf v. Bingaman (298 U.S. 407, 1936), 677
Morris, George M., on judicial councils, 621
Moses, Governor John (N.D.), length of service of, 319
Motion pictures, censorship of, 727–728
Motor vehicles: growth in number of, 439; organization, powers, and duties of department of, 441–444; references on, 453–454; taxes on, 515, 533, 543–544, 550; regulation of use of, 716
Mott, Rodney L.: on due process, 674, 678; on eminent domain, 703
Mount Vernon-Woodberry Cotton Duck Company v. Alabama Interstate Power Company (240 U.S. 30, 1916), 704
Mugler v. Kansas (123 U.S. 623, 1887), 724
Mumford, Lewis, on our overgrown cities, 775–776
Municipal courts, 602–604
Municipal leagues, influence of, on legislation, 167–168
Munro, William B.: on function of the party worker, 97–98; on municipal research, 171; on problems of metropolitan regions, 895
Murdock v. Pennsylvania (319 U.S. 105, 1943), 684
Murphy, Charles F., relations of, with Governor Sulzer, 333
Murray, Governor William H. (Okla.), exercise of removal powers by, 335
Murray v. Hoboken Land and Improvement Company (18 Howard 272, 1855), 673
Myers v. United States (272 U.S. 52, 1926), 334

National Association of Legal Aid Organizations, on essentials of legal aid, 663
National Conference of Commissioners on Uniform State Laws: model act of, for state court administrator, 627–629; organization and work of, 854–856, 857, 861, 862, 866
National Conference on Interstate Trade Barriers, 870–871
National Conference of Judicial Councils: survey of, on administration of justice by, 607; meetings of, 624; survey of, on selection of jurors, 656; survey of, on summing up evidence, 659
National Conference on Street and Highway Safety, initiates movement for uniform motor vehicle laws, 856–857
National Education Association, campaign of, for school district reorganization, 756
National Guard, 398; history and development of, 399–400; theoretical and constitutional basis of, 400; organization of, 400–402; functions of, 402–403; veterans' exemptions for, 417; racial discrimination in, 692; transfer of, to Federal authorities, 881, 882
National Lawyers Guild, legal aid work of, 664
National Municipal League: on value of a constitutional convention as means of civic education, 81–82; work of, on ratification of New York constitution, 87–88; model registration system of, 119; model election administration system of, 135; organization and work of, 161–162; and Citizenship Clearing House, 182; supports home rule, 801; model laws of, 861, 862
National Opinion Research Center, makes study of voter participation, 174
National Reporter System, 637–638
National Resources Board: assists states in planning field, 438, 762; regionalism study of, 892–893
National Security Resources Board: on responsibility of states in civil defense, 404–405; civil defense legislation drafted by, 409
Natural resources: see conservation
Near v. Minnesota (283 U.S. 697, 1931), 681
NEBRASKA: constitutional amendment procedure in, 56; adoption of constitution of, 70; voting population of, 103; voting laws of, 108; convention system in, 121; initiative in, 146; recall in, 152; unicameral legislature in, 191–193, 210, 212; apportionment in, 200; legislative committees in, 225, listed, 226, 227, 228; cost of legislation in, 231; legislative service agencies in, 242, 258, 259, 265, 267, 275; local legislation in, 285; three reading system in, 296, 308; mechanical voting in legislature of, 309; governors' messages in, 337; veto power in, 341; administrative reorganization in, 375, 378; boards and commissions in, 385; administrative procedure legislation in, 393; civil service law in, 464; adopts budget law, 494; growth of debt in, 512, 513; general property tax in, 532; pari-mutuel taxes in, 538; liquor taxes in, 542; gasoline tax in, 544; cigarette tax in, 545; inheritance tax in, 549; equity system in, 571; justice courts in, 600; judicial administration in, 608, 630; selection of judges in, 611; judicial council in, 620; advisory opinions in, 638; publication of judicial opinions in, 645; closed shop amendment in, 701; blood tests in, 715; local government in, 747, 749, 768; power of governor over local units in, 797; home rule in, 801; supervision of the schools in, 816; public welfare administration in, 826; interstate compacts in, 839, 848
Negroes: suffrage of, 106–112; in National Guard units, 402; civil rights of, 688–697
Neuberger, Richard L., on costs of campaigning, 322
NEVADA: adoption of constitution of, 70; voting population of, 103; voting laws of, 108; initiative in, 146; recall in, 152; legislature of, 210, 211; legislative retirement in, 214, 215; special sessions in, 220; legislative committees in, 225; cost

of legislation in, 231; legislative service agencies in, 242, 250, 258, 259, 262, 265, 267, 273, 275; veto power in, 339; administrative reorganization in, 378; agricultural commission in, 435; adopts budget law, 494; power of legislature over budget in, 498; growth of debt in, 512, 513; tax limitation in, 532; liquor taxes in, 542; gasoline tax in, 544; cigarette tax in, 545; inheritance tax in, 549; community property law in, 552; equity system in, 571; judicial administration in, 608; selection of judges in, 611; judicial council in, 620; pre-natal examinations in, 715; local government in, 748, 749, 768; county park systems in, 763; interstate compacts in, 839, 848

New England: local government in, 744; Interstate Flood Control Committee, 848; Council, 864

NEW HAMPSHIRE: early chief executive in, 44; establishes new state government, 46; procedure for constitutional amendment in, 56; adoption of constitution in, 70; voting population of, 103: voting laws of, 104, 108; legislative sessions in, 190, 210, 222–223, 337; apportionment in, 200; legislative membership in, 211; legislative compensation in, 213; legislative committees in, 225; cost of legislation in, 231; legislative service agencies in, 242, 259, 265, 267; adjournment of legislature in, 337; veto power in, 339, 342; functions of attorney general in, 366; governor's council in, 366; administrative reorganization in, 378; military powers of the governor in, 396; bonus legislation in, 416; secretary of state in, 424; adopts budget law, 494; growth of debt in, 512, 513; general property tax in, 532; liquor taxes in, 542; gasoline tax in, 544; cigarette tax in, 545; inheritance tax in, 549; equity system in, 571; judicial review in, 586; justice courts in, 600; judicial administration in, 608; selection of judges in, 611, 612; judicial council in, 620; freedom of speech case in, 678–679, 680; eminent domain in, 703; blood tests in, 715; heart-balm legislation in, 730; public nuisance case in, 735; local government in, 748, 749, 768, 773; county park systems in, 764; power of governor over local officers in, 797; control over local debts in, 808; public welfare administration in, 827; interstate compacts in, 839, 848

NEW JERSEY: disability insurance in, 10; early lack of confidence in popular government in, 49; efforts of, to revise constitution, 56–57, 64; constitutional revision commissions in, 58; interstate cooperation of, with Pennsylvania, 64; adoption of constitution of, 70; preparatory work for constitutional convention in, 74; campaign in, for ratification of constitution, 88–90; voting population of, 103; voting laws of, 108, 115; conduct of elections in, 133; recall in, 152; short ballot in, 154; state-wide civic groups in, 167; zoning legislation in, 168; citizen training of adults in, 178; legislative sessions in, 190, 210, 219, 220; apportionment in, 200, 201, 203; legislative turnover in, 205; legislative membership in, 211, 212; legislative retirement in, 215; legislative committees in, 225, 226; cost of legislation in, 231; legislative service agencies in, 242, 265, 267, 268; local legislation in, 287; sources of legislation in, 291–292; Governor Wilson in, 318; gubernatorial term in, 323; salary of governor in, 324; governor's powers of appointment in, 332–333; seizure of struck properties in, 335; veto power in, 339, 341, 342; administrative reorganization in, 374, 377; boards and commissions in, 387; administrative procedure legislation in, 393; non-segregation policy in, 402; civil defense organization in, 405, 408–409 (charts), 410; veterans' preference in, 418, 476; secretary of state in, 424; organization of social welfare in, 446; management of institutions in, 447; establishment of state university in, 452; early civil service law in, 463, 464; expenditures of, for civil service, 465; civil service administration in, 467, 477–478; budget system in, 493, 494; growth of debt in, 512, 513; general property tax in, 526, 528, 532–533; pari-mutuel taxes in, 538; liquor taxes in, 542; gasoline tax in, 543, 544; cigarette tax in, 545; income tax in, 546; inheritance tax in, 549; equity system in, 571; early judicial review in, 586; abolishes justices of the peace, 599; appellate courts in, 607; court reorganization in, 607; judicial administration in, 608, 626–627, 628, 629, 630; selection of judges in, 611, 612; salaries of judges in, 616; judicial council in, 619, 620, 623, 638; volume of judicial business in, 638, 640; modern court procedure in, 666; school bus case in, 685–686; racial discrimination banned in, 692, 700, 701; blood tests in, 715; sale of fireworks banned in, 719; motion picture censorship in, 727; local government in, 747, 749, 768, 773, 784, 797, 798–799; home rule in, 801; control of local budgets in, 807; control over local debts in, 808; supervision of local accounts in, 811; state-local health relations in, 822; public welfare administration in, 824, 826; state aid for highways in, 827; interstate rendition in, 835; interstate compacts in, 839, 848, 851, 853–854; boundary dispute of, with Delaware, 841; interstate enforcement of gasoline tax by, 865; organizes first Commission on Interstate Cooperation, 869

New Jersey Education Association, program of, for citizen training, 178

NEW MEXICO: test case of use of Federal land grant funds by, 37; constitutional amendment procedure in, 56; adoption of constitution of, 70; constitutional convention procedure in, 71, 86; voting population of, 103; voting laws of, 108, 115; convention system in, 121; referendum authorized in, 143; initiative in, 146; recall in, 152; long ballot in, 155; legislative sessions in, 190, 220; legislative retirement in, 214, 215; legislative committees in, 225; cost of legislation in, 231; legislative service agencies in, 242, 259, 265, 267; salary of governor in, 324; veto power in, 338, 341; gasoline tax in, 439, 543, 544; experience of, with civil service, 463; adopts budget law, 494; growth of debt in, 512, 513; tax limitation in, 532; liquor taxes in, 542; cigarette tax in, 545; income tax in, 548; inheritance tax in, 549; community property law in, 552; equity system in, 571; judicial administration in, 608; selection of judges in, 611; judicial council in, 620; supreme court of, 632; publication of judicial opinions in, 645; anti-peonage law in, 670; prenatal examinations in, 715; local government in, 748, 749, 768; control of local budgets in, 807; control over local debts in, 808; supervision of schools of, 816; mothers' aid in, 827; interstate compacts in, 839, 848, 849, 853; boundary dispute of, with Colorado, 841

New State Ice Company v. Liebmann (285 U.S. 262, 1932), 6–8

NEW YORK: disability insurance in, 10; relations of, with United Nations, 41; early legislative election of governor in, 44; veto power in, 45, 338, 339–340, 341, 342; efforts of, to revise constitution, 57, 64; constitutional revision commissions, 58; use of constitutional amending procedure in, 62–63, 136; constitutional convention in, 69; adoption of constitution of, 70; constitutional convention procedure in, 72, 78, 79, 86–88; preparatory work for constitutional convention in, 74–76, 908; citizen action in, for new constitution, 85–86; party boss in, 100; voting population of, 103; voting laws of, 106, 108, 116, 118–119; convention system in, 121, 128; use of voting machines in, 132; conduct of elections in, 133; corrupt practices legislation in, 137; short ballot in, 154; state-wide civic groups in, 165, 180; league of municipalities in, 167; Freedom Train in, 177; legislative sessions in, 190, 210, 219; apportionment in, 201; legislative turnover in, 205; legislative retirement in, 214, 215; legislative committees in, 225, 226, 245, 246, 247; cost of legislation in, 231, 232, 233, 234, 235–236; legislative service agencies in, 242, 249, 264, 265, 267; abuses of lobby in, 254; law revision in, 269–270, 272; legislative powers in, 281, 282; local legislation in, 287; executive-legislative relations in, 293; legislative procedure in, 304; quantity of legislation in, 310–311; Governors Roosevelt and Hughes in, 317; Governors Smith, Roosevelt, and Lehman of, 318, 345; qualifications for governor in, 321; Governors Lehman and Dewey in, 324; salary of governor in, 324; impeachment of Governor Sulzer in, 327, 333; Governor Roosevelt's policy regarding appointments in, 333; executive clemency in, 348–349; extradition procedure in, 350; functions of attorney general in, 366; civil service law in, 370; administrative reorganization in, 371, 372, 374, 375, 376, 378, 387; management improvement in, 391; administrative procedure legislation in, 393; military powers of governor in, 395–396; governor refuses to use troops in labor dispute, 397; Home Guard in, 398; history of National Guard in, 399; Federal military property in, 401; military training institutions in, 402; non-segregation policy in, 402; civil defense in, 410; bonus legislation in, 416; secretary of state in, 424; establishes a department of banking, 425; investigation of insurance in, 426; organization of insurance department in, 427; organization of labor department in, 427; cost of highway program in, 441; canal system in, 444; department of mental health in, 445; staff of state department of education in, 451; establishes a state university, 452; growth of state personnel in, 458; early spoils system in, 459; establishes civil service system, 462–463, 464; expenditures of, for civil service, 465; constitutional provisions of, on civil service, 465–466; civil service administration in, 467, 473–476, 484; personnel council, 471–472; training programs in, 480; merit award system in, 481–482; budget system in, 493, 494, 498; growth of debt in, 512, 513; general property tax in, 532, 534, 551; corporation taxes in, 535; bank taxes in, 536; pari-mutuel taxes in, 538; liquor taxes in, 542; gasoline tax in, 543, 544; income tax in, 544, 546; cigarette tax in, 545; income tax in, 548; inheritance tax in, 549; equity system in, 571; Baumes fourth offender law in, 579; doctrine of judicial review in, 587, 588; growth of court system of, 592–594; justice courts in, 600; district courts in, 604; appellate courts in, 606; court reorganization in, 607; judicial administration in, 608, 630; selection of judges in, 611; salaries of judges in, 615; impeachment of judges in, 617; judicial council in, 619, 620, 621, 623, 624; advisory opinions in, 638; publication of judicial opinions in, 645; publication of crime and sex stories in, 682–683; discrimination in higher education in, 695; blue ribbon juries in, 697;

protection of right to work in, 699–701; blood tests in, 715; safety legislation in, 718; rent control legislation in, 723; pari-mutuel betting in, 727; motion picture censorship in, 727; billboard nuisance in, 737; local government in, 745, 747, 749, 750, 753, 767, 768, 770, 772, 774, 781, 797; school districts in, 756, 795; local library services in, 762; county planning and zoning in, 762, 763; county forests in, 764; power of governor over local officials in, 797; home rule in, 799–801; local tax powers in, 802, 805–806, 810–811; grants-in-aid in, 809; supervision of accounts in, 811; control over school curriculum in, 818; control over school buildings in, 819; public welfare administration in, 824, 825; interstate rendition in, 835; divorce law in, 836; interstate compacts in, 839, 848, 849, 851, 853–854; pioneers in uniform state laws, 854, 857; interstate enforcement of gasoline tax by, 865; adjustments necessary when Federal Security program began, 881; urban-rural conflict in, 896

New York City: *Bremen* incident in, 40; registration law in, 117; cost of elections in, 137; defects of district system in, 157; Citizens Union of, 169–170; performance budgeting proposed in, 497; assessment procedure in, 526; tax exempt property in, 528; municipal court in, 602–603; bail abuses in, 647; cost of litigation in, 662; legal aid in, 662; voluntary defenders in, 665; enforcement of sanitary code of, 711–712; building inspection in, 716; deaths in, due to fireworks, 719; zero wards in, 758; present size of, 775; Tweed ring in, 777; council in, 778–779; Interstate Sanitation District in, 853; Council of State Governments office in, 866; metropolitan problems of, 895, 896–897

New York ex rel. Lieberman v. Van de Carr (199 U.S. 552, 1905), 711–712

New York State Citizens Council, organization and work of, 180–181

Noble State Bank v. Haskill (219 U.S. 104, 1911), 709

Nominations: systems of, 119–128; by caucus, 119–120; by conventions, 120–121; by direct primary, 121–128; of governor, 321–323

Nonpartisan primary, 123

Nonvoting: reasons for, 173–174; compulsory voting, as remedy for, 174–175

NORTH CAROLINA: state symphony orchestra in, 10; constitutional revision commissions in, 58; adoption of constitution of, 70; voting population of, 103; voting laws of, 108; corrupt practices legislation in, 137; initiative in, 146; recall in, 152; early legislative organization in, 188, 190; apportionment in, 201; legislative compensation in, 213; legislative committees in, 224, 225; cost of legislation in, 231; legislative service agencies in, 242, 250, 265, 267; lobby expenditures in, 254–255; local legislation in, 285; salary of governor in, 324; special sessions in, 337; veto power in, 338; duties of the governor in, 351; administrative reorganization in, 372; administrative procedure legislation in, 393; civil service law in, 464; adopts budget law, 494; debt service in, 511; growth of debt in, 512, 513; general property tax in, 532; liquor taxes in, 542; gasoline tax in, 544; cigarette tax in, 545; inheritance tax in, 549; equity system in, 571; judicial review in, 586; judicial administration in, 608; selection of judges in, 611; salaries of judges in, 616; judicial council in, 619, 622; advisory opinions in, 638; racial discrimination in, 695; closed shop legislation in, 701; eminent domain in, 703; blood tests in, 715; local government in, 748, 768, 772, 773, 774, 781, 797–798, 808; highway function in, 748, 749, 828; local library services in, 762; county liquor stores in, 765; control of local budgets in, 807; control over local debts in, 808; supervision of the schools of, 815, 816; public welfare administration in, 825–826; divorce law in, 836–837; interstate compacts in, 839, 849

NORTH DAKOTA: adoption of constitution of, 70; voting population of, 103; voting laws of, 108, 160; initiative in, 146; recall in, 152; long ballot in, 155; legislative sessions in, 190, 210; apportionment in, 200, 201; legislative committees in, 225; cost of legislation in, 231; legislative service agencies in, 242, 250, 259, 265, 267; Governor Moses of, 319; Governor Frazier, recall of, in, 327; veto power in, 338, 341; administrative reorganization in, 378; administrative procedure legislation in, 393; bonus legislation in, 416; grazing districts in, 436; gasoline tax in, 439, 543, 544; motor vehicle registration fees in, 441; organization of social welfare in, 446; adopts budget law, 494; growth of debt in, 512, 513; liquor taxes in, 542; cigarette tax in, 545; income tax in, 548; inheritance tax in, 549; equity system in, 571; judicial administration in, 608; selection of judges in, 611; judicial council in, 620, 621, 622; integrated bar in, 660; blood tests in, 715; has no small loan law, 729; weights and measures legislation in, 730–731; local government in, 747, 749, 768, 774; county planning in, 762; public welfare administration in, 826; interstate compacts in, 839, 848, 849

Northwest States Development Association, 848

Northwestern Fertilizer Company v. Hyde Park (97 U.S. 650, 1878), 734–735

Obligation of contract, protection of, 697–699

Offenses, criminal, defined, 575; classified, 576–578
Ogg, Frederic A.: on nature of federalism, 15; on representative character of state legislatures, 195
OHIO: adoption of constitution of, 70; constitutional convention procedure in, 78; voting population of, 103; voting laws of, 108; initiative in, 146; recall in, 152; state-wide civic groups in, 165; apportionment in, 199, 201, 203; legislative membership in, 211; legislative retirement in, 214, 215; legislative sessions in, 220, 221, 225; cost of legislation in, 231; legislative service agencies in, 242, 259, 263, 265, 267, 268, 272; sources of legislation in, 292; Governor Bricker of, 319; veto power in, 338, 341; administrative reorganization in, 372, 378, 380, 391; administrative procedure legislation in, 393; use of troops in labor dispute in, 397; bonus legislation in, 416; veterans' preference in, 418, 476; civil service law in, 464; adopts budget law, 494; growth of debt in, 512, 513; general property tax in, 532, 551, 803; corporation taxes in, 534; liquor taxes in, 542; gasoline tax in, 544; cigarette tax in, 545; inheritance tax in, 549; equity system in, 571; justice of the peace system in, 597; judicial administration in, 608, 630; selection of judges in, 611; salaries of judges in, 616; judicial council in, 619, 620, 623; blood tests in, 715; safety legislation in, 718; public convenience regulation in, 721; motion picture censorship in, 727; small loan legislation in, 729; zoning regulations in, 736; land system in, 745; local government in, 747, 749, 768, 774, 780, 781; county park systems in, 764; power of governor over local officers in, 797; home rule in, 799, 800, 801; public welfare administration in, 825; interstate rendition in, 834–835; interstate compacts in, 839, 849, 850–851; interstate enforcement of gasoline tax by, 865
Ohio River Valley Sanitation Commission, 850–851
OKLAHOMA: regulation of ice companies by, 6–8; test case on powers of, to move capitol, 36; length of constitution of, 46; adoption of constitution of, 70; preparatory work for constitutional convention in, 74; constitutional convention procedure in, 86; voting population of, 103; voting laws of, 108, 110, 160; initiative in, 146; long ballot in, 154; preferential voting invalid in, 160; run-off primary in, 160; legislative sessions in, 190; apportionment in, 200, 203; legislative membership in, 211; telecasting legislative procedure in, 217; legislative committees in, 225, 226, 228; cost of legislation in, 231; legislative service agencies in, 242, 259, 265, 267; reasons for defeat of bills in legislature of, 301–302; presession training conferences in, 307; legislative voting in, 309; salary of governor in, 324; impeachment process in, 327; governor's power of removal in, 335; veto power in, 342; functions of attorney general in, 366; motor vehicle registration fees in, 441; motor vehicle operators' licenses in, 443; department of mental health in, 445; adopts budget law, 494; performance budgeting in, 496–497; growth of debt in, 512, 513; general property tax in, 532, 803; liquor taxes in, 542; gasoline tax in, 544; cigarette tax in, 545; income tax in, 548; inheritance tax in, 549; community property law in, 552; equity system in, 571; judicial administration in, 608, 630; selection of judges in, 611; judicial council in, 620; advisory opinions in, 638; racial discrimination in, 693–694; blood tests in, 715; sterilization law in, 720–721; local government in, 747–748, 749, 768, 774; power of governor over local government in, 797; home rule in, 801; audit supervision in, 813; demonstration classes in, 818; interstate compacts in, 839, 848; uniform state laws in, 855
Oleomargarine, regulation of the sale of, 732
Olson, Governor Floyd E. (Minn.), use of troops by, in labor disputes, 396–397
Optional charter plan: in New Jersey, 798–799; originated in New York, 800
Ordinances: power of governor to make, 345–346
OREGON: constitutionality of direct legislation tested in, 21; constitutional initiative in, 59, 71; use of constitutional amending procedure in, 60; adoption of constitution of, 70; voting population of, 103; voting laws of, 108, 116; initiative in, 146; recall in, 150, 152; long ballot in, 155; apportionment in, 203; legislature of, 210; legislative sessions in, 223; legislative committees in, 225, 246; cost of legislation in, 231; legislative service agencies in, 242, 256, 267; gubernatorial succession in, 325; impeachment process in, 327; veto power in, 341; administrative reorganization movement originates in, 370; Little Hoover Commission in, 378; management improvement in, 388; administrative procedure legislation in, 393; bonus legislation in, 416; gasoline tax in, 439, 543, 544; organization of social welfare in, 446; civil service law in, 464; adopts budget law, 494; growth of debt in, 512, 513; general property tax in, 532; liquor taxes in, 542; cigarette tax in, 545; income tax in, 548; inheritance tax in, 549; community property law in, 552; equity system in, 571; justice courts in, 599, 600; judicial administration in, 608, 630; selection of judges in, 611; judicial council in, 620; supreme court of, 632; blood tests in, 715; local govern-

ment in, 748, 749, 768, 773, 774; county planning in, 762; home rule in, 801; vocational education in, 816; public welfare administration in, 826; interstate compacts in, 839, 848, 852; member of PACBIR, 904
Oyama v. California (332 U.S. 633, 1948), 702

Pacific Coast Board of Intergovernmental Relations (PACBIR), organization and functioning of, 904–905
Pacific Marine Fisheries Compact, 852
Pacific States Telephone and Telegraph Company v. Oregon (223 U.S. 118, 1912), 21
Packer Corporation v. Utah (285 U.S. 105, 1932), 737
Pardon, and parole, governor's power of, 347–350
Pari-mutuel betting, regulation and control of, 726–727
Parker, John J., on functions of courts, 637
Parks and forests, as local function, 764
Parties: American system of, 95–101; and elections, 101–141; representation of, in legislatures, 202, 204–205; control of, over legislation, 291
Patterson, Robert P., on organization of National Guard, 400
Pattison, Governor Robert E. (Pa.), reelection of, 324
Patton, Simon N., on weaknesses of the states, 877–878
Paul v. Virginia (8 Wallace 168, 1868), 426
Pecos River: compact, 839, 853; Commission, 849
Pennekamp v. Florida (328 U.S. 331, 1946), 682
PENNSYLVANIA: a commonwealth, 15; early unicameral legislature in, 44, 191; early chief executive in, 44; amending process in, 55, 61–62; efforts of, to revise constitution, 57, 71; need for constitutional revision in, 64–65; constitutional convention in, 69; adoption of constitution of, 70; constitutional convention procedure in, 72–73, 77–78; party boss system in, 100; voting population of, 103; voting laws of, 108, 116; conduct of elections in, 133; election frauds in, 136–137; illustrates defects of district system, 157; state-wide civic groups in, 165, 166, 167; Intercollegiate Conference on Government in, 178; legislative sessions in, 190, 191, 221; representative character of legislature of, 196; apportionment in, 199, 200, 201, 203; legislative turnover in, 205; graft in construction of capitol of, 209; legislative retirement in, 214, 215; legislative committees in, 225, 246, 248; cost of legislation in, 231, 232, 235, 236; legislative service agencies in, 242, 250, 251, 252, 259, 260, 263, 264, 265, 267, 275; graft charges in, 283; restrictions on legislative powers in, 284; local legislation in, 286, 288–289; quantity of legislation in, 289–290; flow chart of bills in legislature of, 295; passage of bills in, 297–299; correction of errors in bills in, 301; presession training in, 307; Governor Pinchot in, 318, 324, 345; qualifications of governor in, 321; Governor Pattison in, 324; salary of governor in, 324; governor's powers of appointment in, 332; governor's powers of removal in, 334, 335; adjournment of legislature in, 337; veto power in, 338, 339, 341; executive board in, 366; administrative reorganization in, 372, 373, 375; boards and commissions in, 386–387; administrative procedure legislation in, 393; Federal military property in, 401; non-segregation policy in, 402; bonus legislation in, 416, 511; veterans' preference in, 418, 476; secretary of the Commonwealth in, 424; establishes department of banking, 425; organization of insurance department in, 427; organization of labor department in, 427; regulation of weights and measures in, 432; legislation on food products in, 434; growth of state highway system in, 440, 828–829; mental health work in, 445; organization of social welfare in, 446; management of institutions in, 447; state-owned hospitals in, 447; higher education in, 452; origins of spoils system in, 459–461; limited use of civil service in, 463; organization for collection of revenue in, 487; disbursements in, 491; budget system in, 493, 494; increase in expenditures in, 501–502, 504; changes in purposes of expenditures in, 503; growth of debt in, 512, 513; income sources in, 517; Prison Labor Fund in, 520; general property tax in, 532, 551, 803; taxes on business in, 539; mercantile tax in, 540; liquor taxes in, 542; gasoline tax in, 544; cigarette tax in, 545; income tax in, 548; inheritance tax in, 548, 549; equity system in, 571; judicial review in, 586; justice of the peace system in, 597, 598, 600; magistrates courts in, 601; district courts in, 604, 611; civil and criminal courts in, 605; appellate courts in, 607; judicial administration in, 608, 630; selection of judges in, 611; judicial tenure in, 615; salaries of judges in, 616; judicial conference in, 619, 620, 623; advisory opinions in, 638; volume of judicial business in, 639; case on distribution of religious literature in, 684; discrimination in employment banned in, 700; blood tests in, 715; safety legislation in, 718; sale of fireworks banned in, 719; early lotteries in, 726; billboard nuisance in, 737; local government in, 745, 747, 748, 749, 751, 767, 768, 773, 774, 798; school districts in, 756, 795; rural zoning in, 763; home rule in, 800, 801; local tax powers in, 802, 804–805; local tax collection in, 806; control over

local debts in, 808; grants-in-aid in, 809; audit supervision in, 812–813; control over school buildings in, 819; system of local health administration in, 820–821, 823; stream pollution control in, 823; public welfare administration in, 824, 825, 826; interstate rendition in, 835; divorce law in, 837; interstate compacts in, 839, 848, 849, 850–851, 852, 854; boundary dispute of, with Maryland, 841; use of Restatements in, 860; interstate enforcement of gasoline tax by, 865; urban-rural conflict in, 896
Pennsylvania Economy League, organization and work of, 167
Pennsylvania Intercollegiate Conference on Government, 178
Performance budgeting, 496–497
Perkins, John A.: on defects of ad interim committees, 249; on management improvement in Michigan, 390
Perry, Stuart H., on judicial primary in Detroit, 610
Personnel: governor's power over, 364; improvement in administration of, 370; growth of, in states, 457–459; spoils system in management of, 459–462; civil service system for, 462–467; merit system for, 467–470; basic problems in administration of, 470–484; supervision of local, 814, 821–822, 830; cooperative use of, 902
Philadelphia: primaries and elections in, 97, 98; long ballot in, 155–156; Committee on Public Affairs in, 169; Committee of Seventy in, 170; Committee of Fifteen in, 171; representation of, in state legislature, 199; magistrates courts in, 601–602; municipal court in, 602, 603; court of common pleas in, 611; powers of judges in, 619; bail abuses in, 647; legal aid in, 662, 664; sale of fireworks banned in, 719; zero wards in, 758; early status of, 774–775; council in, 777, 778; new charter of, 784; tax powers of, 805; debt control in, 807; port development in, 854; metropolitan problems of, 895
Pinchot, Governor Gifford (Pa.): as outstanding leader, 318, 345; reelection of, 324; practice of, regarding appointments, 332; exercise of removal powers by, 335; letters received by, from constituents, 356–357
Pittsburgh: assessment procedure in, 526; tax delinquency in, 530; municipal court in, 602
Placement, in state service, 476–477
Planning: relation of governor to, 364–366; influence of, on administration, 383–384; for management improvement, 390–391; agencies for, 438; financial, 489, 493–500; and zoning, 735–737, 762–763
Plant industry, bureau of, 435
Platt, Thomas C.: state boss in New York, 100; relations of, with Governor Roosevelt, 333
Poletti, Governor Charles (N.Y.): serves as chairman of State Constitutional Convention Committee, 74; resigns judgeship to run for office, 615
Police power: origin of, 707–708; definition of, 708–709; as an emergency power, 710; for protection of public health, 710–715; of public safety, 715–721; of the public convenience, 721–723; of the public morals, 724–728; for prevention of fraud, 728–732; for suppression of public nuisances, 732–739
Poll tax, as prerequisite for voting, 106–107
Pollock, James K.: on election costs, 139; on arguments for short ballot, 156
Popular government: Founders' lack of confidence in, 47, 49; devices for achieving, 142–184; controls over administration in, 382–383
Population: shifts in, create new state problems, 11–12; growth of, in cities, 774–776
Port of New York Authority: 753, 850; organization and program of, 853–854
Porter, Kirk H.: on history of the suffrage, 102; on deserted primary in Iowa, 125; on history of local government, 744; on powers of local government, 759
Potomac Valley Conservancy District, 851–852
Pound, Roscoe: on judicial councils, 619–620; on unified court system, 627; on judicial procedure, 658
Powell, Alden L.: on amendment of the Louisiana constitution, 59–60; on defects of the Louisiana constitution, 66
Preferential voting, 160
Premarital examinations, 714–715
Prenatal examinations, 715
Prescott, Frank W., on veto powers of governor, 338–340
President's Committee on Civil Rights, on recent developments on white primary, 112
Pressure groups: may defeat general constitutional revision, 87; influence of, in constitutional conventions, 83–86; influence of, in ratification of constitutions, 89–90; and selection of legislative subjects, 291–292; power of, to control administration, 383; and tax legislation, 539
Pretrial conferences, 639–641
Primary: white, in Texas, 111–112; elections; see also direct primary
Printing: legislative, 234–236, 308
Private law, and public law, distinguished, 573
Privileges: of members of legislature, 217–218; and immunities of citizens, under Amendment XIV, 670, 835–836
Procurement: improvement of methods of, 389; as phase of fiscal process, 490
Professions: representation of, in legislatures, 194–197; examination and licensing for, 430–433

Prohibition, writ of, defined, 568
Property: management of, as phase of fiscal process, 491; rights, protection of, 697–705
Proportional Representation (P.R.), 157–160; List system of, 158; Hare system of, 158–160; sample ballot used in, 158
Prostitution, control of, under police power, 725
Public accommodation, discrimination in, 690–692
Public assistance (relief), development of program for, 448–449
Public convenience, protection of, under police power, 721–723
Public domain, revenue derived from, 518–519
Public expenditure: see expenditures
Public health: history and development of, 444–445; organization, powers, and duties of department of, 445–446; references on, 455; protection of, under police power, 710–715; as local function, 761; municipal administration of, 785–786; state supervision of, 819–824
Public law, and private law, distinguished, 573
Public morals, protection of, under police power, 724–728
Public nuisances: suppression of, under police power, 732–739; classification of, 733–734; abatement of, 734–735; zoning for control of, 735–737; billboard control under, 737–739
Public opinion: influence of, in selecting legislative subjects, 291–292; power of, in control of administration, 382–383
Public purpose: in taxation, 524; in eminent domain, 703
Public safety: protection of, under police power, 715–721; in municipal administration, 784–785
Public service commissions, powers and duties of, 429–430
Public utilities: commissions for regulation of, 429–430; activities of local governments in, 764–765; municipal administration of, 786–787
Public welfare: see social welfare
Public works: municipal administration of, 787–788; interstate compacts on, 839; postwar needs for, 886
Puerto Rico: reorganization commission in, 377, 378; standards for top management in, 388; National Guard in, 403

Queenside Hills Realty Company v. Saxl (328 U.S. 80, 1946), 716
Quo warranto, writ of, defined, 568

Radio, use of, in political campaigns, 130
Rainmaking, regulation of, 721
Ransone, Coleman B., Jr.: on duties of governor in North Carolina, 351; on daily schedule of governor in Virginia, 355
Rationing, wartime, part of states in, 883
Reapportionment, in legislatures, 199–204
Recall, 150–152; of judicial decisions, 153
Recording: responsibility of states for war, 420; as a local function, 758
Recreation: development of state programs in, 449; as local function, 761–762; municipal administration of, 789
Recruiting, and examining of personnel, 472–473, 476
Referendum: on constitutional amendments, 61–63; of revised constitutions, 86–90; operation of, 149–150
Regionalism: proposals for sub-national, 891–892; progress of, 892–893; merits of, 893–894; metropolitan, 894–897
Registration: for voting, 116–117; periodic, 117; permanent, 117–119
Regular sessions, 219, 237, 303
Reitz v. Mealey (314 U.S. 33, 1941), 716
Removal: of governor, 325–328; governor's powers of, 334–335; in state service, 483; of judges, 615–616
Rendition, interstate, 834–835
Renne, Roland R., on special districts for agricultural purposes, 436
Rent controls, 722–723
Reorganization movement: characteristics of, 369–379; evaluation of, 379–381
Reporting: financial, 491; supervision of local, 813–814
Representation: faults of district system of, 153, 156–157; proportional, 157–160; functional, 256
Republican government: duty of states to maintain, 21; guarantee of, 23, 33
Research: and citizen action, 171–172; in the legislative service, chapter 7; influence of, on administration, 383–384; of judicial councils, 623–625
Restaurants, inspection and control of, 712
Restrictive covenants, 701–702
Retirement: of legislators, 214–216; of public employees, 483; assessments for, 521
Revenue: collection of, 487–488; sources of, 515–521; basic problems on taxes for, 521–525; general property tax for, 525–534; corporation and business taxes for, 534–539; general sales, use, and gross receipts taxes for, 540–541; excise taxes for, 541–544; income taxes for, 544–548; inheritance and estate taxes for, 548–549; current problems regarding, 549–554; references on, 554–555
RHODE ISLAND: disability insurance in, 10; retains previous charter, 46; constitutional revision commissions in, 58; adoption of constitution of, 70; voting population of, 103; voting laws of, 108; convention system in, 121; legislative sessions in, 190, 219; apportionment in, 203; legislative retirement in, 214, 215; legislative committees in, 225; cost of legislation in, 231; legislative service agencies in, 242, 250, 265, 267; salary of governor in, 324; veto power in, 338,

339, 341; personnel organization in, 364; administrative reorganization in, 372; management improvement in, 388; bonus legislation in, 416; civil service law in, 464; adopts budget law, 493, 494; growth of debt in, 512, 513; general property tax in, 532, 803; liquor taxes in, 542; gasoline tax in, 544; cigarette tax in, 545; income tax in, 548; inheritance tax in, 549; equity system in, 571; judicial administration in, 608; selection of judges in, 611, 612; salaries of judges in, 616; judicial council in, 620, 621; supreme court of, 632; advisory opinions in, 638; publication of judicial opinions in, 645; blood tests in, 715; sale of fireworks banned in, 719; local government in, 748, 749, 767, 768; powers of governor over local officers in, 797; home rule in, 801; public welfare administration in, 825; interstate compacts in, 839

Rich, Bennett M., on constitutional revision commissions, 58

Right to work, protection of, 699–701

Riley, Fletcher, on position of the courts, 582

Ritchie, Governor Albert C. (Md.): as outstanding leader, 318; long tenure of, 324

Roman law, influence of, 560–561, 570, 572

Roosevelt, Franklin D.: as outstanding leader, 318, 345; on poor housing, 764; on excessive layers of government, 794–795; sponsors TVA, 847; calls interstate industrial conference, 864; on states' rights, 871; and Federal-municipal relations, 887

Roosevelt, Theodore: advocates recall of judicial decisions, 153; as outstanding leader, 317; practice of, regarding appointments, 333; calls first Governors' Conference, 763, 863; calls White House Conference, 826

Root, Elihu: on California school case, 40; reorganizes military establishment, 399; as chairman of American Law Institute, 859; on future of the states, 910

Roraback, J. Henry, state boss of Connecticut, 100

Rothenberg, Charles, on divorce law, 837

Rules: of legislative procedure, 294–296; power of executive to make, 345–346, 372, 391–393; judicial making of, 623

Rural Electrification Administration, work of, 765

Safety, and health, in public service, 482

Saia v. New York (334 U.S. 558, 1948), 680–681

St. Louis: quadrennial registration in, 117; cost of elections in, 137; long ballot in, 155; Conference of Chief Justices meets in, 607; new charter of, 784; units of local government in, 795

Salaries: legislative, 212–214, 232–234, 238; of governors, 324–325; of judges, 616–617; of public employees, 477–479

Sales taxes, 515, 516, 540–541, 550

Salt Lake City: cost of elections in, 137; long ballot in, 155

Saltonstall, Governor Leverett (Mass.): length of service of, 319

San Francisco: school case in, 39–40; biennial registration in, 117; cost of elections in, 137; use of recall in, 151; garbage disposal in, 713; liquor license ordinance in, 725; Council of State Governments, office in, 866

Sanitary conditions: state control of, 822–823; engineering projects affecting, 823–824; interstate compacts on, 839, 853

Satterfield, Millard H., on county welfare work in Alabama, 760–761; on county forests in West Virginia, 764

Saxe, Martin, on constitutional provisions on taxation, 524

Scace, Homer E., on organization and staffing of governor's office, 363–365

Schacter, Harry W., organizes and directs Committee for Kentucky, 179–180

Scholz, Governor David (Fla.), comment of, on extradition case, 835

Scholz, Karl, on moving average for local debt control, 807

Schools: number of districts for, by states, 749; consolidation of districts for, 756–757; state supervision of, 815–819; control over buildings for, 819

Screws v. United States (325 U.S. 91, 1945), 695

Secretary of state, powers and duties of, 424

Security issues, regulation of, 426

Segregation: of motor funds, 544; racial, in education, 692–695; in procedural rights, 695–697; in property rights, 699–702

Selective Service System, administration of, 882

Senning, John P., on unicameralism in Nebraska, 191–193

Separation: of powers in state constitutions, 43–46; in state service, 483

Sessions, legislative: regular, 219, 237, 303; special, 219–220, 337; split, 220–221; adjourned, 221; executive, 221; weekly schedule of, 221–223; length of, 223; end of, 303–305

Severance taxes, 516, 537, 550

Sewage: disposal of, 713, 823; municipal administration of system for, 788

Shelley v. Kraemer (334 U.S. 1, 1948), 702

Short, Lloyd M., on trends in constitutional changes, 82

Short ballot; principles and use of, 154–156

Shumate, Roger V., on legislative procedure, 306

Sigler, Governor Kim (Mich.), management improvement program of, 390

Sipuel v. Oklahoma (332 U.S. 631, 1948), and related cases, 693

Slaughter House Cases (16 Wallace 36, 1873), 707–708

Sly, John F., on welfare state, 11

Small, Norman J., on community property, 552
Small loans, regulation of business of, 728–729
Smith, Governor Alfred E. (N.Y.): sponsors constitutional amendments, 62–63; as outstanding leader, 318, 345; length of tenure of, 323–324; comment of, on executive clemency, 348–349; comment of, on extradition, 350; on dual function of governor, 356; on state spending program, 494–495
Smith, Bruce, on justice of the peace, 597
Smith, Reginald H., on cost of litigation, 661
Smith v. Allwright (321 U.S. 649, 1944), 111–112
Smith v. Texas (311 U.S. 128, 1940), 696
Snake River Compact, 849
Social Science Research Council, makes study of public service personnel, 468
Social security: scope of Federal-state program for, 449, 760, 786, 825, 827; as applied to public employees, 483; taxes for, 516; postwar extension of, 885
Social welfare: organization, powers, and duties of department of, 446–449; references on, 455–456; as local function, 760–761; municipal administration of, 785–786; state-local relations in, 824–827
Soil conservation, administration of, 436, 764
Solomon, Samuel R., on the governorship, 318–319, 375
SOUTH CAROLINA: terms of legislators in, 44; establishes new state government, 46; early suffrage limitations in, 49; constitutional amendment procedure in, 56; constitutional conventions in, 69; adoption of constitution of, 70; constitutional convention procedure in, 86; voting population of, 103; conditions of suffrage in, 104, 108, 115, 116; white primary in, 112; convention system in, 121; ballot forms in, 131; recall in, 152; legislative sessions in, 190, 219; apportionment in, 200, 201; legislative term in, 212; legislative retirement in, 214, 215; legislative committees in, 224, 225; cost of legislation in, 231; legislative service agencies in, 242, 258, 259, 265, 267, 278; governor's removal powers in, 335; veto power in, 338, 342; requirement of publication of rules in, 372, 393; administrative reorganization in, 378; motor vehicle registration fees in, 441; adopts budget law, 494; growth of debt in, 512, 513; general property tax in, 532; liquor taxes in, 542; gasoline tax in, 544; tobacco taxes in, 544, 545; income tax in, 548; inheritance tax in, 549; equity system in, 571; judicial review in, 586; judicial administration in, 608; selection of judges in, 611, 612; judicial council in, 620; pre-natal examinations in, 715; no small loan legislation in, 729; local government in, 748, 749, 768, 772, 781; county park systems in, 764; rural power distribution in, 765; supervision of the schools of, 816; mothers' aid in, 827; divorce law in, 837; interstate compacts in, 839, 849
SOUTH DAKOTA: adoption of constitution of, 70; voting population of, 103; voting laws of, 108; convention system in, 121; movement for direct legislation originates in, 143; initiative in, 146; recall in, 152; legislative sessions in, 190, 223; legislative committees in, 224, 225, 226, 246; cost of legislation in, 231; legislative service agencies in, 242, 250, 259, 265, 267; veto power in, 338, 341; administrative reorganization in, 372; administrative procedure legislation in, 393; bonus legislation in, 416; grazing districts in, 436; lack of mental health work in, 445; staff of department of education in, 451; adopts budget law, 494; growth of debt in, 512, 513; general property tax in, 532; liquor taxes in, 542; gasoline tax in, 544; cigarette tax in, 545; income tax in, 546, 548; inheritance tax in, 549; equity system in, 571; judicial administration in, 608; selection of judges in, 611; salaries of judges in, 616; judicial council in, 620; advisory opinions in, 638; modern court procedure in, 666; blood tests in, 715; no small loan legislation in, 729; local government in, 747, 749, 768, 773; county park systems in, 764; vocational education in, 816; public welfare administration in, 826; interstate compacts in, 839, 848, 849; uniform state laws in, 855
Southern Regional Education Compact, 845–846
Southern states: Negro suffrage in, 106–112; Reconstruction legislatures in, 188–189
Speaker, powers and duties of, 218
Special assessments, 521
Special districts: for agricultural purposes, 436; number of, by states, 749; discussion of, 750
Special legislation, 239, 283–285
Special sessions, 219–220; power of governor over, 337
Spicer, George W., on state-local fiscal relations, 814–815
Split sessions, 220–221
Sponsler, William A.: on purposes of expenditures, 503–504; on sources of revenues, 517
Staff services: as means of executive supervision, 359; of governor's office, 363–365; for municipalities, 782–784
Stare decisis, importance of doctrine of, 584
Stark, Governor Lloyd (Mo.), in succession controversy, 326
Stassen, Governor Harold E. (Minn.), sponsors management improvement program, 389
State aid: to local units, 808–811, 815–817; see also grants-in-aid

State commissions on interstate cooperation, organization and work of, 858, 869–871
State police: organization, powers, and duties of, 425; work of, in highway safety, 443–444
States: problems of, at mid-century, 3–14; training function of, 4–5; as laboratories, 5–8; fundamental position of, 8–10, 875; new duties and responsibilities of, 10–12; sources of information about, 12–14; relations of, with Federal government, 19–31; limitations on power of, 31–34; admission of new, 34–38; relations of, with foreign governments, 38–42; relations of, with local governments, 793–831; relations of, with each other, 834–873; indictment of, 876–879; in the depression, 879–881; during World War II, 881–885; in the postwar era, 885–886; future of, 908–910
Status, changes of, in public service, 482
Statutes: drafting of, 263–266; codification and revision of, 266–273; relation of, to common law, 565–566
Staunton, Virginia, city manager form originates in, 780
Steele, John, controversy of, over Illinois governorship, 325–326
Steffens, Lincoln, on Governor Oswald West, 322
Sterilization, of criminals in Oklahoma, 720–721
Sterling, Philip, on lawyers as legislators, 197
Stevenson, Governor Adlai E. (Ill.), item veto message of, 342
Studensky, Paul, on referenda on bond issues, 508–509
Substantive law, and adjective law, distinguished, 574
Suffrage: early limitations on, 49; a privilege, not a right, 101; controls over conditions of, 101–102; history of, 102, 104; general qualifications for, 105–107; Negro, 106–112; woman, 112–114; by absentees, 114–116; registration for, 116–119
Sullivan, Rodman, on inheritance taxes, 549
Sulzer, Governor William (N.Y.), impeachment of, 327, 333
Summons, writ of, defined, 569
Sumners-Wilcox Act, for defaulting municipalities, 888
Sumter, South Carolina: early manager government in, 781
Sunderland, Edson R.: on justice of the peace system, 598; on judicial councils, 621, 624–625; on improvement of appellate courts, 629–631; on administration of justice, 666
Supervision: governor's powers of, 329–330; methods of, by governor, 357–360; obstacles to, by governor, 360–361; types of control over, 361; financial, 490
Supreme courts, state, 607–609
Sweatt v. Painter (339 U.S. 629, 1950), 694
Swift v. Tyson (16 Peters 1, 1842), 561
Swisher, Carl B., on California constitutional convention of 1878, 84

Taft, William H.: states objections to recall of judges, 151–152, 617; influence of his Commission on Economy and Efficiency, 370, 371; on judicial procedure, 658; on due process, 678
Talmadge, Governor Eugene (Ga.): 320, 335; use of spoils system by, 462
Talmadge, Governor Herman (Ga.): election controversy of, 326
Taxes: requirements of sound system of, 521–522; distribution of burden of, 522–523; provisions of, in state constitutions, 523–525; escape from, 523; on general property, 525–534; exemptions from, 527–529; delinquency of, 529–530; limitations on, 530–531, 532; declining importance of, on realty, 531–533; on personalty, 533–534; on corporations and business, 534–539; franchise, 536; on banks, 536; on chain stores, 536–537, 538; severance, 537; pari-mutuel, 537–538; state differentials on, 539; sales, use, and gross receipts, 540–541; excise, 541–544; liquor, 541–543; gasoline, 543–544; cigarette and tobacco, 544, 545; income, 544–548; inheritance and estate, 548–549; pattern of, in states, 549–551; broadening base for, 551; community property and, 551–552; double and overlapping, 552–554; state supervision of rates of, 803–806; state supervision of collection of, 806; sharing of, with local units, 809–810
Taxpayers' organizations, 166–167
Taylor v. Alabama (335 U.S. 252, 1948), 697
Taylor v. Mississippi (319 U.S. 583, 1943), 683–684
Teacher certification, 817–818
Television, use of, in political campaigns, 130
TENNESSEE: amending provisions in constitution of, 53, 59, 60; adoption of constitution of, 70; voting population of, 103; effort of, to abolish poll tax, 107; voting laws of, 108; statewide civic groups in, 167; apportionment in, 200; adjourned sessions in, 221; legislative committees in, 225, 226; cost of legislation in, 231, 233; legislative service agencies in, 242, 250, 265, 267; poor legislative drafting in, 264; local legislation in, 285, 286; Governor Cooper of, 319; veto power in, 339, 340, 342; administrative procedure legislation in, 393; secretary of state in, 424; civil service law in, 464; adopts budget law, 494; growth of debt in, 512, 513; liquor taxes in, 542; gasoline tax in, 544; cigarette tax in, 545, 548; inheritance tax in, 549; equity system in, 571; study of justice courts in, 599; ju-